The story of Alderley

CW01496944

MANCHESTER
1824

Manchester University Press

The story of Alderley

Living with the Edge

Edited by A. J. N. W. Prag

With contributions by John Adams, Tristram Besterman, Richard S. W. Braithwaite, Laurence Cook, Roger L. H. Dennis, Nigel Dibben, David P. Earl, John L. Ecclestone, Sean R. Edwards, Alan Garner, David I. Green, Jonathan Guest, M. V. Hounsome, Matthew Hyde, Richard H. Johnson, Carolanne King, Dmitri V. Logunov, Henry McGhie, Jeremy Milln, John R. Nudds, John E. Pollard, Clare Pye, Mike Redfern, Robin Salmon, Jill Smethurst, Edward Stanley, Thomas eighth Lord Stanley of Alderley, Alan Straw, David B. Thompson, Simon Timberlake, Geoffrey Warrington, Jean Wearne, Stephen Wearne, Christopher Widger

Manchester University Press

Published by Manchester University Press
Altrincham Street, Manchester M1 7JA

www.manchesteruniversitypress.co.uk

British Library Cataloguing-in-Publication Data
A catalogue record for this book is available from the British Library

Library of Congress Cataloging-in-Publication Data applied for

ISBN 978 07190 9171 1 hardback

First published 2016

Typeset in Plantin by R. J. Footring Ltd, Derby
Printed and bound by CPI Group (UK) Ltd, Croydon, CR0 4YY

If you're not living on the Edge then you're taking up too much space.
(Graffito seen in Verona Youth Hostel, 2008)

Contents

Plates

The thirty-two-page plates section begins after the preliminary pages.

Figures

Appendices

Tables

A series of large and detailed tables (9.1–9.5) pertaining to surveys of vegetation on Alderley Edge (see pp. 800–2), as well as a table (13.2) recording a survey of butterflies on the Edge (see p. 874), undertaken as part of the Alderley Edge Landscape Project, are provided online, in Excel format, at:

http://www.manchesteruniversitypress.co.uk/
ThestoryofAlderlyAdditionalResources

Contributors

John Adams, Project Manager, Alderley Edge Landscape Project: Heritage and Educational Resources (AELPHER)

Tristram Besterman, Director, Manchester Museum, 1994–2005

Richard S. W. Braithwaite, formerly Senior Lecturer in Chemistry, UMIST and University of Manchester, and Honorary Consultant to the mineral collections at Manchester Museum. Erstwhile Visiting Professor of the University of Salzburg, Honorary Senior Lecturer in the School of Chemistry

Laurence Cook, formerly Reader, School of Life Sciences, University of Manchester; Visiting Professor, Manchester Metropolitan University

Roger L. H. Dennis, Honorary Research Fellow, NERC Centre for Ecology and Hydrology, Monks Wood, Huntingdon, Cambridgeshire, and Visiting Professor, Institute for Environment, Sustainability and Regeneration, Staffordshire University

Nigel Dibben, Derbyshire Caving Club

David P. Earl, Lancashire Environment Record Network (LERN), c/o Lancashire County Council

John L. Ecclestone, MBE, National Trust Volunteer Sound Archivist

Sean R. Edwards, Keeper of Botany, Manchester Museum, and Honorary Senior Lecturer in the School of Biological Sciences (University of Manchester) until 2004

Alan Garner, OBE, author and antiquary

David I. Green, Honorary Research Associate, School of Earth, Atmospheric and Environmental Sciences, University of Manchester, and Honorary Research Associate, Department of Geology, National Museum of Wales

Jonathan Guest, Ecologist

M. V. Hounsome, Keeper of Zoology, Manchester Museum, until 1999

Matthew Hyde, architectural historian; formerly teacher at Manchester Museum

Richard H. Johnson, formerly Senior Lecturer, Department of Geography, University of Manchester

Carolanne King, Archaeologist; formerly Project Surveyor, Alderley Edge Landscape Project

Dmitri V. Logunov, Curator of Arthropods, Manchester Museum

Henry McGhie, Head of Collections and Curator of Zoology, Manchester Museum

Jeremy Milln, National Trust: Regional Archaeologist for Mercia 1988–2002 and for West Midlands 2002–11

John R. Nudds, Senior Lecturer, School of Earth, Atmospheric and Environmental Sciences, University of Manchester; formerly Keeper of Geology, Manchester Museum

John E. Pollard, formerly Senior Lecturer in Geology, School of Earth, Atmospheric and Environmental Sciences, University of Manchester

A. J. N. W. Prag, formerly Keeper of Archaeology and Professor of Archaeological Studies, Manchester Museum; Honorary Professor at Manchester Museum and Professor Emeritus of Classics, University of Manchester; Coordinator, Alderley Edge Landscape Project (Editor)

Clare Pye, Archivist for the Alderley Edge Landscape Project and local historian

Mike Redfern, former National Trust guide, Nether Alderley Mill, and local historian

Robin Salmon, National Trust Volunteer Guide, Alderley Edge

Jill Smethurst, formerly Special Sites Officer, Cheshire Wildlife Trust, Grebe House, Reaseheath, Nantwich, Cheshire

Thomas, eighth Lord Stanley of Alderley

Alan Straw, Ornithologist

David B. Thompson, formerly Fellow of the University of Keele

Simon Timberlake, Senior Researcher, Cambridge Archaeological Unit, Department of Archaeology, University of Cambridge and Member of the McDonald Institute; Excavations Director, Early Mines Research Group; formerly Chief Surveyor, Alderley Edge Landscape Project

Geoffrey Warrington, formerly British Geological Survey; Honorary Visiting Fellow, Department of Geology, University of Leicester; Chartered Geologist and Senior Fellow, Geological Society of London

Jean Wearne, Assistant Archivist, Alderley Edge Landscape Project, and Alderley History Group

Stephen Wearne, Alderley History Group

Christopher Widger, National Trust: Cheshire Countryside Property Manager 2004–09; Countryside Manager, Cheshire and the Wirral 2009 onwards

Foreword

Lord Stanley of Alderley

My family lived at Alderley for over 400 years so I was fascinated, as I am sure you will be, by the detail you will find even from the headings of the various chapters and by the number of people who have been involved in the Alderley project, for it covers a multitude of disciplines and interests, including a separate book on its archaeology. You will be fascinated by the detail of the work done by so many, all of whom have through their work on the project become intimately connected in one way or another with Alderley. There is, however, one thing that unites them, and that is how the social history is intricately tied in with the land itself and the effect it has had on them and on those who live there or indeed visit it.

We live in an age when the importance of belonging to a particular area has been downgraded and perceived as being of little or no value. Globalisation, whatever that means, is the current philosophy but this book points us the other way, to the danger of separating people from their local surroundings and background. Anyone reading this book will soon realise that one of our modern problems has been caused by divorcing people from the place where they live and by a failure to understand the importance of its history and the people who make and have made it. It has made me understand some of the problems caused by my cousin failing to appreciate this simple but important fact when he sold and left Alderley so insensitively some seventy-odd years ago.

Its detailed study of so many aspects of the story of Alderley makes this volume a blueprint for all of us, wherever we live, for how to ap- preciate and learn from our surroundings, so I am left with the strong message that where you live is important and interesting, something that today is sadly missing in our national life. The book has taken many people a lot of time and effort to produce, not least because there was so much to discover, so I hope it will have sequels, for there are always more things to discover and appreciate about where you live, now, and who lived in it yesterday and how it has come to be what it is.

Preface

Tristram Besterman

Come to the edge.
We might fall.
Come to the edge.
It's too high!
Come to the edge!
And they came,
and he pushed,
and they flew.

By Christopher Logue, copyright © Christopher Logue, 1969, Untitled ('Apollinaire said'), in *New Numbers* (London: Cape): 65–6.

Teased out in the pages of this remarkable book is a many-stranded tale of a place and its people. In one sense it might be thought a commonplace: there is surely nothing unique about a landscape defined by nature and reshaped by people whose lives are in turn moulded by it. It is, after all, but one small part of the mosaic of Britain and its people. Yet in other senses it is a narrative without precedent. By turns baleful and benign, Alderley Edge seems uncannily to demand our attention, exerting an extraordinary influence over countless lives through the turn of the centuries. This might help to explain why so many facets of one place have now been subjected to such intense, prolonged and expert scrutiny.

Palimpsest. That was the word that came to mind when I walked the Edge with John Prag and Alan Garner as my guides in 1995. A document from which the original writing has been erased and later overwritten. While not exactly a scraped parchment, Alderley Edge nonetheless teases us with layers of information contained in, on and around it. Information embedded, accreted, disrupted, fragmented – but still there to hear and to read if we have the wit to listen and see. And that is exactly what the Alderley Edge Landscape Project (AELP) set out to do.

This book is one of the more notable offspring of that project. There have been many others, some unforeseen at the outset, but all welcome progeny of creative interactions: an exhibition at Manchester Museum in 1998 (part of which transferred to Alderley Edge); a specialist book in 2005, *The Archaeology of Alderley Edge*; a newsletter; educational events on the Edge that involved, among other things, extracting and smelting copper, Bronze Age style; an award-winning educational website (regrettably no longer extant) that was used by schools all over England as a template for local studies; archaeological investigation; a permanent archive to be lodged with Cheshire Archives and Local Studies, in addition to the excavation archive in Manchester Museum; and data that have informed the National Trust's management and interpretation of the Edge.

As anyone can see from the chapter headings, this book is the collective outcome of many individuals collaborating across a range of disciplines, each contributing specialist expertise and, in many cases, years of hard work, some starting long before the AELP was established. This cooperative endeavour began well before ideas of 'multidisciplinarity' became fashionable in higher education, when a cell biologist working with a geneticist was considered ground-breaking. The buzz of excitement was palpable when a newly uncovered nugget of information appeared at the table, stimulating an unstoppable flow of knowledge and ideas as it was passed from ethnographer to miner to local historian to geologist to local resident to storyteller to botanist to archaeologist and back again. As with all good research, every discovery raised a dozen new questions, pursued in the field, in the library, record office and laboratory.

I thank everyone who contributed to this book, some of whose names are represented as authors, many whose names are not. I am grateful to Manchester Museum's corporate partners, on whose goodwill, active cooperation and financial support the project relied: the University of Manchester, the National Trust and other landowners in the study area, Derbyshire Caving Club, Cheshire County Council, English Heritage and the Heritage Lottery Fund. If I had the privilege of occasionally wielding the conductor's baton, it was John Prag who kept the score and who made sure that everyone and everything came together as it should; it is to him that we owe this book and the success of the AELP. Like some of the enigmatically carved stone Celtic heads of the north-west of England, the AELP faced in many directions. The project looked to the academic as well as to the local community; it studied what was below ground as well as what was at the surface; it seized on fact and myth, on artefact and on nature; it looked to the past and connected it to the future. John channelled that activity and wove those disparate strands into a coherent narrative in a way that exemplifies all that is worthy of Manchester Museum.

This book is written for readers of many kinds. For as many, and more, as have experienced Alderley Edge themselves; for those who are the sons and daughters of the three villages of the Edge, and its villas; for those who live in and around the Edge; for those who work there; and for those who visit: we hope that this book will be the source of interest, delight and inspiration it has been to its many contributors. And for those who may never have been near Alderley, there is resonance in its pages for anyone who is interested in their relationship with the land and how it subtly informs our sense of who we are.

Post scriptum

I now live close to Bodmin Moor, another man-made landscape, scarred above and riddled below with old copper mines. Eighteenth- and nineteenth-century remnants of industry survive, from the towering engine houses to the rust-drilled granite sleepers of mineral railways half overgrown by moorland heath. Prehistoric stones entice us with ritually enigmatic purpose. Common ground, in some ways, with Alderley Edge, but this stark, unforgiving land is quite different geologically and topographically from Cheshire's; its history is distinctive, too. To the west the granite uplands and streams yielded tin to miners from prehistoric times to the late twentieth century, the sound of pick and shovel echoing the winning of copper at Alderley Edge, to which this Cornish landscape must surely have been linked. For the Bronze Age miners who worked the copper ores of Alderley needed Cornish tin to make the alloy they cast for the tools and weapons they used to feed and defend themselves. In more recent times, from South America to Australia and South Africa, they say that where metal was to be had from rock, a Cornish miner was never far away. As Alderley Edge has shown us time and again, the connections are probably there if we look for them, just as others emerge, unsought, in the looking.

Tristram Besterman
Director, Manchester Museum, 1994–2005

Preamble and acknowledgements

A. J. N. W. Prag

Like the story of the Edge itself, this book has taken a long time to put together and for that I must take much of the responsibility. For that too I offer my apologies to all concerned with this project, especially to the contributors and to the long-suffering people of Alderley: but it is a long story and a complicated one and the telling of it has involved many people in many ways.

The Alderley Edge Landscape Project – AELP – was conceived under Tristram Besterman's directorship of Manchester Museum as a multidisciplinary undertaking such as befitted a university museum, even before such things became fashionable: had I realised in 1995 that it would come to take over my life I might have been less keen to follow his enthusiastic lead, but that very multidisciplinarity has of course been a pleasure and an inspiration for us all, and I am grateful to Nick Merriman, the present director of the Museum, for continuing to support the project as we attempt to draw it to a conclusion. Harnessing so many different enthusiasts and enthusiasms is not a recipe for a speedy conclusion, and understandably some of the contributors and some of the funders have occasionally expressed concern over the delays – one even confided to a co-author that he hoped that I would live long enough to see it through to completion. I appreciate his concern and offer my warmest thanks to all my colleagues on the Project and to those who have supported us in so many ways. As we noted in the opening pages of *The Archaeology of Alderley Edge*, the first report on the Project's work (Timberlake and Prag, 2005), this has been a joint project between the Manchester Museum at the University of Manchester and the National Trust, and then, as now, we offer thanks to colleagues in both organisations for their help and advice that often went much further than simply help and advice, and provided encouragement and stimulation. That volume was primarily concerned with the archaeology of the Edge and its associated disciplines; this one covers 'everything else', and thus the opportunities and the requests for help have grown accordingly and exponentially.

So many of the people and the organisations whom we thanked then still deserve our thanks (or deserve them again). If I do not repeat them all here then it is not for lack of gratitude, but simply to keep this preamble within the bounds of reason and perhaps also because their support and their contributions were intended (and appreciated!) chiefly for the Project's archaeological work and or the accompanying exhibition in 1998. However, the Leverhulme Trust's generous award was fundamental to the whole Project on the one hand, and on the other we could have achieved very little without the continuing support and goodwill of the people of Alderley Edge, in particular all those who allowed us access to their property, who offered us items for the Project Archive, and who gave us their time and their memories by allowing us to interview them. It is a mark of their openness and generosity of spirit that there are too many to list them individually here, but many of their names can be found scattered through the chapters that follow. This is their book: we are sorry it has taken so long to produce, but we hope they feel it has been worth the wait.

Through the good offices of Will Spinks, AstraZeneca kindly gave us money to complete the publication and launch of the first book. Further very welcome funding towards the production of this second volume has come from the Alderley Edge Institute (whose secretaries, Kevin Ranshaw and later Ashley Comiskey Dawson, had to be very understanding when the book suffered further delays), from the National Trust (some of it from the fund established in memory of Michael Ford – my thanks to Jeremy Milln for arranging this, some of it from Cheshire property funds, thanks to Christopher Widger), and from the Marc Fitch Fund for additional photography and drawing, for which I thank the late Dr Elaine Paintin.

On the Edge we could have achieved little in recent years without the constant help of both Christopher Widger and David Standen, the National Trust's Countryside Manager and Warden respectively. Without the initiative and passion of Jeremy Milln, the Trust's Regional Archaeologist first for Mercia and then for the West Midlands, AELP would never have happened and I owe him much more than he probably believes. With the reorganisations within the Trust, responsibility for Alderley has now shifted to Jamie Lund, Regional Archaeologist for the North West Region, and it has been good to know that I could rely on his support too. Underneath the Edge we could have done nothing without the commitment and enthusiasm of the Derbyshire Caving Club, whose members I think soon realised that our hearts were in the right place and were liberal with their support, and then with a donation towards the cost of this volume: Nigel Dibben and Stephen Mills in particular have been ever-willing to answer questions, take us into the mines and to provide us with more and more interesting facts. Stephen Mills generously capped this with a gift for the book itself.

In Alderley Edge village, Mandy Parr's knowledge of the ways and means and people has made her a splendid facilitator, and I already miss the sparkling eyes and the fund of stories that were such a part of the late Harold Smith's presence. Chris Jervis's researches provided a mine of information when the story of Philip Jarvis came to light, and we remain delighted that Gill Davies told us so promptly of her finding of Jarvis's gravestone in her garden. It was very good to be able to consult the archives of St Mary's, Nether Alderley, through the kindness of Jenny Youatt, the church archivist, and before her of the late Brian Hobson, while the methodical and willing guidance through the burial records and the burial ground given by Geoff Windsor, chairman of the parish burial board, helped considerably in the final part of Jarvis's story.

Some unfortunate contributors have found themselves on the receiving end of streams of queries from me about parts of the book for which they bore no responsibility as I picked my way through this long and intricate volume. Here I owe very special thanks to Dmitri Logunov, who not only found me somewhere in his department to work after my previous office was absorbed in one of the Museum's reorganisations, but who also expanded and completely rewrote the chapter on the invertebrates (Chapter 13) from a small fragment into a masterly and many-faceted survey, and who after that still had the kindness to help me with illustrations and with questions about other aspects of the Edge's natural history; those people who helped him and provided photographs of the invertebrates are named in that chapter. Laurence Cook kindly brought some order to Part III, on natural history, at an earlier stage in the proceedings. Jonathan Guest revised and updated the pondlife chapter (Chapter 12) after the untimely death of Jill Smethurst and also cast a very helpful eye over the chapter on the birds (Chapter 11). Nigel Dibben did the same for some of Part IV, 'Human history – archaeology and underground', and for Chapter 22, on graffiti (and answered numerous questions with tact and promptness as well as taking endless trouble in improving some of the images reproduced in this book), and Jeremy Milln revised the chapter on the 'large stones and hoary rocks' of historical significance (Chapter 27). Alison Scott (at that time in the Centre for Continuing Education of the University) and Stuart Burley (then at British Gas) read early drafts of the geology chapters (Part II) and Geoffrey Warrington rechecked Part II when I thought it was finished. Lucy Armstrong at the National

Trust kindly gave advice and information on the recent restoration work at Nether Alderley Mill. Jonathan Pepler (the Cheshire County Archivist) and his successor Paul Newman at Cheshire Archives and Local Studies in the Cheshire Record Office provided the image of the *Stanley Notebook* and gave us permission to reproduce this and other items from the Stanley archive (Figures 19.1, 19.5, 19.7–19.9, 19.13–19.15 and 20.8, and Plate 61), such as sections of the 'Crossley' map and the Enclosure Award map and Norman Abbott's map of the feathered singing visitors on the Edge (Figure 11.1). Jonathan Pepler deserves my particular gratitude for patiently answering so many of my questions, and for reading over some of the chapters in their final form.

Others who have borne with my importunities include John Adams, Sean Edwards, Matthew Hyde, Carolanne King, John Nudds, Phyllis Stoddart and Simon Timberlake, my co-editor on the first book. I have badgered colleagues in other parts of the university and elsewhere too: Melanie Giles and Bryan Sitch for advice on Celtic matters, Nick Higham on questions of local history (he also kindly read drafts of some chapters), David Langslow on the etymology of some insect names and Rosie Stoddart (née Pearson) for advice on some of the nicer points of the naming of woodlice and codlice and their possible but unlikely role in cudding or rumination in cattle. My thanks too to Donna Sherman, Assistant Librarian (Maps) in the University of Manchester Library, for help in identifying the sources of some of our maps, and to Mike Nevell and Norman Redhead (formerly directors of the University of Manchester Archaeological Unit and the Greater Manchester Archaeological Unit respectively, and now respectively Head of the Centre for Applied Archaeology and Heritage Management and Director of the Greater Manchester Archaeological Advisory Service at Salford University) for elucidating some obscure aspects of Manchester archaeology. Steve Allen at the York Archaeological Trust provided information on the Brynlow 'goblet', Chris Carlon told me about the Cheshire Basin and the Alderley mines and read drafts of part of the book, and Jill Collens and Mark Leah (now with Cheshire West and Chester Borough Council) and Moya Watson (Cheshire Shared Services) gave welcome advice on matters of planning, footpaths and other such local issues. Numerous other friends and colleagues allowed themselves to be persuaded to read and comment on drafts of chapters, among them George Bankes, Paul Cavill, Alan Garner, Melanie Giles, John Hodgson, Ken Howarth, Matthew Hyde, Jamie Lund, Neil Philip and John Pickin.

Many people have helped us with the illustrations. I have tried to acknowledge them appropriately in the list of figures but there are some who should be mentioned here. My late colleague Barri Jones and after him John Garnons-Williams flew over Alderley for us and generously gave their photographs to the Project archive. Julie Ballard and David I. Green digitised the images for Chapters 5 and 7. John Beswick gave us the photograph used as Figure 19.17. Peter Blore and his colleagues in the Graphic Support Workshop in the University's Media Services department, in particular Dan Wand, provided crucial help with the scanning of the maps in Chapter 1 and elsewhere and in sorting out 'difficult' images. Eleanor Casella allowed us to use a version of the location map (Figure 1.1) for Alderley Edge from her book *The Alderley Sandhills Project* (Casella and Croucher, 2010). Paul Deakin has let us use his magnificent photos of the mines. Harry Fairhurst presented the Project with the 1938 *Sale Catalogue* from which Figures 19.19, 24.1, 24.5 and 24.8 are taken. Jan Hicks, Archives and Information Manager at the Museum of Science and Industry, Manchester (MOSI), tussled with the sources for Figure 16.17. Alan Hulme lent us his collection of old postcards of Alderley to be copied for the Project archive, some of which have been used in Chapter 19 of this book and elsewhere. Lona Jones kindly helped us with a reference to a work in the National Library of Wales. Philip Manning gave assistance with Plate 5. Stephen McCabe, now in the University of Manchester's Communications and Marketing office, digitised and redrew the maps for Chapter 28. Jack Mitchell allowed us to show his magnificent hand axe as Figure 14.6. The photograph used as Figure 10.19 was part of a gift from Sheila Mackie. Bryan Perceval and Stephen Mills provided the photos of Hayman's Quarry and the stone cart (Figure 18.5). Jeremy Milln made the drawings of the seal of Richard of Alderley for Figure 14.12. Thanks to Seán Ó'Brógáin we can use his reconstruction drawings freely (Figures 2.5, 14.2 and 15.5). Ian Roberts, Malcolm Bailey and Rachel Bailey have allowed us to reproduce the photo of Rachel Bailey with the newly discovered coin hoard yet again (Figure 2.4). Mrs Maria Robins-Bailey gave us permission to illustrate the finds made at Alderley by her late husband, David Bailey. Duncan Broomhead kindly provided the photograph for Figure 19.18, and I am grateful to Mary Houseman for permission to reproduce it here. Dr Ian Somerville kindly facilitated permission for us to re-use material from the *Geological Journal*. Thomas, eighth Lord Stanley, allowed us to reproduce portraits of members of his family (Figures 19.2 and 19.11), and his daughter-in-law Lady Stanley kindly gave us the photograph used as Figure 19.2. Elaine Taylor provided us with the photographs of John Evans from the Derbyshire Caving Club archive for the appendix to Chapter 21, and the permission to use them. George Twigg lent us his collection of old photographs of Alderley, some of which are reproduced in Chapters 19, 20 and 23. Roger and Elaine Williams have permitted us to use the plan of Hill Cottage (Figure 23.3). Another long list – but in no way does its length diminish or dilute my gratitude to them all.

My thanks too to the Churches Conservation Trust for permission to reproduce the painting of Charles Roe by Joseph Wright of Derby in Christ Church, Macclesfield (Figure 16.4); to Christie's Images Limited for permission to reproduce the photograph of the Leycester map (Plate 61) and to Francesca Hickin for help in obtaining that permission; to Elsevier Limited for permission to publish figure 132 from R. C. Selley, *An Introduction to Sedimentology* (second edition), London: Academic Press (1982), as Figure 5.5; to HarperCollins Publishers Ltd for permission to reproduce the cover of the *Weirdstone of Brisingamen* (Figure 29.1d); to Philippa Sitters, of David Godwin Associates, Ltd, literary agent of the late Christopher Logue and to Rosemary Hill, Logue's widow, for permission to quote in full the poem known as 'Apollinaire said'; to Manchester Archives and Local Studies for allowing us to use part of the 1807 Stanley estate map from the Stanley estate book (Figure 18.3); and to the Controller of Her Majesty's Stationery Office for permission to reproduce various parts of the 1992 Ordnance Survey 1:25,000 Pathfinder map sheet 759 and some other maps (Figures 1.2, 1.3, 8.1, 10.16, 14.1, 16.7, 16.14, 18.2, 18.11, 19.15, 28.1, 28.2, 28.3; Plates 3a and 20). We have tried to track down all the copyright holders, and if unwittingly we have reproduced any images without permission then I offer our sincere apologies.

When a book has as long a gestation as this one it is inevitable that other works will appear which will supplement or complement it before it sees the light of day. One in particular needs to be mentioned, *Alderley Park Discovered*, by George B. Hill, to be issued by Carnegie Publishing: as its title suggests, this will focus on the story of the Park, which largely lay outside our area of study, and the two books will (we both hope) provide very satisfactory foils for each other. Nonetheless, George Hill has been extremely generous with his knowledge, and has provided us with better versions of some of the illustrations, for which we owe him very warm thanks.

Ralph Footring checked the final text with a masterly, hawk-like eye and pounced on many a wayward slip and inconsistency: his sympathetic and thoughtful reading saved us from all too many sins of omission and commission. We are all very, very grateful to him. The house rules of Manchester University Press discourage authors and editors from naming individual members of their staff – but that need not prevent me from expressing enormous gratitude to the tact and understanding of those who have helped me to put this leviathan of a tale into publishable form, notably our editor Matthew Frost.

It is a great sorrow that some of those who contributed to the book, indeed some who took a leading part, have not lived to see its publication: among them we remember George Bankes, John Ecclestone, Julie Green, Matthew Hyde, Chuff Johnson, Jill Smethurst, Harold Smith,

Thomas eighth Lord Stanley of Alderley, Sarah Whitehead and David Thompson (for whom the geological story of Alderley Edge was such an important part of life).

However, it would be wrong to end on a downbeat note. Without the certainty that I could always call on Alan Garner's innate and passionate knowledge of everything connected with the Edge in any way (and of Griselda's take on that) I would have felt much less confident about what I was doing. And there are two other people who deserve my especial thanks: Clare Pye, who has always been there to answer my endless questions about the story of the Edge and its people quickly, knowledgeably and with unfailing good humour – even when I asked her the same question a few weeks later having in the meantime pigeon-holed her answer and moved on to something else (nominally the Project's archivist, she has been my prop and stay as this book came together); and my wife Kay, who since at least 1996 has had to live with my ever-growing and over-riding obsession with Alderley's story and its people, seemingly to the exclusion of all other interests, and who – an experienced archaeologist and editor herself – even volunteered to read over everything as a means of speeding the book on its way. I hope that she will be as pleased as I to see this saga drawn to a conclusion.

Note on units

Given the wide range of subject matter covered in this volume, the units of measure, imperial or metric, used across the chapters vary with the context. For readers less familiar with one or other system, some conversions are given below:

Length, area, volume

1 inch = 2.5 cm
1 foot = 30.5 cm (12 inches)
1 yard = 0.9 m (3 feet)
1 mile = 1.6 km (1,760 yards)
1 fathom = 1.83 m (6 feet)
1 acre (statute acre) = 0.4 hectare (ha = 10,000 m²), 0.4 ha
1 Cheshire acre = 0.8 ha (2 statute acres)
1 pint = 0.57 litres
1 gallon = 4.5 litres (8 pints)

Weight

1 ounce (oz) = 28 g
1 pound (lb) = 0.45 kg (16 oz)
1 stone = 6.35 kg (14 lb)
1 hundredweight (cwt) = 50.8 kg (112 lb)
1 ton = 1,016 kg (20 cwt; 2,240 lb)

Power

1 horsepower = 746 watts (550 foot-pounds per second)

Currency

In the historical chapters, monetary values are given in the original pounds, shilling and pence, expressed in the format £1.1s.1d. There were twenty shillings in the pound and twelve pence to one shilling. No attempt has been made to indicate the purchasing power in a modern money equivalent.

2.4d (old pence) = 1p in modern terms (not value)
12d or 1 shilling = 5p
20 shillings = £1

Abbreviations

AELP	Alderley Edge Landscape Project
AELPHER	Alderley Edge Landscape Project Heritage and Educational Resources
AEMCL	Alderley Edge Mining Company, Limited
AMC	Alderley Mine Company
AMCL	Alderley Mining Company, Limited
AOD	above Ordnance datum
ArchAE	Timberlake, S. and Prag, A. J. N. W. (eds). 2005. *The Archaeology of Alderley Edge: Survey, Excavation and Experiment in an Ancient Mining Landscape* (British Archaeological Reports, British Series 396). Oxford: John and Erica Hedges.
BGS	British Geological Survey
BP	before present
CALS	Cheshire Archives and Local Studies
CPBF	Chester Pebble Beds Formation
CPI	Conservation Performance Indicator
CRO	Cheshire Record Office (now CALS)
DCC	Derbyshire Caving Club
EVCM	Engine Vein Conglomerate Member
GIS	geographic information system
GPS	Global Positioning System
ha	hectare
HMSO	Her Majesty's Stationery Office
HSF	Helsby Sandstone Formation
MCC	Macclesfield Copper Company
ME	Middle English
NA	Nether Alderley
NASM	Nether Alderley Sandstone Member
NGR	National Grid reference

NT	National Trust
NTSMR	National Trust Sites and Monuments Record
OA	Over Alderley
OE	Old English
OS	Ordnance Survey
PDOP	Position Dilution of Precision. PDOP is an error indicator of the triangulation by which GPS satellites calculate a position. PDOP = 1 indicates good satellite constellation and high-quality data; PDOP ≥ 8 is poor
PRO	Public Records Office
RIGS	Regionally Important Geological and geomorphological Site
Sale Catalogue	John Pritchard and Co. (auctioneers). 1938. *Alderley Park Estates Sale Catalogue* (no place of publication given)
SAM	Scheduled Ancient Monument (now referred to as a Scheduled Monument)
SMR	Sites and Monuments Record
SSSI	Site of Special Scientific Interest
Stanley C7	*Stanley Estate Book, 1800–1808.* Manchester Archives and Local Studies Centre: C7, mf2678.
Stanley Notebook	Stanley, J. T. 1830–44. *Genealogical Manuscript Book* (copy in the AELP archive, item no. 3; original in Cheshire Archives and Local Studies, D 8065/1).
TSF	Tarporley Siltstone Formation
WMCM	Wood Mine Conglomerate or Pebbly Sandstone Member
WMSM	West Mine Sandstone Member
WSF	Wilmslow Sandstone Formation

Plates

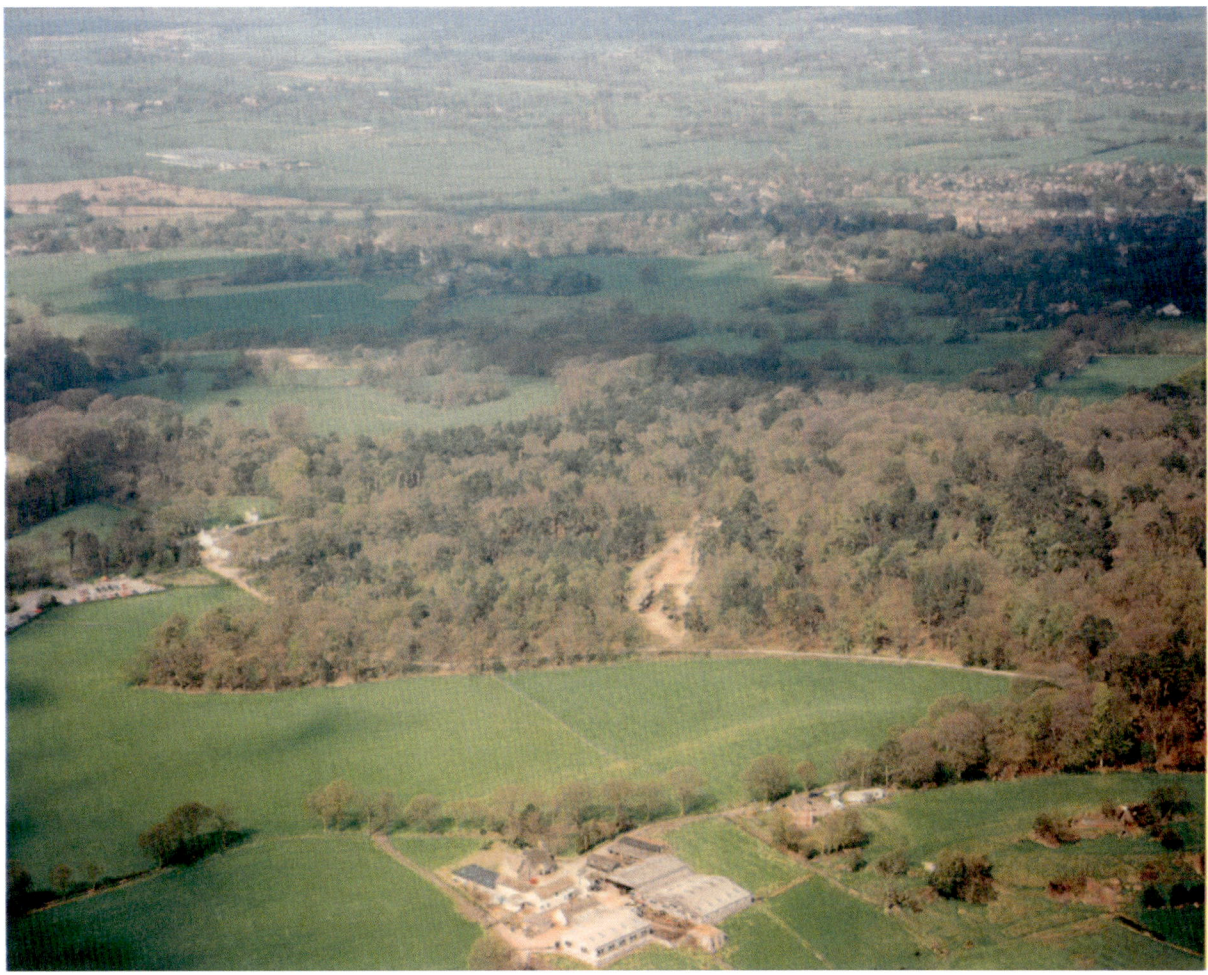

(a)

Plate 1. (a) Aerial view over Alderley Edge looking west, taken in May 1996. Edge House Farm is in the foreground, the National Trust car park and the Wizard are on the left with Artists Lane and Brynlow immediately beyond. Engine Vein shows as a scar in the centre, with Windmill Wood behind and a spur of woodland running down to the Sandhills in the middle distance. Alderley Edge village with its railway is in the background. (b, *over page*) Aerial view over Alderley Edge looking north-west, taken in May 1996. Dickens Wood and Glaze Hill are on the left, the erosion at Stormy Point is in the centre, with Saddlebole to its right and the Hough beyond, and Findlow Bower Farm is just visible on the right. The spire of St Philip's Church in Alderley Edge village can be seen in the background.

Photographs Barri Jones.

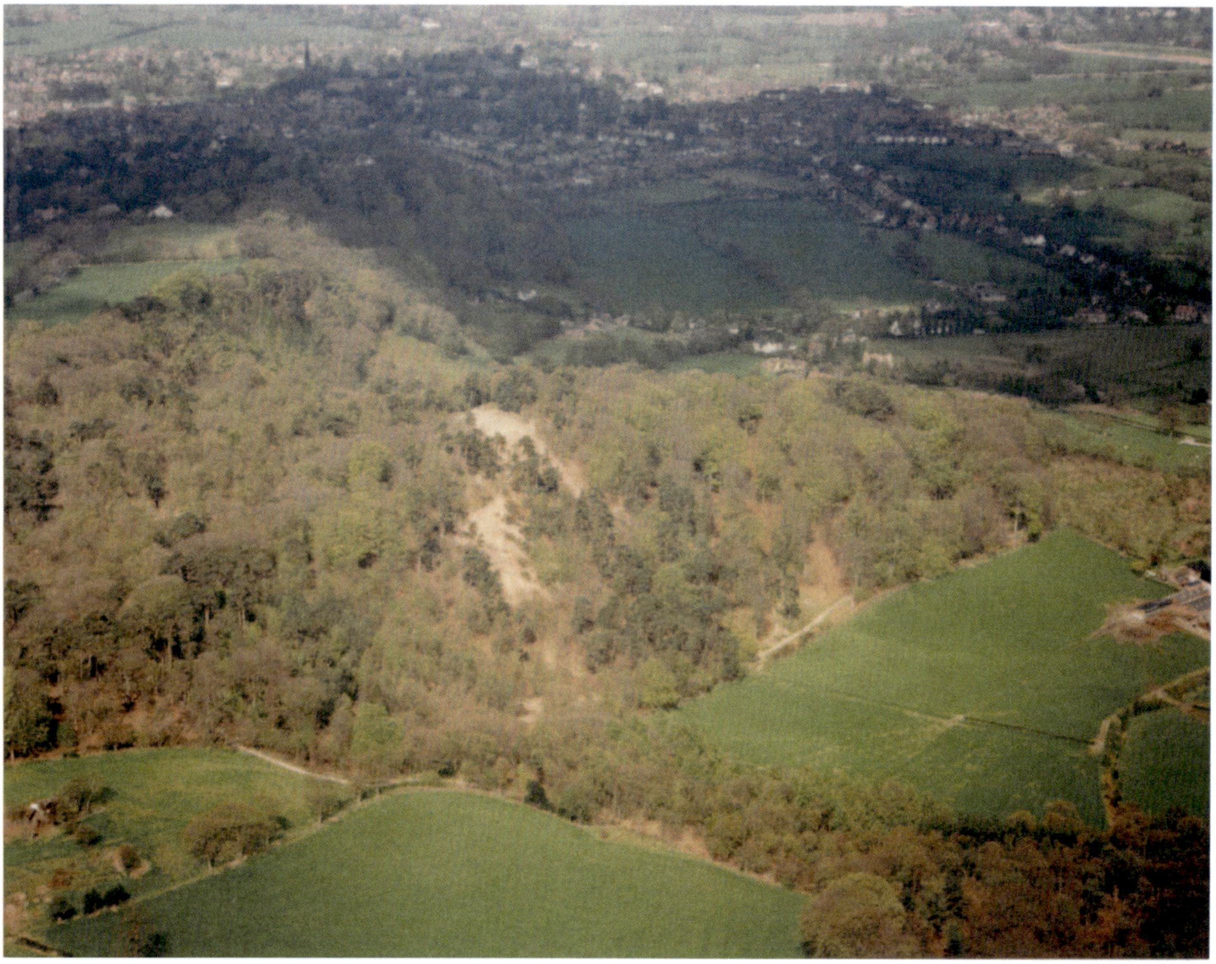

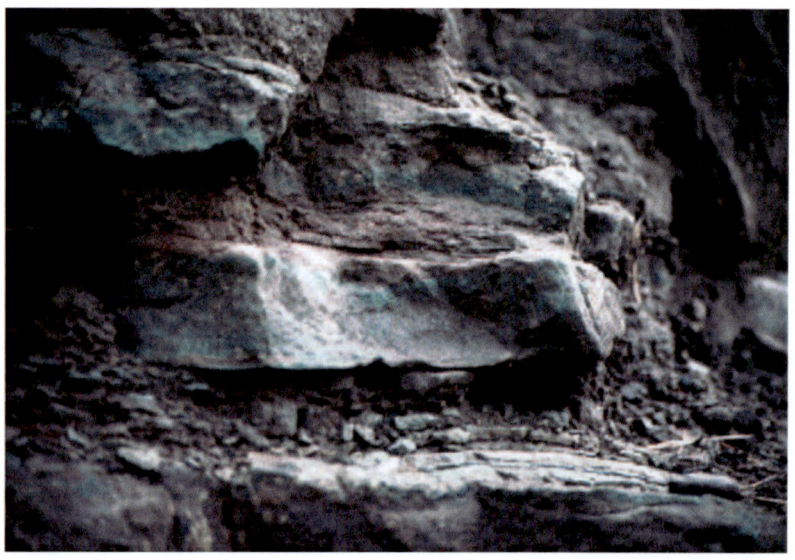

(b)

Plate 2. Cupriferous sandstones in the largely aeolian Wilmslow Sandstone Formation above Pillar Mine. Exposures like these first attracted Bronze Age and perhaps earlier miners to this site. The porous sandstones lying in between and beneath the less permeable red and green mudstones have become the sites of secondary mineral deposition.

Photograph Simon Timberlake.

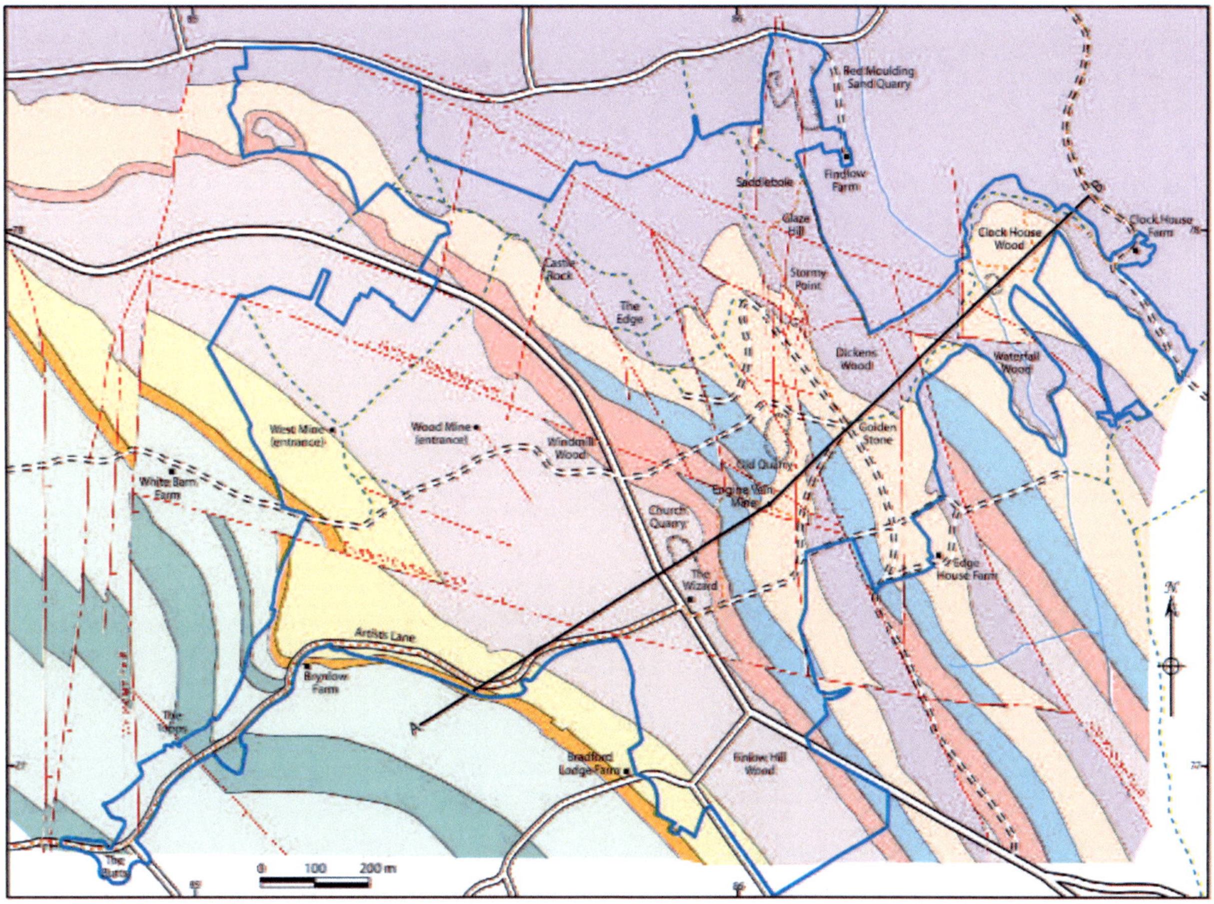

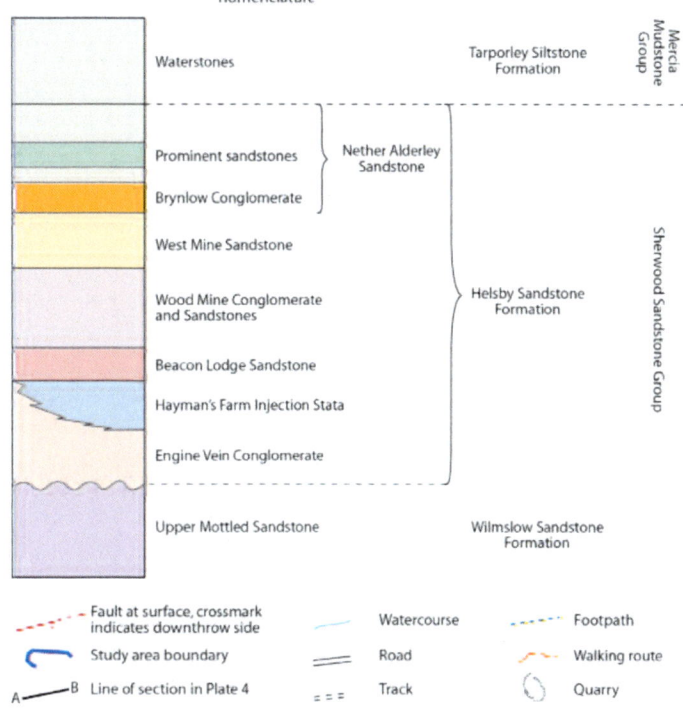

Plate 3. Geological map of the Alderley Edge area (*above*), with key (*right*). Topographical base from Ordnance Survey 1:2,500 maps (2010). Broken red lines, faults; thick black line, line of section in Plate 4; thick blue line, boundary of the AELP core area.

Reproduced with the permission of the Controller of Her Majesty's Stationery Office, Crown copyright October 2013. Geology from mapping by D. B. Thompson (1966).

Local and superseded nomenclature | Current nomenclature

Waterstones — Tarporley Siltstone Formation — Mercia Mudstone Group

Prominent sandstones — Nether Alderley Sandstone

Brynlow Conglomerate

West Mine Sandstone

Wood Mine Conglomerate and Sandstones — Helsby Sandstone Formation — Sherwood Sandstone Group

Beacon Lodge Sandstone

Hayman's Farm Injection Strata

Engine Vein Conglomerate

Upper Mottled Sandstone — Wilmslow Sandstone Formation

- – – Fault at surface, crossmark indicates downthrow side
- Study area boundary
- A —— B Line of section in Plate 4
- Watercourse
- Road
- ≡ ≡ ≡ Track
- – – – Footpath
- Walking route
- Quarry

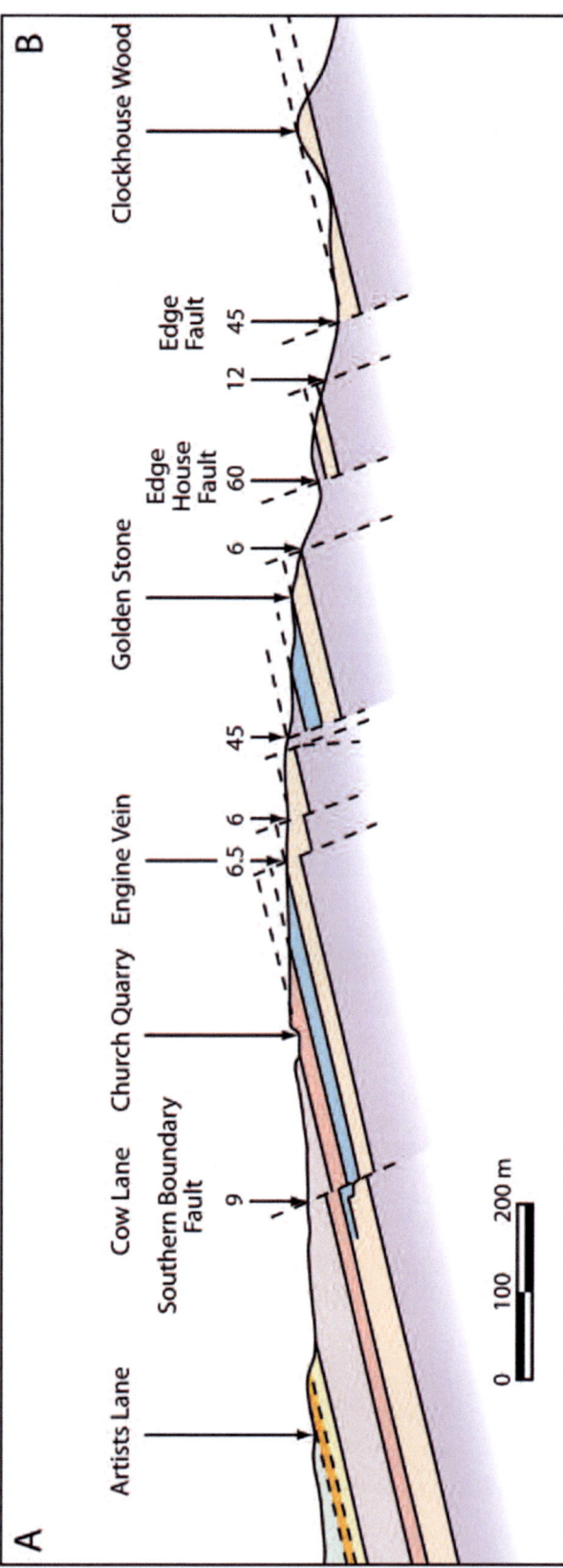

Plate 4. Detailed geological cross-section (north–east to south–west) across the AELP core area (Plate 3a), using local rock unit names and showing the effect of the main fault lines See Plate 3b for key to colours. Numbers indicate the displacement on faults in metres.

After Thompson (1991: 72).

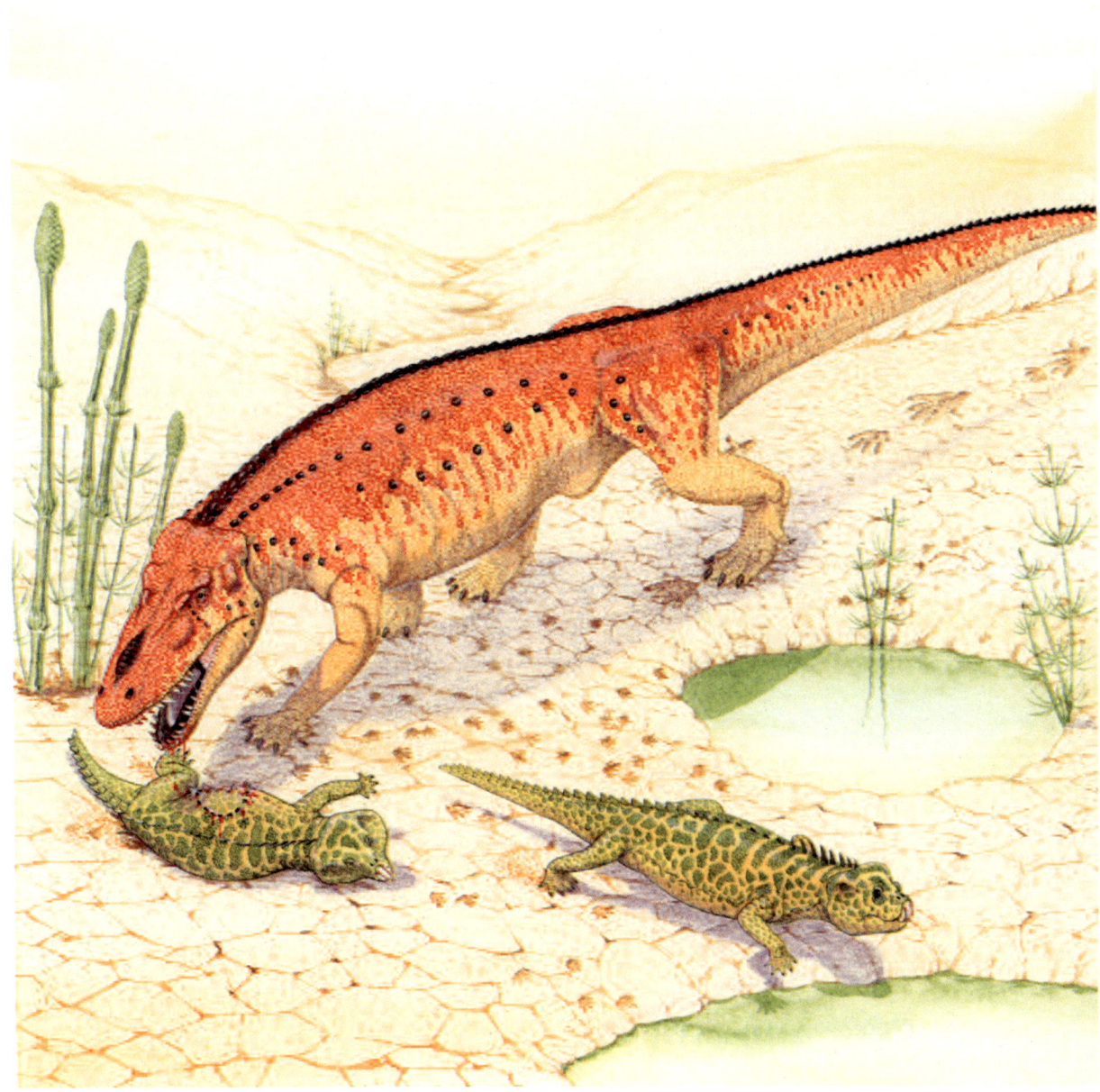

Plate 5. Reconstruction of a carnivorous archosaur (*Ticinosuchus*) attacking a pair of herbivorous rhynchosaurs. The presence of footprints attributed to these creatures (the large, hand-like *Chirotherium* and the smaller *Rhynchosauroides* respectively) in the Alderley Edge area indicates the presence of these reptiles there in Mid Triassic times.

Painting by Graham Rosewarne.

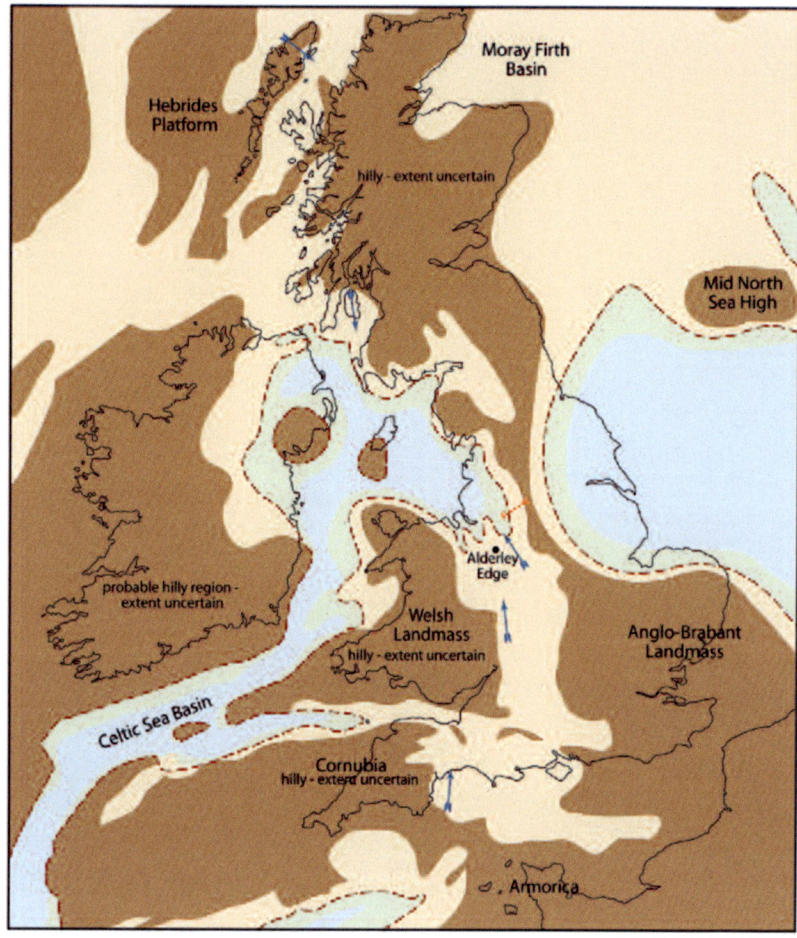

Moray Firth
Basin

Hebrides
Platform

hilly - extent uncertain

Mid North
Sea High

probable hilly region -
extent uncertain

Alderley
Edge

Welsh
Landmass
hilly - extent uncertain

Anglo-Brabant
Landmass

Celtic Sea Basin

Cornubia
hilly - extent uncertain

Armorica

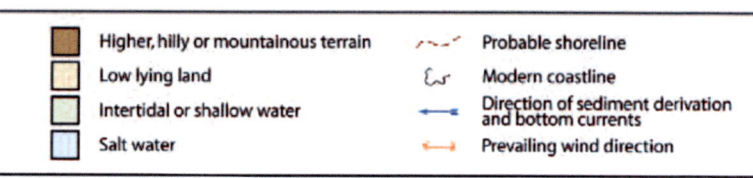

■ Higher, hilly or mountainous terrain	⌇⌇	Probable shoreline
□ Low lying land	ℰ⌇	Modern coastline
□ Intertidal or shallow water	←→	Direction of sediment derivation and bottom currents
□ Salt water	←→	Prevailing wind direction

Plate 6. Regional palaeo-geographical setting of the Cheshire Basin during deposition of the Helsby Sandstone Formation in early Mid Triassic times (*c.* 245 million years ago). The Alderley area is situated in a fluvial system that drained north-westwards into semi-marine environments connected to an oceanic source.

After Warrington and Ivimey-Cook (1992: fig. Tr1b).

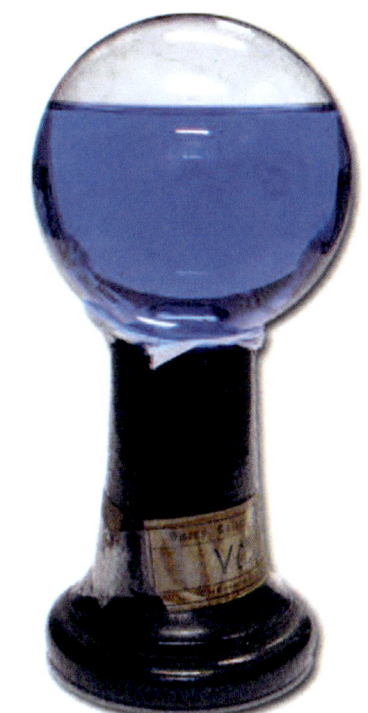

Plate 7. A flask of vanadium-bearing solution prepared from the mine residues at Mottram St Andrew by Sir Henry Roscoe and used in his experiments on vanadium.

Manchester Museum acc. no. N18851. Photograph David I. Green.

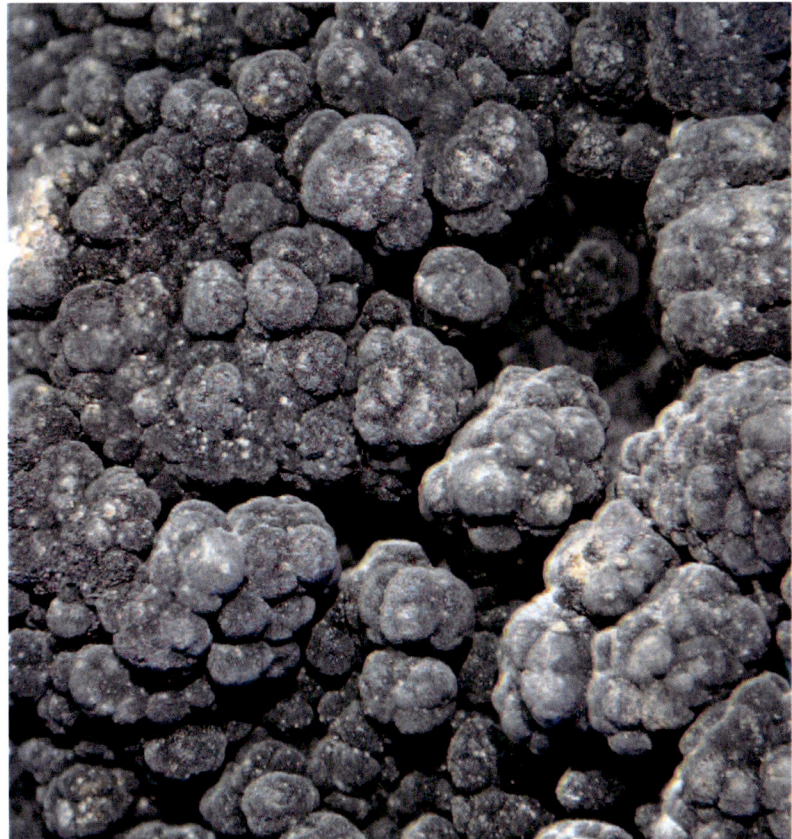

Plate 8. Dark botryoidal mottramite aggregates from Mottram Mine. To this day, some doubt remains as to where the original mottramite specimens came from. Some argue that Pim Hill Mine in Shropshire was the source. Others regard Mottram Mine as the type locality. This specimen, with botryoidal aggregates up to 3 mm across, was collected in 1994 and is definitely from Mottram Mine.

Manchester Museum acc. no. N12134. Photograph David I. Green.

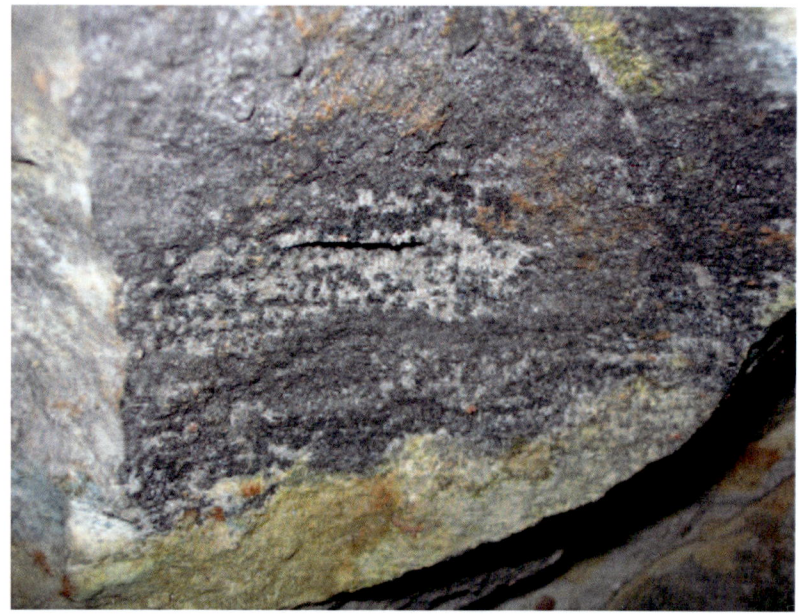

Plate 9. Coarse-grained sandstone from Alderley Edge containing disseminated grey to black copper and lead sulphide ores, with minor alteration to yellow and blue supergene minerals. This type of ore is typical of the Triassic sandstones at the locality.

Photograph David I. Green.

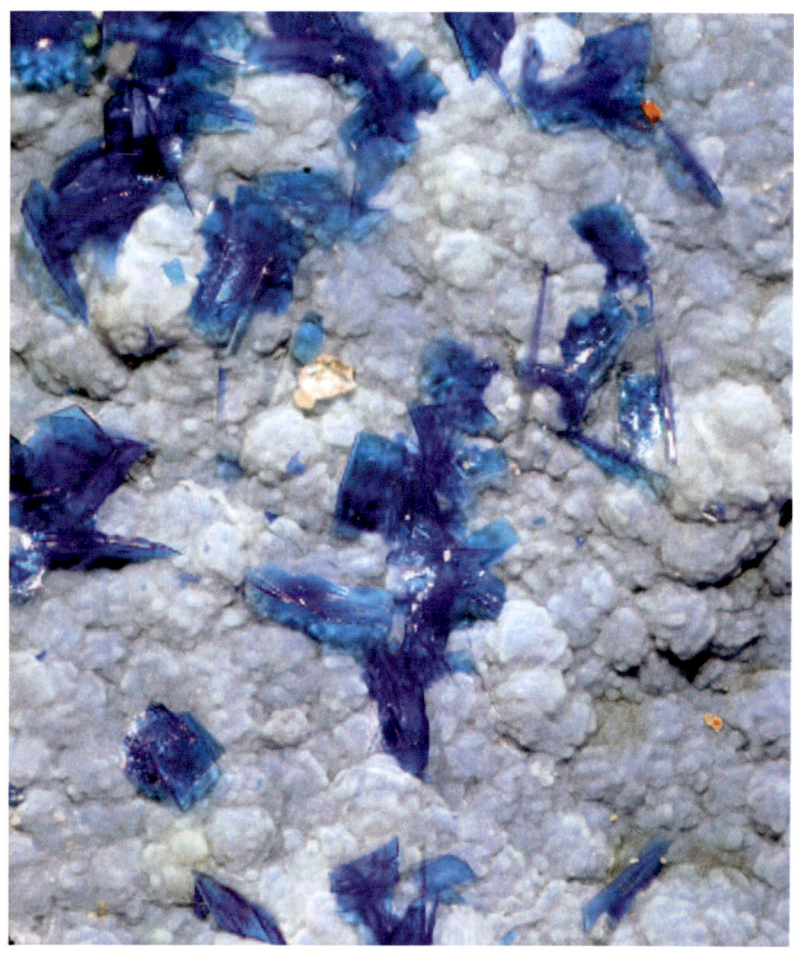

Plate 10. Dark blue azurite crystals, up to 0.8 mm long, of an unusual platy habit from Wood Mine.

Photograph David I. Green.

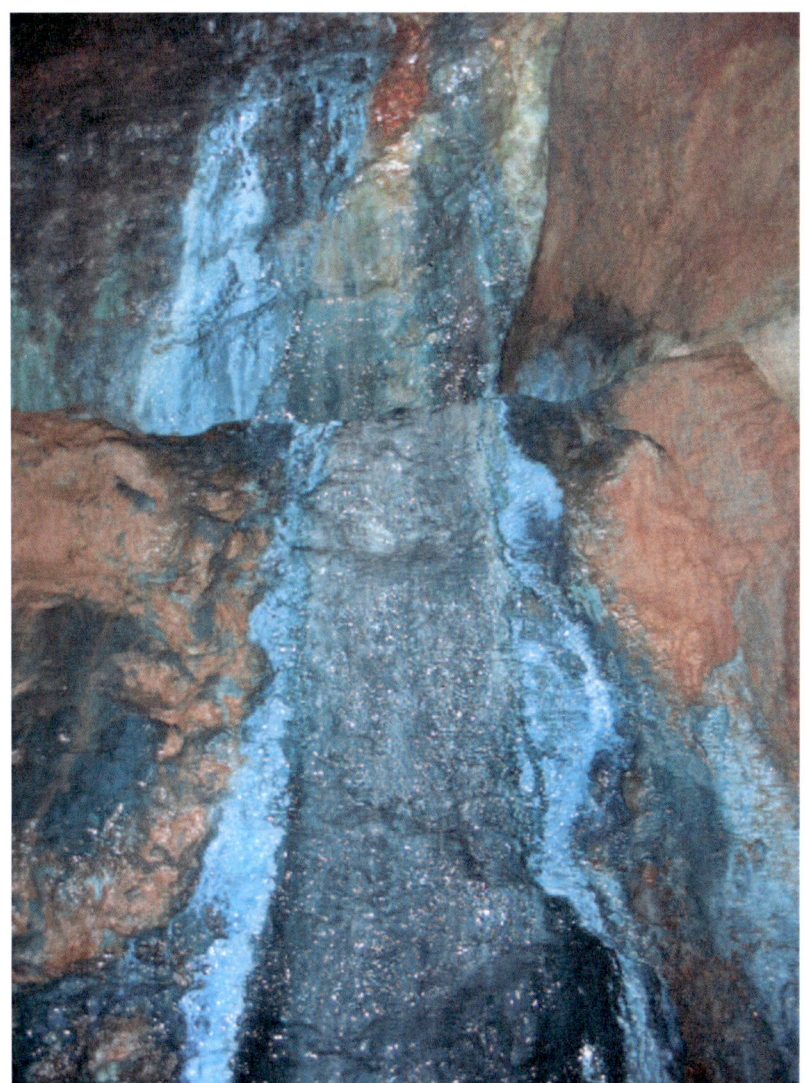

Plate 11. Supergene alteration in action: this blue deposit in Engine Vein Mine ('Blue Shaft') is made up of copper silicate gel which has been dissolved from the overlying ore and is precipitating on the mine walls.

Photograph David I. Green.

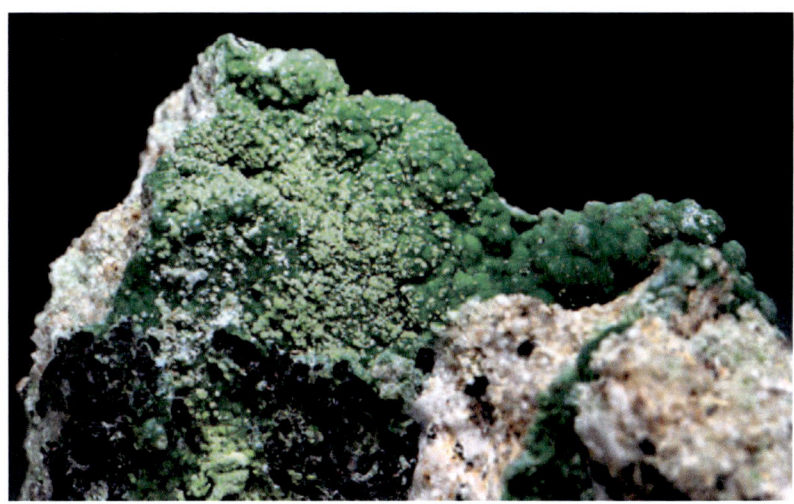

Plate 12. Dark green drusy pyromorphite crusts lining a cavity in sandstone and overgrown by paler pyromorphite pseudomorphs after an unknown mineral. The specimen is 40 mm across and from Engine Vein Mine.

Manchester Museum acc. no. N15613. Photograph David I. Green.

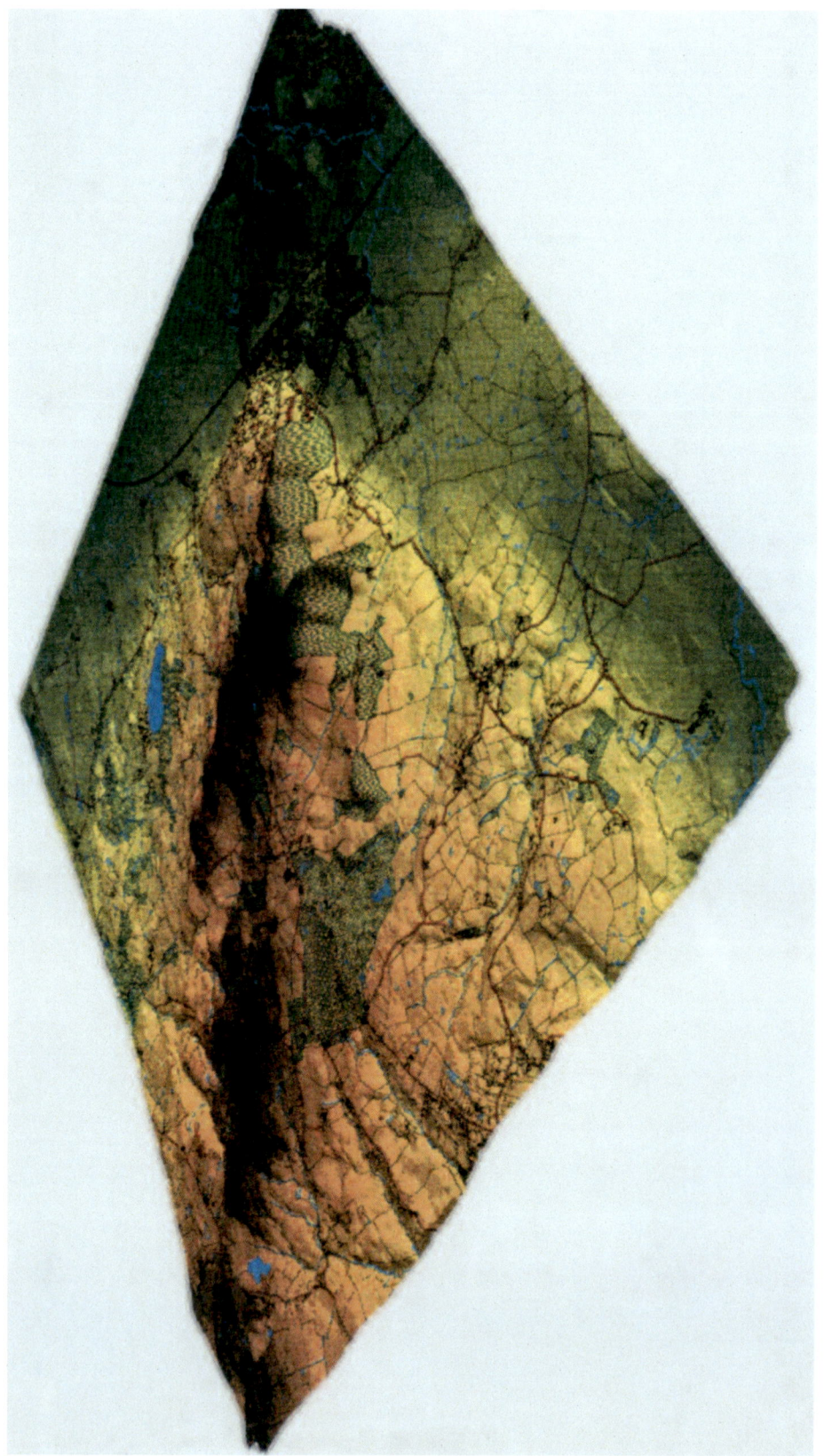

Plate 13. GIS-based MapInfo model of the Alderley Edge area as viewed from the north-east. From the present Bollin river valley at the north-east corner of the model the view extends south-westwards to beyond Radnor Mere. The Edge and the Ridge, partly masked by cloud shadow, form the high relief and along their margins moraines and other glacial landforms can be identified.

Created by Neil Matthews in the Regional Research Laboratory, School of Environment and Development, University of Manchester, based on an aerial photograph of the area defined on Ordnance Survey maps by the coordinates 383 380, 389 380, 389 374, 383 374.

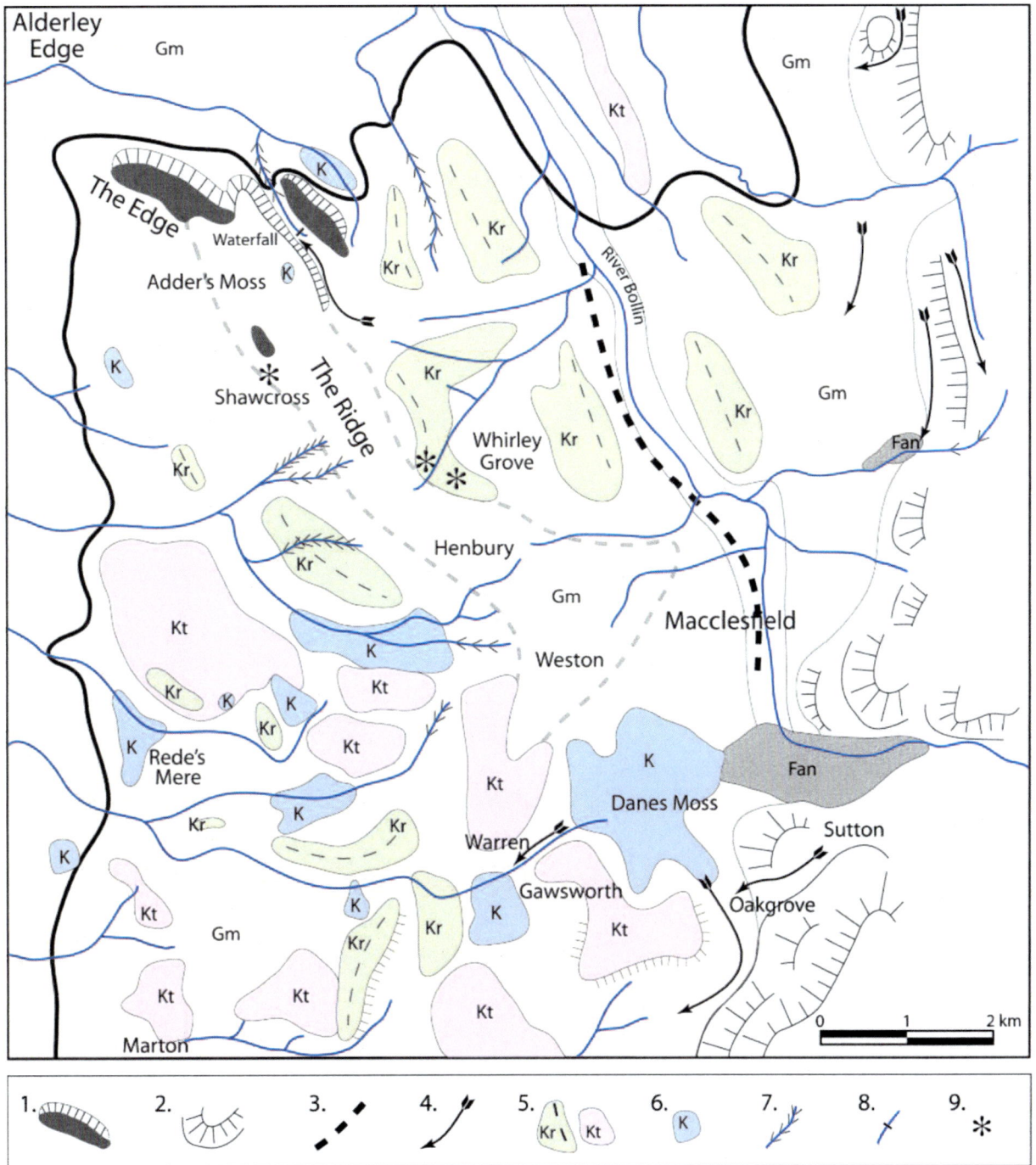

Plate 14. Geomorphological sketch map showing principal landforms associated with the glaciation of the Edge and surrounding area. (1) The Edge and other Permo-Triassic rock outcrops. (2) Pennine Upland scarp features. (3) Alignment of the Bollin buried valley. (4) Meltwater channel. (5) Glacial and glacio-fluvial landforms: Gm, ground moraine/till surface; Kt, kame terrace; Kr, kame or moraine ridges. (6) K, Kettle-hole or former ice-margin lake site. (7) Incised valley or gully. (8) Waterfall. (9) Site of former sand/gravel quarry where deformed strata were observed.

Drawn by the author and digitised by David I. Green and Julie Ballard.

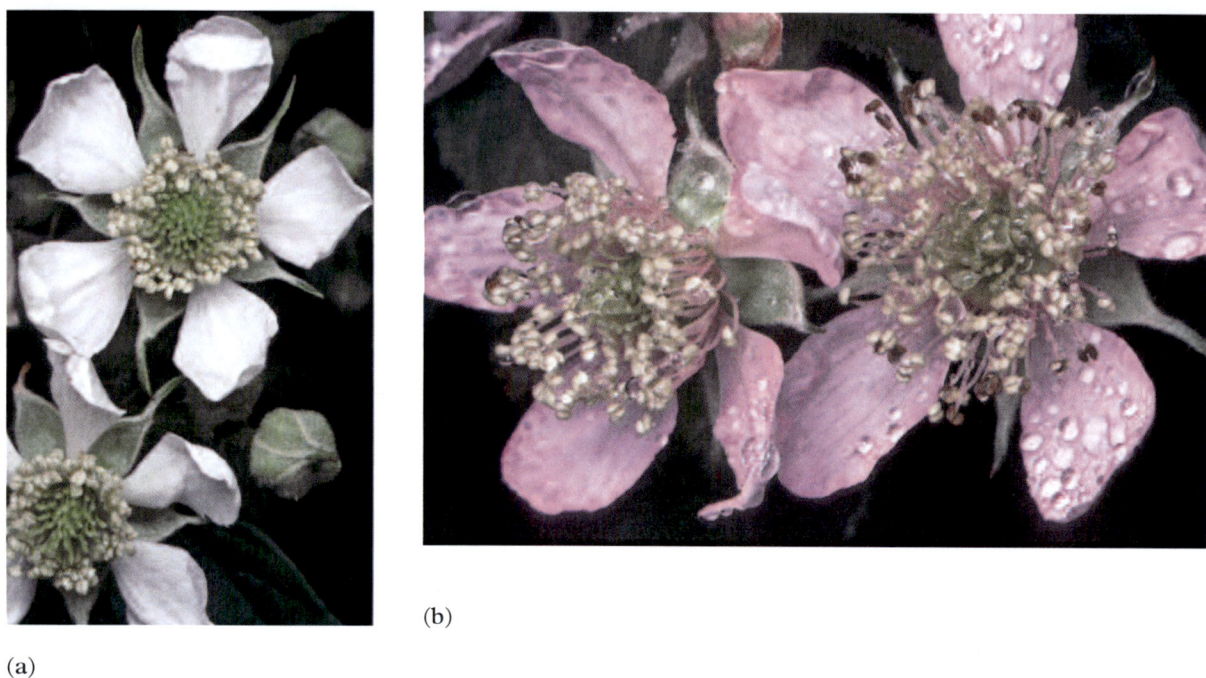

(b)

(a)

Plate 15. (a) Bailey's Bramble (*Rubus baileyi* DP Earl MS). (b) The Alderley Edge Bramble (*Rubus alderleyensis* DP Earl MS).

Photographs Sean Edwards.

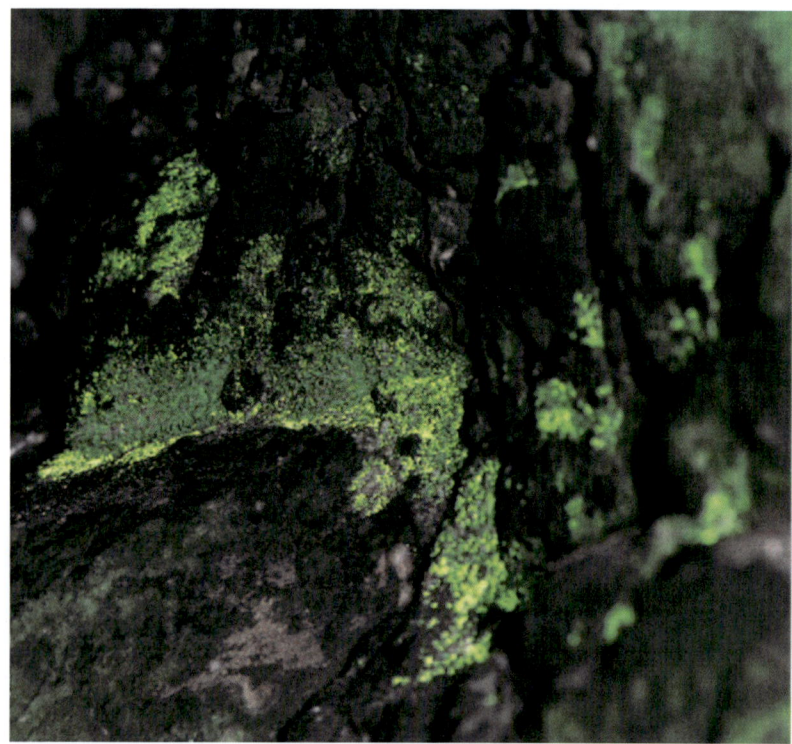

Plate 16. The moss Goblin Gold (*Schistostega pennata*)

Photographs Sean Edwards.

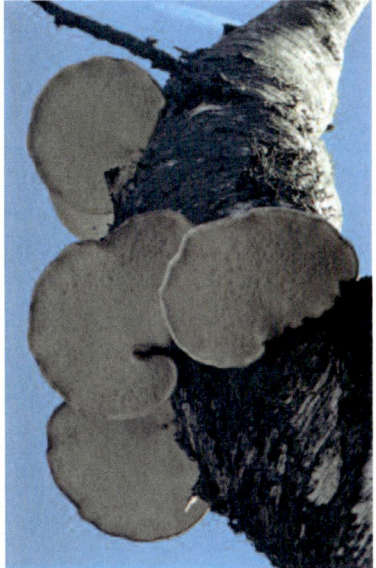 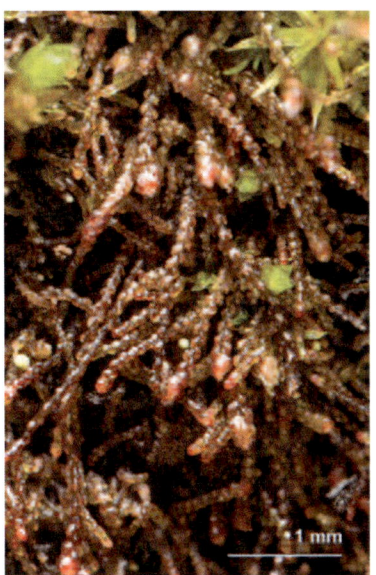

Plate 17. Birch Polypore fungus (*Piptoporus betulinus*)

Photograph Sean Edwards.

Plate 18. The threadwort *Cephaloziella divaricata*

Photograph Sean Edwards.

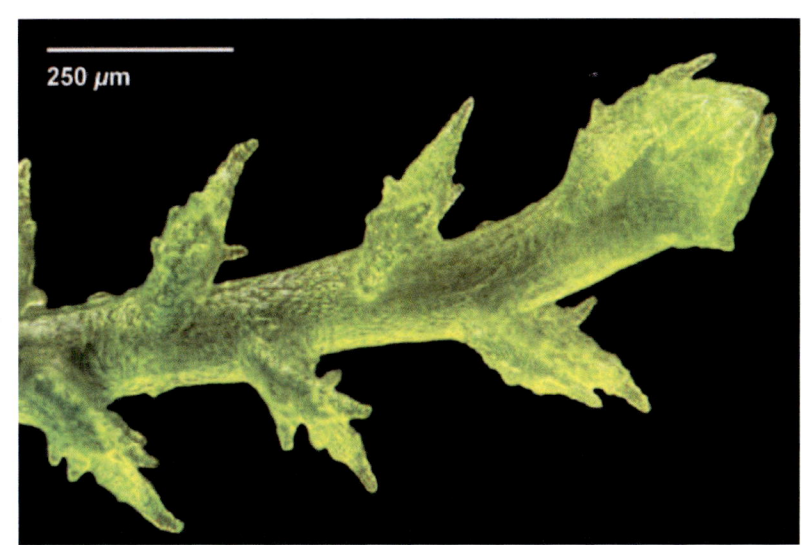

Plate 19. Great Copperwort (*Cephaloziella nicholsonii*) (scale shows 0.25 mm).

Photograph Des Callaghan.

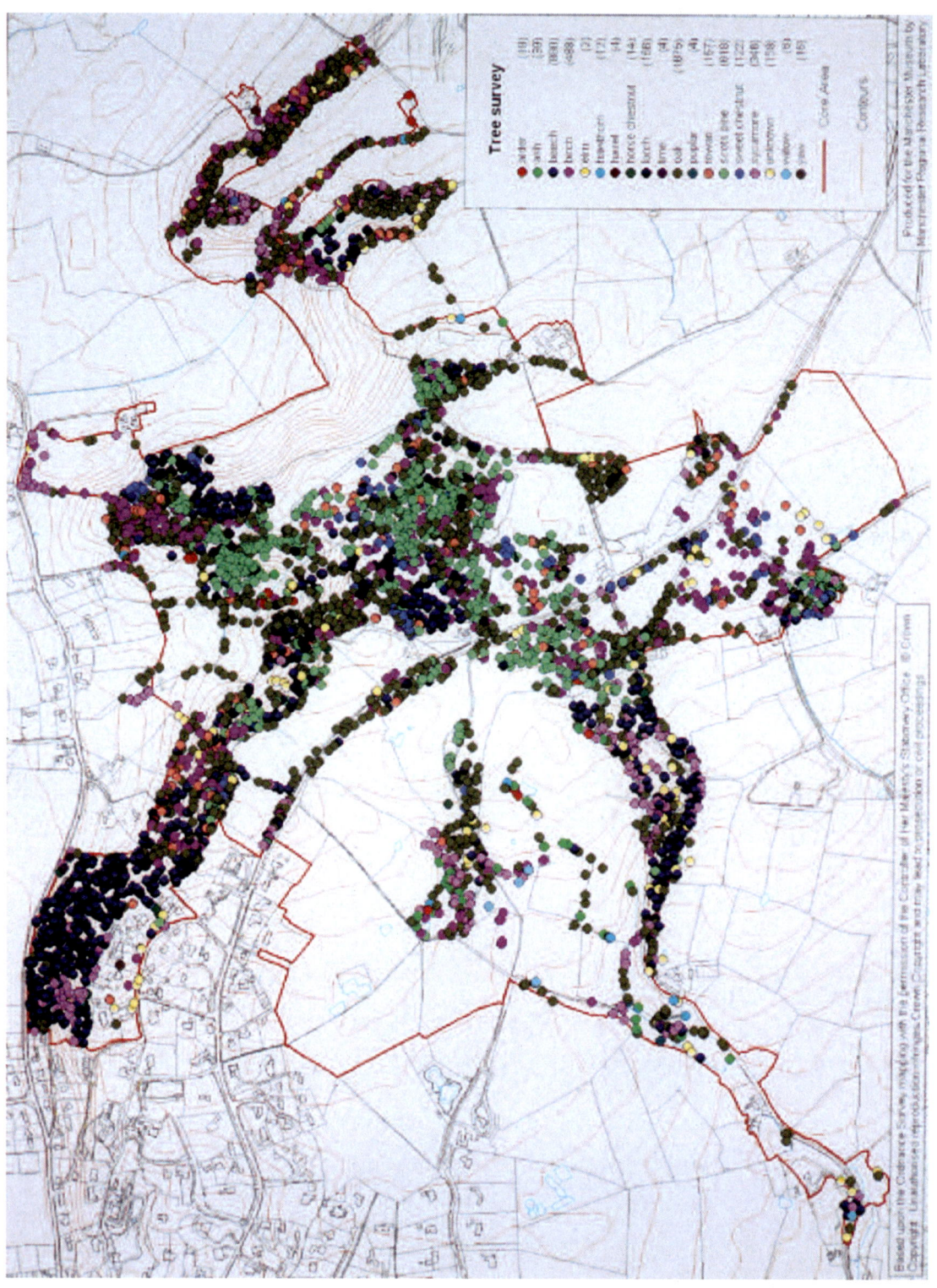

Plate 20. Distribution map of tree species in the AELP core area.

Based on the 1992 Ordnance Survey 1:25,000 Pathfinder map sheet 759, with the permission of the Controller of Her Majesty's Stationery Office, Crown copyright October 2013.

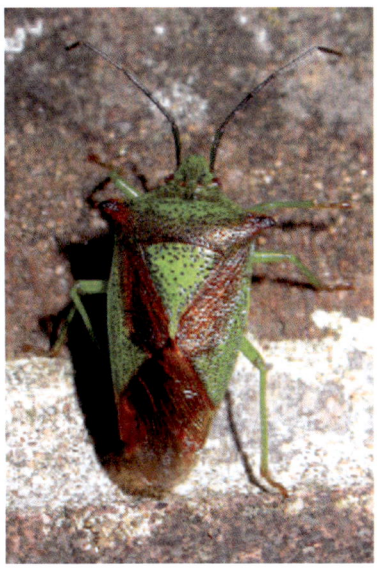

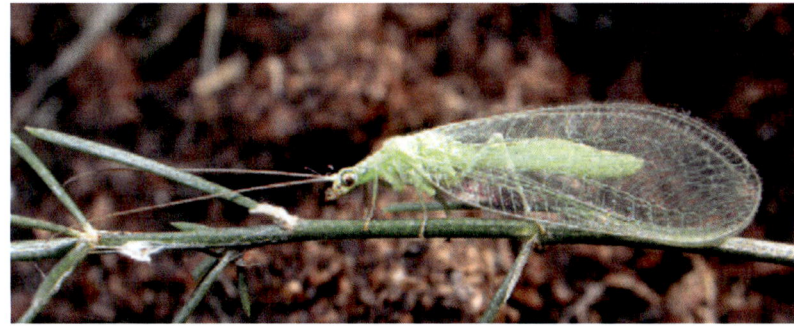

Plate 22. Common Green Lacewing (*Chrysoperla carnea*). Its larvae are fierce predators of greenflies, whiteflies and other garden pests.

Photograph David I. Green.

Plate 21. Hawthorn Shieldbug (*Acanthosoma haemorrhoidale*), widespread and common across Britain in wooded areas.

Photograph David I. Green.

Plate 23. Field Grasshopper (*Chorthippus brunneus*), a medium-sized grasshopper widespread throughout much of the British Isles.

Photograph David I. Green.

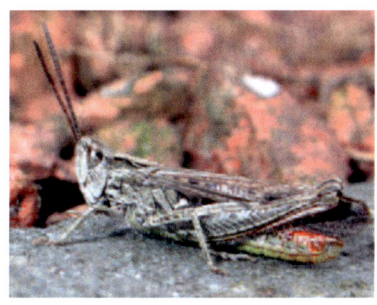

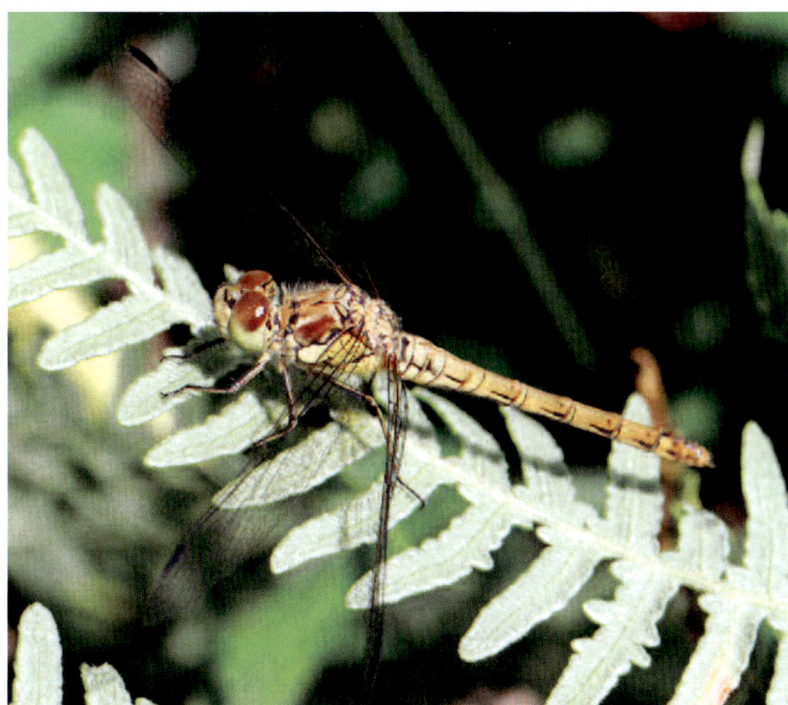

Plate 24. Common Darter (*Sympetrum striolatum*; female).

Photograph David I. Green.

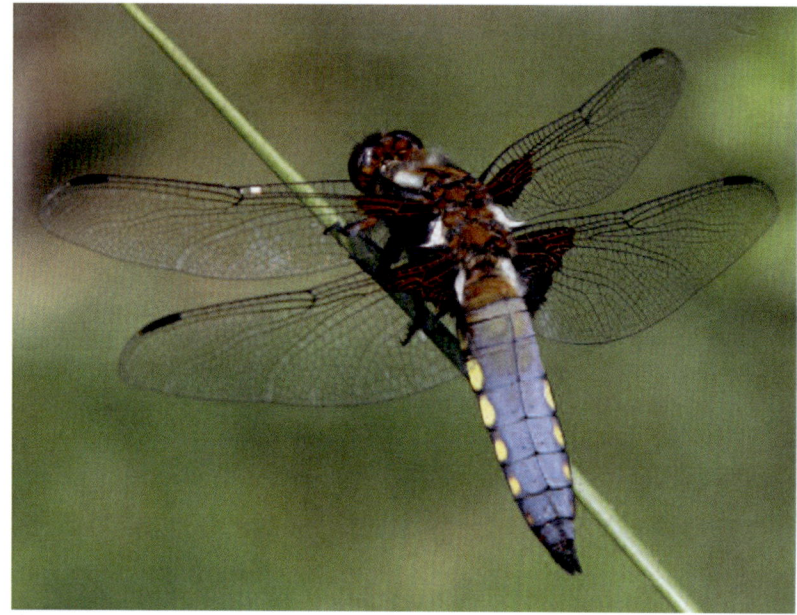

Plate 25. Broad-bodied Chaser (*Libellula depressa*; male), widespread in Cheshire but rare at the Edge.

Photograph David Kitching.

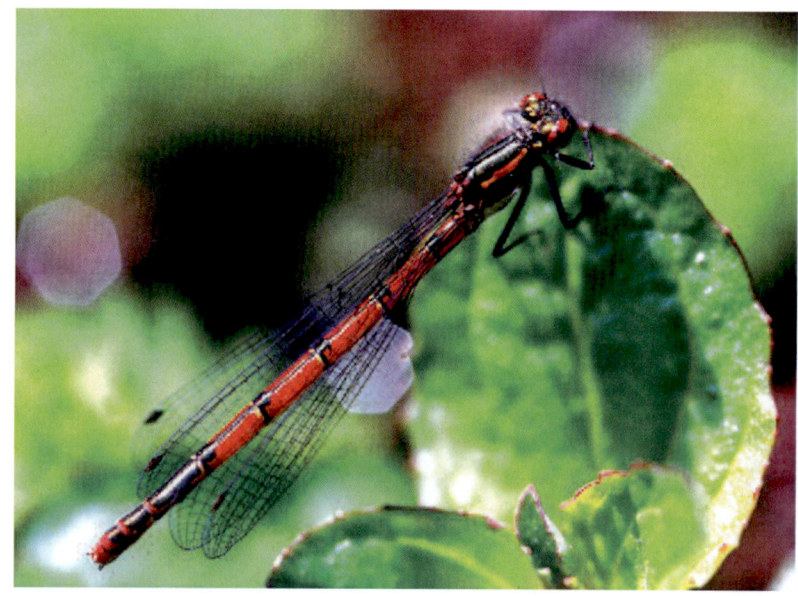

Plate 26. Large Red Damselfly (*Pyrrhosoma nymphula*; female): can be seen in spring and can be found on almost any habitat near water.

Photograph David I. Green.

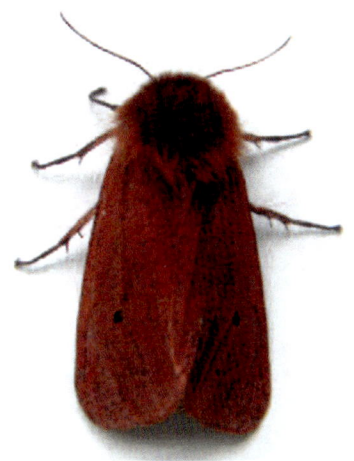

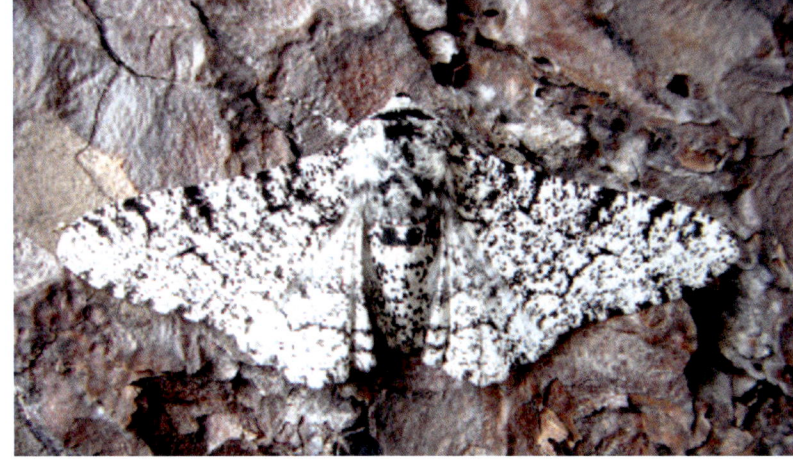

Plate 27. Ruby Tiger Moth (*Phragmatobia fuliginosa*), a common species throughout Britain.

Photograph Michael Dockery.

Plate 28. Peppered Moth (*Biston betularia*; typical form), a favourite of geneticists investigating the problem of industrial melanism.

Photograph Michael Dockery.

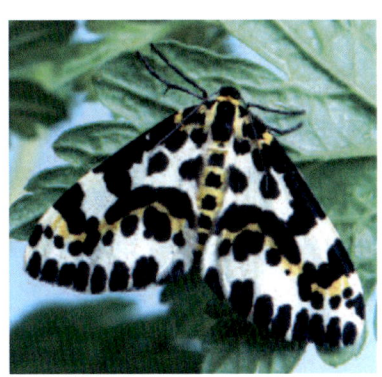

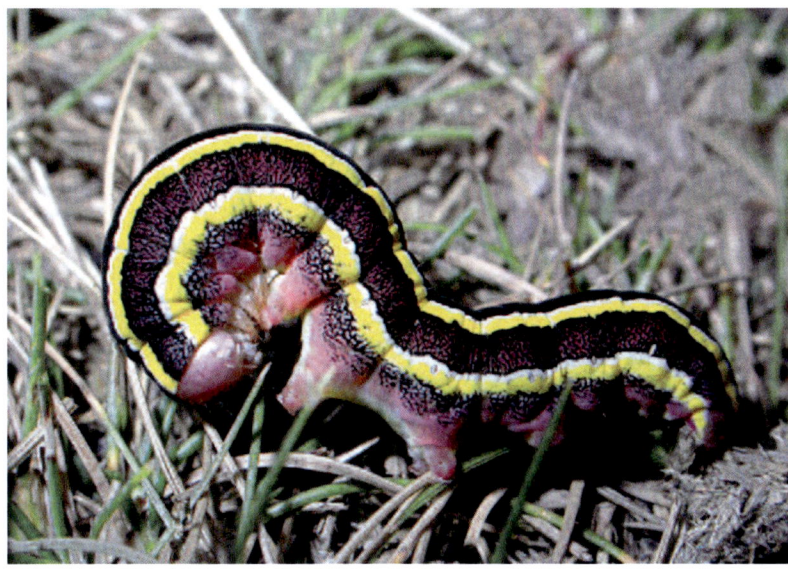

Plate 29. Magpie Moth (*Abraxas grossulariata*), a common garden species whose caterpillars can damage currant and gooseberry bushes.

Photograph Roy Leverton.

Plate 30. Broom Moth caterpillar (*Melanchra pisi*): can be seen in a wide range of habitats, including gardens.

Photograph David I. Green.

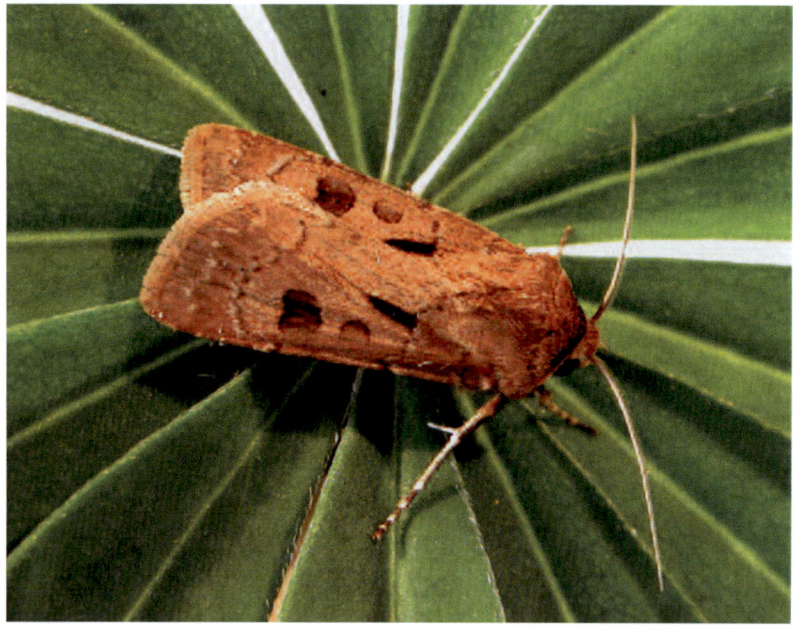

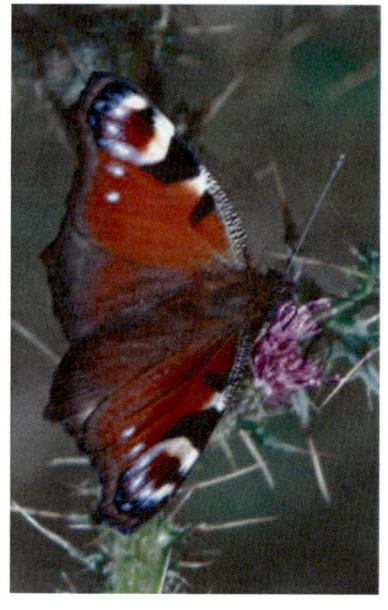

Plate 31. Heart and Dart Moth (*Agrotis exclamationis*), a common species throughout most of Britain.

Photograph Michael Dockery.

Plate 32. Peacock Butterfly (*Aglais io*), a common resident on the Edge.

Photograph Roger Dennis.

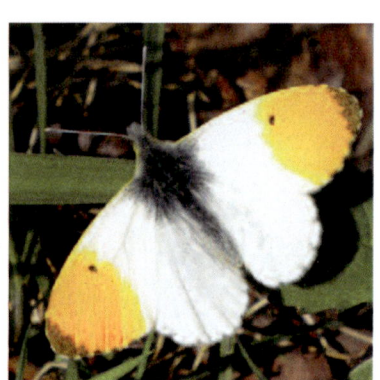

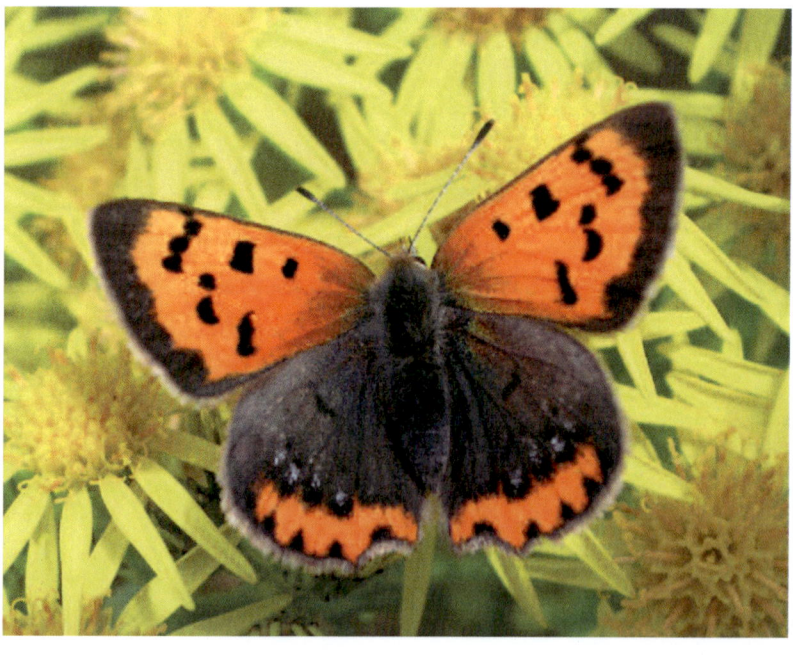

Plate 33. Orange-tip Butterfly (*Anthocharis cardamines*; male), another common resident on the Edge.

Photograph Peter B. Hardy.

Plate 34. Small Copper Butterfly (*Lycaena phlaeas*), an uncommon resident on the Edge.

Photograph Peter B. Hardy.

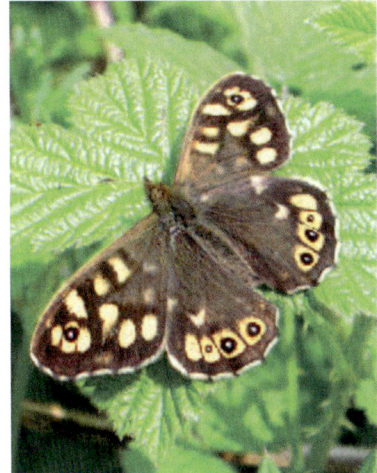

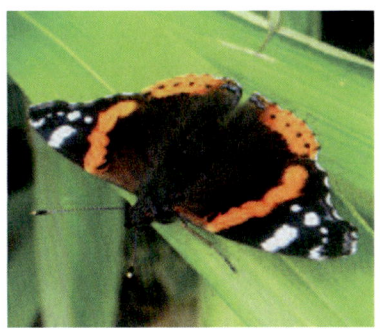

Plate 35. Speckled Wood Butterfly (*Pararge aegeria*; male), a species that has recently colonised the Edge.

Photograph Peter B. Hardy.

Plate 36. Red Admiral Butterfly (*Vanessa atalanta*), a migrant from the Continent.

Photograph Peter B. Hardy.

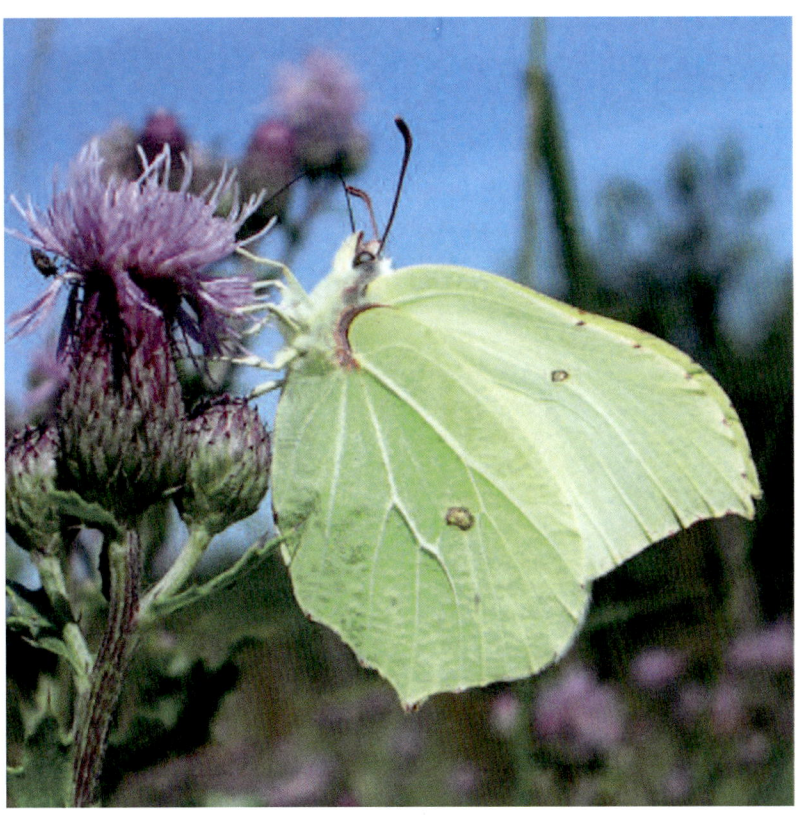

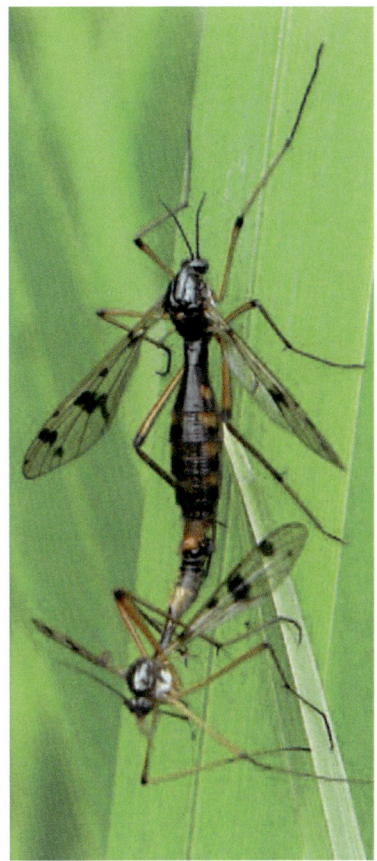

Plate 37. Brimstone Butterfly (*Gonepteryx rhamni*; male), another uncommon resident on the Edge.

Photograph Peter B. Hardy.

Plate 38. A mating pair of the Fold-winged Cranefly (*Ptychoptera contaminata*): the female is the larger.

Photograph Steven Falk.

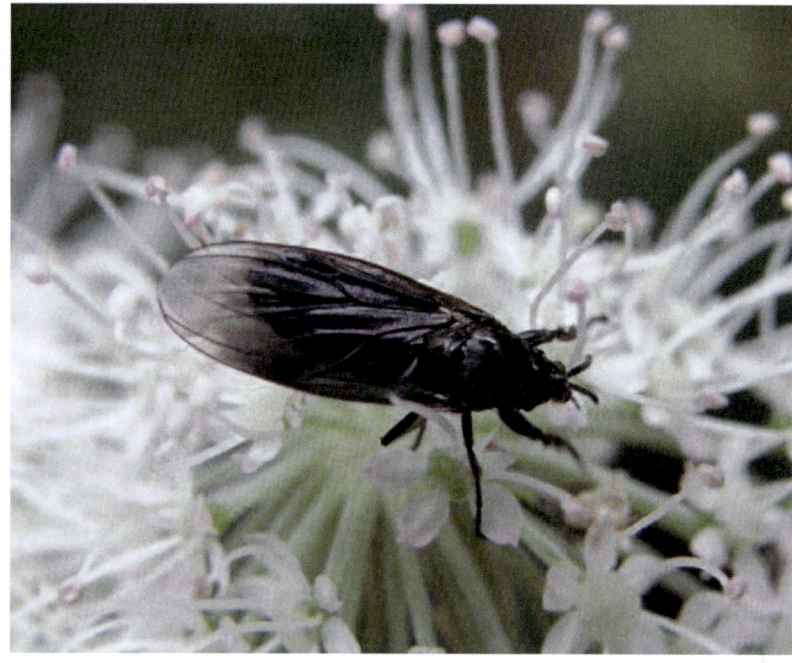

Plate 39. Fever-fly (*Dilophus febrilis*; female). Common and widespread around low vegetation in April and May.

Photograph Steven Falk.

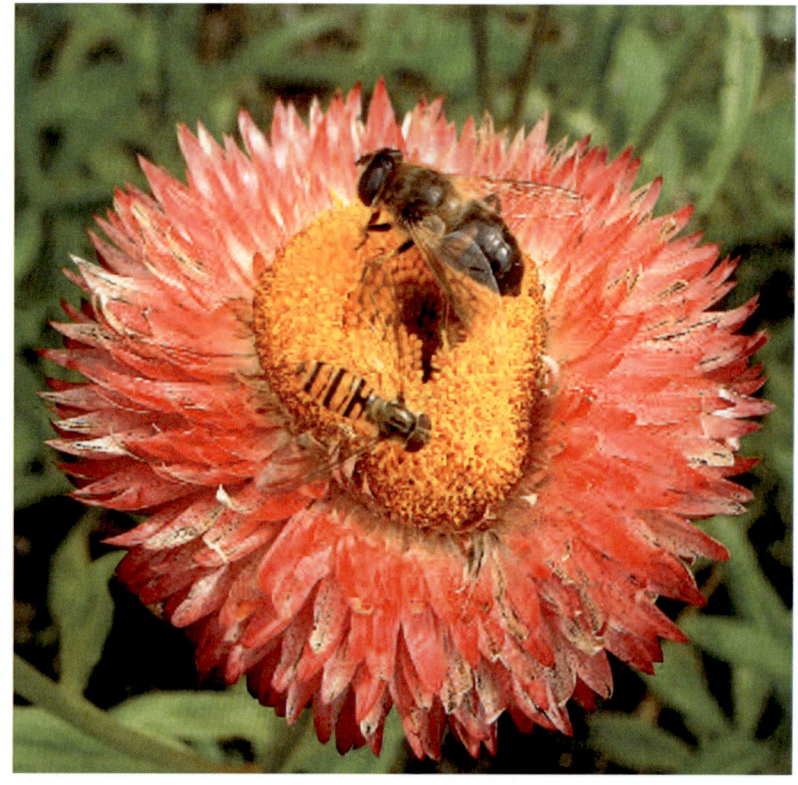

Plate 40. Hoverflies *Eristalis tenax* (Dronefly, larger) and *Episyrphus balteatus* (smaller), two species which can commonly be seen in British gardens.

Photograph Yvonne Golding.

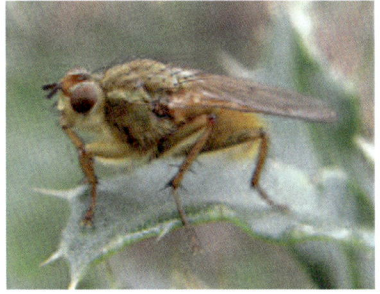

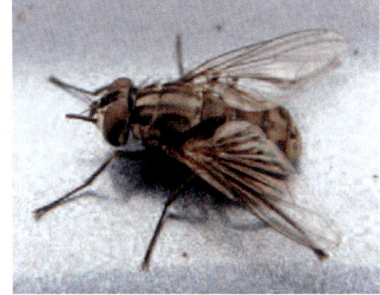

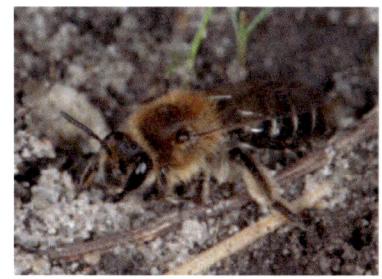

Plate 41. Yellow Dung-fly (*Scathophaga stercoraria*): can be seen on the Edge crowding on pats of cow or horse dung.

Photograph Steven Falk.

Plate 42. Stablefly (*Stomoxys calcitrans*), an obnoxious blood-sucking species that can be seen around open pastures on the Edge and can inflict painful bites.

Photograph Steven Falk.

Plate 43. Mining Bee (*Andrena barbirabris*; female), a common species restricted to places with exposures of sand.

Photograph Mike Edwards.

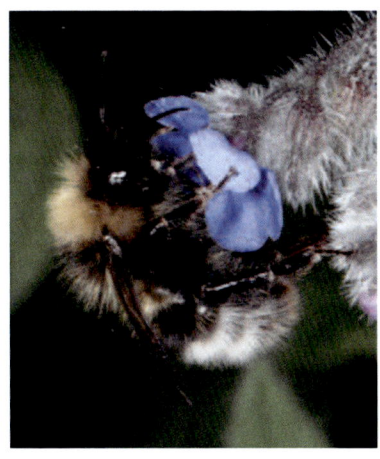

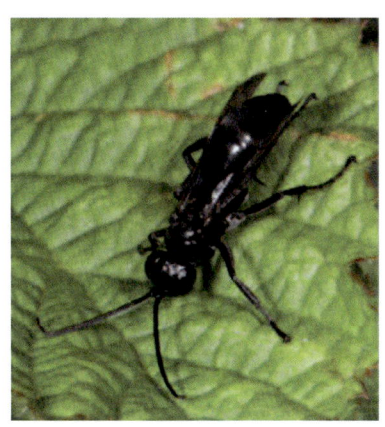

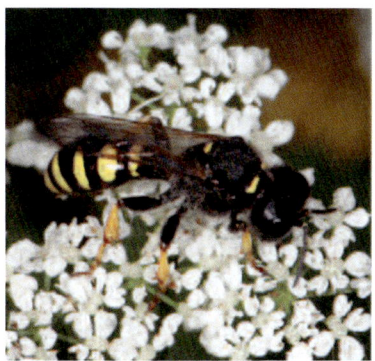

Plate 44. Four-coloured Cuckoo Bee (*Bombus (Psithyrus) sylvestris*), known to aggressively attack colonies of other bumblebees.

Photograph Mike Edwards.

Plate 45. Spider-Hunting Wasp (*Anoplius nigerrimus*), found in a wide range of habitats and reported to prey on Wolf and Nursery-Web Spiders.

Photograph Mike Edwards.

Plate 46. Slender-Bodied Digger Wasp (*Crabro cribrarius*), a large solitary wasp which nests in sandy soil and stocks its burrows with flies.

Photograph Mike Edwards.

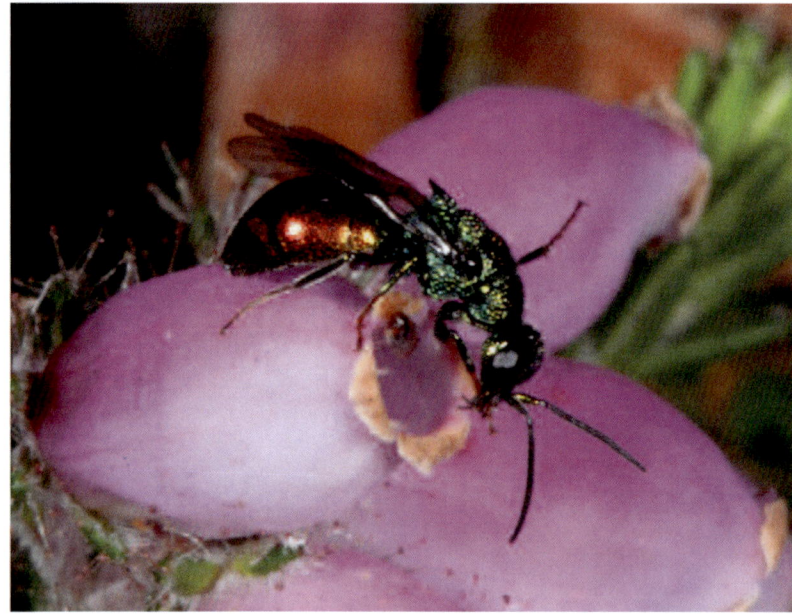

Plate 47. Ruby-tailed Wasp (*Elampus panzeri*), a brood parasite of digger wasps (*Sphecidae*).

Photograph Mike Edwards.

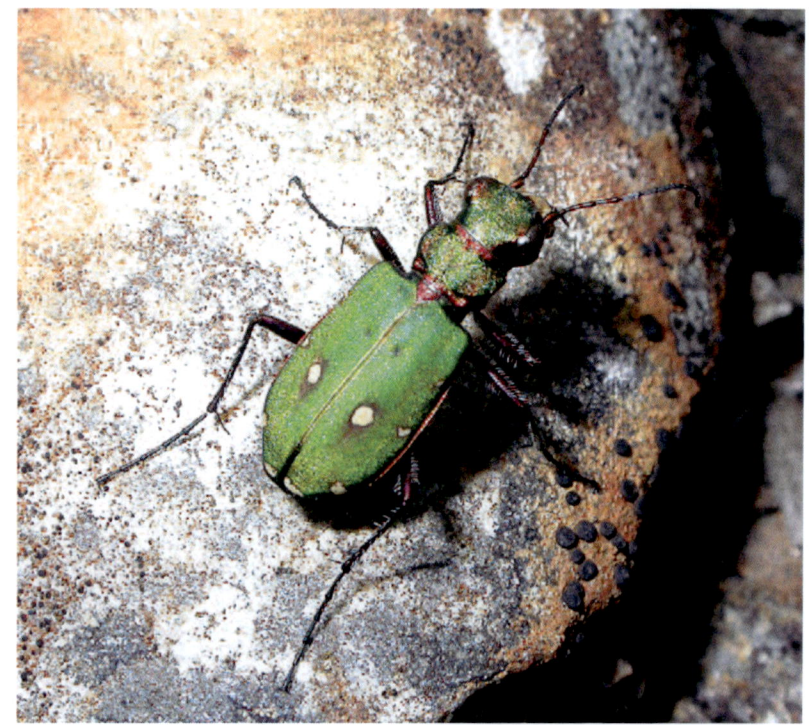

Plate 48. Green Tiger Beetle (*Cicindela campestris*), an active predator, usually seen in early summer on heaths, dunes and sandy places

Photograph David I. Green.

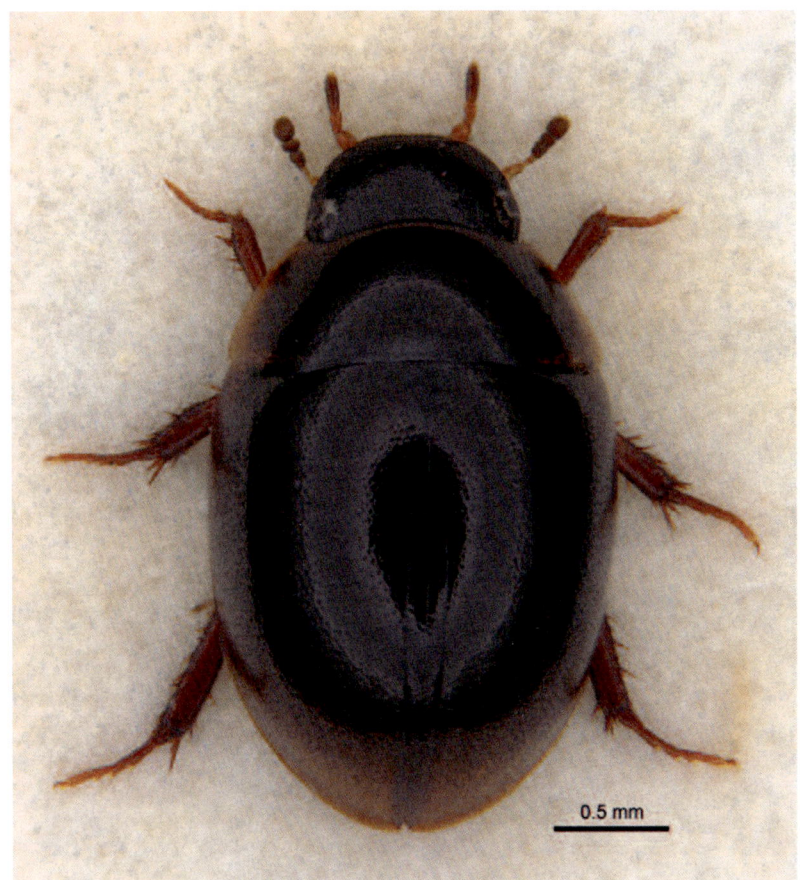

Plate 49. A museum specimen of *Anacaena globulus*, a common representative of the Scavenger Water Beetles, which can be found in rich mud at pond edges

Photograph Katherine Child.

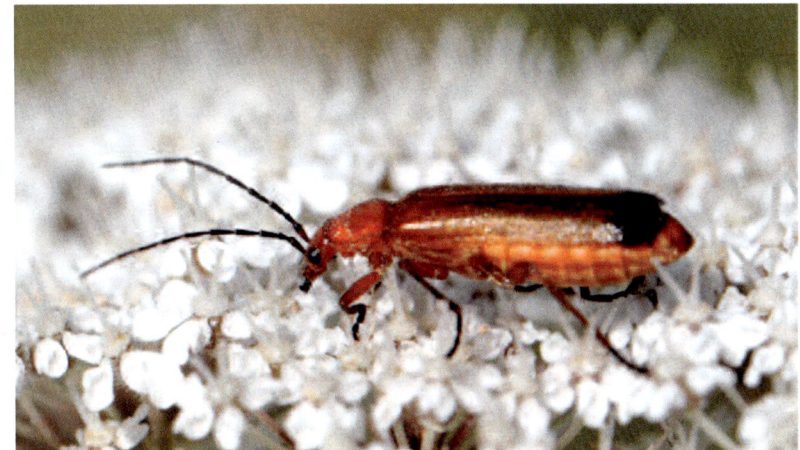

Plate 50. Common Red Soldier Beetle (*Rhagonycha fulva*), a frequent visitor to open-structured flowers such as members of the carrot family.

Photograph David I. Green.

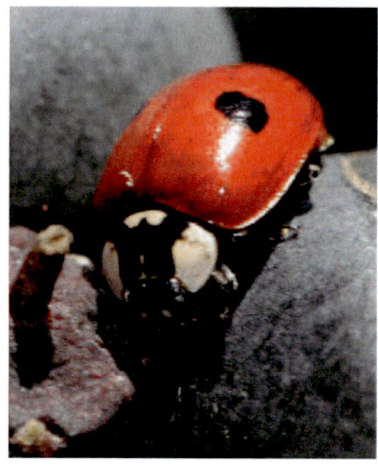

Plate 51. Two-spotted Ladybird (*Adalia bipunctata*), a fairly common species and one of 'England's true guardian angels' (see text, p. 275).

Photograph David I. Green.

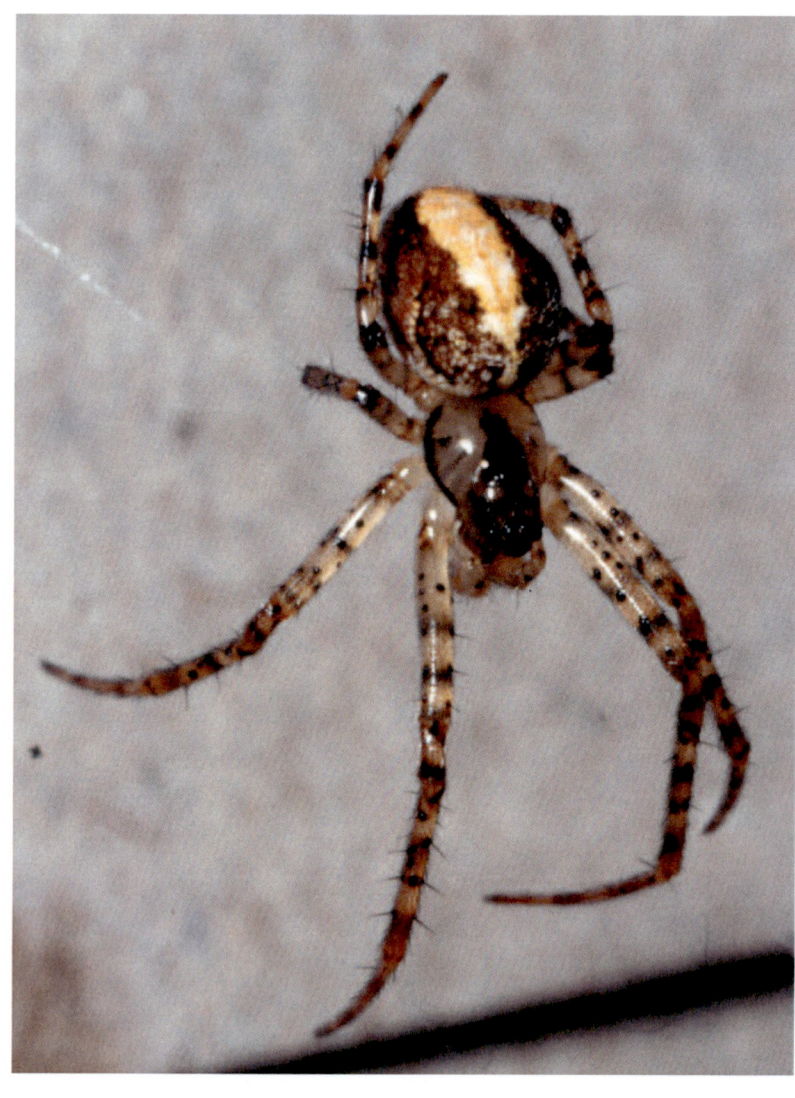

Plate 52. Long-jawed Spider (*Metellina merianae*, colour variety *celata*; female), a common dweller in entrances to old mines.

Photograph Martin Askins.

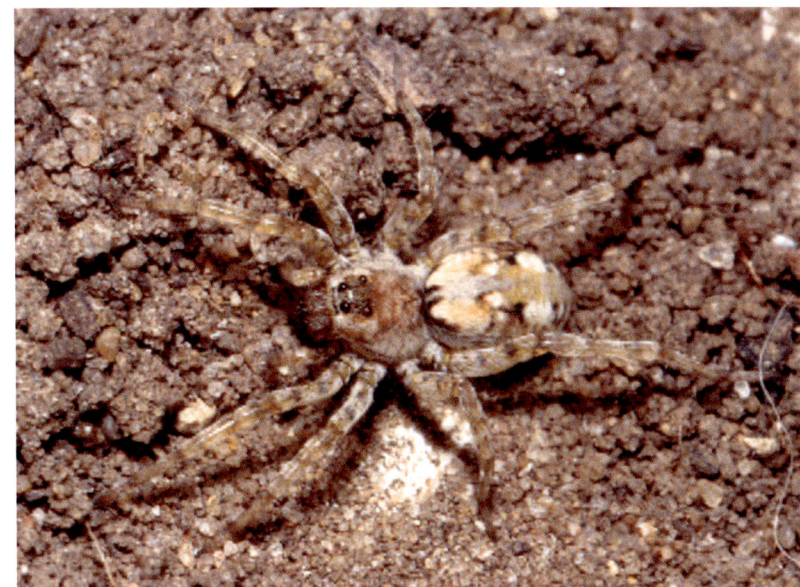

Plate 53. Cryptic Wolf Spider (*Arctosa perita*; female), dwelling in the Sandhills region.

Photograph Martin Askins.

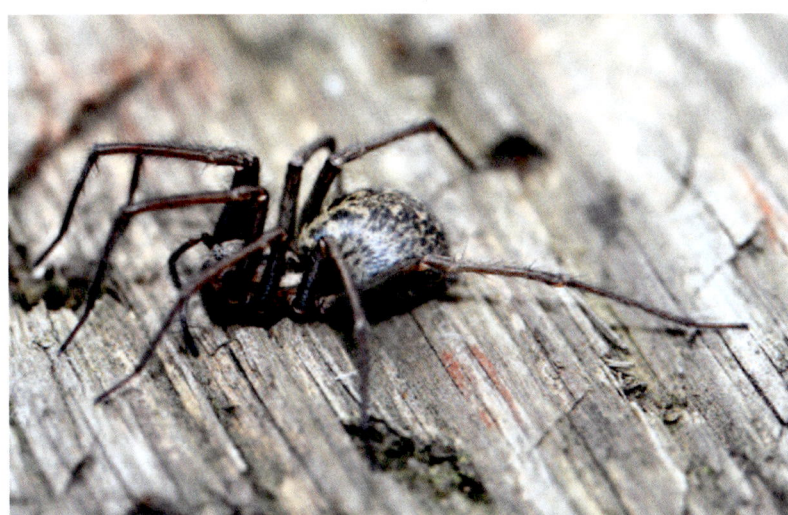

Plate 54. The Giant House Spider (*Tegenaria gigantea*) occurs in houses and out-buildings as well as outside.

Photograph Peter Nicholson.

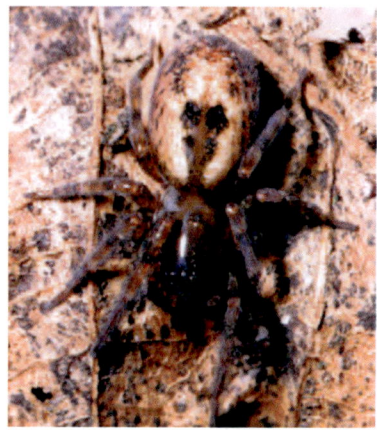

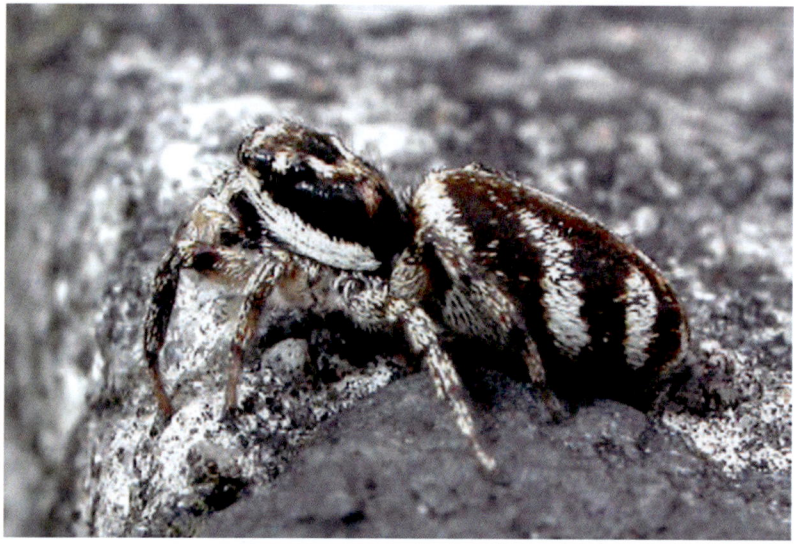

Plate 55. Window Spider
(*Amaurobius fenestralis*: female),
which builds retreats in holes in
rocks and under tree bark.

Photograph Martin Askins.

Plate 56. Zebra Spider (*Salticus scenicus*), a common dweller of stony
walls and rocks.

Photograph David I. Green.

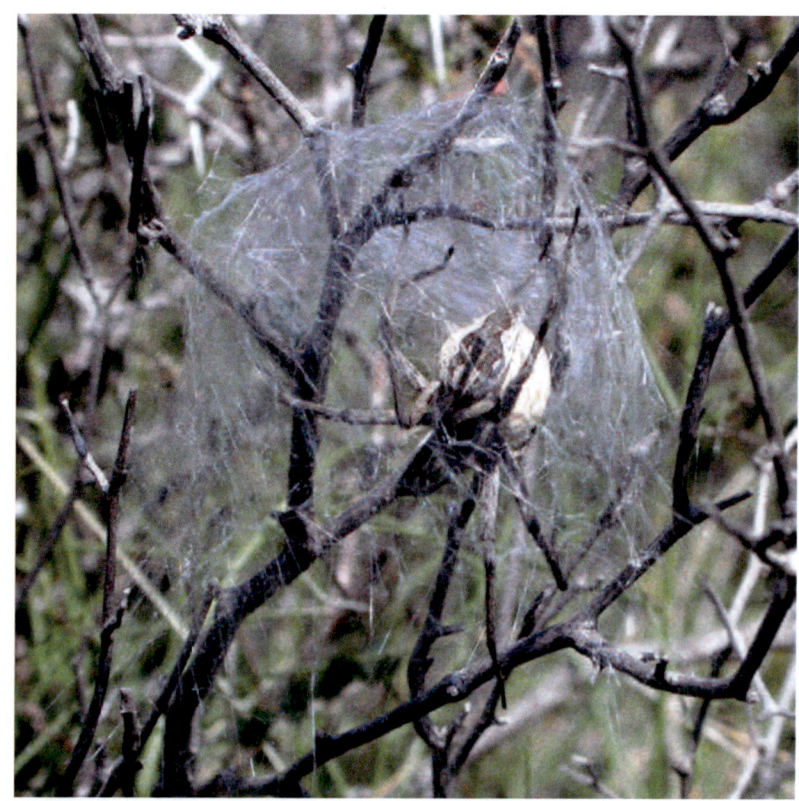

Plate 57. Nursery-web Spider
(*Pisaura mirabilis*; female) with
egg sac inside its nursery web.

Photograph Martin Askins.

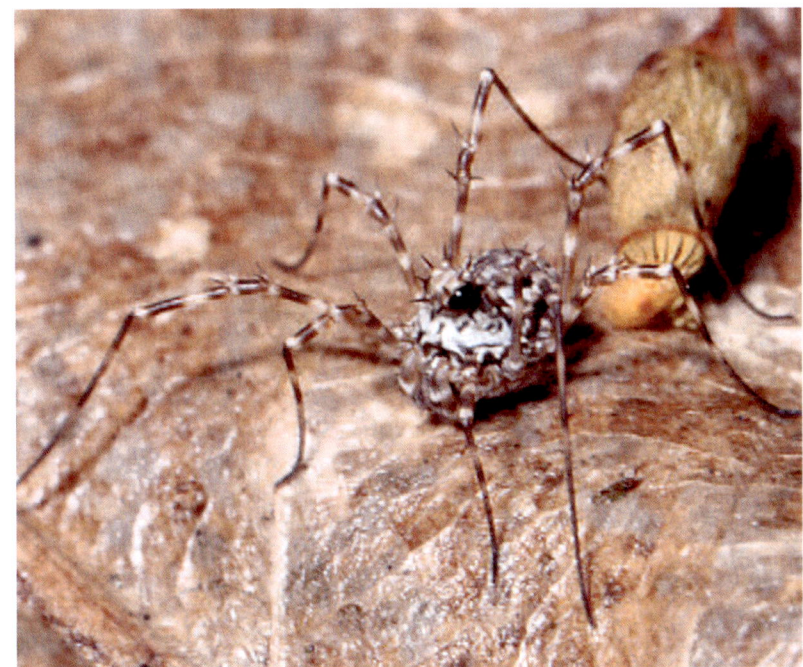

Plate 58. The tiny harvestman *Megabunus diadema* can be found on rocks.

Photograph Martin Askins.

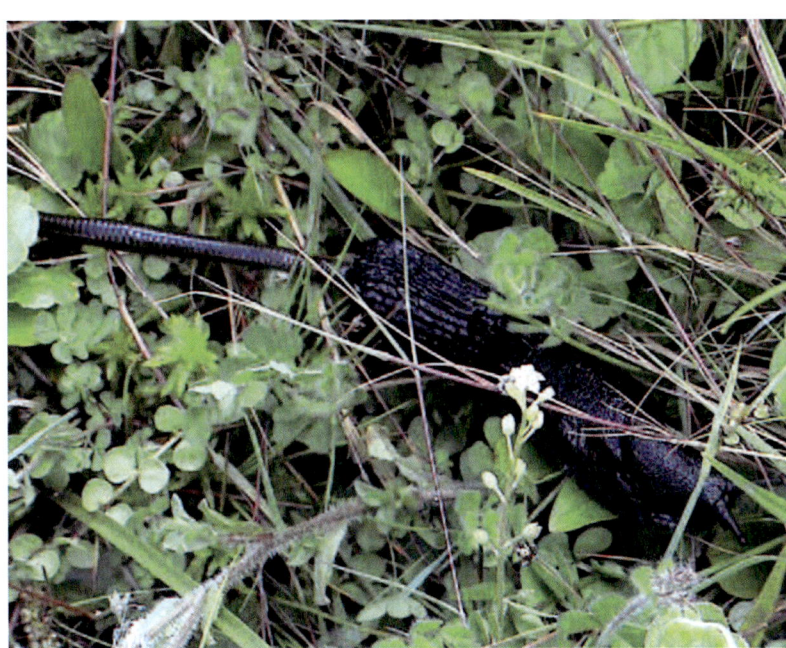

Plate 59. Horse Leech (*Haemopis sanguisuga*, left) attacking a Great Black Slug (*Arion ater*, right).

Photograph John Walters.

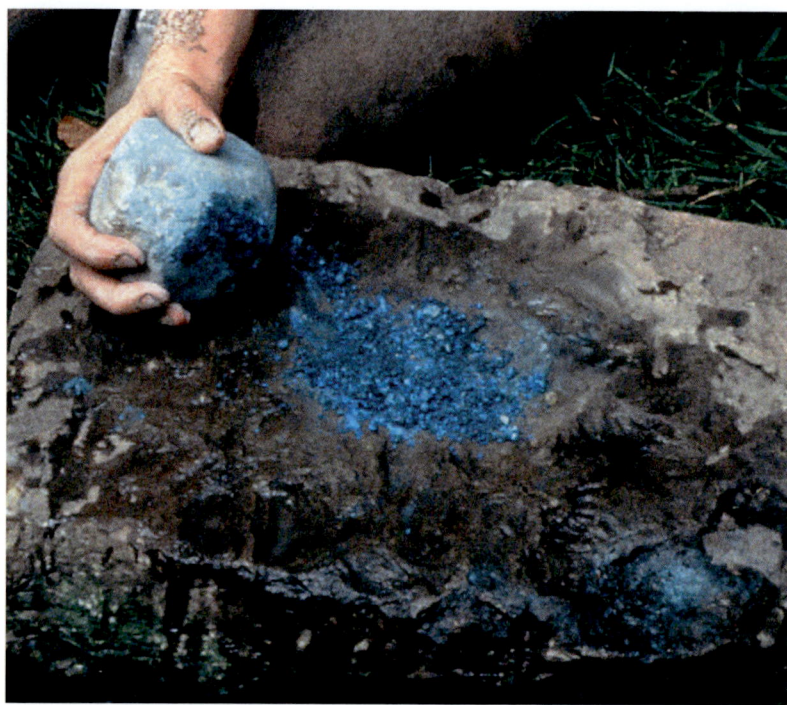

Plate 60. Crushed azurite nodules from Engine Vein.

Photograph Timberlake.

Plate 61 *(page XXIX, opposite)*. Map of Leycester lands by Broadheath, Over Alderley, as surveyed in 1636 by Thomas Hibbert and Henry Overton at the time of one of the quarrels between the Stanleys and the Leycesters over control of Broadheath. The heath is shown as the hatched area in the middle of the Leycester lands. As on some other early maps, south is here at the top.

Image copyright Christie's Images Limited 1999.

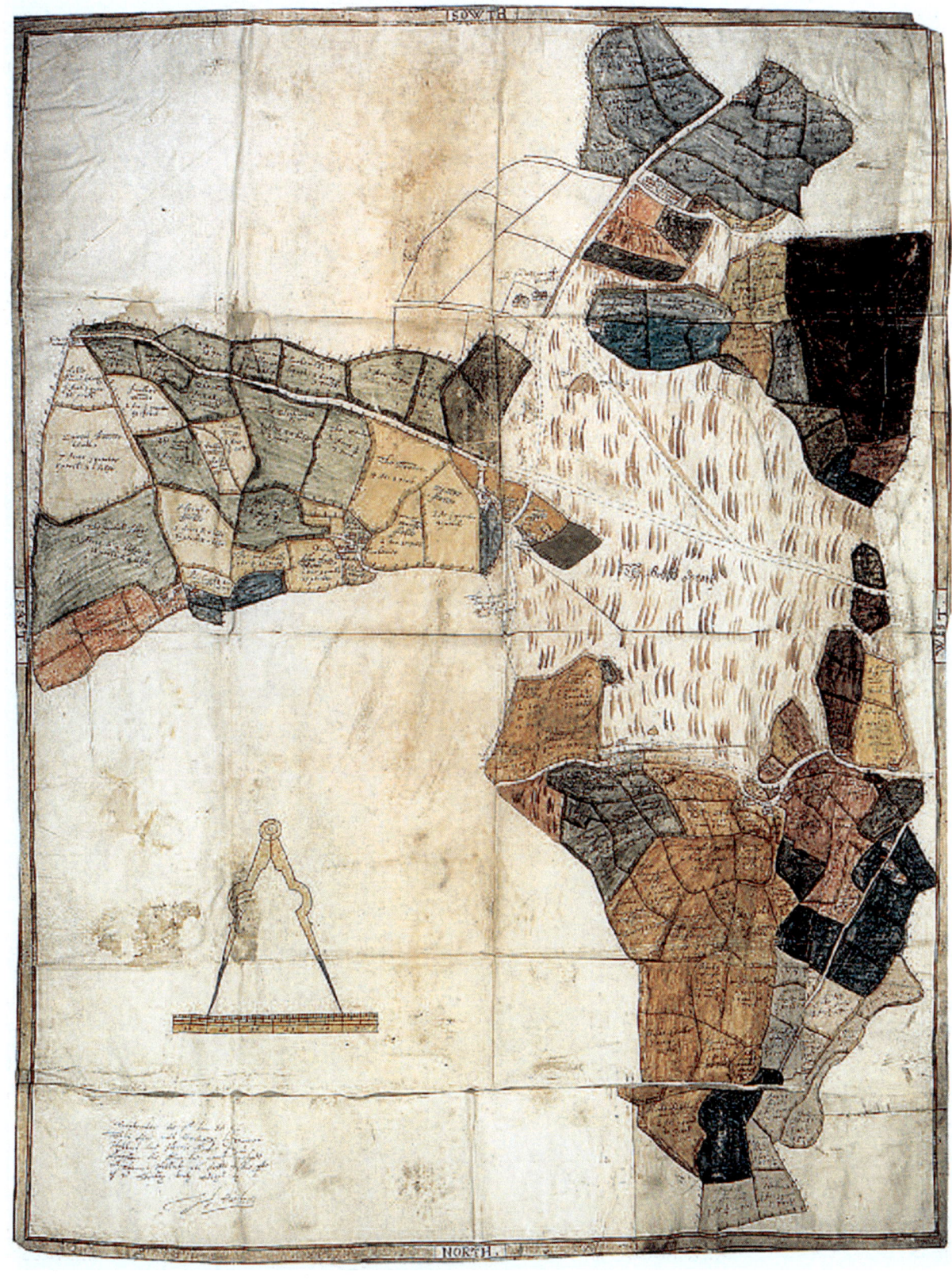

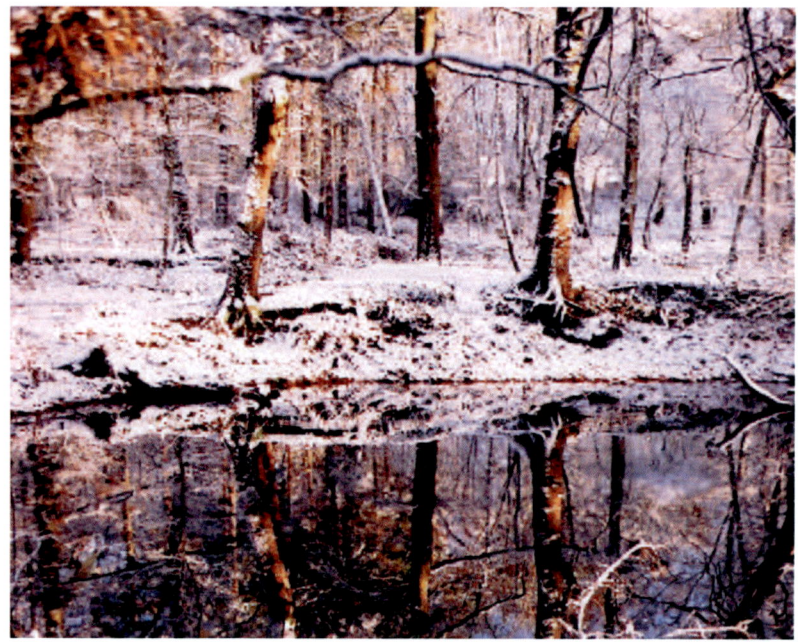

(a)

Plate 62. (a) Naturally
regenerated woodland and
(b) 'landscaped' woodland on
Alderley Edge.

Photographs Christopher Widger.

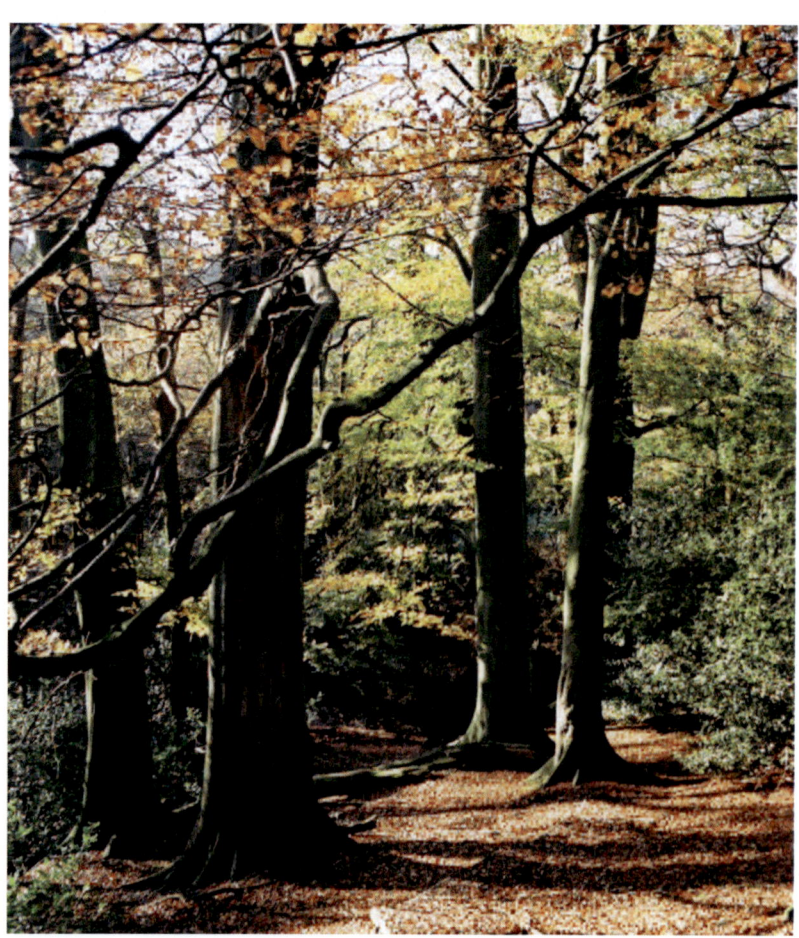

(b)

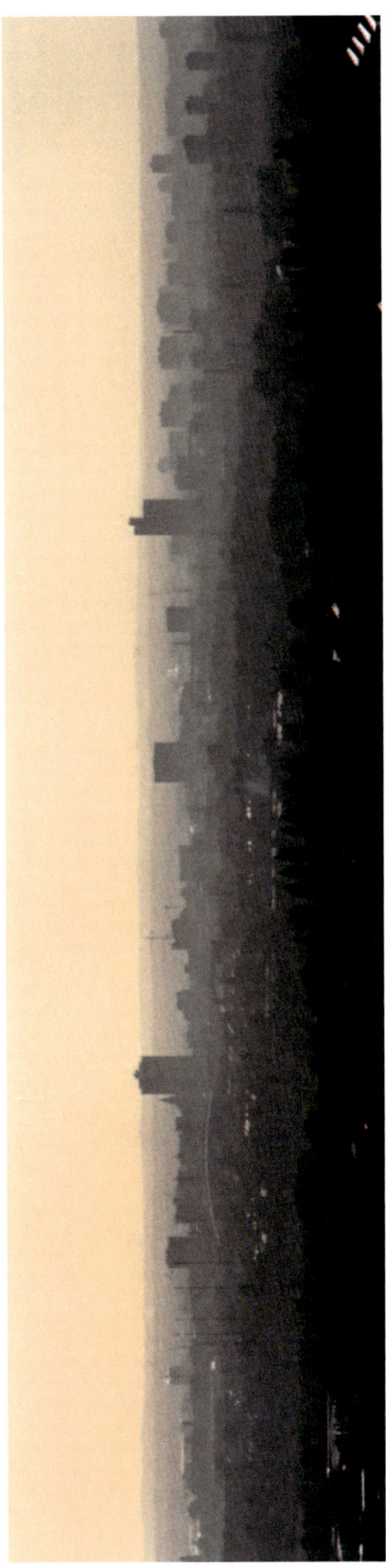

Plate 63. 'Escape': the Manchester cityscape from east of Ashton-under-Lyne.

Photograph Aidan O'Rourke.

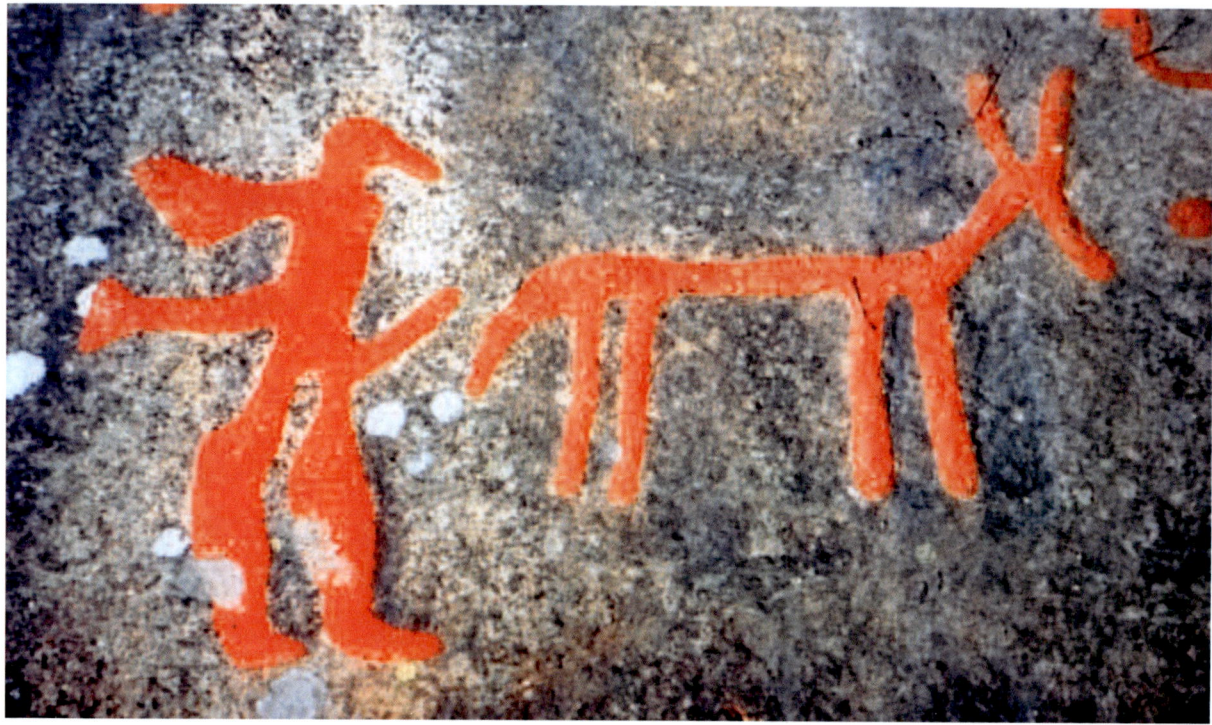

Plate 64. Bronze Age rock painting of a bird-man with mare.

From Johnsen (2005: pl. 58), courtesy of Bogforlaget Frydenlund.

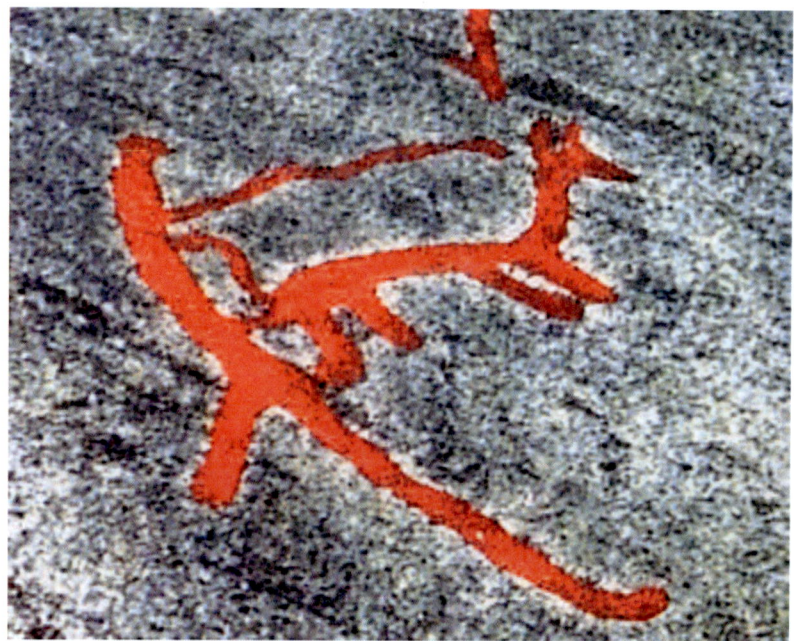

Plate 65. Bronze Age rock painting of a man copulating with a mare.

From Johnsen (2005: pl. 57), courtesy of Bogforlaget Frydenlund.

Part I

Introductory

The background to the Alderley Edge Landscape Project

A. J. N. W. Prag

This is the SHOVEL that dug the COPPER, that fetched the Roman, who sunk the SHAFT that hid the POT till we found it.

These are the RAILS that fetched the MAN from Manchester mills, who built the HOUSE on ALDERLEY EDGE with a garden.

This is the WORT that grew on the HILLS, that the MINER heaped when he hacked the STOPES under the ground of the STANLEYS.

This is the place where the Sleeping Knights lie.
And is this the WIZARD to wake them?

It all started with a shovel, a singer of tales and an archaeologist. The singer of tales found the shovel (it was prehistoric) that had been hidden for very many years, and he told the archaeologist. Together they delved – not alone – and together they began to spin a tale that caught up many others in its spinning and in its telling. That is the tale told in this book, but first it needs a few words of introduction.

When I arrived in Manchester in 1969 as a sadly ignorant southerner to take up the post of Keeper of Archaeology at the Manchester Museum, I found in the Museum collections a small assemblage of crude hammer stones and a few other prehistoric stone implements (see Figure 2.2) from a place called Alderley Edge on the southern outskirts of Manchester (Plate 1, Figure 1.1). I heard stories of early mining there, of Roman and even Bronze Age miners, but any traces of their work seemed to have been largely obscured by later digging and,

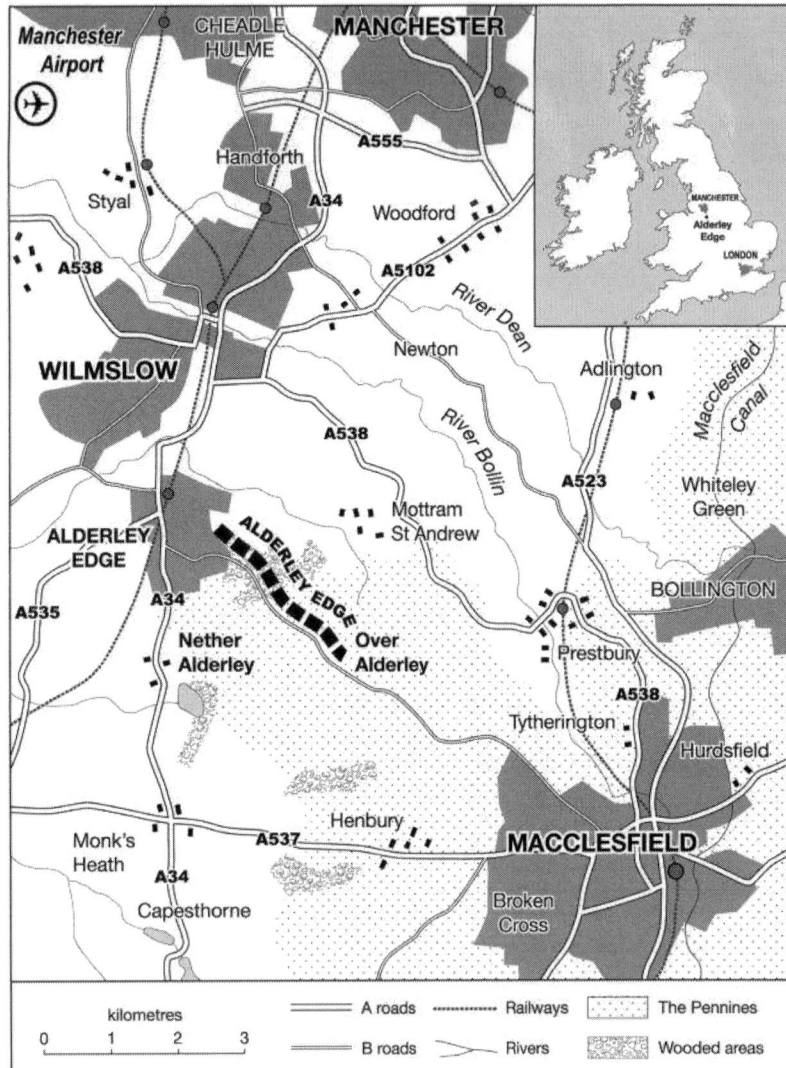

Figure 1.1. Location map of Alderley Edge. The layout and numbering of some of the roads (notably the A34) on this map and on Figures 1.2 and 1.3 have changed slightly since the opening of the Alderley Edge by-pass in November 2010. The naming of the village after the Edge itself is explained at the start of Chapter 23, p. 586.

After Casella and Croucher (2010: fig. 2.1).

besides, I had a huge task on my hands in the Museum and all this really lay outside my area of expertise. Alderley Edge was simply one of many local sites about which I was expected to know and show an interest when occasion demanded. Sometimes members of the public asked me for an opinion on objects found at Alderley; once I was even shown a stone head allegedly spotted in the bank at the roadside by someone whiling away his time waiting for a bus at Over Alderley which – inspired no doubt by those tales of Romans – I identified as the representation of a maenad, a follower of the god Bacchus, dating from the second century AD (wrongly, as I later discovered). As new arrivals, our house-hunting activities soon made it clear that Alderley Edge was not a place in which a young academic could aspire to live but, like many urban

Mancunians, we found the Edge a nice place to walk at the weekend, easily accessible and with stupendous views, as well as that extra layer of archaeology and history and the undercurrent of the legend of a sleeping king and his treasure guarded by a wizard somewhere beneath our feet. Where it was not dotted with the villas of the wealthy, the Edge – some 250 acres of it – was largely owned by the National Trust, whose reputation for stewardship at that time was larded with tales of having had the Territorial Army blow up the entrance to Engine Vein 'in the interests of public safety', and by a general lack of interest or concern for anything other than the fauna and the flora of the place, most notably the trees. In the later 1970s I heard tell of a plan to open West Mine (the only mine whose entrance lay on land not owned by the Trust), on a scale – they said – to rival the burgeoning attractions at Alton Towers, a plan – they said – that was scotched only by the valiant efforts of the villagers (later I found that the facts were otherwise, of course). There were stories of witchery, or at least of unseemly goings-on, on the Edge at Hallowe'en, which the Trust and the local police tried to prevent. As our children grew up we read more about the legend of Alderley in *The Weirdstone of Brisingamen* (1960) and its sequel *The Moon of Gomrath* (1963) by Alan Garner, and there was a memorable day when their author came to address our son's English class at school, memorable not least because of events that unfolded over the ensuing years.

By then I had discovered a little more about Alderley Edge, not least that Manchester Museum had a link that went back to the nineteenth century, starting almost by chance:

> In May, 1874, Mr H. Wilde and myself happened to take a walk to the new excavations which were in progress at the copper mines at Alderley Edge…. While walking over the surface, which was fantastically hollowed, a worked stone happened to catch my eye; and when we examined the stones lying about in the hollow we saw at once that a large number had been used in mining operations; and of these, owing to the kindness of the manager and the captain of the mine, we were able to secure thirty-five, which are now lodged in the Museum at the Owens College [later the University of Manchester]. (Boyd Dawkins, 1875: 74)

In the autumn, Boyd Dawkins went back and collected some more and studied the site further, and then in the 1875 he had to return once again to examine new finds:

> As some miners were at work on the Edge [clearing round an old working at Brynlow], they came upon a large collection of stone implements, consisting of celts or adzes, hammerheads or axes, mauls, etc. from one to two feet below the surface … and others were left in some old diggings of the copper ore, from three to four yards in depth, along with an oak shovel that had been very roughly used. (Sainter, 1878: 47)

Boyd Dawkins concluded, albeit tentatively, that the whole group were of Bronze Age date, although his arguments had to be based simply on the crudeness of the tools he had found. A selection of these stones was for long displayed in the geology galleries of the Museum, along with a model of the stratigraphy and topography of the Edge. The Museum also had finds from the excavations carried out by C. Roeder and F. S. Graves around the turn of the twentieth century, including Mesolithic and Neolithic flint implements as well as more hammer stones, and a large collection of minerals: indeed, *in toto* these formed the largest collection of finds from the Edge in any public collection. In the late 1970s all the Alderley material was recatalogued along with the rest of the Museum's lithic collections as part of a pioneering scheme funded by the government's Manpower Services Commission to put all the Museum's holdings onto a computerised database. This, and the research interests of David Gale of Bradford University, led to a spate of renewed archaeological activity on the Edge from the late 1970s into the early 1990s, which is described more fully in Chapter 14. Meanwhile, underground the Derbyshire Caving Club, the lessee of the mines from the National Trust since 1969, had re-opened Wood Mine in 1970 and has regularly taken parties of visitors underground ever since; over the next twenty or thirty years it extended its underground lease, clearing more mines and making them accessible to visitors as well as holding regular open days (see http://www.derbyscc.org.uk). The year 1979 saw the publication of what is still the only handbook to the mines, C. J. Carlon's *The Alderley Edge Mines* (Carlon, 1979, revised in 2012 with N. J. Dibben), and Alderley and its legend came to feature more and more in local guidebooks, as well as in some of the more fanciful literature and websites (e.g. Pickford, 1992).

This was the setting when in 1991 I had an invitation from Alan Garner to visit his house to look at some items which he wanted to donate to Manchester Museum. To my amazement, chief among them was that oak shovel from Brynlow, which had disappeared from knowledge soon after its publication by Dr Sainter in 1878 and which by a combination of serendipity, childhood memory and sheer persistence he had rediscovered nearly forty years before. How that came about is for him to tell in the next chapter of this book (and to illustrate in Figure 2.3), but for me this was one of those rare moments in a museum curator's life when he does not really believe that he is seeing what is laid before him. One's colleagues, more senescent, more cynical or just less gullible, tended not to believe it. Not, perhaps, a Tudor winnowing fan as the British Museum had once suggested, but very probably a peat-cutter's spade, no older than Medieval, they said. No one argued with the circumstances of the discovery, but the fact remained that the hammer stones on which the context depended were themselves not properly dated, and at least two recent writers had cast serious doubt on the prehistoric date for Alderley and other sites, on the grounds of insufficient evidence (Warrington, 1981; Briggs, 1983). The donor bravely agreed to our seeking a radiocarbon date for the shovel and we submitted an application to the Radiocarbon Accelerator Unit at the Research Laboratory in Oxford. Oxford confirmed Boyd Dawkins' Bronze Age date: at *c.* 1750 ± 90 BC. Thus, the wood from which the shovel was fashioned appeared to belong firmly in the early Middle Bronze Age. At last there was proof positive for Bronze Age activity on the Edge (Sainter, 1878; Garner *et al.*, 1994).

Then in March 1995, while they were making safe on old shaft that had begun to cave in beside Engine Vein, the Derbyshire Caving Club found a coarse-ware pot containing a hoard of over 500 Roman coins, which they promptly and properly reported both to Jeremy Milln, the National Trust's Regional Archaeologist for Mercia, in whose patch Alderley belonged, and to Manchester Museum (Figures 2.4, 14.9). A rapid first study by Keith Sugden, then Keeper of Numismatics at the Museum, established that they were from the time of the emperor Constantine I and his son Constantine II, minted between AD 317 and *c.* 335, and were probably deposited around AD 340. There had been a very few earlier finds of Roman objects from Alderley: for example, in 1901 Charles Roeder recorded some Roman coins that had been found on the Edge, which seem to be the same as the four pieces shown to the Cheshire Museum Service in Northwich in 1978 (Roeder, 1901: 95; *ArchAE*: 106), but this was the first real evidence for Roman occupation at Alderley, and with it came a new danger. The story of the wizard and his treasure were enough in themselves to spark interest in the site among less reputable treasure hunters, and the new find – even though it was a humble hoard consisting entirely of copper coins – could only add fuel to this. Already in 1992 a curious gold bar allegedly found by the side of Artists Lane by a metal-detectorist had been reported to the Museum and, after the treasure trove inquest, stories of another five similar bars found on various sites across the Edge began to appear in the press and on the internet. Although only the first one, now lodged in Manchester Museum, has ever been seen by professional archaeologists (and so far it has not been possible to identify either its date or its origin, despite our best efforts), and despite the fact the use of metal-detectors on its land is contrary to the National Trust's bye-laws, incidents like this pointed to the urgent need for positive action to understand and to protect the archaeology and the history of Alderley Edge.

Not just the archaeology and the history, for the story of Alderley Edge is much longer and wider than that. Geologically, the Edge is of outstanding interest for its mineralisation, and for the relationship of this mineralisation with the Triassic rock strata in which it occurs; indeed, it has been identified as the most important British occurrence of the enrichment of sedimentary rocks by ores of copper and other metals, notably lead and cobalt. As well as the 250 acres of the Edge held inalienably by the National Trust, which include most of the area of mining and early occupation, a similar area – partly overlapping the Trust's holding – had been identified as a geological Site of Special Scientific Interest (SSSI) and a Regionally Important Geological/geomorphological Site (RIGS), largely because the unique combination of geology, geomorphology and human impact has created an unusual environment that has given the flora and fauna a special identity and interest (Figure 1.2; the National Trust's holding on the Edge itself is shown in Figure 14.1). An area of hedgerow trees at Brynlow is protected by a Tree Protection Order, and Cheshire Conservation Trust had marked Waterfall Wood on the Trust's land as a grade C Site of Biological Interest (SBI); while not as significant or as highly protected as an SSSI, this still means that the habitat type and the species to be found living there are of more than local importance. The site had already been recognised as an important candidate for review under the Monuments Protection Programme, which could lead to its scheduling under the Ancient Monuments Act (and this did in fact happen later, but that is looking ahead). The special nature of the geological story had also influenced Alderley's social history. It was once the home of miners and smelters, farmers and craftsmen, swamped since the coming of the railway in 1842 by Manchester commuters, who have their own story, one that is revealed most clearly by the villas which they built. Sufficient 'folk memory' still survived – just – for one to be able to reconstruct something of the chronicle of this double community. Overlying it all is the legend of the wizard, which could provide an opening for an ethnographic study.

But because the Edge is also very beautiful and so rich in legend and history and because it lies only twelve miles south of Manchester, it had become a honeypot for urban folk seeking country air. This was nothing new: early in the twentieth century it was said in Alderley that during holidays you could walk from the railway station to the Edge on the heads of the people, but now they were coming in their cars too. The Cheshire County Structure Plan (1977, updated 1986) recognised the area both as of Special County Value for Landscape and as a priority for countryside recreation facilities, but these two designations do not sit easily together. The National Trust in its turn recognised that Alderley Edge was one of its more sensitive open-space properties: it estimated that it was receiving some 70,000 visits per year and that the numbers were growing. Not surprisingly, some areas were beginning to suffer badly from erosion and hill-wash of the light sandy soils, especially along popular corridors and at the most attractive locations, such as Engine Vein and Stormy Point. While the Trust could manage access up

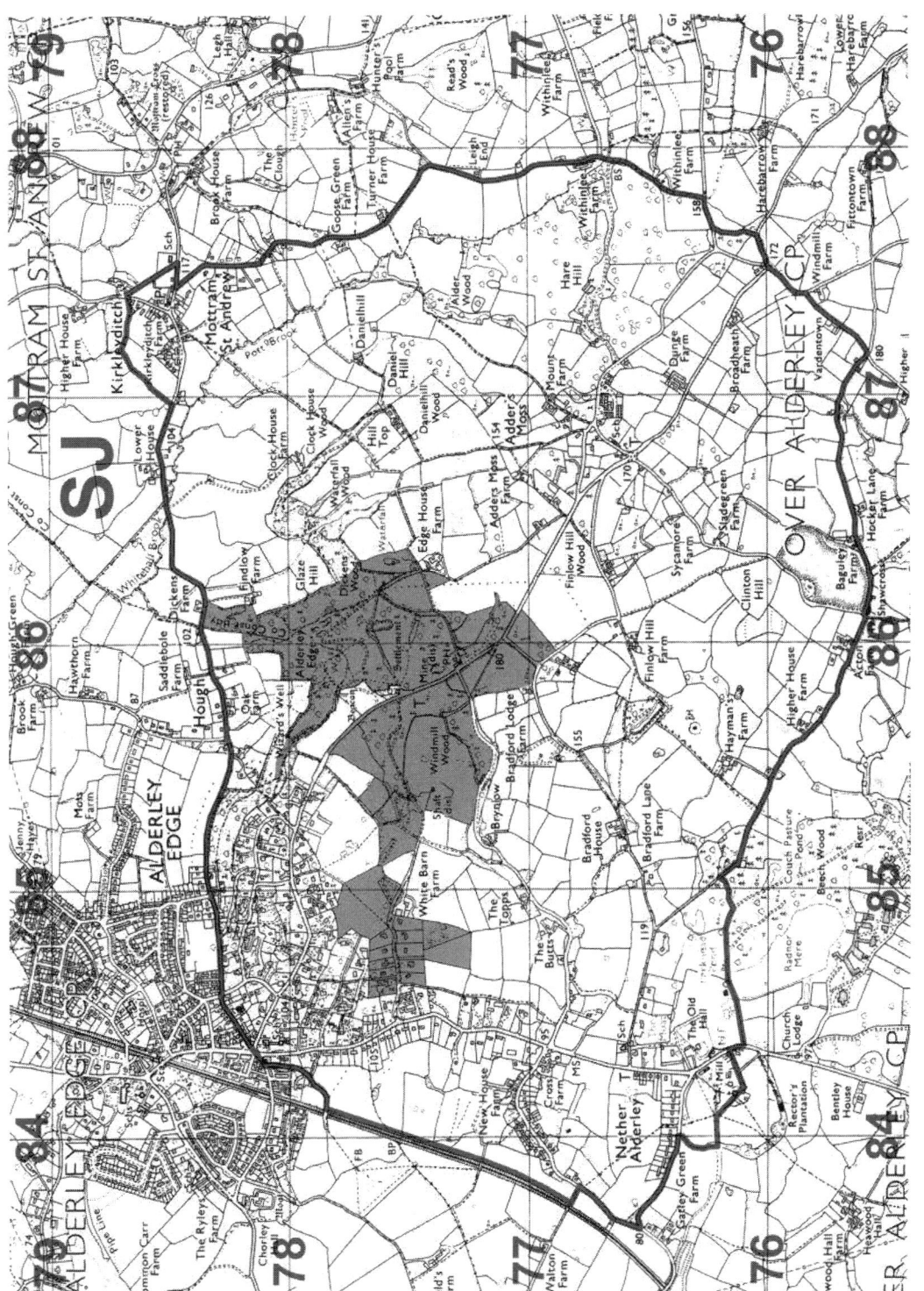

Figure 1.2. Map of Alderley Edge: the area identified as a geological Site of Special Scientific Interest (SSSI) is shaded, and the Regionally Important Geological and geomorphological Site (RIGS) is enclosed in a dark line.

Based on the 1992 Ordnance Survey 1:25,000 Pathfinder map, sheet 759, with the permission of the Controller of Her Majesty's Stationery Office, Crown copyright October 2013.

to a certain degree, the situation really demanded a programme of conservation and of diversifying visitor interest by spreading their impact over a wider area. However, such plans would have to be founded on a full and properly researched understanding of the human and natural history. The discovery of the Roman coin hoard provided the catalyst for action. In April 1995 Jeremy Milln called a site meeting of the interested parties, which involved, among others, representatives from the National Trust, the Department of Archaeology of the University of Manchester, Manchester Museum, Cheshire County Council, Bradford University, the Derbyshire Caving Club, the Early Mines Research Group and the local residents. Further meetings followed during the summer and a Steering Group was set up to draft a proposal for a full historical and topographical survey of the Edge, and to plan the area that would be covered, the topics to be surveyed, the methods of doing so, the bodies that might be involved and, indeed, the destination of any finds and research archives. It was agreed that Manchester Museum was their natural home, in part because of the long history of involvement with the Edge by both University and Museum, and also because in 1992 the Museum had already reached an agreement with Cheshire County Museum Service that all archaeological finds from the site, past and future, should come to the Museum in order to maintain the integrity of the Alderley archive. This agreement did not cover finds from the Trust's land, which are subject to the National Trust Acts, but during 1995 a similar agreement was reached with the Trust for archaeological finds from Alderley. An application for funding to the Heritage Grant Fund of the Department of National Heritage in September 1995 was unsuccessful, but after further discussion and refinement of the plan Manchester Museum submitted a bid to the Leverhulme Trust in the following year on behalf of both organisations for the Alderley Edge Landscape Project. Its objectives were set out as follows:

> The Alderley Edge Landscape Project is a joint venture between the Manchester Museum and the National Trust to make the first complete survey of the story of the Edge. The suite of minerals at the site is both unique and complex: from this geological starting point the project intends to record both the flora and fauna and the traces of man's activity both above and below ground. The further aims of the project include (a) a management plan for the site; (b) an exhibition at the Museum, followed by a longer-term display at the site; (c) opportunities for teaching linked to the National Curriculum; (d) an illustrated guidebook to the Edge as well as a multidisciplinary monograph or series of articles; (e) avenues for possible further research, both archaeological excavation and in the study of the species identified.

The timing of the bid was good. Not only is the site unique archaeologically, but it straddles three major themes of current British archaeological interest which had recently been identified by English Heritage: the archaeology of multi-period landscapes, of industry, and of extraction and processing of non-ferrous minerals (English Heritage, 1991). Moreover, a number of books and articles on early mining in Britain had recently been published which highlighted the need for a proper survey of Alderley (Crew and Crew, 1990; Ford and Willies, 1994; Thackray, 1994). One could say that the Alderley Edge Landscape Project fitted precisely into the interest in landscape studies that was burgeoning in the late twentieth century. Its time had come. The Leverhulme Trustees and their referees were impressed with the Project, especially its holistic approach, and commented that 'if successful, it could well provide a model for future projects of this nature, and reflects a growing feeling that "heritage", archaeological and natural, cannot be considered in isolation'. They awarded the Project nearly £108,000, and over the next two years AELP, as it came to be known, won further funding from a number of other bodies for parts of its work – Cheshire County Council, Rio Tinto plc, Survey Systems Ltd, Zeneca Pharmaceuticals and its successor AstraZeneca, the Mabel Evans Trust, ICL Computers, Gifford and Partners, and National Tyre. As this book takes its course it will become clear how many other individuals and organisations provided help in kind or as colleagues and collaborators, and how essential and integral they became. We give their names in the Preamble and acknowledgments.

Methodologically, one of the attractions of the Landscape Project was its multidisciplinary approach: in this it reflected the range of subjects covered by Manchester Museum, from archaeology to zoology – unlike other departments of the University of Manchester at that time, the Museum embraced a wide variety of disciplines in both the sciences and the humanities, and virtually all my curatorial colleagues became involved in the Landscape Project at various times. At the same time, the Project could and did call on those working in other specialised disciplines available within the University and the National Trust, as well as a remarkable range of skills and interests that became apparent in Alderley village. Nonetheless, it fell to me as the Museum's Keeper of Archaeology to take responsibility for coordinating the Project: we had estimated it might take 25 per cent of my time over two years. If only! For the next two decades – well beyond the original two years of the core research which the Leverhulme Trust funded and indeed well into my official retirement from the Museum – it really took over much of my working life. With some prescience we had included in our application to the Leverhulme Trust the sentence 'since this is primarily a survey, we anticipate that it will raise questions in more than one discipline meriting further research later – but not forming part of this application'. As will become clear from the rest of this book, and from the list of chapter headings and the names of their authors, I was by no means the only one entrapped in this way by the Edge. Although geographically restricted, the range of topics and of questions which the Landscape Project proposed to investigate was so wide that, as time went on, many other people also became involved because of their interest or because of their connections with Alderley. It was interesting to find that no matter how detached, how scientific, how academic one tried to be in one's approach to the work, almost everyone came to agree that in some way Alderley Edge was a special place. The National Trust and others may own the ground of Alderley Edge in a physical sense, but nobody actually 'owns' the Edge – certainly not the Alderley Edge Landscape Project, however possessive some of us may have come to feel about it. Other people are here too: many of them have been here much longer than we have, and they often have a quite different perspective and a different agenda. While it was hardly unexpected that the Landscape Project brought together people from a variety of walks of life who shared a deep interest in the Edge, a remarkable by-product was the way in which it reunited and galvanised some who over the years had reached a point of misunderstanding and non-communication which had stalled further research and prevented practical on-site cooperation. It cannot be said too often that this was a project about people as much as about a place, and to name all those who have helped us in all kinds of ways would fill many, many pages of this book. I hope that they will forgive us if we simply thank them all here as a group united by their interest in the place rather than as discrete individuals, in the middle of a chapter that is trying to set the scene, rather than in a long and ultimately overwhelming list at the beginning of the book. If the story of the people of Alderley in the earlier twentieth century was still one of 'them and us', by the end of the century we all felt that this was *our* story now.

We had already been given a great deal of help, advice and information by the people of Alderley; one of the first things that we did once funding had been confirmed was to arrange a public meeting at St Hilary's School, at which we could tell them of our plans. There was a little suspicion and hostility to the notion that a bunch of academics from Manchester would be moving in on their village, prying into their secrets and publishing them to the world for their own profit, intellectual or otherwise, and that the publicity which such activities would generate would bring in yet more visitors to disturb their peace and increase the threat to their beloved Edge after we had moved out again. It is only fair to say that a significant proportion of this antagonism came from people who were themselves incomers to the village, but it was important to assuage such concerns at the outset, to make it clear that this was the opposite of what we intended, and that we had already given the matter much thought. The representatives of the National Trust made it clear that they would not have been partners in this project if they believed that this was a real risk, and we gave an undertaking, which always remained important in any public activities and in any dissemination of our work, that we would do our best to respect the privacy of the village and the fragility of the Edge itself. One might add that, at this time, television programmes such as *Meet the Ancestors* and *Who Do You Think You Are?*, which fostered and built on people's interest in the past of their homes and towns or the history of their families, had yet to make their appearance, and even *Time Team* was still in its infancy. Tony Blair could claim publicly that history did not matter to the people of New Labour's Britain, and the enthusiasm to know about one's past on which these programmes played was still around the corner. It might well be said that projects like AELP and its offshoots helped nurture it. In fact, the great majority of those attending that first public meeting gave us their warm and enthusiastic support. Names were written down, addresses noted, offers of help and further likely contacts listed. One local resident was heard to say 'you have made us speak to each other again': there could not have been a more heartfelt vote of confidence and, as we found over the following years and months, this was not just something said in the enthusiasm of the moment, for the support and commitment continued all through the life of the Project. But then William Smith, writing *A Treatise on Cheshire* in the seventeenth century, had already noted that 'The people of the country are of a nature very gentle and courteous, ready to help and further one another' (cited in Ormerod, 1882: vol. 1, p. 129).

As we carried out our surveys over the following years we met only one blank refusal from a landowner to allow us access – and he was an absentee landlord; his tenant, by contrast, had been as cooperative as the terms of his lease would allow. The sensitivity and fragility of the Edge as well as the right of the villagers to live without undue disturbance always remained uppermost in our minds, and when in due course an approach from *Time Team* would have enabled us to tackle one of the problems for which we lacked the resources we turned it down because of the great number of visitors it would generate in the months following broadcast. Much later I discovered that this concern was not really shared by the local people themselves.

To make the Landscape Project work, several things needed to be done: a scheme as complex as this needed a proper management structure; the area and the topics to be studied had to be defined; and a Chief Surveyor needed to be appointed together with a support team.

From the outset, the Landscape Project's work was guided by the Steering Group mentioned above. Chaired by the Director of Manchester Museum, coordinated by the Keeper of Archaeology and serviced by the Museum, this group comprised the interested members

of the Museum and National Trust staff and of other University departments, notably Archaeology and Geography, representatives of other
bodies with an interest in Alderley Edge, such as English Heritage, the
Cheshire Wildlife Trust, the Derbyshire Caving Club and St Hilary's
School, and a number of private individuals with a preoccupation with
the Edge's story. Once the Project began work we created a number
of working groups to establish the direction in which particular topics
should be pursued, and later on there were various occasions when sub-
committees were set up to tackle specific issues. By the summer of 1998
the Steering Group had perhaps become too large to make effective
strategic decisions and a small Management Group was created to
take on this role, made up of representatives of the Museum, the Trust
and the Derbyshire Caving Club. The Steering Group nevertheless
continued to act as the main – and very spirited – forum for discussion
and collaboration over the Landscape Project's research, publication
and day-to-day activities: indeed, at the point when the two years of
Leverhulme funding were over and the Steering Group might properly
have been wound up, its members were almost unanimous in reforming
themselves into a 'working group' to allow those with a continuing
interest to have a framework within which to carry out their research. In
this form the group continued to meet and to interact for another seven
years, ceasing to exist formally only when its chairman and coordinator
both retired from the University in 2005. Even at the time of writing,
in 2013, several of its members are still active in their research and
involvement with the Edge, and questions and problems still come in
from researchers, members of the public and sometimes from one of the
various special interest groups at Alderley such as the Edge Association.

Simon Timberlake, a geologist and prehistorian and a founder member
of the Early Mines Research Group as well as its Excavation Director,
was appointed Chief Surveyor to the Landscape Project, taking up his
position on 1 December 1996: this marked the formal starting date
for AELP. Through a very satisfactory arrangement with the Greater
Manchester Archaeological Unit, Tom Burke was seconded to the
Landscape Project as Assistant Surveyor, allowing the Project to call on
the other resources of the Unit when necessary. Later Timberlake took
on the role of Project Consultant, with particular obligations towards the
provision of copy for the exhibition and the writing up of the Landscape
Project's research and was replaced as Project Surveyor by Carolanne
King, who had previously conducted some of the Project's excavations.

An essential part of the Project brief was to create a proper archive,
not only of our own papers but of the various documents and photographs which we anticipated would be lent or given to the Landscape
Project; most opportunely, Karna Bloch, a history and gender studies
student at Aarhus University in Denmark, had come to the Museum

on a six-month placement in February 1997. In the course of this she established the Landscape Project's archive most efficiently, and was then appointed as Research Assistant and Archivist for a further six months. At this point the designated funding for the archive came to an end, and she returned to Aarhus, where she used material from the Landscape Project for her dissertation – surely the only Dane working on the landed families of Cheshire: AELP produced many offshoots, but this must be the most far-flung. However, the archive had proved such a popular and important part of the Project that it could not be abandoned, and its maintenance and expansion were ably undertaken by a number of volunteers and members of the Steering Group. Because the National Trust has built up a tradition of recording the voices and memories of people who have lived or worked on its properties, we also began a programme of recording Alderley voices and memories, and of collecting and copying earlier recordings. These archives are described in Chapters 20 and 21. Like so many aspects of AELP, they seem to have acquired lives of their own, and even ten or twelve years later offers and suggestions for more material were still coming into the Museum. Our first plan was ultimately to deposit all original material in the archive in the John Rylands Library at the University of Manchester, with similar collections from other University projects; however, changes in University policy and funding meant that it became more practical to lodge it with the Cheshire Archives and Local Studies service. This includes the sound recordings made for the oral archive, although copies of these have also been placed in the National Trust archive and in the National Sound Archive in the British Library, in accordance with the Trust's normal practice. The excavation archive, of course, should remain in the Museum.

However, this is looking ahead. Although the intellectual scope of the Landscape Project was very wide (one of the Leverhulme Trust's referees commented 'there is no technique that they do not mention', adding sagely 'perhaps they are being a little over-ambitious') its geographic compass was limited. We divided Alderley Edge into 'core' and 'hinterland' areas for our research (Figure 1.3). The 'core' focused on the parts of the Edge owned by the National Trust and those designated as an SSSI, therefore including the area of the Sandhills and around Whitebarn Farm, beyond the Trust's western boundary, and between Engine Vein and Edge House Farm to the east: here 'every' aspect was to be studied, at least in theory: this area had been the subject of a detailed topographic and archaeological survey and some exploratory excavation (*ArchAE*: ch. 8). However, there are features of archaeological, historical and scientific interest outside these boundaries, so we included a 'hinterland' extending west to the railway line, north to the Mottram Road and incorporating part of the Hough and Kirkleyditch

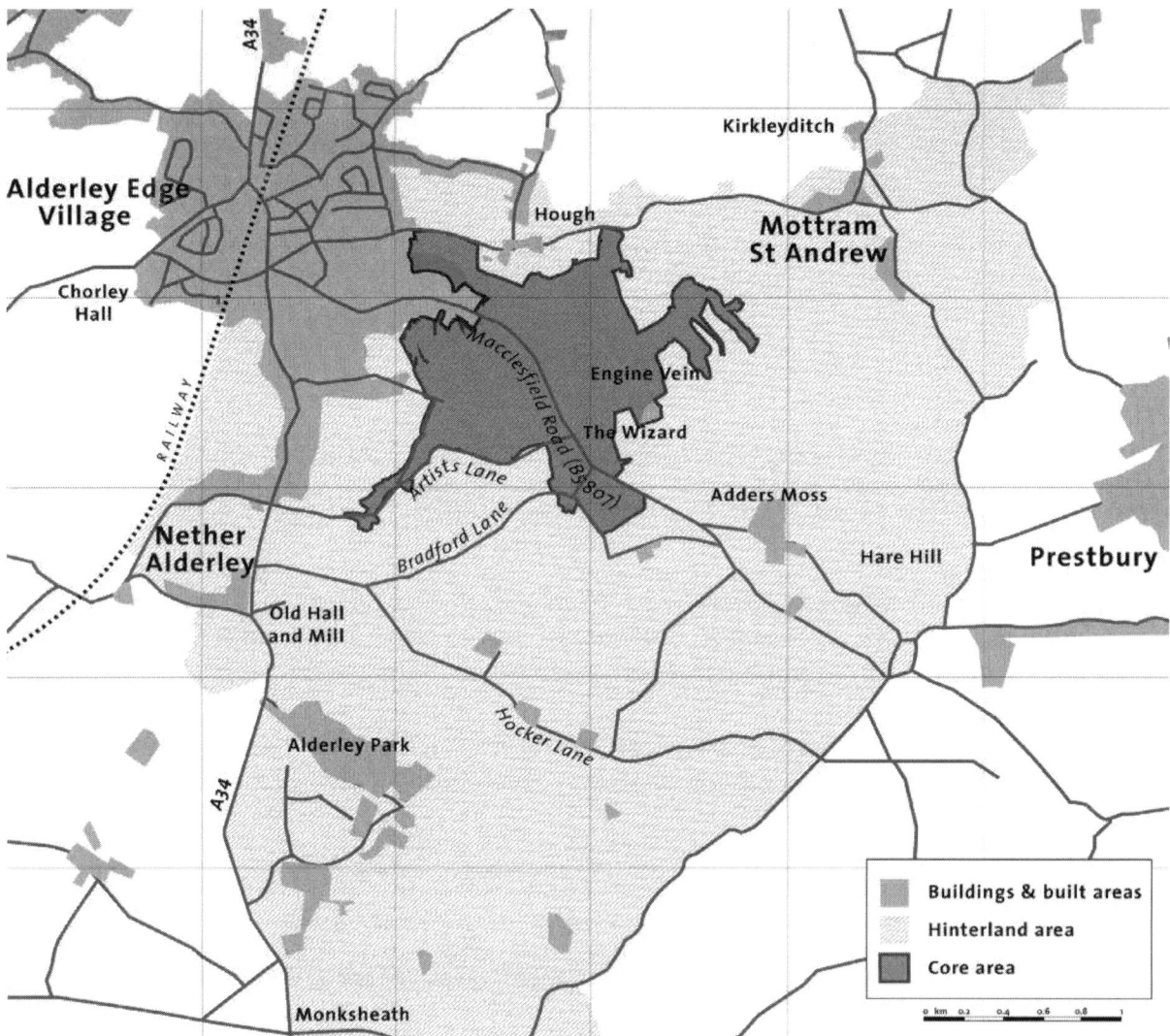

Figure 1.3. Map of Alderley Edge showing the Project's 'core' and 'hinterland' research areas.

Based on the 1992 Ordnance Survey 1:25,000 Pathfinder map, sheet 759, with the permission of the Controller of Her Majesty's Stationery Office, Crown copyright October 2013.

(the site of Mottram Mine) as well as the village of Mottram St Andrew, east to Shaws Lane and Birtles Lane, taking in Adders Moss, and south to the Chelford–Macclesfield Road (the A537) so as to include Alderley Park. In this area research was selective and picked out only items of particular interest or relevance, mostly relating to Alderley's geology, such as the kettle-hole at Adders Moss, and to its topographic and social history – place names, trackways, buildings and the like. This was a slight extension of the hinterland as we had originally conceived it: as this book makes clear, we are of course a long way from being the first to work on story of the Edge, whether on the mines and the minerals, the archaeology, the flora and fauna or indeed the legend. There were many before us on whose shoulders we stand or under whose feet we dug. The proposals to the Department of National Heritage and the Leverhulme Trust were based on a pilot study involving desktop research and searches of the literature, and once the fieldwork began it became clear that a small amount of tweaking to the area we should cover would yield a more coherent picture in the end.

It is also worth saying here that when our Project was conceived, landscape studies of this kind and this breadth were still in their infancy and much of the technology was still relatively untried in the field of archaeology, but this was one of the things that gave the Project its zest and excitement. The fact that 'geofizz' in all its forms could be seen on television every week on *Time Team* showed how far archaeology had progressed in a decade or so, but one should remember that devices using the satellite-based Global Positioning System (GPS), now to be found in almost every new car and in many walkers' hands and on their mobile phones, were then still in their infancy in field archaeology, as was the application of geographic information systems (GISs) to build up a record incorporating all the archaeological, mineralogical and biological data: we had many teething problems to overcome, ranging from heavy tree cover to the error built into the GPS coordinates of the time that was intended to confuse enemy spy planes. As coordinator of the Landscape Project, sitting in my warm office in Manchester, I could sense all too clearly the occasional frustration of the survey team working in the field and in the rain. The survey is described in *ArchAE* (ch. 8) and I have written in that book how much we owe to our colleagues in the Cheshire County Council Geographic Information Unit for their help in solving the difficulties that arose over the GPS survey, but I happily repeat our thanks here. In our final report to the Leverhulme Trust in 2000 we said:

> one of the most exciting aspects of the various surveys has been their integration as separate 'coverages' onto a single computerised MapInfo database through a Geographic Information System: this was achieved thanks to the collaboration of the Regional Research Laboratory in the School of Geography of the University of Manchester, sometimes using technology that did not exist and was thus scarcely anticipated when our Proposal was drafted in 1995. Despite problems of both time and developing technology this gave a whole new dimension to the results, for their collation and interpretation and also for their dissemination.

For this collaboration we owe particular thanks to Dr Robert Barr, the director of the Lab, and to Neil Matthews, the GIS manager.

If the start of the Landscape Project was accompanied by the excitement that goes with nearly every new venture of this kind, what was more unusual was the way in which the Edge seemed to take hold of nearly everyone who became involved, however 'detached' and 'scientific' they believed themselves to be. In part this was undoubtedly the effect of having not just such a wide range of disciplines involved and new technologies to employ, but also such a mix of people, all passionately committed to their particular disciplines but linked on this occasion by their interest in the Edge. Trying to coordinate such a 'team' was sometimes like herding cats or directing a choir composed of prima donnas, but perhaps one of the Landscape Project's achievements was to bring a sense of order and discipline and also of unity of purpose to a wide range of pre-existing interests and discrete groups and individuals. In the end the extent of the Project was limited only by our own efforts to rationalise it (at one point there was even a notion to commission an opera – but we agreed that we needed to complete the written word first). The extent and range of the Project is probably demonstrated most clearly by the titles of the chapters that comprise this book, and also, it must be said, by the different approaches and backgrounds of the various contributors: inevitably there is occasionally overlap or repetition where people come at a question from different disciplines and standpoints. Sometimes there will be inconsistencies, although I have tried to keep these to a minimum – the reader will have to bear with the fact that (for example) sometimes we refer to the Goldenstone and Monksheath as one word and sometimes as two, reflecting variations in usage. (Similarly, we sometimes refer to the project as AELP, but as often happens the acronym assumed a life of its own and so it is also called 'the AELP'.) However, this approach should make it possible for those with a particular interest in part of the story to read just the relevant chapter or section.

Even so, the titles are not a completely accurate reflection of the Project's activities. On the one hand there are chapters that describe work that happened only after the Landscape Project was officially completed, or that never formed part of it, such as Mike Redfern's description of the restoration of Nether Alderley Mill (Chapter 25) or the account of Philip Jarvis speaking to us from a German prisoner-of-war camp in the First World War (Appendix 21.2). On the other there are the activities not recorded in this book but essential to the Project as a whole, such as the research conducted by students not just from Manchester but from universities and colleges as far away as Cumbria and in topics as diverse as geology and leisure management, and the visitor surveys carried out to find out why people visited the Edge and what they expected to find.

One essential strand – and part of the commitment to the funders – was the notion of 'giving something back'. After all, this Landscape Project had sprung from a shovel that seems to have been deliberately buried and a pot of coins that had been hidden, which the Edge had given back to us. We owed it something in return. This bunch of academics from

Manchester (and elsewhere) owed it to the people of Alderley, onto whose patch and into whose lives they were intruding, to let them be among the first to see the fruits of their labours. Therefore we arranged a number of events during and at the end of the Project, ranging from a set of lectures (held in St Hilary's School on a series of amazingly wet evenings but always fully attended), a day-school and finally a farewell event in the village at which the book reporting on the Landscape Project's archaeological work was launched, to an exhibition at Manchester Museum, whose information panels then travelled to local venues before ending up in the information centre on the Edge itself. Although the exhibition – called 'Living on the Edge', with the subtitle 'The Myths, Mines and Merchants of Alderley' – aimed to describe all the different layers of Alderley's story as the Landscape Project was unpeeling them, the feeling of the unexpected and of the strong local traditions that still run through the village was epitomised by a performance by the Alderley Mummers at the opening, repeated at various stages during the exhibition. There were other activities too, perhaps most notably and most usefully the experimental archaeology carried out during the National Archaeology Days in July 1997, when members of the public of all ages were encouraged to take part in practical experiments to make hammer stones and use them in fire-setting to begin a mine adit, and then to assist in some experimental smelting of the local copper ores. One of the most interesting aspects was not just what one learned about the practical aspects of replicating Bronze Age technology (though it was extremely valuable as an academic exercise too), but the way in which it became a group activity which could involve a large proportion of the community (*ArchAE*: chs 10 and 11). The reconstruction of a Bronze Age mining scene depicted in Figure 15.5 illustrates this, and it cannot be chance that the artist has chosen to model several of the 'Bronze Age' figures on people who actually took part in the experiment. And if there were events and involvement for the public, there were also books and articles produced by members of the Landscape Project team that derived from their work at Alderley, even if they did not form part of the formal publication plan, ranging from the semi-popular *The Villas of Alderley Edge* by Matthew Hyde (1999) to specialised articles such as an account by Dr Dmitri Logunov, the Project's spider specialist, of one complete field season spent on Alderley Edge, 'Preliminary Survey of the Spiders, Harvestmen and False-Scorpions of Alderley Edge, Cheshire', published in the *Newsletter of the British Arachnological Society* (Logunov, 2003), or one that brought the story of the famous shovel into the twenty-first century which we wrote for the *Journal of Archaeological Science*, entitled 'Natural Preservation Mechanisms at Play in a Bronze Age Wooden Shovel Found in the Copper Mines of Alderley Edge' (Smith *et al.*, 2011).

However, there was an inevitable focus on the archaeology of Alderley Edge, since, in the end, all the human story of the place derives from that. When it came to putting together the final full publication of the Landscape Project's work there was simply too much archaeology to describe for it to sit comfortably in a single publication with all the rest of the story: this would have become an unbalanced book intellectually, and an impossibly weighty one physically. Therefore the archaeological work was brought together and set in its wider context in a separate volume, entitled *The Archaeology of Alderley Edge (ArchAE)*, edited and largely written by Simon Timberlake together with myself. Aimed at a specialist audience, it was published by John and Erica Hedges in 2005 in the British series of 'British Archaeological Reports', with an identical separate version for sale locally – mostly through Manchester Museum (the book is now distributed by Archaeopress, via Hadrian Books). All the rest of the story, with a summary of the archaeology, is to be found in the present book. One might argue that the geology is also so complicated and so fundamental that it deserves a separate volume too: however, there was a danger that the picture would fragment just when we were trying to put the jigsaw together, so we have tried to divide this book into separate and comprehensible sections that do not distort the overall view, while giving those with a particular interest in one area clear avenues which they can follow.

In the course of its life, AELP became such a vigorous plant that it grew several offshoots which developed lives of their own. The first of these was AELPHER, the 'Alderley Edge Landscape Project Heritage and Educational Resources'. The brainchild of Griselda Greaves and John Adams, it had a twofold purpose: first to make the Project's findings and its archive available to a much wider audience by means of a website (http://www.alderleyedge.manchester.museum; no longer extant but in the British Library's archive – see below and Chapter 20, p. 532); and second to use that web-based archive to create a learning resource that would address the dip suffered by many children as they move from primary to secondary school, and which could be used in tandem by secondary schools and their feeder primaries. It is based on *The Stone Book Quartet*, Alan Garner's account of a single crucial day in the life of a child in four different generations of his own family in Alderley Edge village (Garner, 1979). Because the book celebrates the landscape and the power that landscape has to shape the people within it, it serves to show how an author gathers his material and writes his book, how people belong in their particular setting and how that setting has grown up. In the language of education used on the website:

> the scheme of work consists of integrated Humanities teaching units for English, Geography and History, specifically designed to encourage the development of transferable higher thinking skills across all three subjects.

Each subject unit may be used on its own, but if used together, the units are more than the sum of their parts: they support children in a systematic enquiry into the Geographical and Historical background of the book.

The Project was funded principally by the Heritage Lottery Fund but with further help from bodies such as the Carnegie United Kingdom Trust, Manchester Airport Community Trust Fund and Macclesfield Borough Council, and developed in partnership with the Cheshire Education Authority; it became a model for similar schemes across the county and indeed further afield. However, this rather prosaic account of its development conceals its somewhat turbulent gestation caused by the sizzling high-energy enthusiasm of all the participants. As with so much of our Alderley story, the problem lay in keeping the excitement in check, not in driving it along. It is a great sorrow to us that when the University changed its policy on hosting 'additional' websites a few years later, many of the links in this site were broken, so that although there are plans to re-establish it in a different format, at the time of writing (2013) it is no longer possible to use it to access the Project Archive nor the recordings of interviews. Fortunately, it survives intact as a CD and in the British Library's archive (see Chapter 20, p. 532).

Another of the offshoots was the Alderley Sandhills Project (ASP), an excavation at the site of the Miners' Cottages in the Hagg, conducted in 2003 jointly by the Museum and the University Department of Art History and Archaeology under the direction of Dr Eleanor Casella, with the involvement of local volunteers and schools and funded by the Aggregates Levy Sustainability Fund distributed through English Heritage (the Sandhills at Alderley Edge were, after all, created from mining spoil and the material was later used as aggregate for roads and runways). This was an innovative excavation, employing New World methods, of two pairs of supposedly eighteenth-century cottages that linked the archaeology of the cottages to the memories of three children who had grown up in them but were now in their eighties: it produced some fascinating and revealing mismatches between the facts recollected by the boy and the two girls when compared with the archaeological evidence (Casella and Croucher, 2010).

The story does not end here, however. One of the initial purposes of AELP was to collect information that would provide the National Trust with the basis of a proper management plan for the site. It was clear in the early days that the Trust sometimes found it hard to comprehend the mindset of some of its new partners from the University and to appreciate the disinterested nature of the Landscape Project's research – to understand that those involved were there to help, to be a source of expert advice not readily available to them at most of their properties, and that this was not just another special interest group. However, Chapter 29 of this book ('Close to the Edge – Ensuring the Future of the Edge for Everyone'), written by the Trust's present Countryside Manager for Cheshire and the Wirral, should make it clear how that attitude has not so much changed as made a complete *volte face*. Now that the University-led Landscape Project has drawn to a close, it is the Trust that is driving the archaeological and environmental research on the Edge (with University support) as part of its wide-ranging and innovative conservation and access programme. A plan put together by the Trust and the University to investigate further the archaeology of the landscape has had to be shelved for lack of resources, but it is there to be taken down and put into action when its time comes, while from the University Faculty of Life Sciences and the Museum has come a project to use DNA sequencing of bacterial diversity on the Sandhills and in Windmill Wood as a test-bed for a study of the long-term effects of industrial pollution. Sons of AELP, in fact.

In the village itself there is now the Alderley Edge History Group, founded by the late Harold Smith, who had served on the steering group as one of the village representatives. Its first meeting was in 2006, a year after the launch of *The Archaeology of Alderley Edge* at what was intended to be the 'farewell event' for the Landscape Project. It goes from strength to strength, recruiting its members both from 'old locals' who have lived in Alderley all their lives (and possibly for several genera-tions) and from younger incomers: there is enormous enthusiasm, and regular meetings that seem to be ever more crowded – at the time of writing the Group has had to move to larger premises. At one stage the Project issued a regular newsletter called *Edgewise*, giving information about its work and its plans, largely for the benefit of the village and for the various volunteers who gave their time, and more, for our benefit. However, when it was suggested that the village or one of the existing groups which claimed to care for Edge's interests might take on its pro-duction there was little response. It seems that what was needed here was a pause while everyone sat back and recovered from AELP, took a deep breath, and started again on a new footing.

What of that sentence in our funding application which I quoted earlier: 'since this is primarily a survey, we anticipate that it will raise questions in more than one discipline meriting further research later'? Some of those questions are answered – at least in part – in the chapters that make up this book. Others are still raising their heads a dozen or more years later. There are new insights into the legend that can be only touched on here, for they deserve a whole other book to themselves. What of the 'Roman' mineshaft that we believe we had found? The radiocarbon date for the planks from the bottom of the shaft came out at 360–280 BC or 250 BC–AD 15 (the alternative dates result from the 'flat spot' in the dating curve at this point): this appears to be too early for the tree to have been felled when the Romans advanced into northern

Britain during the later first century AD. We can quite reasonably try to dismiss that by saying that these planks were being re-used by the time they were put into the bottom of the shaft – but as Simon Timberlake asks in Chapter 14, how do we then explain the growing number of Iron Age dates for other mines that had previously been thought to be Roman (*ArchAE*: 88–9)? The Landscape Project began with the rediscovery of a Bronze Age wooden shovel: why did it survive so well in what was clearly not a waterlogged anaerobic context? Perhaps twenty-first-century technology could provide the answer: the shovel was submitted to the Synchrotron Radiation Source at the Science and Technology Facilities Council's Laboratory at Daresbury, near Warrington, as one of the last investigations to be carried out at before its final closure on 4 August 2008. The answer appears to be a very high concentration of copper (no surprises there), along with high levels of lead (again to be expected) and arsenic. While the arsenic is important as the element that binds the copper to the wood – Cuprinol before it was modified to respect current health and safety regulations – the most interesting result of this study was the discovery that the concentrations of copper were markedly higher over working areas of the blade and the unbroken parts of the handle, where it would have been rubbed by the miners' ore-stained hands more than elsewhere: in other words, the copper was forced into the wood while the shovel was being used rather than leaching into it while it was buried in the ground afterwards. In contrast, the Roman planks from the sump in Pot Shaft, which had simply lain in wet if copper-rich conditions for 2,000 years, contained much less copper, and are less well preserved (Smith *et al.*, 2011). There is good evidence that the shovel was deliberately broken ('killed') and sacrificed – we discuss this further in the chapter on the archaeology of the Edge (Chapter 14). Also described in that chapter is the discovery of a wooden goblet in 2005 close to the find-spot of the shovel. The Edge does indeed still have many surprises to catch the unwary or indeed the open-minded.

Alan Garner concludes his 'Approach to the Edge' (Chapter 2) by wondering how much his readers' fingernails have grown in the course of the chapter. The Project coordinator has grown a beard and it has turned grey in the course of this Project, though he has probably not acquired the wisdom that should go with it: even after years of working up there it is still easy to lose one's way on the Edge, for so much is not quite what it seems.

Further reading

Carlon, C. J. 1979. *The Alderley Edge Mines*. Altrincham: John Sherratt and Son.
Carlon, C. J. and Dibben, N. J. 2012. *The Alderley Edge Mines*. Nantwich: Nigel Dibben.
Garner, A. 1979. *The Stone Book Quartet*. London: William Collins (most recent reprint HarperCollins 2010).

2

Approach to the Edge: a personal view

Alan Garner

This chapter was first written as a handbook for the Alderley Edge Landscape Project's exhibition 'Living on the Edge' in 1998, but even then I felt that I could not limit it just to that event, and the editor of this volume has suggested that we reprint a version of it now in the wider context of the full and final publication of the Project's work. Those who would know more about the geology and the water-fleas or the ritual and the chemistry of the shovel's survival or indeed the myriad flora and fauna of the Edge will find some answers in later chapters of the book. The exhibition was a first attempt to give a larger public a sense of what we who grew up in Alderley from childhood have always known: that the Edge is a most special place, and now it is possible for hard evidence to support that inborn knowledge.

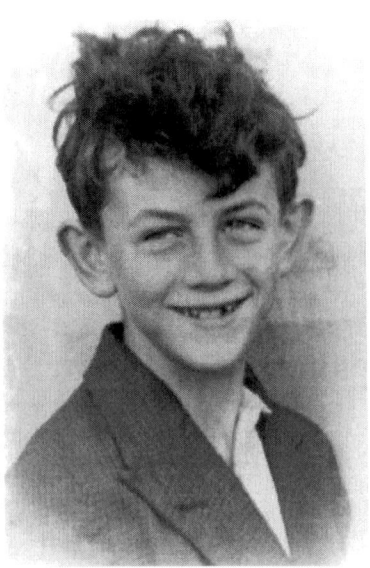

Figure 2.1. Alan Garner in Miss Bratt's class at Alderley Edge Council School, aged six

Photograph courtesy Alan Garner.

The feelings and their truths will remain, for they are permanent, but if the exhibition and now this book do their job, the bringing together of *some* objects, of *some* images out of many hundreds, and of *some* of the stories and facts about the Edge will combine to show how the feelings and the truths came about and how, through unimaginable time, everything connects and has influenced everything else; and that is the greatest of wonders.

For me, this Project started in 1940. I was six years old (Figure 2.1) and in the Infants' Department of Alderley Edge Council School, and my teacher was Miss Bratt.

Miss Bratt always called me Richard, because she had taught my father and his brothers, and I shared with Uncle Dick a frequently employed habit of running away from the Gothic hell-hole of that classroom, with its lancet windows too high to look out from, with uncut evergreens blocking the light so that we were denied even the sky. There was just Miss Bratt, perched at her desk by the blackboard, a coke stove protected by a brass railed wire mesh guard, on which hung the reeking, steaming undergarments of those of us who could not wait until playtime. On the wall there was a cupboard, by the cupboard a nail, and from the nail hung something of no interest whatsoever, except that nobody knew what it was.

So, as my uncle before me, I found myself running down the lane from the school, Miss Bratt panting, 'Richard! Richard!', because she had to catch us before we got to the main road.

The next chapter was the summer of 1953, during my last term at Manchester Grammar School. I had been dispatched to the Central Reference Library to compare differing versions of a Classical text. But I was reading another book, which had the memorable title: *The Jottings of Some Geological, Archaeological, Botanical, Ornithological and Zoological Rambles Round Macclesfield*, by J. D. Sainter, FGS, 1878. Page forty-seven had me hooked. It described the recent findings by miners of a number of grooved stone hammers, or mauls, in an old surface working 'from three to four yards in depth' near the copper mines at Alderley Edge (Figures 2.2, 4.3).

The hammers were quite distinctive. They were used as door stops in the cottages and farms of the area, and I found three myself on the Edge. (In later years, I learnt that such artefacts are common where early metal-working has taken place. Those that I have handled, in Ohio and Armenia, had been found in the first metal cultures of the two places, and although they were separated in time by millennia, they were identical. It is simply that the same problems tend to produce the same answers.) Yet, although the Alderley hammers suggested a Bronze Age occupation, they could not be dated. Flint tools and waste from the Neolithic and Mesolithic periods showed that the Edge had been

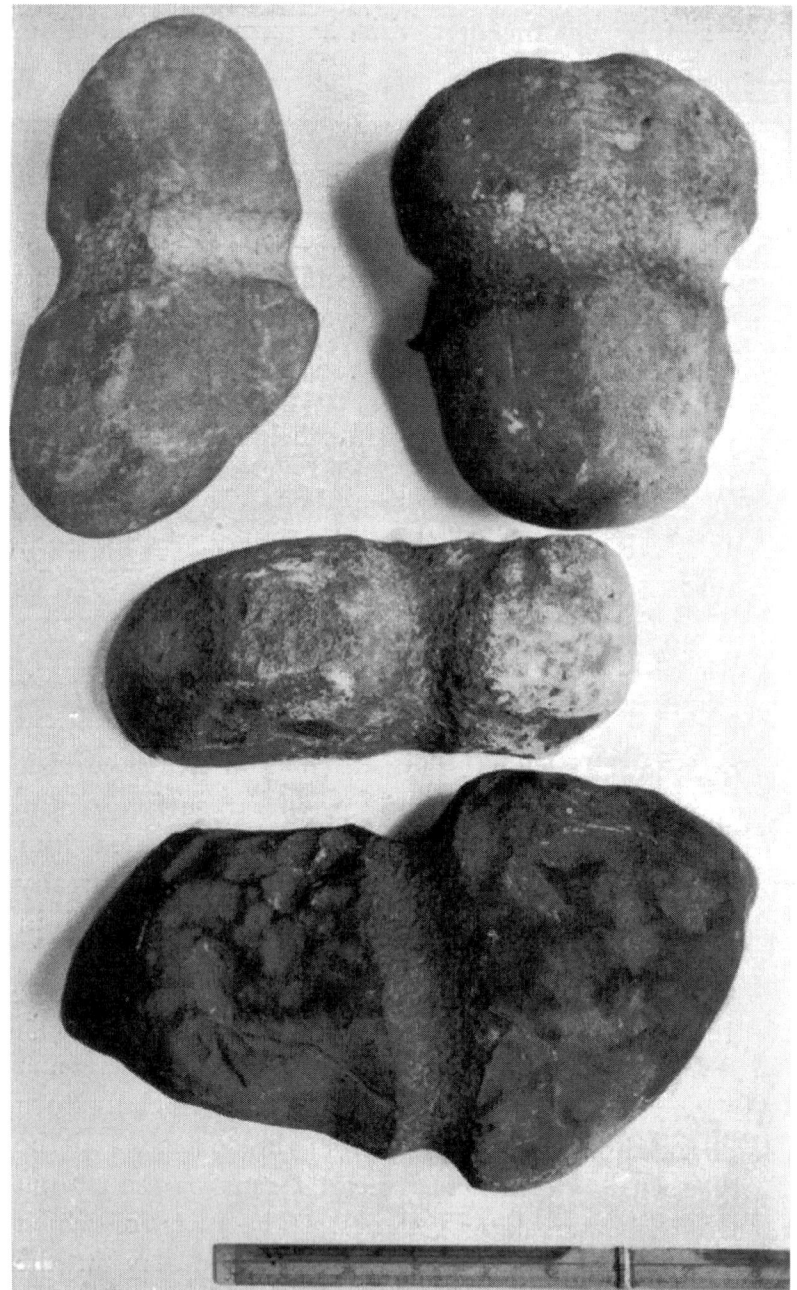

Figure 2.2. A characteristic group of stone hammers from ancient mine pits, Alderley Edge.

After Shone (1911: fig. 35).

occupied for about eight thousand years but what these hammers were, and what they had been used for, could not be proven. Indeed, some archaeologists would not accept that they were more than weights to hold down the roofs of bothies in quite recent mining.

What was so interesting about Sainter's record was that among the hammers lay 'an oak shovel that had been very roughly used'. Sainter

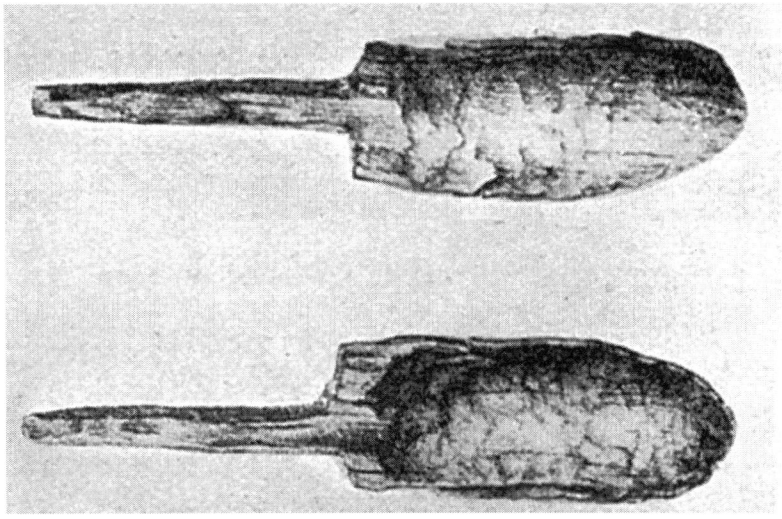

(a)

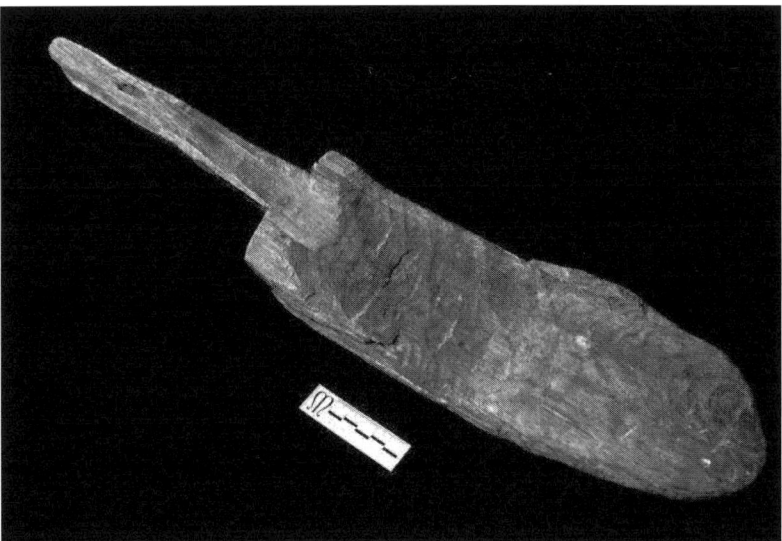

(b)

Figure 2.3. The Alderley
Edge shovel. (a) J. D. Sainter's
drawing, 'Back and Front of
an Oak Spade, Found in the
Ancient Mine Pits, Alderley
Edge'. (b, c) Front and back
views.

(a) After Shone (1911: fig. 39).
(b,c) Manchester Museum acc. no.
1991.85. Photographs Manchester
Museum, University of Manchester.

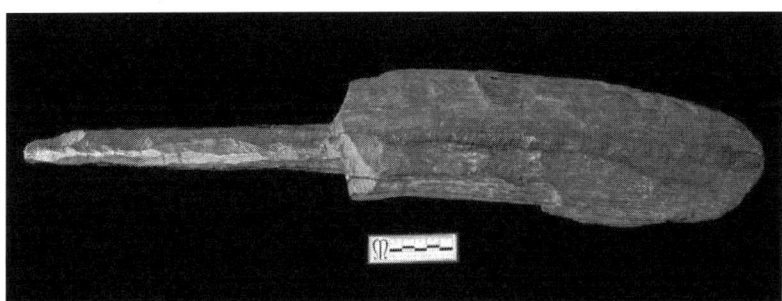

(c)

illustrated the shovel, back and front, opposite page sixty-five (Figure 2.3a), and to my bewilderment I knew that I had seen that 'shovel', and seen it often. But where? I couldn't remember. I knew only that it was familiar.

Days later, in the way that such things happen, I was thinking about something else when I 'saw' the 'shovel' and where it was.

I rushed to Alderley Edge Council School and cornered the head-mistress, Miss Fletcher. She was a formidable authoritarian, with a heart as golden as the plait of the hair of her youth that she wore as a wreath about the equally striking silver of her age.

'The shovel! The shovel in Miss Bratt's room. The shovel!'

Miss Fletcher, used to my manic ways, said, 'I don't know, Alan. Calm down. Let's go and look.'

We went to Miss Bratt's room. Sainter's 'shovel' was the strange thing that had hung above my head and had absorbed much of my attention as I fended off the droning of the eight times table all around me. I am still not happy with the eight times table.

I was even less happy with what I now saw. The cupboard was on the wall. The nail was next to it. But there was nothing on the nail. 'I remember there was something,' said Miss Fletcher. 'We'll ask Mr Ellam.'

We found the caretaker. 'Oh, ay, there was a bit of a thing, wasn't there?' said Billy Ellam. 'But we had a sort-out when Twiggy retired, and most of it went on the tip.' I became hysterical. 'I'll tell you what,' said Billy Ellam. 'If it's not on the tip, it'll be under the stage in the hall.'

I squeezed into the twelve-inch gap below the stage, lighting my way with Billy Ellam's torch. The space was filled with coconut matting, high-jump posts, Miss Bratt's fireguard of mephitic memory (we still use it at home as a towel rail), baskets, boxes, hoops, balls: all the clutter of a village school. I was lost to sight, and Miss Fletcher called after me, but I persevered, turning everything over systematically. Soon contact with the outside world was lost as I worked my way into the dark. Under a rag, at the furthest end of the last corner, was the last object. It was the 'shovel'. Sticking to it was a grubby typed label describing its origin. It was the 'oak shovel that had been very roughly used' (Figure 2.3b,c).

There was no room to turn in. I had to find my way back blind, pulling with my toes and pushing with my one free hand.

'Well!' said Miss Fletcher. 'I think it's "finders keepers". I've never seen anything like that performance in all my born puff!'

I took the 'shovel' to the Manchester Museum. Despite my protestations, there was 'no one available' to comment.

So it began. I felt compelled never to leave the 'shovel' at risk again. It went with me, all through the army, occupying the centre of my kit bag, to the detriment of Her Majesty's property. The British Museum dismissed the 'shovel' as 'possibly a Tudor winnowing fan'.

It was with me at Oxford. The Ashmolean Museum was not interested and declared it to be a 'child's toy spade: Victorian.' The conditions of its finding were ignored. Eventually I stopped asking. There were other things to be done. So I kept the Tudor winnowing fan and Victorian child's spade safe and bided my time. I knew instinctively, and, later, intellectually, that the object was of considerable archaeological importance, and trusted that, one day, it would be recognised. I bided for forty years. And I shall not forget the sense of justification as I formally put the shovel into the hands of John Prag, then Keeper of Archaeology at the Manchester Museum, entrusting it to his care.

Radiocarbon dating was carried out at Oxford. The so-called 'Tudor/Victorian' implement was found to be made of oak that was nearly four thousand years old.

In 1995, the Derbyshire Caving Club, in starting to make safe a shaft that was beginning to collapse at the surface, found a pot holding fourth-century copper Roman coins, fortunately of no great financial worth, and certainly not a question of treasure trove. But the excitement they created was beyond price (Figure 2.4).

Nothing Roman had ever been found on the Edge; which was surprising, since, if anything, Roman remains were the most likely to be expected. But here was evidence, and beyond evidence suggestion: suggestion that, towards the end of the Roman occupation, something had happened that had scared whoever the people were living on the Edge.

The British tribe of this area were the northern Cornovii, relatively peaceful for a part of Britain that was always under military law, which was especially strict where mining of any kind took place. But within a few hours' march were the real bogeymen, the Brigantes.

Everyone, Roman or British, was in trouble if the Brigantes decided to take a stroll down from the Pennines, an area that was never pacified. And, at the time of the digging of Pot Shaft, which turned out to be close to AD 65, the Brigantes were still some five years from being 'conquered', itself a Roman euphemism (research at other sites in Britain and elsewhere carried out since the Project was at work now suggests that Pot Shaft may actually have been dug before the Roman conquest, but it does not affect this discussion – see Chapter 14). Before then, they had been classified as 'precarious', and in AD 69 they were upgraded to 'open enemies', and the Governor of Britain, when called upon to supply troops for troubles nearer home, refused, giving as his reason his inability to manage the Brigantes. The Edge, and its mining, were on the very limit of the controllable Roman Empire. You have only to stand at Pot Shaft and look to the hills to realise that in AD 65 a miner's lot was not a happy one; nor was a Roman soldier's. One of my most intense understandings of Roman Britain came as a schoolboy, when in Brigantine Northumbria, I saw a Roman tile, on which fifty years after

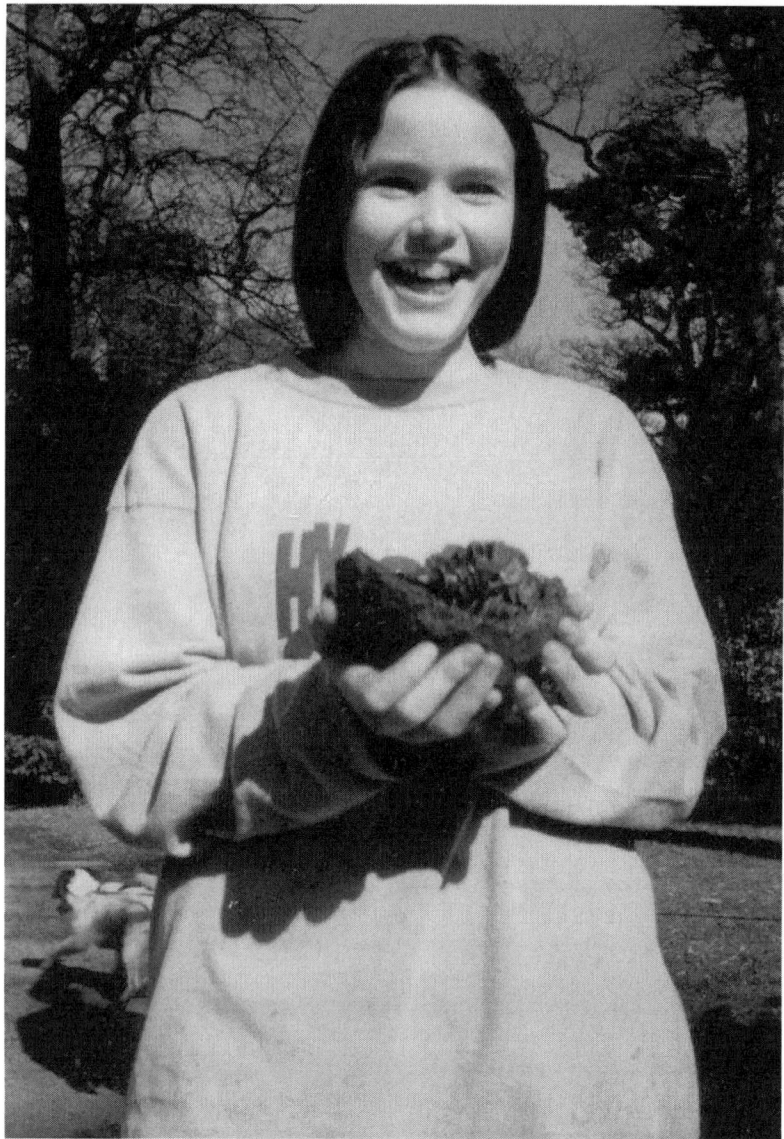

Figure 2.4. The pot containing the hoard of Roman coins, in the hands of Rachel Bailey, immediately after its discovery by her father in April 1995.

Photograph Ian Roberts, courtesy of Ian Roberts, Malcolm Bailey and Rachel Bailey.

Pot Shaft, the maker had scribbled with his finger on the tile before it was fired the Latin equivalent of, 'Oh, shit!'

So it is not unreasonable to suppose that, at a time when the Romans were in the first years of losing their grip, the Brigantes would sniff a chance. The result would be panic. That panic rose up at us in 1995 as we looked down into what is now called Pot Shaft. Someone had been in a hurry to hide the pot and its contents (Figure 2.5). Any old hole would do, so long as it could be found again. And here was a shaft, filled nearly to the top with rubbish and wind-blown sand. Whoever hid the coins almost certainly knew of it and where to come to find them again

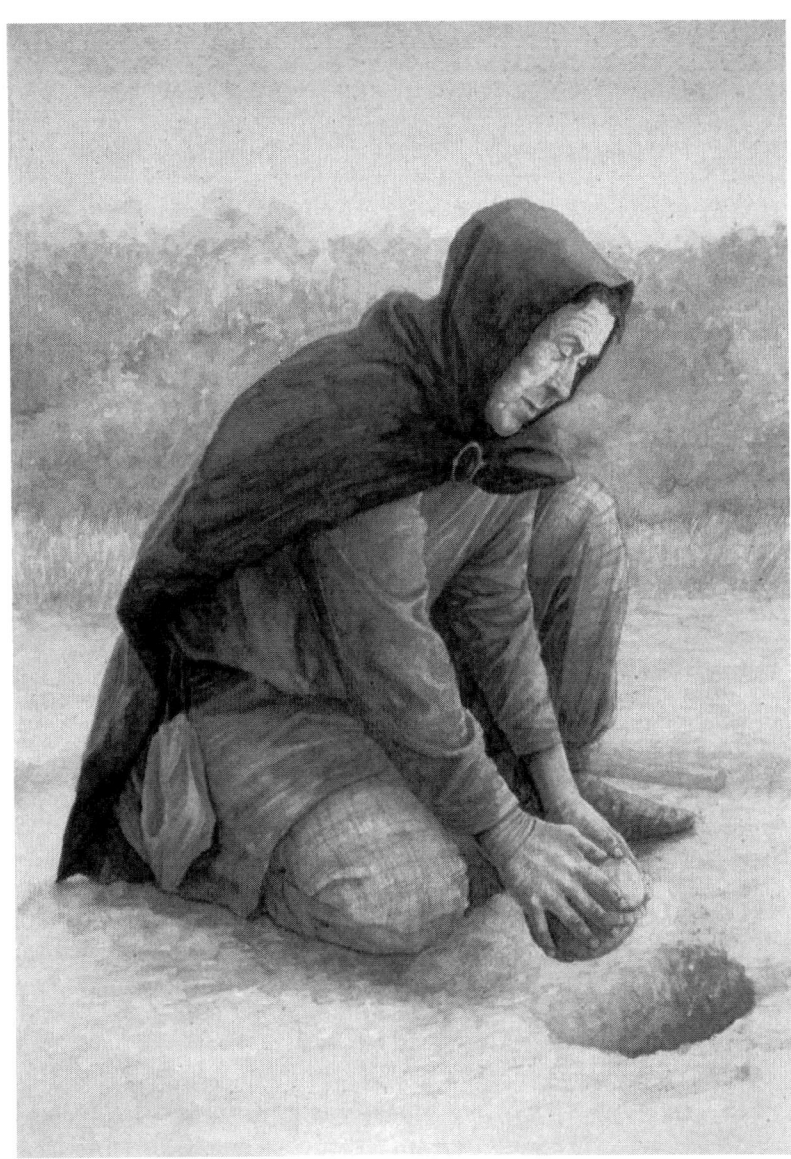

Figure 2.5. Artist's reconstruction of the burial of the coin hoard *c.* AD 340.

Drawing by Seán Ó'Brógáin.

when times were better. But it seems that, for him, time ran out, and stayed out for nearly two thousand years. (Figure 14.9, p. 332, shows the hoard itself.)

When it was excavated in 1997, Pot Shaft proved to be eleven metres deep, a tunnel had been cut from the bottom to reach the copper ore, and there was a wooden construction in perfect condition so that radiocarbon dating at a laboratory in Miami could give evidence for the possible digging of the shaft in about AD 65, less than a quarter of a century after the Roman invasion of southern Britain, and possibly

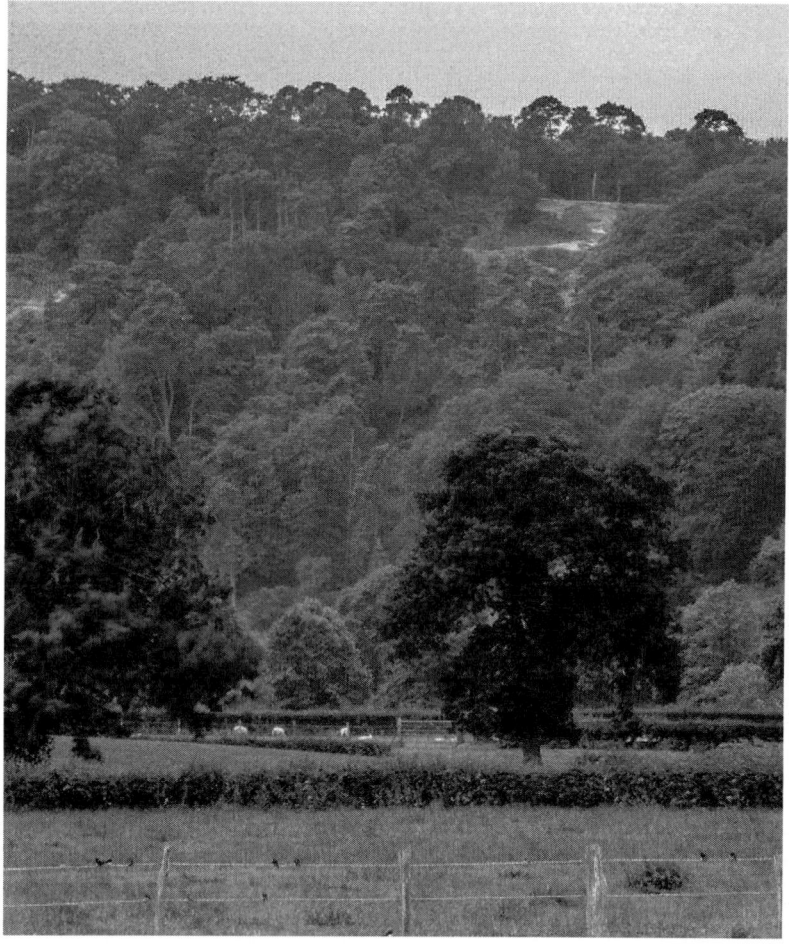

Figure 2.6. Alderley Edge and Stormy Point from the north-east.

Photograph Sean Edwards.

during the reign of the emperor Nero (Figures 14.10, 14.11). It must have been a considerable military operation, and so the next, and not yet proven, matter had to be that of where the soldiers were quartered.

It was as if the Edge had been waiting until people showed that they were worthy of its knowledge, and that it felt that we were ready to be told. A pot of coins, an oak spade twice their age, and now. The gaps were so even, so neat. We were being invited to join in the rhythm of the Edge. The Project's exhibition was some of the first notes of the tune.

Although the Project started for me in 1940, the Edge was earlier in my forming.

Suburban Mottram Road ends at the Woodhill, an abrupt scarp of beech trees above the footpath. A sloping bank only twice my two-year infant height goes up to a level path. Here was my first experience of the struggle with gradient and land; my engagement with the Edge (Figure 2.6; Plate 1).

When I had conquered that little bank, there was the hill above, the ground deep in leaves and twigs, which were the next initiation into weakness, to the body's humbling, in order to reach the flat safety of the ledge of the old quarry road halfway up the hill, which, after the abandoned quarry, resumed its narrow packhorse dimensions, snaggled with roots. It was a learning of textures, a teaching of respect. When those had been engrained, there was granted the main climb, over sand and rocks, and the sticky red clay that was called Tough Tom, to the highest path. Here, as a mark of recognition for what the infant had won, was the greeting of the Wizard's Well, the portals to the Edge itself.

The Wizard's Well is a stone trough below a cliff, dug from the rock, ancient, perhaps prehistoric, and above it the carving of a sombre, bearded face (Figure 2.7). It is family tradition that the face is the work of my great-great-grandfather, Robert. A later hand had written:

DRINK OF
THIS AND
TAKE THY
FILL FOR THE
WATER FALLS
BY THE
WIZHARDS
WILL

And into the trough, every few and regular seconds there falls a single drop of water. It never changes, flood or drought. It has seeped for years in the rock and has no care for Time. Nor has the sandstone it has passed through, an ancient river bed or delta, embedded with rounded pebbles of white quartz.

It is my first memory of awe: that here, six hundred feet high, was a river bed. But what had that river been? And from what hills or mountains had it washed those pebbles? And when?

Before a child's brain could assimilate these questions I had reached Castle Rock, and the eye, protected before by the curtain of trees, was shown the enormity of the world. The Edge, the quest, had been achieved. It had taught much, and demanded more, but here, at Castle Rock, was the reward: the opening of the next challenge. The Edge and the child had been attained, and in the attaining, which had taken months, they had become one.

It is not that for everybody. The Edge is itself, and, being itself, can become whatever is made of it. Having its own truth, it can reflect and enlarge the truth of all who experience it. Being itself, the Edge will tell you who and what you are. It will magnify you, strengths and weaknesses.

It is all in the approach.

Because of the way that I learnt, a strange awareness has emerged over the years. I have always been reasonably fit, can climb mountains,

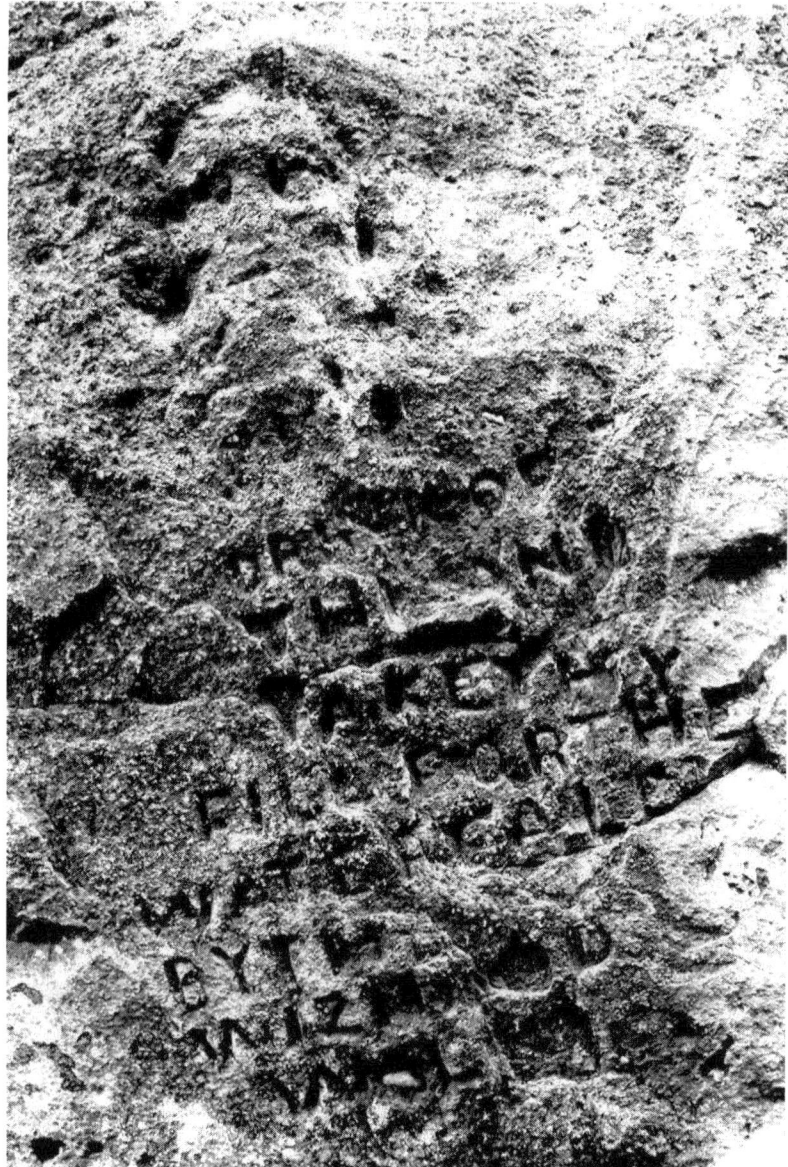

Figure 2.7. The carvings at the Wizard's Well: a bearded face, and below it the inscription DRINK OF THIS AND TAKE THY FILL FOR THE WATER FALLS BY THE WIZHARDS WILL.

Photograph Sean Edwards.

walk hills, and be as out of breath and need to rest as often as anybody; but not on the Edge. I lean into it and go up in one. It's as if that particular gradient of land, known since I was two, has become a part of me. Likewise, when descending, I scree-run, and, provided I don't think about what I'm doing, I don't slip, no stone trips, no root catches.

It was how I found my first Bronze Age hammer. I was climbing the slope below Stormy Point, using hands and feet, so quickly that I was not looking up but moving instinctively. I put my hand on a stone, and couldn't move, dared not lift my head. My hand felt the stone, and was gripping it by the polished groove, worn smooth by a haft of withies three thousand and seven hundred years ago. And no one, probably, had held it since then until now. It was not the first or the last time that the Edge has given me a token, not always physical, but always heart-stopping.

It is in the approach. It depends on what you need of the place and how much effort you are willing to put into it.

If you want to drive your car and to park on level tarmac, pause to buy an ice cream, and then walk by pleasant and easy ways under dappled tree light of a fabled beauty-spot until you come to the lip of the Edge, pause and admire one of the most dramatic of landscape views, and return to your car, you will drive home refreshed. That is what you came to do, and the Edge has obliged. It is the same if you walk your dog.

At the other extreme for the visitor (and I am not talking about the native, to whom none of this will apply), it will be quite another experience, if the approach is made from the north, and especially the north-east. From round about Woodford, if you are driving, you will catch glimpses of what is ahead, until it cannot be avoided. If you come by train, nothing is hinted at before you have left Wilmslow station. Then, for a couple of minutes, you will have the finest of all sights of the Edge. Here there is no doubting that it is a matter that demands recognition. You may even feel that it has recognised you.

However you come, face the Edge. If you choose to forgo the tarmac and to park in the old quarry on Mottram Road, do not rush. You have more than three hundred feet to climb. Watch before you move. You are in the first of many wondrous places (Figure 2.8).

It scarcely looks like England. You are surrounded by foxy-red sandstone. The ground is sand. Pick up the sand and let it run through your fingers. It is smooth. There is a path on the other side of the quarry, leading out and up. The wooded Edge dominates. That climb before you is what you have to achieve. But, before you attempt it, spend a few minutes, or hours, at the east wall of the quarry. It is a simple path, and you need go only a few yards before you realise why it does not look like England. It is not the England of today. This wall shows that the past is indeed another country.

The wall is in part a section through the dunes of a petrified desert. The tops of the dunes have been cut off by sandstorms, and, in turn, fresh dunes have crept over them. The dunes are still so soft that mason bees make their nests there. This soft smoothness is the result of the sand's being swirled in dry winds, so that the sharpness of the grains has worn away.

It is a desert that was formed over two hundred and forty-five million years ago by the Trade Winds, not more than twenty degrees north of the equator, at about the latitude of Arabia, Yemen, Oman, Sudan and

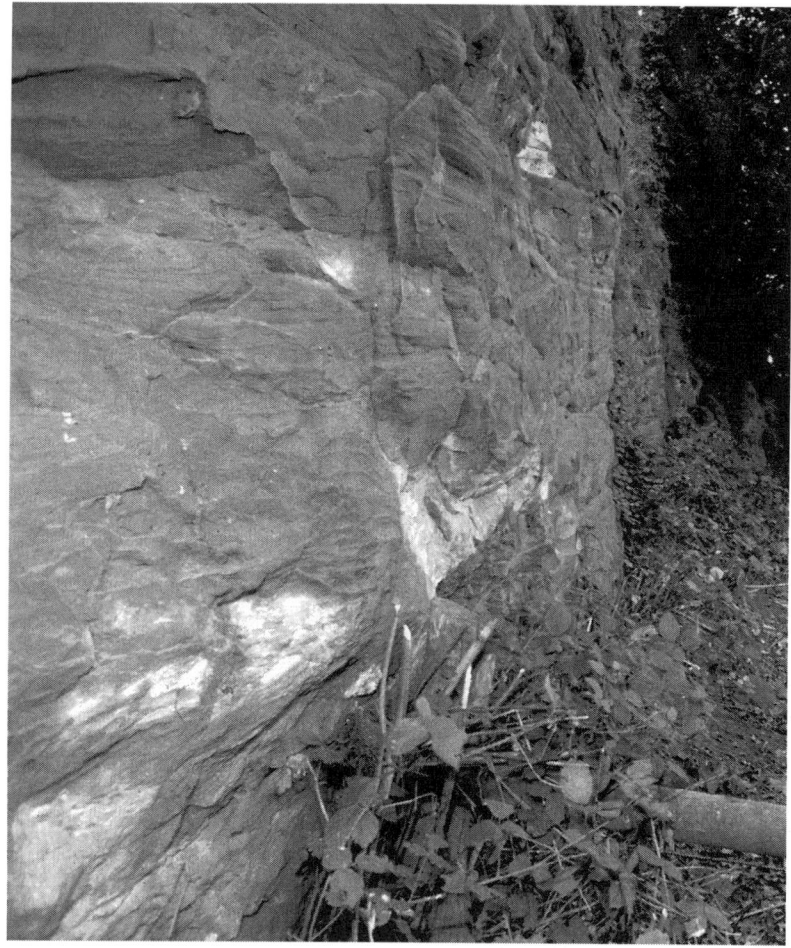

Figure 2.8. Mottram Road sand quarry – a section through the dunes of a petrified desert.

Photograph Sean Edwards.

the Sahara. And, ever since, it has been drifting with the Earth's crust in this direction at the speed at which your fingernails grow. And it is still moving.

Whereabouts on that latitude the desert formed is not known yet. What we do know is something of the animals that inhabited that land from the traces of their passing imprinted in the stone. There are the footprints of reptiles (Figure 5.3, and Figures 5.14, 5.15 in Appendix 5.1): large meat-eaters and small, swift plant-eaters (Plate 5). There are shells the size of a pin head, left by creatures related to fresh-water shrimps which lived in muddy shallows (Figure 5.2).

If you cross the quarry floor and climb up the path, with the field on your right, you will have begun this journey through Time and Space.

When you reach the wood, the desert will be lost under fallen leaves, as it is under the ridge of the field, reappearing as small outcrops and loose stones on the many long-distance trackways that cross and climb the Edge. But if you go straight up the ridge you will be not only on a track but on an old boundary, still existing, that also suggests a land of more than physical power, and hints at a reverence, and a wariness, for the Edge that must have been in people's minds since at least Anglo-Saxon times, thirteen hundred years ago, and even before (Figure 2.9). The names on the boundary may be translations from Welsh and earlier.

The hint survives in an undated grant of land made at some time between AD 1230 and 1250, on the evidence of the signatures, where this boundary is described. The starting point would have coincided with Mottram Road, and then 'climbing up the Green Ridge of the Elf [and an elf then was no quaint thing, but a spirit to be feared] as far as the Sadel [Saddlebole, a Medieval and earlier smelting hearth above a dip in the ridge, which forms the Saddle] and from the Sadel, following a certain road as far as the Great Birch and to the Peaked Burial Mound

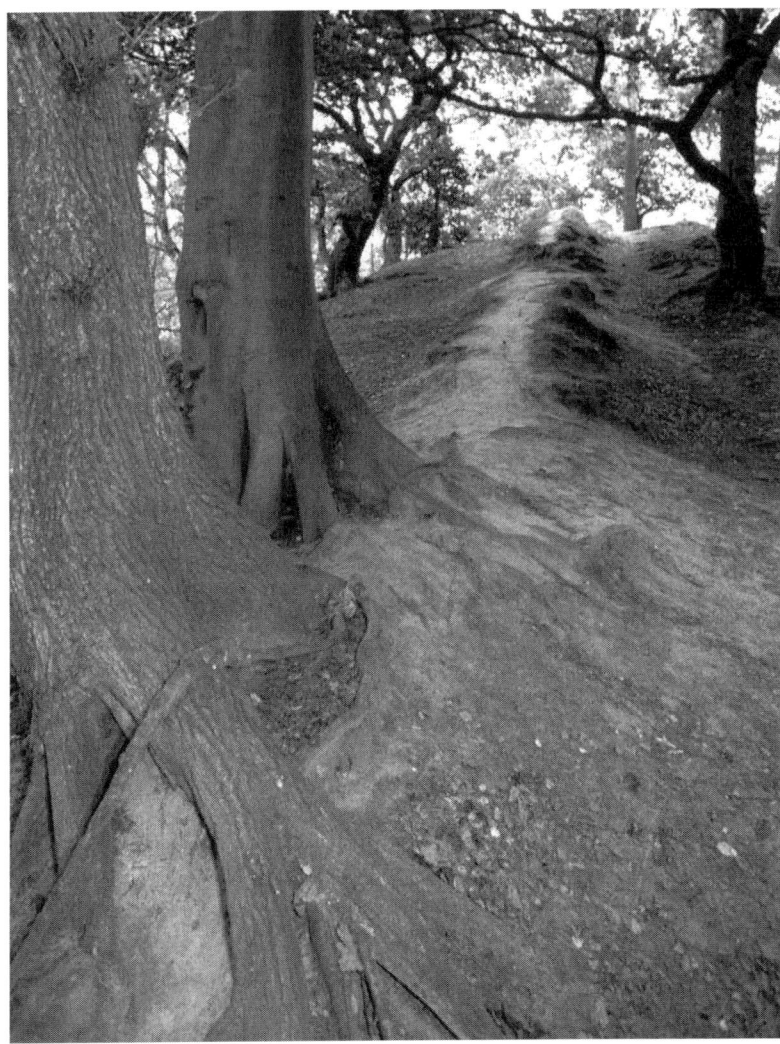

Figure 2.9. Path following the early boundary bank on Saddlebole.

Photograph Sean Edwards.

and the Gate of the Elf Guard'. All the way, you will have followed the low earthen boundary wall, still visible, and at last have arrived, and won the right to stand, at the Devil's Grave on Stormy Point, with panoramic views you will have earned and will appreciate the more.

You are no longer in a desert but on a river bed that came flooding in, sweeping sand and pebbles from long worn-down heights in what are now France, Devon and Cornwall. The sand and the rock are hard, and of a different colour, sharp, the grains quickly deposited by the water that brought them and soon covered up by other layers that protected them from wear.

It has been a long climb, but it took the Edge longer to form it.

Over two hundred and fifty million years ago, the surface of the Earth under what is now Cheshire was being stressed from both west and east. Ireland and Wales were tugged towards becoming a part of America, and England was dragged away from Scandinavia and Northern Europe. Then, for reasons not known, the process stopped. 'Cheshire' did not become an ocean rift like the Red Sea, as it inevitably would have done, but just a sagging basin. It was in this setting that the alternating wind-blown and later the water-borne sands of the Edge were laid down.

About seventy to eighty million years later, the stress pattern went into a long reverse, and the rocks were upfolded. Some of them cracked and flipped up on one side, sloping gently downwards on the other, rather in the manner of a misplaced and fractured paving stone, but in a more complicated form, forcing mineralising and oily solutions to the surface. Over further millions of years, rivers, ice and wind eroded the exposed heights, and in such an epic way the Edge was made, rearing imperceptibly the path from the Green Ridge of the Elf to the Gate of the Elf Guard. And, because you have been looking at the ground before you as you climbed, you will have felt those years in your bones and have seen their force. That is why you will know the Edge in a way that you cannot from a walk made cozy. You will have felt the rhythm. Now it is possible for understanding to begin.

We, the children of my generation who were born to the Edge, played here through all seasons, by day and by night, learning our own ways. The child lore of the Edge was rich, and still is, for the signs of its continuity are to be seen, if you know what they are. It is not my job to betray them here, but to pass them on by word of mouth to the inheritors. Small knowledge and precious. And how old?

We knew where to find the different coloured clays for our war paint. One of the bodies from nearby Lindow Moss was perhaps painted with the same hues two thousand years ago (Pyatt *et al.*, 1995, 70–3; but Smith, 1993, and Cowell and Craddock, 1995, raise the possibility that the raised copper levels in the skin are simply the result of a natural process). Were they from the same clays? We knew the trees, the dangerous, the special, the kindly and the safe. We knew the one thin band of clay, hidden under leaves, that worked as soap to spare us from a good hiding when we got home. However thirsty we were, we still drank from the only pure water on the Edge, and we knew the secret of how to get it.

We knew the secrets and the truths that were not physical. We knew that the Hanging Stone, in 1740, fell and landed on an old woman and her cow with such force that it shook all the houses in the Hough. We knew the ghosts (they were of our own families). But, because of our respect, we were not afraid. The multitude of abandoned, overgrown stone quarries could have killed us, but they did not. Perhaps in some way we were protected by the graceful herringbone pattern left by the quarrymen, our ancestors, where they won the stone and lost their lives. Few of them could expect their lungs to survive beyond the age of forty-six. However, there was one aspect of the Edge that we never tampered with: the mines.

In the Bronze Age and two thousand years later by the Romans, they were worked, as they are known to have been in the historical record from the seventeenth century. It is unknown, as yet, whether they were worked in the periods between; but the story of human discovery tends to show that, once something, be it a skill or a resource, is found it is seldom lost. The main danger, however, was from the workings of the eighteenth to the nineteenth centuries. Until the Derbyshire Caving Club took responsibility for the mines, those mines were open and they injured and killed. But it was always strangers. Locals knew better. Perhaps we had lost too many of our people in making them. While visitors, the women wearing high heeled shoes, tottered into the unknown dark, striking matches as they went, we stayed outside. In doing so, we lived until we could see the double wonder of the Edge.

The surface is archaeologically rich, but the inside of the hill is as great. The Edge has these two splendours: the worlds over and under. When you walk on it, you walk on a sponge. Beneath your feet is a land, brought about by geological forces, which veined the hill with coloured minerals injected from below by pressure. They are more than coloured, they are jewelled and have haunting names: malachite, azurite, pyromorphite, cerussite, galena; and, because of the damp air, they shine in a way that cannot be seen on the surface, where, by comparison, they are just pretty stones.

The result, after the mining, is a labyrinth almost beyond comprehension (see Chapter 17). But I was twenty years old before I went there, and then only after the army had taught me the rudiments of caving and rock climbing. I stood where a roof fall had killed my great-great-uncle Richard. My grandfather, aged ten, in 1886, disgusted by the crude hacking of graffiti in the desert sandstone ('Any fool can be a breaker' he told me, 'but it takes a proper man to be a maker'), had put his name there in Real Writing, cursive script, the only example on the Edge, above the traces of the name of that same Richard. There, in one anecdote, is the truth of the tribal relationship with the land. We are each a part of the other. Australian Aborigines call it 'the bone country.'

That is not a boast. The children of the Edge are fortunate, and fortunate to know it. Which leads me to the final, delicate questions, so nicely balanced that to fall one way is to be a self-affirmed ignoramus, and to fall the other is to be forced to try to explain a reality, born of knowledge and experience, that perhaps may not be spoken, only felt. The questions, so often asked, are: Is the Edge alive? Is it sentient? Does it, too, know? My human reaction is 'Yes' to all. But I would not explain much further, if I could. The frustration is that Western Europe embraced one of the world's few great cultures that would find it necessary to ask the questions when the answers were so evident. Such is the downside of our inheritance of Humanism: William Blake called it 'the Spectre of Reason'. In the end, it becomes a personal question of feeling, experience, interpretation. Yet there is something.

It is obvious, from the contracted Medieval Latin and the Old English names in a document more than seven hundred years old, that the Edge has influenced the beliefs of people for a long time. I have already said that it will be whatever you need it to be. But I must admit, without withdrawing that remark, to a certain exasperation, an exasperation made the more acute by my knowledge of experiences had by people who are not anxious to flaunt them.

The aspect of the Landscape Project that deals with oral memory has come up with the most remarkable information, and in this context a cousin of mine has only now revealed that, as a child in the 1940s, he and the boys he was playing with one night on Stormy Point heard sustained music coming from under the ground. They had not experienced it before, and my cousin has not experienced it since.

Surprisingly little has been written about the Edge. Still amongst the most informative is a slim book, *Alderley Edge and Its Neighbourhood*, written by the Honourable Louisa Dorothea Stanley in 1843, but published anonymously, since she was both a woman and an aristocrat (Stanley, 1843). My cousin did not know that she wrote: 'The people living on the Edge persuade themselves that they hear music sometimes underground. There are some now living who tell a wonderful tale of sounds and sights that they have heard and witnessed'. That it has taken the Project and over fifty years for me to learn of my cousin's experience is diagnostic of a genuine event, whatever the cause. It is the self-aggrandisers with whom I am impatient.

If you want to publish accounts of your mystical visions of blue-robed worshippers at a sacred well, then publish. But you should know that the well, and the hermit's cave behind it, are again traditionally the nineteenth-century work of Robert Garner, my great-great-grandfather, who was content to fulfil the Romantic fantasies of the landowner.

If you want to be a witch, and to have the police make of the Edge a no-go area at Hallowe'en so that you may keep faith with the 'age-old tradition of witchcraft' there, then you should know that the 'tradition' dates from September 1962, when a somewhat disturbed individual, who styled himself 'king of the witches', persuaded *The Manchester Evening News* to witness, and photograph, his 'resurrecting' into new life of a 'dead' man on Stormy Point.

If you elect to worship at the 'prehistoric' Druid Stones, or, in opposition, carve neutralising though inaccurate runes, sacred signs and Christian symbols on them, realise that they are, allegedly, the result of Robert's willingness to place in a circle odd ends of useless stone that a cleverer gentleman than he was willing to pay for so that he could show off to his guests his 'Ancient British Remains' (Figure 2.10). I use the word 'allegedly', because Louisa Stanley has this to say in 1843. 'On the road between Stormy Point and the Beacon, is a circle of stones placed in the form of a Cromlech or Druidical circle. An author, who was writing some account of Cheshire, put down in his book these stones as real remains of antiquity, and was far from being well pleased when he was undeceived.' Robert could have set the stones up, though he would have been a young man to have done so. I report only tradition. My feeling, in this instance, is that, with so many stoneworkers in the family, it may not have been Robert himself, but I do not doubt that the name was Garner. It is common in folk memory for true stories to be remembered as being all associated with one individual. The stones are discussed again in Chapter 27 (pp. 676–7).

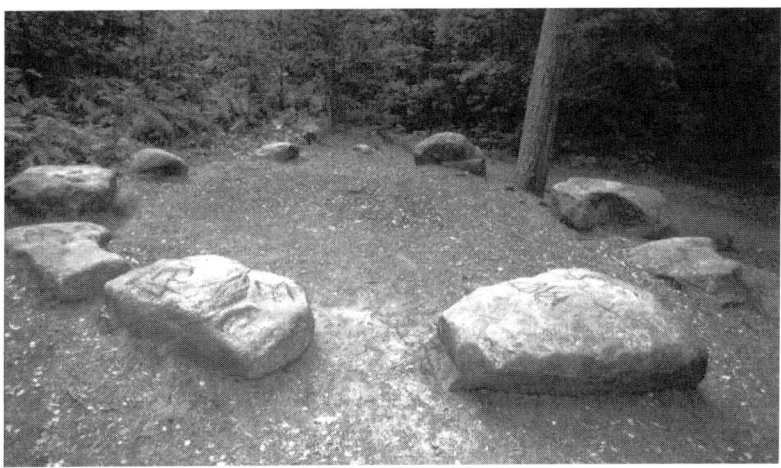

Figure 2.10. The 'prehistoric' Druid Stones.

Photograph Sean Edwards.

There is no point in my saying more, other than that I never know whether to laugh or to cry. Laughter may be cruel, weeping arrogant. But sometimes I do bang my head on the softer sandstones.

If you have mystical vision, if you are a 'witch', if you possess arcane knowledge that is forbidden to all but the chosen, I suppose that you may answer that of course Robert Garner did what he did in the place where he did, because he was being controlled by ancient forces, who directed him to sites that were, and are, 'sacred'. You will say that he had no choice.

The argument is circular. But, along with the Green Ridge of the Elves, it shows that the Edge does affect a sense of 'otherness' in many people, and has for a long time, since there is surely a conflict of sensibilities between those who would dance naked in November and those who could find and tussle with a thirteenth-century version of monkish shorthand. They are not likely to be the same individuals. And that, whatever the reality, is extremely interesting.

I am not in any way seeking to disparage the spiritual. It is the reverse. I am saying that if such people, instead of cavorting around and making the Edge in their own fashion, would instead be quiet and still and listen, then the Edge would express to them a greater truth.

Which at last brings us to the Wizard (Figure 2.11).

The Legend of Alderley is well known, and it will be discussed fully in Chapter 30: its particular importance to the Edge lies in minute details and in order to appreciate it fully it may help to have read the rest of the Edge's story first.

At its briefest, the Alderley Legend is the story of a farmer, who, on his way to market to sell his white mare, is stopped by an old man who wishes to buy the mare. He takes the farmer underground by making a rock open to reveal a pair of iron gates, beyond which a tunnel leads into the hill. The farmer enters a cave where a king is sleeping with his knights, all in silver armour, and each, except for one, accompanied by a white horse. They are waiting to fight the last battle of the world, and the old man needs the mare to make up the number. He pays the farmer with a rich treasure, and takes him back to the upper world. In the Legend of Alderley, the old man is not at first called a wizard, and his name of Merlin and of Arthur for the Sleeping Hero are nineteenth-century decorations, from a romanticised version by James Roscoe, published in *Blackwood's Magazine* in February 1839. In the legend as it was told to me by my grandfather, they were simply an old man and a king. But, although the characters were vague, the time was not. The old man met the farmer 'at dawn on a day at the end of October'.

The legend always intrigued me. There was something wrong about it that was right. The old man met the farmer at the place called Thieves' Hole and took him to the rock of the Iron Gates 'by Seven Firs and

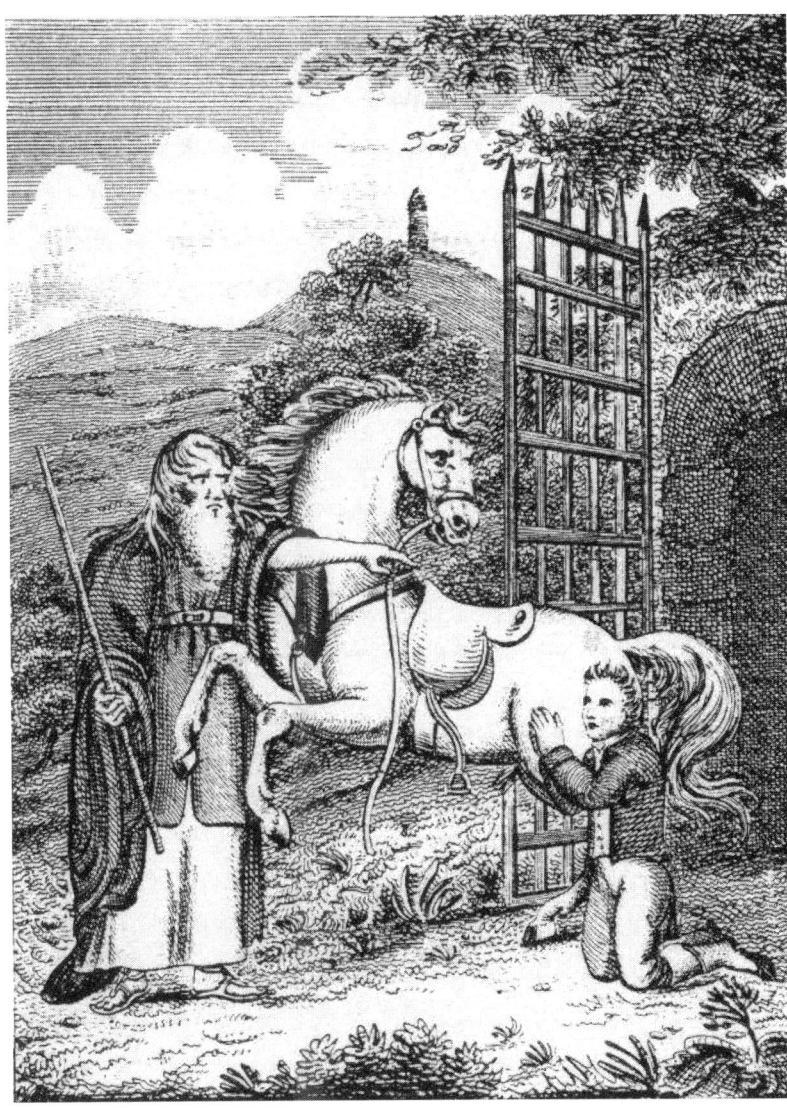

Figure 2.11. The Farmer and the Wizard.

From Stanley (1843).

Goldenstone and Stormy Point and Saddlebole'. The rock of the Iron Gates was by the side of the path just before Saddlebole. For some reason, the old man traipsed the farmer in a meandering line across open ground which increased the journey by about twenty per cent (see Figure 28.3, p. 707). Why? The Edge was not planted with trees until the eighteenth century. Before that, it was described as a 'dreary common'.

I went to look, and at each place mentioned I found man-made structures that appeared to be prehistoric, and suggested especially the Bronze Age of four thousand years ago, although no archaeologist could agree that there was any evidence for the Bronze Age on Alderley. Only the imported flints of the Neolithic and Mesolithic periods, five and

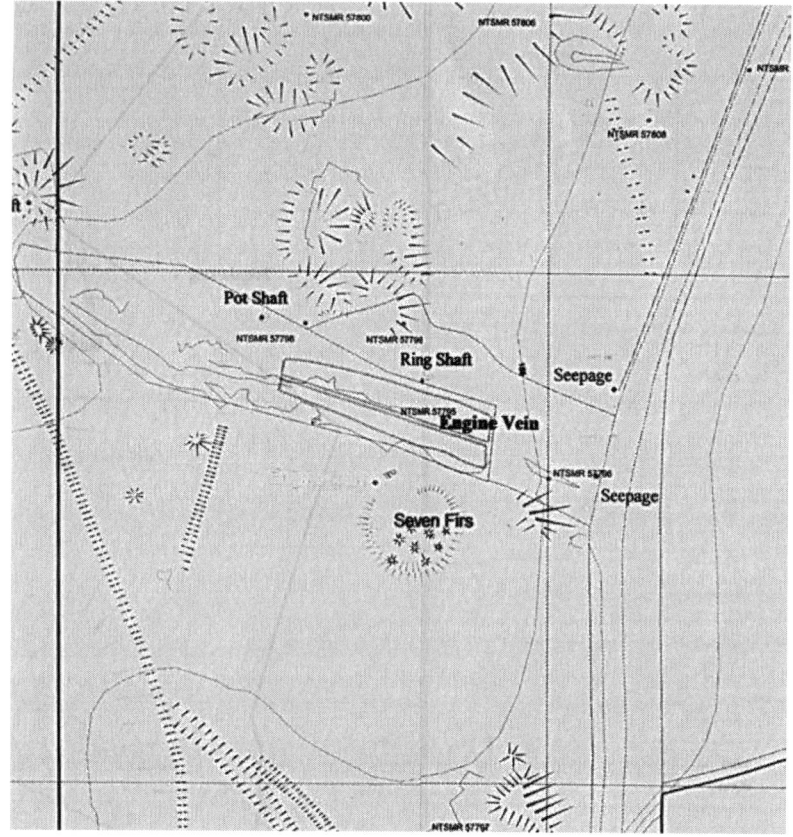

Figure 2.12. GIS-based map of the tree boles at Seven Firs.

eight thousand years ago, were dateable by their style (Figure 14.3). But had my grandfather inherited, and I through him, a truth that had come down as a form of Chinese Whispers over four millennia? There is a Russian riddle that I find most eloquent. 'What is lighter than silk, more enduring than salt? A story'.

The Landscape Project survey of the earthwork at Seven Firs has picked up signals that show what appear to be the remains of the boles of seven trees under the turf (Figure 2.12). The Goldenstone is a big, free-standing block of sandstone, but it does not come from stone immediately to hand (Figure 2.13). It has, at some time and at some effort, been moved to that spot, although stones of apparently equal worth were close by (see Chapters 27 and 30).

I would also argue strongly for the Legend of Alderley to contain evidence for a prehistoric view of Time, and I should like to think (but cannot say more than 'like') that my grandfather, in his teaching of me, was handing down distorted fragments of importance that have endured for perhaps five millennia. More of this, and all that lies behind it, in a later chapter.

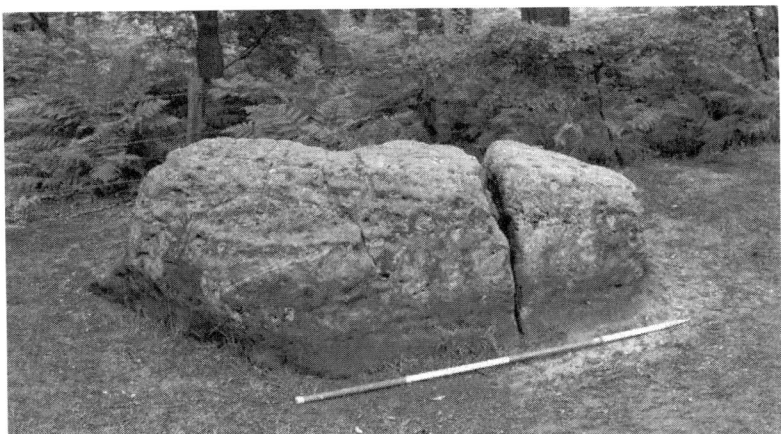

Figure 2.13. The Goldenstone seen from the east, close by the track to Clockhouse Farm.

Photograph Sean Edwards.

What I can say now is that however old the story, I discovered by testing it elements of a Bronze Age prehistory which the Landscape Project has verified. And that is more exciting than would be the meeting with a witch on Stormy Point. The modern seekers after the sensational are, as I see it, denying themselves a greater experience.

In the world of folkloric studies, the elements of the Legend of Alderley also point to the Edge as an important place over a large span of time. Such elements are classified as 'motifs', and here we have three that are basic to the human spirit: the Hollow Hill, the Sleeping Hero, and the Treasure Mountain. All indicate sanctity, especially the sanctity of renewal and of the soul's strength. The bright and shining Hero will wake and return to the light. In the cave (that is, the grave) life has vanished. It is hidden, but not dead. Also hidden is the Treasure. Everywhere in popular legend this Treasure is imagined as being within the earth. The Treasure is frequently not recognised, since it appears as a valueless object. Alchemy was considered to be a useful tool of mining as late as the nineteenth century. A Medieval Latin alchemical poem ascribed to Arnaldus de Villanova (*c.* 1235–1311) published in Frankfurt in 1550 refers to

> This puny stone of little worth,
> Spurned by the fool, honoured by the wise.

'This puny stone' is both the Grail and the alchemist's Philosopher's Stone. Something ancient is at work here.

The Treasure is often protected by a deathless figure. Is it the old man and his Iron Gates? Is he the Elf Guard? The Iron Gates are on the boundary of the thirteenth-century land grant; and remember that an elf was a figure of supernatural power, not a garden ornament.

At Alderley the motifs of the Hollow Hill, the Sleeping Hero and the Treasure Mountain frequently merge, yet they must not be thought to represent the mines. There are no natural caves in the hill. The great caverns are all recent and man-made, and it is not the mineral wealth that is the Treasure. The real Treasure is of the Spirit.

It would seem that the Edge has been at some time, and that time a long time, a place of special activity; and that the evidence of a scientific methodology is more moving than current ersatz and external manifestations, though both exist. The difference is in the approach.

It is for each of us to decide for ourselves. Is the Edge a romanticised 'puny stone of little worth', or is it more? For me, I can say that it has been a womb. But, above all, it is itself, the Edge.

The Landscape Project, after its allotted first two years, recognised that it had but scratched the surface. The Edge has asked more questions than it has answered. In some form the Project must and will continue, not just after the first two years nor even after the all but two decades that it has taken to bring its researches to full publication. This essay was originally intended to give a context to, and to flesh out, an exhibition which could claim to be 'The Story So Far' but not 'The Final Word', and to give a general picture of that which has come to possess so many different specialists. Now, fifteen or so years on, it serves the same purpose for the final volume. All who have worked on the Project have got more than they bargained for and have learnt a lot. Much of what has been discovered was there to be found, but I suspect that each of us has experienced the greatest excitement as a result of what we have been told. A large part of the success of this venture has been the product of the generosity shown by the people of Alderley, and to them go our special thanks.

How much have your fingernails grown while you were reading this?

Part II

The bedrock of the Edge – geology and geography

3

The geological story of Alderley Edge

David B. Thompson and Simon Timberlake

Alderley Edge comprises an uplifted block, 3 km wide, of Triassic sandstones that are about 245 million years old. The block lies between two major north–south fracture zones – the Alderley Fault to the west and Kirkleyditch fault to the east. These downthrow the rocks in adjoining areas to the west and east respectively. The softer, finer Wilmslow Sandstone underlies the harder, coarser, pebbly Helsby Sandstone, which is succeeded by a thick sequence of mudstones and rock salt (halite) that formed between around 242 and 205 million years ago. The sandstones contain trace fossils such as *Rhynchosauroides* and *Chirotherium*, the footprints of precursors of lizards and dinosaurs. These, and the fossil magnetism of the red rocks, indicate an origin in hot, semi-arid to desert environments in tropical latitudes. The rock units that form Alderley Edge lie on the southern flank of the Wilmslow upfold, or anticline. The overall structure of the Edge formed a classic hydrocarbon trap, with impermeable muddy rocks capping porous and permeable host rocks, into which mineral solutions migrated. These were derived from salty groundwaters from Triassic and older rocks in the Cheshire Basin and its underlying Carboniferous rocks. Between about 205 and 175 million years ago copper, lead, zinc, cobalt and vanadium minerals were precipitated from these solutions and now occur between the sand grains and against faults within the block. As a landscape feature, the Edge was formed by differential erosion of all these rock units in the last 2 million years, before, during and after the Ice Age. As a result, a broken escarpment faces north and east, and a dip slope in which copper mines were worked from Bronze Age times extends to the south and west.

Even that summary paragraph demonstrates how complex geological terminology can appear to the non-specialist and how unfathomable its concepts. The wealth of detail necessary to explain the evolution of an area as well studied and as complicated as Alderley Edge can surely appear difficult to digest. Perhaps more than any other part of the Alderley Edge Landscape Project, the study of the Edge's geology has needed the services and expertise of a wide range of specialists. No fewer than eight names appear in the credits to the following four chapters, but one could add several more, those of people who have been involved in putting together the story – and that just in the short period when we have been working on it. Therefore we have compiled a condensed and somewhat simplified version (Chapter 4) as an overview to the specialist reports that form the three succeeding chapters. It is an account written by an archaeologist with a background in geology, and concludes with a geological walk over the Edge. It can be read on its own by those who wish to skip the more detailed and fully referenced discussions of the solid geology, the mineralogy and the geomorphology in the following chapters. Some of the more technical and less immediately obvious terms are included in the geology glossary at the end of the book.

4

Rocks, minerals and landforms: an overview

Simon Timberlake

Note: technical words in this chapter which are explained in the geology glossary (pp. 912–16) are italicised the first time they appear.

Introduction

A good deal of imagination is required to take the sandstone cliffs which today make up the wooded scarp and dip slope of Alderley Edge and to picture them as part of a hot desert basin covering the area of present-day Cheshire, at a time when much of England was exposed as an arid landmass near a tropical sea. However, we know from the measurement of the magnetic field (*palaeomagnetism*) still imprinted upon the red coating of iron oxide which surrounds many of the sand grains within these rocks that some 245 million years ago, during the *Triassic* period, Alderley Edge (and indeed all of Britain) was part of an ancient landmass located some 20° north of the equator and lying within the trade-wind belt. Furthermore, the age of the Alderley rocks can be inferred by comparison with similar rock types elsewhere, through the study of their position within the sequence – the *stratigraphy* – of sedimentary rock layers which accumulated within the Cheshire Basin, and by examination of the limited fossil evidence to hand. Reconstructions of this ancient environment are based on the recognition of the different forms of bedding and the types of sand grains and pebbles included in them (*clasts*), together with many other features of sedimentation. Some of these appear strikingly similar to examples still to be found today in areas of sand dunes, in *braided rivers* and on dried-up riverbeds in most of the desert or semi-arid to arid regions of the world. This evidence helps to provide us with the means to reconstruct with some confidence the earliest chapter in the story of Alderley Edge.

The geological story of the Edge continues with an incursion of the sea, followed by the burial of the desert rocks beneath thick layers of mudstone and rock salt, and then a period of earth movements such as *faulting* accompanied by earthquakes, which left Alderley as an up-standing *block (horst)* of rock within a still-sinking basin. The porous desert sandstones buried within this block later became a potential trap and then a *reservoir* for oil and gas rising up from below, and afterwards for the warm mineralising solutions which deposited *baryte* and then lead and copper ores within the fractures or *faults* in the rock between around 205 and 175 million years ago.

Burial of this Triassic landscape beneath more recent *Jurassic* and *Cretaceous* marine sediments continued to the beginning of the *Tertiary*, about 65 million years ago, when uplift following another phase of the opening of the North Atlantic began to push these buried rocks back up to the surface. Overlying sediments were stripped off and the top of the uplifted 'Alderley Block' was again exposed; the hydrocarbons (oil and gas) leaked away, while erosion then exposed the sandstones, faults and mineral veins to the action of weathering and landform generation. By this time, some 3–4 million years ago, the continents had drifted considerably northwards over the surface of the globe. The Atlantic Ocean had opened up fully and the outline patterns of the continents of America, Africa and Europe would all have been recognisable. Britain and Cheshire were then at approximately the same northerly latitudes as today.

From the beginning of the *Pleistocene*, some 2.6 million years ago, a fluctuating but steadily increasing drop in global temperature, due in part to the changed circulation pattern of ocean currents following continental separation, resulted in the lowering of world sea-levels and a considerable increase in the size of the polar ice caps, with much available water being locked up in the ice, an event which initiated a period of widespread *glaciation* in the northern hemisphere. Between 400,000 and 12,000 years ago, Britain was subjected to six glaciations as the ice-sheets made major advances, interspersed with major (*inter-glacial*) and minor (*interstadial*) periods of climate warming, lasting between 1,000 and 20,000 years. Today, little evidence of these earlier glaciations or of their intervening warm periods is to be found in this area of north-east Cheshire, although the last period of ice advance did leave a thick mantle of glacial *till* and gravels in its wake, a deposit which now covers much of the Cheshire Plain. Alderley Edge remained a topo-graphic high for at least part of this period, and thus towards the end of the last ice age (the *Devensian* glaciation) the somewhat diminished and thinner 'rivers' of ice began to flow around this 'island' of upstanding rock (*nunatak*), depositing till, meltwater sand and gravels and lumps of stagnating ice against its sides, and leaving a ridge of glacial deposits southwards in its wake.

The melting of the ice around the foot of the Edge left behind it a hummocky sand and gravel landscape consisting of *kettle-holes* and sinuous gravel ridges or *kames*, among which we see the development of 'mosses' or peat bogs following the warming of the climate and recolonisation of the area with trees and plants some 10,000 years ago. Many of the erosion features on top of the Edge, such as the *combes* or dry valleys, scarps and *talus* or scree slopes, date from this most recent period, and relate to the annual cycle of freezing and thawing and to changes in the drainage system which accompanied this period of climatic change.

Glaciation exposed the mineral veins first worked by prehistoric people, while the associated glacial till and outwash gravels supplied the flint and fine-grained volcanic rocks exploited by Mesolithic hunters for fashioning knives, scrapers and arrowheads, as well as the cobbles of *greywacke* and Lake District igneous rocks later collected by the Bronze Age copper miners of the Edge for use as mining hammers. Meanwhile, the pollen records of the 'mosses' and peat-filled kettle-holes around the Edge provide us with a record of climate and vegetation change as well as of human activity in the area going back at least to the end of the last ice age.

Structure and strata

The naming and dating of the geological strata which make up the sequence of Lower–Middle Triassic rocks of central England have evolved over the years, and a basic explanation of their relationship is perhaps necessary before beginning a description of the rocks, their structure and the environments in which they were formed. Fortunately, many of the local names given to the rocks of Alderley Edge during the first detailed mapping (see Plate 3) by Wilfred Trotter of the Geological Survey between 1946 and 1951 and by David Thompson between 1962 and 1964 have been retained ever since.

Only the uppermost unit of the Lower Triassic, formerly termed the Bunter Upper Mottled Sandstone, crops out on the Edge, yet this forms both the base and sides of the escarpment, and consists of a sequence of sandstones at least 105 m thick, the *c.* 246 million-year-old Wilmslow Sandstone Formation. This is succeeded by a further 150 m of sandstones, pebbly sandstones and rarely conglomerates, and thin mudstones, which together cap the scarp of the Edge and form the dip slope to the south-west. Formerly treated together as the 'Keuper Sandstone', these beds are now referred to individually (from bottom to top) as the Engine Vein Conglomerate, Hayman's Farm *Injection Strata*, Beacon Lodge Sandstone, Wood Mine Conglomerate, West Mine Sandstone and the Nether Alderley Sandstone, with the Brynlow Conglomerate at its base. These members constitute the Helsby Sandstone Formation, *c.* 245–242 million years old. These are Middle Triassic in age and together with the underlying Wilmslow Sandstone form the upper part of the Sherwood Sandstone Group in the Cheshire Basin. At the very top of the rock sequence in the Alderley area, above the Nether Alderley Sandstone, is the Tarporley Siltstone, 242–240 million years old. Regionally, this lies at the base of the Middle and Upper Triassic Mercia Mudstone Group (*c.* 242–204 million years), which overlies the Sherwood Sandstone.

Overlying all the Triassic beds, except on the exposed summit of the Edge, is a mantle of drift or superficial Pleistocene deposits, which includes boulder clay, some glacial sands and gravels, alluvium and peat.

The succession of beds of the Triassic rocks was originally laid down horizontally, but was then folded and faulted during further deposition and as the buried strata became compacted; the process became more marked during the earth movements in the Jurassic, Cretaceous and Early to Middle Tertiary which followed. These last movements, around 65–55 and 25 million years ago, were responsible for the uplift of the block upon which Alderley Edge now stands. Two north–south faults or fractures, the Alderley Fault and the Kirkleyditch Fault, form the western and eastern boundaries of this block respectively and in some respects define the present area of high ground. Another series of near-parallel faults runs west-north-west to east-south-east across the top of the Edge. The latter give a step-like appearance to the Edge's topography, resulting from differential erosion that has taken place between the hard and soft sandstones juxtaposed on either side of faults. Several periods of stress, fracturing and mineralisation occurred along these faults up to *c.* 175 million years ago, and possibly again in more recent geological time. Underground, in the tunnels of the copper mines, it can be seen that a number of the north–south faults have intersected and displaced (or downthrown) the west-north-west to east-south-east faults and zones of fractured rock (*cataclastites*), and thus appear to postdate them. Furthermore, these north–south faults are often barren of mineral.

Deserts and flash floods – sedimentation and the ancient environment

Thought once to have been formed by river action or by shallow coastal marine currents, the pebbly Triassic sandstones of Alderley Edge are now universally recognised as being the product of terrestrial sedimentation, laid down by both wind and water within an ancient semi-arid to desert environment.

The Wilmslow Sandstone Formation consists for the most part of soft, coarse to fine-grained red sandstones. These were deposited by rivers flowing from higher ground to the south and east of Alderley, the sand probably being produced from the erosion of pre-existing sandstone rocks. Some of these Wilmslow Sandstone beds show evidence of deposition from more substantial river channels, with signs of drifting ripples and/or sand banks (*cross-bedding*), but without any of the pebble bands characteristic of fast water and flood conditions. However, the occasional thin mudstone or sand-silt *laminae* covered with small flakes of mica suggest deposition of suspended clay under quiet conditions following flooding, probably by slightly slower-moving braided streams migrating over a wide riverbed along the margins of the arid plain. Occasionally one also finds horizons with fossilised mud cracks or *desiccation cracks*, suggesting short periods of complete aridity when channels were cut off during times of low water-flow, and the resultant shallow ponds or lakes gradually dried up. The fine sand silts of drying-out mud-flats and inter-dune areas preserved footprints such as *Chirotherium*, probably made by a carnivorous reptile such as the archosaur *Ticinosuchus*, which may have followed the dried-up riverbeds in search of water and food (Plate 5).

Some of the cross-bedded sandstones, especially at the top of the formation, were originally deposited or re-deposited by wind; the trough cross-bedding features are interpreted as those of shifting sand dunes, most probably in a dune field or sand sea lying between the river channels. The consistent westward orientation of the cross-bedding suggests deposition by a steady wind from the east, such as that found in the tropical trade-wind belt of today. Under the microscope we can see the roundness of the wind-transported sand grains, forming the typical 'millet-seed grain'. This type of erosion results from lengthy abrasion of grain by grain and is a common phenomenon in the sands of modern arid areas and sand seas, as is the coating of iron oxide around each individual grain, an effect which has helped to impart the distinctive brick-red colour to the rock.

At the end of the Wilmslow Sandstone deposition the environment changed to that represented by the Helsby Sandstone Formation. Preceding this there may have been a gap of many hundreds of thousands of years, during which time large earth movements caused uplift and as a result erosion, the latter taking the form of river channels flowing much faster in a north-westerly direction and subject to episodic flooding (the so-called 'Alderley River') and which brought considerable quantities of pebbly and coarse sands into the area, creating the deposits of the Engine Vein Conglomerate. These river channels may first have eroded away the top of the underlying Wilmslow Sandstone, although the initial flood deposit appears to have swept with it numerous wind-abraded pebbles or *ventifacts*, which must have been lying in some of these dried-up river channels for some thousands of years beforehand. The flood discharges, perhaps major incidents every few thousand years but including many smaller ones, resulted in repeated cycles of deposition of sediment (from coarse to fine). In reality this reflects the movement of the sand *bars* of the channels over previously laid sediments – for example the deposition of pebbly sandstones or conglomerates within the channels, coarse to fine sandstones towards the channel margins, and the much finer siltstones and red mudstones formed from the sediment which settled out of the standing water left covering the abandoned channels after flash floods, the last most clearly represented by the Hayman's Farm Injection Strata, exposed at the western end of Engine Vein. The gradual drying up of these impermanent ponds resulted in the formation of pools which harboured water-fleas and other life, while ferns and conifers established themselves around the edges, before these too dried up, leaving a plain of mud cracks, with perhaps the occasional reptilian footprint. Rare examples of these desiccation cracks can still be seen on the Edge, usually on the underside of overlying sandstone beds: there are good examples in the Engine Vein Conglomerate near Wizard's Well, and others are exposed in the roofs of mine passages underground, such as inside Engine Vein (Figure 4.1). The detection of spores of ferns and club mosses (*lycopods*) as well as

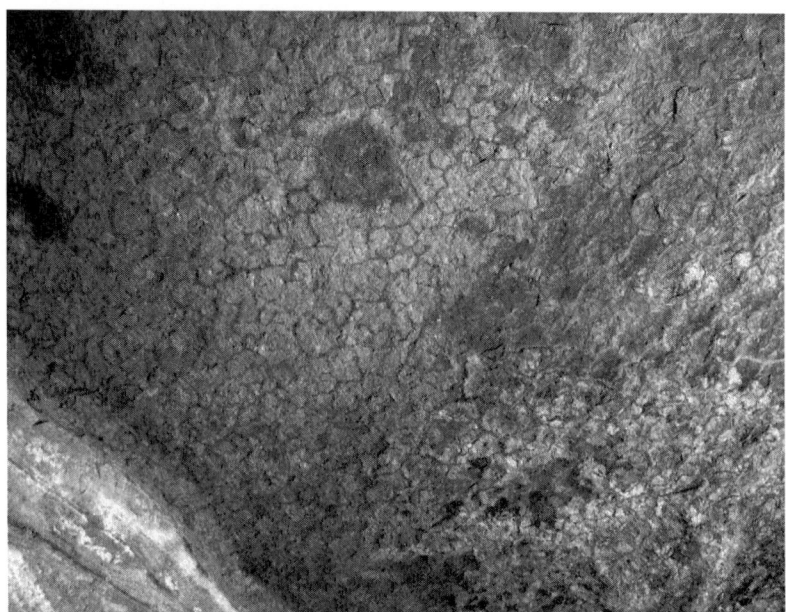

Figure 4.1. Mud cracks on the underside of a bedding plane in the Engine Vein Conglomerate, in the roof of a passage in Engine Vein.

Photograph Nigel Dibben.

conifer pollen within these fine-grained muddy-sandy sediments seems to imply that at certain times adjacent or nearby land areas were fairly well colonised with plants.

A slowing down in the rate and scale of flood discharge from the 'Alderley River', perhaps after some 300,000 years, led to increasing drying out of the river plain, following which the riverbed sands began to be blown once more into *aeolian* dunes. The Beacon Lodge Sandstone is an example of one of these aeolian sands. On Alderley Edge it crops out only alongside the path from Beacon Lodge to Old Alderley Quarry.

Above this level, renewed flooding and deposition of pebbly sandstones of the Wood Mine Conglomerate occurred with reactivation of the 'Alderley River' system and a change in the direction of the channels (now from south to north), perhaps with a new source of sediment. Thicker mudstone beds also indicate an increase in the amount of fine sediment flowing into and settling in the area, but otherwise the type of sedimentation and physical and climatic environment would have been very similar to that 100,000–200,000 years earlier, during the period of deposition of the Engine Vein Conglomerate. *Trace fossils* have been found on the bedding-plane surfaces of some of the finer-grained sediments, reflecting periods when these emerged as mudflats. For example, from borehole cores have come occasional tracks such as *Rhynchosauroides*, the footprint of the small lizard-like herbivorous reptile *Rhynchosaurus* (Appendix 5.1, Figures 5.14–5.16), together with *Planolites* and *Skolithos*, the horizontal and vertical burrows made by worms or colonies of *arthropods*, perhaps even insects (Figure 5.3b, p. 79). On some of the bedding surfaces underground in Wood Mine can be seen the beautifully preserved ripple marks caused by a current that always flowed in the same direction, while on others *prod and scour marks* indicate the variable but often much higher-energy and faster-flowing water conditions that still prevailed within the channels.

The deposition of coarse, non-pebbly sands in the channels of the 'Alderley River' may have continued into the early part of the deposition of the West Mine Sandstone, although the onset of yet another major cycle of drying out meant that masses of river sand were again being blown and re-deposited as shifting aeolian dunes, part of the sand sea that has been traced in the underlying rocks beyond the Wirral to the Douglas Oilfield in the East Irish Sea Basin north of Llandudno. These dune fields or sand seas, called *ergs*, formed in areas between the periodically drying-up and reactivated river channels. Smaller floods of shorter duration resulted in the regular appearance of dried-up river courses and mud cracks, some with evidence of small flourishes of vegetation, such as the growth of the horsetail *Equisetites*, fragments of which – dismembered by floods and then preserved as fossils – can still be seen underground in West Mine on the underside of mudstone/

sandstone bedding planes. These sandstones are only poorly exposed at the surface on the Edge, for example at Brynlow and along the roadside on Artists Lane, yet they are well represented in the Hayman's Farm borehole section and in West Mine itself.

By contrast, the rocks of the overlying Nether Alderley Sandstone appear to be almost wholly fluvial rather than aeolian in origin. The basal beds of these siltstones and sandstones can be seen on the *dip slope* of the Edge in the quarries at Brynlow, Finlow, Bradford Lane and Topps Farm. With the exception of the lowest pebbly layer, these beds consisted mostly of sandy sediments deposited by a much slower-moving and more sinuous river channel. The lower banks of these channels enabled flooding to take place at a much reduced rate of water discharge, leading to a far greater distribution of finer muddy sediments beyond. Trace fossils within these flaggy siltstones and mudstones, which were formerly mudflats, include the burrows of small reptiles and insects as well as that of a probable crustacean, *Cruziana*, whose lifestyle has been compared to that of the present-day brackish-freshwater shrimp *Triops*. This has a short lifespan well adapted to living in small temporary pools; its eggs can also withstand high temperatures and desiccating conditions. As these brackish pools and mudflats dried up, nodules of calcium carbonate and rarely also crystals of salt were precipitated on or just under the surface. The presence of the latter appears to indicate the very earliest formation of saltpans (*evaporites*) – evidence which suggests that this part of the river system was now located much closer to the sea and probably in the midst of a coastal plain.

These beds are succeeded by the former 'Waterstones' strata, now referred to as the Tarporley Siltstone Formation, which lie to the south-west of the Edge and appear for the most part to have been deposited within a more truly inter-tidal environment, perhaps in an area of salt lagoons or in the channels at the mouth of the dried-up river.

Burial, black gold and mineralisation

To understand the processes responsible for introducing minerals into the rocks of Alderley Edge we need first to understand a little of the burial history of the Alderley Block and the evolution of the Cheshire Basin.

The Triassic sandstones of Alderley Edge were deposited on a basement of *Carboniferous* rocks comprising limestone, sandstone, coal and metal-rich organic black shales. The same type of basement underlies rocks of *Permian* to Triassic age in other parts of central and northern England. In most places these are now exposed at the surface, but in the Cheshire Basin and in several similar basins which now lie beneath the

Irish Sea the base of this sequence remains concealed, since these were areas of periodic subsidence and sedimentation for some 200 million years, from the Permian until the beginning of the Tertiary period.

The Cheshire Basin developed as a consequence of east–west extensional forces pulling on this area of the Earth's crust. This both thinned and weakened it, causing fractures and allowing large blocks to move downwards along faults. These north–south fractures formed the sides of a *graben* or rift valley, similar to that of the East African Rift Valley of today. Continental-type sediments, mostly sandstones, then began to infill the growing rift, while continuing fault movements left some large masses of rock standing, either as steps or as free-standing blocks. In this way the Alderley Block (horst) was initiated. As subsidence continued throughout the Triassic, deeper parts of the basin developed, and these then became inundated by the sea some 240 million years ago, in a similar way to the rift valley which lies beneath the present-day Red Sea. However, instead of continuing to extend and becoming an ocean, the sea was intermittently cut off, and within this basin evaporite salt deposits were laid down. Jurassic and Cretaceous rocks accumulated on top and the Triassic rocks beneath were buried deeper and deeper. The maximum depth which the Alderley rocks reached in this basin was probably 2–3 km, during the mid-Jurassic, about 180 million years ago.

Around 200–190 million years ago, and prior to the mineralisation, the Alderley Block, along with other horsts and fault structures in the Cheshire and Irish Sea basins, became a potential trap to rising hydrocarbons – oil and gas – as these migrated upwards through porous sandstones from their source rocks, the most likely candidates for which are the underlying Carboniferous black shales out of which hydrocarbons would have been expelled following the rise in temperature and pressure accompanying deep burial. At that time the porous sandstones of the faulted and tilted Alderley Block, sealed on either side and on top by the impervious capping of Mercia Mudstone, would have provided an ideal *trap*, and with a porosity of about 30 per cent the sandstone potentially became a small reservoir for the accumulation of oil and gas. The former presence of oil in the Alderley rocks is indicated by a residue of bituminous material remaining within microscopic fractures inside samples of *galena* (lead ore), suggesting that but for uplift and erosion and the leaking away of fluids and gas Alderley Edge might well now have been a small producing oilfield, rather similar to some of those now being worked in Morecambe Bay and the east Irish Sea.

As with the hydrocarbons, the Alderley Block probably acted as a trap to warm mineral-laden saline solutions which migrated up-dip through the strata or else along available conduits such as deep-seated faults from a source elsewhere in the basin. The temperature of the rocks at that depth would probably have been sufficient to circulate heated groundwaters, enabling them to dissolve salt and gypsum, as well as leach out heavy metals from the same Carboniferous shales which supplied the hydrocarbons. The resultant brines also appear to have been rich in sulphates derived from the Mercia Mudstone. The mixing of this solution with barium-rich pore waters already present within the Alderley sandstones may well have been responsible for the precipitation of large amounts of baryte within the rocks. It also provided a source of the sulphur which combined with the metals in solution to form the ores galena and *chalcopyrite*. The formation of these sulphide ores requires a chemically *reducing environment*, which the hydrocarbons present within the Alderley rocks may well have provided. Indeed, this environment provides an important link between the genesis of this mineral deposit and the presence of oil and gas.

Temperature studies carried out on small inclusions of fluid remaining within some of these minerals suggests that the ores were deposited at a temperature of between 50–60°C. One important and quite visible side-effect of the passage of these hot mineralising fluids through the rock is the bleaching or colour reduction of the red iron oxide coating around the quartz grains in the sandstone. By mapping this and the distribution of baryte and sulphides and the various fault structures, it has been possible to conclude that the mineral solutions first travelled up one or two conduits (e.g. the deep-seated Alderley and Kirkleyditch faults), then migrated laterally, up-dip, through the more porous beds of the Engine Vein Conglomerate, and the Wood Mine and West Mine Sandstones. They then became concentrated on the underside of the impervious mudstone layers and along pre-existing fault planes running east–south-east to west–north-west, where shale or clay acted as a partial barrier to fluids and encouraged the deposition of minerals. Baryte appears to have been deposited first, both as a crystalline infill within the rock and then in veins, followed by the sulphides pyrite, chalcopyrite (copper iron sulphide), sphalerite (zinc sulphide) and the ubiquitous galena, which is often found on the *footwall* (or upthrow side) of the faults as irregular masses cementing sandstone. More baryte was pre-cipitated later.

A secondary or *supergene* mineralisation of the sandstones occurred at a much later date, following the uplift of the Alderley Block some 65 million years ago (and again at 25 million years), and the subsequent lowering of the water-table, erosion and gradual exposure of the mineral veins before, during and after glaciation. Downward-percolating ground-waters began to oxidise the sulphide minerals, particularly the more reactive pyrite and chalcopyrite, redistributing these metals throughout the porous sandstone beds, and then re-depositing the copper in the form of its green and blue carbonates malachite and azurite, the iron as a rusty brown iron hydroxide (*goethite*) and the less soluble lead as the white and yellow-green *secondary minerals cerussite* and *pyromorphite*. Manganese hydroxide is commonly found as an amorphous black powdery deposit along some of the faults, or else as spots within some of the sandstones, as a result of the decomposition of late-stage iron and manganese carbonate. In places this might contain appreciable amounts of cobalt, and sometimes nickel and even vanadium: it was then referred to by the miners as *asbolane*, a substance which was once mined as a cobalt ore.

In some respects Alderley Edge may be seen as a unique type of ore deposit when compared with other British examples, but it is just one of a number of rather similar lead and copper occurrences around the margins of the Cheshire Basin, all associated with fault structures and most of them within the Helsby Sandstone Formation. These include the mines of Mottram St Andrew on the Kirkleyditch Fault, less than 2 km from Alderley Edge, and Gallantry Bank near Bickerton some 60 km away on the western edge of the basin, while on the south side, just within north Shropshire, are to be found the mines of Hawkstone, Wixhill, Clive, Pim Hill, Eardiston and Yorton Bank. All of these worked the supergene copper ores malachite and azurite, although at a number of the mines galena and also cobalt ore were extracted.

Modified by ice

The uplift of the rocks during the Tertiary appears to have left the Alderley Block as part of a long ridge extending south-east towards Macclesfield, and beyond as far as the edge of the Pennine margin. Prior to the advance of the glaciers from the north, this ridge was breached by the ancestral River Bollin, forming a steep-sided valley more than 50 m deep near Macclesfield. However, we know very little of the subsequent history of the earlier glacial and interglacial periods in this area, since most of the deposits left by the earlier ice-sheets were either swept southwards or mixed up with those left by the last (Devensian) glaciation. Nevertheless, a few deposits remain near Chelford, consisting of boulder clay tills, possibly of the earliest Anglian glaciation (350,000 years ago), and some warm-period interstadial deposits from about 100,000 years ago.

The last ice advance reached its maximum about 20,000 years ago, with flows of ice emanating from the high ground of the Lake District, the Southern Uplands and the Western Highlands of Scotland carving their way across the floor of what is now Morecambe Bay and the Irish Sea to North Wales and the Cheshire Basin. These ice streams would preferentially have taken the easiest route southwards, and thus the greatest thickness and weight of ice would have passed over the Cheshire Plain.

Nevertheless, at the beginning of the ice advance Alderley Edge would have been covered with some hundreds of feet of ice, but as time went by the ridge became more and more of a barrier to the slowly moving ice as the floor of the lowland plain was scoured out and deepened and as the ice-sheets became thinner and started wasting away around 16,000–17,000 years ago. Eventually, the top of the Edge began to protrude above the ice as a small peak or nunatak, while the glaciers continued to flow around it. As these ice streams melted, their rate of progress southwards began to slow. Meltwater rivers flowed down the sides of glaciers and underneath them: their force could carve channels through the rock. At the same time, sediments carried by the ice, including considerable volumes of ground rock or clay and thousands of larger rock *erratics* (many of which were originally plucked from the sides and floors of glaciated valleys in the Lake District) were dumped at the margins of the ice-sheets as these melted. In this way large amounts of *moraine* were deposited around the southern and eastern flanks of Alderley Edge, while the meltwater rivers issuing from the ice sorted these sediments still further, washing away the clay and depositing ridges of gravel and sand (kames) along the course of former channels. Indeed, hundreds of metres of sediments deposited by the ice between the Pennine margin and Alderley Edge formed an extension of the Alderley–Prestbury ridge almost as high as the Edge itself. Within this landform and overlying the earlier glacial till and boulder clay was found the evidence for meltwater lakes and rivers formed in front of the snout of the melting ice-sheets, while above these lay the rapidly deposited mud or earth flows derived from the surface of the subsequently retreating glaciers. However, there is also evidence for further short-lived advances of the ice, in the form of *ice-tectonic structures* (the deformation and crumpling of previously deposited layers of *fluvio-glacial* sands and gravels caused by the weight and 'bulldozing effect' of an advancing glacier); examples of these can be seen in sandpits at Whirley Grove. Such phenomena appear to indicate the temporary return to cold conditions. Furthermore, the presence of 'local' glacial erratics, such as the 'out of place' blocks of Engine Vein Conglomerate occasionally found upon or around the Edge, is also suggestive of small-scale 're-glaciation'.

Continued melting of the ice around the southern edge of the Alderley Edge outcrop as well as along the south-east ridge of the moraine led to further *slumping* within these sediments, and also to the burial of large fragments of stagnating ice beneath sediments derived from more recent meltwater channels. Thereafter, less further sediment accumulated on top (no more moraine was being deposited), while the concealed ice beneath invariably took much longer to melt, the result of which was that collapses or kettle-holes appeared in the landscape in their stead, sometimes years after the final retreat of the ice. In addition to these kettle-holes, the immediate post-glacial landscape also revealed the hummocky terrain of the *kame terrace*, upon whose surface once lay the parallel ridges and troughs of sand and gravel deposited from the braided channels of meltwater streams at the edge of the *downwasting* ice-sheet. The remains of these terraces can be seen around the margins of the Edge, towards Over Alderley, and to the south and east of Alderley Park. One such kettle-hole was formed on the upper kame terrace near Adders Moss, and survives as a small peat-filled basin located just to the north of the Macclesfield Road and about 800 m south-east of Engine Vein. In April 1997 the centre of this depression was cored by the Project's surveyors and proved to be more than 5 m deep in peat, with layers of lime-rich peaty marls indicative of ponded sediments at its base (Shimwell in *ArchAE*: 220–1; Mighal *et al.* in *ArchAE*: 270–5). This suggested the formation of a small lake here following the retreat of the ice from the landscape, a hollow which gradually filled with peat following the natural regeneration of heathland, woodland and the local landscape. It is conceivable therefore that the pollen record from this site may yield a fairly complete record of vegetation changes as well as human activity on and around the Edge from the end of the last ice age, some 12,000 years ago, up to the present.

The former direction of meltwater streams which once flowed across the Edge, parallel to the edge of the northern escarpment abutting the margins of the ice-sheet, appears also to have influenced the current drainage pattern. For instance, the stream (with waterfall) in Waterfall Wood, which now carries an insignificant discharge of water, must once have been a fairly powerful flow. It seems likely that this originally tapped other drainage areas to the east, the course of this river then being diverted northwards by the eroding ice front. This resulted in a cascade and a powerful river which flowed northwards beneath the ice-sheet, steeply *incising* the present valley as the waterfall cut back some 200 m along its present course, in the process undermining the softer Wilmslow Sandstone and resulting in the progressive collapse of the more resistant overlying Engine Vein Conglomerate at the head of the valley (Figure 4.2).

A period of cold conditions and an annual freeze–thaw cycle similar to that now prevailing in the tundra areas of northern Canada and Siberia followed the wasting away of the ice-sheets about 11,000–12,000 years ago. Evidence of *frost pitting* and of wind faceting, also called venti-faceting, can sometimes be seen on the surface of glacial erratic boulders and cobbles which once lay exposed on the surfaces of these freezing kame terraces and moraines, indicating continuing *periglacial* or perma-frost conditions and a tundra-like climate. (However, such pitting did not deter the early miners from fashioning the cobbles into hammers – see Figure 4.3 and Figure 2.2.) Freeze–thaw action would have helped

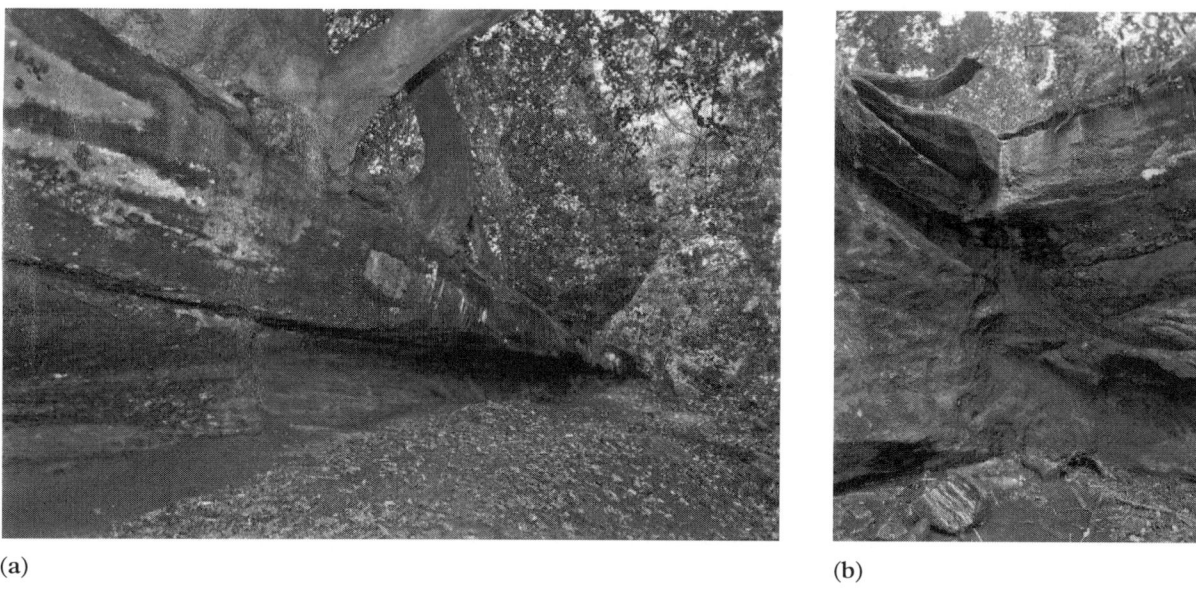

(a)

(b)

Figure 4.2. (a) The hard resistant beds of the Engine Vein Conglomerate overlying the Wilmslow Sandstone, which formed the waterfall in the late glacial/postglacial valley in Waterfall Wood (b), although thanks to changes in the water-table the 'waterfall' is now only a trickle at best.

Photographs Sean Edwards.

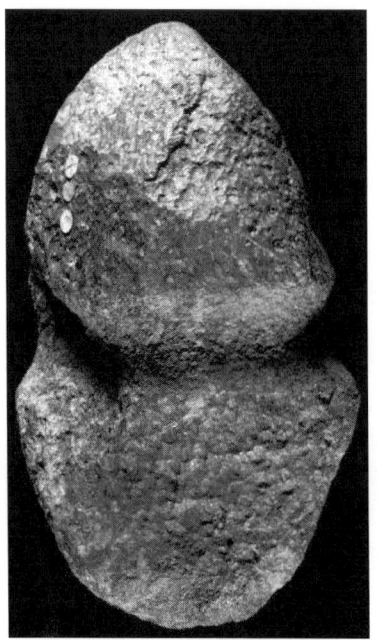

Figure 4.3. Frozen in time – a cobble with an interesting history! This erratic cobble of Ennerdale granophyre was transported to the Edge from the Shap area of the Lake District by ice some 20,000 years ago. It then lay on the surface, exposed to the bitter periglacial winds which post-dated the retreat of the glaciers 13–11,000 years ago, becoming sand-blasted, frost-pitted and polished by the action of sand (a ventifact). During the Early Bronze Age (c. 1700 BC) it was picked up by the earliest miners of the Edge, who pecked and ground a groove around its middle to help attach it to a wooden handle. It was little used before being discarded on a waste heap on the north side of Engine Vein; during the Roman period it was thrown down a shaft after mining was abandoned about 1,900 years ago. It was rediscovered in the Project's excavations in 1997 and is now in the Manchester Museum (acc. no. 1998.42).

Photograph Manchester Museum, University of Manchester.

detach large lumps of rock from the escarpment, particularly where wet conditions prevailed, such as on the *spring line* lying above impermeable clay horizons to which water was channelled along pre-existing faults like those at Wizard's Well and Holy Well. At the latter site this has led to considerable erosion of the escarpment. Summer snow-melt would also have resulted in short-lived but high levels of stream discharge, contributing to the deposition of rock scree and *alluvial fans* of sand and clay at the foot of the Edge. Spring-head erosion such as that described above has continued into more recent times, and has helped to maintain the steep and to some extent unstable scarp face of the Edge, while dry valleys or combes (formed during the immediate post-glacial period by streams that had previously been more active) are to be found at a number of different locations on the shallower dip slope, for example that followed by Artists Lane at Brynlow, and north of Windmill Wood. Below Stormy Point a natural problem of land-slipping and rock falls occurs, one which undoubtedly began many thousands of years ago but which has since been aggravated by Medieval and post-Medieval stone quarrying and to a lesser extent by mining activities since the Bronze Age. It continues to this day, worsened by the footpath erosion that accompanies increased visitor pressure on some areas of this fragile landscape. Meanwhile, the most recent changes to the hydrology or drainage of the Edge, such as the drying up of springs, watercourses and ponds, dates from the onset of more extensive underground mining and the driving of drainage levels during the mid to late nineteenth century.

Walking around the Edge – rocks, minerals and glacial erratics

One hopes that this description of the sedimentary rocks, mineralisation and glaciation of Alderley Edge can provide some sort of synthesis of the geological story so far, but it is perhaps also useful to include simple notes which can be used when visiting the site. This is not intended to be a geological walk for specialists, but aims instead to provide some geological commentary on localities as well as additional facts, both archaeological and historical, which might be of interest (Plate 3 shows the geology of the area, and Figures 14.1, 15.1 and 18.2 indicate the location of the mines and the quarries).

If starting at the main National Trust car park near the Wizard you might well make a short detour to visit Church Quarry, which lies up the footpath behind the restaurant and information centre. Passing the hand pumping-wheel of the disused Wizard Well, the path reaches the quarry entrance and a very unusual small room on the left-hand side hollowed out from behind a quarried face in the Wood Mine

Conglomerate, which is usually described as a gunpowder store. The link with gunpowder becomes more obvious inside the main quarry. Here the overlying pebbly beds have been blasted, and long shot-holes are visible perpendicular to the bedding, while the underlying finer sandstones or *freestones* (the name given to rock which may be worked with equal ease in all directions) were cut by hand during the late eighteenth and early nineteenth centuries, the 'herring-bone' pick-marks being clearly visible. Cross-bedding is visible in the section.

Returning to the Wizard, take the path signposted to the Beacon, until you reach the first clearing, to the east side of which lies the long

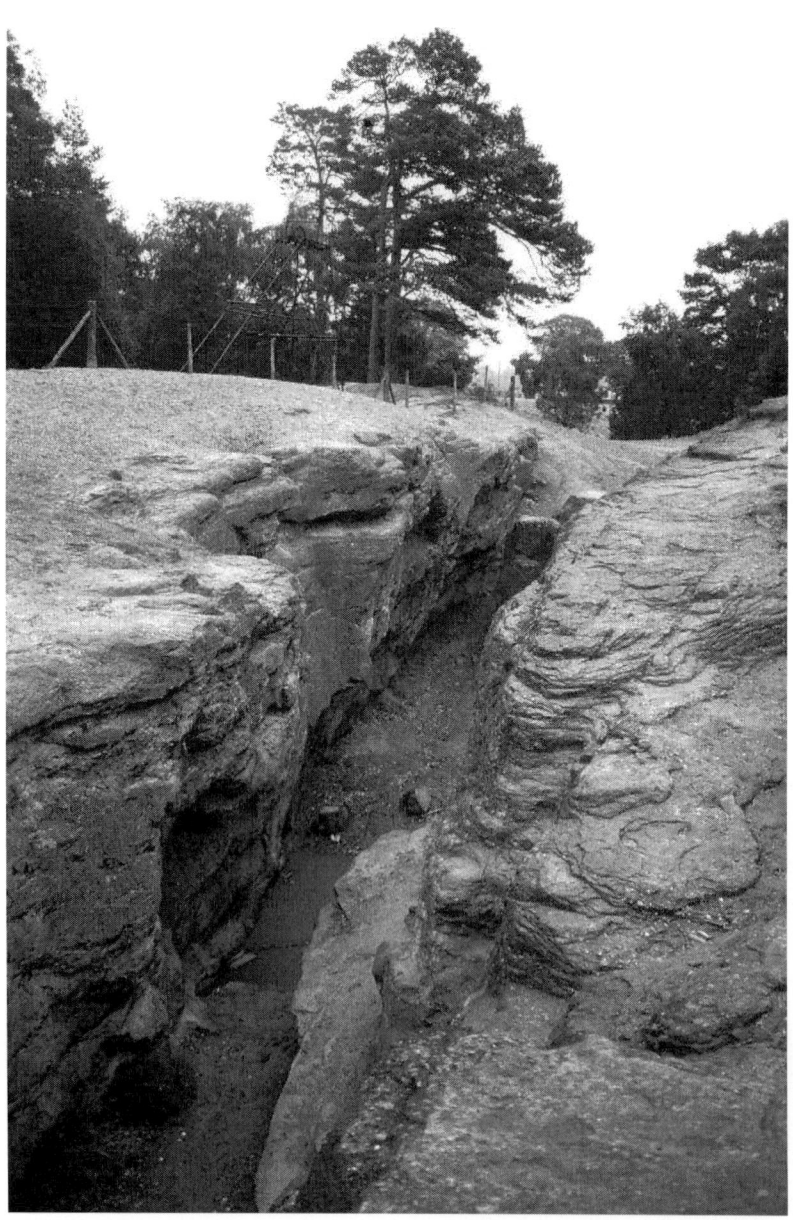

Figure 4.4. The deep chasm of Engine Vein opencut photographed from the west/north-west end. The hanging wall of the fault can be seen on the left-hand side. In the foreground the sandstone beds of the Engine Vein Conglomerate can be seen dipping gently to the south-west, while subsidiary faults and thin baryte veins of the cataclastic fracture zone can be seen running parallel to the working along the main fault in the centre.

Photograph Simon Timberlake.

opencut trench of Engine Vein (Figure 4.4). Erosion is a serious problem here, which the National Trust is attempting to remedy by the ongoing programme of fencing and grass regeneration described in Chapter 29, and thus access arrangements will change from time to time. Descend into the western end of the long shallow gully, on the south side of which it is usually possible to walk along the plane of the Engine Vein Fault, although the deeper and part-flooded opencast beyond is normally fenced off for safety reasons. It is possible here to inspect the footwall of the fault and in places the vertical striations of the *slickensides*, the scratches formed by the sliding of one mass of rock against another. Here the pebbly sandstone of the Engine Vein Conglomerate is exposed, the fault plane being covered by much dull white baryte. On the north side of the fault the geology is quite different, the displacement bringing down beds of soft sandstone and red mudstone of the Hayman's Farm Injection Strata within which *Euestheria* have been found. Walking east, but still on the south side and on the Engine Vein Conglomerate, just above the start of the deep chasm one reaches the remains of a shallow oval-shaped hollow 1.5 m in diameter cut into the surface of one of the dipping sandstone beds. This is an emptied prehistoric mining pit (Figure 4.5). A thin smear of green malachite is just visible around its base. The dimpled effect on its rock sides are the marks of the stone tools of the Bronze Age miners. Examining the rock closely, one can also see nodules and rosettes of small lath-like crystals some 5 mm across growing between and around the sand grains. This is baryte, whose *cementation* and *in situ* crystallisation have helped make the sandstones of the Engine Vein Conglomerate so hard and resistant to erosion. During the mineralisation of these faults baryte was deposited in several phases. Narrow veins of this mineral can also be observed as small upstanding lines or ridges on the surface of the eroded beds of sandstone. The first *miospores* recorded from the Triassic in the Cheshire Basin were recovered from the lowest mudstone in the Engine Vein Conglomerate at the east end of the Engine Vein opencast. Samples of galena and sandstone stained with malachite may be found in the clayey mine spoil between this point and the north–south track to the east which leads to Edge House Farm.

Continuing from the clearing northwards along a small footpath you soon reach the edge of the Old Alderley Quarry, worked for building stone from the mid-eighteenth century or before. Entering this from the north-east side by way of the old quarry road you will get a good view of the north face, with a considerable thickness of cross-bedded sandstones, separated by a prominent red mudstone horizon from which *Euestheria* were once collected. The latter would have been deposited under much quieter conditions of sedimentation within an inter-channel area. Furthermore, in the north-east corner of the quarry

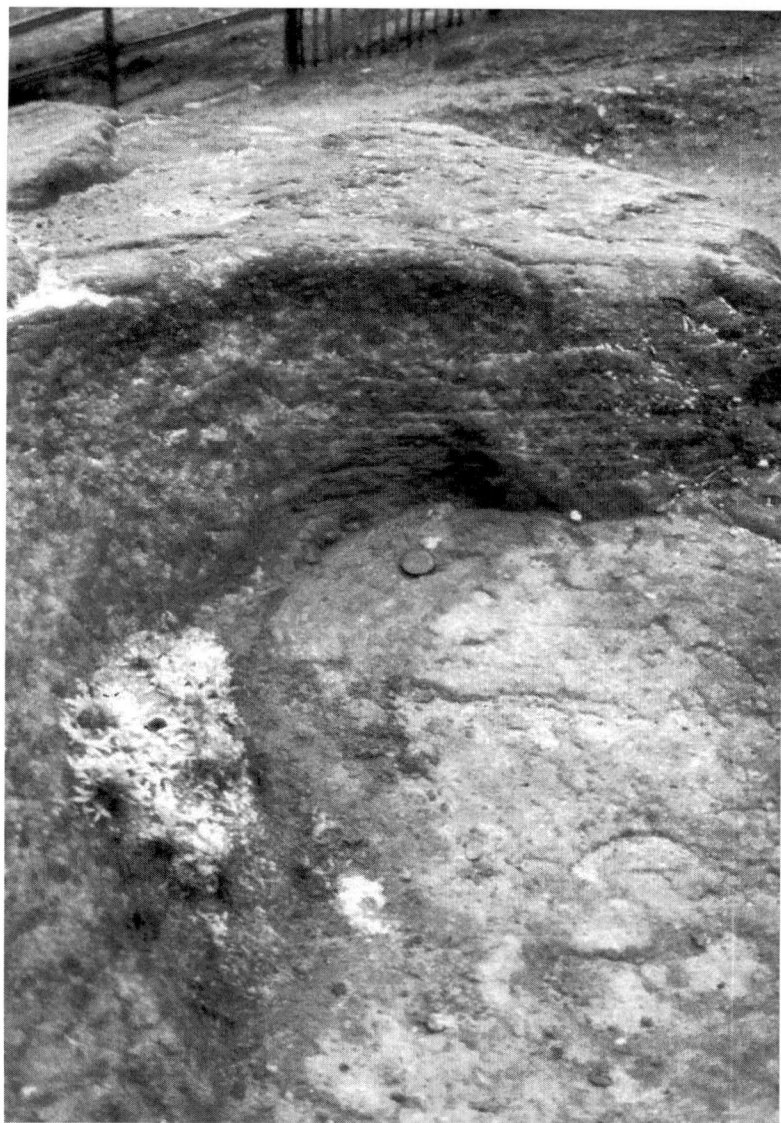

Figure 4.5. An abandoned and subsequently emptied prehistoric mining pit on the south side of Engine Vein. The pockmarks on the wall of the pit are the imprint of stone tools on the surface of the hard barytic sandstone through which it was cut to reach a rather thin smear of malachite lying on top of the underlying bed. (A detail from this photograph highlighting the working of the stone appears as Figure 15.6 on p. 354.)

Photograph Simon Timberlake.

can be seen a good example of a normal fault in cross-section, the short vertical *displacement* of a mudstone bed indicating the small amount of *throw* on the fault. These normal faults were caused by tensional stress (i.e. stretching or extension) of the Earth's crust.

Take a short cut northwards from the quarry, and you will cross more old mine workings, such as the Canyon Opencast, and soon reach the track to Stormy Point. Taking a right fork after about 50 m, follow a small footpath down the slope to the edge of a large cave-like opening: access here may be restricted because of erosion control work by the National Trust. Excavated out of the largely aeolian Wilmslow Sandstone Formation, Pillar Mine (Figure 16.2, p. 375) must be one of the earliest mines on the Edge, but is now rather vandalised: it has lost its central pillar and the soft mineral-impregnated sandstone walls are heavily carved and covered with graffiti. On the long slope of mine spoil beneath, one can often see small fragments rich in malachite as well as pea-shaped nodules of blue azurite formed within the mudstones – although on no account should they be removed from this scheduled and historic site. Hammer stones used by prehistoric miners are occasionally unearthed from beneath the modern layers of spoil, washed out after heavy rainstorms (Figures 2.2 and 4.3 illustrate such hammer stones found elsewhere on the Edge). Most of these have been crudely fashioned from glacial erratic cobbles collected from the local boulder clay which mantles the base of this scarp slope. Typically these are hard greywacke sandstones or volcanic rocks such as *andesites* or *rhyolites* derived from the *Borrowdale Volcanic Series*, and transported here by glaciers from the Lake District (Browne, 1995). Climbing up above the rock fall adjacent to Pillar Mine and level with its roof, the path passes up through the bottom of several exposed Bronze Age mining pits. Just beneath this, within an outcrop of very soft mineralised sandstone (Plate 2), are abundant powdery traces of malachite (green), the lead mineral pyromorphite (yellow), iron ochre or goethite (red-brown) and manganese wad (umber-black). Such evidence makes one think that the Edge could have been a source of mineral pigment long before it was ever mined for copper.

Continue up, passing Doc Mine on your left (cut at the junction of the Wilmslow Sandstone Formation and the Engine Vein Conglomerate) and take the path which climbs up to the right, eventually coming out on the edge of a large clearing at Stormy Point. Below to the north-east is the massive rock fall, while above, beneath a large sandstone overhang and now protected by a grille, is the entrance to Devil's Grave, another early mine working. The earliest miners undercut this coarse pebbly sandstone, presumably the base of another *fining-upwards* sequence of *channel-fill* sandstones in the Engine Vein Conglomerate. Traces of black manganese oxides that may be rich in cobalt can also be seen in the base of a partly excavated fault which forms part of the later entrance to the mine.

Walking northwards, one starts to descend an old saddle road along which blocks of quarried sandstone were once sledged down to the Hough, passing a number of very large toppled blocks of Engine Vein Conglomerate on the way. The path drops down to a col and then rises to the ridge of Saddlebole, upon which rests an *outlier* of the pebbly Engine Vein Conglomerate, surrounded by the underlying Wilmslow Sandstone.

The path descends the northernmost spur of the Edge towards the Hough, passing the more recent Red Moulding Sand Quarry on the right-hand side. This quarry, cut into Wilmslow Sandstone, was once worked for the sand used to make castings for foundry work. The soft sandstone walls are now largely slumped and eroded, and pockmarked with holes drilled by miner bees. Nevertheless, several faults and thin veins of baryte, part of a cataclastic fracture zone, can be seen on the east side, while the cross-bedded *foresets* of the former wind-blown dune sands can still be seen in some places, along with *wave ripple marks* and lamination, sometimes containing thin layers of clay and mud flakes that suggest occasional short-lived flood conditions that created interdune ponds across whose surfaces the wind induced wave motions.

Leave the quarry and turn west along the Mottram–Alderley road as far as the path that leads southwards and up the scarp face at grid reference SJ 854 783. This path is underlain by the soft Wilmslow Sandstone Formation all the way to Wizard's Well and Castle Rock. The path eastwards towards the Beacon may then be followed. You are now following the top of the irregular outcrop of the Engine Vein Conglomerate cut by a number of faults running from north-west to south-east. Two of these define the promontory of rock overhanging Holy Well. A small path runs down one side of this and back up the other side. Properly speaking, this should now be classified as a 'dripping well' or slow seepage of water from the rock face, the issue of water here having much to do with the presence of a perched water-table over the *unconformity* between the Engine Vein Conglomerate and the underlying Wilmslow Sandstone. Water gathers within the porous conglomerate which overlies an impervious bed of mudstone (clay) on the top of the Wilmslow Sandstone, creating a long-standing source of instability and occasional landslip: several very large blocks of conglomerate which were relatively unsupported on the gently dipping and soapy mudstone have collapsed under gravitational force alone. Local legend has it that a large block near here collapsed, killing a woman and a cow at some time during the eighteenth century (see Chapter 2). Some metres to the south and west of Holy Well is a more powerful *chalybeate* spring (one rich in iron) which issues from the fault itself and tumbles into a carved stone basin known as De Trafford's Well. There are two valleys on either side of this promontory, whose origins probably derive from the outcrop of two sub-parallel faults.

Passing just below the site of the Beacon, of which nothing now remains except a few stone foundations on a much earlier mound, follow the base of the cliff-face of Engine Vein Conglomerate along the top of the western scarp. As one approaches Castle Rock the junction with the underlying Wilmslow Sandstone appears (Figure 4.6). The mainly *trough cross-beds* of the overlying pebbly to coarse to fine sandstone succession can be seen resting upon a series of channels cut into its upper surface. Just above the junction some of these pebbles show evidence

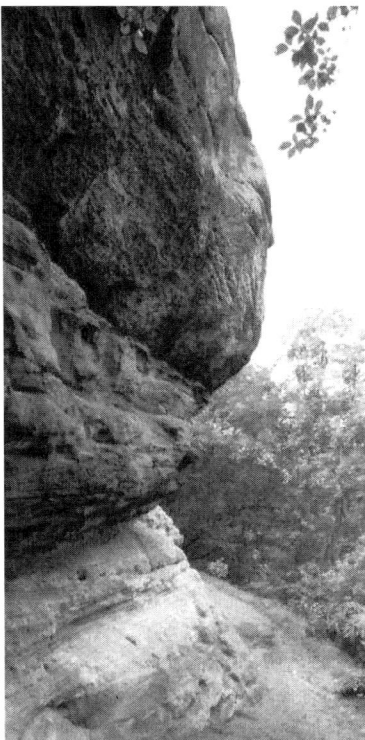

Figure 4.6. Cliff face beneath Castle Rock composed of fluvial channel-fill pebbly sandstones of the Helsby Sandstone Formation (Engine Vein Conglomerate Member) and trough cross-bedded sandstones unconformably overlying the soft red Wilmslow Sandstone.

Photograph Sean Edwards.

of wind-faceting as *dreikanters*, while *rolled-mud clasts* are also common. By climbing up to the summit of Castle Rock one can examine the top of one of these pebbly sandstone units in detail. Some of the pebble clasts within this are composed of white vein quartz, while many others are probably of Carboniferous gritstone. These reworked pebbles are of Chester Pebble Beds type, a formation which was probably deposited on the flanks of the Southern Pennines in early Triassic times and, as a result of the earth movements which gave rise to the *Hardegsen unconformity*, were uplifted and eroded and so incorporated into the Helsby Sandstone Formation. Considerable amounts of baryte have replaced some of the original cements of these sandstone capping rocks on the Alderley Edge ridge. For instance, an estimated 30–50 per cent of parts of this rock on Castle Rock is now composed of baryte. The resistance of these barytised rocks to erosion in part explains the formation of a prominent scarp at this location.

Tool-making debris found on the top of the dip slope beneath the field just to the south of Castle Rock confirmed that here is the site of an important Mesolithic hunting camp. First attracted no doubt by the prospect of viewing the movement of game on the plains below, these people also exploited sources of suitable stone which they found among the local glacial erratics as well as nodules of flint or chert brought with them to flake into scrapers and composite points for arrows (see Chapter 14, and Cowell in *ArchAE*: ch. 3).

The path beneath the scarp top may be followed westwards as far as Wizard's Well and Mottram Wood. Some hundred metres along the path one passes a very small and old outcrop quarry on the left-hand side. With the eye of faith, fossilised mud-cracks can be seen here on the underside of a sandstone bed, where the interleaved mudstone has since been eroded and picked out. This is also where a reptilian footprint (*Chirotherium*) was found (Figure 5.3a). Wizard's Well is another dripping well, and on the right-hand side of this rock lies the outcrop of a north–south fault, along which an exploratory adit level was once driven.

This route forms the basis of an introduction to the geology and scenery of Alderley Edge, but various detours can be made to explore some of the less-visited areas. Windmill Wood was the centre of nineteenth-century mining on the Edge. It lies on the outcrop of the Wood Mine Conglomerate. A path may be followed from the west side of the Macclesfield Road, starting opposite the car park adjacent to Beacon Lodge and leading through the woods as far as the first big clearing. This was the site of both opencast and shaft workings and also of an early nineteenth-century windmill used for ore crushing. All that now remains is the crushed mine waste, yet at the bottom of some of the rain-wash gullies one can still find heavy fragments of ore rich in galena and also cerussite (a lead carbonate mineral).

On the east side of the Edge, Waterfall Wood is also worth exploring. This incised valley with the waterfall at its southern end, formed by the hard resistant Engine Vein Conglomerate overlying the readily erodable aeolian Wilmslow Sandstone Formation, is one of the most impressive but least visited natural features of the Edge (see Figure 4.2).

A minimum of three to four hours is recommended to complete the main geological route at a fairly leisurely pace. A long walk, but a short time to contemplate some 245 million years of events which have helped to shape this sandstone escarpment and dip slope, not the least of which have been the activities of people who have hunted, lived, farmed, mined and quarried the surface of the Edge, and even now, through conserving it, continue to influence the landscape.

Further reading

Armstrong, A. and Brasier, M. 2004. *Microfossils* (2nd edition). Oxford: Blackwell.
Kearey, P. 2003. *Penguin Dictionary of Geology.* Harmondsworth: Penguin Books.

5

The solid geology of Alderley Edge

David B. Thompson, Geoffrey Warrington, John E. Pollard and John R. Nudds

An introduction to the geological maps and cross-section

David B. Thompson

An appreciation of the geological nature and origin of the Edge depends upon an understanding of events at least 250 million years ago and across the whole of the Cheshire Basin (Plant *et al.*, 1999). An idea of the general structure of the Wilmslow–Alderley area may be gained by undertaking short journeys across it, from north to south and east to west. The first might be southward from Styal to Nether Alderley. The featureless nature of the route along the modern B5166 and B5369 (formerly the A34) reflects the thick cover of glacial river sands and stony clays which were laid down 24,000–13,000 years ago, during the Ice Age, and river and lake sediments that were subsequently deposited on top. The underlying harder Triassic rocks exposed near the mill and car park at Quarry Bank, Styal, were originally laid down horizontally but are now gently inclined to the north-west, but at Alderley Edge rocks of equivalent age dip to the south-west: these opposing dips result from later folding that produced the Wilmslow Anticline, whose axis trends east-north-east to west-south-west (Figure 5.1). Approaching Alderley village, the Edge, which extends eastwards for 3 km, has a north-facing escarpment caused by differential erosion of sandstones of varying hardness before, during and after the Ice Age, the high ground being due to the durability of Triassic pebbly sandstones that are widely mineralised by baryte (barium sulphate; $BaSO_4$). Any former glacial deposits have been largely swept clear of this upland area. The route of

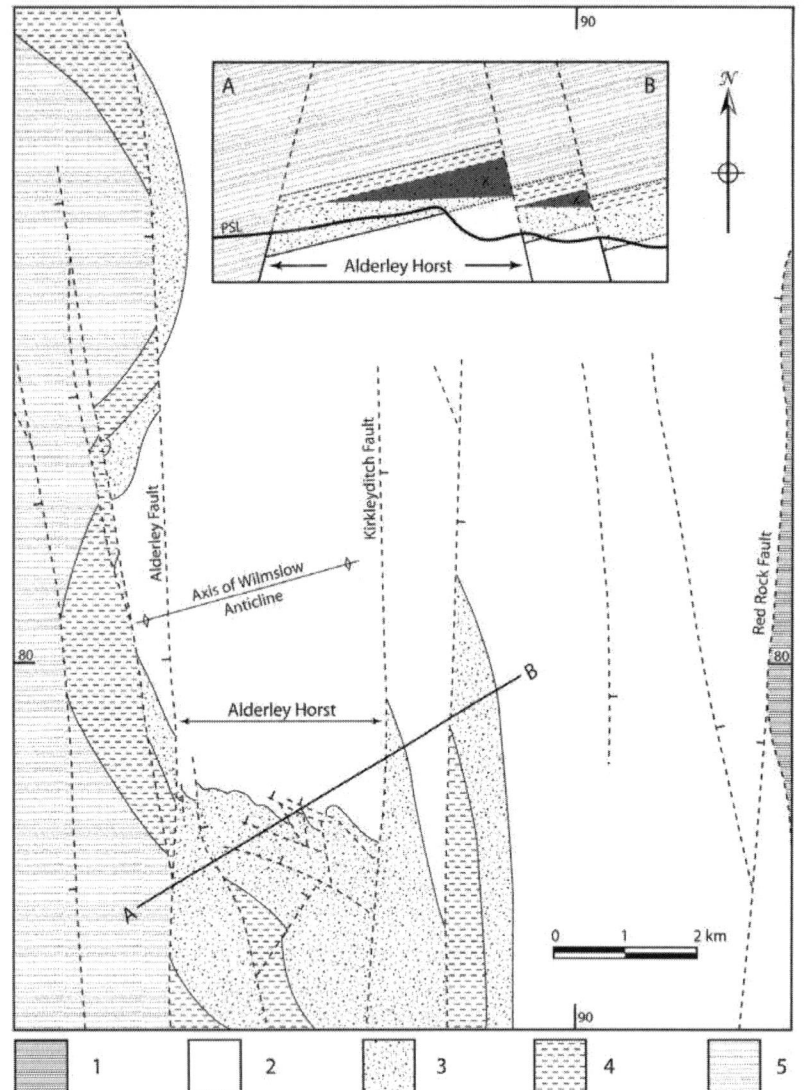

Figure 5.1. Outline solid geology and structure of the Alderley–Wilmslow–Styal district. Inset: Schematic section on line A–B on the geological map, showing potential structural traps (x) for hydrocarbons and other fluids in the Helsby Sandstone Formation beneath a cap-rock of the Mercia Mudstone Group. Key: 1, Carboniferous; 2, Sherwood Sandstone Group (Wilmslow Sandstone and older formations); 3, Sherwood Sandstone Group (Helsby Sandstone Formation); 4, Mercia Mudstone Group (Tarporley Siltstone Formation); 5, higher Mercia Mudstone Group formations (see Figure 5.8 for equivalent superseded terms used in pre-1980 literature).

After Warrington (1980: fig. 1).

the B5369 (formerly A34) to the south of the town climbs the western end of this scarp as far as Whitebarn Road and then runs down and across its dip slope. The road runs parallel to, and east of, a west-facing scarp that is the result of differential erosion of the rocks adjacent to a large north-to-south trending fracture zone known as the Alderley Fault (Figure 5.1). This fault resulted in the downward displacement of rocks to the west by as much as 1,000 m (Chadwick, 1997), so that younger, softer mudstones of the late Mid and Late Triassic Mercia Mudstone Group are now juxtaposed with the older, harder sandstones of the Early and early Mid Triassic Sherwood Sandstone Group that form the Edge to the east. Further to the south, the roadside at Nether Alderley Mill is cut in yellow-orange sandstone lying in the Alderley Block, to the east of the Alderley Fault. Two boreholes drilled a short distance to the east of the entrance to Alderley Park in 1971 for ICI Pharmaceutical Division showed that faulted, mineralised sandstone is present hereabouts and is affected by part of the same fracture zone (Alderley Park 1 and 2, SJ 8447 7583 and 8432 7477, British Geological Survey (BGS) nos SJ 87 NW/10–11).

A journey eastwards, along the foot of the Edge from Alderley to Mottram St Andrew, takes one over glacial and post-glacial deposits at a height of about 90 m above Ordnance datum (AOD). To the right one can glimpse the site of Alderley Beacon at over 180 m AOD on top of the scarp to the south and, farther on, the former Alderley Red Moulding Sand Quarry on the low ground below Saddlebole hill. On nearing Kirkleyditch, the Edge is seen to terminate eastwards beyond Clockhouse Wood and Daniel Hill. Equivalent rocks to those of the top of the Edge occur low down in Kirkleyditch village, and form a subdued scarp at a height of 120 m AOD. This runs north-west to south-east through the old mineral quarries and shafts in the grounds of Kirkley Mount and Copperfields. The termination of the ridge is due to the presence of another major north–south fracture zone, the Kirkleyditch Fault; this forms the eastern boundary of the Alderley Block and has displaced the rocks to the east downwards by c. 200–250 m (Figure 5.1).

Travelling southwards from Kirkleyditch, across glacial and post-glacial deposits and roughly parallel to the line of the Kirkleyditch Fault, one comes to the road from Macclesfield to Alderley Edge (B5087). Turning right towards Alderley, as height is gained the land generally slopes north-east to south-west so that one is travelling along the top of the Edge and across hard Triassic sandstones which dip south-westwards. Since the dip of the rocks is steeper than the fall of the land, younger and younger beds outcrop to the south (see Figure 5.1 and Plate 3). The important Hayman's Farm Borehole, drilled for Macclesfield Water Board in 1964, lies 0.75 km across the fields to the south (SJ 8563 7633, BGS no. SJ 87 NE/2); nearly 306 m deep, it revealed the whole of the Triassic succession that is exposed on Alderley Edge. Many of the mineralised areas and mines lie on either side the road: the Cobalt Mine between Finlow Wood and the Wizard restaurant with, farther on, Engine Vein Mine to the right, and Wood Mine and West Mine under woods and fields to the left. The last part of the journey by-passes the Mesolithic site on the top of Castle Rock, to the north, and descends westwards into the area of the old quarries from which the villas of the 'Cottentots' were built, and into Alderley Edge village. These journeys will have revealed that the Edge has developed on the south side of the Wilmslow Anticline and in a large upstanding block of rock (a horst) lying between two major fault zones (Figure 5.1). The copper and other mines lie largely within this block.

For a more detailed appreciation of this geological setting, the visitor should walk south-westwards from Kirkleyditch along the public footpaths marked on the geological and Ordnance Survey maps (Plate 3). The route is via Clockhouse Farm, Waterfall Wood, Dickens Wood, Stormy Point mines, Engine Vein Mine, Church Quarry, Brynlow valley and mines, Artists Lane and Topps and Butts quarries, to Nether Alderley Mill and the entrance to Alderley Park. Such a journey reveals the succession of Triassic rocks in the upper part of the Sherwood Sandstone Group, from the oldest exposed (the Wilmslow Sandstone Formation), seen at the foot of the Edge, through successive members of the overlying Helsby Sandstone Formation, to the lowest unit in the Mercia Mudstone Group, the muddy Tarporley Siltstone Formation. The visitor will also gain an idea of the internal structure of the Alderley Block, and will understand that its many mini-escarpments and dip slopes are repeated no less than eight times (Plates 3 and 4). Most of these are due to the repetitions of outcrops of the Engine Vein Conglomerate, the lowest member of the Helsby Sandstone Formation, which reflect internal faulting of the horst, principally along west-north-west to east-south-east and north-west to south-east directions. By this time, the visitor will have noticed shafts and tunnels that are surface indications of extensive mine workings from which copper, lead and cobalt ores were wrested at various times since the Bronze Age. 'Wealth from the ground' is the basis of the development of the man-made landscape of the Edge from the earliest times.

By now some questions will have been raised in the enquiring mind:

- When, and in what sequence of latitudes, climates and environments, was the succession of sandstone rocks deposited?
- What was the subsequent history of the Cheshire Basin as these rocks were buried?
- By what forces, on how many occasions and at what times were the rock units folded and faulted?
- When did the mineralisation occur?
- What and where were the sources of the baryte, copper, lead and cobalt?
- How did these elements migrate into, become trapped and then precipitated in the sandstones and against the fault zones?
- When was the cover of younger, softer Triassic rocks worn off?
- What was the nature and sequence of the pre-glacial, glacial and post-glacial events?

Some at least of these questions will be considered in the following sections of this chapter and in the two chapters that follow.

Palaeontology: the dating and correlation of the Triassic rock formations

Geoffrey Warrington, John E. Pollard, David B. Thompson and John R. Nudds

Within the 'core area' of the Alderley Edge Landscape Project only the Helsby Sandstone Formation has yielded fossils. These comprise miospores (spores and pollen of land plants), conchostracan crustaceans (water-fleas living in fresh–brackish water) and the tracks of land vertebrates. Only the miospores are of value for dating and correlating the rocks within and beyond the Cheshire Basin; however, the crustaceans and the tracks of reptiles provide important information about the successive climates and environments of Triassic times.

The first miospores recorded from the Triassic in the Cheshire Basin were recovered by Warrington from the mudstone overlying the lowest conglomerate in the Engine Vein Conglomerate Member at the east end of the Engine Vein Mine opencast. The assemblage comprises pteridophyte and lycopsid spores, including *Calamospora tener*, *Cyclotriletes microgranifer*, *Densoisporites nejburgii*, *Punctatisporites triassicus*, *Saturnisporites praevius*, *Verrucosisporites applanatus* and *V. morulae*, and conifer pollen, including *Alisporites grauvogeli*, *Angustisulcites klausii*, *Illinites chitonoides*, *Protodiploxypinus doubingeri*, *P. fastidiosus*, *P. sittleri*, *Triadispora falcata*, *T. staplini*, *Vitreisporites signatus* and *Voltziaceaesporites heteromorpha*, and possibly *I. kosankei* and *T. crassa* as well. Other samples from the core area, from other levels in the Helsby Sandstone Formation and from the Wilmslow Sandstone Formation, have proved barren (Warrington, 1970; Warrington, personal records). Conchostracan crustaceans (*Euestheria*) have been recovered from mudstones in the Engine Vein Conglomerate Member in the Old Alderley Quarry and at the west end of the openworks of Engine Vein Mine (de Rance, in Brockbank, 1891a, 1891b; Warrington, 1963) (Figure 5.2). A footprint (Figure 5.3a), originally interpreted as tridactyl but now considered referable to *Chirotherium*, was discovered by Warrington on the under-surface of a pebbly sandstone in the Engine Vein Conglomerate Member near Wizard's Well (Thompson, 1970c: 48; Warrington and Thompson, 1971: 70; Sarjeant, 1974: 312). Plant fragments have been found in sandstones in Wood Mine and also in West Mine, where they probably comprise equisetalean (horsetail) remains. Several horizons of vertical *Skolithos* burrows occur in West Mine (Figure 5.3b). Pebbles in the Engine Vein Conglomerate Member contain fossils, mostly rugose corals identified by Nudds (1998) as *Siphonodendron martini*, *Amplexizaphrentis enniskilleni* and *Caninia* sp., and possibly *Dibunophyllum* sp., derived from rocks of Early Carboniferous age.

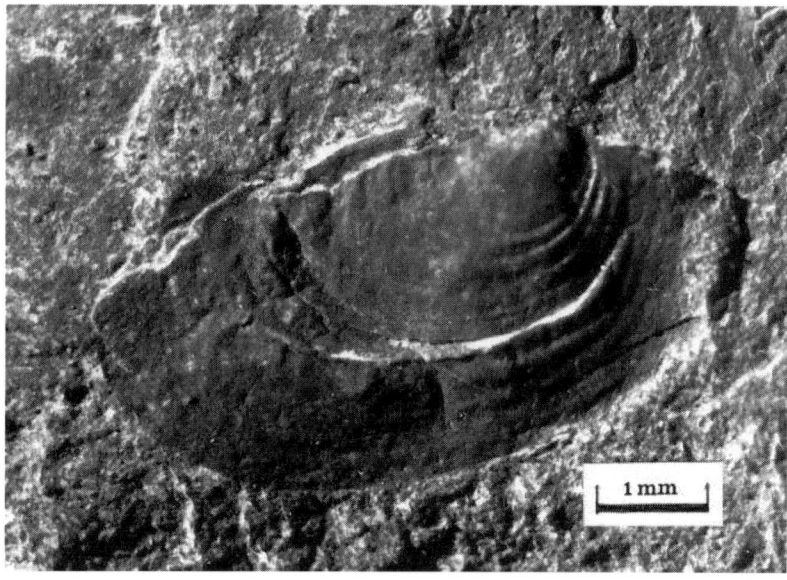

(a)

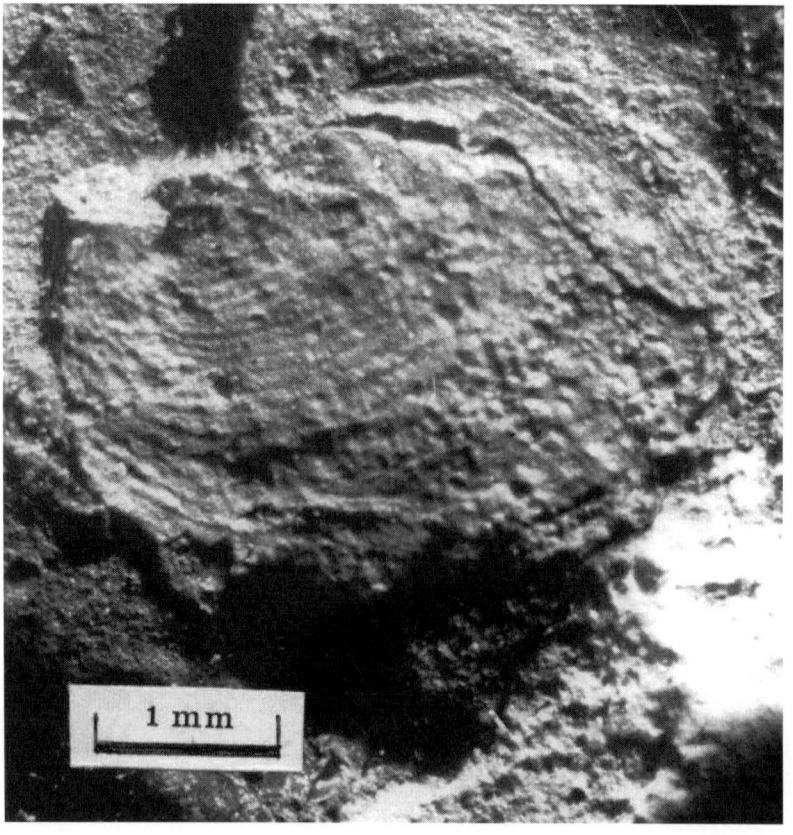

(b)

Figure 5.2. Fossil conchostracan crustaceans (*Euestheria*) from the Engine Vein Conglomerate, Helsby Sandstone Formation. (a) Specimen collected by C. E. de Rance from mudstone in the Engine Vein Conglomerate, Old Alderley Quarry. (b) Specimen collected by G. Warrington from injection strata in the Engine Vein Conglomerate (Figure 5.7), at the hanging wall of the Engine Vein Fault at the west end of the Engine Vein openworks.

(a) Warrington (1963); Manchester Museum: collection number L.12113. (b) Warrington (1963); British Geological Survey: collection number GSM 108095.

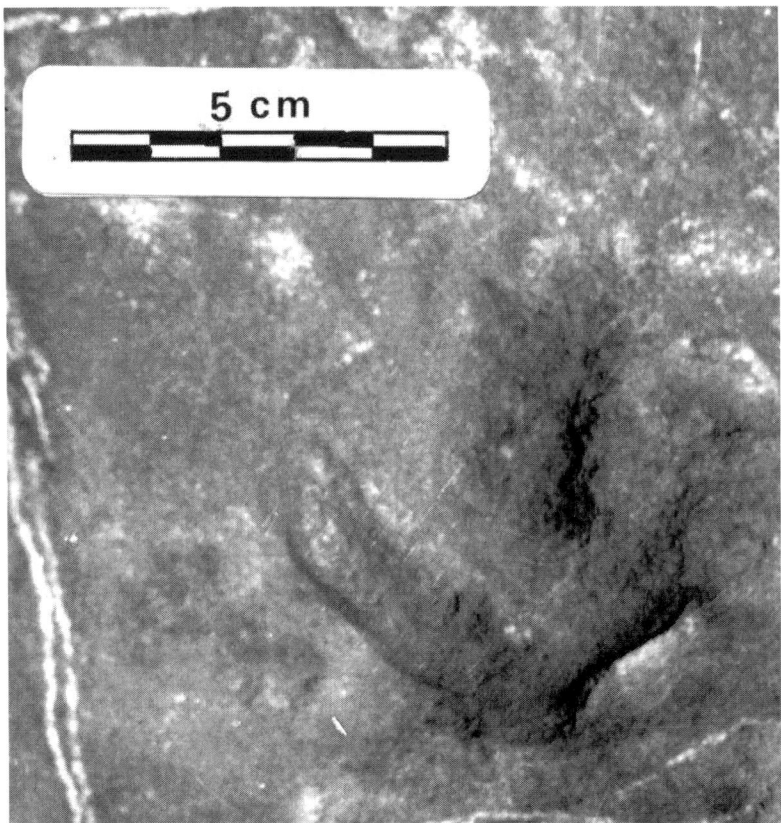

(a)

Figure 5.3. Trace fossils.
(a) Reptile footprint
(*Chirotherium* sp.); sandstone
cast of imperfect impression
in mudstone (now removed);
under-surface of sandstone bed
at the base of the second cycle in
the Engine Vein Conglomerate,
c. 96 m west of Castle Rock,
Alderley Edge. (b) Burrows
(*Skolithos* spp.): West Mine
Sandstone Member, Helsby
Sandstone Formation, west
side of stope in West Mine,
c. 360 m west-south-west of
the original entrance to the
underground workings. The
dark (orange-brown), tubular
burrows in low-angled cross-
bedded or laminated, grey-white
and orange-brown sandstones,
comprise isolated, test-tube-
shaped forms, sometimes with
a laminated infill, 10–15 mm
diameter and up to 50 mm
deep, and abundant, oblique
or vertically sinuous forms,
3–5 mm in diameter and
20–80 mm deep. Both probably
reflect opportunistic insect
colonisation of sands marginal to
fluvial channels under subaerial
conditions, during periods of
little or no sedimentation (pencil
scale bottom left – 12 cm).

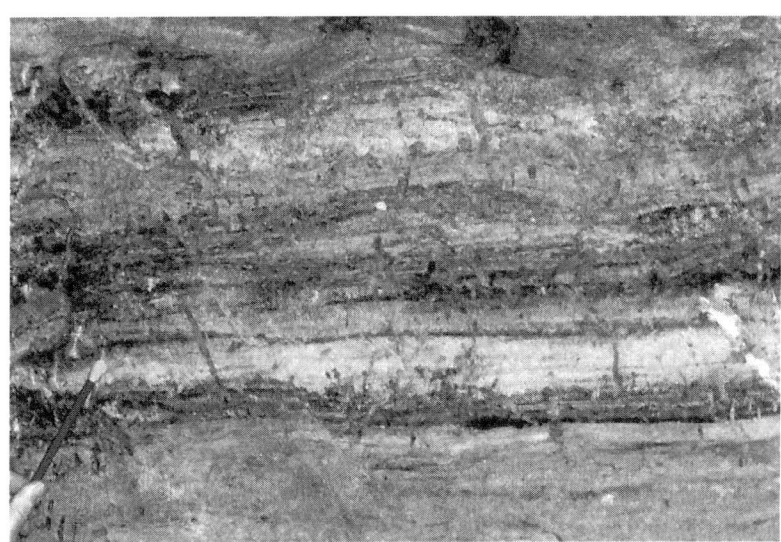

(b)

Within the hinterland of the Landscape Project and beyond, a single print of *Chirotherium storetonense* (now in Stockport Museum, with a cast of the specimen in Manchester Museum) was found in beds now assigned to the Wilmslow Sandstone Formation in Wilmslow No. 3 Water Borehole (at 201 m), drilled for Stockport Corporation Waterworks in 1912 (deepened in 1931: site SJ 849 815; BGS no. SJ 88 SW/7) (Alty, 1926: 278; Taylor *et al.*, 1963: 61, 155; Thompson, 1966). In addition, several footprints of *Rhynchosauroides rectipes* (now in Manchester Museum) were found in the Hayman's Farm Borehole (at *c.* 119.5 m) in the Wood Mine Conglomerate Member (Thompson, 1966: 185; see Figures 5.14–5.16 in Appendix 5.1), where arthropod burrows referable to *Planolites* and *Skolithos* are also common.

A rich but very poorly preserved miospore assemblage recovered from the Nether Alderley Sandstone Member at 63.68 m in the Hayman's Farm Borehole is dominated by very poorly preserved conifer pollen; the few determinable specimens are referable to *Alisporites grauvogeli*, *A. toralis*, *Lunatisporites* sp. and *Stellapollenites thiergartii*. Another rich but slightly better-preserved assemblage from the same member at 56.01 m in the same borehole includes a few spores (*Calamospora* sp., possibly *Verrucosisporites contactus*) but is dominated by rather poorly preserved bisaccate pollen, mostly referable to the genus *Alisporites* (Figure 5.4); determinable specimens include *Alisporites grauvogeli*, *A. toralis*, *Angustisulcites gorpii*, *A. grandis*, *A. klausii*, *Illinites kosankei*, *Lunatisporites* sp., *Protodiploxypinus* sp., *Striatoabieites balmei*, *Triadispora crassa* and *Voltziaceaesporites heteromorpha*. Poorly preserved conifer pollen was also recovered from four higher levels in the same member, from 46.63 m to 55.58 m in the borehole (Warrington, personal records). The Nether Alderley Sandstone Member has also yielded trace fossils, including *Planolites* and *Skolithos*, and possibly *Diplocraterion*, and one record of *Cruziana* (*Isopodichnus*) *problematica* from Bradford Lane Quarry (Tony Browne, personal communication). Only the pollen from 56.01 m and 63.68 m in the Hayman's Farm Borehole are useful for dating and, like those from the base of the Helsby Sandstone Formation at Engine Vein Mine (see above), are indicative of an Anisian (early Mid Triassic) age.

Elsewhere in the Cheshire Basin, miospores indicate that the succession up to a level above the Northwich Halite Formation in the Mercia Mudstone Group (see Figure 5.8, below) is Anisian (i.e. Mid Triassic) in age (Warrington, in Benton *et al.*, 1994: 154; Warrington *et al.*, 1999: 37); no miospores have been recovered from beds below the Helsby Sandstone Formation. Other fossils recorded from similar rock units elsewhere in the Cheshire Basin include indeterminate plant remains, conchostracan crustaceans, reptile remains and trace fossils (from both invertebrates and vertebrates). Of these, only the remains of

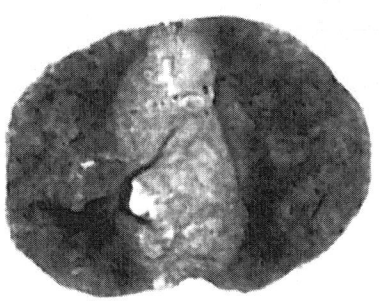

Figure 5.4. Bisaccate conifer pollen (*Alisporites* sp.) from the Nether Alderley Sandstone, Hayman's Farm Borehole (56.01 m; Figure 5.7).

Specimen from slide MPA 48353/2, palynology collection, British Geological Survey, Keyworth, Nottingham. Size (maximum width in microns) – 67 μm; colour orange-brown.

lizard-like reptiles (*Rhynchosaurus articeps*) from the Tarporley Siltstone Formation and underlying sandstones at Grinshill, north Shropshire, have stratigraphical value: these indicate a Mid Triassic age compatible with that of the miospores from the Helsby Sandstone Formation and the lower part of the Mercia Mudstone Group farther north in the basin (Benton, 1990; Benton *et al.*, 1994; Warrington *et al.*, 1999: 37).

Lithostratigraphy and palaeogeography: the ancient environments and geographic origins of the rock formations

David B. Thompson, Geoffrey Warrington and John E. Pollard

The description and interpretation of the rocks of the Edge have a long and contrasting history. Bakewell (1813) believed them to have been formed by alluvial (i.e. river) processes. The discovery in the 1830s of the footprints of vertebrates within rocks of comparable age in the Wirral–Liverpool and north Shropshire areas added to this picture. The animals which produced both the large *Chirotherium* footprint (the 'hand beast', a two-metre-long carnivorous archosaur – i.e. a precursor of the dinosaurs) and the small *Rhynchosauroides* footprints (produced by a lizard-like creature some 25 cm long) (Plate 5) were believed to have lived either along drying-out river courses (Cunningham, 1839) or on sandbanks within inter-tidal areas on the coast (Buckland, in Cunningham, 1839; see Tresise and Sarjeant, 1997). Despite these ideas, the first Geological Survey officers (Hull, 1860, 1869; Hull and Green, 1866) considered that all the cross-bedded sandstone rocks originated from shifting shallow-marine currents and all the pebble beds from high-energy coastal environments between the tide marks, the footprints of land animals presumably belonging to the more elevated parts of the latter areas. The discovery of water-fleas (*Euestheria*; Figure 5.2) at Alderley Old Quarry (de Rance, in Brockbank, 1891a, 1891b) and the Engine Vein Mine opencast (Warrington, 1963) invited a reappraisal of these ideas, for at the present day these invertebrates are known to occupy stagnant fresh to brackish or salty water, especially interior continental, but never seawater (Lomas, 1905; Kobayashi, 1954). This reinterpretation has been developed since the early 1960s by several of the authors of this chapter (Warrington, 1963, 1970; Thompson, 1966, 1970a, 1970b, 1970c, 1984, 1991; Warrington and Thompson, 1971; Warrington *et al.*, 1980; Pollard, 1981, 1985; Warrington and Ivimey-Cook, 1992; see further below).

The Wilmslow Sandstone Formation is now interpreted as a largely low-sinuosity, braided-river deposit formed more than 245 million years ago. Upwards through this unit there is increasing evidence of aeolian (wind-generated) processes and deposition in a semi-arid area. It is overlain by the Helsby Sandstone Formation, which is interpreted as deposited in an ephemeral, low-sinuosity, strongly flood-prone, braided-river system (Figure 5.5) some 245 million years ago. Deposition

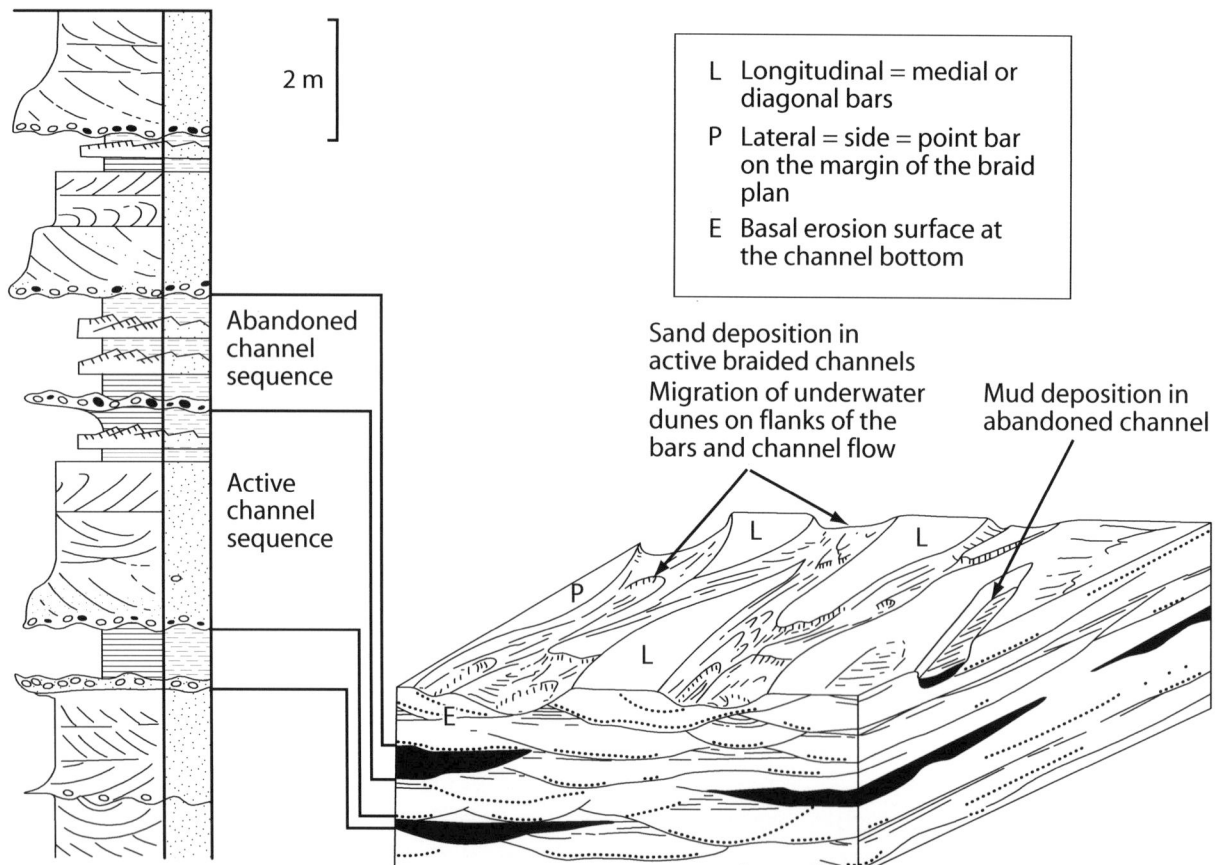

Figure 5.5. The physiography, processes and sedimentary facies of a braided alluvial channel system. From Selley (1982: 274, fig. 132).

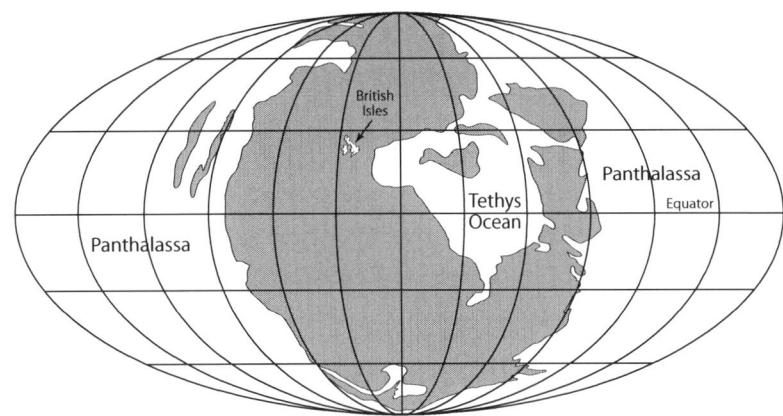

Figure 5.6. Global palaeo-geography for Mid Triassic times, showing the position of the UK in relation to the contemporary equator.

of sediments was probably dominated (at least in terms of time) by arid intervals, when aeolian processes and deposits developed. These conditions were succeeded imperceptibly by further riverine and inter-tidal deposits and events, to which evaporitic, soil and salt-pan-forming processes were added. Evidence for these latter interpretations, relating to around 242 million years ago, is seen in the Tarporley Siltstone Formation, which outcrops in the Nether Alderley region of the Project hinterland. The palaeomagnetism – i.e. the traces of the original (contemporary Triassic) magnetic field – in the red sandstone rocks at Styal (Clegg *et al.*, 1954) confirms that these events took place in the tropical trade-wind belt, *c.* 20° north of the equator (Figure 5.6). The regional palaeogeographical setting of the Cheshire Basin area at this time is depicted in Plate 6. More details are given in the succeeding sections, but some readers may prefer to make do with this outline summary and go forward to the next chapter, which describes the mineralogy of the Edge.

Geological mapping (Hull, 1861; de Rance, 1890; Eagar and Broadhurst, 1959; Trotter and Taylor, 1963; Thompson, 1966) and detailed descriptive (graphic) logging of successions at outcrop and in mines (Warrington, 1963, 1965; Thompson, 1966) and in boreholes at Hayman's Farm and Alderley Park by Thompson in 1963–64 and 1971, and elsewhere (Taylor *et al.*, 1963) have revealed the detailed nature of the Wilmslow Sandstone and Helsby Sandstone formations (Figure 5.7) (as well as the Tarporley Siltstone Formation). The Helsby Sandstone is divided into several local rock units, or members, which can be correlated across the Cheshire Basin (Figure 5.8). Descriptions and interpretations of these formations and members in the Project core and hinterland areas are given below.

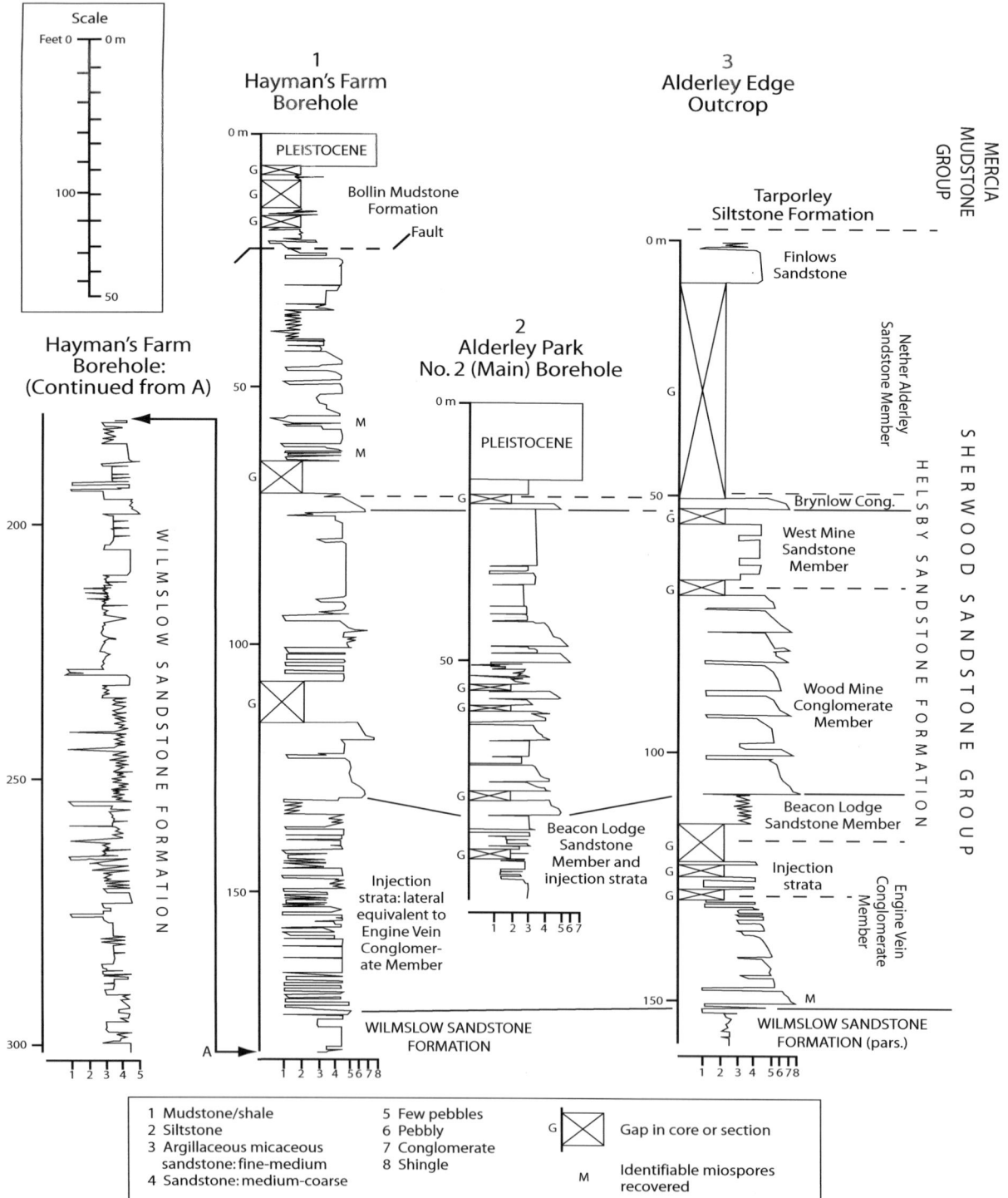

Figure 5.7. The succession proved in the Hayman's Farm Borehole correlated with those in the Alderley Park No. 2 (Main) Borehole and seen at surface and underground in the core area. Borehole sections logged by D. B. Thompson. Succession in the core area from surface sections logged by D. B. Thompson, and the section of the Wood Mine Conglomerate Member logged in Wood Mine by G. Warrington and N. J. Hunter.

SYSTEM	SERIES	STAGE	AGE (at base)[1]	FORMER NOMENCLATURE (pre-1980)	NOMENCLATURE (post-1980; with abbreviations used in text)					SEDIMENTOLOGY & PALAEOENVIRONMENT
					Cheshire Basin (general succession)[2]			Alderley - Styal area succession[3]		
					GROUP	Formation	Member	Formation	Member	
JURASSIC		Toarcian	183	Lias	Lias	(> 627m)				Shallow marine
		Pliens-bachian	189.6							
		Sine-murian	196.5							
		Hettan-gian	199.6							
TRIASSIC	Upper	Rhaetian		Rhaetic Beds	Penarth	Lilstock (5.77m)	Langport? (<0.15m)			Semi-marine and marine; coastal and littoral
			203.6				Cotham (c.5.75m)			
						Westbury (7.8m)				
		Norian		Upper Keuper Marl	Mercia Mudstone		Blue Anchor (18m)			Playas and inland sabkha environments terminated by a marine transgression
			216.5				Branscombe Mudstone (205m)			
		Carnian	228.7	Upper Keuper Saliferous Beds			Wilkesley Halite (404m)			Hypersaline salinas; marine input
	Middle	Ladin-ian	237	Middle Keuper Marl		Sidmouth Mudstone (>1500m)	Wych Mudstone (186m)			Playas and inland sabkhas; aeolian and water-lain sediments
							Byley Mudstone (182m)			
		Anisian		Lower Keuper Saliferous Beds			Northwich Halite (283m)	Sidmouth Mudstone (pars.)	Solution breccia ?	Hypersaline salinas; marine-sourced
				Lower Keuper Marl			Bollin Mudstone (>500m)		Bollin Mudstone	Wide coastal plains or sabkhas; periodic marine incursions
				Waterstones		Tarporley Siltstone (TSF: c.120m)		Tarporley Siltstone (TSF: c.120m)		Fluvial to lagoonal and marine intertidal; brackish to hypersaline
				Lower Keuper Sandstone	Sherwood Sandstone	Helsby Sandstone (HSF: 100-150m)	Frodsham Soft Sandstone (FSSM: c.30m)	Helsby Sandstone (HSF: c.132m)	Nether Alderley Sandstone (NASM: c.51m); Brynlow Conglomerate (c.3m) at base	Fluvial: rivers with moderate sinuosity
									West Mine Sandstone (WMSM: c.17m)	Aeolian >> fluvial
							Delamere Pebbly Sandstone (DPSM: c.30m)		Wood Mine Conglomerate (WMCM: c.40m)	Fluvial: low sinuosity rivers
							Thurstaston Soft Sandstone (TSSM: c.30m); Thurstaston Hard Sandstone (c.3m) at base		Beacon Lodge Sandstone (12m)	Aeolian > fluvial
			245.9						Engine Vein Conglomerate (EVCM: 30m)	Fluvial: ephemeral low sinuosity rivers
	Lower	Olen-ekian	249.5	Bunter Upper Mottled Sandstone		Wilmslow Sandstone (WSF: c.300m)		Wilmslow Sandstone (WSF: c.300m)		Aeolian > fluvial in upper part Fluvial > aeolian in lower part
		Induan	251	Bunter Pebble Beds		Chester Pebble Beds (CPBF: c.200m)		Chester Pebble Beds (CPBF: c.200m)		Fluvial: low sinuosity braided rivers; very high discharges
PERMIAN		Lopin-gian	260.4	Manchester Marl / Bunter Lower Mottled Sandstone	Cumbrian Coast	Manchester Marl	Kinnerton & Bridgnorth Sandstones (c.350m)	Manchester Marl (40 100m)		Marine to brackish; restricted faunas / Aeolian -
		Guad-alupian	270.6	Collyhurst Sandstone	Appleby	Collyhurst Sandstone		Collyhurst Sandstone (150-175m)		inland sand sea with dunes, draa and dry interdune areas
		Cis-uralian	299							
PRE-PERMIAN					Lower Palaeozoic and Carboniferous			Carboniferous		

Figure 5.8. The succession of rock units in the Cheshire Basin: lithostratigraphic nomenclature, ages and interpreted depositional environments. (1) Age of stage base, in millions of years; from International Stratigraphic Chart, International Commission on Stratigraphy, 2009. Mundil *et al.* (2010) propose slightly different ages, with the base and top of the Anisian Stage dated at 247.2 and 242.0 million years, for example. (2) Nomenclature from Thompson (1970a), Warrington *et al.* (1980), Wilson (1993), Howard *et al.* (2008). (3) Nomenclature from Warrington (1965), Thompson (1970a), Warrington and Thompson (1971), Warrington *et al.* (1980), Wilson (1993), Howard *et al.* (2008). Vertical line ornament – strata not represented. Peck-and-dot lines mark unconformities, reflecting periods of non-deposition or uplift and erosion.

The Wilmslow Sandstone Formation

These foxy-red sandy rocks, some 300 m thick, are best seen on the surface in the former Alderley Red Moulding Sand Quarry (Figure 5.9), at Castle Rock (Figure 5.10), Pillar Mine and Waterfall Wood, and underground in the Hough Level and Engine Vein Mine. They are soft, easily eroded and vary in grain size from fine to coarse sand. They are either cross-bedded or flat-bedded. Where they are micaceous and rich in clay minerals (forming draping ripple marks or torn-up flakes or thin mudstone bands), they are undoubtedly of fluvial origin. Where details of ancient fluvial flow directions are measured (palaeocurrent data being derived from the sandstone cross-beds; Figure 5.11), the orientations are towards the north-west (Figure 5.12). The fluvial beds are interpreted as having formed in low-sinuosity, moderate- to low-energy, braided streams (Figure 5.5). Where interbedded red silty-mudstone and sandstone bands show rare horizons of desiccation cracks lying between repeated current ripple flows (as in the Hough Level and Engine Vein Mine), episodic but complete aridity, sub-aerial exposure and aeolian reworking of sands are indicated. The latter comprise cross-beds and flat-beds that are clearly visible at the foot of Castle Rock (Figure 5.10b), for example:

- low-angle 'pin-stripe' laminations, bearing reverse grading (attributable to the migration of wind ripples on the lower slopes of dunes or in interdune areas);
- high-angle wedges of coarse, very rounded sand grains, graded with the coarsest grains downslope (caused by avalanching of grains down the frontal slopes of sand dunes);
- zig-zag and brittle-fracture deformations of cross-beds (produced experimentally only in damp aeolian dune sands) (McKee and Bigarella, 1972);
- rhythmically developed patches of highly polished, sand-blasted 'pebbles' (mini-ventifacts) of granule size (2–4 mm).

Wavy bedding is common and may be promoted by: (1) early cementation of sand grains by evaporitic minerals; (2) differing adhesion of sand grains on half-wet, half-dry surfaces; (3) partial algal binding of sand grains and (4) true wave-ripple generation (Herries, 1997). Current directions in such rocks are directed towards the west (Figure 5.12), signifying a steady effective wind from the east, as in the tropical trade-wind belt of today. The single *Chirotherium* underprint from this formation in the Wilmslow No. 3 Water Borehole was found in wave-rippled, micaceous, fine-grained, flat-bedded interdune sandstones (Thompson, 1966). It is, however, often very difficult to assign individual cross-beds or flat-beds either to fluvial or to aeolian processes and origins.

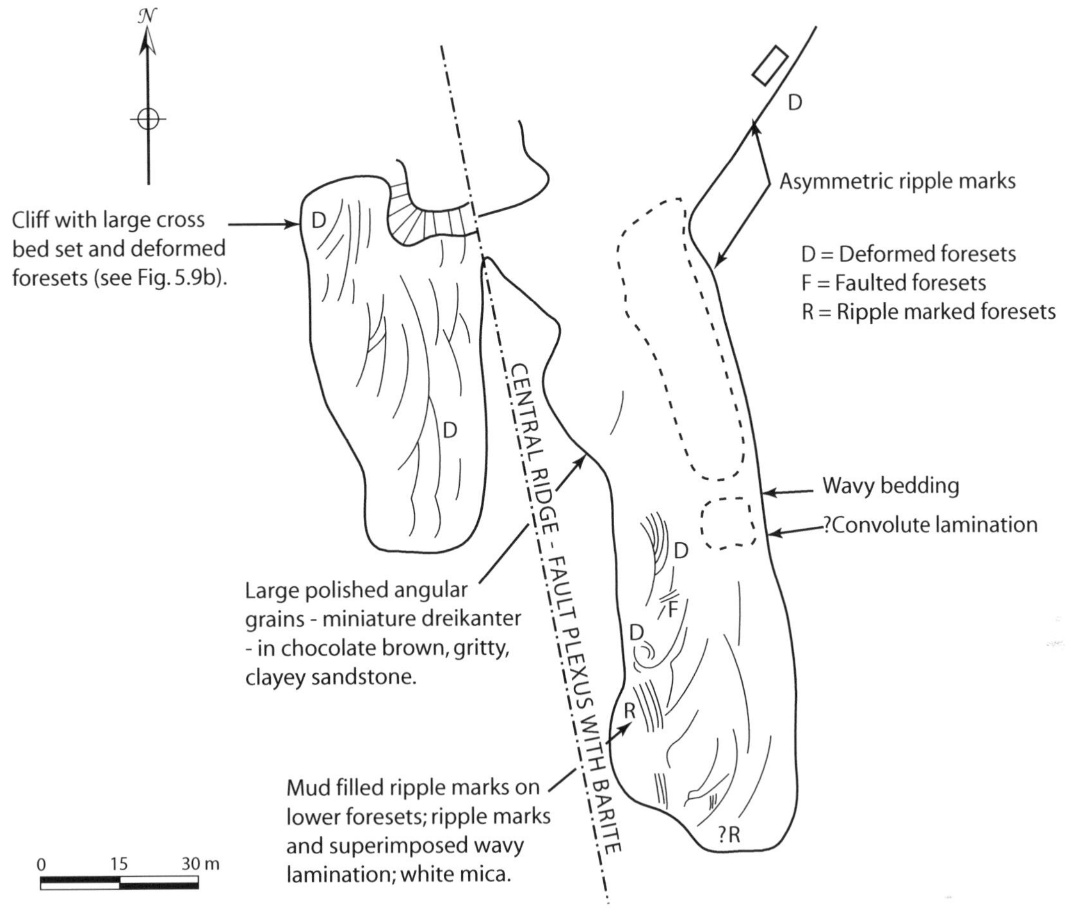

N

Cliff with large cross bed set and deformed foresets (see Fig. 5.9b).

CENTRAL RIDGE – FAULT PLEXUS WITH BARITE

Large polished angular grains - miniature dreikanter - in chocolate brown, gritty, clayey sandstone.

Mud filled ripple marks on lower foresets; ripple marks and superimposed wavy lamination; white mica.

0   15   30 m

Asymmetric ripple marks

D = Deformed foresets
F = Faulted foresets
R = Ripple marked foresets

Wavy bedding
?Convolute lamination

(a)

Figure 5.9. Features of the Wilmslow Sandstone Formation, in the Alderley Red Moulding Sand Quarry. (a) Plan of cross-bed foresets in the Wilmslow Sandstone Formation in the quarry floor, and disposition of other sedimentary features. (b) Detail of deformed cross-bedding in the north-west corner of the quarry (see Figure 5.9a).

(a) From Thompson (1966: fig. 37).
(b) From Thompson (1966), fig. 85A, from field sketches and a photograph by G. Warrington (1963).

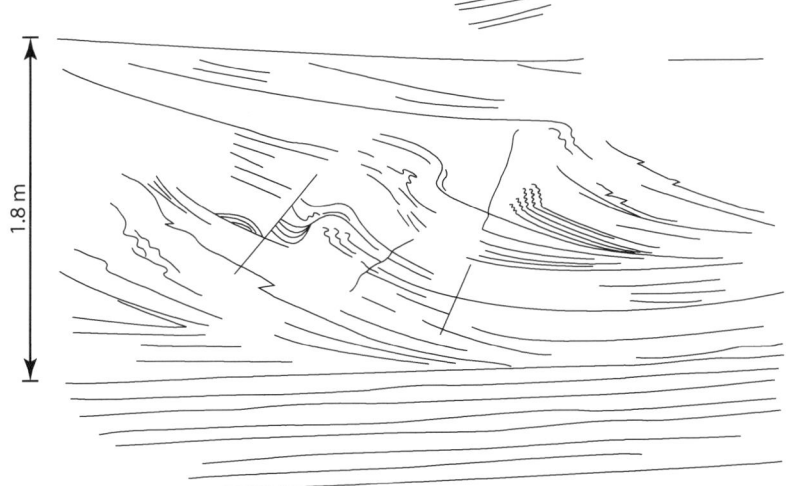

1.8 m

(b)

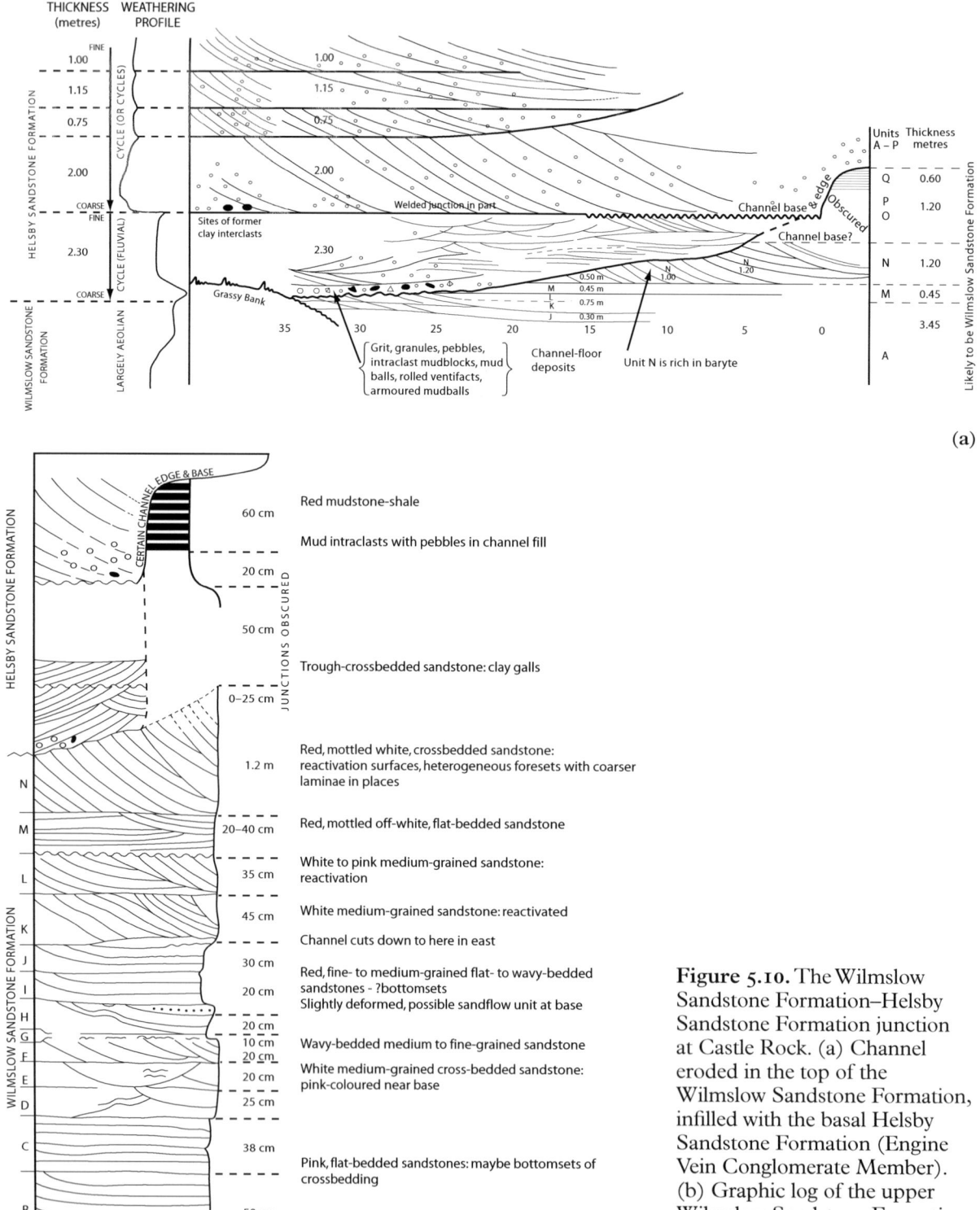

Figure 5.10. The Wilmslow Sandstone Formation–Helsby Sandstone Formation junction at Castle Rock. (a) Channel eroded in the top of the Wilmslow Sandstone Formation, infilled with the basal Helsby Sandstone Formation (Engine Vein Conglomerate Member). (b) Graphic log of the upper Wilmslow Sandstone Formation and its junction with the Helsby Sandstone Formation.

From Thompson (1985: figs 21 and 22 respectively).

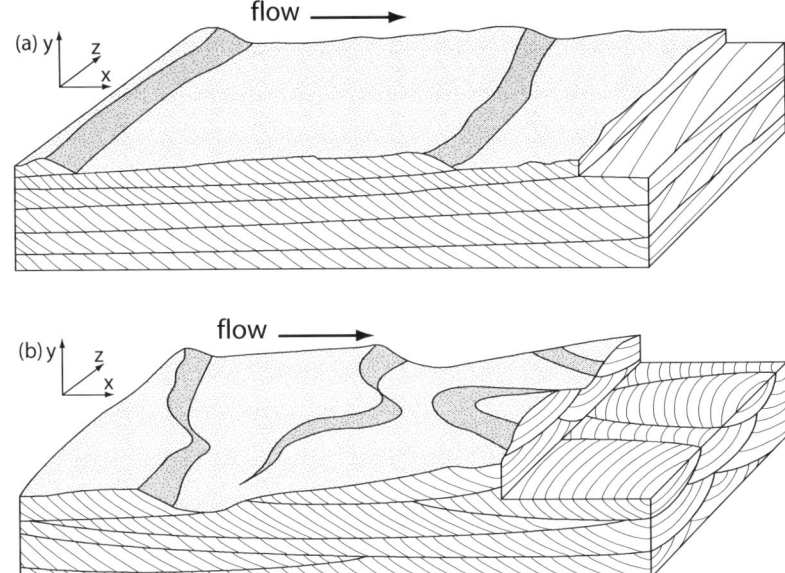

Figure 5.11. Patterns of cross-bedding generated by the migration of dunes with different morphologies. (a) Straight-crested dunes generate sets of planar cross-bedding, which exhibit relatively little variability in sections parallel to the dune crest. (b) Sinuous-crested dunes generate sets of trough cross-bedding in which trough- or scallop-shaped scours filled with foresets are evident in sections parallel to the dune crest.

Courtesy of N. P. Mountney, from Collinson *et al.* (2006).

The palaeogeography of Wilmslow Sandstone times suggests a semi-arid environment within a long-standing, landlocked Permo-Triassic Cheshire Basin. It was dominated by episodic inputs of sandy rivers from the south-east, between which there was much reworking of the river sands by desiccating easterly winds at a latitude *c.* 20° north of the equator. The carnivorous reptiles that made the *Chirotherium* tracks roamed interdune areas and the drying-out river courses. The tracks of such animals imply the existence of a food chain, including plants, invertebrates and herbivorous animals, of which no trace remains, and that the contemporary landscape was, like modern deserts, far from devoid of life. Sand supplies were derived from the erosion by water and wind of previously deposited sedimentary rocks lying to the south-east and east. When considered in relation to the underlying Chester Pebble Beds Formation (Figure 5.8), a unit formed from very vigorous and frequent river floods directed to the north-west (Steel and Thompson, 1983), but which is not exposed at Alderley Edge, the Wilmslow Sandstone can be assigned to a series of braided river plains that were of waning energy and were gradually becoming more arid. The 600 m of the Chester Pebble Beds and Wilmslow Sandstone Formation together form a very long-lasting megacycle of largely climatic origin which may have been controlled by slowly changing cosmic events related to the

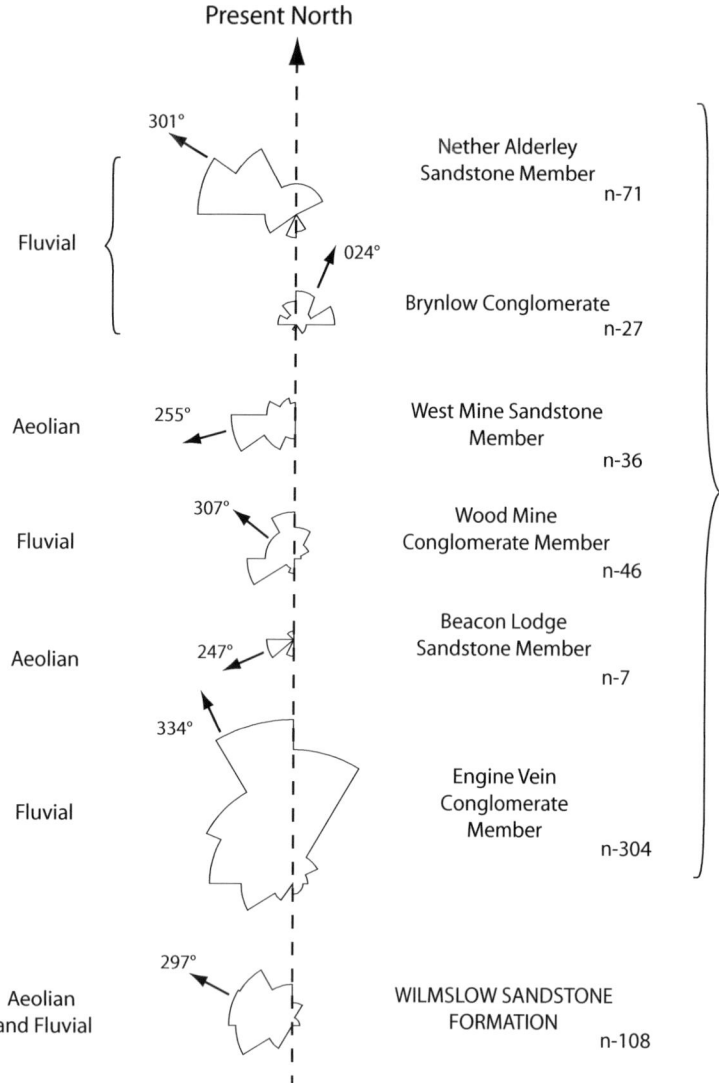

Present North

301° — Nether Alderley Sandstone Member n-71

Fluvial

024° — Brynlow Conglomerate n-27

Aeolian — 255° — West Mine Sandstone Member n-36

Fluvial — 307° — Wood Mine Conglomerate Member n-46

Aeolian — 247° — Beacon Lodge Sandstone Member n-7

334° —

Fluvial — Engine Vein Conglomerate Member n-304

Aeolian and Fluvial — 297° — WILMSLOW SANDSTONE FORMATION n-108

HELSBY SANDSTONE FORMATION

Figure 5.12. Palaeocurrent data from the Wilmslow Sandstone Formation and the successive members in the Helsby Sandstone Formation at Alderley Edge. These illustrate the contrasting directions of sediment transport in aeolian units (dominantly west in the Wilmslow, Beacon Lodge and West Mine Sandstones) and fluvial and mixed aeolian and fluvial units (dominantly to the north-west) (based on Thompson, 1966: figs 137a, 138a,b, 139a–c; Thompson, 1985: fig. 11). The data are also representative of the palaeocurrents in those facies within the Cheshire Basin (Thompson, 1966: figs 137b, c, 138c–l, 139d–g, 140; Thompson, 1985, figs 9–11). The 'rose diagrams' show the number of cross-bedding azimuth measurements in 20° intervals; arrowed bearings indicate the mean transport direction; n-values are the number of measurements from each unit.

Drawn by David I. Green and Julie Ballard.

completion of one eccentric cycle of the orbit of the Earth around the Sun (Clemmensen *et al.*, 1994). Such long cycles are believed to take around 400,000 years.

The Helsby Sandstone Formation

This rock unit has been divided into five members (Thompson, 1970a; Warrington and Thompson, 1971) (Plate 3; Figure 5.8).

The Engine Vein Conglomerate Member

After the deposition of the Wilmslow Sandstone Formation there followed a period of non-deposition of unknown extent and duration (Figure 5.8). This is reflected in a disconformity at the base of the Engine Vein Conglomerate Member, which is best seen in the rocks at the foot of Castle Rock (Figure 5.10). After this hiatus in sedimentation, the area was inundated by the deposition of around 30 m of potentially much harder sandstones, forming a unit that comprises around ten cycles of conglomerate and pebbly sandstone, separated by beds of mudstone (Figure 5.7). The first five events and cycles are well seen in the Castle Rock–Wizard's Well and Engine Vein areas. Their generality and details are modelled in cycle type A, shown in Figure 5.13b. Measurements of the palaeocurrents suggest the presence of strong low-sinuosity braided-river flows directed to the north-west (Figure 5.12). Upwards through the succession, pebbly material diminishes in abundance and greater numbers of interbedded mudstones are developed, as modelled in cycle type B (Figure 5.13c). Multiple repetitions of such muddy-topped cycles are characteristic of the whole of the Engine Vein Conglomerate Member in the Hayman's Farm Borehole (Figure 5.7), 1.5 km south of the Edge. The muddy interbeds are characterised by repeated levels with desiccation cracks and the upward injection of sand through such cracks. Areas where injection strata occur are likely to represent the marginal, higher and/or abandoned parts of the braid-plain, into which muddy flood waters and gentle sandy flows frequently but gently lapped (Figure 5.5). Upon sudden rises of discharge, such as those produced by violent local thunderstorms, flash floods developed; water-tables rose rapidly, driving air and water before them in the subsurface. Up-currents of air, water and sand repeatedly filled and injected the mud-cracks, some no doubt giving rise to sand volcanoes at the surface. The possible presence of isolated aeolian rock units generated by easterly winds has been noted in places at the top of the Engine Vein Conglomerate Member, thus adding to the evidence for a series of drying-upward events.

The first event of each of these cycles (Figures 5.10a, 5.13) is interpreted as a major flood episode that caused a channel cut or sharp erosion surface; this was followed, during the waning of discharge, by the deposition of braided river sand bars within the major channels. Finally, there was a widespread settling out of mud within the river-plain. Within the first cycle the sediments produced by these events covered the uppermost aeolian sand dunes of the Wilmslow Sandstone Formation (Figure 5.10a), and the muddy waters then spread outside the braid channels and into the interdune areas. These flood discharges swept up previously wind-fashioned pebbles (ventifacts) which had

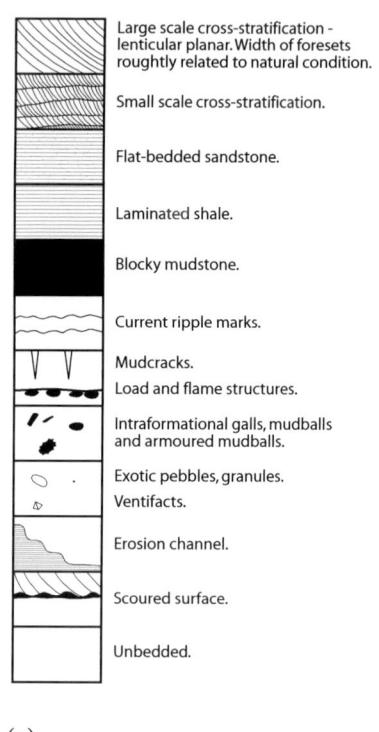

(a)

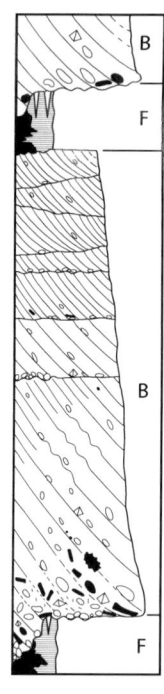

(b)

Facies F

Red, micaceous, well- and poorly-sorted silty mudstones formed by vertical accretion under low-flow regime and tranquil conditions in cut-offs and channel swales in a low-sinuosity river plain environment. Mudcracks indicate subaerial exposure. *Euestheria* may be present. Top usually channelled and eroded below overlying facies B but may bear footprints of vertebrates.

Facies B

Red, secondarily(?) buff or grey, medium- to coarse-grained, poorly-sorted sandstone, pebbly sandstone or rare conglomerate, deposited in river channel, point and lateral bars, generally under upper low flow regime conditions with sand and gravel transported as bedload and finer sediment carried away in suspension. The bars may have lag surfaces on their tops. Flow surges deform cross bedding; high flow causes loss of bedding definition. Migrating low sinuosity braided channels may cut through bars. Floods may uproot vegetation around channels and erode vertical accretion deposits from swales, cut-offs and the topstratum, producing intraformational clasts that become rounded or armoured if transported in bedload. Extraclasts include quartz and igneous and sedimentary rocks. Cross bedding foresets poorly defined at the base and well defined at the top; set thickness and grain size often decrease upwards. Top usually sharp and flat, reflecting relatively sudden cessation of flood and bed load traction. Base an uneven scoured surface resulting from erosion of underlying facies F by high flow regime currents.

Summary description based on Thompson (1970b: fig. 7).

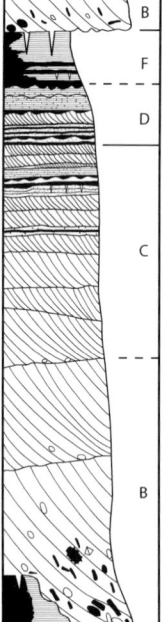

(c)

Facies D and F

Fluvial riverplain topstratum deposits formed largely by vertical accretion under dominantly tranquil conditions after high stage overbank flooding, with a less abrupt transition than in the example in Fig. 5.13b. They comprise interbedded dark chocolate red, occasionally green, micaceous shale, mudstone, siltstone and sandstone; the last, commonest in the lower part and mostly fine-grained, was deposited under low flow, ripple-inducing conditions. Coarser sandstones, some with pebbles or clay galls, are rare. Top channelled and usually partially eroded below uneven base of overlying facies B. Desiccation surfaces, some with mudcurls, and plant remains, *Euestheria* and trace fossils, including tracks of vertebrates, may occur.

Facies B and C

Channel fill and lateral accretion deposits comprising trough cross-bedded, pink-red, medium- and fine-grained micaceous sandstones deposited in bars and from migrating megaripples; some deformed cross-bedding. Fluctuating strong currents in the high flow regime at the base but generally steady, upper low flow regime conditions with decreasing strength and water depth, and a decrease in grain-size, upwards through the unit. Base uneven; migrating channels cut into underlying facies F, locally producing sole marks on the surface of scoured hydroplastic sediment. Rarely a thin basal lag gravel.

Summary description based on Thompson (1970b: fig. 8).

Figure 5.13. (a–c) Characteristic features of the repeated rock units in the Helsby Sandstone Formation and their interpretation. (a) Key to parts b and c. (b) Cycle type A. (c) Cycle type B.

After Thompson (1970b: figs 7, 8).

formed within dried-out river courses or on rocky landscapes upstream, perhaps over periods as long as 10,000 years (Thompson and Worsley, 1967). Succeeding cycles of deposition at the top of the Engine Vein Conglomerate Member represent much shorter-lived events, such as channel cuts and fills produced by the gentler flows of braided rivers.

The deposition of underwater sand bars and sand dunes was separated by longer periods of unknown duration involving the settling of suspended matter from still waters and periods of complete aridity. These are marked by red mudstones with desiccation cracks. During these periods vegetation was re-established, water-fleas colonised temporary pools and lived their short active life phases before adopting a resting state which may have lasted many years, while reptiles of undetermined type, but possibly *Ticinosuchus*, the creature which is thought to have left the prints known as *Chirotherium* (see Tresise and Sarjeant, 1997: 142–9), wandered around the drying-up pools of the river courses. Miospores, the only evidence from this member of a contemporary vegetation, are dispersed by wind and water and may therefore have come from plants in the region or farther afield. In addition to the productive sample from Engine Vein Mine (see above), six levels in this member in the Hayman's Farm Borehole were examined for miospores but only indeterminate pollen was recovered, from 162.74 m and 160.33 m (Warrington, personal records).

The palaeogeography of the Engine Vein Conglomerate period suggests that these deposits may be related to the establishment of a relatively long-lived early Mid Triassic 'Alderley River' which was fed from the south-east, probably via the Leek–Rudyard–Rushton Spencer palaeovalley (Thompson, 1984; Chisholm *et al.*, 1988). It occupied the eastern part of the Cheshire Basin, a landlocked continental basin formed tectonically by east–west extension (Plate 6). Such small cycles of interbedded fluvial–aeolian sedimentation have been interpreted as possibly reflecting Milankovitch precession cycles of some 26,000 years' duration, which resulted from variations in the tilt and direction of the Earth's axis in relation to the plane of its orbit around the sun (Clemmensen *et al.*, 1994). Counts of pebble type and measurements of palaeocurrent directions based on the cross-bedding suggest that uplifted rocks of the underlying Chester Pebble Beds Formation located upstream on the south-east margins of the basin could have been reworked in order to supply all these sandy sediments. This was first suggested by Hull (1860, 1869), substantiated by Thompson (1966, 1970b) and re-emphasised by Evans *et al.* (1993: fig. 10), and is supported by the presence of derived fossils of Lower Carboniferous age, identified by Nudds (1998). However, there is no evidence that the rocks of this member represent a local alluvial fan derived from the former eastern (Palaeo-Pennine) margin of the basin (Evans *et al.*, 1993).

The Beacon Lodge Sandstone Member

The log of the Hayman's Farm Borehole (Figure 5.7) shows *c.* 11–12 m of pin-striped, laminated, notably round-grained and cross-bedded sandstone interbedded with ripple- or wavy-bedded sandstones bearing mud-cracked and mud-curled laminae (Figure 5.13c). Outcrops near Beacon Lodge display soft sandstone cross-beds around an adit entrance; these are interpreted as aeolian sand dunes derived unidirectionally from the east. Palaeogeographically, the indications are that floods were gentler, that the river-plain often dried out, and that river-bed sands were quickly blown into dunes by the ruling trade winds. The Engine Vein Conglomerate and Beacon Lodge Sandstone members together represent a relatively thick (*c.* 42 m) drying-upwards cycle, perhaps referable to an eccentricity cycle of 100,000 or 400,000 years' length (Clemmensen *et al.*, 1994). A sample from this unit at 139.75 m in the Hayman's Farm Borehole was barren of miospores (Warrington, personal records).

The Wood Mine Conglomerate or Pebbly Sandstone Member

The base of this unit is not seen at outcrop and it is hard to judge whether an angular unconformity, and hence a major break in sedimentation, exists at this horizon, as claimed by Evans *et al.* (1993). In Church Quarry, north of the Wizard restaurant, the lowest two or three thick fluvial pebbly-sandstone cycles of type A (Figure 5.13b) are very well exposed and the lowest unit has provided a fine, hard freestone which was used in the construction of many major buildings locally, while the upper beds were largely used for walling on the Alderley Estate. Upwards, a further seven to eight somewhat thinner cycles of both types, A and B (Figure 5.13), are exposed in Wood Mine and part of West Mine (Figure 5.7). The whole sequence of the Wood Mine Conglomerate Member is very well recorded and was proven in the main borehole (No. 2) at Alderley Park (SJ 8432 7577) (Figure 5.7). Indeed, the nature and origin of the rocks is similar to that of the Engine Vein Conglomerate Member. They represent major fluvial floods at the base and smaller but still significant ones at the top. Pauses between the flood cycles, allowing the drying out of the braid-plain and the formation of ventifacts, are of unknown duration. New features observed in the Wood Mine Conglomerate Member are the presence, at a depth of about 120 m in the Hayman's Farm Borehole, of a surface covered with multiple footprints of *Rhynchosauroides rectipes* Maidwell now preserved in Manchester Museum, described and interpreted by Thompson (1966: 185–93) and further discussed in Appendix 5.1 (Figures 5.14–5.16, Plate 5), as well as the incoming of frequent burrows referable to *Planolites* and *Skolithos*. The former relate to herbivorous reptiles (Benton, 1990); it is likely that the latter reflect the activity of established colonies of arthropods, probably insects (JEP, personal communication). Three samples, from 124.36 to 98.84 m in Hayman's Farm Borehole, were investigated for miospores but proved barren (GW, MS records). The fluvial palaeocurrents of the Wood Mine Conglomerate Member are directed between west-south-west and north-north-west (Figure 5.12). Palaeogeographically, the whole of the inland Cheshire Basin was now more often covered by river floods and less subject to local drying out. The increasing appearance and preservation of mudstones upwards in the sequence provides greater numbers of low-permeability barriers to migrating mineral-bearing solutions which much later (around 205–180 million years ago) were ponded below such horizons (Warrington, 1980, 2010; Plant *et al.*, 1999: 220).

The West Mine Sandstone Member

This unit, some 17 m thick, is currently poorly exposed in the Brynlow valley but the sequence was fully recorded in the Hayman's Farm and Alderley Park Boreholes (Figure 5.7). In West Mine the formation is divisible into three units, the 'bottom', 'middle' and 'top' beds. The beds are composed of closely laminated, fine to coarse, non-pebbly, cross-bedded sandstone. These sandstones are interbedded with finer, thin, cross-bed units, one bearing fragments of equisetalean plants (horsetails), and several horizons of vertical *Skolithos* burrows close to a wind-rippled unit (Figure 5.3b). There are also mud-cracked and mud-curled horizons. The thicker sandstone units are likely to be at least partly aeolian, and to correlate with the spectacular aeolian Frodsham Member (Figure 5.8) seen at Styal, Lymm and comparable areas across the East Irish Sea Basin at least as far as the reservoirs of the Douglas Oilfield (Thompson, 1969, 1970a; Yaliz, 1997). Palaeogeographically, this represents a basin-wide sand sea (or erg) generated by steady easterly winds (Figure 5.12). The finer interbeds suggest gentler fluvial floods and the settling of muds, interspersed with periods of desiccation; stands of horsetail plants existed in the interdune areas.

Taken together, the Wood Mine Conglomerate and West Mine Sandstone Members represent a third large drying-upwards cycle of events within this landlocked Mid Triassic basin (cf. Mountney and Thompson, 2002). The roundness and coarseness of many sand grains contribute to the high porosity and permeability of the rocks, which, in turn, allowed them to be migration routes for basinal fluids and ultimately to be host rocks to sulphide mineralisation and, potentially, hydrocarbons (Warrington, 1980, 2010; Plant *et al.*, 1999: 220) (Figure 5.1, section). No miospores have been recovered from a thin desiccated mudstone exposed in West Mine, despite the presence of possible traces of equisetalean plants in the immediately overlying sandstone (Warrington, personal records).

The Nether Alderley Sandstone Member

This unit is at least 51 m thick but has not been fully cored. It comprises between ten and twenty less well defined cycles of type B (Figure 5.13c) and is best seen in quarries at Finlow, Bradford Lane, Brynlow, Topps Farm and the Butts. The lowest unit is a grey pebbly sandstone cycle – the Brynlow 'Conglomerate' Bed – which is well exposed on Artists Lane; succeeding units are coarse to fine, rather flaggy, clayey, micaceous sandstones, succeeded by interbedded ripple cross-laminated, micaceous, mud-cracked silty mudstones (Figure 5.7). Horizons with calcite (calcium carbonate; $CaCO_3$) nodules are found. Apart from the lack of pebbles, such units resemble cycles of type B and the interbedded strata resemble the beds formerly termed 'Waterstones'. However, one characteristic feature of the latter rocks, the frequent presence of cubic pseudomorphs after 'hopper' crystals of halite (sodium chloride; $NaCl$), indicating fully evaporitic, possibly marine-intertidal conditions, has been seen only once. Miospores have been recovered from this unit in the Hayman's Farm Borehole (see above). Trace fossils include horizontal and vertical burrows (*Planolites* and *Skolithos*, and possibly *Diplocraterion*) and *Cruziana* (*Isopodichnus*). The producer of this last trace is compared with the present-day *Triops*, a notostracan arthropod (a shrimp) that lives in clear shallow brackish or freshwater ponds with soft muddy bottoms which are prone to seasonal drying out. Desiccation increases its viability and eggs may hatch in temperatures as high as 80°C. Larvae grow rapidly, with daily moulting, and reach maturity in sixteen to twenty days. Its life span is only twenty-five to thirty-five days, even if the pools survive longer (Pollard, 1985).

Fluvial palaeocurrents evident in this member are directed north-westwards (Figure 5.12). These rocks represent the continuation of river flows, but with reduced rates of discharge, longer continuity and higher fallout of suspended silt and clay minerals. The rivers now formed part of a coastal plain rather than an inland semi-arid basin. The under-water dunes and ripples topping the bars that filled the channels were of smaller size and hence the fine sediments were more frequently deposited as much in dried-out channels as beyond the stream banks. Evidence for a drying-upwards tendency is still present, but is expressed in terms of evaporitic processes (pseudomorphs after halite crystals that formed in drying salt pans, and carbonate nodules developing within possible fossil soil profiles) as much as in mud-cracking. If ever developed, aeolian beds are not preserved hereabouts, as they are in the Malpas area further south in the Cheshire Basin. This is the fourth drying-upwards megacycle that is possibly due to cosmic control.

Palaeogeographically, this sandstone member may pass laterally to the north-west into the Tarporley Siltstone Formation (Figure 5.8), which shows more evidence of having been deposited in a coastal plain subject to marine incursions, inter-tidal sedimentation and evaporation in salt lagoons (Ireland *et al.*, 1978; Pollard, 1981) (Plate 6). The east of the Cheshire Basin and the Alderley area were still the site of a fairly permanent south–north-flowing 'Alderley River' which, as demonstrated for the Engine Vein Conglomerate Member, was present episodically in earlier times.

The greater silty-muddy nature of the Nether Alderley Sandstone Member serves as a general upward seal to the migration of mineralising fluids and hydrocarbons (Figure 5.1, section), as will be explained in the next chapter. Indeed, these rocks remain red precisely because such reducing solutions have not greatly penetrated them and removed their haematitic grain coatings.

Further reading

Aitkenhead, N., Barclay, W. J., Brandon, A., Chadwick, R. A., Chisholm, J. I., Cooper, A. H. and Johnson, E. W. 2002. *British Regional Geology: The Pennines and Adjacent Areas* (4th edition). Keyworth: British Geological Survey.

6

The minerals of the Edge

David I. Green, Richard S. W. Braithwaite,
David B. Thompson and Geoffrey Warrington

It is hard to walk more than a few hundred metres in the woodlands at Alderley Edge without coming across some evidence of mining activity. Engine Vein Mine cuts a deep scar across the top of the Edge and other workings have left conspicuous spoil heaps. Below the surface, galleries and tunnels were cut through the rock in search of lead and copper ores. People have exploited the minerals here for thousands of years.

There are two substantial workings, Engine Vein Mine and Wood Mine, beneath the National Trust woodlands on the Edge and a third, West Mine, under adjoining land. These mines are surrounded by smaller trials, pits and levels, some conspicuous, some hidden, which bear mute testimony to the mineral wealth concealed within the sandstone rocks.

The mines were worked primarily for copper. Some lead and a little silver were also produced. Cobalt ore was mined for a short time in the early nineteenth century and the small workings that lie beneath the Alderley Edge information centre and the nearby car park are known as the Cobalt Mine. Zinc-, manganese-, arsenic- and vanadium-bearing minerals are found in small quantities, but have not been worked as ores.

A little-known but historically important working, Mottram Mine, lies largely forgotten beneath the village of Mottram St Andrew, about a mile to the north-east of Stormy Point. Mottram Mine achieved a measure of scientific fame in the 1860s when Henry Roscoe, Professor of Chemistry at Owens College in Manchester, refined the element vanadium from residues he obtained from the processing works (Plate 7). He later described the lead-copper vanadate mineral mottramite, which is named in honour of the locality (Plate 8).

The Alderley Edge district is notified as a geological Site of Special Scientific Interest (SSSI) for its minerals and the geological and geo-chemical processes that they record (Warrington, 2010). It is uniquely accessible and of international importance for both educational and scientific reasons. One of the aims of the Alderley Edge Landscape Project was to provide as comprehensive a record of the natural history of the area as possible. This chapter gives a brief overview of the mineralisation processes that took place in the area. Appendix 6.1 provides a tabulation of the minerals that have been recorded at the Alderley Edge mines. There is a display of some of the species, including the rare mineral mottramite, which is named for the village of Mottram St Andrew, in the Rocks and Minerals Gallery at Manchester Museum.

The rocks that form Alderley Edge

The Alderley ore deposits lie near the north-eastern edge of the Cheshire Basin. This underlies much of Cheshire and northern Shropshire and is the most important large-scale geological feature in the region (Plant *et al.*, 1999). The basin opened along a line of weakness in the Earth's crust in Permian and Triassic times, when east–west extensional forces pulled the rocks apart, allowing large blocks of Carboniferous and older Palaeozoic rocks to move downward along faults, creating a subsiding area in which sediment accumulated. As further down-faulting occurred, successive layers of sediment were buried and eventually lithified, becoming the Permian and Triassic conglomerates, sandstones and silt-stones that we know today. These rocks rest on limestone, sandstone, coal and metal-rich black shales of Carboniferous age and, locally, on older Palaeozoic rocks.

The rocks that form Alderley Edge are sandstones and conglomer-ates of Early to Mid Triassic age. They are part of a large body of sedimentary rocks known as the Sherwood Sandstone Group and form a tilted block, 3 km wide, which is bounded to the east and west by north–south trending fracture zones and is known as the Alderley Block. The interior of the Alderley Block is criss-crossed by numerous small faults with relative displacements of less than 10 m, which are typically oriented north to south or east-south-east to west-north-west.

For most of the time since they were deposited, the rocks that make up the Alderley Block were buried beneath impermeable mudstones of the younger Mercia Mudstone Group. It is only in the recent geological past that these have been eroded away and the rocks that make up the core of the Block have been exhumed.

Origin of the ore bodies

To understand the origin of the Alderley mineral deposits it is worthwhile reviewing the way ore deposits form in general terms. Copper, lead and other valuable metals are, on average, present in minute concentrations in the rocks of the Earth's crust. To form ores that are rich enough to be mined, natural chemical processes must concentrate them. It is axiomatic that, compared with the size of the ore deposit, a large volume of rock is required as a source.

The metals and other chemical elements that go to make up an ore body are usually physically dispersed and chemically bonded to the source rock. They are typically released by 'stewing' a large volume of the source rock in a solvent such as water for a long period of time. This produces a body of hot, metal-rich fluid, which is described as a hydrothermal solution. If this fluid flows to a site where conditions are favourable for mineral deposition, usually a cooler area with suitable open spaces, ore-bearing minerals may be precipitated to form an ore deposit. This process occurs in many different ways and gives rise to many different types of ore deposit, but the principle remains the same.

The Alderley ore deposits include some vein-like bodies associated with faults, as at Stormy Point and Engine Vein, but the majority are disseminations in the host sandstones, with the ore minerals occupying the spaces between sand grains (Plate 9). It was once thought that the ore minerals were deposited at the same time as the sandstone rocks. Subsequent research has shown that they were in fact introduced long after those rocks had been lithified. Fluids circulating in the Cheshire Basin leached minerals from the sediments in the Basin and deposited them in the Alderley Block, possibly in the presence of hydrocarbons trapped in the same structure. This process, suggested by Warrington (1980), has been substantiated and elaborated by subsequent workers. A short summary of the mineralising process is provided below; more detailed information is given by Ixer and Vaughan (1982), Holmes *et al.* (1983), Naylor *et al.* (1989), Rowe and Burley (1997), Milodowski *et al.* (1999), Plant *et al.* (1999) and Warrington (2010).

The sediments that make up the rocks at Alderley Edge were rapidly buried, reaching a depth of more than 2 km about 180 million years ago (Chadwick *et al.*, 1999). By this time, the rocks were extensively faulted and the Alderley Block had been tilted beneath an impermeable mudstone cap to produce a classic trap structure in which hydrothermal fluids could gather (Warrington, 2010).

As the sediments were buried, the temperature of the fluid contained within them increased and metals such as copper and lead began to come into solution. A large body of warm, metal-bearing, hydrothermal fluid accumulated. The major faults running through the basin directed the flow of this fluid. When it entered the Alderley Block a range of sulphide ores was deposited. It seems likely that small faults within the Alderley Block acted as baffles, ponding the fluids in certain areas to produce some of the ore bodies we see today. Mudstone beds in parts of the succession also influenced fluid flow, resulting in smaller, more irregular mineral disseminations, such as those in Wood Mine, in contrast to the larger, more extensive disseminations that formed in beds with almost no mudstones, such as those in West Mine.

Several episodes of mineralisation, with precipitation from different fluids, are required to account for the Alderley Edge ore deposits. The primary minerals, including the sulphide ores galena and sphalerite, together with baryte, iron-rich calcite and a few others, were deposited by saline, metal-bearing, hydrothermal solutions. The secondary minerals were produced by the action of downward percolating oxygenated groundwater on the primary minerals. They include the attractive blue and green copper carbonates azurite and malachite.

Primary minerals

Detailed investigations of outcrops in the mines, and studies of cut and polished sections, have shown that the primary mineralisation is complex. The first primary mineral to crystallise was, in most cases, a pink-coloured baryte. This was followed by sulphide ore minerals, typically in the sequence pyrite–chalcopyrite–sphalerite–galena, and then by a second generation of baryte, together with late-stage, iron-rich calcite. These minerals (and a number of uncommon sulphides, listed in Tables 6.1–6.8 in Appendix 6.1) make up the primary mineralisation at Alderley Edge.

Fluid inclusions that were trapped within the crystals during their formation provide important information about the origin of the primary minerals. Analyses of inclusions trapped in the baryte and calcite indicate that they crystallised from highly saline sulphate-rich brines, at a temperature of about 50–60 °C. This temperature suggests a burial depth of at least 2 km, a conclusion that is corroborated by investigations of the chemistry and mineralogy of the ore minerals. Since baryte is highly insoluble in sulphate-rich solutions, it probably formed as a result of the mixing of two distinct fluids, one sulphate-rich and the other barium-rich. Further information about the origin of the primary minerals can be gleaned by examining their isotopic signatures and comparing these with the surrounding rocks. Applying this technique to the sulphur present in baryte indicates that it probably originated from rocks of the Mercia Mudstone Group that overlie the Sherwood Sandstone Group in the Cheshire Basin.

Since the fluid inclusion studies show that the minerals crystallised from warm, saline, hydrothermal fluids, it is reasonable to ask where they came from. The passage of large volumes of fluid can bleach sandstone rocks. The core from a borehole drilled at Alderley Park, 200 metres east of the position of the Alderley Fault, as determined by the British

Geological Survey, revealed highly faulted sandstone with pyrite and baryte mineralisation. Parts of the Wood Mine Conglomerate and the whole of the West Mine Sandstone in this borehole are bleached, suggesting that this structure was a major fluid conduit. It seems likely, therefore, that the major faults that delineate the Alderley Block were conduits for the mineralising fluids.

The sulphide ores formed some time after the initial baryte mineralisation. The origin of the hydrothermal fluids that formed the sulphide ores is open to conjecture, as sulphur isotope studies have proved inconclusive. One possible source is the Carboniferous sediments that underlie much of the Cheshire Basin. These contain black, metal-rich shales, which are rich in hydrocarbons. Being buried rather more deeply than the sandstones, they would have been hotter, certainly hot enough to dissolve significant quantities of lead and copper. Whatever their source, metal-rich fluids moved laterally along faults towards the edge of the basin. Chemical reactions, perhaps with hydrocarbons, caused sulphide ores to be deposited. The presence of abundant hydrocarbon inclusions in some of the galena from Alderley Edge certainly suggests that it crystallised in an environment rich in hydrocarbons.

Secondary minerals

The highly coloured secondary minerals such as azurite (Plate 10) and malachite, that are so conspicuous in the mines today, are a more recent addition to the mineralogy and were produced by an entirely separate process. Uplift, beginning in earnest in the Early Tertiary, some 65 million years ago, gradually removed the overlying sediments, allowing almost all the hydrocarbons trapped in the rocks to dissipate. Eventually the primary minerals were raised above the water-table. Oxidising groundwaters then began to react with the ores, chemically changing them in a process known as supergene oxidation (Plate 11). This produced the unusual and brightly coloured minerals, such as malachite, azurite, pyromorphite (Plate 12) and erythrite, for which Alderley Edge is known today. Although these secondary minerals have nothing to do with the original process of ore formation, they are conspicuous in the rock outcrops and easily smelted to produce metals. It is likely that they first attracted Bronze Age people to the area.

Further reading

Tindle, A. G. 2008. *Minerals of Britain and Ireland.* Harpenden: Terra Publishing.
Woodcock, N. H. and Strachan, R. 2000. *Geological History of Britain and Ireland.* Oxford: Blackwell.

7

Geomorphology: the evolution of the landscape

Richard H. Johnson and David B. Thompson

The Edge at Alderley is located 8 km west from the Pennine Hills at Kerridge. Its summit is *c.* 180 m above sea level and is formed of Triassic rocks which crop out over 3 km² (Plate 13). The history of the Edge can be divided into three periods of distinctly different duration. The first, and by far the largest, antedated the Ice Age and its events were responsible for the general form of the escarpment seen today. A second took place when the area was covered at times by ice-sheets, which left glacial landforms and sediments that did not completely bury the scarp, but changed its relief dramatically. The third period includes events which caused significant but small changes to the landscape in the post-glacial period.

Before the Ice Age

A Pennine upland and Cheshire Basin lowland had developed by the end of the Tertiary period and the sandstone outcrops of the Alderley Block (horst) were higher than the surrounding areas, which were underlain by mudstones (Taylor *et al.*, 1963). To the east of the Edge, the area of high undulating relief separating the catchment areas of the Rivers Dane and Bollin contains a considerable thickness of glacial deposits, but with small inliers of Triassic bedrock. From the evidence of the inliers and from borehole data, Pocock (1906) traced the extension of the Edge eastwards and southwards as a rock barrier – hereafter referred to as the Ridge – underlying the glacial sediments (Figure 7.1). He suggested that this Ridge had been breached by an ancestral River Bollin some time prior to the last glacial events around the Edge (Plate 14; also Figure 7.2). In Macclesfield, the pre-glacial Bollin valley has been infilled

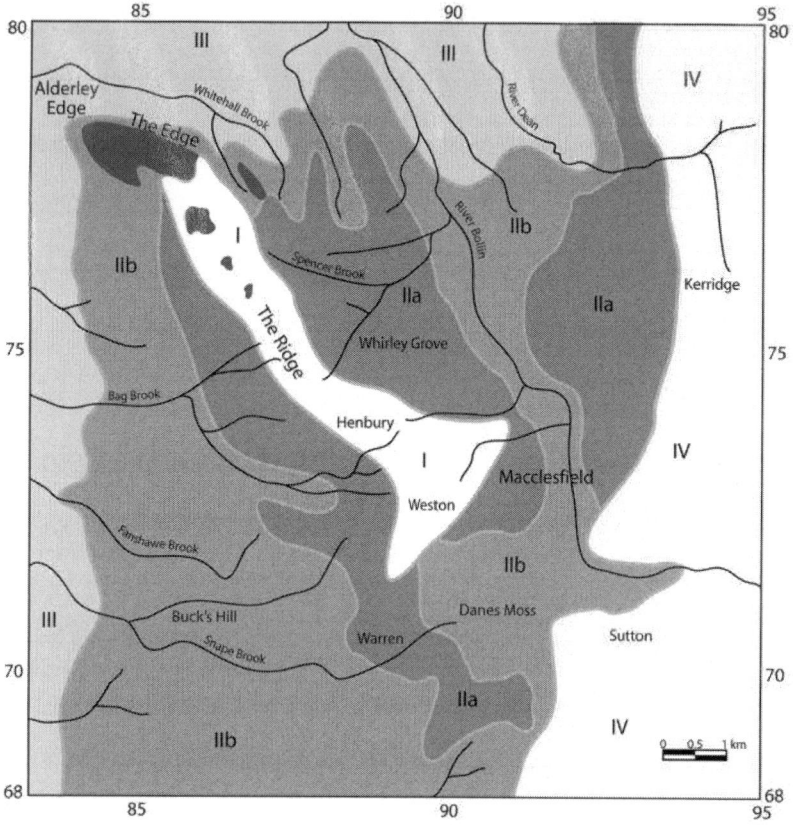

Figure 7.1. Sketch map showing the general distribution of glacial deposits and topographic relief in the area surrounding the Edge. The distribution of glacial sediments has been generalised from data on 1:50,000 scale maps published by the British Geological Survey. The boundary line separating the largely till-covered relief of the lowlands (III) from the higher areas mantled with both glacial and glacio-fluvial deposits (IIb) is also shown in Figure 7.2.
I. The Edge and the Ridge (Permo-Triassic outcrops not covered by glacial tills also indicated).
IIa. The upper slopes of the Ridge covered largely by sand and gravels but with some ground moraine also present.
IIb. The lower slopes of the Ridge and the Edge where glacial sands and gravels and flow-tills are important elements of a hummocky moraine topography.
III. The Cheshire lowlands whose ground moraine topography is formed by glacial sediments derived from the basal layers of the ice-sheet. Modern river terrace gravels, alluvium and peat mosses are not shown.
IV. The Pennine hills east of the Edge. Largely formed of Carboniferous rocks but mantled with glacial tills on the lower slopes.

Drawn by David I. Green and Julie Ballard.

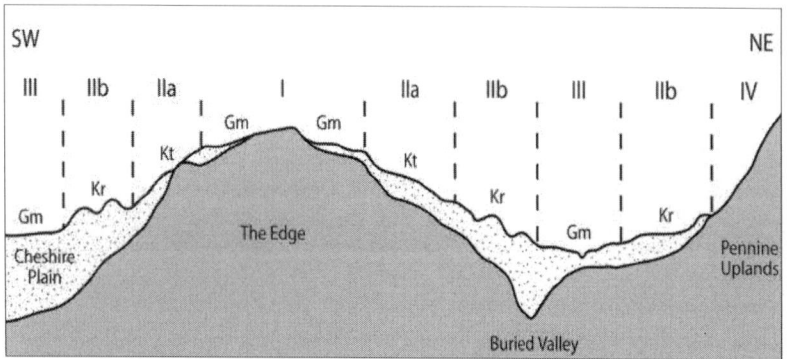

Figure 7.2. Schematic section south-west to north-east across the Edge and the Ridge to the western edge of the Pennines. The approximate position of the rockhead surface exposed or underlying the glacial deposits is shown together with the landform division (for key see Figure 7.1; see also Plate 14).

Drawn by David I. Green and Julie Ballard.

with glacial sediments over 70 m thick. The old valley floor at 103 m above Ordnance datum underlies the more westerly parts of the town, and has steep valley sides 40 m high on its west flank (Pocock, 1938).

Events during the Ice Age

To the west of Alderley, a break in relief along the line of the Alderley Fault separates the hummocky terrain of the upland from the lowland. The Cheshire Plain is mantled by Pleistocene deposits of glacial origin associated with the Last Glacial Maximum (Devensian) ice-sheets *c.* 22,000–15,000 BP (Delaney, 2003) (Figure 7.1, 111, and Figure 7.3). This ground moraine cover overlies the Mercian Mudstone Group bedrock and occasionally older glacial deposits. At Chelford, 5 km from the Edge, interstadial deposits formed *c.* 100,000 BP are revealed in quarry exposures and in boreholes together with tills that are either Early Devensian (*c.* 110,000 BP) or more probably Anglian (*c.* 350,000 BP) (Worsley, 1985, 1991, 1992, 2005). These deposits antedate glacial events related to the Edge itself.

During the Last Glacial Maximum, *c.* 20,000 BP, the Edge was a more prominent feature than today, a consequence of glacial erosion of the surrounding low-lying Cheshire Plain. At the Glacial Maximum, ice streams emanating from the southern Lake District were confined to the eastern parts of the composite ice-sheet by the larger glaciers originating in the west and north of the Lake District, the Southern Uplands and the western Highlands of Scotland. These Irish Sea glaciers were deflected south-eastwards onto the Cheshire Plain while within the west Pennine marginal zone, of which the Edge is a part, the flow

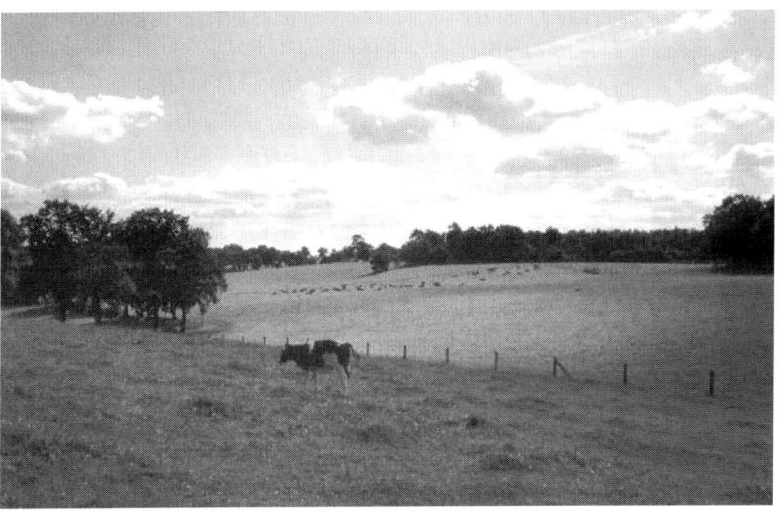

Figure 7.3. The 'Ridge' as seen from near the Engine Vein pit on the top of the Edge (see Plate 14). Glacial deposits similar to those which form much of the Cheshire lowland plain here form a surface cover overlying the Ridge, which extends south-eastwards towards Macclesfield.

Photograph R. H. Johnson.

was more directly southwards. This glacial history is inferred from the distribution of erratics, striations and glacial sediments, and they show that the former ice streams emanated from the inner Lake District, the eastern Fells and areas of Carboniferous limestone in the southern Lake District. At some stage, however, some west Cumbrian granites and Irish Sea floor erratics, including the enigmatic 'Macclesfield' marine molluscan fauna, were transported by the larger western glacier streams entering the Alderley Edge region (Thompson and Worsley, 1966; Evans *et al.*, 1968).

It is clear that the Edge was buried under a considerable thickness of ice and offered little obstruction to this generally southerly ice-sheet movement; its upper surface would have been abraded, although its rocks are too soft to have preserved glacial striae. To the east, the ice-sheet glacier streams moved southwards passing over the Ridge, and their ground moraine deposits form a gently undulating relief well above the level of the glaciated plain elsewhere.

Last glaciation deposits and landforms

Glacial deposits are usually characterised by their texture, lithological composition and original position within an ice-sheet or glacier. Sediments transported at the sole of a glacier are termed *tills* or *diamicts*, which are subglacial in origin. They are usually poorly sorted and range in size from clay to large boulders and when melted out form a gently undulating ground moraine topography. Englacial and supraglacial deposits are derived from materials transported either within the ice or upon the ice surface. At an ice-sheet margin or front the ice layers become stressed and much basal debris is moved upwards, to be incorporated into the englacial or supraglacial zones. Deformation and shearing within the ice here caused debris from the base and interior of the ice to be thrust upwards to mix with sediments being deposited upon the stagnant 'dead' ice. The up-thrust basal tills would then have run as mudflows or flow tills off the front of the ice, where abundant meltwaters would re-sort some of these and other glacial sediments into *glacio-fluvial* sands and gravels or *lacustrine* deposits. These sediments are poorly sorted, but less compacted than the basal diamict debris, and as a consequence may be more subject to either mass slippage and flowage, or to re-sorting by meltwater streams active at the time of ice decay.

The lower relief of the Cheshire Plain, where ultimately the ice-sheet stagnated *in situ*, is largely mantled with diamicts or till deposits which have been modified by ice, meltwater streams or modern streams to form the present topography (Figure 7.1, 1). However, a much more complex depositional history resulted where the major ice stream flows from the Irish Sea still impinged upon the west flank of the Pennines. Here, initial downwasting resulted in the removal of ice from the higher slopes and, at the same time, with the release of meltwaters a succession of meltwater channels was eroded along the Pennine hill slopes, either at the ice margin or subglacially, that is, beneath the ice itself (Johnson, 1965, 1985).

At a much later stage in the history of the decaying ice-sheet the ice front became obstructed by the lower hill barriers, for example the Rossendale Hills (Crofts *et al.*, 2005) and the Edge/Ridge upland. These barriers impeded the flow of the ice and led to its eventual stagnation along their margins. However, unimpeded and still mobile Irish Sea ice streams penetrated into the lowlands south and south-east of the Edge/Ridge. On the higher parts of these uplands the ice was sufficiently mobile both to transport and to deform any glacial sediment present at its margin, but eventually the ice lobe downwasted and retreated downslope, leaving a series of moraines and other glacial landforms. As the ice melted away its meltwater streams played a major role in depositing the sediments which for the most part shape the landforms where the ice margin had once stood. As a result, a complex topography of 'hummocky' moraines and kames was preserved in the vicinity of the Edge, and comprises part of one of the largest 'hummocky' moraine areas to be found in the British Isles (Hambrey, 1994: 142). East of the Edge the moraines, some 50 km^2 in area, extend through to Prestbury and southwards to Buck's Hill and Marton, with the highest parts being east of Edge House through Whirley Barn and Henbury to Weston and Warren (Figure 7.1 IIa and IIb, also Figure 7.2). East of Henbury the ridges have a west–east alignment but further west the glacial landforms become aligned in a north-west to south-east direction.

The higher parts of this hummocky terrain were exploited for sand and gravel in the middle part of the last century in pits near Whirley Grove and at White Barn and Shaw Cross. Photographs of the strata taken at the time by Worsley and Johnson showed thick sands with lenses of silt and gravels deposited by south-westerly flowing streams with sedimentary structures indicative of fast summer-melt flows (Figure 7.4). Sections at the top of the quarries displayed flow tills which had partially destroyed and disturbed the upper sandy strata. At the two Whirley Grove sandpits the sandy strata were affected by slumping and faulting (Taylor, 1958) or were deformed by ice movements. In the eastern pit, a large monoclinal fold was exposed, 'whose fold axis was aligned 150–330° N with the overturn to the east in an 11 m thick sequence' (P. Worsley, personal communication). The monocline was exposed on the east face and other parts of the fold could be traced along the south face and into the western face, where there was a complete overturned lower limb. A small anticlinal flexure was to be

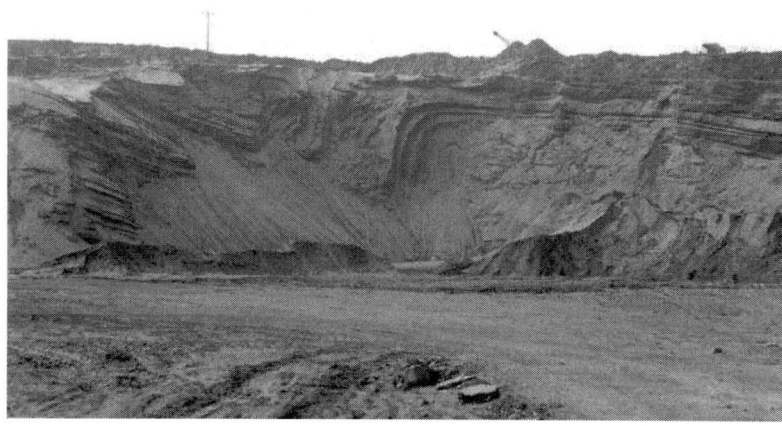

(a)

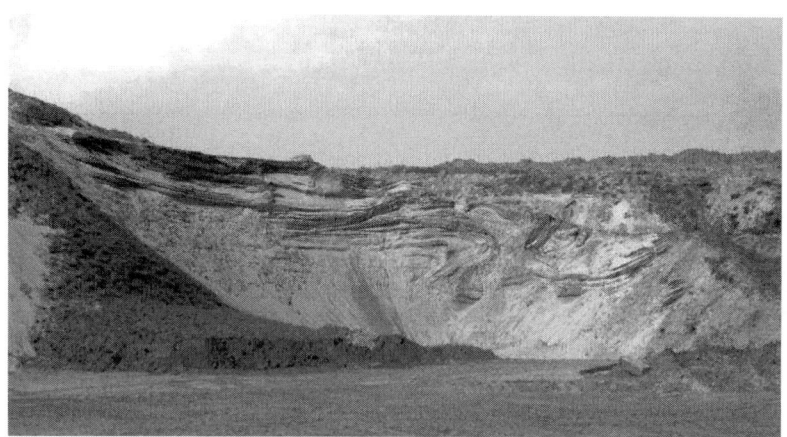

(b)

Figure 7.4. Whirley Grove sand and gravel pit. These photographs, taken in 1964, show where sand and gravels deposited in a small lake delta or channel bed at a former ice margin were subsequently overridden and deformed by ice transgressing northwards from lowland areas south of the Ridge. (a) The former exposures located on the east flank of the pit; (b) those on the south and west.

Photograph R. H. Johnson.

seen exposed in the western quarry. These features were formed either as a result of adjacent ice movement when the still-active ice front to the south of the Ridge advanced against the relatively gently inclined slope, causing folding to develop within the sands, or by mass (slide) movements related to downwasting of the ice-sheet margin to the north. Massive detached blocks of pebbly Helsby Sandstone were noted at Whirley Grove by Johnson (1965) and at Shaw Cross by Thompson and Worsley (1966), where there were also curved thrust planes related to movements of ice close to its margin. Fold structures were also noted by Evans *et al.* (1968) at a pit near Warren and this deformation was probably caused by ice-thrust movements directed towards the southern flank of the Ridge.

Moraines, kames and kettle-hole topography

Good exposures of the glacial deposits are now rare but temporary sections and borehole records in this terrain have revealed sequences of *pro-glacial* lacustrine and glacio-fluvial sediments, which occasionally overlie more compact till from the basal ice-sheet layers. More commonly, the sands and gravels are overlain by material derived directly from the ice surface which had been released and transported in mud or earth flows – that is, flow tills. These latter deposits are poorly sorted, and such a sequence (basal till → glacial sands, gravels and/or lacustrine sediments → flow tills) indicates that almost all the deposits were laid down pene-contemporaneously and in close proximity to a downwasting ice front. Clearly, glacial meltwaters and flow tills played a major part in the construction of these hummocky moraines, and the chaotic assemblage of post-glacial landforms reflect their original environments (Bennett and Glasser, 1996).

The topographic ridges of sand and gravel capped by flow tills (*kame ridges/moraines*) mark the former presence of the ice edge as it shifted in the course of time. With the removal of the 'dead ice' from beneath the outwash sediments, ponds and topographic depressions known as *kettles* were formed. Much of the northern part around Henbury, now drained by the headwaters of Bag Brook, is marked by a series of parallel ridges, kame terraces and kettles which were aligned along the edge of the wasting and shifting ice margin. Many of the kettles have since become drained and infilled with peat or mud and are integrated into the general drainage system, although the largest kettle, at Redes Mere, may be related to salt subsidence (Figure 7.5). Flat terrace levels (*kame terraces*) indicate the former courses of meltwater streams, which sometimes formed deltas in small but ephemeral lakes within the moraine belt: wherever there was a shift of the ice-sheet margin new drainage lines were created and others abandoned.

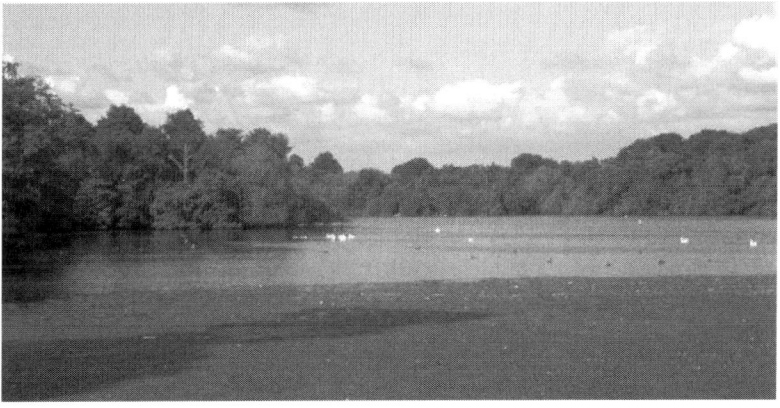

Figure 7.5. Redes Mere. Although located in an area of possible salt subsidence this attractive mere is an area where kettle holes are a distinctive feature of the glacial topography to the south of the Edge and were formed when the ice-sheet began to downwaste and decay.

Photograph R. H. Johnson.

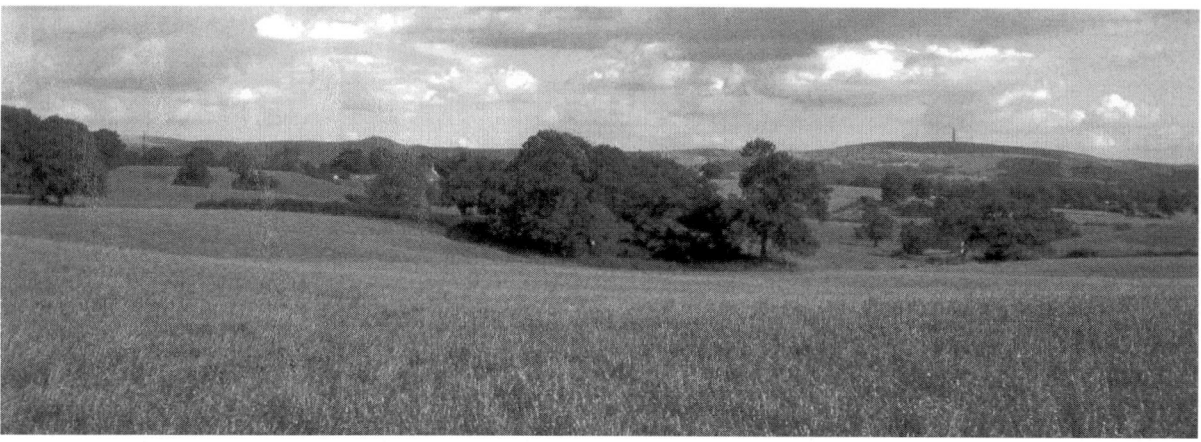

Figure 7.6. Lower Pexhill. The local relief here is characterised by low morainic hills or ridges separated by former meltwater stream channel courses, which in the present landscape appear as flat valley floors or terraces.

Photograph R. H. Johnson.

A lower and more hummocky moraine terrain was created between Alderley Park and Marton, and eastwards to Henbury (Figure 7.6). Other ridge features, near Warren, are aligned south of east and extend eastwards to Danes Moss. Here a broad kame terrace was also constructed where the slopes of the local hill and ice-sheet margins were also less steeply inclined. With ice stagnant in the Bollin valley at Macclesfield and with the hummocky terrain forming a barrier to the west, the Danes Moss pro-glacial lake drainage was diverted first through an outlet channel to Gawsworth (Evans *et al.*, 1968) and then via a deep channel near Oakgrove (Plate 14). Later, with the ice melted to the north of Macclesfield, this moss became part of the present Bollin catchment.

Other glacial ridges marking possible still-stands in the later stages of downwasting are recognised in the areas to the north of the Edge and Ridge. A crescentic lobe of ridges and terraces extends from the Edge eastwards to the Prestbury area (where it is now dissected by the Spencer Brook and its tributaries) and on across the Bollin valley north of Macclesfield to Kerridge on the Pennine margin. A large kettle or possible glacial lake hollow is located at Adders Moss, close to the boundary between the undulating hummocky relief and the higher ground of the Edge itself (Mighal *et al.*, in *ArchAE*); other kettles occur close to the foot of the northern escarpment and along the western margin of the Edge.

On the northern scarp erosion too has played a prominent role in forming the topography, with meltwaters eroding valleys aligned east to west and along the north margins of the Edge and the Ridge. The waterfall in Waterfall Wood is of particular interest as a small cascade, about 3 m high but with its flow now much reduced, occurs at a point where the geology, morphology and direction of the valley change (SJ 866 774) (see Figure 4.2b). The waterfall is formed at the outcrop of Helsby Sandstone (Engine Vein Conglomerate) and is partly masked by a cover of glacial till which overlies the valley floor to the east. Upstream the catchment is small and its discharge insignificant, but at its head there is a low col allowing access to other drainage areas to the east. Below the fall, in softer Wilmslow Sandstone, the valley is steep-sided and incised over a length of 200 m to a depth of nearly 40 m below the scarp crest. It is suggested that when ice was still abutting the scarp face, the upper valley functioned as part of a meltwater course for streams flowing along the scarp face, but that these meltwater streams were diverted to a lower level within the adjacent ice-sheet, with consequent headward erosion and downcutting.

The end of the Pleistocene glacial period and the beginning of the Holocene (Recent) period

The end of the Last Glacial Maximum incursion (Devensian) in Cheshire saw the development of integrated drainage systems within the whole region of north-west England. The lowland landforms of glacial origin developed a land surface which in general sloped towards Liverpool Bay and the north part of the Irish Sea. This was a consequence of glacial-isostatic loading with a tilt towards the area where the ice-sheet had been at its maximum thickness (Lambeck, 1995). As a result, the Dee and the Mersey with its tributaries, including the Weaver–Dane and Dean–Bollin, now flow towards Liverpool Bay and the streams draining both flanks of the Edge and Ridge are now included in much larger river catchments, but with their direction determined by their past glacial history.

On the higher parts of the Alderley Edge escarpment and in the upper kame area (Figure 7.1 and Plate 14) downcutting took place, and small but deep valleys were created, for example by the headwaters of the Bag and Spencer Brooks. Along the northern edge of the escarpment several large, broad, open combe-like features were and are being developed, which owe their form in part to structural weaknesses such as faults like the Holy Well Fault, and to the erosional conditions which occurred towards and at the end of the Pleistocene period. This was when a periglacial climate prevailed in Cheshire, which caused the sub-soils to be permanently frozen and freeze–thaw cycles to be extremely active in the ground surface layer. In such a regime, summer snowmelt and stream discharges were exceptionally high, leading to active downcutting and backwasting of the slopes. A mantle of scree formed on the steeper part of the Edge and strong periglacial winds acting on unvegetated ground led to the facetting of many pebbles and cobbles (Thompson and Worsley, 1967).

With improvement of the climate and a return to warmer conditions there has been a decrease in the rate of erosion, which has led to a general slope stability and the formation of soils with their associated vegetation cover. Only the steepest parts of the scarp faces remain uncovered, and in some instances rock falls have taken place. There has also been some landslipping to the north-east of Stormy Point, which is currently being addressed by the National Trust (Thompson, 1991; see also Chapter 29). Spring-head erosion is still active within the combes and in some instances perched water-tables, held up by laterally discrete mudstone strata (for example at Wizard's Well and twice at Holy Well), are maintaining the morphology of the scarp.

Acknowledgements

The authors would like to thank the late Dr Fred Broadhurst for his critical appraisal of the manuscript and Professor P. Worsley for his comments and fieldwork observations.

Further reading

Hambrey, M. J. and Alean, J. 2004. *Glaciers* (2nd edition). Cambridge: Cambridge University Press.
Harvey, A. 2012. *Introducing Geomorphology: A Guide to Landforms and Processes*. Edinburgh: Dunedin Academic Press.
Summerfield, M. A. 1991. *Global Geomorphology*. Harlow: Longman Scientific and Technical.

Part III

Natural history – the flora and fauna

8

The natural history of Alderley: an introduction

A. J. N. W. Prag with Sean R. Edwards, Simon Timberlake and Laurence Cook

> The largest number that have ever assembled took their departure from the station, but heavy rain unfortunately began to fall as the train approached Alderley, and only about thirty persons, including five or six ladies, adventured upon the projected walk. The reward, nevertheless, was great. Ferns, including the *Polypodium Dryopteris*, were collected in abundance, and tea was the more enjoyed from the inclemency of the afternoon. The Manchester Madrigal Society, led by Mr Shore, kindly accepted the invitation of the M.F.N.S., to join them in this trip, and after tea favoured the company at intervals, with their classic and delightful music.

These words, taken from the *Report and Proceedings* of the Manchester Field-Naturalists' and Archaeologists' Society for September 1861, show that Alderley Edge has long been a favoured site for botanising excursions. Founded by two well known Manchester naturalists, Leo Grindon and Joseph Sidebotham, and supported by a distinguished list of patrons, the Society did much to foster an interest in rural areas in the vicinity of the city (Kargon, 1977). That interest has continued ever since, and at the weekends the Edge continues to attract many visitors, braving whatever the weather may bring. The Victorian passion for collecting ferns contributed however to the loss of the oak fern, *Gymnocarpium* (= *Polypodium*) *dryopteris*, from Alderley and, indeed, from Cheshire as a whole.

The site consists of fairly exposed sandstone, bordered to the west by the Cheshire Plain and to the east by the higher land of the south Pennines. These factors determine the general character of the flora and fauna. Since the area is rich in metals, the flora contains metal-tolerant plant species. These sometimes act as indicators to metal prospectors and may also raise problems of adaptation and of colonisation. Changes in land use in the eighteenth century converted much of the area from heath to closed woodland, creating some spectacular scenery, and we should expect to find indications of the transition among both plants and animals, with relicts of the earlier habitat remaining among newer elements associated with the trees. All aspects of the Edge inter-relate and should not be looked at in isolation. For example, birds may eat grubs that are found in moss that lives on a particular geological substrate that attracted miners, who gave rise to major aspects of the Edge's social history, and this in turn goes full circle to affect the landscape and the natural history it supports.

Unlike some of the other aspects of its story, the Edge did not immediately present any ready-made natural history projects. In contrast to the geology and the human history, and despite its status as a Site of Special Scientific Interest, the flora and fauna of the Edge proved to be surprisingly ordinary: there were no evident questions to answer nor any obvious and exciting discoveries to follow up. This inevitably affected the scope and the depth of this side of the Project's research.

But this is looking ahead a little. The first thing that a natural historian should do when presented with a new area is to find out what is there, in other words to make a straightforward survey or inventory. Then the questions will reveal themselves. Therefore members of the Landscape Project began by making detailed studies of the botany, zoology, entomology and ecology of the area. The first step was a survey and inventory to establish a framework for future ecological analysis and to allow changes and developments on the site to be monitored. A considerable amount of information was assembled in data files, now held at Manchester Museum and by the National Trust's office at Alderley Edge, creating a resource for future study. The site is not unique, however, but has a profile that is characteristic of north-east Cheshire on the borders of the Pennines: therefore the bias in the following chapters is towards those features of the survey which have a bearing on the other concerns of this volume – human utilisation, exploitation and appreciation of landscape.

In order to approach a place as large as the Edge with limited resources, it was necessary to define a core area for intensive study, as described in Chapter 1. The natural historians then divided this core into land 'parcels' or 'compartments', each as uniform as possible and consisting of, for example, a single field or wood. Species associations could then be examined within the parcels. A preliminary examination led to the choice of fifty-four parcels, sufficient to allow statistical comparisons to be made but each small enough to be reasonably uniform; however, as the work progressed it sometimes became clear that parcels should be further subdivided, or that subdivisions should be merged – as for example in the case of parcel 17 (Figure 8.1 and Table 8.1; see also Figure 1.2).

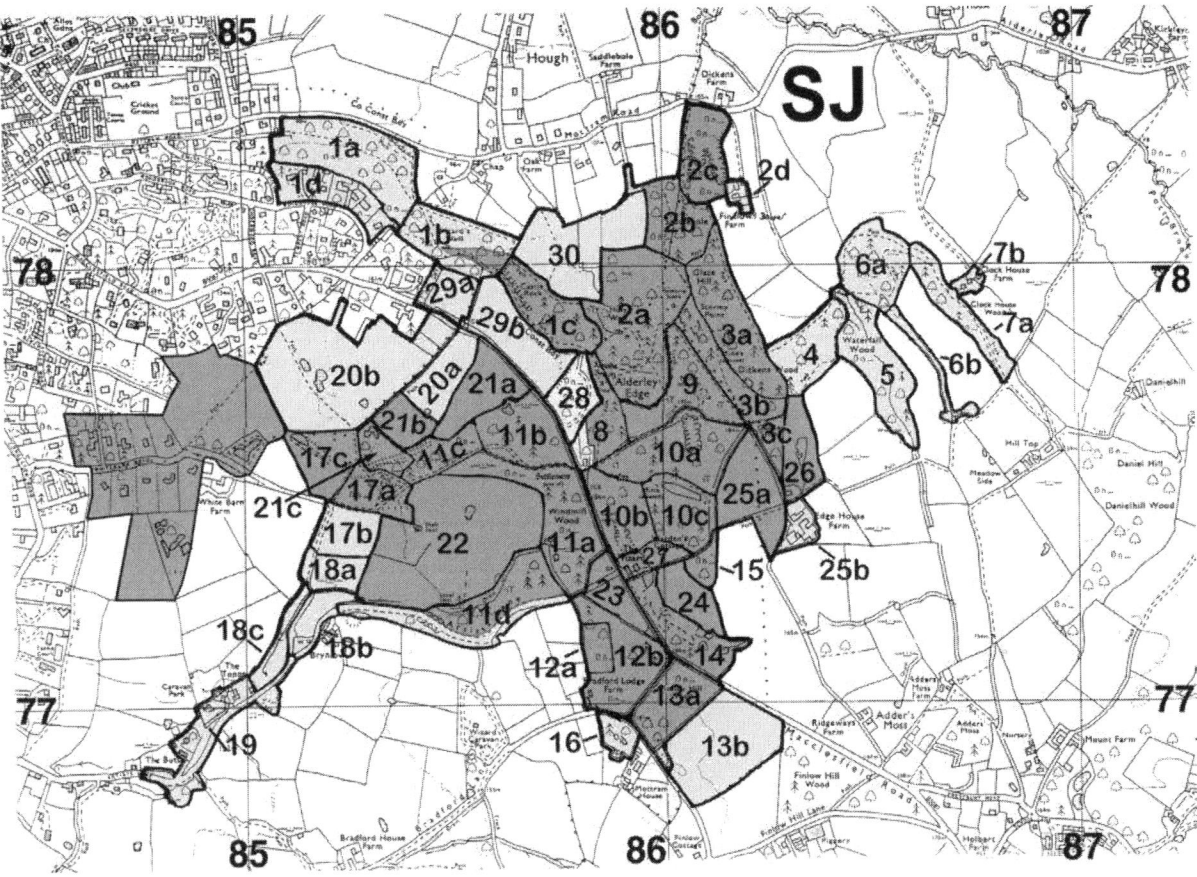

Figure 8.1. Map of the Project's core area divided into 'parcels' for recording the flora and fauna. The dark shading marks the area identified as a Site of Special Scientific Interest.

Based on the 1992 Ordnance Survey 1:25,000 Pathfinder map, sheet 759, with the permission of the Controller of Her Majesty's Stationery Office, Crown copyright October 2013.

While the two years of funding from the Leverhulme Trust were sufficient to allow – in theory at least – a thorough study of the human history of the Edge, by its very nature a proper account of the natural history requires several seasons' survey and analysis, which were beyond our scope. Nonetheless, when it came to the final stages of writing up the project a decade and more later, the potential of the data we had gathered was such that we felt that many gaps in the fieldwork could and should be filled from desk-based analysis of surveys carried out by other teams – something which will be particularly apparent in the account of the insects and other invertebrates in Chapter 13. The resulting picture is inevitably a little uneven – in the case of the birds we have even used the work of the Reverend Edward Stanley in the nineteenth century as a foil for recent surveys, and the story of the mammals remains a

Table 8.1. Working names for the biological recording parcels

Parcel no.	Parcel name	Parcel no.	Parcel name
1a	Mottram Wood	13a	Finlow Hill Wood
1b	Wizard's Well	13b	Finlow Hill Field
1c	Castle Rock Woods	14	Car Park Wood South
1d	Woodbrook Road North	15	Car Park Wood North
2a	Holy Well Memorial Stone Woods	16	Bradford Lodge Farm Wood South
2b	Saddlebole Wood	17a	Sandhills East
2c	Saddlebole Quarry	17b	Sandhills South
2d	Finlow Bowers Farm House	17c	Sandhills North
3a	Glaze Hill/Dickens Wood North	18a	Brynlow North
3b	Glaze Hill/Dickens Wood West	18b	Brynlow South
3c	Golden Stone	18c	Brynlow West
4	Dickens Wood East	19	Whitebarn SSSI/Topps and Butts
5	Waterfall Wood South	20a	Southern NT Meadows East
6a	Waterfall Wood North	20b	Southern NT Meadows West
6b	Bilberry Hill Hollow Lane	21a	Northern Meadows East
7a	Clock House Wood	21b	Northern Meadows Central
7b	Clock House Farm House	21c	Northern Meadows West
8	Armada Beacon Wood	22	Southern Meadows
9	Opencast Mine Wood	23	Wizard Verges
10a	Alderley Quarry Wood	24	Car Park Meadows
10b	Church Quarry Wood	25a	Edge House SSSI Meadows West
10c	Engine Vein Wood	25b	Edge House SSSI Meadows East/Edge House Farm House
11a	Windmill Wood South	26	Edge House North-East Meadows
11b	Windmill Wood North	27	Wizard Warden's Cottage Grounds
11c	Windmill Wood North-West	28	House Grounds
11d	Artists Lane Woods/Brynlow Dell	29a	Northern NT Meadows West
12a	Bradford Lodge Farm Wood West	29b	Northern NT Meadows East
12b	Bradford Lodge Farm Wood East	30	Hough Settlement

blank in our book, as it appears to do in most other surveys of Alderley Edge. Time had passed since the Project's original surveys of 1996–98 and most of the Project's natural historians had moved on, so much of this ordering and re-assessment of the data was carried out by other naturalists with an interest in the story of Alderley. As coordinator of the Landscape Project and editor of this volume – and a mere archaeologist quite unfamiliar with the language and methodology of natural history – I owe them a great debt of thanks, for without this extra contribution our story of the Edge would have been much poorer.

A number of different surveys have also been carried out by or on behalf of the National Trust; that of Clements, Scruby and Lutley (1985) was updated following a renewed visit of the Trust's survey team in 1997 (Jackson and Alexander, 1998); at the time of writing, further updating is anticipated for 2015–16. These reports provide a brief synopsis of woodland composition and are primarily concerned with the ground flora and the insects, birds, mammals and amphibia.

For readers unfamiliar with the details of the taxonomic system that is fundamental to understanding the natural world we have provided an explanation in the preamble to Appendix 13.1 (p. 821).

Acknowledgements

Aside from those whose names appear in the text of these chapters, many other people deserve our thanks for help with the research into the natural history of the Edge, and we should here record our thanks to them. If any names have been omitted from among those who got wet and cold in the name of AELP we can assure them it is not deliberate. We are grateful to Tom Burke (UMAU), who worked on every aspect of the tree survey, and in addition spent many months on Alderley Edge in all weather conditions without losing his sense of humour and tolerance. Among the numerous volunteer surveyors we would like to thank in particular Phil West (UMAU), Carolanne King, Dave Cartilage and Christine Comer, and T. Jarvis and D. Brown, who led the tree survey volunteers under the overall direction of Jeremy Milln with the support of Richard Littleton, the National Trust Warden at the time. Carl Davis and John Taylor played important parts in early stages of the surveys of the spiders and fungi respectively, and Dr Martha E. Newton helped with the vascular plants, mosses and liverworts. Professor Ed Bellinger's knowledge of the algae was invaluable and without the vast knowledge of the late Professor Brian Fox our list of the lichens on the Edge would have been far smaller. We are indebted to Adrian Tindall and Cheshire County Council for providing us with grant assistance to continue with the surveying work, and for providing GPS equipment and expertise through their Geographic Information Unit (GIU) at County Hall, Chester. In particular, we are grateful to Chris Young and Jill Morris of Cheshire GIU for carrying out the corrections to the data. The work would not have been possible either without the involvement of Dr (now Professor) Robert Barr and the Regional Research Laboratory of the School of Environment and Development, University of Manchester: particular thanks are due to Neil Matthews, who produced all the GIS tree maps.

9

The vegetation of the Edge

Sean R. Edwards, Simon Timberlake and Jonathan Guest

Introduction

The DAFOR system

Unlike the fauna of the Edge but like the archaeological remains, plants tend not to move around, but unlike the archaeology they vary from season to season, and thus recording them needs its own methodology. The Project's botany surveyors used the blunt but effective system known as DAFOR, an acronym for the names of five classes used to score relative frequency. In descending order, these are:

D   Dominant ('the most noticeable species', but has a size factor as well as frequency);
A   Abundant ('all over the place');
F   Frequent ('quite a lot about');
O   Occasional ('here and there', or 'a few scattered occurrences');
R   Rare ('only one or two small patches').

These categories involve subjective judgements, but they have the virtue of allowing not only the presence of a given species to be noted but also a rapid assessment of abundance to be made, providing good indications of the overall patterns of occupancy. An analogous system in which wind is recorded as force 9 (strong gale), force 5 (fresh breeze), and so on, known as the Beaufort Scale, was developed in the early nineteenth century and is still useful as a quick and effective way to convey information about weather conditions – we can hear it in daily use on the BBC shipping forecasts. The method has little scientific credibility, but it is widely used by naturalists, as a web search for 'DAFOR' will show. It provides much information very quickly, with virtually no extra work: instead of marking a tick or a cross, the surveyor records, for example, a D or an A. No information is lost by using DAFOR: it can still be reduced to a presence or absence survey, but on the other hand assigning numerical values to the frequency classes renders it ideal for computer analysis, allowing one to look, for instance, for associations between species or with other survey information. At Alderley the surveyors elaborated the DAFOR scale with phrases and quantified each class to aid consistency between recorders and interpretation, and to enable comparative calculations to be made for the whole site afterwards: Dominant ($= 100$; 'the most noticeable species'); Abundant ($= 30$; 'all over the place'); Frequent ($= 10$; 'quite a lot about'); Occasional ($= 3$; 'here and there'); Rare ($= 1$; 'only 1 or 2 small patches in parcel'); # or + (depending on surveyor), unspecified/unquantified 'present' ($= 1$); h, marginal (i.e. arguable as to whether it occurred in the parcel or not) ($= 1$).

Issues arising from the survey

Plants are static and many of them reproduce vegetatively rather than sexually. For many, the abundance scale is therefore an appropriate way of measuring cover. Trees are relatively large and, even when vegetatively propagated, can be scored and measured as individuals, and a comprehensive survey of the larger species made. The eighteenth-century afforestation was a sufficiently important part of the history of the Edge to make it appropriate also to examine the distribution of some selected species.

Given that survey parcels (see Figure 8.1 and Table 8.1) were defined by anthropogenic rather than ecological boundaries, it comes as no surprise that different vegetation communities were found within certain of them. A statistical comparison of plant lists from what are essentially land-use parcels can be misleading. For example, both Gorse and Birch are present as pairs of species which are superficially similar. The two Gorse species *Ulex europaeus* and *U. gallii* are almost equally common on the Edge, the former being in seven parcels (17, 18b, 18c, 20a, 20b, 22, 26) and the latter (to be seen in Figure 10.3) in six (2c, 10b, 11d, 12b, 25a, 26); but only in parcel 26 have both been recorded. If the distribution between the fifty-four parcels examined were random, we should expect $6 \times 7/54 = 0.78$ cases of overlap, so that these figures do not suggest a tendency to be mutually exclusive. On a British scale, however, the summer-flowering *U. gallii* has a more limited western distribution than the widespread winter–spring-flowering *U. europaeus*. It is less likely to be found on calcium-rich soils. As such, its presence on the Edge represents a fading echo of the lost heathland.

Of the two birches in the area, Silver Birch (*Betula pendula*) occurs in twenty-one parcels and Downy Birch (*B. pubescens*) in thirty-four, of which fifteen parcels have both: they can be distinguished by the more 'double-jaggedy' deltoid leaves, flat across the base, of *Betula pendula*, whose young twigs are rough-scaly (Figure 9.1; see also Figure 10.3), while *Betula pubescens* has more evenly toothed, rounded leaves, lacking the flat base, and has young twigs that are pubescent-hairy (Figure 9.2). This distribution too (to which we shall revert in the next chapter) meets the random expectation. *B. pubescens* is, however, more tolerant of wet and cold conditions. As with Gorse, further study of the distribution maps in the core area may give some indication of the relation between tolerances and success. There are many aspects of the survey of vascular plants which have thrown up problems of this kind that are worthy of detailed study. It is with the trees, however, that we see patterns which

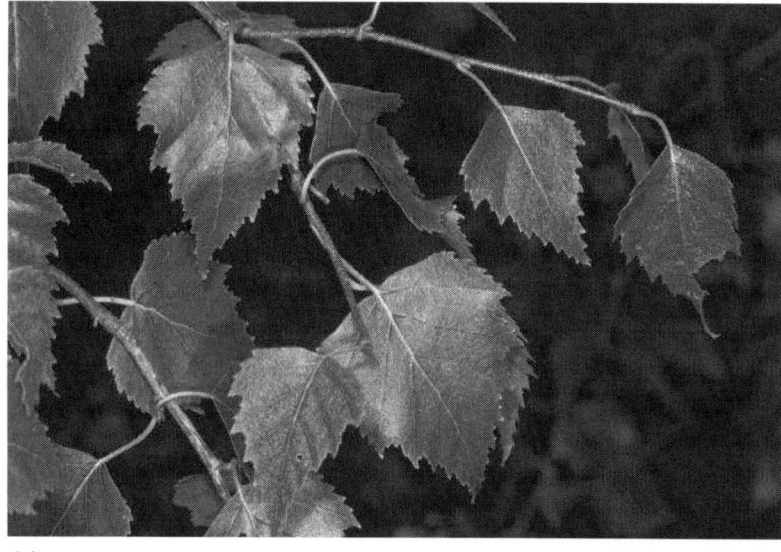

(a)

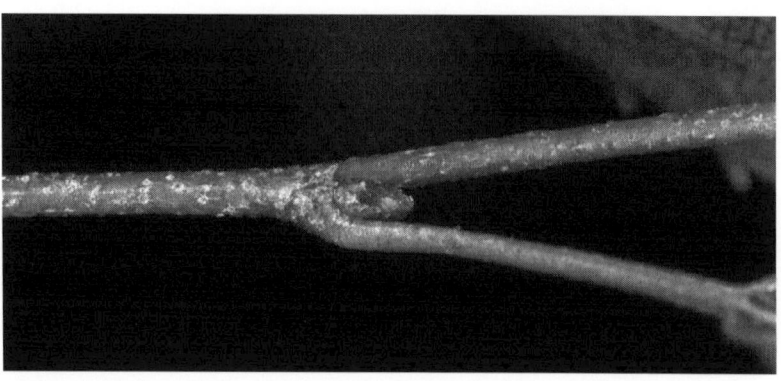

(b)

Figure 9.1. The leaves (a) and stem (b) of Silver Birch (*Betula pendula*).

Photographs Sean Edwards.

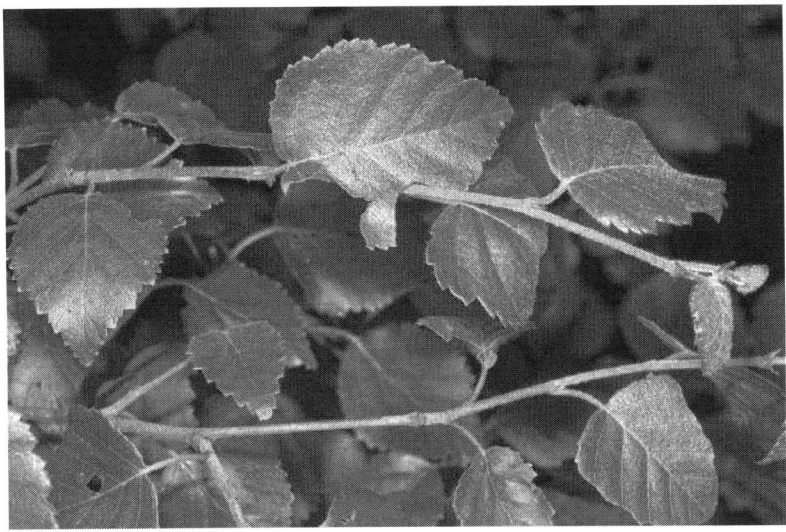

(a)

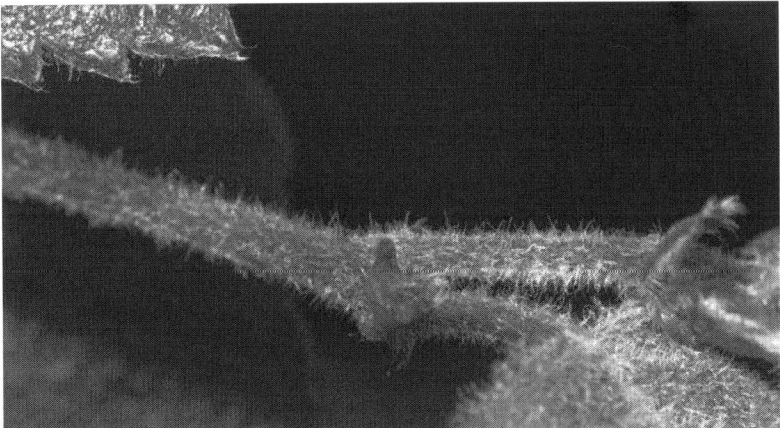

Figure 9.2. The leaves (a) and stem (b) of Downy Birch (*Betula pubescens*).

Photographs Sean Edwards.

(b)

characterise the area and can trace the changes which led to the present diversity: they are discussed more fully in the following chapter, but it is the discovery of these patterns that explains the efforts devoted to surveying them properly.

The botanical land parcel survey produced 5,826 records of 1,023 species. The vascular plants include all flowering plants (which, of course, include most trees), and also the conifers and yews, ferns and horsetails; from this group, 3,004 records were made of 351 species, with 90.9 per cent of the parcels surveyed to a reasonable level. The results of the vegetation survey are presented as Table 9.1 in Appendix 9.1. Brambles are taxonomically complex. Detailed study of the forms occurring at the Edge and in its hinterland has produced some very interesting data (see Table 9.2, Appendix 9.1; brambles are discussed further below and in Appendix 9.2, by David P. Earl).

The following descriptive section on the vegetation draws on the present survey and on historical records, chiefly de Tabley's posthumously published *Flora of Cheshire* (de Tabley, 1899), and includes accounts of the brambles, mosses, liverworts and algae, fungi and lichens.

Vegetation at the Edge

As William Webb approached Alderley from the south in the middle of the seventeenth century, he was struck by the conspicuous Beacon, up on the Edge (quoted in Ormerod, 1882: vol. 3, p. 545). This was an installation of critical military importance, not to be obscured by trees. The rather infertile, acidic soils that developed over the sandstone support only a limited diversity of higher plants, and traditional management of this vegetation as heathland was a convenient way of maintaining the strategic, open aspect of the hill. Heathland had long been a valued resource for grazing and for the harvesting of Bracken (*Pteridium aquilinum*) for bedding for animals and of Gorse (*Ulex* spp.) for bakers' and other ovens, so it may not have occurred to anyone that the hill could be planted with trees.

The natural vegetation of the Edge, however, without human intervention, would have been woodland dominated by Oak (*Quercus* spp.) but probably with glades maintained by the grazing and browsing of deer and wild cattle, or by the wallowing of wild pigs in the peaty areas. Birch (*Betula* spp.) would quickly invade such clearings if grazing pressure eased. Rowan (*Sorbus aucuparia*) and Holly (*Ilex aquifolium*) would be scattered throughout as an understorey, with occasional Aspen (*Populus tremula*). Then as now, ferns would have been a conspicuous component of the field layer. Wood Sage (*Teucrium chamaedrys*), Climbing Corydalis (*Ceratocapnos claviculata*) and Bluebell (*Hyacinthoides non-scripta*) may also be assumed to have grown here in antiquity. Many now familiar tree species, however, such as Beech (*Fagus sylvatica*), Hornbeam (*Carpinus betulus*), Scots Pine (*Pinus sylvestris*), Larch (*Larix* spp.), Sycamore (*Acer pseudoplatanus*) and Sweet Chestnut (*Castanea sativa*), are not native to the Edge. The original woodland certainly contained fewer tree species than are now present but its character would have been quite distinct from woods on the clay of the Cheshire Plain and more akin to the oakwoods of the Pennines.

As we describe in the next chapter, the native woodland on the sandstone was cleared by the early Medieval period, but elements of the ground flora survived on the heathland that developed in its place. Wavy Hair-grass (*Deschampsia flexuosa*) and Bilberry (*Vaccinium myrtillus*) are equally at home in light woodland or on heaths. Indeed, these two species may be assumed to have been constantly present on the Edge since prehistory. Into recent centuries a chain of heaths and mosslands extended from the Pennine moors way out onto the Cheshire Plain, allowing plants associated with such habitats to disperse across the landscape. The Western Gorse (*Ulex gallii*) is particularly associated with heaths and other infertile soils throughout Wales and western England. Western Gorse still grows in more open parts of the Edge and must have characterised the former heath. It would also have been ideal for firing the Beacon.

What might be described as a southern element in the flora consists of small, often ephemeral species that grow and flower on thin, sandy soils before they become parched in summer. In the 1970s J. Guest found Annual Knawel (*Scleranthus annuus*), Birdsfoot (*Ornithopus perpusillus*), Silver Hair-grass (*Aira caryophyllea*) and Early Hair-grass (*A. praecox*) growing on sandstone detritus in the old quarry at the Hough. All but the Silver Hair-grass survived here and were recorded the recent survey. The Squirreltail Fescue (*Vulpia bromoides*) was reported from the Edge by de Tabley (1899) in his *Flora of Cheshire*.

The Alderley escarpment lies within sight of the Cheshire Pennines, the southern tip of upland northern Britain. The Crowberry (*Empetrum nigrum*), present on the Edge in the nineteenth century, remains common on the Pennine moors but has largely vanished from lowland Cheshire. It represents a boreal (northern) floral element. Other plants associated with heathy grassland, noted around Alderley by de Tabley or his informants but since lost, were the Green-ribbed Sedge (*Carex binervis*) and the Pill Sedge (*Carex pilulifera*). The Marsh Violet (*Viola palustris*) and Bulbous Rush (*Juncus bulbosus*) are northern species that still occur in wet heathy patches and the Round-leaved Crowfoot (*Ranunculus omiophyllus*) is characteristic of runnels and seepages in upland pastures.

The heathland component descended from and replaced the native woodland over the sandstone. On the slopes below the Edge, however, where clay prevented the draining away of water and the leaching of plant nutrients, there would have been an abrupt change in the character of the ancient woodland. Oak would have remained dominant, but perhaps with Alder (*Alnus glutinosa*), Ash (*Fraxinus excelsior*), Hazel (*Corylus avellana*), Sallows (*Salix* spp.) and a more varied field layer. The presence of Primroses (*Primula vulgaris*) in the railway cutting southwards from Alderley station hints at the character of the lost woodlands on these lower slopes.

On the gentle slopes to south-east of the escarpment, the change from sandy soils to clays would have been less abrupt, showing a gradation in recent centuries from perhaps Heather (*Calluna vulgaris*), Bilberry,

Wavy Hair-grass and Western Gorse to grassland with Common Bent (*Agrostis capillaris*), Catsear (*Hypochaeris radicata*), Pignut (*Conopodium majus*), Heath Bedstraw (*Galium saxatile*) and Tormentil (*Potentilla erecta*), and low scrub of Common Gorse (*Ulex europaeus*), Brambles (*Rubus* spp.) and Bracken. The Wild Daffodil (*Narcissus pseudonarcissus*), recorded from Alderley by de Tabley in the nineteenth century, and still present a short distance to the south of the study area, probably belongs in such a setting.

A part of the process of breaking in such 'waste' for agriculture was marling (see Timberlake *et al.* in *ArchAE*: 133–4). The resulting availability of calcium and other nutrients allowed many plant species to grow that had formerly been rare or absent in the vicinity. The pastures within the study area are characterised by Meadow Foxtail (*Alopecurus pratensis*), Sweet Vernal-grass (*Anthoxanthum odoratum*), Crested Dogstail (*Cynosurus cristatus*) and other grasses, together with wildflowers, including Lady's Smock (*Cardamine pratensis*), Meadow Buttercup (*Ranunculus acris*) and Yarrow (*Achillea millefolium*). The majority of these were presumably sown onto newly marled land, perhaps as seed gathered from hay fields already existing. Meadow plants, that is, species discouraged by spring grazing, such as Knapweed (*Centaurea nigra*), Meadow Vetchling (*Lathyrus pratensis*) or Ox-eye Daisy (*Leucanthemum vulgare*), are now scarce within the study area. That Corncrakes formerly occurred on the Edge suggests however that hay crops were produced here into the twentieth century (see Chapter 11). The normally calcicolous Yellow-wort (*Blackstonia perfoliata*), found in the nineteenth century 'in a pasture under the Edge' (de Tabley, 1899: 202), may indicate elevated calcium availability following marling.

Marling also allowed the production of arable crops. The Corn Buttercup (*Ranunculus arvensis*), now extinct in the region, was found in 1873 'in a cornfield on Alderley Edge' (de Tabley, 1899: 10). The Large-flowered Hemp-nettle (*Galeopsis speciosa*), another weed of arable fields, was recorded from the area at about this time. During the present survey it was found in the field above Castle Rock.

The Bladder Campion (*Silene vulgaris*) also favours disturbed ground. It was not found during the present survey but de Tabley reported that a Miss Hopps had found it, 'Abundant in the wash-fields surrounding the new copper-mine at Alderley'. This same Miss Hopps, together with a Miss Beacall, found the Oak-fern (*Gymnocarpium dryopteris*) 'in the wood near the moss-house by the Wizard Inn' (de Tabley). This was the '*Polypodium Dryopteris*' mentioned by the Manchester Field-Naturalists in 1861 (see opening of Chapter 8). Collecting by naturalists and others hastened its extinction in the county.

The species list from the present vascular plant survey (see Table 9.1, Appendix 9.1) includes a large number of plants that have escaped from cultivation. Many are familiar but over-vigorous garden plants that have been dumped into the woods over the decades, such as Lady's Mantle (*Alchemilla mollis*), Perennial Cornflower (*Centaurea montana*), Cranesbill (*Geranium endressii*), Welsh Poppy (*Meconopsis cambrica*), Dotted Loosestrife (*Lysimachia punctata*) and Green Alkanet (*Pentaglottis sempervirens*), or culinary plants such as Horseradish (*Armoracia rusticana*) or Spearmint (*Mentha spicata*). A few, such as Tutsan (*Hypericum androsaemum*), Redcurrant (*Ribes rubrum*) and Swedish Whitebeam (*Sorbus intermedia*), may have been sown by birds.

Brambles (Rubus sp.)

> Life is short and brambles are interminable. (de Tabley, 1899: xxvii)

Bramble and Blackberry are two names for the same plants. They are sometimes cursed by archaeologists and casual visitors to the Edge for their powers of thorny obstruction, but they provide useful botanical and historical indicators. Whatever your point of view, they are common and important plants of the Edge, providing sanctuary for many animal species, from small insects to birds and mammals, and their fruit is sought by all in autumn.

Brambles are of course flowering plants, but they are particularly difficult to distinguish and for the general survey they were all recorded in the common terminology as *Rubus fruticosus* aggregate. The observant rambler round the Edge will notice, however, that the bramble bushes are not all the same. Some, such as the abundant Blousy Bramble (*Rubus tuberculatus*), have big white blousy flowers, while others, such as Sprengel's Bramble (*Rubus sprengelii*), have intense neat pink flowers; some have stems with a few large backward-pointing thorns, while others are covered densely with fine needles, and the fruit may be tart and hard to pull off or luscious and soft. The description of these different types presents problems which have to do with reproduction, taxonomy and the definition of species.

According to the modern definition, a species (in sexually reproducing organisms) is a group of individuals which will interbreed but are reproductively isolated from the next most similar group. For those which reproduce asexually or by forming vegetative clones this definition has obvious drawbacks. The taxonomist may then define as a species a group with a set of traits which are distinctive and inherited and do not merge via intermediates with other similar groups. The principles of taxonomic hierarchy are explained more fully in Appendix 13.1.

Brambles generally reproduce in a surprising way. The flowers may be pollinated by insects, but fertilisation does not usually take place, and the pips are not seeds or fruit at all; they germinate into identical clones of the bush that bore them. Other plants which present the same difficulties are the dandelions (genus *Taraxacum*) and the hawkweeds (genus *Hieracium*). In his standard modern *Flora*, Stace (1997) records the brambles as a series of sections which may be relatively easily separated, and describes the attendant taxonomic problems as 'notorious', but there are specialists who divide them into a large number of taxa (see, for example, Edees and Newton, 1988). The Alderley Edge Landscape Project was fortunate in having the services of David P. Earl, one of the few batologists, or bramble experts, in the country. Using the DAFOR system, he has recorded brambles from the Edge and its hinterland: his conclusions are set out in Appendix 9.2. The area has thirty-five species in all, an increase from the twenty previously recorded, and thirty-one of these are found on the Edge (Table 9.2, Appendix 9.1). Six are present in the majority of the fifty-four parcels sampled, four in about half and the rest are rare and sporadic.

Two local bramble species are a feature of the Alderley Edge landscape, and are described in Appendix 9.2; the first had previously been referred to *pro tempore* as the Cheshire Glandular Accrescens but is now known as Bailey's Bramble (*Rubus baileyi*), after the great Victorian Manchester botanist Charles Bailey, whose valuable collection of 300,000 specimens is housed at Manchester Museum (Plate 15a). The second, known as the Alderley Edge Bramble and now called *Rubus alderleyensis*, is known to occur in any abundance only at Alderley and Poynton, with isolated populations occurring on the banks of the River Tame, Ashton-Under-Lyne and on a railway embankment at Cheddleton, near Leek (Plate 15b). The survey has also revealed a new southern limit for the Manchester Bramble, *Rubus mancuniensis*, also awaiting description.

Bramble distribution and history

The distribution of brambles may relate to the distribution of animals, and it also indicates historical changes, for example when woodland species are found in open habitats.

Before the Alderley Edge landscape was transformed by the activities of people, the vegetation would have been predominantly woodland (e.g. *ArchAE*: 7, 9, 10–11). On the shallow sandy soils covering the sandstones the woodlands would probably have been of oak and birch, an ideal habitat for three species of bramble that are still a feature of the oak and birch woodlands today, *Rubus sprengelii*, *R. accrescens* and *R. distractiformis*. In addition to the existence of the woodland, we know from the place names such as Adder's Moss that peat mosses were a feature of the landscape. These mosses were later drained and only fragments of them now remain, but several brambles associated with the margins of old peat mosses do occur at Alderley Edge. Examples include the raspberry-like *Rubus scissus* growing with Purple Moor Grass at Finlow Hill, and *R. euryanthemus* growing under birch trees by Macclesfield Road near Dunge Farm. The latter species also grows in great abundance along the margins of Danes Moss to the south of Macclesfield.

Much of the original woodland was cleared for agriculture and a new landscape developed, but as can be seen today at some of the old fields of Alderley Edge, bramble species can persist among thickets and rough pastures provided grazing pressure is not too intense. Once hedgerows became a feature of the landscape, a new habitat providing a refuge for a number of species of brambles was created. Hocker Lane and Slade Lane are exceptionally noteworthy because along these lanes brambles occur which at present have no scientific name. Along Slade Lane the 'Alderley Edge Bramble', with its most attractive pink flowers, occurs in abundance. In the vicinity of Hocker Lane at least three very localised brambles with no scientific name occur in the hedgerows and hedge banks, stressing the significance of the survival of such historic landscape features for the development of new life on Earth.

Alderley Edge is famed for its industrial archaeology and one of the features of the mining spoil areas with a high mineral content is that brambles are noticeably absent. Some species do however thrive on the associated disturbed ground nearby: thus, at the Sandhills *Rubus tuberculatus*, the champion coloniser of bare open disturbed ground, occurs in abundance.

Within very recent times a number of allotment brambles have become naturalised at Alderley. One species, *Rubus armeniacus* (sold as the blackberry-producing Himalayan Giant), is a very aggressive invader of the countryside, and is often referred to as the 'Japanese Knotweed of the bramble flora'. Conservation measures need to be taken to ensure this species is kept at bay, as indeed they need to be for Japanese Knotweed itself.

Native species of bramble are associated with the people of Alderley Edge. At the Hough (parcel 30) there are remains of an old settlement and here a few plants of *Rubus nemoralis* occur. Although this species has probably recently begun to re-colonise the hillside at parcel 30, it should be noted that *R. nemoralis* is an excellent provider of berries. Therefore it is highly likely that early settlers and their descendants would have gathered the berries of this species during the late summer from the hillsides of Alderley Edge. Even today, people cherish their own areas for picking wild blackberries, and in the past the maintenance of bramble bushes may have been essential to the very survival of the people of Alderley Edge.

Mosses, liverworts and algae

This section encompasses several plant groups belonging to the cryptogams, or flowerless plants, but excludes the ferns and their allies, which
were surveyed as part of the vascular plant survey, and the lichens, which
had their own survey (described in a separate section below). Fungi
(discussed in the next section) used to be included in the cryptogams,
but are now not regarded as true plants at all and are also dealt with
separately. In all, 1,412 records were made of 169 species of mosses,
liverworts and algae (Table 9.3, Appendix 9.1).

Mosses and liverworts, like lichens, provide many good indicator
species. For example, the north-eastern section of Windmill Wood
appears at first sight to be a fairly uniform broadleaf woodland scattered
with ponds, in which several *Sphagnum* (bog-moss) species occur. In
the more northerly of the ponds the *Sphagnum* species included the
expected *S. palustre* and *S. squarrosum*, which are adapted to mineral-
poor water, whereas the more southerly pond by Cow Lane contained *S.
fimbriatum*, which indicates higher mineral availability. Investigation by
the archaeologists indicates why there should be a difference in ecology:
the more northerly ponds were probably marlpits, while the Cow Lane
pond was a mining scrape. Another indicator species of interest is a
liverwort known as the Greater Copperwort, *Cephaloziella nicholsonii*;
there was one confirmed find from one tiny site in the Sandhills area
(discussed in the section on Sandhills, below). As its name implies, it is
associated with copper-rich soil.

Finally, the mosses could not be considered without mentioning a secretive plant that is scattered about the Edge in the back and
sides of caves and small holes, where it forms luminous patches. The
Manchester Field-Naturalists found it when they returned to the Edge
in 1874, describing it as 'glowing like emerald, the beautiful, shining
cavern-moss' (Plate 16). Common names are Goblin Gold, Fairy Gold
and Rabbits' Candle. Many things in caves and holes can look ghostly
pale, such as the lichen *Lepraria*, but this plant, *Schistostega pennata*, is
much the most striking. Looking into a cave, a visitor to the Edge may
see a bright shimmering light that has an almost emerald sparkle, but
then vanishes. Its glow, as Tolkien's Gollum would say, is 'tricksy'. Go in
to find it, and there is nothing there but a dingy mossy wall.

The very specialised part of the plant that glows was once thought
to be an alga and not recognised as part of the moss itself, which had
been described in 1785 under the name *Schistostega*. The glowing part
was named as an alga *Catoptridium smaragdinum* in 1827, which can be
translated as 'emerald lightbender', giving a clue to two strange aspects
of its real nature. It is in fact part of the moss, the first threads produced
by germinating spores and known as the protonema. These pear-shaped

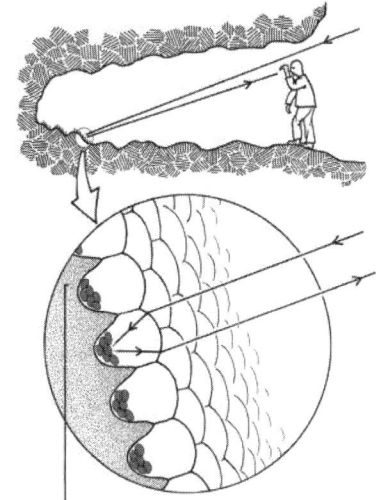

Figure 9.3. Drawing of the light-bending protonema of Goblin Gold (*Schistostega pennata*).

Drawn by Sean Edwards.

structures act like thousands of microscopic catseyes. The light entering a deep recess such as a rabbit hole is not bright enough to support most plants, so the cells form miniature lenses focusing what little light there is onto the chloroplasts, which are packed into the narrow part of the pear-shaped structure. Most plants are perceived as green because they use colours other than green, which is reflected unused. In this case the brightly lit chloroplasts shine back through the same optical system that illuminated them, giving the luminous effect (Figure 9.3). So noticeable is the glow that people have tried to grasp the 'emeralds' only to find they vanish when taken into the light. This is because the effect, like catseyes, works only when the eyes are close to a narrow source of light, as when looking down a hole; in the open, in omni-directional light, the emeralds are magicked away, leaving nothing but brown-green earth.

Only plants with specialised light-bending protonema can survive in really dark locations – moss plants without them become established nearer the light, although with changing conditions there is inevitably some overlap. The protonema can even reproduce itself without producing moss plants, by means of little sticky gemmae (vegetative propagules) that are distributed by insects that rest on the moss at night. Towards the lighter parts of caves the plant develops like other mosses which fruit and produce spores, although these spores are unusual in being sticky and insect-distributed, rather than distributed by the wind. *Schistostega* is a local species with a distributional bias to the south-west of Great Britain. Its fairly common presence on the Edge is a welcome part of the flora.

Fungi

Fungi have always held a fascination for people, providing both food and poison, as well as plenty of myth and magic. Three hundred and ninety-one species were recorded during this survey (Table 9.4, Appendix 9.1). Fungus recording is a specialised process. If a tree or even a moss is recorded one year, the chances are that it will be there next year, not to mention next week. The fungus may be gone and not reappear for years; it may still be present, but hidden underground or inside a rotting tree, until it next fruits. Micro-fungi such as moulds are abundant on the Edge, but not usually seen. Other types, such as Birch Polypore (*Piptoporus betulinus*), remain very visible throughout the year, although they may be few in number (Plate 17). For these reasons, a quantitative survey presents special difficulties, although it can be carried out in particular cases.

Many of the macro-fungi at the Edge are associated with particular tree species, either growing symbiotically as mycorrhizas on the roots of trees or as saprophytes, devouring dead twigs, branches or heartwood. Thus, Fly Agaric (*Amanita muscaria*), Tawny Grisette (*Amanitopsis fulva*), Ugly Milk-cap (*Lactarius turpis*) and Brown Birch Bolete (*Leccinum scabrum*) are chiefly to be found under birches. In damper settings the bright yellow *Russula claroflava* and the uncommon *Leccinum holopus* have been found beneath Downy Birch. Oak has many associated species. The milk-cap *Lactarius quietus* is particularly common. The red-stemmed *Boletus erythropus* has yellowish flesh that turns rapidly to a startling blue when the cap is broken. The Beefsteak Fungus (*Fistulina hepatica*) turns the heartwood of oak to a reddish colour. Its fruit-body resembles raw fibrous meat with a watery red juice. *Ciboria batschiana* feeds on acorns. Blackened, split acorns strewn beneath the trees may show the dark brown fruiting cups of this fungus.

Introduced tree species have their own associated fungi. The first beeches planted in Alderley Park are reputed to have been grown from seed brought from Worcestershire, in which case fungi are unlikely to have been imported with them. It may well be that some trees were bought in as saplings from nurseries in the south, or perhaps the spores of such mycorrhizal associates as the Beechwood Sickener (*Russula mairei*) or the Slimy Milk-cap (*Lactarius blennius*) have blown in since the trees were planted. Certain mycorrhizal fungi, such as the Blusher (*Amanita rubescens*) or the Common Yellow Russule (*Russula ochroleuca*), may be found under oak or beech. The False Death-cap (*Amanita citrina*), with its distinctive smell of raw potato, grows especially among Wavy Hair-grass beneath either tree species.

One conspicuous fungus to be found especially on acid soils in woodland and heaths is the Common Earth-ball (*Scleroderma citrinum*).

This is not a puff-ball. As it matures it simply cracks open and the spore mass within is carried about by invertebrates. The Parasitic Bolete (*Xerocomus parasiticus*) was found during the present survey near Castle Rock and has also been recorded from Finlow Hill Wood. It grows exclusively on earth-balls, which then have a deflated appearance. Unlike most agarics and boletes, whose gills or pores lie perpendicular to the ground so that their sticky spores can fall free from the cap before drifting off on the breeze, the toadstools of Parasitic Boletes stick out at all angles from their host, such that spores can seldom if ever be released.

Gardeners will be familiar with the black flattened boot-lace rhizomes of the Honey Fungus, *Armillaria mellea sensu lato*, which occurs under the bark of doomed shrubs and trees. Underground, in the mine workings, the rhizomes become rounded in section and adopt strange coral-like branching shapes; Honey Fungus is an avid utiliser of dead wood as nutrient, and must have become rarer with the reduction in number of pit props. It is common enough above ground on the Edge.

Serpula himantioides is the wild relative of Dry-rot, and is established on a couple of pine trees at one location. This species does not invade houses, and the true Dry-rot, *Serpula lacrymans*, is found in the wild only in Asia.

False truffles, of the genus *Elaphomyces*, may not be rare, but are most difficult to find since they develop hidden in slowly decomposing leaf mould (Figure 9.4). We were assisted in our search by a squirrel who left one, partially eaten, on its tree-stump table. It is said that in China *Elaphomyces* was worth its weight in gold as an aphrodisiac, a point to note considering the abundance of squirrels on the Edge. The agaric *Laccaria tortilis* and bolete *Tylopilus felleus* are rarely seen in the region, but have both been recorded on the Edge.

Few grassland fungi are included in the list; however, one species, *Entoloma poliopus* var. *parvisporigerum*, only recently recognised to occur in Britain, was found on the unfertilised ('unimproved') grassland, which may reveal further species in a good fruiting season.

The Edge is also rich in many of the smaller species, such as the slime moulds. These fungi, which are probably not closely related to the macro-fungi, move about as communal masses of amoeba-like cells which mature from time to time into solid fruiting bodies full of spores. Most are small and easily missed, but when examined closely many are exceptionally attractive in both colour and detail. Some are very large, such as *Brefeldia maxima*; this was not recorded in the survey but is common enough in Cheshire and probably occurs on the Edge. One specimen at Sunbank Woods in the Bollin valley weighed 20 kg, the standard air-line baggage allowance; this is impressive for an organism that crawls about in the woods feeding on bacteria.

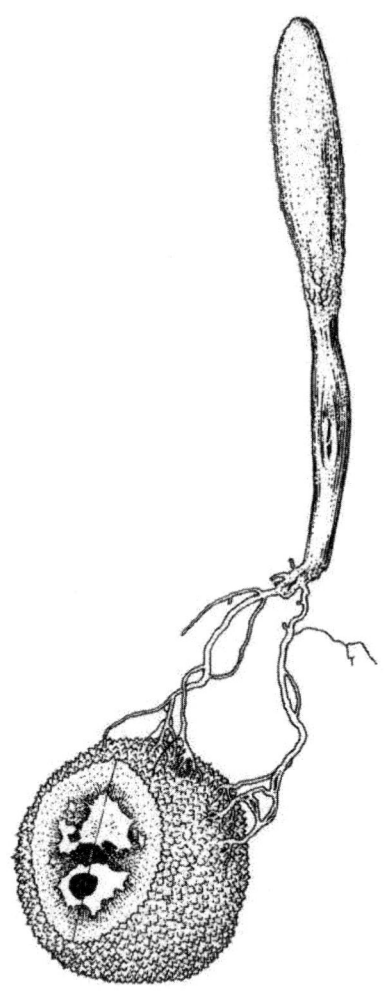

Figure 9.4. Drawing (with section cut out) of the False Truffle (*Elaphomyces granulatus*) being parasitised by the sac fungus (*Cordyceps ophioglossoides*).

Drawn by Sean Edwards.

We have not here touched on the fungal life to be found below ground on the Edge, since it is not readily accessible and visible to most visitors, but the constant and high humidity in the mines provides a favourable environment for many species (see e.g. Taylor and Beck, 1976); further details can be found on the website of the Derbyshire Caving Club (www.derbyscc.org.uk/alderley/geology_biology.php).

Lichens

Professor Brian Fox began collecting samples at Alderley with the intention of producing a report for a specialist journal such as the *Lichenologist* or the *Bulletin of the British Lichen Society*. His survey was the first to complete all fifty-four parcels, but sadly he died on 29 March 1999, before he could write any assessment. His fine recording will provide future workers the basis to investigate this further. An account of some of his experimental work can be found on pp. 238–9 of *ArchAE*. The present account is based on his records (Table 9.5, Appendix 9.1) and on *The Lichen Flora of Cheshire and Wirral* (Fox and Guest, 2003). Note that the Alderley records were not available during preparation of the *Lichen Flora*.

Lichens consist of a fungus, which gives its name to the lichen, and usually one (occasionally more) species of alga. An algal species may appear as a component of more than one lichen. Many lichen species are vulnerable to atmospheric pollution, especially from sulphur dioxide and the acids derived therefrom. Historical records from the southern Pennines show that the lichen flora of the region was once rich, but now tree lungworts (*Lobaria* spp.) and other species are restricted to the clean air districts of Highland Scotland, Ireland or Wales. The Industrial Revolution, concentrated as it was along the Mersey valley and into the Pennines, all within view of the Edge, led to severe smoke and sulphur pollution and the rapid disappearance of most lichen species. A single species, *Lecanora conizaeoides*, bucked the trend and increased from a position of great rarity to become by far the commonest lichen across midland England. It has since been found beside volcanic springs in Iceland and may have evolved in that hostile environment. During the recent survey it was still the commonest lichen at the Edge, forming a grey-green crust on the bark of oak, beech and other trees. However, the algivorous fungus *Athelia arachnoidea* also occurred very commonly, appearing as bleached rings of dying alga and causing *L. conizaeoides* to die back. This was observed throughout the Cheshire region, especially from the 1980s onwards, as patterns of pollution changed, smoke and sulphur pollution having been brought under control. This improvement in air quality allowed many lichens to move back into industrial regions. During the Alderley survey, *Evernia prunastri*, *Parmelia subaurifera*, *P. sulcata* and *Usnea subfloridana* were found – all species that would have been absent twenty years previously and all still restricted to the slopes to south-west of the Macclesfield Road. North-west winds brought dirty air from the Mersey valley and blasted the scarp face of the Edge.

The regional flora continues to change rapidly and a repeat survey now would certainly reveal more epiphytic species that have arrived in the past decade. There has also been a large increase in nitrogen pollution, which, together with traffic dust, has brought a great increase in *Physcia* and *Xanthoria* lichens.

In antiquity, the lichenological interest of the Edge lay in its metallophytic lichens. We can only guess at which species may have occurred. A particular assemblage may even have guided prehistoric specialists prospecting for copper. Among the few saxicolous types that survived twentieth-century smogs, *Rhizocarpon furfurosum* is especially characteristic of old mine workings. It is said to indicate iron sulphide. *Micarea bauschiana* is tolerant of copper and grows both at Alderley and at Raw Head in southern Cheshire, close to another old copper mine.

Two contrasting areas

The Sandhills

[As already noted, the Sandhills have recovered remarkably in the years between the survey and its writing up, and the publication of this book, and so some of the descriptions below are no longer fully accurate. Ed.]

The Sandhills region, known as parcel 17b, rapidly became the familiar focus of most surveyors. This is the south-facing area some 100 m × 100 m that was left after the giant sandhills themselves, 20 m high (being the spoil from the acid-leaching ore-processing from the mines described in Chapters 16 and 17), were removed in the mid-twentieth century. Even in the variety of the Edge, it is distinct and apparently out of place, something that is particularly striking when seen from the air (Figure 9.5). Coming into it from the woodland is surprising; there are expanses of open heathy sand, though no heather. Although it owes its

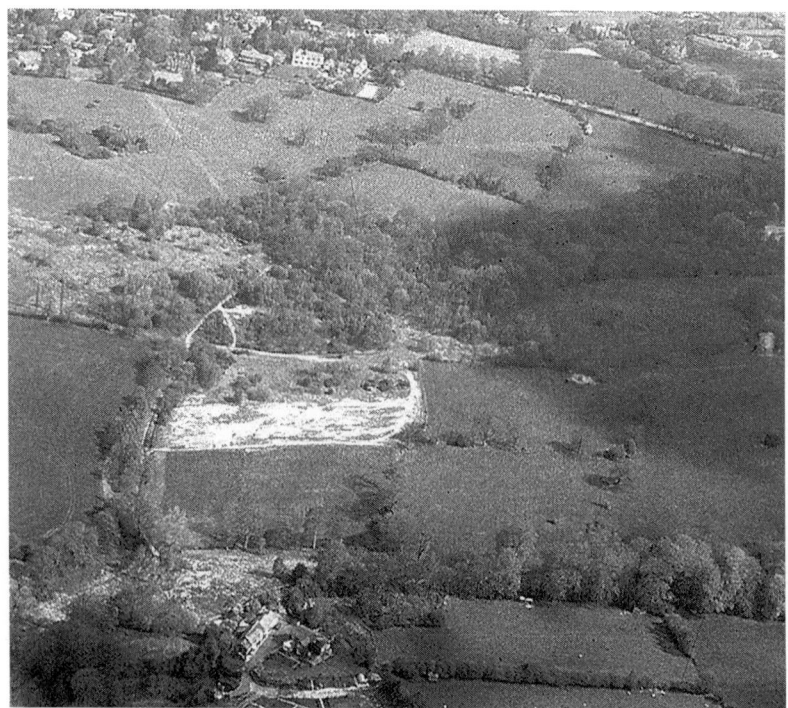

Figure 9.5. Looking north over the Sandhills. The photograph was taken in May 1996, since when much of the vegetation on the Sandhills has regenerated.

Photograph Barri Jones.

existence to the industrial processes associated with mining, it probably gives a good impression of the appearance of the area before the tree-planting programme began. On the other hand, it is a testament to the resilience of nature that even in the years that have elapsed since the survey was carried out (1997–2003) and the publication of this volume, the appearance of the Sandhills has changed noticeably as it begins to recover and to revert to a flora similar to the adjoining parcels.

Sites such as this, with high concentrations of heavy metals and high acidity, might be expected to be inhospitable, and indeed the most striking characteristic of parcel 17b is the large area of apparently bare sandy soil, with scattered patches of low grassy vegetation. However, closer inspection shows that the sandy surface is largely covered with a thin crust, varying in colour from sandy, through bluey-green, to almost black, depending on the time of year and the weather. In dry times, the crust cracks and lifts at the edges, looking rather like those familiar pictures of cracked dry mud in droughts (Figure 9.6). The composition

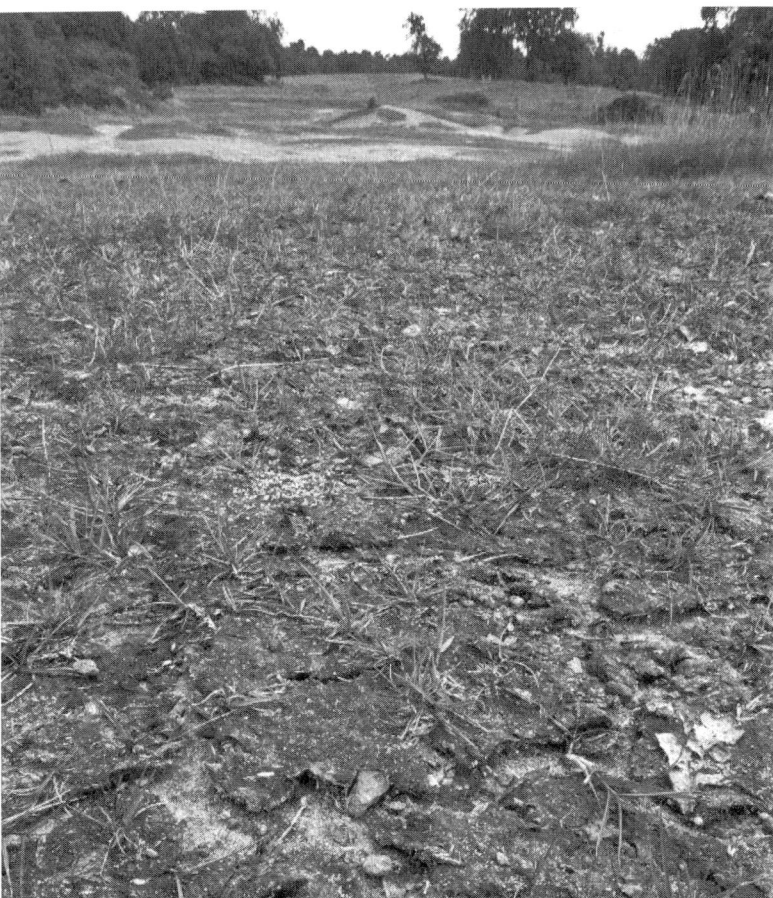

Figure 9.6. Looking north over the Sandhills towards Windmill Wood: the algal crust formed over the sand by *Microspora amoena* is clearly visible.

Photograph Sean Edwards.

of these crusts varies around the world, and in many places they are protected because they form a remarkable plant community that holds the desert sands together, absorbs moisture, provides nutrients and provides seed-beds in which other plants can grow. Intermixed blue-green algae, or cyanobacteria, provide valuable nitrogen fixation to enrich the soil. The crusts are called variously Cryptobiotic ('hidden life'), Microbiotic ('very small life') or Cryptogamic (referring to the cryptogamic or flowerless plants that constitute them) Crusts.

Microscopic examination shows the Sandhills crust to consist largely of algal threads, in particular the green alga *Microspora amoena*, together with other algae and cryptogamic plants such as mosses, liverworts and lichens. The threadworts, which are small thread-like liverworts of the genus *Cephaloziella*, mainly *Cephaloziella divaricata* (Plate 18), thrive in the Sandhills crust.

The Sandhills also turned up a number of rarities. Parcel 17b possesses several species characteristic of mining spoil, and in particular the find of the small, delicate and rare Greater Copperwort, *Cephaloziella nicholsonii* (Plate 19), from the edge of the crust. This is a minute plant (only a few millimetres in size), so named because the Lesser Copperwort is even smaller. It occurs among the similar and widespread threadworts that form the crust, including the less common *C. stellulifera*. Both these species are western in distribution in Britain, and although *C. stellulifera* also occurs in the Pennines and Cheshire, *C. nicholsonii* was previously known only from the West Country and does not occur outside Britain (Hill *et al.*, 1991; Paton, 1999). Both plants tolerate high acidity and are largely or exclusively confined to ore deposits and mine waste (Smith, 1982).

Plants which are not restricted to regions high in heavy metals sometimes behave differently on the Sandhills, probably due to the metal concentration or high acidity. Minerals flushed from the ground in the spring cause many species to lose their normal green colouration, a process known as chlorosis: examples are Bird's-foot Trefoil and grasses, whose pale yellowish plants are clearly visible to the casual walker. The crust also yielded a moss, by mining spoil seepage, that was tentatively named as a rare montane plant. After 18 years it was finally identified as an extreme metallophyte form (*gemmiclada*) of the common *Pohlia nutans*.

Far from being an impoverished site with a few oddities, parcel 17b turns out to be an altogether rich and varied locality. So far, there are 179 species of vascular plants (with the next richest site being parcel 20b, with 122), plus seventy-four species of mosses, liverworts and algae (the next best being fifty in parcel 3a). It is the second-best site for lichens, with twenty species (the best being twenty-seven in parcel 12b) (Tables 9.1, 9.3, 9.5, Appendix 9.1). Fifty-seven species of spider have been recorded from parcel 17 (the next best being twenty-one) and seventy-six species of insect (again the highest), although it must be noted that this site received more survey effort than the others by the zoologists, who also included records from the woodland and grassland parcels 17a and 17c.

The Sandhills in the broad sense (parcel 17) suffers from introductions, such as Japanese Knotweed (*Fallopia japonica*) (Figure 9.7): there are various accounts of how this was introduced at this spot (parcel 17c) – that it was planted to mark the visit of the 'Satsuma Students' from Japan in 1865 described in Chapter 16, or to hide a shaft at West

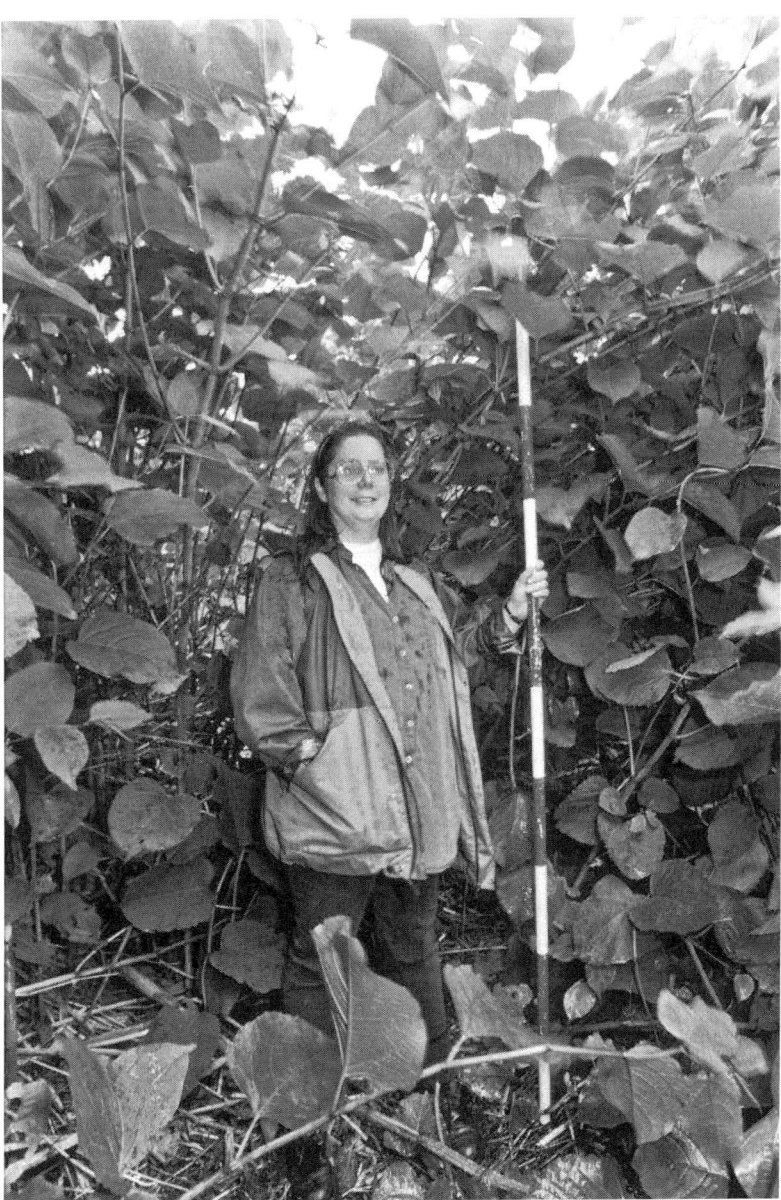

Figure 9.7. Japanese Knotweed (*Fallopia japonica*) at the entrance to West Mine.

Photograph Sean Edwards.

Mine, or that it simply arrived naturally. Picturesque though some of these stories may be, the history of the West Mine entrance, backed by aerial photographs, confirms that the third explanation must be the correct one (Paul Sorensen, personal communication). Having established itself, this invasive pest is spreading rapidly and is causing serious management problems elsewhere on the Edge. Further, the Pigmy Pondweed (*Crassula helmsii*), from New Zealand, has been introduced into the pond in parcel 17a, and on its past track-record will swamp it; it is further discussed in the context of the pondlife of the Edge (Chapter 12).

Waterfall Wood

Cheshire retains a much lower proportion of its area as woodland than most English counties; Waterfall Wood, especially the northern parcel (6a), is characteristic of rare (possibly ancient) semi-natural woodland that is typical of relatively undisturbed Cheshire countryside, although even this area owes much of its fauna, flora and character to human activity (Figure 9.8). It has (or had, before the felling of what the birds would regard as some of the best trees) the highest bird and invertebrate densities of the parcels surveyed, but is not notable for large numbers of species in other animal groups. Waterfall Wood is not as greatly used by the general public as the areas near the roads, and in terms of its woodland habitat value it is the best area of the site; as such, it benefits from low-level management. From the wildlife point of view, the growth of large dominant trees is to be encouraged, with the emphasis on allowing a natural succession to take place and the only intervention focused on the safety of visitors on main paths. The National Trust has a 'usage zone' policy that sets the level of response to potentially hazardous trees, which aims to retain trees for as long as possible, for ecological reasons; the retention of dead wood, whether standing or fallen, is a very important part of this policy, as it encourages the growth of fungi, mosses, lichens, insects and other organisms, which in turn offer opportunity for birds and mammals, while there is also some discreet manipulation of fallen timber to reduce soil erosion. A few trees may be removed to open up the canopy a little along the main footpaths, to allow more light and air to penetrate, but otherwise the only felling (apart from removal of non-native species, such as sycamore, which suppress native regeneration) is where trees are threatening known archaeological features. The management of Waterfall Wood – and of all the woodland – is described further in Chapter 29.

Waterfall Wood South (parcel 5) is an attractive wooded valley, which was expected to provide some of the more interesting results from the

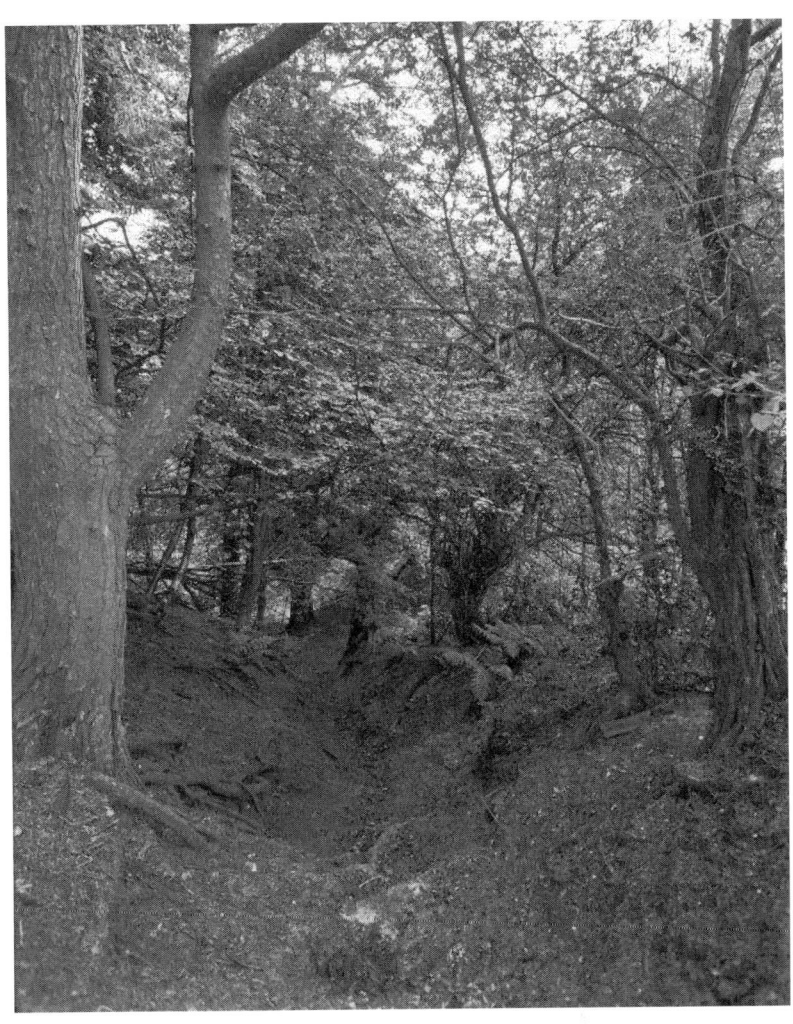

Figure 9.8. A hollow way
running through Waterfall Wood.

Photograph Sean Edwards.

botanical surveys. In fact, it was no more than average in species richness. There were forty-seven species of vascular plants, with twenty-four of the other parcels yielding at least as many, and five parcels having over 100 (179 in the Sandhills). The thirty-four species of moss, liverwort and algae made it seventeenth in richness, the list headed again by the Sandhills, with seventy-four species. For fungi it ranked fourth, with forty-two species, but well below the 135 species recorded in the un-improved grassland of parcel 30. The count of ten bramble species was high for the Edge, possibly because of the large marginal area bordering fields, but there were twelve other parcels with at least as many species. The lichen count of five was definitely low. First impressions are not always confirmed and lack of disturbance does not necessarily lead to abundance and diversity.

Conclusions

The vegetation and natural history of the Edge are of interest in three respects in connection with the subject matter of this volume.

In the first place, they were often the original stimulus which brought visitors to the area and resulted in further enquiry and research.

Secondly, examination of the present vegetation and its accompanying fauna provides an opportunity to retrace to some extent the ecological history of the site. Over the past 1,000 years it has changed from being open heath and grassland given over to common grazing and exploitation to enclosure and planting as useful but also deliberately picturesque woodland. Evidence of the change can be seen in the distribution of trees noted above and in the persistence of open-ground species in areas like Findlow Hill Wood, such as Heather (*Calluna vulgaris*) and Bilberry, along with Bracken, Wavy Hair-grass and Bramble.

Thirdly, the vegetation of an area sometimes gives clues to mineral composition and other physical characteristics of the soil and geological formations on which it stands. Some plant species, known as metallophytes, are associated with the presence of particular metals. A survey by the Department of the Environment published in 1994 lists fifteen vascular plant species, twelve bryophyte species and thirty-one lichens in this category. Where the information is known, the association is usually with lead and zinc, more rarely with copper or iron. Of the vascular plant species, one flowering plant (*Epipactis helleborine*) is found at Alderley and one fern, the Moonwort (*Botrichium lunaria*), is represented by a nineteenth-century unsubstantiated report. Of the thirty-one metal-tolerating lichens on the list, four (*Peltigera neckeri, Rhizocarpon furfurosum, Stereocaulon dactylophyllum* and *S. pileatum*) are to be found among the eighty lichens in total recorded at Alderley (Fox and Timberlake in *ArchAE*: 238-9). Among the bryophytes, the copperworts (*Cephaloziella*) have already been noted. Five species are regarded as metallophytes (Paton, 1999), two or three of which are present at Alderley, as well as the two mosses *Weissia controversa* and *Pohlia nutans* form *gemmiclada*. Thus, few plants proclaim the presence of metals in the soils. Those which do are noteworthy, however, and some may have been evident indicators to miners in the past.

Addendum

Over five days in September 2014 and January 2015, Dr Des Callaghan conducted a further survey and assessment of the bryophites of the Sandhills on behalf of Natural England. His main objective was to determine the present status of *Cephaloziella nicholsonii* (Greater

Copperwort) and *Orthodontium gracile* (Slender Thread-moss) at Alderley Edge, but he also carried out a full bryophyte survey and an assessment of the site, and it was he who finally identified the extreme metalophyte *Pohlia nutans* form *gemmiclada*. The spot where Dr Newton had located *C. nicholsonii* for AELP in 1997 had since been colonised by grasses and other coarse vegetation, and although some colonies of *C. stellulifera* survive there Dr Callaghan found no evidence of *C. nicholsonii* itself either there or at any other location on the Edge. He concluded that 'it is a typical story of rare metallophyte populations in Britain, which were dependent on active mining and the dumping of metalliferous spoil in order to provide an on-going supply of fresh substrates' (Callaghan, 2015).

Further reading

Mabey, R. 1997. *Flora Britannica* (2nd edition). London: Chatto and Windus.
Newton, A. 1971. *Flora of Cheshire*. Chester: Cheshire Community Council Publications Trust.
Newton, A. 1990. *Supplement to the Flora of Cheshire*. Leamington Spa: Alan Newton.
Stace, C. A. 1997. *A New Flora of the British Isles* (2nd edition). Cambridge: Cambridge University Press.

10

The trees of Alderley Edge

Simon Timberlake and Sean R. Edwards

As described in the previous chapter, trees were recorded using the land parcel (Chapter 8) and DAFOR system (Chapter 9) as part of the general survey of vegetation. The basis of this chapter is an additional survey of the trees of Alderley that utilised the Global Positioning System (GPS), carried out by Simon Timberlake and Tom Burke with the support of Sean Edwards; in order to keep the story of the trees together, the results of both surveys as well as other research conducted in the woodlands are included here, and there are links with the work on birds and trees presented in the next chapter.

A GPS tree survey of woodland on Alderley Edge

Between March and August 1997 a survey of the trees in the core area of the Alderley Edge Landscape Project (AELP) was carried out by the project surveyors with the help of volunteers, using a data logger and the Asset Surveyor software program linked to GPS to record the location of these trees together with a host of other relevant data, ranging from species, size, health and management criteria, down to the dates of graffiti cut into their trunks. Up to 5,000 trees of more 1.35 m girth at chest height (1.5 m) were logged in the 60 ha of National Trust woodlands, covering some 95 per cent of the mature trees.

From the corrected GPS data a number of thematic Geographic Information System (GIS) maps were produced for the Landscape Project by the University of Manchester's Regional Research Laboratory, some of which are interpreted here. Spreadsheets summarising some of the data were downloaded onto CDs and deposited in the AELP archive and at the Trust's Property Office at Alderley Edge. We also give a brief historical background to the planting and management of woodland on Alderley Edge, along with a photographic record of some of the Alderley trees, of which a complete set has been deposited in the AELP archive, and we describe a number of individual trees, some of historic note, located in both the core area and hinterland of the Project (see Figure 1.3, p. 16).

The archaeological evidence – tree cover during the prehistoric and Roman periods

A small amount of palaeo-environmental evidence relating to the tree and shrub cover of the Edge during the Early Bronze Age and again during the late Roman period is available as a result of limited archaeological excavation work at Engine Vein and at Pot Shaft (*ArchAE*: 45–6, Timberlake and King citing Shimwell and Hradil, 1998; *ArchAE*: 101–3, Brayshay and Shimwell). Pollen samples, and to a lesser extent plant macro-fossils, have provided us with a snap-shot of the vegetation cover in this part of the Edge.

During the Early Bronze Age, open woodland appears to dominate, with a minor oak canopy, and a dominant birch and hazel understorey and marginal scrub. The woodland was apparently not particularly dense, with many clearings dominated by heather and bracken. Similar woodland conditions persisted into Roman times – if anything, the woodland component of the pollen spectra increases. Within these areas the open hazel scrub dominates, with a slightly reduced oak canopy, and a birch, hazel and alder understorey. Lesser woodland species included holly, ivy, ash, yew and willow.

The historical background of planting and woodland management

There appears to be little or no record for tree cover on Alderley Edge from the Early Medieval period up until the eighteenth century, suggesting that post-Roman clearances were followed by the increased use of this area as common grazing land. Grazing effectively prevented the regeneration of the woodland.

Beech trees are mentioned in the neighbouring Alderley Park, among them those planted during the mid-seventeenth century by Sir Thomas Stanley, the first baronet, from beech mast which came from the park belonging to the father of his wife, Elizabeth Pyte or Pytt, at Kyre in Worcestershire – a possible seed source for later Stanley plantings on Alderley Edge; the part that tree-planting at Alderley played in the story of the Stanleys is described in the account of the history of the Edge (Chapter 19). However, at this time the Edge itself appears to have been rough grazing land; the only references to be found concern the illegal cutting of gorse for kindling and the like and of fern for animal bedding, mentioned by John, first Lord Stanley, in his notebooks (*Stanley Notebook*: p. 158, 1610; p. 283, 1611; p. 282, 1610). A companion notebook in the Stanley archive held by Cheshire Archives and Local Studies (CALS) refers in general terms to the first plantings of hundreds of Scots pines on the 'highest point' of the Edge between 1745 and 1755, before which time 'it does not appear that a single tree grew on it' (CALS DSA 3752/1, p. 65). While this last comment might be an exaggeration, it is nonetheless suggestive of fairly heavy grazing pressure at the time.

More specifically, there are references to the planting of firs (probably Scots pine) above Church Quarry and between the Quarry and Glaze Hill by Sir James Stanley around 1740 (CALS DSA 3752/1, p. 73). The plantations referred to here may be the same as those shown on the map of the 1775 Enclosure Award (CALS DSA 1919/33; Figure 19.7), and thus clearly represent plantings by the Stanleys within an area of what was otherwise common land. By 1760 we find a reference to the planting of Brynlow Wood or Nursery and also the trees on Beacon Piece, and in 1780–82 the planting of a fir wood on Glaze Hill by Sir John Thomas Stanley. A note dating from 1780 concerning the wages paid to labourers (CALS DSA 3752/1, p. 74) indicates that many parts of the Edge were sown with acorns at around this time, and that afterwards several of these areas were repeatedly set on fire, presumably by the disgruntled commoners in an attempt to destroy the seedlings. Even after enclosure, in 1799 plantings were still being destroyed by successive firings of the gorse heath, and in 1798 several acres of plantation behind Bradford Lodge and Finlow Hill Piece were burnt. Elsewhere on the Edge it is recorded in the *Stanley Notebook* that the rest of the 'waste land in the Hough' was planted out in 1798.

The 1787 Crossley map of the Stanley estates in Over Alderley, Nether Alderley and Chorley shows additional parts of the Edge under woodland (CALS P143/14/1; see e.g. Figure 19.9). One can probably assume that this is mature or semi-mature woodland; apart from those areas already mentioned like Brynlow Wood, Church Quarry, the Beacon and Glaze Hill, other plantations are shown, such as a long strip between the Old Alderley Quarry and Stormy Point (also shown on the 1775 Enclosure Award map), together with more extensive woodland in the areas of Dickens Wood (equivalent to AELP recording parcel 4 – see Figure 8.1), parts of Waterfall Wood and Clockhouse Wood. The latter evidence is interesting, suggesting that all or parts of some of these valley or slope-land woods away from the main escarpment of the Edge may in fact pre-date the mid- to late-eighteenth-century plantings. West of the Macclesfield Road some of the post-enclosure field boundaries, marked for the first time on this 1787 map, are shown with accompanying copses of trees.

By the early 1800s tree encroachment on the Edge is much more evident. The *Stanley Notebook* in Chester provides a lot of detail about John Stanley's planting programme on the Edge around 1800 (CALS DSA 5/10): it indicates that the main trees planted were pines and larches (the latter as cash crops), together with oaks and beeches for their landscape value. On an 1807–08 Stanley estate map, more or less the whole of the eastern escarpment between the Golden Stone and Glaze Hill now appears to be under trees, while both Finlow and Bradford Lodge Woods appear to be covering a considerably larger area than at present. However, the top of the Edge still remains largely treeless. The area of Mottram Wood is not shown, this being on de Trafford land, but it is tempting to suggest that these relatively elderly beech trees had already been planted out by this time. By 1841 (the date of an informative tithe map, CALS IR 30/5, discussed in Chapter 19 and elsewhere), this picture of woodland coverage had changed once again. On the twenty-five-inch first edition of the Ordnance Survey map of Cheshire, published in 1872, the greater part of the area on the Edge under woodland at the end of the twentieth century was already covered with trees, most of them more likely self-set than deliberately planted. This included all of Windmill Wood, the top of the Edge, Mottram Wood and the greater part of the escarpment. Only the slope margins above the fields of the Hough, parts of the escarpment to the west of Castle Rock and the western slope of Saddlebole are shown as rough grazing, or else as a mixture of grazing and open woodland.

A somewhat *laissez-faire* approach characterised woodland management during much of the twentieth century, resulting in a good deal of natural regeneration in the less visited areas. Since the National Trust made its first acquisition here in 1947, it has sought to reintroduce traditional broadleaf woodland and a more structured approach to management. The Trust's prescriptive Woodland Plan for 1983–87 and through subsequent five-year periods provides a history of this woodland activity (Clements *et al.*, 1985). Between the 1950s and 1980s under-planting was carried out across some thirty acres (twelve hectares) of the property so as to restore a balanced age structure to areas of woodland of similarly aged trees. This was grant-aided under the Forestry Commission's Approved Woodlands Scheme and involved a mixture of species, including coppiceable hazel and sweet chestnut (for sticks, posts and cleft rails) and standards like larch, Scots pine and beech. Elsewhere there has been thinning of scrub and understorey to benefit the woodland flora. A good deal of effort has been devoted to the care of the ageing beech and to safety work, especially close to footpaths. Where they do not represent a potential hazard to the public, diseased or dead trees have been allowed to collapse and decay to provide much-needed deadwood habitat. Thinning has been practised more selectively, with the removal of particular species such as sycamore within some significant patches of beech or oak woodland. However, during the 1980s, management in Clockhouse Wood involved the felling of a number of mature oaks, a rare opportunity to achieve an economic return from the woodland. Much of the small-scale woodland work on the Edge is undertaken by the National Trust's countryside staff with the assistance of numerous volunteers, although outside contractors are brought in for larger projects and for safety-related remedial tree work. Enjoyed by so many, the primary aims are to manage for amenity, conservation and biodiversity, rather than for a financial return. So, for example, the Trust has been working with the Forestry Commission to remove trees from locations identified in the National Trust Sites and Monuments Record (NTSMR) in order to reduce potential damage to archaeological features. Conversely, in some areas such as Stormy Point, part of which has been fenced off as it suffers erosion, the presence of some trees is seen as beneficial in stabilising the thin soil cover (see Chapter 29 and Plate 62).

The staggering of the original plantings of beech and Scots pine as well as most of the re-plantings up to the 1980s, combined with the effects of natural regeneration of our native broadleaves once common grazing and mining pressure had ceased, has resulted in a considerable mixture of age classes. However, in some areas, such as those with stands of open, high-canopy mature beech woodland, typically on the north-western slopes and to a small extent near Beacon Lodge, this mixture of ages is much less evident and a scheme is under way to remove a number of mature beech trees selectively so as to create the conditions necessary to promote natural regeneration of beech as well as other native species. The long-term aim in such areas is to increase the age range of trees and thus to avoid a similar situation in future. In this context, two non-native invasive species give cause for real concern: Japanese knotweed and the grey squirrel. The threat from the former has been mentioned in the previous chapter (see Figure 9.7); it is the latter that constitutes a real threat in a woodland setting, for these creatures threaten the perpetuation of beech trees as a feature of the site. The grey squirrel will strip the bark from beech saplings and trees of up to a couple of decades in age to such a degree that these specimens never reach the maturity which makes them such significant features of the landscape. The Trust actively controls the squirrels, but without similar control on neighbouring land removal here tends to create a 'sink' of new territory for others from outside to colonise. Thus the problem continues. Thinning the trees should create the conditions necessary for the natural regeneration of beech and other native species, in part because the Trust recognises that thanks to the grey squirrels one cannot realistically expect beech to be the sole species to prevail, certainly not if we wish to see the high-canopy, mature specimens foreseen and realised by Lord Stanley, but also because the Trust's current aim is to see the development of a broader ecological value on the Edge, as present in a mixed native woodland.

Previous woodland surveys

A number of surveys have been carried out by or on behalf of the National Trust. Biological surveys are carried out periodically on the Trust's estates by a small team of botanists and ecologists now based at the headquarters in Swindon. One such survey was carried out in 1985 and updated in 1997, with follow-ups planned when resources permit (Clements *et al.*, 1985; Jackson *et al.*, 1997). These reports provide only a brief synopsis of woodland composition and are primarily concerned with the ground flora and insect, bird, mammal and amphibian fauna. Biological surveys have also been carried out at the Butts Farm since the Trust acquired it in 2007.

Between August and November 1996, recorders from the Manchester Group of National Trust Volunteers carried out a more detailed tree-by-tree survey of an area encompassing the central or most heavily visited part of the Trust's woodlands, also referred to as the 'core' area of the Edge, although not identical with the Project's 'core'. This was divided into nine recording compartments (unrelated to those of the AELP survey), lying inside a line drawn between the Beacon, Stormy Point, Pillar Mine, the Golden Stone, the road to Thieves Hollow, the Wizard, Beacon Lodge and back to the Beacon. Details of species, canopy and trunk size, health and density index were recorded, along with exact girth measurements, and every tree was numbered and marked with a small metal number tag for future reference. What could not be recorded so easily was the exact location of each tree – something which was clearly impossible within what was in most cases dense woodland with few if any diagnostic landmarks or mapped features. However, within this area details of some 939 trees were gathered. Most of these were Scots pine (338), with similar numbers of oaks (290), but fewer birch (103), beech (90) and sweet chestnut (41). The tagging of these trees with labels has proved immensely useful for monitoring and management work: applied to the Trust's tree safety policy, it has produced one of the best monitoring systems available for this kind of property.

Smaller areas of woodland have been surveyed in different ways for quite different reasons. Linked to the AELP surveys have been several studies carried out as student projects under the direction of Dr M. V. Hounsome, then Keeper of Zoology at Manchester Museum. Several monitored bird and squirrel populations in particular areas of the Edge; the bird survey is discussed in the next chapter. As part of one of these studies it became necessary to record the location and size of *all* trees and saplings, as well as the width of both the understorey and overstorey canopy cover; the discussion of aspects of surveying in the previous chapter makes the point that not every creature sees a 'tree' in the same way.

The 1997 tree survey – method and data

The operation and use of GPS recorders

For the purpose of locating trees during the 1997 survey, two GPS recorders were hired from the Geographic Information Unit of Cheshire County Council. These consisted of a back-pack mounted Trimble Pathfinder Pro-XL (illustrated in *ArchAE*: 126, fig. 8.2) and a hand-held Trimble Geo-Explorer. The methodology has already been described in the account of the Project's topographical and archaeological survey of the Edge (*ArchAE*: 124–5). One should remember that in 1997 the civilian use of GPS was still being developed, and furthermore that until 2000 the signal available for civilian use was intentionally degraded by the US military so that it was accurate only to 100 m at best. Data for each tree, including the uncorrected GPS coordinates, were collected on a data logger using Asset Surveyor software. At the end of every day or every other day, the files for each 'job' were downloaded as ntf/dxf files directly into a PC. Disks containing the files were then sent to County Hall in Chester, where the degraded signal was corrected using the GPS data gathered by the Trimble Community Base Station receiver.

In the field, signals were picked up by the antennae of the mobile receivers from a number of GPS transmitting satellites. Usually, reception from four to six different satellites was required, the ability of the GPS to configure coordinates depending upon the PDOP (Position Dilution of Precision) value, or the trigonometry of the satellite positions and their orbits. If the satellite number and PDOP value were good enough, it took a minimum of about thirty seconds to record enough signals for an accurate coordinate to be obtained. The in-built spoiler error of the GPS signals needed to be corrected if one wanted to use GPS to map or survey features in the field (using the Community Base Station, it was possible to back-calculate the true position of each record taken). For the purposes of the current survey, an error of 2–4 m after correction was considered sufficiently accurate for mapping tree positions. Inevitably the tree surveyor needed to stand several metres back from the trunk of the tree or else to walk around it in order to receive sufficient signals anyway, and thus a coordinate error of this magnitude appeared quite acceptable.

During the course of the six-month survey a number of difficulties were encountered with the use of GPS in this hilly and wooded environment, which towards the end of this period slowed the rate of progress considerably. Blind spots from which it was difficult if not impossible to obtain a satellite reading exist at several places on the Edge, most often in the bottom of deep or incised valleys like Waterfall Wood or at the base of steep cliffs or overhangs such as Castle Rock. Temporary blind spots are common, which relate to obscuring rock outcrops or else the blocking effect of large tree trunks, from which it was often possible to escape by moving a metre or so to either side. The time of day was often important in this respect. High PDOP values were common during the middle of the day and satellite reception proved difficult at this time. The PDOP threshold was that much more difficult to overcome within topographically problematical or densely wooded areas of the Edge. The onset of spring and the burgeoning of the leaf canopy in the woodland made signal reception more and more difficult as summer progressed. During the winter months we found that an experienced surveyor might record the positions of anything up to 150–200 trees a day, but by July would be lucky to record more than fifty or sixty.

Problems with data capture resulting from operator error or equipment failure or else due to the signal reception being too poor to allow a coordinate fix probably resulted in the loss of no more than 1–2 per cent of collected/collectable records over the six-month period. A more serious loss of records from parcels 3a, 4 and 20, forming an estimated 5 per cent of the total, resulted from the misallocation of tree files already recorded and sent for correction. It was this loss of data, which occurred during April 1998, that is responsible for some of the gaps in the colour-coded map of the distribution of tree species in the Alderley Edge core (Plate 20). If need be, this could be rectified by re-recording several days' work, but even without these data we can be confident of having produced a map which is by and large correct and 93–95 per cent complete.

Recording tree data

A menu of tree data that was easy both to understand and to use was prepared for loading onto each data logger. We hoped that in spite of its necessary simplicity this menu would enable us to record as comprehensive a record of tree size, condition and anthropogenic factors as might be obtained using a manual recording system, such as filling in record sheets with short free-text descriptions. By providing the data menu with bracket ranges (i.e. <5 m; 5–10 m; 10–15 m; 15–20 m; >20 m) for recording the various tree dimensions such as girth, height and canopy width, we hoped that after a learning period we would be able to make quick but accurate estimates of significant variables that were otherwise difficult to measure. Other types of data would inevitably be more sub-jectively determined, but by its very nature this was intended to be only a quick visual survey.

The data menu record allowed for the inclusion of details such as *NT tree number* (where appropriate); the record of *tree species* (nineteen categories, arranged alphabetically under common names, alder to yew, but including a category of 'unknown'); *trunk girth* or circumference at chest height (1.35–2 m; 2.5–3 m; 3.5–4 m; >4 m); estimated *tree height* (<5 m ; 5–10 m; 10–15 m; 15–20 m; >20 m); and estimated *canopy width* (<5 m; 5–10 m; 10–15 m; 15–20 m; >20 m).

Most of the remaining features recorded related to tree condition and health, the bulk of which could be fairly easily assessed visually. These included simple tick lists under such headings as *plant growths* (plant galls) – canker (trunk excrescences or tumours), witches' broom (bunches of twiggy growths from a trunk), or none; *fungus*, e.g. bracket fungus, other, or none; *general condition*, i.e. healthy, diseased, old (some rotten), or dead; *angle* (angle of trunk), i.e. upright, leaning, or prone; *damage* (physical damage), i.e. split trunk, top trunk missing, top trunk and limbs missing, limbs missing, branch damage, or lightning strike; *roots*, i.e. roots part exposed, standing and roots exposed (cavities or hollows between roots – therefore evidence of soil erosion), or uprooted; and finally *trunk condition*, i.e. solid, cavities, part hollow, fully hollow, and stump only.

A final category related to anthropogenic issues such as tree manage-ment and tree graffiti, the latter a common and oftentimes interesting feature of many of the older trees on the Edge. *Graffiti* were recorded in general terms as either pre-1960 or post-1960, a factor which made it possible to record large amounts of graffiti quickly, often because much of this was illegible anyway, and because such a threshold date proved somewhat easier to estimate. However, a further data field labelled *graffiti comment* allowed for the free-text insertion of rather more in-formative and specific details, such as names, dates and comments (this had a maximum length of twenty-six characters), as well as permitting reference to illustrations. Some trees were so heavily covered with graffiti that the data menu was set up to record several graffiti fields, 'graffiti 1', 'graffiti 2' and 'graffiti 3'. Discussion of these graffiti belongs with the social history of the Edge (Chapter 22) rather than its arboriculture. The *management* field in the 'anthropogenic' category included the following options – old coppice, recent pruning, recent felling, stump regrowth (something which may have management implications) and 'pulled out' (referring to roots). A *comments* field allowed the inclusion of other information in the form of free text. Some of this was anthropogenic in nature, the most common references being to the presence of functional or damaged bird boxes on the tree, the use of rope swings and the like, and the marking of the tree with paint spots for management purposes. The tree record itself and thus the approximate location of the tree (in the form of GPS coordinates and with a corrected error range of 2–4 m, as noted above) could be identified by means of the precise *time of collection*, automatically entered in the data menu.

The Trimble GPS equipment and data loggers from Cheshire County Council had already been used for mapping and recording trees in the Granada Arboretum at Jodrell Bank nearby, for which they had performed well. The Alderley Edge tree condition survey was to be basically similar in format but rather more comprehensive.

The survey results

The distribution of common woodland trees

The thematic map in Plate 20 shows the distribution of mature trees of the commoner species within the AELP core area (some 70 per cent of this area consists of National Trust woodland). The general impression is one of mixed oak–birch–beech–Scots pine woodland associated with a lesser amount of mature rowan, and small areas of sycamore, chestnut and larch planting. Landscape planting of Scots pine and beech can be recognised in some of the older areas of woodland. Notes on the common species are given below, in alphabetical order of common English name.

Unknown species

In total, 159 trees were recorded as 'unknown'. However, this number included many of the thirty-one holly trees, which were recorded separately.

Alder, Alnus *spp.*

Only nineteen mature trees (>1.35 m girth) were recorded during the survey. None of these were long-lived examples, the oldest probably being fifty to sixty years at the most. The majority were found growing around the edges of the old marlpit ponds, such as near Hill Top Farm (SJ 867 776) and Higher Croft field at Brynlow (SJ 855 774); occasionally they had been planted along field boundaries in slightly damper areas of grassland, for example at the eastern end of parcel 30 above the Hough (SJ 859 780). The latter are Grey Alder (*A. incana*) as opposed to the Common Alder (*A. glutinosa*), which most of the other identified specimens appear to be. Alder is very rarely found in the area of mixed woodland up on the Edge. An exception is a fairly large tree found growing below Holy Well (SJ 858 778). However, there is a younger growth of alder saplings in this area of boggy woodland, following the course of the Holy Well Slack.

It is tempting to interpret the place name 'Alderley' as *alder* [*aller*] *ley* (or alder meadow(s)), perhaps referring to the land around the Edge, but that this is a false etymology is shown in Chapter 28.

Ash, Fraxinus *spp.*

Ash rarely occurs in heavily wooded areas of the Edge, and its occasional appearance along field boundaries and on the sides of roads and tracks in the area is much more typical of this tree's open woodland habitat (only thirty-nine recorded in the core area).

Mature trees are very rare on the eastern side of the Edge, one of the few examples being the old and almost dead tree located on the side of the track below Edge House Farm (SJ 863 775) close to the site of Old Edge House (Figure 10.1). To the west of the Macclesfield Road there are several large examples growing upon old and now redundant field banks in open grazing land at Brynlow (e.g. SJ 853 773). There are also a number of large ash trees in a sheltered and much damper location on the other side of the small valley and stream near Brynlow Farm (SJ 851 772) as well as behind the Topps water mill.

Beech, Fagus sylvatica

Together with Scots pine, beech is one of the 'classic' trees of the Alderley Edge woodlands. It is perhaps the memory of these beech woods which leaves its mark most clearly imprinted upon the mind of the adventurous visitor.

Beech is the second most common mature tree on the Edge (880 recorded, compared with 1,675 oaks). It forms 25–30 per cent of the woodland of Alderley Edge, being absent from some parts such as Clockhouse Wood, the west side of Saddlebole and Finlow Wood. Elsewhere, beech woods, consisting of old and magnificently tall stands of trees, dominate the steep slopes of the Edge (Figure 10.2). Mottram Wood (also known as the Beech Wood) forms the largest overstorey canopy of ancient beech (up to 350 trees), although some of those on Artists Lane and the Brynlow valley (SJ 858 777), at the north end of Waterfall Wood (SJ 864 777), and along the east slopes of Glaze Hill

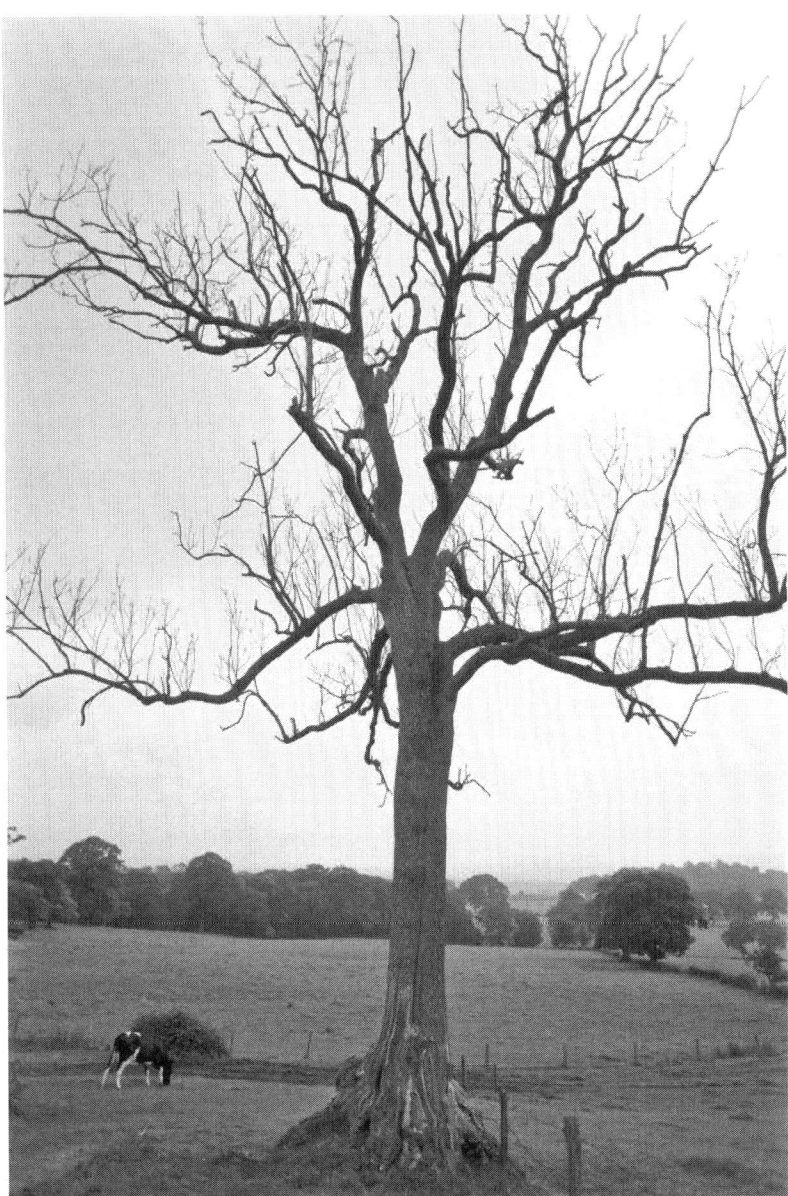

Figure 10.1. Dying ash tree (*Fraxinus excelsior*) below Edge House Farm.

Photograph Sean Edwards.

and Saddlebole (up to 100 trees in squares SJ 860 779/780) form finer and probably much older stands. Some are probably more than 150 years old. An avenue of ancient beeches above Artists Lane have Tree Preservation Orders attached; otherwise, there is little recording, monitoring or protection provided for individual trees on the Edge.

Regeneration of beech can be seen on the upper slopes of Mottram Wood and on the east side of the track between the Golden Stone and Stormy Point (SJ 861 777). In other places the high and dense leaf canopy formed by old trees has blocked much of the available light, thus

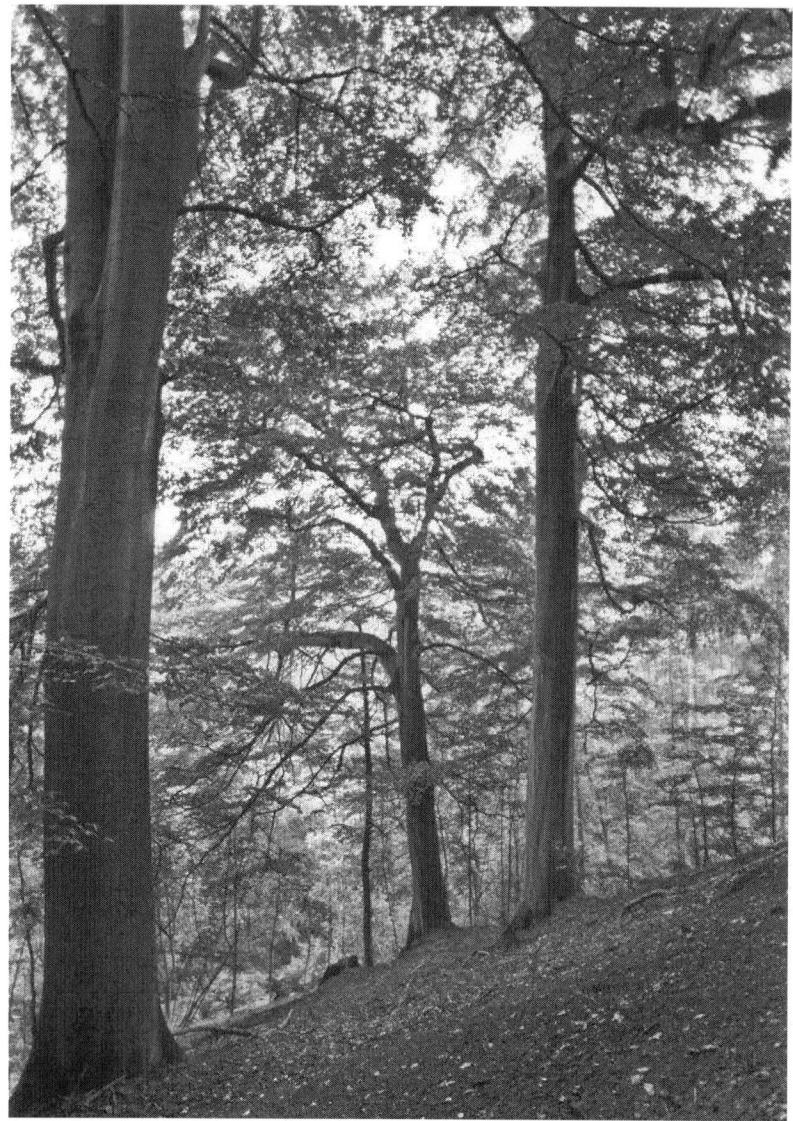

Figure 10.2. Beech trees (*Fagus sylvatica*) on the slopes of Waterfall Wood.

Photograph Sean Edwards.

limiting the undergrowth and stifling tree seedlings, in particular those of other species. For this reason, mature beech is dominant, leaving a spacious, open woodland floor. However, in some of the older beech woods in shallow soil on steep slopes, for instance Mottram Wood, fallen, dead or dying trees are much more common than elsewhere on the Edge.

Self-seeded beeches are common in areas of disturbed ground such as the patches of woodland in the area of Wood Mine/West Mine spoil (SJ 8533 7757) and around the northern margin of the Alderley Red Moulding Sand Quarry on the Mottram Road (SJ 8607 7835).

Birch, Betula *spp.*

Birch or silver birch tends to be a slender-trunk tree, so that the 488 individuals recorded during this survey may not accurately reflect the true number of mature trees in the woodlands of the Edge (Figure 10.3). We have already touched on the distribution of birch in the previous chapter: it closely accompanies that of oak, except in the youngest areas of regenerated woodland such as Finlow Hill Wood (parcel 13a) and Bradford Lane (parcel 12b).

The association of birch and oak in the absence of beech or Scots pine may indicate 'natural' as opposed to planted and landscaped woodland. This is certainly the case in the north part of Waterfall Wood and Clockhouse Wood, where many of the oldest birches are to be found. However, even these may only be eighty or ninety years old, although

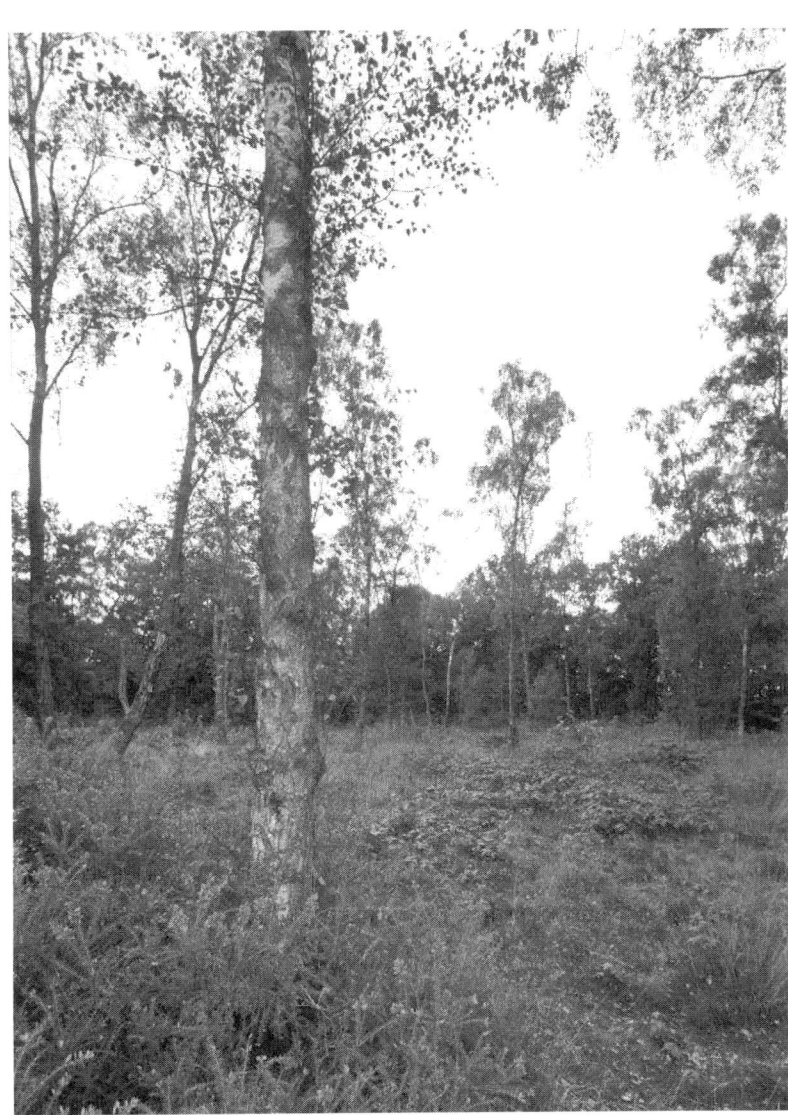

Figure 10.3. Silver birch (*Betula pendula*) with gorse (*Ulex gallii*) growing beneath.

Photograph Sean Edwards.

some are fallen, split, twisted and gnarled (Figure 10.4). Most of this area is now secondary woodland. The patch of wood on the western side of Saddlebole (parcel 2b) most clearly reflects the type of woodland colonisation which would have occurred naturally on the flanks of the sandstone ridge. The birch and oaks here are much closer in age. It is noteworthy that this was one of the very few areas of rough grazing land and scrub remaining by 1872. Other important areas of birch woodland include the tract between Castle Rock and Wizard's Well. Today, good examples of immature birch woodland are to be found in the Hagg, in the area of more recent disturbance around West Mine, and on the patch of heathland on the north side of Bradford Lane (parcel 12b).

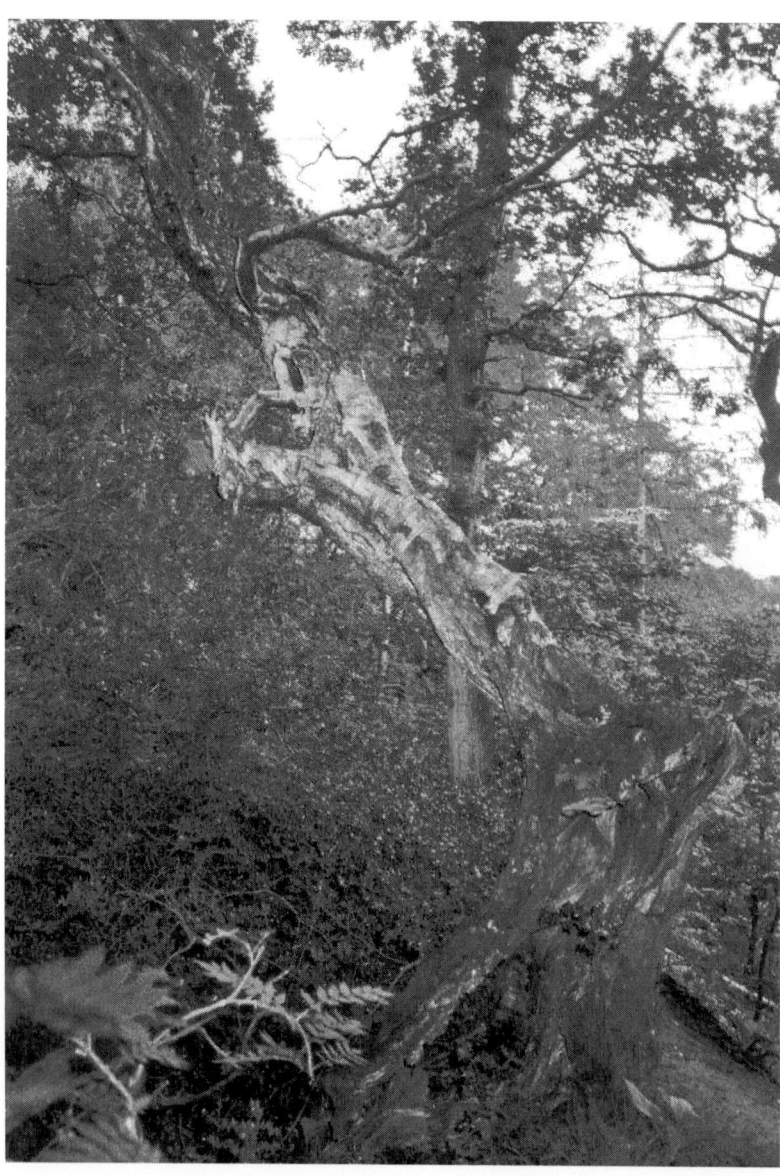

Figure 10.4. Ancient twisted birch, Waterfall Wood.

Photograph Sean Edwards.

Elm, Ulmus *spp.*

Only two elms were recorded during the survey. One of these is close to the Butts Farm (SJ 848 768). It seems most unlikely that elms were ever common in this area, but their absence along field boundaries and roadsides, in the sorts of places where they might be expected, is almost certainly a consequence of the ravages of Dutch elm disease since the 1960s.

Hawthorn, Crataegus monogyna

While hawthorn is common along the woodland edge and hedgerows, the trunks of mature trees rarely exceed 1.35 m in girth. The twelve examples recorded from the Edge are probably fairly ancient. The majority are in open fields, either on disused and ancient field banks such as those of the Riddings and Higher Croft at Brynlow, or at current field margins associated with the remains of old hedgerows, such as below Edge House Farm (SJ 863 775). Within the woodland, hawthorn rarely grows to any size, nor does it seem to be long-lived, presumably because of competition with tall trees with a wide canopy.

Hazel, Corylus avellana

Uncoppiced hazel forms part of the understorey scrub in some areas of the Edge, such as Windmill Wood, parts of Dickens Wood and to the east of the Old Alderley Quarry. Although very much a woodland tree, it rarely seems to be old. Even the occasional example derived from stools of old coppice exceeded the minimum girth recorded only if it was the central pole of the stool. Only four hazel trees of this girth were recorded, almost certainly isolated remnants of coppiced woodland.

Holly, Ilex aquifolium

Holly is not uncommon, particularly in some of the older semi-naturalised woodland such as Clockhouse Wood and the southern half of Waterfall Wood. Some 70–80 per cent of these bushes or trees are less than 1.35 m in trunk girth. Many occur in the densest woodland, where they form clumps or thickets as part of the understorey. A quite different association occurs on the margins of some of the older woodland, and along the lines of ancient hedgerows, particularly old tracks or hollow ways such as that between Waterfall and Clockhouse Woods (SJ 866 778). An interesting group of ancient hollies is to be found at the top of the eastern slope at the southern end of the incised valley of Waterfall Wood. These trees overhang the lip of the rock cliff above the footpath and waterfall

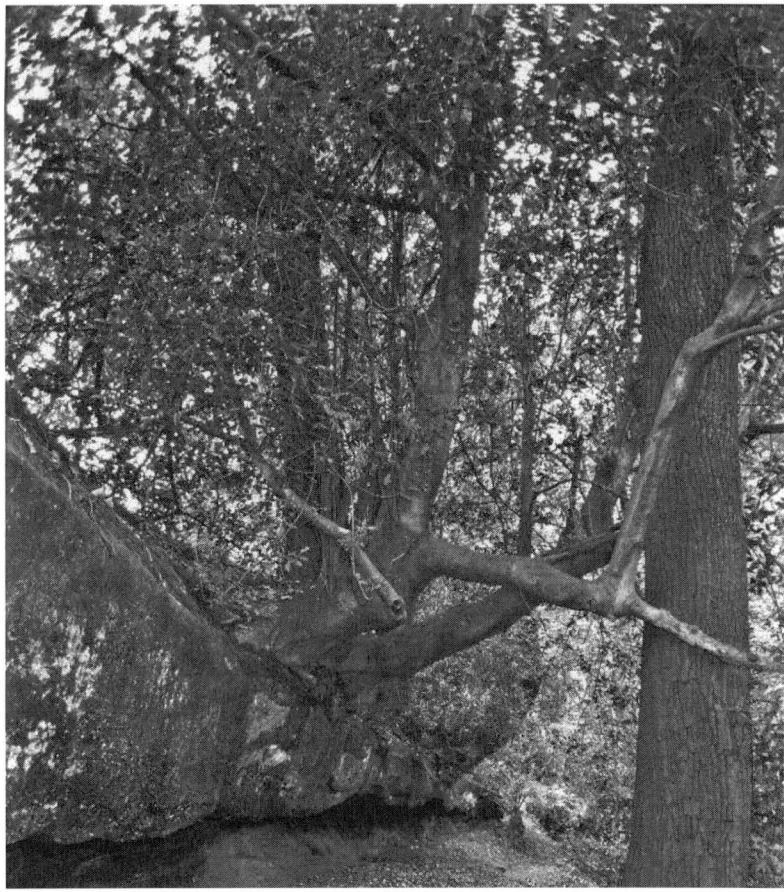

Figure 10.5. Old holly trees (*Ilex aquifolium*), centre, clinging to the edge of a rock ledge, Waterfall Wood.

Photograph Sean Edwards.

(Figure 10.5). Several are more than 2 m in girth, and are associated and sometimes intertwined with ancient oaks. One or two may be more than 150 years old, and the presence of holly along this woodland edge may be much older. There is no clear evidence for coppicing here but the line of the trees suggests that they may have been planted. In all, thirty-one 'ancient' holly trees have been recorded from the Edge.

Traditionally holly was used as a shelter tree for livestock and also as foliage for winter browsing (a practice apparently common in the Lancashire–Cheshire Pennine margin). Being evergreen and long-lived, hollies may sometimes have been used as guide or marker trees for tracks or drove roads in areas of open landscape (Mabey, 1996). There is little doubt that some pre-date the enclosure of common land on the Edge.

Hornbeam, Carpinus betulus

Several individuals were recorded throughout the woodland area. Hornbeam is sometimes thought of as an indicator of ancient woodland,

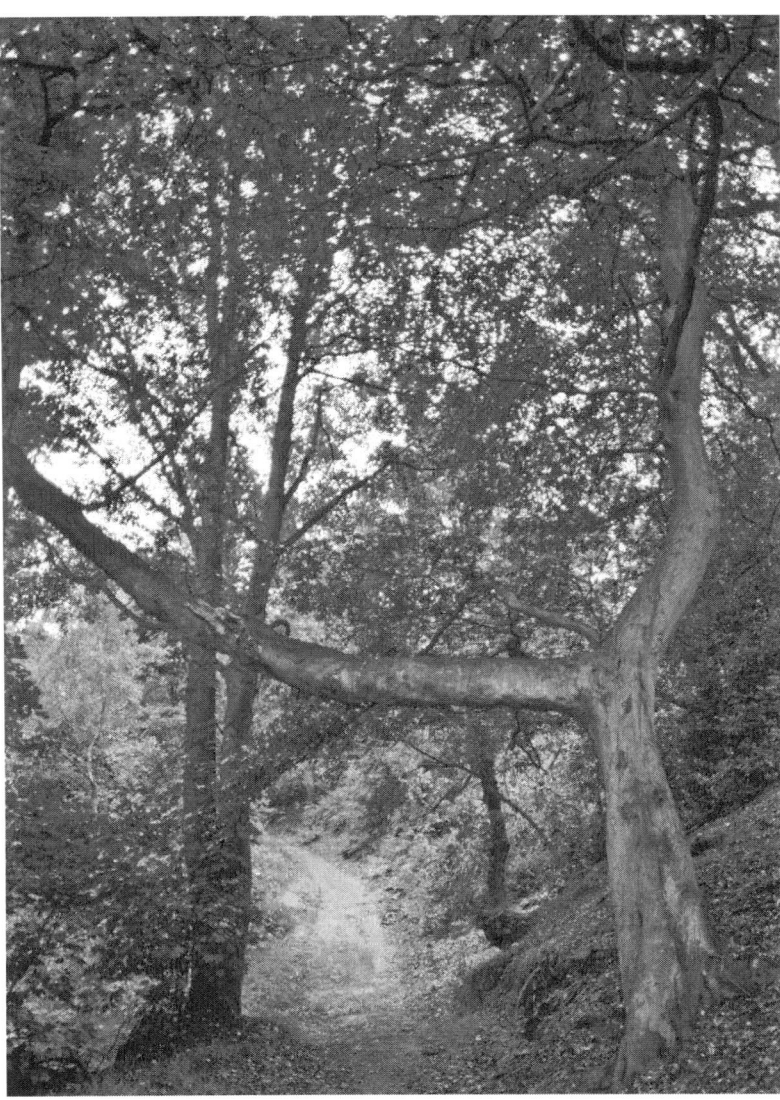

Figure 10.6. Hornbeam (*Carpinus betulus*), right, in Clockhouse Wood.

Photograph Sean Edwards.

so that its presence on Alderley Edge is not to be expected. It is not a typical woodland tree in the north-west, being most abundant in parts of southern and eastern England. One mature individual is in the mixed oak woodland north of Clockhouse Farm (SJ 8668 7795), in what appears to be the oldest and least disturbed patch of woodland (Figure 10.6).

Horse chestnut, Aesculus hippocastanum

Fourteen mature horse chestnut trees were recorded, most of which were found in the central and densest part of the woodlands, such as in parcels 10b (to the east of Church Quarry), 10a (Old Alderley Quarry), 9 (Canyon Mine) and the southern part of 2a (above Holy Well). Horse

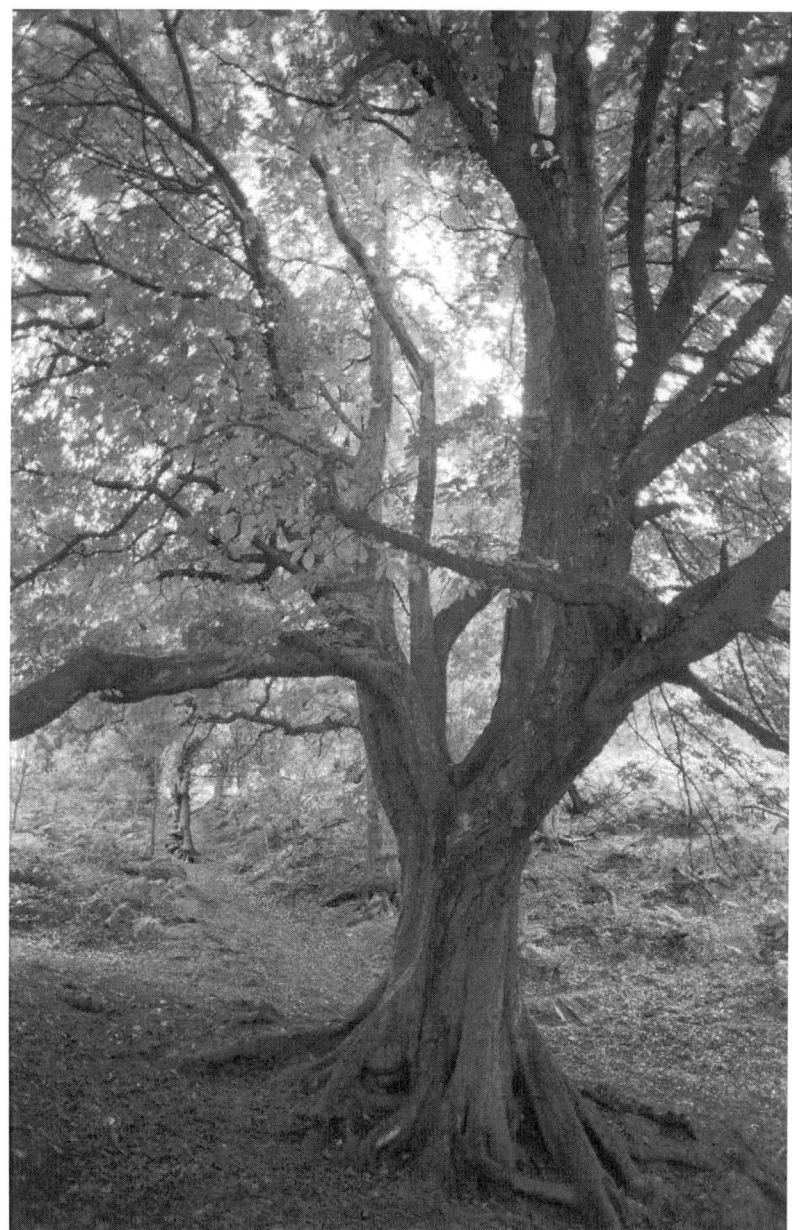

Figure 10.7. The broad boughs and low canopy of an old horse chestnut tree (*Aesculus hippo-castanum*) in Dickens Wood, growing close to one of the many ancient tracks which criss-cross the Edge.

Photograph Sean Edwards.

chestnuts thrive in open wooded or garden environments where the canopy can spread, but are rarely found on field boundaries in the core area. The mid-wood location probably reflects 'fill-in' planting to replace fallen or removed trees of other species (Figure 10.7). The early flowering and leaf budding of the chestnut gives this tree an advantage over the otherwise dominant beech and oak, both of which bud up to a month later. A few trees are probably more than seventy to eighty years old.

Larch, Larix *spp.*

Mature larch trees are scattered throughout the central woodland, commonly associated with Scots pine; some appear to have been planted to replace the Scots pine. Before the bequest of the woodlands to the National Trust, larch would almost certainly have been planted as a cash crop or as windbreaks. Good stands of large trees grow on the east of Waterfall Wood, among conifers (SJ 865 777), and there are many mature specimens, some more than 2 m in girth, in Dickens Wood, below Stormy Point and to the west of Waterfall Wood (parcels 3a and 4).

Lime, Tilia *spp.*

Lime trees are rare. Only four mature examples were recorded, although there are probably more young saplings. In the old roadside quarry east of Mottram Wood they are associated with younger sycamore (SJ 853 772).

Oak, Quercus robur

This is the commonest species present (1,675 mature trees), some large examples being among the oldest inhabitants of the woodland. The main concentrations of mature trees are to be found in Clockhouse Wood (200–300 trees), in Dickens Wood between the Beacon and Castle Rock (e.g. in SJ 858 778), on Glaze Hill ridge (known as 'Oak Hill' in 1787) (SJ 860 771) and the west end of Windmill Wood (SJ 855 775). In dense slope woodland there is usually natural regeneration from seed. Old oaks on the top of the escarpment, for example on the wind-exposed ridge of Glaze Hill between Stormy Point and Saddlebole, are stunted compared with those on the slopes, particularly where the latter compete for light with the higher beech canopy.

The oldest oaks probably grow along the hedge lines of earlier field boundaries, such as those drawn on the 1787 Crossley map (e.g. Figure 19.9). Many of these were banks, ditches or paths associated with still older enclosures. One example is a field boundary and ditch forming the current boundary between parcels 20b and 20a/21b (at SJ 854 777). Some ancient gnarled and leaning specimens, at least one of which is fully hollow, are all that survives of an ancient hedgerow (Figure 10.8). These trees are likely to have been present at the time of the 1787 map, and one or two may be at least 300–400 years old. An avenue of trees shown on this plan lining the Macclesfield Road between the Wizard and Castle Rock, as well as groups of hedgerow trees at the margins of Higher and Lower Riddings at Brynlow, survive today as ancient field oaks, although none of them is the age of the field boundary to the south of Armstrong Farm.

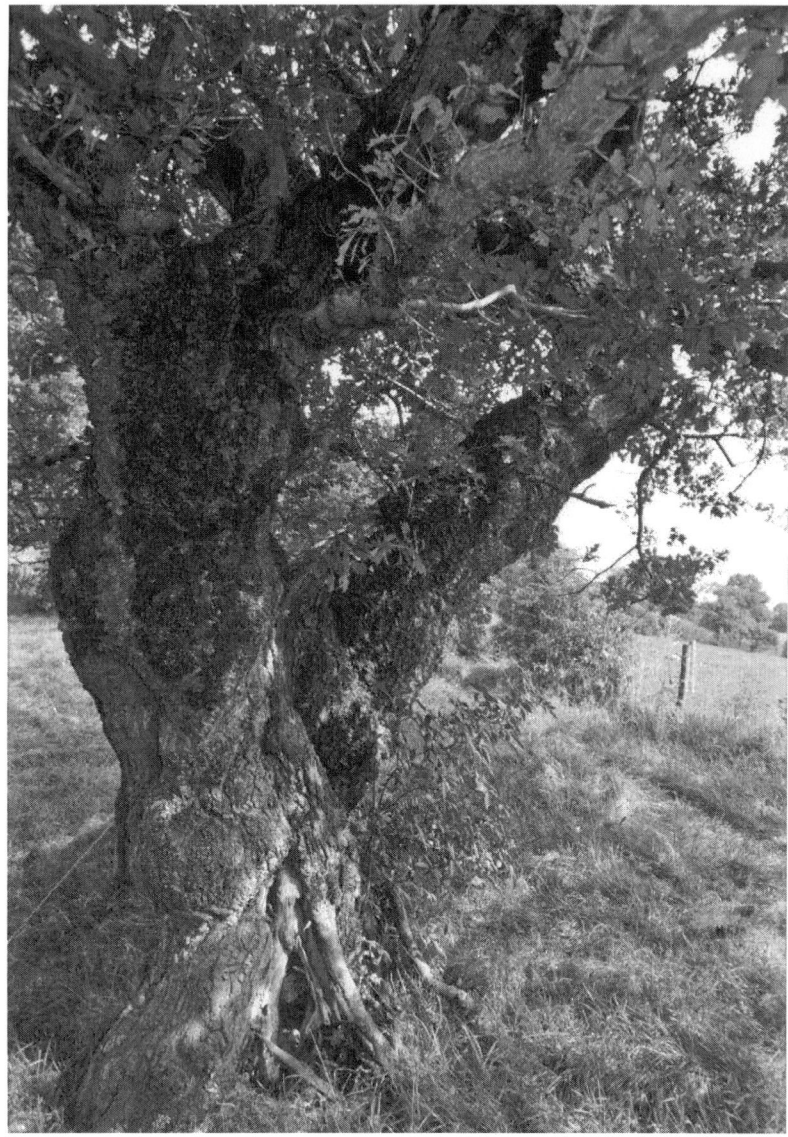

Figure 10.8. An ancient oak (*Quercus robur*) with split trunk and hollow fork by a footpath near Armstrong Farm – all that remains of an eighteenth-century hedgerow.

Photograph Sean Edwards.

Poplar, Populus *spp.*

The hybrid referred to as the Railway Poplar (*Populus* × *canadensis* 'Regenerata') is a variety of the Black Poplar, so-called because of its habit of colonising railway embankments. There is a local form referred to as the Alderley Poplar (*Populus* × *canadensis* 'Alderley'), to be found on the lands of the old Stanley estate to the south of Alderley Edge. It was planted by the Stanleys on their estate farms, and examples are to be found down Bradford and Hocker Lanes and on the floor of the valley followed by Artists Lane, between the Butts Farm and Alderley

Cross. These trees prefer open field valley or damp sites, and do better at such locations even when planted. Standing on their own they form distinctive landmark features, which is probably why the Stanleys chose them during their landscape improvements in the last century. Richard Mabey (1996) refers to the distinctive Black Poplars of Alderley Edge whose bark 'for once, merits the description "black"'. No trees were found either in or around the edges of the woodland of the core area, although four mature individuals were recorded on its south-western margin. These included several close to the old mill pond above the Topps (SJ 850 771) and one within the area of old enclosed fields, on the field bank of Higher Riddings (SJ 8542 7735). A typical example can be seen in the middle of the valley down Artists Lane (SJ 846 768) (Figure 10.9).

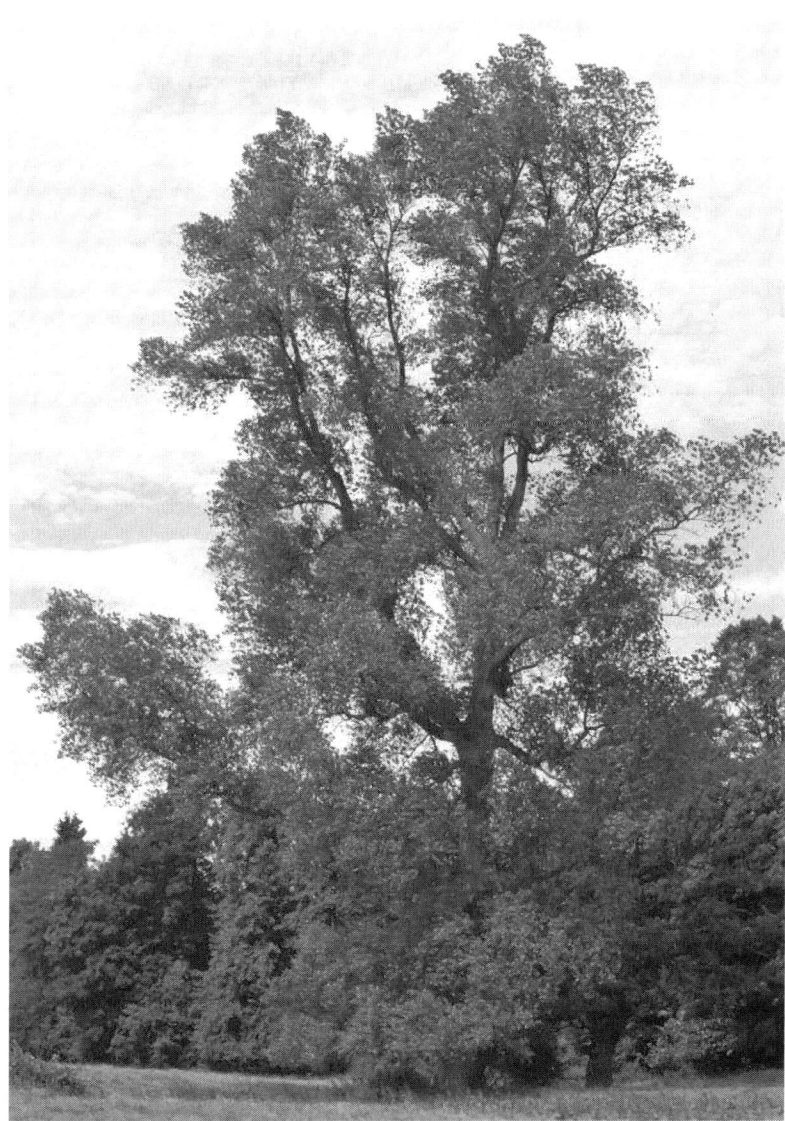

Figure 10.9. One of the 'Alderley poplars' (*Populus × canadensis* 'Alderley') planted by the Stanleys – a landmark tree at the lower end of Artists Lane.

Photograph Sean Edwards.

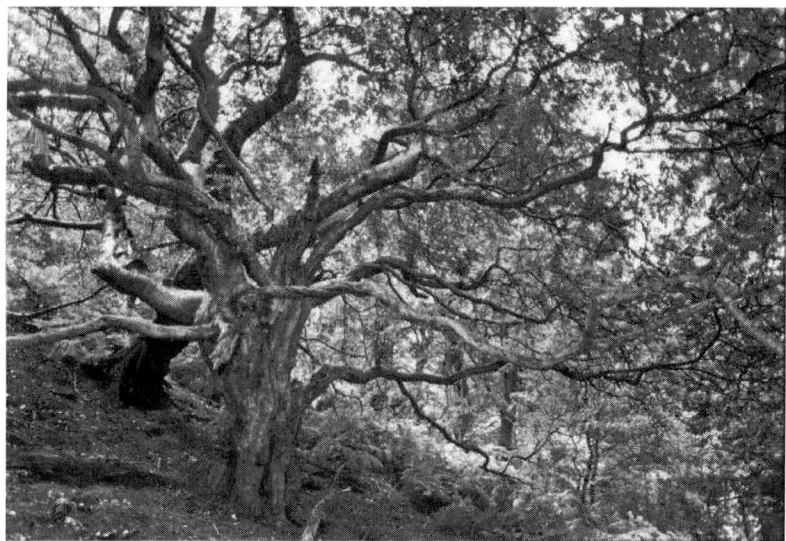

Figure 10.10. Ancient rowan tree (*Sorbus aucuparia*), Clockhouse Wood.

Photograph Sean Edwards.

Rowan, Sorbus aucuparia

The rowan or mountain ash is surprisingly common in some of the mixed birch–oak woodland, in particular in parts of Waterfall Wood, Clockhouse Wood and neighbouring areas (parcels 4, 5, 6a, 6b, 7a). Large examples also occurred in the oak woodland below Wizard's Well (SJ 854 780), on Glaze Hill and below Stormy Point. In all, 157 were recorded, but many more fell below the minimum recording size.

The oldest, many leaning or with split boughs and some having hollow cavities, occurred in or near Clockhouse Wood. A particularly fine example, possibly in excess of 150 years old, is hidden among old oaks and birches in the far north end of the wood (in SJ 865 780) (Figure 10.10). While there is some regeneration, the canopy here is too dense for it to proliferate. Given its fairly even scatter through the oldest oak woodland, it is unlikely that rowan was ever deliberately planted. More probably the berries were distributed by birds, and with birch it may have been a natural coloniser of open heath when it was managed as common land. Rowan probably favoured the valley sides and steeper slopes, with birch on the open heath of the tops.

Scots pine, Pinus sylvestris

Scots pine is perhaps the most visible or noticed tree on the Edge (Figure 10.11), although there are fewer than would be expected, given their domineering presence on the skyline (618 mature trees). There have been few recent replacements, and the majority are large, having a girth of 1.35 m or more.

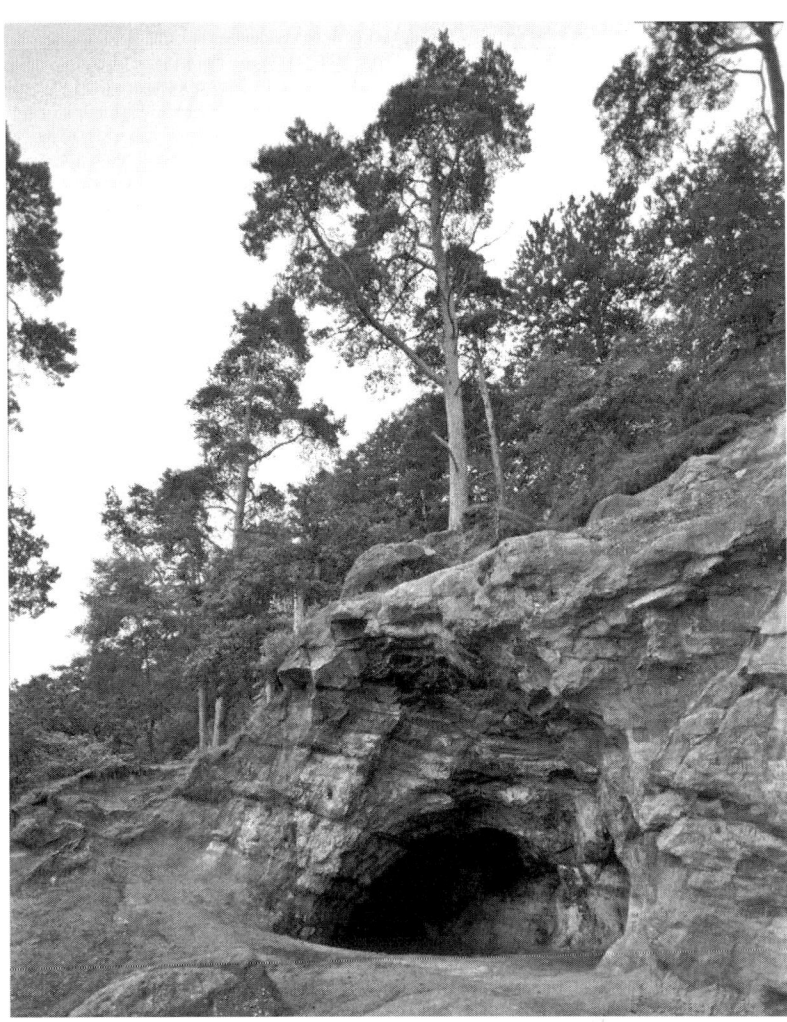

Figure 10.11. Scots pine (*Pinus sylvestris*) behind Pillar Mine.

Photograph Sean Edwards.

The majority of plantings are in the central area of the Edge, with the densest concentration of large mature trees in parcels 10a and 10c, between the Golden Stone and the Old Alderley Quarry. Elsewhere, slightly smaller trees are to be found at the east end of Windmill Wood, with other important concentrations below Saddlebole (SJ 859 779) overlooking the Hough, and on the slopes below Pillar Mine and Stormy Point. The latter two sites form the pine-covered ridge seen when approaching the Edge from the north (Wilmslow and Alderley) and east (Mottram St Andrew). Many of these plantings are distinctively landscaped, and in some cases have not changed since the end of the eighteenth century. The habitat of the pine woods, as typified by the area north of Engine Vein, is very different from that of the oak and birch woodland. In places the woodland floor has a bramble and fern undergrowth, but it usually lacks an understorey of younger trees.

In a number of landscape plantings, the ground is uneven due to the presence of un-rotted tree stumps or boles just below the surface of the soil, many of which appear to be of Scots pine (e.g. at 'Seven Firs', where the remains of seven old trees survive as low mounds). Some stumps may be over 200 years old, although it is doubtful whether the living pines themselves are of this age. A few may be a century old or more. Many of those clinging to the rock edge on the escarpment are shallow-rooted and have suffered a good deal from recent soil erosion.

Sweet chestnut, Castanea sativa

Sweet chestnut (also known as Spanish chestnut) is to be found scattered throughout the woodland on the Edge. It is considerably more common (122 trees) than its non-edible counterpart the horse chestnut, and a

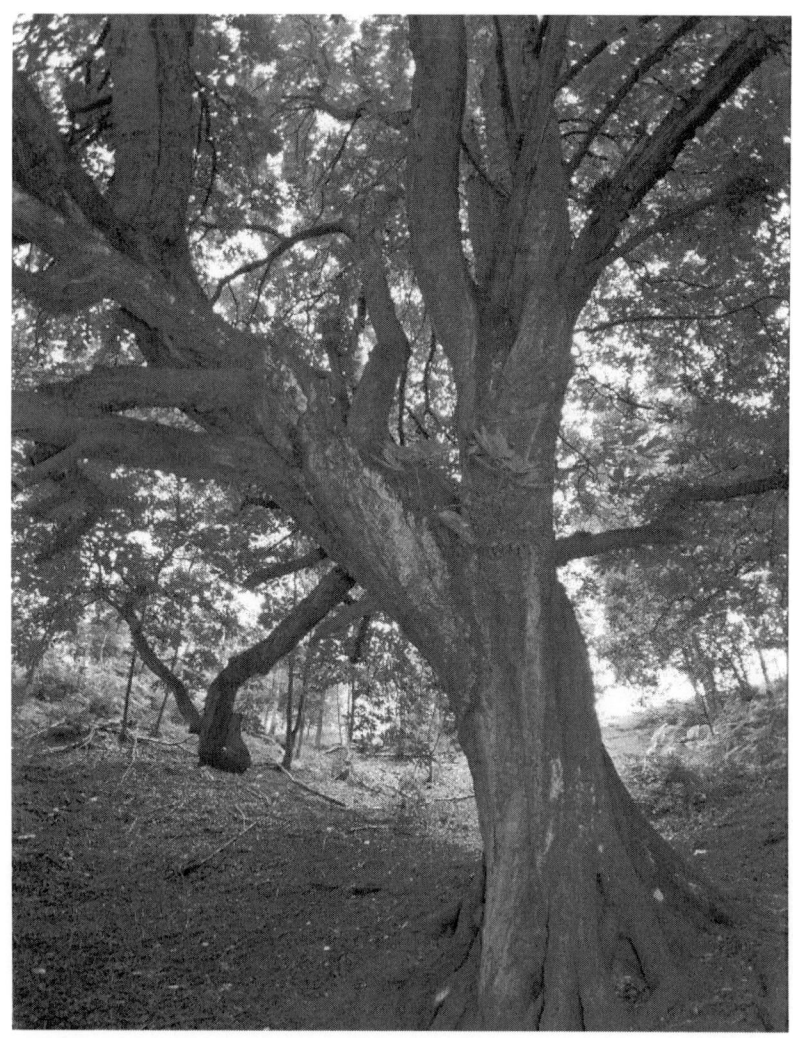

Figure 10.12. Old sweet chestnut (*Castanea sativa*), Clockhouse Wood.

Photograph Sean Edwards.

few ancient-looking individuals, such as the gnarled and contorted specimen 3.5–4 m in girth recorded from the north end of Clockhouse Wood (SJ 8657 7797), may be among the oldest surviving woodland trees on the Edge (Figure 10.12).

In many cases the sweet chestnut is associated with old birch woodland. There are mature trees on both sides of the core area. They often occur in groups, such as those found near the Beacon (SJ 8583 7777), in Finlow Wood (SJ 860 770) and in the wood south of Bradford Lodge Farm (parcel 16; SJ 858 769). Some (up to sixty or seventy years in age) show unmistakable signs of coppicing (Figure 10.13). Younger plantings are to be found in Windmill Wood and in other specific locations, such as in the small roadside quarry to the south of Topps Mill (SJ 850 770).

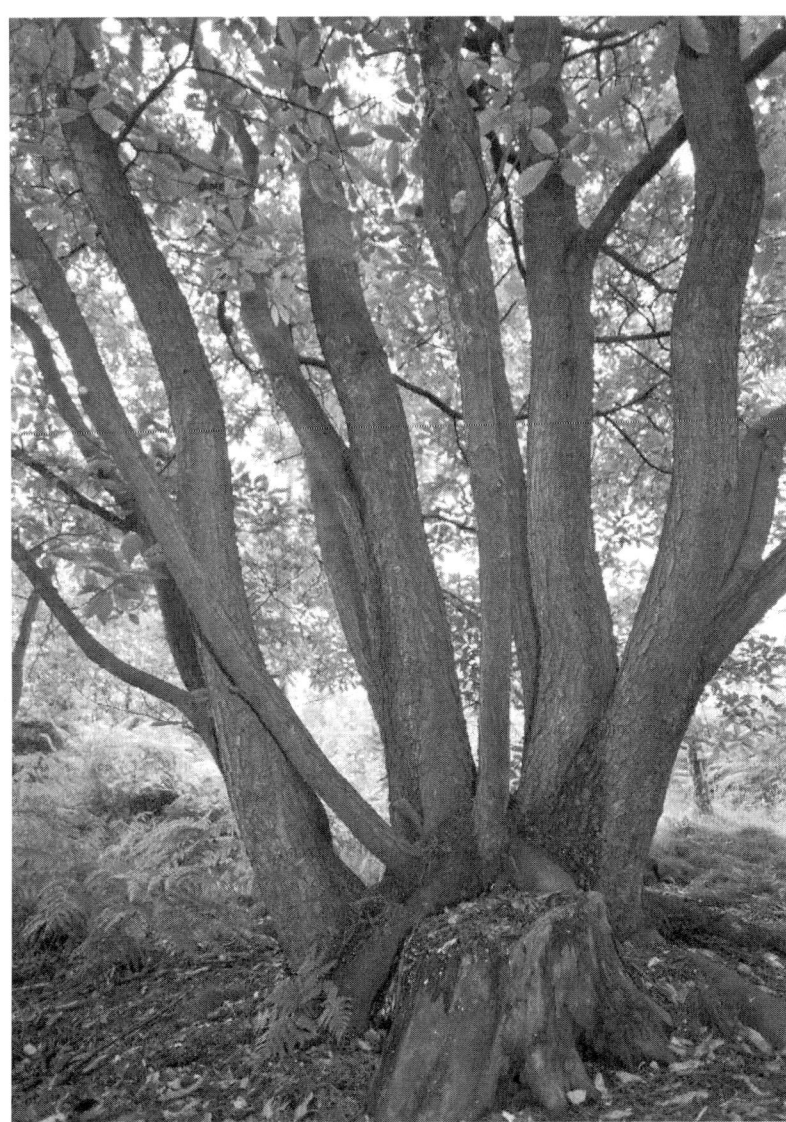

Figure 10.13. Sweet chestnut (*Castanea sativa*) regenerated from coppice.

Photograph Sean Edwards.

Sycamore, Acer pseudoplatanus

The sycamore is not uncommon (346 mature trees), although it has probably never been encouraged. It is opportunistic and grows quickly to fill clearings in the woods in the absence of replacement planting. The mosaic growth is particularly noticeable in some ancient beech woods such as Mottram Wood (e.g. at SJ 8516 7827). To a lesser extent it can be seen in some of the semi-naturalised oak woods, such as the old clearings on higher ground in parcel 6a, at the north ends of Clockhouse and Waterfall Woods (e.g. SJ 8656 7717). Mature sycamores in the latter area, some of which may be forty to fifty years old, have recently been felled to allow oak to regenerate once more.

More than sixty mature sycamores are scattered through the ancient beech wood in the Brynlow valley (Artists Lane), possibly one of the largest accumulations in the National Trust woodland. In this case some may have been planted forty to fifty years ago to provide quick-growing replacements for fallen beeches.

Willow, Salix *spp.*

No more than half a dozen mature trees (> 1.35 m in girth) were recorded from the core area. At least four are in damp areas of recently disturbed ground in the West Mine area, near the site of the Miners' Cottages in the Hagg (SJ 8538 7746). Younger saplings are common in this area, around the site of the Wood Mine Engine House, and elsewhere on the Edge on the margins of some of the marlpits where the soil is damper and more clay-rich. Willow is more or less unknown in the woods.

Yew, Taxus baccata

Yew is comparatively rare on the Edge (fifteen trees) and there appear to be no examples of ancient or even perceptibly old trees growing in the woodland itself. Some of the small trees or bushes found in the heart of the woods may have been seeded from berries brought in by birds. However, the two small trees growing on the rocks above Holy Well (SJ 8592 7785) suggest deliberate planting. At least one of them has been there for more than sixty years (Alan Garner, personal communication).

The oldest yew tree in the boundary of the core area is at the south end of Clockhouse Farmhouse. It is a female tree with a central trunk of less than 2 m in girth. A photograph of the farmhouse taken around 1900 shows it only marginally smaller than it appears today, which seems to imply that the tree is more than 300 years old (Figures 10.14, 10.15). As to its origins, the farmer incumbent at the time of the survey, Malcolm Eley, reported only that it was planted on the south side in order 'to

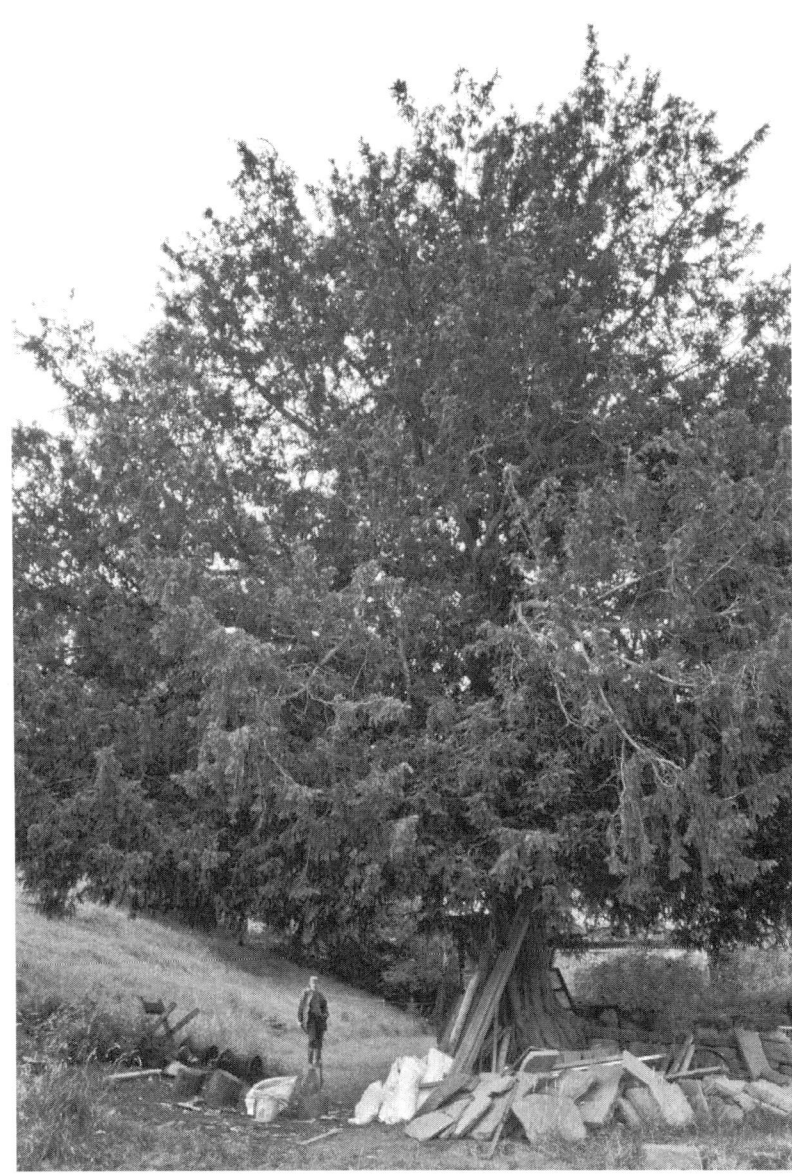

Figure 10.14. Yew tree (*Taxus baccata*), Clockhouse Farm, August 1997.

Photograph Sean Edwards.

ward off evil spirits' and to protect the farm. In previous years its foliage was pruned to prevent the cattle grazing on it and taking its poisonous berries. In living memory it has been well cared for and protected.

Some characteristics of the woodland trees

It was possible to use the survey information to map the distribution of trees under headings such as 'old trees', 'tall trees', 'broad canopy trees', 'healthy/leaning trees', 'diseased trees', 'felled trees and tree stumps'

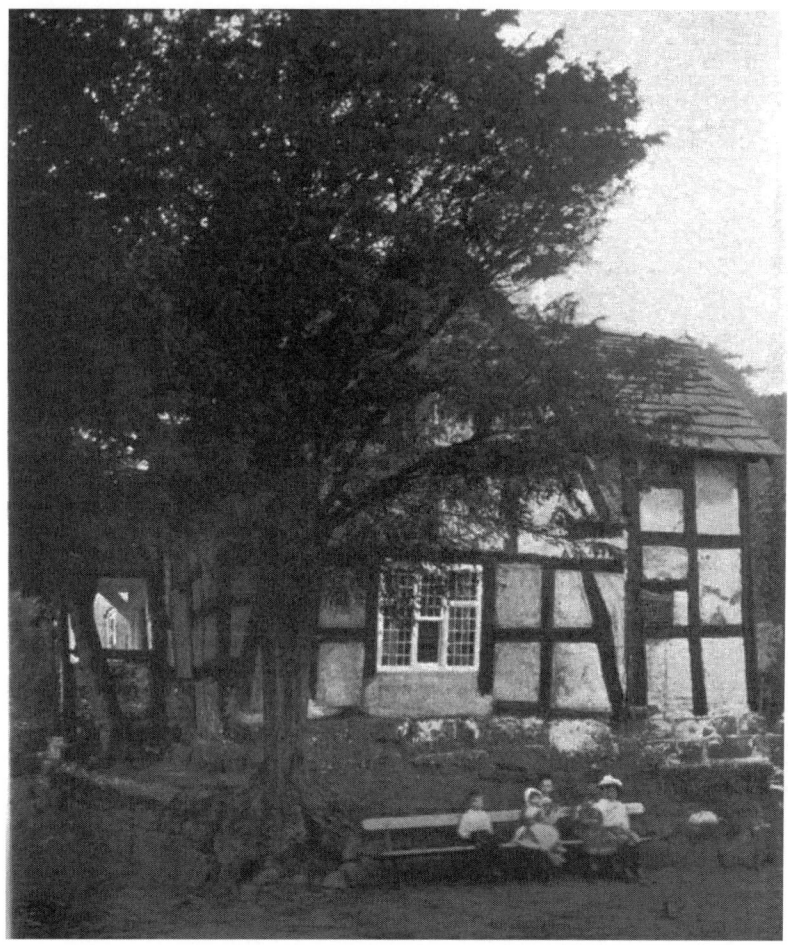

Figure 10.15. Photograph of the yew tree shown in Figure 10.14 taken *c.* 1900.

From Moss (1903).

and 'pruned and coppiced trees': such thematic mapping should help in planning future woodland management. The information gleaned from these maps about the distribution and dates of graffiti cut into the trees really forms part of the social history of the Edge, and so is discussed in Chapter 22.

In terms of age, one can say that trees with a girth of 2.5 m or more are likely to be a century old or more. However, rate of growth or trunk increment per year is difficult to gauge. Growth rate varies between individual trees and is strongly affected by location. Growth rate also varies between different tree species, so that a fast-growing sycamore, for example, cannot be compared easily with a yew tree. Whatever the exact yardstick, we can be certain that, in relative terms, the plotting in Figure 10.16 shows the distribution pattern of the *oldest* trees or *earliest surviving* plantings on the Edge.

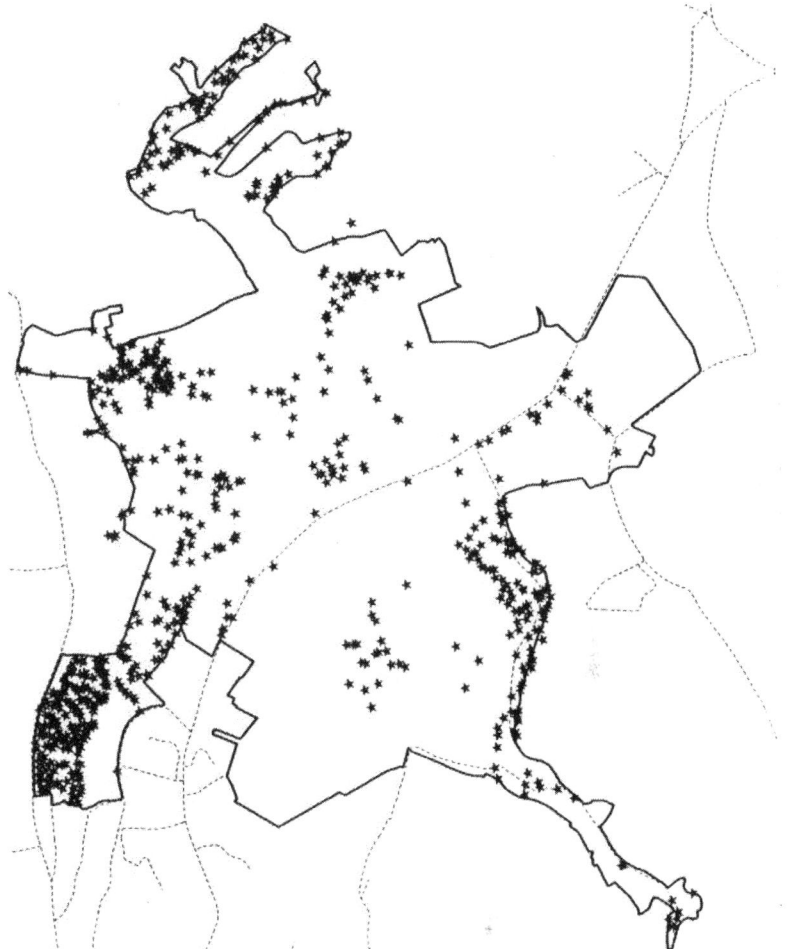

Figure 10.16. Map of old trees (i.e. those with a girth > 2.5 m) in the core area.

Based on the 1992 Ordnance Survey 1:25,000 Pathfinder map, sheet 759, with the permission of the Controller of Her Majesty's Stationery Office, Crown copyright October 2013.

The clearest correlation between age and tree type is to be found in the ancient beech wood, notably the whole of Mottram Wood (parcel 1a), the Beacon plantation, the eastern slopes of Glaze Hill and Saddlebole, and much of Brynlow valley. The large trees scattered diffusely over the central part of the Edge turn out almost without exception to be oaks. Perhaps the most interesting pattern to emerge is the outline of old field boundaries or roads indicated by the older field oaks. The outlines of old field boundaries (House Field, Bent Field, Low Meadow, Higher Meadow) become evident in the Hough (parcel 30), as well as in the central part of the Edge (e.g. the 1787 boundary between Church Quarry and the west end of Engine Vein in SJ 859 774). The disused routes of the 1775 Brynlow Lane (SJ 859 771), Bradford Lane and Old Hall Road, and the Macclesfield Road as far as the Wizard can be determined in the same way.

The oldest Scots pines are also the tallest (more than 20 m in height). This association of age and height also operates for beech, and to a lesser extent oak, particularly in the central part of the Edge. In the outlying areas, where competition from beech or pine is not so strong, other species such as sycamore rapidly grow as tall.

The distribution of broad-canopy trees (>15 m in width) is more difficult to interpret, but field oaks at least (i.e. mature oak trees in more open woodland situations) tend to be broad. This is true of the oaks at the west end of Windmill Wood (the Hagg) (SJ 853/854 775), Thieves Hollow (SJ 860 773), Saddlebole ridge, Wizard's Well and across the central part of the Edge. The outline of Old Alderley Quarry can also be seen in this distribution, as well as many of the older field boundaries. Roadside avenues of mature oaks show up well, such as the plantings on either side of the Macclesfield Road. In some areas, such as along Artists Lane, ancient beech trees form wide leaf canopies. Elsewhere, for example in Mottram beech wood, the trees are relatively closely spaced and correspondingly constricted.

In some parts of the woodland there are large numbers of still healthy but leaning or part-fallen trees; old and tall trees are often overcrowded and form a hazard on steep valley sides. This pattern may be seen on the edges of Waterfall Wood and parts of Clockhouse Wood, on the steep and shallow soil-covered slopes of Saddlebole, in Dickens Wood below Wizard's Well and throughout much of Mottram Wood. In the last, the collapse of dead beech trees from up-slope has affected the growth of healthy trees below. The highest incidence of tree-lean is to be found in the mixed birch/oak woodland on the north-western slope of Saddlebole. Few of these trees are more than 20 m high, but the woodland here is relatively unmanaged and overcrowded. The inherent lean and awkward angles of these trees may have something to do with competition for light.

Disease in trees, identifiable through the presence of plant galls (including witches' broom), canker (Figure 10.17), wood rot and loss of bark, was detected in some 140 individuals throughout the core area. The highest incidence of disease was found in the mixed oak woodland of parcels 6a and 7a (Clockhouse Wood). It was rare in the woodland to the west of the Macclesfield Road, while isolated pockets of diseased trees appear around the Beacon, at Saddlebole and in the south end of Waterfall Wood. Mottram Wood appears to be the most diseased area of ancient beech woodland. This may indicate stress from overcrowding, as well as the presence of many old trees nearing the end of their active growing lives. The surviving beeches in Brynlow Wood seem quite healthy by comparison.

Tree stumps survive from a wide range of dates. They usually indicate felling but may result from natural decay, tree-fall, wind-blow

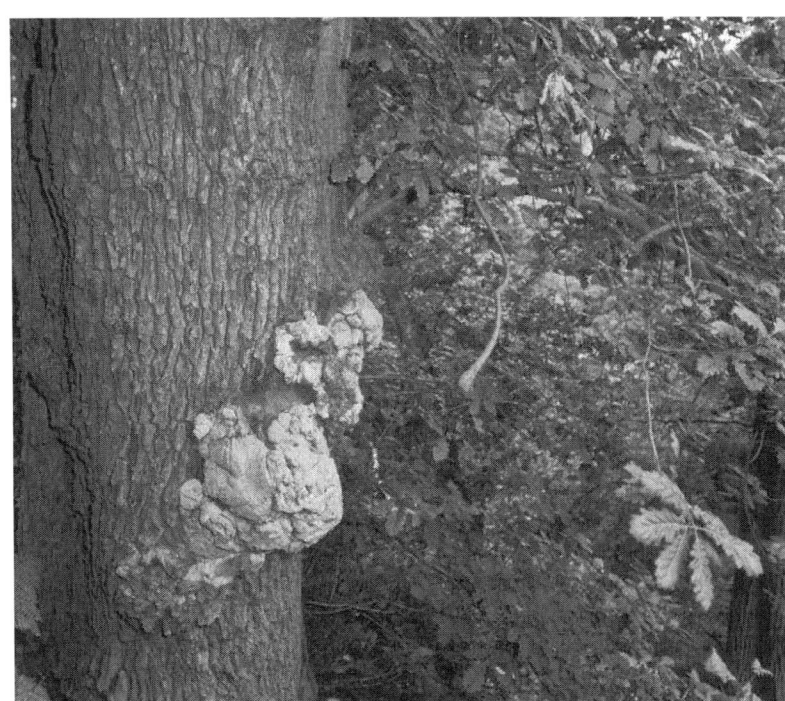

Figure 10.17. Canker on the trunk of an old oak tree (*Quercus robur*) in Waterfall Wood.

Photograph Sean Edwards.

and the like. The evidence from Brynlow Wood appears to show recent felling at its eastern end (of more than twenty-five trees, some of them sycamores) but with the suggestion of former management or death of some of the larger beeches, particularly those of the beech avenue on the south side of Artists Lane. Similarly, Mottram Wood shows evidence for much more felling or tree-fall in the past. The correlation between stumps and the detection of felling operations in Clockhouse Wood is good, confirming that most if not all the management here was recent.

As with the record of felling, the survey provides useful geographical data on recent woodland management. Pruning is much more common than coppicing. There is evidence for pruning both in the woodland itself and along the surrounding field margins. An example can be traced in a curved line between Thieves Hollow (SJ 860 57733) and Edge House Farm (SJ 8626 7735). Pruning of the large oaks either side of the Macclesfield Road was probably carried out by the local authority. Bridleways in the woodland have been pruned, for instance around the edge of Old Alderley Quarry to Stormy Point (SJ 860 777). National Trust pruning work aimed at reducing the risk of falling limbs or branches from partly dead trees is to be seen in Mottram Wood, and to a lesser extent in Brynlow Wood and the western end of Windmill Wood.

Trees of note in the core and hinterland areas of Alderley Edge

The Butts Oak (SJ 8484 7685) (Figure 10.18)

This is an old oak of unusually wide girth, located in the corner of a field at the point at which the track to the Butts Farm meets Artists Lane. Its trunk, though solid, proved to be more than 6 m in girth, and it is thus among the largest oaks in east Cheshire, and possibly upwards of 400 years old.

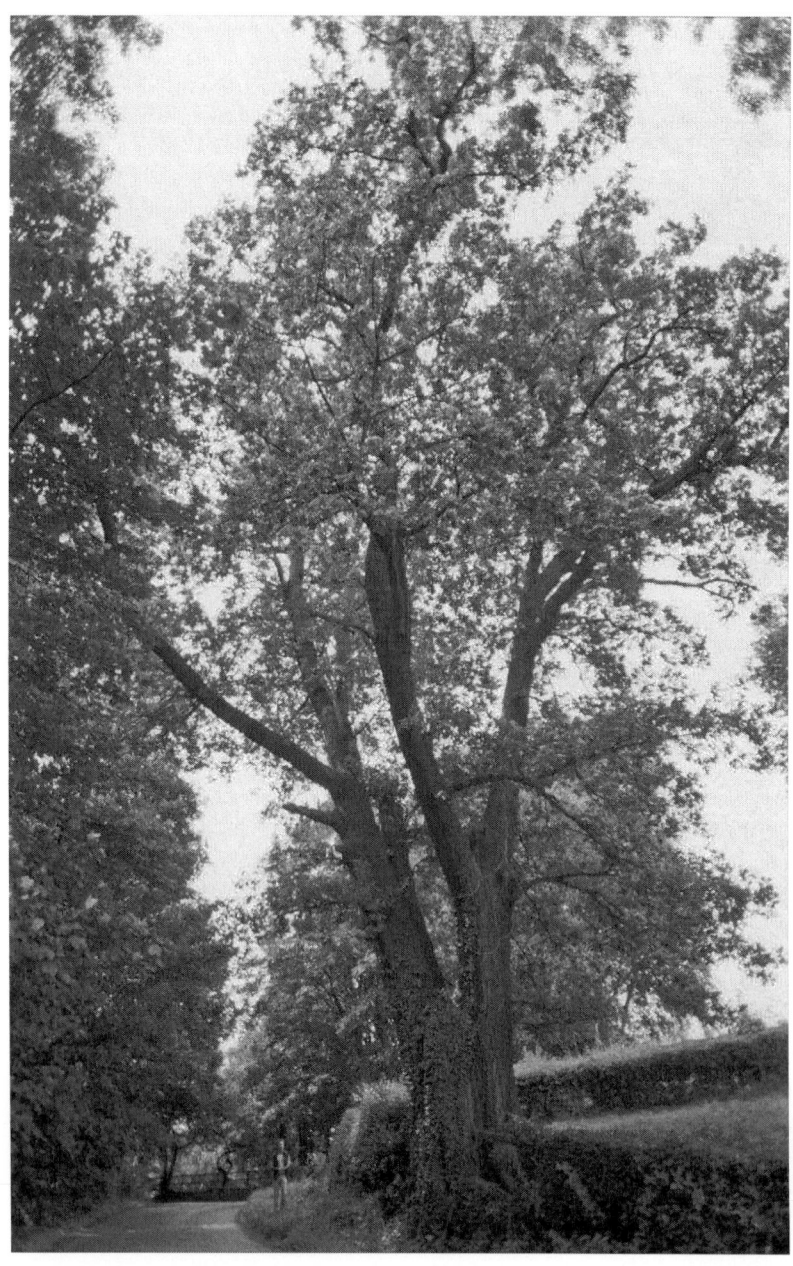

Figure 10.18. The Butts Oak, Butts Farm.

Photograph Sean Edwards.

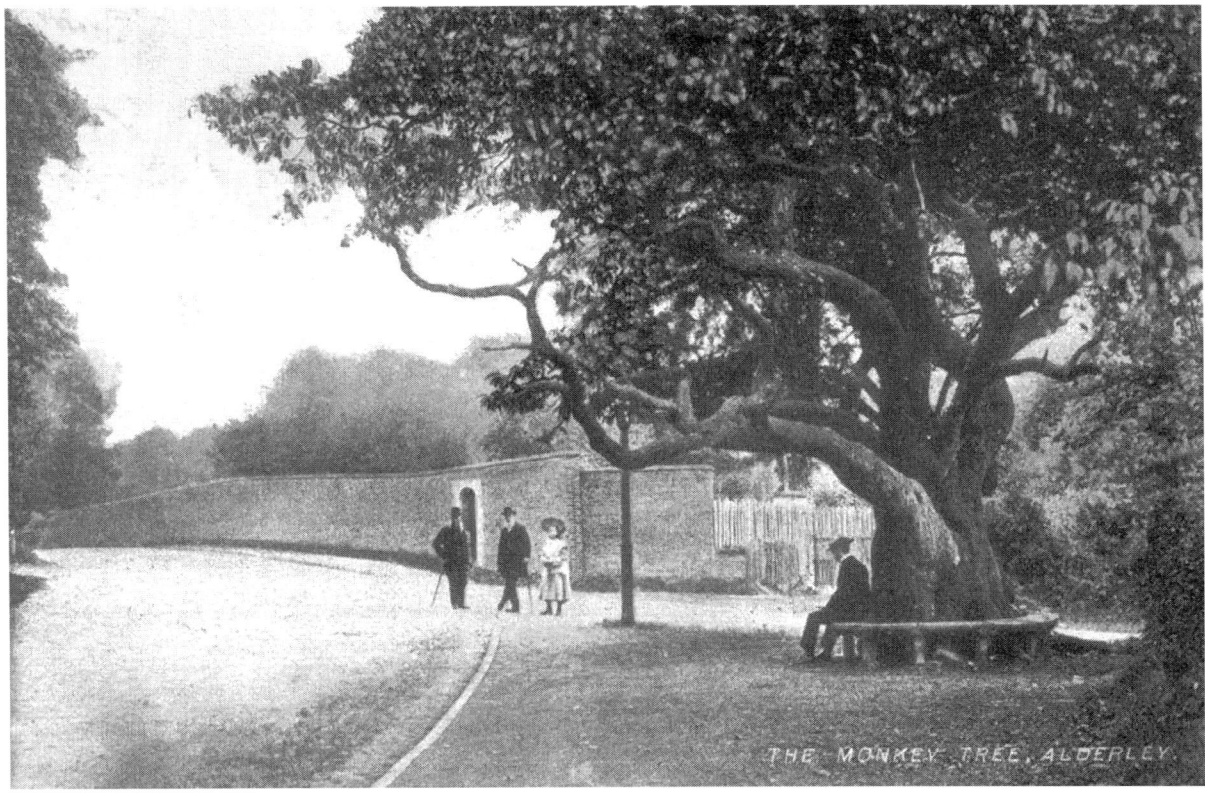

Figure 10.19. The Monkey Tree, Sand Lane.

From a series of postcards collected by Miss Jenny Simpson, who was in service in Cheshire before the First World War, and lent to the Project by her grand-daughter, Mrs Sheila Mackey.

The Monkey Tree Sand Lane, Nether Alderley (SJ 843 763)
(Figure 10.19)

A sweet chestnut has stood at the corner of Sand Lane and the Congleton Road for several hundred years. The tree is still alive, although the top part of the trunk is dead and it has been heavily pruned in the past. It lives on, bathed in diesel fumes and shaken by traffic from the adjacent main road, the former A34. A wooden bench has surrounded it for longer than anyone can remember. The origin of the tree's name remains a mystery, although the tradition that it is frequented by courting couples may have something to do with it. While we cannot be sure that it is marked on the Crossley map of 1787, the spot marks an important junction: it was once the point where four roads met around the entrance to the Old Hall at the north end of Alderley Park, and it seems quite possible that the tree was planted at or before this time.

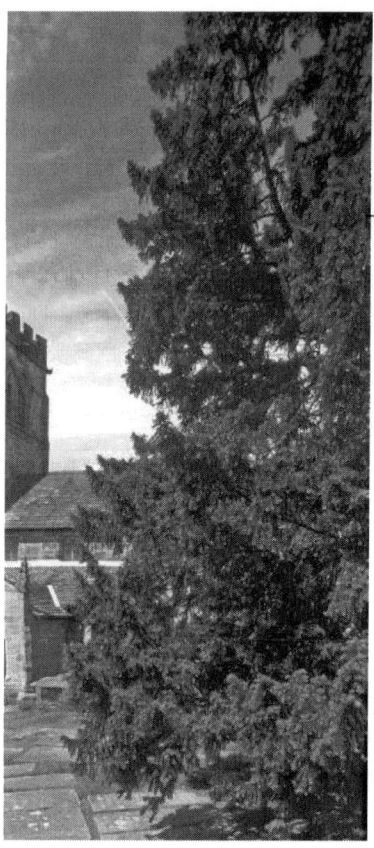

Figure 10.20. Ancient yew (*Taxus baccata*), Nether Alderley Church.
Photograph Sean Edwards.

The Nether Alderley Yew Nether Alderley Church (SJ 842 761) (Figure 10.20)

A healthy looking and reputedly ancient yew tree is to be found in the south-east end of Nether Alderley churchyard. Although it has not been dated scientifically, specialists from the Conservation Foundation in London reckon the tree to be more than 1,000 years old, suggesting that it pre-dates the current church building (*c.* 1300 AD) by at least 300 years (Brian Hobson, personal communication). If the yew had already been planted at the time of the church's foundation, this would give support to the theory that there was a much earlier Saxon church at the site. In the later nineteenth century, several yews sprouting from the base of the main trunk were transplanted to the back of the church.

The Waterloo Tree Old Rectory, Nether Alderley (SJ 843 762)

A rhododendron tree growing in the garden at the back of the Old Rectory, next to Nether Alderley church, is known as 'the Waterloo

Tree', reputedly having been planted in 1817 to commemorate the Battle of Waterloo (N. Hamilton, personal communication). If this is true, then the tree is of historic importance, since rhododendrons were first introduced into this country only two years before.

Many of the old trees surrounding Nether Alderley Church were recorded as part of the current survey, including those in the Rector's Plantation, whose planting was recorded in some detail by the Reverend Edward Stanley in the 1820s.

Birds and trees

The trees that grow on the Edge, large or small and old or young, do of course have an important role in sustaining and sheltering its bird life; this is an aspect we explore a little further in the next chapter.

Further reading

Johnson, O. (illus. More, D.). 2006. *Collins Tree Guide*. London: Collins.
Sterry, P. 2007. *Collins Complete Guide to British Trees*. London: Collins.

11

The birds of Alderley Edge

Jonathan Guest, M. V. Hounsome and Edward Stanley
with John Adams, Alan Straw and Henry McGhie

The zoologists who formed part of the team investigating the flora and fauna of the Edge had an interest in trees as a habitat for birds, and in Chapter 9 we describe the rationale and methodology of the botanical survey, which included trees, while Chapter 10 reports the results of that and other surveys in relation specifically to the trees. The second section of the present chapter, 'Birds and trees', by M. V. Hounsome, reports the results and conclusions of survey work on birds carried out mainly during the winters of 1996–97 and 1997–98. Copies of the detailed results of this survey were lodged at Manchester Museum and with the National Trust. However, it requires more than one or two seasons and more intensive study than the resources of the Alderley Edge Landscape Project (AELP) could spare to produce a proper account of the birds of Alderley: the first section, contributed by Jonathan Guest, therefore sets the scene with a review of the breeding birds of the Edge over the past 100 years or so. The next part of the chapter takes the story back to the earlier part of the nineteenth century, with a reprint of the sections on Alderley from Edward Stanley's *A Familiar History of Birds*, first published in 1835. Local results of Cheshire-wide breeding bird surveys in 1978–84 and 2004–06 are summarised in Appendix 11.1. The chapter concludes with 'Alderley: a bird and iron bottle', a nineteenth-century tale of marital jealousy and haunting, in which Stanley appears in another guise, that of an exorcist, in the strange tale of the iron bottle – still perhaps safely located at the bottom of Radnor Mere in Alderley Park, with its ghostly spirit only occasionally released as a small bird. It is taken (with slight adaptation) from Peter Portland, *Around Haunted Manchester* (Purley: AMCD Books, 2002).

A century of change

Jonathan Guest

Following prehistoric clearance of woodland and up until the eighteenth century, when trees were first planted on the Edge, the sandy soils over the escarpment would have supported a heathland vegetation of wiry grasses and gorse, interspersed with patches of turf closely grazed by cattle, sheep and rabbits. Further tree planting, the cessation of grazing and natural regeneration of trees led to a spread of increasingly dense woodland during the nineteenth and twentieth centuries, with a corresponding loss of heathland. This change from open heathland to closed woodland is mirrored by changes in the avifauna.

The composition of the heathland bird populations prior to the eighteenth century can partly be reconstructed from later evidence. It is fairly certain that species such as the Linnet and Long-tailed Tit, which often nest in gorse, would have been common on the heath. Red-backed Shrikes nested at Alderley in about 1869 (Coward and Oldham, 1910) and may therefore have done so more frequently in the more distant past. Coward and Oldham also named the Edge as a breeding locality for the Long-eared Owl in about 1900. These owls might have nested in clumps of pines, from where they might fly out to hunt over heathland and rough pastures. At this same time, a few pairs of Green Woodpeckers nested. Especially during the summer, this woodpecker feeds largely on the ground, extracting ants and their grubs from their nests in closely grazed turf. The presence of nesting Green Woodpeckers is further evidence of heathland survival at the start of the twentieth century, when one other characteristic inhabitant of heathland, the Nightjar, is known to have nested on the Edge. Norman Abbott plotted three churring birds here in 1919 on his map of singing summer visitors (Guest *et al.*, 1992, on which much of this account is based). At the beginning of the twentieth century, when there were few if any cars and no aircraft to drown the nocturnal chorus of amphibians or birds, Coward heard Nightjars churring from the firs on the Edge as he pedalled back from Chorley Hall to his hotel in Alderley Village (Coward, 1903).

In the absence of grazing, and without the planting of alien tree species such as beech or sweet chestnut, the natural vegetation of the Edge would be woodland composed of oak and birch with rowan and holly. As such, it would resemble woodlands in the Pennine foothills or in the hills of Wales. All these tree species are found among the imported beeches and sweet chestnuts on the Edge. A characteristic assemblage of breeding birds typical of upland oakwoods did in fact occur here into the 1980s. Wood Warblers and Tree Pipits then nested annually, with Redstarts in most years. Pied Flycatchers nested in 1957 and were seen in several other years. Both Wood Warblers and Tree Pipits nest on the ground, here among fern tussocks, wavy hair-grass and leaf-litter. By 1978, when I estimated twelve Wood Warbler territories in the Alderley Woods, it was considered that the trampling of visitors to the Edge might be keeping glades in the woodland sufficiently open to maintain the small breeding population of Tree Pipits but subsequently these have disappeared. The sheer number of human visitors, and especially of their dogs, which sniff out nests at ground level, presumably accounts for the loss of the upland bird fauna. The Redstart and Tree Pipit favour open woodland, often where this grades into heathland or rough pasture. The thickening and maturation of woodland on the Edge during the twentieth century also rendered the habitat less suitable for these species. In addition to these negative influences, migrant birds encounter problems along their migration routes and in their winter quarters, chiefly linked to environmental degradation and agricultural intensification.

The beech is probably not native to Cheshire, at least in recent centuries. It arrived on the Edge by human agency. Beech does not fruit well every year but when it does its mast is sought during the ensuing winter by many bird species, especially Great Tits, Coal Tits and Nuthatches. Bramblings fly in from northern Europe each autumn but only when there is a heavy crop of mast do they appear in flocks under the beeches, as in Artists Lane.

The spread of woodland on the Edge, both as plantation and through natural succession, certainly displaced many bird species but it also allowed others to move in. Perhaps the most striking change in this respect concerns a pair of closely related species, the Willow Warbler and the Chiffchaff. As a nesting species, the Willow Warbler favours tall scrub and young or regenerating woodland. The Chiffchaff, on the other hand, nests in mature woodland, often one with a closed canopy. In 1919 Norman Abbott of Davenport Green mapped singing summer visitors on the Edge. After his death his daughter gave his birdwatching diaries covering the years 1911–30 to the (now defunct) Manchester Ornithological Society, which made the diaries available for the preparation during the 1980s of *The Breeding Bird Atlas of Cheshire and Wirral* under the aegis of the Cheshire Ornithological Association, later superseded by the Cheshire and Wirral Ornithological Society (CAWOS) (Guest *et al.*, 1992). In August 2015 the diaries were held on behalf of CAWOS with the possibility that they will be placed in the long-term care of Cheshire Archives and Local Studies (CALS). Abbott's map (Figure 11.1) shows seventy-seven Willow Warblers but no Chiffchaff. He noted that he had not heard a single Chiffchaff on the Edge all summer. The relative fortunes of the two species have reversed since the middle of the twentieth century as woodlands across the region have matured in the absence of timber extraction and as former heaths and

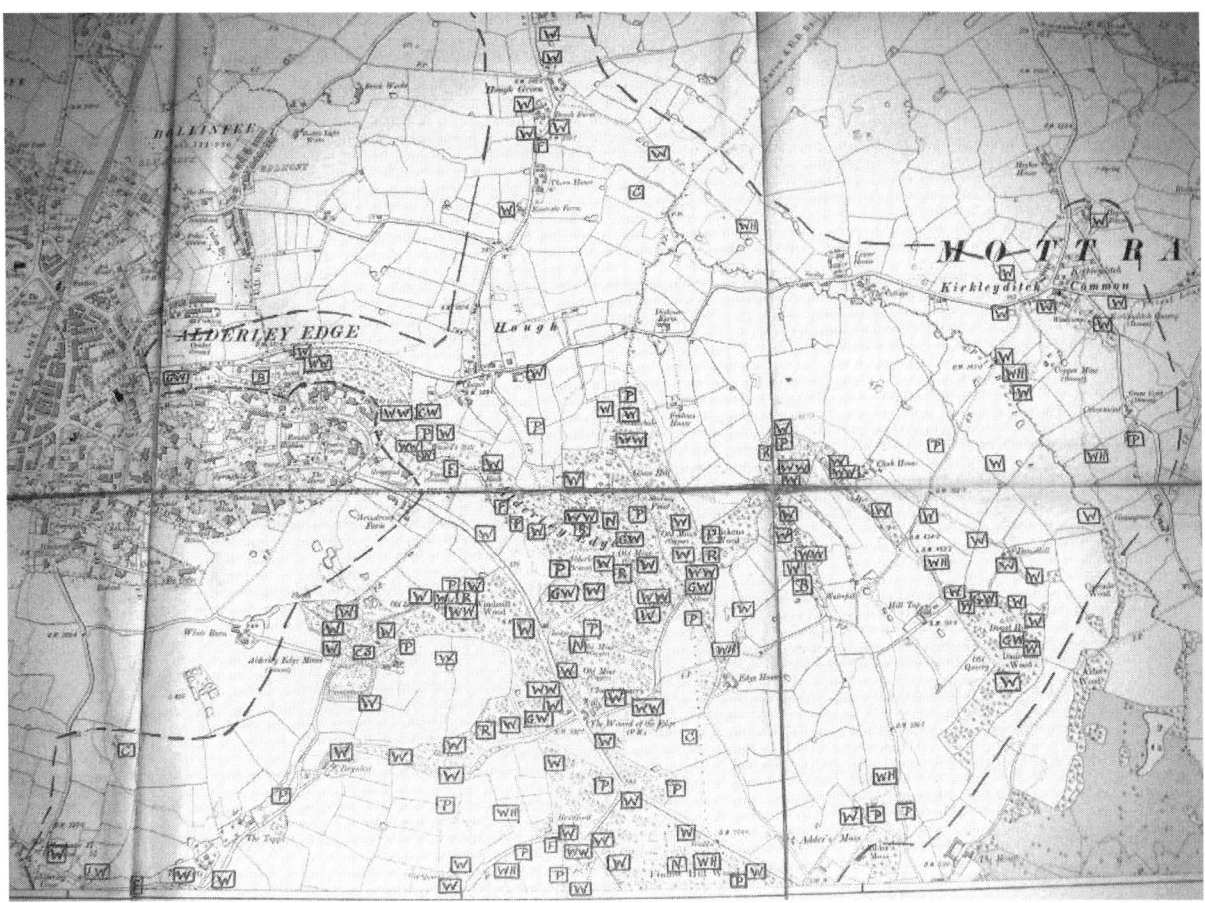

Figure 11.1. Norman Abbott's 1919 map of singing summer visitors on the Edge. B, Blackcap (2); C, Corncrake (3); CS, Common Sandpiper (1); F, Spotted Flycatcher (4); GW, Garden Warbler (8); LW, Lesser Whitethroat (1); N, Nightjar (3); P, Tree Pipit (22); R, Redstart (6); W, Willow Warbler (74); WH, Whitethroat (8); WW, Wood Warbler (14). WN, shown south-east of Clockhouse Wood, was probably a Whinchat (the species was excluded from the key). Note the scarcity of Blackcaps and the absence of Chiffchaffs, inhabitants of closed-canopy woodlands, now the two commonest warbler species in the area.

Abbott diaries held by CALS.

mosslands have become overgrown. The ratio of eight Garden Warblers to one Blackcap in 1919 has also reversed, the former species requiring tall scrub, the latter mature woodland. Another woodland bird that has extended its range as hardwood plantations from the eighteenth and nineteenth centuries have aged is the Nuthatch. A century ago the Nuthatch was absent from eastern Cheshire, spreading into the area during the 1930s and 1940s. Just when it reached Alderley is not known but it was common here by the late 1960s. At that time birds were seen inspecting cavities in a quarried sandstone face and it was suspected that they might adopt this as a nest site, after the fashion of Rock Nuthatches in Mediterranean lands, but this was never proven, although Coal Tits did later nest in such a cavity.

The planting of Scots pine (Scotch fir) and larch from the middle of the eighteenth century allowed a few additional bird species to move onto the Edge, most notably the Coal Tit and Goldcrest. Given that these two species almost invariably nest where conifers grow, both must have been rare in, or absent from, the region as breeding species, the Goldcrest at least occurring primarily in winter. After planting, it took several decades for the trees to mature and it may have taken longer for an associated invertebrate fauna to become established. In 1919 Abbott sought Goldcrests on the Edge throughout the summer but saw none until two in October. The Coal Tit was also scarce a century ago. In recent decades both species have nested frequently.

Despite its name, the Corncrake was primarily an inhabitant of hay meadows. The presence of a calling bird east of the Wizard suggests that at least some of this farmland was then under hay.

One of Norman Abbott's records that would seem inconceivable nowadays was the presence of Common Sandpipers at the West Mine. There were then perhaps shallow pools in an open landscape, reminiscent of certain of the sand quarries around Chelford where Common Sandpipers nested in later decades. A similarly freakish record would be the House Martins prospecting for nest sites under the grassy overhang above a face of exposed sand at Hocker Lane sand quarry in 1980. The West Mine site rapidly developed a cover of vegetation during the 1960s and 1970s. Grasshopper Warblers reeled in some years from the thickets of willowherb and bramble, while Whitethroats sang over the gorse bushes. Later, Willow Warblers increased and Garden Warblers appeared as aspen and other scrub grew taller. In time, this area too may become closed woodland with nesting Blackcaps and Chiffchaffs.

The twentieth century saw great changes in the local landscape, the general trend here, as throughout the region, being one of simplification, with blocks of tall woodland ending abruptly at the edge of farmland. Heath, scrubland and woodland glades are all too scarce.

Birds and trees: AELP survey results

M. V. Hounsome

Trees are usually good indicators of the general environment for birds. For the bird survey, points were chosen central to each of the parcels described in Chapter 8 (see Figure 8.1 and Table 8.1), and all trees within 18 m of each bird recording point were identified and had their girth measured, along with their distances from the central point. The first question to be answered was 'what is a tree'? A moment's thought makes one realise that the question is not straightforward. The definition used in this study was 'a woody plant whose girth at chest height (*c.* 1.3 m) is at least 10 cm and which does not branch lower than this height'. This rules out bushes and tall green plants, but a strict interpretation would also rule out some willows (*Salix* spp.) and rowans (*Sorbus aucuparia*), so a degree of latitude was allowed. Density per hectare, regularity of spacing and uniformity of age were estimated from these measurements. Of the eleven species recorded, birch was the most common, closely followed by rowan. Oak, Scots pine and beech were the other common trees. The overall density of trees in the fourteen parcels where birds were recorded was 461 per hectare, or a tree every 4.7 m. This density varied from 70 per hectare in parcel 3a (Glaze Hill/Dickens Wood North) to 990 in parcel 16 (Bradford Lodge Farm Wood South).

All individual birds detected in the tenths of a hectare around the survey points in four ten-minute periods within a one-hour sample were recorded, together with their estimated distances from the central point. In total, 129 visits were made to fourteen of the core parcels in the winters of 1996/97 and 1997/98. A total of 2,557 birds belonging to twenty-seven species were recorded during this period.

From these data it is possible to estimate the density of each species in each parcel. The methods used for recording trees have been described in the previous chapter; in addition, an index known as Shannon's Diversity was scored for the stands of trees and their associations of birds. This is a measure used in quantitative ecology; the index is high when there are many species, all represented by similar frequencies. It falls as species number goes down and if one or a few species predominate while others are very rare. It is therefore a composite measure of both numbers of species and their relative abundance (Magurran, 1991; see also Cook, 2008).

Parcels varied from having only one species of tree, for example 3a, where they were all beeches, to considerable diversity, as in 11a (Windmill Wood South). In parcel 6a (Waterfall Wood North) forty-two specimens of five species stood within 18 m of the survey point before the larger trees were felled between the two winters of the survey (1997 and 1998). In the year following the felling of the best trees the bird diversity dropped and density fell from 33.1 to 8.4 birds per hectare. Occupancy by birds is affected by tree diversity, and there is now an opportunity to record the changes which take place as this parcel recovers.

None of the bird species recorded was unexpected (even Ravens are now becoming commonplace) and the assemblage was typical of the seasonal patterns of Cheshire wood and farmland. During the winter period, when surveys were carried out, the commonest birds were the tits: the Blue Tit, Great Tit, Long-tailed Tit and Coal Tit, in descending order of abundance, were all at densities of more than 2 per hectare. The Goldcrest, Robin, Treecreeper and Wren occurred at densities of between 1 and 1.2 birds per hectare. There were fewer Coal Tits and Goldcrests than might have been expected considering the abundance of conifers.

Contrary to expectations, there were no meaningful correlations between the tree measurements and bird diversity or density, probably because birds are so mobile. There were, however, correlations between the numbers of the various tree species and the densities of some species of bird. For example, Wrens, Wood Pigeons and Crows were at high densities where there were large numbers of sycamores and willows, but Crow density was negatively correlated with numbers of rowans. Goldcrests and Treecreepers, on the other hand, seemed to like rowans, not Scots pine or larch, as their habits elsewhere would lead one to expect. Treecreepers were also associated with oak, as were Magpies. Song Thrushes were associated with beech, Blue Tits with beech and sycamore. Robins, Great Spotted Woodpeckers and Mistle Thrushes were associated with larch.

The overall winter density for all the parcels was 16.6 birds per hectare, or a bird every 24 m. This is on the low side, but well in the normal range for a Cheshire wood. The two parcels with the most abundant winter birds were 6a and 16 (Waterfall Wood North and Bradford Lodge Farm Wood South). Birds in winter are much less territorial than they are in the breeding season and they are very mobile creatures, so it is not surprising that there is little systematic variation in their density across parcels; the whole area is a single entity as far as they are concerned. There were a few exceptions – Long-tailed Tits were particularly abundant in parcels 6a and 16, and Goldcrests in 10c and 11a (Engine Vein Wood and Windmill Wood South).

The Familiar Birds of Alderley Edge, by Edward Stanley

Edited by John Adams (JA) with Alan Straw (AS)

Edward Stanley's *A Familiar History of Birds* was first published in 1835 and ran to many editions, the last dated 1902; it is still available in print-on-demand format. These extracts and the illustrations are taken from the ninth edition of his work, revised by Stanley before his death and published posthumously in 1881 by Longmans, Green and Co. in London. They were republished in 2005 as *The Familiar Birds of Alderley and Alderley Edge in 1835* by AMCD (Publishers) Limited, Purley, with the original illustrations, and with an introduction by John Adams and notes on the ornithology by Alan Straw, a local ornithologist, which have now been largely incorporated into Appendix 11.1 by Jonathan Guest. What follows is a slightly revised and updated version of that book (which is now out of print), with some further notes on the birds by Henry McGhie, Head of Collections and Curator of Zoology at the Manchester Museum. Edward Stanley's words and style remain his own, and are many years out of copyright, but he is the true author of this section. Editorial comments are enclosed in square brackets.

Foreword to the 2005 edition, by JA

Edward Stanley DD, FRS (1779–1849), younger brother of the Sir John who became the first Lord Stanley of Alderley, was Rector of Alderley from 1805 to 1837 and then Lord Bishop of Norwich until his death. His *Familiar History of Birds* ran through many editions from the first in 1835 and the posthumous edition as late as 1892. Stanley himself revised and added to the text, which covers not only his period at the rectory at St Mary's, Alderley, but also avian anecdotes from his time at the Bishop's Palace in Norwich. His personal gamut therefore runs from the pastureland of Cheshire and the more rocky heights of Alderley Edge to the reed beds of the fens of Cambridgeshire and Lincolnshire.

This present selection brings together those sections which can be shown to have been written about Alderley and Alderley Edge in the period 1805 to 1837, when Edward Stanley was Rector. The scope of Stanley's *Familiar History* – the worldwide families of birds – is much wider, though plainly built on his love of birds and personal observation at several locations, such as Anglesey, where his mother had estates. Stanley was widely travelled in France, and other parts of his book refer to observations of birds there, for example at Fécamp in Normandy. We have included one observation from his time as Bishop of Norwich, since the story of the Christmas Robin in the Cathedral has the charming – and to us perhaps distant – sensibility of the first Victorian Christmas cards.

Stanley was however something more than a country parson: he was connected through his family to national events. He travelled through France three times, in 1802, 1814 and 1816 – sketching a new-fangled guillotine at Verdun and recording his emotions on seeing it used. He was a witness, at an upstairs window, to the events of the 'Peterloo Massacre' in Manchester in 1819. He was of the Whig or reforming mentality and forthright in his views.

It may be worth pointing out that in his treatment of Eagles, Stanley chooses to cite an unusual Anglo-Saxon version of the Stanley family's 'Eagle and Child' legend. His careful wording states 'one of their [Stanley] ancestors, when a child, having been carried off by an Eagle'. This legend is, or was, known locally at Alderley under two other names: 'the Brid and Babby' and 'the Brid and Bastard'. It was probably too much for a mid-Victorian Lord Bishop of high radical principle to advertise a story pointing to the barrenness of an ancestor's wife and the introduction of an illegitimate child as the lawful heir [see Chapter 28, p. 713, where there is a further brief discussion]. In fact, the 'Eagle and Child' motif forms part of the arms of all the Stanley families, including the Earls of Derby, and refers to the story that a distant childless ancestor acquired an heir by finding a child at the foot of an eagle's eyrie. When the Stanley estates at Alderley were sold, almost all of the stone Eagles on the gate columns were removed on the orders of the then Lord Stanley, and buried. They were of a particularly white stone, from a designated quarry, reserved to the use of the Stanleys (S. Mills, personal communication).

There was no lack of courage in the man: his son records a vivid description of him breaking up a bare-knuckle fight organised by the unruly copper-miners of Alderley somewhere on the Edge:

> The whole field was filled, and all the trees round about.... I saw the Rector coming up the road on his little black horse quick as lightning, and I trembled for fear they should harm him. He rode into the field and just looked quick around (as if he thought the same) to see who there was that would be on his side. But it was not needed – he rode into the midst of the crowd, and in one moment it was all over; there was a great calm; the blows stopped; it was as if they would all have wished to cover themselves up in the earth – all from the trees fell down directly – no one said a word, all went away humbled. (Stanley, 1880: 13)

But Stanley also sits in the great Victorian tradition of not just observation of but also philosophising about natural history, and indeed about geology, in which he also took a close interest. These were inexpensive and ostensibly blameless diversions for a clergyman with a large family and small income. Stanley lived a generation before Lyell and Darwin, when these two disciplines became suspect in religious terms; although he pre-dates these doubts, he is evidently troubled by some of the Creator's less manifest purposes: why, for example, he asks, do the 'Canary-bird' and the Raven fail to show parental instinct?

There are other sources for birds at Alderley, including the notebooks of Edward's older brother, the first Lord Stanley. Here we find mention of Red Kites or Gledes at Radnor Mere, in the grounds of Alderley Park, in 1791. A century later, when Coward and Oldham came to write their *Birds of Cheshire* in 1900, they remarked that the Alderley Kites were long gone, and it may be significant that Edward Stanley makes no mention of them, despite his long residency (Coward and Oldham, 1900).

Several of the present selections refer directly to the rectory next to St Mary's Parish Church, where Stanley had an aviary with Canaries and Goldfinches. He also had birdcages suspended from the first-floor veranda, outside the bedrooms, holding not only Nightingales, but Redstarts and Flycatchers. Other cages were at times suspended outside rectory 'offices' – here meaning pantry and kitchen.

Stanley lived most of his life at the rectory in Alderley. This is described by Augustus Hare, the adopted son of Mrs Augustus Hare, née Maria Leycester, sister of Edward Stanley's wife, Kitty Leycester (Hare, 1872):

> A low house, with a verandah forming a wide balcony for the upper storey, where bird cages hung among the roses; its rooms and passages filled with pictures, books, and old carved furniture. In a country where the flat pasture lands of Cheshire rise suddenly to the rocky ridge of Alderley Edge, with the Holy Well under an overhanging cliff; its gnarled pine trees, its storm beaten beacon tower ready to give notice of an invasion and looking far over the green plain to the smoke which indicates in the horizon the presence of the great manufacturing towns.

Alderley fought off two major threats to encroachment on this rural idyll – in the 1840s it narrowly escaped becoming a rail junction like Crewe, centred on St Mary's Church, and in the 1930s it was planned to sell off the Edge for housing. Stanley's rectory is still standing and still has the inscription, perhaps cut by himself, 'Deus Nobis Haec Otia Fecit' – 'God has given us this leisure': a suitable motto for all birdwatchers.

Extracts from Stanley's 1881 text (ninth edition)

The Eagle [Figure 11.2]

The well-known crest of the Eagle and Child borne by the Stanley family is supposed to have been founded upon a tradition of one of their ancestors, when a child, having been carried off by an Eagle; and a story is told in a very old book of English history, which, whether true or not in all its particulars, proves at least the prevailing belief that eagles occasionally flew away with children; indeed, there was an ancient Act of Parliament 'anent the slaying of the Erne', that is concerning the slaying of the Erne, the name of a particular species of Eagle (the White-tailed Eagle) in which, on account of its being 'a terror to farmers, from fowls to children' a reward should be granted to the person who should destroy a nest or a bird [Figure 11.2]. The story alluded to from the above mentioned old book is as follows:

> Alfred, king of the West Saxons went out one day a-hunting, and passing by a certain wood heard, as he supposed the cry of an infant from the top of a

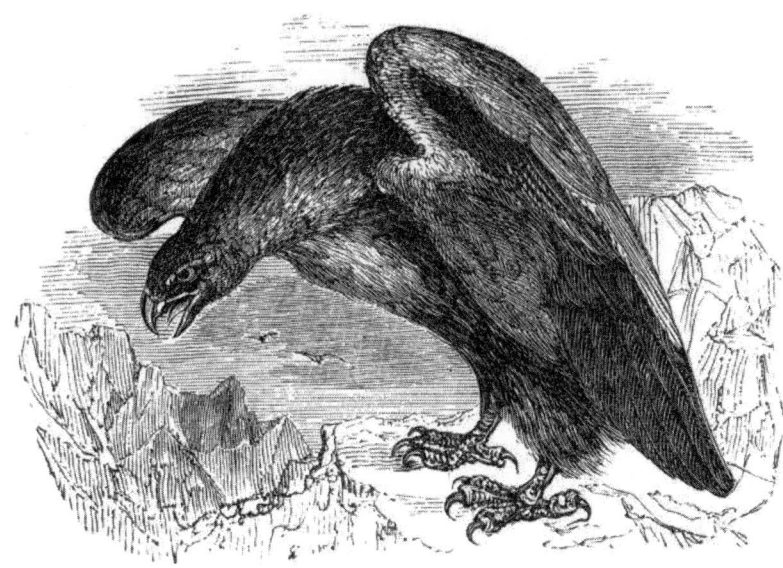

Figure 11.2. The eagle.

From Stanley (1881: 100).

tree, and forthwith diligently inquiring of the huntsmen what that doleful sound could be, commanded one of them to climb the tree, when in the top of the tree it was found an Eagle's nest, and lo! Therein a pretty sweet-faced infant wrapped up in a purple mantle, and upon each arm a bracelet of gold, a clear sign that he was born of noble parents. Whereupon, the king took charge of him, and caused him to be baptised; and because he was found in a nest, he gave him the name of Nestingum, and in after times, having nobly educated him, he advanced him to the dignity of an earl.

[Stanley refers this story to 'Monast. Ang. vol. 1', presumably *Monasticon Anglicanum, sive, Pandectæ coenobiorum Benedictinorum, Cluniacensium, Cisterciensium, Carthusianorum a primordiis ad eorum usque dissolutionem*, published by Sir William Dugdale and Roger Dodsworth in 1655, with the first English translation appearing in 1693 (*Monasticon anglicanum, or, The history of the ancient abbies, and other monasteries, hospitals, cathedral and collegiate churches, in England and Wales: with divers French, Irish, and Scotch monasteries formerly relating to England*). Numerous subsequent editions followed in both Latin and English, down to at least 1846. We have not been able to track down the exact reference, but Stanley's description of it as an 'old book' suggests he may have been using the 1693 edition.]

The Blackbird

We have a curious instance, … considering the nearness of the parties involved, [which] fell under our observation a season or two ago – namely a Blackbird's nest on the ground, in a tuft of grass or rushes close to the seat of a rabbit, the tail in fact of the rabbit being in contact with the nest. As the seat as well as the nest were both occupied, these two companions must have sat meditating together for many a day, in perfect peace and good fellowship. We do not know whether the Blackbird ever sings on its nest....

The Raven

With us the Raven may be called the herald of the year; for as early as the latter end of January, if the weather be mild, or at all events in the beginning of February, some faithful pair (for the union of the male and female is for life) may be seen looking into the state of their nursery-tenement, usually constructed on the upper and most inaccessible branching fork of some high tree, where they have been known to build beyond the memory of the most ancient chronicler of the parish. Probably most of our readers have, if not within their own precincts, at least within their knowledge, a venerable establishment of this description.

The Jackdaw [Figure 11.3]

Ours is a noble beech about ninety feet in height, in the centre of a beautiful wood, – from time immemorial called the Raven-tree. At one extremity of this wood, a noisy troop of Jackdaws have long been accustomed to rear their progeny unmolested, provided they venture not too near the sacred tree of the Ravens, – in which case, one or other of

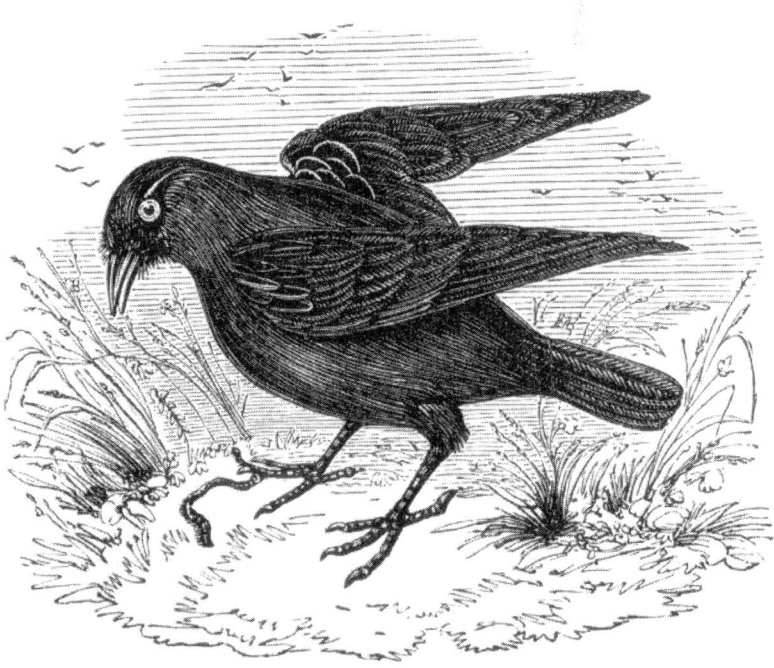

Figure 11.3. The jackdaw.

From Stanley (1881: 201).

the old birds dashes upon the intruders, and the wood is in an uproar until the incautious bird is driven off.

Few have dared to scale the heights of this famed tree; but the names of one or two individuals are on record, who have accomplished the perilous undertaking and carried off the contents of the nest.

Some years ago the wife of a neighbouring farmer made such loud complaints, on the diminution of a fine brood of young Turkeys, which occasionally wandered from her farmyard into some fields adjacent to the wood, that one of the old ones was shot; it proved to be the female, whose young ones had unfortunately been hatched, and were then nearly fledged. For some time the surviving parent hovered about the nest, uttering loud and menacing croakings whenever anybody approached. At length, however, he disappeared and absented himself for two or three days, and then returned with another mate; when a strange scene occurred. The poor half-starved fledglings were attacked by the stepmother; who, after severely wounding, precipitated them from the nest; two however were found at the foot of the tree with signs of life, and with great care and attention reared at the rectory about half a mile distant, and, after being slightly pinioned, were allowed their liberty; but they seldom quitted the lawn or offices, roosting in a tree in the shrubbery. Here they were soon discovered by their unnatural parents, who, for a long time, used to come at early dawn and pounce upon them with fierce cries. Their antipathy to their young (which by several authors has been considered as peculiar to Ravens) has been remarked by many, who have not only known them to show great indifference to any young ones accidentally thrown out of the nest, but have further ascertained that the parents actually devour them....

At all events, while sitting or rearing its progeny, the Raven deserves the highest credit for persevering attachment, having been known (though one of the shyest and most suspicious of birds) to die rather than desert its post.... But constant or affectionate as they may be to their brood, it lasts but for a time; and as is the case with Eagles, and indeed with almost all birds, when the young ones are sufficiently matured to take care of themselves, the old ones almost invariably drive them away and live independently.

The Canary-bird

We do not believe this want of feeling to be peculiar to Ravens; on the contrary, in an aviary where several Canaries build annually, instances repeatedly occur of young birds falling out of the nest, when, if they are of very tender age, the old ones seem to show no uneasiness whatever; hopping and flying over them, with the greatest unconcern, though the poor naked birds may be struggling for life.

We have yet, indeed, much to learn respecting the real extent and quality of the affection of animals for their young; for in the case of Canaries we have known if wet or cold weather chanced to continue for a day or two, not only nests containing eggs, but others with nearly fully fledged nestlings, requiring all a mother's care, to be at once abandoned, and left to perish by cold or hunger.

On the 2d of June 1833, a Canary-bird in an aviary was unexpectedly drenched, having built her nest, during dry weather, in a spot exposed to rain, which fell in a heavy shower on that day. On the following day she accordingly quitted her nest, and appeared so unwell that it was deemed expedient to remove her into a small cage, and place her in a warmer situation. But to our great surprise a Goldfinch, which had been in confinement with the Canary-birds for three or four years, without paying any attention to the nests, immediately took her place, and continued to sit very closely, though uselessly, over the chilled and lifeless eggs, which were completely addled.

It is surprising, too with what rapidity, in cases of emergency, small birds can build a nest. A Canary was observed to commence her labours about five o'clock in the morning, from which time till near seven o'clock she worked so hard, that it was completely finished; she had often been disturbed, in consequence of building in inconvenient places, which probably induced her to use more than ordinary despatch in this nest, availing herself of early hours, before people were likely to see and interfere.

The mysterious assemblage of birds

The following instance of the mysterious assemblage of birds may be justly classed amongst their most extraordinary instinctive habits. In the month of February, we recollect once seeing a prodigious number of Magpies in a field; some hopping about near the edge, others secreted in the hedges, and no less than twenty-seven perched on a small ash tree. At first the presence of a fox was suspected, knowing it to be a constant practice of these birds to collect, if Reynard shows himself; but as they did not appear to be hovering over any particular spot, as if a concealed enemy were lurking near, we inclined to the opinion that some private concerns of their own had brought them together. The chattering was incessant, and when disturbed and under the necessity of beating a retreat, they flew nearly in the same direction, as if disposed to adjourn their meeting to a more retired spot, than with a view to break it up.

A singular habit, somewhat similar, little known or noticed, though uncommon, prevails among Starlings. If carefully watched, they may be seen occasionally to alight in a regular circular form. A numerous flock was once seen to divide itself into two companies, each forming a distinct circle. If undisturbed, they will remain a considerable time in the same place, uttering the same twittering note upon the ground as when perched on trees or reeds. This habit is usually observable in pastures; sometimes though rarely in stubble-fields; but never upon fallow or new-ploughed land.

The Rook [Figure 11.4]

We now come to an important question respecting Rooks, in the settlement of which the world is much divided. Are they beneficial or injurious to man? Is the farmer a gainer or a loser, by being subjected to the daily visits of two or three hundred of these birds from a rookery?

In former days there can be no question of public opinion being entirely against them, and that the destruction of Rooks was regular and systematic – an inference which may be fairly drawn from the following entry among certain presentments concerning the parish of Alderley, in Cheshire, in 1598, being the fortieth of Queen Elizabeth's reign: 'We find that there is no Crownett [crow net] in the parish, a payne that one be bought in the charge of the parish'.

As in most cases, so in this, we are inclined to think that a great deal may be said on both sides; for as the Rook cannot be altogether acquitted of the charge of doing some harm, so neither is he to be found guilty of doing nothing but mischief. We will examine, first the unfavourable

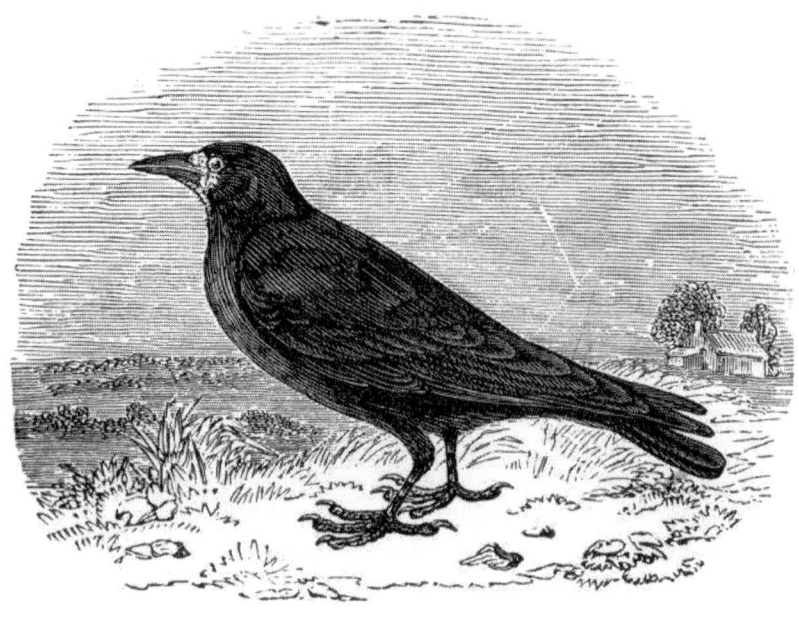

Figure 11.4. The rook.

From Stanley (1881: 188).

side. A Rook, which we kept for some time, was after a night's fast, fed entirely on oats, of which it ate in twenty four hours, two ounces of sixteen ounces to the pound; while another, under similar circumstances, consumed two ounces and a half of bread. [English measures were not fully standardised until the 1820s. Until then a series of local measures were used.]

This certainly would bear strongly against them, was there nothing to be said in mitigation; but it should be remembered that the above consumption is founded upon the assumption that Rooks live entirely upon grain, which so far from being the case is very much the reverse, for they prefer an insect diet, if not altogether, at least to a great extent....

We remember, a few years ago, seeing for several days, a flight of Rooks regularly resorting to a field close to the house; and, on walking over it, observed that the whole surface was covered with uprooted stems of one particular plant and on looking more narrowly it was ascertained that many of those still untouched were of an unhealthy yellow appearance, and that to these alone the Rooks seemed to direct their attention; and, on still closer attention, the roots of each of these unhealthy plants were found to have been attacked by a small grub, which at once accounted for the daily presence of these sable visitants.

Could we dive into all the mysteries of a rookery, a page in the book of nature would be opened filled with much that 'man's philosophy hath never dreamed of'. Without any assignable cause, a party will secede from an old-fashioned rookery and form a new one. A case of this sort occurred some years ago, in the parish of Alderley in Cheshire. Seven pairs of Rooks, supposed to have come from an old rookery about two miles distant, where an extent of wood admitted an unlimited accommodation, took up their residence in a clump of trees, and proceeded to build; there they have continued ever since, the number of nests increasing as follows: – in 1828 there were seven nests; in 1829, nine; in 1830, thirteen; in 1831, twenty-four; in 1832, thirty-three; in 1833 upwards of fifty; and in this latter year there was a proportionate increase, with colonies settling in adjacent trees.

The Starling

The Starling, although closely resembling the Thrush and Blackbird in some respects, differs from them essentially in others; as its beak, on examination, will be found to be without a notch on its extremity, it may be decidedly placed amongst the conirostral tribes [i.e. including for example larks, tits, finches, sparrows, crows and linnets].

Of some birds it is difficult, from their retired habits, to give any clear or accurate account. Not so our friend the Starling. When it suits his purpose, he comes fearlessly under our observation and invites us to learn his history. For many and many a year we have watched him from month to month, with the exception of a certain season, when, for reasons best known to himself, he altogether disappears, and leaves us to wonder what is become of him.

Close before the window of our scene of observation, a well-mown short-grassed lawn is spread before him – it is his dining room; there in the spring he is allowed to revel, but seldom molested, on the plentiful supply of worms, which he collects pretty much in the same manner as the Thrush. Close at hand, within half a stone's throw, stands an ivy-mantled parish church [evidently the rectory and church of St Mary, Alderley] with its massy grey tower, from the turreted pinnacle of which rises a tall flag-staff, crowned by its weathercock; under the eaves and within the hollows and chinks of the masonry of this tower are his nursery establishments. On the battlements and projecting grotesque tracery of its gothic ornaments he retires to enjoy himself, looking down on the rural world below; while, at other times, a still more elevated party will crowd together on the letters of the weathercock, or accustomed to its motion, sociably twitter away their chattering song, as the vane creaks slowly round with every change of the wind.

We will give a journal of our Starlings' lives. At the close of January, one or two unconnected birds now and then make their appearance on this weathercock; at first but for a few minutes as if without an assignable reason they had merely touched upon it as an inviting resting-place, in their unsettled course. In February, if the weather happens to be mild, the number of idlers may now and then increase; but still the visit seems to be the mere passing call of a few strangers, without a leading object. In March, however, about the first or second week, according to the state of the weather, things begin to assume a more bustling and serious appearance. Hitherto but one or two, or at the most three or four, may have dropped in, as if to say 'here we are; the winter is past and gone and a happier season is at hand'. But now the flights increase, the three and four are multiplied to fourteen or sixteen, and the song becomes a little chorus, more loud and more joyous than before; and occasion-ally, though with some circumspection and hesitation, one or two of the boldest will let themselves gently fall from their airy height and glide down upon the lawn, as if to inquire into the state of their future larder; for they scarcely take time to taste the hidden treasures below the sod, but looking suspiciously about, are on the wing in a moment if an inmate approached the window, or a door is heard to shut or open.

About the latter end of the second week, affairs begin to be placed on a more regular footing; the parties on or about the battlements and weathercock seem as if they had determined on a permanent estab-lishment. From early dawn till about ten, there they remain carolling away their communications; at that hour, however, off they go, and till four or five o'clock are seen no more throughout the greater part of the day; being absent in the fields, where they may be seen chattering in company with the inhabitants of a neighbouring rookery, or a noisy set of Jackdaws, who have from time out of mind, been the undisputed tenants of a certain portion of ancient beech wood at no great distance.

About the third week the plot begins to thicken still more. The field, the lawn, and the weathercock are no longer the only objects of interest. Detachments may now be seen prowling busily over the roof, cautiously creeping in and out from under the projecting eaves, and by the end of the month, the regular establishment amounting to about thirty, has assembled, and the grand work of the year commences. From this time all is bustle; straws and nest-furniture are seen flying through the air in beaks, contriving, nevertheless, to announce their comings and goings by particular harsh or low muttering cries, according as they think they are watched or not. They are cunning birds and discover in an instant whether a passer-by has an eye to their movements, and perfectly aware whether he is following his own business or theirs. If he steps onwards, without troubling himself about them, they go in and out with perfect unconcern; but if a glance of curiosity or observation is directed to their motions, they are all upon the alert; the bearer of a tuft to the nest wheels to the right-about, and perching on the naked upper twig of a small beech tree, or the projecting point of a gable end, sits there, uttering a particular note, which seems to give, as well as words could do, intimations to a mate to be on its guard, as a spy is at hand.

If the weather is tolerably favourable, everything goes on smoothly and regularly; but (and we have in the journal of our Starlings' proceedings, many instances on record) should a severe and sudden change occur, a violent storm of snow, or continuance of chilling winds, all operations are suspended; not only the eaves and nests but even the tower itself, battlements, weathercock, and all, are deserted, till a return of fine weather, when the Starlings too return and the work again proceeds. At length the nests are built, the eggs laid, and the young ones hatched, then a new scene of noise and activity, and bustle commences, increasing of course as the nestlings become older and more voracious. Then it is that the lawn becomes a favourite resort; hitherto a few idlers may have hopped and pecked up a stray worm or two, but now the search is a matter of serious occupation.

Down they come, the sober-coloured hen, and the cock with the sun glittering on its spangled feathers, with claws and beaks as busily employed as if their very existence depended upon it. All however in good social harmony, never quarrelling with the shy and less intrusive Thrush or Blackbird; or with the lively Wagtails, contenting themselves with the lighter fare of the myriads of minute flies and beetles hovering over the fresh mown turf.

The noise and bustle go on incessantly, till the young ones are fledged, when for a day or two they may be seen fluttering about the building, or taking short flights. At length, their strength being matured, old and young collect on the tower, and then wheel away over the neighbouring fields, as practising for future and more important evolutions. But still the evening finds them roosting near the place of their birth. At last, however, a day comes when all is hushed. No hungry guests are feasting on the lawn, no clamorous throats are calling aloud for food, no twitterings are heard from bough or battlement, not even a straggler is to be seen on the pinnacle of the weathercock.

The joyous assembly is broken up. The Starlings are gone, and till the Autumn, with scarcely an exception, we shall see them no more. The abandonment of their breeding-place depends, of course, upon the season. In 1833, the month of May having been remarkably warm, it occurred on the 6th of June; but we have known it to be delayed to the second week of July; the whole of June having been very unseasonable and stormy. Then, about the third week in September, again on their favourite perch, the weathercock, one, or two, or three, may chance to appear towards evening, not with the merry note of spring, but uttering that momentous, plaintive, long-drawn whistling cry, as cheerless as the cheerless season for which they seem to bid us to prepare. That these and the few other stragglers occupying the same post, are our spring friends is most probable; for a lame Starling was observed for eight years to return to the same nest, and every observation we have made tends to prove that this is a general instinctive custom of, we believe, every bird whatever.

Having thus given some report of our Starlings for the greater part of the year, we will endeavour to follow the main body for the remaining months as yet unaccounted for. To do this effectually would be no easy matter, as we believe that they are partially migratory, *i.e.*, quitting one part of the kingdom for another more suited for their usual mode of life: nevertheless, enough remain within the sphere of our observation, and are to be met with in little flocks during the summer in favourite meadows, where food is plentiful, associating with their old friends, the Crows, Rooks, and Jackdaws.

As winter approaches they follow the example of some other birds, such as Larks, Buntings &c, and congregate in larger quantities. Not far from the Church we have mentioned there is a considerable sheet of water, occupying nearly thirty acres, flanked and feathered on the eastern side by the old beech wood, already spoken of as the abiding place of the Jackdaws. Its western margin is bounded an artificial dam, which, as the water is on a much higher level, commands an extensive view over the flat rich country, the horizon terminated by the faint outline of the first range of Welsh mountains. [This may be Radnor

Mere and the Beech Wood: it covers only around eleven acres, which has led to suggestions that Lymm Dam or Tatton Mere are intended, but these are too far away, and the topography of Radnor Mere matches Stanley's description.]

This dam, on the finer evenings of November, was once the favourite resort of many persons, who found an additional attraction in watching the gradual assemblage of the Starlings. About an hour before sunset, little flocks, by twenties or fifties, kept gradually dropping in, their numbers increasing as daylight waned, till one vast flight formed, amounting to thousands, and at times we might almost say to millions. Nothing could be more interesting or beautiful than to witness their graceful evolutions.

At first they might be seen advancing high in the air, like a dark cloud, which in an instant, as if by magic, became almost invisible, the whole body by some mysterious watchword or signal, changing their course, and presenting their wings to view edgeways, instead of exposing, as before, their fully-expanded spread. Again, in another moment, the cloud might be seen descending in a graceful sweep, so as to almost brush the earth as they glanced along. Then once more they were seen spiring in wide circles on high; till at length with one simultaneous rush, down they glide, with a roaring noise of wing, till the vast mass buried itself unseen, but not unheard, amidst a bed of reeds projecting from a bank adjacent to the wood. For no sooner were they perched than every throat seemed to open itself, forming one incessant confusion of tongues.

If nothing disturbed them, there they would most likely remain; but if a stone was thrown, a shout raised, or more especially if a gun was fired, up again would rise the mass, with one unbroken, rushing sound, as if the whole body were possessed but of one wing to bear them in their upward flight.

In the fens of Cambridgeshire and Lincolnshire, where reeds are of considerable value for various purposes, the mischief they occasion is often very considerable, by beating down and breaking them as many as can find a grasping hold clinging to the same slender stem, which, of course bends, plunging them into the water, from whence they rise to join some other neighbours, whose reed is still able to bear their weight. This perpetual jostling and breaking down is the probable cause of the incessant chatter, which continues for a considerable time; indeed, till all procured dry beds and a firm footing.

Their favourite dormitory of reeds, indeed, has dwindled gradually away, since the dam was raised, and the depth of water increased, which may partly account for the diminution; but still reeds are left in sufficient abundance for the accommodation of ten times the number that are ever assembled in the neighbourhood of which we speak.

The Christmas Robin

We can remember indeed a Robin hopping more than once, familiarly, as if aware how safe from peril it was at such a moment, upon our own Bible, as it lay open before us reading the lessons on a Christmas Day.

The Swallow

The same church steeple [St Mary's] which has enabled us year after year to watch the Starlings was formerly a source of equal interest respecting Swallows; their nests were snugly concealed in sheltered nooks, the belfry itself being a favourite resort, notwithstanding the frequent peals which might have shaken the nerves of less determined birds; and a few days before their final departure, it was pleasant to watch them marshalling their newly-fledged broods along the projecting dripstones and mouldings on the eastern side of the old grey tower, enjoying the morning sun. As the numbers collected seemed far to exceed those which were reared there, it appears as if the united broods of the neighbourhood had, by common consent, fixed upon it as a favoured central rendezvous. All was exhilaration – a perpetual twittering was kept up; a few of the old ones would, after flying in circles around the battlements, pass screaming by the reposing ranks of the young ones, and then, as if by word of command, the whole body would sweep from their resting places, and in loud chorus take a wider circuit, as if to try their powers, and then in an instant crowd again together, and rest as before.

The flight of the common Swallow has been computed at 90 miles [per hour], that of the Swift has been conjectured to be nearly 180 miles per hour. We can scarcely, indeed, calculate or limit the speed which can be produced by the effort of a wing's vibrations. That a small insect can with ease accomplish forty or fifty miles an hour, and probably much more, we know to be a fact, from our own experience on the Liverpool and Manchester railroad; for, when rolling along at the rate of about thirty miles an hour we saw bees and flies, sometimes hovering round the carriages, sometimes settling, then when disturbed, flying to the right or left in an irregular course, but still keeping up, without the slightest appearance of extra exertion; and often when tired of continuing with the train, shooting forward, and in an instant leaving us far behind, and this, too, in opposition to a fresh breeze heading them.

If any of our regular migratory birds are kept in an aviary or cage, when the usual time arrives for the departure of the rest of their species, these prisoners, without having any communication with their companions, will nevertheless manifest great uneasiness and often die if detained. We have seen this repeatedly in the Redstart and the Flycatcher, which, though carefully supplied with the same food on which they have thriven for weeks before, and been quiet and apparently satisfied with their lot, will, early in September, begin to show great impatience, flying about and striking against the bars of the aviary, and usually dying after a few days spent in ineffectual endeavours to escape.

The Vanishing Woodcock

There was a time when Woodcocks might be almost said to be as plentiful as Wood-Pigeons are now – at least, they abounded to such a degree that catching them was a regular trade; and about a hundred years ago, they used to be sold at the moderate rate of from six to seven pence a couple; but, like Starlings, Wood-Pigeons, and several other birds, they have since diminished in numbers.

As far as concerns Woodcocks, this indeed may easily be accounted for. In the first place, the demand not for the full-grown birds merely, but for the eggs, has greatly increased in Sweden, where they are highly esteemed, and therefore as diligently sought for as Plovers' eggs with us. Thus, not a twentieth part of the former abundant numbers may now be reared, and of course, our natural winter supply must proportionably decrease. But other causes have operated, in this country, still further to diminish the number of those which under former circumstances, might be inclined to come over – namely the great decrease in our woodlands; the improvements in agriculture, by which their haunts have been drained or broken up; and lastly, the increase of population, which, more than we are aware of deters shy and solitary birds from remaining in neighbourhoods to which they formerly resorted.

It was a favourite amusement, in former days, to catch Woodcocks by dozens, of a night, in places where now not a dozen could be taken in a whole season. Large openings were left, or rather made in woods, which at night were filled with wide-spreading nets, fastened with pulleys to tall branches; a man stood concealed on one side, with a rope running through the pulleys, who, the instant he felt a cock touch the net, let it go, and the net falling over the bird secured the prize.

In the fine old beech woods we have more than once alluded to, numbers were formerly taken, in a wide space still known as the Woodcock-glade, where many a winter's night might now be spent unprofitably and possibly without meeting a single bird. Another form of trapping was by springes – a sort of trap, formed of an elastic stick, to which was fastened a horsehair noose, put through a hole in a peg, fastened into the ground, to which a trigger was annexed; and in order to induce the Woodcock to walk towards the noose, a little fence was extended on each side by small sticks, set up close enough to prevent the bird passing between: these all met at the trap; so that, by this funnel-shaped fence, the Woodcock in feeding is compelled to pass through the narrow passage with every chance of being caught by the legs. The elastic stick in flying up, of course, draws the noose quite tight, and effectually secures the Woodcock; but a common horse-hair noose will often answer the purpose, particularly if the little avenue fence is placed to lead the birds to the snare.

The faithful Goose and the frightened farmer [Figure 11.5]

We frankly own, that so strange and so improbable do some stories [concerning Geese] appear, that we should neither have inserted nor paid them the slightest attention, had we not the following testimony to their credibility, for the accuracy of which we can vouch; and deeply do we regret, that a better fate did not await so extraordinary a bird, which, under more intelligent observers, might have afforded opportunities of ascertaining the extent of so unusual a development of affection.

A farmer in Cheshire possessed a flock of Geese, one of which, at the end of about three years, without any apparent cause, began to show a peculiar partiality for its master. It first appeared on the bird's quitting its companions in the barnyard or pond and stalking after him. These symptoms became daily stronger, and in a short time, wherever the farmer went, whether to the mill or the blacksmith's shop, or through the bustling streets of a neighbouring manufacturing town, the Goose was at his heels. So perseveringly did it follow his steps, that if he wished to go out alone, he was under the necessity of fastening up the bird.

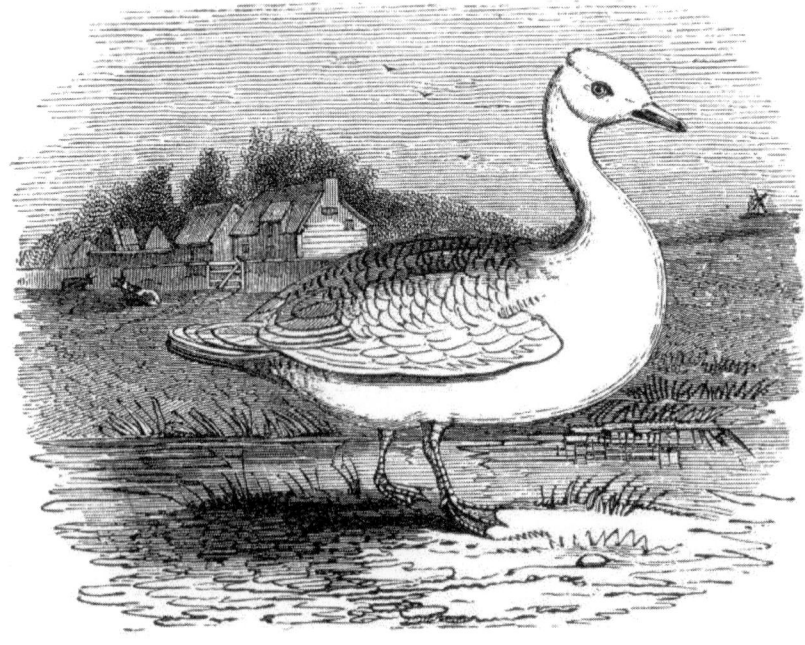

Figure 11.5. The goose.
From Stanley (1881: 335).

The farmer was in the habit of holding his own plough ... and on these occasions, the Goose as regularly passed the day in the ploughing field, walking sedately, not with the usual waddling pace of its fellow Geese, but with a firm step, head elevated and neck erect, a short way before him in the line of the furrows, frequently turning around and fixing its eyes intently upon him. When the length of one furrow was accomplished and the plough turned, the Goose, without losing its step, adroitly wheeled about, and thus continued its attendance till the evening and then followed its master home; and if permitted would mount upon his lap as he sat by the fire after dark, showing the strongest signs of affection, and nestling his head in his bosom, or preening the hair of his head with its beak as it was wont to do with its own feathers.

Sometimes the farmer would go out shooting, and no sooner had he shouldered his gun, than his companion was [at] its post, following him as before in spite of every obstacle; – 'getting over' to use the man's own words, 'the fences as well as I could myself'."All this it should be observed, continued not only without any encouragement on the part of the farmer, but even in spite of every discouragement on his part. How long it would have continued, or to what extent, we lament to add, he effectually precluded the world from knowing; for, with an unpardonable inattention to so truly a wonderful a case, in addition to equally unpardonable superstitious fear, he took it into his head that this mysterious affection of the poor Goose foreboded some evil; and in a moment of alarm he killed the faithful bird.

The Nightingale and other birds

In the year 1837 an instance came under our observation rather at variance with what has been stated [above, under 'The Swallow'] in the case of a Nightingale, reared from the nest in the spring of 1835. It soon became tame, and was kept in a cage till May 1837, singing always in the winter from Christmas till April, and feeding readily upon minced pieces of meat and meal-worms, and showing no symptoms of impatience at the usual period of migration. It was silent the rest of the year. In May it was permitted to go out of its cage, which was hung up open at the door of the offices [kitchen, pantry etc.]. At first it returned regularly in the evening to its cage, and was taken into the pantry, and released again the next morning. As the season advanced, it sometimes stayed out all night, in the shrubberies and pleasure grounds, but if called by any of the servants, whose voice it knew, would return, and feed out of their hand.

For a day or two, towards the close of summer, it seemed rather uneasy, getting into the coal hole and cellar; but this soon wore off. As the season still further advanced, it was to be permanently housed, and was expected to sing again at Christmas.

One other very remarkable fact connected with these long journeys undertaken by birds over seas and lands, is that they are gifted with some secret power, enabling them not only to find their way to and from the distant countries that they visit, but actually guiding them to the very same place from whence they came, and the very same spots for building their nests. This has been proved by marking the claws of Swallows, which were in the habit of building in sheds or outhouses, where they could easily be retaken on their return in the spring, and examined. An instance came under our own observation, of a pair of swallows returning to build for three years in a small closet in a school-house [presumably the Old School House in the grounds of the churchyard of St Mary's Church], entering by a broken pane in the casement, and forming their nests in a corner above the window; and as they were never disturbed, the female would remain sitting and the male fly in and out in our presence. But though several broods were hatched, the old birds allowed no intruders, and not a single young bird was ever seen to return to the place of its birth after it had once quitted the nest.

It has been observed that the time of departure of certain birds is by no means so exact as that of their arrival; which may be accounted for by a natural disinclination on the part of the old ones to desert the nests of young ones still requiring their care. But even this most powerful of all instincts, the attachment of a parent to its young, is not in all cases strong enough to conquer the still stronger impulse for migration; for Swallows will actually desert their nests, and leave helpless little ones to perish by hunger, rather than remain long after their companions. A pair of Martins which had deserted their family in the autumn, on returning in the spring, were observed to draw out the dead bodies of three nearly fully-fledged nestlings. Another pair acted in a different manner; after vainly endeavouring to drag out the bodies, which had most probably formed a dried mass with the wool and feathers in the interior, they entirely closed up the opening of the nest with clay, and leaving them thus entombed, proceeded to build another nursery.

Arrivals and departures

As much interest and amusement may be derived from watching and expecting the arrival and departure of our migratory birds, a list of a few of the most common are provided ... with the earliest and latest dates which have come under our observation.

[At this point in his text Stanley presents a table, reproduced here as Table 11.2. We assume that the dates he gives apply to Alderley in the period of Stanley's residency, from 1805 to 1837. Sand Martins are now one of the first migrants and birders will daily visit prime sites to record the first birds arriving. In 2003 the first record was 8 March, with the recent average being 9 March. Their last departure is about 10 October. So, these days the martins arrive nearly three weeks earlier and depart about three weeks later. Swallows and swifts are now behaving in a roughly similar fashion. (AS)]

Table 11.2. Dates of the arrival and departure of migratory birds at Alderley according to Edward Stanley's observations, probably covering the years 1805–37

Species	Date of appearance	Date of departure
Sand Martin	27 March	21 September
Chimney Swallow	11 April	20 October
Redstart	6 April	5 September
Whitethroat	6 April	8 September
Cuckoo	10 April	30 June
Redwing	26 September	3 April
Fieldfare	29 September	2 May
Woodcock	25 October	2 April

Source: Stanley (1881: 90)

'Magpie hawking' (Figure 11.6) (JA)

This curious illustration (see over) to Stanley's *Familiar History of Birds*, probably from 1826 and chosen by the publisher, seems to show a long-abandoned sport, which Stanley at no point mentions in his text, but whose revival merits consideration, in view of the present proliferation and habits of the Magpie, *Pica pica*.

> The magpie shifts with great cunning and dexterity to avoid the stoop; and when hard pressed, owing to the bushes being rather far apart, will pass under the bellies of the horses, flutter along a cart rut, and avail himself of every little inequality of the ground in order to escape. (*Observations on Hawking* by Sir J. Sebright, first published in 1596 and re-issued in 1826)

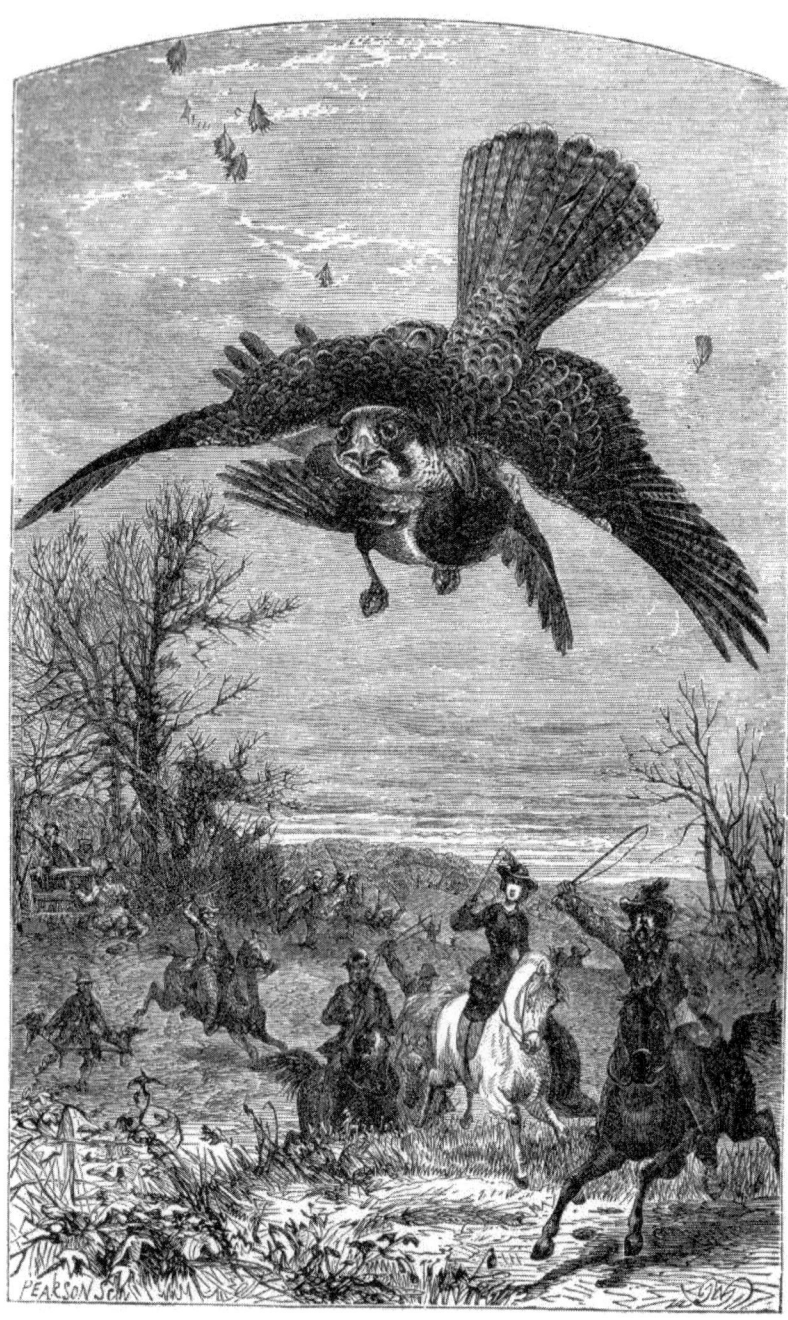

Figure 11.6. Magpie hawking.
From Stanley (1881: frontispiece).

Alderley: a bird and iron bottle

From Peter Portland, Around Haunted Manchester
(Purley: AMCD Books, 2002)

This tale from Alderley is of rural infidelity, which is the motivation for a haunting – many ghosts seem to appear for no good reason. It occurs in *Cheshire Notes and Queries* for March 1881, over the initials TJ – whom we have presumed to be Thomas Jarman of Stockport. Jarman claims here to have grown up in Alderley and imbibed the folklore 'in the chimney corner of an old cottage which yet stands between the Soss Moss and the Beech wood'.

The tale must be set somewhere between the 1810s and 1830s. Jarman heard that a few years before he sat in that inglenook as a child, there was a gamekeeper called Firbank, who lived in the area with his wife. Jarman is coy, but Mrs Firbank seems to have fallen in love with another – the 'green-eyed monster' made its appearance and 'domestic felicity was ended'. Firbank fell ill, and realising he was dying, he made his wife promise that she would not marry the cause of his jealousy – a promise she did not keep.

Old people declared that following the new marriage, Firbank could not rest in his grave, and began to play tricks on the newly-weds. As they sat by the fire, a third unwelcome chair would be drawn up to the hearth, and by degrees the outline and then the accusatory figure of Firbank would appear, glaring at them, but never speaking a word.

The couple made their way to the rectory – almost certainly to see Edward Stanley (Jarman describes it as the sweetest spot on earth). Stanley upbraided them for what seemed to him verification of Firbank's suspicions, but his professional interest was doubtless engaged and he agreed to 'lay' the ghost.

He first visited Henshall, the local blacksmith, at his smithy near to the beech wood, and asked him to make a large cast-iron bottle. In order to avoid being labelled as the 'ghost-bottler' ('in country places nicknames were more easily acquired than got rid of') the smith decided to make the bottle at midnight. It was delivered to the house of the deceased Firbank. The rector went through the form of words, and the ghost was laid with surprising ease in the iron bottle, which was screwed shut and buried in St Mary's churchyard.

But Firbank rose again the following night with hideous noises, to haunt the couple. They fled to the rector, who realised that the making of the bottle in the dead of night had been an error. Firbank, 'always a shrewd and far-seeing man', knew that the bottle was flawed in some way, and had allowed himself to be laid far too easily. Now he would be more difficult to deal with.

Henshall made a second bottle, of better iron, and this time in the daylight. Firbank's spirit saw that more serious preparations were underway, and begged the rector for some modicum of liberty. After parleying, he was permitted to appear at certain times as a small bird, flitting only a certain distance round a particular tree in the beech wood. He was once again secured, in this second iron bottle, which was then buried in the wood, so that he could annoy the living no more.

The laying of ghosts was no idle occupation for a parson. Fletcher Moss has this addition to the Alderley Tale: 'A gamekeeper with a black dog used to walk at Authorley, till th' passon laid 'im; but th' passon's yure [hair] wur as black as a crow th' day afore, an in th' morn it wur as grey as a badger; so he mun a bin rarely feart ["he must have been really afraid"]' (Moss, 1898: 135). There is no place I can find called Authorley, although, as discussed in Chapter 28, at least one source cites it as a form of 'Alderley'.

The portraits we have of Edward Stanley show him as dark-haired and strikingly handsome: he was himself made of cast iron, and seems to have come in to Alderley as a reforming minister, caring for the sick and the poor, opposing public drunkenness and, as we have already seen, on one occasion stopping single-handed a prize fight between miners.

Local research in 2002 produced the following interesting commentary on the Firbank tale:

> In my family's *oral* tradition, the transference of the ghost into a bird was not known, nor were the *two* bottles. Edward Stanley simply conjured the ghost of Firbank into an iron bottle, made by the blacksmith, and threw it into Radnor Mere [in the present Alderley Park]. The gamekeeper's house still stands, on Hocker Lane.
>
> The incident of the iron bottle is so rare in English folklore that I suspect that it was an historical event, perhaps given force by the wider knowledge of folklore and great understanding of Edward Stanley. He would have known the power of the dramatic gesture. (Alan Garner, personal communication)

Further reading

Cocker, M. and Mabey, R. 2005. *Birds Britannica*. London: Chatto and Windus.
Holloway, S. 2002. *The Historical Atlas of Breeding Birds in Britain and Ireland: 1875–1900*. London: T. and A. D. Poyser.
Norman, D. 2008. *Birds in Cheshire and Wirral*. Liverpool: Liverpool University Press.

12

Alderley Edge pondlife

Jonathan Guest and Jill Smethurst

The Alderley Edge Landscape Project (AELP) coincided with a regional survey of 1,000 ponds in north-western England, namely the Pond*Life* Critical Biodiversity Survey, supported by the European Union's Life Fund and conducted by Jonathan Guest on behalf of Liverpool John Moores University. As part of this survey, several ponds within the study area of the Landscape Project were examined (see Figures 1.3 and 8.1) and, at the instigation of the late Jill Smethurst (Cheshire Wildlife Trust), the findings were summarised and have been made available here.

In the early years of the twentieth century, the presence of a frog in the well at Jarman's Farm on Hocker Lane was taken as evidence that the water was fit to drink. Otherwise little was known about the distribution of amphibians in the area around Alderley Edge, although a few ponds had been surveyed by members of Cheshire Wildlife Trust and a small amount of information had been collected during other surveys. A request for information in the AELP newsletter, *Edgewise*, elicited only one response concerning frogs in a garden pond. In fact, despite the abundance of ponds in lowland Cheshire, little was known about their fauna until very recently. Between 1995 and 1998, however, the Pond*Life* Critical Biodiversity Survey studied plant, amphibian and invertebrate life in 1,000 ponds across north-western England, with some 500 of these lying in Cheshire. The Pond*Life* project was based at Liverpool John Moores University and funded by the Life fund of the European Community and by various statutory bodies and local authorities. In 1998, twenty-two ponds within and adjacent to the core area of the Landscape Project were included in that survey, and the information gathered was kindly made available to the Alderley Project. This contributed to a total of 676 records made of 145 invertebrate species or groups (see Table 12.1).

Four species of amphibians were found: Common Frog (*Rana temporaria*), Common Toad (*Bufo bufo*), Smooth Newt (*Triturus vulgaris*) and Great Crested or Warty Newt (*Triturus cristatus*).

Table 12.1. Invertebrate species or groups recorded by the Pond*Life* Critical Biodiversity Survey within and adjacent to the AELP core area in 1998

	No. of species	No. of records
Tricladida (flatworms)	2	17
Hirudinea (leeches)	7	38
Mollusca (snails and mussels)	17	79
Malacostraca (shrimps and hoglice)	4	28
Ephemeroptera (mayflies)	1	13
Plecoptera (stoneflies)	1	1
Megaloptera (alderflies)	1	4
Odonata (dragonflies)	9	29
Hemiptera (bugs)	19	84
Lepidoptera (China mark moths)	2	9
Trichoptera (caddisflies)	9	25
Coleoptera (beetles)	73	349

Many of the pond creatures present on the Edge are presumed to have moved in since pools were created by human activities. As with many other animals, it is difficult to see where they could have lived in an ancient wooded landscape. Ponds could not have formed on the freely draining sandstone on top of the Edge and the heathland that developed there must have been inhospitable to amphibians, although itinerant frogs and toads may have refreshed themselves at the Wizard's Well and Holy Well at intervals down the centuries. Where clay covers the rock, we can conjecture that springs and flushes may have been scraped out by wallowing deer (as today in Macclesfield Forest) or wild pigs (as today in mainland Europe) to form small pools, especially in peaty areas. Natural depressions in the clay, left on the lower slopes by the action of ice, would have filled with water and such shallow pools might have been kept open by the trampling and browsing of wild or feral cattle. Early humans must have dug out clay, albeit on a small scale, for daubing onto wattle buildings or for making pots. (Clay will have been used in the wattle-and-daub panels of the fourteenth-century barn at Clock House Farm.) Clay was dug on a larger scale for making bricks or to spread onto the sandy heathland soils to improve them for agriculture. On the clay lands of the Cheshire Plain, marlpits often occur singly. (Note that the word 'marl' has been appropriated by geologists and given a narrower meaning than it had in colloquial use.) Clay was spread onto sandy soils to improve their physical properties and there are many localities in Cheshire where groups of pits occur side by side at the edge of pockets of glacial sands or beside sandstone outcrops. These groups of ponds have generally developed a surround of woodland which casts heavy shade over the ponds (Figure 12.1). Some of the ponds on the Edge originated in this manner, to improve

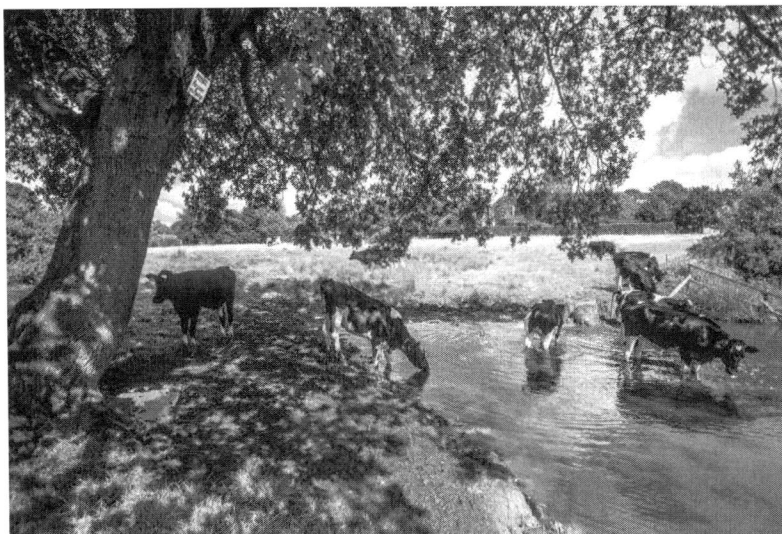

Figure 12.1. Marlpit in Oldham's Field on Armstrong Farm. Note the overhanging tree and the cows drinking from the pond.

Photograph Sean Edwards.

soils for agriculture, such as the shaded pits at the south-eastern end of the Wizard car park. This same agriculture would have levelled out the surface of farmland, ploughing and the trampling of cattle progressively wearing down the higher points while hollows were deliberately drained.

Invertebrates

One ancient type of habitat would be in the holes left when trees fall, the root-plate tearing out small hollows which, in wet ground, would fill with water. A small pool in woodland near Bradford Lane resembles such a root-hole. Although only 2 m in diameter, it was found to contain six species of water beetle. Large numbers of such small wetland features may have been more important to many species of insects than the few, larger wetland features in the ancient landscape.

Several of the water beetles found at the Edge have a localised distribution within Cheshire, as they shun the more alkaline ponds of the agricultural plain and are confined to acidic pools on heathland. These include the peatland species *Agabus affinis*, *Hydroporus obscurus* and *H. incognitus*. *Hydroporus erythrocephalus*, *H. gyllenhalii* and *H. pubescens* are slightly more widespread in Cheshire in ponds acidified by accumulating plant debris. The survival of all these species at the Edge is a pointer to its former status as heathland. *Hydroporus neglectus* is a nationally scarce beetle found in the accumulations of floating twigs at the sides of shaded, woodland ponds, especially where there is a little vegetation such as Woody Nightshade or floating grasses.

Another ancient type of habitat is the spring. On Cross Farm, Nether Alderley, pits, presumably for marl, were dug on the spring-line where groundwater from the Edge surfaces. One of these is ringed by Common Alder trees, this being a frequent feature of spring-fed ponds in other parts of Cheshire, for example at Bexton and Carden. The freshwater shrimp *Gammarus pulex* is a typical inhabitant of spring-fed ponds, but how it finds its way to remote trickles is a mystery. The beetle *Agabus paludosus* dwells in grassy streams and springs and the snail *Euconulus alderi* is found in woodland springs and flushes. The stonefly *Nemoura cinerea* lives in springs and headwaters. It might have been found more widely at the Edge if the survey had included running waters.

Ponds consist of numerous micro-habitats. One of these, most productive of beetles, is mud, especially where admixed with cow muck. The arrival of the latter in a pond is quite an event. To *Anacaena globulus*, less than 3 mm long (Plate 49), the arrival of several pounds of steaming dung from several feet above might appear catastrophic, but the beetle is well adapted to cope with the splashing and churning of hooves when cattle visit a pond to drink. Dabble with a pond-net through the rich mud at the edge of such a pond. As the detritus settles back against the fabric of the net it forms a ball. Drop this into a sorting tray and watch. A succession of scavenger beetles tunnel out, including several species that are globular in shape. At the Edge these include species of *Anacaena*, *Cercyon*, *Cryptopleurum* and *Laccobius*.

At the other extreme, open water may be beneficial to fish, but few invertebrates live there because of the lack of shelter from predators, including those same fish. The caterpillar of the Brown China Mark Moth (*Nymphula nymphaeata*) lives in a floating case cut from the leaves of Broad-leaved Pondweed or similar vegetation. Such protection is essential. Fish such as carp nose up to lily pads or other floating leaves and pick snail eggs or exposed caterpillars off the undersides.

Once ponds had been dug (whether for marl or some other purpose), they were often stocked with fish. Moving fish in this way helped spread several species of invertebrate around the region. *Dugesia* flatworms are commonly found in fishponds, and there was one record at the Edge from the survey. The Great Ramshorn Snail *Planorbarius corneus* is not native to the area but had been introduced by accident or design to four of the ponds surveyed. The American shrimp *Crangonyx pseudogracilis* was found in twelve of the twenty-two ponds and is now one of the commonest pond creatures in the area, occurring even in shaded woodland ponds.

Seven species of leech were found. Among the British leeches, only two rare species, neither now known in the region, are capable of piercing human skin. The Medicinal Leech (*Hirudo medicinalis*) may formerly have occurred in Cheshire; it would be interesting to learn the extent of its past employment and how sated animals were disposed of. The Horse Leech (*Haemopsis sanguisuga*) is the largest leech found in the present survey. It is amphibious, leaving ponds by night or in wet weather to travel overland in search of earthworms and other invertebrate prey (Plate 59). Squashed and disabled worms are often found where cattle or horses have trampled, and it is these worms, not the horses, which attract the leeches. Horse Leeches are most easily found by turning over logs and stones lying at or just above the water's edge in ponds. They cannot pierce human skin. The Fish Leech (*Hemiclepsis marginata*) is uncommon in the region but is present in one pond to the south of Castle Rock. Despite their loathsome reputation, several species of leech, including *Helobdella stagnalis*, *Glossiphonia complanata* and *G. heteroclita*, carry their young attached to their bellies and brood them protectively.

The fauna of a pond changes rapidly in the early years after its formation. A pond by the West Mine was almost devoid of vegetation in the late 1980s. Nutrients released from the bottom of the pond during its construction fed aquatic algae, which then formed dense floating wefts. Such algal mats are sought out by egg-laying chaser dragonflies. The highly mobile Broad-bodied Chaser (*Libellula depressa*) (Plate 25) was then known only from two breeding ponds in Cheshire, including one by the Middlewood Way, near Poynton (although it occurred commonly further south in England). In about 1988 a dragonfly of this species was seen depositing its eggs into the algae in the West Mine pond (J. Guest, personal observation). Nymphs of the species were found soon afterwards in a large puddle formed during construction of the Silk Road north of Macclesfield. Subsequently, the Broad-bodied Chaser has become widespread in Cheshire but it appears no longer to breed at the Edge. The West Mine pond is now densely vegetated and no longer suitable.

Amphibians

Amphibians have, by definition, a life cycle which requires them to return to water to breed, although they spend much of the year on land. Frogs lay their clumps of spawn in various shallow water bodies such as ponds, ditches, temporary rainwater pools and wheel ruts. Most Cheshire frogspawn is laid in March, although a few animals may spawn in February. Earlier spawning, linked to climatic changes, is now being reported in other parts of the country. Toads move to their traditional breeding ponds in March and stay for only a few days, draping their spawn in long strings around vegetation near to the surface. These are often deeper ponds, well oxygenated and likely to contain fish. Newts

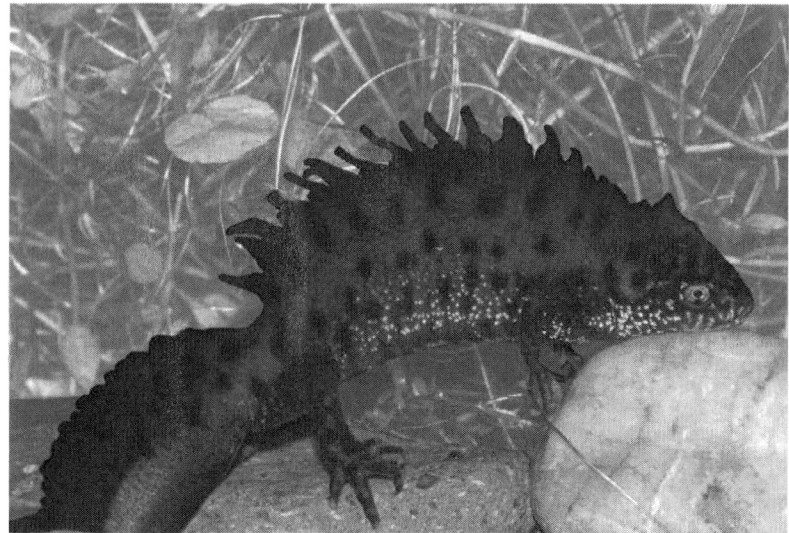

Figure 12.2. Great crested newt.
Photograph Matt Wilson.

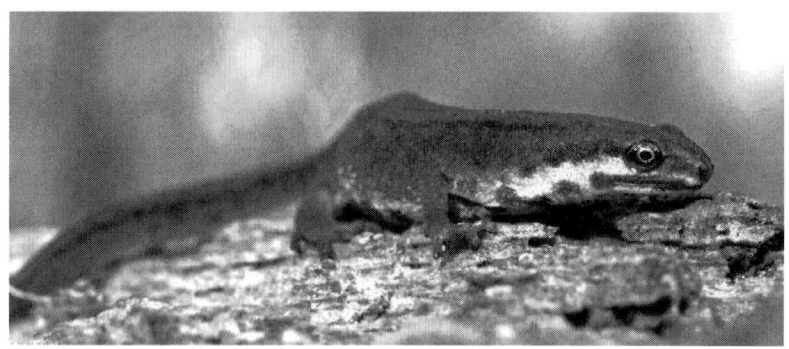

Figure 12.3. Smooth newt.
Photograph Matt Wilson.

fold their eggs individually into the leaves of pond plants. A few are laid
in March, most between April and June, while on rare occasions newt
eggs may be found outside this season. Great Crested Newts (Figure
12.2) in Cheshire have been found to deposit their eggs into the leaves of
more than fifty species of plants (J. Guest, personal observation). These
can be aquatic plants or submerged terrestrial species. All that matters is
that the leaves are smooth and flexible. In the Alderley ponds surveyed,
eggs were found folded into leaves of Brooklime (*Veronica beccabunga*),
Tufted Forgetmenot (*Myosotis laxa*), Floating Sweet-grass (*Glyceria
fluitans*) and Water-plantain (*Alisma plantago-aquatica*). Smooth Newts
(Figure 12.3) also fold their eggs into submerged leaves, generally those
of smaller dimensions. They also suspend eggs among algae or on the

undersides of duckweed. All the amphibians spawn in shallow water, where sunlight can provide sufficient warmth to aid development. Later, tadpoles and larvae may be seen. Frog and toad tadpoles are superficially similar. Common Toad tadpoles may be recognised by their blacker colour, shorter tails and the fact that the membranous crest along the back and tail is clear and not mottled as in the tadpoles of Common Frogs. Newt larvae are very different in appearance from the tadpoles of frogs and toads. They look like miniature adult newts but with filamentous gills protruding from the sides of the neck.

The Great Crested Newt flourishes in the clay-based ponds of the Cheshire Plain. It has declined greatly throughout its mainland European range, which extends to Russia and the northern half of France, and has been given legal protection in the UK under schedule 5 of the Wildlife and Countryside Act 1981 and under the Conservation (Natural Habitats, etc.) Regulations 1994. Interest in the species having been thus aroused, it has recently been found to be relatively common in Cheshire, surviving there because there are so many ponds between which the newts can move. Boothby (1997) counted some 14,000 ponds in the county from aerial photographs. Jonathan Guest found Great Crested Newts in more than 250 Cheshire ponds out of some 800 that he surveyed. The Great Crested Newt has legal protection, so a licence from Natural England is needed to catch or disturb the species or to disturb its habitat. Great Crested Newts will wander up to several hundred metres from their breeding ponds. On intensive Cheshire dairy farms they have been found breeding in small numbers in ponds set in closely cropped pasture with very little cover available once the amphibians leave the water. In such settings it is assumed that they migrate for considerable distances across the open grassland to the shelter of hedgerows or woodlands. If, however, a pond is fenced from cattle and surrounded by even a narrow belt of rank grassland, the breeding population of newts is likely to be much bigger. The newts forage among rough herbage, following vole runs in which invertebrates such as spiders, small earthworms and insects are easily caught. Just as moles check their tunnels for worms which have fallen in, so the newts can feed in vole runs. To escape from summer drought and winter cold they crawl beneath debris or follow the runs of small mammals down into their subterranean nests. Soil cavities are also occupied, such as those formed by the rotting of dead tree roots. When assessing the suitability of a site for Great Crested Newts, it is not only the aquatic and terrestrial conditions that should be considered but also the subterranean habitat. Ponds suitable for Great Crested Newts should ideally have a good extent of rough grassland, tall herbage or woodland close by to shelter the animals during the terrestrial part of their lives. The soil within all these terrestrial habitats will have remained untouched for some years, during which time mice, moles and other agencies will have caused the formation of cavities in the ground. While adult newts perform their mating displays in open water, and will dive into the depths to escape from predators, the larvae are very vulnerable to predation by fish and birds (and cannibalistic adult newts) and so stand more chance of survival if fish are absent or if there is plenty of submerged vegetation among which they can shelter.

The Smooth or Common Newt occurs widely, as its name implies, and is found throughout much of Cheshire. It is generally commoner than its larger relative, occupying a wider range of types of ponds. It will breed, for example, in shallower, more temporary pools and in small garden ponds such as those with pre-formed liners. Because its larvae hide in vegetation more than those of the Great Crested Newt, they are more likely to escape the attentions of predatory fish, and so the Smooth Newt breeds successfully in many fish ponds. Once they leave the ponds, they will also wander for hundreds of metres. They spend the winter underground and are sometimes dug up by gardeners, having burrowed into the soft soil of flowerbeds and vegetable plots.

The Palmate Newt (*Triturus helveticus*) is found in upland or acidic ponds. Its continental range is much more restricted than that of the Great Crested Newt, extending from northern Iberia through France and into western Germany. In Britain it has a scattered distribution in lowland areas but extends to the north coast of Scotland. In Cheshire it is confined to flooded quarries, mill lodges and other ponds in the sandstone areas of the Pennine fringe and to a few heathland areas on glacial sands or peat in places such as Delamere Forest, Rudheath and Lindow Moss. Given the historical presence of heathland on Alderley Edge and its proximity to the Pennine fringe, it was considered possible that Palmate Newts were present. No evidence was found. The sandstone itself and the 'brown sand' soils developed over the rock are porous. Pools form only where there is an impermeable clay base, in the areas now occupied by 'brown earth' soils (for more information on the soils of Alderley Edge see e.g. Shimwell in *ArchAE*: 217–22). Lowland heaths where Palmate Newts breed invariably have a high water-table. Palmate Newts may yet be found in the Bradford Lane area but the wet heath there lacks open pools.

Plants

During the botanical survey of the twenty-two ponds, fifteen aquatic plant taxa and seventy-seven 'emergent' plant species (those with leaves above the water surface) were recorded, with a total of 354 records. As would be expected from its geographical setting, the Edge supports several plant species which are common in the Pennine fringes of Cheshire yet scarce or absent on the Plain. These include Round-leaved Crowfoot (*Ranunculus omiophyllus*) at Hill Top Farm and Lesser Spearwort (*Ranunculus flammula*) in at least four ponds. The Crowfoot has long been confined to springs seeping from acidic rocks in the uplands but the Spearwort, once common throughout Cheshire, has retreated to the hills as twentieth-century drainage techniques have destroyed many of its lowland haunts. Short-fruited Willowherb (*Epilobium obscurum*) also shows a preference for the Pennine fringes.

Downy Birch (*Betula pubescens*) hybridises freely with Silver Birch (*Betula pendula*), both species and their intermediates being common on the Edge (Figures 9.1, 9.2, pp. 122 123). Downy Birch picks out wetter, peaty areas and is a typical heathland tree. It shaded two of the ponds surveyed. Bulbous Rush (*Juncus bulbosus*) is another heathland plant, hanging on in the Bradford Lane area where former wet heathland is vanishing under trees. Water-pepper (*Persicaria hydropiper*) and the Water-starwort (*Callitriche stagnalis*) grow in seasonally damp wheel-ruts and sloughs as well as around ponds. Both are commonest in mildly acidic areas. The bog-moss *Sphagnum fimbriatum* is abundant in one shaded pond formed in a flooded mineshaft.

Historical trends

The formation and retention of heathland on the Edge must have been associated over many centuries with grazing by livestock. There is a symbiotic association between livestock and many pond-dwelling plants and animals. Where cattle wade into a pond to drink, they create a distinctive habitat by browsing the vegetation, churning the muddy margins and fouling the water (Figure 12.1). Ivy-leaved Crowfoot (*Ranunculus hederaceus*) grows in such ponds, especially where a slight upwelling of water (as from a field drain) keeps the mud in a very liquid state. This crowfoot still occurs widely across the Cheshire Plain but the arrival of piped water and the fencing of ponds have caused some loss of suitable sites. It was found in three of the ponds surveyed. Much scarcer in the region is Water-purslane (*Lythrum portula*), a low-growing, unobtrusive plant which is found only rarely around the margins of ponds, among floating grasses bitten short by cattle. It is present in two ponds at the Edge but is otherwise rare in Cheshire.

Shaded, woodland ponds are poor breeding sites for amphibians. Accumulations of tannin-filled oak leaves and twigs in ponds make them inhospitable habitats to many aquatic invertebrates. There are uncommon species among seldom-studied invertebrate groups such as craneflies and empid flies, which breed in mud and rotting wood in and by ponds, but these have not been studied at the Edge. The closing of the woodland canopy at the Edge within the last fifty years must have been accompanied by great changes in the aquatic fauna as well as the documented changes among terrestrial fauna.

Submerged waterweeds are in decline throughout England. A major cause of the decline appears to be the increase of plant nutrients in groundwater. In ponds this causes algae to grow over the submerged leaves of higher plants, reducing their ability to photosynthesise. In the twenty-two ponds surveyed, there were only single records of Various-leaved Water-starwort (*Callitriche platycarpa*), Small Pondweed (*Potamogeton berchtoldii*) and Blunt-leaved Pondweed (*P. obtusifolius*). Canadian Waterweed (*Elodea canadensis*) was found in two ponds. This plant was brought into Cheshire from North America in the late nineteenth century and has been moved between ponds by anglers and others as an oxygenator. It may also be spread by birds. Water-violet (*Hottonia palustris*), a native British species, occurs in two ponds near the site of the West Mine. It arrived in one pond very soon after its formation in the 1980s and had evidently been deliberately introduced.

The mechanisms by which many plant species move between ponds remain a mystery. In some cases, as with the Lesser Spearwort mentioned earlier, the loss of ditches and wet areas as the water-table has fallen in response to deeper agricultural drainage may now prevent them from moving between ponds, hence their decline. The growth in sales of aquatic plants from garden centres is leading to changes in the pond flora of the Edge. When Canadian Waterweed first became naturalised in Britain, fears were expressed that it might displace native species. Whether it has actually done so we cannot tell, historical records being too sparse. Two newly arrived species are now competing with the native and naturalised plants in local ponds. These are the New Zealand Pigmyweed (*Crassula helmsii*) and the Least Duckweed (*Lemna minuta*). The Pigmyweed grows either on damp mud at the edges of ponds or submerged in up to 60 cm or more of water. It has thin, rigid leaves which offer little worthwhile shelter to aquatic invertebrates and which are too inflexible and narrow to be used as egg-laying sites by newts. It is now well established in a pond near the site of the West Mine. Elsewhere in Cheshire there is documentary evidence that it is displacing uncommon native plants, including Alternate-leaved Water-milfoil (*Myriophyllum alterniflorum*) and Lesser Water-plantain (*Baldellia ranunculoides*). There is a risk that it will spread at the Edge into the two shallow ponds with Water-purslane. Least Duckweed is an American species, which has now become established in ponds scattered widely across lowland Cheshire. It was found in three ponds at the Edge. Although there is experimental evidence that it can displace the native duckweeds, it coexists with these in many ponds.

Common Duckweed (*Lemna minor*) remains the commonest aquatic plant in the study area, being noted at seventeen of the twenty-two ponds in the survey.

Both Pigmyweed and Least Duckweed are found commonly as contaminants in pots of pond plants sold by garden centres, despite the potential threats they pose to native wildlife. Gardeners are generally humane people who try to help frogs by distributing what they consider to be a surplus of spawn, carrying it in buckets from their gardens to ponds in the countryside. Country parks have been the starting point for the liberation of alien pond plants into the Cheshire landscape. Although it is illegal to release alien species 'into the wild', 'the wild' exists only in the minds of bureaucrats. It cannot, in reality, be separated from the human environment. Human activities will continue to shape the ecology of the ponds at Alderley Edge.

Acknowledgements

Thanks are due to the National Trust and to the various private landowners who permitted access to their ponds for the purposes of this survey. We also wish to thank the Pond*Life* Project, 15–21 Webster Street, Liverpool L3 2ET, for permission to use records gathered during the Pond*Life* Critical Biodiversity Survey of North-Western England.

13

The insects and other invertebrates of Alderley Edge

Dmitri V. Logunov and Roger L. H. Dennis

Introduction

Dmitri V. Logunov

> Insects glistened in the sunshine,
> Insects skated on the water,
> Filled the drowsy air with buzzing.
> H. W. Longfellow (1856), *Hiawatha*, Pt 2, XVIII, The Death of Kwasind

From every point of view, 'bugs' – the insects and other invertebrates – represent the most diverse group of organisms both locally on Alderley Edge and nationally in the British Isles. The total number of bugs recorded from the Edge by the Alderley Edge Landscape Project (AELP) is 1,732 species: they are listed in Appendix 13.1. The total numbers of the eight groups of bugs recorded on the Edge is summarised in Table 13.1. The best-represented are the harvestmen, with their total accounting for 44 per cent of the British species; the least represented are the Hymenoptera, at 1.7 per cent. As a whole, the groups given in Table 13.1 make up about 7 per cent of the British list of invertebrate species. The total of 1,732 species for Alderley Edge is by no means exhaustive because for many practical reasons only selected groups were surveyed and identified. For instance, the soil fauna remains totally unknown. Given that over 2,135 species of insects and other invertebrates have been found in just a single ordinary suburban garden in Leicester (although collected

Table 13.1. Numbers of species in selected groups of invertebrates recorded on Alderley Edge and in the British Isles as a whole

Taxonomic group	Alderley Edge	British Isles	% of British Isles
True Bugs (Hemiptera)	134	c. 1,830	7.3
Beetles (Coleoptera)	363	4,034	9.0
Butterflies and moths (Lepidoptera)	616	2,717	23.0
True flies (Diptera)	216	7,035	3.1
Ants, wasps, bees (Hymenoptera)	128	7,517	1.7
Spiders (Araneae)	137	649	21.1
Harvestmen (Opiliones)	11	25	44.0
Centipedes and millipedes (Myriapoda)	17	156	10.9

Note. The term 'True Bugs' is in different contexts used to denote the entire order of Hemiptera but alternatively specifically the suborder Heteroptera.
Source: author generated; total counts of species of each order in the British fauna were taken from various sources.

over a period of thirty years: see Owen, 2010), the number of bugs from the Edge is indicative of how poorly their real diversity over the site is currently known: the figure should at least be trebled.

For instance, to date, the best-studied and therefore the richest insect fauna of Alderley Edge is that of the Lepidoptera (butterflies and moths), with 616 recorded species (Table 13.1). In the UK there are 2,717 recorded Lepidopteran species (see Kimber, 2014), accounting for 11 per cent of the entire British list of insects (c. 25,054 species). By extrapolating this proportion, as 616 species representing about 11 per cent of the entire insect diversity of the Edge, one could estimate its diversity as about 5,600 species of insects. An estimate of about 4,600 insect species can be calculated if one uses the spiders, which are relatively well studied on the Edge, as a proportional value. However, the real diversity of the entire fauna of invertebrates of Alderley Edge must be even greater.

Some readers might think that with a few exceptions creepy-crawlies, so often referred to as 'pests', are not worthy of all this attention and discussion. We all are rather happy with showy butterflies flapping around us or birds singing in the air and obviously doing it for our own pleasure. As T. Turpin (2009) remarked, 'one reason for insects is, no doubt, to give poets something to write about!' However, myriads of unnoticeable bugs are the cornerstones of all existing ecosystems, providing vital ecological services on which humans depend: they pollinate flowers and crops, recycle our wastes and do many other invisible jobs in our gardens. Insect pollinators such as honeybees, bumblebees, butterflies and hoverflies are thought to contribute to one in every three mouthfuls of the food that we eat. As Losey and Vaughan (2006) put it, 'love them or hate them, we need insects for global survival!', and therefore bugs deserve our special attention. One can only agree with Jennifer Owen, the author of *The Ecology of a Garden* (1991), who argued that 'there are no pests, because everything in my garden is a source of interest and enjoyment'. Therefore let us talk a little about the interest and enjoyment that our diminutive neighbours can generate if we pay a little attention to them.

The brief essays that make up the rest of Chapter 13 are devoted to various groups of bugs and are written in a manner that will (we hope) make them interesting for non-entomologists; the intention is to arouse readers' enthusiasm rather than overloading them with technical details and terms. For this reason they are better used in conjunction with the more detailed and specialised literature devoted to each of the groups we discuss and which we mention in its context, and with the excellent account of the cultural stories of the British invertebrates called *Bugs Britannica*, by Marren and Mabey (2010). At the same time it is also our hope that these essays and especially the checklist in Appendix 13.1 will draw the attention of local entomological enthusiasts to the bug fauna of Alderley Edge and to the need for a thorough inventory. Further progress in the study of this fauna will certainly depend on those individual enthusiasts who are ready to take on this challenge.

To help the reader identify the insects mentioned in this chapter, the *Collins Pocket Guide to the Insects of Britain and Western Europe* by Chinery (1986, and subsequent editions) and the comprehensive field guide by Brock (2014) are recommended. Some of the more detailed guides to particular groups of British insects are mentioned in the relevant sections and in Appendix 13.1. For a comprehensive account of specialised literature on British insects and other invertebrates see Barnard (1999, 2011).

A. True Bugs (Hemiptera) and smaller orders of insect

Dmitri V. Logunov

> Yet let me flap this bug with gilded wings,
> This painted child of dirt that stinks and stings.
> Alexander Pope (1735), 'Epistles to Several Persons: Epistle to Dr. Arbuthnot'

The Hemiptera, or True Bugs, constitute a diverse group of insects with incomplete metamorphosis in which the young bugs (nymphs) develop gradually, resemble miniature wingless adults and do not undergo a pupal stage. The word 'bug' is thought to derive from the Middle English word *bugge*, meaning a 'spirit' or 'ghost' (Schaefer, 2003): should one awake in the morning with small, red itching welts and swellings, these marks were mistakenly attributed to a malevolent spirit called a *bugge*; yet the real culprit was in fact the Bedbug (*Cimex lectularius*). Thus the 'bad' habits of one creature gave its name to the whole group of its 'better' relatives. All True Bugs are characterised by piercing mouth parts (termed the rostrum), like a tiny hypodermic needle, which they use to suck up liquid food: juices from plants or body fluids from other insects, or even the blood of vertebrates (e.g. the already mentioned Bedbug, not yet formally recorded from the Edge). Some plant-feeding bugs such as Greenflies are all too familiar. A total of 134 species of the Hemiptera have been found on Alderley Edge, while some 1,830 species are known nationally (see Appendix 13.1; Table 13.1; Bantock and Botting, 2010).

Traditionally, the Hemiptera were subdivided in two suborders: the Heteroptera (True Bugs) defined by the forewings lying flat over the body and partially sclerotised (horny at the base and membranous at the apex); and the Homoptera (Froghoppers, Leafhoppers, Greenflies, etc.), in which both pairs of wings are membranous and uniform in texture and are held roof-like over the body. However, recent morphological studies and DNA analysis strongly suggest that the Homoptera is not a natural taxonomic unit and consists of at least four suborders (see Henry, 2009, for a discussion; Barnard, 2011). In the present section, the information is presented in the traditional way (Heteroptera and Homopteran bugs), whereas the checklist of recorded species in Appendix 13.1 is given according to the modern taxonomic classification. This section is best used in conjunction with the comprehensive synopsis on the British Heteroptera by Southwood and Leston (1959; see Nau, 2006, for the corrected bug names used in the latest books) and with the good introduction to the biology and ecology of the British Hemiptera with identification keys to families by Dolling (1991). Useful general information on the True Bugs can also be found in Schuh and Slater (1995); aquatic groups of bugs are briefly covered by Greenhalgh and Ovenden (2007); and an illustrative identification guide to the British Hemiptera with many impressive colour images has been assembled by Bantock and Botting (2010).

Although the known diversity of the Hemiptera of Alderley Edge may seem impressive (134 species), it is much less than the diversity yet to be discovered. One of the obvious reasons why the True Bugs are so diverse is that many of them (the Homopterans in particular) are food plant specific and therefore their diversity on the Edge should be equal to or more than that of the vascular plants (351 species; see Chapter 9). The diversity of bugs and their lifestyles can explain why insect enthusiasts find them so fascinating to study and observe. Even gardeners should learn more about their habits in order to see that not all of them are foes.

Heteroptera

The Heteroptera (True Bugs) represent the largest and wonderfully diverse group of bugs, with 563 species found in the UK (Nau, 2006) and some 42,350 species worldwide (Henry, 2009). The currently known fauna of True Bugs of Alderley Edge is modest, numbering eighty-nine species only (Appendix 13.1). Nevertheless, the fauna contains a number of species with interesting lifestyles. In the text that follows, the counts of British species in various Heteropteran families follow Nau (2006).

The most familiar and easily recognisable group of the True Bugs seem to be Shield Bugs of the families Acanthosomatidae (three species, five nationally) and Pentatomidae (two species, nineteen nationally). Usually, these are relatively large insects, often shield-shaped, exhibiting a great diversity in colouration. The majority of the Shield Bugs are plant feeders, with a distinct preference for immature fruits and seeds. For instance, the commonest of them, the Hawthorn Shieldbug (*Acanthosoma haemorrhoidale*; Plate 21) feeds on hawthorn, but can also be found on bramble and other fruiting shrubs (parcels 17 and 20b of the biological survey done as part of the Alderley Edge Landscape Project – see Chapter 8), from where one can occasionally pick it up together with berries and then be unpleasantly surprised by the reaction of the bug: when disturbed, Shield Bugs emit an unpleasant pungent scent, sometimes smelling mildly of almonds, hence their other vernacular name of Stinkbug. Interestingly, the stinky smell produced by the Shield Bugs seems to protect them not only from vertebrates but also from ants.

One of the striking biological features of Shield Bugs is their maternal care, which is sometimes even reflected in their names. For instance, the female of the Parent Bug (*Elasmucha grisea*), a common dweller in birch trees throughout the Edge, lays between thirty and forty eggs in a compact mass which is completely covered by her body, so that she can protect the eggs and newly hatched youngsters from predators and parasitoids (see section E for a discussion of parasitoids). A few species of Shield Bug are entirely carnivorous, for instance *Picromerus bidens*, which is found on low vegetation along woodland edges and marsh margins (parcel 17). This species can attack only slow-moving insects which are not equipped to defend themselves, such as moth caterpillars.

Compared with the clumsy carnivorous Shield Bugs, the Assassin Bugs (Reduviidae; one species on the Edge, seven nationally) are far more effective predators, capable of subduing a wide array of prey among other arthropods, which they actively seek out and seize. The only species of the so-called Thread-legged Assassin Bugs (*Empicoris vagabundus*) recorded from the Edge uses only the two hind pairs of its very long and delicate legs for walking. The first pair of legs is raptorial, as in the Mantids, and is used to hold down its prey – various soft-bodied insects such as Booklice. This Assassin Bug is a cryptically coloured ambusher, commonly found on the trunks and branches of trees.

The small (about 4 mm long or less) and predatory Flower Bugs (Anthocoridae; four common species on the Edge, thirty-four nationally) can be found on almost any plant in parcels 3a, 5, 11d, 17, preferring lower vegetation. The commonest of them is *Anthocoris nemorum*. One of the Flower Bugs (*Tetraphleps bicuspis*) is more specific and is associated with the larch (parcels 4, 20b); adults of this species hide under the bark and the nymphs are normally seen in July and August. A striking biological peculiarity of the Flower Bugs is the so-called 'traumatic insemination', also known in the Bedbugs, that is, the mating practice in which the male pierces the female's abdomen with its sharp penis in order to deposit its semen. How that cruel 'love practice' could have evolved is a matter of debate, but some call it a sexual conflict.

An interesting group of predacious bugs, often flightless, are the Damsel Bugs (Nabidae; four species on the Edge, twelve nationally), of which all of the recorded species prefer a range of open habitats, including grassland, marshy places and ruderal communities (parcels 17, 18). Some species have shortened (in *Nabis flavomarginatus*) or very short (in *Nabis limbatus*) wings and look almost like ants. Even better ant-mimics are the females of the *Loricula* species (Microphysidae, or Minute Bugs; two species on Alderley Edge, eight nationally): these are tiny (1.5–2 mm long), virtually wingless creatures with a narrow orange anterior part of the body and a greatly broadened and rounded dark brown abdomen. *Loricula* species are also notable for their distinctive sexual dimorphism, for the males have normally developed wings. Both *Loricula* species found on the Edge live on the bark of various trees, mostly hiding in the crevices among the lichen on tree trunks, where they hunt Mites, Springtails and fly larvae. Another interesting and rarely encountered bug living beneath the bark of birch and oak trees and feeding on bracket fungi (*Polyporus*) is *Aradus depressus*, the only representative of Flat Bugs (or Bark Bugs) found on the Edge (Aradidae; seven nationally). These bugs have a very flattened body, shortened legs and, what is particularly striking, unlike other True Bugs, their mouth parts are very long and narrow and stored coiled within the head.

There are several medium-sized farmland ponds on Alderley Edge (parcels 11d, 20b, 22) which support a good variety of common water bugs (fifteen species; Appendix 13.1) and other insects (see below); for a general account of the Alderley Edge pondlife see Chapter 12. Most aquatic bugs are predators; perhaps the best-known are Pond Skaters (e.g. *Gerris lacustris*) and the Common Backswimmer (*Notonecta glauca*). The latter species is a highly evolved predator that can readily attack the fry of fish, tadpoles and aquatic insects, immobilising them with a toxic bite. This bug will even stab a person's fingers painfully if handled. Even so, it is worth trying to grab the bug since the old wisdom teaches us that 'if you can catch a lucky bug out of water, you will have fine luck'. Due to its remarkable 'tail' (a respiratory siphon), the Water Scorpion (*Nepa cinerea*) is another easily recognisable bug of the Edge's ponds; it prefers shallow muddy waters at the margins. They are notable for having a set of three pairs of hydrostatic organs: these detectors of water pressure allow the bug to orient itself in relation to depth, and also give an indication of the deviation of its body from the horizontal. Two species of Water-cricket found on the Edge (*Microvelia reticulata* and *Velia caprai*) are daytime predators, snatching up insects or spiders that fall on the water surface, on which they can walk. Large prey is usually conveyed to the land for consumption. Unlike other water bugs, Water Boatmen (Corixidae; thirty-three species in the UK) are herbivorous, feeding on bottom algae. In order to gather algae they use the modified, spoon-shaped tarsi of their first legs. Another unusual biological feature of the corixids is a courting song produced by males of many species (e.g. *Corixa punctata*) by rubbing the special sound-pegs of their front femora against the resonant head margin, the process called stridulation (as in Grasshoppers). Water Boatmen 'sing' after dusk and their 'songs' can be heard from a few metres away.

An interesting group of bugs which can be collected from the margins of ponds, ditches and slow streams (parcels 17, 18, 20b) is the Shore Bugs (Saldidae; three species on the Edge, twenty-one nationally). Shore Bugs are active predators that have good visual acuity and detect their prey by sight. They are ovoid in outline and are notable for their agility through a combination of fast movements, jumping and flight. Some species (e.g. *Saldula saltatoria*) occur in saltmarshes or small temporarily flooded hollows, always on firm mud; others (e.g. *Chartoscirta cincta*) can be found among reeds and rushes. If truly terrestrial, like *Saldula orthochila*, they prefer acid grassland, sandy heaths and paths on sandy soil (parcel 17b).

Beautiful Lace Bugs (Tingidae; two species on the Edge, twenty-three nationally) are easily recognisable by their bizarre flat bodies and the lace-like reticulation of their pronotum and forewings. Both species found on Alderley Edge (parcels 17a, 18) feed on the underside of leaves of a single host plant or a group of closely related species: the common Gorse Lacebug (*Dictyonota strichnocera*) occurs on gorse and also on broom; *Tingis ampliata*, one of the most frequently encountered Lace Bugs, can be predominantly found on creeping thistle (*Cirsium arvense*).

Over a half of the True Bugs recorded on Alderley Edge belong to two large and diverse families of the Ground or Seed Bugs (Lygaeidae; eight species of eighty-two known nationally) and of the Capsid Bugs (Miridae; forty-five species of 216 known nationally). Most species of the

Lygaeidae are ground-living insects, feeding on mature seeds – hence their two common names. Two of the recorded species are uncommon in northern England: *Kleidocerys ericae*, a heather-feeding bug which is found mainly on heathland in England; and *Cymus claviculus*, a bug preferring drier open habitats such as sandy heaths and dry meadows, where it is associated with knotgrass and toad rush. The Birch Catkin Bug (*Kleidocerys resedae*) is a noisy and smelly bug that in June can swarm on catkins and seed heads of birches and alders (parcels 17, 20b). It can produce a sound by rubbing forewings and hindwings together, which can be heard by the human ear, especially if an insect is placed in a small vial and then shaken – who would not 'sing' when caged!

The Capsid Bugs (Miridae) constitute the largest family of True Bugs, containing nearly one-third of all the True Bugs, with some 10,400 species described worldwide (Henry, 2009). The family consists of soft, delicate-looking bugs of variable size and appearance: their varied colouration can blend well with the foliage, flowers or bark on which they rest or feed. Capsid Bugs easily shed their legs by muscular action if seized by a predator or trapped in a film of moisture (Dolling, 1991). Most Capsid Bugs are herbivorous, feeding largely on developing fruits and seeds and therefore some species may get into conflict with gardeners. For instance, the Potato Bug (*Closterotomus norvegicus*) can occasionally be a pest of crop and garden plants; the polyphagous *Lygocoris* species (e.g. the Common Green Capsids – *Lygocoris pabulinus*) can not only feed on various garden plants but also damage them by injecting their toxic saliva, which kills off tiny areas of plant tissue. A common sign of Capsid damage is distorted, crinkly leaves full of small, brown-ringed holes, while flower buds may never open. On apples they leave raised bumps and scabby patches. Some Capsid Bugs are partly (e.g. the *Phylus* species) or entirely (e.g. *Deraeocoris lutescens*) predacious. All the three *Phytocoris* species found on the Edge not only have a distinctive appearance, due to their long hind femora and very long first antennal segment, but are also predominantly carnivorous. They occur on the trunks and branches of a range of deciduous trees all over Alderley Edge, feeding on small insects and mites. Among predacious Capsid Bugs found on the Edge there are species with rather specialised feeding habits; for example, *Campyloneura virgula* feeds predominantly on Barklice of the family Psocidae.

Identification of the Capsid Bugs is difficult, not only because of their overwhelming diversity but also because many species are wing-polymorphic, in other words, individuals of the same species exist in distinct long-winged and short-winged forms. Such wing polymorphism is especially widespread in the bugs associated with grasses, and it is known in at least seventy-five British Heteroptera species (Waloff, 1983). This phenomenon is also well known in Pond Skaters (Gerridae).

Although factors underlying the wing polymorphism in True Bugs have not been fully understood, it is agreed that a complex hormonal regulation in combination with environmental factors such as density of population, host plant condition and temperature is involved. Of the species recorded from Alderley Edge, the Fern Bug (*Bryocoris pteridis*), occurring on various woodland ferns (parcel 3a), shows strong wing polymorphism in both males and females. The same holds true for *Dicyphus pallicornis*, a garden species commonly found on foxgloves.

Homoptera

Only forty-five Homopteran bugs have been recorded from Alderley Edge to date (Appendix 13.1). The majority of Homopterans are plant feeders that are usually restricted to a single host plant or to a few related plant species. However, there are exceptions: for example, the Common Froghopper (*Philaenus spumarius*), found on the Edge, with over 500 documented food plants, has the broadest known host range of any plant-feeding insect. It is one of the three Froghopper species (Aphrophoridae) found on the Edge (nine species in the UK: Bantock and Botting, 2010). Although most readers will probably not have seen adult Froghoppers, many (if not all) will be familiar with the frothy masses, commonly known as 'cuckoo spits', which can be seen on grassy plants around Alderley Edge in spring and early summer. The name 'cuckoo spit' seems to originate from antiquity, when Aristotle taught that instead of laying eggs like other birds cuckoos spat their young into the world, and the tiny being inside the spit was a baby cuckoo (see Marren and Mabey, 2010). Contrary to the opinion of the great Aristotle, we now know that the spits are actually produced by baby Froghoppers (nymphs), which sit inside them. This is why another common name of these creatures is Spittlebugs. If you are not sure of this, please visit the Edge in late spring and check for yourself! The frothy mass is created to protect nymphs from predators and desiccation and to insulate them from temperature extremes.

An interesting Homopteran group found on Alderley Edge (parcel 17) is the beautiful lace-winged Planthoppers (Cixiidae; two species on the Edge, twelve in the UK), which are distinguished by their transparent membranous forewings with well defined contrasting veins and often with reticulate brownish markings. Nymphs of some Planthoppers (e.g. *Tachycixius pilosus*) develop at the base of grasses in dry, sunny places and can be found in the litter layer throughout the winter. A group of small plant-sucking hoppers of the family Delphacidae (three species on the Edge, seventy-six in the UK) is characterised by the presence of a large movable spur at the apex of the hind tibia and by the well expressed wing polymorphism in most species. The Delphacidae are slow-moving bugs, with the majority living and feeding exclusively on grasses, sedges or rushes, never trees or shrubs (e.g. *Conomelus anceps* feeds only on rushes).

The majority of the Homopterans found on Alderley Edge belong to the large family Cicadellidae commonly referred to as Leafhoppers (twenty-six species on the Edge of the 288 known in the UK; Bantock and Botting, 2010). The most familiar of them is the Green Leafhopper (*Cicadella viridis*), a bright green and eye-catching Leafhopper that can be found elsewhere on grasses and rushes in marshy places. In gardens it is common on emergent rushes and sedges at the margins of garden ponds. Most Leafhoppers have only a single food plant or a narrow range of them, and therefore are usually confined to a particular habitat. For instance, the very variably coloured Leafhopper *Oncopsis flavicollis* feeds only on birch; the heavily built green or brown Leafhopper *Iassus lanio* is usually found on oaks, although occasionally on other trees; and the very distinct *Ulopa reticulata*, with strongly convex and coarsely punctured forewings, can be found exclusively on heather (both *Erica* and *Calluna*), normally at the bases of the plants. It is worth mentioning that Leafhoppers and Planthoppers can cause damage to the structure of the food plant as they pierce it for feeding and, even more important, they can transmit viruses or bacterial pathogens from one plant to another; some countries go so far as to categorise them as agricultural pests.

A unique feature of the Leafhoppers among all insects is the production of a distinctive hydrophobic biomaterial, known as brochosomes (protein-lipid granules). Brochosomes constitute an excretory product that is expelled from the anus with the liquid faeces and used for covering Leafhoppers' bodies with a hydrophobic coating. This coating makes the body surface highly repellent to water and protects the creatures from wetting by water and their own liquid excreta (Rakitov, 2009).

Unfortunately, identification of Leafhoppers can be complex, depending on venation of both wings, detailed facial features and internal male genitalia, and requires extensive training because many species are very variable and also sexually dimorphic. Besides, about 16 per cent of the British Homopterans associated with grasses and forbs display wing-polymorphism, as mentioned above (see Waloff, 1983). Identification guides (e.g. Le Quesne and Payne, 1981) to the British Homopterans are still limited (see Barnard, 1999, for further references).

Several families of the Homopterans are commonly called Aphids, better known as Greenflies (suborder Sternorrhyncha; see Appendix 13.1). These are tiny, soft-bodied and pear-shaped insects of varying colours and shades, many of which are troublesome garden pests. Most

Aphid species are restricted to a few food plants: for example, *Aphis epilobii* feeds only on leaves or shoots of willowherbs (*Epilobium* spp.), while the Grey Pine Aphid (*Schizolachnus pineti*) feeds exclusively on pine needles. Consequently there may be almost as many species of aphids on Alderley Edge as there are native and cultivated vascular plants (351 species; see Chapter 9), yet only eight of them have been recorded to date (of some 600 aphid species known nationally and over 4,500 species described worldwide; Forero, 2008). Some Aphid species can subsist on several food plants, which are sometimes alternated during the season. For instance, as its name indicates, the Willow-carrot Aphid (*Cavariella aegopodii*) subsists on two kinds of food plants: its primary host is willow (*Salix* spp.), on which it feeds during the spring and autumn, and the secondary hosts are various umbellifers such as carrot, celeriac, parsnip and others, on which it feeds during the summer.

All British Aphids have several generations per year. Their life cycles are generally complex, and they reproduce both asexually and sexually. Another hallmark of the aphids is that they are often 'farmed' and guarded by ants for their sweet excrement, known as honeydew. About 25 per cent of British aphids are ant attended (Hopkins and Thacker, 1999) and both parties seem to benefit from the interaction. Ants not only 'milk' Aphids as dairy cows but also protect them, fighting off Ladybirds and other predators. Of the Aphid species recorded from the Edge, *Aphis epilobii*, as well as other species of *Aphis* which have not been formally recorded from the Edge (e.g. the Black Bean Aphid – *Aphis fabae*), are known to be associated with the Black Garden Ant (*Lasius niger*). The European Birch Aphid (*Euceraphis punctipennis*) is known to be tended by Wood Ants of the genus *Formica*. Since most Aphid species are quite polymorphic (i.e. they occur in several different forms and morphs), their identification is difficult and usually requires microscopic examination and extensive training. Furthermore, as a consequence of their specialised feeding habits, reliable identification of Aphids inevitably requires reasonable knowledge of their food plants. A good introduction to the British Aphids is the book by Blackman (1974); see also Barnard (1999, 2011) for further references.

Only two species of the Jumping Plant Lice (superfamily Psylloidea) of the eighty species known nationally (Barnard, 1999, 2011) have been found on the Edge to date. These are small plant-feeding insects re-sembling diminutive cicadas and ranging in length from 1.5 to 4.5 mm. Their common name reflects the ability of adults to jump backwards when disturbed. As with the Greenflies, the Jumping Plant Lice are host plant specific, being associated with just one or two host plant species; consequently their likely species number on the Edge is to be multi-plied many times. The Jumping Plant Lice is one of the least studied groups of British Homopterans and the most difficult set of species to identify (many species require dissection to distinguish them). For those who are interested in studying Psyllidae, the identification guide by Hodkinson and White (1979) and the online resource by Bantock and Botting (2010) can be recommended.

As an additional sign of the incompleteness of our knowledge of the Edge's Homopterans one can mention a total lack of records for the Whiteflies (Aleyrodoidea; nineteen species nationally; Kloet and Hinks, 1964) and especially for the Scale Insects (Coccoidea; 107 species nationally; Barnard, 1999). The Whiteflies are tiny insects with waxy white wings; they resemble minute moths. They usually feed on the underside of leaves and may be familiar to many gardeners, both in greenhouses and outdoors, because their adults often appear in hordes of hundreds flying away from the foliage of a favoured host plant. The Scale Insects constitute a large group of the Homopterans with a great variety of forms and lifestyles, that are usually small (less than 5 mm long) and often cryptic in habit. Although their reproduction is thought to be sexual, the males of many species, which look like tiny flies with a single pair of forewings, have not yet been found and described.

Smaller orders of insect

Insect groups presented in this section do not constitute a natural taxonomic grouping. Their common feature is a comparatively low number of recorded/known species on both a regional (Alderley Edge) and a national scale, and for this reason all such groups are briefly discussed together.

Some of the insect groups with only a few representatives found on the Edge simply remain under-recorded. For instance, virtually nothing is known about the soil-dwelling, primitive, wingless insects such as the Springtails (order Collembola; one species on the Edge, of the 304 known nationally; Kloet and Hinks, 1964) and the Two-pronged Bristletails (order Diplura; one species of the twelve native species). As with the soil mites and other soil invertebrates (see section G), these insect groups remain practically unstudied on Alderley Edge. Other groups, such as the Scorpion Flies (order Mecoptera; four species nationally), the Alder Flies (order Megaloptera; seven species nationally), the Green Lacewings (order Neuroptera; sixty species in the UK; Plate 22 shows a species photographed on the Edge), Grasshoppers (order Orthoptera; thirty-three known nationally; Plate 23 shows a species photographed on the Edge) and the Earwigs (order Dermaptera; four native species), are poorly represented overall in the UK and thus it not surprising that only one or two of the commonest species have been found on Alderley Edge.

Earwigs (Dermaptera) are almost too well known to require description: elongate insects with a pair of large terminal, pincer-like appendages. The only species found on the Edge is the Common Earwig (*Forficula auricularia*). This species is a harmless scavenger, although it can chew flower petals and thus cause a little damage in gardens. The word 'earwig' is of historical significance on account of the widespread belief that these creatures are liable to crawl into the human ear and wreak havoc. Yet how earwigs became associated with ears is uncertain – some blame Pliny the Elder, the Roman natural historian, for bringing this idea up: see Berenbaum (2009) for further details – and this notion is just a common misconception which has never been proven.

Four smaller orders represent semi-aquatic groups, whose larvae or nymphs live in water while adults are terrestrial (flying) forms. The most dazzling of these insects are of course the Dragonflies and Damselflies (order Odonata; Plate 24 shows a female Common Darter, *Sympetrum striolatum*, from the Edge), with nine species recorded from the Edge of the twenty-one known in north-west England (Bentley, 2008) and fifty nationally (see the website of the British Dragonfly Society, http://www.british-dragonflies.org.uk/). Those recorded locally include some spectacular species, such as the large Southern Hawker (*Aeshna cyanea*), which can be up to 70 mm long; the species is brightly coloured, with apple-green marks on a dark background, and can be seen swinging or darting to and fro over ponds around parcels 20b and 22. This species breeds in well vegetated small ponds, often those in gardens. The Brown Hawker (*Aeshna grandis*) can be distinguished by its golden-brown wings; interestingly, the record of this species is near its northern limit in the UK. The Broad-bodied Chaser (*Libellula depressa*; Plate 25) is another easily recognisable species of the Edge. It has a very broad, flattened abdomen, which is blue in males and golden brown in females. Out of four common Damselflies found on the Edge, it is worth mentioning the Large Red Damselfly (*Pyrrhosoma nymphula*; Plate 26), an active, deep-red damselfly with black legs, which can be found elsewhere near ponds or slow-moving water. The Odonata of Cheshire have been fully surveyed by Gabb and Kitching (1992). A very interesting account of Dragonflies and Damselflies and their cultural associations has been provided by Lucas (2002; see also Marren and Mabey, 2010).

Two other groups of semi-aquatic insects, the Stoneflies (Plecoptera; thirty-four British species) and the Mayflies (order Ephemeroptera; forty-seven British species) are represented on the Edge by a single species only (see Appendix 13.1). The main reason for this may be not an under-recording, as in the case of the soil-dwelling groups mentioned above, but rather the low water quality of the Edge's ponds and slow-moving streams. All species of Stoneflies are intolerant of water pollution. The same holds true for the Mayflies, which are routinely used for monitoring water quality because their presence and, even more importantly, their species diversity can be valuable indicators of water quality. Incidentally, the nymphs of the only Mayfly species found on the Edge (*Cloeon dipterum*) are notable for their high resistance to a low level or a significant decrease of oxygen, which may be why this species is able to exist on the Edge. This Mayfly is also famous for its ovoviviparity (a unique feature among the European Mayflies), that is, a mode of reproduction in which embryos develop inside eggs that are retained within mother's body until they are ready to hatch.

Caddisflies (order Trichoptera) are superficially similar to moths and, unlike the aforementioned groups of semi-aquatic insects, they have a complete metamorphosis, and pass through a pupa stage. Caddisfly larvae are famous for constructing portable protective cases made of vegetable fragments or sand grains joined together by silk; the shape and structure of these cases are often species specific and can be used for identification. Only thirteen of the 198 British species of Caddisflies have been found on Alderley Edge (see Appendix 13.1), less than half of the species recorded from north-west England (fifty species; Bentley, 2008). Adults rarely feed; they can form mating swarms, are usually active at night and thus can be collected by light traps, as can moths. Identification of Caddisflies requires training, as it is based on examination of their genitalia under a microscope and of the fine venation of their wings (see Barnard, 1999, for references to useful identification guides).

A large number of good introductory books exist on British freshwater life, for instance a well illustrated guide by Greenhalgh and Ovenden (2007). A complete list of aquatic invertebrates in north-west England ponds has been provided by Bentley (2008).

An interesting group of the Barklice (order Psocoptera) is represented on the Edge by only five of about seventy known in the UK (New, 2005) and is certainly under-recorded here. For comparison one can mention that fourteen species of Psocoptera were found in just a single garden in Leicestershire by Owen (1991). Barklice are small to minute insects, often wingless, that occur on the foliage of trees, on and beneath bark or in leaf litter, where they graze on organic debris, algae or mildewed leaves. Some species occur indoors, where they feed on stored dried products and moulds on damp books, hence their second common name – Booklice. Because none of the Booklice can tolerate desiccation, a single session with the fan heater will easily solve the problem of domestic Booklice.

A limited number of parasitic insects have been recorded from Alderley Edge to date: seven species of the True Lice (order Phtiraptera; about 550 in the UK – see Barnard, 1999) and nine species of Fleas (order Siphonaptera; sixty-two in the UK – see Whitaker, 2007). The real number of species of True Lice on the Edge must actually be many times greater than this.

Overall, the clear under-recording of some insect groups on the Edge mentioned above and a total absence of records of others, such as Bristletails (Thysanura; seven species in the UK) and Thrips (Thysanoptera; 160 species in the UK), are clear indications of how poorly the insect fauna of Alderley Edge has been studied so far. There is a lot of room for any enthusiasts who would like to conduct their own research on any of the insect groups mentioned here, or on those to be discussed in the following sections of this chapter.

B. Order Lepidoptera – micromoths and macromoths

Dmitri V. Logunov

> And here and younder a flaky butterfly
>   Was doubting in the air, scarlet and blue.
> G. MacDonald (1893), 'A Manchester Poem'

Butterflies and moths are grouped in the order Lepidoptera ('scale wings'), also called Lepidopterans, an artificial, non-scientific division. They are the insects to which people are generally first attracted, undoubtedly because of their beautiful colouration and variable patterns. Poets have called them 'pretty genii of the flowers' or 'daughters of the air' (Faulkiner, 1931). However, such epithets are likely to have been inspired by a relatively low number of better-known and showy butterflies, which are culturally seen as joyful spirits: happy, frivolous and carefree (see Marren and Mabey, 2010). As with other insect groups, the majority of Lepidopterans are tiny and inconspicuous, difficult to observe and to catch.

A total of 616 species of Lepidoptera (259 micromoths and 357 macromoths – see below) has been recorded from Alderley Edge (see Table 13.1), accounting for 23 per cent of the British fauna (2,717 species; see Kimber, 2014). The status of the current knowledge of Lepidoptera could be considered reasonable, but still incomplete. The checklist in Appendix 13.1 contains no species of the 'bagworms' of the family Psychidae (twenty-one species in the UK). There is only one recorded species of the Clearwing Moths from Alderley Edge, the Currant Clearwing (*Synanthedon tipuliformis*, of the family Sesiidae; sixteen species in the UK), but adults of these moths are difficult to find except shortly after emerging. Only two species of the Eggars (Lasiocampidae; twelve species in the UK) have been recorded to date. Even such common species as the Drinker (*Euthrix potatoria*), the Small Eggar (*Eriogaster lanestris*) and the Fox Moth (*Macrothylacia rubi*) (and others) have not been recorded yet, but all are likely to occur on the Edge. It is safe to assume that the recorded number of Lepidoptera species is around 80 per cent of the entire fauna.

Except for a limited number of butterflies (see section C) no specific bionomic data based on the local studies of the Lepidoptera of Alderley Edge are available. Therefore the listed species remain known to a large extent by name only, along with the data in the published literature on their larval preferred food plants and flying seasons. The following overview of the Lepidoptera of Alderley Edge is thus intended as a very general introduction and it is better used in conjunction with three recent field guides to the British Lepidoptera, by Manley (2009), Skinner (2009) and Waring and Towsend (2003), the classic two-volume synopsis by South (1973), and the comprehensive online resource on the UK moths by Kimber (2014). The last resource also contains the latest and most complete checklist of the British Lepidoptera.

Twenty butterfly species of the Hesperiidae (Skippers), the Lycaenidae (Gossamer-winged Butterflies), the Pieridae (Yellows and Whites) and the Nymphalidae ('Brush-footed' Butterflies) are considered in detail by Roger Dennis in section C (see also Anon., 2011) and are not included in the following overview. A complete list of the Lepidoptera recorded to date from Alderley Edge is given in Appendix 13.1. Lepidoptera have been conventionally subdivided in two large groups, micromoths and macromoths, depending on the size of their wingspan rather than on any scientific basis. Generally speaking, macromoths are larger than micromoths (but there are exceptions) and almost all of them have English common names, whereas most of the micromoths do not. The present overview follows this conventional subdivision.

Micromoths

Almost half the moths recorded from Alderley Edge (259 species out of 616) are small-sized, with a wingspan usually 3–20 mm, and are commonly known as micromoths. They rarely come to the attention of visitors to the Edge, who are more likely to notice their caterpillars, which may live communally and spin silken webs or mine leaves in a distinctive way. Micromoths are difficult to identify: close examination of their genitalia is often the only method, although sometimes the structure of larval leaf-mines is the primary basis (which in practice can be examined only if the moths are bred in captivity), as in the case of the Gracillaridae described below. Micromoths have a wide variety of feeding habits in both larval and adult life stages, and can be found in both terrestrial and freshwater aquatic habitats (some of the Pyralidae are a case in point, as described below).

Most peculiar are the Micropterigidae, the most archaic group of Lepidoptera, because they have normally developed mandibles (jaws), whereas all other Lepidopterans possess only a proboscis – a tube-like mouth-part used for feeding. Adults are diurnal and feed on pollen. Larvae of the Case-bearing Moths possess rather long antennae which are most unusual for the Lepidopterans; they live in mosses and lichens, feeding on fungal hyphae. Of the five species known in the UK only one, *Micropterix aruncella*, was recorded from the Edge.

Some micromoths are very distinctive in their general appearance. For instance, the luxuriously coloured Cosmopterigidae can be recognised by the lanceolate (pointed) forewings, often with a metallic pattern consisting of raised scale tufts. The Honeysuckle Moth (*Ypsolopha dentella*; Yponomeutidae) and other representatives of the genus *Ypsolopha* recorded from the Edge have tips of their forewings extended and raised up, hence their common name 'sickle-winged moths'. The Longhorns (Adelidae) are easily recognisable by their very long antennae, especially in males, reaching two and half or even three times their forewing length. Males of some Longhorns (e.g. *Adela reaumurella*) form small summer swarms in the same way as do Midges or Gnats (Garland, 1985); females are usually to be found resting on leaves nearby.

Two other unusual-looking moths of the Edge are both commonly called 'Plume Moths', despite being unrelated to each other. The Twenty-plume Moth (*Alucita hexadactyla*) is the only representative of the family Alucitidae in the UK; each of its wings is split into six plumes, whence the scientific name. The true Plume Moths (the family Pterophoridae) are represented on Alderley Edge by three species (*Amblyptilia acanthadactyla*, *Gillmeria pallidactyla* and *Emmelina monodactyla*), compared with forty-three species in the UK fauna as a whole. Its wings are deeply divided into several 'fingers', each of which is finely feathered, or plumed. Because of this wing structure the Plume Moths do not look like moths at all, for with a T-shaped body they can be confused with large Mosquitoes or Craneflies. None of the British Plume Moths is a pest.

Some species of micromoths are difficult to distinguish visually, but they can easily be recognised by their constructions. For instance, caterpillars of several species of the Yponomeutidae (known as Ermines because the adults resemble a stoat in its winter coat) are notable for living in large communal web-nests that are spun for protection from wasps and birds before they pupate. The famous Bird-cherry Ermine (*Yponomeuta evonymella*) can occur in pest numbers and if this happens its larvae can produce a huge web-nest completely covering a medium-sized bird-cherry tree and even a car parked nearby (see *Daily Mail*, 28 May 2009). However, such outbreaks of this species seem never to have been observed on Alderley Edge.

Many of the micromoths are leaf-miners. Their tiny larvae are usually flattened in the dorso-ventral direction and feed inside the leaves, mining cavities which appear as discoloured blotches and meandering lines where the internal tissues have been eaten away. The structure of such mines is an important or sometimes the only means of their identification. Nepticulidae is a family of the smallest leaf-mining moths, with a wingspan of approximately 3–6 mm, and characterised by scaly eyecaps over the eyes. Over 100 species are known from the UK, with twenty-eight of them having been found on the Edge. *Stigmella aurella*, recorded from the Edge, is one of the commonest British leaf-miners. Its larvae excavate serpentine-shaped tunnels just under the surface of bramble leaves. They spend the winter in their mines and then come out of the leaf to pupate. Some leaf-miners, such as members of the family Gracillariidae (thirty-four species in the Edge, almost a half of the British fauna), can seriously damage host plants by spoiling the external appearance of leaves. For instance, larvae of the Nut Leaf Blister Moth (*Phyllonorycter coryli*) mine blotches on hazel leaves, causing the leaf to contort. Their mines are very visible in late summer and autumn.

A very interesting group of micromoths of Alderley Edge is the family Coleophoridae, collectively known as Case-bearers or Case-bearing Moths. The common names of the Coleophoridae refer to the fact that their caterpillars live in portable protective cases made of silk, plant material and frass. Cases are discarded and built anew as caterpillars grow and moult, in the same way as the aquatic larvae of the caddisflies. Ten species of the case-bearers have been recorded from the Edge, of about 110 known in the UK. Moths of this group are tiny and similar in appearance, having pale, long and slender wings. Genitalia examination is usually required for a positive identification of these micromoths.

Only ten species of the large family Gelechiidae have been found on the Edge out of 150 in the UK and about 4,500 worldwide. These are usually very small moths with narrow, fringed wings, and with the front end of the body often being raised when at rest. Caterpillars feed on various parts of their host plants, sometimes causing galls. It is worth mentioning the larvae of the three *Bryotropha* species occurring on the Edge, which specialise in feeding on mosses growing on rocks or stony walls, of which the Edge has plenty. The larvae of one of these, *Bryotropha domestica*, live in silken galleries.

Moths of the family Oecophoridae are distinct in having wide and often brightly coloured forewings, which are folded flat when at rest. Many oecophorid species are the most colourful and attractive micromoths in the UK. Eleven of about ninety British species have been recorded from the Edge, all of them common. The majority of oecophorids overwinter as adults. Caterpillars show a great diversity of lifestyles and food preferences, and some are indoor pests: for instance, larvae of the Brown

House Moth (*Hofmannophila pseudospretella*), which was introduced from Asia to Europe in the 1840s, feed on detritus and other organic material, including old wool and leather. Overall, many species of the micromoths can cause severe damage to plants as well as to fabrics and other man-made goods or stored products. The best known of them is of course the clothes moth (*Tineola bisselliella*), which, surprisingly, has not yet been formally recorded from the Edge, although its wild counterpart, *Tinea trinotella*, a common scavenger in birds' nests, does occur there. However, the majority of economically significant pests come from two families, Tortricidae and Pyralidae, both of them well represented at Alderley Edge.

The Tortricidae is the largest family of micromoths, with sixty-one species being recorded from the Edge, of some 350 species in the UK and almost 9,500 worldwide. These moths are commonly known as Leaf-rollers, because their caterpillars roll themselves up into the tips of leaves and flowers. They feed and pupate within the protective shelter of rolled-up leaves. Some of the Leaf-rollers can become pests, being unwelcome guests in gardens and orchards. One of these is the Light Brown Apple Moth (*Epiphyas postvittana*). In the 1930s this species was accidentally introduced into the southern part of the UK from Australia, where it causes serious damage to orchards, and it has spread quickly northwards. It is a polyphagous species, for its larvae can feed on about 2,000 different plants, and therefore the potential threat from this moth is high. As the name suggests, larvae of the Garden Rose Tortrix (*Acleris variegana*) feed on rose bushes, including cultivated kinds. The Cyclamen Tortrix (*Clepsis spectrana*) can damage such cultivated plants as cyclamen, strawberry, hops and brideworts. Sometimes larvae of the tortricid moths develop inside fruits; the best-known is the Codling Moth (*Cydia pomonella*), which is considered a pest because of the larval habit of feeding inside the fruits of apple, pear and other wild and cultivated fruits.

The family Pyralidae is an impressively diverse group of micromoths, with thirty-two species being recorded from the Edge, of some 200 in the UK and over 6,200 worldwide. The pyralid moths come in a wide range of sizes, with some species such as the Mother of Pearl (*Pleuroptya ruralis*) having a wingspan up to 40 mm, reaching the point when they can hardly be called micromoths anymore. The feeding habits of Pyralidae vary significantly, from the Bee Moth (*Aphomia sociella*), which attacks the honeycomb inside bee and wasp nests, to the Meal Moth (*Pyralis farinalis*), found in grain products stored in barns and warehouses. At least thirty resident pyralid species which are now indoor pests of stored products have been imported into the UK with plant material. Some pyralid species such as the Garden Pebble (*Evergestis forficalis*) can be a pest in gardens and allotments, feeding on cultivated crucifers.

Particularly interesting are (semi-)aquatic pyralid moths. For example, larvae of the Small China-mark (*Cataclysta lemnata*) are semi-aquatic, building floating cases made of fragments of the duckweed on which they feed. They acquired their common name because of a supposed resemblance to the potter's marks on antique porcelain. The caterpillars of the Water Veneer (*Acentria ephemerella*) are fully aquatic, feeding on submerged freshwater plants such as pondweeds and Canadian waterweed. Furthermore, there are two forms of the Water Veneer's female, winged and wingless, of which the wingless ones remain under water after emergence, mating at the surface with fully winged males.

Macromoths

Several groups of macromoths are absolutely unmistakable if encountered on Alderley Edge or elsewhere. Easiest to recognise are the Tiger Moths (Erebidae; ten species in the Edge, of thirty-eight in the UK; they are alternatively called Ermines, but that term is also used to denote a group of micromoths, as above). True Tigers have fluffy and brightly coloured bodies and wings, either monochrome, as in the case of the Ruby Tiger (*Phragmatobia fuliginosa*; Plate 27), or with numerous dark spots on a red, yellow or white background, as in the White Ermine (*Spilosoma lubricipeda*). The Hook-tips (family Drepanidae) also cannot be confused with other moths, as the majority have hooked tips to the forewings. Nine species of the Hook-tips of the sixteen recorded in the UK have been found on the Edge; of these, the Pebble Hook-tip (*Drepana falcataria*) closely resembles a dead leaf when resting. The Leopard Moth (*Zeuzera pyrina*; family Cossidae) has a fluffy white body and pale wings with a span of about 5 cm, covered with numerous black or dark-blue spots (whence the common name). This spectacular moth is the only representative of the Cossidae recorded on the Edge, of three found in the UK. The moth is associated with woodland, gardens and orchards. Its larvae bore into the stems of trees and cause damage by eating the heartwood. A fully grown larva can reach a length of 5 cm and is white, fleshy and apparently tasty, like the edible larvae of several Australian relatives of the Leopard Moth known as witchetty grubs. But who in this country would dare to taste them?

The Hawk Moths (Sphingidae; eight species from the Edge, of the twenty-six recorded in the UK) are easy to recognise by their streamlined appearance. These medium to large moths are powerful fliers, capable of hovering in front of flowers and sipping the nectar with their long proboscis, looking like humming birds. Indeed, the best-known is the Humming-bird Hawk-moth (*Macroglossum stellatarum*), a common visitor in gardens and parks all over Britain. Many species of Hawk

Moths actively migrate to the UK from as far as North Africa and the Canary Islands. For instance, the Convolvulus Hawk-moth (*Agrius convolvuli*) regularly migrates from southern Europe in late summer and autumn, and at dusk can be seen feeding on garden flowers, especially those of the tobacco plant. A much scarcer visitor from North Africa is the Silver-striped Hawk-moth (*Hippotion celerio*), also recorded from the Edge. This species usually arrives in autumn and can be seen as far north as Scotland.

The majority of macromoth species found on Alderley Edge belong to two families, Geometridae (148) and Noctuidae (169), accounting for 51 per cent of the entire Lepidopteran fauna of the site. It is hardly surprising as both groups represent the two largest moth families in the world and in the UK: the Geometridae number 21,093 species worldwide, with over 300 in the UK, and the Noctuidae 42,030 species worldwide, over 400 of them in the UK.

Moths of the family Geometridae, commonly known as the Geometers, have broad butterfly-like wings that are large relative to their slender bodies. The wings are flat and outstretched when at rest, with the hindwings visible, having a radial wavy pattern consisting of contrasting lines or bands coming across both pairs of wings and the body. Moths usually rest on a similar-looking substrate and so tend to blend into the background. However, many species are quite spectacular, which is reflected in their poetic and wonderfully picturesque names, for instance the Feathered Thorn (*Colotois pennaria*), a rich reddish-brown moth whose males have feathery antennae; the Lilac Beauty (*Apeira syringaria*), a moth of a crumpled leaf-like appearance; and the Small Phoenix (*Ecliptopera silaceata*), which has a wing colour pattern resembling a rare kind of marble. The name Geometridae means 'earth-measurer': they are so named because of the walking pattern of their caterpillars, which do not have legs in the middle portion of the body and move by arching and then straightening their bodies, creating the impression of measuring their journey. This is why the caterpillars are called 'measuring worms' or 'loopers'.

The majority of the Geometers recorded from the Edge are common, although some are mainly distributed in the southern half of England, becoming gradually scarcer or absent further north and in Scotland – for instance, the attractive greenish Blotched Emerald (*Comibaena bajularia*), the Small Yellow Wave (*Hydrelia flammeolaria*) and the Blood-vein (*Timandra comae*). However, a few species are indeed rare. For instance, the Cloaked Pug (*Eupithecia abietaria*) is included in the *British Red Data Book* (Shirt, 1987) under category 3 (rare species). This scarce species is a suspected migrant that was once resident in a range of scattered locations throughout Britain but became almost extinct at the beginning of the twentieth century. Since then it has been rediscovered in parts of England, Wales and Scotland. Its larvae feed internally on the cones of Norway spruce, Sitka spruce and noble fir, of which none has been recorded within the surveyed territory (see Chapter 10). It is possible, however, that the food plants of the Cloaked Pug occur in some private gardens on Alderley Edge.

Many species of the Geometers are polyphagous, that is, capable of feeding on many kinds of plants. Of the species recorded from the Edge, the most famous one of this kind is the Peppered Moth (*Biston betularia*; Plate 28), which can feed even on the poisonous leaves of oleander. This species has been the subject of numerous genetic studies investigating the problem of industrial melanism, where all-dark individuals became the dominant form in industrial and polluted regions of northern England. Nowadays the melanic form is declining again in these areas due to changes in the ecological situation. Other Geometrid groups are specialised feeders. For instance, larvae of *Eupithecia* species (twenty-three on the Edge), commonly known as Pugs, feed on the flowers and seeds of their food plants rather than the foliage. Many of them demonstrate a particular specialisation: for example, the larvae of the Foxglove Pug (*Eupithecia pulchellata*) feed inside the flowers of foxglove, while those of the Larch Pug (*Eupithecia lariciata*) specialise on the needles of larch. Some Geometer species are considered garden pests because of their feeding habits, such as the Magpie (*Abraxas grossulariata*; Plate 29, from the Edge) and the Phoenix (*Eulithis prunata*), whose caterpillars can swarm over currant and gooseberry bushes and damage them. See Owen (1983) for a useful popular overview of moth pests in British gardens.

The family Noctuidae, or the Noctuids, is an extensive assemblage of moths characterised by an incredible diversity of feeding preferences and lifestyles, from those living on rotten or withered leaves like the Fan-foot (*Zanclognatha tarsipennalis*) to classical foliage feeders such as the Gothic (*Naenia typica*). Most Noctuids are plain-looking moths usually with brownish forewings, which have given them the common name of Owlet Moths. The colour pattern of their forewings is simple, usually consisting of a spot shaped like a kidney bean and a further spot nearby. However, the relative size, colour and arrangement of these spots are important diagnostic characters that help to distinguish similar species. Hindwings of some noctuid moths such as the Red Underwing (*Catocala nupta*) or the *Noctua* species are brightly coloured: red, orange or yellow, with a wide brown band. Some species are quite peculiar: the Spectacle (*Abrostola tripartita*) possesses raised tufts of scales on its thorax which resemble a pair of spectacles when viewed from the front. Some of the noctuid species recorded from the Edge are common migrants, for instance the Silver Y (*Autographa gamma*) and the Scarce Bordered Straw (*Helicoverpa armigera*). It is worth mentioning one of the classic invasive species recorded from the Edge, the Golden Plusia (*Polychrysia moneta*). This moth was first recorded in Britain in 1890, since when it has spread rapidly north-westwards thanks to plentiful supply of such garden food plants as delphiniums and monkshood.

With a few exceptions, the noctuid moths fly only at night and in order to capture them one has to use a light trap (see Martin, 1977, for details). During the day their larvae usually hide on the ground (Plate 30, photographed on the Edge), among low herbage or in spun-together leaves, and generally leave their retreats only at night, to feed. Nonetheless, larvae of some noctuid species like the Flounced Rustic (*Luperina testacea*) feed underground in the bases of grass stems and among the roots. The food preferences of some Noctuids are very specific. For instance, larvae of the Beautiful Yellow Underwing (*Anarta myrtilli*) and the Neglected Rustic (*Xestia castanea*) feed mainly on heather and heath, and therefore both species have a very scattered distribution over most of Britain, chiefly occurring on heaths and moors.

Many Noctuids are important agricultural and garden pests. Caterpillars of some species, such as those of the Heart and Dart Moth (*Agrotis exclamationis*; Plate 31, photographed on the Edge) and of the Large Yellow Underwing (*Noctua pronuba*), are known as 'cutworms' and feed on virtually all types of grasses, including cereal crops. They emerge at night, cut off seedlings at ground level and then devour them. Larvae of the aptly named Cabbage Moth (*Mamestra brassicae*), as well as those of the geometrid Garden Carpet (*Xanthorhoe fluctuata*) and the tiny Diamond-back Moth (*Plutella xylostella*), are pests on cabbage and related crops. One species, the Angle Shades (*Phlogophora meticulosa*), is rather special, for its green caterpillars can be found feeding on house plants such as pelargoniums that have been brought inside for the winter after female moths laid their eggs on them during the autumn (Garland, 1985).

In this brief section it is impossible to discuss all the recorded species of Lepidoptera of Alderley Edge, even the most interesting ones, but see South (1973) and Kimber (2014) for details. Although the majority of these species are common, each can be seen more clearly through the magnifying lens of your own curiosity. This alone can turn a diminutive and dull micromoth into a spectacular creature of many wonders. People like to watch birds in nature and bird-watching a very popular hobby. But so is butterfly-watching! However, just as in a sport, the more you know about the game the more enjoyable it is to watch. Look round and you can see 'daughters of the air' flapping above flowers or resting in secluded corners. With a little patience you can discover that many of them are distinctive and can be identified by the way they look.

Finally, there is no need to go to your nearest butterfly-house to watch and interact with the Lepidopterans. This can be done on Alderley Edge free of charge and with no time limits; it can even be done at night. Many moths can be attracted by lamp-light and can be observed in your own garden (see Owen, 1983, for useful hints). Possibly one of the more unusual techniques is to use so-called 'sugar baits' that attract many night-flying moths (see Garland, 1985). A mixture of black treacle, sugar and stale beer is painted onto the vertical surface of trees and then these sites are searched by torchlight during the night. 'Sugar baits' and light traps are best used in combination because certain moths rarely come to lights but are common on sugar, and vice versa. Sugaring is certainly an ingenious method used by moth hunters who do not intend to kill the moths but want to watch them: fun, and easy!

C. Order Lepidoptera – butterflies

Roger L. H. Dennis

In memory of the late Charles Ian Rutherford, 1919–2008, Alderley Edge's lepidopterist

Introduction: butterflies on Alderley Edge – resources, habitats and changes

Compared with other arthropods, the butterfly fauna of Britain is small, comprising some sixty species that breed in the islands or are regular immigrants from the Continent (Thomas, 2007). The fraction on Alderley Edge is smaller still, with only twenty breeding species recorded (Dennis, 2000a); Appendix 13.2 describes the detailed survey results. Even so, the interest they generate far exceeds their number; colourful, easily recognisable, aesthetically pleasing creatures, they form valuable indicators of landscape – and thus human – health and of environmental changes, especially those associated with climate and biotope fragmentation. This section provides a brief overview of research done on Alderley Edge butterflies, a guide to where particular species may be observed on the escarpment and the conditions that influence their presence.

Surveys

Four sets of butterfly survey have been undertaken on Alderley Edge since the mid-1990s, though not as part of the AELP. The purpose of three of these was largely scientific, to explore vagrancy (occurrence of individuals at sites lacking their host plants) and the use of resources outside 'habitats' in the so-called 'matrix'; even so, they reveal important aspects of butterfly geography on the escarpment. Work on Alderley Edge butterflies has been instrumental in refining the notion of 'habitat' from its traditional usage as a biotope (vegetation unit) to that of the 'resource-based habitat'. The resource-based habitat is broadly defined as the conjunction of a number of distinct resources and conditions (e.g. light, temperature) essential for the survival, reproduction and the development of individuals – in butterflies during their different stages as eggs, larvae, pupae and imagos (adults) – and thus for the persistence of a population (Dennis, 2010).

The 1996–99 survey of squares

Butterfly records were obtained from thirty 1 ha units in the Alderley Edge Site of Special Scientific Interest (SSSI), the corners of which had been pegged for topographic survey. The squares, located north-east to south-west over the escarpment from base to summit, were evenly distributed over woodland and open ground (mean wood cover 81.6 per cent and 22.1 per cent respectively). Data were collected from thirty-eight three-hourly visits using a fixed transect covering each square over four seasons. Data were independently collected on biotopes and two butterfly resources (larval host plants, nectar flowers used by adults) (Dennis, 2000a).

Parcel survey

A broad survey in September 1999 was conducted of all parcels for butterfly larval host plants (Appendix 13.2). No attempt was made to distinguish use or condition of the host plants, the data merely indicating potential for habitat restoration with suitable management. Records obtained on butterfly early stages and adults from casual observation over several years, and dedicated surveys, are added to this record, providing the basis for information on butterfly distributions on the escarpment.

2003 and 2004 transect surveys

Two surveys were conducted by the author in consecutive years of resource use over different substrates and biotopes. The first was on the satyrines (browns), the Meadow Brown (*Maniola jurtina*), Gatekeeper (*Pyronia tithonus*) and Speckled Wood (*Pararge aegeria*), the second on the pierines (whites), the Large White (*Pieris brassicae*), Small White (*Pieris rapae*) and the Green-veined White (*Pieris napi*). The first followed a fixed transect south-west of the Macclesfield Road in parcels 11b, 11c, 17, 18a, 20b, 21c and the track and path bisecting the fields towards unit 20b from Whitebarn Farm. The second applied random transects over much of the escarpment. The spontaneous behaviour of each individual was recorded in relation to substrate, biotope and weather conditions (Dennis, 2004; Dennis and Hardy, 2007).

2006 nettle patch surveys

Larval host-plant suitability for the Peacock (*Aglais io*; Plate 32) and Small Tortoiseshell (*Aglais urticae*) butterflies were assessed using two surveys in 2006 on the Alderley escarpment (Dennis, 2008). The first involved sampling ninety-three nettle patches within a 5 m box of a 5 km transect route over the escarpment, evenly located over wood and open ground. The second survey, conducted immediately after the first, focused on a random sample of 24 ha stratified for woodland and open biotopes. Nettle patch dimensions, butterfly larval batches and environmental conditions were recorded.

Comparison of two basic biotopes

Two surveys (1996–99, 2006) on Alderley Edge reveal sharp contrasts between woodland and open biotopes (100 m squares) for butterflies (see Figure 13.1). British woodlands can be especially rich biotopes, despite the fact that most British butterfly species (83 per cent) feed on herbaceous host plants (Greatorex-Davies *et al.*, 1993; Fox and Waring, 1999; Kemp *et al.*, 2008). However, this is not the case for Alderley Edge. The Alderley woods contain significantly fewer host plants and nectar sources for butterflies than the surrounding open ground, particularly the Sandhills, the unimproved pasture and Saddlebole Quarry. More than twice the number of butterfly species is recorded for squares with open biotopes than woodland biotopes (means: 14.6 versus 6.5 respectively after thirty-eight visits). Over 1 ha squares, there is a loss rate of one species for every 7.8 per cent increase in woodland cover (one breeding species for every 6.7 per cent increase). This pattern is also reflected in the number of butterfly individuals encountered (Dennis, 2000a). Of the eighteen species for which sufficient data were available for testing differences, only two were observed to be more abundant in woodland than in open biotopes, Speckled Wood and Red Admiral (*Vanessa atalanta*). Regression analyses on each species separately demonstrated that contrasting abundances for specific host plants and nectar sources accounted respectively for the incidence of fifteen and seventeen of the eighteen species in squares. The only species lacking a

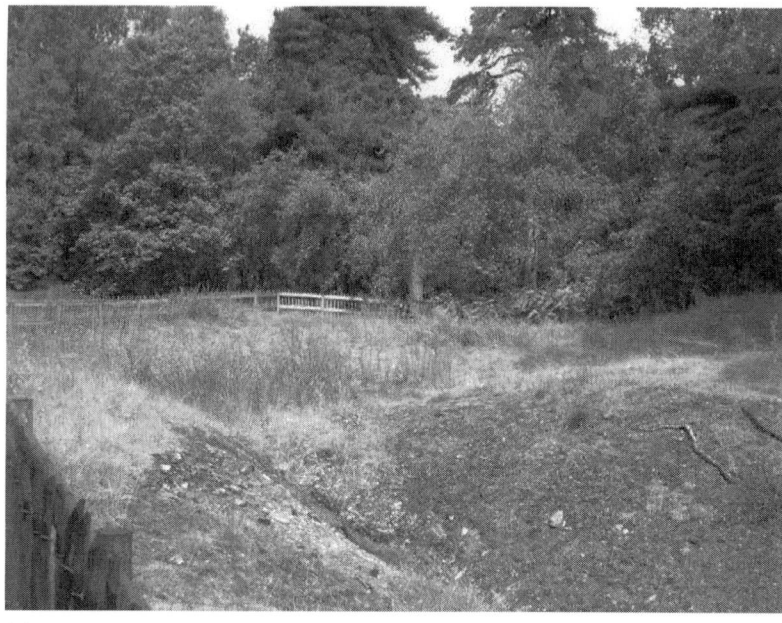

(a)

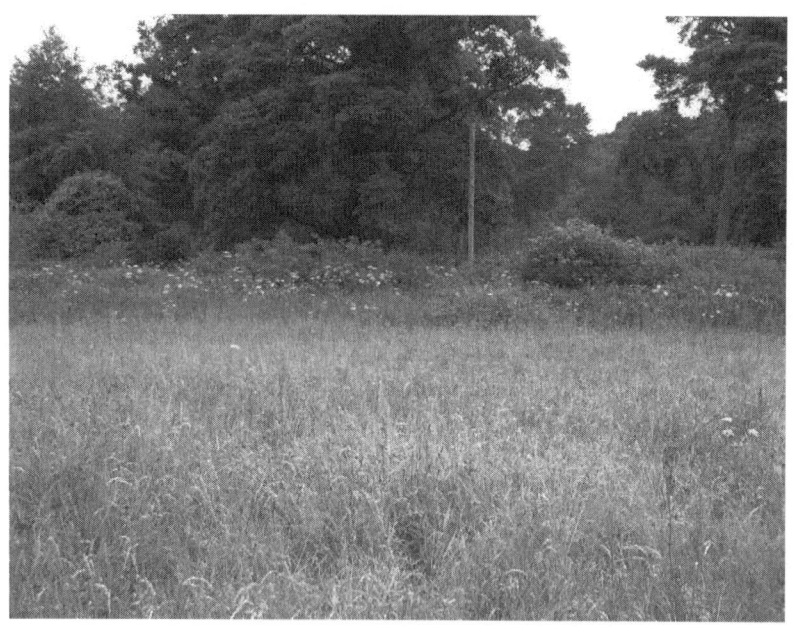

(b)

Figure 13.1. Open biotopes (foreground) and wood biotopes (background) on Alderley Edge. (a) The west end of Engine Vein. Since fenced off and seeded, this open area has become one of the butterfly hot spots in the wood. (b) The field adjoining the car park (parcel 24). With increasing conversion to unimproved pasture, this area is becoming a valuable butterfly biotope with a wide range of flowering plants and mixed grasses.

Photographs Roger L. H. Dennis.

significant association with either its host plant or nectar sources is the Red Admiral, a butterfly which is most evident when it uses landscape high points and woodland sunspots for locating mates (Dennis and Dennis, 2008). The Speckled Wood defends territories in the woodland and has long been known to do this by occupying sunspots on the woodland floor (Davies, 1978). More recently, this butterfly has been found exploiting territories higher in the canopy on Alderley Edge (Dennis *et al.*, 2009); the females adopt a possum-like behaviour when harassed (Dennis, 2003b; Shreeve *et al.*, 2006).

Apart from the Speckled Wood and Red Admiral, three other butterflies have host plant sources in the woods. The Purple Hairstreak (*Favonius quercus*) uses oak; it has not been seen in the main woodland but has been observed on the Sandhills oaks. There is now plentiful holly and ivy for the Holly Blue (*Celastrina argiolus*) in the woodland, but much of it inappropriately under shade, and the butterfly has only been seen in open biotopes and ecotones (wood edges) on Alderley Edge, although during 2012 ivy was cut off many trees and substantially reduced (indeed, the vegetation on the Edge has undergone some substantial changes since the surveys described elsewhere in Part III of the book). The Green-veined White feeds on small and immature crucifers (Dennis, 1985); it is seen flying through the woods and can use hairy bitter-cress (*Cardamine hirsuta*) in dappled shade, which occurs sparingly along the paths, and Jack-by-the-hedge (*Alliaria petiolata*) along wooded sections of Macclesfield Road and Artists Lane (parcel 11) and the track from Thieves Hollow to the Goldenstone (parcel 10a).

A further interesting contrast between woodland and open biotopes is found in the occurrence of breeding and vagrant butterfly species. Inevitably, the cumulative distribution of new species for squares increases with the number of visits; this tends to flatten out for the thirty squares on Alderley Edge after twenty visits. However, the number of vagrant species is significantly higher in woodland than in squares with open biotopes and, interestingly, vagrant species increase at a faster rate in woodland squares. The reason is not difficult to find. There is a marked contrast between species in butterflies' capacity to migrate between habitat patches. Woodland squares, lacking habitat patches, have a larger pool of vagrant species to draw on over time; eventually, even the most sedentary of species crosses into woodland squares in seeking out new habitats (e.g. in 2009, the Gatekeeper was observed in the Armada Beacon hilltop opening in the woodland). In an ancillary study it was shown that degree of vagrancy identified in this way (individuals of species occurring in squares lacking host plants) corresponded with other independent measures of butterfly migration capacity (Cook *et al.*, 2001).

In 2006, a separate study concentrated on the exploitation of nettle patches by the nettle-feeding nymphalids, the Small Tortoiseshell and Peacock (Dennis, 2008), two species which are capable of migrating over large distances and are seen both in the woods and on open ground. Although sufficiently large nettle patches used by these butterflies, which lay their eggs in batches, are found in most squares over Alderley Edge in both woodland and open biotopes, only one larval batch was found within the woodland and a further seventeen on nettle patches outside the woods or wood/open space ecotone. Egg batches are laid only on large, dense nettle patches (typically having a diameter over 200 cm) in sunlight, and patches in shade are ignored; the nettle patch used in the woods had a south-facing aspect at the wood edge.

Resources and habitats

The comparison of woodland and non-woodland areas on Alderley Edge suggests a dichotomy of the landscape: the woodland would be considered as non-habitat or 'matrix' by ecologists, as it is the open spaces (habitat) that are butterfly rich and the woodland as butterfly impoverished. This view of habitat and matrix emerges largely owing to a preoccupation by ecologists with a limited set of resources for organisms (Dennis *et al.*, 2008). Studies in 2003 and 2006, on three 'browns' and three 'whites', indicate that resource use is much more complex among butterflies. For instance, they require sites for roosts, basking, resting, finding mates, escaping enemies, pupation and hibernation among other more specialised conditions of heat, light and moisture. It has long been known, however, that butterflies are picky and exploit a fraction of the available substrates for a particular resource. In some cases the reasons are obvious, as in the case of the nettle-feeding nymphalids discussed above. The later studies disclosed that butterflies often use fragmentary, tiny resource units in the so-called matrix (Dennis, 2004); a nice example was a larval batch of Large Whites on Jack-by-the-hedge on the neatly mown margin of the National Trust car park (Dennis and Hardy, 2006b), an attractive butterfly better known for infesting cabbage patches. The 'whites' search for resources in biotopes, for instance roosts and mates in the wood canopy, where no resources were previously thought to exist (Dennis and Hardy, 2007). Inevitably some butterflies search for resources (host plants) in examples of biotopes where they are expected to exist even when they do not; a classic example was a Comma (*Polygonia c-album*) female searching for the host plants, nettle or elm, within woodland parcel 10a. For this reason, visitors to the Edge should not be surprised to find butterfly species in unexpected situations doing unusual things; delightful surprises have been a non-territorial Painted Lady (*Vanessa cardui*) in a woodland clearing surrounded by bilberry basking on a dead log, Red Admirals vigorously defending a territory on a dying birch trunk near the memorial stone, Holly Blues well away from their holly and ivy host plants, feeding on heather at Stormy Point, and two Peacocks diving into the same rabbit run at the base of a gorse bush for shelter during a rain storm (Dennis, 2005b).

A resource-based definition of a butterfly habitat (Dennis, 2010) draws attention to significant parcels on Alderley Edge where species are found but in very small populations, scattered at low density. The classic cases are the unimproved pastures (parcels 20b and 22); here, Meadow Browns, Orange-tips (*Anthocharis cardamines*) (Plate 33) and Green-veined Whites, Small Coppers (*Lycaena phlaeas*) (Plate 34), Common Blues (*Polyommatus icarus*) and other species all breed, but are few in number. These areas, vital for plants and insects, have in the past been too heavily grazed or grazed at the wrong time of the year and also have received occasional herbicide treatment (e.g. 21 May 2007; Dennis, personal observation). In effect, resources are available but are being suppressed or eradicated, as in the case of a nettle patch which had a Peacock larval batch treated with herbicide in parcel 20b in May 2007. Other nymphalid larval batches have been destroyed in parcel 24 near the car park by cutting in 2007 (for hay) and 2008 (accidentally during an archaeology experiment). Contrasts in the size and density of butterfly populations are not evident in Appendix 13.2 but the differences can be marked, as for instance between parcels 20b and 18a; in the latter, the population density of several butterfly species is high, as it is (but decreasingly) on marginal land outside farming in parcel 17 of the Sandhills. As parcel 18a comes under more intensive use its butterfly population is decreasing.

Changes over time

A prominent feature of observations on butterflies at Alderley Edge has been the changes in butterfly populations and turnover of species over time. These are probably associated with three main factors: climate, vegetation succession and land-use practices.

Significant fluctuations in the butterfly populations are expected from year to year relating to changes in fecundity and survival (Warren, 1992); climate is a key agent (Dennis, 1993). Regular visitors to the Edge will be aware of large fluctuations in numbers of migrants from the Continent (e.g. Painted Lady, Red Admiral); this feature was most evident in the surveys of the thirty 1 ha squares between 1996 and 1999, and 2009 was a year for Painted Lady butterflies. But seasonal weather can have more subtle influences, affecting for instance the interaction of butterflies with their resources and providing further insight into the specialist demands of butterfly species. In the cool spring weather of 2005 Orange-tips loaded many eggs onto few shoots of cuckoo flower. Usually, because the larvae are cannibalistic, females lay one egg per shoot and avoid plants that have already received eggs; as the larvae feed on the flower heads the adults pick large shoots with more buds. In 2005, emergence of the butterfly and growth of the plant were poorly syn-chronised, and because conditions were too cold and cloudy for longer flights in areas lacking shelter, fewer females left the Sandhills to exploit other hosts (e.g. Jack-by-the-hedge) along the roadsides. Some plants became overloaded with eggs, one receiving eight, seven of which were consumed after the first larva appeared (Dennis and Hardy, 2006a).

Since the mid-1990s there have been some notable changes in species, associated with a warming climate (Dennis, 1993; Hill *et al.*, 2002). The Wall Brown (*Lasiommata megera*), once abundant on the Sandhills, as over Cheshire generally, has become very scarce (Dennis and Dennis, 2006); the Speckled Wood (Plate 35), Gatekeeper and Small Skipper (*Thymelicus sylvestris*), not recorded on the Edge in the early 1980s, became abundant components of the fauna in the early 1990s (Hardy *et al.*, 1993; Hardy and Dennis, 1997) and remain so. The Ringlet (*Aphantopus hyperantus*) was found by the author in the Goyt Valley to the east of Alderley Edge in 2008, in Macclesfield Forest in 2011 (Dennis *et al.*, 2011) and on the Edge itself (but outside the National Trust property) in 2015. The Meadow Brown increasingly invaded the woods, even laying eggs on tree trunks (Dennis, 2003a), and long-distance migrants that hitherto survived only at the coastal fringe, over-wintering as adults, have started to survive deeper into the British countryside; evidence of this was a record of a Red Admiral (Plate 36) on Alderley Edge in February 2000 (Dennis, 2000b). Woodland shade may also be important for nectar sources (e.g. bramble flowers) during hot summers; woodland butterflies like the Speckled Wood can use other food, such as cuckoo spit (Dennis, 2005a).

One noticeable change has been the decline of the Common Blue. This was found throughout the Sandhills (parcel 17) in the 1980s. However, vegetation succession has moved on apace, scrub, saplings and tall dense herbs crowding out the bird's foot trefoil (*Lotus corniculatus*) and lesser bird's foot trefoil (*Lotus pedunculatus*), and the population of the butterfly in consequence has been reduced to single figures through-out the current century. The biotopes at the Sandhills have shifted from being most suitable for Wall Browns, Common Blues and Small Coppers to ones that favour Meadow Browns and Small Skippers, ultimately providing habitats for Gatekeepers and Speckled Woods. A similar process has affected Saddlebole Quarry. Some recent clearance of scrub such as broom has reversed conditions on the higher slopes.

Managing future butterfly resources

From the various surveys of butterflies, indications have emerged of what can be achieved for the National Trust area; instigating change is of huge importance for the Edge and its farming and urban surrounds. Currently, butterfly populations on the Edge are small and some species that could occur are missing, reflecting a lack of habitat for them. Yet for butterflies Alderley Edge functions as a refuge or source for the multiplicity of tiny resource patches dotted over the surrounding Cheshire countryside. From the viewing points on the Edge, Cheshire looks green and lush, but from a butterfly standpoint the largest part of it is in fact a green desert, intensively farmed. Essentially, large areas on the Edge can be enhanced for butterflies and other wildlife, rapidly and at low cost. The proviso is that evidence-based ecology, the science that underlies any suggestions (Pullin and Knight, 2001), is currently poorly developed; consequently, experimental approaches need careful advance planning and monitoring of changes since land use, National Trust revenue and other aspects of the flora and fauna may be affected. This is particularly the case for grazing regimes; evidence regarding interactions between grazing intensity and livestock type is distinctly lacking, frustrating prediction regarding the impacts of different types of livestock at given stocking intensities (Stewart and Pullin, 2008). A well established system, the Butterfly Monitoring Scheme (Pollard and Yates, 1993), applied to over 100 sites now for over thirty years and extended recently to many hundreds more, provides a foundation for monitoring changes in management; ideally, monitoring needs to be put into action before any large-scale changes are made.

Most butterflies on the Edge require open conditions but also a range of substrates, from bare ground to short and tall herb-rich grassland and patchy scrub. The conditions required for any species are both varied and dynamic (Asher *et al.*, 2001; Dennis *et al.*, 2003); key biotopes in the successional sequence of vegetation types are only too short-lived (less than five years). The fenced-off area around Engine Vein produced a valuable herb biotope for several butterflies in 2009 (e.g. Green-veined White, Small Copper, Meadow Brown, Gatekeeper), but this could easily be lost to birch scrub development without management, and during 2012 scrub was removed here. In the present state of knowledge, management is best conducted for a mosaic in biotopes (Oates, 1993), including a focus on dry sandy ground used by the Common Blue and Small Copper and on wetlands such as the marlpits valuable for Orange-tips and Green-veined Whites. Currently, the key areas on the Edge with the greatest potential for housing butterfly populations, the unimproved and semi-improved grassland parcels (parcels 20b, 22, 23, 24 and 30), are overgrazed and receive excessive nutrients. Intermittent ground disturbance is vital for producing conditions for a number of species (e.g. Common Blue, Small Copper) but is adverse when continuously applied. Moves towards selecting appropriate grazing animals, smaller herds and a greater bias towards winter as opposed to summer grazing should restore much of the plant and insect diversity in the grassland regimes that are being planned (Oates, 1993 – but see Stewart and Pullin, 2008; C. Widger, personal communication). Where this is not possible, dividing up the ground into sectors in which land use is cycled will help to generate a biotope mosaic.

Management of the woodlands for butterflies is a difficult matter; it can take centuries to produce mature deciduous woodland (Merryweather, 2007) and many open spaces on the Edge, like the viewing spots such as Stormy Point, are intensively used by visitors and thus suffer from erosion. Even so, important steps are being taken to improve conditions for arthropods dependent on mature and dead timber and to open up some woodland (C. Widger, personal communication). Valuable steps that can be undertaken are relatively simple: increasing exposure of holly and ivy at sunny edges to light; renewing coppice cycles where feasible; and planting tree and shrub host plants. Stripping of ivy (as was done during 2012) is beneficial for the trees but it has implications for birds as well as insects. Elm (*Ulmus* sp.) is scarce on the Edge and planting it in opportune locations along field boundaries will in years to come support the White-letter Hairstreak (*Satyrium w-album*), which has been observed near Wilmslow. Planting up sunlit wood edges and clearings as well as hedges with alder buckthorn (*Frangula alnus*), already started by the National Trust staff, will reap more immediate benefits. This is the host plant for the Brimstone Butterfly (*Gonepteryx rhamni*) (Plate 37), which lays its eggs on young as well as mature plants, but essentially on those in sunlight. There is little difficulty in butterflies finding these new resources; vagrants fly into the National Trust area from considerable distances. Even sedentary butterflies, such as the Green Hairstreak (*Callophrys rubi*) and the Small Heath (*Coenonympha pamphilus*), species reminiscent of a time before 1800 when the Edge was under heath, may find their way to the Edge from the Pennine foothills (however, these records are not from the present surveys and so do not appear in Appendix 13.2). In the 1980s, a Green Hairstreak was observed in a garden off Macclesfield Road (C. Rutherford, personal communication) and a Small Heath was seen by the author in what was then a barley field (parcel 25a). Reminders of earlier times are still apparent, such as the ling at Stormy Point and the bilberry in Bradford Lodge Wood (parcel 12b), the latter of which, if extended, may be a large enough patch to sustain populations of Green Hairstreaks.

Some important contributions are easily made. Crucially, use of herbicide should be restricted. In one survey 45.2 per cent of areas studied outside the National Trust area and 4.7 per cent of unimproved pastures and verges within it had been recently treated with herbicide (Dennis, 2000a). Herbicide drift in the top field (parcel 29b) has caused dieback of marginal trees and kills off host plants for the Orange-tip and Green-veined White in the roadside hedgerow such as Jack-by-the-hedge. More care over mowing during the period April to August, especially leaving nettle patches in direct sunlight, will also benefit our nymphalid butterflies.

Conclusions

Alderley Edge provides habitats for some twenty butterfly species and acts as a refuge for butterflies in the surrounding countryside. Currently, butterfly populations tend to be small but can be greatly improved with changes in management, at the same time providing an increasing source of interest for visitors to the Edge. With these visitors in mind, the National Trust has produced a colour brochure illustrating nearly all the butterflies found there, which is normally available in the main car park.

D. True Flies (Diptera)

Dmitri V. Logunov

> A fly, Sir, may sting a stately horse and make him wince; but one is but an insect, and the other is a horse still.
> J. Boswell, *Life of Samuel Johnson* (1791)

True Flies are members of the order Diptera (= two-winged) and are a familiar group of insects which includes Mosquitoes, Midges, Hoverflies, Fruit Flies and many others. It is the second-largest order of the British insects, with 7,035 species known nationally (Chandler, 2010) and over 150,000 species worldwide (Courtney *et al.*, 2009). To date, only 216 species of true flies have been recorded from Alderley Edge (see Table 13.1 and Appendix 13.1), which beyond doubt represent just a fraction of their real diversity over the site. For instance, only a single species of the Gall Midges (Cecidomyiidae; 652 species nationally), three species of the Black Fungus Gnats (Sciaridae; 266 species nationally) and no species of Agromyzidae (a group of specialised leaf-miners; 392 species nationally) have been recorded from the Edge to date. Here and elsewhere in the following report, the counts of British species in various Diptera families are given on the basis of the 2010 edition of *A Dipterist's Handbook* (Chandler, 2010), which is the most up-to-date and comprehensive account of information and specialised literature on British flies. The following brief report is best used in conjunction with this *Handbook*, and with the checklist by Chandler (1998) and the excellent, classical account by Colyer and Hammond (1951).

Traditionally, the Diptera are subdivided in two groups (suborders): Lower Diptera (formerly called Nematocera), recognised by filamentous, multi-segmented antennae which may be plumose in males, and Brachycera, recognised by shorter antennae, usually no longer than the head.

Lower Diptera (= Nematocera)

The Nematocera, collectively termed Threadhorns, are a group of flies that includes Mosquitoes, Midges, Gnats, Craneflies and some others. The majority of them develop in water. Their free-living larvae can dwell on the water surface (e.g. Meniscus Midges – Dixidae), swim (e.g. Mosquitoes – Culicidae), crawl on the bottom (e.g. Non-biting Midges – Chironomidae) or even tunnel actively in muddy sediments (e.g. Craneflies – Ptychopteridae and some Tipulidae). A common feature of the lower Diptera, particularly of Phantom Midges and Non-biting Midges, is the formation of dense mating swarms, generally composed of males that dance up and down to attract females. The swarms are formed in areas of moist vegetation or over dark areas of damp earth, and can be observed all around Alderley Edge on warm and quiet spring or summer days. When a female enters the swarm, coupling quickly takes place. Once the female is fertilised, she is no longer receptive to the males and will fly away to lay eggs.

Six nematocerous families are loosely called Craneflies (twenty-seven species recorded from Alderley Edge and about 435 nationally). Craneflies, with their rather leggy appearance, are probably familiar to most people as Daddy-long-legs (in fact few Cranefly species have English common names). Typical Daddy-long-legs (*Tipula*-type) can be encountered on the Edge from April (e.g. *Tipula vittata*; a dweller of shaded and open situations in woodland) to autumn (e.g. *Tipula staegeri*; a species widespread in wet and damp woodland). Some species are fairly common and widespread (e.g. *Tipula oleracea*) and can come into houses on warm summer evenings, being attracted to light. Despite all Daddy-long-legs being non-venomous, non-biting and unable to harm humans in any way, a common urban myth is that these creatures have poisonous fangs and could be the most poisonous animals of all (Marren and Mabey, 2010). In fact Craneflies barely eat as adults. Their larvae are usually scavengers of decaying matter, occurring on wet pastures and water margins, often under water. Nevertheless, some species, such as *Nephrotoma appendiculata* (Spotted Cranefly), *Tipula oleracea* and *Tipula paludosa* (the commonest Cranefly, not yet formally recorded from the Edge) are deemed to be horticultural and agricultural pests. Their larvae – tough-skinned grubs – feed on grass roots and are known to gardeners and farmers as 'Leatherjackets'. It is worth remembering that both larvae and adults of most if not all Craneflies constitute the major food source for bats and birds.

Of the Cranefly species found on the Edge, *Dolichopeza albipes* of the family of Long-palped Craneflies (Tipulidae) is known as the White Footed Ghost (see Boardman, 2007). It is an entirely black Cranefly, except with shining white ends to its legs. The creature prefers densely shaded places under fallen trees or rocks along streams (e.g. parcel 11d). When disturbed it flies out of the darkness, displaying its white leg segments to confuse predators. Its larvae live in patches of liverwort along densely shaded stream banks.

The group of Short-palped Craneflies (Limoniidae) comprises quite small and elegant flies, representing the most numerous and diverse group of Craneflies, with twelve species on the Edge and some 215 nationally. Some of the species recorded from the Edge (e.g. *Cheilotrichia cinerascens* and *Ormosia hederae*) have two generations per year and fly in early spring and again in late summer/autumn. Many species (e.g. *Dicranomyia modesta* and *Erioconopa trivialis*) occur virtually anywhere that presents wet soil. However, some dwell in rather unexpected habitats: for instance, *Limonia duplicata* breeds in dung, and so is common in cattle-rearing areas (parcels 20b or 22), and *Limonia nubeculosa* is abundant in sand dunes and sand heaths (parcel 17b), with its larvae living in leaf litter. Some species (e.g. *Rhypholophus varius*) prefer acid substrates such as carr and seepages.

Winter Gnats of the family Trichoceridae, with three common species found on the Edge, are abundant throughout the year, but more so in late autumn and winter, and this is why they acquired their common name. All the recorded species of Winter Gnats are potentially ubiquitous; the males can be seen swarming in sheltered spots in gardens, woodland clearings or along footpaths. The Fold-winged Craneflies (family Ptychopteridae) are represented on the Edge by two common species (*Ptychoptera albimana* and *P. contaminata*; Plate 38). Both are small attractive flies with spotted wings and the abdomen visibly constricted in its middle part. Larvae burrow into soft sediment or live among dead leaves at the bottom of ponds and streams, and breathe through long tubes. According to Stubbs (1993), ptychopterid species are good indicators of the quality of aquatic habitats.

Of other nematocerous flies found on the Edge it is worth mentioning Window Gnats (Anisopodidae). One of the two recorded species, *Sylvicola fenestralis*, breeds in a variety of decaying wood or vegetation, animal manure, mud and fermenting sap. Its larvae have even been reported as being capable of causing damage to honeycombs, cider and homemade wines. However, the fly enters houses accidentally, especially in springtime, being attracted to light, and can be found near windows (hence its English common name). This species is one of a number of True Flies collectively known as 'Filter Flies' (Hickin, 1964). They breed in sewage filters, preventing the fungal mat (on which the larvae feed) becoming too dense and clogging the filter beds in sewage works.

If you are a mushroom hunter, you know how disappointing it can be to pick up a wild mushroom that is full of wormholes and white 'worms'. In fact these 'worms' are the larvae of various True Flies that develop in fungi known as fungicolous flies. Two groups of flies found on the Edge are definitely in this league, the Fungus Gnats of the families Mycetophilidae (twenty-nine species on the Edge, 471 nationally) and Bolitophilidae (four on the Edge, seventeen nationally). Many groups of the Mycetophilidae are oligophagous and develop only in a particular kind of mushroom, such as *Mycetophila formosa*, which develops only in the Wrinkle Crust (*Phlebia radiata*). Larvae of others are less choosy and can develop in various mushrooms. For instance, *Allodia lugens* and *Mycetophila fungorum* inhabit living agarics, boletes, Pezizales and some other kinds. All four *Bolitophila* species recorded on the Edge develop in agarics, the most common group of mushrooms. Their larvae are gregarious and develop internally in soft fungi. Larvae of the Black Fungus Gnats (Sciaridae; three species on the Edge) develop in decaying detritus, but some, such as *Lycoriella ingenua*, also in agarics and polypores, such as bracket fungi, which are often found on Alderley Edge on rotting logs. As a whole, the world of flies associated with fungi is quite diverse and is likely to exceed 800 species in the UK alone. A detailed account of which British Diptera species occur in fungi and how to collect and to study them is given by Chandler (2010).

While walking over wet meadows on Alderley Edge (parcels 17a–17c) on a warm spring day it is difficult to avoid black, slow-moving and absolutely harmless St Mark's Flies (Bibionidae; two species on the Edge, eighteen nationally), so named because they often appear close to St Mark's Day (25 April). Some species (e.g. the Fever-fly, *Dilophus febrilis*; Plate 39) can swarm on flowers, where flies will be seen doubled up during copulation, the habit that resulted in another country name, 'Love Bugs'. These flies breed in soil and rotting vegetation. Another easily recognisable family is the Moth-flies (Psychodidae; ninety-nine species nationally), small flies with short, hairy bodies and wings giving them a 'fluffy' appearance. They develop in moss and damp vegetable matter. Unfortunately, the fauna of Moth-flies of Alderley Edge remains practically unknown, with a single finding of aquatic larva of an undetermined *Psychoda* species.

The only group of blood-sucking Lower Diptera recorded from the Edge to date is the Mosquitoes (Culicidae) (three species locally, thirty-four nationally). Females of two species (*Aedes punctor* and *Culex pipiens*) feed on a range of mammals, including humans, and bite readily, while those of *Culiseta morsitans* mostly feed on birds (see Snow, 1990). The *molestus* form of *Culex pipiens* is famous because its larvae occur underground, for example in flooded cellars or in the underground railway systems of large cities.

Brachycera

The suborder Brachycera, collectively termed 'Shorthorns', contains various groups that we think of as typical flies, such as Hoverflies, Houseflies and Bluebottles. Hoverflies (the family Syrphidae; twenty-one species on the Edge and 276 nationally) are among the best-known Diptera and almost universally liked by the general public because of their bright colour and effortless hovering around garden flowers (Plate 40 shows two species recorded on the Edge). Hovering by males seems to be a strategy for attracting females. For this reason males tend to hold small territories in loose swarms and chase off rivals.

Adults of the majority of Hoverflies feed on nectar and pollen in different proportions when visiting flowers. Many of them look like bees and wasps, including a similarity in colour, morphology and even behaviour. For instance, the Dronefly *Eristalis pertinax* and the Hoverfly *Cheilosia illustrata* resemble the Honeybee; the black and white Hoverflies *Syrphus vitripennis* and *Myathropa florea* resemble social wasps (*Vespula vulgaris* and related species); the furry black and yellow and white Hoverfly *Eristalis intricarius* looks very much like a Bumblebee; the orange and black hoverfly *Xylota segnis* resembles an Ichneumon wasp. Such similarity, known as mimicry, protects Hoverflies from predators (birds in particular) that are deceived into mistaking the harmless fly for a noxious insect and do not attack it (see Edmunds, 2008). Some Hoverflies not only look like social wasps and bees, but their larvae also live in wasps' nests, usually as scavengers. For instance, *Volucella pellucens*, of which adults can be seen hovering above the ground in woodland clearings on Alderley Edge, lays its eggs in the nests of social wasps in early autumn, when the wasp colony is about to die out; the Hoverfly larvae then feed on nest debris until next spring.

The larvae of many Hoverflies (e.g. *Epistrophe grossulariae*, *Melanostoma scalare* and *Platycheirus albimanus*) feed on Aphids and thus are friends to the gardener, alongside such predatory groups of insects as Lacewings, Ladybirds and Ground Beetles (see section F). Larvae of others (e.g. *Cheilosia illustrata* and other members of the same genus) are herbivorous, mining in the stems and roots of plants, and are associated with large umbellifers such as hogweed, on which the adults are typically seen. Larvae of *Eristalis* species are of the rat-tailed maggot type and occur in drains and ponds rich in the decaying organic matter on which they subsist. Larvae of *Xylota sylvarum* feed on dead rotting wood and occur under rotten bark.

Many other flies are also convincing mimics of other Hymenoptera, for instance of the Ichneumon wasps. Adults of the only species of Awl-flies recorded from the Edge (*Xylophagus ater*; Xylophagidae) are delicate-looking flies which can be found by examining standing, freshly dead broad-leaved timber or fallen logs, on which eggs are laid, mainly in May and June. Males move and look very much like an Ichneumon wasp. Larvae of *Xylophagus ater* live in dead wood, sub-cortically (between the bark and the dead sapwood), but are carnivorous, preying on other larvae. Another mimic of the Ichneumon wasp is *Loxocera albiseta* (Psilidae; twenty-six species in the UK), an elongate red and black fly that lays eggs into plants on which the larvae feed.

Many flies, such as *Acidia cognata*, the sole representative of the Picture-winged Flies (Tephritidae) found on the Edge (seventy-six species in the UK), have delicately patterned wings. The wings are used in courtship, but also provide a form of camouflage. Larvae of *Acidia cognata* are leaf-miners of the coltsfoot (*Tussilago farfara*), cutting semicircular slits under the leaf epidermis. It is worth noticing that the fly leaf-miners and stem-miners of Alderley Edge remain virtually unstudied, though there are over 350 native British species (Pitkin *et al.*, 2015). For instance, only two species of the Opomyzidae (sixteen nationally), whose larvae bore grass stems, and two species of the Shore-flies (Ephydridae; 151 in the UK), whose larvae mine leaves or stems of aquatic plants, have been found on Alderley Edge.

Our remoter forebears were right in assuming that flies could be generated from decaying organic matter (but not spontane-ously as they thought). Two important groups of the kind are the Blowflies (Calliphoridae; two species on the Edge) and the Flesh-flies (Sarcophagidae; three species on the Edge). Larvae (i.e. maggots) of certain species (e.g. *Calliphora vicina*) feed on decaying animal material, being the dominant group of insects that decompose large carcasses. Maggots can occur in huge numbers, as each female lays about 300 eggs, and hatched maggots complete their development in less than two weeks. If fly maggots are present, 90 per cent of the available soft tissue on the carcass is gone within approximately six days. *Calliphora vicina* seems to be one of the most important fly species in the field of forensic entomology because of its consistent time of arrival and colonisation of the corpse, which it finds by odour. However, maggots of other species, known as Bird Blowflies (e.g. *Protocalliphora azurea*), are obligate external parasites of birds; they are found in the nests of birds and suck the blood of nestlings. Furthermore, some Sarcophagidae species (e.g. *Metopia argyrocephala*) are associated with nests of solitary bees (Apidae) and wasps (Sphecidae and Pompilidae), where fly larvae subsist on the food store intended for the owner's offspring. Adults can be found in dry sandy places such as sand heath (parcel 17b), where their hosts nest.

Many Diptera species are associated with dung and play an important role in its recycling. In the UK at least 201 fly species develop in cow dung (P. Skidmore, in Chandler, 2010), forming an important part of what is collectively termed as the 'cow-dung community' (see also section F). These flies are well represented on the Edge because of the availability of permanent pastures (parcels 20b, 22). Some of them are exclusively dung-breeders, for instance the family Sphaeroceridae or Lesser Dung-flies, with eight species found on the Edge of the 137 known in the UK. These black and usually small flies are most often found in samples of cow dung. Most unusual is that the flies can penetrate below the dung surface, using the tunnels made by larger insects (Skidmore, 1991). Many species (e.g. *Copromyza atra*, *Crumomyia nigra* and *Sphaerocera curvipes*) can also utilise horse, pig and sheep dung, and are common in farmyard dung or compost heaps. Far more interesting, though, are the Scathophagidae, a group of exclusively dung-breeders loosely called the Yellow Dung-flies (fifty-four species nationally), with two common species found on Alderley Edge (Plate 41). Both of them belong to the genus *Scatophaga*, meaning 'dung-eater'. These bright yellow and orange furry flies are highly predacious and can attack much larger insects, including the Craneflies. In springtime, males of *Scatophaga* species can be seen on the Edge (parcels 5, 11d, 22) crowding on pats of cow dung. Males are territorial and try to defend their own space on the dung against rivals. The winner of a particular dung space, usually the largest male, is visited by a female that mates with him and then deposits her eggs.

The dung of poultry is also populated by flies, for instance by *Sepsis violacea*, a small bright black fly – a representative of the small family of Black Scavenger Flies (Sepsidae; four species on the Edge and twenty-nine nationally). Other species of the Sepsidae (e.g. *Sepsis fulgens*) are notable because they can form large swarms of adults, especially in the late winter.

However, in its association with human concerns the most famous group of dung-breeding flies is the family Muscidae (Houseflies). Because of the strong association of these flies with dung and decaying matter, many people assume that *all* flies feed on and develop in excrement of some sort. The main public accusation of the Housefly was brilliantly articulated by T. Crew in his 'The Song of the Fly' (1931):

Straight from the rubbish heap I come,
I never wash my feet,
And every single chance I get
I walk on what you eat.

It is an unfortunate but well known fact that, for instance, the Common Housefly (*Musca domestica*), which has not yet been formally recorded from the Edge, is not only an obnoxious home pest but can also be a mechanical vector of human diseases such as typhoid, dysentery, summer diarrhoea and others (Hickin, 1964). A comprehensive account of the Common Housefly and anti-housefly campaigns in the UK, where it was once called 'one of man's greatest enemies', was provided by Clark (2009).

For the sake of accuracy, it is worth stressing that larvae of many muscids (e.g. of *Hydrotaea cyrtoneurina*, *H. irritans* and *Polietes lardarius*), even if they occur in dung, are predators feeding on other fly larvae. Many muscids are indeed dung-breeders, for instance *Coenosia tigrina*, *Hebecnema umbratica* and *Mesembrina meridiana*, which are typically found around cattle pastures (parcels 11, 17, 20). Of these, *Mesembrina meridiana* is rather showy and can be identified in the field: it is a large shiny black fly with conspicuous orange-yellow bases to its wings. Adults can be seen sunbathing on logs, fences or bare sunny ground; this is why it is sometimes named the Noon Fly. Other muscid flies (e.g. *Thricops semicinerea* and *Phaonia basalis*) are frequent visitors to flowers, especially hogweed. Many species of the Muscidae such as *Phaonia subventa* are widespread and common, and can be found on the Edge from March until it freezes. Others are common visitors to our houses. For instance, the shiny green fly *Eudasyphora cyanella* sometimes overwinters indoors and is among those flies which are collectively known as 'Cluster Flies'. This fly is one of the first to appear each year, and individuals can be seen sunning themselves outside on walls.

Two species of Housefly recorded from Alderley Edge are particularly notorious. One of them is known as the Sheep Headfly or Sweat Fly (*Hydrotaea irritans*). It is a typical cattle-nuisance fly which bothers farm animals by swarming around their heads, feeding on saliva and mucous secretion, with a preference for blood. In Scotland, the fly can cause economic damage and it has been suggested that it is a vector for summer mastitis, a bovine bacterial infection. Another obnoxious species of the Edge is the Stablefly or Biting Housefly (*Stomoxys calcitrans*; Plate 42). It appears to be closely connected with horses and therefore can be found near stables, whence its common name. The fly resembles the Common Housefly, but it is a blood-sucker. It mainly attacks horses and cattle, choosing the lower part of the legs as the spot to feed, but (what a surprise!) it can also attack people. It is almost embarrassing to think that if methods for their total eradication are discovered we shall show no mercy towards Stableflies, nor towards the other Houseflies that commonly enter houses. But my personal heresy is that really we should not fight against nature, even if it comes to us in the appearance of a fly. Despite our deep animosity towards flies, it is worth remembering a bit of popular wisdom that 'if you kill a fly, two more will come to its funeral'; we shall never win!

There are many other Diptera groups which can be found indoors at Alderley Edge, for they are likely to be attracted to light. Many are difficult for non-specialists to distinguish, for instance the small and dull-coloured *Heleomyza serrata* (Heleomyzidae) and *Palloptera ustulata* (Pallopteridae) and *Opomyza germinationis* (Opomyzidae) – a small yellowish fly with strongly marked wings. The latter species is abundant in grassy habitats, for its larvae are stem-borers in grasses. Some species of the Lauxaniidae (e.g. *Lyciella rorida*, a small yellow fly with orange eyes) can also be found indoors. Larvae in this family develop in decaying vegetable matter, including compost heaps, whereas adults prefer shady situations and this is why they may enter houses. Even some Soldier-flies (Stratiomyidae; five species on the Edge of forty-eight known in the UK) such as the Twin-spot Centurion (*Sargus bipunctatus*) may enter houses. The latter is an autumn species and a typical garden-dweller which can be seen from August to early November; its larvae breed in dung. Adults of the Soldier-flies are usually associated with wetlands (parcels 17a, 18c, 20b) and can be collected by sweeping waterside vegetation, on which they congregate and rest. Their common name is due to their bright (often metallic green or vivid yellow) body coloration, which is thought to be reminiscent of the soldiers' uniforms of long ago.

Many flies are parasitoids (i.e. parasites that kill their host; see also section E). The most diverse of such flies are the Tachinidae or Parasite Flies, with eight species found on the Edge (261 in the UK). These are usually medium-sized, dull-coloured flies, often resembling the Houseflies but more bristly. Tachinid larvae are almost without exception solitary internal parasitoids of other insects, especially of Lepidoptera and Coleoptera (Askew, 1971). For instance, larvae of *Dexiosoma caninum* parasitise larvae of the Cockchafer (*Melolontha* spp.), and those of *Eriothrix rufomaculata* and *Tachina fera* develop inside caterpillars of Arctiidae and Noctuidae. The host usually does not die until the larval development of the parasite is complete. Compared with the parasitoid Hymenoptera, larvae of the parasite flies are less specific and some of them can attack many hosts. The Thick-headed Flies (Conopidae; four species recorded from the Edge, twenty-three nationally) are another family that is exclusively parasitic. They attack adult bees or wasps: *Conops quadrifasciatus* is a parasitoid of the White-Tailed Bumble Bee (*Bombus lucorum*) and *Physocephala rufipes* is a bee-killing fly, its larvae being parasitoids of adult bees. Adults of the Thick-headed Flies are nice-looking creatures, with a wasp-like or bee-like appearance (often striped black and yellow), typically found in woodland glades and edges, meadows and sand heath (e.g. parcels 17a, 17c), visiting flowers, especially umbels and composites, where their hosts are likely to be found. The family of Big-headed Flies (Pipunculidae; two species on the Edge and ninety-five nationally) includes small, dull-coloured flies that earn their common name from their disproportionately large heads, which are composed mostly of the enormous eyes. Another hallmark of the family is that they are exquisite fliers, capable of hovering just like the true Hoverflies (see above). Larvae of the Big-headed Flies are internal parasitoids of Homoptera, especially of Leafhoppers (Cicadellidae) and Froghoppers (Cercopidae) (discussed in section A).

Most unusual are the Keds or Louse Flies (Hippoboscidae; one species on the Edge of fourteen known in the UK), whose adults are external blood-sucking parasites of birds and mammals other than bats. These flies have flattened bodies and are often wingless. Instead of laying eggs, a female produces a fully grown larva, which pupates immediately. Only one larva is carried at a time, and one female can produce ten to twelve larvae during its life (Askew, 1971). The only species recorded from the Edge is *Stenepteryx hirundinis*, taken from the house martin, but the fauna of Hippoboscidae should include more species, for instance the Forest Fly (*Hippobosca equina*), a parasite of horses and cattle, and *Ornithomyia avicularia*, a parasite of a wide range of woodland birds, and others.

Some of the Edge's flies, notably the Dance-flies of the families Empididae and Hybotidae, can surprise an attentive spectator by their elaborate courtship rituals. At first glance everything seems ordinary: on a sunny spring or summer day, elegant small to medium-sized flies, non-metallic and rather bristly, form aerial mating swarms, in a similar manner to the Non-biting Midges (see above). However, the males exhibit unique mating behaviour. Each male carries some prey (usually other flies), which is given to the female during courting as a 'nuptial gift'. Sometimes males prey on rival males of their own species and use them as gifts. In the swarms, males advertise their gifts by a rapid side-to-side 'dance', as if swaying on a pendulum, which explains their common name of Dance-flies. Females seem to choose the male with the most enticing offering. Mating does not take place until the female accepts the fly and feeds on it (a kind of a parental investment from the male); see Preston-Mafham and Preston-Mafham (1993) for more details of sexual rituals in the Dance-flies. Similar courtship ritual is described for the Nursery-web Spider (*Pisaura mirabilis*), but there it is performed for a different reason (see section G).

The fauna of the Dance-flies of Alderley Edge remain poorly studied, with only nine species of the Empididae (208 nationally), six species of the Hybotidae (178 nationally) and one species of the Brachystomatidae (four nationally) recorded to date. Nevertheless, one of the recorded species (*Rhamphomyia caliginosa*; Empididae) is nationally scarce, and two others (*Empis hyalipennis* and *Hilara monedula*; both Empididae) are rare in northern England. Despite the unusual courtship ritual of Dance-flies, many aspects of their biology remain to be explored. Even in some common species recorded from the Edge, such as *Empis punctata*, *Hybos culiciformis* and *Platypalpus pallidiventris*, the larval biology is still unknown, and in others (e.g. *Trichopeza longicornis*) even habitat requirements have not been established. All Dance-flies are predators, having a conspicuous down-pointing proboscis, which is used for piercing the prey: other flies, Caddisflies, Mayflies and Moths. This is why another common name for the Empididae is Dagger-flies.

Of the Diptera groups occurring on Alderley Edge, one cannot omit the large family of Long-legged Flies (Dolichopodidae), close relatives of the Dance-flies, with ten species found on the Edge and 296 nationally. Members of the family are easy to recognise: all are medium to small slender flies with green or copper metallic-coloured bodies and long legs. However, identification of individual species is very difficult, because many are similar. Long-legged Flies have a short proboscis and prey on other small insects. Males demonstrate the elaborate courtship behaviour, which involves visual communication between sexes. Males show dynamic flight manoeuvres and/or display their leg modifications (called 'badgers' in scientific jargon) by waving them in front of the female. Adults of the common Long-legged Flies found on the Edge (e.g. *Dolichopus trivialis*, *D. ungulates*, *Hercostomus aerosus*, *H. cupreus*) prefer damp situations and wetlands; the carnivorous larvae develop in damp soil or mud.

It is worth mentioning a few more of the remaining groups of flies on Alderley Edge. The Common Clegg (*Haematopota pluvialis*) is the sole representative of the Horseflies (Tabanidae; thirty species nationally) found on the Edge. It is a greyish biting fly that is associated with marshes and damp woodlands, like other local species of Horseflies. Females bite mammals, including humans (especially around parcels 17b, 20b and 22), and the bites hurt. Certain representatives of the predatory Snipe-flies (Rhagionidae), such as *Rhagio scolopacea*, can be recognised by their habit of perching head-downward on tree trunks, from whence they make short flights at passing prey (other soft-bodied insects). This is the reason for their other common name – 'Downlookers'. Some of the Brachycera flies are associated with fungi, for example *Suillia bicolor* (Heleomyzidae; eight species on the Edge, fifty-six nationally), whose larvae inhabit agarics and boletes. Larvae of the Snail-killing Flies (Sciomyzidae; one species on the Edge, seventy nationally) are specialist predators of snails and slugs.

Although it is possible to continue telling more interesting stories and facts about what could be seen by some as the all-too-common flies occurring on Alderley Edge, this brief report cannot cover all of them. Therefore why don't you just choose a warm, sunny spring or summer day and visit the Edge yourself? Myriads of flying minibeasts of which little or nothing is known are still there to be looked at and studied. For observation nothing is required but patience, a pocket lens and goodwill. Whether you are a nature-lover or a rigorous scientist, you might be the one who will discover something unusual about our neighbourhood flies or challenge what seems to be a well known fact about them.

E. Wasps, ants, bees and allies (Hymenoptera)

Dmitri V. Logunov

> The roving bee proclaims aloud
>   Her flight by vocal wings.
> W. Wordsworth (1888), 'Gold and Silver Fishes in a Vase'

The order Hymenoptera is the third largest group of insects after the Coleoptera (beetles) and Lepidoptera (butterflies and moths), numbering over 145,000 species described worldwide (Huber, 2009). In the UK it is the largest insect order, with 7,517 species (G. Broad, personal communication). The group gets its name from the Greek words *hymen* and *pteron*, and means 'membrane-winged'. Hymenoptera are characterised by usually having two pairs of membranous wings. However, fore- and hindwings are tightly interlocked by a line of small hooks and hence during flight the pair of wings on each side acts as a single membrane. There are two main taxonomic groups of Hymenoptera: the Symphyta (sawflies and wood wasps), which are broad-waisted, and the Apocrita, which usually have a pinched waist and include all the remaining Hymenoptera, themselves traditionally considered in two groups: the Parasitica (parasitoid wasps) and the Aculeata (those groups that can sting: bees, wasps and ants).

The most widely recognised hymenopterans – bees, ants and wasps – have long been part of art, ritual, folklore and literature worldwide – to take just one unforgettable comment by A. A. Milne's Winnie-the-Pooh: 'The only reason for being a bee that I know of is making honey ... and the only reason for making honey is so I can eat it'. Whatever the reasons for 'being a bee' might be according to Winnie-the-Pooh, many hymenopterans do indeed provide themselves and especially their offspring with nutritious food, either animal-based (paralysed insects) as in the case of wasps, or plant-based (seeds, pollen, honey, etc.), as do the ants and bees. In the latter case, a poorer food resource such as nectar is usually modified into a better one such as honey.

The regional fauna of the Hymenoptera of Alderley Edge remain poorly known, with only 128 species being recorded to date (see

Appendix 13.1, Table 13.1). This number is even less than the number of collected species of flies (216) or spiders (137). It is mainly due to the notably low number of recorded parasitoid wasps, the most diverse and the least-known group of the Hymenoptera. These wasps are called 'parasitoids' because, technically speaking, they are not 'parasites'. True parasites, like helminths, subsist at the expense of their host and rarely or never kill it, whereas young parasitoids develop inside the host, consuming it entirely apart from the skin, and always kill it. Nearly 10 per cent of described insect species are parasitoids, but they are in fact likely to represent 20–25 per cent of all insect species (Mills, 2003); yet most of them belong to poorly known groups such as parasitoid wasps (over 64,000 known species worldwide).

Only twenty-two of the parasitoid wasp species (Braconidae, Ichneumonidae and Proctotrupidae) out of over 5,500 known in the UK have been recorded from the Edge, mainly on the basis of the old card index of faunistic records of insects of Lancashire and Cheshire compiled in 1920–54 by the famous British entomologist Harry Britten and held in Manchester Museum. Yet the parasitoid wasps are likely to be one of the most abundant flying insects in British gardens, far more numerous than moths or even flies (Thompson, 2006), and thus it is hardly an exaggeration to say that the fauna of parasitoid Hymenoptera of Alderley Edge still remain practically unexplored.

Of the Parasitica recorded from the Edge, it is worth mentioning the huge family of Ichneumon Wasps (Ichneumonidae), the parasitoids of butterfly and moth caterpillars or pupae in which they lay their eggs. For instance, the large, Black Ichneumon *Amblyjoppa proteus* is reared in caterpillars of the Elephant Hawk-moth, a common species of the Edge. Although the great majority of the Ichneumon Wasps have fully developed wings and are very active in flight, females of some species, particularly of the genus *Gelis* (three species of which have been found on the Edge), are wingless, looking like elegant ants. They can attack spider cocoons. Some parasitoid wasps develop inside aphids. For instance, *Ephedrus plagiator* (Braconidae) attacks the Black Bean Aphid (*Aphis fabae*; see Askew, 1971), which forms large colonies on many host plants. Surprisingly enough this aphid species has not yet been formally recorded from the Edge – another sign of how incomplete is our current knowledge of the insects of Alderley Edge.

Only a single species of the gall wasps (*Andricus kollari*, Cynipidae) has been recorded from Alderley Edge. A gall is an abnormal swelling of plant tissues induced by various organisms, including the grub-like larvae of gall wasps. Gall provides nourishment and shelter for the gall maker. *Andricus kollari* is well known for developing spherical and woody Oak Marble Galls, which were used as dye-source for cloth and ink until 1860. This is why this gall wasp, which is a native of the Middle East, was introduced to Devon during the 1830s and by 1860 had spread as far northwards as Scotland (see Redfern and Askew, 1992). Herbalists also used gall extract as remedy to cure rheums, dysentery and other fluxes.

The Sawflies and Wood Wasps (Symphyta) of Alderley Edge remain poorly known and include only eleven of the 470 species recorded in the UK (Archer, 2002). They are more familiar as grubs, for the caterpillar-like larvae, some of which attack certain garden plants such as currants and roses, are often gregarious (Owen, 1983, 1991). Sawflies get their name from the saw-like ovipositor used by females for cutting plant tissues and laying eggs. Sawflies are most numerous in woodlands. The most spectacular and largest British species is the Birch Sawfly (*Cimbex femoratus*; up to 25 mm long), of which spectacular fast-flying adults can be collected from May to August; its greenish, solitary grubs feed on birch. Only slightly smaller (15–20 mm long) is *Trichosoma lucorum*, which at first glance could be easily mistaken for a bee; its grubs also subsist on birch leaves. Representatives of the large family Tenthredinidae (nine species on the Edge) are much smaller and often difficult to identify; their grubs are usually gregarious.

Alderley Edge is regionally important for the Aculeata (about 570 species in the UK; see Archer, 2002), primarily due to the easy availability of open habitats, such as sandy heaths, grasslands, heathlands and exposed soil along the edges of paths (parcels 3b, 12b, 17, 20b, 22, etc.), whose soil provides suitable nesting sites for solitary bees and wasps, such as Andrenidae, Halictidae, Pompilidae and some Sphecidae. Many of these groups are strongly habitat-associated and therefore local, with a very patchy distribution. Two species, the Hairy Sand Wasp (*Podalonia hirsuta*, Sphecidae) and the Spider-hunting Wasp (*Priocnemis schioedtei*, Pompilidae), are nationally scarce. One species, *Nomada lathburiana* (Anthophoridae), is listed in the *British Red Data Book* (Shirt, 1987) as a rare species (category 3), which means the species is extremely localised within the UK and seems to be at risk of extinction. It is a Cuckoo Bee that resembles a wasp (striped in yellow, black and red), being a nest parasite of the Grey Mining Bee (*Andrena cineraria*). The female enters the open cell of the host and lays its egg. When it emerges the larva kills the egg or young larva of the host and feeds on the stock of pollen that forms its stored provisions.

Of the solitary bees, two groups are best-represented at the Edge: the Mining Bees (Andrenidae; thirteen species) and the Sweat Bees (Halictidae; thirteen species) (nationally thirty-two and fifty-seven species respectively). The Mining Bees are small to large subterranean-nesting bees, brown or blackish in colour, and look superficially like honey bees. As with all solitary bees, it is the female Mining Bees that dig and provision the nest. Generally a nest consists of an entrance leading to a main burrow with shorter lateral burrows, each ending in a cell or cluster of cells lined with a wax-like substance. All the recorded species are common and widespread, but some, such as *Andrena fucata* and *A. barbilabris* (Plate 43), are local in distribution, being restricted to places with exposures of sand or light sandy soils, including landslips and sandy heaths (parcel 17). Other species are strongly associated with a particular plant, for instance *Andrena lapponica* with the bilberry (*Vaccinnium* spp.; parcels 3b, 12b), from which the females collect pollen. The nests of all *Andrena* species are sometimes taken over by Cuckoo Bees of the family Anthophoridae (five species on the Edge, nationally thirty-two). Female Cuckoo Bees resemble wasps, do not construct their own nests, and lay their eggs in the nests of Mining Bees, as described above for *Nomada lathburiana*, behaviour reminiscent of cuckoo birds. In professional jargon, Cuckoo Bees are named cleptoparasites.

The Sweat Bees (Halictidae) are small to medium-size subterranean-nesting bees, usually dark-coloured and often metallic in appearance (e.g. the metallic bronzy-green *Halictus tumulorum*). These bees may be solitary (as are all the *Lasioglossum* species recorded from the Edge) or primitively eusocial (*Halictus tumulorum*). In the latter case, the female that has established a nest becomes the queen. She rears a first brood, some of which remain in the nest when they become adults, as workers helping the queen to take care of the second brood. All species of *Sphecodes* (four on the Edge) are cleptoparasites of either *Halictus* or *Lasioglossum* bees, usually with no particular specialisation. They can even attack the Mining Bees. For instance, the black and red *Sphecodes pellucidus* is known to parasitise the nests of *Andrena barbilabris*.

Solitary bees of the Edge also include Leaf-cutting Bees (Megachilidae). One of the two species recorded from the Edge (*Megachile willughbiella*) is notorious for making neat, semi-circular holes in rose leaves, which are cut from the leaf margins by the female bees and used to create nest walls. On the other hand, Leaf-cutting Bees are important as pollinators.

All groups of bees are efficient pollinators of fruit crops and garden flowers, and are capable of enhancing a garden (see Owen, 1983). Crops such as apples, pears and berries are entirely dependent on pollinators for fruit production. Various measures such as bee nesting boxes, bamboo canes and the like can be used to attract the bees to gardens and orchards (see Thompson, 2006). The most famous of the pollinators are social bees (Apidae), Bumblebees (*Bombus* spp.) and the Honey Bee, with organised societies and elaborate honeycombs. It is about them that the early seventeenth-century English proverb says that 'where bees are, there is honey'. Eight species of Apidae have been found on the Edge out of the twenty-five British species (250 worldwide: Huber, 2009). All British Bumblebees live socially in colonies throughout their lives. They nest underground, often in old mouse or vole nests, and can have from 30–50 up to 150–200 bees in the colony (e.g. *Bombus terrestris*). Bumblebees forage on a wide range of plants, feeding on pollen and nectar and rearing their grubs on the same diet. Bumblebee colonies are annual affairs: they die out each autumn, leaving only young mated queens to survive the winter and start new colonies each spring. Many British bumblebee species are in serious decline, causing what is known as 'pollination deficit', and a number of measures need to be taken to conserve and protect them (see Marren and Mabey, 2010). Two of the Apidae species recorded on the Edge are Cuckoo Bees, which belong to the subgenus *Psithyrus* of the genus *Bombus* (Plate 44 shows one of these two) and which may take over a substantial part of the colonies of other *Bombus* species, giving them their common name (see Prŷs-Jones and Corbet, 1987). The *Psithyrus* female crawls into a bumblebee nest, often kills the host queen and starts laying her eggs in the host nest. As a result, its larvae are reared by workers of the host bumblebee species. One of these Cuckoo Bees (*Bombus vestalis*) is regionally notable in northern England, and otherwise common.

Of the solitary wasps recorded from Alderley Edge, it is worth mentioning Spider-hunting Wasps (Pompilidae; seven species) and Digger Wasps (Sphecidae; twenty-four species) (44 and 120 British species respectively). A common feature is that the female wasps make individual nests, dug in sandy soil or excavated in plant stems, and then provision them with paralysed prey such as spiders, caterpillars or other insects as food for their offspring. Several dozen insects or spiders can be collected for each larva: see Yeo and Corbet (1983) for a useful account on the general biology of and identification key to the British solitary wasps. All the Spider-hunting Wasps recorded on the Edge are common but local in distribution. As the name suggests, these wasps usually prey on spiders, particularly on ground-dwelling Wolf Spiders (Lycosidae), and are commonly seen running erratically on sand and bare earth. Some groups such as the *Priocnemis* species excavate multi-celled burrows, often in natural cavities; others like *Anoplius nigerrimus* (Plate 45) make their nest cells in deserted burrows, including those of other Aculeata, or sometimes even in snail shells. There are even nest parasites among the Pompilidae. For instance, *Evagetes crassicornis* is a brood parasite on other subterranean nesting species of the family such as *Arachnospila anceps* and *Anoplius nigerrimus*; the latter was recorded from the Edge.

The Digger Wasps represent a rather diverse group (731 species worldwide; Huber, 2009), with a wide array of habits and prey used for their larvae. For instance, the large yellow and black Slender-bodied Digger Wasp (*Crabro cribrarius*; Plate 46) as well as other *Crabro* and also *Crossocerus* species provision their young with flies of various families (Asilidae, Empididae, Muscidae, Syrphidae, Therevidae, etc.); species of the genus *Psen* stock their nests with cicadellid leaf-hoppers;

the *Pemphredon* species, commonly nesting in rotten wood or in broken plant stems, prey on Aphids; females of the nationally scarce species *Podalonia hirsuta* provision their nest with caterpillars. A few sphecid species such as *Passaloecus corniger* have adopted a parasitic lifestyle, stealing aphid prey of other *Passaloecus* species and from *Psenulus pallipes*, which is most unusual for Digger Wasps.

As a stock of paralysed insects represents a valuable food source, all solitary wasps have their own cleptoparasites, which lay their eggs in the host's nest cells and their larvae then eat the rightful brood, like the Cuckoo Bees (see above). For instance, the Cuckoo Wasp *Elampus panzeri* (Chrysididae; Plate 47) recorded on the Edge parasitises Digger Wasps of the genus *Psen* (Sphecidae). The adults of this and other species of Chrysididae are bright, metallic-coloured insects (hence their second English common name – Ruby-tailed Wasps), which feed on nectar and pollen, often on garden flowers.

However, the most familiar to everyone are the Social Wasps (Vespidae), with five species reported from Alderley Edge of the nine known in the UK (4,918 worldwide; Huber, 2009). In various regions of Britain, these wasps are known as Apple-bees, Sow-wasps, Jaspers, Yellow Jackets, etc. (see Marren and Mabey, 2010); the last name is due to their black and yellow banded bodies. All Social Wasps build complex nests made of chewed wood pulp, a kind of papier mâché, which is obtained from dead trees, fences, etc. Nests are usually suspended in enclosed spaces such as bird boxes, hollow trees, roof spaces or cavity walls, as in the case of the *Dolichovespula* species, or the wasps form colonies underground, as does the Common Wasp (*Vespula vulgaris*). Young are reared on meat of other insects or scraps of carrion. The adults feed on nectar, fruits and honeydew or steal honey from colonies of Bumblebees.

Seven species of Ants have been found on the Edge, out of some fifty British species (see Skinner and Allen, 1996). Ants are best known for living in well organised eusocial colonies. In children's popular literature Ants are frequently affirmed to be the cleverest, most organised and hardest-working creatures, living in kingdoms at their own disposal. As the Book of Proverbs suggests (vi.6), 'Go to the ant, thou sluggard; consider her ways, and be wise'. The majority of Ants are omnivorous, although many of them tend their own colonies of Greenflies and regularly 'milk' them for honeydew. For instance, the Black Garden Ant (*Lasius niger*), the commonest species of the Edge, farms Greenflies on garden plants and also eats ripe fruit, causing problems for gardeners. It is abundant everywhere, under pavements and garden paths, and frequently builds its nests in the insulation layers of houses; colonies average 5,500 individuals. Because Ants are the evolutionary cousins of bees and wasps, some of them are vicious stingers. Four species of the kind have been found on Alderley Edge, all from the genus *Myrmica*. Their generic name originated from the Greek word *myrmex*, meaning 'ant', which the ancients thought had the same root as the Myrmidons, the followers of the hero Achilles who moved in battle as one mass like soldier ants (see Sleigh, 2003). The commonest of the stingers is the Red Ant (*Myrmica rubra*), which may be found in gardens and woodlands and nesting in colonies under stones and in rotting wood. This ant is a generalist predator and scavenger. The uncommon *Myrmica lobicornis* can be found occasionally, restricted to warm and dry isolated sites.

Although overall the Hymenoptera fauna of Alderley Edge may appear rather ordinary (see Appendix 13.1), it contains a great number of species, particularly of the more charismatic solitary wasps and bees, whose behaviour and natural history still conceal many surprises and unknown facts. Whether you are a child or an interested adult, few things can be more fascinating than observing how a Mason Wasp (Eumenidae) is constructing its jug-like nest out of clay, how a Spider-hunting Wasp (Pompilidae) is hauling off a paralysed spider to its nest, or how Yellow Jackets (Vespidae) are making their own papier mâché. Such curious observations and discoveries are very educational and can easily be made on Alderley Edge. There is no end to discovering and learning of new facts about wasps, bees or ants, if you take the time to visit the site and to observe them carefully.

F. Beetles (order Coleoptera)

Dmitri V. Logunov

> There ought to be a moral in Beetles but I haven't found it.
> (G. Taylor, 1948: 30)

Beetles (Coleoptera, 'sheath-wings'), with approximately 357,000 species described worldwide (Bouchard *et al.*, 2009), are the largest group of animals in the world, representing one-fifth of all known living organisms and about a quarter of all named species in the plant and animal kingdoms. As the famous British scholar J. B. Haldane exclaimed, 'the Creator, if he exists, must have an inordinate fondness for beetles' (see Marren and Mabey, 2010: 331). Beetles are easily recognised by their forewings, which have modified into hardened wing cases (elytra), covering and protecting the second pair of membranous flight wings. Some groups of beetles have no hindwings and are therefore flightless. Most beetles have mouthparts clearly adapted for chewing, with four main types of feeding: on plant tissues, on fungi, on decaying animal/plant matter, and as predators. The following brief overview of the beetles of Alderley Edge is intended for a general reader and is better used in conjunction with *A Coleopterist's Handbook* by Cooter and Barclay (2006), the field guide by Harde (1999) and the checklist of British beetles by Duff (2008). The latter checklist is also available online on the website of *The Coleopterist* journal, http://www.coleopterist.org.uk. For general reading on the biology of beetles the book by Evans (1975) remains one of the best.

With 4,034 species recorded to date (see Duff, 2008), the beetle diversity of the British Isles comes third, being surpassed by Diptera (true flies, 7,035 species; Chandler, 2010) and Hymenoptera (bees, wasps, ants, sawflies, 7,517 species; G. Broad, personal communication; and see sections B and D, as well as Table 13.1). On Alderley Edge a total of 363 beetle species has been recorded to date (see Appendix 13.1, Table 13.1). This number constitutes only about 9.0 per cent of the entire British fauna and is by no means complete. The lack of some beetle groups which are restricted to the south of the country, such as Jewel Beetles (Buprestidae) or Thick-legged Flower Beetles (Oedemeridae), can partly be explained by the unsuitable conditions of the Atlantic climate of the Edge (high rainfall and cool summers) and partly by a secondary character of the site's woody vegetation, which is basically an old plantation. Nonetheless, the low diversity of such groups as Leaf Beetles (Chrysomelidae), Seed Weevils (Apionidae) or True Weevils (Curculionidae) is definitely due to under-collecting (see p. 276). No representative of the Tortoise Beetles (*Cassida* spp.) has been found (fourteen species nationally). Even common garden species, such as the Violet Ground Beetle (*Carabus violaceus*; Carabidae), are absent from the current checklist. A conservative estimate is that at least the same number as has already been recorded from the Edge is still awaiting discovery.

Of the beetles recorded, the Ground Beetles (Carabidae) are one of the most popular research subjects for both amateur and professional coleopterists. They occur in all terrestrial habitats and demonstrate diverse modes of life. Although some Ground Beetles are vegetarians (e.g. *Pterostichus melanarius*, which occasionally attacks soft fruits such as strawberries), the majority are ground-living predators or scavengers. As many carabids are easy to collect in pitfall traps, they are commonly used by researchers as sensitive bio-indicators of various environmental conditions and processes, including pollution by heavy metals and the like. The distinctively coloured Green Tiger Beetle (*Cicindela campestris*; Plate 48) is undoubtedly one of most remarkable Ground Beetles of the Edge. It occurs in sandy heath conditions such as the Sandhills at Alderley (parcel 17) and is a diurnal predator that hunts by sight, being active and fast in sunny conditions and always flying away promptly when disturbed. Its larvae live in burrows and wait for prey passing close to the entrances of their burrows. The shining jet-black

Black Clock (*Pterostichus madidus*) is very common where the land has been disturbed and in areas associated with people, such as gardens (parcels 2c, 17). More interestingly, the beetle is noted for its 'forecasting capabilities'. According to children's folklore, stepping on a Black Clock brings rain. However, this species, like *Nebria brevicollis*, has been reported to be an important predator of caterpillars and even slugs in gardens or agricultural crops. A kind of 'green snail killer', not one you can buy in a garden centre, is the Snail Hunter (*Cychrus caraboides*). This very distinctive beetle has a pear-shaped body with an elongated head designed for entering snail shells, especially those of the small *Oxychilis* snails (Zonitidae), to eat their flesh. Widespread throughout the British Isles, it is usually found under logs or bark where it is damp. Some ground beetles such as the shiny bronze *Notiophilus biguttatus* or the metallic-coloured *Elaphrus cupreus* prefer damp situations and on the Edge can be collected in wet meadows from under stones and tussocks of rush (parcels 1, 5). The former is a sun-loving beetle, with large, very conspicuous bulbous eyes used in hunting small-sized insects on the ground, especially Springtails. There is one riparian species (*Nebria rufescens*), which can primarily be collected under streamside stones (parcels 4, 5). In wood litter and under tree bark (parcels 2c, 11d, 14) various species of the large genera *Bembidion* and *Leistus* can be found. Common species of the British ground beetles can be identified by means of the guide by Forsythe (1987).

There are at least two ponds (parcels 11ab, 20b, 22) and a stream (parcel 5) on the Edge, together with some damp areas with slowly running water (parcels 17, 18c, 19). These habitats harbour a number of aquatic beetles, of which the Diving Beetles (Dytiscidae) and the Scavenger Water Beetles (Hydrophilidae) are most diverse, with thirty and nineteen species respectively. These figures account for about a half of the recorded diversity of Diving and Scavenger Water Beetles in north-west England (seventy and forty-seven species respectively; Bentley, 2008). The Diving Beetles are much modified for life in water, with their streamlined bodies and oar-shaped hind legs. Most can be found throughout the year. Both adults and larvae are carnivorous. Some species (e.g. *Agabus bipustulatus*, common in Britain) are remarkable for their abilities to colonise all forms of aquatic habitat. Small diving beetles of the genus *Hydroporus* are very common in all kinds of still water, but prefer shallow bog habitats. The Scavenger Water Beetles contain both aquatic (subfamily Hydrophylinae) and terrestrial (subfamily Sphaeridiinae) species. The former group includes poor swimmers that are usually omnivorous scavengers (Plate 49 shows the hydrophyline *Anacaena globulus*, found on the Edge). The latter includes species associated with dung (*Sphaeridium* and *Cercyon* spp., Sphaeridiinae found in parcels 15, 18a).

Some water beetles are unusual in their lifestyle. For instance, pupation of the Burrowing Water Beetle (*Noterus clavicornis*; Noteridae) takes place in cocoons attached to the roots of aquatic plants. Even more peculiar adaptation to aquatic life is demonstrated by the Reed Beetle *Donacia vulgaris* (Chrysomelidae). Its soft and grub-like larvae feed on the roots of aquatic plants, but they have no gills. They inhale air by means of two hollow spine-like tubes that pierce air reservoirs in the roots. Pupae are attached to aquatic plants in the same way. A single species of the Whirligig Beetles (*Gyrinus substriatus*) was found in the Edge, of the twelve known in the UK (Duff, 2008). These are small, shiny black beetles that live in small groups on the surface of the water. When disturbed, the Whirligigs quickly scud over the water's surface, leaving circular ripples; this is the reason for their common name. The beetles can see both above and below water, and subsist on dead or dying insects that have fallen on the water. For a general account of the pondlife of the Edge see Chapter 12. A well illustrated introduction to the freshwater life of Britain was produced by Greenhalgh and Ovenden (2007). A very useful identification key to aquatic beetles is that by Friday (1988).

Some common but notable beetles have been found on Alderley Edge. The Rhinoceros Beetle (*Sinodenron cylindricum*; Lucanidae) is the only Stag Beetle found there (parcel 18a), out of the four species recorded in the UK. It is known to breed in rotting stumps, especially of beech, the second commonest tree species on the Edge (see Chapter 10, pp. 154–6). The species gets its name from the pointed projection on the front of the head of the males, which gives it a rhinoceros-like appearance. The Cockchafer (*Melolontha melolontha*; Scarabaeidae) is most familiar as a night-flier that often comes crashing into lighted windows on warm dusks in early summer. Its larvae feed on the roots of a number of plants, especially of grasses and cereals. The Garden Chafer (*Phyllopertha horticola*) is the smaller relative of the Cockchafer, which can be found throughout the UK in June and July. Both chafers are related to a distinct group of beetles that make their lives from utilising dung. A total of 275 insect species has been reported to occur in the dung of cattle in Britain (Skidmore, 1991). The majority of dung beetles are Scarabs and Dor Beetles, which feed directly on dung, but on the Edge their diversity is low. For instance, only five species of *Aphodius* (Scarabaeidae), the most diverse genus in the UK (forty-two species), have been recorded to date (parcel 18a). The main reason for this is likely to be current agricultural practice elsewhere in the UK, such as the treatment of livestock with persistent anti-helminthic drugs. Residues of these drugs can persist in the dung and are lethal to the beetles. The Dumble-dor, otherwise known as 'Lousy Watchman' (*Geotrupes stercorarius*; Geotrupidae), is common on grazing pastures, where a pair of beetles dig out a nesting tunnel under suitable dung and furnish it with dung for the larvae to feed on. Despite a clumsy manner of walking, Dumble-dors are good fliers. Having taken off, they fly with a low rasping droning buzz that can be heard several metres away ('dor' was an old word for 'drone' – the beetle's buzzing flight): hence the name dor beetles. The nickname 'Lousy Watchman' was earned because in a close-up view one can see that these beetles carry lots of tiny copper-coloured mites on their ventral sides. In 1959 the entomologist Hyatt recorded 488 mites on a single Dor Beetle, belonging to seven different species. The majority are predatory mites (predators of other mites and small invertebrates) that are simply using the beetles as a common means of dispersal, the phenomenon known as phoresy. A similar association with mites is also known for the Burying Beetles (Silphidae), which feed on carcasses of small dead animals and birds, performing the very important role of sanitary officers of the fields. However, the only species of Silphidae found in the Edge, the Beet Carrion Beetle (*Aclypea opaca*), is known to be a vegetarian, reported as a pest of beet and turnip crops.

The Rove Beetles (Staphylinidae), or 'staphs' in coleopterists' jargon, form the largest and most diverse beetle family in the UK, with 1,087 recorded species (over 50,000 species worldwide). Rove Beetles are usually small and slim. They are characterised by having greatly shortened wing cases, leaving most of the abdomen exposed, with their flying wings much folded underneath the elytra. This gives 'staphs' narrow flexible bodies that allow them to chase their prey rapidly through complex narrow spaces such as densely matted grass or leaf litter. Most species fly well. The most common and best-known of the staphs is the large and black Devil's Coach-horse (*Ocypus olens*), especially in Ireland, where it was believed to have magic power and to be able to kill merely by a look. On the other hand the beetle's power could be turned to advantage: if the beetle was imprisoned within the handles of someone's scythe, their skill would improve (see Marren and Mabey, 2010).

Although many 'staphs' are scavengers, the majority are ground-living predators, feeding on small invertebrates. Some, like the *Tachyporus* species, specialise in feeding on Aphids. To date, ninety species of 'staphs' have been found on Alderley Edge (all over the site), collected from leaf litter, decaying fungi/detritus, under the bark of dead trees and dung. As with the money spiders (see pp. 279–80), the sieving of leaf or moss litter and detritus and using special extracting equipment such as Berlese extraction funnels or Winkler selectors are the best methods of collecting 'staphs' (see Martin, 1977; Cooter and Barclay, 2006). With some exceptions the identification of Rove Beetles requires the dissection of their genitalia and extensive training.

A few of the beetles that frequent flowers or that can be collected by sweeping from blossoming shrubs and grasses can be mentioned here. *Malachius bipustulatus* is 'the only representative collected from the Edge (parcel 15) of the small family of Soft-wing Flower Beetles (Malachiidae; sixteen species in the UK), one of the most common species of the family known from the UK and Europe. It is metallic green with a bright scarlet spot at the end of each wing case. The beetle feeds on the pollen of grasses and flowers, but its larvae feed on other insect larvae such as caterpillars and maggots living under the loose bark of trees. Of the forty-one species of the Soldier Beetles (Cantharidae) registered in the UK, ten have been found on Alderley Edge (parcels 4, 11b, 15). They are called Soldier Beetles because of their slender and straight bodies coloured red, black or yellow, reminiscent of military uniforms. The adult beetles sit on flower heads, waiting for other flower-visiting insects, on which they prey, but also feeding on nectar themselves. Some of the Soldier Beetles, such as the Common Red Soldier Beetle (*Rhagonycha fulva*; Plate 50) (parcel 2c), have acquired a bad reputation, presumably because of their reddish colour: many people mistakenly believe that these beetles are bloodsuckers, though they are quite harmless. Large groups of small, elongate yellowish-brown beetles with variable black markings can be seen on hawthorn or elder blossoms in June (parcels 3c, 4, 10a, 15, 18a). These are Tumbling Flower Beetles (Scraptiidae), which feed on pollen. When disturbed they promptly drop down to the ground to confuse predators. Some species of Nitidulidae, including the commonest, Rape Blossom Beetle (*Meligethes aeneus*) and *Epuraea melanocephala*, can be found feeding as larvae and adults on the unopened buds and flowers of many plants (parcels 1a, 11b, 15, 18a, 29a). They are important pollinators. But others, such as *Carpophilus marginellus* and *Epuraea biguttata* (parcel 4), are known to be associated with tree sap. Due to this duality of food preferences, the family is called Pollen or Sap Beetles.

Although it is impossible to mention all the groups of beetles and other insects visiting flowers for feeding or for preying upon other visitors to the flowers, there is one group that cannot be neglected. It is the Ladybirds (Coccinellidae), familiar to and beloved by most people. What about the simple little saying: 'My dear, have you heard of that nice Lady Bird who yet is no lady, and yet is no bird?' (for some, perhaps, a reminiscence of their own, hopefully happy, childhood). Ladybirds were once called 'England's true guardian angels', because of their effective work in ridding garden plants of Aphids and Greenflies (Owen, 1983). However, scholars are confident that the Ladybird was in fact named after and dedicated to Our Lady (the Virgin Mary) (see Kritsky and Cherry, 2000). This is why Ladybirds are regarded as bringers of good fortune, particularly to the person on whom they alight. Fifteen of the fifty-three species of Ladybirds in the British Isles have been found on the Edge, including the common Two-spotted Ladybird (*Adalia bipunctata*; Plate 51).

Some beetle families demonstrate a clear disparity between their general high diversity worldwide and in the UK and the surprisingly low number of species recorded on Alderley Edge: this is a clear sign of the incompleteness of our knowledge of the Edge's beetles. The Click Beetles (Elateridae) have yielded five species on the Edge (seventy-three in the UK and over 7,000 worldwide). These beetles get their common name from the distinctive click that they make as they flip themselves upwards when disturbed, employing a special mechanism that uses powerful muscles in the thorax. The larvae of Click Beetles have a long thin body and are collectively called 'wireworms'. Some of them, such as the larvae of the *Agriotes* and *Athous* species, are pests of cereals like wheat, barley and oats and of root crops, as they damage the plant roots on which they feed. The adults are omnivorous, the larvae strictly vegetarian. Only four species of the Long-horn Beetles (Cerambycidae) have been encountered on the Edge, of sixty-five in the British list (the world total is well over 20,000 species). Of these, the Wasp Beetle (*Clytus arietis*) is the only representative of the Long-horn Beetles commonly occurring on flowers, particularly on umbellifers. The beetle is a perfect wasp mimic, dark brown to black, with bright yellow transverse stripes resembling the colour pattern in jacket wasps. This species can also be seen scuttling over tree trunks, especially of beeches, in whose wood its larvae develop. The Leaf Beetles (Chrysomelidae) are represented by twelve species on Alderley Edge, of the 271 species recognised in the UK and over 35,000 worldwide; almost all are leaf-eaters. Approximately half of the British fauna of Leaf Beetles belongs to the Flea Beetles, which are small and difficult both to catch and to identify. Some Leaf Beetles can be recognised by the characteristic damage they cause to the leaves on which they feed; for instance, the *Oulema* species cut short longitudinal strips in parallel lines 1 mm wide, completely perforating the leaf blade.

To date, a single species of the Seed Weevils (*Exapion ulicis*, Apionidae) has been collected from the Edge (parcel 17), yet there are eighty-eight species on the British list (some 900 species in the Palaearctic region), many of which are quite common and widespread. The majority of Seed Weevils are closely associated with particular host plants, sometimes with just a few or even one, on which they feed and breed. For instance, *Taeniapion urticarum* feeds only on the common stinging nettle. As 351 species of vascular plants were recorded in the survey of the Edge described in Chapter 9, one can expect the number of the Edge Seed Weevils to be multiplied many times (at least a dozen species can be expected). The same holds true for the True Weevils (Curculionidae), of which only twenty-five species have been found on Alderley Edge. This number reflects only a small proportion of their real diversity here. Of these, the Clay-coloured Weevil (*Otiorhynchus singularis*) specialises in the needles of pine trees, but its adults can also be seen on hawthorn blossoms (parcels 7, 27). It is worth mentioning that there are more species of the True Weevil in the UK (476 in total) than of birds, mammals, reptiles and amphibians combined (336 species). Their world diversity is over 60,000 described species (Bouchard *et al.*, 2009). For those who want to study weevils, a reasonable working knowledge of botany, particularly of the names of their host plants, will be of great help. A useful starting guide to the weevils is that by Morris (1991).

Members of the family of Pill Beetles (Byrrhidae; thirteen British species) are hard-bodied, convex and black. When disturbed, they retract their legs and antennae into ventral recesses, forming a compact 'pill', hence the common name. Adults and larvae feed on plants, sometimes on tender hair roots. *Simplocaria semistriata* is the most widespread, and the only species of Pill Beetles recorded from the Edge (parcel 4). This species occurs elsewhere in large numbers. The single finding of Museum Beetle (*Anthrenus museorum*; Dermestidae) picked up from a *Heracleum* flower (parcel 10a) is of some interest. This species is more evident indoors, where it is a serious pest, damaging materials containing chitin and keratin, but adults also feed on pollen. As its common name implies, museum zoological collections are always under threat. It is the main concern of any entomology curator.

Fungi provide a very attractive habitat for many groups of beetles that feed on the fungi themselves or prey upon other invertebrate inhabitants, as some Rove Beetles do. On Alderley Edge, a number of such fungus-dwellers have been collected. For instance, the metallic blue and red *Tetratoma fulgorum* can be found in fungal fruiting bodies, especially when they are in advanced stages of decay (parcels 1b, 8). Representatives of the Minute Tree-fungus Beetles (Ciidae), such as the tiny *Cis boletus* (and other *Cis* species), can commonly be found tunnelling into old dry birch bracket fungi (*Piptoporus betulinus*) (parcels 1, 5, 6, 11d; see Plate 17). Many more species feed on the parts of fungi not usually seen. A typical example is the black orange-spotted *Mycetophagus quadripustulatus* and other species of the Hairy Fungus Beetles, which feed on the hyphae or fungal root structures penetrating the bark and the wood of old trees (parcels 2a, 6).

Many beetles are associated with nests of animals and birds. They either scavenge the nest or prey on Fleas and their larvae which are usually present. To date, only three nest-dwelling beetles have been found on Alderley Edge. The tiny *Gnathoncus rotundatus*, the only representative of the Clown Beetles (Histeridae; fifty British species) recorded from the Edge, was collected from under a great tit nest (parcel 15). One species of the Feather-winged Beetles (*Ptenidium laevigatum*; Ptiliidae) was found in an old hedgehog nest. The Rove Beetle *Haploglossa nidicola* was collected from a sand martin nest. A great diversity of beetles of various families are associated with ants' nests (Wood Ants in particular), but none of them has yet been collected from Alderley Edge.

Some small beetles live quietly and usually unseen unless special methods of collecting are used or a collector knows exactly where to search for them. For instance, the Silken Fungus Beetles (Cryptophagidae; 113 British species) are usually small, inconspicuous (black/brown) and difficult to identify. Some of these (e.g. *Atomaria* spp.) can be found in grass tussocks, leaf litter and compost, where they feed on decaying plant material and fungi. Others, such as the *Cryptophagus* species, are dwellers in birds' nests, squirrel dreys and even the nests of ground-dwelling bees and wasps. Representatives of the small family of Root-eating Beetles (Monotomidae; twenty-three British species) can be found all over Alderley Edge, under the sappy bark of dead and dying trees, sometimes two or three species together (parcels 1a, 3c, 5, 7, 10a, etc.). The large family of Feather-winged Beetles (Ptiliidae; seventy-five species in the UK) consists of tiny beetles, none of them longer than 1 mm. These beetles feed on fungal hyphae and spores and can be collected from a variety of habitats, including rotting vegetation and wood, under bark, and dung. As with the 'staphs', in order to collect all these small beetles, special equipment needs to be used, such as a sifter (like a kitchen sieve but with collecting bags attached to it), baited pitfall traps or special laboratory extractors such as Berlese extraction funnels or Winkler selectors (see Martin, 1977, for further details).

Although the recorded beetle fauna of Alderley Edge (listed in Appendix 13.1) may seem to some to be quite ordinary, particularly in terms of notable species or rarities, it does not mean that the site does not have its potential. The majority of recorded beetles on Alderley Edge, leaving on one side those which are yet to be found there, are still known to a large extent by name only. At best, we are more or less aware of how common they are, where they have been recorded in the UK and what their preferred habitats are. Yet few or no details of their general biology, feeding or mating habits, life cycles, interactions with other insects or with plants have been recorded. One cannot say better than Shakespeare that 'in Nature's infinite book of secrecy / a little I can read' (*Antony and Cleopatra*, act 1, scene 2). Believe it or not, there is no need to go to the tropics to be a true discoverer. The wonderful world of beetles and other insects, with all its wonders and surprises, is awaiting you on Alderley Edge.

G. Invertebrates other than insects

Dmitri V. Logunov

Spiders (Araneae)

> With spiders I had friendship made
>   And watch'd them in their sullen trade.
> Byron, *The Prisoner of Chillon*, XIV, 16–17

In total, 137 spider species from Alderley Edge have been recorded to date (see Table 13.1 and Appendix 13.1), which account for 21 per cent of the 649 species that comprise the entire spider fauna of the British mainland. It is hardly a bad score when one takes into account the relatively small size of the Edge and the secondary character of its vegetation – as described in Chapters 9 and 29, it is secondary woodland, planted in the middle of the eighteenth century and now largely replacing the earlier heathland. However, as with all the animal groups but particularly with invertebrates, there is still a lot of surveying to be done. A clear indication of the incompleteness of our knowledge of the spiders of the Edge is the absence from the final checklist of certain groups which are nevertheless highly likely to occur here, such as Pirate Spiders (Mimetidae), common species of *Hahnia* (Hahniidae), Goblin Spiders (Oonopidae), more species of the Funnel-web Spiders (Agelenidae), and many others. The fact that only one member of the Hackled-web Spiders (*Dictyna arundinacea*, Dictynidae) has been collected from the Edge is another indication that its spider diversity is still incompletely known. It is safe to assume that the recorded number of spider species (137) is around 70 per cent of the entire spider fauna. A complete checklist of the British spider fauna is available in the *Member's Handbook* of the British Arachnological Society (Russell-Smith, 2008) and also online on the Society's website, at http://www.britishspiders. org.uk/html/bas.php. Distribution maps and notes on habitat preferences for all British spider species are given in the *Provisional Atlas of British Spiders* by Harvey *et al.* (2002). The following overview is intended for the general reader, and is better used in conjunction with these two books and also with the field guide to British spiders by Roberts (1995).

Sixty per cent (eighty-three species) of the spiders recorded from Alderley Edge belong to the family Linyphiidae (Money Spiders), the second-largest spider family in the world. In the UK, these spiders are so called because of the superstition that if you see such a spider running over you it means financial good fortune. The high proportion of Linyphiidae on the Edge is not surprising: in all local spider faunas of the temperate zone of the northern hemisphere, Money Spiders account for roughly half the registered species. The commonest of all the Edge's Money Spiders is *Microneta viaria*, found in nearly every sample of leaf litter taken from the Edge. The species is widespread throughout the British Isles. Most species of Money Spiders are very small, less than 3 mm long, and cannot be identified in the field: identification is based on a study of their genitalia under a microscope and requires special skills and training. Money Spiders make small catching sheet-webs in leaf litter, grass or on bushes, and usually live unnoticed by people. The best time for non-specialists to encounter them seems to be late summer or early autumn, when the tiny creatures can be seen ballooning on fine silk threads (gossamer) in warm and dry weather. Such a spider landing on your clothes is absolutely harmless and it seems appropriate to recall the famous saying that 'if you wish to live and thrive, let a spider run alive': this is about Money Spiders – and let it be so! For those who would like to collect and study Money Spiders, one of the best methods of collecting them is sieving foliage, leaf litter or rotting wood, using a special device called a sifter (see Martin, 1977, for further details).

Although most of the spider species of the Edge are fairly common, some records are worthy of special attention. The finding of *Entelecara congenera* and *Crustulina guttata* represents their most northerly records in the UK. The former is a tiny Money Spider, collected by shaking them off the twigs of gorse bushes (parcel 17a). This species' status is currently recognised as nationally scarce, but it is likely that it has been simply under-recorded. The latter belongs to a very distinctive genus of the Comb-footed Spiders (Theridiidae), which is characterised by tiny warty granulations on the carapace and sternum. This species occurs in grass tussocks and detritus, and is widespread but generally scarce.

The most diverse and interesting spider habitats are the heathers that represent the remains of the original vegetation of the Edge. Originally, the Edge was covered with sparse woodland whose clearings were dominated by heather and bracken. Nowadays the heather habitats occur in at least two variants: heather–stony slope (parcel 3a) and the moss–heather–bilberry heath in birch coppice (parcel 12b), both impacted by human activity. A total of forty-eight spider species has been recorded from the heathland, sixteen of which were not collected outside it. As usual, Money Spiders (Linyphiidae) predominate in the heather habitats, with some records being of especial interest. For instance, *Minyriolus pusillus* is a common species in Scotland but scattered elsewhere in Britain, and *Saaristoa firma* is a very local and scarce species. The heath in birch coppice was the only site from which two interesting litter dwellers were collected. One is *Neon reticulatus*, a tiny Jumping Spider (Salticidae) with very large anterior eyes and recognisable reticulate brown colouration of the body; another is *Zora spinimana*, the only representative of Spiny-leg Spiders (Zoridae) found on the Edge. The latter species is easily recognised by the long spines on the ventral surfaces of its leg tibia and the contrasting stripes on the carapace. Though common on the Edge, elsewhere both species have only scattered populations.

The second most diverse habitat on Alderley Edge is the damp meadows with rush and moss (parcels 18c, 20b), which almost certainly belong to one of the original vegetation types. This habitat is occupied by forty-two spider species, of which twenty-six (or 62 per cent) are Money Spiders. Notable is the fact that six of the eight species of Long-jawed Spiders (Tetragnathidae) recorded from the Edge occur in damp meadows. Most species are long-legged and thin-bodied. The feature shared by them all is that the males have disproportionately elongated and divergent chelicerae (the fang-like mouthparts found in spiders and their relatives) which they use for locking up the chelicerae of the female during mating, thereby avoiding being bitten. Such a 'love bite' would be fatal, for if a female spider bites the male he will be poisoned and paralysed or killed. Representatives of the genera *Tetragnatha* and *Metellina* spin delicate orb-webs, which are often inhabited by male and female together. By contrast, adult *Pachygnatha* species are ground dwellers and free hunters.

One species of the Long-jawed Spider, *Metellina merianae*, is a common dweller at the entrances of old mines (e.g. parcel 10b), where it makes its orb-webs at the ceilings of tunnels (Plate 52). This fact recalls the famous Scottish legend about Robert the Bruce, king of Scots, who took courage from watching a spider. During the Scottish wars of independence, Bruce was hiding in a cave on Rathlin Island. There he watched a spider trying again and again to place a web across a space in the roof. After six failed attempts, the spider finally succeeded. At the time Robert the Bruce had lost six battles against the English but this incident inspired him and his supporters to continue the campaign for an independent Scotland. The only spider suspect that could occur in that cave and could have been seen by Robert the Bruce is *Metellina merianae*. On the Edge one can easily observe *Metellina* at the entrances of old mines with the aid of torchlight. Go and see the spider that impressed the king with its resilience and persistence (for more details of this legend and its possible relation to the biblical story of David and Saul, see Marren and Mabey, 2010: 98).

The Sandhills region (parcel 17b) is composed of bare sandy soil covered with patchy low grassy vegetation. It is quite different from the rest the Edge, and it is not surprising that its spider fauna turned up some rarities, such as the cryptic Wolf Spider *Arctosa perita* (Lycosidae): 'cryptic' here means similar to the background, camouflaged (Plate 53). This species is strongly associated with sandy coasts; inland it is widespread but local, confined to old sand pits and sparsely vegetated mine spoils. The species builds a burrow in which it hides, emerging to catch prey during daytime. One can easily recognise it by its bright and variegated colouration, consisting of white to yellow spots over the greyish background of the body, camouflaging the species on the sandy soil. Adults can be collected from mid-June. If one is prepared to bend down and take a close look at the low grassy vegetation of the Sandhills, some species of Money Spider can be found that are generally infrequent and scattered elsewhere, among them *Walckenaeria vigilax*, occurring in wet moss and grass, and *Pelecopsis parallela*, which is usually common in calcareous and acid grasslands. The Sandhills is bordered on one of its sides by a dry sand ditch; here one can find funnel webs of the Giant House Spider, *Tegenaria gigantea* (Agelenidae) (Plate 54), a relative of the Hairy House Spider. Males of several *Tegenaria* species often enter houses in search of females in late August–September. All are absolutely harmless and do not, as some mistakenly believe, turn up in the bath from sewer pipes.

Waterfall Wood (parcel 5) is considered by botanists to be an example of relatively undisturbed Cheshire woodland (see Chapter 9). The survey of the fauna here yielded only seventeen species, mostly common species of spiders and harvestmen, a figure that hardly describes its real diversity. The reason for the low spider diversity reported in Waterfall Wood seems to be that only sieving and hand-collecting were used in the fieldwork; for a full account of collecting methods of spiders see Martin (1977) and Roberts (1995). Nevertheless, there were some interesting finds. For instance, *Cryphoeca silvicola* is a relatively common species in northern England and Scotland, but is absent from most of east and south-east England. It is a representative of the Funnel-weavers (Agelenidae).

The interesting habitats of the Edge's woodland are: rocks, where spiders can be collected from under dry ferns and grass clumps, leaf litter, moss and lichen (parcels 5, 10b, 11d); and standing dead trees or fallen logs, where they can be found under loose bark. Both habitats are characterised by a small but rather specialised fauna, of which the most common is surely *Amaurobius fenestralis*, a dark brown spider with a prominent pale oval ring marking (Plate 55). It belongs to the family of Window Spiders (Amaurobiidae), so called because they frequently build retreats in the crevices around doors and windows. In nature they construct retreats within holes in rocks and under tree bark, where the spiders spend the daytime. It is believed that the spider can be attracted from its retreat by holding a sounding tuning fork against its web, presumably resembling the sound of a trapped insect. The rare Sac-spider *Clubiona corticalis* (Clubionidae) was collected from under the loose bark of dead standing trees, which is indeed its common habitat. This find lies at the northernmost limits of the species' distribution in the

UK. The species can also be found in birds' nests and squirrel dreys. The common European Money Spider *Labulla thoracica* (Linyphiidae) has been collected only from rocks. The species has a very distinctive appearance, with a group of white spots easily seen on the underside of the abdomen, just in front of the spinnerets.

The spider fauna of stone field and house walls is related to the one just described, as some species (e.g. *Amaurobius fenestralis*) can also be collected there, and it contains a number of really peculiar spiders. One of them is the Six-eyed Tunnel Spider *Segestria senoculata* (Segestriidae), which makes its tubular retreat within holes in walls and bark, each with a silken collar at the rim and a number of short straight lines of silk radiating out from the entrance. These solitary spiders normally sit near the entrance, waiting for their prey. Another interesting species is the Jumping Spider *Salticus scenicus* (Salticidae), better known as the Zebra Spider, remarkable for the black and white stripy pattern of its body (Plate 56). It is common in southern Britain but becoming scarce in Scotland. The species can often be observed on the sunny walls of buildings. As with all Jumping Spiders, the Zebra Spider has excellent binocular vision and it can jump, either when pouncing on its prey or when escaping its own enemies.

Grassland habitats are best represented in parcels 17a and c, but also occur patchily elsewhere on the Edge. Thirty-four spider species have been found there. Half of the nationally recorded Orb-weavers (Araneidae) have been found in the Alderley grasslands, including the commonest, the Garden Cross Spider (*Araneus diadematus*). Most of these species mature in late summer, when one can see large females sitting in the centre of their orbicular aerial webs, or hiding with their egg cocoons in silk retreats at some distance from the web, as with *Larinioides cornutus*. Spiders react to the tensing and vibration of threads in the web when prey is caught. The Long-jawed Spiders (Tetragnathidae) are also common in grassland, especially in the wetter parts. A number of larger species of Linyphiidae, such as *Linyphia triangularis*, *Microlinyphia pusilla* and *Neriene montana*, can be encountered in the grasslands in late summer. The creatures make their sheet-webs on grasses and bushes, hanging upside down below them. Compared with other Money Spiders, these species are distinguishable by their distinct black-and-white dorsal pattern, even making it possible to identify them in the field with a magnifying lens. On drier parts of the grassland one can see females of the common Wolf Spider *Pardosa pullata* carrying their globular egg sacs attached to their spinnerets. By carrying the cocoons or newly hatched spiderlings on their backs, female Wolf Spiders protect their brood and help the youngsters in distribution. Another example of brood-care behaviour is demonstrated by the Nursery-web Spider (*Pisaura mirabilis*), a relatively large spider (up to 15 mm long) which can be found in grassland in late June–July. The female carries the very large egg sac in her chelicerae underneath the body for about four weeks. Before the spiderlings emerge she weaves a tent-shaped nursery-web, where the youngsters stay for some time, guarded by their mother (Plate 57). It is worth mentioning another hallmark of the Nursery-web Spider, which is its elaborate courtship ritual. A courting male offers a female a 'nuptial gift', which is an insect prey caught by the male and wrapped up in silk. Mating does not begin until the female has accepted the gift. It has been suggested that the role of the 'nuptial gift' is protection for the male spider from being eaten by a hungry female during courtship and mating. Several groups of True Flies, such as Dance-flies (Empididae), are also known to offer 'nuptial gifts' to the females during a ritual courting (see section D, pp. 262–3).

An even more sophisticated example of brood-care behaviour is displayed by two Comb-footed Spiders (Theridiidae), namely *Phylloneta impressa* and *Phylloneta sisyphia*. Both are common and widespread throughout Britain, being easily recognisable in the field by their body colour pattern, consisting of white stripes and two sub-parallel inter-rupted brown bands. Yet to separate these species one has to examine their genitalia under a microscope. Each species constructs inverted a cup-shaped retreat covered with plant debris and below it the tangled catching web typical of all the Comb-footed Spiders. *P. sisyphia* inhabits bushes, especially gorse, whereas *P. impressa* prefers lower vegetation. The blue-green egg sac is attached to the retreat from beneath and is protected by the female. Later, she feeds the emergent spiderlings orally by regurgitation and even shares large prey with them. When the mother dies, her body is effectively sucked out by the spiderlings; this kind of 'parental investment' is known in several groups of spiders. In general terms, the behaviour of these *Phylloneta* species is called 'periodic social', referring to the fact that the spiders live in small family groups for some time. Some tropical Comb-footed Spiders are famous for their more advanced social behaviour, when a large group of spiders of various ages and generations live and prey together in very large tent-shaped webs. However, none of the British Theridiidae has reached such high levels of social behaviour.

Because of their irregular three-dimensional webs, the Theridiidae are sometimes called 'Cobweb Weavers', and their web a 'cobweb'. This name calls to mind the *Critical Essay upon the Faculties of the Mind* by Jonathan Swift, who wrote that 'laws are like cobwebs, which may catch small flies, but let wasps and hornets break through'. One can only guess why it is that spiders usually provoke such negative associations in humans: most likely it is because we do not know them well enough and therefore fear them. For the sake of scientific accuracy, one can add that the cobweb of Theridiidae is strong enough to allow spiders to catch prey almost twice their own size and weight. I cannot help myself but to quote once more from Shakespeare, where in *A Midsummer Night's Dream* Bottom the Weaver says 'I shall desire you of more acquaintance, good Master Cobweb' (act III, scene I).

A story of the Edge's spiders cannot be limited to these brief notes. Should you be interested in the spiders of Alderley Edge, one of the finest natural history monuments of Britain, just pick up your wellies and go. The amazing world of spiders and other creepy-crawlies awaits you there.

Harvestmen (Opiliones) and False-scorpions (Pseudoscorpiones)

Harvestmen and False-scorpions are related to spiders but are much less diverse groups. The British fauna of Harvestmen numbers only twenty-five species (see Hillyard, 2005), while False-scorpions run to twenty-seven species (see Legg and Jones, 1988), compared with the 649 registered spider species. The Harvestmen (Opiliones) are non-venomous arachnids with a small rounded body and very long thin legs, of which the 'Harvest Spider' – also known rather confusingly as Daddy-long-legs, a name also given to Craneflies and one group of spiders (Pholcidae) – is archetypical and the most familiar to the majority of people. Harvestmen are omnivorous, either preying upon small insects or feeding on various plant materials, fungi or even dead organisms and dung. The False-scorpions (Pseudoscorpiones) are small arachnids (2–3 mm long) resembling a tailless scorpion. Most of them are dwellers of litter and under-bark or under-stone spaces, but some can be found even in libraries among old papers and are therefore called Book Scorpions. These False-scorpions feed on tiny invertebrates like springtails or bristletails and are absolutely harmless to humans.

A total of eleven Harvestman and one False-scorpion species have been recorded from Alderley Edge (see Appendix 13.1 and Table 13.1); seventeen species of Harvestman were recorded in Cheshire and Lancashire by Mackie (1968). The commonest Harvestman has been *Nemastoma bimaculatum*, which occurs in most ground habitats studied throughout the country. This tiny species is easily recognised in the field by its dark brown or black body with a pair of prominent silvery white spots. This is the reason for its Latin species name, stemming from *bis*, meaning 'twice', and *macula*, meaning 'spot', in other words 'two-spotted'. Adults of this species occur all year round. This is also true for *Mitostoma chrysomelas* (see Hillyard, 2005), a very tiny and delicate species with long legs, which was collected once from the heather–stony slope of Alderley Edge (parcel 3a). Adults of most of the Edge's Harvestmen appear in late summer, but the exception is *Platybunus triangularis*, whose season of maturity is unusually early, from April to July.

An interesting dweller in rocks (among lichen) and fallen and standing trees (on or under bark) is the harvestman *Megabunus diadema* (Phalangiidae) (Plate 58). It is a common but narrowly distributed species, which is remarkable for the two rows of exceptionally long spines situated above its eyes on the ocular tubercle and looking like a crown. This feature is flagged up in the name of the species, as the Latin word *diadema* means 'royal fillet or crown'.

The only False-scorpion found on the Edge is *Neobisium muscorum*, the commonest and most widespread species in the UK, which was collected by sieving from leaf litter and from the moss–heather–bilberry heath (parcels 10b, 13a). It is clear that other common British species of False-scorpions such as *Chtonius ischnocheles* will also be found on Alderley Edge in the future.

Ticks and Mites (Acarina)

As with many other groups of invertebrates, the Ticks and Mites (Acarina) of Alderley Edge remain poorly studied, with only twenty species recorded to date (see Appendix 13.1). Many groups of Acarina, even common species of the Velvet Mites (Trombidiidae) which definitely occur on the Edge, remain to be formally recorded.

Ticks (suborder Ixodida), known in Scotland as 'keds' or 'taigs', are all blood-feeding ectoparasites of vertebrates and can survive only by sucking the blood of their hosts. Twenty-six species of Ticks are known from the British Isles (Hillyard, 1996), five of which have been recorded in Lancashire and Cheshire (Thompson, 1972), but only one, the Hedgehog Tick (*Ixodes hexagonus*), has been found on the Edge. This Tick is very common on hedgehogs and in their nests, but can frequently be picked up by many other animals, including dogs. It can even bite humans and is known to be capable of transmitting pathogens of several diseases such as human babesiosis, Lyme disease and even tick-borne encephalitis.

The most important group of soil Mites are the Oribatida, known also as Beetle Mites. They are the world's most numerous arthropods living in soil, and are abundant everywhere, including the soil of our back gardens, yet only one of them (*Hermannia scabra*) has been recorded from the Edge to date. The abundance and diversity of Oribatida in a particular soil serve as a good indicator of its 'health'.

A useful general account of the British fauna of Ticks and Mites, but with out-of-date nomenclature, remains the synopsis by Turk (1953).

Other litter/soil invertebrates

Twenty-seven species of litter-dwelling invertebrates have been found on Alderley Edge: nine species of Millipedes (Diplopoda), eight species of Centipedes (Chilopoda), three species of Woodlice (Isopoda) and ten species of land snails and slugs (Pulmonata). For a checklist of these species see Appendix 13.1.

The Millipede *Proteroiulus fuscus* was present in large numbers. It is the sixth commonest millipede of the British Isles (Blower, 1985), found typically under the bark of fallen logs and stumps of both coniferous and deciduous trees. Another common species was the White-legged Snake Millipede (*Tachypodoiulus niger*), which is easily recognised by its narrow black cylindrical body with contrasting white legs (around 100, not the huge number that many people assume). It is a common and widespread species, found in gardens, woodlands and anywhere with rocks or rotting trees under which it can hide. This species subsists on encrusting algae as well as on decaying detritus. *Polydesmus angustus* is the most frequently seen of the Flat-backed Millipedes: this is a flattened, brownish Millipede, with off-white legs with heavy mottling and sculpturing on its back. This species, as well as other Millipedes, normally feeds on dead leaves and other rotting plant material. Unlike other Millipedes, the Pill Millipede (*Glomeris marginata*) is capable of rolling itself up into a ball, just like a pill-bug. It is a common European species, with short body, either dark brown or black. This Millipede occurs in leaf litter, and is often active on bright, sunny days. On the Edge it was found in parcels 3a and 5.

Geophilomorpha are known as the Earth Centipedes, because they usually occur in the soil or in leaf matter. These are slender and very long Centipedes, 2–6 cm long. All of them, like the common Luminous Centipede (*Geophilus carpophagus*) found on the Edge, can easily be recognised by their habit of repeatedly knotting and unknotting their slender bodies. Earth Centipedes are predators, feeding on soil invertebrates, in particular small earthworms. In contrast to the Earth Centipedes, Lithobiomorpha are surface-active feeders and therefore called Stone Centipedes. They are voracious predators, feeding on ground-dwelling invertebrates, including creatures larger than themselves. All species recorded on the Edge are widespread, especially in woodland; a good example is the Variegated Centipede (*Lithobius variegates*). This species is red-brown but its legs are conspicuously banded with brown or purple rings.

Only nine species of land molluscs of the 140 recorded in Cheshire and Lancashire (Pettitt, 1975) have been found on the Edge. Of these the Discus Snail (*Discus rotundatus*) is rather beautiful when seen under magnification. It is fairly small, with a lens-shaped, tightly coiled and densely ribbed shell. The species is very common, occurring in almost any type of cover provided by leaf litter, stones, logs and the like. It feeds on detritus and fungus. The rather large Yellow Slug *Limax flavus* is beautifully coloured, usually yellow overlaid with greyish mottling and with pale blue tentacles. It is Mediterranean in origin and therefore in Britain it is synanthropic, that is, it is strongly associated with human habitation, such as gardens, out-houses and damp cellars. On Alderley Edge, it has been collected several times in rotting wood and litter (parcels 3a and 3b) near private houses. Fairly common slugs of the Edge are the Southern Garden Slug (*Arion hortensis*) and related forms, usually found under the loose bark of fallen logs and in litter. Nonetheless, a proper identification of all these forms requires dissection and special skills. Commonest of all slugs is the Great Black Slug (*Arion ater*; Plate 59). As its name suggests, the slug is generally black, but in nature its colouration varies; this slug can even be orange or white. It is an omnivorous species, eating carrion and dung as well as vegetable matter. The Great Black Slug prefers rotting vegetation to living plants and therefore rarely does much harm in the garden. Of the pest species recorded from the Edge, it is worth mentioning the Dusky Slug (*Arion subfuscus*), the species that can cause some damage to garden flowers. Really pestilential species, such as the Netted Slug (*Deroceras reticulatum*) and the Keeled Slugs (*Milax budapestensis* or *M. sowerbyi*), have not yet been formally recorded from Alderley Edge, but may well occur there. The best field guide to slugs and land snails is the book by Kerney and Cameron (1979).

Of the thirty-five woodlouse species recorded in the UK (Hopkin, 1991), only three common ones have been found in the Edge to date. Woodlice are not insects but crustaceans, related to crabs and shrimps. They form the suborder Oniscidea, within the order Isopoda. Woodlice typically inhabit damp soil and leaf litter in woodland but can also be found in nearly every other temperate habitat, including grasslands, sparsely vegetated fields, spaces under the bark of fallen logs or even basements of buildings. In different parts of the UK woodlice are referred to by a surprising variety of local names – at least sixty-five have been recorded, from 'Sink-lice' in Lancashire, 'Bible bugs' in Stafford to 'Cod-worms' in Shropshire. This last name came about because of the local belief that woodlice, if thrust down the throat of a cow, can be beneficial in promoting the restoration of rumination and cudding in a sick cow (Cloudsley-Thompson, 1958: 5). Various woodlouse remedies (for example using them against such disorders as jaundice or kidney stones) are mentioned by Marren and Mabey (2010). On Alderley Edge, the commonest woodlouse is *Porcellio scaber*, otherwise known as the Common Rough Woodlouse or the Potato Bug, which can be found particularly beneath the dry loose bark of vertical trunks of living or dead trees. It can be recognised by the transverse rows of small tubercles that cover the back of the head and body. The Common Pygmy Woodlouse (*Trichoniscus pusillus*) can be extracted from the topsoil and litter of beech woodland, particularly from moist sites with the decaying leaf litter on which it feeds. It is abundant elsewhere, although the animals can be overlooked owing to their small size and dark colouration. This species normally produces two distinct generations per year, breeding taking place between May and September; an interesting fact is that in Britain the species usually occurs in parthenogenetic populations, that is, those composed almost entirely of females.

Unfortunately, nothing is yet known about the soil animals of Alderley Edge, such as the Earthworms, Potworms (Enchytraeidae) and Nematoda, of which many are small enough to be easily overlooked. However, it is known that the top 15 cm of soil beneath 1 m² of permanent grassland can contain hundreds of Earthworms, over 100,000 Mites and up to 200,000 Potworms, not to mention also millions of Nematoda (see Owen, 1983). Some soil organisms are true herbivores, because they feed directly on the roots of living plants, or are carnivorous or parasites, but most subsist upon detritus, microbes, fungi and algae associated with dead plant matter, or a combination of these. As such, soil organisms play a vital role in the breakdown and recycling of organic matter. For instance, Aristotle – who understood the role of Earthworms in the decomposition of organic matter – called them 'the intestines of the earth'. Earthworms are also of prime importance for maintenance of soil texture, ploughing and aerating the soil. Thirty-seven species of the Earthworms are known from the UK (Sims and Gerard, 1999), but none has so far been formally recorded from Alderley Edge. For those who might be interested in reading about soil animals or surveying them on Alderley Edge, the first book to read might be *Fundamentals of Soil Ecology* by Coleman *et al.* (2004).

Aquatic invertebrates

Several medium-sized farmland ponds of Alderley Edge (parcels 11d, 20b, 22) support a variety of common aquatic invertebrates, of which Leeches (class Hirudinea) and freshwater Molluscs are best represented and known (see Appendix 13.1); for a general account of the Alderley Edge pondlife see section F for the water beetles and also Chapter 12.

Of the sixteen British species of leeches (Elliott and Mann, 1979), seven have been found at the Edge, which is almost equal to the total number of Leeches recorded from ponds across north-west England (nine species; Bentley, 2008). In Old English, 'leech' is a word for cure or healing (see Marren and Mabey, 2010): so someone skilled in healing was called a leech. The name was shared with a bloodsucking worm known now as the Medicinal Leech (*Hirudo medicinalis*), a species which has not yet been formally recorded from the Edge (but search in the nearest pharmacy where you may indeed find them because they are coming back into fashion as a therapeutic aid, as are maggots for cleaning infected wounds).

Leeches are closely related to Earthworms and Potworms but, unlike those groups, which subsist on decaying organic matter, the majority of them are voracious predators (such as the Horse Leech – *Haemopis sanguisuga*; see Plate 59), feeding on insect larvae, various worms, including other Leeches of smaller size, and even molluscs; smaller prey is usually swallowed whole. Some predacious Leeches (e.g. *Erpobdella octoculata*) can also feed on moribund or dead animals and even on plants. Leeches devour their prey using three toothed jaws situated around the mouth, but some (e.g. all representatives of the family Glossiphoniidae) lack jaws and instead have an eversible proboscis that is used to penetrate the tissues of their prey or host. Some Leeches of the latter group became bloodsucking ectoparasites of tadpoles and fish (the Fish Leech, *Hemiclepsis marginata*) or water birds (the Duck Leech, *Theromyzon tessulatum*, a small, matchstick-sized leech which usually enters the bird's nostrils).

Sixteen species of freshwater molluscs have been recorded at Alderley Edge, rather fewer than the total recorded in north-west England (forty-five species; Bentley, 2008). It is interesting to note that the fauna of the Edge's molluscs includes both the so-called hard-water species, those that prefer water with a high concentration of calcium (e.g. *Anisus vortex*, *Lymnaea stagnalis*, *Planorbis carinatus*), and those which can occur both in hard and in soft waters (e.g. *Bathyomphalus contortus* and *Gyraulus* species) (see Macan, 1977, for further explanations). This fact seems to be rather surprising, as the site of Alderley Edge is known to be formed on the sandstones (see Chapters 4 and 5), which seems to mean that the water is low in dissolved salts and is therefore soft. Yet the presence of the Lake Limpet (*Acroloxus lacustris*), for instance, which prefers the ponds and lakes on chalk or limestone, seems to contradict this assumption. The latter species is a small and inconspicuous snail with a low cone-shaped shell (about 2 mm in height), which can be found attached to vegetation such as the stems of the common reed (*Phragmites*).

Of the relatively large and showy freshwater snails of the Edge, it is worth mentioning two: the Great Pond Snail (*Lymnaea stagnalis*), the largest species (35–50 mm high, 18–25 mm wide); and the Great Ramshorn (*Planorbarius corneus corneus*), a large snail (up to 12 mm in diameter) that is common in garden ponds.

Some Pond Snails (family Lymnaeidae) can be found not only in water but also in damp places in fields. One such species, the Dwarf

Pond Snail (*Galba truncatula*), is even regarded as not truly aquatic (see Macan, 1977). Apparently as a consequence of such habitat preferences, the Dwarf Pond Snail became involved in the life cycle of a dangerous parasitic worm known as the Common Liver Fluke (*Fasciola hepatica*). The Snail is the intermediate host in which the parasite's larvae, called *cercariae*, develop. In the UK, the Fluke can be found in a variety of mammals, including humans, frequently causing the disease known as fascioliasis, which leads to the destruction of the host's liver tissue and bile ducts. Farm livestock (cattle and sheep) become infected by grazing in low-lying, marshy pastures, where the Snail occurs.

An interesting group of freshwater molluscs is the Pea Mussels (family Sphaeriidae), of which five species have been found in the Edge. These molluscs are often abundant, but can be overlooked because they normally remain buried in the pond mud or sandy bottoms (Greenhalgh and Ovenden, 2007). However, these bivalves can spin slime threads, which are attached to the leaves of water plants, and the molluscs can be seen climbing up and down these threads. Most interesting is that many of these molluscs, such as the Horny Orb Mussel (*Sphaerium corneum*), are ovoviviparous species: that is, their eggs develop inside the gills, in special brood-pouches, and the young (usually between six and thirty of them) when extruded are completely developed and look like miniatures of the adult mussels (Ellis, 1978).

Although currently pond Snails and Leeches seem to maintain a rather low profile among naturalists, many aspects of their biology and interactions with other freshwater organisms remain poorly understood – something to look into for those who have a garden pond or a freshwater aquarium.

Acknowledgements

We wish to express our warmest thanks to the following colleagues:

- Mr Martin Askins (Swindon, UK) for providing us with the images of spiders (Plates 52, 53, 55, 57, 58).
- Dr Peter Chandler (Melksham, UK) for commenting on and correcting of the checklist of Diptera and for providing us with images of True Flies.
- Ms Katherine Child (Oxford University Natural History Museum) for providing us with the image of the Scavenger Beetle (Plate 49).
- Dr Jon Cooter (Oxford Natural History Museum, UK) for commenting on the earlier draft of the Coleoptera section.
- Dr Michael Dockery (Manchester, UK), for providing us with the images of moths (Plates 27, 28, 31).

- Dr Vladimir Dubatolov (Siberian Zoological Museum, Novosibirsk, Russia) for comments and useful suggestions for the Lepidoptera section.
- Dr Roman Dudko (Siberian Zoological Museum, Novosibirsk, Russia) for the identification of the Carabidae collected by DL in Alderley Edge in 2002.
- Dr Jason Dunlop (Museum für Naturkunde at the Humboldt University, Berlin, Germany) for a consultation regarding the Acarina classification.
- Mr Mike Edwards (Secretary of the Bee, Wasps and Ants Recording Society, UK) for providing us with the images of Hymenoptera (Plates 43–47).
- Mr Shane Farrell (Data Officer of the Cheshire Moth Group, UK) for allowing us to use his unpublished list of the Lepidoptera of Alderley Edge.
- Dr Yvonne Golding (Buxton, UK) for providing us with the image of Hoverflies (Plate 40).
- Dr David I. Green (University of Manchester, Manchester, UK) for providing us with images of various insects (Plates 21–24, 26, 30, 48, 50, 51, 56).
- Dr Jonathan Guest (Kronach, Germany) for providing us with the results of his 1998 aquatic invertebrate survey of Alderley Edge.
- Dr Steve Hind (Cheshire (VC58) county micro-moth recorder) for providing us with a list of the Lepidoptera of Alderley Edge.
- Mr Tom Hunt (rECOrd, the Biodiversity Information System for Cheshire, Chester, UK) for the data on the invertebrates of Alderley Edge released at our request from their information centre.
- Mr Colin Johnson (Glossop, UK) for allowing us to use his unpublished report on the terrestrial Coleoptera of Alderley Edge.
- Dr Steve Judd (Director, World Museum Liverpool, UK) for allowing us to use the unpublished report prepared by the Liverpool Museum staff and associates resulting from the Alderley Edge Invertebrate Survey undertaken by them in 1996.
- Dr David Kitching (Cheshire County recorder for Odonata, UK) for providing us with a list of Odonata recorded by him from Alderley Edge and for the image of the Broad-bodied Chaser (Plate 25).
- Mr Roy Leverton (Manchester, UK), for providing us with the image of the Magpie Moth (Plate 29).
- Mr Darren Mann (Oxford University Natural History Museum) for help in providing the image of the Scavenger Water Beetle (Plate 49).
- Mr Kevin McCabe (Alderley Edge) for providing us with his list of the Lepidoptera of the Edge.

- Mr Peter Nicholson (Hoveton, UK) for providing us with the image of the Giant House Spider (Plate 54).
- Mr Graham Proudlove (Manchester Museum, UK) for the identification of Myriapoda collected by DL in Alderley Edge in 2002.
- Mr Phillip Rispin (Manchester Museum, UK) for the help in extracting data from the Lancashire and Cheshire Card Index by Harry Britten held in the Manchester Museum.
- Mr Don Stenhouse (Cheshire County recorder for Coleoptera, Bolton Museum, UK) for giving us a list of the beetles collected by him from Alderley Edge.
- Dr Ian Wallace (Curator of Molluscs and Aquatic Invertebrates, National Museums Liverpool, UK) for providing us with the results of his 1996 aquatic invertebrate survey of Alderley Edge.
- Mr John Walters for providing us with the image of the Horse Leech (Plate 59).

With specific reference to the butterflies section (C), grateful thanks to Chris Widger, David Standen and Tim Ryan for details of management on Alderley Edge, and future plans; also to Peter B. Hardy for so kindly providing photographs of butterflies. Explanations of specialist terms relating to butterflies in the General Glossary are based on definitions given in Collin (1988), Dennis (2010) and Hanski and Gilpin (1997).

Bibliography

Chapter 13 covers a somewhat specialised topic and thus its bibliographic references are also specialised and are linked more closely to the discussion in the text than elsewhere in this book. For that reason they appear here rather than with the main list of references at the end of the volume. Books for general reading on invertebrates are also mentioned in the text of each section.

Abbreviations used in this list:

FBA   Freshwater Biological Association
FSC   Field Studies Council
LCES   Lancashire and Cheshire Entomological Society
LCFS   Lancashire and Cheshire Fauna Society
RES   Royal Entomological Society

Agassiz, D. J. L., Beavan, S. D. and Heckford, R. J. (eds). 2013. *Checklist of the Lepidoptera of the British Isles*. St Albans: RES.
Anderson, R. 2011. Annotated list of the non-marine Mollusca of Britain and Ireland. At http://www.conchsoc.org/resources/Anderson-2008.pdf (accessed 11 April 2011).
Anon. 2011. *Butterflies on Alderley Edge*. Macclesfield: Irlen Centre NW.

Archer, M. E. 2002. *The Wasps, Ants and Bees of Watsonian Yorkshire*. Weymouth: Yorkshire Naturalists' Union.

Asher, J., Warren, M., Fox, R., Harding, P., Jeffcoate, G. and Jeffcoate, S. 2001. *The Millennium Atlas of Butterflies in Britain and Ireland*. Oxford: Oxford University Press.

Askew, R. R. 1971. *Parasitic Insects*. London: Heinemann Educational Books.

Askew, R. R. 1981. Pompiloidea (Hymenoptera Aculeata) in Lancashire and Cheshire. In *LCFS Publication No. 78*: 5–8. LCFS.

Bantock, T. and Botting, J. 2010. British Bugs: An Online Identification Guide to UK Hemiptera. At http://www.britishbugs.org.uk/systematic.html (accessed 27 March 2011).

Barber, A. D. 2008. *Key to the Identification of British Centipedes* (Shrewsbury: FSC Occasional Publication 130). Shrewsbury: FSC.

Barnard, P. (ed.). 1999. *Identifying British Insects and Arachnids: An Annotated Bibliography of Key Works*. Cambridge: Cambridge University Press.

Barnard, P. 2011. *The Royal Entomological Society Book of British Insects*. Oxford: Wiley-Blackwell.

Bentley, D. 2008. Aquatic Invertebrates in North West England Ponds – Regional Status Review. At http://www.davebentleyecology.co.uk/18.html (accessed 28 April 2011).

Berenbaum, M. R. 2009. *The Earwig's Tail: A Modern Bestiary of Multi-legged Legends*. Cambridge, MA: Harvard University Press.

Blackman, R. 1974. *Aphids*. London: Ginn and Co.

Blower, J. G. 1985. *Millipedes* (Synopses of the British Fauna (New Series) 35). Shrewsbury: FSC.

Blower, J. G. 1987. The Myriapoda of Lancashire and Cheshire. In *LCFS Publication No. 80*: 15–26. LCFS.

Boardman, P. 2007. *A Provisional Account and Atlas of the Craneflies of Shropshire*. Weston Rhyn: Pete Boardman.

Bouchard, P., Grebennikov V. V., Smith A. B. T. and Douglas, H. 2009. Biodiversity of Coleoptera. In Foottit, R. G. and Adler, P. H. (eds), *Insect Biodiversity: Science and Society*, 265–301. Oxford: Blackwell.

Bradley, J. D. 2000. *Checklist of Lepidoptera Recorded from the British Isles*. Chippenham: Antony Rowe.

Brindle, A. 1971. The Grasshoppers, Earwigs and Cockroaches of Lancashire and Cheshire. In *LCFS Publication No. 59*: 23–31. LCFS.

Britten, H. 1947. Insecta in 1943 and 1945. Additions to the Lancashire and Cheshire Lists. In *Twenty-Seventh Report and Reports of the Recorders for 1943–46*: 23–9, 36–41. Lancashire and Cheshire Fauna Committee.

Britten, H. 1950. Insects and Acari in 1948–1949. Additions to the Lancashire and Cheshire lists. In *Twenty-Ninth Report and Reports of the Recorders for 1949*: 93–107. Lancashire and Cheshire Fauna Committee.

Broad, G. R. (ed., in prep.), Checklist of British and Irish Ichneumonidae (Hymenoptera). At http://www.brc.ac.uk/downloads/Ichneumonidae_checklist.pdf (to be published by St Albans: RES).

Brock, P. D. 2014. *A Comprehensive Guide to Insects of Britain and Ireland*. Newbury: Pisces Publications.

Chandler, P. J. 1991. Some Corrections to the Fungus Gnats (Diptera, Mycetophiloidea) of Lancashire and Cheshire. *LCES Annual Report and Proceedings*, 114: 38–53.

Chandler, P. (ed.). 1998. *Checklists of Insects of the British Isles (New Series). Part 1: Diptera* (Handbooks for the Identification of British Insects No. 12). London: RES.

Chandler, P. (ed.). 2010. *A Dipterist's Handbook* (Amateur Entomologist Vol. 15). Orpington: AES.

Chinery, M. 1986. *Collins Pocket Guide to the Insects of Britain and Western Europe*. London: Collins.

Clark, J. F. M. 2009. *Bugs and the Victorians*. New Haven, CT: Yale University Press.

Cloudsley-Thompson, J. L. 1958. *Spiders, Scorpions, Centipedes and Mites: The Ecology and Natural History of Woodlice, 'Myriapods' and Arachnids*. London: Pergamon Press.

Coleman, D. C., Crossley, D. A. and Hendrix, P. F. 2004. *Fundamentals of Soil Ecology*. Oxford: Elsevier Academic Press.

Collin, P. H. 1988. *Dictionary of Ecology and the Environment*. Teddington: Peter Collin.

Colyer, C. N. and Hammond, C. O. 1951. *Flies of the British Isles*. London: Frederick Warne and Co.

Cook, L. M., Dennis, R. L. H. and Hardy, P. B. 2001. Butterfly–Hostplant Fidelity, Vagrancy and a Measurement of Mobility from Distribution Maps. *Ecography*, 24: 497–504.

Cooter, J. and Barclay, M. V. L. 2006. *A Coleopterist's Handbook* (4th edition) (Amateur Entomologist 11). Orpington: AES.

Courtney, G. W., Pape, T., Skevington, J. H. and Sinclair, B. J. 2009. Biodiversity of Diptera. In Foottit, R. G. and Adler, P. H. (eds), *Insect Biodiversity: Science and Society*, 185–222. Chichester: Wiley-Blackwell.

Davies, N. B. 1978. Territorial Defence in the Speckled Wood Butterfly (*Pararge aegeria*): The Resident Always Wins. *Animal Behaviour*, 26: 138–47.

Dennis, R. L. H. 1985. Small Plants Attract Attention! Choice of Egglaying Sites in the Greenveined White Butterfly (*Artogeia napi*) (L.) (Lep., Pieridae). *Bulletin of the Amateur Entomologists' Society*, 44: 77–82.

Dennis, R. L. H. 1993. *Butterflies and Climate Change*. Manchester: Manchester University Press.

Dennis, R. L. H. 2000a. Contrasts in Status of Butterfly Species Among Open and Woodland Biotopes of a Northern English SSSI. *Entomologist's Gazette*, 51: 257–73.

Dennis, R. L. H. 2000b. Early Red Admiral. *Entomologist's Record and Journal of Variation*, 112: 130.

Dennis, R. L. H. 2001. Progressive Bias in Species Status Is Symptomatic of Fine-Grained Mapping Units Subject to Repeated Sampling. *Biodiversity and Conservation*, 10: 483–94.

Dennis, R. L. H. 2003a. Arboreal Substrate for an Egglaying Meadow Brown. *Entomologist's Record and Journal of Variation*, 115: 241–2.

Dennis, R. L. H. 2003b. Playing Possum as an Alternative to Mate-Refusal Posture in *Pararge aegeria* (L.), Satyrinae. *Entomologist's Record and Journal of Variation*, 115: 293.

Dennis, R. L. H. 2004. Butterfly Habitats, Broad Scale Biotope Affiliations and Structural Exploitation of Vegetation at Finer Scales: The Matrix Revisited. *Ecological Entomology*, 29: 744–5.

Dennis, R. L. H. 2005a. Alternative to a Nectar Source for a Thirsty *Pararge aegeria* Linnaeus (Satyrinae). *Entomologist's Record and Journal of Variation*, 117: 150.

Dennis, R. L. H. 2005b. Retreats for Peacock Butterflies *Inachis io* Linnaeus (Nymphalidae) in Changing Weather Conditions. *Entomologist's Record and Journal of Variation*, 117: 175.

Dennis, R. L. H. 2008. How Abundant Are Key Resources for Common Butterflies? Insights from Nymphalid Butterflies in a Conservation Area. *Entomologist's Gazette*, 59: 79–84.

Dennis, R. L. H. 2010. *A Resource-Based Habitat View for Conservation. Butterflies in the British Landscape*. Oxford: Wiley-Blackwell.

Dennis, R. L. H. and Dennis, M. P. 2006. Hill-Topping in British Butterflies: Incidence and Cues in a Cool, Windy Climate? *Entomologist's Gazette*, 57: 17–20.

Dennis, R. L. H. and Dennis, M. P. 2008. Territorial Hill Topping in British Butterflies: High Summits Present a Special Case. *Entomologist's Gazette*, 59: 227–32.

Dennis, R. L. H. and Hardy, P. B. 2006a. Excessive *Anthocharis cardamines* (L.) (Pieridae) Egg Load on Cuckoo Flower Hostplants. *Entomologist's Gazette*, 57: 13–15.

Dennis, R. L. H. and Hardy, P. B. 2006b. What Host-Plants Does *Pieris brassicae* (Linnaeus, 1758) (Lepidoptera: Pieridae) Use Most Frequently Away From Urban Environments and Crucifer Crops? *Entomologist's Gazette*, 57: 205–6.

Dennis, R. L. H. and Hardy, P. B. 2007. Support for Mending the Matrix: Resource Seeking by Butterflies in Apparent Non-resource Zones. *Journal of Insect Conservation*, 11: 157–68.

Dennis, R. L. H., Shreeve, T. G. and Van Dyck, H. 2003. Towards a Resource-Based Concept for Habitat: A Butterfly Biology Viewpoint. *Oikos*, 102: 417–26.

Dennis, R. L. H., Shreeve, T. G. and Van Dyck, H. 2006. Habitats and Resources: The Need for a Resource-Based Definition to Conserve Butterflies. Extinction Risk Issue. *Biodiversity and Conservation*, 15: 1943–66.

Dennis, R. L. H., Hardy, P. B. and Shreeve, T. G. 2008. The Importance of Resource Databanks for Conserving Insects: A Butterfly Biology Perspective. *Journal of Insect Conservation*, 12: 711–19.

Dennis, R. L. H., Hardy, P. B. and Kinder, P. M. 2009. A High Level Territorial Perch in *Pararge aegeria* L. (Satyrinae) in a British Woodland. *Entomologist's Gazette*, 60: 84.

Dennis, R. L. H., Dennis, M. P., Hardy, P. B., Kinder, P. M. 2011. Range Extension in Butterflies: Dispersal Capacity, Colonisation Potential and Geographical Outliers in the Distribution of *Aphantopus hyperantus* (Linnaeus, 1758) (Lepidoptera: Nymphalidae, Satyrinae). *Entomologist's Gazette*, 62: 83–7.

Dennis, R. L. H., Dapporto, L. and Dover, J. W. 2014. Ten Years of the Resource-Based Habitat Paradigm: The Biotope–Habitat Issue and Implications for Conserving Butterfly Diversity. *Journal of Insect Biodiversity*, 2(8): 1–32. Available at http://www.insectbiodiversity.org/index.php/jib/article/view/55/pdf_20 (accessed June 2015).

Dolling, W. R. 1991. *The Hemiptera*. Oxford: Oxford University Press.

Duff, A. G. (ed.). 2008. *Checklist of Beetles of the British Isles: 2008 Edition*. Wells: A. G. Duff.

Dunlop, J. A. and Alberti, G. 2008. The Affinities of Mites and Ticks: A Review. *Journal of Zoological Systematics and Evolutionary Research*, 46(1): 1–18.

Edmunds, M. 2008. Hoverflies: The Garden Mimics. *Biologists*, 55(4): 202–7.

Elliot, J. M. and Mann, K. H. 1979. *A Key to the British Freshwater Leeches, with Notes on Their Life Cycles and Ecology* (FBA Scientific Publication No. 40). Ambleside: FBA.

Ellis, A. E. 1978. *British Freshwater Bivalve Mollusca* (Synopses of the British Fauna (New Series) 11). London: Linnean Society.

Ellis, J. W. 1940. *The Lepidopterous Fauna of Lancashire and Cheshire* (revised by Mansbridge, W.). Published by the Lancashire and Cheshire Entomological Society in its occasional Annual Report and Proceedings series.

Emmet, A. M. 1991. *The Scientific Names of the British Lepiodoptera, Their History and Meaning*. Colchester: Harley Books.

Evans, G. 1975. *The Life of Beetles*. New York: Hafner Press.

Faulkiner, P. E. 1931. Insects in English Poetry. *Scientific Monthly*, 33(1–2): 53–73, 148–63.

Fitton, M. G., Graham, M. W. R. de V., Bouček, Z. R. J., Fergusson, N. D. M., Huddleston, T., Quinlan, J. and Richards, O. W. 1978. *A Check List of British Insects* (Handbooks for the Identification of British Insects, 11(4)). London: RES.

Forero, D. 2008. The Systematics of the Hemiptera. *Revista Colombiana de Entomología*, 34(1): 1–21.

Forsythe, T. G. 1987. *Common Ground Beetles* (Naturalists' Handbook 8). Richmond: Richmond Publishing.

Fox, B. W. and Waring, P. 1999. The Butterflies and Moths of Bentley Wood and Blackmore Copse on the Borders of Wiltshire and Hampshire. *Entomologist's Gazette*, 50: 261–79.

Friday, L. E. 1988. *A Key to the Adults of British Water Beetles* (FSC Publication No. 7). Shrewsbury: FSC.

Gabb, R. and Kitching, D. 1992. *The Dragonflies and Damselflies of Cheshire*. Liverpool: National Museums and Galleries on Merseyside.

Garland, S. P. 1985. Butterflies and Moths (Lepidoptera). In Whiteley, D. (ed.), *The Natural History of the Sheffield Area and the Peak District*, 135–50. Sheffield: Sorby Natural History Society.

Gledhill, T., Sutcliffe, D. E. and Williams, W. D. 1993. *British Freshwater Crustacea Malacostraca: A Key with Ecological Notes* (FBA Scientific Publication No. 52). Ambleside: FBA.

Greatorex-Davies, J. N., Sparks, T. H., Hall, M. L. and Marrs, R. H. 1993. The Influence of Shade on Butterflies in Rides of Coniferized Lowland Woods in Southern England and Implications for Conservation Management. *Biological Conservation*, 63: 31–41.

Greenhalgh, M. and Ovenden, D. 2007. *Freshwater Life: Britain and Northern Europe*. London: Collins Pocket Guide.

Hallan, J. 2008. Biology Catalogue. At http://bug.tamu.edu/research/collection/hallan (accessed August 2015).

Hanski, I. A. and Gilpin, M. E. 1997. *Metapopulation Biology: Ecology, Genetics, and Evolution*. London: Academic Press.

Harde, K. W. 1999. *A Field Guide in Colour to Beetles*. Leicester: Blitz Editions.

Hardy, P. B. and Dennis, R. L. H. 1997. Butterfly Range-Extension into Greater Manchester: The Role of Climate Change and Habitat Patches. *Urban Nature Magazine*, 3: 6–8.

Hardy, P. B., Hind, S. H. and Dennis, R. L. H. 1993. Range Extension and Distribution-Infilling Among Selected Butterfly Species in North-West England. Evidence for Inter-Habitat Movements. *Entomologist's Gazette*, 44: 247–55.

Harvey, P. R., Nellist, D. R. and Telfer, M. G. 2002. *Provisional Atlas of British Spiders (Arachnida, Araneae), Vols 1 and 2*. Huntington: Biological Records Centre.

Henry, T. J. 2009. Biodiversity of Heteroptera. In Foottit, R.G. and Adler, P.H. (eds), *Insect Biodiversity: Science and Society*, 223–63. Oxford: Blackwell.

Hickin, N. E. 1964. *Household Insect Pests: An Outline of the Identification, Biology and Control of the Common Insect Pests Found in the Home*. London: Hutchinson.

Hill, J. K., Thomas, C. D., Fox, R., Telfer, M. G., Willis, S. G., Asher, J. and Huntley, B. 2002. Responses of Butterflies to Twentieth Century Climate Warming: Implications for Future Ranges. *Proceedings of the Royal Society, London B*, 269: 2163–71.

Hillyard, P. D. 1996. *Ticks of North-West Europe* (Synopses of the British Fauna (New Series) 52). Shrewsbury: FSC.

Hillyard, P. D. 2005. *Harvestmen* (Synopses of the British Fauna (New Series) 4). Shrewsbury: FSC.

Hodkinson, I. D. and White, I. M. 1979. *Homoptera, Psylloidea* (Handbooks for the Identification of British Insects, 2(5a)). London: RES.

Hopkin, S. 1991. *A Key to the Woodlice of Britain and Ireland*. Shrewsbury: FSC.

Hopkins, G. W. and Thacker, J. I. 1999. Ants and Habitat Specificity in Aphids. *Journal of Insect Conservation*, 3: 25–31.

Huber, J. T. 2009. Biodiversity of Hymenoptera. In Foottit, R. G. and Adler, P. H. (eds), *Insect Biodiversity: Science and Society*, 303–23. Oxford: Blackwell.

Judd, S. 2009/10. First Lancashire and Cheshire Records of True Bugs (Hemiptera: Heteroptera) with Revised County Checklists. *Journal of the Lancashire and Cheshire Entomological Society*, 133, 134 (2009, 2010): 51–61.

Kemp, R., Hardy, P. B., Roy, D. and Dennis, R. L. H. 2008. The Relative Exploitation of Annuals as Larval Host Plants by Phytophagous Lepidoptera. *Journal of Natural History*, 42: 1079–93.

Kerney, M. P. and Cameron, R. A. D. 1979. *A Field Guide to the Land Snails of Britain and North-West Europe*. London: Collins.

Kidd, L. N. and Brindle, A. 1959. *The Diptera of Lancashire and Cheshire. Part 1. Lancashire and Cheshire Fauna Committee*. Arbroath: T. Buncle and Co.

Kimber, I. 2014. UK Moths: Your Guide to the Moths of Great Britain and Ireland. At http://ukmoths.org.uk/index.php (accessed 28 November 2014).

Kloet, G. S. and Hinks, W. D. 1964. *A Checklist of British Insects. Part 1: Small Orders and Hemiptera* (Handbooks for the Identification of British Insects, 11(1)). London: RES.

Kritsky, G. and Cherry R. 2000. *Insect Mythology*. San Jose, CA: Writers Club Press.

Lee, P. 2006. *Atlas of the Millipedes (Diplopoda) of Britain and Ireland*. Sofia: Pensoft.

Legg, G. and Jones, R. E. 1988. *Pseudoscorpiones* (Synopses of the British Fauna (New Series) 40). Shrewsbury: FSC.

Le Quesne, W. J. and Payne, K. R. 1981. *Cicadellidae (Typhlocybinae) with a Checklist of the British Auchenorhyncha (Hemiptera, Homoptera)* (Handbooks for the Identification of British Insects, 2(2c)). London: RES.

Logunov, D. V. 2003. Preliminary Survey of the Spiders, Harvestmen and False-Scorpions of Alderley Edge, Cheshire. *Newsletter of the British Arachnological Society*, 98: 4–5.

Losey, J. E. and Vaughan, M. 2006. The Economic Value of Ecological Services Provided by Insects. *BioScience*, 56(4): 311–22.

Lucas, M. J. 2002. *Spinning Jenny and Devil's Darting Needle*. Huddersfield: The Author.

Macan, T. T. 1977. *Fresh- and Brackish-Water Gastropods, with Notes on their Ecology* (FBA Scientific Publication No. 13). Ambleside: FBA.

Mackie, D. W. 1968. Harvestmen (Opiliones) in Lancashire and Cheshire. In *LCFS Publication No. 53*, 24–6. LCFS.

Manley, C. 2009. *British Moths and Butterflies: A Photographic Guide*. London: A. and C. Black.

Marren, P. and Mabey, R. 2010. *Bugs Brittanica*. London: Chatto and Windus.

Marshall, J. A. and Haes, E. C. M. 1988. *Grasshoppers and Allied Insects of Great Britain and Ireland*. Colchester: Harley Books.

Martin, J. E. H. 1977. *Collecting, Preparing and Preserving Insects, Mites, and Spiders* (Insects and Arachnids of Canada, Part 1. Publ. 1643). Ottawa: Research Branch, Canada Department of Agriculture.

Merryweather, J. 2007. Planting Trees or Woodlands? An Ecologist's Perspective. *British Wildlife*, 18: 250–8.

Miller, P. L. 1987. *Dragonflies* (Naturalists' Handbook 7). Cambridge: Cambridge University Press.

Mills, N. 2003. Parasitoids. In Resh, V. H. and Cardé, R. T. (eds), *Encyclopedia of Insects*, 845–8. San Diego, CA: Academic Press.

Morris, M. G. 1991. *Weevils* (Naturalists' Handbook 16). Surrey: Richmond Publishing.

Nau, B. 2006. Current Names of Southwood and Leston (1959) Heteroptera Species. At http://www.britishbugs.org.uk/systematic_het.html (accessed 27 March 2011).

New, T. R. 2005. *Psocids, Psocoptera (Booklice and Barklice)* (2nd edition) (Handbooks for the Identification of British Insects, 1(7)). London: RES.

Oates, M. R. 1993. Butterfly Conservation Within the Management of Grassland Habitats. In Pullin, A. S. (ed.), *Ecology and Conservation of Butterflies*, 98–112. London: Chapman and Hall.

Owen, J. 1983. *Garden Life*. London: Hogarth Press.

Owen, J. 1991. *The Ecology of a Garden: The First Fifteen Years*. Cambridge: Cambridge University Press.

Owen, J. 2010. *Wildlife of a Garden: A Thirty-Year Study*. Peterborough: Royal Horticultural Society.

Parker, J. R. 1982. What's in a Name? The Harvestmen. *Newsletter of the British Arachnological Society*, 33: 1–2.

Parker, J. R. 1993. Names of Spiders. In *Member's Handbook*, 1–17. St Neots: British Arachnological Society.

Patterson, R. 1838. *Letters on the Natural History of the Insects Mentioned in Shakspeare's Plays. With Incidental Notices of the Entomology of Ireland*. London: Wm S. Orr and Co.

Pettitt, C. 1975. A Check-List of the Non-Marine Mollusca of Lancashire and Cheshire. In *LCFS Publication No. 67*: 9–12. LCFS.

Pitkin, B., Ellis, W., Plant, C. and Edmunds, R. 2015. The Leaf and Stem Mines of British Flies and Other Insects. At http://www.ukflymines.co.uk (accessed June 2015).

Pollard, E. and Yates, T. J. 1993. *Monitoring Butterflies for Ecology and Conservation*. London: Chapman and Hall.

Preston-Mafham, R. and Preston-Mafham, K. 1993. *The Encyclopedia of Land Invertebrate Behaviour*. Cambridge, MA: MIT Press.

Price, R. D., Hellenthal, R. A., Palma, R. L., Johnson, K. P. and Clayton, D. H. 2003. *The Chewing Lice: World Checklist and Biological Overview* (Illinois Natural History Survey Special Publication No. 24). Champaign, IL: Illinois Natural History Survey.

Prŷs-Jones, O. E. and Corbet, S. A. 1987. *Bumblebees* (Naturalists' Handbooks 6). Cambridge: Cambridge University Press.

Pullin, A. S. and Knight T. M. 2001. Effectiveness in Conservation Practice. Pointers from Medicine and Public Health. *Conservation Biology*, 15: 50–4.

Rakitov, R. A. 2009. Brochosomal Coatings of the Integument of Leafhoppers (Hemiptera, Cicadellidae). In Gorb, S. N. (ed.), *Functional Surfaces in Biology: Little Structures with Big Effects, Vol. 1*, 113–37. Berlin: Springer Science and Business Media B.V.

Redfern, M. and Askew, R. R. 1992. *Plant Galls* (Naturalists' Handbooks 17). Slough: Richmond Publishing.

Reynoldson, T. B. and Young, J. O. 2000. *A Key to the Freshwater Triclads of Britain and Ireland, with Notes on their Ecology* (FBA Scientific Publication No. 58). Ambleside: FBA.

Roberts, M. J. 1995. *Collins Field Guide: Spiders of Britain and Northern Europe*. London: HarperCollins.

Russell-Smith, A. (ed.). 2008. *Member's Handbook*. St Neots: British Arachnological Society.

Schaefer, C. W. 2003. Prosorrhyncha (Heteroptera and Coleorrhyncha). In Resh, V. H. and Cardé, R. T. (eds), *Encyclopedia of Insects*, 947–65. San Diego, CA: Academic Press.

Schuh, R. T. and Slater, J. A. 1995. *True Bugs of the World (Hemiptera: Heteroptera), Classification and Natural History*. Ithaca, NY: Comstock Publishing.

Shirt, D. B. (ed.). 1987. *British Red Data Books: 2. Insects*. UK: Nature Conservation Council.

Shreeve, T. G., Dennis, R. L. H. and Wakeham-Dawson, A. 2006. Phylogenetic Habitat and Behavioural Aspects of Possum Behaviour in European Lepidoptera. *Journal of Research on the Lepidoptera*, 39: 80–5.

Sims, R. W and Gerard, B. M. 1999. *Earthworms* (Synopses of the British Fauna (New Series) 31). Shrewsbury: FSC.

Skidmore, P. 1991. *Insects of the British Cow-Dung Community* (FSC Occasional Publication No. 21, FSC AIDGAP Project). Shrewsbury: FSC.

Skinner, B. 2009. *Colour Identification Guide to Moths of the British Isles* (3rd edition). Stenstrup: Apollo Books.

Skinner, G. J. and Allen, G. W. 1996. *Ants* (Naturalists' Handbook 24). Slough: Richmond Publishing for the Company of Biologists.

Sleigh, C. 2003. *Ant*. London: Reaktion Books.

Snow, K. R. 1990. *Mosquitoes* (Naturalists' Handbook 14). Slough: Richmond Publishing.

South, R. 1973. *The Moths of the British Isles* (Edelsten, H. M., *et al.*, eds) (Series 1 and 2). London: Frederick Warne and Co.

Southwood, T. R. E. and Leston, D. 1959. *Land and Water Bugs of the British Isles*. London: Frederick Warne and Co.

Stewart, G. B. and Pullin, A. S. 2008. The Relative Importance of Grazing Stock Type and Grazing Intensity for Conservation of Mesotrophic 'Old Meadow' Pasture. *Journal of Nature Conservation*, 16: 175–85.

Stubbs, A. E. 1993. *Provisional Atlas of the Ptychopterid Craneflies (Diptera: Ptychopteridae) of Britain and Ireland*. Huntingdon: NERC.

Taylor, G. 1948. *Some British Beetles*. London: Penguin Books.

Thomas, J. A. 2007. *Guide to Butterflies of Britain and Ireland*. London: Philip's.

Thompson, G. B. 1972. Records of Ticks (Ixodoidea) from Lancashire and Cheshire. In *LCFS Publication No. 61*: 22–5. LCFS.

Thompson, K. 2006. *No Nettles Required: The Reassuring Truth About Wildlife Gardening*. London: Eden Project Books.

Turk, F. A. 1953. A Synonymic Catalogue of British Acari. *Annals and Magazine of Natural History*, 6(12): 1–26, 81–99.

Turpin, T. 2009. *What's Buggin' You Now? Bee's Knees, Bug Lites, and Beetles*. West Lafayette, IN: Purdue University Press.

Waloff, N. 1983. Absence of Wing Polymorphism in the Arboreal, Phytophagous Species of Some Taxa of Temperate Hemiptera: An Hypothesis. *Ecological Entomology*, 8: 229–32.

Waring, P. and Towsend, M. 2003. *Field Guide to the Moths of Great Britain and Ireland*. Hook: British Wildlife Publishing.

Warren, M. S. 1992. Butterfly Populations. In Dennis R. L. H. (ed), *Ecology of Butterflies in Britain*, 73–92. Oxford: Oxford University Press.

Whitaker, A. P. 2007. *Fleas (Siphonaptera)* (Handbooks for the Identification of British Insects, 1(16)). London: RES.

Winston, J. E. 1999. *Describing Species: Practical Taxonomic Procedure for Biologists*. New York: Columbia University Press.

Yeo, P. F. and Corbet, S. A. 1983. *Solitary Wasps* (Naturalists' Handbook 3). Cambridge: Cambridge University Press.

Part IV

Human history – archaeology and underground

14

The archaeology of Alderley Edge

A. J. N. W. Prag and Simon Timberlake

When we first considered how we should write up the story of the Alderley Edge Landscape Project (AELP) the obvious course was to produce a single volume that would cover all the aspects of the Edge's story. However, it soon became clear that because we had approached the Edge first and foremost as archaeologists we had a much longer, more detailed and more specialised story to tell about its archaeology, and that such a single volume would become both unbalanced and in every sense of the word unwieldy. Therefore the archaeology became a separate book, *The Archaeology of Alderley Edge*, edited by the two authors of this chapter and published in 2005 as no. 396 in the British series of British Archaeological Reports, with a separate but identical 'local' edition published at the same time by J. & E. Hedges for the Manchester Museum and the National Trust (hereafter *ArchAE*): that volume covers the many different facets of the Edge's archaeology studied by the Landscape Project, from a summary of Alderley Edge's place in the north-east Cheshire hinterland and a detailed topographical survey of the Edge, to reports on excavations of Bronze Age, Roman and even the Industrial periods, accounts of experimental mining and smelting, and analyses of the soils and the groundwaters. The reader who is interested in pursuing those topics further is encouraged to look at that book. However, you cannot tell the rest of the story of Alderley without saying something about the archaeology, and so this chapter is basically a summary of the digging and the finds, and the history (generally the prehistory) that they illuminate, with the aim of providing a foundation for the human story of the Edge. Since so much of the early history is essentially the story of the mines, there is inevitably some overlap between this chapter and the ones that follow describing the mining and quarrying, but we hope that together they provide a picture of the beginnings of human activity at Alderley. Archaeological work on the Edge did not cease altogether with the ending of the Landscape Project, and so this chapter also includes references to more recent work carried out for the National Trust, at Stormy Point and elsewhere.

Alderley Edge is the kind of place to have attracted a certain amount of unofficial (and unsanctioned) digging, most of it unrecorded, at various times and places by treasure-hunters, over-enthusiastic amateurs and folk who just wanted to satisfy their curiosity. The Derbyshire Caving Club has done and continues to do sterling work in the field of industrial archaeology in clearing and recording the mines, as described in Chapter 17. There have also been several formal excavations that have looked at the prehistory, the history and even the modern periods of Alderley's story.

First came Professor William Boyd Dawkins from Owens College, later the University of Manchester, in 1874 and 1875, in response to discoveries at Brynlow by the Victorian miners of hammer stones and of the now-celebrated wooden shovel. Between 1899 and 1905 C. Roeder and F. S. Graves surveyed parts of the Edge and conducted diggings at Engine Vein and elsewhere, written up in the *Transactions of the Lancashire and Cheshire Antiquarian Society* (Roeder, 1901; Roeder and Graves, 1905a). In 1979 a team from Manchester Museum funded by the Manpower Services Commission carried out a survey of the earthworks and mine-workings around Engine Vein during a programme to catalogue the Museum's collection of lithics, but a plan to excavate one of the pit-workings foundered for lack of funds. In the mid-1980s David Gale from the University of Bradford carried out a further survey of three of the pits dug by Graves, and then in 1991 he led a team from Bradford supported by Manchester Museum to investigate sites near Wood Mine, at Brynlow, along the Engine Vein Fault and at Engine Vein itself (Gale, 1986, 1989, 1993, 1994; Timberlake and King in *ArchAE*: 33–6). In 1997–98 Simon Timberlake made a detailed survey of the 'core area' of the Edge for the Landscape Project (see Figure 14.1) and carried out excavations on the north side of Engine Vein adjacent to the pits surveyed by Roeder and later by Gale, and on the south side of Engine Vein at the location of an undisturbed prehistoric pit-working shown in photographs taken by Roeder but otherwise not examined by him. At the same time, this team from the Landscape Project helped to clear and record Pot Shaft, with the close involvement of the Derbyshire Caving Club. These recent excavations are described in full in Chapters 4 and 6 of *The Archaeology of Alderley Edge* (*ArchAE*; Timberlake and Prag, 2005), and their implications are discussed further in the next chapter of the present volume.

The National Trust's policy is generally against intrusive excavation without a compelling reason; over the years it has carried out small

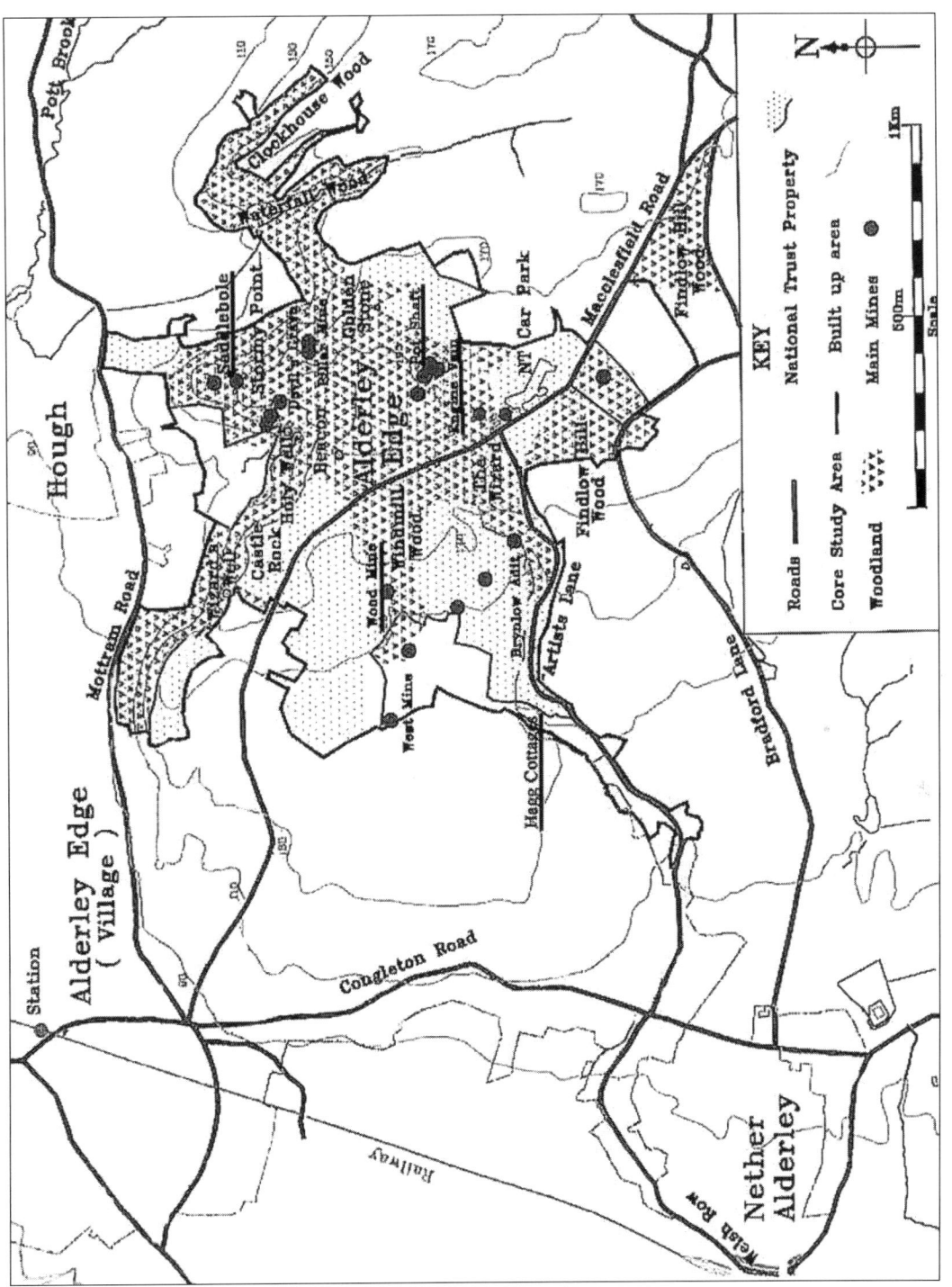

Figure 14.1. Map of the Edge showing the core study area and the mines. The core area effectively coincides with the National Trust property; the names of mines where the Project carried out excavations are underlined.

Based on the 1992 Ordnance Survey 1:25,000 Pathfinder Map, sheet 759, with the permission of the Controller of Her Majesty's Stationery Office, Crown copyright October 2013.

digs at various times as part of its routine conservation and repair work on the Edge, and in 1999, when illegal 'excavation' on the Saddlebole ridge was causing damage and was becoming a danger to the public, Jeremy Milln, then responsible for the Edge as the Trust's Regional Archaeologist for Mercia, worked with the Derbyshire Caving Club on the boundary bank and the mine as well as on the quarry road nearby as part of the Landscape Project's programme (Milln *et al.* in *ArchAE*: 169–87) (Figure 14.1, fully detailed map of the survey based on GIS mapping, can be found at *ArchAE*, plates 3–16).

Apart from some of the work at Saddlebole, the principal aim of all these excavations was to try to find answers to questions about the early mining history of the Edge, and either to locate working areas and find dating evidence or, in the case of Pot Shaft, to give a context for the finding of the hoard of Roman coins in 1995. A completely different purpose lay behind the Alderley Sandhills Project in 2003. This was a separate scheme under the overall direction of Dr Eleanor Casella of the University of Manchester that grew out of the original Landscape Project and was funded largely by the government's Aggregates Levy Sustainability Fund: its object was to use the methods of New World archaeology to excavate the 'Miners' Cottages' which lay just outside the National Trust land, in the area known as the Hagg on the edge of the Sandhills, and which were thought to have been built in the mid-eighteenth century and demolished in the 1950s. Even though almost all trace of the cottages had gone except in their gardens, there were numerous photographs of the two buildings and their setting, and three people who had lived in the cottages as children were still alive and had recorded their memories of growing up there. There was thus a chance to combine the approaches of excavation, anthropology and oral history to elucidate the story of domestic housing from the later eighteenth to early twentieth centuries, a period when archaeologists have until recently tended to concentrate on the more public buildings and works that typify 'industrial archaeology' (Casella and Croucher, 2010).

The place of the Edge in the wider prehistory of Cheshire is described in *ArchAE* (ch. 2), while the topography and possible significance of the various humps and bumps on the Edge are surveyed in the same book (ch. 8), which also contains detailed descriptions of the Landscape Project's own excavations at Engine Vein, Pot Shaft and Saddlebole; it also gives a full bibliography, to which we would refer the reader who wants to pursue the topic in detail. We shall not as a rule repeat those accounts or their supporting references here, but rather shall try to summarise Alderley's archaeological story. It is, however, worth re-iterating the caution expressed there that the Edge is surprisingly poorly endowed with archaeological remains, despite its prominent situation on the margin of the hills and on what would seem to be a useful route from south to north and east to west: aside from some rather specialised Mesolithic occupation, and mining in the Early Bronze Age, on a small scale in or around the Roman period, and again from at least the late sixteenth century on, there is – at least for the present – little to be seen on or in the ground. As we shall see, there are surprisingly few prehistoric burial mounds on the Edge, despite their frequency in the surrounding countryside.

Palaeolithic and Mesolithic

Evidence for Palaeolithic occupation in Cheshire is at best sparse, and so far there is none for Alderley Edge. The story really begins in the Mesolithic, the period of hunter-gatherers lasting from around 8500 BC until *c.* 4000 BC. As Cowell has pointed out (*ArchAE*: 21, 29–32), it was the location and the topography of the Edge that made it attractive to Mesolithic hunters (the present section is based almost entirely on Cowell's account). Alderley Edge lies at the north-western edge of the belt of Triassic sandstone hills that stretch westwards from the Pennines out over the Cheshire Plain, and forms a scarp that overlooks what is now rolling farmland to the north, although 10,000 years ago it was probably covered with scrub and later with trees. From this scarp three

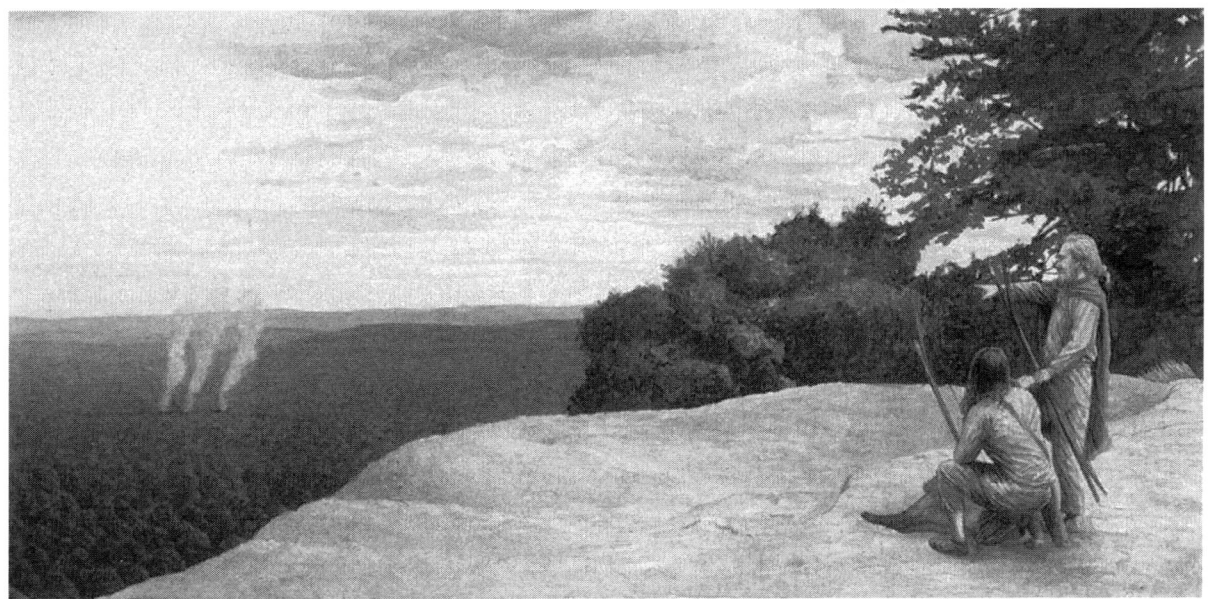

Figure 14.2. The view looking north from Castle Rock, in the Mesolithic period.
Drawing by Seán Ó'Brógáin.

spurs project northwards: the easternmost, running to Prestbury, is the lowest and is divided by the River Bollin from the Mottram St Andrew ridge, beyond which the small Pott Brook forms a valley before the main ridge of Alderley Edge itself, which here forms a virtual cliff face rising nearly 100 m above the plain to some 180 m above sea level. Where modern visitors admire the view and try to pick out familiar landmarks, for early hunters this gave a strategic viewpoint from where they could watch for approaching game on the open land to the north and also for returning forage parties or indeed for intruders (Figure 14.2).

That it was used in this way is borne out by the finds of Mesolithic tools, made from both flint and chert (Figure 14.3). A few have been found on Saddlebole ridge, and significant quantities at Engine Vein, on what is a small plateau (though it is not so easy to make this out today) about 180 m above sea level overlooking the eastern slopes of the escarpment; however, by far the greatest quantity come from Castle Rock, some 600 m to the north, from an area around 40 m in from the cliff edge which commands the best view over the plain. It is interesting

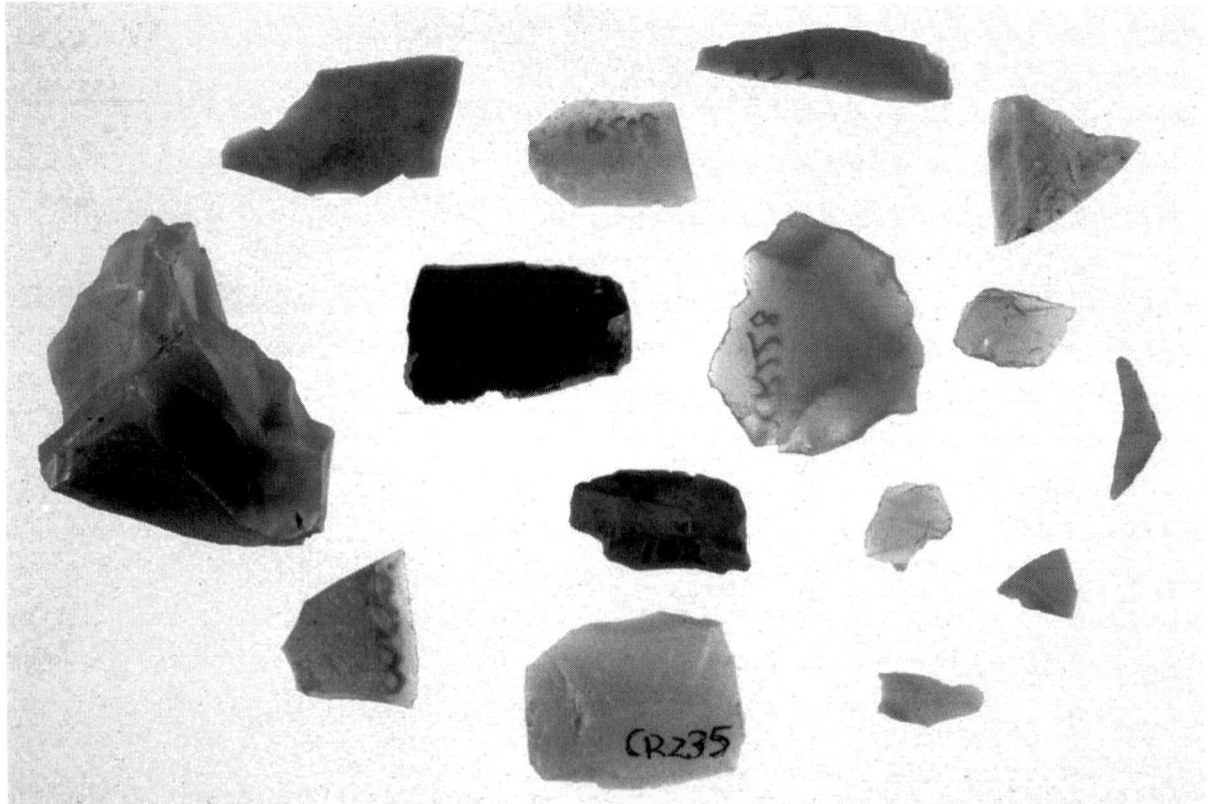

Figure 14.3. A selection of Mesolithic tools from Castle Rock, from the collection at Manchester Museum.
Photograph Manchester Museum, University of Manchester.

to note that a small number have also been found at Whitebarn Farm on a small terrace about 150 m above sea level, on the gentler western slope of the ridge that gives a view in the other direction.

Mesolithic technology involved the use of large numbers of small blades and associated tools such as microliths, and perhaps the most striking feature of any Mesolithic site is the huge number of tiny pieces of flint and chert that seem to leak out of the ground. This of course presents considerable logistical problems for any excavation if the finds are to be processed properly. It was not part of the Landscape Project's brief to excavate Castle Rock, though it remains on the wish-list for a future occasion, and our interpretation of Mesolithic life at Alderley is based on Cowell's analysis of the collections in Manchester Museum, which comprise largely finds made on the surface by Roeder and Graves a little over 100 years ago, augmented by a small group collected by the Project's own archaeologists in a small controlled area at Castle Rock (496 pieces) or found in the excavations at Engine Vein in 1997 (136 pieces). The total is a very small figure by the standards of Mesolithic archaeology, and it is inevitably skewed because the very small fragments of waste are easily overlooked in surface collections, particularly at the time when Roeder and Graves were working, when their full significance was not yet appreciated, but a useful picture emerges nonetheless.

By comparing colour, texture and lustre it has been possible to identify numerous different categories of flint and chert among the Mesolithic implements at Alderley Edge, along with other types of stone (though very small in proportion), probably the volcanic rock rhyolite. Around two-thirds of the flints are from nodules occurring in the glacially deposited boulder clay, which are found quite commonly in the beds of the local rivers and streams. They are mostly different shades of grey but a small proportion is of a translucent brown. There is perhaps nothing surprising in this, but the remaining third of the flints tells a more interesting story: these are of a white or whitish-grey flint, often with a patina, which is also found on Early Mesolithic sites in the Yorkshire Pennines and which probably originates in the Lincolnshire Wolds. Similar flint has been noted recently at Tatton, and Cowell has concluded that during the Early Mesolithic period Alderley was possibly part of a distribution network that stretched from the eastern English lowlands into and over the Pennines, perhaps even linking up with groups living in the Wirral. The Pennine sites of the later Mesolithic show a greater variety of flint types than do the early ones, often with a bias to grey or brown flint; the range of flint types at Alderley reflects this, and suggests that the occupation stretched into the later Mesolithic here too.

However, not all the implements at Alderley Edge are made from flint: in the Landscape Project's samples, 47 per cent of those from Engine

Vein and 29 per cent of those found at Castle Rock are of chert, a less fine-grained material than true flint, which is found in limestone and shales and which, particularly in the later Mesolithic, was sometimes used in preference to flint in part because of its range of colour and texture and also, as we shall see, because of its availability. Five basic varieties of chert have been detected at Alderley, none of them the 'pebble chert' which would have been available locally as glacial erratics in the boulder clay; at least one variety, a dark grey or black chert, was most likely brought down from the Sheldon area of Derbyshire.

The material from which the tools are made suggests, then, that at any rate in the early period, our Mesolithic hunters were ranging over a wide territory and had contacts that stretched much of the way across northern England; at least for their tools and weapons they had no need to restrict themselves to locally available raw material, but were prepared to trade and to carry with them the best or the most attractive (the two may, of course, have been the same).

Turning now to the actual function of the tools, the material can be divided into four main groups that reflect the technological sequence in manufacture and subsequent use: first, the primary shaping into manageable chunks of flint or chert; then, the working of these nuclei into usable blanks; third, retouching the blanks to make various kinds of implements; and finally the actual use and eventual discard of those implements. Since each stage of the knapping process produces its own distinctive waste, establishing the relative quantities of each kind in the total assemblage should provide the basis for a study of the activities on the site. In terms of actual objects, we are dealing with: *cores* – the remnants of the original nodules or pebbles which have been worked down to produce suitable blanks for the implements; *removals* – the flakes and blades detached from the cores; *debitage* – mostly very small debris resulting from the various stages in tool production; and finally the *implements* themselves.

Any interpretation that is based only on surface finds of the stone tools without excavation either to give them a stratified context or to identify any possible structures or encampments can only be tentative. It could be that comments about the Mesolithic use of the Edge also apply to the early Neolithic after *c.* 4000 BC: in both periods people used a blade technology, making it difficult to distinguish between them from surface lithic assemblages alone. Thus a number of tools at both sites, and by implication the waste from making them, may belong to the period after 4000 BC. The publication of the recent excavations at Manchester Airport further emphasises this point and additionally shows for the first time that blade technology was a feature of Early Bronze Age tool-making (Garner *et al.*, 2007). This makes it likely that the Early Bronze Age component of the stone tool assemblage, particularly perhaps at Engine Vein, is potentially greater than was originally thought. However, some of the tool types and the raw materials used do suggest that human occupation of the Edge started in the early Mesolithic, around 8000 BC, or a little earlier, and stretched into the later part of the period from 7000 BC on, when fashions or the availability of flints and cherts changed.

One should see this interpretation of the archaeological evidence in the context of what we know of the changing environment: the climate grew warmer after the end of the last Ice Age, around 9400 BC. For the next thousand years the arctic scrubland was gradually replaced by trees such as birches, and by the middle of the eighth millennium BC the lower land was dominated by hazel scrub. Between around 7000 and 5700 BC the weather continued to get warmer and wetter and sea levels rose, so that the coastline, which during the early Mesolithic had lain to the west of Anglesey, moved almost to its present position. Forests of birch, pine and oak spread over the Pennines up to around the 525 m contour and the higher land was covered with birch, willow and hazel scrub. As the soil became waterlogged and more acid there developed a shifting pattern of forest, scrub, bog and eventually heathland on the higher ground; in the lowlands dense forest remained dominant, with an understorey of alder, but now with large areas of swampy peat and fen appearing on the lower ground and in the hollows. Although foraging for plants was important for their diet, Mesolithic peoples must have welcomed the animal life that flourished in the new forests, even if movement through them was difficult, and campsites got smaller but increased in number as the people adapted and responded to the new environment. It probably became more difficult to predict the movement of game as conditions and terrain changed, and we are perhaps seeing a shift to year-round 'encounter' hunting rather than a seasonal following of the animals. Long-distance travel and trade must have become more difficult: as the much-prized white flint from Lincolnshire became hard to get in the west, people had to turn to materials that were available locally. This explains the change which we have seen take place at Alderley Edge.

Since all the finds at Alderley come from surface collection or from surface levels in excavations rather than from stratified excavation of sites, one cannot say how many visits to the Edge by Mesolithic people those finds represent, nor how long each stay lasted, nor indeed whether the purpose of each visit was the same. For instance, the fact that many of the retouched and worked implements from Castle Rock seem to use pieces of knapping debris in a rather opportunistic way suggests that hunters were there only for a short stop, unless they were filling in time between other activities during a longer stay. There are eighteen cores in the collection analysed by Cowell, ten of them from Castle Rock, but relatively little of the waste that one would expect from the initial working-down of the basic nodules or pebbles, implying that most of the basic preparation took place somewhere else, most probably near the actual sources of the flint and chert. However, most of the other production stages are better represented, and there is a good variety of different tool types, which suggests that the Edge was being used for a variety of different activities: if it was being visited solely in the course of hunting, we would expect a preponderance of microliths, the tips made from the very small blades that were used to make up spears and arrows; rather, they provide evidence for a whole range of domestic activities, such as preparing hides, antlers, wood and other plant material. The presence of unfinished pieces, waste and burnt flints suggests that tools were indeed being made here, and that whoever was here made fires: many short visits over a long period of time, a few long-stay occupations, or a combination of both? Without excavation we cannot tell.

The evidence from Cheshire as a whole is still patchy, but if this interpretation of the Alderley material is correct, then the Edge can be seen as part of a pattern of Mesolithic sites spreading from the Wirral coast and the Dee valley through sites such as Frodsham and Ashton in central Cheshire to Tatton Mere and thence up onto the moors. Perhaps rather surprisingly, Mesolithic sites in northern England are concentrated in the central Pennines, especially in the quite small and narrow upland area between Saddleworth and Marsden. Alderley is thus a foothill site between the lowlands to the west and north, notably the well drained gravels of the Bollin valley, and the Pennine hills, which rise 10 km or so to the east. One can take this as evidence for migration as Mesolithic people followed the spread of the forest and its fauna inland, or – perhaps more likely – for a seasonal camping site for collecting parties or for hunting groups in pursuit of game such as red and roe deer, aurochs and boar. There seem to have been two basic strategies used by such groups, which varied according to factors such as the mobility of the group as well as the plentifulness or otherwise of their prey: there was 'residential foraging', where the whole group moved on once the resources round their campsite began to run low; and 'logistical foraging', where the core of the group – one assumes the women and children – remained for longer periods at what one might see as a base camp while small bands of hunters and gatherers and perhaps even traders ranged far afield. We have no evidence, but it is tempting to speculate that the shallow caves formed under some of the sandstone outcrops on the Edge may well have provided them with shelter, making the site doubly attractive.

There is one other resource on the Edge which may have been of interest to visiting Mesolithic peoples – mineral pigments. It is not inconceivable that the softer bands of sandstone impregnated with green and blue malachite and azurite or the same nodules in the marl bands outcropping near Engine Vein and Stormy Point may once have been dug out for use as body pigments or as paint, using wooden prise sticks or stone tools. The sands impregnated with yellow-coloured arsentian pyromorphite (a lead and arsenic mineral), iron oxide (brown) and manganese oxide (black) may also have been used, as indeed they could have been later on, during the Neolithic, Bronze and even Iron Ages. However, there is as yet no evidence for this, just an apparent correspondence between some of the campsites (demonstrated by the concentrations of flint) and mineral outcrops such as those at Engine Vein and Whitebarn Farm/West Mine. Quite possibly this is a complete coincidence, yet it does raise interesting questions concerning the importance of Alderley Edge and its resources within the wider early prehistoric landscape.

There may have been more to the choice of site than a simple combination of environmental and economic factors. The availability of plant and animal food as well as raw material already made the Edge attractive. The strategic element furnished by the prospect over the plain and towards the hills not only strengthened the ability of anyone living there to predict those resources – crucial for the economic as well as for the social life of this hunter-gatherer society – but also made it possible to anticipate the arrival of other human groups, as well as of animals. Cowell has suggested that there might have been social reasons too for the Edge's importance to Mesolithic people. We are deep in prehistory here and far from any written record, but ethnographic parallels suggest that such a significant and striking feature in the landscape might become a focus for memories and associations with earlier generations of hunter-gatherers, so that for them it became not just a landmark in the physical landscape but also a mythological one to which a spiritual meaning might be anchored.

Neolithic

By contrast, evidence for Neolithic occupation on Alderley Edge is at best sparse. Roeder and Graves wrote of Neolithic encampments and Neolithic hunters at Castle Rock and Engine Vein, but Cowell's analysis of the lithics from these sites has shown that most, if not all, are Mesolithic, though he adds the rider that some of the later Mesolithic blade-based technology continues almost unchanged into the Early Neolithic. The Neolithic revolution that began in Britain around 4000 BC saw a change from a hunter-gatherer economy to a way of life based on land-clearance and farming, although it is becoming clear that the different elements of the new way of life, such as the domestication of plants, the new stone technology and the new ceremonial monuments, were not necessarily introduced in the same sequence and at the same time in different areas. The break will not have been a sharp one, and it is likely that a significant degree of seasonal and nomadic life continued in Neolithic society (references to further discussions are given by Brennand, 2006: 29). We have seen how in the later Mesolithic the forests encroached on western Cheshire and it seems likely that a site on the edge of the hills became less attractive. Unfortunately, the lowest (pre-Early Bronze Age) section of a core taken through the peat-filled kettle-hole at Adders Moss, on the eastern flank of Alderley Edge, less than 1 km from Engine Vein, was not sampled as part of the study reported by Mighall *et al.* (*ArchAE*: 272–3, 274). There is little clear evidence of settlement in this part of eastern Cheshire: down on the plain we know of two sand islands in the peat, at Lindow Moss and a much larger one at Oversley Farm in the valley of the Bollin, now under Runway 2 at Manchester Airport (SJ 825 815 and 816 886). While the latter yielded many thousands of early Neolithic implements lying over a small Mesolithic collection, and implies a longer-lived settlement that lasted into the Early Bronze Age, the former produced only a small scatter of Early Neolithic flints and was probably no more than a short-lived clearance of elms and other woodland for growing cereals and pasturing animals. This is echoed at other such sites on the edges of the Cheshire wetlands, such as Tatton Park, where finds can be radiocarbon dated to *c.* 3500–2945 BC, and probably the very few Neolithic flints that have been found at Alderley simply confirm this picture of low-intensity pastoralism and hunting in eastern Cheshire (Leah *et al.*, 1997: 148–51; Garner *et al.*, 2007: 12–28).

There are perhaps half a dozen Neolithic axes from the area surrounding Alderley, including one in the Manchester Museum collections from Sandle Bridge, 2 km to the west, in the parish of Great Warford. It is noteworthy that most of the twenty-eight or so Neolithic stone axes recorded from Cheshire as a whole have been found away from just those lighter sands and gravels of the Central Mid-Cheshire Ridge and the Pennine fringes which the Neolithic farmers would have preferred. One is led to ask whether Alderley Edge still had a special significance in the landscape.

Early Bronze Age

The most important aspect of the Early Bronze Age at Alderley is of course the copper mining that we now know to have begun around 1900 BC. This is really part of the long story of the Alderley Edge mines, and so we discuss it separately in the next chapter. Here we shall touch on it only as it is relevant to the Edge's archaeological history, and summarise it in the following paragraphs.

It seems likely that the Bronze Age prospectors first became aware of the copper deposits of the Edge through the erosion and exposure of the sandstone cliff faces at Stormy Point and Pillar Mine, and perhaps also at Engine Vein, where a seasonal run-off channel had eroded the bedrock, to expose the colourful surface deposits of malachite at the top of the fault. At many of these sites the natural undercutting of the soft marl beds will have resulted in the collapse of some of the mineralised sandstone conglomerate beds and also washed out tiny nodules of malachite and azurite from the mudstone, depositing these in the small clay fans around the outcrops, much as we find on a smaller scale today. This period of increased erosion and exposure of the cupriferous beds in the Early Bronze Age may correspond to the phase of deforestation of the natural oak, birch, alder and hazel forest on and around the Edge, which seems to have begun about 1900–1800 BC, and which is recorded in the pollen core from Adders Moss (Mighall *et al.* in *ArchAE*: 270–5). The small rise in cereal pollen around this time attests to the presence of cultivation and probably also small-scale settlement close to the Edge, but still more important is the evidence for burning indicated by a peak in charcoal in that core. The exploitation of the copper deposits and the use of felled timber and brushwood in fire-setting and perhaps also in smelting is likely to correspond with this woodland clearance; a similar phenomenon has been suggested at sites of Early Bronze Age mining in mid-Wales such as Copa Hill in Cwmystwyth (Timberlake, 2003). Interestingly there is also a copper pollution peak recorded in the peat at Adders Moss, but this is slightly later (perhaps around 1500–1400 BC), suggesting the deposition of naturally copper-rich soil, or of soil which had been contaminated by mining but which had subsequently eroded away.

The archaeological evidence suggests that the exploitation of the easily winnable ores of malachite and azurite took place in the cliff-like outcrops of the copper beds, where natural overhangs were mined (as at Devil's Grave) and the soft mineralised sandstones hollowed out (for example at Pillar Mine). Elsewhere shallow pits were dug through these soft layers and the harder barytised sandstone beds in order to reach the richer lenses of malachite sandwiched between the sandstones and shales beneath. Mining was undertaken using a combination of hafted hammer stones and chisels made of broken cobbles; fire was used to break up the rocks. Examples have been identified above Pillar Mine and at Stormy Point, Engine Vein and Brynlow. The largest area of these pit-workings (seemingly the most abundant and favoured method of extraction) was uncovered in 1874, during mining operations in the Field Opencast at Brynlow. Here a 'hollowed-out surface of rubbish-filled pits', some of them 2–3 m wide and as many deep, contained the remains of discarded cobble hammer stones, many of which were grooved. From one of these pits came a crudely carved oak shovel (Figure 2.3a–c; Boyd Dawkins, 1875; Sainter, 1878). Almost by a miracle this artefact seems to have survived the ravages of time and the lack of any conservation treatment. The post-excavation story of its survival is a difficult one to beat: we have told it briefly in Chapters 1 and 2 (see also Garner et al., 1994; Smith et al., 2011). Crucially, its radiocarbon dating to about 1750 BC provided confirmation of Bronze Age mining on Alderley Edge, making this the earliest metal-mining site known in England at the time. Radiocarbon dates from wood found during the Landscape Project's own excavations at Engine Vein in 1998 later pushed the date for the first occupation at the Alderley mines back to c. 1900 BC. Meanwhile, Damian Goodburn at the Museum of London identified the tool-marks on the shovel as having been made by Bronze Age implements, but hopes of getting a more accurate date for the shovel using tree-ring dating (kindly carried out for us by Dr Cathy Tyers in the Dendrochronology Laboratory at the University of Sheffield) were frustrated when she found that an insufficient number of clear rings survived to give her a definite answer.

Hammer stones and pit-workings were first identified at Engine Vein by Roeder and Graves in the early 1900s (Roeder, 1901), while they also found similar tools and workings at Pillar Mine and the Hagg (Roeder and Graves, 1905a, 1905b). They described the method of using these grooved stone hammers in some detail, and suggested techniques of early mining. Fortunately, Roeder and Graves missed at least one of the Engine Vein pits during their diggings in the 1900s. This was discovered and excavated by modern archaeological methods by the AELP in 1997–98. A shallow hourglass-shaped pit (approximately 1.8 m long and 1.3 m wide) had been excavated by the prehistoric miners along the dip of the bedding plane, following the traces of malachite ore. The small amount of ore present here suggests that this could have been intended only for prospection, most probably in advance of the actual discovery of the mineralised fault and ore in Engine Vein. Following archaeological excavation a radiocarbon date from fire-set debris in the base of this pit provided a date for its digging sometime between 1955 and 1760 BC. Above the floor of the pit had been placed some broken but joining fragments of hammer stone, and overlying this was a layer of mineral, wood and sediment washed in from the surroundings of the pit. This contained fragments of crushed ore, abundant organic material, along with numerous splinters and flakes from a knapped hammer stone of rhyolite, a glassy-flinty volcanic rock of Lake District origin. Following its abandonment, the pit was re-used as a hearth sometime around 1700 BC, though clearly contemporary with mining of the vein (see Timberlake in ArchAE: 56). The earliest date obtained from archaeological excavations undertaken on the north side of the vein came from the soil layer lying immediately beneath the earliest identifiable mining horizon. The dating of charcoal from here indicates some sort of activity, possibly mining, on the site between 2280 and 1890 BC.

In June 2007, archaeological evaluation carried out at Stormy Point by the University of Manchester Archaeological Unit revealed probable further evidence for Early Bronze Age and perhaps also later prehistoric mining, in the form of at least two prospection pits, one of which also seems to have been used as a hearth and then deliberately backfilled with material also containing charcoal, from which a date of 1690–1510 CAL BC was obtained (Mottershead and Wright, 2008). Other mining or ore-processing features thought to belong to the Bronze Age were also identified in some of the test pits, though none of these could be dated. Most interestingly there also seemed to be evidence here for a larger mine-working of the collapsed rock-shelter type, linked to the Devil's Grave and the mining of the malachite nodule bed. Despite this, significant spreads of malachite ore associated with some of these features on Stormy Point appear never to have been mined. Might the copper ores have been brought to this spot for smelting in crude wind-blown furnaces? This notion looks increasingly likely as we begin to eliminate the more complex smelting procedures through experimental reconstruction, while also re-examining the existing meagre archaeological evidence and taking the implications of its absence into consideration (Craddock, 2007; Craddock *et al.*, 2007). Much still waits to be unravelled, while the potential for further discovery here remains high.

It seems that as little as two to three tons of ore may have been removed from the entire Engine Vein workings during the whole of the Early Bronze Age. In total this may have yielded as little as 100–200 kg of copper metal. However, considerably more copper may have been mined from Brynlow, a site which revealed a considerably larger area of pits when excavated by William Boyd Dawkins in 1874–75, some of them up to 2 m deep. Whatever the actual level of production in prehistory, Alderley Edge must have been an important local source of metal during the Early Bronze Age.

When we examine the dating of this site in the context of all British Bronze Age mines, an interesting pattern emerges. Bayesian statistical analysis carried out on more than 100 radiocarbon dates from the British mines suggests a pattern of exploitation which may have begun in West Wales at Copa Hill, Cwmystwyth, moving perhaps to North Wales (Parys Mountain, Anglesey) and then eastwards to Alderley Edge some time around the end of the third or the beginning of the second millennium BC (P. Marshall, personal communication). This eastward movement in prospecting activity culminated in the exploitation of the Ecton Mines in Staffordshire (Timberlake, 2010) yet, following this, we then see a period of much more intensive mining on the Great Orme in North Wales. Here, the acme of production was achieved at the beginning of the Middle Bronze Age, when mining reached depths of over 30 m below surface, with narrow, labyrinthine galleries extending for over 2.4 km through the mineralised limestone (Lewis, 1990a, 1996; Timberlake, 2009). Alderley Edge by comparison was just a small series of mines worked and abandoned in the Early Bronze Age.

For students of early mining, one of the most significant aspects of Bronze Age exploitation on Alderley Edge is the use of grooved hammer stones, some of them with very complex hafting. At all other such sites in Britain apart from the neighbouring mine of Mottram St Andrew, grooved hammer stones are rare. It has been suggested that the limited number of suitable cobbles that could be collected from the local glacial drift, together with the softness of the sandstone outcrop and the length of time these efficient hard rock tools could be used, may be reasons enough to explain this (see Timberlake and Pickin in *ArchAE*: 58–78).

Mining here seems to have spanned some 300–400 years, and was very probably an intermittent activity. There is no conclusive evidence for local smelting. However, our experimental work on the processing and smelting of Alderley ores (Timberlake and Craddock in *ArchAE*: 188–97) shows that, often, little remains of these ephemeral poorly reducing furnaces to find its way into the archaeological record, other than charcoal.

The burial monuments that are so often a feature of the Neolithic landscape are notable by their absence in this part of Cheshire (e.g. Hodgson and Brennand, 2006: 39–40), and the Early–Middle Bronze Age burial mounds in the county cluster along the Mid-Cheshire Ridge (marginal land with a sandstone substrate), and then re-appear on the Pennine fringe. Various reasons have been suggested for this – that they were associated with important features in the landscape or at least with topographic eminences, or more prosaically that they were deliberately placed on marginal terrain to spare the good agricultural land (Longley, 1987: 61; Leah *et al.*, 1997: 150–1).

Circular earthworks of various kinds appear as a familiar feature among the trees of the Edge (Timblerlake *et al.* in *ArchAE*: 156–60, 165–8, with further references) and it is natural to assume that they mark the remains of barrow mounds or of the banks or palisades that surrounded such mounds. Not surprisingly, there is a long-standing belief both locally and among academics that they must be pre-historic: the fact that barrow cemeteries are to be found on similar ridges between Alderley and Macclesfield would seem to confirm this. Some fifty barrows or inurned cremation burials are to be found in the area enclosed by Ordnance Survey 1:25,000 Pathfinder map no. 759, which covers Alderley Edge and extends to Jodrell Bank a little to the south-west, Gawsworth and Sutton to the south, Macclesfield Forest and Kettleshulme on the east, and Wilmslow and Adlington to the north. The known burial mounds and cremation urns in the Alderley–Macclesfield area are set out in in *ArchAE* (13, table 2.1); a reasonably comprehensive listing of Cheshire barrows can be found in the *Victoria History* for Cheshire (Longley, 1987: 82–6), although more recent excavation and dating evidence from some of these sites is still unpublished at the time of writing. The nearest Early Bronze Age burial site to the Edge to have been dated appears to be that near Birtles Hall in Over Alderley (SJ 856 746) (Longley, 1987: 70; Ormerod, 1882: vol. 3, p. 536), but very few of these barrows have been excavated and still fewer dated. Nonetheless, it seems most likely that they belong to the period before 1500 BC, and it is therefore perfectly conceivable that the period of occupation of this part of north-east Cheshire suggested by the cluster of monuments and the distribution of stray finds coincided with the earliest mining activity on Alderley Edge.

However, there is very little hard archaeological evidence for either date or function for the earthworks on the Edge itself. In 1905 Roeder and Graves mapped the density of sites around Alderley Edge, and noted the correspondence between the location of tumuli and the lines of old trackways. When they excavated the now-destroyed earth circle by the Macclesfield Road in 1904 they found no artefacts at all, and so far no others have been excavated, nor has there been any trace of pottery. In their present form, some of the Alderley 'mounds' still resemble real mounds, for example that under the Beacon and those near the Goldenstone, at Pykedlow and in Finlow Hill Wood; that at Stormy Point appears as a simple raised platform, while those in Windmill Wood and at Seven Firs are now shallow circular earth banks. The siting of many of these corresponds with the visible high points on the Edge, and most do indeed lie close to or on either side of the trackway that runs along the ridge from east to west. All this evidence, though circumstantial, strengthens the case that they are from the Bronze Age. The fact that their diameters vary can be paralleled in other burial groups in the region. However, one should note that there are no similar 'embanked circles' in this part of Cheshire: the closest parallels are to be found in the ring-bank barrows of the Dark Peak in Derbyshire, and this leads to the question of whether these were really barrows which had been modified, as seems to have happened for instance in landscaping projects at Capesthorne and at Birtles (Timberlake *et al.*, *ArchAE*: 10–11, 156–9). The fact that some of the circles are marked as small round plantations on the 1775 Enclosure Award map (Figure 19.7) can be taken to show either that they were creations of the landscaping carried out on the Edge by the Stanleys in the mid-eighteenth century, or equally that these were pre-existing features which were then emphasised by tree-planting, for which there are parallels in many parts of the country. As Louisa Stanley wrote in the middle of the following century, 'Alderley Edge was a dreary Common till the year 1779, when it was enclosed, together with all the other waste lands of Alderley. Some hundreds of Scotch firs were planted on the highest points by Sir James and Sir Edward Stanley, between the years 1745 and 1755. Before that time, it does not appear that a single tree grew upon it' (Stanley, 1843: 5–6).

The Pykedlow mound (also known as Pikelow and Peaked Lowe) deserves special mention, in part because it appears to have a special historic role as the meeting-point of three parish boundaries and is mentioned in a land grant of around AD 1230–50: on this, see further Alan Garner's discussion in Chapter 30 of this book, and Timberlake *et al.* and Milln *et al.* in *ArchAE* (pp. 154 and 158, and 175, respectively). It is eroding badly, revealing that the central core of the mound was built up from heaped sand, sandstone fragments and pebbles and dark layers of local turf. In 2007 a broken and reworked Neolithic point (still in private possession) was found in soil washed out of the mound, but without excavation there is no way of telling whether this comes from a proper stratified context or merely from material brought in to build up the mound, perhaps during landscaping by the Stanleys (Alan Garner, personal communication). The mound was never large or high, estimated at less than 10 m in diameter when built, and there is no trace that it was ever surrounded by an earthen bank.

The mound on which the 'Armada Beacon' stood is obscured both by the trees that surround it now and by the amount of modification which it has undergone in the post-Medieval period, making it difficult to interpret. It seems fair to assume that it began life as a prehistoric tumulus, yet a magnetometer survey carried out by the Landscape Project in 1997 failed to reveal either a ditch or any other features.

Roeder described these mounds as 'entrenched earth circles', and one explanation for their present hollow form would be that they have been robbed or quarried for the good topsoil and turf from which they were constructed. The practice is known from areas of poor sandstone and from upland terrain such the Peak District: it could have taken place at Alderley, and might explain the partial mound and circle near the Goldenstone, but the great majority of circles on the Edge are unbroken, and it hardly seems likely that someone would go to the trouble of digging out the mound without breaking an entrance way into the surrounding bank. Perhaps they were further modified afterwards by the Stanleys as part of the Romantic landscape they were trying to create on the Edge (Timberlake *et al.* in *ArchAE*: 159).

One further feature on the Edge that should be mentioned here is the series of three earthen banks that surround Church Quarry Hill to form an asymmetric multiple enclosure, which appears not to have had an entrance unless it was on the south, where the later quarry seems to have cut through the outer bank; the banks are not immediately obvious on the ground because of the heavy vegetation, but they show clearly on the survey map (*ArchAE*: plate 11). The outer bank may once have enclosed up to three-quarters of a hectare; the middle one, which was earlier and encircled the summit of the hill, had a diameter of about 50 m; little survives of the third, which formed a small circular bank or raised platform no more than 25 m across. Unusual too is the fact that the outer and middle banks appear to overlap and combine along the eastern side. One would like to see here evidence for a Late Bronze Age palisaded enclosure or an Iron Age hill-fort, or else a Medieval motte or ring-work, all of which are found on the Mid-Cheshire Ridge, on the Pennine margins and in the Dark Peak, but in each case some aspect does not fit, be it size, shape or contours. Again, it is very possible that their present form if not their origin lay in the landscaping activities of the Stanleys: excavation may yield a different answer, but on present evidence this seems the most convincing explanation.

When we turn to the archaeologist's staple, the pottery of the period, it transpires that no recognisable Bronze Age pottery has ever been reported from Alderley Edge itself, although Roeder and Graves (1905b) reproduce a drawing of three fragments of a rudimentary 'smelting pot' collected by J. J. Phelps in June 1885 from near the Hagg Opencast in Windmill Wood, close to the spot where hammer stones were later discovered (*ArchAE*: 12, fig. 2.5). The sherds are now lost, but Roeder and Graves imply that they were ancient, and contemporary with the hammer stones, although this seems extremely unlikely: their drawings are unlike collared urns or indeed any Bronze Age pottery we have seen. On page 36 of the first volume of the *Proceedings of the Society of Antiquaries* (1843–49) Lord Stanley reported the discovery of a collared urn 'whilst gravel digging close to the Macclesfield Road' in 1844 but its exact find-spot is unknown (see Longley, 1987: 70, 82). There are other equally vague references to finds of 'Bronze Age' burial urns, such as that in the Reverend Edward Stanley's handwritten *Account Book* for Nether Alderley Church for the years 1805 to 1817, which mentions the discovery on 4 January 1816 of an urn containing burnt bones while digging close to the site of the present rectory (Stanley, 1805–17: 18). A few miles to the north what appears to have been a small barrow cemetery on Wilmslow Common, close to the site of the present railway station, disappeared beneath the urban spread which followed the arrival of the railway in the 1840s.

On the other hand, the excavations of the Early Bronze Age agricultural settlement at Oversley Farm at Manchester Airport in 1997 yielded what is probably the largest single collection of sherds of 'Beaker' phase

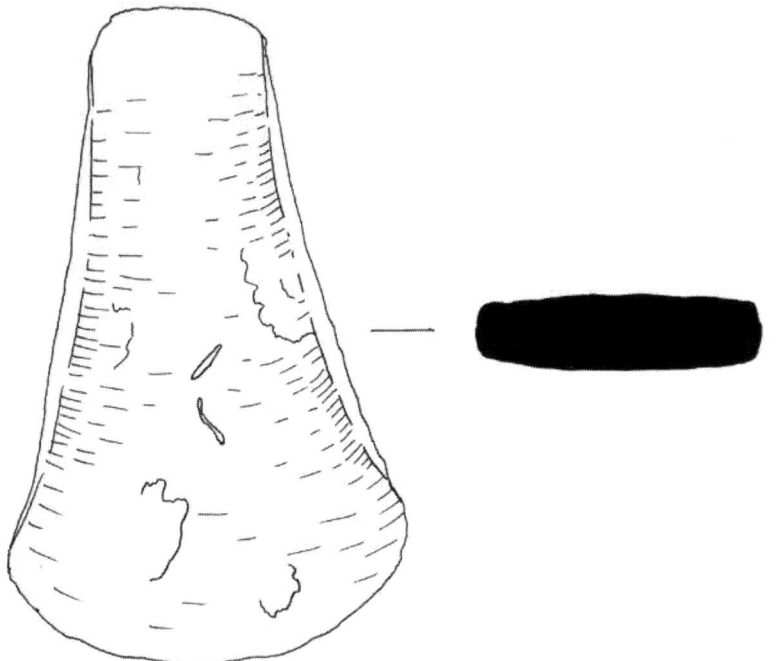

Figure 14.4. Early Bronze Age bronze flat axe found at Hunter's Pool, south-east of Mottram St Andrew.

Drawing, Manchester Museum.

and Early Bronze Age pottery to have been found in north-west England (Garner, 2001, and personal communication). Other artefacts of the earliest Bronze Age, such as barbed and tanged arrowheads, are not particularly common, though several have been found at Macclesfield, and others are associated with the burials at Sutton and Langley. Early examples of metalwork are rare. Rowley (1982: 34) mentions the story of a 'brass weapon of war' found under Soldier's Hill, Monksheath: presumably this is the Early Bronze Age tumulus at Sodger's Hump (*ArchAE*: 13, table 2.1). A late Early Bronze Age tanged dagger was found in one of the barrows on Wilmslow Common mentioned above (*ArchAE*: fig. 2.8) and a flat bronze axe found at Hunter's Pool, south-east of Mottram St Andrew and perhaps a mile from Alderley Edge, could well belong to the beginning of the Early Bronze Age (Figure 14.4). However, this was a chance find, made in what was almost certainly a secondary deposit; although it has not been possible to examine the site, no other finds have been reported. Like the Early Bronze Age 'Beaker' burials at Gawsworth and Langley in the upper Bollin valley, these finds appear to be contemporary with the earliest date for prospection on the Edge and at Mottram itself, namely around 1900 BC, but it is going well beyond our present evidence to link the two.

Stone shaft-hole implements, consisting of mace heads, battle axes and axe hammers, fabricated largely of Lake District rocks, are characteristic artefacts of the earliest Bronze Age, and are common in Cheshire, though most are stray finds and do not provide further information on settlement or other activity. In particular, finds of stone axe hammers appear to be distributed in some numbers along the Pennine margin between the 60 m and 120 m contours; a significant grouping of these and other shaft-hole implements is to be found in the Alderley area, the vast majority of them apparently manufactured from Lake District greywacke (Council for British Archaeology implement petrology Group XV: see Coope *et al.*, 1988).

Cobbles of the same rock type are sometimes found in the local glacial drift on and around Alderley Edge, and by the Bronze Age the makers of grooved hammers came to prefer them (see Timberlake in *ArchAE*: ch. 5). Leahy (1986: 147–9) and Roe (1967: 69; 1979: 29) both suggest that axe hammers could have been used in copper mining, but they are more common in the hills and away from mining contexts, so it seems more likely that they were used by farmers and others for felling trees and splitting timber. A small fragment of a broken axe hammer which seems to have been used or re-used as a mining tool was recently discovered below Pillar Mine on Alderley Edge, apparently found in secure association with grooved stone hammers and buried in early mining spoil (see Pickin in *ArchAE*: 75–8, fig. 5.16). There is another such implement noted to come from 'Alderley Edge' (but not apparently associated with mining) in the Manchester Museum collections (*ArchAE*: 12, fig. 2.7), while a further much finer polished axe hammer of the Early–Middle Bronze Age, now in private possession, was found near the Goldenstone,

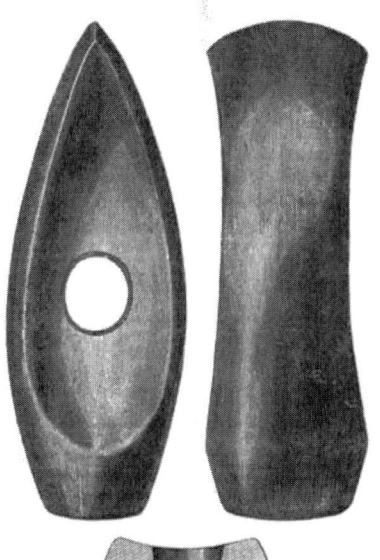

Figure 14.5. Three views of an Early–Middle Bronze Age axe hammer from Kirklington, north Yorkshire, the twin of that found near the Goldenstone in the mid-twentieth century.

From Evans (1897: fig. 137).

measuring some 23 cm long, with a maximum width and depth of 7.5 cm and an hour-glass perforation that is just over 3 cm in diameter at the surface; its optical twin is depicted here as Figure 14.5. There are also other references to shaft-hole implements from Alderley Edge. One is in the Grosvenor Museum in Chester and others are reported from private collections. Roeder (1901: 99) also refers to one from Blackshaw Farm, Nether Alderley, and from further afield come examples from Mottram St Andrew, Macclesfield, Chelford, Withington, Siddington and Styal, while the discovery of two part-perforated 'hammer stones' in the quarry ditch of the barrow at Woodhouse End, Gawsworth, further reinforces the likely association between this group of implement types and the earliest Bronze Age industry and activity in the area.

Perhaps the most spectacular stone implement from the Early Bronze Age from the area is a massive axe of most unusual form, 20.7 cm long and reaching a maximum width of 12.5 cm and a maximum thickness of 4.7 cm, found in the upper reaches of the River Bollin between Langley and Macclesfield in 2000 and still in private possession (Figure 14.6). Although at first sight it resembles a Palaeolithic hand axe, the hammered and ground technique and the material of which it is made place it much later, probably in the Early Bronze Age. It is manufactured from Eskdale granite rather than the volcanic tuffs from Borrowdale, which are more usual for axes from east Cheshire, and its size and shape imply that it may have had a ceremonial purpose rather than a practical one. Indeed, the question whether such axes were primarily intended as symbols of status or ritual rather than for a practical role in tree-cutting and land-clearance remains open, for many show little damage or wear.

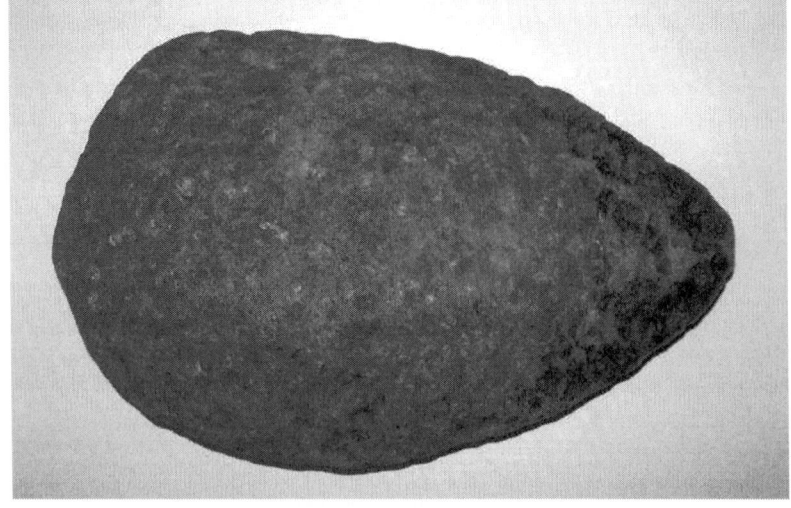

Figure 14.6. Early Bronze Age hand axe of granite from the River Bollin.

Courtesy of Jack Mitchell.

Middle–Late Bronze Age

There is little evidence of occupation in the Alderley–Macclesfield area after 1500 BC. This may well be linked to the decline of arable agriculture in the Pennine uplands and the upland margins that resulted from a deteriorating climate. The higher altitudes were invaded by blanket bog, and the areas of lowland mire such as Lindow Moss, Soss Moss and Lifeless Moss which surround the Edge will also have been affected by the increased rainfall. Climate deterioration may have even have played a part in the change from a concern with religious and burial practice to increased secular activity. Certainly, considerably fewer burial mounds were erected in the area from 1400 BC on, although there is evidence that some were re-used and that satellite burials within or around the circumference of the barrows continued until the beginning of the Late Bronze Age; however, there is as yet no evidence for this on Alderley Edge itself.

On the other hand, during the Middle Bronze Age we find a new practice of ritual deposition of metalwork in rivers and other watery contexts, which may signify a change in allegiance from the celestial deities of the Early Bronze Age to those of rivers, streams and lakes, a belief for which we have artefactual evidence from the Late Bronze Age, and later the documentary evidence of the early Roman historians for the Iron Age. On the other hand, Richard Bradley (1984) has suggested that the new practice might relate in some way to the abundance of metal in circulation and a desire or a need to control it. The evidence is still fragmentary and tentative, but here the Edge enters the picture again with two recent finds of Middle Bronze Age bronze 'shield' palstaves (so called from the shield-shaped hollow in front of the stop ridge) which appear to have been deposited in or adjacent to water on the low ground on its northern side. One of these, a shield palstave that is still in private possession, was found at Common Carr Farm to the west of Alderley Edge village in 1937, close to the course of a stream which flowed towards Lindow Moss (Figure 14.7a). The other, now in the Manchester Museum (acc. no. 2000.1), was unearthed in 1991 while digging a pond in the garden at Holly Trees in Hough Lane, immediately at the foot of the Edge escarpment (Figure 14.7b) (drawings of both pieces can be found in *ArchAE*: 15, fig. 2.9a–b). A third such palstave was found in 1994 in marshy ground east of the Bollin at Prestbury (Figure 14.7c). There is nothing to link any of these axes to the mining of copper on the Edge, and it has been suggested that they form part of the Acton Park industry (*c*. 1500–1300 BC) and thus may originate from north or north-east Wales. Indeed, all the evidence so far suggests that mining had ceased at Alderley by the end of the Early Bronze Age, presumably as metal began to circulate much more widely and extracting the ores

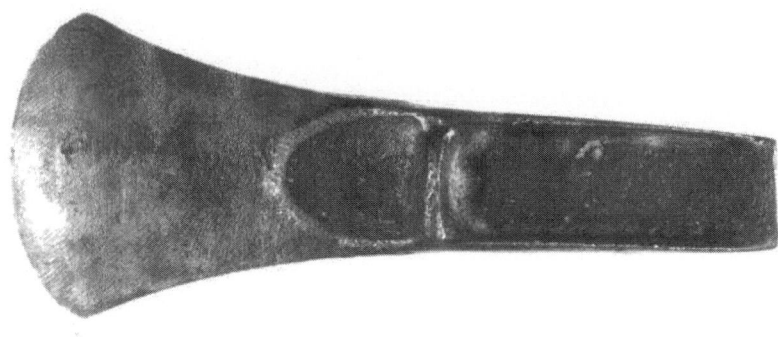

(a)

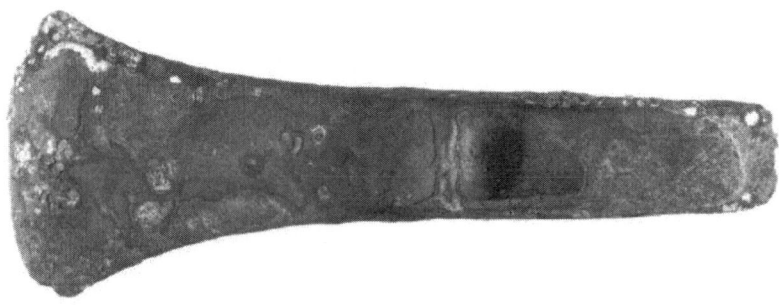

(b)

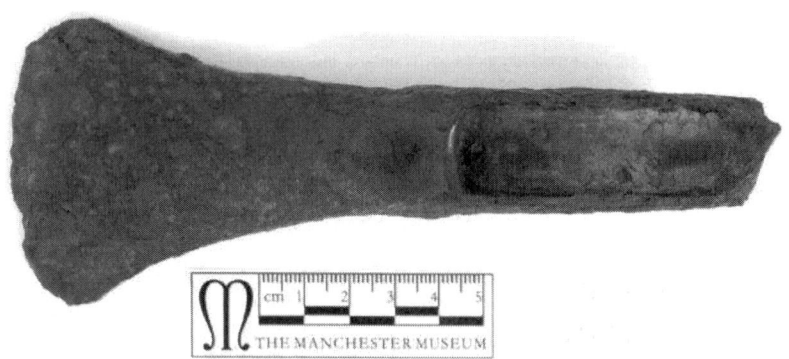

(c)

Figure 14.7. Middle Bronze Age palstaves (*c.* 1500–1300 BC) from the Alderley Edge area. (a) Specimen from Common Carr Farm, Alderley Edge. (b) Specimen from the Hough (Manchester Museum acc. no. 2000.1). (c) Specimen found near Prestbury.

(a) Courtesy of Roy Pearson. (b) Photograph Manchester Museum, University of Manchester. (c) Courtesy of the late David Bailey.

at Alderley was no longer viable (see Chapter 15). A small hoard of several looped palstaves deposited not far away at Wilmslow at some time towards the end of the Middle Bronze Age are almost certainly not local products and are much more likely to be of Continental origin, perhaps originating in Brittany (Needham, 1980). Two further such palstaves, found in 1912 while repairing a hedge bank on the railway

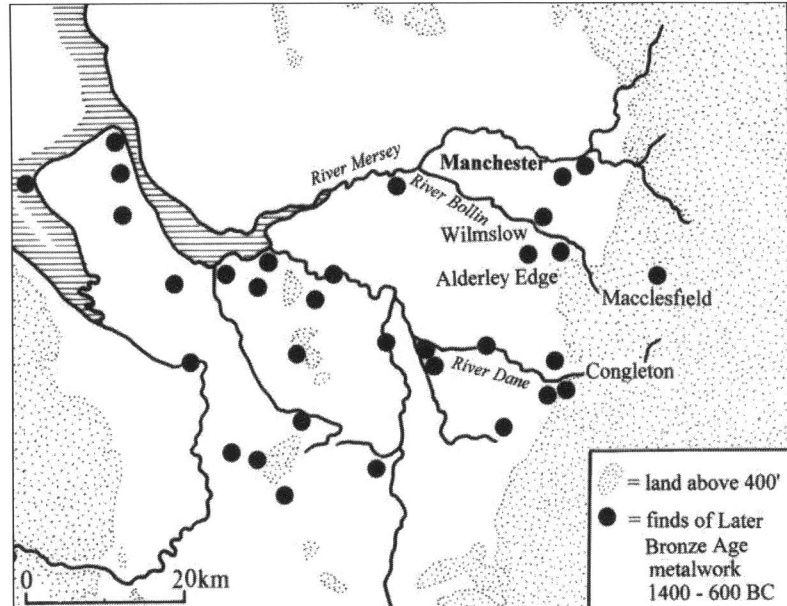

Figure 14.8. The distribution of Later Bronze Age metalwork in Cheshire.

Drawn by Brenda Craddock and Simon Timberlake, after Longley (1987: 95).

at Stanneylands, between Wilmslow and Styal, are now in Stockport Museum (Davey and Forster, 1975: 54–5; Longley, 1987: 103).

The map of later Bronze Age metalwork from Cheshire shows isolated finds and hoards of bronze distributed along the lowlands and the river valleys, and also down the Mid-Cheshire Ridge, where most of the county's hillforts and enclosures from the Late Bronze and Iron Ages are to be found (Figure 14.8). In contrast to the significant amounts of metalwork deposited during the Middle and Late Bronze Ages and the Iron Age at sites in the East Anglian wetlands, such as Flag Fen in Cambridgeshire, and in the Iron Age at Llyn Fawr in Glamorgan and at Llyn Cerrig Bach in Anglesey, there are no specific reports of Late Bronze Age metalwork from the sites of former meres in Cheshire. Finds of Late Bronze Age metalwork lying close or adjacent to their presumed place of manufacture can sometimes suggest the presence of a minor local metalworking industry. One such instance is the socketed axes associated with a metalworker's crucible and fragments of a clay mould discovered inside the perimeter of the Iron Age fort at Beeston on the Mid-Cheshire Ridge. Alderley Edge has been suggested as a source for the lead and/or copper used here, but as a local source the copper deposits at nearby Bickerton are just as plausible (Blick, 1991: 71; Rohl and Needham, 1998). Indeed, it is just as likely that the Bickerton smiths followed the common practice of Late Bronze Age metalworkers and re-used ingots or scrap bronze, which were often more readily available than newly smelted ore.

The only evidence – if evidence it be – for Late Bronze Age activity on Alderley Edge is a mystery piece, the sword of Wilburton Type B known as 'Merlin's Wand' (Tindall, 1995, has a sketch). It was reputedly found on Alderley Edge in 1871 – the period of the most active mining and ground disturbance – on 1 November. Its exact provenance is unknown, and the alleged find-date happens to coincide with the Celtic winter festival of Samhain, dedicated to the gods of the underworld. Indeed, its subsequent history seems deliberately 'mysterious': there is a story that it was subsequently used each Hallowe'en, which is the eve of Samhain, in the ritual celebration of the Celtic New Year. The present owner acquired it at a house sale at Alderley Edge, and although a drawing exists the sword itself has unfortunately not been available for study.

The Iron Age

From this discussion it will have become clear that although there is a wealth of detail for the surrounding area, aside from the all-important mining we have very little evidence for what was taking place on the Edge itself during the Bronze Age. It is not much better for the next few centuries either. Nevell (1999), in a re-assessment of the Roman and immediately pre-Roman occupation and land use in Cheshire, paints a picture of fairly marginal agriculture and settlement in the infertile and wet lowlands from the middle of the first millennium BC on, with little or no land in cultivation along the Pennine margin above the 250 m contour. This general decline appears to be linked to a worsening climate at the beginning of the first millennium, and even a minor recovery in the weather at the end of the millennium and for the first few centuries AD does not seem to have led to any significant improvement in land use. The general picture for the region as a whole is one of limited settlement and agriculture in and around the mosslands, a picture not unlike that in the East Anglian Fens and the Somerset Levels at this time. Few recognisable Iron Age finds have been recorded from the mosslands around Alderley Edge, the only possible examples, noted by Rowley (1982), being two rotary querns found on Danes Moss in 1848, although these could equally have been Romano-British or later. More recently, limited evidence of activity between the Late Bronze Age and the Iron Age, in the form of pits with a possible domestic or agricultural function, has been found overlying the Early Bronze Age settlement deposits at the Oversley Farm site at Manchester Airport, perhaps 5 km from Lindow Moss.

Despite the deficiencies in the current palaeo-environmental record for the Iron Age, there is undoubtedly artefactual as well as environmental evidence for occupation elsewhere in the Cheshire wetlands. The most striking instances are the bog bodies from the Cheshire and Lancashire mosses, of which the best-known is Lindow Man, who belongs at the very end of the Iron Age and may have been sacrificed to placate the gods as the Romans advanced northwards (Stead *et al.*, 1986; Turner and Scaife, 1995, especially the chapters by Briggs, Garland, Magilton and Turner; Joy, 2009); at the time of writing (2015) the head described by Garland (in Turner and Scaife, 1995) from Chat Moss and known as Worsley Man is undergoing intensive cross-disciplinary study at Manchester Museum. Those Iron Age peoples hunting and farming along the moss edge at Lindow may have been culturally or even racially isolated groups, divorced from the more settled communities occupying the cultivated landscapes of the Mersey basin and Mid-Cheshire Ridge (Nevell, 1999); there appears to have been a history of indigenous races inhabiting the mosslands of north-east Cheshire, and the descriptions of these people left us by William Norbury, writing in 1884 and recorded from the living memory of Alderley inhabitants, might well refer to peoples whose place and way of life had changed little since the Iron Age: 'they are a very ancient race … with long heads and projecting eyebrows, high cheek bones and strong coarse limbs … and were sly and suspicious as aboriginal races always are, apparently very harmless, but not so safe as they appeared' (cited by Roeder, 1901: 102; see also Hyde and Pemberton, 2002). Whether the people who still lived in benders and tents on the mosslands during the early years of the nineteenth century were the actual descendants of Lindow Man, or of those who put him to death, is of course a matter for speculation. What seems rather more likely is that those who lived within sight of Alderley Edge could have had reason to visit it regularly, either as a vantage point and for communication, or as a possible source of food, timber, stone, pigment and perhaps even of metal ore; however, if they did so no traces of their presence have yet been found, beyond one hint in the radiocarbon dates for Pot Shaft, to which we shall return shortly, and another in the Legend of Alderley, which forms the subject of Chapter 30.

The Roman period

The regional picture for Cheshire and north-west England during the first few centuries AD is still one of fairly marginal agriculture and settlement (Nevell, 1999), with predominantly native Romano-British management of the landscape outside the main garrison towns like Manchester and Chester. However, the pollen record for north-east

Cheshire and the Pennine margin at this period does provide us with an indication of an upturn in agricultural output and thus of an increase in rural population: more land was cleared for pasture and arable farming, reaching a peak in the third and fourth centuries AD. We can assume that the Alderley Edge hinterland benefited from this rural growth, and its geographical position must have continued to give it a strategic and economic importance: it lay on the fringe of the tribal *civitas* of the Cornovii south and east of Chester and was sandwiched between the Deceangli in north-east Wales and the powerful Brigantes on the north and east, and although relatively thinly populated this territory continued to control the east–west corridor between the Pennine uplands and the northern Welsh marches, as it had done since the Mesolithic (Longley, 1987: 115). However, the evidence of the actual finds does not suggest that the picture of a settled, populated and well managed (or for that matter a militarily occupied) Roman landscape around Alderley Edge necessarily holds good for much of the period.

Indeed, there is little tangible evidence for any significant military use of the area between Macclesfield and Alderley Edge, and no major routes appear to pass through it. The Roman roads around the Edge are discussed more fully in Chapter 26 (see p. 468), and Timberlake considers the wider regional picture in *ArchAE* (pp. 17–18, 79–80), but although one can draw a map of the Roman road network in much of Cheshire, the actual evidence at Alderley itself is slender and relies mainly on names such as 'Street Lane' (the old name for what became the A34 until the opening of the by-pass in 2010) in Alderley Edge Village and Nether Alderley, and 'Devil's Lane' running east of Hayman's Farm in Over Alderley. In neither case is there any archaeological proof: local reports of excavations through the embankment or *agger* of 'Street Lane' with finds of Roman artefacts in the vicinity of Nether Alderley School cannot be substantiated, and what appears to be a Roman *agger* running through Alderley Park is probably the embankment of the eighteenth-century turnpike.

Until 1995 no traces had been found of Roman structures and – apart from a few scattered finds to which we shall return – no real evidence for Roman occupation on Alderley Edge. This did not prevent a local tradition that there had been Roman mining here. Partly this is no doubt due to the widespread habit of referring anything old or ancient to 'the Romans', particularly if it involves technology or engineering. The *Mining Magazine* for 16 October 1858 carries a report by Samuel Higgs on the Alderley mines, which had just been reopened by James Michell and the Alderley Edge Mining Company: Higgs notes that 'lead was supposed to have been worked here from the time of the Romans up until 150 years ago' (1858: 692). Roeder and Graves argued that the pit-workings and hammer stones at Engine Vein, which we now know to be symptomatic of prehistoric mining, were of Roman date; their argument was based entirely on the discovery of what they described as an 'iron pick' on the 'central part of the excavated floor' of a pit on the western side of Engine Vein. The pick, 30.5 cm long and just over 2 cm in diameter, is now in the Manchester Museum (acc. no. 28775), and still attached to it is the splendid old label 'prehistoric iron pick'; as Warrington rightly says, it is in fact a piece of boring rod of a type which was still in use as recently as the later nineteenth century (Roeder and Graves, 1905a: 23; Warrington, 1981: 51).

Then, on 12 March 1995 the unearthing of a hoard of 564 Roman coins and the subsequent finding of the first Roman mineshaft to be discovered in Britain, at Pot Shaft, burst onto this rather bare scene like a rocket. The discoveries are described in full in *ArchAE* (chs 6, 7), and there is an account of the shaft in the context of early mining on the Edge in Chapter 15 of the present book, so here we merely give a summary.

Members of the Derbyshire Caving Club, which leases the mines from the National Trust and maintains them on the Trust's behalf, were removing fill from the top of a hitherto unknown shaft which had begun to subside prior to capping it to make it safe, when they found a coarse-ware pot containing silver-washed copper coins. They immediately alerted both the National Trust's Regional Archaeologist and Manchester Museum. The coins were identified as Roman, from the reigns of the emperors Constantine I and his son Constantine II, and apart from making the shaft secure further clearance was suspended. The members of the Caving Club are to be congratulated on the promptness of their reaction, the skill and care of their excavation – and the sharpness of eye of the finder, Malcolm Bailey: all the loose coins and all of the surviving parts of the pot were retrieved intact, including fragments that had become detached while it was in the ground. When the pot (probably of Severn Valley ware) was later emptied by Dr Mike Nevell of the University of Manchester Archaeological Unit in a micro-excavation at Manchester Museum, it appeared that one side had been damaged in antiquity and that the neck had been broken off to make it easier to insert the coins. The mouth of the pot had been covered by a piece of cloth, possibly linen. There proved to be 564 coins in all, minted between AD 317 and 335, suggesting the hoard had been buried by around AD 340. It seems to have been a poor person's hoard, put together not over time (as savings) but in panic during the unrest that followed Constantine's withdrawal of many of the Roman troops from Britain to support his bid for the Roman throne (*ArchAE*: ch. 7). There was nothing to suggest any other occupation or use of the area by the Romans at the time, and the shaft must have been long out of use, even if it still provided what the owner thought was a spot which could be

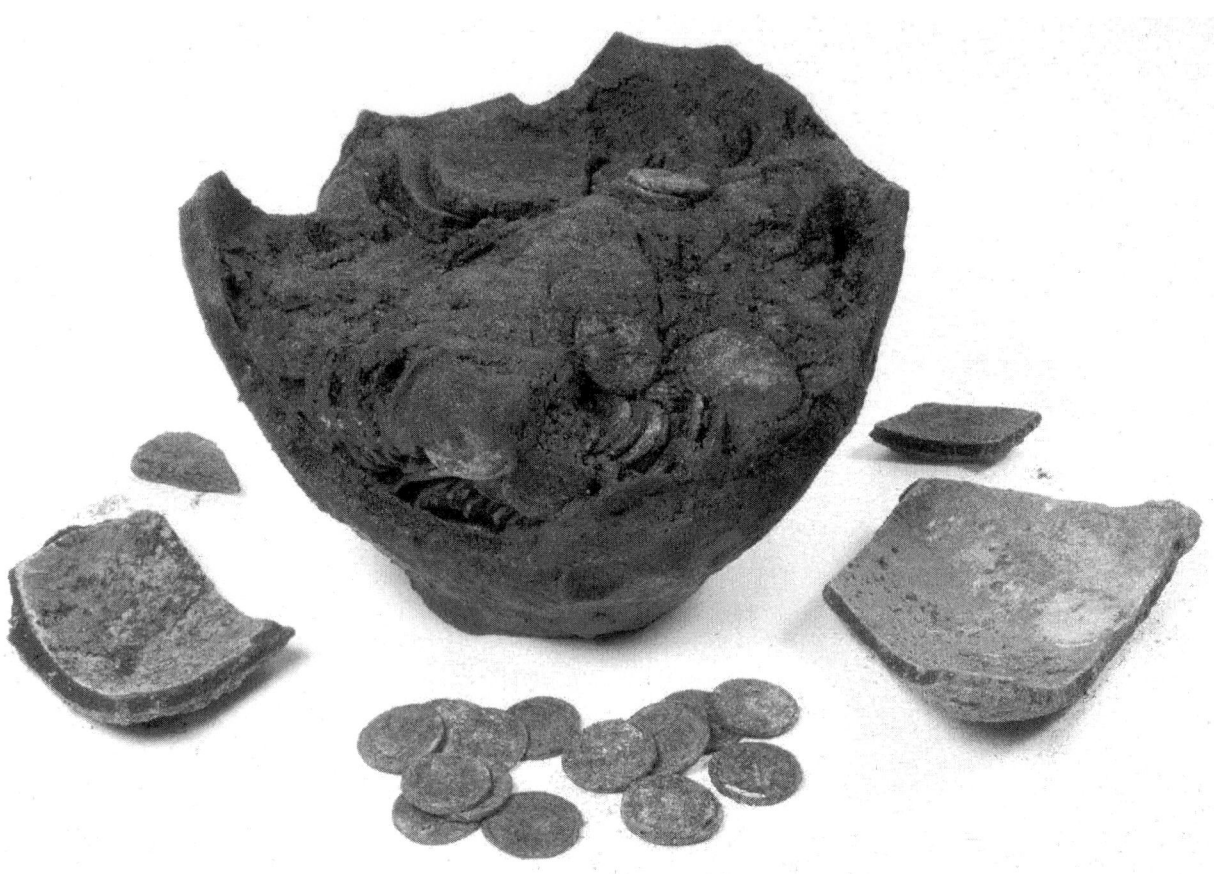

Figure 14.9. The Alderley hoard, as found.

Photograph Manchester Museum, University of Manchester.

remembered and so returned to later. At that time, the last metre or so of the shaft had not yet been filled up; the upper two-thirds of the exterior of the pot and the interior down to the level of the cloth and the coins are noticeably weathered, which suggests that the person who buried it took the risk of leaving it partly exposed, or else was disturbed in the act of burying it. In the event, they never came back, and the pot was quickly covered as silt and sand washed into the shaft from the spoil heaps and erosion gullies surrounding it (Figure 14.9 shows the hoard as found; the burying of the pot is illustrated in Figure 2.5).

The shaft was cleared between October and December 1997 by the Caving Club working together with the Landscape Project. Digging out a mineshaft is rather different from a conventional archaeological excavation, not merely because of the logistical and safety elements in clearing a narrow and very deep 'trench' but also because the nature of the fill will be very different. Rather than a series of differentiated occupation layers, like any hole in the ground a mineshaft normally becomes filled by a steady build-up of sediments, either tipped in deliberately after the abandonment of the mine or gradually washed in by the weather. Any objects from the fill are likely to tell one more about the surrounding area than the history of the shaft itself, although, since many shafts are at least partly waterlogged, they often contain a high proportion of organic material. Since much of the fill is likely to come from nearby mine dumps, it may give information about the mining process.

Pot Shaft, as it was named by the Caving Club, is 12 m deep from the present ground surface, but this includes 1 m of surface build-up and its ancient depth was only 11 m metres, of which around 10 m is filled with historically significant material. This fill contains enough in the way of discarded hammer stones and blocks of weathered lead ore ignored by the early miners to show that, even if no mining was actually taking place when the Romans arrived at the site, there was plenty of evidence literally lying around to indicate the history and the potential of the place to their engineers. Nothing remains of the Roman ground surface to show traces of their lifting equipment or spoil heaps, but the shaft itself is almost square and measures 1.9 m across. The coarse pick-marks and rounded corners find good parallels in Roman mines in Spain and at Dolaucothi in Wales. None of this has been seen on any of the shafts from the later historic period on Alderley Edge. Particularly idiosyncratic is the way the shaft twists gently through some 35° on its vertical axis and narrows slightly as it goes down. There are no traces of stemple holes to support ladders or staging, but instead two noticeable changes in the profile of the shaft on the way down, at intervals of approximately 3.4 m, must be for the insertion of such staging and climbing ladders, dividing the shaft into three sections. The curious twist is the result of right-handed pickmen working their way down without being able to refer to daylight above them to keep their exact orientation (Figure 14.10). Timberlake discusses this quirk and other technical aspects of the shaft in greater detail in the next chapter, and in *ArchAE*: ch. 6).

A few centimetres above the bottom of the shaft a level runs southwards for some 7 m towards the ore-bearing stratum at Engine Vein. This was clearly the reason for sinking the shaft, and the accuracy of its positioning makes it clear that the miners knew well the layout of the ore-bearing veins. The level is cut in the same style and exhibits the same tool-marks as the shaft. In contrast to the 'coffin levels' of the later mining, this one has the shape of a rounded trapezium, narrower at the top than at the bottom: this is characteristic of the Roman mines at Sounion in Greece and Rio Tinto in Spain and elsewhere (Davies, 1935; Willies, 1997). It is 1.8 m or 6 Roman feet high at the arch-like portal,

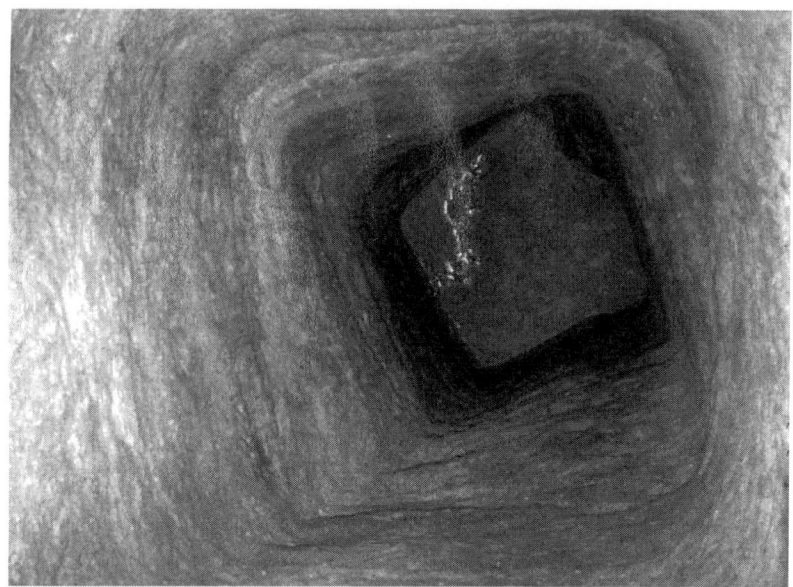

Figure 14.10. Pot Shaft: looking down the Roman mineshaft from the surface, with light reflecting on the water in the sump.

Photograph Malcolm Bailey.

dropping to 1.6 m where it meets the fault; the width varies between just under 1 m to 1.3 m. It is in fact as large as many modern workings; one might also say it is typical of the (Roman) army to cut a textbook level so precisely and to cut away so much more stone than a simple coffin level would demand (Figure 14.11). At the bottom of the shaft was a sump to catch water that seeped into the shaft; in the sump were three carefully worked oak planks, probably re-used from somewhere else. Their purpose was most probably to provide a walkway over the sump or a stand for a bucket, but axe-marks in the centre of one of the planks have suggested that they had been used as a crude method of surveying the sinking of the shaft. For the archaeologist, much the most important aspect of the planks was that a sample from one of them provided a radiocarbon date of 360–280 BC or 250 BC–AD 15 (the two calibration ranges at *c.* 95 per cent probability reflect the squiggle on the carbon-14 calibration curve at this period).

At first sight this takes us back into the Iron Age, but of course this is the felling date for the tree(s): there is good evidence that all three planks came from trees that were between 100 and 200 years old at the time of felling, perhaps more, and that by the time they came to be in the sump of the shaft they had been through other uses. Thus it seems likely that Pot Shaft was being worked during the later part of the first century AD, just the period when the Romans were making their major push northwards; a radiocarbon date of around AD 50 from one

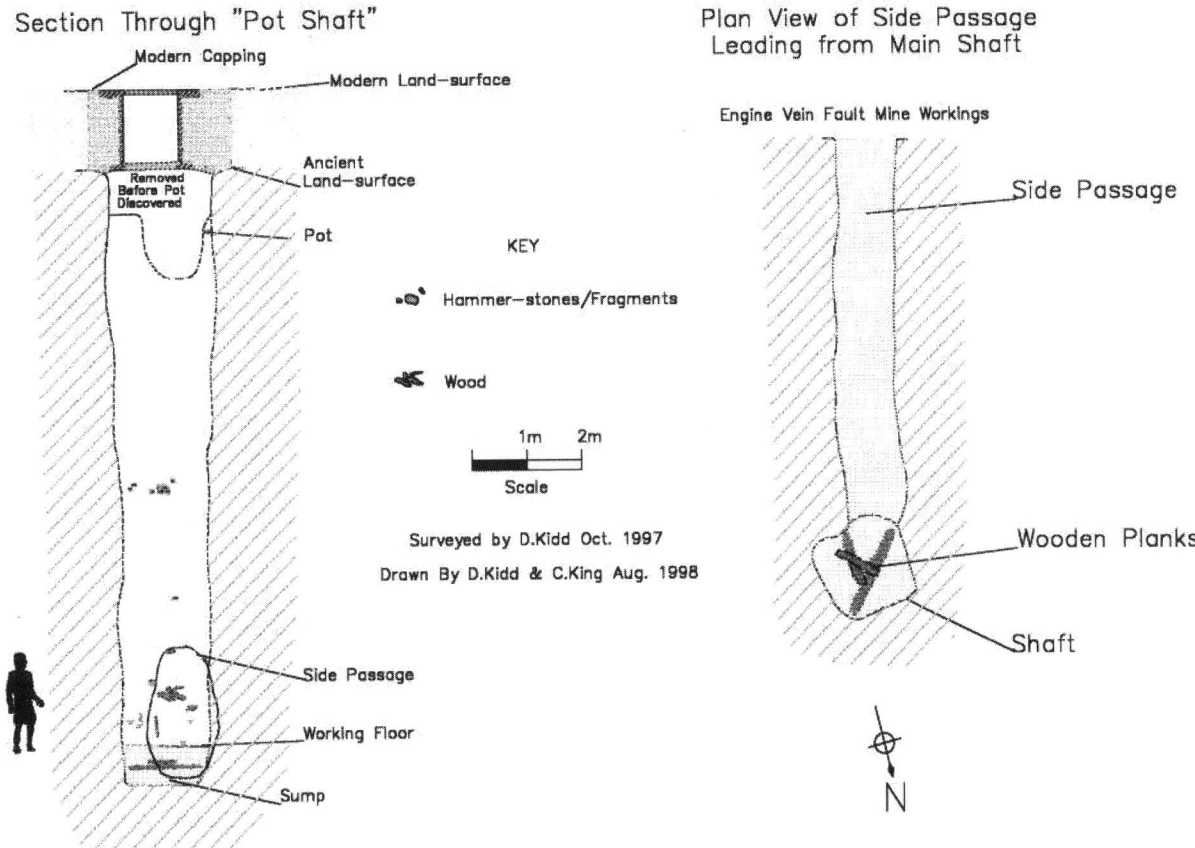

Figure 14.11. Section of the Roman mineshaft and level (side passage).

Drawing by Doug Kidd, Carolanne King and Simon Timberlake.

of the charcoal samples recovered from the fill of the shaft would seem to confirm this. However, one should remember that the value of this second sample for dating the shaft is limited, since, unlike the planks, it was just part of the debris thrown in following its abandonment, and that debris also contained Bronze Age mining spoil.

There is no other confirmed evidence of Roman workings on the Edge, but there are a number of features on the southern side of the Engine Vein opencast which show similarities to the methods used at Pot Shaft, including traces of a second shaft, but they are hard to find among the later workings, which have mostly destroyed or obscured them. Members of the Caving Club also report having seen traces of similar working elsewhere under the Edge, but they too have been largely swept away by the later miners. There is growing evidence from elsewhere of the Romans working pre-existing mines immediately after the conquest of Britain in AD 43, presumably at the very least with military support – which of course leaves one wondering whether at Alderley we have simply missed the traces of Iron Age mining. What is interesting is the growing number of Late Iron Age or very early Roman dates (in particular radiocarbon but also pottery dates) associated with these British mines. This is certainly the case with the Roman lead and silver mining at Charterhouse on Mendip, which seems to have been active during the period AD 50–80, with possible pre-conquest origins (Todd, 1996), while similar Iron Age and early Roman dates have been obtained from recent excavations carried out in the mill area at the Dolaucothi gold mines near Lampeter in mid-Wales (Burnham, 1994) and from a major site of lead smelting discovered more recently on the edges of Borth Bog close to the Erglodd Roman fort at Talybont, some 50 km or more further north (Page, 2005). It seems possible, if not likely, that at Alderley, as at other sites in Britain, the Romans were merely taking over smaller native-worked mines. The consecutive nature of these (probable) military operations may have meant that little of the immediately preceding workings survived.

Whatever the case, it seems clear that the Romans did not stay long, and Pot Shaft had been abandoned by AD 100. Indeed, the whole thing may not have been more than a prospecting exercise, perhaps for lead rather than copper. Nonetheless, one is left asking 'where did these people live?' Even if the mines were worked by local people living in simple huts which may have escaped detection, there ought to have been some military camp or evidence of Roman settlement nearby.

There is no certain archaeological evidence of Roman occupation and settlement anywhere in the hinterland of Alderley, neither military nor civilian, nor any trace of Romano-British farmsteads, but we do have clear indications that somewhere in the area agriculture and the associated rural settlement were expanding during this period. The most likely location for such activity is in the surrounding lowlands, perhaps on the flood plain of the River Bollin. There are a very few finds of Roman objects from the Edge: a miniature bronze Dolphin brooch of Polden Hill type was recovered in the Hough in 1999 and reported by David Bailey, the finder, to Manchester Museum; it was probably made in the third quarter of the first century AD, which matches the mining dates nicely. About 2.5 km to the south, in Over Alderley Mr Bailey later found another brooch, of trumpet type, and dating between 50 and 150 AD, along with a *sestertius* of the emperor Trajan minted in Rome in 105 AD (Mattingly and Sydenham, 1926: 564); the coin is very worn and must have been long in circulation before it was lost. Roeder reported some Roman coins that been found 'in a pot hole' on Alderley Edge (1901: 95), and in 1978 four coins that had apparently been found on the Edge around 1900 were handed in at Weaver Hall Museum in Northwich. It seems safe to assume that they are the same. They were minted under the emperors Elagabalus (AD 218–22), Postumus (AD 259–68), Crispus as Caesar (AD 317–26) and Valentinian I (AD 364–75) (Sugden in *ArchAE*: 106, appendix 4), but although they overlap with the Pot Shaft hoard of *c.* 340 AD the presence of the coin of Valentinian shows that the Roman story of the Edge lasted at least into the later fourth century.

Medieval

In the 1980s a stone head, allegedly found at the side of School Lane in Over Alderley many years previously by someone waiting for a bus, was brought into Manchester Museum for identification: young and perhaps over-enthusiastic, one of the authors of this chapter, in his role as Keeper of Archaeology at the Museum (AJNWP), identified it as Roman, probably of the second century AD, and perhaps representing a maenad. Since then wiser counsels have prevailed, and we now believe the head to be Medieval, though at present we have no idea from which building it might have come. Indeed, the archaeological evidence for activity on Alderley Edge during the Medieval period or indeed for any period between the burying of the coin hoard and the seventeenth and eighteenth centuries is negligible. The needs of conservation provided an opportunity for the Landscape Project to carry out excavations at Saddlebole in 1999, which might throw light on the history of the boundary bank, and which would investigate the evidence for mining and for the story of a wind-blown smelter at this col on the Edge. While it is very likely that the bank does go back to the Medieval period, the archaeology could not prove it beyond doubt. Similarly, some of the toolmarks in the mines here are not incompatible with Medieval practices, but there were no supporting finds and this interpretation could easily have been wrongly suggested by the softness of the rock. When it came to the smelter, no evidence could be found at all on Saddlebole. It seems possible that a smelter was located on Glaze Hill, between here and Stormy Point, or perhaps even on Stormy Point itself: in fact, suggestions of wind-powered smelting (of both copper and lead ores) were found during recent excavations carried out at this site, although the dating and proof of this still remain to be resolved. The excavation of Saddlebole bank and mine is fully described by Jeremy Milln and others in *ArchAE* (ch. 9); in the present book, the Saddlebole Mine is discussed in greater detail by Timberlake in Chapter 15. The story of the boundaries is part of the Medieval history of Alderley, and this really depends not on the archaeology but on the literary sources, which are more plentiful and informative. This story is set out by Clare Pye in Chapter 19, together with a discussion of the castle which

Thomas Ridgeway in the eighteenth century and others before and since believed lay underneath Castle Stone Field south of Castle Rock (also Timberlake *et al.* in *ArchAE*: 159–60).

There can be no doubt that the quarries on Alderley Edge were worked during the Medieval and post-Medieval periods, but here the evidence is largely 'second-hand': cut stones identified as from Alderley have been found in Medieval contexts at Toad Hall, Blackden, some 11 km to the south-west (Alan Garner, personal communication), and St Oswald's in Lower Peover is not the only Cheshire church to have been improved with Alderley sandstone in the sixteenth century. The story of the Alderley quarries is discussed in detail by Nigel Dibben in Chapter 18, while the merestones in the area are considered in Chapter 27. The Landscape Project also carried out excavations at Wood Mine and West Mine in 1997 but these, like the probable Medieval iron bloomery on the north side of Bradford Lane, form part of the story of the mining on the Edge rather than its archaeology (Chapter 15; see also Timberlake *et al.* in *ArchAE*: 140–4).

However, it would be wrong to end this archaeological chapter in a minor key. There are of course scattered finds from the succeeding centuries from Alderley Edge, admittedly none for the Anglo-Saxon period, which is also a blank in the literature, but there have been some interesting Medieval items, notably those found in recent years by the late David Bailey and reported most diligently to the Portable Antiquities Service. Mr Bailey's finds have featured before in this chapter, and one should add that none comes from National Trust land, where metal-detecting is forbidden by the Trust's bye-laws, and in every case he pursued his search with the consent of the appropriate landowner; some of his finds he presented to Manchester Museum. The pieces listed below all come from Over Alderley.

Two Medieval items stand out, found in 2001–02. The first is a bronze oval seal matrix from the Hough, still with part of its handle on the back and measuring 26 mm by 18 mm (Manchester Museum acc. no. 2002.3: Figure 14.12). The main image is a bird with its wings pointing downwards and with a crescent above its head. In Medieval Lombardic script it carries the inscription 'RICARD[I D]E ALDER[LEGH?]' (Richard of Alderley). It is especially interesting because it leads us to the name of a real person. While we cannot identify him for certain, the only Richard of Alderley for whom we have any written evidence is recorded in documents of the early years of the reign of Edward II (1307–27) (Ormerod, 1882: vol. 3, p. 582). The Alderleys were connected with the Actons of Over Alderley, whose best memorial in the landscape is Acton Farm on Hocker Lane, a couple of miles to the south across the Edge from where the seal was found. Stylistically it can be dated between AD 1200 and 1350. The bird may be an eagle, which forms part of the

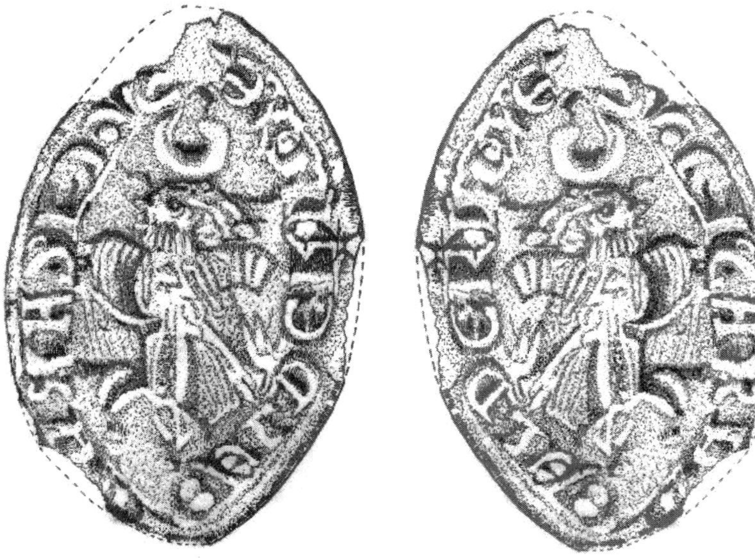

Figure 14.12. The seal
of Richard of Alderley,
AD 1200–1350: (a) original and
(b) impression (Manchester
Museum acc. no. 2002.3).

Drawn by Jeremy Milln from photographs in the Portable Antiquities
database and by Phillip Rispin.

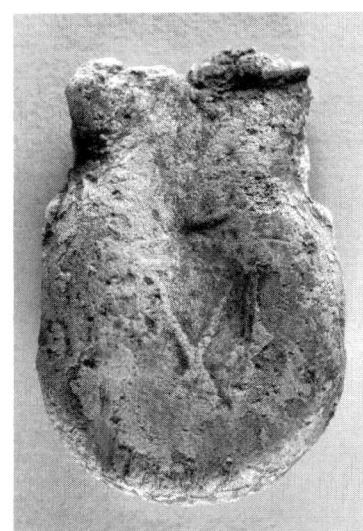

(a)   (b)

emblem of the Stanleys, but it is much too early for that family's links
with Alderley, for the Stanleys appear here only in the early fifteenth
century (see Chapter 19). At another site Mr Bailey found a second seal
matrix, this time of lead and unfortunately scarcely legible, along with
other Medieval items, including a thimble and two lead spindle-whorls.

Almost as intriguing is a little holy-water flask or *ampulla* made of lead
measuring 42 mm by 28 mm, and dating from the thirteenth or fourteenth century, from Hocker Lane (Figure 14.13). It is nearly complete,
and has a cross on one side and – rather faintly – what appears to be a

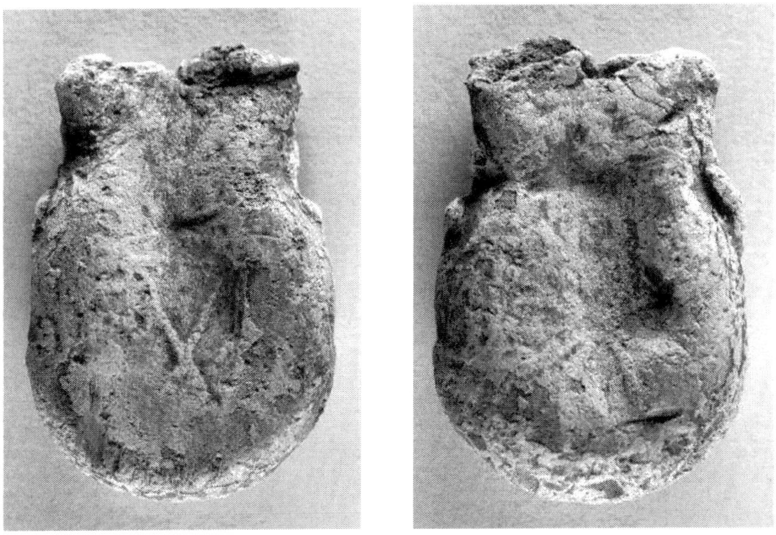

Figure 14.13. Lead ampulla
(holy-water flask) found by
David Bailey at Over Alderley,
thirteenth or fourteenth
century AD: (a) front; (b) back.

Photographs Manchester Museum,
University of Manchester.

(a)   (b)

daisy on the other. Miniature flasks of this kind were used by pilgrims to bring back holy water from the shrines which they visited. There is no saint's emblem on the Alderley flask to show whence it came: the shrine of St Winifred at Holywell in Flintshire is the closest, but those of the Virgin at Walsingham in Norfolk or St Thomas à Becket at Canterbury were also very popular at the time.

Post-Medieval

Many other small items have been picked up on and around the Edge over the years, from coins of Elizabeth I and fragments of post-Medieval pottery to the Second World War shrapnel described by Alan Garner in *Tom Fobble's Day* (it was worth more as a swap if it was still warm when you picked it up) (Garner, 1992 edition: 172); one of the oddest is probably the mysterious gold bar allegedly found by the side of Artists Lane on 24 May 1992, whose real origins and indeed authenticity are still in doubt. Perhaps the last find that should be mentioned here is one that came up at the end of the Landscape Project's work. At the very last meeting of the Project's Working Group, on 25 May 2005, Stephen Mills from the Derbyshire Caving Club laid on the table a box containing what appeared to be a wooden goblet or chalice measuring 13.8 cm high and with a rim diameter of 9.8 cm, which he had found two weeks earlier while clearing a pond and making a drainage channel

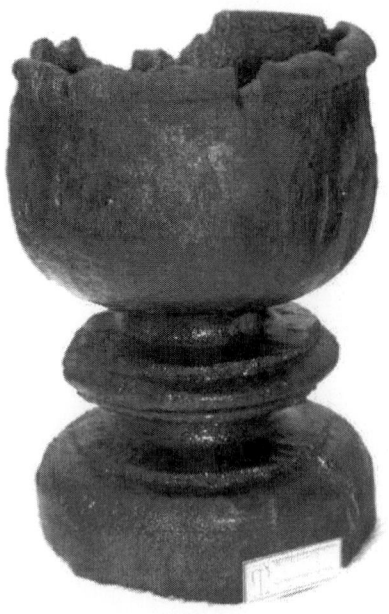

Figure 14.14. Wooden 'goblet' found at Brynlow in 2005 (Manchester Museum acc. no. 2011.2). The scale at the base measures 5 cm.

Photograph Manchester Museum, University of Manchester.

at Brynlow, not far from where the wooden shovel had been discovered seventy years earlier. He presented it to the Museum through the National Trust, in accordance with the agreement then in force. After cleaning and conservation in the specialist laboratory of the York Archaeological Trust, it has been put on display in the 'conservation' section of the Ancient Worlds galleries in Manchester Museum (acc. no 2011.2; Figure 14.14). The specialists in York identified it is as a block of ash heartwood (*Fraxinus excelsior L.*), turned on a lathe into the shape of a small goblet. However, they noted that the interior – the 'cup' – is not fully hollowed: it is only 4 cm deep, so it would not hold much liquid; and that in any case the way it has been carved from the parent tree might make it leak badly through splits. There is a large blind hole in the flat base, slightly off-centre, which might well have served to receive a pin or dowel, leading them to suggest that unless it were a stage prop and not actually intended for practical use (a possibility that has also been suggested with local Christmas productions in mind) it is perhaps a turned decorative fitting made to look like a goblet, and might once have adorned a sculpture, decorative panel or building, although they could not be more specific. No other items were found with it, and it is very difficult to give it a date on stylistic grounds: although the upper part, especially the bowl, recall seventeenth- or even sixteenth-century forms, the shape of the foot is more at home in the nineteenth century. As with so many aspects of this story, the final chapter has not yet been written.

Further reading

Timberlake, S. and Prag, A. J. N. W. (eds). 2005. *The Archaeology of Alderley Edge: Survey, Excavation and Experiment in an Ancient Mining Landscape* (British Archaeological Reports, British Series 396). Oxford: John and Erica Hedges (abbreviated throughout the text as *ArchAE*).

15

Early mining: the evidence before 1598

Simon Timberlake

The following account provides a brief discussion of the evidence for prehistoric, Roman and early Medieval mining on the Edge (Figure 15.1). This includes all those sites thought to have been in operation at or before 1598, the date of the earliest recorded perambulation of the parish boundaries (recorded in the *Stanley Notebook* – Stanley, 1830–44). That there is overlap with the chapters on the archaeology and the history of the Edge and with that on the later mining is probably unavoidable: one hopes that there are no actual contradictions, and that it makes each story more complete.

Prehistoric mining

Sites of prehistoric mining on and around Alderley Edge

In 1874 a fragment of prehistoric mining landscape, now thought to be Early Bronze Age in date, was uncovered at Brynlow during the course of modern mining activity. The early workings here were first recognised by Boyd Dawkins (1875), who inspected the site on numerous occasions in the company of other leading archaeologists. The stone tools found here were later described by Roeder (1901), Roeder and Graves (1905a) and Shone (1911). Accompanying these tools was a Bronze Age wooden shovel, which was recorded by Sainter (1878) as having been found within one of these early mine pits, and which has just recently been radiocarbon dated to *c.* 1750 BC: its story is told elsewhere in this book (Chapter 1, pp. 6–7, and Chapter 2, pp. 27–8, including Figure 2.3).

Elsewhere on the Edge, particularly at Engine Vein but also in Dickens Wood and Windmill Wood, and at Mottram St Andrew, a

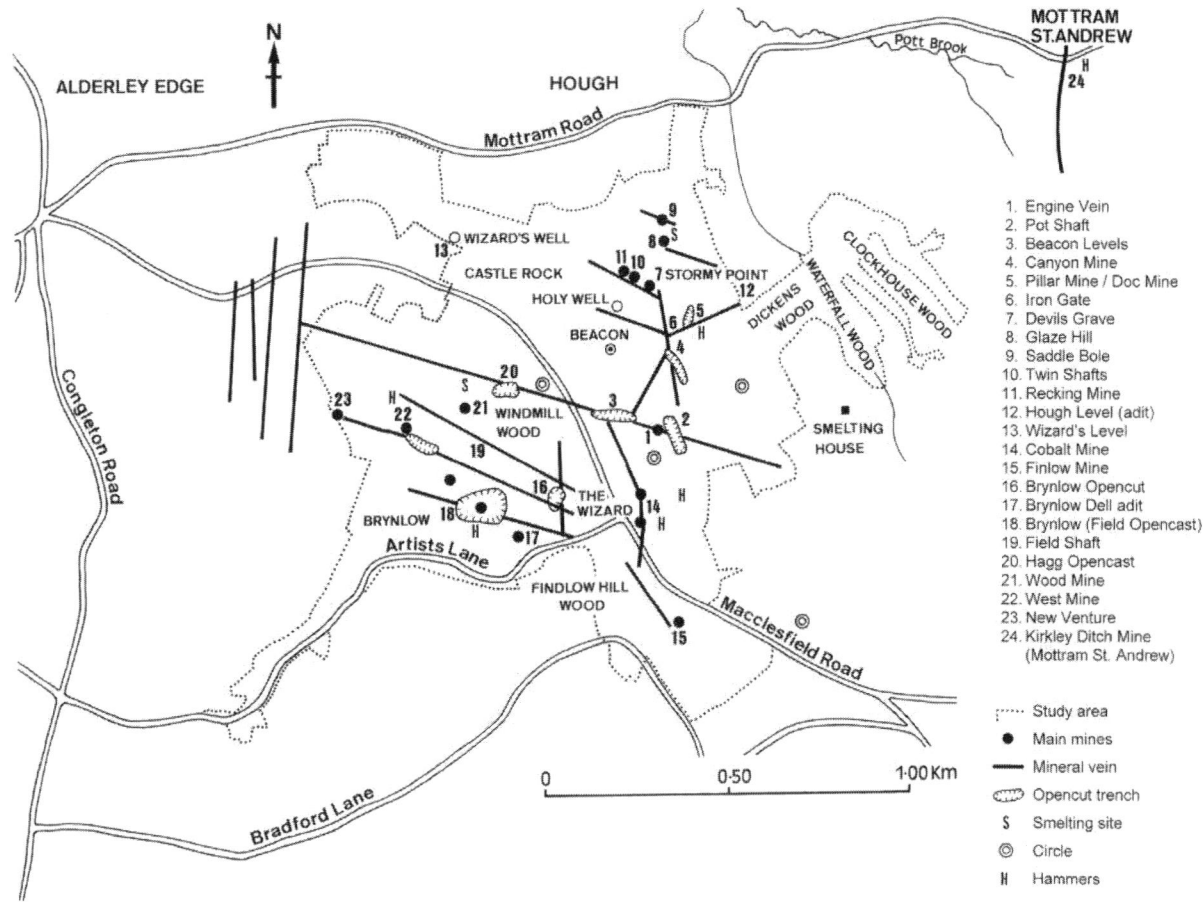

Figure 15.1. Map of Alderley Edge showing pre-1598 mines: Bronze Age, Roman and early Medieval.
Drawing by Brenda Craddock.

kilometre or so to the east, mining sites of a similar type were examined
by Roeder in 1901, by Roeder and Graves (1905a), then mentioned
by Oliver Davies (1935), Carlon (1979), Warrington (1965, 1981) and
others. More recently, those surviving and still recognisable sites such
as Dickens Wood (Pillar Mine) and the Engine Vein Opencast were
re-examined by Pickin (1990, 1991) and Gale (1989, 1993, 1995), and
finally by Timberlake as part of the Landscape Project's survey in 1997
(*ArchAE*: 135–44). Following the last of these, a previously unknown
pit-working was excavated close to the south-west end of Engine Vein:
its life can now be ascribed with some certainty to the period 100–150
years just before or after 1900 BC (Timberlake and King in *ArchAE*:
ch. 4). Archaeological evaluation carried out at Stormy Point by the
University of Manchester Archaeological Unit in 2007 seems to have

revealed further evidence for Early Bronze Age and perhaps later pre-historic mining in the form of at least two prospection pits, one of which was dated to 1690–1510 BC (Mottershead and Wright, 2008).

An association of Mesolithic flint with known areas of mineralisation such as Engine Vein and West Mine raises the question as to whether there was any contemporary exploitation of some of the colourful secondary minerals as pigments. This is suggested by the presence of soft sandstone or marl horizons on the Edge impregnated with oxidised minerals, resulting in the formation of rocks stained green (malachite/chrysocolla), blue (azurite), yellow (pyromorphite) and brown-black (manganese/cobalt wad or asbolane). The rocks in these mineralised horizons may have been discovered and used for the extraction of colourful pigment long before their value as metal ores was appreci-ated. One of these sites of possible pigment extraction is to be found at Pillar Mine. However, given the fact that these minerals were probably collected from the surface of outcrops that have now largely weathered away, the best method of confirming such activity would be to examine one of the possible Mesolithic campsites, such as Castle Rock, located some distance away from the nearest source of mineralisation and mining (for discussion of traces of worked and used mineral pigment see Timberlake in *ArchAE*: 223–55). Archaeological investigation here or elsewhere may yet show whether these peoples were extracting minerals from the Edge.

There are yet further suggestions of mining on the Edge earlier than the Bronze Age, including a couple of anomalously early radiocarbon dates associated with the infill of the excavated pit-working EVB1 at Engine Vein, together with finds of Neolithic–Early Bronze Age flints associated with this working, which may or may not be residual (Cowell in *ArchAE*: 20–32, especially 29). Such evidence begs the question whether there was still earlier Bronze Age activity at Engine Vein, *c.* 2300–2000 BC or before. This earlier phase of working may have been for copper ore and thus for metal, or for pigment. A much more comprehensive investigation of the south side of Engine Vein would be needed to answer this question.

Field Opencast, Brynlow

An unspecified number of small pit-workings were uncovered when the old ground surface beneath an area of open meadow at Brynlow above the Sandhills was exposed during mining operations carried out in 1874. The area was then examined by Professor William Boyd Dawkins in May that year. Boyd Dawkins (1875) states that the old ground surface here was 'laid bare' as miners worked their way up to the surface in search of low-grade copper ore in the form of malachite. He described the area as being 'fantastically hollowed'. From this spot he recovered some thirty-five hammer stones, and then later in the year another 100 or so grooved or partially grooved hammer stones. For the most part these were found lying in the bottom of the irregular hollows or pits, some of which were around 3 m deep. Boyd Dawkins (1875) likened this to a 'wheelbarrow formation', worked from above, following what appeared to be low-grade ore. The stone hammers were thrown back along with other debris following the abandonment of the working; Roeder (1901) considered the mixture of well used alongside unused hammers at the base of these workings to be indicative of a sudden abandonment. The exact location of these pits was never indicated by Boyd Dawkins, although we do know that they were exposed within the confines of the opencast, the edges of which can still be located today. Roeder's field map of *c.* 1901 and an accompanying photograph (both now kept with the Roeder and Graves MSS in Manchester Central Reference Library: Roeder and Graves, 1905b) suggest that the pits were grouped along the east side of the opencast, mostly within the 100 m square SJ 855 773. A sketch section first drawn by Boyd Dawkins and later reproduced by Roeder shows the side of the Field Opencast with the very irregular hollows cut away and the approximate positions of the hammer stones marked (Figure 15.2). Very little remains to be seen at this site today, given that much of the area of the opencast was filled in during the nineteenth century. Most (if not all) of the hammer stones were removed and the majority are now in Manchester Museum.

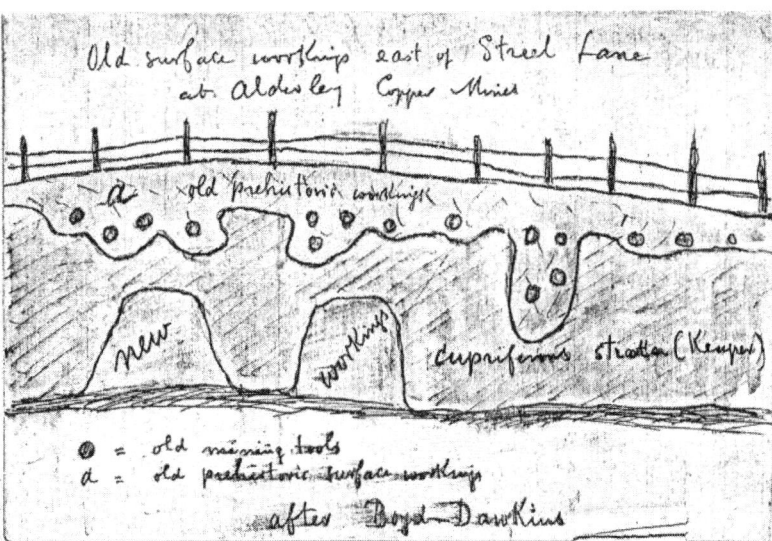

Figure 15.2. Diagrammatic section of pit-workings in the side of the Brynlow Opencast.

Drawing by Roeder after an original by W. Boyd Dawkins.

West Mine Opencast

Roeder and Graves (1905a: 24) refer to 'a large hollow filled with big boulders, stored ready for use' (as hammer stones) close to the edge of this modern opencast. The grid reference for this presumed ancient site was given as approximately SJ 8523 7752. However, there is no real reason for believing that this hollow and its associated collection of boulders had anything to do with Bronze Age mining. All this area now lies beneath re-deposited mine spoil, rubble and infill. Although we have no specific reference to the presence of surface pits in the area of West Mine, it seems possible that early prospection pitting could have continued over to the area of outcropping cupriferous sandstone present on this side of the opencast. Here there was also an area of rock outcrop with some evidence of Mesolithic or later prehistoric activity or settlement, judging from the finds of flint tools and wasters. Indeed, there is a suggestion of some early mining, thought to be Roman, somewhere in this vicinity, since a number of shallow workings which could have been fire-set were discovered here during the earliest excavation of the Victorian mine and opencast entrance (Higgs, 1858).

The Hagg, Windmill Wood

This small (and now infilled) opencast referred to by Roeder and Graves as the site of an ancient mine lies in the northern part of Windmill Wood, at the junction of the Northern Boundary fault and another fault striking south-south-west to north-north-east which heads off towards Castle Rock (SJ 8557 7767). No description survives of the type of working that was once here, and the site itself was backfilled by the local council for safety reasons some time during the twentieth century; the area is now covered with dense vegetation. It was here that Frederick Graves found the fragments of a smelting pot which he implied was of prehistoric origin. Three 'slagged sherds' of this crucible are illustrated in a sketch in the Roeder and Graves papers (reproduced in *ArchAE*: 12, fig. 2.3). However, none of the artefacts have been traced and they are now believed to be lost. Another two or three hammer stones were found mixed up in 'modern' (eighteenth- or nineteenth-century) mine spoil deposited at the foot of a level a little way to the east (at approximately SJ 8550 7755). No hammer stones have been found in this area of the Edge in recent times.

Pillar Mine, Dickens Wood

On one of the sandstone ledges which outcrops above and to the north of the large entrance to Pillar Mine, Roeder and Graves (1905a) describe yet another shallow pit, in which they found the remains of charcoal, calcined lead ore and hammer stones. However, some of the hammer stones were found lying adjacent to or downslope of this point. Today the remains of about three bisected pits are still visible; they are rather weathered and eroded by the passage of feet and water, yet at least one of them still retains small areas of the original rock surface, which features pecking or batter marks resulting from the use of stone tools. Several larger indented hollows or 'eyes' in the sides of these pits indicate those places from which the enriched pods of malachite-cemented sandstone had been scraped in the distant past (see Gale, 1989). The most obvious pit here is about 1 m in diameter and 1.5 m deep, and has been worked vertically into the sandstone from a thin malachite-enriched horizon above (SJ 8612 7783). There may also be traces of other shallow pits on the bedding plane surfaces above and below this layer, but later mining and erosion have taken their toll here and they are now difficult to see. The large entrance to Pillar Mine (see Figure 16.2, p. 375) has also been referred to as a Bronze Age working (Richardson, 1974: 82, plate 15). When this suggestion was made, it was probably just a poorly informed guess, yet it may not be far off the mark. Some 30–50 m downslope of this large opening, hammers occasionally come to the surface in the gradually eroding spoil and scree, particularly after bouts of heavy rain, when gully erosion exposes earlier horizons of buried tips downslope and to the south-east of the Pillar Mine entrance (SJ 8614 7783 – 8618 7783). The number of hammers collected here since 1901 implies that there was once a much larger area of prehistoric working exposed than the small number of pits which are evident today. For example, the shape of the existing rock outcrop suggests the former existence of a small prehistoric opencast some 10 m long, associated with an east–west fault and formed a now largely destroyed mine-working to which the surviving pit-workings and Pillar Mine entrance are related.

Devil's Grave, Stormy Point

The mine-workings at Devil's Grave consist of a number of shallow-dipping galleries underlying the top of the rock outcrop at Stormy Point (SJ 8620 7787). The mine entrance is cut by a narrow trench and shaft, and beneath this the early miners excavated away a thin mineralised mudstone horizon which lies between the sandstone and conglomerate beds, working down-dip from the outcrop.

The upper parts of the rock slide at Stormy Point may represent similar collapsed workings. For instance, during the archaeological evaluation carried out by the University of Manchester Archaeological Unit in June 2007, evidence for the collapse of mine-workings of large rock-shelter type on the slope in front of Devil's Grave was recovered, in the form of buried fragments of the roof overhang. This same eroded area also revealed evidence of Early Bronze Age and perhaps later pre-historic mining, in the form of at least two prospection pits dug on some small baryte veins, one of which also seems to have been used as a hearth. These had been deliberately backfilled with material containing charcoal, from which a date of 1690–1510 CAL BC was obtained (Mottershead and Wright, 2008). Other mining or ore-processing features thought to have been of Bronze Age date were also identified in nearby archaeological test pits. Rather surprisingly, the significant spreads of malachite-rich rock found associated with some of these features appear not to have been mined. Most likely the object of the mining operation at Devil's Grave to the west of these pits was the recovery of the filmy malachite and pea-sized nodules of azurite present in the intervening clay; a rather similar ore was worked for pigment in the upper mudstone beds of Engine Vein.

In conclusion, the surviving mine galleries at Devil's Grave could be of Bronze Age date, although as yet there is little evidence to support this, stone tools being conspicuous by their absence. However, one should ask whether such tools would really be needed if it was only the soft clay and the mineral that were being removed.

Engine Vein Opencast

In 1998 an archaeological excavation of an undisturbed pit-working on the south side of Engine Vein, carried out by the Landscape Project, provided the first conclusive dates for prehistoric mining on the Edge. Charcoal from fire-setting in the base of pit EVB1 was radiocarbon-dated to the Early Bronze Age (beta-115606: 3550±70 BP = 2035–1690 CAL BC at 95 per cent probability) (for further dates and discussion see Timberlake and King in *ArchAE*: 33–57). Examples of both heavily fractured but also unbroken grooved hammer stones were found during these Engine Vein excavations (Figure 4.3, p. 64).

The location and type(s) of early pit-workings exposed in the sides of this large opencast trench are described by Roeder (1901), Gale (1986, 1989), Timberlake and King in *ArchAE*, and Mottershead and King (2005). A sketch section drawn by Graves in 1902 (in Roeder and Graves, 1905b) shows the remains of five pits plus a number of smaller hollows along the side of the fault, while Gale produced an elevation plan of this face showing the detail of tooling marks as well as various hollows or 'eyes' where rock as well as pockets of mineral had been removed from the sides of the pits (Gale, 1989: fig.1; reproduced in *ArchAE*: 34, fig. 4.1b). Roeder and Graves (1905a: 8–9) mention their investigation of some smaller pits on the south side of the vein. Here they found evidence for hearths, calcined lead ore, hammer stones and what they took to be a Roman iron pick (in fact the boring rod

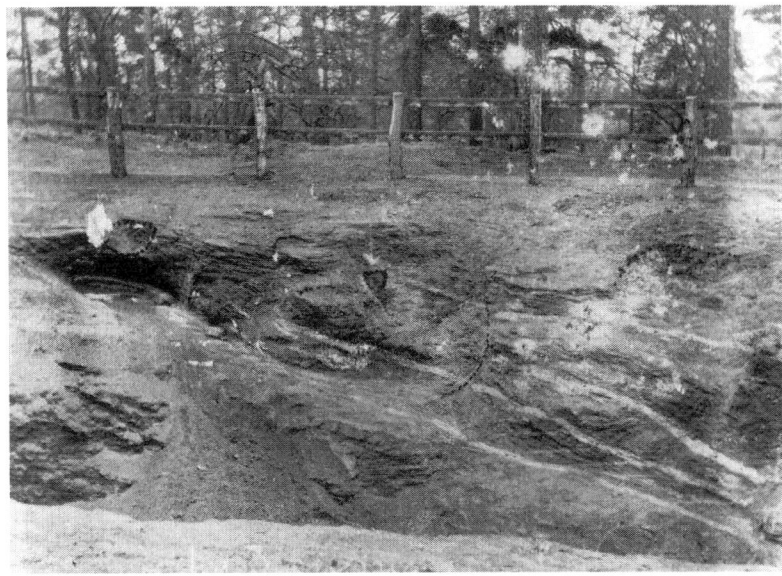

(a)

Figure 15.3. Small pit-working exposed at the south-west end of Engine Vein. (a) Photograph from the Roeder and Graves archive, Manchester Museum, *c.* 1900. (b) The same view in 1997, showing the position of the excavated pit EVB1 a short distance above.

Photograph Simon Timberlake.

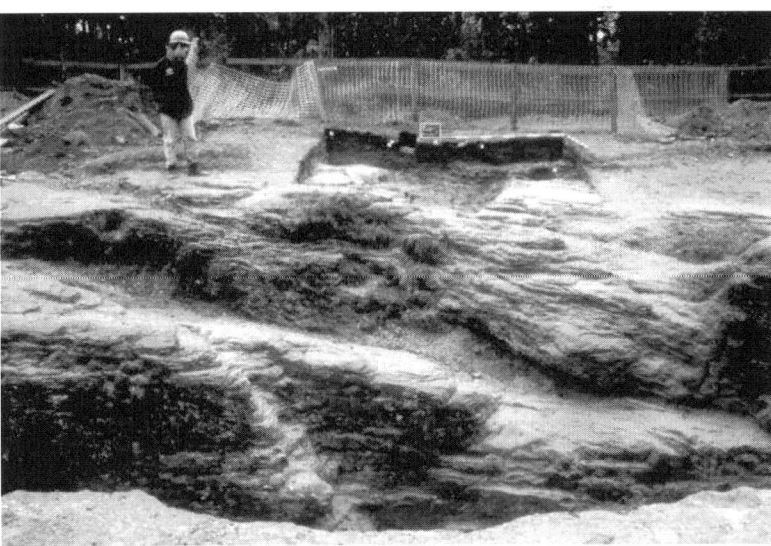

(b)

from a seventeenth- to nineteenth-century hand drill). A few of the pits are shown on an unlabelled photograph in Manchester Museum (Figure 15.3a). It was the rediscovery of this photograph in the Museum archives that enabled us to locate the virgin pit-working excavated in 1998 as EVB1 (Figure 15.3b). This may represent some of the earliest mineral prospection carried out at Engine Vein (*c.* 1900 BC), with the abandoned pit then being used as a working hollow for crushing ore and as a shelter, and finally backfilled following later mining activity on the fault itself (Timberlake and King in *ArchAE*: 33–57).

Roeder and Graves (1905a: 9) mention the evidence for smelting, referring to a hearth at the far western end of the workings, with remains of copper slag and smelted copper mixed in the mine spoil. A sample of smelted copper, claimed to be from Engine Vein, was deposited in the Manchester Museum mineral collections. However, it seems unlikely that this represents prehistoric activity. In recent years a hammer stone was found at the far west end of Engine Vein (SJ 8596 7754), at a spot close to a series of old shafts but possibly overlying an earlier small opencut trench (Gale, 1994), while during the 1900s, well before agricultural improvement had begun to conceal other areas of early workings, Roeder (1901: p. 79) recorded finding stone tools both above and below the Edge House Farm Road (at SJ 8611 7746 and 8613 7740), as well as along the footpath which passed through a field between Thieves' Hole and the Macclesfield Road (at SJ 8603 7727). Thus hammer stones were still being found in the early twentieth century some distance away from Engine Vein and other known mineral workings, which would seem to suggest a wider area of prehistoric mining or processing to the south and west of the main mining site. The results of recent geochemical prospection suggest one possible site of early processing activity centring on SJ 8605 7740, perhaps a location for the dressing or even smelting of ores in an area now covered by woodland (Timberlake in *ArchAE*: 237).

Alongside the prospection and small-scale extraction of lens-like deposits of malachite and azurite formed along the bedding planes of the south-dipping sandstone and conglomerate beds which lie just to the south of the Engine Vein Fault, richer carbonate ores, oxides – including native (i.e. pure) copper – and even sulphides were being extracted from the mineralisation present along the fault itself. Still other sources of ore could have been the pisolith spheroidal nodules of rich azurite and

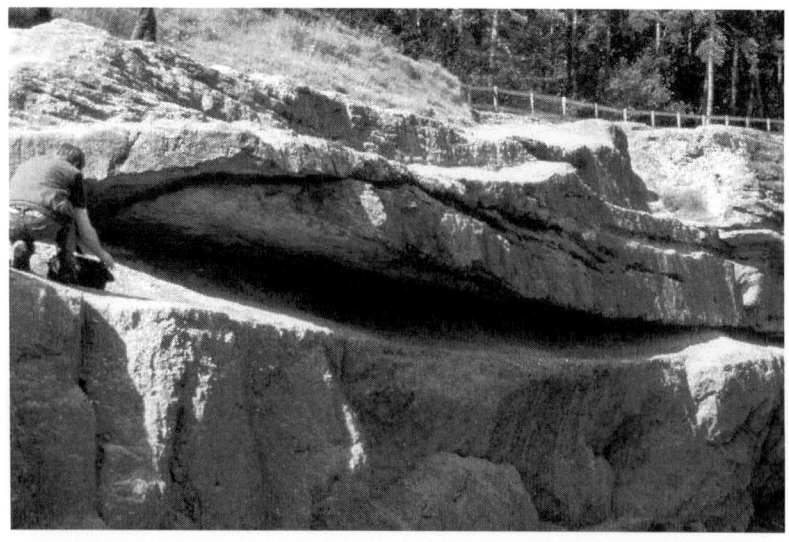

Figure 15.4. A possible prehistoric extraction for azurite and malachite pigment from the mudstone bed on the south side of the Engine Vein Fault.

Photograph Simon Timberlake.

chrysocolla obtained from the outcropping red and green clay-mudstone bed(s) exposed on the southern side of the fault (Thompson, 1970c). The mudstone here has been almost completely removed, perhaps a pre-historic extraction for blue and green pigment (Figure 15.4; Plate 60).

Mottram St Andrew

Roeder and Graves (1905a: 10) reported finding stone tools re-deposited among surface disturbance and modern mine spoil at the Mottram Mine. They also mention finding the remains of a hearth (undated), though they failed to locate the actual prehistoric workings. Presumably these were shallow pit-workings rather similar to the ones they found at Engine Vein. Their map indicates the approximate position of the hearth (SJ 740 840) and also the finds of hammer stones (SJ 730 850). These were located either side of the quarry shown on the plan of the Mine and Treatment Works of *c.* 1872 (see Carlon, 1979: 115). Since most of the tools which they found were either completely unmodified cobbles or only partly modified for use as mining implements, they considered the earliest miners of Mottram to be of 'inferior status' to those of Alderley Edge, habitually using much more primitive tools and techniques. Subsequent finds do not suggest this was the case at all. Hammer stones recently collected from this site and now in Manchester Museum show evidence of very similar grooving.

Much of the Mottram Mine has now been built over and the area of prehistoric extraction and processing has been all but obliterated. However, collapses into old shafts and workings are not uncommon along the fringes of the residential area around Kirkleyditch. Recently a number of hammer stones were recovered from this area (e.g. from SJ 740 830) following disturbance caused by the subsidence of a garden and subsequent restoration work, while others have been found near Kirkleyditch Farm (SJ 730 840) (Tony Browne, personal communication; Mr Browne presented his finds to Manchester Museum in 2005, shortly before his death). This supports the original observation that the area of prehistoric extraction lay mostly to the east of the Treatment Works, and was therefore probably associated with mineralisation on the North Lode.

The typology and identification of Early Bronze Age mining

Recent excavations described in the previous chapter suggest that the Bronze Age miners were first prospecting for copper following the showings of malachite in surface rock outcrops. They began by excavating shallow pits using grooved and hafted stone hammers of various weights and sizes to break up and remove the overlying sandstone and conglomerate beds in pursuit of films and lenses of visible but relatively poor ore present along joints and bedding planes. Soon they would have made the connection that this could guide them to pockets of much richer material. By doing this the miners may have ended up following the outcrop or sub-crop showings of ore coursing in the same direction or perhaps towards the major mineral veins, sometimes for distances of over 20 m. On reaching the larger mineral veins such as the Engine Vein Fault, deeper and sometimes interconnected pits would be sunk at intervals on the vein, a process known as incipient opencasting; it is very unlikely that any of these pits reached depths of more than 3 m. Eventually the mineralised ground on the productive side(s) of the fault will have been worked in steps or benches, the faces of which were formed as a result of working back along the bedding planes in search of further ore. Access to the deeper pits may have been by way of rock-cut steps or ledges, obviating the need for ladders: such an access route has

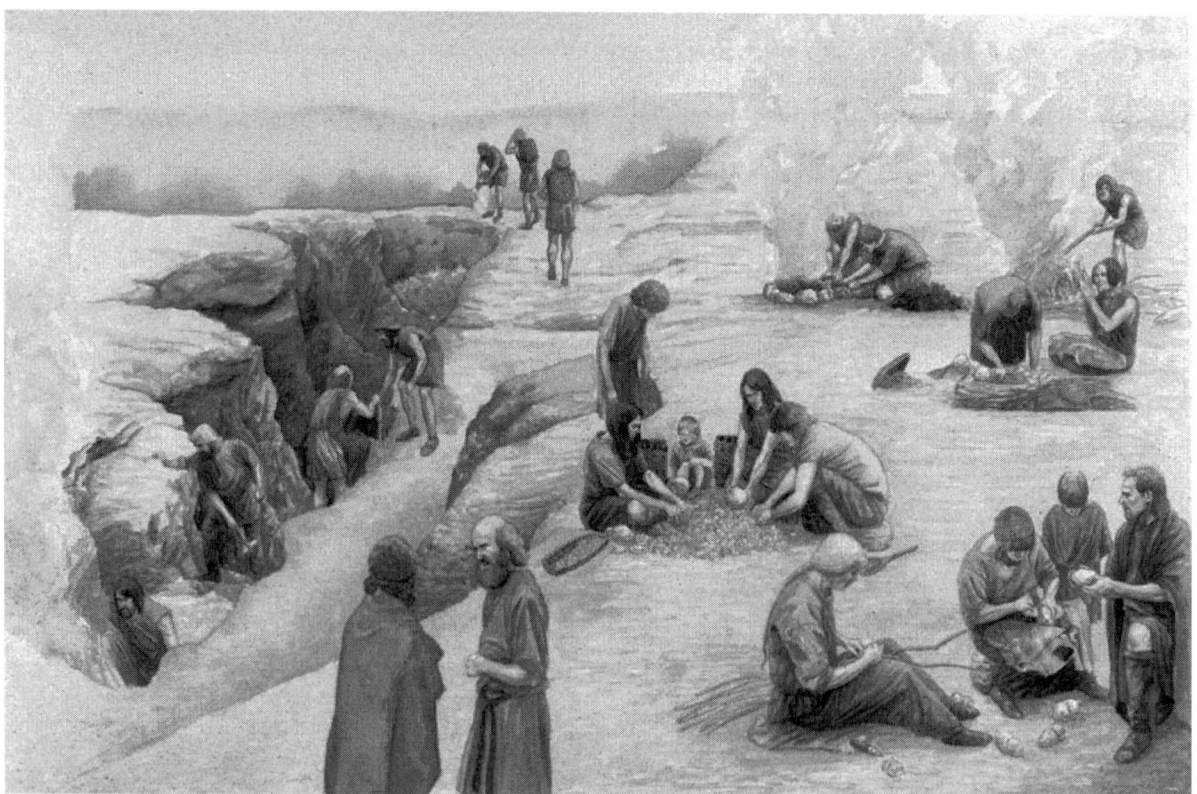

Figure 15.5. Reconstruction of mining and ore-processing at Engine Vein during the Early Bronze Age. Drawing by Seán Ó'Brógáin.

been identified at the south-west end of the Engine Vein Opencast. The whole process of Bronze Age mining and ore preparation is illustrated in Figure 15.5.

Water would have been one of the limiting factors governing the feasible depth of working. This could have been a reason why mining may even have been a seasonal activity. If this was the case, then the deepest pits or 'sump' of the interconnected workings, be they pits or opencast, needed to be drained before each new period of mining commenced.

Fire-setting was employed to a greater or lesser extent during the excavation of these workings, together with the use of hafted stone tools, wooden shovels and possibly also antler picks and hammers. Indeed, we might expect to find charcoal, unburnt wood and burnt stone alongside broken stone hammers and flakes in almost any of the pit-workings. As regards the stone hammers, there appears to be some evidence for the careful selection of the implements used. For example, small hand-crushing stones have been found alongside mortar or anvil stones in some of the shallowest abandoned pits, the latter being suitable sites for use as shelters (Figure 15.3b) where the various stages of ore processing may have been carried out subsequently.

The pecking or dimple marks produced by the impact of stone hammers against some of the harder barytised sandstone beds are quite distinctive features, as are the rounded profiles of the pit walls and the hollows of the 'eyes' cut into them (Gale, 1989: 269, phase 1a). In general, the exposure of these worked rock surfaces to long periods of weathering has considerably reduced their detail; in most cases it has enhanced the smooth rounded appearance of the walls – a common phenomenon at both Pillar Mine and Engine Vein. However, this loss of detail may not be universal. Some of the pits were quickly filled in after their abandonment and have remained so up to the present day. One such working which was excavated through hard barytised sandstone has survived high up on the south-west rim of the opencast, close to the site of the excavated pit EVB1 (Figure 15.6). Its pristine condition may be due to the presence of an original infill which protected the sides of the pit right up until the early 1900s, when it was emptied and examined by Roeder and Graves (1905a: 6).

Where the faults and mineralised sandstone beds outcrop on the steep scarp slopes of the Edge we may be seeing a slightly different form of early mining; examples include the short 'cave-like' galleries with larger entrances, such as those worked in the softer sandstone beds that we find at Pillar Mine, or the excavation in the underground bedding-plane, dug through the soft mudstone band sandwiched between sandstone or conglomerate units, such as we find at Devil's Grave or along the southern side of Engine Vein.

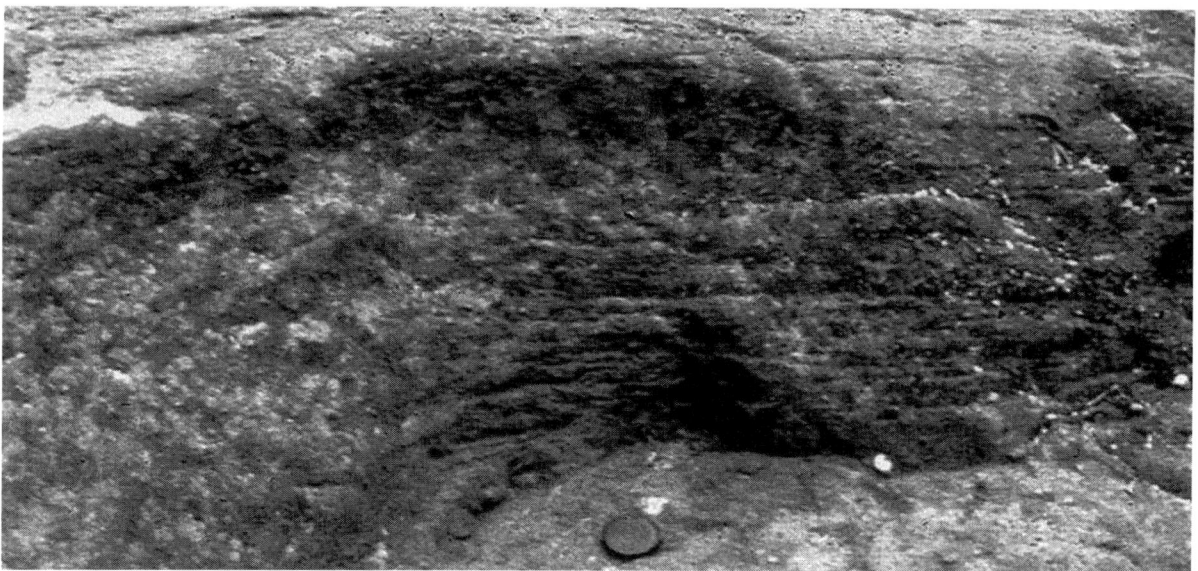

Figure 15.6. Surviving pitting or dimple marks produced by hammer-stones on the side of an emptied Bronze Age mining pit excavated through a hard barytic sandstone layer at the south-east end of the main opencast at Engine Vein. (Detail from Figure 4.5, p. 68, which shows more of the pit.)

Photograph Simon Timberlake.

The production of copper and perhaps also a small amount of lead during this 100–200-year period may never have exceeded twenty tons of hand-picked and cobbed (i.e. crushed and dressed) ore. Given this relatively small amount, it seems plausible to suggest that the copper was smelted locally here on the Edge, yet no evidence for this has ever been found. The possible techniques used in the preparation and smelting of the ore are discussed in more detail elsewhere (Craddock *et al.*, 2007; Timberlake, 2007). Some of the experiments described were undertaken during the National Archaeology Days at Alderley Edge during September 1997 and July 1998 (Timberlake in *ArchAE*: 198–216). These involved the construction of small ephemeral bowl furnaces fired with charcoal and wood, employing simple bag-bellows or blow-pipes to create a forced draught and the reducing conditions necessary to carry out a basic and probably rather inefficient smelt.

Almost certainly there are areas of prehistoric mining and prospecting on Alderley Edge which remain to be found. Some sites worthy of further investigation include the mineralised area between Pillar Mine and Stormy Point (SJ 8611 7787), the area of woodland to the south-west of Engine Vein and the buried outcrop along the line of the Northern Boundary Fault (SJ 8540 7776).

Most Bronze Age sites uncovered as a result of later mining are easily recognised and identified. Unfortunately, the level of recognition of mining carried out during the Roman and early Medieval periods is far lower. More importantly, little evidence has emerged of mining or metallurgical activity during the intervening Late Bronze Age–Iron Age. One exception to this is the possibility of late Iron Age origins for the 'Roman' Pot Shaft. It could be argued that the radiocarbon dates of the wood recovered from the base of this shaft suggest the presence of mining before the Roman conquest (Timberlake and Kidd in *ArchAE*: 79–97); however, we discuss this further in the next section and conclude that the evidence is not convincing.

Before moving on to later mining, we should perhaps mention that Alderley Edge no longer stands on its own as a site of Early Bronze Age copper mining in central England. Between 2008 and 2009 the Early Mines Research Group excavated several sites on the summit of Ecton Hill, a historic copper mine located on the eastern side of the Manifold Valley in Staffordshire, in view of the gritstone hills of Macclesfield and only around 30 km from Alderley Edge as the crow flies (Timberlake, 2010). The geological setting of Ecton with its Carboniferous limestone and pipe veins is quite different to Alderley Edge, yet here the Bronze Age miners were also working malachite, using bone tools to scrape the ore from the soft weathered limestone, and antler picks and cobbles obtained from the river bed to fracture and lever off this rock in both surface and shallow underground workings (Barnatt and Thomas, 1998; Timberlake, 2014). The proximity of this site to Alderley Edge suggests some sort of link. For instance, the slightly later dates at Ecton (*c.* 1800–1700 BC) might imply that prospection spread across the Pennines from west to east, although the complete absence of grooved stone tools at the latter site (only one notched hammer stone was found at Ecton) suggests that mining developed on Alderley Edge during the Bronze Age in a really quite special way.

Roman mining

Roman mining on Alderley Edge was first discussed by Roeder (1901) and Roeder and Graves (1905a), based largely on the evidence of the primitive workings at Engine Vein, though the existence of Roman galleries here was suggested as long ago as 1858 (Higgs, 1858: 692). The subject was looked at again by Carlon (1979), and then by Warrington (1981). However, it was not until the discovery in March 1995 of an early fourth-century AD coin hoard in the top of an infilled and previously unknown shaft on Engine Vein (Nevell, 1996b; Nevell *et al.* in *ArchAE*: 98–123) that the possibility of Roman mining was seriously entertained. Following this discovery, work on the shaft was halted until a full excavation could be undertaken by a team from the Derbyshire

Caving Club and the Landscape Project in October 1997 (Timberlake and Kidd in *ArchAE*: 79–97). This archaeological investigation revealed an abandoned Roman shaft 11 m deep and a cross-cut level which connected to the open stope working of Engine Vein (see Chapter 14).

The 2 m × 2 m square shaft is large by Roman standards, yet the method of sinking and of driving the 7 m long level from its base shows clear similarities with Roman workings recorded in Spain and elsewhere. The shaft, which apparently dates from the first half of the first century AD, is unique to Britain, yet the style of pick-work on its walls is reminiscent of another Roman mine-working, the Penlanwen Adit at the Dolaucothi Gold Mine in South Wales (Manning, 1968; Lewis, 1977).

'Pot Shaft', as it was named by the Derbyshire Caving Club after the coarse-ware pot inside which the coins had been buried, seems to have been used as a means of laddered access into a series of underground workings excavated on the vein itself. A similar shaft, of which only two corners and an edge remain, can be found about 20 m from Pot Shaft on the south side of the Engine Vein Opencast (SJ 8605 7748) (*ArchAE*: 92, fig. 6.8). This appears to be associated with an inclined walkway cut through the rock, with vertical slots cut into its side some 4 m back from the shaft edge, perhaps in order to fix a primitive wooden windlass or capstan. These fixings suggest that this working may once have been a haulage shaft. Meanwhile, 20–30 m to the east and preserved in the north wall of the opencast are traces of another shaft and perhaps also a gallery, the latter truncating the bisected pits associated with the much earlier Bronze Age workings.

Unfortunately, there is as yet no conclusive evidence that any of these other features described are actually Roman in date. Nor is there any evidence for an adit level or surface spreads of Roman mine spoil, nor any archaeological traces of the foundations of buildings or processing areas which one might presume to find associated with them. It seems possible therefore that the Roman mine at Engine Vein never amounted to much: perhaps a small mine or trial dug to sample this vein properly for lead, silver or copper, the strategy being to test the unexploited vein lying beneath the much earlier Bronze Age workings.

The range of radiocarbon dates obtained from timbers found *in situ* in the base of Pot Shaft does not preclude a pre-conquest date (i.e. late pre-Roman Iron Age) for this mine, yet, based on the particular style of working, an Iron Age origin seems unlikely. It is more appropriate perhaps to consider the date when the wood was actually used. This could be Roman (mid-first century AD), particularly if one assumes that the radiocarbon-dated sample of sawn oak timber (beta 115611: 2120 +/- 60 years BP [360–280 CAL BC or 250–15 CAL BC/AD]) might have included heartwood, and/or if this was an old timber re-used.

Unfortunately, dendrochronological analysis undertaken on this wood proved unsuccessful, and no Roman pottery or other artefacts were recovered from this working. If early Roman in date, then it seems more than likely that mining was carried out here under military control, perhaps even by the Twentieth Legion from their base at Chester (Timberlake and Kidd in *ArchAE*: 94). In any event, it was probably only a short-lived affair, lasting little more than twenty years.

Although there is no clear evidence for Roman mining elsewhere on the Edge, the presence of a number of shallow buried opencuts between Engine Vein and Beacon Lodge and at several locations round the head of the Brynlow valley may indicate other Roman or early Medieval workings. Interestingly, shallow opencut rakes are believed to be more typical of the type of Roman workings found in Derbyshire and the Mendips (Todd, 1996; Barnatt, 1999). We should also be aware of the fact that Artists Lane, which follows the route of a much earlier saddle road up the side of Brynlow Dell, would have been the most direct route between Street Lane (the suggested course of a Roman road between Alderley Edge and Congleton) and the mining area of Engine Vein. This route may well have linked other Roman prospecting with prospecting sites on the Edge.

There is one final comparison that needs to be made with the Roman workings we have found at Engine Vein and Pot Shaft. This is the uncanny resemblance to the workings of a second- to fourth-century AD underground mine recently excavated by the Deutsches Bergbau Museum at St Barbara, Wallerfangen, in the Saar in Germany (Korlin, 2010; Martin Strassburger, personal communication). During the late Roman period, this mine was extensively dug to extract azurite. As at Engine Vein, the mineral was found as small pisolith nodules within the mudstone bands lying between much thicker beds of Triassic sandstone. It appears that azurite was highly prized by the Romans as a pigment to make paint for applying to wall plaster. The pigment, also known as Egyptian Blue, was a valuable commodity in the provinces of Germania and the three Gauls (Belgica, Lugdunensis, Aquitania), the recipe and sources being described in some detail by Vitruvius (*De Architectura* 7.11.1; see Heck, 2005). If Engine Vein was another (earlier) mine worked for pigment, we should perhaps note that the Roman level meets the fault in the immediate vicinity of the azurite-rich mudstone band.

The typology of Roman workings

Some of the characteristics of these shaft-and-level workings have already been mentioned, such as large square shafts and coarsely picked walls. On the basis of current evidence it would appear that the walls of these Roman shafts were deliberately cut smooth *without* the use of slots or holes to hold in place wooden climbing stemples or staging. In this respect they differ from post-Medieval workings. In fact, we find that most of the seventeenth- to early nineteenth-century shafts on the Edge are narrower, more rectangular and generally more rounded in shape than the Roman example. In addition, the post-Medieval shafts are regularly cut with (stemple) beam slots and have finely picked walls (often this pick-work follows a 'herring-bone' pattern). A more distinctive feature of this Roman shaft-working is the rather significant twist of up to 90° in its axis and the variation in width over its depth

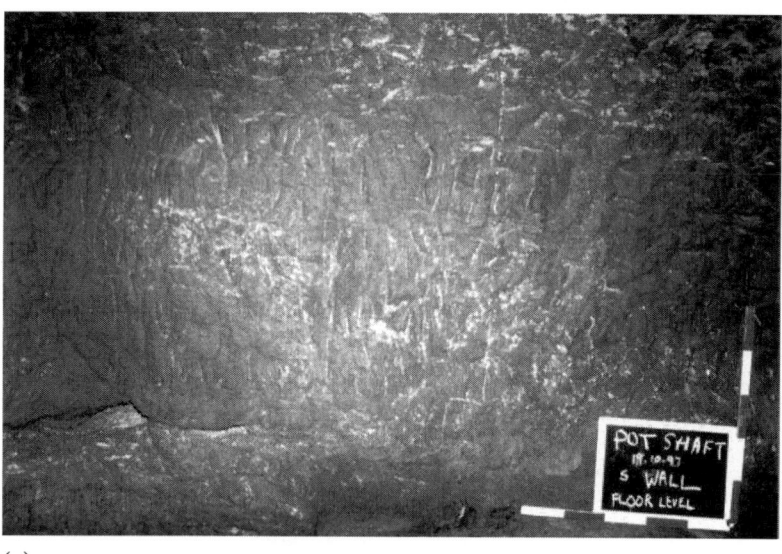

(a)

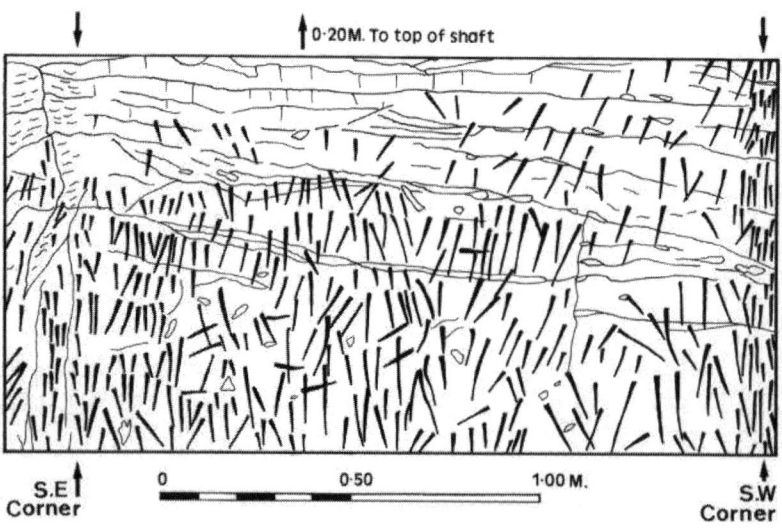

(b)

Figure 15.7. The pick-marks on the wall of Pot Shaft. (a) Photograph of detail. (b) Drawing of the same pick-marks.

Photograph Norman Rowcroft. Drawing Simon Timberlake.

of 13 m (Figures 14.10, 14.11). Certainly this twist is more than one would expect to find in a post-Medieval example. Of particular note are the crudely rounded corners to the shaft, and the almost vertical and coarsely executed pick-and-gad cuts upon the walls (Figure 15.7). These are unique and are not to be seen in later mining works on the Edge.

If further Roman shafts are uncovered on the Edge it is very likely that they will be of a similar design, or that the pick-and-gad tooling techniques will be comparable. However, finds of Roman artefacts such as pottery in the fill of these shafts are unlikely to be at all common. Much more probable is the inclusion of remnants of earlier mining debris, for example Bronze Age hammer stones, charcoal and calcined ore re-deposited within these later sediments. Roman levels are likely to be short, square or possibly rectangular in cross-section, in contrast to the tall, narrow and arched style typical of the seventeenth and eighteenth centuries. These levels would have been driven in order to work the higher-grade lead and copper ores present along the faults themselves, rather than the lower-grade mineralisation found in the malachite-cemented sandstones which we find on either side.

Medieval

There is no real evidence for any mining activity on the Edge during the Saxon or later early Medieval periods, but one can perhaps speculate that people may have been aware of the minerals beneath the surface and of their potential value.

The Domesday Book, compiled in 1086–87, describes part of the two 'Aldredelies' (Over Alderley and Nether Alderley) as being 'waste'. While this may mean no more than that the dues on the land had been withheld or attached to another manor, it is most likely that it refers to the desolation that followed the Harrying of the North in 1069; the account mentions both woodland and open ground, the latter perhaps reduced to heathland (Morris, 1978; Williams and Martin, 2003: 728–30; see also Chapter 19, especially p. 467). In this environment the presence of hollows and spoil left as a result of Roman and earlier mining would presumably still have been visible to those using and crossing the escarpment, perhaps even from some distance away, and we would expect the same to have been true of the scar formed by the earlier workings on Stormy Point for those approaching the Edge from the north or the east.

The actual amount of prospecting work carried out on the Edge before the sixteenth century will have been influenced as much by local demand for metal as by the restrictions or indeed stimulus provided by the supply of lead from the neighbouring mining fields such as those of

Wirksworth–Bakewell–Ashover and Matlock in the White Peak. Mining at Wirksworth was of considerable importance to the abbey of Repton during the ninth century, while a minimum of seven lead works were recorded as being at work in Derbyshire in 1086, with mining becoming a very important part of the local economy and legislature of the Peak from 1280 onwards (Ford and Rieuwerts, 1968).

The Flintshire mining field which lay just to the east of the Wirral on the Dee estuary may also have exerted an influence on local mining activity in Cheshire. For example, in 1301 we hear that merchants from Chester were providing a ready market for Welsh lead, and by 1312 lead (including perhaps Cheshire lead) was being locally smelted (Lewis, 1967). Depopulation in the later fourteenth century following the Black Death and the consequent demand for an agricultural labour throughout this period will have had a negative effect on the ability of local people to engage in mining. In fact, most early records of mining activity both in Wales and in England relate to disputes over land, the disturbance to property and livestock and watercourses, the felling of trees, and the damaging effects of smelting. However, around Alderley we hear only of disputes relating to turbary rights and to the burning of gorse, and this only from the late sixteenth century on: actual mining is never mentioned in the Court Leets at this time. The situation is described in greater detail in Chapter 19.

The Court Leet for 1598 refers to 'myne holes': this is the first written evidence for any mining activity at Alderley, but it would seem to suggest that these workings were already old by this time, and furthermore their distribution sparse; most likely they were of much less significance than the more recently worked marlpits or stone quarries. In fact, the first *direct* reference to mining does not appear until 1693; at this time we hear of mining being carried out under the direction of Thomas Legh of 'The Ridge' and his partners (*Quarter Sessions County Palatine of Chester 1559–1760*: 195; see Carlon, 1979: 46); this episode and the later history of the mines is described fully in the next chapter. This apparent lack of interest in mining during the Medieval period may well have been because the top of the Edge was still considered to be a 'waste'. Except for the purposes of rough grazing, little interest appears to have been shown in this common land before the seventeenth century.

Possible sites of Medieval mining

Saddlebole (SJ 860 780)

Roeder and Graves (1905a) suggest that the name Saddlebole refers to the presence of a 'bole' – a wind-blown (i.e. naturally draughted) lead-smelting furnace oriented to face the prevailing wind. They believed this furnace was located somewhere towards the end of the ridge, north of Stormy Point. Within this area they claimed to have found 'abundant' specimens of calcined lead ore (Roeder, 1901: 107), yet at no point do they provide any details of its location, or any description of the site itself. In fact, a recent geophysical and geochemical survey, field-walking and archaeological excavation have all but failed to find any traces of a lead-smelting site on the top of this hill (Timberlake and King in *ArchAE*: 33–57; Kidd and Taylor in *ArchAE*: 177–83; Timberlake in *ArchAE*: 223–55).

Nonetheless, on the summit of Saddlebole ridge, just to the east of the boundary bank (SJ 8603 7807), we find some of the shallowest and smallest levels on the Edge (Figure 15.8). These form a maze of small hand-picked and probably fire-set tunnels, without any true shafts and showing very little evidence of the minerals worked. As with other primitive-looking mine openings on the Edge, in the past these have been referred to as 'caves' (Roeder and Graves, 1905a). On the other hand, some traces of the lead mineral pyromorphite and of baryte veining suggest that these could have been early and probably unsuccessful trials for lead; to some extent this has been confirmed by an examination of the recent soil geochemistry (Timberlake in *ArchAE*: 235). However, immediately below these ancient-looking workings were a series of larger levels reminiscent of early nineteenth-century cobalt workings. Recent archaeological excavation of these galleries suggests

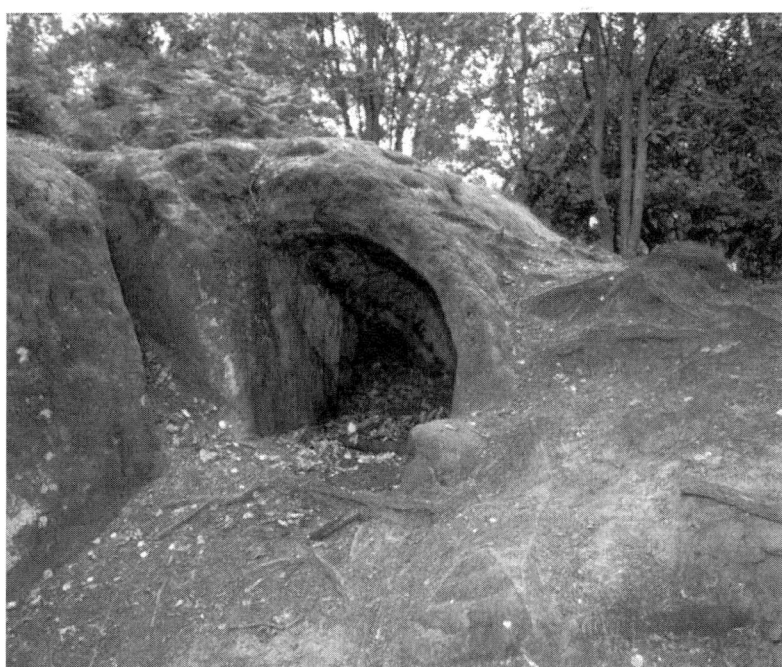

Figure 15.8. Arched adit entrance below Saddlebole ridge.

Photograph Sean Edwards.

that during the eighteenth or early nineteenth centuries the mine may have been (re-)worked for manganese ochre, used as a colorant in glass production (Kidd and Taylor in *ArchAE*: 183). Downslope from here, larger and more modern-looking tips suggest a considerable amount of mining undertaken over the years. On typological grounds alone, it would appear that the uppermost workings remain a promising contender for Medieval mining. In fact, Saddlebole ('Saddle boule') is mentioned in the 1598 perambulation, although the existence of any 'myne holes' here is not, either on or below the ridge.

Glaze Hill and Devils Grave (SJ 859 779 – 860 779)

Here we are dealing with circumstantial and etymological evidence and little else (the possible origin of the name 'Glaze Hill' is discussed in Chapter 28, p. 710). Throughout the Medieval and early post-Medieval periods a particular form of soft but non-silver-bearing lead ore was often described as 'potter's ore', referring to the use to which it was put on pots in the production of lead glaze – the familiar green glaze of Medieval wares (Bick and Wyn Davies, 1994).

There are mine entrances and lead mineralisation on both sides of Glaze Hill (including Rock Shaft, Twin Shafts and Reeking Mine), although none of the workings inspected by the author are thought likely to have had a Medieval origin. However, there are other workings in this general area of Stormy Point, such as Devil's Grave, which may be the mines referred to in the 1598 perambulation of the Edge: 'and so to the Mere Stone on top of ye hill and from thence on the north side the *Myne holes* directly to the Saddle boule' (our italics).

Rock Shelter (Wizard's Cave Mine or Iron Gates)

This is a small gallery (approximately 1–1.5 m high) cut into a bed of soft, partly mineralised Wilmslow Sandstone. The low-lying entrance (Figure 15.9) leads into a similar small chamber some 3–4 m wide with two rock-cut pillars left to support the roof. The working lies beneath the eastern edge of the earthwork circle on Stormy Point, with its entrance at approximately SJ 8607 7784. As with Saddlebole, this mine may have been an early trial for lead. It has clearly been worked with metal tools.

Graves describes and illustrates this working in 1901 (Roeder and Graves, 1905b) and refers to it as the rediscovered 'Iron Gates'. This and another small trial level some 10 m to the north might also be included among the 'myne holes' of the 1598 perambulation. The latter level, no more than 2 m long, has been driven on a fault, and has the appearance of a lop-sided arch, similar in some ways to the early mine entrance on the top of Saddlebole.

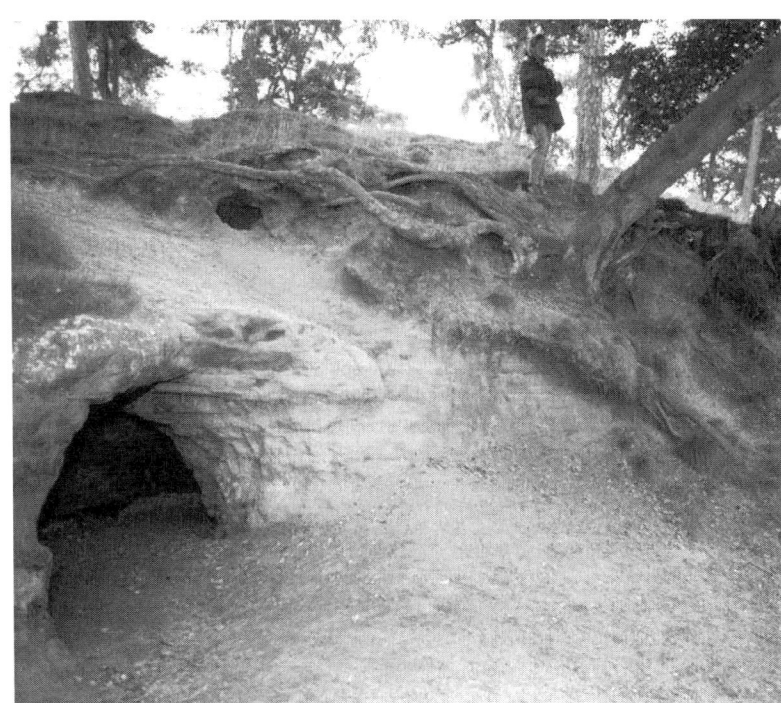

Figure 15.9. Entrance to 'Wizard's Cave' below Stormy Point.

Photograph Sean Edwards.

Canyon Mine opencast and rake (SJ 860 777 – 861 776)

Canyon Mine is an earlier opencast which was re-worked during the eighteenth and nineteenth centuries. This widening of the opencast (worked by pick as well as with explosives) has truncated five earlier workings. These are all small shallow opencuts or levels 1–3 m long that have been cut with iron tools, yet within them there is evidence for at least two different phases or types of working. Among the original features which survive are some that match descriptions to be expected of Medieval mining. All are in pebbly sandstone/conglomerates, their locations representing the junctions between several lead and copper veins running north-north-west to south-south-east and one running east to west. To the south-east the workings continue as an infilled rake or opencast, the latter associated with numerous small shafts. While some of these workings are clearly post-Medieval, other parts maybe significantly older than this still open section of opencast visible at its north-west end. This could not be the mine referred to in 1598. Although the track from 'Lingard's to the Beacon' mentioned in the perambulation is almost certainly the one just to the south of here, the actual 'trackway to the Myne holes' along which the perambulation was clearly taking place is undoubtedly the one which leads from the Goldenstone to Stormy Point.

Other possible sites

The large opening and internal galleries of Pillar Mine (SJ 8612 7783) may have been worked or re-worked during the Medieval period. There is a little but not much evidence for the use of metal tools, and possibly also for fire-setting, but unfortunately there are few original surfaces left to examine within the main entrance chamber.

It seems likely that there was mining at Engine Vein during the seventeenth century. Furthermore, some of the undated features referred to as Roman could be Medieval or early post-Medieval in date.

A flooded opencast and its northward continuation in the form of a buried trench or rake is located at the east end of Windmill Wood (SJ 8573 7736). This was already a drowned working in 1760, whose de-watering was supposedly the main reason for driving an adit in from the head of Brynlow Dell. This level was driven by Charles Roe of Macclesfield and his miners, yet it was abandoned some 50 m short of its target. The age of the flooded mine is unknown, but it may well pre-date the seventeenth century.

None of the workings described in this section can be assigned with any degree of certainty to the Medieval or even early post-Medieval periods. Excavation and dating of mining deposits at one or other of these sites may allow a better typology to be created. The field evidence would seem to suggest that many of the earliest workings were in fact trials, and it also seems that lead was the mineral being sought. This matches the picture one might expect for Medieval mining on the Edge.

A typology of Medieval and early post-Medieval working

There are several distinct types of early mine-working on the Edge which seem neither to be prehistoric or Roman nor to be similar to workings dateable to the eighteenth and nineteenth centuries. Likewise, these features do not match the descriptions of seventeenth-century mining, such as the works under way in 1693 under the direction of Thomas Legh of Ridge (see above, p. 360, and Carlon, 1979: 46).

These include shallow opencast trenches or rakes, most of them less than a few metres wide and with little evidence of tool marks on the walls. Moreover, where short lengths of tunnel have been driven along these faults, they are commonly irregular in profile, sometimes appearing as a lop-sided arch with the slickenside plane of the fault forming one wall, the other pick-cut wall curving over to meet it at about 90°. These workings could have been fire-set. Examples of this type of mining can be seen at Saddlebole, close to Wizard's Cave, and on the Canyon Mine rake. While such features cannot be thought of as symptomatic of Medieval mining, levels of very similar shape have been recorded from late Medieval lead and silver mines in Europe, such as those at Sainte-Marie-aux-Mines in the Vosges, France (Fluck, 1993). Other examples of similar but clearly fire-set workings have been seen by the author in a Medieval mine at Bouco-Payrol, Aveyron, in France. Unfortunately, similar features observed elsewhere in Britain remain undated. However, note the form of the early Medieval Lumbern Leat associated with the Bere Ferrers Mines in south Devon which is securely dated, and similarly shaped (Claughton, 1996). Nevertheless, one should be cautious in ascribing all fire-set adits to Medieval mining, for it is now known that some areas of the Peak District had a strong tradition of using coal fire-setting to work the mines, none of which appear to date from much before the seventeenth century (Barnatt and Worthington, 2006). 'Coffin levels' are, however, typologically different. These are typically narrow, meandering and carefully chisel-cut, as well as being slightly broader (over 0.5 m) at chest or shoulder height. Some could be late Medieval, yet by and large these levels are common in mines worked from the Elizabethan period up to the mid-eighteenth century (Smyth, 1846: 667).

The style of pick-work or grooves to be found on the walls of these pre-seventeenth-century workings are widely spaced and shallow, yet they are quite different again from the kind found in the Roman workings at Engine Vein. It is possible that this type of tooling represents hammer-and-gad rather than pick-work. Furthermore, all the workings identified were found at shallow depths, rarely more than 1 or 2 m from surface, most being of irregular height with sloping roofs and some very constricted sections of passage. In places very clear indications of fire-setting were found, such as at Saddlebole and Pillar Mine. This included reddening of the rock, a sign of burning, as well as the presence of smooth arched walls and roofs that progressively decrease in height, sloping downwards at the forefield or working end of the level. However, the presence or absence of fire-setting is something that is quite difficult to prove, particularly where the profile of the mine level has been considerably modified through the use of iron tools.

A slightly different kind of working is to be found at Wizard's Cave and Pillar Mine. These workings have the appearance of being excavated 'caves', with much larger areas of domed or flat roof supported by pillars. Mining excavations following along minor faults may have produced some of the walls of these galleries. Typically they were excavated into beds of softer sandstone, usually with disseminated copper mineralisation. Where visible, the tooling marks found here are generally quite similar to those described above. However, in other respects it is not easy to ascribe these workings to the same period or type of mining as that found on Saddlebole, Glaze Hill and at Canyon Mine.

Conclusion

There is good evidence at both Alderley Edge and Mottram St Andrew for localised prospection and mining for copper during the Early Bronze Age. Alderley Edge is one of twelve confirmed Bronze Age copper-mining sites in Britain, worked between 2100 and 800 BC, the most recently excavated example being at Ecton Hill in Staffordshire, only around 30 km from the Edge but exploited just marginally later (Timberlake, 2014). Like the majority of the British Bronze Age mines, Alderley Edge was exploited and then abandoned during the Early Bronze Age. This is in stark contrast to the much larger mine of the Great Orme in North Wales, which continued working right up till the end of the Middle Bronze Age. On the Great Orme, the malachite ore was considerably more abundant than at Alderley Edge and the limestone free-draining, allowing mining to extend to depths of over 30 m below surface, with a total prehistoric production variously estimated at between 25 and 1769 tons of copper metal (Timberlake, 2010).

The characteristics of these Bronze Age mining campaigns are now well recognised and documented. Nevertheless, there may have been an earlier exploitation of the colourful secondary minerals on Alderley Edge for use as pigments during the Mesolithic–Neolithic–Bronze Age, although the precise evidence for this is still lacking.

As with Bronze Age activity, the features of late Iron Age–Roman mining are likely to be quite distinctive. At the moment the only evidence comes from Engine Vein and most probably dates from the first century AD. It seems that this was a comparatively short-lived operation, yet it was sophisticated enough in terms of its mining engineering to suggest military control. Copper alongside lead and possibly also silver were most probably the metals sought. However, there is another possibility. This small-scale and probably short-lived operation could have had as its goal a more prestigious prize, the azurite pigment known as Egyptian Blue, a substance sought for the manufacture of a paint used in the decoration of wall plaster. A rather similar mine with beds also containing azurite nodules was recently excavated at Wallerfangen in the Saar in south-west Germany.

The evidence for Medieval mining on the Edge is rather less clear-cut. It is perhaps best to classify these features simply as examples of post-Roman and pre-seventeenth-century mining. On typological grounds alone it appears likely that some features relate to Medieval prospection, with lead probably being sought in preference to copper. Moreover, the evidence for early historical mining appears to be confined to the top of the Edge and straddles the parish boundary between Over and Nether Alderley. Most likely the ore extracted here was used in the manufacture of ceramic glaze ('potter's ore'), rather than in the production of metal.

Further reading

The most convenient work in which to pursue the topic of early mining on the Edge is:

Timberlake, S. and Prag, A. J. N. W. (eds). 2005. *The Archaeology of Alderley Edge: Survey, Excavation and Experiment in an Ancient Mining Landscape* (British Archaeological Reports, British Series 396). Oxford: John and Erica Hedges (abbreviated throughout the text as *ArchAE*).

16

Mining in the Alderley district: the documented period

Geoffrey Warrington

The Alderley mining district ('the district') in north-east Cheshire comprises land on Alderley Edge, in the northern parts of the parishes of Nether and Over Alderley, and to the north-east, around Kirkleyditch, in the adjacent parish of Mottram St Andrew (Figure 16.1). This chapter covers almost 330 years, from what is presently the earliest known written notice of mines, in 1598, until the dissolution, in 1927, of Alderley Copper, Limited, the last company to work mines in the district. (Imperial measures are therefore drawn upon in this chapter, but a note on metric equivalents is given on p. xlv.)

The mineralisation occurs in sedimentary rocks of Mid Triassic age. It consists largely of disseminations that are stratiform (concordant with the bedding of the host rocks), although some vein-like bodies occur, associated with faults. It is found almost exclusively in three conglomerate and sandstone units within the Helsby Sandstone Formation, the lowest of which is seen at Mottram St Andrew and on the northern and north-eastern sides of Alderley Edge (see Chapter 5; also Warrington, 2010). Successively higher units appear progressively in a westerly to south-westerly direction on Alderley Edge, where, during the period covered, the focus of mining appears to have moved broadly westwards, and upwards through the ore-bearing succession.

The principal metallic ores in the district are those of copper, an element that has long been of commercial and strategic importance (see Chapter 6; also Warrington, 2010). For example, from Tudor times, when, for want of indigenous expertise, German miners were brought to England, it was in demand for the production of 'battery' or brass for

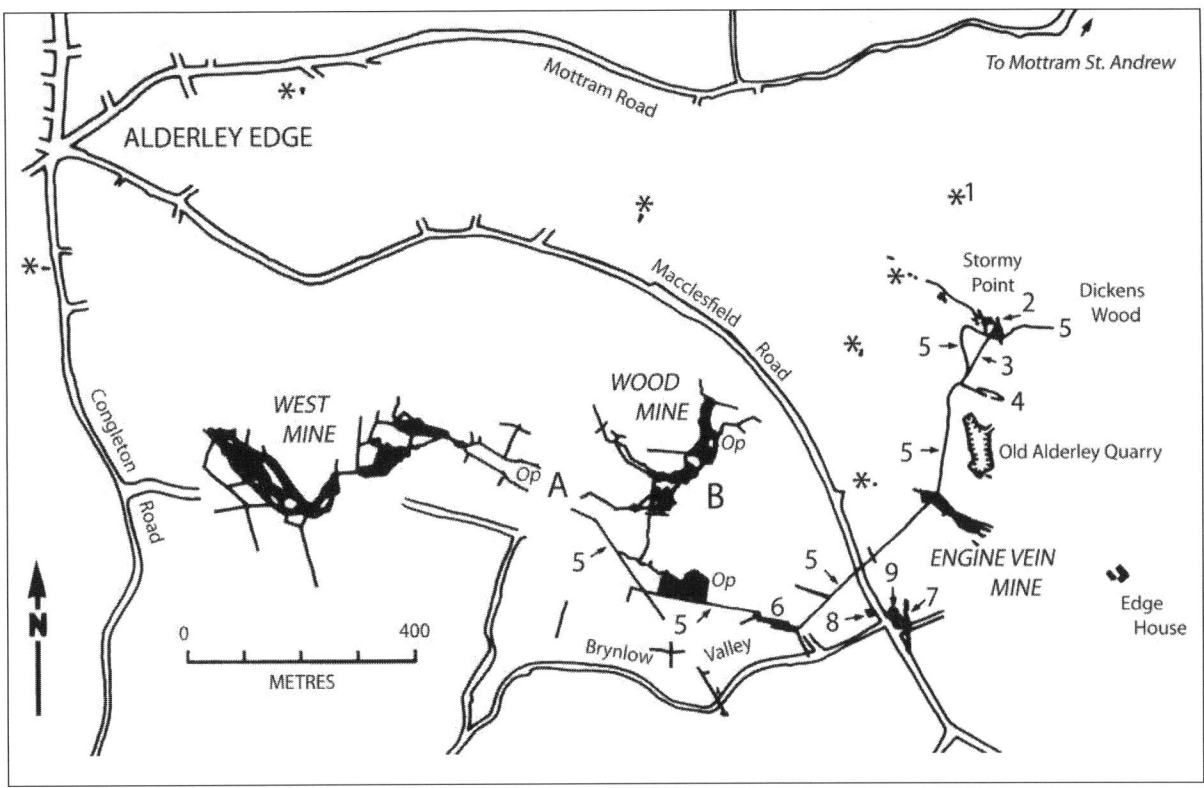

Figure 16.1. Mine workings at Alderley Edge. Full black – principal known workings, including opencast sites (Op: now infilled); ★ isolated minor workings or trials. A, site of the Alderley Mine Company's smelting house and steam engine (early nineteenth century) and the process works of the Alderley Edge Mining Company, Limited (mid-nineteenth century); B, approximate site of the Alderley Mine Company's windmill and ore crusher. 1, Saddlebole Mine; 2, Pillar Mine entrance (see Figure 16.2); 3, possible 'Abbadine' tunnel (see Figure 16.3); 4, Canyon Opencast; 5, 'Hough Level'; 6, Brynlow Mine; 7, 'Cobalt Mine'; 8, the 'Surgery'; 9, Wizard of the Edge restaurant (formerly the Miner Inn; see Figure 16.6).

After Warrington (1981: fig.2, with the addition of more recent underground observations).

ordnance (cannon). It supported the first leg of the 'triangular' trade, in which copper 'guinea bars' were shipped to west Africa, from where cargoes of humans were transported across the Atlantic to work in the colonies that provided commodities such as sugar, tobacco and cotton for the third, return leg, to the European market. In the late eighteenth century, copper sheathing of ships' hulls, which enhanced speed by combating fouling, created a fresh demand. During the Industrial Revolution copper was required not only as a raw material for brass manufacture and, in its own right, for rapidly diversifying industrial applications, but also for the coinage needed to pay the increasing numbers of workers attracted to the industrial areas. The development of electricity created new applications and broadened demands in the later nineteenth century.

In 1768, while operating mines at Alderley Edge and elsewhere, the Macclesfield-based enterprise of Chas Roe and Co. discovered a major body of copper ore at Parys Mountain, Anglesey, which later in the eighteenth century was the site of the largest copper mine in the world (Bevins and Mason, 2010: 264). Prior to that time, when most British copper mines were relatively small in scale, those in the Alderley district were probably no less significant than many of their contemporaries. However, they subsequently declined in importance until the mid-nineteenth century, when a method of treating their distinctive low-grade ore profitably was introduced at a time when many other British mines were closing in the face of competition from 'giant' producers in other countries.

The principal mining legacy in the district is at least eight miles of underground workings that are presently known in Alderley Edge (Figure 16.1) and which are largely accessible, as a consequence of the support of a local landowner and the National Trust for the efforts of the Derbyshire Caving Club (DCC). They constitute a unique geological and historical asset that contributed to the designation of the area as a geological Site of Special Scientific Interest (SSSI) and its inclusion in the Geological Conservation Review (Warrington, 2010). Surface expressions of mining and the remains of some related structures exist (see Timberlake in *ArchAE*: 135–44) but are not always obvious; implements and ephemera have survived from various parts of the documented period.

Sources on the chronology of mining in the Alderley district

An early contribution by the writer (Warrington, 1965) dealt largely with geological aspects of the district but included a summary of the mining history that was drawn from secondary sources and is un-satisfactory. In researching this subject further the writer has, wherever possible, used original sources or the earliest available authority. This research was made public in a Manchester Museum lecture (1977) and in one at the Grosvenor Museum, Chester (14 January 1978; recorded), and appeared in a publication (Warrington, 1981). Unless otherwise indicated, information in the present chapter is derived from that account and the sources noted therein, which are cited again only where necessary for clarity. The opportunity has been taken to expand or update parts of that earlier account and to introduce new material. An account of the effect of the mines on the life of the district, and of the part played by the Stanleys in their development or otherwise, will be found in Chapter 19.

The first notice of mines in the Alderley district

The Domesday surveys of 'Aldredelie' (Nether Alderley and Over Alderley) and 'Motre' (Mottram St Andrew) mention 'waste' but include no reference to mines (Earwaker, 1877: 4, 5; Tait, 1916). The earliest known written mention of mines in the district is in an account of a perambulation of the Nether Alderley–Over Alderley parish boundary in 1598 (*Stanley Notebook*). This was traced from the Goldenstone (SJ 8622 7763) to a 'mere Stone in the Track way Towards the Myne holes, and so To the mere Stone on the top of ye hill and from thence on the North side the Myne holes directly to the Saddle boule'. Whether these 'Myne holes' were active is not indicated, but mining evidently occurred there in or before 1598. The 'Myne holes' are among workings in the highest beds in the Wilmslow Sandstone Formation and the lowest in the overlying Helsby Sandstone Formation (see Chapter 5; also Warrington, 2010), around Stormy Point; some of these have been classed as 'Medieval' and 'post-Medieval' (Timberlake *et al.* in *ArchAE*: 165–6). A mine at the 'Saddle boule' (SJ 8603 7807), in the same geological situation, was not mentioned in 1598; following excavations in 1999 this is thought to be part Medieval, part nineteenth century (Kidd and Taylor in *ArchAE*: 182; see also Chapter 15 of the present volume).

Cheshire was included in the grant made by Elizabeth I in 1565 to venturers who in 1568 were incorporated as the Society of Mineral and Battery Works. Prior to 1565 other monarchs had granted rights to mine for metallic ores in various counties, with one made by Henry VII on 27 February in the first year of his reign (1485) covering 'all his Mines of Gold, Silver, Tin, Lead and Copper in England and Wales' and thus including Cheshire (Pettus, 1670: 19). The 'Myne holes' recorded in 1598 may reflect activity carried out under one or more of these grants. There appears to have been only limited interest in mining for copper in Cheshire during the existence of the Society of Mineral and Battery Works. In 1582, for example, the county was considered a potential market for, rather than a producer of, the metal (Donald, 1955: 214). Camden's *Britannnia* was first published in Latin in 1586 and the entry for Cheshire, as translated in the fourth edition, included mention of the county having 'salt-pits, mines, and metals' (Camden, 1772: 479). In 1624 Edmund Nicholson of London sought renewal of a lease previously held by him on mines in the Chester palatinate but whether these were at Alderley, and whether any mining had taken place there, is not known (Rees, 1968: 633). It is unlikely that any took place subsequently, for the renewal had still not been confirmed in 1630 and payment of rent due under the lease, though later remitted by the Society, was still being demanded in 1637. Pettus noted that 'Copper Mines containing some Gold and Silver are in ... Cheshire', and 'The best Lead oar containing Silver are [sic] in ... Cheshire' (1670: 6, 7). The only other copper mine in the county is at Bickerton, in the Peckforton Hills, some twelve miles south of Chester; the earliest documented mining there was in 1690, though shafts may have existed at the site before 1679 (Carlon, 1981: 28).

Legh and partners v. Crosse and partners, 1696

The earliest known contemporary record of mining activity in the district is in court records of a dispute over mine ownership in 1696 (Cheshire Archives and Local Studies (CALS), Quarter Sessions files, QJF 124/2, documents 88–93; see Bennett and Dewhurst, 1940: 195–7).

Thomas Legh, of 'The Ridge', an estate in Sutton Township about two miles south-east of Macclesfield, had by the 1690s sufficient capital to enter into partnership with two others and begin mining at Alderley Edge (Camden, 1772: map between pp. 478 and 479; Earwaker, 1880: 447, 449; Bentley Smith, 2005: 40). On 14 May 1696 one Timothy Mason testified that this partnership had been 'in quiet and peaceable' possession of copper mines in Nether Alderley for 'three yeares & a quarter or upwards' (i.e. probably since the beginning of 1693), until 'a forcible Entry was made upon them ... about three weekes agoe' (i.e. about 21 April 1696) by employees of Thomas Crosse and his partners, John Applebey (or Appleby) and Daniel Kingston. Anthony Goodman, steward and agent for the latter partnership for about a year, had stated on 11 May 1696 that it was 'Entituled to Certaine Copper Mines and a Smelting Milne in Over Alderley ... under a Lease for a great Many yeares yett to come from Sir Tho: Stanley Barr[tt]'; Goodman's time in this position suggests that this lease commenced early in 1695. On the same day, one Thomas Lowe stated that he had been employed at copper mines in Nether Alderley by Crosse and others 'for Sev'all Monthes Last past', suggesting that mining was being carried out by the Crosse partnership early in 1696, at the latest.

Legh and his partners had disputed the right of the Crosse partnership to work the mines. On or about 27 April, William Redditch, an employee of Legh ('who p'tends Some Interest in the Sd Mines'), threatened to murder Lowe if he worked for the Crosse concern, other employees of which were also intimidated. On 8 May, Goodman overheard two of Legh's employees plotting to gain possession of the mines, apparently at Legh's instigation. This attempt, on Saturday 9

May, was unsuccessful, as Goodman had locked the mine doors and placed workmen on guard. However, around 2 a.m. on Monday 11 May, Legh's men broke in and replaced the doors. On the following day these men were violently evicted from the workings and the Crosse interest was, presumably, re-established.

At the Quarter Sessions in Nantwich on 14 July 1696, those implicated on both sides of the dispute were 'bound to be of good behaviour', which seems lenient in view of the threats and damage reported (CALS Quarter Sessions files, QJB 3/5; see Bennett and Dewhurst, 1940: 197).

The testimonies record that the mine entrances could be locked and that equipment included a windlass and picks. However, the site of the workings is uncertain, as most statements refer to mines in Nether Alderley parish but Goodman referred to mines and a smelting mill in Over Alderley parish. Possible sites are where workings are close to or pass beneath the parish boundary in the Stormy Point area, or between there and the Engine Vein Mine (Figure 16.1). Bentley Smith (2005: 41–2) suggested that the dispute may have arisen because of legal uncertainties or an assumption by Legh and his partners that Derbyshire customs regarding lead mining also applied to what was then common land at Alderley. Support for the latter may be found in the use of the term 'Groves' or 'Grooves' in references to the mines by witnesses with allegiance to Legh, but not by those connected with Crosse. Also, the Legh concern may have ceased mining temporarily, and the opportunity then been taken by Sir Thomas Stanley, third Baronet (1652–1721) of the Old Hall, Alderley, to grant a formal lease to the Crosse partnership.

Thomas Crosse was a merchant of Liverpool and Chorley. Bentley Smith (2005: 207, 208) stated that his mother, Ann, was from the Yate family of Whitchurch, Shropshire, and suggested the possibility of a connection with early eighteenth-century mining by 'Abbadine' (see below) on behalf of a 'Shropshire gentleman'. However, this appears unlikely, as, in the pedigree of Crosse of Crosse Hall and Shaw Hill (Foster, 1873), Thomas's mother is recorded as 'Anne, eldest daughter of the Rev. Samuel Yate, of Middleton Cheney, co. North Hants'.

Applebey and Kingston were London merchants and businessmen with considerable interests in the copper trade. On 24 December 1697, 'John: Applebee' (*sic*) was one of twenty-three signatories to 'The humble Petition of The Brassiors, Workers and Traders in Copper, As also the Masters of the Copper Mills, in and about the Citty of London, whose names are hereunto subscribed' presented to the Lords Commissioners of His Majesty's Treasury (*Calendar of Treasury Papers*, 1697–1701: 120). William Hatch, another London merchant who signed this petition, was soon to be involved with Alderley. Legh and Crosse both appear to have moved away from mining shortly after the dispute in 1696. The former became the MP for Newton, near Warrington, in

1698 and died in 1703. The latter left the partnership with Applebey and Kingston and was replaced by 'William Hath' (*sic*) (Bentley Smith, 2005: 42); he died in 1706 (Foster, 1873). A copper works survived at Alderley after the events of 1696, for on 28 May 1698 William Hatch was signatory for 'self & Partners in ye Copper Workes of Alderlyedge in Chesshire' to 'The Humble petition of the Corporation of Copper miners in England, and Divers others concerned in the makeing of English Copper' (*Manuscripts of the House of Lords*, new series 3: 244, and original manuscript). This document gives no information about the Alderley mines but the partnership was evidently significant because the other signatories represented the important copper works at Bristol, 'Corbeck [*sic*: Caldbeck?] in Cumberland', and Redbrook (Gloucestershire), and the Governor and Company of Copper Miners in England. In the same year, Celia Fiennes, who made observations on mines and manufactories on her journey around the country, passed through Cheshire en route from Manchester to Northwich (Morris, 1949: 224), but made no mention of Alderley, perhaps implying that the 'Copper Workes of Alderlyedge' were inactive at that time.

The elusive Mr Abbadine

Henry Holland, in his survey of Cheshire that was largely compiled between July and September 1806, when he was still only eighteen years of age (Meteyard, 1871: 309, 363), recorded that mining had been carried out at Alderley Edge about 100 years previously, by a 'Mr. Abbadine', who was described as a Shropshire gentleman (Holland, 1808: 16) but whose identity is not yet established satisfactorily. Bentley Smith (2005: 84, 207–8) has reasoned that his name may have been Hibberdine, that he represented a Mr Yate of Whitchurch in Shropshire, and that the activity referred to took place in the early 1730s. This connection was based upon Ann Yate, the mother of Thomas Crosse, being from Whitchurch, Shropshire, but is unlikely, as her family was from Northamptonshire (see above).

In 1843 Louisa Dorothea Stanley (1799–1877), third daughter of John Thomas (1766–1850), first Lord Stanley of Alderley (1807–50), and Lady Maria Josepha Stanley (1771–1863), née Holroyd, wrote that William Faringdon, an old Alderley Park labourer alive in 1805, 're-membered the mines having once been taken on some kind of agreement by a Mr Abbadine, of Shropshire'. 'Abbadine' had a tunnel five feet high and three feet wide driven in sandstone from Dickens Wood to the engine-shaft near the great quarry and obtained sufficient ore to warrant construction of a smelting house near Edge House (see Timberlake in *ArchAE*: 235–6) but was ruined by his speculations (Stanley, 1843:

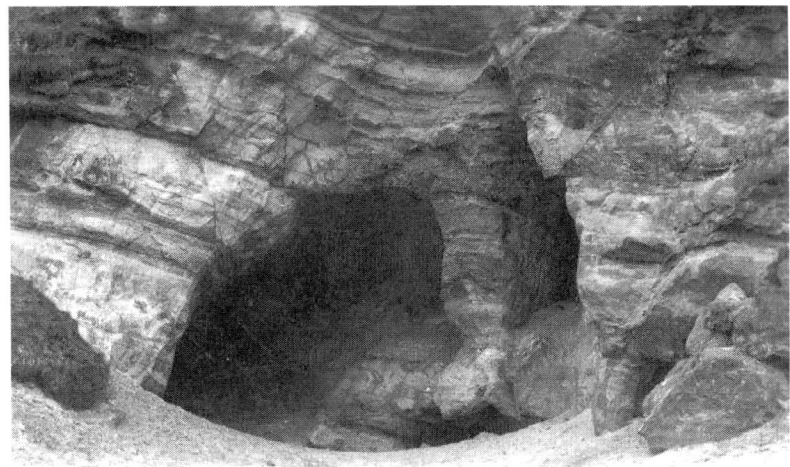

Figure 16.2. Old postcard showing the entrance to Pillar Mine, excavated in the Wilmslow Sandstone Formation; access to what some consider to be the 'Abbadine' tunnel (e.g. Carlon, 1979: 53) is visible at the lower right (see Figure 16.1).

Photographer unknown; author's collection.

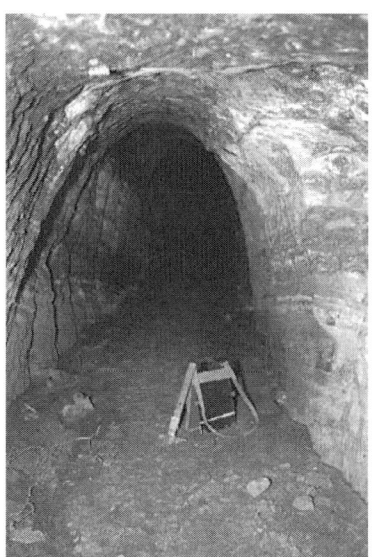

Figure 16.3. Inside what may be the 'Abbadine' tunnel (see Figures 16.1, 16.2).

Photograph Geoffrey Warrington, 1963.

33), though when that happened was not recorded. Holland (1808: 16–17) described the same tunnel, possibly from the same source, and added that it had been driven about thirty yards below the surface 'half through the hill' until it reached 'the centre', where it was found that 'the valuable part of the ore was considerably below the level of his tunnel' and the enterprise was abandoned. Though Faringdon was 'old' in 1805 (Stanley, 1843: 33) his testimony concerning events variously dated 70–100 years before that time must be based on hearsay.

The engine-shaft near the great quarry may be that at SJ 8606 7773, about 125 feet north-west of the Canyon Opencast (Figure 16.1;

ArchAE: plate 8). It is intersected at a depth of 86 feet by a tunnel that runs north-eastwards to Pillar Mine (S. Mills, personal communication, October 2008). The shaft extends down to 178 feet to join the 'Hough Level' (P. Deakin, personal communication, April 2006), an adit that runs from Dickens Wood (SJ 8619 7783) to Engine Vein, the Brynlow mines and Wood Mine (Figure 16.1). Warrington (1965: 113), writing when this shaft was infilled and depths could not be ascertained directly, regarded the northern part of this adit as the 'Abbadine' tunnel. Its entrance in Dickens Wood corresponds with Stanley's description (1843: 33) but it is now known to be at a greater depth than reported for that tunnel by Holland (1808: 16). Carlon (1979: 53) noted that the tunnel connecting the shaft with Pillar Mine (SJ 8613 7782; Figures 16.2, 16.3) was generally considered to be Abbadine's tunnel; if so, it was not driven about 1780, as stated by him. Though intersecting the shaft at a depth close to that reported by Holland (1808: 16) for Abbadine's tunnel, it did not encounter any ore bodies and would not have justified construction of a smelter. A nineteenth-century date has been suggested for this tunnel (Dibben cited by Pickin in *ArchAE*: 77).

Neither the Hough Level nor the 'Pillar Mine' tunnel appears to fit the limited hearsay descriptions of Abbadine's tunnel, which may, like one said to surface near Edge House Farm (Timberlake in *ArchAE*: 228), be as yet undiscovered and run to a presently unexcavated or unknown shaft near the 'great quarry' or the Canyon Opencast, or even towards Engine Vein Mine.

'Oar from Alderley Edge Mine', presented before 1740 to the Reverend John Pointer, MA, by Richard Dyer, a Fellow of Oriel College, Oxford, was described as 'Oar without mixture, & runs Copper ye first melting' (Gunther, 1925: 498); it may be representative of ore obtained there by 'Abbadine' and others prior to that date, when smelting was the method of treatment.

Holland (1808: 17) stated that since Abbadine's time, other companies had 'driven tunnels, and sunk shafts into various parts of the hill, but without finding an ore sufficiently pure to render the mine valuable. The last company … was that of which Mr Rowe [*sic*], of Macclesfield, was at the head'.

Chas Roe and Co. of Macclesfield

This enterprise in which Charles Roe (1715–81; Figure 16.4) was the principal partner obtained a lease to mine at Alderley Edge around 1755, either from Sir Edward Stanley, fifth Baronet (died 1755), or Sir John Stanley, the sixth Baronet (1735–1807), who succeeded him in that year (Stanley, 1843: 33–5). At that time the Edge was 'a wild dreary Common,

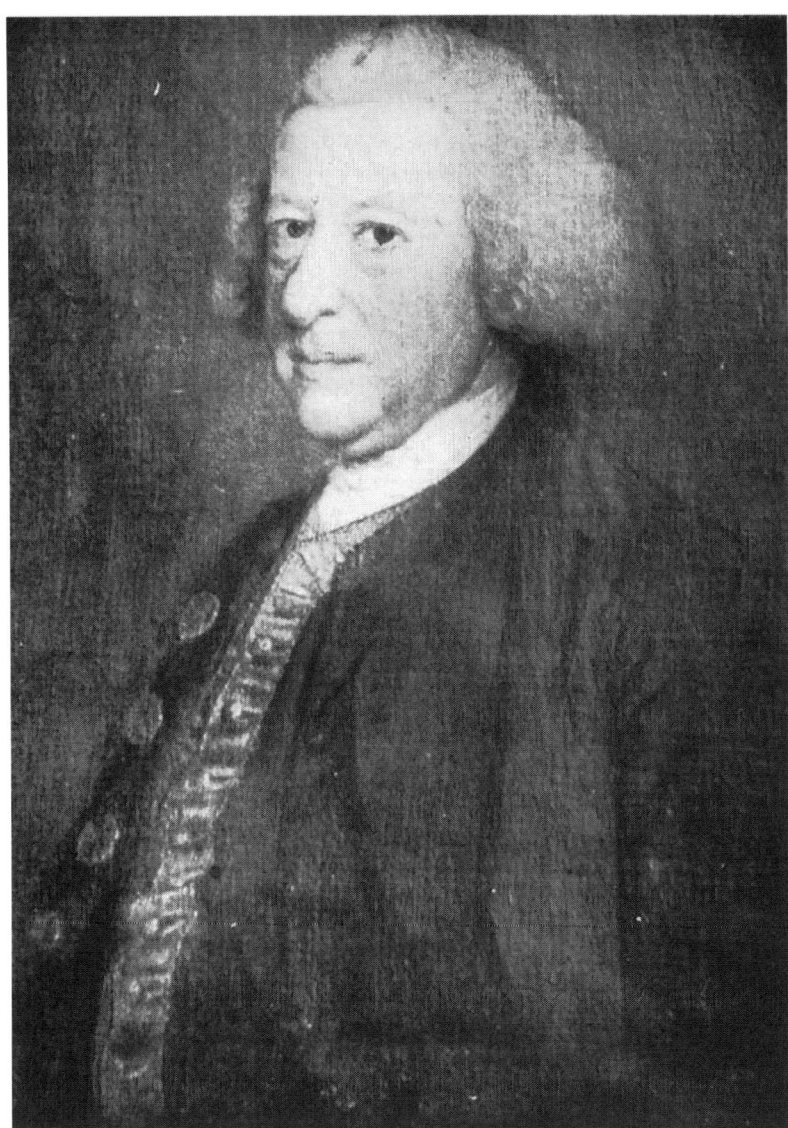

Figure 16.4. Charles Roe (1769), from the painting by Joseph Wright of Derby.

Christ Church, Macclesfield: photograph courtesy of the Churches Conservation Trust.

without any sign of cultivation, except the few clumps of hardy fir trees … planted … between … 1745 and 1755' (Croston, 1883: 78), a period enlivened, on 1 December 1745, by the Jacobite army passing just east of the district on its way to Derby (Stanley, 1843: 31). Before the firs were planted by Sir James Stanley, fourth Baronet (died 1746) and by Sir Edward, the Edge appears to have been devoid of trees, and it remained a 'dreary Common' until enclosed in 1779 (Stanley, 1843: 5–6).

Chas Roe and Co. had an important copper manufactory at Macclesfield and mined at Alderley Edge for some fifteen years, from around 1755 until about 1770, and, as the Macclesfield Copper Company (see below), returned there between *c.* 1788 and 1791 (Bentley Smith, 2005: 515–16). Chaloner (1953: 141) suggested that the company may also have mined at Kirkleyditch, Mottram St Andrew, but this is not supported by the authority cited (Earwaker, 1880: 357).

Holland (1808: 17) stated that Roe 'was at one time very sanguine in his expectations of success, and kept not less than forty or fifty men constantly employed'. Stanley (1843: 35) recorded that the company 'opened the tunnel in the Brinlow dell [*sic*]' (Figure 16.1) to drain water from old shafts, and 'kept twenty or thirty men at work, and for a time got a considerable quantity of ore, so much, it was said, as to give them a clear profit of £50 a week. Their tunnel, however, was not carried as far as they intended by twenty yards'.

Davies (1961: 115) referred, without clearly identifying the source of the information, to the miners staging a 'stay-in' strike, because they were paid less than quarrymen, but continuing in Roe's employ when the Alderley mines were abandoned.

The Roe company evidently carried out a significant amount of mining at Alderley but the only work specifically attributed to it is an unfinished adit in 'Brinlow dell', indicating that, in the middle of the eighteenth century, mining was taking place west of the Alderley–Macclesfield road. Excavations by the DCC in the Brynlow valley have given access to a small but complex mine, and may have located the unfinished adit (Johnson, 1984a: 10). An inscription ('I.W. 1764') in these workings (Johnson, 1984a: 12) indicates that they pre-date, or date from, the time of the Roe company. Bentley Smith (2005: 246, 252–3) has attributed this inscription to Josiah Wagstaffe, who was brought from the company's Coniston mine to deal with problems at Alderley, where flooding had occurred at Engine Vein Mine in 1763 (see also Chapter 22, pp. 576, 584–5 and Figure 22.2a, p. 573). The Brynlow Mine is considered to comprise eighteenth-century workings slightly modified by nineteenth-century activity (Johnson, 1984a: 12). The original levels are of coffin-type, and stoped areas are narrow and directly on a fault; similar features are seen in parts of the Engine Vein and Stormy Point workings (Figure 16.1) and may indicate that the Roe company carried out mining in those areas also. The ore body mined at Brynlow was probably first found in shallow surface pits, some of which were intersected by later mining (Johnson, 1984a: 12).

In 1768 the Roe company made a major discovery at Parys Mountain, Anglesey (Chaloner, 1954: 56), and its activities at Alderley ceased around 1770 (Bentley Smith, 2005: 331, 515). It had become a complex organisation which, following the signing of 'Articles of Partnership between Charles Roe Gentleman and other Partners in the Copper Company' on 7 August 1774, became the Macclesfield Copper Company (MCC) (Bentley Smith, 2005: 342–3). Alderley business lingered on, however, for at a general meeting in Macclesfield on 17 August 1774 it was directed, as Order 32, 'that Mr John Stafford's acc^{nt} be made out and delivered to him immediately', and on 19 August it was resolved, as Order 27, 'That it is desired that Mr Chas Roe & Mr Robt Hodgson do go to Mr Stafford & endeavour to settle with him the Debt due from him to the Co on y^e Alderley Edge mine. Acc^n £40 – 7 – 10^{2}/$_4$' (*Committee Book of the Macclesfield Copper Company 1774–1833*: English MS 1344, John Rylands Library, University of Manchester). Stafford had long been an associate of Roe, and prominent in Macclesfield affairs, but was declared bankrupt in 1773 and tragically ended his life in 1775 (Bentley Smith, 2005: 348, 373).

Whitfield and Heaton, Mr Patten of Warrington, and the return of the MCC

William Faringdon (see above) recalled that, *after* the MCC abandoned the Alderley mines, 'a Mr. Whitfield and a Mr. Heaton, from London, searched the Edge for ore' (Stanley, 1843: 35–6). This account by Faringdon relates to events in the thirty-five years prior to 1805 and is therefore more likely to have been from personal knowledge than that concerning 'Abbadine'. The Whitfield of this account may have been Joseph Whitfield, who from 1735 until 1776 was the London Lead Company's agent in Derbyshire (Raistrick, 1977: 153); the Heaton referred to may have been John Heaton, who around 1781 was the agent for the Duke of Devonshire (Bentley Smith, 2005: 434). According to Faringdon's chronology, Whitfield and Heaton's 'search' would have been between *c.* 1770 and 1776; interest by the important London Lead Company would have gratified the Stanleys but there was no report of any mining resulting. In spring 1779, the Old Hall in Alderley Park was burnt down, with the loss of records that may have been held there (Croston, 1883: 68; see also Chapter 19). However, new evidence (Carlon and Dibben, 2012: 51–2) suggests that Whitfield and Heaton's activity *preceded* that of the MCC and that the London Lead Company mined briefly at Alderley around 1736.

Faringdon recounted, again possibly from personal knowledge, that *after* Whitfield and Heaton abandoned their search, the mines were worked 'with some profit' by Mr Patten of Warrington (Stanley, 1843: 36; but see above). The Patten family had established a copper-smelting works at Bank Quay, Warrington, about 1717, and a brass works at Cheadle, Staffordshire, around 1725, to which a copper-smelting works was added before 1794; around 1790 the firm acquired a former tinplate works at Oakamoor, Staffordshire, for use as a copper rolling and slitting mill (Plant, 1881: 36; Keys and North Staffordshire Railway Society,

1974: 17). After the cessation of the MCC's operations at Alderley around 1770, the lease was taken up by the Cheadle Company, which worked there until 1 February 1787. Thomas Patten entered into a partnership with William Dumbell and Thomas Watkins in 1775; 'twelve copper furnaces were built on a new site at Warrington, Alderley ore was being treated and the mines were being worked with some profit' (Carlon, 1979: 48), but operations at Warrington ceased early in 1787 (Carlon, 1979: 48; Carlon and Dibben, 2012: 53). The MCC then appears to have conducted further work at Alderley, until about 1791. In that year a Mr Radcliffe reported to Sir John Stanley that 'The mine goes on well, but the lead ore is out in one place. The copper continues good. Yesterday I saw a quantity of rich copper ore drawn out; eight women are employed in dressing it, and a woman came out of Derbyshire to wash the lead' (Stanley, 1843: 36). Derbyshire methods of washing lead ore around this time have been described by Willies (1975). Radcliffe may have been the Stanley family steward of that name who died at Alderley Park in 1804 (Stanley, 1843: 51), some thirteen years after his report and three years before Sir John's death. If so, it is unlikely that he was the manager of the mine, as suggested by Roeder (1901: 109), or that he worked it (Carlon and Dibben, 2012: 53) or held the lease (Bentley Smith, 2005: 515–16) during what was probably the closing phase of the MCC's activity at Alderley.

Jonathan Aikin (1795: 49–50) noted that the copper and lead ore at Alderley, though found near the surface, 'is of too poor a quality to pay the expence of getting and smelting. It was attempted to be worked many years ago, and the attempt was not long since renewed, but without success'. Reference to the 'attempt ... not long since renewed' was probably an allusion to the activity reported in 1791 (see above) rather than to working in 1795, as stated by Carlon (Carlon and Dibben, 2012: 53). Charles Hatchett toured England and Scotland in 1796, visiting mines and manufactories and, like Celia Fiennes ninety-eight years earlier, passed through Cheshire (Raistrick, 1967: 108). En route from Manchester to Northwich he broke his journey in 'Altringham ... a small Town', less than ten miles from Alderley, which was not mentioned, possibly signifying that mines there were inactive in 1796. They were also probably inactive in 1799, when evidence was gathered for the 1803 *Report from the Committee appointed to enquire into the State of the Copper Mines and Copper Trade of this Kingdom (Great Britain)*, which made no reference to Alderley (*Reports from Committees of the House of Commons*, 1803, vol. X (miscellaneous subjects): 651–728).

Robert Bakewell noted, during a visit in the summer of 1810, that 'Copper ore was formerly got here in large quantities, as appears by the scoriæ or slagg which remains', but stated, incorrectly, that 'The works have been discontinued during nearly forty years' (Bakewell, 1811: 8).

The Alderley Mine Company

In 1806 Holland noted that, following 'the unexpected discovery of a few veins of good ore at the extremity of the old works, some gentlemen of Stockport were induced to recommence the speculation. Their prospect of success appears, at present, good; large quantities, both of copper and lead ore have been obtained, and they are now engaged in the erection of works for preparing and smelting it' (reported in Holland, 1808: 17). Lysons and Lysons (1810: 413) stated, in a broadly similar account, that in '1803 some gentlemen of Stockport were induced, from the discovery of a good vein at the extremity of the old works, to open a mine … and buildings have been erected for crushing and smelting the lead ore'; however, the date given in this account appears incorrect (see below).

These observations relate to activity that followed investigations made in 1804 by one James Ashton, described as a Derbyshire miner, as a result of which the Alderley mines were leased by Sir John Stanley for fourteen years from 1 January 1805 to a partnership that, according to Louisa Dorothea Stanley (1843: 36), included Ashton, Messrs Bury and Dodge of Stockport, Messrs Horne and Stackhouse, Dr Jarrold and others, and was known as the 'Alderley Mine Company' (AMC) (*Stanley Estate Book, 1800–1808, C7*; hereafter *Stanley C7*). The lease, to Bury and Dodge, stipulated a royalty of 10 per cent of the merchantable ore (National Library of Wales manuscript 15475 D; hereafter NLW 15475 D). However, according to an agreement made on 1 January 1808 (kindly made available to the writer by N. J. Dibben, October 2006), the original partnership comprised only Jeremiah Bury of Heaton Norris, 'Cotton Manufacturer', Samuel Dodge of Stockport, 'Mercer', and James Ashton of Over Alderley, 'Labourer'. Bury and Dodge had a good opinion of the 'Skill Honesty and Diligence' of Ashton and his inclusion was to relieve them of the 'Trouble of the Attendance and Management of the whole Business'. The AMC was a joint stock enterprise of £1,000, in which the three partners were each liable for £250, to be paid as and when required; the remaining £250 was covenanted by John Thomas, first Lord Stanley of Alderley. Ashton, however, could defer his payments and have his salary of £1.11s.6d per week, for managing and superintending the enterprise, withheld until any outstanding liabilities were discharged. By 1808 about £4,000 had been expended on the mine, and individual liabilities had increased to £1,000. Ashton appears not to have made any contributions, as about £245.14s.0d in salary had been withheld. His outstanding liability, of about £754.6s.0d, was reduced to about £254.6s.0d when, by the agreement made in January 1808, Thomas Jarrold of Manchester, 'Doctor of physic', took half (£500) of Ashton's share in the joint stock and was admitted to the partnership.

The AMC rented properties known as 'Chantlers or Topps', and 'Timperleys or the Hagg' (NLW 15475 D; *Stanley C7*), west of the Alderley–Macclesfield road, and probably mined largely in the Windmill Wood and Brynlow areas. In 1807–08 the rents on these properties were £9 and £40, respectively (*Stanley C7*: 57–8, 65–6). In addition to these properties the company had, at some time, '2 Cottages near the Mottram Pitts, The Windmill, The Smelting house, a Cottage near the Windmill on the Edge, Plowes Cottage & weighing Machine, and Land' (NLW 15475 D). The windmill, situated in Windmill Wood (*Stanley C7*; *ArchAE*: fig. 8.10a – see Figure 18.3, p. 442), was used to drive an ore crusher until superseded by a steam engine (Stanley, 1843: 32; see also below); 'Plowes Cottage & weighing Machine' were connected with the early phases of mining for cobalt ore (see below). The *Stanley Notebook* (pp. 243–5) records that a small dwelling adjoining Mottram House (SJ 859 768) was built by the AMC, and that James Ashton, the company's agent, occupied 'Topps', a tenement on the 'Brinlow' (*sic*) road (SJ 8497 7702). In 1807 Ashton occupied the latter property, as 'Chantlers', under a lease for the life of Samuel Topps (died 1810), and at a rent of £1.2s.6d (*Stanley C7*: 61–2). A house at the Hagg (SJ 8538 7744) was built about 1746 by Daniel Deane, whose daughter married Frank Timperley; after Timperley left it was converted by the AMC into dwellings for its labourers. A smelting house erected on waste ground behind and above this house was later 'pulled down and re-erected in almost the old form at the End of the Park wood', where, as Beechtree Lodge (SJ 8513 7614), it was occupied by two families. A windmill erected on the same ground (Figure 16.1; *c.* SJ 856 776) to crush ore proved inadequate and was moved to Winnington for brine pumping; it was replaced by a steam engine (see below) erected on the Hagg tenement, and there were troughs for washing the crushed residue.

The expenditure incurred between the inception of the AMC in 1806 and the enlargement of the partnership in 1808 suggests that, despite the initial optimism, the enterprise had little or no success. The situation evidently did not improve, for, in the summer of 1810,

> an attempt was made again to get the ore, and a furnace erected for reducing it. I was there the day after the trial, which had not succeeded, owing to the poorness of the ore, and want of skill in the persons employed. (Bakewell, 1811: 8)

The 'scoriae or slagg' Bakewell observed then may have been partly the product of these early nineteenth-century activities.

The AMC appears to have been dissolved before August 1812, probably shortly after the abortive attempt to smelt copper ore reported by Bakewell, and despite the recognition, within the first two years of the company's existence, of cobalt ore at Alderley.

The Alderley-based cobalt industry

A pulverised glass, produced by fusing blue cobalt oxide, powdered flint and potash, and known as 'smalt', was used for ornamenting porcelain, staining glass and as an early 'blue-whitener' for tinting writing paper and in the powder and stone blue used in laundries. Indigenous sources of cobalt oxide were limited and when supplies of smalt from mainland Europe were interrupted during the Napoleonic wars the discovery of cobalt ore in Cheshire elicited considerable commercial interest. This discovery was probably made at Mottram St Andrew (see below), where the ore had been noted before Holland compiled his survey of Cheshire in 1806 (Holland, 1808: 17), and is attributed to a miner who had seen cobalt ore in Saxony (Bakewell, 1811: 8). The ore was also recognised at Alderley Edge, allegedly by James Ashton (see above; Adeane, 1899: 322) or by 'Mr Plowes, of the Pontefract company' (Stanley, 1843: 36), and on 11 October 1806 was mentioned by Peter Holland, father of Henry Holland, to Josiah Wedgwood II (Wedgwood MSS L2-266, Wedgwood Museum, Barlaston). Samples were sent to Wedgwood for examination but Peter Holland, writing to Wedgwood on 7 January 1807, noted 'From your report of Mr Stanley's ore of Cobalt, I am afraid he has no reason to expect it to be of much value' (Wedgwood MSS L2-269). Nonetheless, on 1 October 1807, Maria Josepha, Lady Stanley, informed Louisa Stanley that £1,000 per annum, plus a tonnage payment for all in excess of a certain amount, had been offered for the Alderley cobalt ore; she hoped that 'this year the concern will begin to be profitable, though I do not expect my diamond necklace quite yet; when the Man has made 5,000*l* by the mine, I am to have a very handsome one' (Adeane, 1899: 297–8). The cause of this optimism soon became apparent.

On 8 April 1808 Peter Holland informed Wedgwood that supplies of cobalt ore from Alderley had been 'let a few weeks ago to some gentlemen concerned in a pottery at Ferry bridge, for 2,000*l* p ann., exclusive of his lord's share, which will amount to about 400*l* p ann. in addition. – Seaton & Plough is the name of the firm who have taken it – They are limited as to the quantity of ore, & are to pay in the same ratio for all above this quantity.... They were very anxious to have the contract signed; but keep, for the present, secret their intended application of it' (Wedgwood MSS L2-278). This agreement, which appears to have been finalised early in 1808, was made with a Mr Plowes (Stanley, 1843: 36), who is commonly cited as from 'the Pontefract company'. He was, however, John Plowes Jr, of Tomlinson, Plowes and Company of the Ferrybridge Pottery, Yorkshire (Figure 16.5), who was to be paid travelling expenses and may have become a representative of that firm (Lawrence, 1974: 149). Reference to 'Plowes Cottage & weighing Machine' in the Alderley estate records (NLW 15475 D) reflects a direct

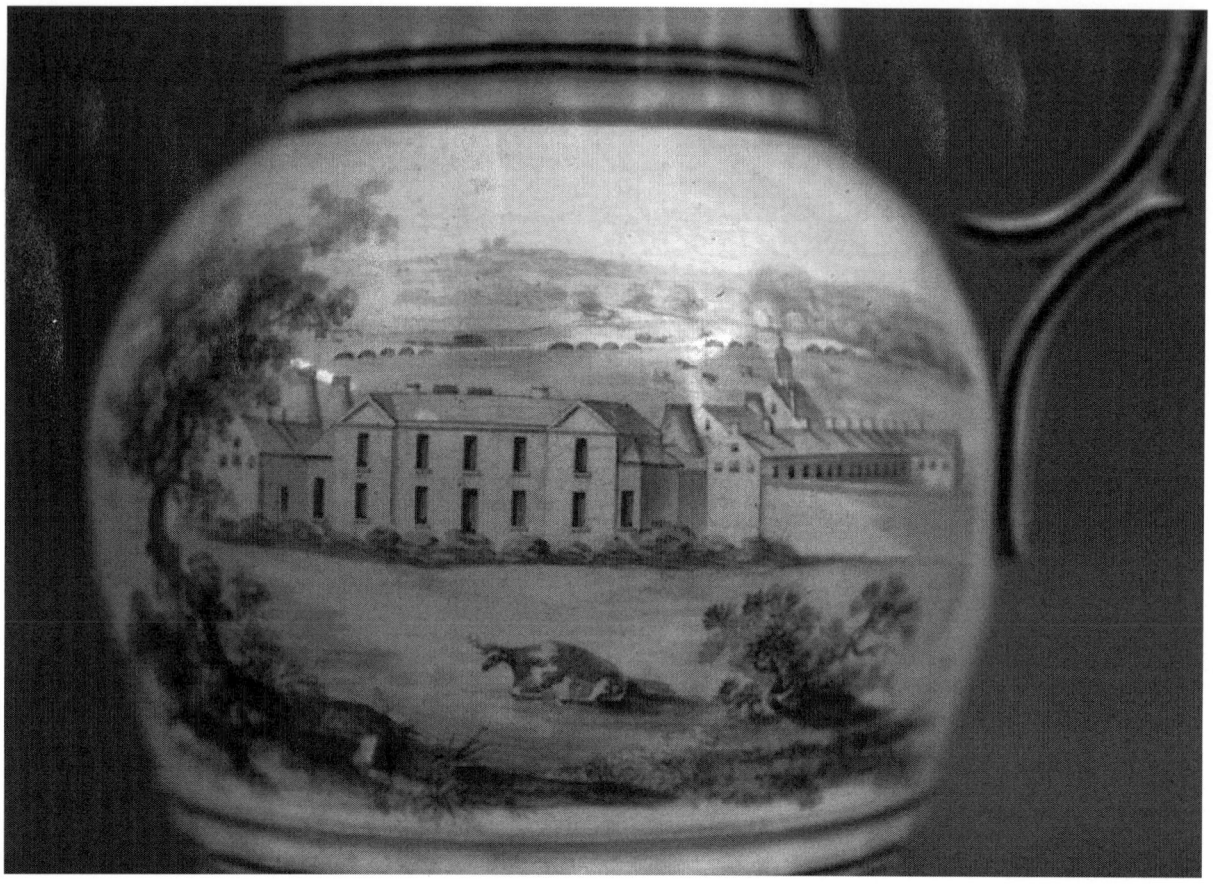

Figure 16.5. The Ferrybridge pottery, depicted on the 'Cambrian Pottery' jug (identification by Bidgood, 1978).

National Museum of Wales Cardiff, registered number 2353; Morton-Nance Bequest. Photograph Geoffrey Warrington, 1976.

involvement by the Ferrybridge concern in securing a supply of cobalt ore from Alderley. The ore, described as blue-black grains, similar to gunpowder, disseminated in red sandstone or lying in thin seams, was 'got out in thin pieces, and separated afterwards as much as possible from the stone; it is then packed in tubs and sent near Pontefract, where it is manufactured into smalt' (Bakewell, 1811: 8). According to John Thomas, first Lord Stanley of Alderley, a considerable quantity of this material was conveyed to Ferrybridge, where it was turned into smalt 'little inferior in colour to that imported from Saxony' (Lysons and Lysons, 1810: 413). However, the agreement with the Ferrybridge company appears to have been terminated after little more than one year, probably because of financial or other difficulties that resulted in work at Ferrybridge being suspended at the end of 1810 (Bakewell, 1811: 9; Lawrence, 1974: 150), rather than deficiencies in the supply or quality of the Alderley ore. Indeed, cobalt ore production continued at Alderley and a treatment works was established at Wallasey; this was operated by the Secombe Cobalt Company (NLW 15476 D). Experiments there were observed by Lord Stanley in October 1809, after which Maria Josepha, Lady Stanley, wrote to Louisa Stanley that 'Nothing can be more agreeable than the prospect of the riches held out to us' (Adeane, 1899: 322). In the following month 'The labourers had a shilling each' in recognition of the jubilee of George III on 13 November, and the Stanleys 'went to the Edge to see the miners eat and drink' (Adeane, 1899: 323), a spectacle possibly witnessed in anticipation of the wealth to be derived from their efforts. At this time Holland (1811: 40, fig. 1) recorded 'masses of sulphate of barytes' and lead, copper and cobalt ores at Alderley Edge. The cobalt ore was illustrated by Sowerby (1811: facing p. 69), who hoped 'for the owner's sake, this may become more profitable than hitherto, and lead to the acquisition of the more perfect substance. This is so mixed with Sand, Oxide of Copper, Manganese, &c, that it is of but little value as an Ore of Cobalt' (Sowerby, 1811: 69). Nevertheless, in August 1812 Maria Josepha, Lady Stanley, informed her aunt Sarah Martha Holroyd that 'We have been at Liverpool and seen the cobalt works going on very prosperously … pale smalts are in great demand among the linen-bleachers of Ireland. The Seacombe Company [*sic*] can provide this article equal in goodness and … sell it at a lower price than the foreign market, even if the trade with Holland becomes free again' (Adeane, 1899; 337–8). However, this company was probably the Secombe Cobalt Co. (NLW 15476 D: 218), which was interpreted as manufacturing glass without a licence and was charged by the Excise for unpaid duty, a demand which, though subsequently dropped, seriously affected the business (Bakewell, 1813: 347–8; Hunt, 1884: 162, 259) and resulted in its dissolution in 1814 (NLW 15476 D: 218). It was succeeded by the Seacombe Company, which, as the Seacombe Smalt Company (NLW 15476 D: 218), lasted only until July 1817 (Warrington, 1981: 57), when, under competition following the resumption of imports from Europe after the Napoleonic wars, the enterprise was abandoned, its property sold and the profits divided among the partners (Stanley, 1843: 37). Timberlake *et al.* (*ArchAE*: 144) suggested that no more than 300 tons of cobalt-rich concentrate may have been produced from workings on Alderley Edge.

Workings thought to be those from which the cobalt ore supplied to the Ferrybridge and Wallasey works was obtained were discovered adjacent to the Wizard of the Edge restaurant (SJ 8591 7731) (Figure 16.1) in May 1984 (Johnson, 1984b). They were named the Wizard's Well Mine after being first accessed via a well (SJ 8594 7731) to the rear of the

restaurant (Johnson, 1984b: 17), but are now generally known as the
Cobalt Mine (e.g. Timberlake and Mills, 2003), to avoid confusion with
the Wizard's Well (SJ 8548 7803), about half a mile to the north-north-
west, on the north face of Alderley Edge. The workings follow a fault
zone that trends north–south and have been explored for some 165 feet
north and 265 feet south of 'Tom's Shaft' (Timberlake and Mills, 2003:
fig. 3), situated (SJ 8593 7731) under the National Trust information
centre adjacent to the Wizard restaurant, and may extend further in
each direction (Timberlake and Mills, 2003: 42). When cobalt ore was
being mined, the restaurant was a public house, built around 1780, that
was known as Pogmores or the Miner Inn or the Miner on ye Edge and
was rented to John Pogmore (NLW 15475 D; *Stanley C7*); the rents in
1807–08, 1809 and 1810 were £12, £30 and £9 respectively (*Stanley C7*:

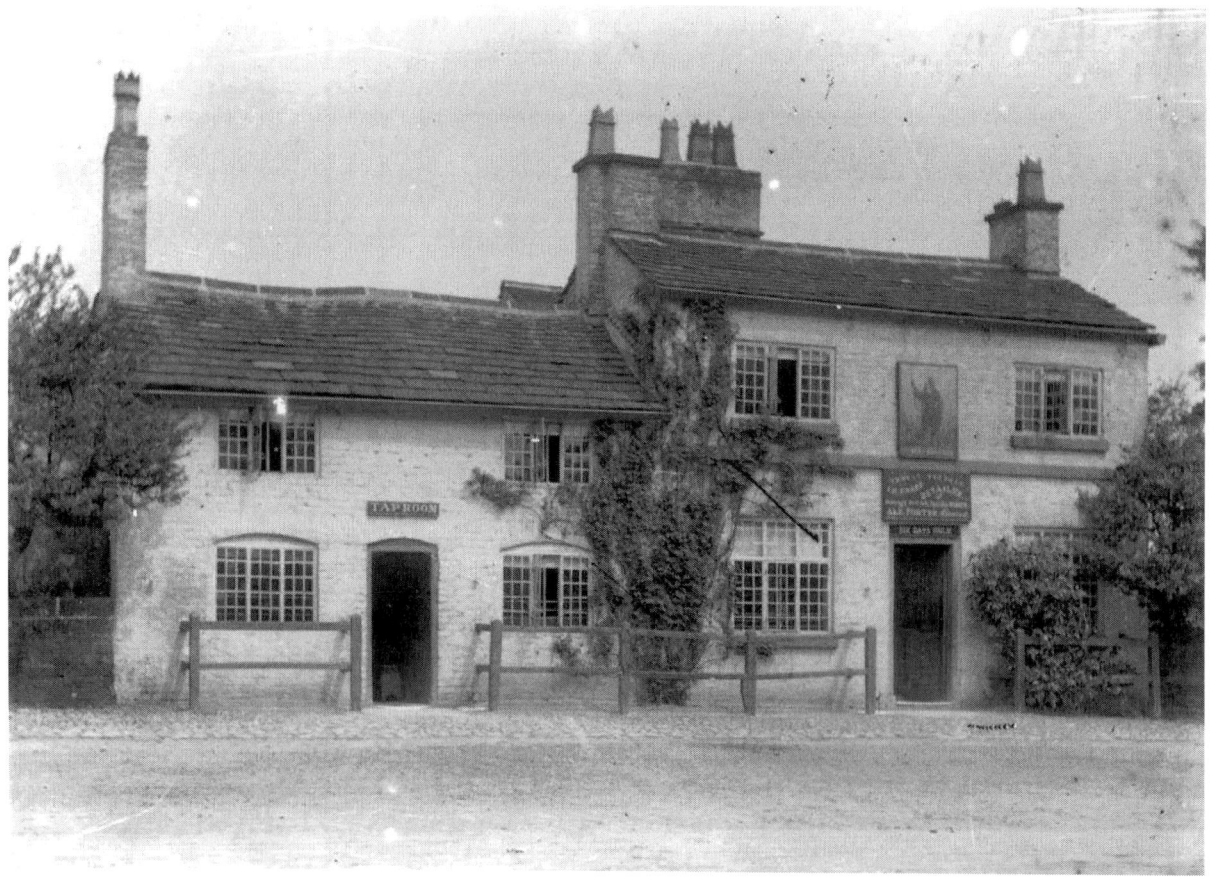

Figure 16.6. Old photograph of the public house formerly known as Pogmores or the Miner Inn and
sometimes as the Miner on ye Edge, and in more recent times as the Wizard of the Edge (a restaurant) (for
its location see point 9 in Figure 16.1).

Photographer unknown. Author's collection.

71–2). The AMC held meetings in this building which was extended for that purpose at that company's expense (*Stanley Notebook*: 243). Of interest is the identification of other buildings associated with the mining activity at that time, particularly 'Plowes Cottage & weighing Machine'. A contemporary map (*Stanley C7*) shows structures identifiable as the windmill, the smelting house and a cottage near the windmill. However, a building (SJ 8587 7733) across the Macclesfield road from the public house, and therefore close to the adjacent mine, remains unattributed and may be Plowes' Cottage. This building is not marked on Crossley's plan of the Stanley estate (1787) but is shown on a derivative of that map (in *Stanley C7*). It is now known as 'The Surgery' (Figure 16.1) and used by the DCC. A Mr Lawton, a tenant of the public house around 1850, by which time the inn (Figure 16.6) had become a temperance establishment and renamed the Wizard of the Edge, was described as a 'veterinary surgeon' (Anon., 1913: 11).

The Alderley steam engine

The Industrial Revolution may be said to have reached Alderley in 1807, rather later than elsewhere in north Cheshire. On 1 October that year, Maria Josepha, Lady Stanley, informed Louisa Stanley that 'The Edge has become a very busy scene. The steam-engine is finished and set to work' (Adeane, 1899: 297). The engine was erected near the smelting house and cottages at the Hagg (Stanley, 1843: 32). A contemporary map (*Stanley C7*; *ArchAE*: fig. 8.10a) shows a building with a smoking chimney in this area (*c.* SJ 8527 7750) (Figure 16.1), in the southern part of a field known as Lower Oldham (see below). There is no other contemporary information about this engine, which was introduced by the AMC to drive an ore crusher that had previously been powered by a windmill at a site some 1,150 feet to the east-north-east (see above, and Stanley, 1843: 32). However, research by the writer suggests that it was a ten-horsepower Boulton and Watt machine made for Alexander Hunt and installed in his Stockport cotton mill in 1792. This engine was transferred to Messrs Randall and Allcock in 1801 and used in brick-pits at Stockport; in 1806 it was acquired by Samuel Dodge of Stockport. The Boulton and Watt papers (Central Library, Birmingham) contain no reference to Alderley (Cheshire) or the AMC. The suggestion that this machine was the one erected at Alderley in 1807 is based upon the likelihood that Samuel Dodge, the last recorded user of the engine, and the Samuel Dodge of the AMC are one and the same. If so, Jeremiah Bury, who had erected an eight-horsepower Boulton and Watt machine, only the second steam engine in Stockport, in his cotton mill in 1792, and installed a larger (thirty-horsepower) machine there in 1799, may have influenced Dodge, his partner in the AMC, to replace the inadequate power source of the windmill at Alderley with the steam engine he had acquired in 1806.

Later nineteenth-century activity

Following the demise of the indigenous cobalt industry, the Alderley mines appear to have been abandoned for around forty years, until James Michell, a Cornishman, initiated what was probably their single most productive and profitable phase. Around the mid-point of this interregnum Alderley Edge was noted as a locality for 'Indurated black cobalt ochre, in red sandstone; iron; blue carbonate of copper; lead' (Tooke, 1837: 40), and Norbury recalled some forty years later that it had been 'a black hill covered with the earlier forms of vegetation, mosses, ferns, brambles, larches, etc., and … only a house on the top for the Keeper and one or two cottages on the western slope' (*Alderley, Wilmslow and District Advertiser*, 20 January 1877). In May or June 1841 Maria Josepha, Lady Stanley, wrote to Henrietta Maria Stanley that 'My Lord seems quite happy with Sir Philip [Sir Philip de Malpas Grey Egerton] geologising and mineralogising' (Mitford, 1938: 9) but her correspondence in 1848 and 1849 revealed darker aspects of those times at Alderley, including occurrences of smallpox and cholera (Mitford, 1938: 158, 207).

After 1856, mining in the district was carried out largely by companies established under the Joint Stock Companies Acts of 1856 and 1857, or subsequent statutes. Their records, together with Robert Hunt's *Mineral Statistics of the United Kingdom*, published annually from 1855, and, from 1 January 1873, the returns and inspectors' reports required under the Metalliferous Mines Regulation Act of 1872, comprise valuable formal contemporary documentation. These resources and other contemporary material, including mine accounts books, trade periodicals and scientific and other publications, have enabled the compilation of a relatively comprehensive, though inevitably still incomplete, account of the last seventy years of the mining history of the district (see Warrington, 1981, and below).

James Michell (1796–1862) and the Alderley Edge Mining Company, Limited

The Alderley Edge Mining Company, Limited (AEMCL) was formed following investigations by James Michell, who, in the summer of 1857, entered into an agreement concerning mining on the Alderley estate with Edward (1802–69), second Lord Stanley of Alderley (1850–69). Initial trials were successful and a lease covering mining from the Stormy Point–Engine Vein area westwards towards the Alderley–Congleton road (Figure 16.1) was granted on 12 April 1858; a supplementary grant was made on 5 May 1859. These interests were transferred to the AEMCL, which was incorporated on 13 August 1859, with a nominal capital of £10,000 in £10 shares which were initially held by Michell and seven others, all of whom were of West Country origin; Michell was the principal shareholder and a director of the company. The company established its process works near the Hagg cottages, where the AMC

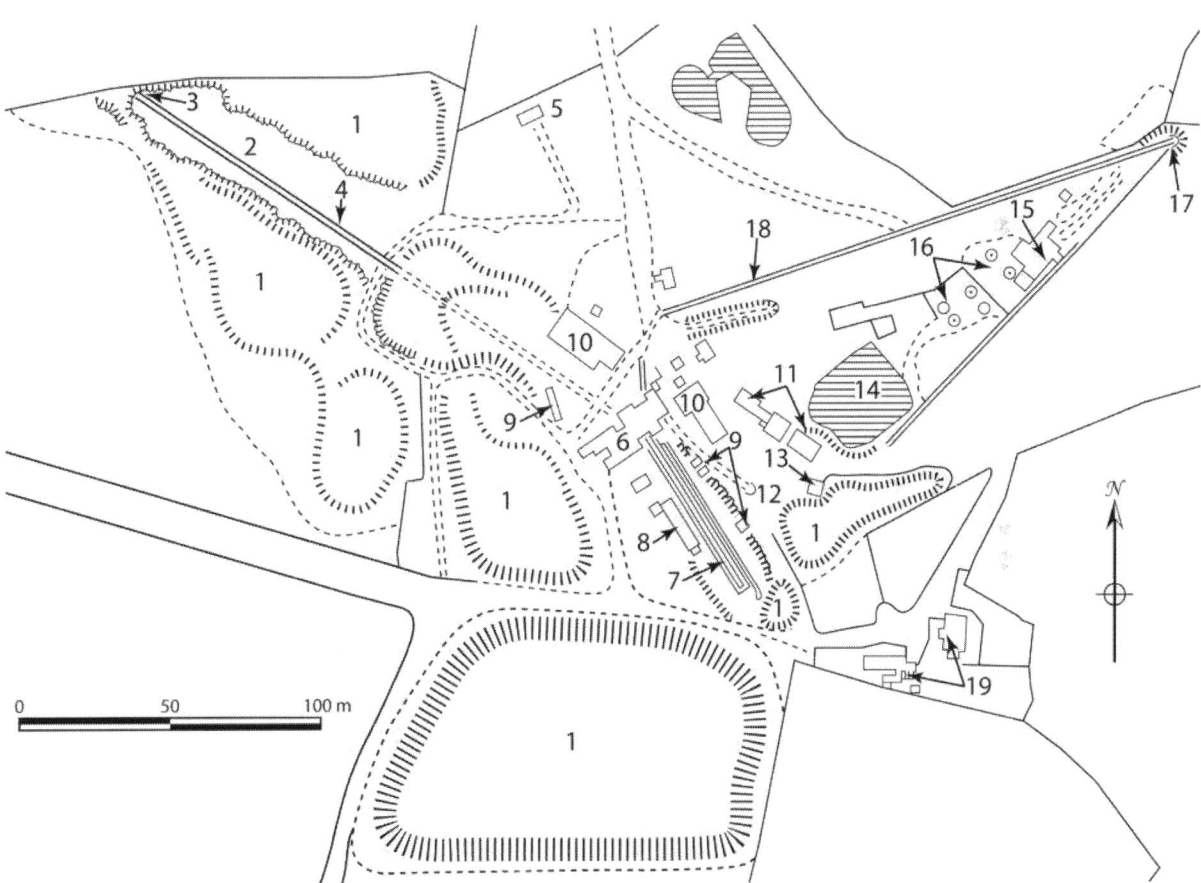

Figure 16.7. Layout of the works of the Alderley Edge Mining Company, Limited (see Figure 16.1). 1, spoil from mine and process works; 2, opencast; 3, entrance to underground workings of West Mine; 4, haulage incline; 5, explosives store (?); 6, haulage engine (with boiler(s)) and ore crusher; 7, leaching tanks (under tramway); 8, precipitation tanks; 9, other tanks (purpose unspecified); 10, workshops and chemical stores (?); 11, laboratory (?) and offices; 12, 'Hough Level' portal; 13, condensing tower (?); 14, reservoir; 15, engine house (see Timberlake *et al.* in *ArchAE*: fig. 8.11b); 16, circular buddles (see Timberlake *et al.* in *ArchAE*: 142); 17, Wood Mine adit portal; 18, haulage way (see Timberlake *et al.* in *ArchAE*: fig. 8.12); 19, the Hagg cottages; horizontal ruling, water bodies.

From Ordnance Survey twenty-five-inch to the mile sheet Cheshire XXVIII/13, first edition, surveyed 1872.

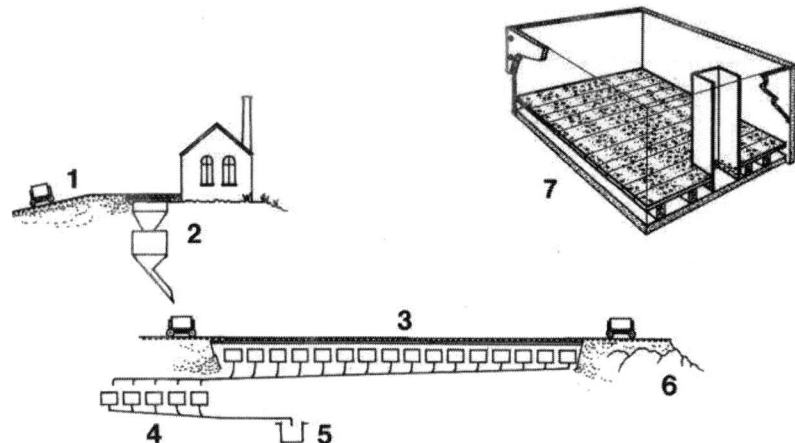

Figure 16.8. The process works (schematic) of the Alderley Edge Mining Company, Limited: 1, incline and tramway from West Mine; 2, winding engine house and ore crusher; 3, tramway over leaching tanks; 4, precipitation tanks; 5, reservoir for solutions from 4; 6, spoil dumps; 7, isometric view of a leaching tank, illustrating construction, with the pump housing extending down into the sump below the perforated wooden floor.

Drawn by Geoffrey Warrington.

had earlier erected a steam engine. In 1824 this area, the southern third (about one Cheshire acre or two statute acres, around 0.8 ha) of the field known as Lower Oldham, was recorded as 'spoild by the Miners' (*Book of Reference to the Stanley Estate Plan*; CALS DSA 238), perhaps as a result of the activities of the AMC, or earlier enterprises. This division of Lower Oldham is indicated on Crossley's plan of the Stanley estate (1787) and the Tithe Apportionment map of 1842. The works built there by the AEMCL (Figures 16.7, 16.8) were, however, unlike anything previously seen in the district.

The AEMCL mined in several parts of its leased area, including parts of Wood Mine and near Stormy Point, where what may have been rail tracks leading from the 'Hough' Level and Pillar Mine and adjacent workings were recorded when the survey for that part of Ordnance Survey twenty-five-inch to the mile sheet Cheshire XXVIII/14 was carried out in 1872. Its principal operations were, however, directed westwards from the process works site. Here the company started an opencast excavation which, in 1858, was some 90 feet long, 27–30 feet wide and up to 30 feet deep (Higgs, 1858); it ultimately extended west-north-westwards for about 600 feet and was 100 feet wide and up to 60 feet deep. Before September 1861 underground mining had commenced westwards from this pit (Figure 16.9) and by 1863 had extended some 720 feet farther west, to a point where the ore bodies were found to be dislocated by a major geological fault. This impediment was quickly surmounted and the underground workings finally extended to a point some 1,525 feet west of the opencast. Ore was taken to the process works in wagons hauled up an incline. Railton recalled watching, as a child, 'the small, rickety trucks rushing down the sloping, narrow-guage [*sic*] line into the awe-inspiring tunnel that led to the underground workings' and

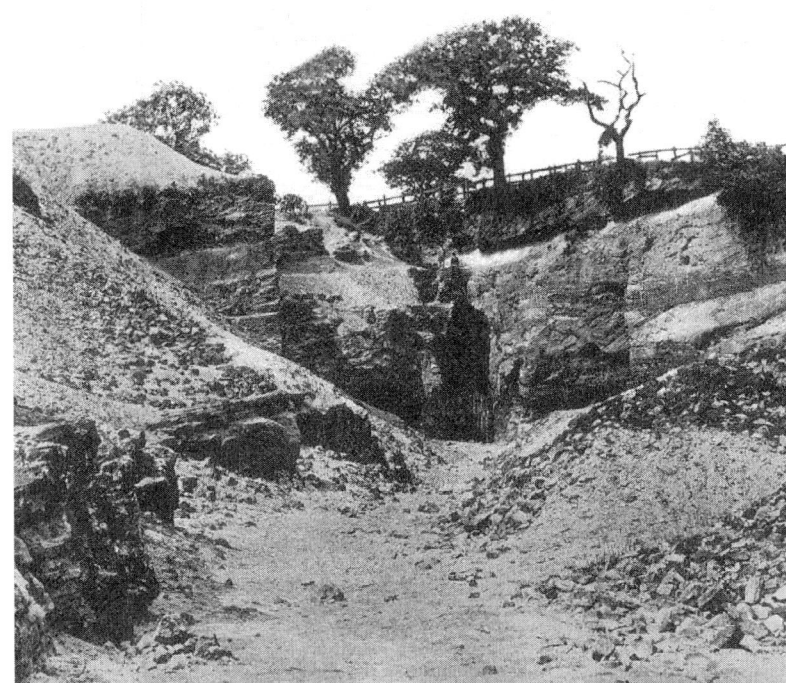

Figure 16.9. The western half of the opencast part of the West Mine workings (see Figures 16.1 and 16.7); the scale is given by a figure standing on a ledge above the entrance to the underground part of the mine.

Photographer unknown. Author's collection.

throwing 'bunches of wild flowers into the empty trucks as they rushed by, for the benefit of the miner far away in the bowels of the earth'. That this account relates to the AEMCL period is confirmed by mention of a 'Captain' Leeman (*sic*), an employee of that company (Railton, 1935: 18). These workings, together with small additions made by other companies in the early twentieth century, constitute what is now known as West Mine (Figure 16.1).

The AEMCL went into voluntary liquidation in 1878 but, unlike many of its contemporaries, the company was a commercial success between its incorporation in 1859 and 1877, when a boiler explosion caused extensive damage to the surface plant. Work carried out prior to its incorporation had produced 820 tons 17 hundredweights of ore, with a yield of 24 tons of copper, in 1857, and 8,007 tons of ore in 1858. In 1859 over 10,200 tons of ore were produced and from 1864 until 1868, inclusive, recorded output exceeded 14,600 tons per annum, with a peak of 15,152 tons in 1867. In 1870 output declined abruptly to about half that achieved throughout much of the previous decade, and from then until mining ceased (in 1877) averaged around 7,500 tons per annum (Warrington, 1981: fig. 4). The significance of this output in a national context, even when production fell after 1869, is impressive. In 1875, for example, Cheshire (i.e. Alderley) produced 8,336 tons of copper ore, or

11.65 per cent of the United Kingdom total, a contribution greater than either Anglesey or Ireland and exceeded only by those of Cornwall and Devon (Bainbridge, 1878: 743).

The company's financial record was equally remarkable. It remained solvent throughout its existence and in addition to operating costs and substantial royalties, which in 1865 alone amounted to £2,000 (Anon., 1865a), disbursed £18,875 to its shareholders, with £15,500 being paid out in twenty-seven dividends declared between 1860 and 1876 (Warrington, 1981: fig. 4). The value of the original £10 shares was repaid in five years and when the final dividend was paid in 1876 nearly £16 had been returned on those shares. It was the only company involved with mines in the district after 1856 known to have paid dividends.

This success was due to a combination of factors. The ore bodies exploited in West Mine occurred in the relatively soft, homogeneous West Mine Sandstone Member of the Helsby Sandstone Formation. They were worked with comparative ease by underhand stoping and were larger, and more extensive and continuous than those lower in the geological succession in, for example, Wood Mine (see Chapter 5; also Warrington, 2010). Mineralisation was variably developed at three levels in the host-rock unit, some sixty feet thick. When working first extended underground from the opencast, the full thickness of this unit was mined in a very large stope (see Figure 17.6, p. 432); in the more distant central and western parts of the mine the three ore-bearing levels were worked separately. The host-rock unit dips gently to the south-west and workings less than 150 feet below the surface were accessed via an incline, thus avoiding the expense of deep shaft operations. The nature of the sandstone ensured that the workings were largely free from drainage problems and attendant pumping costs. Finally, the processing method used was particularly appropriate for the low-grade ore disseminated in the sandstone host rock (Chapter 6; Warrington, 2010).

Previous operators had attempted to extract copper by smelting but only the richer ores could be treated in this manner, a factor reflected in the nature, scale and, sometimes, the lack of success of the earlier operations (e.g. Bakewell, 1811: 8). Michell introduced a process based upon one patented in 1857 by William Henderson, who was the chemist at the company's works until the autumn of 1861, and which proved highly effective and economical (Henderson, 1860b, 1860c).

Ore was treated by leaching with hydrochloric acid in tanks made of three-inch wooden planks or, in some cases, flagstones. Each tank had a sump beneath a perforated wooden floor that rested on notched six-inch joists and was covered with brushwood and straw; a pump was fitted into a wooden housing that extended down into the sump at one end of the tank (Figure 16.8). Stone tanks of this type, from Clive Mine, north Shropshire, which also operated the Henderson process, are preserved at the Bryntail Mine site near Llanidloes, Powys, Wales (Morgan Rees, 1975: 138; Bick, 1977: 37; Warrington, 1995: 23–4; Shaw, 2009: fig. 14.2). A series of sixteen closely spaced leaching tanks, each with internal dimensions of eleven feet by eight and about four feet deep, extended south-eastwards from a building that housed an engine connected to a crushing mill (Figure 16.7). Trucks were hauled up an incline from the mine by a cable wound on a drum attached to the main shaft of this engine (Phillips, 1896: 269). After passing through the crusher, the ore was carried to the leaching tanks in wagons that ran on a tramway over the tanks (Figure 16.8), each of which held nine tons of ore. Five tanks in which copper was precipitated from solutions produced in the leaching tanks were adjacent to those tanks and were of the same size.

Originally, the treatment of the ore involved the following operations (Henderson, 1860b), as numbered on Figure 16.10:

1	Leaching Tank A was loaded with crushed ore to within three inches of its top and the surface of the fill levelled.
2	Sufficient hydrochloric acid to dissolve 75 per cent of the ore minerals was run quickly onto the ore until it was completely covered; wooden shovels were used to level it under the acid.
3	When this first acid charge had percolated completely into the crushed ore, washings from a tank (B) that had reached a later stage in the process were pumped onto the ore in Tank A until that was full to within two inches of its top.
4	Liquid from the sump in Tank A was then pumped over the ore in that tank, a process repeated about every two hours, until the concentration of the copper-rich solution ceased to increase.
5	The liquid was then run or pumped into a precipitation tank, and Tank A and its partially exhausted contents became (broken arrow) a 'Tank B'.
6	An excess of fresh acid was run onto the contents of Tank B, with more washings.
7	Liquid in the Tank B sump was recycled by pumping.
8	The solution resulting from (7) was then pumped (3) to another tank that had just received its first charge of acid and was at the 'Tank A' stage of the process.

When the ore in Tank B was exhausted it was covered with water, which filtered down into the sump. After draining sufficiently, a spade's depth of the leached sand was removed and the surface of the remainder loosened with a fork. More water was added and further layers removed until the false bottom was reached; a new charge of ore was introduced

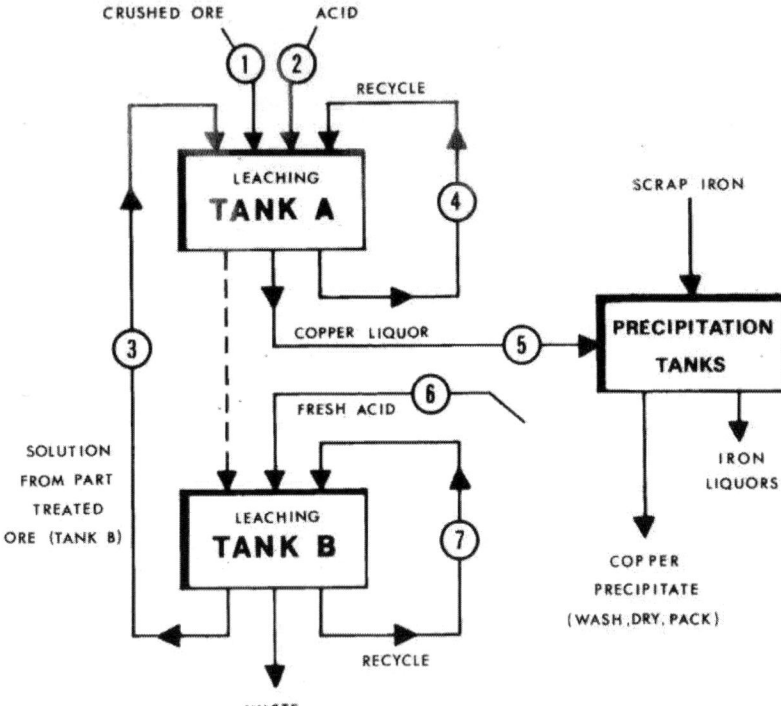

Figure 16.10. Flow diagram of the original copper ore treatment process at West Mine. Steps 1–8 are explained in the text.

Drawn by Geoffrey Warrington.

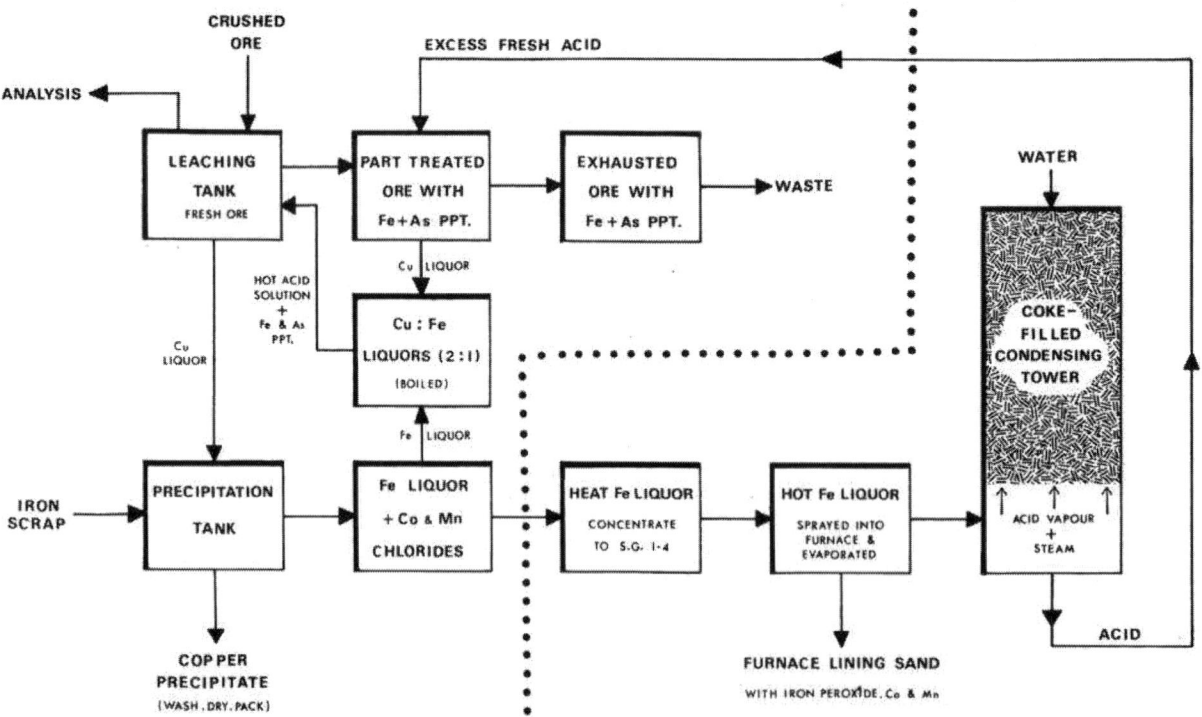

Figure 16.11. Flow diagram of the improved copper ore treatment process at West Mine.

Drawn by Geoffrey Warrington.

after loose sand had been shaken from the brushwood and straw. The leached sand was discharged at the south-east end of the row of tanks and removed to spoil heaps. The copper-rich solutions were discharged into the precipitating tanks, which contained a quantity of light scrap iron that required constant replenishment. Copper metal was precipitated and the resulting solution of iron and other chlorides drained off into receiving tanks. The precipitating tanks were cleaned out each month, the fine particles of copper metal being sifted from fragments of scrap iron, then washed, dried and packed in barrels. The produce had, on average, a fine-copper content of over 75 per cent.

A modified process (Figure 16.11) that overcame problems caused by the high arsenic content of the ore and was capable of reclaiming acid and producing a residue containing cobalt was introduced in 1860 (Henderson, 1860b). Boiling a two-to-one mixture of copper- and iron-rich solutions produced a dense white precipitate of arsenic and iron compounds. The hot, very acidic, supernatant liquid was then used as the first treatment for a tank of fresh ore and when fully saturated was tapped directly to the precipitation tanks. Treatment of the ore was then completed with excess acid; the solution from this second treatment was mixed with an iron-rich solution in the ratio of two to one and, after boiling and the precipitation of arsenic and iron compounds, the hot, acidic liquid was again applied to a fresh tank of ore. This innovation resulted in a reduction of the consumption of acid by one-third and improved the quality of the copper precipitate.

Around 20,000 gallons of iron-rich solutions, which also contained manganese chloride and cobalt chloride, were obtained from the precipitation tanks each week. These solutions were concentrated to a specific gravity of about 1.4 by boiling in wrought-iron pans, then sprayed over sand-covered tiles heated from below in a furnace at dull red heat; metallic oxides, which accumulated in the sand, and hydrochloric acid vapour and steam were produced. The gases were conducted through a stoneware pipe in the roof of the furnace to the base of a condensing tower. This was some sixty feet high, filled with hard coke and topped by a cistern from which water constantly descended, condensing the rising vapours into acid, which flowed from the base of the tower into a tank and was re-used. However, this reclamation had little cost advantage over the purchase of 'strong' fresh acid (at 5s.5d per ton of ore processed) and it was suspended until cobalt present in the residue in the furnace but mixed with manganese could be recovered profitably.

The entire process, from initial filling, through treatment and emptying to refilling, took, on average, about three days (Henderson, 1860b). Its efficiency was illustrated by the result obtained from the 24,155 tons of ore processed in the first three years. Assays by 'experienced' Cornishmen had indicated a copper content of only about

0.75 per cent, but analyses showed the average from the ore treated in those years to be 1.58 per cent, and the recovery achieved was 1.534 per cent (Henderson, 1860c).

Ore as mined was in pieces up to as large as a miner could lift. These were broken down by others, who loaded the ore into wagons, drew these out of the mine to the crusher, and crushed the ore. One person filled the leaching tanks, while others attended to the acid treatment, filled, managed and emptied the precipitation tanks, and discharged and removed the residual sand. Each tank was sampled as it was filled and samples from all tanks were analysed daily in the laboratory. The process works evidently operated twenty-four hours a day, seven days a week, as there were day- and night-shift foremen who dispensed acid, tested the iron solutions and kept account of work done, and were responsible for the efficient running of the plant; they had a weekly wage but others were paid by tonnage (Henderson, 1860c). Other day- and night-shift workers would have included those attending to the leaching tanks, which required pumping every two hours (see above), and others tending boilers. Remains of some structures associated with these works, including foundations of an engine house and lead-washing floors, were located during the survey by the Alderley Edge Landscape Project, and the site of a laboratory may have been identified (*ArchAE*: 141–3).

In 1860 the treatment cost, after mining, of one ton of ore was 9s.½d, of which acid was the largest item. Henderson (1860c) reports the other elements in the cost as follows:

Spalling, tramming, and crushing ore	7½d
Engine costs, wages, coal, grease, oil &c.	3½d
Filling tanks	1¼d
Working tanks, precipitating and removing waste	9¾d
Iron for precipitation	6½d
Washing, drying, weighing and packing precipitate	3d
Management, foremen and laboratory expenses	7½d
Materials, tools, wear and tear	4½d
Sub-total	3s.7½d
Plus acid	5s.5d
Total	9s.½d

Coal for the boilers and furnaces was 7s.6d to 8s.6d per ton. The supply of water to the works was discussed by Timberlake *et al.* (*ArchAE*: 143). Hull and Green (1866: 39) indicated that a clay-lined excavation 40 feet deep and 180 feet across in the centre of the works was used as a reservoir (Figure 16.7).

In the first three years of operations, processing 24,155 tons of ore had yielded 573 tons 5 hundredweight of copper precipitate at a cost of £10,920.1s.6d. This was said to be equivalent to 369 tons 11 hundredweight of fine copper, which, at an average price of £95 per ton, was worth £35,107.5s.0d. After deducting the cost of producing the precipitate, this left £24,187.3s.6d, from which, after deduction of unstated mining costs, over £10,000 remained as profit. Part of this was to be used to increase the capacity of the plant and the remainder distributed in dividends (Henderson, 1860c).

There are no records of the consumption of hydrochloric acid and scrap iron at Alderley but a contemporary works in Germany used 400 lb of 16 per cent hydrochloric acid, diluted to 10 per cent, to leach one ton of copper ore, and 1.25 tons of scrap iron to precipitate one ton of copper metal (Hunt, 1875: 935). On this basis the Alderley works may have used around 2,600 tons of acid at 16 per cent strength, or more at 10 per cent, and, depending upon the grade of copper precipitate produced (see below), consumed between 130 and 185 tons of scrap iron per annum during the period of highest recorded output (1864–68). The acid was essentially a waste product from chemical works at St Helens (Collins, 1893–94: 17) and its transport to Alderley would have been the main cost to the AEMCL. The introduction of the 'improved' process (Figure 16.11) in 1860 reduced the quantities of acid that had to be brought to the site and thus the attendant costs by about one-third. However, the company still required supplies from elsewhere and when, in 1864, there were delays in delivery by rail, it considered using 'six large trucks of their own, and 360 gutta-percha carboys, which is a rolling-stock sufficient for the transit of one-fourth more acid than is required' (Anon., 1864). Alderley station (Figure 19.16) had opened for passenger and goods traffic from the north on 10 May 1842, and from the south, beyond Sandbach, on 10 August 1842 (Jeuda, 1984: 3, 61). In 1866 a daily Birmingham–Manchester goods train was scheduled to call there at 3.50 p.m. to leave wagons 'when required … for the Alderley Mining Co.' (London and North Western Railway working timetable; B. Jeuda, personal communication, January 1983). The AEMCL appears to have had six private-owner wagons in 1864 (Anon., 1864), of which four were among the items advertised for auction when the company wound up in 1878 (Warrington, 1981: appendix 1).

Throughout the year, large volumes of acid would have been conveyed from the station yard in Alderley, via the main street and the Congleton or Macclesfield roads, and then along wayleaves to the process works. Other substantial traffic on these routes would have included coal for boilers at the works (see below), scrap iron and timber, while the produce of the works provided return freight. At the works there would have been a constant reek of chemicals, especially when hot acid was used or solutions boiled, and noise from the engines, crusher and other machinery at the plant, which operated continually and would have required illumination at night.

An indication of the extensive nature of the works (Figures 16.7, 16.8) is given by the list of items advertised for sale by auction when the AEMCL went into liquidation in 1878 (Warrington, 1981: appendix 1). In addition to the leaching and precipitating tanks and numerous sundry items, these included two horizontal steam engines (one lacking a boiler; presumably as a result of the explosion in 1877), a twenty-two-inch beam engine, a double-flued boiler twenty-four feet long and six feet in diameter, a large ore crusher, and a stone condensing tower eight feet square and about eighty feet high. The works also included a smithy and other workshops, an assay office, and premises fitted out as a boardroom.

From 1857 until 1877 the staple produce of the AEMCL was copper precipitate, which was sold as No. 1 and No. 2 grades, containing at least 80 per cent and 60 per cent copper respectively. In 1858 most of this was purchased by Bibby, Sons, and Company, copper smelters, of Seacombe on the Wirral; subsequent production went to smelters at St Helens and Swansea, and to Bouck and Company of Manchester. The total ore production between 1857 and 1877 was, from known and estimated output (Warrington, 1981: fig. 4), likely to have been about 220,000 tons; the copper metal recovered between 1857 and 1878 was recorded as 3,202 tons (*Report of the Controller of the Department for the Development of Mineral Resources in the United Kingdom, presented to the Minister of Munitions*, 1918: 39). This yield, of about 1.455 per cent over the twenty-year period, is slightly less than achieved in the first three years of operations (Henderson, 1860b, 1860c, and above) but close to the average copper content of the ore and underlines again the effectiveness of the treatment process.

Lead ore was mined on a small scale: 273 tons 18 hundredweight, which yielded 98 tons 7 hundredweight of lead and 290 oz of silver were produced in the years 1859–61. In October 1863 the AEMCL had stocks of lead ore and slimes, cobalt and nickel speiss and cobalt precipitate valued at £2,575. By January 1864 stocks of lead carbonate being held for the Patent White Lead Company, Limited, of Macclesfield, had reached an 'inconvenient' level. Production of cobalt and nickel speiss was terminated early in 1864 after 357 tons of precipitate containing those metals had been smelted and 10 tons 11 hundredweight 2 quarters of speiss, with an estimated value of £650 to £700, had been recovered (Warrington, 1981: 61).

The principals involved in Michell's venture and, subsequently, in the AEMCL were experienced in the techniques and management of large-scale mining and mineral processing in south-west England and elsewhere. The surface and underground operations were supervised by separate 'captains', and tasks were bargained for between 'pares', or groups of workers, 'set' on a weekly basis, and recorded in accounts books.

The 1861 Census returns for townships in the parishes of Alderley, Prestbury and Wilmslow list 101 persons as involved directly with mining; some of these were employed at the then active mine at Mottram St Andrew (see below) but the majority worked for the AEMCL. The corresponding 1871 returns list fifty-one people involved with mining, all of whom were then employed by the AEMCL as the Mottram St Andrew mine closed before that date. More information is available for 1872 and subsequent years, when returns of employees became required under the Metalliferous Mines Regulation Act. These show a gradual decline in the numbers employed by the AEMCL, from fifty-one in 1872 and 1873, to thirty-five in 1877. In 1873 and 1877 the numbers of underground workers were thirty-eight and twenty-two respectively. In 1878 only seven people were employed, all above ground (Warrington, 1981: fig. 4).

Reports (e.g. Hull, 1864: 68) that all the miners were of Cornish origin, or that they were from Cornwall and North Wales (e.g. E.E.L., 1913: 20), are incorrect. Of the 101 persons recorded as employed in the mines and process works in the 1861 Census, sixty-three originated from Cheshire, thirteen from Cornwall, nine from Devon and sixteen from other places, including two unspecified; the corresponding numbers for 1871 are thirty-four from Cheshire, twelve from Cornwall, three from Devon and two from other places. Neither Census recorded miners of Welsh origin. In 1861 the employees' ages ranged from ten to seventy, with one unknown. Seven were under fifteen, and ten, including one of seventy years, were aged over forty-five; the remaining eighty-three consisted of fifteen- to forty-five-year-olds and included twenty between the ages of twenty and twenty-five. In 1871 the ages ranged from ten to sixty-five, with one unknown; eight were under fifteen years and nine over forty-five years; the remaining thirty-three consisted of fifteen- to forty-five-year-olds and included eleven between the ages of thirty and thirty-five (Warrington, 1981: fig. 5).

The writer has researched the biographies of the shareholders, workers and others connected with the AEMCL and other companies. This information is beyond the scope of the present account but the following notes on James Michell are included because of his important place in the history of mining at Alderley and because of inaccuracies in what little has been published about him. Michell was born at Tresavean, Gwennap, Cornwall, in 1796 (Boase and Courtney, 1874: 351). Prior to his activity at Alderley he appears to have been involved exclusively with lead mines and lead smelting and in 1835 was, as 'James Michell, of Truro … Gentleman', author of a patent (no. 6853) for smelting argentiferous lead ores. After working in south-east Spain (Michell, 1846) he returned to England and is credited with the introduction of the Spanish slag hearth to Britain, erecting the first at Stonedge Cupola, Derbyshire, probably just before 1850 (Willies, 1990: 3, 11). In 1851 he was living at Chesterfield, but moved to Westbury-on-Trym, near Bristol, before becoming involved with Alderley. Despite the distance, and the fact that he was then over sixty, he appears to have been frequently at the mines, something made possible by the railway which had opened from Crewe in August 1842 (Jeuda, 1984: 3). However, on the morning of 27 November 1862, during an inspection of the underground workings there, he fell thirty feet and died within an hour, his only utterance being 'Oh, I am hurt' (*Bristol Mirror and General Advertiser*, 6 December 1862). He was buried at Westbury-on-Trym on 2 December 1862.

The end of the innovative and productive activities of the AEMCL was precipitated by the explosion of a boiler in 1877. This resulted from wasting of the boiler plates under a feed pipe and caused extensive damage to the surface plant, but no loss of life. Following this event, and in recognition of the proximity of the end of its lease, and other factors, the company resolved, on 24 May 1878, to wind up voluntarily. The effects were auctioned on 5 and 6 June 1878, and the final winding-up meeting on 9 October 1878 ended twenty years of sustained and profitable activity, and the last significant mining operation in the district.

Associated enterprises and other ventures

Two companies were established to utilise raw materials produced by the AEMCL (Warrington, 1981: 63–4).

The Patent White Lead Company, Limited (PWLCL), was incorporated in July 1862, with the object of manufacturing white lead and other products. In October 1863 the removal of raw material from the Alderley mines was reported to be delayed, pending completion of an extension of the company's works at Macclesfield, and by January 1864 the stocks of lead carbonate at the mine had reached an 'inconvenient' level. In September 1864, however, the PWLCL resolved to wind up voluntarily, on the grounds that the supply of lead carbonate from Alderley had failed unexpectedly and no substitute could be found at a satisfactory price.

The Macclesfield Patent Sulphate of Copper Company, Limited (MPSCCL), was incorporated in December 1862, with the objective of producing copper sulphate from solutions from the AEMCL works. In October 1863 the AEMCL was optimistic that this company would eventually take all its copper solutions. In 1865 copper sulphate produced by the MPSCCL was reported to be used extensively on the Continent as a preservative for telegraph posts and railway sleepers (*Macclesfield Courier and Herald*, 16 September 1865). However, the company resolved to wind up voluntarily in October 1869.

A third concern, the Alderley Edge, Copper, Lead, and Cobalt Mining and Land Company Limited, was incorporated on 26 July 1864. Its objectives included the purchase of land, with mining rights, in Chorley and 'Bolton fee' (*sic*; Bollin Fee) townships, and the sale of the land or of houses built thereon. Despite the emphasis on mining in its title this company was probably conceived to carry on business largely, if not entirely, in land and property development. Nothing is known of it following its incorporation, and it was dissolved on 23 January 1883 (Warrington, 1981: 64).

Japanese visitors

The unique features of the mines and process works of the AEMCL attracted many visitors but one by a Japanese delegation on 9 September 1865 created a sensation locally and was reported in the *Macclesfield Courier and Herald* on 16 September 1865, in the florid style of the time. Three Japanese people, under the care of Mr Ryle Holme of Yokohama (Figure 16.12), were accompanied by Mr Edward Clarke, the Portuguese Consul in Kanagawa, Japan. A large party gathered at the mines and an underground visit, with the workings illuminated with magnesium wire (see below) and other pyrotechnics, was attended by Henrietta Maria, Lady Stanley, née Dillon (1808–96). Then followed a 'sumptuous repast' at the Queen's Hotel adjacent to Alderley railway station, during which the Japanese visitors, to the evident surprise of the reporter, 'handled their knives and forks, and both eat [*sic*] and drank, like men who, in their lives had never performed those ceremonies in any other fashion'. The identity and purpose of these visitors, if known, would have been equally surprising. They had been sent to Europe in 1865 by the *daimyō* (feudal baron) of Satsuma, in the southern part of the southern Japanese island of Kyushu, to gather technical, commercial and political intelligence; their journey was illegal and all travelled under false names. The leader of the group was not named in the report of the visit to Alderley. He was Niirō Gyōbu (1832–89), alias Ishigaki Einosuke (Cobbing, 2000: 34); his brief was to observe the British cotton industry, order spinning machinery and engage Western engineers to superintend its installation and operation in Japan (Hunter, 1982: 26). Later, as Niiro Hisanobu, he became governor of Ōshima, one of the Ryūkyū islands, and finally retired to Kagoshima (Cobbing, 2000: 125). 'Mr Shekki' of the report was Godai Saisuke (1835–85), alias Seki Kenzō and known later as Godai Tomoatsu (Cobbing, 2000: 34). He was a former Satsuma naval officer sent to investigate manufacturing and commerce in Western Europe. He became an influential figure in commercial and other developments in Kagoshima and Osaka

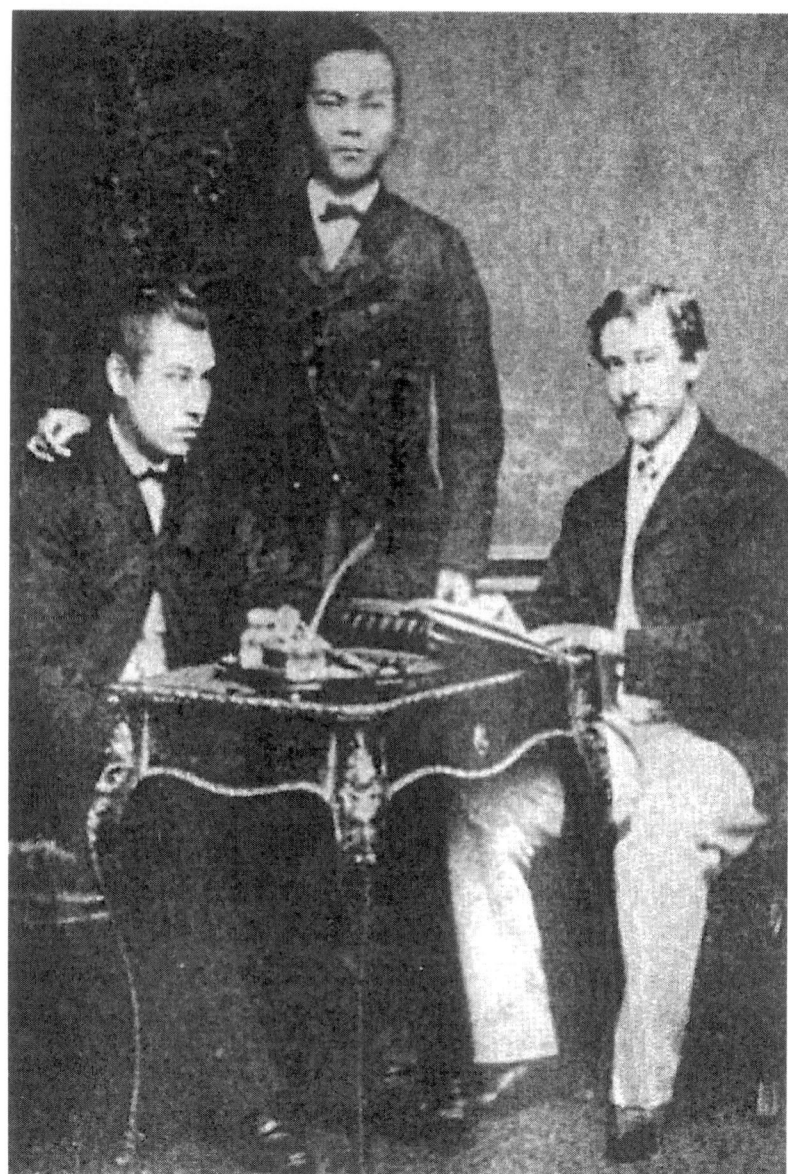

Figure 16.12. Ryle Holme (seated, right), with two of the Japanese visitors to the Alderley mines in 1865, Godai Tomoatsu (centre) and Hori Takayuki (seated, left).

Courtesy of Dr A. Cobbing, whose work leading to the current knowledge of the Satsuma delegation was carried out in Japan after he was introduced to the 1865 *Macclesfield Courier and Herald* article by the writer (Cobbing, 2000: xvi).

(Cobbing, 2000: 126–9). 'Mr Takaki', the interpreter in the report, was Hori Sōjūrō, later Hori Takayuki (Cobbing, 2000: 34, 129). On 19 August 1865 the group had visited the silk spinning plant of Messrs I. and T. Brocklehurst in Macclesfield, where they met C. E. Proctor, the chairman of the AEMCL, who invited them to the Alderley mines (*London and China Telegraph*, 28 August 1865). From Macclesfield the group had returned to Manchester, where the engineering firm of Platt and Co. was commissioned to supply spinning machinery for what became the first Western-style cotton mill in Kagoshima (Hunter, 1982: 26–7; Cobbing, 2000: 82, fig. 11).

Boyd Dawkins and the 'Bronze Age' mining tools

In May 1874 Professor William Boyd Dawkins (1837–1929), from Owens College (which became the University of Manchester), visited excavations being carried out by the AEMCL 'on the hillside immediately above the heaps of refuse near the reducing tanks' (Boyd Dawkins, 1875: 74). The exposed rock surface was 'fantastically hollowed' and fashioned stones, mostly with one or more grooves, were noticed in the hollows; additional finds were made later in 1874 and in 1875, and by others in subsequent years (Chapters 1 and 14; see also Timberlake in *ArchAE*: 58–75;). Boyd Dawkins 'did not attempt to assign a date to the mining operations' involving these artefacts, but concluded only that they implied 'a ruder phase of ... mining' than previously known in the Manchester region, 'a phase which *may point back to the bronze*

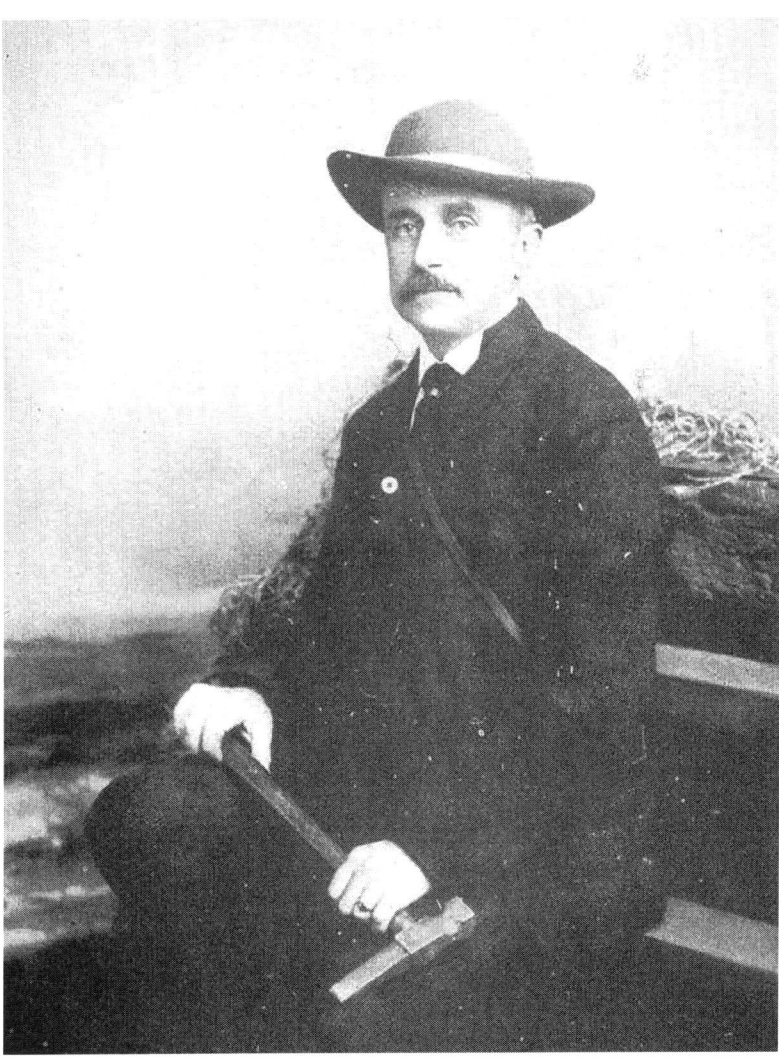

Figure 16.13. William Boyd Dawkins (aged thirty), taken *c.* 1868, six years before his report of stone artefacts from Alderley.

From Jackson (1966).

age' (emphasis added). This cautious assessment has been taken, un-critically, as fact in most subsequent literature. But Boyd Dawkins' publication is inadequate and ambiguous on all critical points: the location of the original discovery is not precisely known, nor is there adequate documentation of the context in which the artefacts were found. These deficiencies were also recognised by Timberlake and King (*ArchAE*: 33) and are particularly regrettable because only Boyd Dawkins (Figure 16.13) and those who accompanied him in 1874 had the opportunity to examine the occurrences and their context when freshly exhumed. Boyd Dawkins' notebook for 1874 (Manchester Museum) contains only one relevant entry, for 8 September, which comprises a crude sketch of a pit, some dimensions of seven pits, minerals observed, and a comment that the workings may have been for iron. Warrington (1981: 51, 53) urged caution in the acceptance of a Bronze Age date solely on the basis of the stone artefacts but neither rejected nor dismissed that possibility (cf. Gale, 1989: 268, 270; Craddock, 1986: 108). Since 1981, stone artefacts, mostly broken, have been found *in situ* in association with charcoal in trench EVB1 at the south side of the Engine Vein Mine Opencast. Radiocarbon dating suggests an age of 3,550 ± 70 years from the charcoal, which indicates their association with some activity in Bronze Age times (Timberlake and King in *ArchAE*: 42–4). This work, however, underlines Warrington's point, that the stone artefacts *alone* are not indicative of such an age. Indeed, such implements are still used at the present day (Worthington and Craddock, 1996) and may have continued in use at Alderley in post-Bronze Age times.

The Mottram St Andrew Mine

Kirkleyditch, just under a mile to the east-north-east of Stormy Point, Alderley Edge, is the site of the poorly known and now largely in-accessible workings generally known as the Mottram St Andrew Mine (Warrington, 1965: 122; Ward, 1982). The ore-bearing units there appear to be the same as in the eastern part of Alderley Edge and were worked in an opencast (Figures 16.14–16.16) and underground in a mine that may be similar in character to those at Stormy Point and Engine Vein but for which there is no known complete plan. Greenwell (1864: 48–9) and Hull (1864: 67–8) gave brief contemporary accounts of the mine, Ward (1982) and Rowe and Burley (1997: 331) reported underground observations, and known features of the workings are reviewed by Carlon and Dibben (2012).

Bentley Smith (2005: 220) suggested that mining activity on Alderley Edge from the late seventeenth century onwards may have stimulated trials at Mottram St Andrew in the early to mid-eighteenth century.

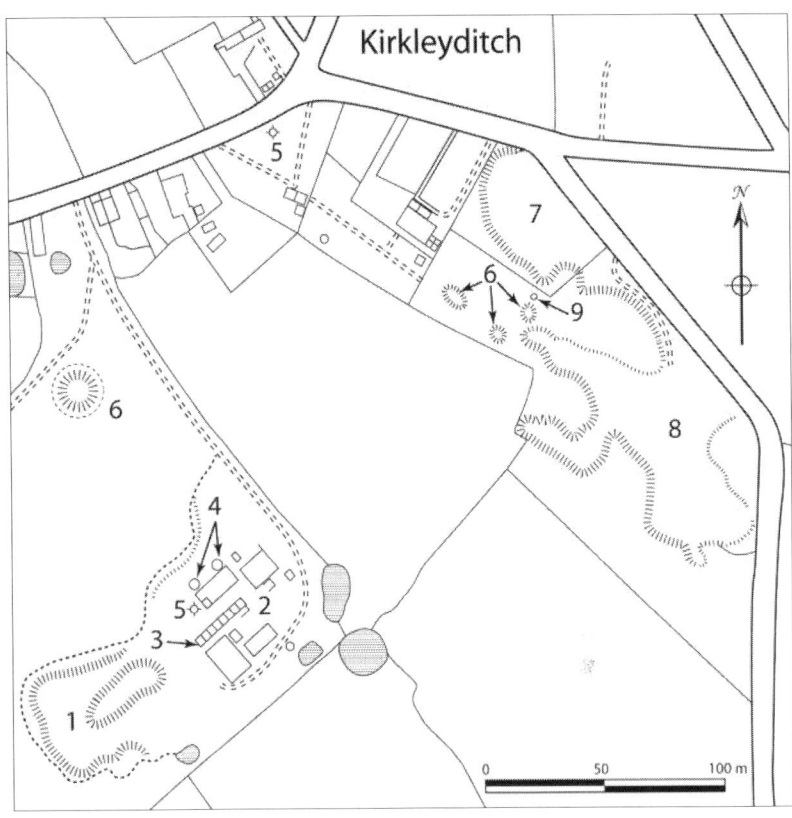

Figure 16.14. Layout of the works at the Mottram St Andrew Mine. 1, spoil from process works; 2, process works (the purpose of individual buildings cannot be determined but machinery on the site included a horizontal steam engine, two boilers and a twelve-head stamps – see Warrington, 1981: appendix 2); 3, leaching tanks; 4, tanks (unspecified purpose); 5, shafts marked on sheet XXVIII/14, first edition; 6, spoil from shafts (?); 7, northern part of opencast workings (see Figure 16.15); 8, southern part of opencast workings (see Figure 16.16); 9, shaft at site of wind-pump (from sheet XXVIII/14, third edition; see Figure 16.16); horizontal ruling, water bodies.

From Ordnance Survey twenty-five-inch to the mile sheets Cheshire XXVIII/10 and 14, first edition, surveyed 1871.

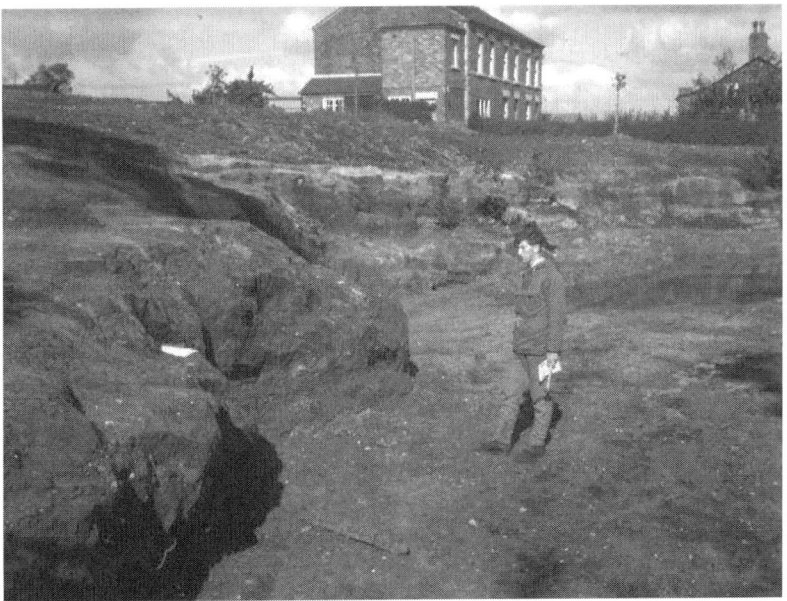

Figure 16.15. The northern part of opencast workings at the Mottram St Andrew Mine, Kirkleyditch, looking west; the site (7 in Figure 16.14) is now part of an ornamental garden.

Photograph Geoffrey Warrington, 1962.

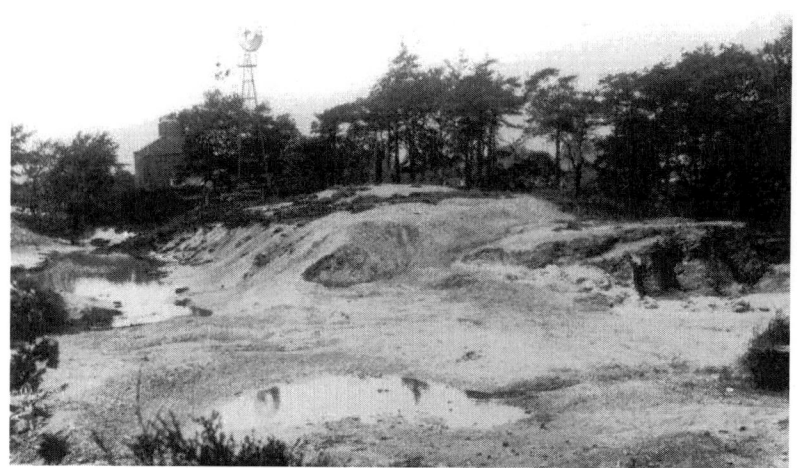

Figure 16.16. The southern part of opencast workings at the Mottram St Andrew Mine, Kirkleyditch, looking north-west (*c.* 1917). The site (8 in Figure 16.14) is now occupied by a house; Carlon (1979: plate 30) described this as 'Mottram Mine treatment works' but the process works at that mine (Figure 16.14) was 200 m to the south-west. The wind-pump was situated over or by a shaft (9 in Figure 16.14).

From a print held in Manchester Museum.

However, a deed executed in 1728, when the manor of 'Mottram Andrew' was sold to William Wright, contains no mention of mines (Anon., 1949: 8). Chaloner (1953: 141) suggested that Roe's Macclesfield company may have mined at Mottram St Andrew in the eighteenth century but this is not supported by the authority cited (Earwaker, 1880: 357).

In the early nineteenth century the locality was the scene of activity contemporary with that of the Alderley Mine Company. Lead and copper ores had been noted (Holland, 1808: 17) and a smelting house was erected near 'Keighley Ditch' (*sic*; Kirkleyditch) by Lawrence Wright in 1807 (Roeder, 1901: 111), apparently to treat lead ore. A quantity of lead was obtained but the enterprise was unremunerative (Stanley, 1843: 33). Cobalt ore had also been recognised there before Holland compiled his survey of Cheshire in 1806, but the amounts were 'not sufficient to render it an object worthy of attention' (Holland, 1808: 17) and it was probably not worked at Mottram at this time. However, this appears to be the site, on an 'adjoining estate', where it was discovered before being recognised on Alderley Edge (see above, and Bakewell, 1811: 8–9).

Interest in this locality was revived by James Michell and activity recommenced during 1860. With John Bibby, of the eponymous Liverpool shipping line and the Seacombe copper-smelting works, Michell obtained a mining lease and erected a process works. These interests were transferred to the Mottram St Andrew Mining Company, Limited (MSAMCL), which was incorporated on 24 January 1861, with a capital of £10,000 in £10 shares. Of the seven initial subscribers, five, including Michell, were also involved with the AEMCL. The

Mottram company was fully capitalised by 14 August 1861, when £2,000 remained in hand after the purchase of Michell's and Bibby's interests. However, this balance appears to have dissipated within a year because a proposal to raise further capital by the issue of 500 preference shares of £10 was confirmed on 20 August 1862. This issue was also fully subscribed but in less than three years the company had accumulated liabilities estimated at £1,000, and on 13 April 1865 it resolved to wind up, despite the recent discovery of vanadium (see below). In an attempt to sell the mine as a going concern, the liquidator continued operations after that date and a company styled the East Alderley Edge Mine, Limited (EAEML) was incorporated on 29 June 1865, with a capital of £6,000 in £5 shares. Its objectives included the purchase, for £4,350, of the interests, rights and effects of the MSAMCL. However, though not formally dissolved until 23 January 1883, the EAEML does not appear to have progressed beyond incorporation, and did not take over the mine. After this attempt at disposal of the property, the liquidator of the MSAMCL advertised its effects for auction on 30 August 1866; this event realised £643.5s.10d and effectively marked the end of mining at Mottram St Andrew, though the company was not formally dissolved until 7 March 1882 (Warrington, 1981: appendix 2). In 1881 the process works site was rented as a brickfield, and an option on the property held by Hide and Jacobs, and subsequently by Alderley Copper, Limited, early in the twentieth century (see below) was probably never exercised (Warrington, 1981: 65).

In comparison with that of its contemporary, the AEMCL, little is known of the output of the MSAMCL; 500–600 tons of ore were mined prior to October 1860 and an estimated 1,000 tons of copper ore in 1864. In the EAEML prospectus it was asserted that the works had produced about five tons of copper precipitate per month, and that £15,000 worth of copper, lead and cobalt had been sold. The process works established by Michell at Mottram St Andrew operated on the same principle as that used by the AEMCL but was smaller in scale; only eight leaching tanks are shown on the first edition of Ordnance Survey twenty-five inch to the mile sheet Cheshire XXVIII/14, the survey for this part of which was carried out in 1871 (Figure 16.14). However, in contrast to the Alderley Edge mines, the Mottram workings suffered from water influx, sometimes on a significant scale, and pumping costs doubtless contributed to the failure of the company (*Report to the Directors of the Mottram Mines*, 20 August 1862; Warrington, 1981: 65). Of those identified as mine workers in the 1861 Census, the number working in the Mottram St Andrew Mine is not known. However, of the twenty-six living in that area in 1861, twenty-two had left mining by the time of the 1871 Census, perhaps giving an indication of the number involved with that mine and affected by its closure.

Vanadium and Henry Enfield Roscoe (1833–1915)

A dark-blue solution produced at the MSAMCL process works was recognised by Henry Enfield Roscoe (1833–1915) as containing vanadium (Plate 7 and Figure 16.17; Roscoe, 1868a: 288). This discovery, though pre-dating the winding-up resolution of the MSAMCL, did not influence its fortunes, nor the future of the mine, but did ensure the locality a permanent place in the history of chemistry and mineralogy. A residue from the preparation of cobalt was found to contain about 2 per cent of vanadium and several tons of this material were secured by Roscoe in February 1865 and used in his classic research on vanadium and its compounds. Though Roscoe clearly specified 'Mottram St. Andrews' as the source of the material, he erroneously attributed the operation to the 'Alderley Edge Copper Mining Company' and illustrated the ore-bearing succession with Hull's account of that then being worked in West Mine, at a higher level in the sequence on Alderley Edge (Hull, 1864: 68; Roscoe, 1868b: 4).

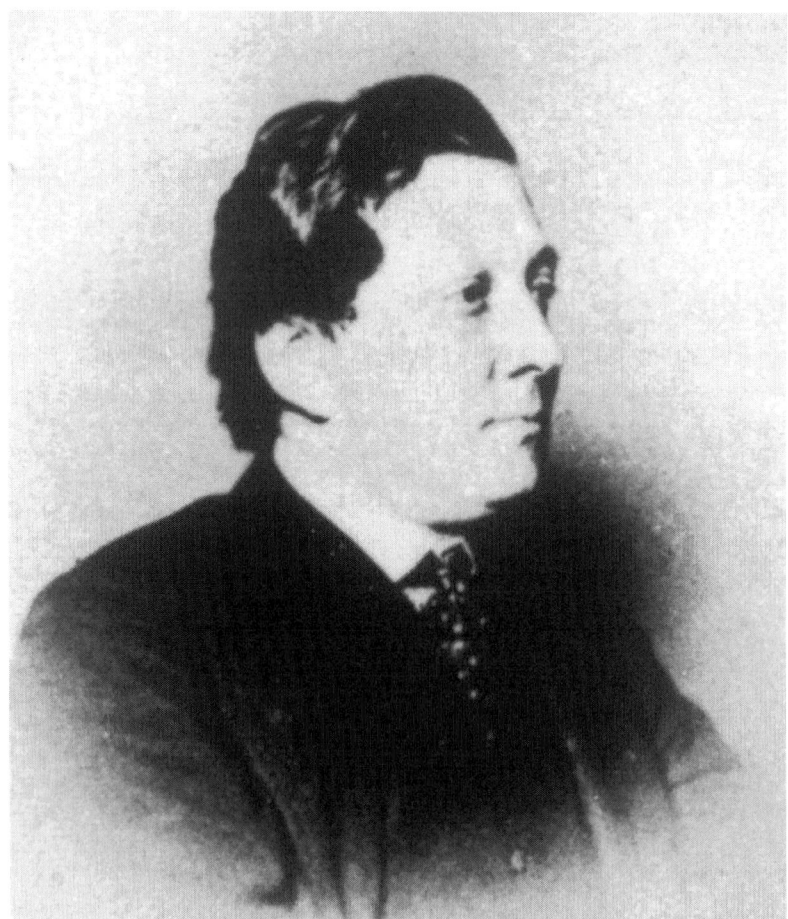

Figure 16.17. Henry Enfield Roscoe (aged thirty-two). Photograph taken by A. Brothers on 22 February 1864, one of the earliest photographs taken by magnesium light, one year before vanadium was recognised at Mottram St Andrew.

From a transparency of a copy taken in the Manchester Museum of Science and Technology, now the Museum of Science and Industry (MOSI). The location of the original is currently unknown.

The correct valency of vanadium was determined using material from Mottram St Andrew (Roscoe, 1868a; 1868b: 4–5). To Roscoe this was 'certainly the best piece of scientific work I ever did, and I do not know that I ever enjoyed anything of an intellectual kind more thoroughly' (Roscoe, 1906: 143). The mineral mottramite, a vanadate of lead and copper, was identified by Roscoe (1876a) and named after Mottram St Andrew, though the type material may not have been from that locality (Braithwaite, 1994: 92–4; Warrington, 2010; see also Chapter 6 and Plates 7, 8).

Vanadium was used in the manufacture of permanent black inks and, by the Magnesium Metal Company, Limited (MMCL), of Patricroft, near Manchester, of permanent black dyes for printing textiles (Roscoe, 1876b: 229). The MMCL used raw material 'collected' from Mottram St Andrew and a site near Shrewsbury (Schunck, 1897: 589). Only very small quantities of vanadium were required and this stock was sufficient to satisfy commercial demands for several years. Roeder (1901: 111) suggested that the MMCL re-opened the Mottram St Andrew Mine around 1865 but this is unlikely as that site was not vacated until after the sale of the effects of the MSAMCL in August 1866 (see above). The MMCL probably provided the magnesium wire used to illuminate West Mine during the visit by the three Japanese men in 1865 (see above).

The last phase: 1909–27

Following the liquidation of the AEMCL in 1878, mines in the district were abandoned until negotiations in 1909 resulted in a lease to mine for minerals, other than gold, being granted to Messrs Richardson and Rollason on 12 February 1910 by Lyulph (1839–1929), fourth Lord Stanley of Alderley (1903–29). This lease, for twenty-one years from 25 December 1909 and covering an area of about 209 acres on Alderley Edge, led to a resumption of mining in 1911. On 27 March 1911 Richardson and Rollason agreed to sell their lease to a company to be formed by the S.E.D. Syndicate, Limited; this was the 'large and influential London Syndicate [that] had decided to reopen the mines' (E.E.L., 1913: 19). The lease was sold on 31 March 1911 to the Alderley Mining Company, Limited (AMCL), which had been incorporated on 28 March 1911, with a capital of £55,000 in 10s shares. The company's prospectus, published on 1 April 1911, proposed the direct production of copper sulphate by the treatment of copper ore with sulphuric acid, and claimed that an estimated 5.25 million tons of ore, containing over 2 per cent copper, existed in the ground leased. An output of 3,000 tons of ore per month was envisaged, and an annual profit of at least £25,000 anticipated. Initial work involved the clearance of debris from

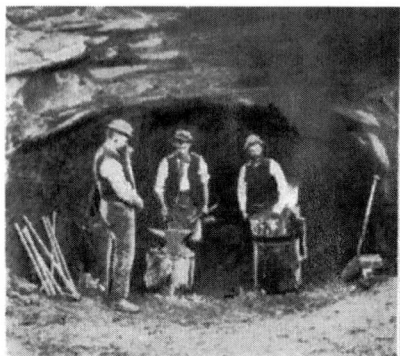
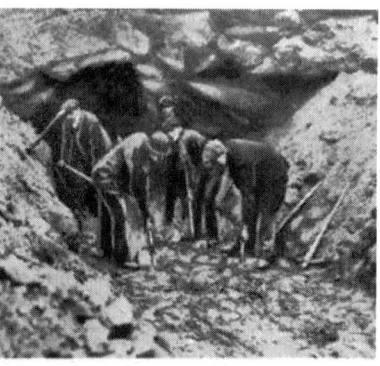

WORKMEN FORGING DRILLS FOR THE PURPOSE   THE ACTUAL WORK OF OPENING UP
OF CLEARING A WAY TO THE MINE.   THE ENTRANCE.

Figure 16.18. Re-opening work by the Alderley Mining Company, Limited (May–June 1911).

From E.E.L. (1913: 23).

mine entrances in the area between the Macclesfield Road and Artists Lane, including what may have been an entrance to Wood Mine or the Hough Level (Figure 16.18). It was, however, understood that the first mining would be in the direction of 'the wood in which the old beacon stands', that is, farther north-east (E.E.L., 1913: 20). The AMCL promotion was not well received, on the grounds that the ore reserves were not adequately proven. By 27 June 1911 only 3,942 shares had been issued and £1,103.15s.0d received from calls. Expenditure comprised £264.13s.4d for 'preliminary expenses', £175 for plant, tools and development work and £360.11s.6d for rent, royalty, insurance, wages, stores, printing, stationery and general charges; £303.10s.2d remained in hand. No further shares were taken up but £781.5s.0d was received between June 1911 and January 1913 from calls made on those already issued (Warrington, 1981: 66).

Rollason became a director of the AMCL and was named as the mine owner in 1911. Work ceased before 1913 and the mine was reported as suspended, but not abandoned, during that year. In December 1914 the company secretary stated that it had no assets and could not conduct any business; it could not pay for liquidation and, in fact, had nothing to liquidate; it was dissolved on 17 December 1915.

The output, if any, of the AMCL is not known, and the small scale of its operations is reflected in the numbers of employees, all of whom were stated to work underground; in 1911 and 1912 the numbers employed were twelve and ten respectively (Warrington, 1981: fig. 6).

Following the cessation of work by the AMCL, but before its dissolution, the Alderley mines were let to Allan Gibb. The lease, made on 18 December 1913, was for twenty-one years from 25 December 1913 and covered about 258 acres on Alderley Edge, with surface rights to over nine acres and leave to appropriate up to ten more acres, if required, for waste disposal. Gibb erected a small process works that included an acid-leaching plant (Figures 16.19, 16.20); 300 tons of ore valued at

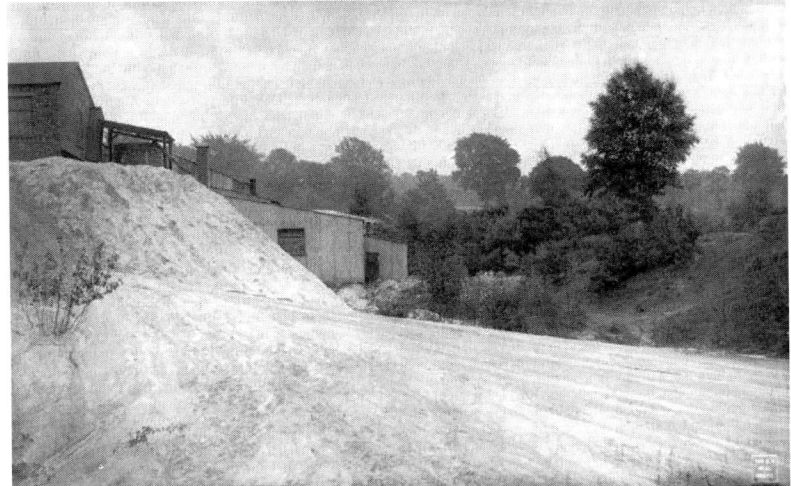

Figure 16.19. The process works erected by Allan Gibb at West Mine and used by Alderley Copper, Limited, in 1918 and 1919, looking east.

Thompson's postcard. Author's collection.

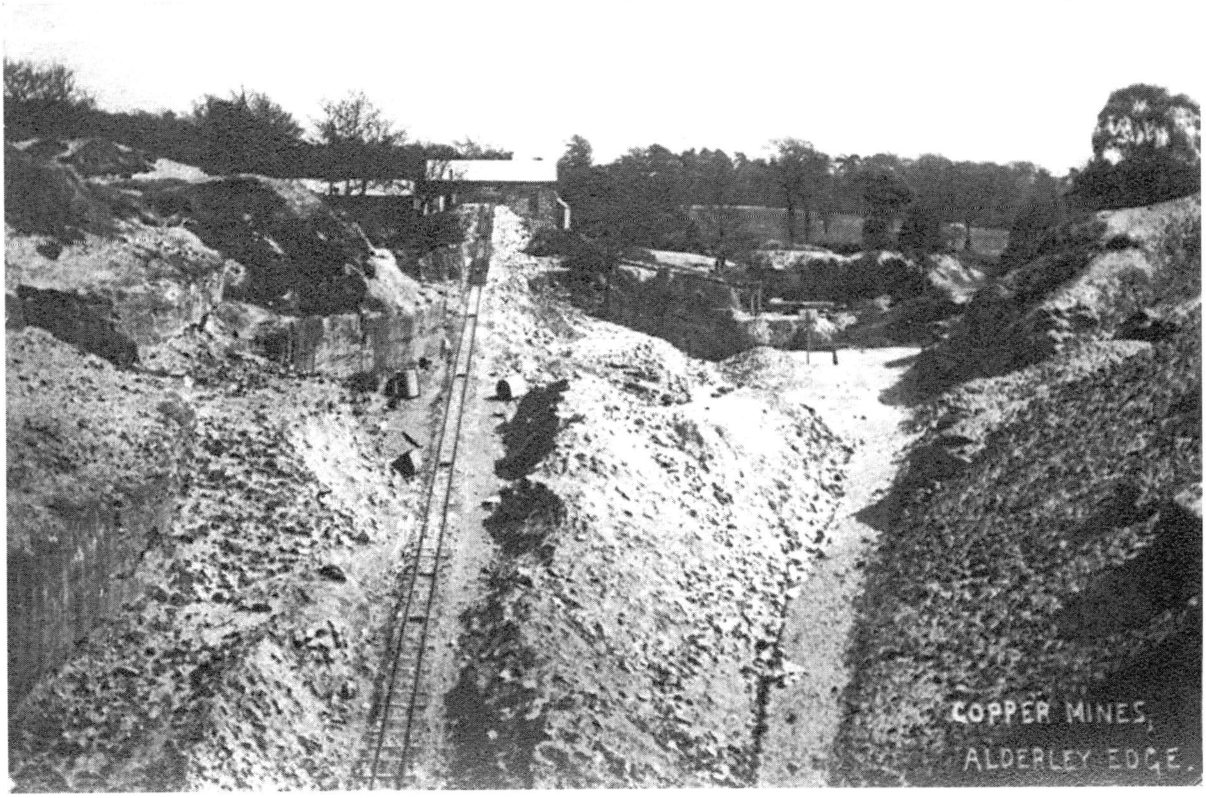

Figure 16.20. The opencast at West Mine, looking east towards Gibb's process works at the top of the incline.

From a print held in Manchester Museum.

£129 were produced in 1914 and 35 tons of precipitate, valued at £1,600, and with a copper content of 22 tons in 1915. In 1914 eight people were employed above ground and five below; the corresponding numbers in 1915 were six and five (Warrington, 1981: fig. 6). Work was suspended during 1916 and 1917 but one person remained as caretaker. In 1917 Gibb was an army officer serving abroad and had, before 21 January 1918, sold his interest in the mines and plant to Arthur Comings Hide (Warrington, 1981: 67), who also held a lease on the other Cheshire copper mine, at Bickerton, for three years from 2 November 1917 (Carlon, 1981: 37).

Early in 1917, Hide, with a Montagu Jacobs, held options on Gibb's property and others on the neighbouring de Trafford estate and at Mottram St Andrew. On 23 March 1917, they agreed with Messrs J. S. Ross and G. L. Crump, owners of the rights to an acid treatment process, on the creation of a company to take over those options and work the mines involved. H. F. Collins made reports on the mine in June and November 1917, when it was noted that 'private enterprise is now testing the property' (*Report of the Controller of the Department for the Development of Mineral Resources in the United Kingdom, presented to the Minister of Munitions*, 1918: 39). Hide took up the option on Gibb's property between 23 March 1917 and 21 January 1918 and the company established through the agreement between Hide and Jacobs and Ross and Crump was styled Alderley Copper, Limited (ACL). This company was incorporated on 8 January 1918, with a capital of £40,000 in £1 shares; its directors included Hide and Ross. On 21 January 1918 ACL agreed to purchase for £3,500 the effects purchased by Hide from Gibb (Warrington, 1981: appendix 3), and to take over the other options held by Hide and Jacobs. Though said to own the Alderley mines in 1917, the ACL cannot have done so prior to this agreement.

The operations of ACL were similar in scale to those conducted by Gibb. In 1918, 250 tons of copper ore valued at £300, and with a metal content of four tons, were produced, together with twenty tons of lead ore valued at £139 and with a metal content of seven tons; this is the last recorded production from mines in the district. In 1918 ten people were employed above ground and five below; when work was suspended in 1919 the corresponding numbers were two and four (Warrington, 1981: fig. 6). On 12 February 1919, when Sir Arthur Russell visited the site, the workforce comprised nine men, who received £2.5s.0d per week for a working day of nine and half hours, and five boys, who received between 17s.6d and £1.0s.6d; all were local and unskilled (Russell MSS, Natural History Museum, London, and Manchester Museum). The plant, which had been taken over from Allan Gibb, included a crusher, ball mill, three leaching tanks each with a capacity of fifteen tons, three precipitating tanks and a precipitate drainer, and storage vats; power was provided by a thirty-five-horsepower oil engine. The leaching and precipitating tanks were made of reinforced concrete and lined with tiles and asphalt, respectively; the fragment of a 'ceramic cistern' and traces of foundations noted by Timberlake *et al.* (*ArchAE*: 142) may relate to this plant. Ore from the West Mine was being used to produce a copper precipitate and copper oxide, and the production of copper sulphate, using 5 per cent sulphuric acid, was being investigated. The lead ore produced in 1918 had been sold to the St Helens Smelting Company.

The brevity of its existence, and the small number of workers, make it unlikely that ACL exercised its options to mine on de Trafford property and at Mottram St Andrew. Carlon (1979: 79) stated that the mine was finally abandoned in 1923, with the plant being sold for scrap, and rail track and reduction tanks removed, but its effects, including these items, were actually advertised for auction on 30 June 1926 (Warrington, 1981: appendix 4). Commercial involvement with the mines in the district ended with the formal dissolution of this company on 11 October 1927 (Warrington, 1981: 67).

Acknowledgements

The writer is indebted to his wife, Christina, whose patient support over many years has made this contribution possible. Thanks are also due to (in alphabetical order) Helen Chadwick, Dr Olive Checkland, Dr Andrew Cobbing, Nigel Dibben, Roger Flindall, Basil Jeuda, Richard F. May, Stephen Mills, Professor Noburu Oba, Professor A. J. N. W. Prag, Paul Sorensen, Professor Hugh Torrens and Lynn Willies, and individuals named in the earlier contribution, for their interest and for welcome advice and discussions on this subject over many years. Dr David Green kindly prepared Figures 16.7 and 16.14 from the author's drafts. The writer introduced Andrew Cobbing to the subject of the Satsuma delegation by showing him the 1865 *Macclesfield Courier and Herald* article before he embarked upon postgraduate studies in Japan that led the current state of knowledge of that group.

Further reading

Carter, C. F. (ed.). 1962. *Manchester and Its Region* (a survey prepared for the British Association for the Advancement of Science Manchester meeting, 1962). Manchester: Manchester University Press.

Warrington, G. 2010. Alderley Edge District, Cheshire. In Bevins, R. E., Young, B., Mason, J. S., Manning, D. A. C. and Symes, R. F. (eds), *Mineralization of England and Wales* (Geological Conservation Review Series **36**), 182–90. Peterborough: Joint Nature Conservation Committee.

17

Working the mines at Alderley Edge: a contemporary perspective

Nigel Dibben

An outline history of the mines

The history of the working of the Alderley mines is poorly documented but from evidence available it appears to have been spasmodic. The most detailed work on unravelling the history has been carried out by Geoffrey Warrington (see Chapter 16; see also Warrington, 1981). More recently, David Gale conducted an archaeological excavation, which was the first notable work in this field since that by Charles Roeder (Gale, 1990; Roeder, 1901; Roeder and Graves, 1905a, 1905b). Gale's excavation was scientifically organised but was too brief to be conclusive. In 1993, the wood of a shovel, found in the nineteenth century, was dated to the Bronze Age (1750 ± 50 BC) (Garner *et al.*, 1994) and in 1995 the Derbyshire Caving Club (DCC) found a hoard of fourth-century Roman coins in the top of a shaft at Engine Vein Mine. Wood preserved in the base of the shaft was radiocarbon dated as described by Simon Timberlake in Chapter 15 of this publication. The work of the Alderley Edge Landscape Project (AELP) has built on the limited knowledge in two useful ways: firstly, by practical exploration, it provided the Roman dating and obtained evidence of earlier Bronze Age work dating from around 1900 BC; and secondly, it brought to light documentary evidence of the nineteenth- and twentieth-century working.

There is a hint at Medieval mining in the sixteenth century but this is inconclusive. There is, however, documentary evidence of mining in the 1690s, when a disturbance occurred at the Edge between two rival groups of miners. The court report indicates that mining might have started in 1693, which, given the repeal of the Mines Royal Acts in 1689 and 1694, is plausible (see Chapter 16, p. 372). There are hearsay records of sporadic exploratory workings in the first two decades of the eighteenth century, although the precise dating is difficult, given that the reference to this period of mining occurs in a nineteenth-century report (Holland, 1808). In the mid-eighteenth century there was a period of working from 1758 to 1768, when Charles Roe of Macclesfield worked Alderley Edge. Shortly afterwards, he moved on to the Parys Mountain mines in Anglesey (Chaloner, 1953). Part of the workings of the mine known today as Brynlow Mine are identified with this period on the basis of the passage shape and the engraving on the wall of initials (IW) in eighteenth-century style ('I' crossed through and double 'V') and the date, 1764 (see also Chapter 16, p. 378, and the note at the end of Chapter 22, pp. 584–5).

Early in the nineteenth century, the mines were worked on and off for lead, copper and cobalt. The last is still found in at least two locations (mines now known as Wood Mine and the Cobalt Mine) and the locality was worked as a source of cobalt smalt, principally cobalt oxide, which was used to provide blue colouring to glass, pottery and paper. The most extensive mining took place between 1857 and 1877. In 1857, James Michell investigated the area and in April 1858 he took a lease from Lord Stanley to work the mines. The first stage of development was in the opencast workings at the entrance to West Mine, which were soon followed by underground workings. By 1861, when the British Association was meeting in Manchester, the workings were large enough and of sufficient interest to justify the organisation of a visit to the main stope (Anon., 1861). By 1870 the venture was obviously becoming more difficult to keep in profit and it is probable that working in the deeper sections of Engine Vein Mine was taking place. In 1877 the mine was closed and all the mining and processing equipment was sold in the following year.

In the early twentieth century, a final attempt was made to work the mines, with West and Wood Mines being re-equipped (the exact extent of re-equipping is not known) and a treatment plant being built. By 1919, work had ceased and in 1926 all of the equipment was sold. Geoffrey Warrington (1981) reproduces the list of effects offered for auction in 1878 and 1926.

Putting aside the mining history, the mines have developed a reputation, good and bad, as a place to visit. There are at least three accounts of visits to the mines for pleasure or education in the nineteenth century (see Railton and Maltby, 1971) and there is well documented evidence of visitors in the 1920s and 1930s (for example Fitzpatrick, 1935). By the 1940s, the mines were becoming very popular at weekends and in the 1950s and 1960s the irresponsible behaviour of visitors had become a major issue, as it had led to a number of fatalities (Lovelock, 1963). In 1964 Wood Mine was sealed by blasting (Anon., 1964). By about 1965 most of the mines had been sealed.

In 1969, members of the Derbyshire Caving Club (formed *c.* 1961) and geologists from the University of Manchester convinced the National Trust, which had owned most of the mines since 1948, that opening on a limited scale was technically possible and highly desirable on scientific grounds. Since 1970 many more of the mines on National Trust and adjoining land have been re-opened. The Derbyshire Caving Club now leases most of the mines from the National Trust and controls access, arranges visits to the mines by specialists and general-interest groups and re-excavates blocked shafts and passages. These activities are carried out within the terms of arrangements with Natural England (in respect of the Site of Special Scientific Interest) and Historic England (in respect of the Scheduled Monuments at Engine Vein and the treatment works), as well as the Health and Safety Executive (in respect of mine management legislation).

The mines in the AELP core area

There are over a hundred adits, shafts and superficial features of note around the Edge; Figure 16.1 (p. 369) shows the locations of a number of these and Table 17.1 (at the end of this chapter) provides a listing. Within this total, it is possible to identify eight distinct groups of entrances and associated workings. The Derbyshire Caving Club has been active on Alderley Edge since the late 1960s and has restored access to the majority of the known workings. Initially, the Club members' interest was limited purely to access but interests have broadened and a major objective is now to expose the full extent of the mines and to understand how and why they developed into their present form. This section gives a brief description and outlines the geology of each mine, before exploitation of the mines is discussed in the following section. Of the mines included below, all except West Mine are on the National Trust property. In addition to the mines listed, one mine has been re-entered by the Derbyshire Caving Club at Kirkleyditch, which lies in the AELP hinterland area. For a fuller description, the reader with an interest in exploring the mines is referred to the cavers' guide to caves and mines of the area (Barker and Beck, 2010) and to the revised edition of *The Alderley Edge Mines* (Carlon and Dibben, 2012). The current names of mines are used here as the historical names are not known in most cases (but see also Chapter 28, pp. 708–11).

West Mine (SJ 8509 7760)

Length of stopes and tunnels *c.* 10,000 m, depth 50 m.

Description

West Mine comprises an extensive series of stopes, tunnels and shafts over three levels. The largest stope is some 140 m long, 15 m high and up to 30 m wide in places. This mine was principally worked in the nineteenth century but with some twentieth-century workings near the entrance and was probably known as the Western Mine in the nineteenth century.

Geology

The mine is developed mostly in the West Mine Sandstone Member of the Helsby Sandstone Formation (HSF). The stopes and tunnels are cut by three north–south faults with relatively small displacements. Its relationship to the faults and the extent of the disseminations are quite different to those of other mines (see the cross-section in British Geological Survey, 1999).

Wood Mine (SJ 8544 7760)

Length *c.* 2,400 m, depth 30 m.

Description

Wood Mine is less extensive than West Mine and contains smaller stopes but is no less interesting, because of the variety of minerals and geological structures exposed in the mine. The main underground workings are mid-nineteenth century, although there is documentary evidence of early nineteenth-century working in the vicinity. A small section was worked in the twentieth century when the adit was re-equipped with flat-bottomed rails. This mine was probably referred to by Stephen Osborne (underground manager) in the nineteenth century as 'Windmill' (Anon., 1864a, 1864b) and as part of the Eastern Mine. It was referred to as 'Wood Tunnel' in 1911 (Public Record Office, record BT31/13561/114940).

Geology

The mine is developed wholly in the Wood Mine Conglomerate Member of the HSF, between and along two faults running west-north-west to east-south-east. The structure of the mine is detailed in Warrington (1965), Carlon and Dibben (2012) and Rowe and Burley (1997).

Brynlow Mine (SJ 8555 7723)

Length *c.* 300 m, depth 25 m.

Description

The adit entrance and one shaft entrance show signs of being eighteenth-century workings. Above the adit, the mine may be of nineteenth- or eighteenth-century origins or even earlier. Below the adit, the mine was drained in the nineteenth century by the Hough Level, which also served as the main route for ore removal in the nineteenth century. There is a section of the mine below the Hough Level, which is now flooded.

Geology

The mine is developed in the Wood Mine Conglomerate Member of the West Mine Sandstone Member of the HSF and particularly along the Brynlow Fault.

Engine Vein Mine (SJ 8605 7747)

Length *c.* 750 m, depth 60 m.

Description

The surface workings are obvious and show evidence of Bronze Age and Roman development as well as eighteenth- and nineteenth-century work. Underground, the various ages of parts of the mine are apparent, as will be discussed below. At the bottom, the mine is connected to the Hough Level for drainage (to the north) and ore transport (to the south). The name 'Engine Vein' is found in a nineteenth-century reference to the fault when encountered in Wood Mine (Anon., 1864b), although it is strictly a misnomer; the mineralisation is disseminated and is not along a true vein.

Geology

The mine is developed in the top of the Wilmslow Sandstone Formation (WLSF) and the Engine Vein Conglomerate Member of the HSF. The

HSF was formerly known as the Keuper Sandstone and the WLSF was formerly the (Bunter) Upper Mottled Sandstone. The structure of the mine is depicted by Warrington (1965), Thompson (1970c, 1991), Carlon and Dibben (2012) and Rowe and Burley (1997).

Stormy Point Mines (SJ 8610 7783)

Length *c.* 150 m, depth 20 m.

Description

There are a number of mining sites on Stormy Point but the longest mine, mostly inaccessible at the time of writing, is Doc Mine, which appears to be a nineteenth-century development of an older working. On the same level as the main section of Doc Mine is Pillar Mine, which consists of a main gallery into the hillside with a branch passage at the end. The entrance of Pillar Mine (see Figure 16.2, p. 375) was divided by a rock pillar until vandalised in the 1970s. The name 'Doc Mine' originated in the 1940s or 1950s.

Geology

The mines are developed in the WLSF and in the Engine Vein Conglomerate Member of the HSF. All are close to the Stormy Point Fault, which trends west-north-west to east-south-east.

Hough Level (from SJ 8622 7781)

Length *c.* 1,500 m, maximum depth below surface 60 m.

Description

The Hough Level links all of the mines listed above except West Mine to a portal near the treatment works of the 1857–77 period. In the nineteenth century, the level was probably known as Oakes Level (Anon., 1864a) and in the early twentieth century it was Yard Level (Russell, 1919).

Geology

The mine was cut in the mainly unmineralised part of the WLSF to the north. The level crosses many of the west-north-west faults of the area at depth.

Saddlebole Mine (SJ 8602 7611)

Length and depth minimal.

Description

Saddlebole is an outlier of the Engine Vein Conglomerate to the north of Stormy Point. Just below the surface at the top of the hill is a small mine in two levels, hand-picked and appearing to date from the eighteenth century or earlier. Excavation work in 1999 has shown that the mine is of various ages and parts of it extend further down the hill on the north face.

Geology

The upper tunnels are cut through the WLSF in its topmost parts. The tunnels do not appear to be influenced by the north–south fault which cuts through the outlier at the top of the rise, although further excavation work may establish a connection.

'Cobalt' Mine (SJ 8594 7727)

Length c. 1,000 m, depth 16 m.

Description

This mine is quite different to the mines named above in that it is shallow, follows the north–south Wizard Fault rather than an east–west fault, contains circular rather than rectangular shafts and shows little evidence of copper mineralisation. It is probable that the mine was worked separately for cobalt in the soft sandstone from which the workings have been excavated; it has been named recently on the basis of this supposition.

Geology

The mine is developed in the Beacon Lodge Sandstone Member of the Wood Mine Conglomerate Member of the HSF. It is developed along the line of a fault complex (Johnson, 1984b).

Exploitation of the Alderley Edge mines

Mining involves a number of steps: discovery of the ore body, exploration, development, extraction and ore processing. In addition, the miners usually have to obtain permissions from landowners and speculative funding in order to open the mines. There is evidence of every step at Alderley Edge. Permissions and funding are not covered here as these are part of the economic history of the site covered in the previous chapter.

Discovery

One can only speculate as to how the Bronze Age miners found the deposits; it is probable that disseminations associated with Engine Vein Mine were exposed at the surface as a gossan. A gossan is a distinctive linear capping of rusty-looking ground flecked with green and blue malachite and azurite where the primary ores have been oxidised. The same is presumed to have been true of the deposits at Brynlow Dell and in the Brynlow Field, where Bronze Age workings are also known. What was visible at West Mine before the entrance area was infilled in the 1960s is unknown, although some pictures appear to show stone-quarrying in the entrance gorge. Once an ore body had been discovered, finding its extent is part of exploration.

Exploration

Early exploration would have been limited to excavation of the immediately obvious ore. A vertical shaft from the surface into the HSF is the most probable technique at Engine Vein Mine. This may, however, have developed into horizontal excavations, as evidence at Great Orme in North Wales (mentioned in Chapter 15) shows a complex Bronze Age mine system in rock which is sometimes harder than at Alderley Edge.

The extent of Roman working has not yet been determined. However, the evidence of the 10 m shaft (Pot Shaft) and 10 m passage into the Engine Vein Conglomerate at Engine Vein Mine shows that the Romans were prepared to drive through unproductive ground to reach the ore body. There is no reason to suppose that Pot Shaft is the only Roman working at Alderley Edge.

Later miners had better tools at their disposal and the opening of Brynlow Mine (Figure 17.1) and the more thorough exploration of Engine Vein Mine since its capping in 1982 have revealed hand-picked levels through virgin ground. These passages show that short straight

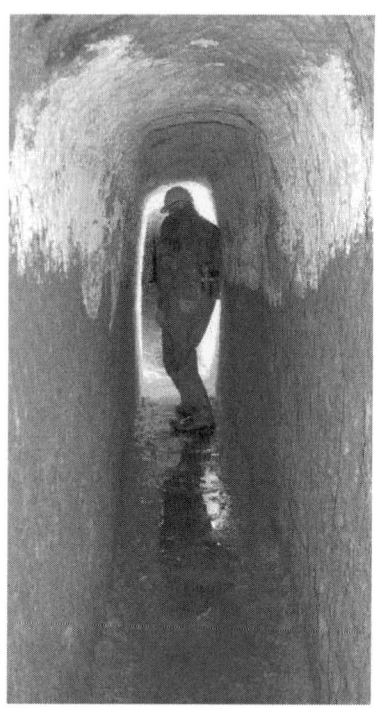

Figure 17.1. Brynlow adit, a typical eighteenth-century passage known as a coffin level.

Photograph Nigel Dibben.

levels were often driven to look for ore and that not all of these trials were successful. It is notable that in Engine Vein Mine (on the cross fault at the western end), the Hough Level (at Square Shaft) and Brynlow Mine (entrance adit extension) these trial hand-picked levels are very small, the smallest being about 900 mm high and 400 mm wide. All levels through which regular access was gained seem to have been driven larger or enlarged later.

During the late nineteenth century, levels driven off the main workings were more or less the same size as standard access levels: 1.5 m high by about 1.3 m wide (Figure 17.2). One innovation of the nineteenth century was the use of surface boreholes to obtain samples without the expense of driving levels. The mine abandonment plan (Mining Records Office, 1878) shows boreholes at the periphery of the site and one can be observed underground in Wood Mine, where it has cut or been cut by a trial level. The borehole is approximately 50 mm in diameter and about 30 m deep. It is also known from contemporary reports (Anon., 1863) that boreholes were sunk ahead of drives. Analysis by the author of the direction of shot-holing in Wood Mine has suggested that the mine was initially explored from four shafts at regular intervals along a line away from the Northern Boundary Fault running west-north-west to east-south-east. Passages were driven to connect the shafts once

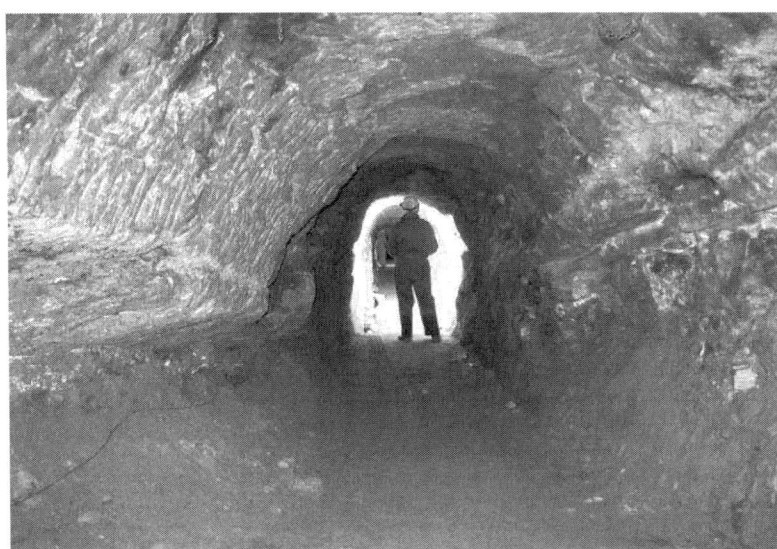

Figure 17.2. Wood Mine adit, driven by gunpowder in the nineteenth century, with a typical arched cross-section.

Photograph Nigel Dibben.

ore locations had been proved. These shafts are marked as A to D on Figure 17.3. The fifth shaft, marked E on Figure 17.3, appears to be related to development of the mine (see below).

Exploration underground was also carried out by winze and sump – there are two examples in Wood Mine, above Blue Lake and the Roadworks Shaft. The latter is distinctive by being rectangular and driven downwards within a nineteenth-century level; most shafts of the period were roughly circular and driven upwards from temporary staging, as shown clearly by the notches in their walls (e.g. in Junction Shaft). The difference is probably because of the difficulty of hand-drilling vertically downwards.

Finally, ore bodies were sometimes found when not expected in the course of driving an access level. This appears to have been the case in the Hough Level between Brynlow and Engine Vein Mine.

Development

Once the ore body had been located, it may not have been worked immediately; most mining requires the development of access tunnels and means of removing the ore before the extraction commences in earnest. In some cases drainage will be required as well. In the Bronze Age, it would be unlikely that much work was done before ore was extracted, either for access or for drainage. Development was probably limited to enlarging the access to the ore concentration.

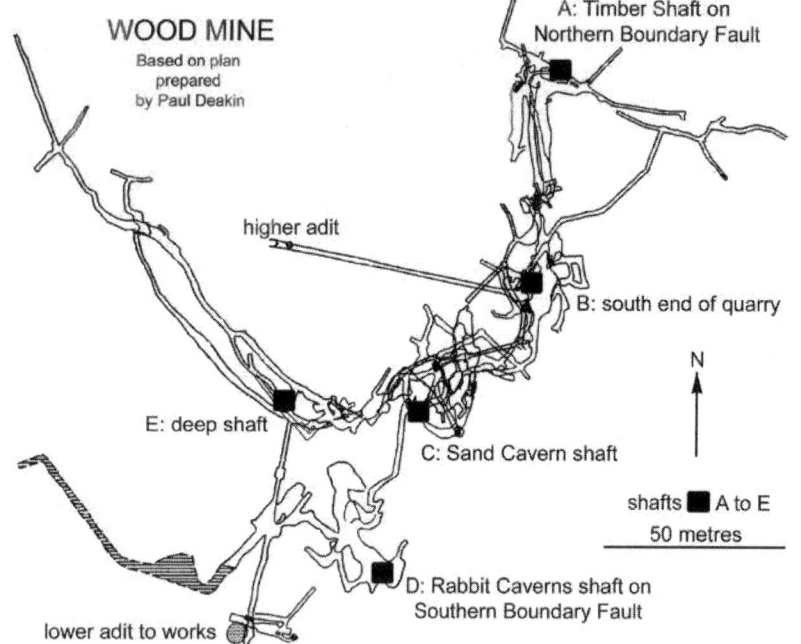

WOOD MINE
Based on plan
prepared
by Paul Deakin

A: Timber Shaft on
Northern Boundary Fault

higher adit

B: south end of quarry

N

E: deep shaft

C: Sand Cavern shaft

shafts ■ A to E
50 metres

D: Rabbit Caverns shaft on
Southern Boundary Fault

lower adit to works

Figure 17.3. Plan of Wood Mine showing locations of main shafts.

From a plan surveyed and drawn by Paul Deakin.

The Roman evidence at Alderley Edge is interesting because all we have so far identified is purely development work. It is probable that the Romans had prior knowledge of the extent and inclination of the Engine Vein Fault and decided that a vertical shaft and horizontal level into the mine presented a more workable alternative than mining down the slope of the 'vein'. We cannot tell at this stage whether they were working to get into a known body of ore or to cut beneath it and therefore to increase the amount of ore available. It is also possible that the shaft was used to remove water as, even at that time, it is probable that Engine Vein Mine would collect rainwater and seepage from the surface. At the base of the shaft, a shallow sump about 50 cm deep was found, which would support the use of the shaft for drainage with buckets hauled up the shaft.

In the eighteenth-century and earlier mines, a series of short shafts and levels were usually driven to gain access to the ore which was extracted from veins. Good examples can be seen in Engine Vein Mine, where, near Bear Pit (a later shaft 55 m deep), a descent to the 30 m level was made in three shafts of about 10 m each. From the bottom of each of the shafts, short tunnels would be driven to intercept the ore body. As a result, development was limited in lateral extent. The same sort of development is visible in the Cobalt Mine, in which five shafts have been identified at intervals of about 20 m along the ore deposit. Working probably moved from shaft to shaft so that the working face was never more than 10 m from a point of access to the surface.

In the mid-nineteenth century, Henderson (1860a, 1860b, 1860c) described the way in which the Alderley Edge ore bodies were worked at that time. Recent exploration and study of the workings bears this out. Once an ore body had been located, the first development took place at its top. When the lateral extent of the ore body had been proved, working continued outwards and downwards using a technique known as underhand stoping, until all the ore had been removed. If the ore body were lost, the pilot tunnel would be driven forwards or sideways to try to intercept the ore again. These features can be seen in most mines, for example in North End Chambers in Wood Mine. Here, the roof of the pilot tunnel is discernible in the roof of the chamber and the benches of rock where the ore was taken out in layers are still visible. In addition, trial tunnels can be seen driving along and perpendicular to the Northern Boundary Fault. In West Mine, a development tunnel can be traced from the entrance as far as the stopes above the Cavern of the Twisted Pillar. It is even possible that the Scout Hole formed the entrance to the proto-West Mine.

After access to the ore had been achieved, the next aspect of development is the creation of easy routes for removal of ore to the surface. As stated above, in early workings the same route was used to get to the workings and to remove the ore. The short shafts were equipped with steps for climbing and windlasses for hauling up the ore. In horizontal levels, it is probable that boxes, baskets or possibly sleds were used. The remains of a sled have been found in Engine Vein Mine and are believed to date from the early nineteenth century.

In the mid-nineteenth century, the extraction routes were developed systematically to converge on the treatment works at the West Mine entrance. In most stopes, a route was developed from the ore body down into a tunnel into which the railway was installed. This would involve driving a tunnel under the ore body and then connecting it to the working area with ore chutes (or box holes). The rail access tunnel was graded downwards to a low point in the mine, from which a direct route was made to the surface. As an example, ore from most of the lower levels of Wood Mine was dropped into a railway level which extends from the north to the south of the mine, linking the principal stopes. The level slopes down to a point where there used to be a shaft to the surface (shaft E on Figure 17.3). Judging from the size of the spoil heap adjacent to this shaft, it served its purpose for some time. Later, however, a level was driven from the surface with two inclines to intercept the workings at the shaft bottom. The first of the inclines is near the surface and was operated by ropes or chains from a steam engine, while the second incline is underground and was almost certainly operated by a two-handed windlass in a chamber where the rock has been cut out in a circular fashion. Between the inclines, the passage is nearly level. The Engine Vein Mine was worked in a similar manner using two ore chutes in the mine itself. These discharged into trucks on two branches of the Hough Level, which met together near the bottom of the Bear Pit in Engine Vein Mine. From there to the treatment works was a gentle downward-sloping passage to the same steam-operated incline as has been referred to above. Interestingly, this level was driven from both ends and meets halfway between Brynlow and Engine Vein Mine. At the meeting point, there was a vertical error of about 0.5 m and a horizontal error of about 1.5 m, necessitating a widening of the passage to provide room for re-alignment of the rail track.

The systematic working of the nineteenth century is praised by Russell (1919), who refers to the Hough Level (for which his name is the 'Yard Level') as 'a most convenient if somewhat devious means of access to the greater part of the workings, numerous rises having been put through to the upper beds and in some cases to the surface'. We can today identify at least nine sites of ore chutes on or near this level. Counting from the east and using modern names, these locations are:

- Square Shaft, serving Pillar Mine, Doc Mine, Opencast;
- Bear Pit, serving Engine Vein Mine (West);
- Ring Shaft, serving Engine Vein Mine (East);
- no name, serving Stope between Engine Vein Mine and Brynlow;
- Boot Hill, Brynlow, serving Brynlow Mine (there may have been two chutes in Brynlow);
- branch passage, serving Opencast in the Field;
- Field Shaft, serving Opencast in the Field (not confirmed);
- Hough Level Junction, serving Opencast in the Field;
- Stump Shaft, serving Probationers' Series/Opencast in the Field.

And of course Wood Mine connects at Stump Shaft.

Drainage has always been a problem in mining and Alderley was no exception, despite the shallowness of the workings and the porosity of the country rock. Driving drainage levels is an expensive operation for sometimes uncertain return. At Alderley, it was long believed that drainage was by natural methods. For instance, Russell (1919) mentions 'the absolute freedom from water; the whole of the workings being above the natural water level'. However, when the Hough Level between Engine Vein Mine and Stormy Point was re-opened in 1985, it was obvious that it had been driven in the eighteenth century (or possibly the early nineteenth) to drain Engine Vein Mine. The level is a hand-picked passage starting at the lowest point in Engine Vein Mine, at the bottom of an inclined shaft on the vein itself. The shaft and the level continue to carry substantial flows of water in all conditions. Interestingly, the level was widened in the nineteenth century over its full length, most probably to continue to function as a drainage level, although it also provided a route for ore from Stormy Point and may have served for some time as a route for the extraction of spoil during the driving of the Hough Level from Engine Vein Mine to Brynlow.

Extraction

The general plan of working has been described above. Once the ore body had been exposed, the ore had to be broken out and reduced in size to pieces that could be moved from the working face through the mine passages to the surface. In the earliest mining period, extraction and size reduction was probably carried out by fire-setting and use of the hammer stones which have been found so widely around Alderley Edge. Experiments by the Early Mines Research Group at Great Orme, North Wales, show how successful hammer stones can be in removing ore and rock (Lewis, 1990b). The ore would be loaded into baskets and carried or lifted by ropes to the surface. Roman and Medieval mining followed a similar pattern, except that iron tools replaced the stone mauls. In addition, the Medieval miners may have used 'plug-and-feathers' (drilling a hole and then inserting wedges to split the rock). In the seventeenth century, use of explosives was first reported in mining in England (Anon., 1665) and there is a report of explosives being used at Gallantry Bank in Cheshire before the end of the century (Carlon, 1981). Most of the early passages at Alderley Edge show little evidence of the use of explosives but a few, such as the Brynlow Mine adit, contain small drill-holes. Because of the restricted width of horizontal access tunnels, ore must have been removed in baskets or boxes carried by the miners.

Drill-holes, mostly triangular from hand drilling, are very common in the nineteenth-century workings. If a level was being driven, eight or so holes would be made in a regular pattern which forced a wedge of rock out at the bottom of the level and then brought the upper part of the heading down. It is probable that each drilling extended the level about 1–1.5 m. From data in the mine setting book for 1864 (Anon., 1864a), it would appear that two to three fathoms a week was common, depending upon conditions. One team of two men and two boys achieved three fathoms and four feet in a week.

Stopes were opened by drilling downwards and outwards from an initial tunnel using the same drilling technique as for levels (Figure 17.4). Ore was broken and sorted near the working face and then transported to the nearest exit or railway tunnel by metal-tyred wheelbarrow. In

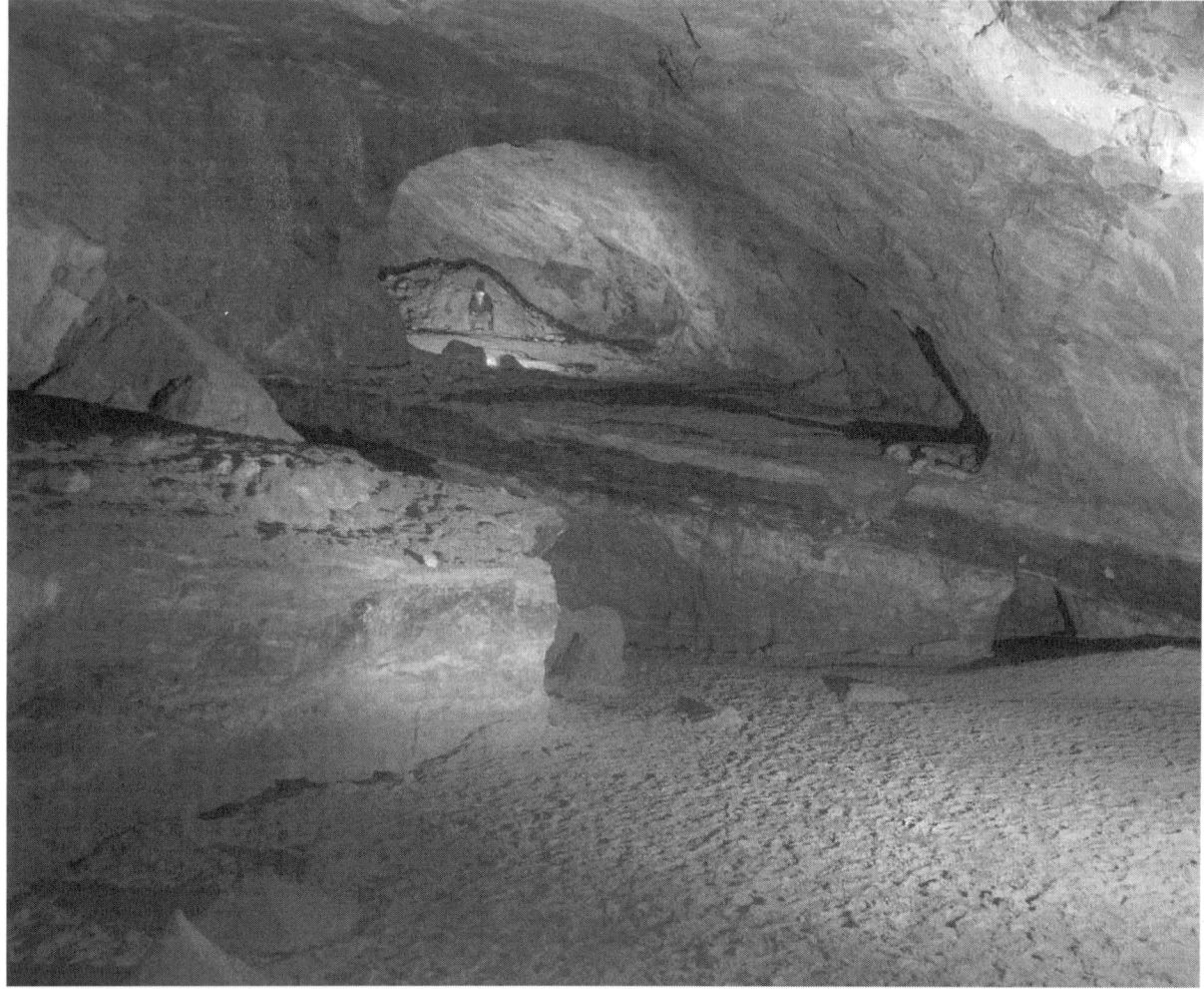

Figure 17.4. West Mine: Sphinx Chamber, showing the extensive workings above and below a barren bed of sandstone.

Photograph Nigel Dibben.

many places in the mines the tracks of wheelbarrows can be found and boards are still in place that were laid to make wheeling them easier. Remains of wheelbarrows are also found. The wheelbarrow routes usually lead to the top of an ore chute above a railway tunnel. Many ore chutes have been located, including four complete with their timberwork. If the timberwork has collapsed and disappeared, evidence is usually present in the form of a sloping line of stemple holes on which the chute was supported. Often the rock of the shaft above the chute will be well smoothed from the passage of rock down the chute. At the

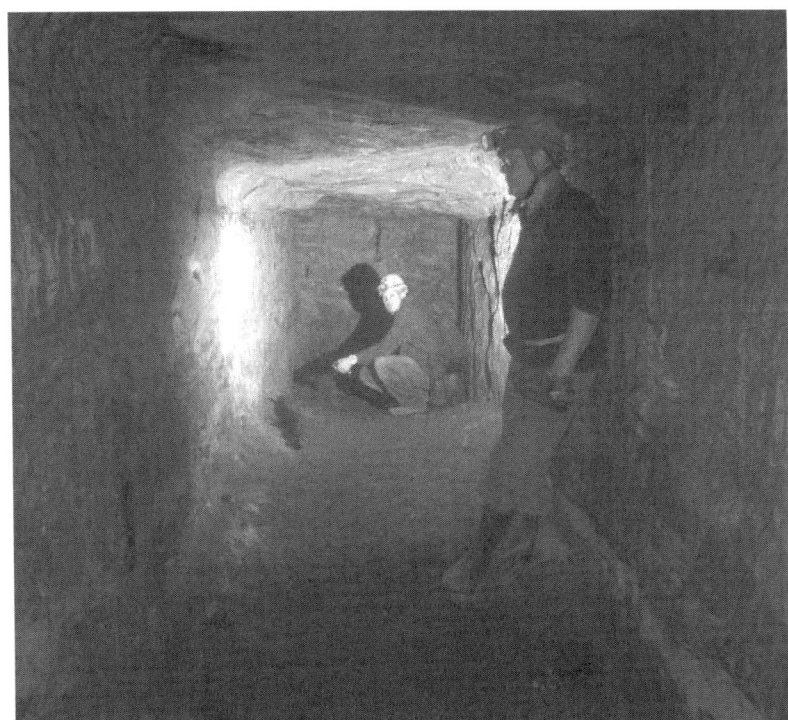

Figure 17.5. West Mine: twentieth-century working near the entrance with the characteristic rectangular shape from the use of high explosives.

Photograph Nigel Dibben.

bottom of the chute, the miner's job was to release a measured amount of ore into each tub. To help him, the miner could block the bottom of the chute with boards or use a long-handled rake to pull out the ore. At one chute in Engine Vein Mine the miner's stance can clearly be seen from the candle soot on the roof above his position and from the recess in the wall behind that saved him from banging his elbow as he raked out the ore!

The final product of the extraction work up to the early twentieth century ranges from small vein-like workings in Engine Vein Mine to the massive stopes of West Mine.

In the last phase of workings, in the twentieth century, high explosives were used and the passages take on a distinctive rectangular shape (Figure 17.5).

Processing

Once the ore had been brought to surface, it was necessary to extract the metal from it. There is evidence of three methods at Alderley, which have been described in more detail in the preceding chapters.

In the Bronze Age, it is probable that the miners worked the secondary ores, such as azurite and malachite, each being about 55 per cent copper by weight. Being copper carbonate, there was no sulphur to be removed and smelting with charcoal in a reducing atmosphere produces copper in one step. This has been proved in practical experiments by Simon Timberlake and the Early Mines Research Group as part of the Alderley Edge Landscape Project (see Chapter 15).

The Medieval miners, and probably the Romans before them, are likely to have processed the primary sulphide ores found in the disseminations such as in Engine Vein Mine. The ore would be dressed to remove waste material and the concentrated lead or copper sulphide would be roasted in air to remove the sulphur. After roasting, the oxide ore would be smelted in a reducing atmosphere with charcoal to produce a crude copper cake. This was then refined further to produce fine copper.

In the period of the Alderley Edge Mining Company, from 1859 to 1877, Henderson's wet process was used to extract copper from the rock by reaction between the carbonate and hydrochloric acid. This had the advantage of being a low-energy process using a waste product from another Cheshire industry, the manufacture of soda from salt by the Le Blanc process. Lead was extracted by physical separation and was sold to make white paint in Macclesfield (see Chapter 16), while a cobalt/ nickel residue was obtained from an acid recycling process. There is no record of the cobalt residue having any real economic value at the time.

The twentieth-century plant used the same technique as above to extract copper, but for at least part of the working period the site was manufacturing copper sulphate crystals by using sulphuric acid in place of hydrochloric acid.

Other features

There are many other features of the mining history that can be interpreted at Alderley Edge. Two in particular are lighting and ventilation.

No one can say what lighting was used in prehistoric or Roman times, although animal-fat or oil lamps are probable. In the mines at Rio Tinto (Spain), typical pottery oil lamps have been found (Fundación Rio Tinto, 1994). Lighting throughout the historic life of the mines has been by candle. Miners would place a candle on their hats or near their workplace and would fix one to the front of a tub when tramming. In Wood Mine, at least four candle stubs have been found attached to the wall of the mine by clay. At junctions and the bottom of shafts it appears that candles may have been left for longer periods, as there is very often a sooty area just above a recess in the wall. We know that in the nineteenth century electricity was not used (Henderson, 1860a). In the pictures of West Mine in the 1920s, poles are visible alongside the rail track into the mine, so either there was electrical signalling or electric lighting at key points (Carlon, 1979: 77). The only other lighting recorded was magnesium strip used to light the mines for visitors (Anon., 1865b; see also Chapter 16, pp. 401, 409).

Ventilation is a constant problem in mines and although no special study has yet been made of the ventilation of the Alderley Edge mines it is possible to say a considerable amount about ventilation from field evidence. Wherever possible, miners would exploit natural ventilation, which can be induced simply by using two entrances. For example, at Wood Mine there is evidence that there was a door at the inner end of the adit entrance on the branch towards the northern end, which would have prevented air from taking the shortest route through the mine. In West Mine, we now think that some of the narrower passages were specifically driven to provide ventilation routes linking parts of the mine that would otherwise accumulate stagnant air and fumes. In 'blind headings', passages driven out from the workings for exploration, one can see where the nineteenth-century miner has modified the passage to accommodate air trunking to feed fresh air to the face workers. Often the existence of such marks can indicate the sequence of working in the mine, as there appears to have been a fairly rigid policy of fitting the trunking (or 'bagging' as it is also called) in the roof on the right-hand side of the passage, looking in. This can help to link field observations with contemporary reports.

Conclusions

The mines at Alderley Edge can provide valuable examples of mining and mineral-working methods from all periods up to the twentieth century. Evidence of Bronze Age working is found alongside Roman, late Medieval, eighteenth- and nineteenth-century mining. The working methods have been developed for the special conditions at Alderley Edge (relatively shallow workings, soft rock and good drainage) but share much in common with workings elsewhere in Britain and Ireland. The final result is a fascinating and extensive range of mine workings ranging from Bronze Age to twentieth century and from body-sized to vast (Figure 17.6).

In the four decades since the National Trust first allowed the re-opening of the mines at Alderley Edge, work by the Derbyshire Caving Club has made exploration and study much easier than was possible before. From the tens of thousands of man-hours spent by the Club members in the mines, it has been possible to interpret the history and

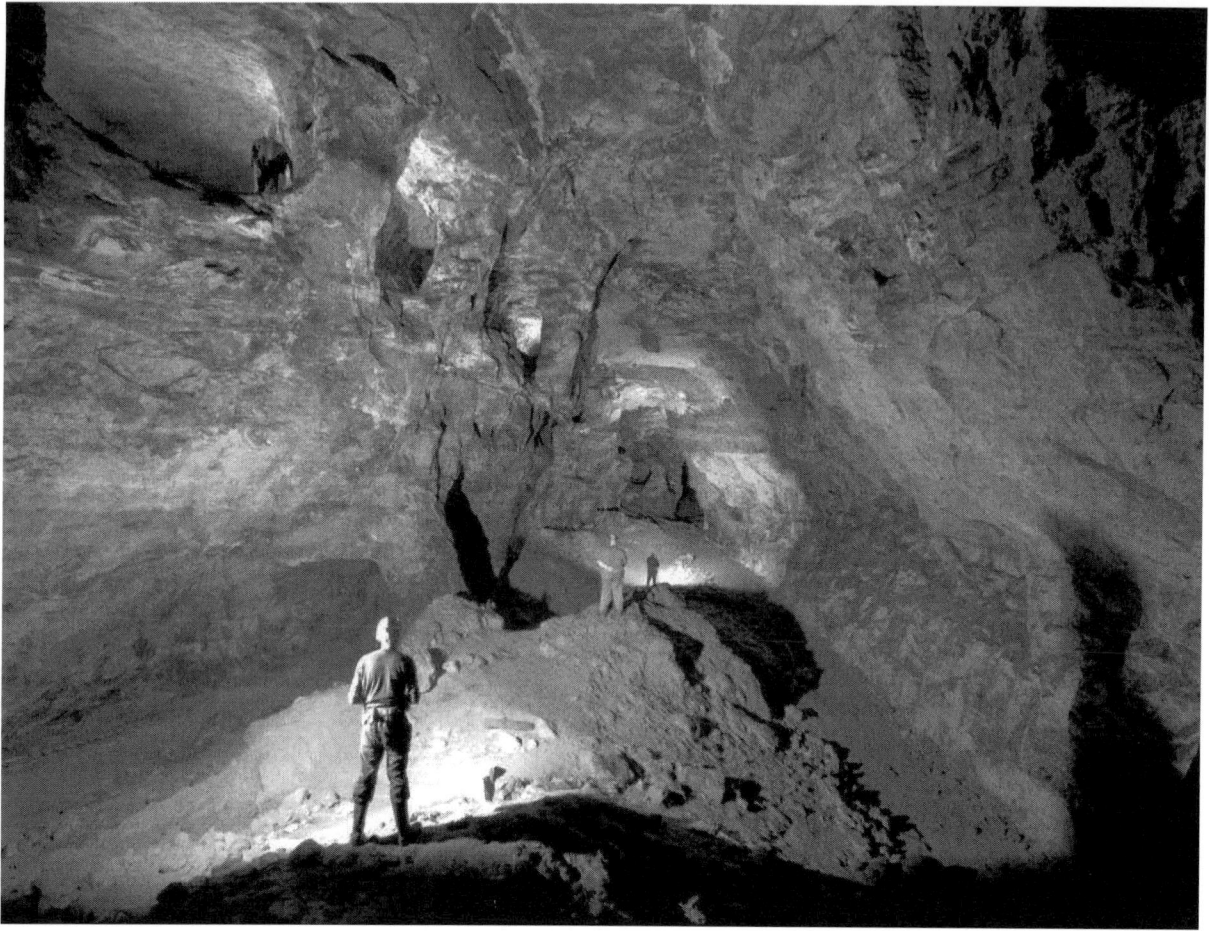

Figure 17.6. Main chamber of West Mine, showing the vast stopes created in the second half of the nineteenth century.

Photograph Ed Coghlan.

working practices of the mines and miners in ways which are not possible from the literature alone. By attempting to reconstruct the features of the mine that have long disappeared, such as the railway from Engine Vein Mine to the Hough, the Club members have not only achieved their objective of opening passages blocked for decades but have also been able to suggest more about mining techniques than is possible from written and oral accounts of mining at Alderley and elsewhere. This chapter has merely scratched the surface and readers interested in more detail are referred to Carlon and Dibben (2012) and to Geoffrey Warrington's account in Chapter 16 of this volume, together with the further references cited there.

Table 17.1. List of mine sites

Name	Grid reference	Shaft (S), level (L) or opencast (O)
Alderley Cottage Adit	SJ 8430 7760	L
Doctor's Shaft	SJ 8468 7759	S
Sphinx Shaft	SJ 8492 7758	S
Sitting Down Shaft	SJ 8498 7760	S
White Shaft	SJ 8501 7764	S
Main Chamber	SJ 8505 7765	S
Top Gallery Shaft	SJ 8505 7766	S
First Shaft	SJ 8508 7762	S
18-Acre Shaft	SJ 8509 7763	S
Over West Shaft	SJ 8510 7762	S
Fireman's Entrance	SJ 8510 7762	L
SW Mine	SJ 8510 7762	L
Side Entrance	SJ 8510 7762	L
Over West Level	SJ 8510 7762	L
Main Entrance	SJ 8510 7762	L
South Mine	SJ 8510 7761	L
North Mine	SJ 8511 7763	L
Block End	SJ 8513 7763	L
New Venture I Level	SJ 8517 7758	L
New Venture II Level	SJ 8521 7753	L
New Venture I Shaft	SJ 8522 7764	S
New Venture II Shaft	SJ 8523 7756	S
Scout Hole	SJ 8528 7755	L
Lost Adit	SJ 8529 7725	L
Hough Level West Entrance	SJ 8531 7748	L
None	SJ 8534 7747	S
Field Boundary Shaft	SJ 8536 7741	S
Stump Shaft	SJ 8540 7740	S
Hough Covered Shaft	SJ 8540 7736	S
Sand Shaft	SJ 8541 7740	S
Hough Cross Roads south entrance	SJ 8543 7733	S
Cromlech Shaft	SJ 8543 7739	S
Temple Shaft	SJ 8544 7746	S
Hough Cross Roads north entrance	SJ 8544 7734	S
Wood Mine Adit	SJ 8545 7760	
Deep Shaft	SJ 8545 7753	S
Wood Mine Adit manhole	SJ 8545 7760	L
Opencast to Probationers west	SJ 8546 7736	O
Pillar and Post	SJ 8546 7746	S
Field Opencast	SJ 8547 7736	S
Opencast to Probationers east	SJ 8547 7735	O
Christmas Shaft	SJ 8547 7736	S
Field Shaft	SJ 8547 7732	S
Field Shaft ore chute	SJ 8548 7733	S
Wizard's Well Level	SJ 8548 7803	L
End of Hough Branch	SJ 8548 7727	S
Cross Mine Level	SJ 8548 7721	L
Cross Mineshaft	SJ 8548 7723	S
Wood Mine possible adit	SJ 8548 7759	A
None	SJ 8549 7728	S
Rabbit Cavern	SJ 8549 7748	S
Greenhat Shaft	SJ 8550 7734	S
None	SJ 8550 7733	S
Squeedle Shaft	SJ 8550 7754	S
None	SJ 8550 7732	S
Opencast ore chute	SJ 8552 7735	S
Straight Mine	SJ 8553 7720	L

Name	Grid reference	Shaft (S), level (L) or opencast (O)
Hagg Opencast	SJ 8556 7760	O
Graffiti Chamber	SJ 8556 7762	S
North End Chamber or Timber Shaft	SJ 8556 7765	S
Brinlow Adit	SJ 8559 7724	L
Brinlow End Entrance / Trembling Den	SJ 8561 7727	L
Car Shaft	SJ 8563 7726	S
Windmill Wood Shaft 4	SJ 8564 7758	S
Windmill Wood Shaft 3	SJ 8564 7758	S
Windmill Wood Shaft 2	SJ 8565 7757	S
Windmill Wood Shaft 1	SJ 8565 7755	S
Cow Lane Shaft 4	SJ 8569 7733	S
Brinlow Roadside Shaft	SJ 8569 7724	S
Cow Lane Shaft 3	SJ 8569 7732	S
Cow Lane Shaft 2	SJ 8570 7732	S
Cow Lane Shaft 1	SJ 8571 7730	S
Brinlow Other Road Side Shaft	SJ 8571 7723	S
Shaft in Windmill Wood	SJ 8572 7744	S
Brinlow Topless Shaft (Norweb)	SJ 8572 7724	S
Shaft in Windmill Wood	SJ 8573 7742	S
Holy Well – Near Trial	SJ 8585 7778	L
Beacon Lodge Level	SJ 8586 7756	L
Church Quarry Mine	SJ 8587 7741	L
Beacon Lodge Shaft	SJ 8587 7756	S
Holy Well Level	SJ 8589 7785	L
Reeking Mine	SJ 8591 7794	L
Possible Level below Holy Well	SJ 8592 7788	L
Cobalt N Shaft 4	SJ 8592 7738	S
Cobalt N Shaft 1	SJ 8592 7736	S
Cobalt N Shaft 3	SJ 8592 7737	S
Cobalt N Shaft 2	SJ 8593 7737	S
Car Park Entrance	SJ 8593 7734	S
West End Shaft No. 2	SJ 8593 7753	S
Tom's Shaft	SJ 8593 7731	S
Holly [Root] Shaft / Hole	SJ 8593 7727	S
Reeking Shaft	SJ 8593 7793	S
Cobalt N Shaft 6	SJ 8594 7744	S
Cobalt N Shaft 5	SJ 8594 7741	S
Well Shaft	SJ 8594 7733	S
Twin Shafts	SJ 8595 7794	O
West End Shaft No. 1 = Santa's Shaft	SJ 8595 7752	S
Subsidence	SJ 8595 7720	S
Cobalt N Shaft 7	SJ 8595 7747	S
Subsidence	SJ 8596 7724	S
Balloon Shaft	SJ 8596 7752	S
Rock Shaft Level	SJ 8597 7790	L
Rock Shaft	SJ 8597 7790	S
Engine Vein Top Level Shaft	SJ 8598 7750	S
Stormy Point Shaft	SJ 8598 7791	S
Bradford Lane Shaft	SJ 8598 7709	S
Bear Shaft / Pit	SJ 8599 7751	S
Devil's Grave	SJ 8601 7788	L
Shaft 3 west of Canyon Opencast	SJ 8602 7775	S
Saddlebole Level 2	SJ 8602 7805	L
Shaft 2 west of Canyon Opencast	SJ 8602 7774	S
Saddlebole Level 3	SJ 8602 7803	L
Finlow Wood Mine	SJ 8603 7697	S
Saddlebole Tunnel 1	SJ 8603 7807	L
Saddlebole Tunnel 2	SJ 8603 7807	L

Name	Grid reference	Shaft (S), level (L) or opencast (O)
Saddlebole Side 1	SJ 8603 7808	L
Saddlebole Level 1	SJ 8603 7805	L
Finlow Hill Shaft	SJ 8603 7697	S
Shaft 1 west of Canyon Opencast	SJ 8603 7773	S
Garner's Grope Shaft	SJ 8603 7807	S
Saddlebole Main	SJ 8603 7808	L
Engine Vein	SJ 8604 7747	L
Engine Vein – Pot Shaft	SJ 8604 7749	S
Saddlebole Side 2	SJ 8604 7807	L
Engine Vein Side Entrance	SJ 8606 7746	L
Square Shaft	SJ 8606 7773	S
Shaft	SJ 8606 7785	S
Trial	SJ 8607 7785	L
Engine Vein – Plan B Shaft (No. 4)	SJ 8607 7747	S
Ring Shaft	SJ 8607 7748	S
Saddlebole Lower Level	SJ 8607 7806	L
Shaft	SJ 8607 7786	S
Shelter	SJ 8607 7784	L
Rock Shelter/Iron Gates	SJ 8607 7783	L
No. 3 Shaft	SJ 8608 7747	S
Shaft 1 near path to Canyon Opencast	SJ 8608 7777	S
Shaft 2 near path to Canyon Opencast	SJ 8608 7775	S
Pit	SJ 8608 7783	S
Shaft	SJ 8608 7784	S
No. 2 Shaft	SJ 8608 7747	S
Engine Trial	SJ 8610 7745	L
No. 1 Shaft	SJ 8610 7746	S
Quarry Opencast	SJ 8610 7762	O
Canyon Opencast	SJ 8610 7770	O
Shelter above Doc Mine	SJ 8610 7782	L
North Engine Vein Level	SJ 8610 7754	L
Doc Mineshaft	SJ 8610 7784	S
Ed's Tunnel	SJ 8611 7759	L
Round Shaft	SJ 8611 7769	S
Silver Shaft	SJ 8611 7766	S
Pillar Mine	SJ 8612 7783	L
Trial	SJ 8612 7758	L
Doc Mine	SJ 8612 7781	L
Shaft 1 east of Canyon Opencast	SJ 8612 7769	S
Doc Mine Lower	SJ 8612 7782	S
Abbadine's Level	SJ 8613 7781	L
Shaft 2 east of Canyon Opencast	SJ 8613 7768	S
Pine Shaft	SJ 8615 7767	S
Pine Adit	SJ 8615 7767	L
Hough End Shaft	SJ 8616 7783	S
Hough Level	SJ 8619 7782	L

The sites are listed in grid reference order reading from west to east and north to south.
Source: author generated.

18

The quarries of Alderley Edge

Nigel Dibben (based on original text by Simon Timberlake, Tom Burke and Clare Pye)

Evidence for quarrying of stone, sand and marl at Alderley Edge has been obtained from maps and field observation. Sadly, there is no contemporary documentary information capable of linking particular quarries to particular periods, with the exception of the Red Moulding Sand Quarry. This chapter therefore starts by summarising the available evidence before discussing the probable ages and uses of the various quarries.

The report from the Alderley Edge Landscape Project (AELP) on the archaeology of Alderley Edge (*ArchAE*) identified and listed more than twenty sites within the study area as quarry locations, although it is believed that the number could be considerably greater if we include every place where stone was won. A number of the locations were newly identified by the AELP, while others were identified in the National Trust Sites and Monuments Record (NTSMR). The complete NTSMR is reproduced in *ArchAE* (pp. 165–8) but an extract relevant to the topics in this chapter is presented in Table 18.1: references to this table will be found in the text using the abbreviation NTSMR and a five-figure number. This table includes the National Grid reference (NGR) of each record (not only each quarry but also the other sites and monuments on the Trust's land).

During the AELP, various experiments were carried out, including one in the Church Quarry in 1997 which showed the effectiveness of fire-setting (*ArchAE*: 188–92). The evidence from that experiment can be used to demonstrate the sort of rock surfaces that might be symptomatic of fire-setting.

Table 18.1. Locations of quarries, wells and associated features in the Sites and Monuments Record with National Grid references (NGRs)

SMR no.	Site	NGR	Monument type	Period
57700	Hollow way, Waterfall Wood	SJ 8643 7906	Hollow way	
57703	Excavated hollow, Waterfall Wood	SJ 8958 7763	Hollow	
57704	Graffiti, Waterfall Wood	SJ 8656 7764	Graffiti	
57705	Rock carvings, Waterfall Wood	SJ 8656 7765	Rock carving	
57707	Stone quarry, Borehole, Waterfall Wood	SJ 8643 7795	Stone quarry	
57708	Stone quarry, Waterfall Wood	SJ 8656 7781	Stone quarry	
57709	Stone quarry, Waterfall Wood	SJ 8644 7779	Stone quarry	
57710	Stone quarry, Clock House Wood	SJ 8668 7795	Stone quarry	
57711	Stone quarry spoil heap, Dickens Wood	SJ 8635 7773	Spoil heap	
57729	Stone dressing floor, Devil's Grave	SJ 8601 7789	Stone dressing floor	
57733	Stone, Memorial Stone	SJ 8602 7791	Commemorative	Modern: 1930–39
57734	Stone quarry, Stormy Point	SJ 8603 7788	Stone quarry	
57735	Stone quarry, Stormy Point	SJ 8602 7791	Stone quarry	
57740	Mine (Adit), Glaze Hill	SJ 8608 7793	Graffiti	Post-Medieval: 1540–1888
57747	Sandstone quarry, near Dickens Farm	SJ 8610 7830	Sandstone quarry	Post-Medieval to modern: 1872–1965
57748	Quarry, Glaze Hill	SJ 8598 7798	Quarry	
57752	Well, Holy Well	SJ 8591 7786	Well	
57753	Stones, Holy Well	SJ 8591 7788	Well	
57754	Well, de Trafford's Well	SJ 8588 7786	Well	Post-Medieval: 1540–1900
57756	Stone quarry, Well Rocks	SJ 8593 7785	Graffiti	Modern: 1901–2050
57756	Stone quarry, Well Rocks	SJ 8593 7785	Stone quarry	
57757	Stone quarry, near Holy Well	SJ 8594 7779	Stone quarry	
57762	Graffiti, Castle Rock	SJ 8560 7798	Graffiti	Post-Medieval: 1540–1900
57764	Stone quarry, Castle Rock	SJ 8555 7797	Stone quarry	
57765	Stone quarry near Wizard's Well	SJ 8553 7803	Stone quarry	Post-Medieval: 1540–1900
57766	Well, Wizard's Well	SJ 8548 7803	Graffiti, well	Post-Medieval: 1540–1900
57768	Sandstone quarry, Mottram Road	SJ 8537 7827	Sandstone quarry	Post-Medieval: 1540–1900
57785	Stone quarry, Church Quarry	SJ 8589 7740	Stone quarry	Post-Medieval: 1540–1900
57785	Stone quarry, Church Quarry	SJ 8589 7740	Graffiti	Post-Medieval: 1750–1850
57786	Powder Magazine, Church Quarry	SJ 8592 7736	Powder magazine	Post-Medieval: 1540–1900
57788	Well, Wizard Inn	SJ 8596 7734	Well	Modern: 1901–49
57791	Marlpits, NT Visitors' Car Park	SJ 8614 7713	Marlpit	
57792	Stone quarry, Thieves' Hole	SJ 8608 7730	Stone quarry	Post-Medieval: 1540–1900
57793	Well, Warden's Cottage	SJ 8598 7739	Well	
57794	Stone quarry, near Warden's Cottage	SJ 8605 7735	Stone quarry	
57797	Stone quarry, near Engine Vein	SJ 8609 7739	Stone quarry	Post-Medieval: 1540–1900
57799	Stone quarry, Engine Vein	SJ 8607 7749	Stone quarry	Post-Medieval: 1700–1900
57800	Stone quarry, near Engine Vein	SJ 8605 7755	Stone quarry	Post-Medieval: 1540–1900
57801	Stone quarry, Old Quarry	SJ 8607 7764	Stone quarry	Post-Medieval: 1540–1900
57802	Road, Old Quarry	SJ 8605 7767	Road	Post-Medieval: 1540–1900
57807	Graffiti, near Engine Vein	SJ 8614 7754	Graffiti	Modern: 1940–50
57809	Recumbent stone circle, near Old Quarry	SJ 8602 7774	Stone circle	Post-Medieval: 1540–1900
57812	Possible reservoirs, Windmill Wood,	SJ 8563 7767	Reservoir	Post-Medieval: 1540–1900
57827	Well, Brynlow	SJ 8514 7714	Well	
57831	Possible marlpit, Artists Lane	SJ 8559 7715	Marlpit	
57834	Mine (adit), Brynlow Dell	SJ 8553 7721	Graffiti	Post-Medieval: 1540–1900
57834	Mine (adit), Brynlow Dell	SJ 8553 7721	Graffiti	Post-Medieval: 1540–1900
57849	Possible marlpits, Brynlow Field	SJ 8553 7745	Marlpit	Post-Medieval: 1540–1900
57858	Marlpits, near West Mine	SJ 8515 7775	Marlpit	Post-Medieval: 1850–1900
57889	Mine-workings, Engine Vein	SJ 8605 7749	Rock carving	
57890	Stone quarry, Engine Vein	SJ 8605 7749	Stone quarry	

Source: Extract from National Trust Sites and Monuments Record.

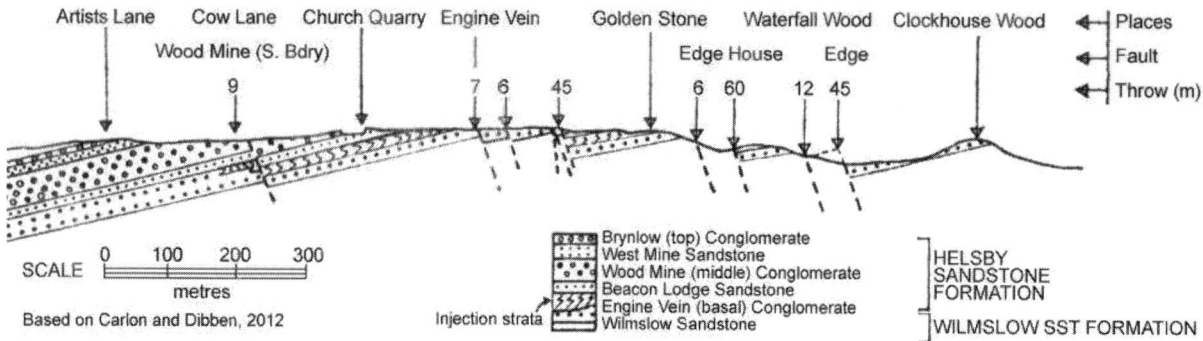

Figure 18.1. Cross-section of Alderley Edge from west to east showing the outcropping of the various sandstone and conglomerate beds.

From Carlon and Dibben (2012: 29, fig. 7), with courtesy of the Geologists' Association.

Outline of geology

The section through Alderley Edge shown in Figure 18.1 (taken from Carlon and Dibben, 2012: 29, fig. 7) shows how the beds of rock in the Helsby and Wilmslow Sandstones, part of the Sherwood formation, dip down along the natural slope from east to west. The dip at Alderley Edge is steeper than the slope of the present land surface. The quarries of building stone lie in the sandstone beds (e.g. Beacon Lodge Sandstone, Wood Mine Sandstone) and not in the conglomerates, which are too hard to be easily shaped. For instance, Church Quarry lies in the Beacon Lodge Sandstone, although the overburden is the Wood Mine Conglomerate, as can be clearly seen on the west wall of the quarry. The Red Moulding Sand Quarry lies in the more clayey and unmineralised Wilmslow Sandstone (Figure 18.1).

Stone quarrying

Field walking and surveying on the Edge during the Landscape Project revealed evidence for at least four different types of stone quarry. These differences relate to scale as well as style of working, and may reflect the duration and complexity or indeed the simplicity of the extraction as much as the chronology of stone exploitation itself (Figure 18.2).

The quarries individually identified in the survey and shown on the map in Figure 18.2 are:

- Old Alderley Quarry;
- Church Quarry;
1 Saddlebole – weathered boulder and outcrop, possibly Medieval;

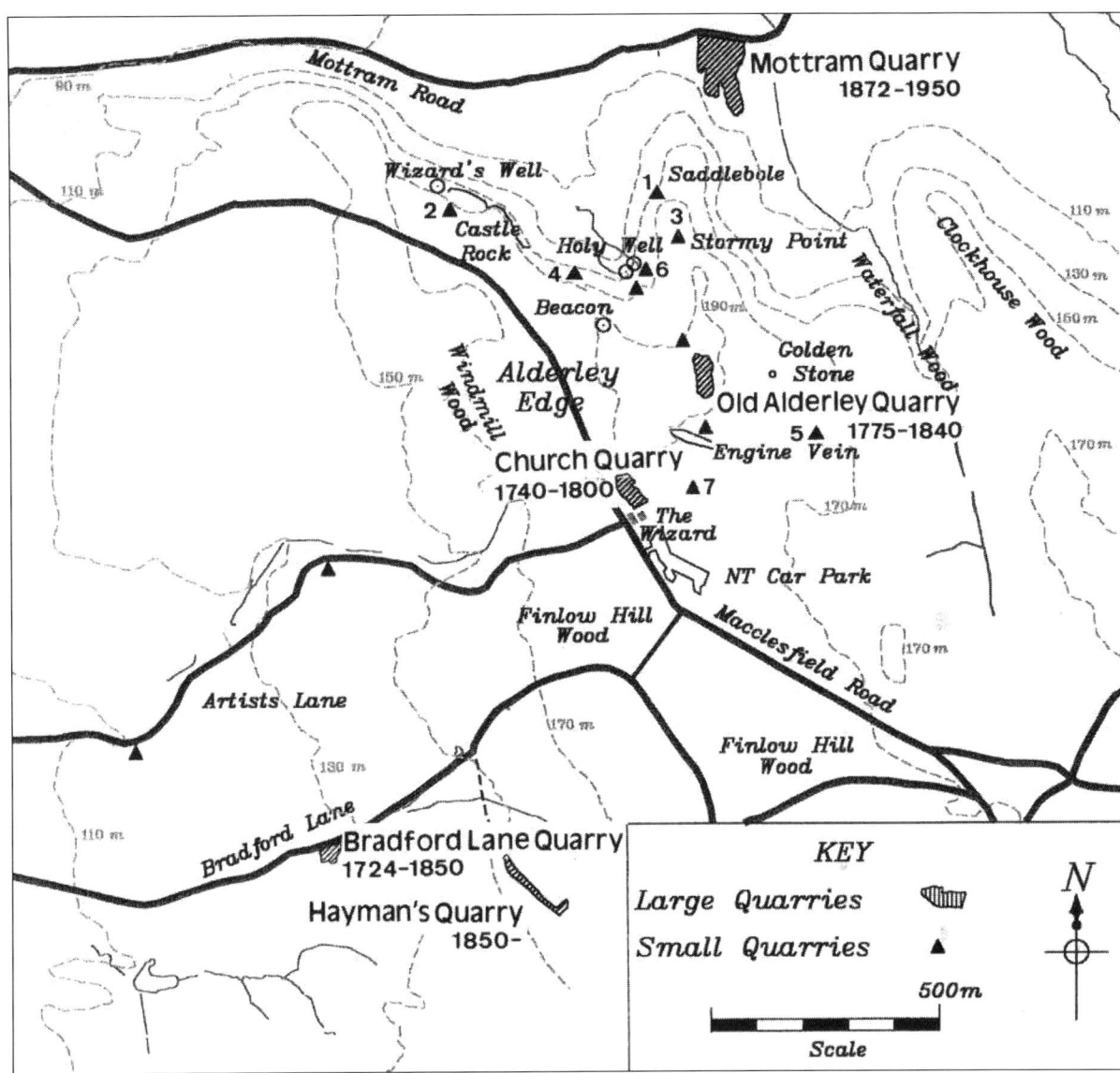

Figure 18.2. Sketch map showing quarry sites and periods: shaded areas showing locations of Old Alderley Quarry and Church Quarry (and others); 1, Saddlebole – weathered boulder and outcrop, possibly Medieval; 2, Wizard's Well – block slot and outcrop quarry; 3, Stormy Point – block slot and outcrop quarry, possibly Medieval; 4, Fitton's Chair – block slot and outcrop quarry, pre-eighteenth century; 5, Old Edge House Farm – small quarry, seventeenth to eighteenth century; 6, Holy Well – small quarry; 7, Thieves' Hole – possibly pre-eighteenth century.

Drawn by Simon Timberlake and Brenda Craddock, based on the 1992 Ordnance Survey 1:25,000 Pathfinder map, sheet 759, with the permission of the Controller of Her Majesty's Stationery Office, Crown Copyright October 2013.

2 Wizard's Well – block slot and outcrop quarry;
3 Stormy Point – block slot and outcrop quarry, possibly Medieval;
4 Fitton's Chair – block slot and outcrop quarry, pre-eighteenth century;
5 Old Edge House Farm – small quarry, seventeenth to eighteenth century;
6 Holy Well – small quarry;
7 Thieves' Hole – possibly pre-eighteenth century.

Photographic evidence from the mid-twentieth century strongly suggests that West Mine opencast was also worked as a stone quarry. In addition, there are estimated to be more than 100 other quarrying locations on a small scale.

There can be little doubt that Alderley Edge was an important local source of stone from at least the Medieval period onwards. Unfortunately, few if any records survive which refer to this industry prior to 1775, and it is particularly sad that most of the early Stanley estate papers, many of which must at the very least have referred to disputes over quarrying and the carriage of stone from the Edge, were destroyed in the fire of 1799 at the Old Hall. Sir Peter Leycester is clear that the common land at Alderley Edge was seen as a source of building stone in the sixteenth and seventeenth centuries (Leycester, 1589).

The earliest reference to stone quarrying on the Edge appears in the 1598 perambulation of the parish boundaries following the merestones, some of which can still be recognised today (see Chapter 19, p. 477, quoting the *Stanley Notebook*). The 'great quarry' located somewhere above the 'stone that lyeth in the slack [stream, i.e. Holy Well Slack] which is reputed the merestone towards Chorley' is not easily identifiable today, but it appears that this description must have been referring to one of the quarries now to be found in the gardens of the villas between Castle Rock and Alderley Edge village.

Early references

Possibly the earliest reference to a named quarry on the Edge is in the mid-eighteenth century, to 'Church Quarry'. It is generally assumed that Church Quarry is the one behind the Wizard restaurant, although it is just possible that it is another reference to the Old Alderley Quarry. It has often been suggested that Church Quarry was so named because it was the source for building stone for churches in the area as early as the Medieval period, such as St Mary's at Nether Alderley, where the earliest stonework is from the fourteenth century, and perhaps other Medieval churches too. At St Wilfrid's in Mobberley the present building (not the first on the site) is largely fourteenth or fifteenth century, and in Prestbury churchyard there is a Norman chapel (*c.* 1190–99) while the present church itself, although heavily restored in the nineteenth century, still has a thirteenth-century interior. In 1582 the tower of the fourteenth-century timber-framed church at Lower Peover was replaced in Alderley stone, showing that there was a good tradition of getting stone for local churches from the Edge. Among the Stanley estate papers deposited at the Cheshire Record Office (CALS DSA 3752/1) there is a reference to Sir James Stanley planting 'firs on the Edge above Church Quarry and between the Quarry and Glaze Hill' in about 1740. Such plantings may well have been carried out to hide or to landscape encroaching spoil tips. There are specific mentions of other plantings here in 1779, while the outline of the present quarry area is shown on the 1775 Enclosure Award map (CALS DSA 1919/33; see Figure 19.7, p. 480). The shape of the plantation shown enclosed within the older earthworks alongside this suggests that a portion of this had already been destroyed by quarrying.

The largest quarry on the Edge ('the Great Quarry', now known as the Old Alderley Quarry) is not mentioned by name in the Stanley estate papers or in the 1768 perambulation of the Edge. We know for certain that exploitation of the Old Alderley Quarry had been organised by 1775, since the Enclosure Award refers to the recent laying of the Quarry Road from the Macclesfield Road, near to what is now Beacon Lodge (on the history of the road see *ArchAE*: 184–7), and the 1775 Enclosure Award map shows 'Stone Quarry' in this location, but at only a fraction of its current size. However, it appears as a slightly larger area on the 1787 Crossley estate map (CALS P143/14/1; Figure 19.9, p. 484) and by this time the continuation of the Quarry Road is shown, joining up with the old road between Edge House, the Goldenstone and Stormy Point. The field on the west side of this quarry is numbered on the Crossley map and listed as 'Quarry Field', while the field on the east is named 'Further Quarry Field' in the 1800 Stanley records (*Stanley C7*), which may suggest agreements to expand the quarrying activities in this direction. Certainly, the maps for Stanley and Holland's *Survey and Valuation of Nether Alderley* in the 1807 estate rental book indicate considerable expansion of this quarry (*Stanley C7*) (Figure 18.3). In 1808, when Henry Holland published his *General View of the Agriculture of Cheshire*, he reported that the 'stone is in great repute for building' although inclined to contain lumps of marl (Holland, 1808). The pattern of development is slightly confused by the appearance of the quarry on the 1842 tithe map (CALS IR/30/5) in the same shape as in 1775 and 1787, smaller than in 1805, but this might be explained by the tithe map maker not having access to the 1805 plan. Evidence on the latter suggests that it is a more accurate representation. The mid-nineteenth century

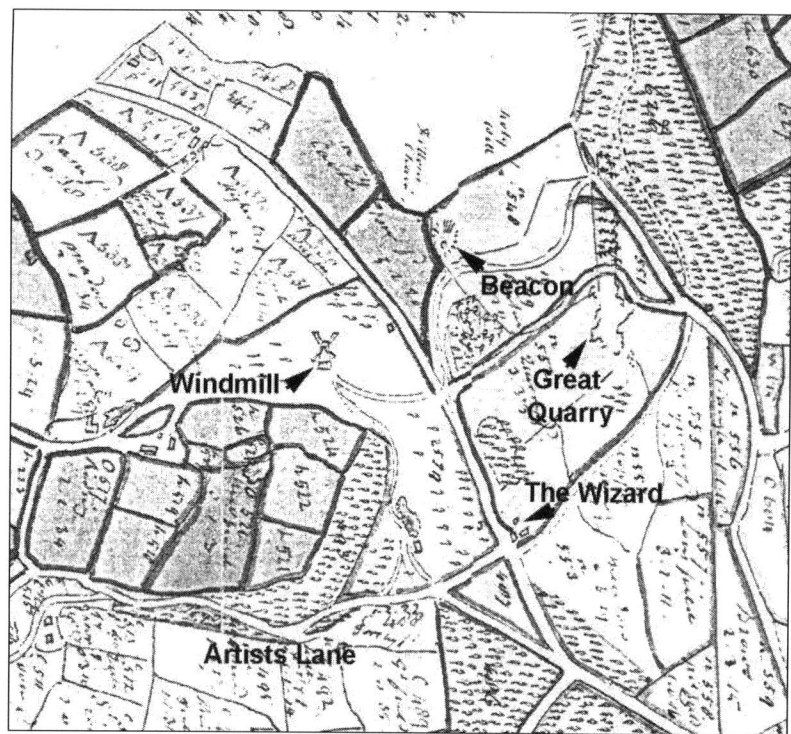

Figure 18.3. Section of the 1807 estate map showing the Great Quarry on the right, inside the sharp bend in the road. The map also shows the windmill in Windmill Piece and sundry other buildings west of the main road which are believed to be related to mining, such as the Surgery opposite the Wizard restaurant.

Courtesy of Manchester Libraries, Information and Archives, Manchester City Council.

appears to mark the end of exploitation of this quarry. In the absence of records it is difficult to be certain, but a late eighteenth-century or possibly early nineteenth-century date for the period of greatest activity is backed up by the evidence of the archaeological survey. As corroboration, it is possible to see that by the time the mines were working in the period 1858–78, the track to the quarry from Beacon Lodge had been disrupted by trial work on the continuation westwards of the Engine Vein fault. These workings probably started as early as 1805–10, when James Ashton was active at the Edge (see Chapter 16, pp. 381–2). The mine known as Beacon Lodge Mine, with a shaft and adjacent level entrance, interrupts the Quarry Road. The 1872 Ordnance Survey map shows this section of the track as unfenced and a diversionary route had been created even before the 1805 map was drawn.

By the middle of the nineteenth century the easily extractable and good-quality sandstone of the Edge had been all but exhausted, and the main focus of quarrying operations had already moved off the escarpment to locations such as Hayman's Farm, a site from which the transport of large amounts of stone by cart on a well laid cobbled quarry road (Bradford Lane) of much gentler incline proved to be an altogether easier and more efficient operation. Hayman's Farm Quarry may have provided the stone for the construction of St Philip's Church (1851–52, with the south aisle and steeple added and various improvements

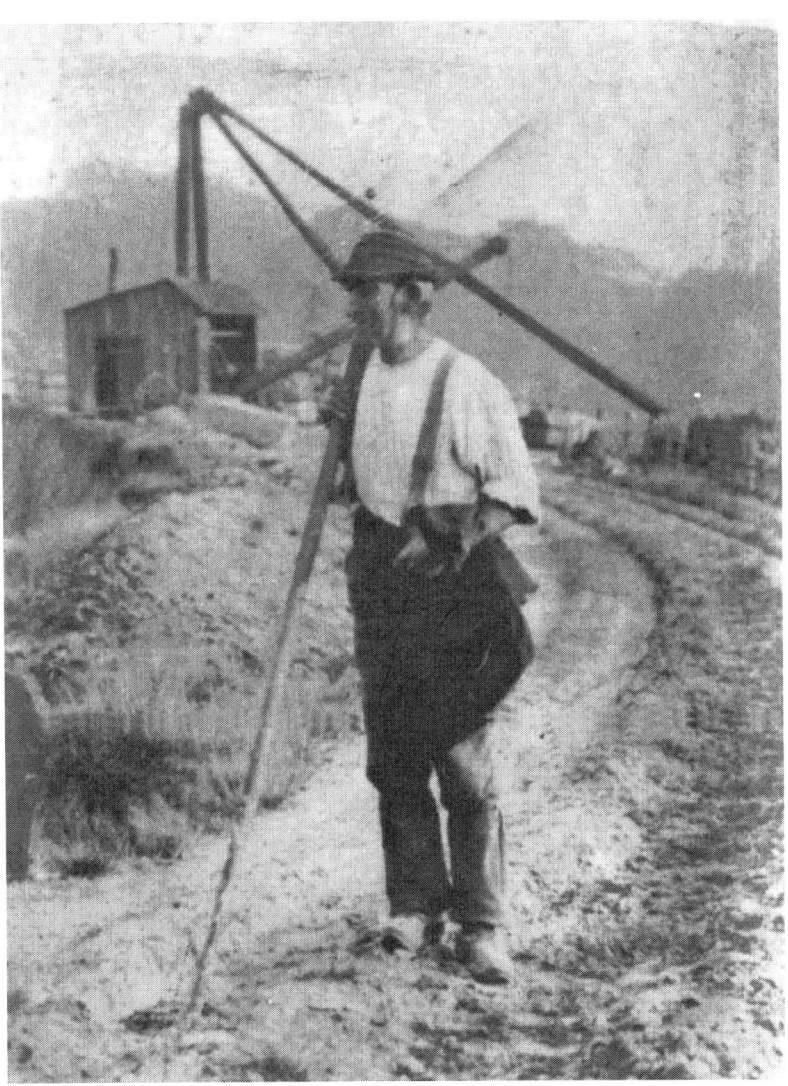

Figure 18.4. Quarryman believed to be Joseph Powell (b. 1840) at Hayman's Farm Quarry.

Photograph courtesy of Stewart Powell.

made in 1857; see Chapter 23, p. 594) and other municipal buildings in Alderley Edge. In 1839, the Turnpike Trust was worried about the damage being done to the road surface from heavy carts hauling stone from Hayman's Farm Quarry (Figure 18.4) to rebuild Capesthorne Hall, a few miles to the south of Alderley (CALS DCB 1179/71/1). In the 1841 Census, stone-getters were lodging at the Hagg Cottages while they took stone out of Hayman's for the railway and there were also a stonemason (James Summerfield) and stone-getter (William Bowers) in Bradford Lodge (Census record reference HO 107/99/2, pp. 1, 15). The operation of this deep quarry continued into the twentieth century, and extraction, though still largely carried out by hand with the aid of some explosives, was considerably more mechanised, with the use of cranes and winches (Figures 18.5) and an incline to the road.

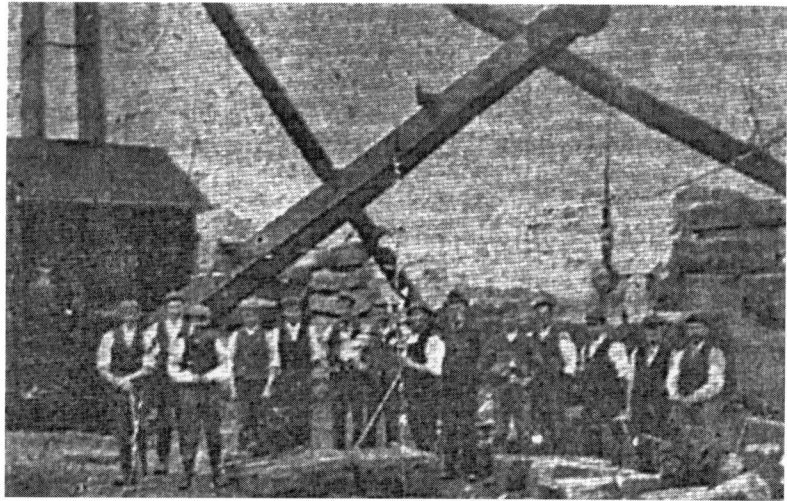

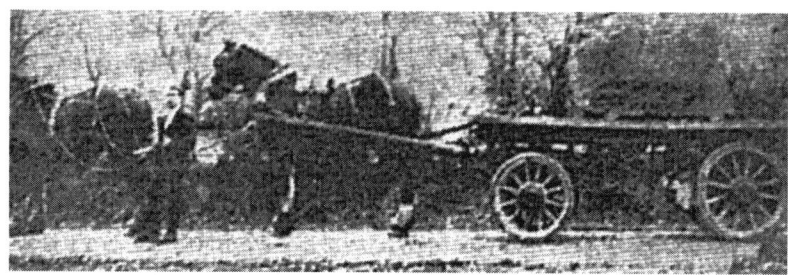

Figure 18.5. Pictures from the 'Do You Remember?' series (nos 191, 192) in the *Alderley and Wilmslow Advertiser*. (a) Group of workmen at Hayman's Quarry with cranes in the background. (b) Cart loaded with stone, probably at Nether Alderley.

Both parts from the 'Do you remember?' series (nos 191, 192) in the *Alderley and Wilmslow Advertiser*.

No other quarries at Alderley Edge are identifiable from documentary references, although there are many small workings scattered across the open land.

Details of quarrying

The main type of stone sought on the Edge was good-quality workable 'freestone' for building. Commonly, the stone is poorly jointed and therefore easily cut and shaped. It is found in beds of medium- to fine-grained non-pebbly sandstone, such as that found in between the pebbly horizons of the Engine Vein Conglomerate (as at the Old Alderley Quarry), the Wood Mine Conglomerate (Church Quarry), Nether Alderley Sandstone (at Topps Farm and the Butts) and occasionally in the basal Wilmslow Sandstone (as at Mottram Road). The conglomeratic sandstone, which is harder to extract and face, was quarried to a lesser extent for use as foundation stone or 'floorstone' in the footings of buildings or walls. Possible examples of this work may be seen in Church Quarry. More commonly, however (and this is found particularly in the later quarries), these beds were quarried away simply to get at the more valuable freestone.

Some stone was extracted for road repair, as can be seen on the accounts of the Surveyor of the Highways. It is perhaps significant that while stone was 'had from Alderley Edge to the Suffs [probably drains, as in 'soughs'] at the Cross', flagstones were also being drawn from Kerridge, near Bollington (Highways Accounts, 1775). This suggests that the Alderley Edge stone was not of suitable quality for some aspects of road repair.

One might hazard a guess at the tonnage of rock extracted as a result of quarrying for building stone on the Edge. It could have been as much as 90,000–100,000 tons (not all of which would have been removed as usable stone) prior to 1850, of which at least 40,000 tons were probably extracted before the end of the eighteenth century. This at least gives some idea of the scale of activity and traffic taking place, and the importance which stone might have had as a common resource before the enclosure of the Edge.

The last quarrying to take place on the Edge was in the Alderley Red Moulding Sand Quarry on the south side of the Mottram Road opposite Dickens Farm. A small 'gravel' quarry is shown marked on this spot on the 1872 twenty-five inches to the mile Ordnance Survey map and in 1909 the quarry is shown with two small open-sided buildings. However, the main period of working appears to be between 1940 and 1960, as will be described later.

Types and areas of quarry working

Weathered boulders and outcrop excavations

A possible area of early stone extraction on the Edge, where the type of quarrying is stylistically the most primitive, is to be found in an area of uneven ground surrounding a number of large perched boulders and weathered outcrops of pebbly sandstone of the Engine Vein Conglomerate on Glaze Hill (NTSMR 57748). Some of the disturbance here is undoubtedly natural, caused by some of these large weathered blocks of conglomerate slipping downhill on the clay-rich interface with the underlying Wilmslow Sandstone. The occasional presence of quarry hollows (e.g. at grid reference SJ 8597 7796) may suggest the removal of blocks which had been split where they were found. However, no tool marks such as pick or wedge cuts are visible on the rock, nor is there any obvious quarrying waste in the area. Some suitably sized blocks may have been levered out and perhaps crudely worked on the spot, or else simply rolled downhill towards the Hough and worked away from their source.

One of the large blocks which forms the feature known as 'the Iron Gates' (at the foot of which a later Medieval sledding or stone-haulage route has been cut) appears to have fallen or else to have rolled from one of these 'quarry areas' above, suggesting the antiquity of any extraction work here. There is also a possibility that the large blocks in this area may be the 'Great Stones' mentioned in the 1598 perambulation of the Edge (*Stanley Notebook*). However, in the absence of further survey or archaeological work, it can only be said that the evidence for this being a Medieval or still earlier working is somewhat ambiguous and inconclusive.

Block (slot) or outcrop quarries

Survey work during the AELP provided considerable evidence for small-scale quarrying of sandstone blocks at outcrops. In many cases these 'slot quarries' produced only one slab or at the most two slabs of stone, often carefully channelled out and cut from the top of an exposed or projecting bed of suitable rock. Commonly such excavations produce little in the way of spoil, although small quarry pits (2–3 m wide) surrounded by shallow banks (less than 1 m high) are sometimes to be found where this extraction has been carried out at ground level at the foot of an outcrop (e.g. NTSMR 57711). Some examples of these cuttings show evidence for a considerable period of weathering, while others appear to be relict features destroyed by later quarrying, and thus by inference are themselves relatively early.

A great many of these are located on rock outcrops close to the hollow ways or saddle roads of the Edge (e.g. NTSMR 57700 and 57711) such as the incline which descends the hill obliquely below Castle Rock, suggesting that blocks were sledged away downhill from source. Others, such as the Church Quarry, were near anciently used ridge routes such as that followed by the present-day Macclesfield Road. Another common association is with old field boundaries on the brows of valleys or at the tops of slopes. In this case, the blocks of stone may have been moved along the sides of the flat fields on temporary cart-ways to the saddle roads, as would have been the case above Dickens, Waterfall and Clockhouse Woods, serving the fields of Intake, Bilberry Hill and Clockhouse Hill indicated on the 1787 Crossley map.

At least ten examples of this early form of quarrying have been located on the Edge, all of which are located to the east of the Macclesfield Road. Concentrations are to be found around the previously mentioned sites of Waterfall Wood and Clockhouse Wood, and between Castle Rock and Wizard's Well. Some are associated with significant topographic features, such as the rock pinnacle immediately above Holy Well and the cutting known as Fitton's Chair on the top of the escarpment between the Beacon and Castle Stone Field. The latter site is mentioned in the perambulation of the boundaries of the Edge referred to in the 1768 Court Leet presentment in the Stanley papers (CALS DSA 3752/1).

Successive sandstone beds outcropping above the top of the rock slide at Stormy Point (NTSMR 57734) and to a lesser extent at Pillar Mine also appear to have been worked in the piecemeal fashion which has been described above, perhaps over a considerable period of time. Some detached and part-worked blocks of stone may still be seen at the top of the rock slide below Stormy Point. It is now difficult to assess how much of this has been removed by quarrying, mining or simply natural slippage. Such quarrying activity as is recognisable shows little sign of any organisation or systematic exploitation, and most likely reflects short-lived forages for stone on numerous different occasions by individuals or small gangs of workmen, perhaps at the start of local building projects. The large upright stones visible in the gable end wall of Findlow Bowers Farm below Stormy Point may well be examples of this practice.

The thinly bedded sandstone outcrops at Stormy Point and elsewhere were undoubtedly one of the most easily workable and transportable sources of stone on the common lands of Alderley, for they could readily have been sledged downhill along the saddle roads. While evidence for such small-scale quarrying on the Edge appears to be widespread, the Stormy Point area may well have been the scene of some of the earliest, possibly Medieval, quarrying activity, which undoubtedly continued into the post-Medieval period. Such informal methods of extraction of stone on the Edge are probably implied in seventeenth-century references to the gaining of freestone 'on the wastes of Over Alderley', as in Piers Leycester's deposition made in 1589 concerning the interest shown in Alderley Edge and Over Alderley as a common resource of freestone (Leycester, 1589). The tool-working on the 'channelled' cut face of the stone suggests the use of wedges as well as iron picks: the pick-work on some of these appears on typological grounds to be earlier – there is crude vertical picking similar to that found in places on Stormy Point. However, nearby examples of narrower, diagonal pick-work suggest a mixture of techniques and periods of working. This supports the idea that we are dealing here with Medieval or early post-Medieval as well as later post-Medieval extraction of freestone. While it is possible that outcrop quarrying continued into the period when the large quarries were being worked, it seems likely that this style of working had all but ceased by the middle of the eighteenth century.

Undoubtedly this piecemeal removal of stone at outcrops from Stormy Point, in combination with the early extraction of malachite and azurite from the interbedded clay bands in between, has greatly contributed to the formation of the rock slide and the subsequent problems of erosion that we see today. Indeed, this point brings into question the very assumption that this rock fall is a 'natural' phenomenon at all. The removal of less than 300 tons of quarried stone at outcrops from this side of the Edge escarpment might still have left a considerable scar on the landscape.

Small quarries with working faces

At least eight other small quarries have been identified on the eastern side of the Edge. These all provide evidence of extraction carried out over a longer period of time, but commonly as a single continuous phase of activity. Some of the cut quarry faces – typically between 5 and 20 m long in total, but rarely more than 2 m high – show evidence of minor benching along the strike of a suitable sandstone bed, and sharp right-angled corners defined by alternating layers of 'herring-bone' diagonal pick-cuts on the rock face, both left- and right-handed, suggesting that channel cutting and systematic removal of stone blocks was carried out in an organised way. Most of these sites are also associated with prominent upstanding outcrops, and no undercutting or extraction below the level of the track entrance seems ever to have been attempted. An example can be seen at Stormy Point (Figure 18.6), although it is not implausible that this excavation was primarily intended as the foundations of a building.

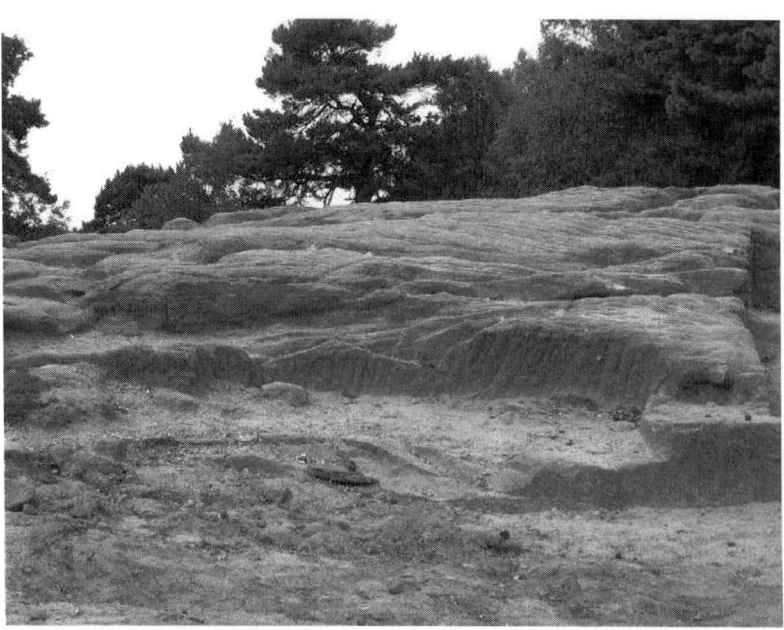

Figure 18.6. Hand-cut rock face on Stormy Point, about 300–600 mm high.

Photograph Nigel Dibben.

Cart tracks, commonly recognisable now as footpaths, can often be traced between these quarries and recognisable roads on the Edge, most of which appear to be related to tracks already in existence by 1775. Spoil tipping took the form of now-overgrown low spoil banks, some of which were deposited in groups of small mounds or ridges, and which appear to be infilling one side of the quarried area as backfill.

It seems doubtful whether many of these pits ever produced more than 100 tons of rock, and the probable working life of most was between one and five years. However, it is possible that they were used as an occasional source of stone thereafter. Some may have been worked during the later Medieval period, although most were probably dug between the seventeenth and the end of the eighteenth century, by which time the more efficient operation of the larger quarries would in all likelihood have made many of these smaller quarries redundant. However, one must be cautious here: the freedom to quarry stone on common land probably meant that small-scale extraction for the needs of local farms continued until the common land was taken in by the Stanley estate.

A good example of one of these small quarries, now covered in woodland, is to be seen along the top of the promontory between the lower path from the Beacon to Stormy Point and the top of the cliff above Holy Well (NTSMR 57757). A slightly larger quarry is to be found in the side of the bank to the north of the original site of the Old Edge House Farm. Its wall is 20 m or more high and has on one face the remains of square hole-settings for wooden beams, together with a hearth site and a chimney, perhaps for a small shelter or dressing-shed. Possibly this was a stone quarry for the farm or the site of the lead and copper smelter of the early 1700s known as Abbadine's smelter, constructed a short distance beneath (*ArchAE*: 235–6).

Examples of still smaller quarries, covering areas of as little as 25–100 m², may be found on Glaze Hill (NTSMR 57733), to the west of Castle Rock (NTSMR 57764), to the west of Canyon Mine (NTSMR 57809), at the back of Engine Vein, above the Wizard – Edge House Farm road to the west of Engine Vein (NTSMR 57797) and near the present warden's cottage (Forester's Lodge, NTSMR 57794). The much larger area of quarried ground (approximately 2,000 m²) located at Thieves' Hollow or Thieves' Hole (NTSMR 57792) is anomalous in this respect, and appears to consist of a whole series of shallow quarry workings excavated one upon the other, with numerous spoil mounds covering quarry faces and infilling earlier workings. This may well be an example of an area of small-scale 'unofficial' working carried out on common land. This large area of quarrying is not indicated on the 1787 Crossley map, although the Edge House Farm road, first shown on the 1807 estate map, was constructed above the northern extremity of these infilled pits, and the site may therefore be very old.

To the north of Engine Vein an area of numerous small pits and spoil mounds may form the prelude to the main working of the Old Alderley Quarry, if not representing a search for new stone following the exhaustion of the main pit.

Large quarries

The locations and origin of the two main quarry sites on the Edge (Old Alderley Quarry and Church Quarry) have already been described but they are not the only sizeable quarries on the Edge. The topography of all these sites was mapped in some detail during the course of the AELP survey, while the detail of the rock faces, some of which included evidence for contemporary graffiti, masons' marks and beam slots, was documented during the recording of the rock outcrops.

Old Alderley Quarry

The earliest identified area of working in this quarry appears to be around the entrance reached by means of a descending cart-way from the 1775 Quarry Road. The pick-cut quarry face along this corridor is less than 2 m high and is rather more weathered in appearance than some of the other faces. These walls appear to have been roughly shaped around the narrowest part of the entrance, with several beam holes and a long vertical slot in the rock, presumably to take a gatepost. On a west-facing wall to the south of the entrance is evidence for what appears to be a contemporary graffito in the form of a name and date carved in 'copper-plate' style. Unfortunately, this is now more or less illegible but could be the name 'Wright'. The northern end of this quarry, worked at a lower level still, seems to have been in existence in 1775.

The working face here is high (up to 5 m tall) and the sides are square, while an excavated or else washed-out clay band halfway up forms an obvious ledge around its circumference (Figure 18.7). Some beam slots can be seen in its walls, presumably to hold up scaffolding or staging, although the method of working here rarely involved renewed extraction from the top of a vertical face. Instead, the dimensions of the area to be quarried must have been planned in advance, and then areas of rock were taken out by a series of stepped benches. South of the entrance, in an area worked before 1800, there are the remains of substantial beam holes in one particular area of the eastern wall (map reference SJ 8608 7765). Possibly this indicates the construction of a wooden shelter or dressing shed (Figure 18.8). In the same area is a clearly carved set of initials reading JS (where the J is represented by an I with a cross-bar) (Figure 18.9).

The greatest volume of extraction appears to have taken place in this southern part of the quarry. A cart road descends from the entrance and

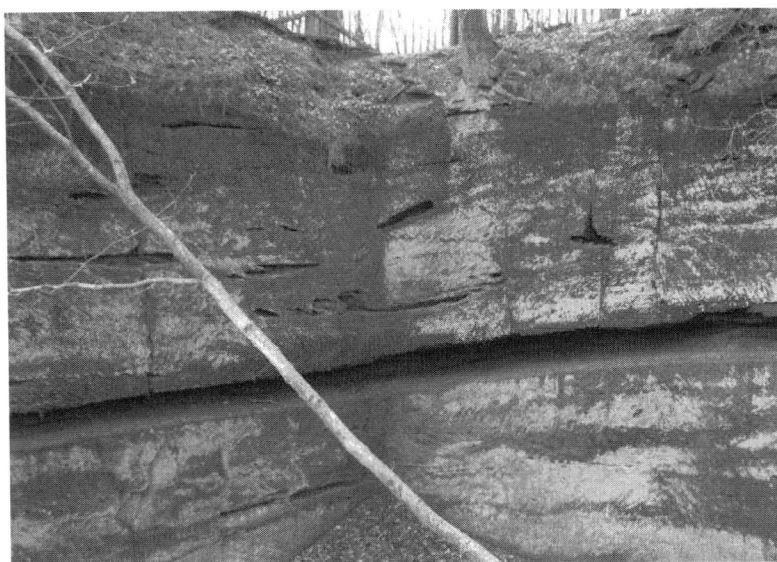

Figure 18.7. North-west corner of the Old Alderley Quarry in the section quarried after the Beacon Lodge–Golden Stone road had been diverted westwards. The dark patches and ledge around the quarry represent clay lenses and layers that have washed out since quarrying.

Photograph Nigel Dibben.

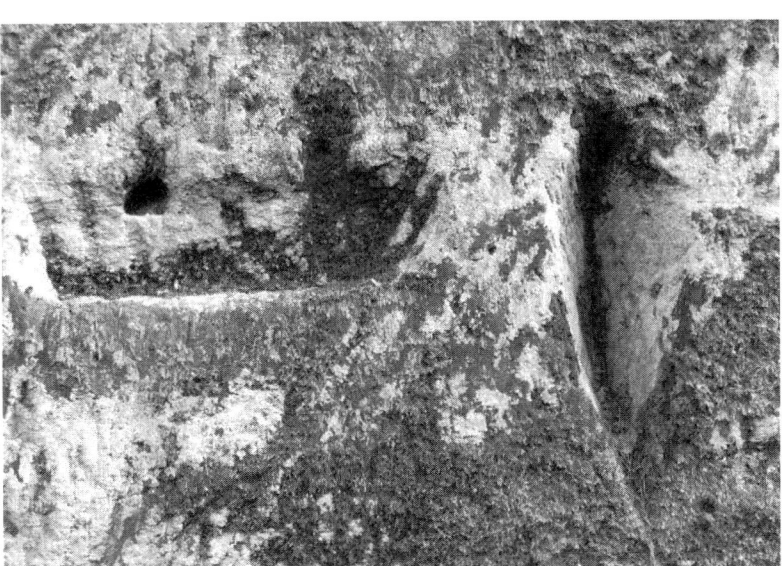

Figure 18.8. Beam slot in wall of Old Alderley Quarry.

Photograph Nigel Dibben.

runs alongside and then round and down into the lowest level (some 5 m down), probably the last area to have been worked prior to 1840. The rock bed at the southernmost end of the quarry is truncated by a north-west to south-east mineralised fault. There appears to be no evidence for the use of explosives in this quarry, the beds of freestone here being extraordinarily thick, with relatively little overburden or conglomerate bands. The facing and channel-cutting skills of the quarrymen, represented here by several vertical rock faces 8–10 m high formed from the cutting of successive tiers of 'herring-bone' pick-work, are among the best examples to be seen on the Edge.

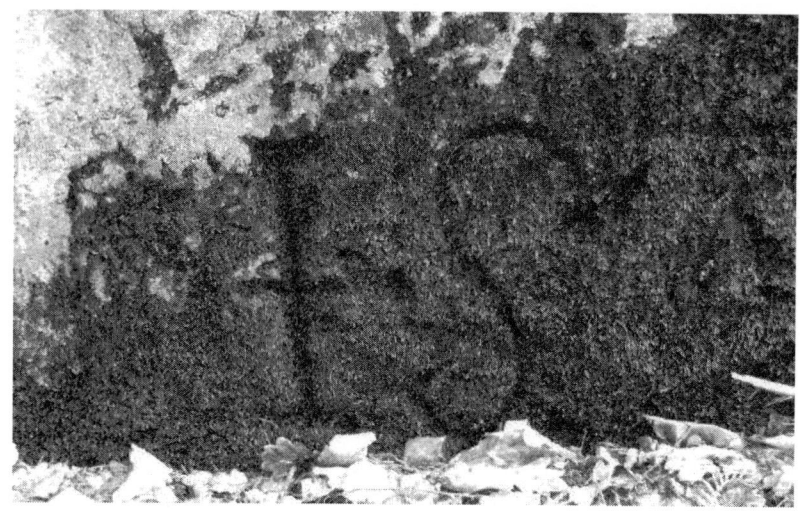

Figure 18.9. 'J·S' carved in east wall of Old Alderley Quarry.

Photograph Nigel Dibben.

The spoil tips surround the margins of the quarry but have been tipped preferentially downslope to the east. Much of this waste probably consists of overburden removed to uncover the top of the sandstone bed before quarrying. The shallowness of the overburden can be seen in Figure 18.7.

It is interesting to note that the shape of the whole area between the north end of the Old Alderley Quarry by way of Engine Vein to Thieves' Hole (as defined by quarry pits, spoil and disturbance) corresponds to that of the original field or enclosed land parcel no. 554n on the Crossley estate map of 1787. Such an arrangement may imply former common rights to stone within this boundary, or otherwise limitations on the quarrying taking place outside it.

Church Quarry

The style of working in Church Quarry, although similar in parts to the Old Alderley Quarry, displays a marked contrast in other respects. Examination of the quarry suggests that there are two distinct periods of working (Figure 18.10). The first may extend up to the point where the floor dips down into the open section of quarry and this would correspond with the area shown on the earlier maps. This includes: the approach, off which is constructed the rock-cut shelter; the branch towards the road, now infilled; and possibly some of the area climbing the slope to the east. This part shows no signs of shot holes. The second phase would be the further quarry with the vertical west face and the clear signs of the removal of a substantial layer of conglomerate overburden by use of explosives. The style of blasting closely resembles that used in Wood Mine and West Mine in the 1860s, which is not found in

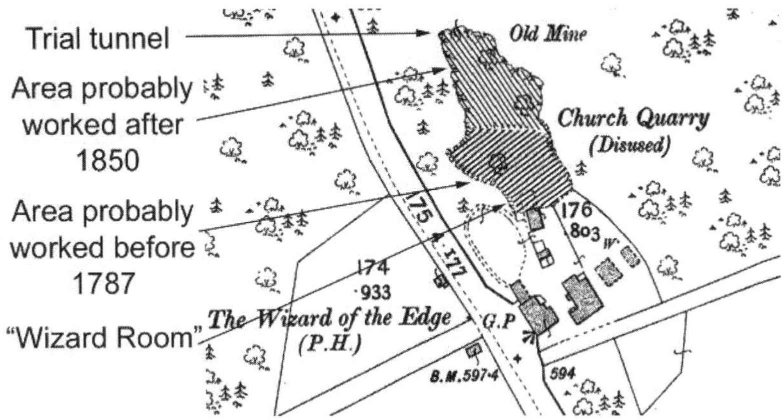

Figure 18.10. Map of Church Quarry showing areas believed to pre-date and post-date 1787.

Based on the 1907 Ordnance Survey map.

earlier mining, such as Scout Hole and the pilot drive through the upper levels of West Mine. Triangular shot holes 3–4 cm in diameter and up to 1 m long were hand-bored at approximately 1 m intervals, generally from the upper surface of this bed, and blasting was carried out using black powder.

In the first phase, the freestone outcropped and was more easily removed in the same manner as seen in the Old Alderley Quarry. In the second phase, the method was different, as the upper bed, up to 2 m above ground level within the excavated section of the quarry, is composed of hard Wood Mine Conglomerate, below which we find beds of Brynlow freestone: it was removed as described above. The contrasting beds can clearly be seen in Figure 18.11.

A room has been cut out of the rock in the outer (and earlier) part of the quarry. It has been suggested that this may be a magazine for the storage of explosives (Figure 18.12). Although the plan of this small store shows some of the features of nineteenth-century dry-stone or brick powder stores such as an L-shaped room and a shielded doorway as safety additions to deflect blast, it does not of course have a wooden roof (normal in powder stores to prevent sideways explosion). Alternatively, it may have been used as a tool store or shelter from the time prior to enclosure. At that time, it was not permissible to erect a building on common land but a rock-cut shelter was not deemed to be a building.

In the wall near the back of the Church Quarry at the north-west end (SJ 8587 7743), there is a single graffito which may be an 'I' or 'J' carved onto the cut face of this bed (Figure 18.13). This is similar to other eighteenth-century carvings (e.g. Figure 18.9) although not sufficiently so to be convincing and it might be 'modern'. It is also in an area believed to have been cut in the nineteenth century.

At the back of the quarry, a short tunnel is driven into the conglomerate. This may be the feature labelled as an 'Entrance to Mine' on the

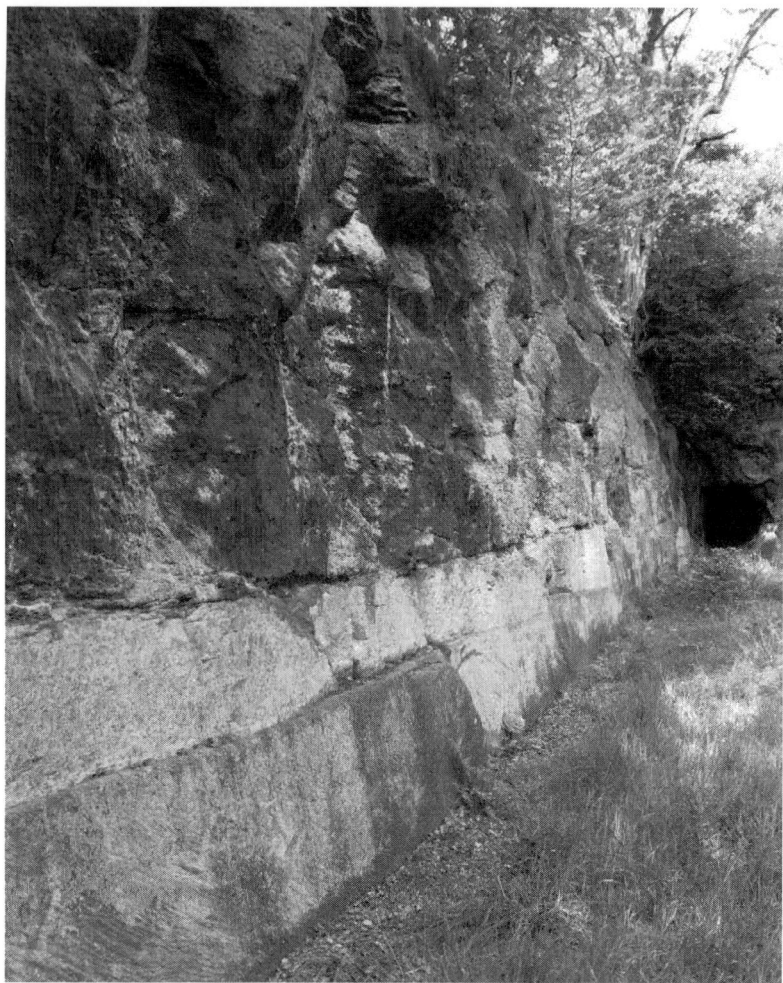

Figure 18.11. Face of the inner part of Church Quarry showing blasted section above and tooled section below.

Photograph Nigel Dibben.

1872 Ordnance Survey map and as 'Old Copper Mine' on the 1907 Ordnance Survey map, although these could also refer to sections of the cobalt mine that comes to surface in the same area. However, it follows the join between the conglomerate and sandstone, so is almost certainly a trial level driven a short distance to sample the rock beyond.

The considerable amount of spoil, mostly sand overburden, surrounding the rim of the quarry on Church Quarry Hill reflects some of the earliest eighteenth-century working here: where this covers and obscures the earthworks ringing its summit, it provides a suitable indication of the latest possible date for these earlier features.

Bradford Lane Quarry
Located just outside the 'core area' of the Landscape Project (see Chapter 1) and close to the caravan park near Bradford Lodge Farm is

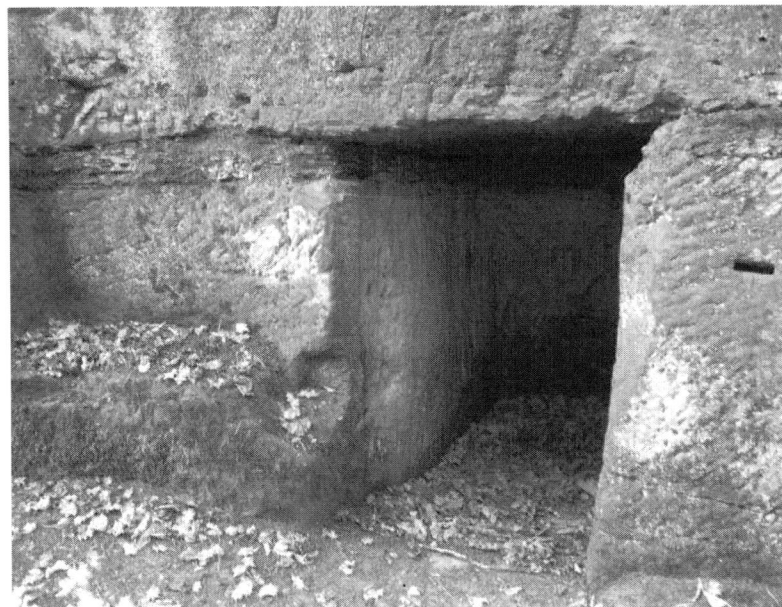

Figure 18.12. The stone-cut room between the Wizard restaurant and Church Quarry.

Photograph Nigel Dibben.

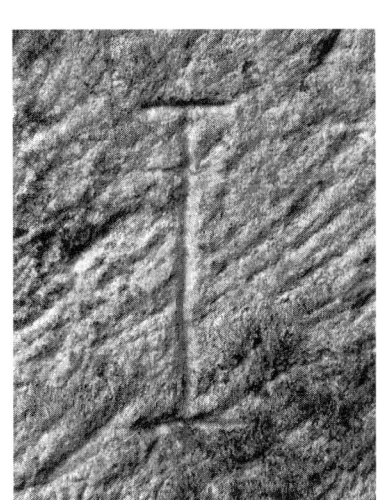

Figure 18.13. Graffito carved in the lower wall of Church Quarry.

Photograph Nigel Dibben.

a quarry which appears to have had a much longer history of working. The most recent, nineteenth-century extraction is from a now flooded section, although higher up there survive some earlier working faces, on one of which has been found carved the date 1727. Little else is known about this quarry and it was not surveyed for the Project.

Hayman's Farm Quarry
This site has already been mentioned briefly. It consists of a very deep and now flooded elongated pit (as at Bradford Lane Quarry) located on a wooded hilltop to the north-east of Hayman's Farm. During the latter

half of the nineteenth century and the early part of the twentieth, stone blocks were quarried and lifted by winch and crane (see Figure 18.5a) to be taken by cart along a specially laid cobble road (Bradford Lane) to the Alderley–Congleton turnpike road and thence to Alderley Edge village (see Figure 18.5b).

Transporting the rock

Apart from the ease of locating and working the freestone at Alderley Edge, one advantage was that it could be transported downhill to buildings in a wide area. The sandstone could be moved on carts or sledges and it is thought that part of the saddle road down from Glaze Hill to the Mottram road was a sledgeway. Another possible incline or sledgeway is located just north-west of Castle Rock near the Wizard's Well. The route is no longer used as a path but the clear line of a man-made route can be seen sloping obliquely down the hillside. This route roughly corresponds with Wilmslow path number 71, which is marked on the definitive maps but not on the maps with a scale of six inches to one mile. Stone from the Old Alderley Quarry could be carted along the 'Quarry Road' to Beacon Lodge and thence to Chorley or Macclesfield and stone from Church Quarry could be taken straight onto the road.

Red Moulding Sand

The twentieth-century Red Moulding Sand Quarry (NTSMR 57747), also known as Mottram Quarry, the largest on the Edge, was surveyed only superficially during the AELP.

This was a large quarry (about 1.5 ha worked over a vertical distance of at least 15 m) and last operated in the late 1940s or early 1950s. In its earliest form, the quarry appears to have been a small 'gravel' quarry, as shown marked on this spot on the 1872 twenty-five-inch Ordnance Survey map. The soft red Wilmslow Sandstone outcrop, where the sand grains are richly coated in kaolinite clay, was subsequently worked as a quarry for moulding sand, a specialist product used for the casting of large objects such as bells. The quarry was worked on two main levels, as well as on a number of different sub-levels. Few features which relate to the original working techniques and machinery survive here on the soft sandstone quarry walls. There is however an anonymous account of these techniques on the internet:

> the quarry was worked from 1940–1963 producing Wilmslow red sand for the metal casting industry. The method of working was by explosives.

To drill the shot holes, a 10 foot twist drill with tungsten carbide tip was driven by hand-held electric motor, the type used in coal mines to drill the coal face. Explosive used was polar ammon gelignite fired by No 6 electric detonators. The soft sandstone was drilled into at an angle at the base. The layout of the Quarry was that as you entered off the Mottram road, the office and weighbridge were on your right, straight on there was a small shed and then the sand hopper with roof in the centre of the Quarry; behind the office and up a path was the magazine set back into the sand hill. ('The Red Moulding Sand Quarry', at http://www.alderley.org.uk/redquarry.html, accessed July 2015; minor editorial amendments have been made but left unmarked for ease of reading)

Marlpits and marling

Marling – the digging of marlpits and the spreading of marl (lime-rich clay) on infertile sandy soils – has long been recognised as an important agricultural practice in Cheshire (Rackham, 1994: 174). The word 'loampit' (probably referring to marl) occurs in Anglo-Saxon charters, and by the thirteenth century marling and even disused marlpits are often documented. Locally there are numerous references in the early Court Leet records to the granting of licences to local individuals to dig and take out marl for laying on heath fields on or around Alderley Edge (for instance in the Stanley papers, such as CALS DSA 3752/1).

The earliest mention of the existence of marlpits on the Edge comes in the account of the 1598 perambulation of the parish boundaries, which refers to the 'pit on the commons that Linguard had marl out of' (quoted in Chapter 19, p. 477), presumably Linguard (Lyngard) of Old Edge House, and thus one must assume either the marlpit at SJ 8652 7720 or perhaps one at SJ 8637 7717. In Stanley's transcription of the Court Leet of the same date we hear mention of a licence given to Edward Fallows to make a marlpit at the lower end of Sandleheath, and a request by Edward Germane to dig for marl on Monksheath, which was granted on condition that the pit was backfilled with 'claugh' (clay). On the Edge itself, Thomas Dane of Brynlow was granted permission to dig for marl from a pit on the lane below his house (possibly the now-flooded square pit alongside Artists Lane at SJ 8525 7720) for the purpose of marling his fields up on the Edge.

From the sixteenth to the eighteenth century the rights to turf, peat and pasturage on common lands were of similar importance in the local economy, but one cannot explain the storms over illicit peat-cutting simply in terms of growing threats of enclosure and the resulting pressures on the use of common land. The class system in Alderley was much more complicated than simple landowner and tenant. Enclosure of peat mosses in the sixteenth and seventeenth centuries was often welcomed by the tenancy as it released land for rental at a time when there was pressure of population on limited resources. The most vociferous defenders of commoners' rights and privileges were the established free-holders or copy-holders, resisting encroachment by poorer cottagers who did not have these common rights: the details of the quarrel between Stanley and Leycester over Broadheath make this abundantly clear (Leycester, 1589).

The great majority of the marlpits to be found in those rural areas which already had a tradition of this practice may have been created as a result of the renewed fashion for marling in the eighteenth and nineteenth centuries (Rackham, 1994: 174). The results of archaeological survey work along with the study of eighteenth- and nineteenth-century maps suggests that this may also have been the case on Alderley Edge, as new areas of heathland were brought into cultivation following the enclosures of 1775 and 1799. A second Stanley notebook (CALS DSA 3752/1, section 3752/5) refers to John Stanley's description of the marlers' customs on the Edge c. 1799–1800, including the election of a leader or 'lord of the pit' from among themselves in order to help coordinate the cooperative effort of its excavation (see Chapter 19, p. 490). The amount of work involved in the digging of marlpits and the shifting of wet clay in carts should never be underestimated.

Most of the pits identifiable on the Edge today were probably excavated over the seventy-five years between 1775 and 1850, while still earlier ones may have been filled in or else considerably enlarged. The former locations of some of these are now detectable only through irregularities in old field boundaries (e.g. at SJ 855 770). Aerial photographs of the Edge and the lowland landscape to the north bring into focus the scale of marl digging over the centuries and the probable importance of this effort to the local economy. The combined acreage of marlpits within the core area is equivalent to some 2–3 ha (c. 1.5 per cent of the land area), while the density of marlpits off the Edge is even greater. On balance, the former agricultural lands of the Edge would have been gross users rather than producers of marl, and at Alderley it may therefore have been transported over much greater distances than was usual elsewhere.

The identification and locations of marlpits

Locally to Alderley Edge, marl was extracted from the overlying drift or glacial boulder clay, deposits of which irregularly drape parts of the dip slope and flanks of the sandstone escarpment, particularly in the lands to the west of the Macclesfield Road (Finlow Hill), the top of Bradford Lane, Brynlow, the upper part of Windmill Wood and the lands around

Armstrong Farm, but also to the south, west and east of Edge House Farm, and to the north and south of Waterfall Wood (Hilltop Farm) – see further Chapter 4. Both the boulder clay and the upper sands and gravels derived from the Irish Sea Drift contain shells of marine molluscs (Thompson and Worsley, 1966) and this incorporation of lime-rich material and other nutrients within the boulder clay sub-soil acts as a natural fertiliser when mixed with the leached and mineral-poor humic horizon or topsoil overlying the sandstone. Typically a marlpit would be dug in the centre of a field or group of interconnected fields that required marling. Even soils overlying boulder clay benefited from the spreading of marl, and thus the excavation of a pit in the centre of the area to be treated reduced the cost of cartage and spreading. The fertility of fields on the Edge appears to have varied enormously, as implied by names such as 'Starvation Field' (information from Mrs Redgrave, Edge House Farm), suggesting that marl usage may have been very selective. In Chapter 28 J. S. Adams has noted many references to marl in the names of the fields and other topographical features of the Edge.

Examples of centrally located marlpits with steep sides and ramp entrances for cartage in and out of the pits may be seen in a number of places around the Edge. The more recent late eighteenth-century or early nineteenth-century pits (all now flooded), often consisting of two interconnected pairs of pits with surrounding banks, have commonly preserved their square or rectangular outlines. Small banks of spoil or overburden, often containing large cobbles or erratic boulders removed from the boulder clay prior to spreading, can sometimes be found alongside the edges of these ponds; there is a good instance surrounding the marlpit on the edge of Finlow Hill Wood at SJ 8599 7687, where it accompanies boulders from the field clearance.

A good example of a group of flooded pits is to be found west of Armstrong Farm (NTSMR 57858) with a ramp and cart-way approaching from the east (see Figure 12.1, p. 211), while the very regular construction of some of these nineteenth-century marl excavations is perhaps best seen in the group of partially drained pits to be found at the north-east end of Windmill Wood (NTSMR 57812), which may have later served as reservoirs for the nineteenth-century mine works. A pre-1787 example is the large pit clearly to be seen on the Crossley map, located in the centre of an area of fields and former common land at Brynlow (NTSMR 57849). Its age is uncertain, but the irregular shape of this pit would suggest that it is older; the fact that the ramp access and the route of an old cart track towards the gateway into Cow Lane are still detectable suggests that it was used both for the original pit and for later enlargements of it. Analysis of the soil geochemical maps of the Edge shows elevated levels of calcium in soils on the fields surrounding this pit at Brynlow; other anomalies appear to surround

Brynlow Farm, Whitebarn Farm (near which there are several large marlpits) and Armstrong Farm. Particularly high levels of calcium are to be found close to the flooded pits south of the Wizard (National Trust car park) and in the fields to the north, west and east of Edge House Farm. During the course of the survey some twenty-two confirmed or suspected marlpits were recorded within the boundary of the core study area, and a further 170 marlpits were located from the study of maps of the hinterland area.

Sand quarrying

There is evidence that in Nether Alderley sand was excavated from sandpits around the parish for repair of roads. Records in the Alderley parish register (Highways Accounts, 1821) show that sand was collected from various places, including Edward Wyche's land at Soss Moss. Is it possible that some of the shallow pits close to the roads were sandpits rather than marlpits – such as those opposite the Bradford Lane junction on the Macclesfield Road? Further evidence for this business, although off the Edge proper, lies in road names such as Sand Lane (which joins the Congleton road near the old Eagle and Child pub), Sandhole Farm (between Marton and Congleton) and Sandleheath. The Crossley list of field names also includes some interesting names such as Great Sandhole, Little Sandhole, Sandhole Field and Sand Hill Field, but these are outside the core study area.

Further reading

Stanier, P. 1985. *Quarries and Quarrying*. Princes Risborough: Shire Publications. Reprinted 2000 as Shire Album 134, with a list of further reading.
Stanier, P. 2000. *Stone Quarry Landscapes*. Stroud: Tempus Publishing.

Part V

Human history – overground: the social history

19

The history of Alderley Edge

Clare Pye

The Edge at Alderley has long been a great local divide. North and west are Wilmslow, the Hough, Chorley and the modern village of Alderley Edge, part of the Bollin Fee since the Norman conquest and the domain of the Traffords, whose vast archive in the Lancashire County Record Office in Preston has yet to be catalogued. South and east is the original Alderley parish, including the two townships of Over Alderley and Nether Alderley, dominated by the Stanleys since the fifteenth century and where the Landscape Project concentrated its work.

The burning of the Old Hall at Nether Alderley (Figure 19.1) in 1779 complicates any research into the history of Alderley, its Edge and its owners. Nearly all the Stanley estate documents, dealing with most of Nether Alderley and parts of Over Alderley and going back to the Middle Ages, were destroyed in the blaze. When the fire broke out Sir John Stanley's steward, Mr Stockton, refused to authorise the clearing of the estate office, but as the flames quickly took hold, the molten lead running down from the roof prevented anyone from making a last-minute rescue (CALS DSA 5/10; primary sources are listed at the end of the chapter).

Certainly Sir John's son, the first Lord Stanley of Alderley (also John; Figure 19.2), with his scientific and antiquarian interests, regretted the loss of these documents and did his best to piece together the history of Alderley and his family's involvement in the area. The result is a series of notebooks, dating from about 1800 to the 1840s, now in the collection of Cheshire Archives and Local Studies (CALS, based at the Cheshire Record Office), in which he recorded his findings (Stanley, 1830–44; henceforth *Stanley Notebook*), often with the help of his daughter, Louisa. Apart from his own boyhood memories, John Lord Stanley used such documents as remained, particularly those that had come into the family when they bought land in Over Alderley from the Leicesters of Tabley in 1797, as well as the Randle Holmes collection in the Harleian Miscellany in the British Museum. He also consulted

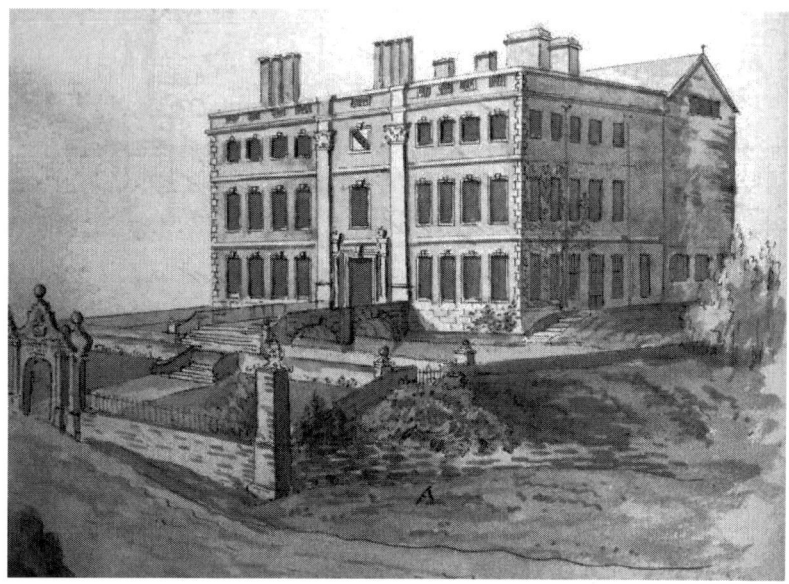

(a)

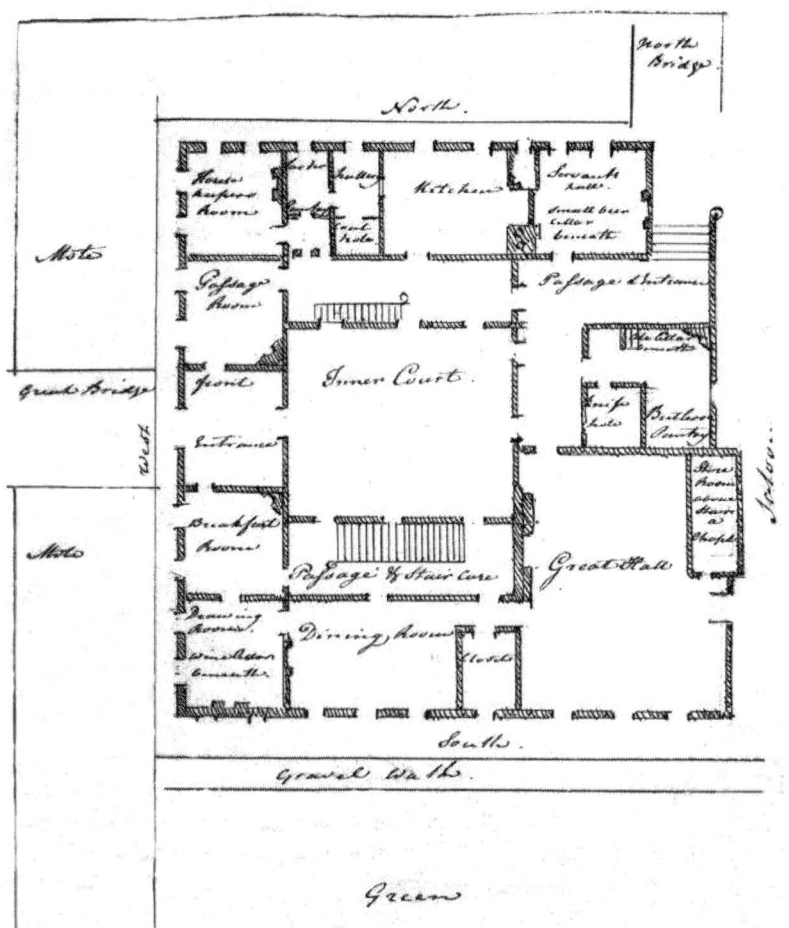

(b)

Figure 19.1. Alderley Old Hall. (a) Drawing from memory (in the top right-hand corner of the page – not shown – he had noted 'Alderley Hall burnt March 1779') and (b) plan drawn from memory by the first Lord Stanley.

Courtesy of Cheshire Archives and Local Studies (DSA 3752/1).

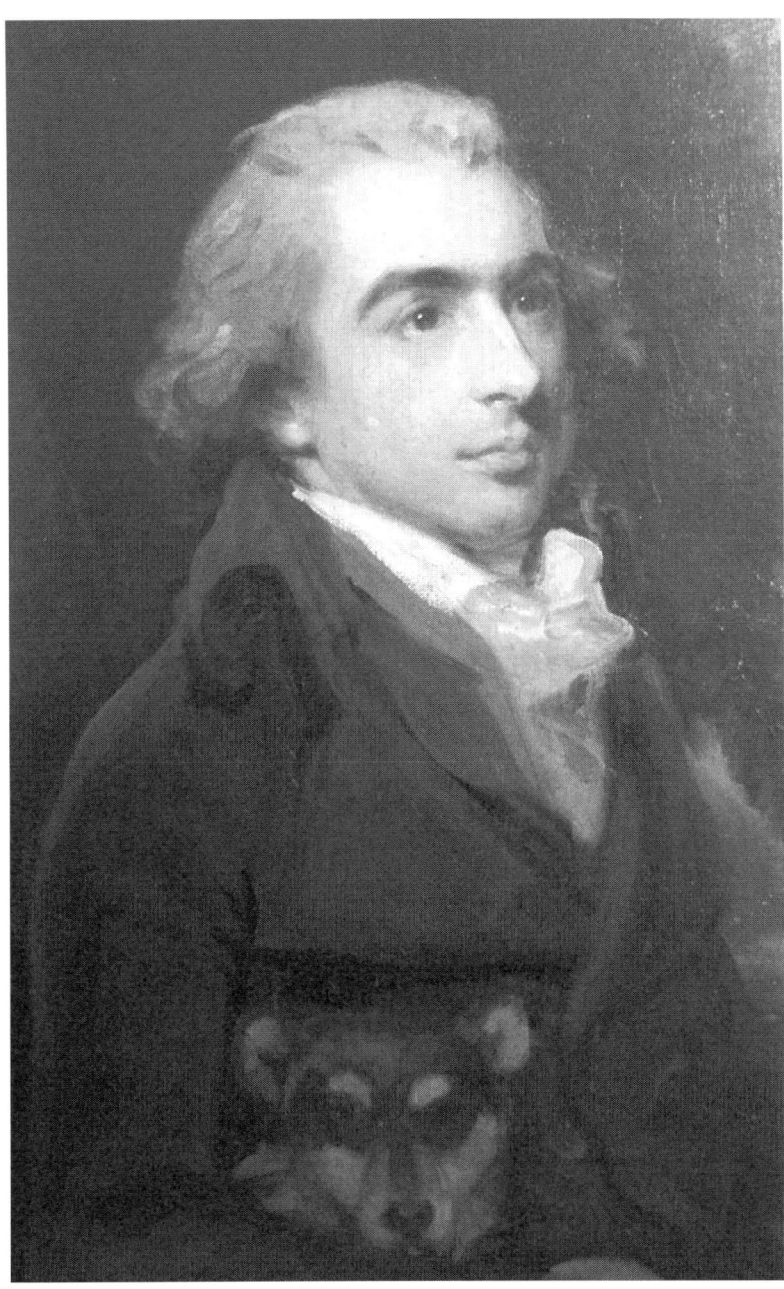

Figure 19.2. John, first Lord Stanley, by John Hoppner, *c.* 1800.

Courtesy of Lord Stanley.

court records and diocesan records in Chester, and the recollections of ancient inhabitants of the parish who could remember the area earlier in the eighteenth century. These were the sources that Louisa Stanley used when she published *Alderley Edge and Its Neighbourhood* in 1843 (Stanley, 1843).

Lord Stanley also relied on Ormerod's *The History of Cheshire*, first published in 1817. Ormerod himself took as one of his main sources the work of the seventeenth-century antiquarian Sir Peter Leycester of Tabley. (This family spelled its name 'Leycester' until the late seventeenth century and then changed to 'Leicester' – see Appendix 19.1.) After 1779, documentation is wider and more complete. Apart from newspapers, estate records and official documents, we have the edited collections of Stanley letters, particularly from the women in the family, published by their descendants: Jane Adeane's *The Early Married Life of Maria Josepha Holroyd, Lady Stanley* (1899) and Nancy Mitford's *The Ladies of Alderley* (1938) and *The Stanleys of Alderley* (1939). Both these editors were more interested in the quirks of family character than details of estate business and the history of the community. J. P. Earwaker's *History of the Hundred of Macclesfield* (in two volumes, published 1877 and 1880) draws on his own antiquarian interests as well as on Ormerod.

All of these have a 'gentry' bias, concentrating on the details of the descent of property, with family trees and armorial quarterings to the fore; as an aristocrat and landowner it is not surprising that Lord Stanley approached his research from this angle. In any age before mass education, the wealthy and well educated will always be better recorded, but an account that attempts to go beyond this, to try to understand the lives of ordinary people before mass literacy, faces the problem that their stories are often not recorded by themselves, but have to be seen through the filter of official documents (often when the people are in trouble with the authorities) and the observations of their social superiors. However, to trace the history of the whole community, a fascinating mixture of farmers and miners, with the inter-reaction of people and their landscape, the Plain and the Edge, one has to try to do just this.

The earliest documentary mention of Alderley is in the Domesday Book (1086). Although the name is Saxon, we have nothing from those times relating to Alderley; this is not surprising, as east Cheshire was debateable land, first between the Romano-Britons and the Saxons, then between Mercia and Northumbria, and finally between Saxons and Vikings. Higham (1993: 174) suggests that, although the parish of Prestbury is of long standing, the Hamestan (Macclesfield) Hundred appears to have been subject to major reorganisation in the late Saxon period. This obscures any earlier arrangements of the land.

However, Alderley appears twice in the Domesday Book. Most historians have suggested these two entries refer to the two townships of Nether Alderley and Over Alderley.

Nether Alderley

In Macclesfield Hundred, Aldredelie. Bigot of Loges holds it.
Godwin held it as a free man. 1 hide paying tax. Land for 8 ploughs. In lordship, 1, with 2 ploughmen;

3 villagers and 1 rider with 1 plough.
Meadow, 1 acre; woodland 1½ leagues long and 1 league wide; 2 enclosures.
Value before 1066, 20s., now 10s.; found waste.

Over Alderley
In Macclesfield Hundred, Aldredlie. William son of Nigel holds it.
William holds Aldelret from the Earl. Brown held it, he was a free man.
1 hide paying tax. Land for 4 ploughs. It was and is waste.
Woodland, 2 leagues long and 2 wide.
Value before 1066. 10s.

(Morris, 1978)

These laconic entries referring to uncultivated land and the reduction in taxable value are clear indications of the damage caused in east Cheshire twenty years before. After the Northern Rebellion of 1069, when the Conqueror's forces laid Yorkshire to waste, they returned south through east Cheshire and Staffordshire, destroying property as they went. In 1086 Over Alderley still, apparently, had no people living there, although the pre-conquest Brown may have given his name to Brynlow (on this see also Chapter 28). Nether Alderley was also under-populated. Dorothy Sylvester (1956: 14–15) suggested the lack of pressure on land resources helps to explain the ease with which the gentry in east Cheshire were able to empark their land in the Middle Ages. Alderley Park is but one of many private Medieval parks in east Cheshire, while the west of the county has relatively few. Like the rest of Cheshire, Alderley was probably 'barren and unproductive of cereals … but abounding in beasts and fish. The natives delight in milk and butter' wrote William of Malmesbury in the *De Gestis Regum Anglorum* in about 1125. Evidence from Macclesfield shows an early specialisation in the area in pastoral farming (Hallam, 1981: 224).

The history of the ownership of the Chorley and Hough side of Alderley Edge is comparatively uncomplicated. Originally part of the Earl of Chester's holding of Macclesfield, Wilmslow, or rather Bollin Fee, was granted to the Fitton family at the end of the twelfth century. They created the independent parish of Wilmslow in the late thirteenth century. The main Fitton line ended in 1370, when Joanna Fitton married Richard Venables. When their grandson, another Richard, died childless in 1415, the lands were split between his sisters, Dulcia, who married into the Booth family of Dunham Massey, and Alice, who married Edmund Trafford. Alice took Chorley and most of Pownall Fee as her share of the inheritance. The Traffords continued to hold these lands until the nineteenth and twentieth centuries, although their main residence was at Trafford Park near Manchester (Angus-Butterworth, 1932: 163; Ormerod, 1882: vol. 3, pp. 593–4).

In the thirteenth century, Alderley itself was owned by the Arderne family. Locally powerful, like many landowners of the time they were intent on exploiting the commercial potential of their estates. In 1243 Sir Walklyn de Arderne was granted charters to establish markets at Alderley and at Aldford, near Chester. In Alderley he gained the right to hold a weekly market on Saturdays and an annual fair or wake in August, at the time of the feast of St Lawrence. The plans for a market did not succeed, as both Knutsford and Congleton already had established markets on a Saturday and Macclesfield on a Monday; these three towns were chartered boroughs, which also gave them an advantage over Alderley (Crosby, 1996: 50). The cross beside the junction of Congleton Road, Artists Lane and Welsh Row (just south of Alderley) is perhaps the only reminder of this failed speculation, but the community of Alderley parish continued to hold their wakes in the second or third week of August (Figure 19.3; Jeremy Milln in Chapter 27 suggests it was a preaching cross). Until the mid-nineteenth century the wake celebrations were centred on St Mary's Church, Nether Alderley, when they moved up the Edge to the Wizard Inn and where they continued to be held until the outbreak of war in 1939 (CALS DSA 5/10).

The timing of the fair to St Lawrence-tide reflects the original dedication of St Mary's Church, Nether Alderley (Figure 19.4); the date of the market charter, 1243, suggests that a chapel of ease for local funerals and burials had already been built in the village before the independent parish of Alderley was created around 1300. It is not surprising that Alderley and Wilmslow parishes were created around the same time. The Fittons and the Ardernes would have wanted to define their mutual boundaries and the foundation of Wilmslow parish could easily have sparked off the creation of Alderley parish next door.

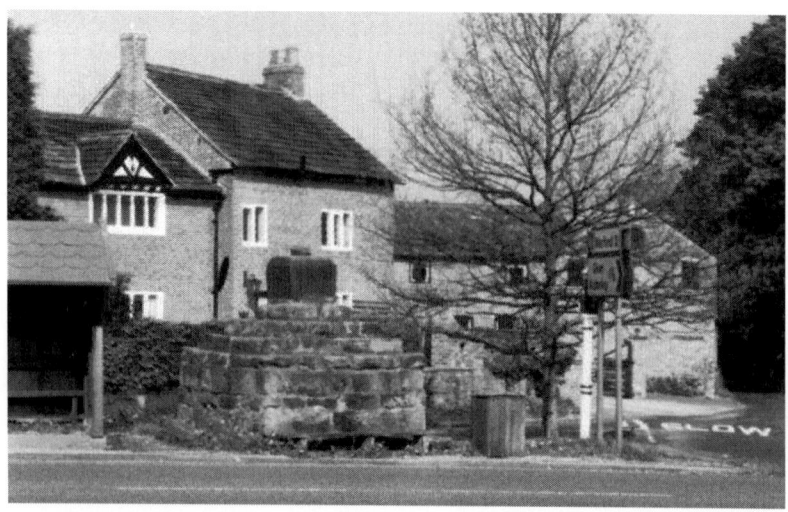

Figure 19.3. The old cross (weathered to a stump) at the crossroads of Welsh Row with Congleton Road (the former A34).

Photograph Clare Pye.

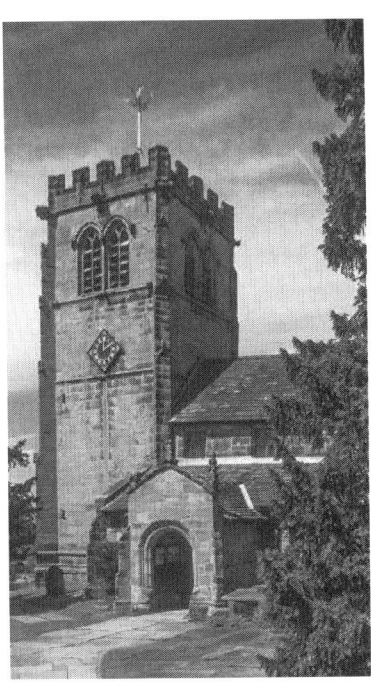

Figure 19.4. St Mary's Church, Nether Alderley.

Photograph Sean Edwards.

The first record in Alderley is the death of an incumbent priest, Robert Bieran or Byron, in 1328. The new parish of Alderley, comprising the townships of Nether Alderley and Over Alderley and Great Warford, was carved out of the original immense parish of Prestbury. Parish and township boundaries usually follow obvious physical features, such as the Pott Brook on the north side of Over Alderley, but where there are no such clear demarcations any deviations can provide an insight into the area at this time, as they were probably respecting existing boundaries or land divisions.

In particular, there is an anomaly in the boundary between Nether Alderley and Chorley, where, as can be seen on the map, a tongue of Alderley land comes down off the Edge to the modern main road (Figure 19.5). A large banked ditch can be seen by the Congleton Road between the two nineteenth-century villas, Westwood and Barnfield, presently part of St Hilary's Park. This feature was investigated when a housing development went ahead in 2001. No clear dating evidence emerged, although there were signs of Medieval iron-working under one of the banks (Owen, 2001). Where one finds boundary anomalies like this they may be respecting different landholdings or assets within a previously common area (Rackham, 1994: 19, 176–7). Although the classic three-field system was rare in the county, it was not uncommon for Cheshire townships to share a common field (Sylvester, 1956: 20). Field-name evidence in the area from the 1841 tithe map such as Town

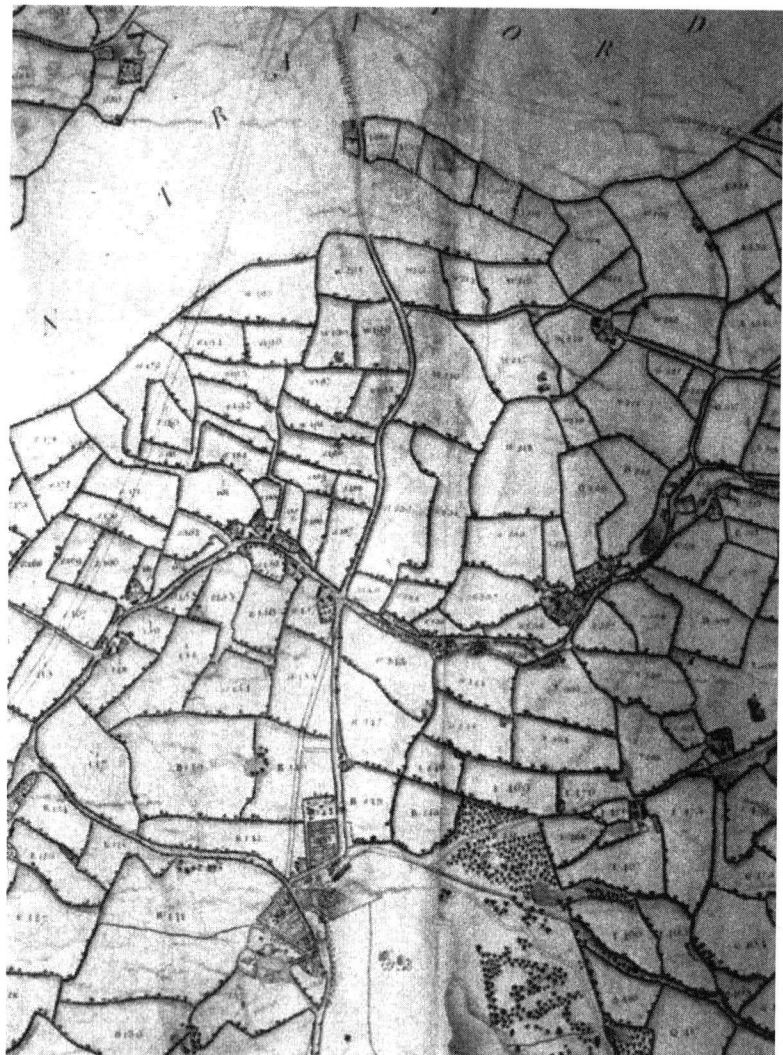

Figure 19.5. Detail from William Crossley's map of the Stanley estates, 1787, showing the boundary anomaly by Barnfield House – the 'Stanley finger' protruding from the rest of the Stanley lands at the top of the map. The division between the Stanley and Trafford lands goes back to Domesday, but the boundary was defined by 1300 after the separate parishes were created.

Courtesy of Cheshire Archives and Local Studies (P 143/14/1).

Field Meadow also suggests a common field between Welsh Row and Sand Lane (CALS IR 30/5). The tongue of land at Barnfield House may also have been there to give both parishes access to the Edge; footpaths once went up to the Edge along both sides of the boundary.

On the Edge itself there is a similar anomaly in the township boundary between Nether Alderley and Over Alderley. Coming south from Saddlebole, it follows the Edge until the Goldenstone, strikes straight out across the shared common land, and then curves round to Finlow Lane. It then deviates, following the field boundaries south of Mottram House, where it makes a series of sharp turns until it runs south-east, past Hayman's Farm to Alderley Park, where it again deviates round the park boundary until it reaches and follows the stream. Until the sixteenth century, when the land began to be sold off (CALS DLT A75/5), this formed part of the boundary of the lands belonging to the Acton family, whose main memorial today is Acton Farm on Hocker Lane. However, the sharp changes in direction on the top of Finlow Hill suggest enclosures already existed in 1300. This is supported by the evidence of an agreement to assart land on the Edge in 1294 (*Stanley Notebook*), which clearly refers to land on the boundary of Nether Alderley and Over Alderley. Interestingly, it says that these new fields are placed next to some pre-existing enclosures, and that the new fields are to be marked out with merestones. Along the boundary by Hayman's Farm are the vestiges of a large bank reminiscent of the bank by Congleton Road. At these banks we may even be looking at the remnants of the two enclosures mentioned in Domesday. Early enclosure is also suggested by the curved bank and ditch between Windmill Wood and the Sandhills area on Brynlow Hill, which defined the boundary of the common land until enclosure in 1775.

Certainly, by the time we can investigate manor and parish records in the sixteenth century, we see a typical Cheshire landscape of separate holdings and enclosed fields with areas of common heath and mossland. Soss Moss, Sandle Heath, Monks Heath, Broadheath and in particular Alderley Edge are all important areas of common land within Alderley parish. The common on the Edge had a typical concave outline, with tracks and paths creating funnel shapes as they come onto the heath (Rackham, 1994: 144). There were probably no defined tracks at this time across the common land; people would come up onto the Edge and then strike out across it to their destination. In the sixteenth century, the common land on the Edge still extended eastwards into Broadheath in Over Alderley. This heath included the area of the nineteenth-century park at Hare Hill.

The Stanleys and the Leycesters of Tabley were the two main landowners in Over Alderley at this time; they had an acrimonious legal wrangle from the 1570s to the early 1660s over common rights in the manor, in particular over the control of Broadheath, used by the local farmers for peat cutting, but which by the mid-sixteenth century was being steadily encroached on as cottagers made enclosures. Both landowners wanted to control this and if possible profit from it (Plate 61 shows the map drawn to support the Leycester case; see also Appendix 19.1 and Chapters 26, p. 652, and 27, p. 673). The quarrel reached its climax in the 1650s over Jackson's Cottage on Broadheath. The case was heard in 1656 by Thomas Marbury, one of Major-General Worsley's Commissioners of the Peace and Peter Leycester's cousin. He divided the manor two to one between Stanley and Leycester, and effectively gave the latter control over Broadheath. The bitterness of the rivalry can be seen in its epilogue in 1658–60: Leycester had evicted the squatters, the Ridgeway family, from Jackson's Cottage and, to prevent them moving back, had demolished the cottage and removed the timbers to Tabley. The Ridgeways looked to Stanley for help and in the resulting court case Leycester was ordered to restore both cottage and Ridgeways. However, he still retained control of Broadheath; his ownership was confirmed after the Restoration and Leycester had the area enclosed completely in 1662 (CALS DLT A75/5). As the Stanley tenants no longer had access to Broadheath, at the 1669 Nether Alderley Court Leet (i.e. the local manorial court) it was ordered that they make their boundary clear, and a sturdy iron gate was erected at Adshead Green to prevent the Leycester tenants from using Alderley Edge to graze their animals (*Stanley Notebook*). The smallholdings and enclosures in Slade Lane and School Lane may be encroachments on the common land allowed by the landowners as they helped to define their respective territories, and the boundary between the two can still be seen along the western edge of Danielhill Wood.

The Stanley involvement with Alderley goes back to the early fifteenth century, but it has a complicated history, as the family has a number of branches (Figure 19.6). In the mid-fourteenth century, the Arderne family split their land in Alderley between two brothers: the elder, John, inherited most of Nether Alderley together with the rest of the Arderne lands in Cheshire; the younger son, Peter, got Fernhill in Nether Alderley and land and manorial rights in Over Alderley. Peter's daughter and heiress, Margaret, married Richard Weever, and their descendant Elizabeth Weever married John Stanley, a brother of the first Earl of Derby, in the mid-fifteenth century, bringing the Alderley and Weever lands with her as her dowry. This branch of the Stanleys settled into their lands in Over Alderley and Nether Alderley, although their estate headquarters were at Weever. Stanley men married respectably endowed women from local gentry families, and generally established themselves in the area. By 1580, however, Thomas Stanley, who died in 1592, had transferred the family headquarters to Alderley, after he built the Old Hall on a moated site beside the main road. The service wing of this house survived the 1779 fire and is still standing. His grandson, another Thomas, inherited the estate in 1595 (Ormerod, 1882: vol. 3, p. 577). (The various residences of the Stanleys at Alderley and elsewhere are also described by John Adams in Chapter 28.)

Meanwhile, the elder branch of the Arderne family also ended with an heiress; Thomas of Arderne's daughter Matilda married a Sir Thomas Stanley in the early fifteenth century, and this branch of the Stanleys held Nether Alderley with the rest of the Arderne inheritance for the next 100 years. However, the John Stanley who held the land in the late fifteenth century, faced with the problem of three daughters and the

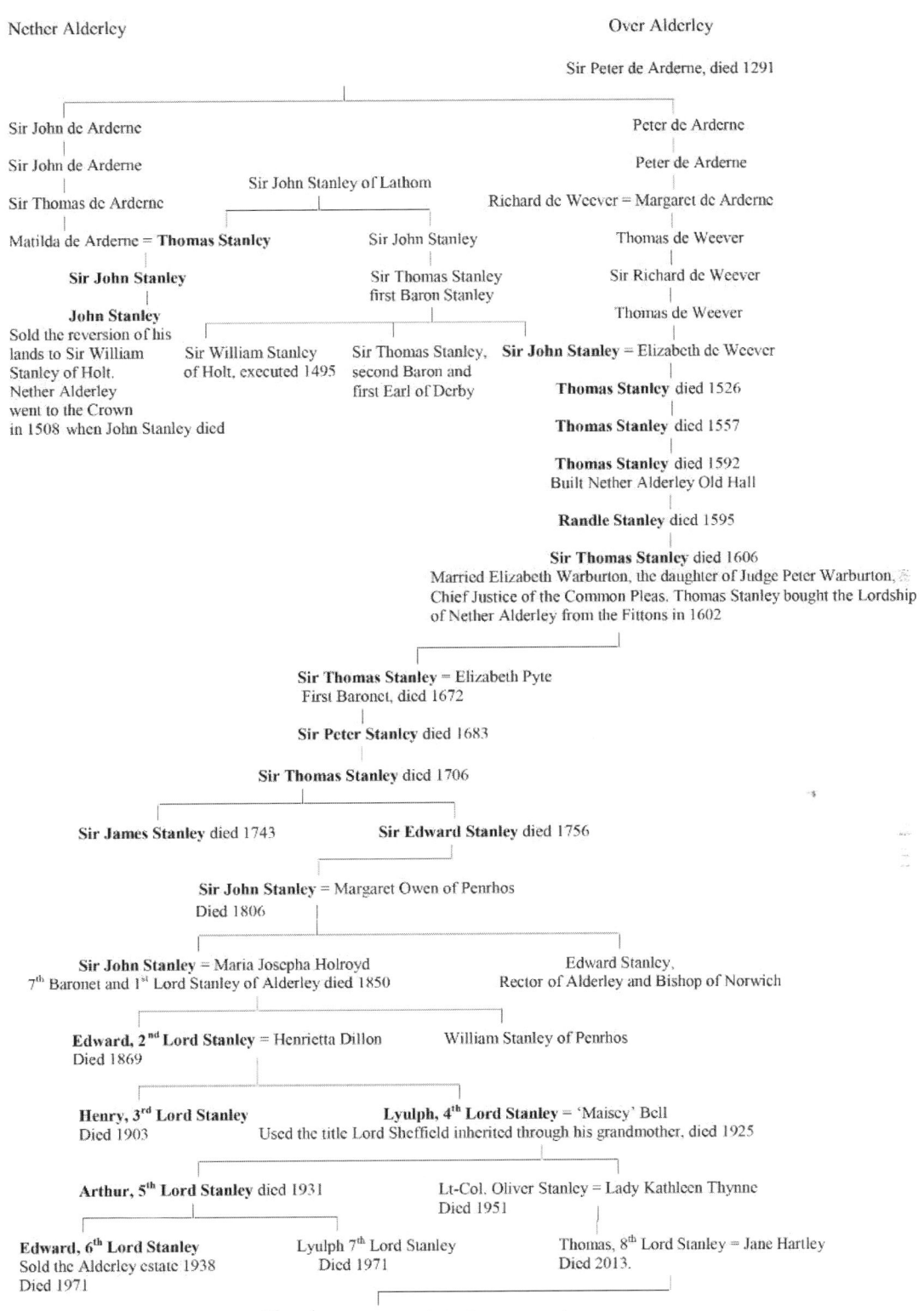

Nether Alderley

Over Alderley

Sir Peter de Arderne, died 1291

Sir John de Arderne — Peter de Arderne

Sir John de Arderne — Peter de Arderne

Sir John Stanley of Lathom

Sir Thomas de Arderne — Richard de Weever = Margaret de Arderne

Matilda de Arderne = **Thomas Stanley** — Sir John Stanley — Thomas de Weever

Sir John Stanley — Sir Thomas Stanley first Baron Stanley — Sir Richard de Weever

John Stanley
Sold the reversion of his
lands to Sir William
Stanley of Holt.
Nether Alderley
went to the Crown
in 1508 when John Stanley died

Sir William Stanley
of Holt, executed 1495

Sir Thomas Stanley,
second Baron and
first Earl of Derby

Thomas de Weever

Sir John Stanley = Elizabeth de Weever

Thomas Stanley died 1526

Thomas Stanley died 1557

Thomas Stanley died 1592
Built Nether Alderley Old Hall

Randle Stanley died 1595

Sir Thomas Stanley died 1606
Married Elizabeth Warburton, the daughter of Judge Peter Warburton,
Chief Justice of the Common Pleas. Thomas Stanley bought the Lordship
of Nether Alderley from the Fittons in 1602

Sir Thomas Stanley = Elizabeth Pyte
First Baronet, died 1672

Sir Peter Stanley died 1683

Sir Thomas Stanley died 1706

Sir James Stanley died 1743 — **Sir Edward Stanley** died 1756

Sir John Stanley = Margaret Owen of Penrhos
Died 1806

Sir John Stanley = Maria Josepha Holroyd
7th Baronet and 1st Lord Stanley of Alderley died 1850

Edward Stanley,
Rector of Alderley and Bishop of Norwich

Edward, 2nd Lord Stanley = Henrietta Dillon
Died 1869

William Stanley of Penrhos

Henry, 3rd Lord Stanley
Died 1903

Lyulph, 4th Lord Stanley = 'Maiscy' Bell
Used the title Lord Sheffield inherited through his grandmother, died 1925

Arthur, 5th Lord Stanley died 1931

Lt-Col. Oliver Stanley = Lady Kathleen Thynne
Died 1951

Edward, 6th Lord Stanley
Sold the Alderley estate 1938
Died 1971

Lyulph 7th Lord Stanley
Died 1971

Thomas, 8th Lord Stanley = Jane Hartley
Died 2013.

Richard, 9th Lord Stanley, born 1956 = Carla McKenzie

Figure 19.6. The Stanley family tree and Alderley (see text). Owners of Alderley are indicated in bold.

After Ormerod (1882) and Stanley (2002: 65–8).

estate being split between them, sold the reversion of his lands to his cousin, Sir William Stanley of Holt. Unfortunately, Sir William, backing the wrong side during Perkin Warbeck's rebellion in 1495, was attainted as a traitor on Warbeck's execution four years later. Consequently, when John Stanley died in 1508 his lands were confiscated by the Crown. Alderley was later granted to Sir William Brereton, but reverted to the Crown when he too fell foul of Tudor politics, in 1536 (see Ives, 1976). In 1556 the Crown sold the Manor of Nether Alderley to Sir Edward Fitton, and it was the Fittons who sold the lands and the Lordship of Nether Alderley to Thomas Stanley of Over Alderley for £2,000 in 1602. Thomas Stanley had already improved the family finances by marrying Elizabeth, Sir Peter Warburton's daughter and heiress, and his position was consolidated when he was knighted by James I in 1603 (Ormerod, 1882: vol. 3, p. 577; Earwaker, 1880: 598–600).

Unfortunately, Sir Thomas Stanley died at the age of twenty-nine in 1606, only three years after he was knighted, leaving a seven-year-old son, another Thomas, to inherit. Lady Stanley remarried, taking the Alderley rents with her as her dowry. Young Thomas's lands were in wardship until 1618, and he did not come into his full inheritance until his mother died in 1631. This was the same year he married Elizabeth Pyte of Worcestershire and started to live at the Old Hall, where he began a programme of beautifying the Park, introducing the beech trees that were such a feature of Alderley Park until they were felled during the Second World War.

Thomas pursued a prudent course through the troubled years of the mid-seventeenth century. Appointed to the bench when he was quite young, he was made Sheriff in 1631 and would have been responsible for collecting taxes for the Crown and organising any Parliamentary elections. However, by 1640, he had become vociferous in his opposition to Charles I's Ship Money Tax, and in the Civil Wars that broke out two years later he was part of the Parliamentary leadership in Cheshire, being especially concerned with raising taxes for the Parliamentary side (Morrill, 1974). The Royalist historian Clarendon had to admit that the Cheshire Parliamentary leaders executed their responsibilities 'with notable sobriety and indefatigable industry' (quoted in Dore, 1966: 16). As part of the original moderate leadership of the county, siding with old Sir George Booth of Dunham Massey against the more hard-line local army leader Sir William Brereton, he disliked the military radicals who emerged towards the end of the First Civil War. The correspondence between Stanley and Brereton show the latter desperate for money to pay the troops, while Stanley argued he could not tax the county any harder; the people 'are so far exhausted betwixt free quartering of our own and plundering by the enemy' (10 April 1645, Stanley to Brereton: see Dore, 1983–84: letter 202).

Although the First Civil War officially finished in 1646, the Parliamentary army was kept in force pending a constitutional settlement. The soldiers still did not receive their arrears of pay, and in May 1647 a group of soldiers occupied Alderley Old Hall until they were paid off with £50. In July the moderate gentry leadership, including Stanley, were rounded up by the soldiers and imprisoned in Chester Castle until money was found to pay them. Chester was just emerging from an appalling siege the year before and from an outbreak of plague; the room where the magistrates were imprisoned lacked even the basic amenities of sanitation, so with much protest they gave in to the soldiers' demands and issued promissory notes on their own recognisances (Morrill, 1974: 201).

During the crisis of the Second Civil War and the King's trial and execution, Stanley kept a low profile, but was sufficiently in favour with the new regime to be a magistrate by March 1649, again involved in running the county, especially on the financial side. He proved himself a diligent local magistrate, prominent in organising the new civil marriages that were introduced in 1653. The parish records for St Mary's Church include several of these; apparently, notice was given either by posting banns in the church porch or by announcing them at market day in Macclesfield. As one of the 'Gentry Confederates', he was against the introduction of the Major-Generals in 1656, as they would challenge the magistrates' running of local government, but he was not part of the group, later to be the participants in the Royalist Booth's Rising, which opposed the election as MP of John Bradshaw, the radical judge from Congleton who had been president of the court that had tried Charles I. During Booth's Rising in 1659 Stanley went into hiding, whether to avoid arrest by the insurgents or merely to see what the outcome was before committing himself we do not know, but he was sufficiently under suspicion to be questioned in London after the Restoration, and he was sufficiently worried about the outcome to make his will before going south. However, Stanley kept his seat on the bench and in 1660 even emerged with a baronetcy from Charles II, the first Cheshire man to be so honoured, probably because the King recognised his long administrative experience in the county and fundamental acceptance of the realities of power. Royalists such as Peter Leycester, who was also made a baronet at this time, were quite disgusted at the honour done to their old enemy (Angus-Butterworth, 1932: 201).

If one looks at St Mary's Church at this period, Sir Thomas's Puritan sympathies are evident. In 1630, Samuel Shipton, the son of the previous Rector, was presented to the living. He was an Oxford don at Brasenose, where he had tutored the Royalist Peter Leycester. In 1643 he was ejected from the living as a supporter of the King and Nicholas Steventon became Rector: Steventon's religious affiliations are clear as he signed the Presbyterian *Attestation of Cheshire Ministers* in 1648, and he was himself thrown out of the living in 1660, when Shipton returned. However, Steventon must have been canonically ordained, as he was compensated with the living of St Mary on the Hill, Chester. After Shipton died in 1670, James, Sir Thomas's fourth son, already Vicar of Mobberley, became Rector. However, he survived only another four years and is buried in his old parish. His widow, Elizabeth Byron of Macclesfield, on her death in 1703 left money to the minister of the Nonconformist chapel in King Edward Street, which had been her customary place of worship for many years (Earwaker, 1880: 633–6).

The second baronet, Sir Peter Stanley, was a Whig supporter, attending the Duke of Monmouth's reception at Dunham Massey in 1682, when the latter was invited to Cheshire by the Booths to canvas support during the Exclusion Crisis. However, both his son and grandson, Sir Thomas and Sir James Stanley, were Catholics; perhaps they were displaying early the Stanleys' cussedness over religion that was to come to the fore in the nineteenth century. Sir Thomas was tried at Chester in 1694, accused of plotting to restore James II; but the case was thrown out for lack of evidence, to much local rejoicing (Hodson, 1978: 18). The fifth baronet, Sir Edward, who succeeded to the title in 1746, reverted to the norm of conforming Anglicanism.

Meanwhile, their ladies were proving themselves formidable house-keepers. Cheshire Archives and Local Studies has their still-room receipt book, containing recipes for medicines and preserves. It was started by Elizabeth Stanley in 1653, and continued in other hands until the eight-eenth century. It is clear that the lady of the house, not the servants, was expected to be practically skilled in herbal medicine, capable of physicking not only her own household but also the whole neighbour-hood. There are numerous prescriptions for alleviating consumption and bad chests, dealing with the effects of smallpox, 'cleaning the blood' (through the use of general tonics with purgative effects) and even one, probably dating from 1665, for preventing the plague; all of these point to common health problems. One receipt for a tonic pill was copied from a source in the Vatican Library around 1700, during the time of the Catholic third and fourth baronets. Seemingly the provenance of the prescription was as important as its content. Some of the receipts are more folk remedies than herbal prescriptions, for example:

> For deafness in the head.
> Take Rue, stampe it and strain it, boile this in the breast milk of a woman that give suck to a girle, strain it and in the water dip black wool and put it in the ears, and keep the head warm. (CALS DDX 361)

During all these vicissitudes the community of Nether Alderley continued its traditional way of life. The Court Leet records from the late sixteenth to the early eighteenth century reveal an active, self-regulating community, well aware of the individual's rights and responsibilities within it and pursuing the township's customary rights and obligations. One of the fullest early records comes from 1598, when the Fittons still held the manor. The Court was concerned that everyone contributed to the upkeep of the parish pinfold (animal pound) up at The Butts, near the boundary of the common on the Edge; it also dealt with sheep-worrying, dogs out of control, affrays between villagers, the rights of turbary on Soss Moss, the repair of highways and the licensing of marlpits. These are typical concerns of any Court Leet, but in 1598 the jurors were especially concerned with defining the parish boundaries up on the Edge and with inspecting the 'new-builded' mill. Nether Alderley Mill is an Elizabethan building but it replaced an earlier structure; its history is discussed in Chapter 25. The jurors appointed a time later in the Whitsun week to deal with both matters.

When the parish jurors came to inspect the boundaries, their 1598 perambulation followed a route that can still be traced today:

> On Thursday Whitsun week, as before rehearsed, the jury did walk the meres on Alderley Edge and did begin at Findlow Hill, the mere there and so to the great stone and so to the merestone at the bottom of the sides of the old and so up the old ditch to another merestone which many of the jury do remember stood on the end and is now fallen down. From thence to the great merestone in the intake and so from that stone straight through to another stone in the bottom near the pit on the commons that Linguard had marl out of. And so lineally by the merestone to the top of the bank by Linguard's house and so to a great stone called the Golden Stone [Figures 2.13, 26.5] on the north side of the wain way that cometh from Linguards to the Beacon. And so lineally to a little merestone in the track way towards the myneholes and so to the merestone at the top of the hill and from thence on the north side the mynehole directly to the Saddlebole and so from the Saddlebole along under the two great stones after the crest. And so back after the crest by the great stones to the two stones lying together over against the hanging stone on the slack and from the hanging stone after the crest up the path towards the Beacon to a stone lying in the same siche [syke, or ditch]. And so following the hillside from crest to crest as they show themselves to the Castle Stone and so along after the crest of the Castle Stone and from thence after the crest all along the hill to a stone that lyeth in the slack which is reputed the merestone towards Chorley beneath the great quarry. And so from that stone turning south westward to the hedge between the lane and the inheritance of Sir Edward Fitton and the lands of Edward Trafford Esq.... All of which several meres and merestones the jury do find and agree by relation of witnesses and the ancient knowledge and reports of those amongst them to be the true meres of Nether Alderley on Alderley Edge and no other between Nether Alderley and Over Alderley, Nether Alderley and the Hough and Chorley. (*Stanley Notebook*)

The merestones of the Edge are described and illustrated more fully in Chapter 27. According to Peter Leycester, most of those defining the parish or township boundaries across the common lands of both Alderleys had been laid out in the mid-sixteenth century, about the time when encroachment on the commons had started to be a serious problem (CALS DLT A75/5). The reference to 'myneholes' is the earliest written evidence of mining on the Edge. Clearly, they were recognised and long-standing landmarks, probably what we now know as Pillar Mine and the Devil's Grave. There is no reference in the Court Leets at this time to mining as an activity, although some of the mineshafts on the Edge, especially near Saddlebole, are thought to be Medieval. The Hanging Stone was above the Holy Well; according to old men interviewed by John Stanley about 1800, it fell down in 1740, making the houses in the nearby Hough shake with the impact (CALS DSA 5/10).

It is possible by reading the Court Leet records to follow families through the generations. The Mottersheads were long-time residents on Brynlow, at what is now known as White Barn Farm. Reynold Mottershead was paid 6s in 1534 for grazing two stray horses found on the Edge (Ives, 1976: 175). Reginald or Randle Mottershead appears in the Court Leets frequently about 1600; he seems to have followed his own independent, if not troublesome, line. In 1598 he was fined for keeping a greyhound bitch and for fighting John Grastie; in 1610 he was still keeping greyhounds, but he had also a net to poach fish in the Stanley moat, and a capon, stolen from Lady Stanley, was found in his house. In 1611 he had neglected to keep his ditches clear up on the Edge and he had been fighting again, this time with his brother Thomas. The 1610 and 1611 Court Leet records are full of such misdemeanours; the first Sir Thomas Stanley had died, his widow was running the manor for their young son and some of the villagers seem to have tried to take advantage of the situation (*Stanley Notebook*). The Brynlow Hill area of Alderley does appear to have been the rough end of the village at the end of the sixteenth century. Not only was Randle Mottershead in trouble in 1598, his neighbour Edward Oldham, from what is now Armstrong Farm, was fined for gambling with his friends at bowls, and Thomas Deane of Brynlow had illegally burnt furze on the Edge (*Stanley Notebook*).

Randle Mottershead's son Robert was in trouble in 1623 for burning furze on the Edge, and in 1651 his grandson Thomas was fined for trespassing on Will Bradford's land (*Stanley Notebook*). Interestingly, the Mottersheads' many infractions of the local laws did not stop them acting as jurors at the Court; as one of the established farming families in the area, they would have known the customary law and their neighbours trusted their judgement in such matters. The 1684 Terrier (the report on the parish church's property and rights) shows that Thomas's son, another Reginald, signing immediately after the gentry in the parish, had a surprisingly Italianate signature, suggesting he was well educated

(Parish Records, CALS m/f 65/1). The Mottersheads moved away to Fitton Town at the eastern end of Over Alderley in the early eighteenth century, but their old farm continued to be known as Mottersheads until after Sir Edward Stanley had a barn built there in about 1750. Whitewashed, its visibility as a landmark led the farm itself to be known as White Barn Farm and later to give its name to the road leading up to it (*Stanley Notebook*).

This traditional way of life, regulated by the Court Leets, remained until the common land was enclosed in the late 1770s. After this, the villagers no longer had any communal land, rights and responsibilities to administer, and the Court Leets lost their importance. Besides the enclosure documents establishing the new order, we have the Court Leet records for 1763 and 1768 and the 1772 Terrier, which all together give us a picture of the old community. The Terrier is particularly useful, as it lists farms and cottages by name, giving not only the owner and leaseholder, but the occupier as well. Many farms took their names from the people who lived there, and in many cases these eighteenth-century names persist today. Elizabeth Topp, the widow of John Topp, held the lease of Topps Farm, James Finney was at Finneys, Samuel Gatley at Gatley Green, Ralph Armstrong at Armstrong; Richard Finlow had lived at Finlow Bower earlier in the eighteenth century (CALS DSA 211). When Armstrong Farm had been occupied by the Oldham family early in the seventeenth century, the holding had been known as Oldham's, and in 1763 some people still knew it as such; their name persisted in 1841, when the tithe map names Higher and Lower Oldham Fields on the farm (CALS IR 30/5). Enclosure was to establish the landscape, and many place names became fixed as well.

Other farms take their names from the area – Finlow Hill Farm and Brynlow Farm – or from distinctive features – such as White Barn Farm. Monks Heath is so called because this area, most of which was common land in the eighteenth century, once belonged to Dieulacres Abbey near Leek (on the history and the names see Chapter 28). The history of its ownership since the Dissolution of the monasteries was complicated and research into it occupied John Stanley a great deal, but he came to no firm conclusions about it.

In 1763, the villagers of Nether Alderley again walked the parish boundary on the common land, this time between Nether Alderley and Chorley. They assembled down on the Hough road, where two Trafford agents and some Chorley tenants met them, clearly intent that all should be above board. They came up Red Lane (by the nineteenth-century Mottram Quarry) to Saddlebole and Glaze Hill, along the top of the Edge above Holy Well to the Beacon, then along to Castle Rock and over the road to the top of Armstrong farm. Thomas Ridgeway, who farmed Castle Stone Field and the Mountain of Poverty, was one of the witnesses; he said at Castle Rock it was usual for the Alderley men to keep to the top path, while the Chorley contingent walked below (*Stanley Notebook*).

One aspect that is clear is that enclosure did not destroy or create new farming units, although the long-time squatters on Monks Heath were given cottages in the area by the present crossroads. The 1775 enclosure was solely concerned with Alderley's commons and heaths. Besides Alderley Edge, then mostly used according to Stanley for grazing villagers' sheep, the common lands were at Monks Heath, Sandle Heath and some small pockets of land at the parish pinfold by the Butts. Soss Moss was not included in the 1775 enclosure as it was already divided up by merestones into 'moss rooms' for the freeholders. Alderley Edge, however, with its mineral rights was specifically allotted to Sir John Stanley. The stated reason for enclosure was to improve the land, and Stanley's pre-existing plantations on the Edge were allowed by the lawyers (CALS DSA 1919/33) (Figure 19.7).

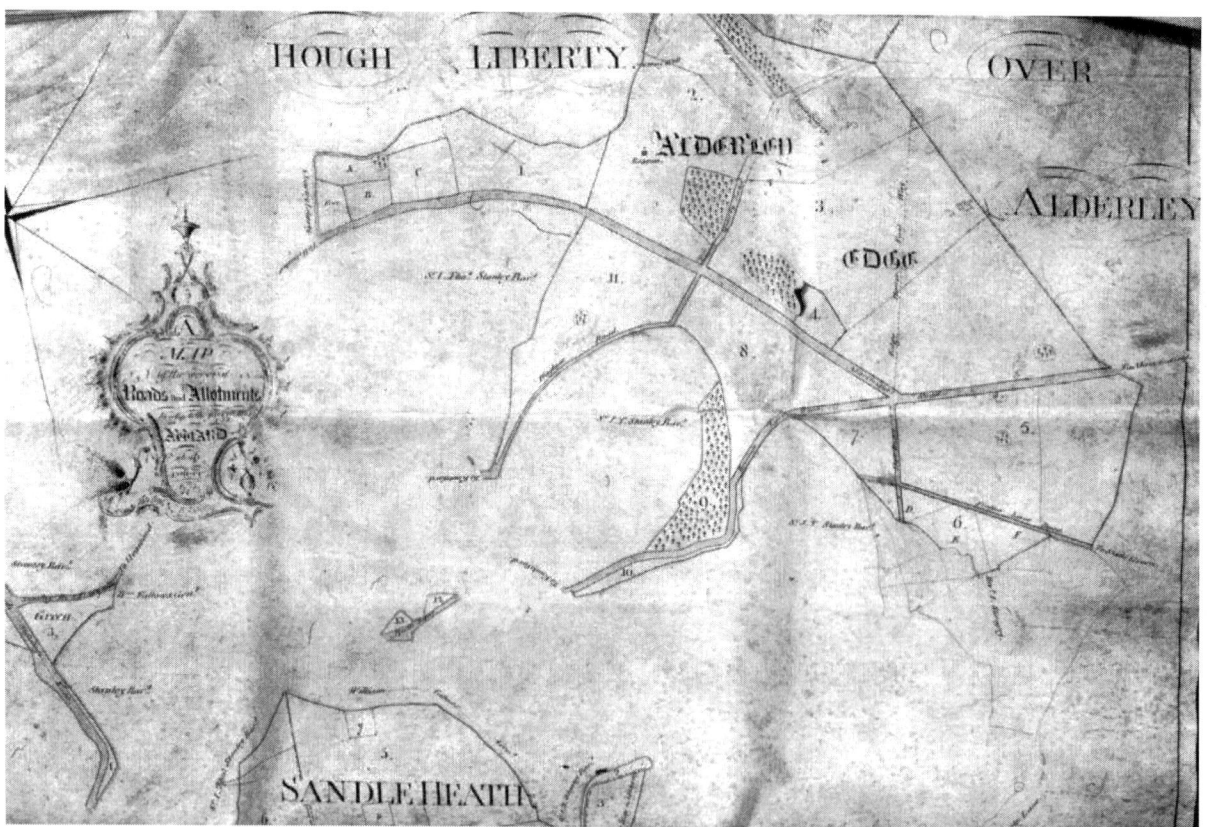

Figure 19.7. The Enclosure Award map for Alderley Edge, 1775.

Crown copyright, Courtesy of Cheshire Archives and Local Studies (CALS) (DSA 1919/33).

The road system over the Edge was largely defined by the enclosure, and the 1775 Enclosure Award document gave precise details:

> Upon that part of the said common or waste ground called Alderley Edge, one Highway or road Twelve yards wide and ditches on each side excluded leading from Wilmslow and beginning northwardly at the boundary of the Township of Chorley adjoining the south side of the ancient enclosed lands of the said Sir John Thomas Stanley [Castle Stone Field and Mountain of Poverty], and of the Inclosures and Allotments marked out in the said Map or Plan Number 1 and the letters b and c and proceeding to the South side of the Allotments Number 2, 3 and 4 and from thence in towards the east between Allotments Number 3 and 5 and leading eastwardly towards Macclesfield and called or distinguished on the said map or plan by the name of Macclesfield Road. (CALS DSA 1919/33)

Other named roads were also created. Quarry Road 'proceeding NE on the South side of Allotment Number 2 to the Stone Quarry in Allotment Number 3', Hag Lane and Hall Road were all to be eight yards wide. Brynlow Lane Road was to go 'Eastwardly along the ancient inclosures to the West of the Common', and Finlow Lane Road 'over the common and waste land within Over Alderley towards Slade Green'. On the Edge, Glaze Hill Road was to be a bridle path from Quarry Road to Glaze Hill, and a footway was to be created from the Macclesfield Road to the Edge House tenements (CALS DSA 1919/33). The ditches and their accompanying banks still define the roads across the Edge, although the modern road system does not follow the 1775 pattern exactly; as this was an enclosure by agreement rather than an Act of Parliament and the Stanleys owned all the land in the area, they were able to make slight alterations.

In order to get total control over the common land, over the next few years Sir John Stanley had to buy out the leaseholders and other small-holders who had common rights on the Edge and elsewhere. It cost him less than £200 to purchase these rights in Nether Alderley and Over Alderley in 1777 and 1778 (CALS DSA 1919/33). However, one deal he made, with Samuel Shrigley of Findlow Hill, was by nature of barter. Samuel's brother the late Reverend John Shrigley, curate of Alderley, had taken a lease on the farm in 1748 and had encroached on about an acre of the common next to his holding; Samuel was able to keep this land in return for surrendering his common rights (CALS DSA 212). The whole area was still undeveloped when young John Stanley first visited Alderley Edge in 1778, just before the Old Hall burnt down the following year. He remembered 'the beechwood, the mere, the adjacent country of the Edge being a common and of Soss Moss only three clumps of trees, and of prison bars played in the open spaces in between' (J. T. Stanley, *Praeterita*, in Adeane, 1899: 4). ('Prison bars' is the Cheshire name for the traditional game of prisoners' base.)

The main turnpike road system was created in the mid-eighteenth century. The Knutsford–Macclesfield road over Monks Heath was improved in about 1740, when John Darcy took a 'pavement of stone' from Castle Stone Field to provide hardcore (CALS DSA 5/10). The north–south turnpike was also reinforced with Alderley stone; in 1780, the burnt remains of the Old Hall were sold off for this purpose (CALS DSA 5/10). The original line of this turnpike ran straight north from Monks Heath. When the Old Hall was largely destroyed, the family removed to Park House in the south of Alderley Park; this modest house was gradually enlarged and rebuilt over the next fifty years to become the family's main residence. Feeling their privacy was threatened by the proximity of the road, its route was altered westwards in 1818 to its present position (see Figure 19.13, p. 489). The line of the original turnpike can still be seen in the park by Church Lodge, at the entrance to the present research complex in Alderley Park.

The 'pavement of stone' from Castle Stone Field has puzzled historians and archaeologists. Thomas Ridgeway, whose family farmed the land, believed the traditional legend that it was the foundation of an unfinished Medieval castle. When he dug a ditch there in about 1770 he found handfuls of what he identified as 'gunflints'. This led Stanley to think this pavement was the remains of a Civil War fortification, and he drew a sketch of the lumps and bumps in the field to support his idea (CALS DSA 3752/1; Figure 19.8).

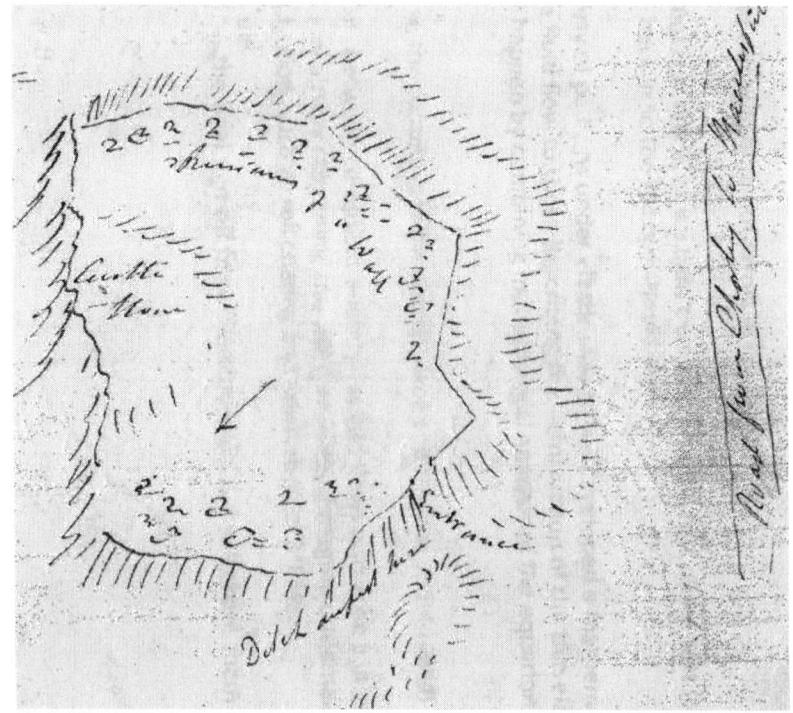

Figure 19.8. Lord Stanley's sketch of the humps and bumps on Castle Stone Field, attempting to prove there was once a seventeenth-century fort there.

Courtesy of Cheshire Archives and Local Studies: DSA 3752/1.

We now know these gunflints were almost certainly Mesolithic micro-liths, and there is no record of seventeenth-century fortifications in this area. However, modern surveys have been inconclusive in dating the humps and bumps in Castle Stone Field (*ArchAE*: 164). Ridgeway was one of Stanley's sources for local stories and legends. As a boy, in about 1740, he claimed he was a fellow-servant at Fallowes Hall with Ellen Beck, a girl who said she saw the legendary Iron Gates on the Edge, but could not find them again. Slighted in love, she committed suicide and, denied consecrated ground, was buried on Armstrong Farm (CALS DSA 5/10).

According to Ridgeway, the existence of the Iron Gates was generally believed by local people. It forms part of the Alderley Legend, first appearing in an account by 'a Perambulator' in the *Manchester Mail*, 19 May 1805. The author said that he was told the story by 'Daddy' Thomas Broadbent, an ancient Stanley retainer who said his informant was Parson Shrigley (d. 1776), who was relating a general belief which 'placed the event about eighty years before his time'. This is typical of oral tradition; it is within a person's comprehension and the hearer feels in touch with the events, but the original source is dead so the story cannot be challenged: see also the account of the Legend by Alan Garner in Chapter 30.

The mid-eighteenth century seems to be the time when many aspects of Alderley life, legend and landscape became settled. Around 1740, the Hanging Stone fell, Ellen Beck died, Castle Stone Field pavement was cleared and Sir James Stanley began planting trees on the Edge. The 1763 perambulation has the first documented mention of the Holy Well, although it must have been a familiar feature by then to be used to mark the boundary. In the 1770s Sir John Stanley repaired the Beacon, heightening it and giving it a new pyramidal roof; it is described in Appendix 19.2. By 1780 the Edge ceased to be common land; it had become part of the private domain of the Stanleys, who were interested in beautifying the place. Louisa Stanley is quite open about the Druids' Circle being a manufactured feature of no mythic importance (Stanley, 1843: 18; this source is quoted in Chapter 2, p. 41; see also Chapter 27, pp. 676–7).

Looking at William Crossley's map (CALS P143/14/1), the Stanley estate map surveyed in 1787 and in use in the estate office until the mid-nineteenth century, we can see the immediate developments after enclosure and the changes made later (Figure 19.9). By 1787 the Wizard Inn, then known as the Miners' Inn, had been built (see also Chapter 16, p. 386) and a road to it was already made, cutting through from the Brynlow Lane road, which is now the top of the modern Artists Lane (Figure 19.10): eventually this would become the main route and the original line of Brynlow Lane, coming out onto the Macclesfield Road

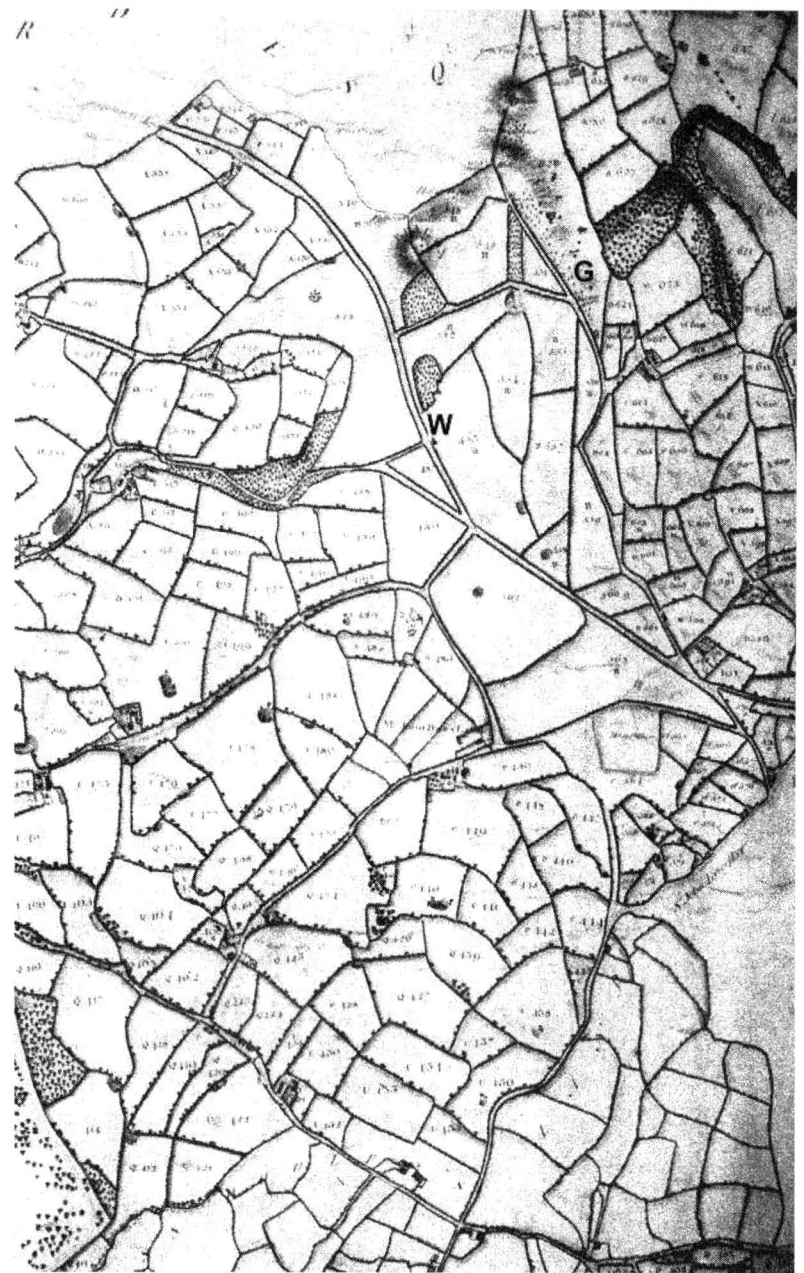

Figure 19.9. Detail from William Crossley's map of the Stanley estates, 1787, showing the top of the Edge. The hostelry now known as the Wizard Inn or the Wizard restaurant (marked W) at the top of Artists Lane is the only building on the Edge, but the new lane, the present top of Artists Lane forming a triangle in the centre of this extract, has appeared since the Enclosure Award map of twelve years before (Figure 19.7). A track curving gently north-east from the Wizard (marked W) past Engine Vein to the Goldenstone (marked G) was marked in pencil on the original, but it is now too faint to reproduce here.

Courtesy of Cheshire Archives and Local Studies: P 143/14/1.

at the top of Hall Lane (Finlow Hill Lane), declined into a bridle path. Instead of making a straight footpath across to Edge House, the estate later decided to build a road from the new ale house, skirting Engine Vein, towards the Golden Stone. This route suggests access was needed to the workings at Engine Vein at about 1800. All this is shown in pencil on the map, as is the line of the 1842 railway.

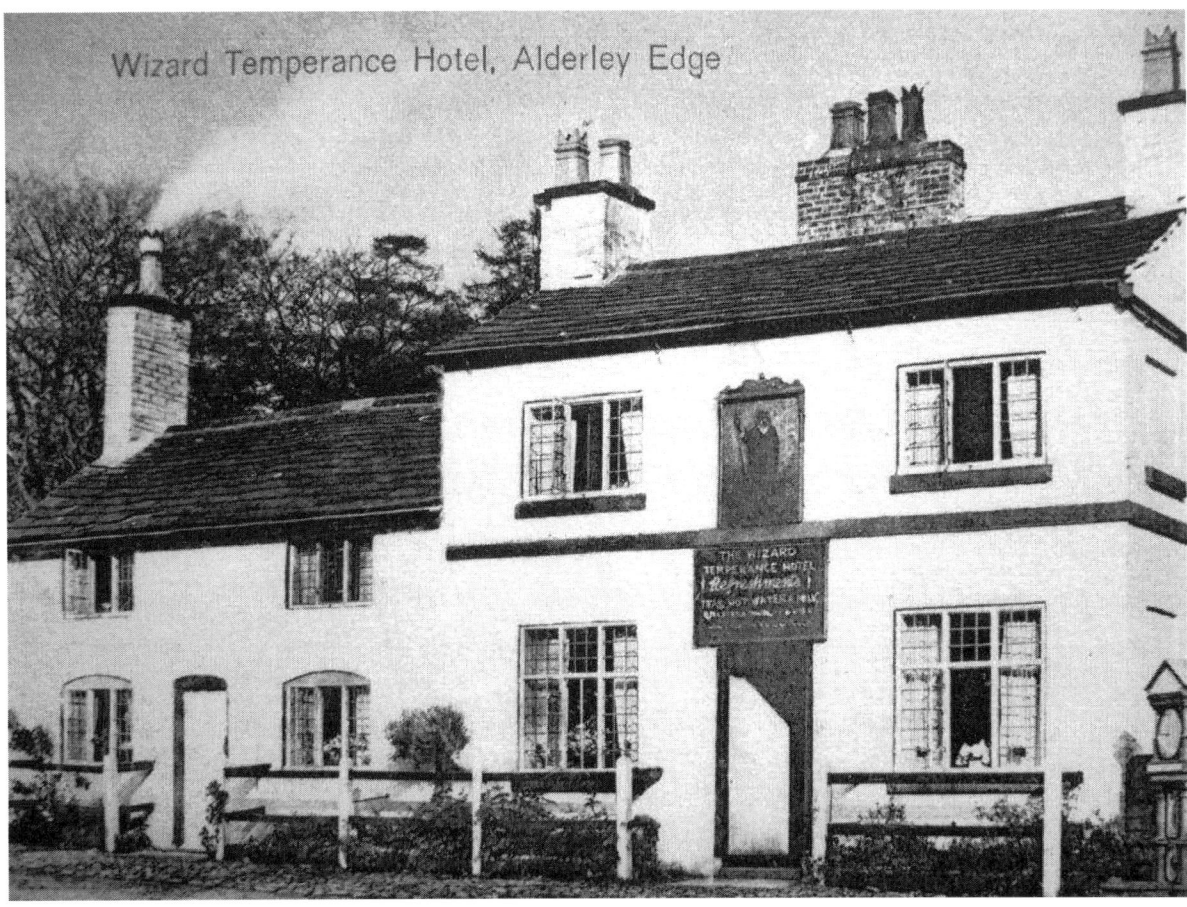

Figure 19.10. An old postcard showing the Wizard Inn on Alderley Edge in its days as the Wizard Temperance Hotel. The sign offers 'Teas, Hot Water & Milk'. Previously known as Pogmores, the Miner Inn, the Miner on ye Edge and then the Miner Inn, by 1831 it was the Miners Arms. In 1843 it was the Wizard, and it has undergone variations on that name ever since.

Even before enclosure gave them the right, the Stanleys had already started to plant trees on Alderley Edge. The first Stanley to show any aesthetic appreciation of the place was Sir James Stanley, the fourth baronet, who had a carriage road made up to the Edge about 1740; he went up there almost every day. He also planted the first trees on the Edge, by Church Quarry and at Glaze Hill about the same time. The Beacon Piece was planted about 1760 by Sir John Stanley and Brynlow Wood was created as a nursery. These plantations can be seen on the Enclosure Award map. Once enclosure had gone through, planting went on apace. The wage book for 1780 shows that workers were scattering acorns all over the Edge to encourage oak tree generation; Finlow Hill Piece and the area behind Bradford Lodge were also planted (CALS DSA 5/10).

There was a strong movement in the late eighteenth century, encouraged by the government, to plant oaks, Spanish chestnuts and fir trees for strategic reasons – to build ships for the navy (Schama, 1995: 168–9). Sir John Evelyn's highly influential *Silva* (1776) was edited and republished by H. Hunter of York in 1786. In his notes Hunter mentions that firs were particularly suitable for 'Mancunian mosses' and that 'in some of the northern counties of this kingdom, the practice of sowing their wastelands with Acorns, Chestnuts, Beechmast, Firseeds, Ashkeys etc is much to be recommended' (Evelyn, 1786: 86). The Stanleys were not among the original subscribers to this edition, but the first Lord Stanley probably saw one of his father-in-law's copies.

However, 'the trees produced from there were mostly destroyed by several successive firings of the gorse and heath. And about 1798, several acres of the plantations at Bradford Lodge and the Finlow Hill Piece were burnt. It could never be discovered whether the fires were accidental or malicious' ('second' *Stanley Notebook*, CALS DSA 3752/1). If the fires were malicious, it suggests there was some local resentment of the Stanleys' takeover of the old common land on the Edge, and that the tension between the Stanleys and those wanting greater access to the area pre-dates the influx of 'Railroadians' in the nineteenth century. The danger of fire still existed in 1804, when, during the French invasion scare before the battle of Trafalgar, it was decided not to store wood or furze beside the Beacon in case it was set alight and caused a false alarm (CALS DSA 5/10).

It took some time for trees to grow up on the Edge. In the 1841 tithe map apportionment (CALS IR 30/5), although many of the enclosures on the Edge are officially plantations, they were still being used for pasture and even for arable farming. In the 1850s the view from the Beacon was still relatively unobstructed by trees; people could easily see Lyme Cage (Barlow, 1853: 123).

The great storms of 1802 and 1803 did damage to the plantations. 'The trees on the Edge are tossed about in a most curious manner, and scarce a fir has escaped without some wound. We rode a tour of the estate the next day and saw nothing but mischief' (Maria Stanley to her sister, Louisa Clinton, 28 January 1802, reproduced in Adeane, 1899: 229). Planting continued; in 1802 John Stanley obtained some seed from his brother-in-law, William Clinton, and planted Clinton Hill on Finlow. This was a cash crop: the firs and larches were harvested in 1830 and the area is no longer wooded.

By this time John Stanley and his wife, Maria Josepha Holroyd, and their rapidly expanding family (Figure 19.11) had been settled at Alderley for several years. When John came of age in 1789, old Sir John Stanley had made the leases of Fernhill and the Dales Farm over to him (CALS DSA 208), and on their marriage in 1796 the young couple set

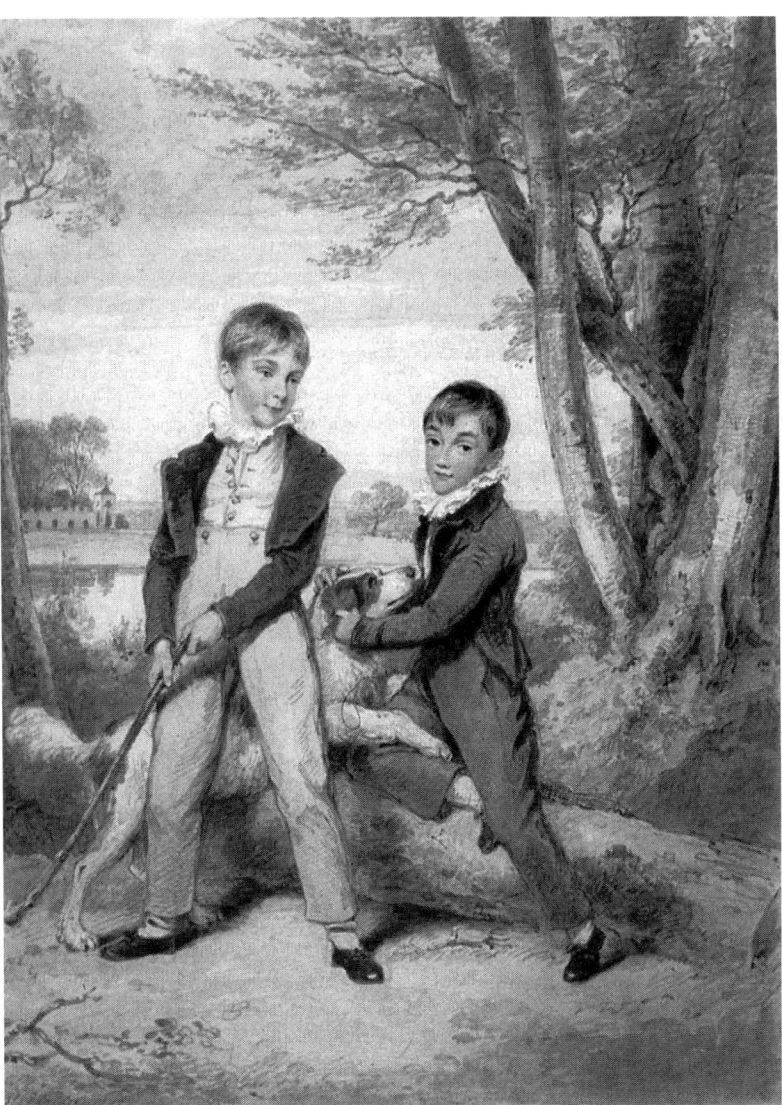

Figure 19.11. Edward and William Stanley, the first Lord Stanley's twin sons, in Alderley Park. The deer house and the beech trees for which the park was famous are in the background. Both these features have now gone.

Courtesy of Lord Stanley.

up residence at the Park House (Figure 19.12), staying there until Lord Stanley's death in 1850. John's father seems to have largely abandoned his central Cheshire estates to live in London, where he was a Gentleman of the Bedchamber to George III, or at his new development at Hoylake on the Wirral, while his mother, Margaret Owen, stayed mainly on her own estate of Penrhos near Holyhead on Anglesey. This meant John and Maria were in charge at Alderley. Maria's letters to her relations, particularly to her aunt, Serena Holroyd, and her sister, Louisa Clinton, give a valuable insight into life in Alderley in the early nineteenth century, after the upheaval of enclosure and the fire at the Old Hall, but before the coming of the railway changed the area completely (Figure 19.13).

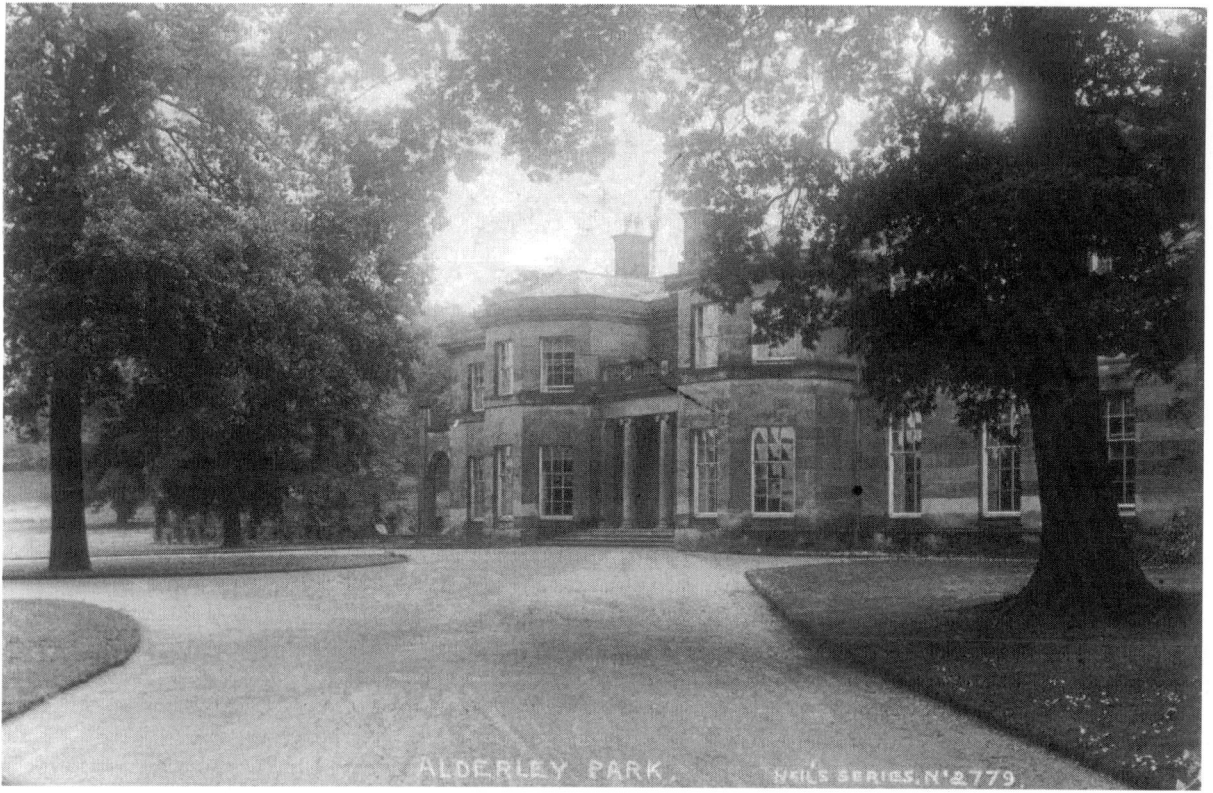

Figure 19.12. An old postcard of Alderley Park House, the Stanley family home, in about 1900. It was largely burnt down in 1931, but the stable area and Tenants' Hall are still there.

Alderley was still an agricultural community, aware of the political and economic changes elsewhere in the country, but as yet relatively untouched by them. The rhythms of the agricultural year were the main determinants of life, and Maria especially enjoyed providing the traditional hospitality expected of the squire and his family:

> We had yesterday what is generally called a harvest home supper, but here a 'shutting', and I really do not think the grandest Lord Mayor's feast with turtle and venison and the finest court ball afterwards could have given me so much pleasure. All the labourers, carpenters, bricklayers and weeding women, to the number of about two or three and twenty had their meal on a long table placed in the coach house, at five o'clock. We went to see them eat, and drank their health in a bumper of ale which they then obligingly returned. Old Peter ... the old labourer who has worked on the estate for forty years, and served four generations of Stanleys, danced the Cheshire Round with Charlotte Alcock, one of the women. They all played afterwards at prison bars in the park until it was quite dark, and then came to the house to sing and dance over a bowl of punch. I believe as happy a party as ever assembled. (8 September 1798, Maria to Serena, in Adeane, 1899: 165)

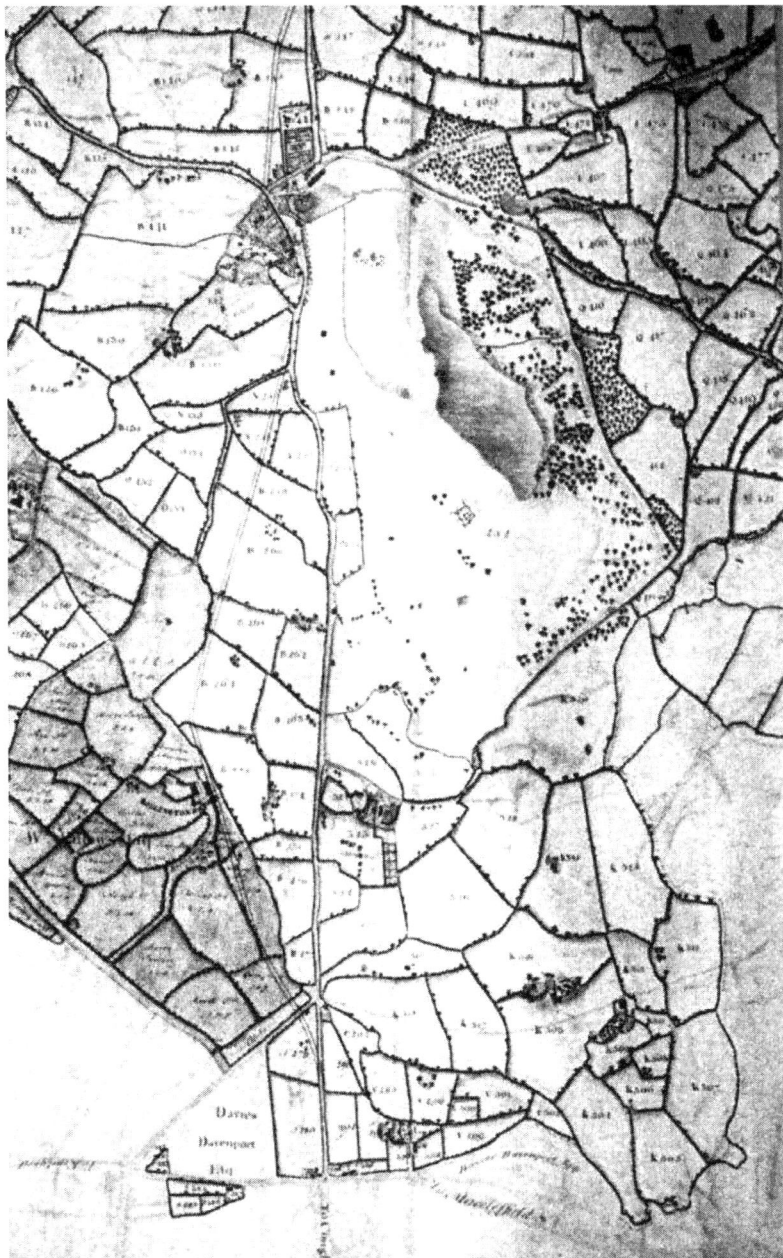

Figure 19.13. Detail from William Crossley's map of the Stanley estates, showing the road system in 1787, before the Stanleys changed it in the early nineteenth century. Their alterations both to the turnpike by the Park House and to Bradford Lane and the northern end of Alderley Park can just be seen marked in pencil. The new course of the road is shown in pencil, visible to the west of the straight line of the old route as two parallel lines.

Courtesy of Cheshire Archives and Local Studies (P 143/14/1).

She also wrote about the customs that were still followed in Alderley at this time, including the north-western custom of Easter 'chairing' or 'lifting'. On Easter Monday, 'the men dressed a chair very fine with ribands and flowers, and when I came down for breakfast offered me a ride, which of course I declined; but as was expected, bought myself off with half a guinea. On Tuesday the maids did actually lift the Man [Stanley] in the chair, he gave them a guinea' (16 July 1800, Maria to

Serena, in Adeane, 1899: 199). John Stanley also remembered the wakes at this time, when they were centred on St Mary's Church; everyone appeared in their best clothes, took very little interest in the service, being more concerned in looking at their neighbours, then went to the Eagle and Child, where the publican usually provided everyone with ribands for the game of prison bars. Frumenty was the traditional dish served to visitors (CALS DSA 5/10).

John Stanley also records the Alderley marlers' customs. Digging a marlpit (Figure 12.1) was a cooperative effort, and the team elected a leader or 'lord of the pit' from among themselves to coordinate the work. When they had finished, they expected payment, usually from Stanley. After they had been paid, they gave a great shout, the volume of the noise depending on the amount of money they got; this cash then paid for rounds of drinks in the pub on the Saturday. Funerals had their own customs. When mourners came to the wake, besides other refreshments they were given a piece of cake to eat wrapped up with a sprig of rosemary. The rosemary was either put into the coffin before it was closed or thrown into the grave at the burial (CALS DSA 5/10).

The Stanleys were intent on improving Alderley; John was outdoors almost all the time, superintending operations, especially afforestation of the old common land, while Maria started a school for girls in the village in 1799 and organised smallpox vaccinations for all the children in 1802 (Adeane, 1899: 175, 228). However, life was not idyllic, especially for the ordinary people. Agricultural wages in Cheshire were low; men's rates increased from 1s.3d to 1s.6d a day during the late 1790s (CALS DSA 3588, 241/1) but appalling harvests in 1799 and 1800, followed by severe winters, caused high food prices and problems for the poor in the parish. While the wages they paid were no higher than the average (CALS DSA 2451/1A), the Stanleys were aware of their obligations in such conditions, and helped to buy in grain for re-sale at a subsidised rate and organised a soup kitchen (2 January 1800, Maria to Serena, in Adeane, 1899: 208); they limited their household consumption the next winter. In November 1800 Maria said that the farmers were reluctant to go to the market in Macclesfield as there were often riots over food prices. In January 1801 she wrote to Louisa, 'I have no dairymaid, and Hassall and the kitchen maid are not a little occupied in cooking for the poor, the labourers and eighteen school children that frequently come twice a week to eat their dinner here' (Adeane, 1899: 211).

They were friends of Humphrey Davy and William Wilberforce and politically were staunch Whigs. They supported Catholic Emancipation in the early nineteenth century, welcomed peace in 1801 and reluctantly accepted the renewal of the French Wars in 1803. Maria's comments to her sister Louisa about George III's Jubilee in 1810 are in her best ironic tone: 'The Jubilee was celebrated rather less from loyalty than from the fear of being thought disloyal, but it was a pleasure to see a great many of His Majesty's subjects eating a better dinner than they could treat themselves under his present government. 208 regaled here and I had the pleasure of seeing them stuff…. The labourers had a shilling each and we went to the Edge to see the miners eat and drink' (Adeane, 1899: 324). They deplored Peterloo in 1819, especially as the way the troops behaved encouraged public opinion to support the more extreme Radicals.

The paternalistic tone of the Stanleys' comments about the villagers in Alderley are what one would expect from them: taking the traditional social divisions of village society for granted, the Stanleys were the squires; *noblesse oblige* required them to be concerned about and charitable towards their dependants, providing they received the respect they thought their due. During the Chartist problems in 1842, about 250 unemployed weavers came out to the Park House, begging at the door; they were given bread, cheese and diluted small beer. Lady Stanley did not know where they came from and she watched them from behind the curtains; clearly they made her nervous (Mitford, 1938: 41). At the same time, Lord Stanley was swearing in special constables in the parish to counter any rioting in local towns. The following year, a man was convicted for stealing wood from the Stanley estate. The gamekeeper, Fleetwood, knowing Lord Stanley would not want the man to be transported, put the value of the wood at a shilling, so the thief was only sent to prison for a month (Mitford, 1938: 58).

Certainly Lady Stanley assumed she had a duty to organise people for their own good. In 1848 there was an outbreak of smallpox at the top of Welsh Row. 'Another of the Ridgeways caught the smallpox & so I am afraid it will spread; the people are so stupid…. I find several small children in that neighbourhood have never been vaccinated and some think it too much trouble to have it done now' (Lady Stanley to Henrietta Stanley, in Mitford, 1938: 188). She intended to rectify the situation immediately. The Ridgeways continued to exasperate Lady Stanley. One of the older boys, Richard, was given the chance to be a footman in the London house, but refused it: 'The Ridgeways are a soft-witted family…. This is folly beyond the usual Alderley folly, but the cat-like attachment to the customary hearth is wonderful' (Lady Stanley to Henrietta, 18 November 1848, in Mitford, 1938: 256).

However, whether because of or despite the Stanley high-handedness, Alderley parish does seem to have been able to look after its own. In 1863 new workhouse buildings were opened in Macclesfield and for the next few years the records detail the parishes responsible for those admitted or discharged. During this period only two old men, Joseph Bailey and Joseph Bankes, were admitted from Alderley, after they declared themselves unable to find work to support themselves. During the same period, there were many more admissions from Chorley parish (which contained the new Alderley Edge village), including a frequent recidivist, Joseph Kitchen, who would abscond from the workhouse about every six months, presumably to taste freedom for a short time, only to return within the week unable to support himself. This is perhaps evidence to suggest that the more stable agricultural community of Alderley, with its associated family networks, was usually better able to care for its vulnerable members (CALS LGM 1/1).

The reference to miners in the description of the 1810 celebrations for George III's Jubilee is one of the few in the Stanley archive. Considering the Stanleys' reputation in the nineteenth century of preferring mines to people, this is perhaps surprising. Similarly, the Court Leet records we have in John Stanley's notebooks are either silent about the mines or mention them in passing, as in the 1598 perambulation of the parish boundaries. Mining has left obvious evidence on the Edge itself, where it had a great impact on the environment, but it was only one aspect of the economy of the whole of Alderley.

That mining was quite extensive on the Edge by the end of the seventeenth century is apparent when one reads the report of a riot among the miners in 1696, after which about twenty men were bound over to keep the peace at the Quarter Sessions that June. There was a dispute between two lessees, Thomas Legh of the Ridge and Thomas Crosse, who both claimed Sir Thomas Stanley had granted them the right to work the mines. When Crosse's miners forcibly evicted Legh's men from the diggings, there was a serious incident, and one of Legh's miners, John Thompson, was lucky not to have been strangled by the rope down the shaft. The references to a shaft and a windlass show the mines were well developed for the time. Most of the men came from established families in Over Alderley; William Gibbon, working for Legh, came from Harebarrow, and John Hough, the ringleader for Thomas Crosse, was from the Finlow Hill area. Everyone was well acquainted with each other and readily identified the men involved in the fracas, even though it was dark at the time (*Quarter Sessions*, 1559–1760 – see Bennett and Dewhurst, 1940: 195–7; on this and details of other mining activities at this time see Chapter 16).

As lords of the manor, the Stanleys had the right to exploit the mineral rights under the common land even before enclosure. The involvement of Charles Roe, the Macclesfield businessman, in mining copper on the Edge lasted from 1758 to 1771, before enclosure, and before the Old Hall was burnt down. Any Stanley documents relating to Roe's work on the Edge are likely to have been destroyed in this fire. According to Henry Holland, who acknowledged his debt to John Stanley for information in the preface to his *General View of the Agriculture of Cheshire*, Roe was 'at one time very sanguine in his expectations of success …

40 or 50 men were constantly employed', but Roe abandoned Alderley once Parys Mountain on Anglesey became available. From the tone of the context, Holland seems to suggest Roe had great hopes and plans, but was disappointed (Holland, 1808: 15–18). After Roe left, mining continued on the Edge. John Stanley says his father usually allowed businessmen to prospect on the Edge on their own account, but occasionally financed some of the explorations himself. He goes on to say, however, that 'it was not worked during the past century with any spirit', as the copper, though always present, was never rich enough to sustain viable exploitation for any length of time (CALS DSA 5/10).

However, such mining as there was did leave some evidence on the Edge. The present Wizard Inn was built as an alehouse for the miners in the 1780s, and was extended so that the mining company could use it for their meetings. The Hagg, rebuilt as a small farmhouse in 1747, was later used by the mining company to house labourers (Appendix 19.3). The company also built a steam engine to crush the ore, troughs to wash it afterwards and a smelting house above the Hagg. This smelter was later dismantled and rebuilt at the end of Park Wood, but then was demolished and the stone used to build Beechtree Lodge in 1828 (CALS DSA 5/10).

The one mining venture Stanley does mention in some detail is the attempt to extract cobalt, which he set up in 1807. One of the miners on the Edge, James Ashton, from Derbyshire, who according to Stanley had already built a windmill on the site of the original smelter above the Hagg, recognised the ore, having seen it in Saxony. Cobalt was an important dye in the china, paper and textile industries but during the French Wars it was extremely difficult to import from the usual European sources because of the Napoleonic blockade, so prices for home-produced cobalt were high. John Stanley clearly hoped for great things, copying out an optimistic article from *The Monthly Magazine* published in 1811 (CALS DSA 5/10), but Maria was less sanguine. She wrote to Louisa with the news that the steam engine was working, but she did not expect a diamond necklace just yet. In 1812 they were thinking of exporting the cobalt to the linen bleachers in Ireland (Adeane, 1899: 338). However, the coming of peace in 1815 and the return of cheaper, better-quality cobalt from the Continent ended the speculation.

The most sustained period of mining on the Edge was from 1857 to 1877, when a new acidic process made the low-yielding copper ores of Alderley economic to exploit. The mining complex on Brynlow, where Wood and West Mines were worked as one unit, was quite extensive. The processing, with its advanced chemical technology, attracted much attention, including a visit by a Japanese delegation in 1865, when the mines were lit up with magnesium flares, as described in Chapter 16 (Figure 16.12, p. 402).

The mines relied on a mixture of local labour and imported specialists from Derbyshire and the West Country, as is revealed in the Census
returns for 1861 and 1871. There was a high mobility of labour: out of
forty-one men working in the mines in 1861, only four were there in 1871.
One of them was John Chyneworth, who had come with his brother and
their families from Cornwall. In 1861, they lived with the other West
Country miners in West Street in Alderley Edge Village. Ten years later
his first wife and one of his children had died, but John had remarried,
a local widow with a child, and they lived with their own three children
at Mottram Cottage on the top of the Edge. He had become part of the
local community and in the early 1900s an A. S. Chynoweth (*sic*) was
teaching Group II at the Alderley Edge Council School: he is named
in the teaching and reading plan for 1909/10 (AELP Archive 107). The
West Country miners were a sizeable group, representing 25–33 per cent
of the total workforce; they found accommodation in the working-class
areas of Chorley parish, where the expanding Alderley Edge village had
housing available for rent. In 1871 they had replaced the Derbyshire
miners who in 1861 had lived at the Hagg Cottages, the only housing
in Alderley controlled by the mining company and used by them to accommodate key workers. The mines agent, Jonathan Downes, also from
Cornwall, lived up Brynlow too, in the Butts farmhouse (as recorded
in the Census returns, CALS, m/f 234/8 (1861), m/f 24/14, 15 (1871)).

The majority of the miners were always local. A significant group
were the sons or sons-in-law of smallholders, men who would otherwise
have had to become agricultural labourers or move out of the area
to find work if they were not in the mines. For example, in 1861 John
Hague, aged twenty-five, was a copper miner; he lived with his wife and
widowed mother-in-law, Mary Norbury, a smallholder with ten acres,
on Welsh Row in Nether Alderley. Up at the Edge Houses in Over
Alderley, Martha Hatton, another widow, with three acres, had two sons
and a son-in-law working in the mines. Some of the miners were very
young; two lads aged fifteen or under were employed in 1861 and in
1871 seven boys of this age group were working there, some of them
with their fathers. However, in all the communities, Nether Alderley,
Over Alderley and Chorley, the mines never employed more than a
small minority; in 1861, sixteen out of a population of 617 in Nether
Alderley, nine out of 421 in Over Alderley (CALS Census returns).

By this time, the dormitory village of Alderley Edge was well established. The story of how this came about is curious. When the Manchester
to Birmingham Railway Company obtained its private Act of Parliament
to build a railway through east Cheshire in 1837, it originally intended
the main line to go south, through Congleton and the Potteries, with
a branch line going from Alderley to Crewe. Consequently, it planned
a station just north of this junction at the point where the line crossed

the turnpike road. However, five years later and after an amalgamation with the Grand Junction Railway Company, the original main line was abandoned and the sole line to be built was the one to Crewe. Now that there was to be no junction, the railway company needed to create some justification for the newly built station in the sparsely populated and economically deprived township of Chorley (see Chapter 23).

It was from this unpromising situation that Manchester's first railway commuter community was created. Mr Easted and Mr Waddington of the Manchester to Birmingham Railway Company and the de Trafford family, who owned Chorley but did not themselves live there, formed a plan to release land for development. Developers could take a head lease of about five acres and build villas on the site, leasing them out under restrictive conditions that forbade the commercial use of the houses apart from the occasional doctors' premises. Comparison of the

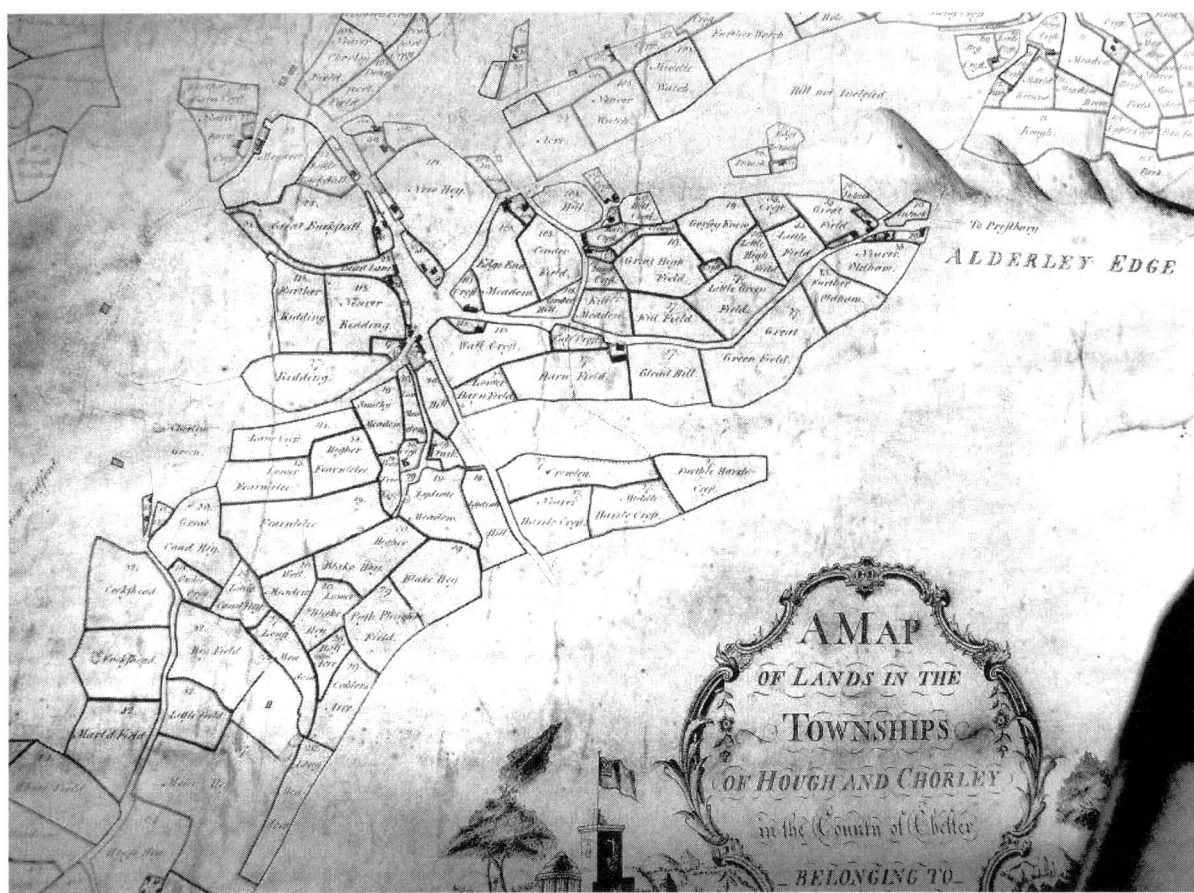

Figure 19.14. Detail of James Heyes' map of the Trafford estates in Chorley and the Hough, 1771, showing the Hill. Note that the curving Trafford Road in the upper centre of the map was already there before the area was developed.

Courtesy of Cheshire Archives and Local Studies (DDT 1405/360/1).

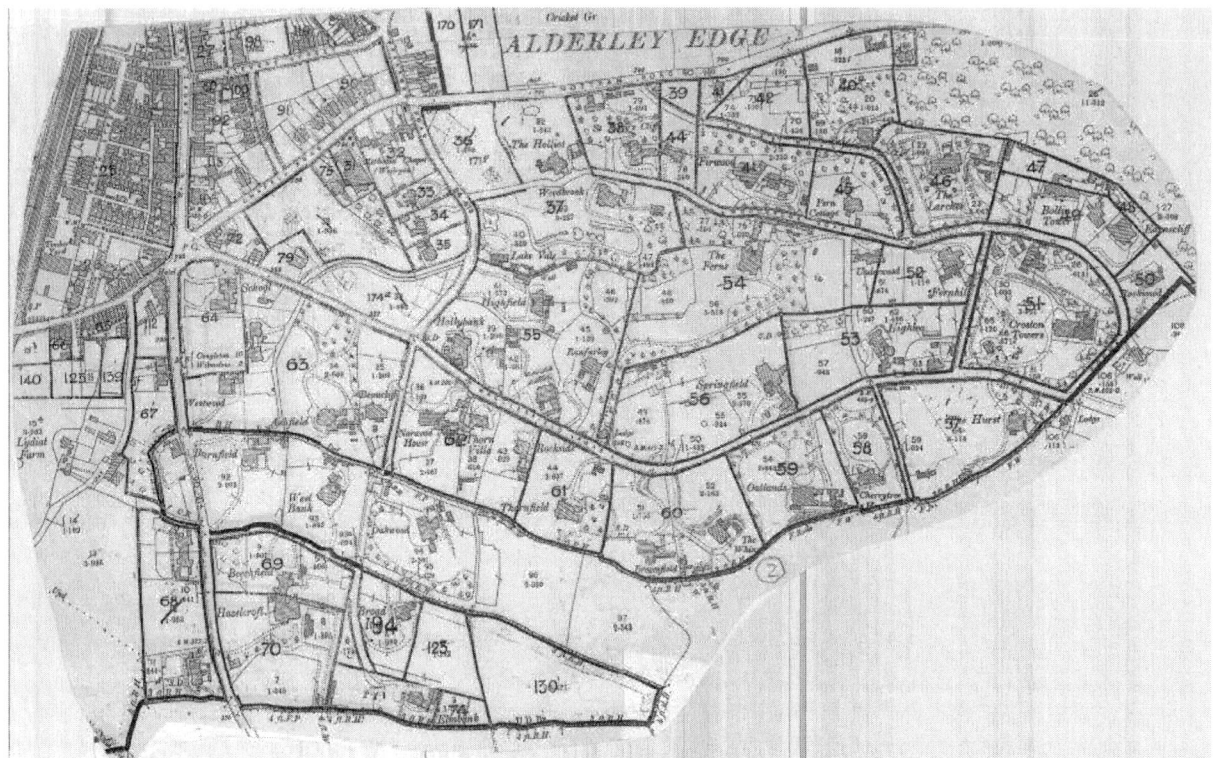

Figure 19.15. Map of the villas on the Edge, based on a late nineteenth-century Ordnance Survey map. The similarities and the differences between the de Trafford development and the Stanley estates can clearly be seen, as can the terrace 'backstreets' between the railway and London Road.

Courtesy of Cheshire Archives and Local Studies (DSA 5/9a).

eighteenth-century map of the Trafford lands in Chorley (CALS DDT 1405/360/1; Figure 19.14) with the Ordnance Survey map of the late nineteenth-century village (Figure 19.15) reveals that the road system in the area was not greatly changed, and in some cases the building plots use the same fields. Relatively few of the original rural cottages remain. Anyway, according to Lord Stanley, their inhabitants had often been destitute and could be expected to benefit from the development as they might be able to find steady employment in the new houses (CALS DSA 5/9a).

Building started in earnest in about 1845 and the villas were deliberately designed to appeal to the newly rich Lancashire industrialists and their families. Generally built with three reception rooms, four or five good bedrooms, extensive offices and servants' accommodation, they sat in about an acre of landscaped gardens. As an incentive, the railway company agreed to give a twenty-one-year first-class pass from Alderley to Manchester for the head of the household, providing the house was worth at least £50 a year rateable value. This gentleman was expected

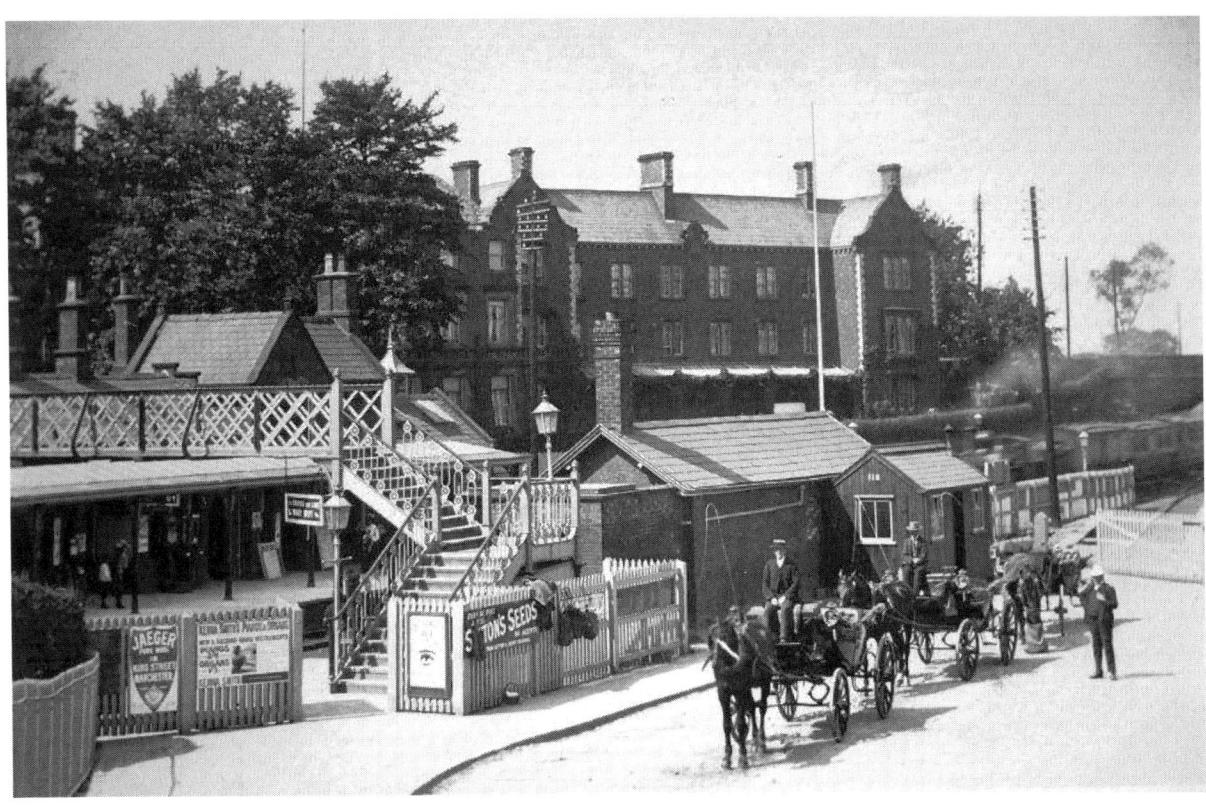

Figure 19.16. An old postcard of the station in Alderley Edge village, with the Queen's Hotel behind. The carriages are waiting by the 'up' platform to collect the Manchester commuters at the end of the day.

to commute to Manchester to work, leaving his wife and family in the healthy air of Alderley (Figure 19.16).

The villas are built in two main areas, near the station around Brook Lane and up the hill on the Edge itself. In between these two villa areas, and between the main London Road and the railway line in the village itself, were built the 'Back Streets', closely packed terrace houses, two up two down, for the service community, gardeners and the like, who worked for the villa households. Along the London Road itself were the shops. The village also contained a new Anglican church, St Philip's, designed by J. S. Crowther, a Methodist Church in Chapel Road and a school for the village children. It was a highly stratified community; literally, everyone knew their place, as people's addresses immediately identified their social class and position in the community. The villas and the village are described in Chapter 23.

The Traffords were willing to see the value of their estates increase with this new development, but the Stanleys stood firm against these changes, despite their agent telling them it would make money (Mitford, 1938: letter 98). They particularly resented the railway company's assumption of the name of their home, Alderley, for the new station and community. They released very little of their land for residential development in the mid-nineteenth century and steadily resisted all persuasion to give the public greater access to the Edge than they were ready to allow. They were happy to allow a mass excursion of Sunday school pupils from Manchester to walk on the Edge in 1853 (Mitford, 1938: letter 72) and to open up the Edge for the public on certain other days, but 'the Manchester gentry are much more annoying to ones comfort and enjoyment than operatives, as one can neither handcuff or great dog them if they are intrusive or offensive' (Lady Stanley to Lord Stanley, September 1853, in Mitford, 1938: letter 84). The Manchester gentry, or Cottentots as the Stanleys called them, did not want to come on public days with everybody else; they wanted exclusive entry on their own days and were ready to be very polite to the Stanleys if they met them. From the persistent way Mr Easted and Mr Waddington approached Lord Stanley, the new community's developers would have dearly liked to have been able to advertise exclusive access to the Edge as one of the incentives to prospective purchasers, alongside the twenty-one-year season ticket to Manchester (Mitford, 1938: letter 84).

The Stanleys hated this attempted intrusion into their privacy and took great pleasure in informing enquirers that Alderley Park itself was never open to visitors. Cottentots and their manners were 'just like Americans, so free and easy' (Henrietta Stanley to Lady Stanley, August 1843, Mitford, 1938: letter 83). The Stanleys were especially jealous of their game: 'Fancy Edward's horror at the idea of *people* loose among his beloved pheasants' (*ibid.*, original emphasis). Edward, second Lord Stanley, was most particular about the new community encroaching on the old Alderley; when he became Postmaster General in 1860, he gave orders that all letters wrongly addressed to Alderley should either be re-addressed to 'Chorley' or put in the dead-letter box (Moss, 1903: 1–2; the topic is also discussed in the context of the place names of Alderley in Chapter 28). Edward Stanley was not the only local to be sensitive on this topic. Katherine Chorley, who grew up at The Ferns, a villa on the Edge, remembered that as a girl if she inadvertently referred to her home being in Alderley when in the company of any original inhabitants, she was quickly corrected (Chorley, 1950: 147).

The second Lord Stanley's eight surviving children were remarkable for their intelligence and strong and varied opinions. One of the younger girls, Kate, became the mother of Bertrand Russell, but unfortunately died young. Her two elder brothers, successively third and fourth Lord Stanley, did not get on. Henry, the elder, was deaf and converted to Islam when travelling in the East. He was responsible for closing all the licensed premises on the estate, although he allowed the Wizard to re-open as a teetotal tearoom for the walkers on the Edge (compare

Figures 16.6, p. 386, and 19.10, p. 485). He had a Spanish wife, Fabia, whom he married three times, by Muslim, Catholic and Anglican rites, but none of these ceremonies were valid, as Fabia's husband was still living. He waited until after his father died to tell his mother that he had been married for seven years and so caused an irreparable rift in the family, especially with his younger brother Lyulph. Fortunately, the marriage was childless. However, due to his dislike of his brother, Henry left as much property as he could away from his heir, thus breaking up the integrity of the estate and starting the decline in the Stanley fortunes. Lyulph, the fourth Lord Stanley, was a Radical in politics and a fierce agnostic in religion. He had the mausoleum at St Mary's Nether Alderley built just outside the churchyard so that he could avoid being buried in consecrated ground (Figure 19.17). Only he and his wife, Maisey Bell, are inside this mausoleum. Nonetheless, he did allow some residential development in Alderley Edge village; the Arts-and-Crafts style villas along the Congleton Road and up Whitebarn Road are on what was Stanley land.

However, agriculture remained the predominant occupation in Nether Alderley and Over Alderley until the sale of the Stanley estate in 1938, and the contrast between this settled traditional life and the newer suburban community of Alderley Edge village remained distinct.

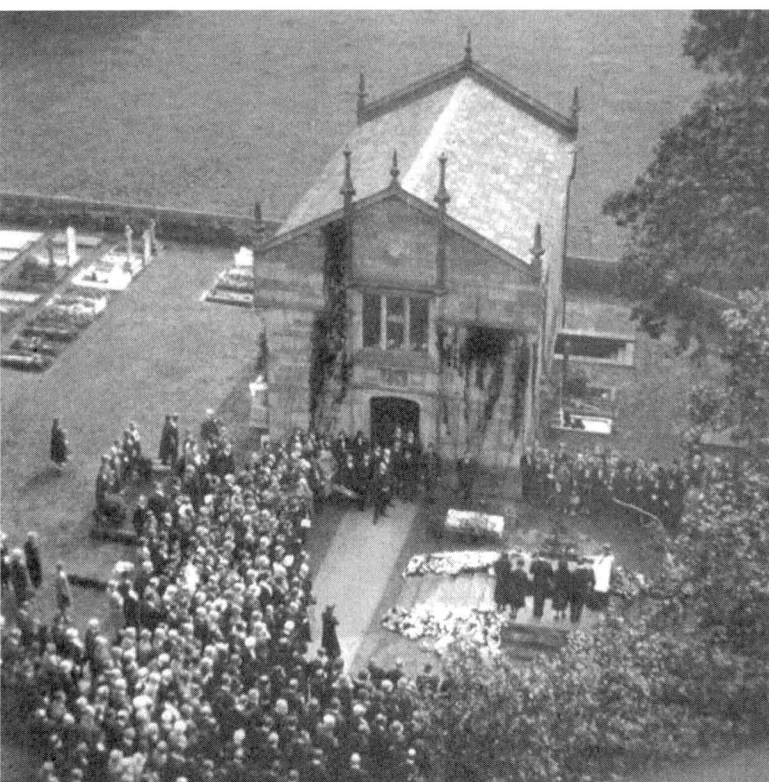

Figure 19.17. The funeral of the fifth Lord Stanley, 1931, seen from the top of St Mary's Church tower. The Stanley mausoleum was built by the fourth Lord on what was then unconsecrated land. The church-yard was later extended, so that the fifth Lord's funeral in front of the mausoleum is taking place in consecrated ground.

Courtesy John Beswick.

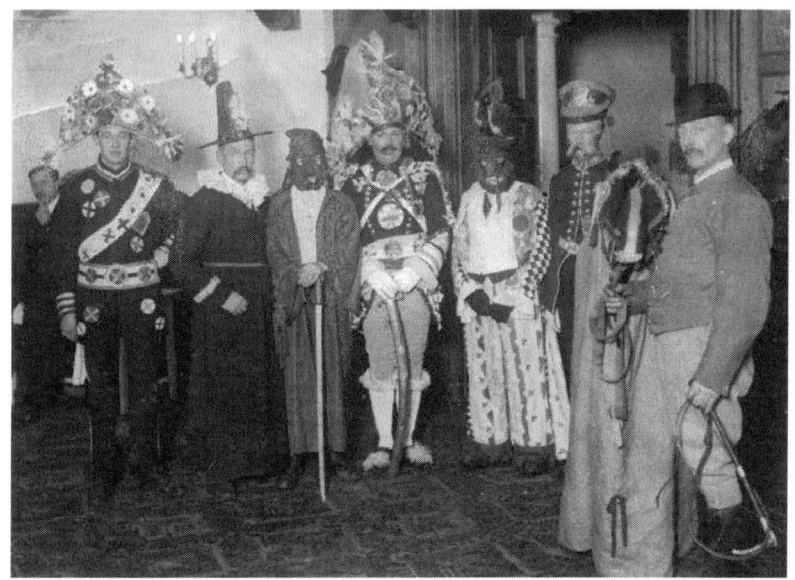

Figure 19.18. The mummers in 1920. All the mummers belonged to the Barber family.

Courtesy Mary Houseman.

The sense of interdependence between the Stanleys and their tenants persisted into the 1920s and 1930s, when both Edna Younger and Margaret Shaak remember the splendid Christmas parties given for the tenants' children at Alderley Park during the time of the fifth Lord Stanley. 'The children belonged; we were sort of belonging to them' (AELP Oral Archive 17003: E. Younger). Sheila Mackie remembers playing in the Park as a child; the only forbidden area was the rose garden when the family was in residence (personal communication). The highlight of these Christmas parties was a performance of the mummers' play (Figure 19.18), where all the parts were played by members of one extended Alderley family, the Barbers. The Alderley mummers' play ceased in 1939, but it has recently been revived and is now performed again regularly in the Alderley area.

When the sixth Lord Stanley succeeded to the title in 1931 at the early age of twenty-three, he faced two lots of death duties, for his grandfather had died only six years before, in 1925. Edward Stanley had lots of charm, but did not have the character to buckle down and see this straitened time through, and he had expensive habits. 'He drank, he gambled and he womanised and he was no good at any of it', was the judgement of his cousin, the eighth Lord Stanley (AELP Oral Archive 17116). However, his decision to sell the Alderley estate in 1938 came as a great shock, especially to his tenants and dependants. Although sales of landed estates were common in the years between the wars, it was more usual for families to offload subsidiary lands rather than the main estate from which the family took its title. This shock and sense of betrayal was made worse as Stanley sold the complete estate to a development company. The first thing most Alderley people knew about the sale was when the sale catalogue appeared and the auctioneers started putting up lot numbers on the properties, having divided up the whole estate in the hope of selling most of it off for residential development (see *Sale Catalogue*, and Figure 19.19, and the further discussion by Matthew Hyde in Chapter 24).

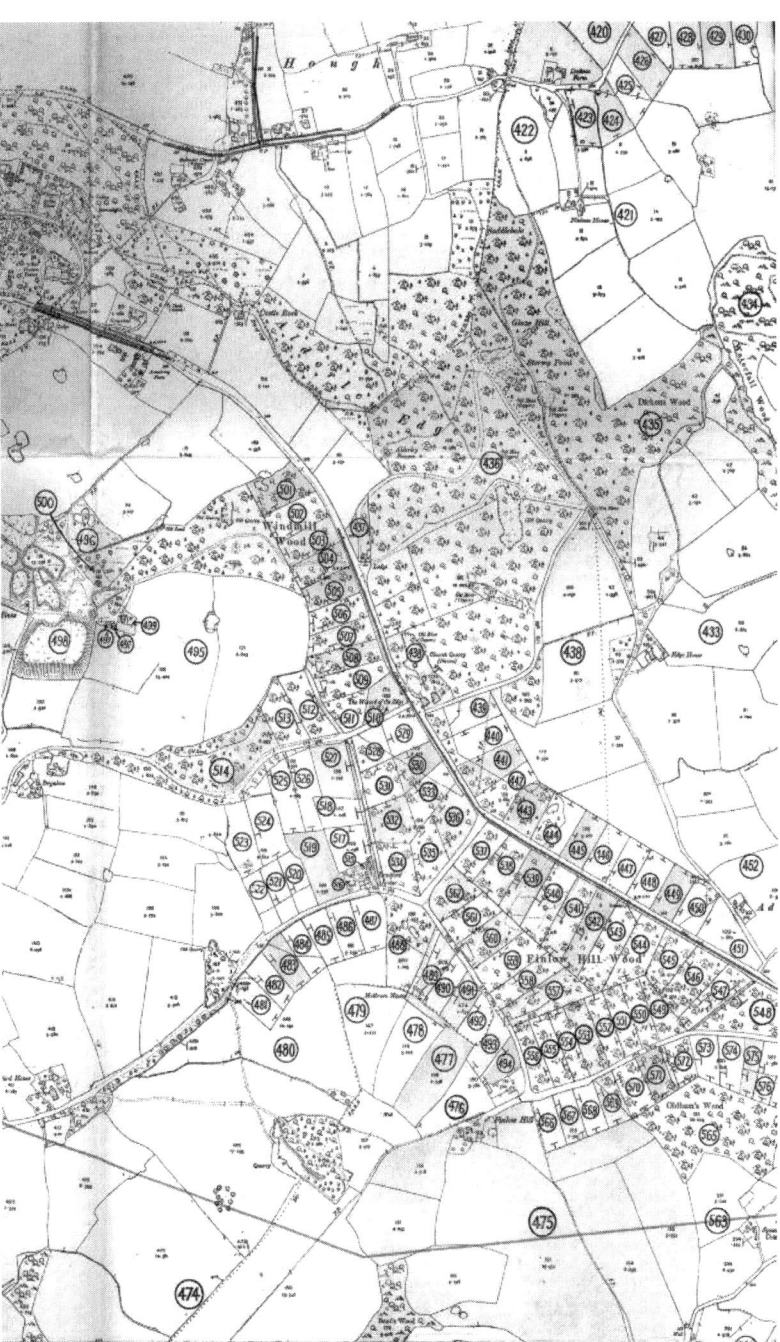

Figure 19.19. Detail of the *Sale Catalogue* (plan no. 2) for the Alderley estate, 1938, showing how the auctioneers hoped to divide up the Edge for residential development.

This shock goes some way to explain the failure of the original auction in Macclesfield, when less than 10 per cent of the lots were sold. People who went to this sale remember the bidding creeping up, only to stop short of the reserve price, and so the lots were withdrawn. Many tenants could not afford the inflated prices expected of potentially desirable residences. 'Our cottage, we couldn't afford it, well none of us could on the estate. I don't think any of them bought their own cottage' (Margaret Shaak, AELP Oral Archive 17010). The timing of the sale, October 1938, may also have been a factor in its failure; few people were thinking of speculative residential development just after the Munich Crisis. There was another sale, in January 1939 in Crewe, when many of the tenant farmers were able to buy their own land at more reasonable prices.

However, the failure of the original intended residential development meant the Misses Pilkington and others were able to organise the protection of the wooded areas of the Edge and in 1948 these lands formed the nucleus of the property given to the National Trust, which opened up the area to the public once again. Nonetheless, although the Edge and the physical landscape have survived, the farming community that created and supported it over the centuries has largely disintegrated. This is a continuing process; the agricultural depression that began at the end of the twentieth century is one of the reasons behind the sale of farms which have ceased to be working family enterprises, such as that of Hill Top in 1999. The land may still be cultivated, with increasing areas owned by the National Trust and managed according to sound ecological principles, but the people living in the old farmhouses and cottages are no longer farmers and miners, but professionals and business executives. The suburban takeover of Alderley, which started with the railway arriving in 1842, is now almost complete.

Primary sources

The Stanley estate records are the most important primary sources for the history of Alderley. The majority of these are in the Stanley of Alderley archive in Cheshire Archives and Local Studies (CALS) at the Cheshire Record Office (CRO), with the label DSA. They include the notebooks compiled by the first Lord Stanley, which are described further in Chapter 20.

Also in the Cheshire Record Office are:

- Elizabeth Stanley's *Receipt Book*, started 1653 (CALS DDX 361);
- parish records for Alderley and Chorley (CALS m/f 65/1);
- Census records for Alderley and Chorley (CALS m/f 234/8 (1861), m/f 24/14, 15 (1871);

- Poor Law records for Macclesfield Workhouse (CALS LGM 1/1);
- William Crossley's map of the Stanley estate, 1787 (most other detailed maps until 1872 derive from this map) (CALS P143/14/1);
- tithe maps, Alderley and Chorley, 1841 (CALS IR EDT 179/3);
- James Heyes' map of the Trafford estate in Hough and Chorley (CALS DDT 1405/360/1);
- Leicester of Tabley collection (CALS DLT).

Other sources have been collected by the Alderley Edge Landscape Project (AELP Archive – see Chapter 20).

Published works are cited in the text and detailed in the list of references (pp. 934–52).

Further reading

Garner, A. 1979. *The Stone Book Quartet*. London: William Collins (most recent reprint HarperCollins, 2010).

Mitford, N. (ed.). 1938. *The Ladies of Alderley, Being the Letters Between Maria Josepha, Lady Stanley and Her Daughter-in-Law, Henrietta Maria Stanley (1841–1850)*. London: Chapman and Hall (2nd edition, London: Hamish Hamilton, 1967, from which quotes in the text are taken).

Mitford, N. (ed.). 1939. *The Stanleys of Alderley. Their Letters Between the Years 1851–1865*. London: Chapman and Hall (2nd edition, London: Hamish Hamilton, 1968, from which quotes in the text are taken).

20

The Archive

Jean Wearne

The Alderley Edge Landscape Project (AELP) acquired a large amount of documentary material about the area, its people, employment and social life. For the duration of the Project the Archive was housed in the Archaeology Department of Manchester Museum; the plan is that ultimately it will be deposited with Cheshire Archives and Local Studies (CALS).

Origins and purpose

The catalyst for the setting up of the Archive was Alan Garner. He produced from his miscellaneous collection of papers about Alderley Edge a mines 'setting' book, detailing the week-to-week running of the mines. This prompted the thought that, scattered about in cupboards and attics, there were probably many more records of the life and history of Alderley Edge which were of potential historical interest. Some of these were in danger of being lost. Others would be of much more value if they could be viewed alongside similar material. We were anxious to make as much use as possible of records and memorabilia made available by local residents, and so that anybody with an interest in Alderley Edge could find relevant material it was decided to compile an archive on computer.

Compiling the database

A standard computer database program would have been sufficient to log each piece of material under an index-labelled system, but the Archive was also to contain all the recorded interviews which would eventually be transcribed (see Chapter 21). Each of these ranged over a variety of subjects and it would have been impossible to index each entry according to every subject matter contained within it. As people might be interested in different aspects of the interviews, potential future users of the Archive would have had a problem – searching them for specific subjects would have been very difficult. A solution to this problem was to use a more flexible database, designed with just this problem in mind, named FolioVIEWS. With this we also compiled a catalogue of newspaper stories about the Edge.

Apart from the Archive catalogue and the interviews, we also compiled an extensive bibliography of the archaeological and historical books relating to Alderley Edge, and this too has been entered in FolioVIEWS.

Setting up a database from scratch needs careful consideration. It was decided to categorise each catalogue entry according to the following criteria: description of the content, date if possible, from whom we had received it, the nature of the material (e.g. a map, letter, notebook, ledger etc.), its condition and, finally, a short title. This should give the researcher enough information to identify the document in which he or she may be interested.

Volunteers were recruited as a result of the initial meeting at St Hilary's School in the summer of 1997 and another at the Museum in September that year. They were needed particularly for two tasks: firstly, to help with searching the local newspapers for stories about events in Alderley Edge; and secondly, to help with transcribing a large nineteenth-century manuscript book which had been lent to the Museum. Thus a team of five people worked on the newspapers and half a dozen on the manuscript transcription, so as to split the work of transcribing.

The data

As of 1999, the documents in the Archive contained over 500 items, grouped into eight categories as set out in Table 20.1, in addition to

Table 20.1. The contents of the document archive

Material	Number	Span of dates	Majority of dates
Pictorial images	240	1850–1999	1900–50
Maps	28	1577–1999	1700–1900
Letters	30	1801–1999	1974–76
Press cuttings	193	1839–1999	1929–33 and 1960–80
Legal documents	10	1691–1976	1800–1900
Diagrams/charts	13	1775–1999	
Reports	8	1836–1996	
Miscellaneous (booklets, catalogues, notebooks, programmes and notes etc.)	50	1805–1999	

those produced by the Project itself. Apart from the gifts of the Jaffrey and Bilsborough archives mentioned below, it has not grown significantly since, although, as mentioned later, thanks to various loans and donations, the pictorial part of the Archive has continued to expand in digital form with the addition of many scanned items.

The record catalogue

The record catalogue includes details of all the written, drawn and photographic material deposited with the Museum for this project. This covers a vast range of subject matter. The sub-headings of the following sections indicate their scope, but in content there is overlap between them.

Topography

Alderley Edge has always been a popular subject for picture postcards and several people have lent us their collections to copy or have provided scans, notably George Twigg and Alan Hulme; a number have been used as illustrations in this book. These can give a historical view of the changing topography of the village. Postcards and photographs in the Archive, AELP Archive 348 and 367 for instance, show the walled front gardens in London Road (Figures 20.1 and 20.2d). These are the origins of the particularly wide pavements which are a feature of the village and the reason for the shopkeepers being allowed to place sandwich boards on 'their' part of the pavement or use it as an extension to their premises. There are also sketches of Alderley from earlier periods, for example AELP Archive 10, dating from 1889, and several postcards which show the changing appearance of the copper mines and of the Sandhills, which used to be such a well known landmark. We also have copies of a series of postcards showing the Wizard Inn at various dates, which were lent to us by John Beswick; a typical example of such a card (in this instance lent by Alan Hulme) is shown in Figure 19.10 (p. 485). John Beswick had the distinction of being born in the Wizard Inn.

Land use

Documents such as leases can give useful historical information on land use and ownership. One such in the Archive is a copy of an 1894 counterpart lease for the sale of the property 'Oakwood' by Edward John Stanley of Alderley (AELP Archive 9) on a 999-year lease. Another

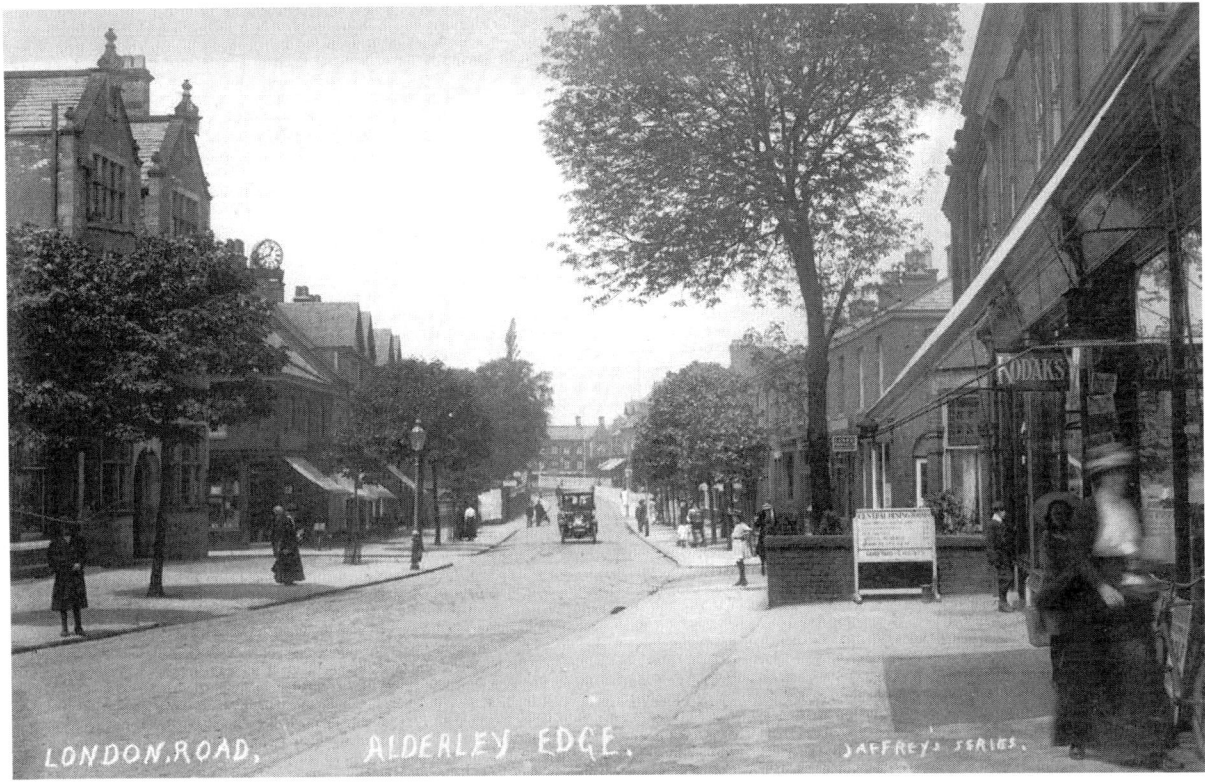

LONDON.ROAD,   ALDERLEY EDGE,   JAFFREY'S SERIES.

Figure 20.1. Postcard in Jaffrey's series, 1905, showing the walled front gardens of London Road, with the Queen's Hotel in the distance. The shop on the right selling Kodak became Boots the Chemists. The menu board for Toft's Central Dining Rooms is readable on the original: a 'good dinner from the joint' 1 shilling and 'a good plain tea' 9 pence, and a 'good yard for cyclists'. George Twigg, who provided the image, commented in 1999 that 'Toft's Dining Rooms were still going in the 1930s. The walled garden existed into my living memory as did a similar garden between Bilsborough's shop and the District Bank. The Union Bank of Manchester, with the clock, became Barclays in the 1950s. Ruth Toft, who owned the tearoom, started work as a housemaid at Westwood and appears on the 1871 Census.'

is an indenture lease relating to the working of the Alderley mine in 1808. We also have a copy of a rent agreement of 1680 (AELP Archive 21) whereby the tenancy of Shawcross, Over Alderley, was secured by payment of rent of 'a pair of white gloves or eight pence'.

Historical maps are of course a rich source of information on land use but the maps in the Archive are covered in more detail in Chapter 26.

Social life

A series of photographs sent in by George Twigg (AELP Archive 320–89) show processions and bands marching through Alderley Edge in the early years of the century (Figure 20.2). These are of interest not

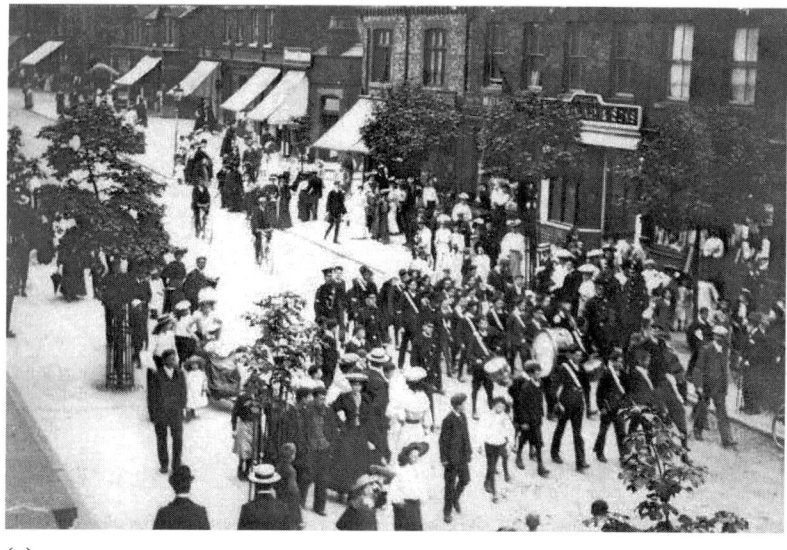

(a)

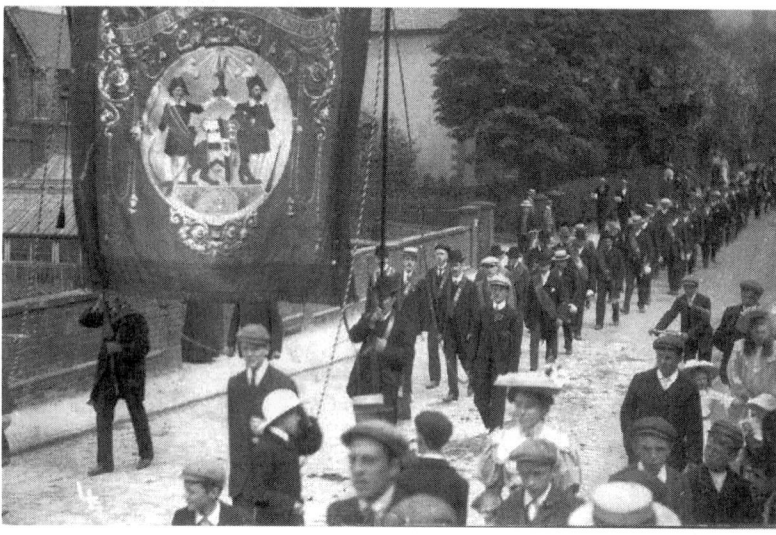

(b)

Figure 20.2. Processions and bands marching through Alderley Edge. (a) Postcard in the 'Prince Series' of a procession with the Church Lads Brigade in London Road, 1905. In the background are the shops with their awnings out, wide pavements and street trees. (b) Procession with Foresters' banner in Trafford Road, 1905. No band is shown, but men, women and children walk alongside, the boys all in flat caps, the women and girls in smart hats and dresses. *Opposite* (c) Church Lads Brigade procession in London Road, 1914, taken nearly opposite the Church Institute, with Barclays Bank building and clock visible in the background. The sailor-hatted group appear to be the juniors, and the man in the white cap with a bus-conductor's badge is probably Daniel, father of George Twigg, who donated the image. (d) A band forming up outside the Church Institute on a Sunday, *c.* 1914. The caps suggest it is St Philip's band. Note the walled gardens extending onto the pavement.

Photographer unknown for all four parts.

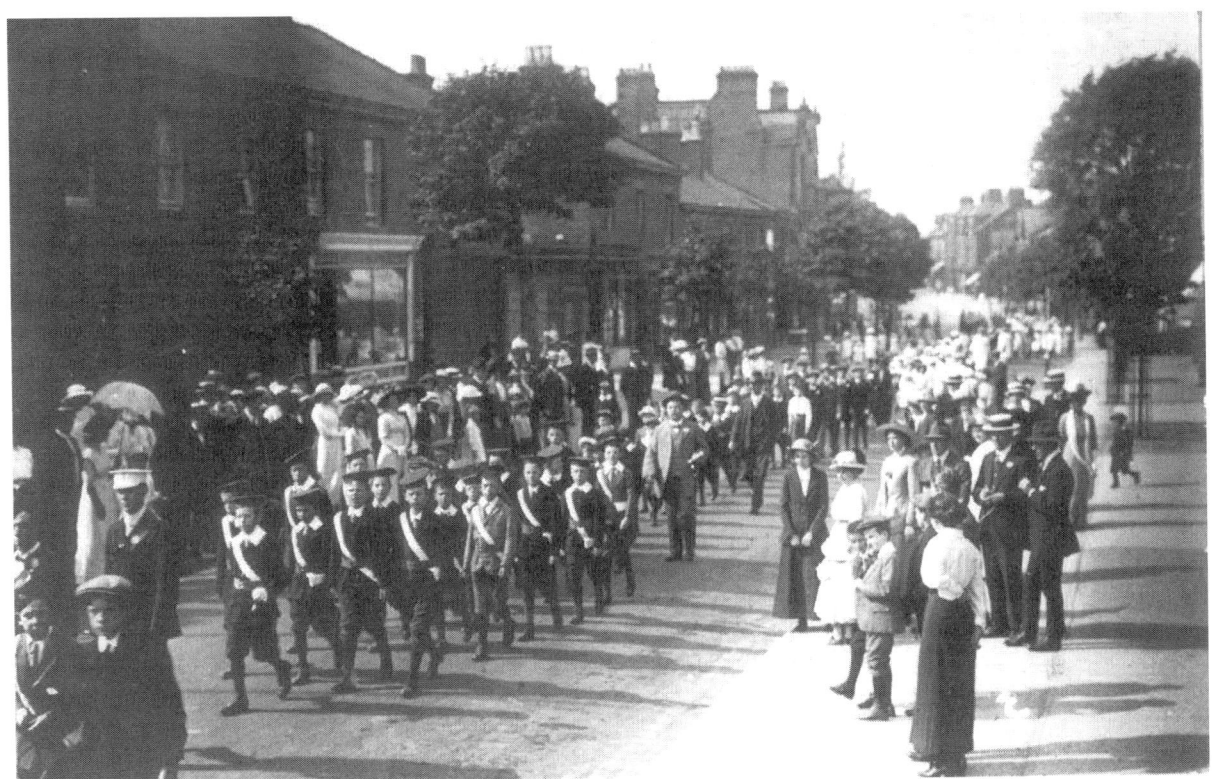

(c)

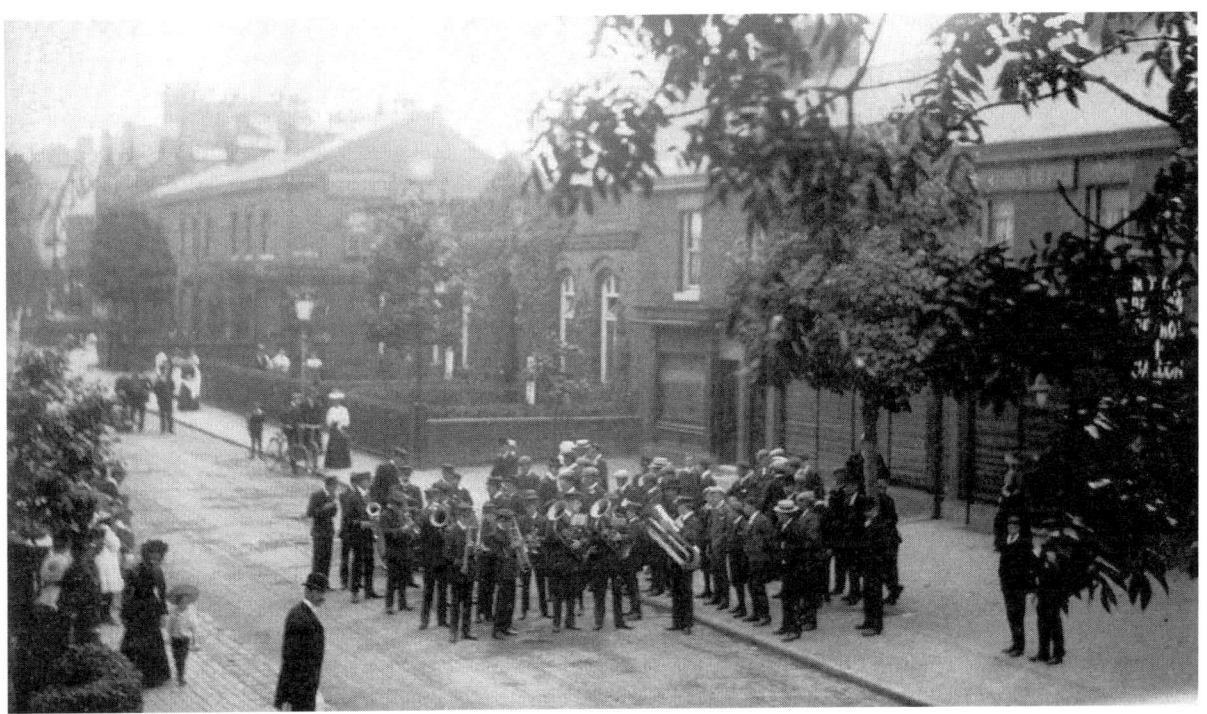

(d)

only for their topographical detail but also for the glimpse they give of the different tempo of life and the different forms of amusement and styles of clothing worn by people seen in what is recognisably the same village street which we know today.

Other items indicative of a vanished society include a splendid photograph of the funeral of Arthur Lyulph Stanley in 1931, a copy of an Alderley Wakes programme from 1891 and a member's score card of the Alderley Edge Archers from 1877. The last shows that archery was a social activity open to both women and men. This may seem surprising for that date but we understand from Wendy Hodkinson, the Honorary Curator of the Simon Archery Collections at Manchester Museum, that mixed archery goes back to the eighteenth century and was seen as a good social occasion, providing opportunities for match making as well as match winning.

Schools

The backbone of the record catalogue is a large collection of photographs and other material either donated or lent for copying by Alan Garner. These include more than fifty photographs (AELP Archive 136–86) of children and staff at what is now Alderley Edge County Primary School, with dates varying from the early years of the twentieth century to about the 1950s, together with other papers relating to the school and the history of education there (especially AELP Archive 102–8) (Figure 20.3). These include, for instance: the curriculum of 1912 (AELP Archive 104), showing that the children were taught a variety of subjects, many of which were gender marked, as well as arts and crafts; and a document detailing the procedure for reporting corporal punishment (AELP Archive 62).

A copy of an illustrated booklet on the history of St Hilary's School, which was merged with Mount Carmel School to form the Alderley Edge School for Girls in 1999, has also been deposited (AELP Archive 396) and this makes an interesting comparison.

Administration

Two seventeenth-century documents of which we have copies give an insight into the way in which the law was administered at that time. One, a Poor Law removal order (AELP Archive 67), refers to the moving on of families from one parish to the next (Box 20.1). This was a way of 'passing the buck' when someone was likely to become a charge on the parish.

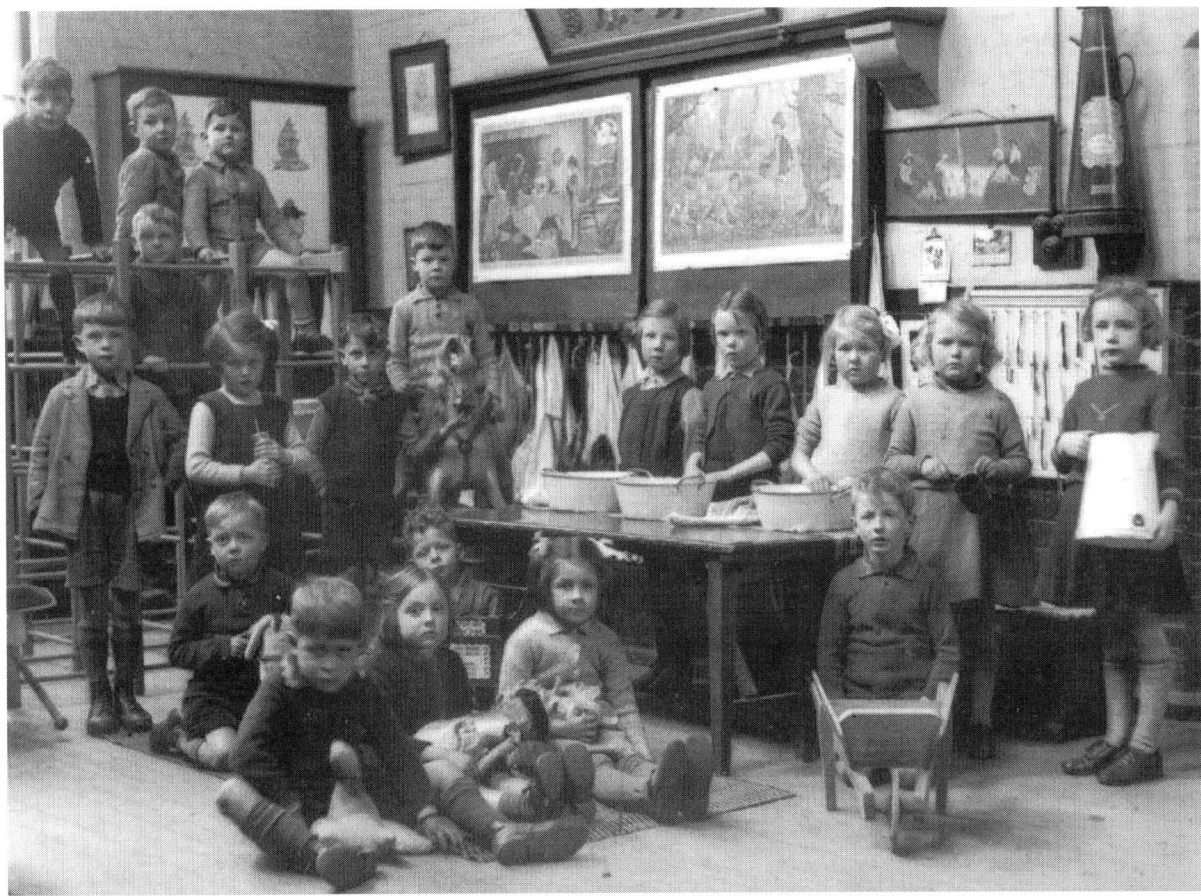

Figure 20.3. Group picture of Alderley Edge Infants' School, 1940. Boys and girls in their classroom, the boys with wheelbarrows, horses and other animals, and the girls mostly with washing up bowls and dolls. The second girl from right, standing with her hands together, is Joan King. The boy kneeling behind a barrow is Ronald Fitchett. The third girl standing on the right is Brenda Hale; the girl next to her with her hands in a bowl is Jean Thompson. The boy on the horse is John Pickford, next to him in a very dark sweater and with curly hair is Desmond Baguley.

Photographer unknown.

Box 20.1. Thomas Gibson

In 1694 Thomas Gibson was ordered to be safely removed with his wife and family from the township of Over Alderley to the township of Henbury. The order was signed by the Constables and Overseers of the Poor in the township of Over Alderley.

Another (AELP Archive 70) is concerned with the assessment and collection of money from local landowners under an Act of Parliament (Box 20.2). Both these documents were found by Alan Garner in 1952 either propping up a corner of the altar in St Mary's Church or under a table runner in the Rectory.

Box 20.2. Hugh Byron and Henry Barlow

In 1695 these two yeomen of Over Alderley were assessors appointed under an Act of Parliament for
the collection of money to maintain the army and navy. The sum granted to His Majesty for the whole
country was £1,484,015.15s.11¾ d but after they had agreed to take on this task the assessment for
their area had been increased and for this reason they protested. A legal document was drawn up
stating that in the event of their imprisonment the signatories, two women and fifteen men, would
look after their estates for them. It is not known whether this was an unusual or common practice.

Employment and shopping

There are several items in the Archive which throw light on the employment patterns of the early 1900s. Among these is a photograph of the
staff of Isaac Massey's, the builders, taken in the early 1900s which shows
sixty-eight men (Figure 20.4; AELP Archive 418). Note that there are
only men and boys in the picture – the child in a skirt in the front row
is actually one of the Massey family, Isaac Massey's grandson. A photograph (AELP Archive 321) of the Gardeners' Society taken outside

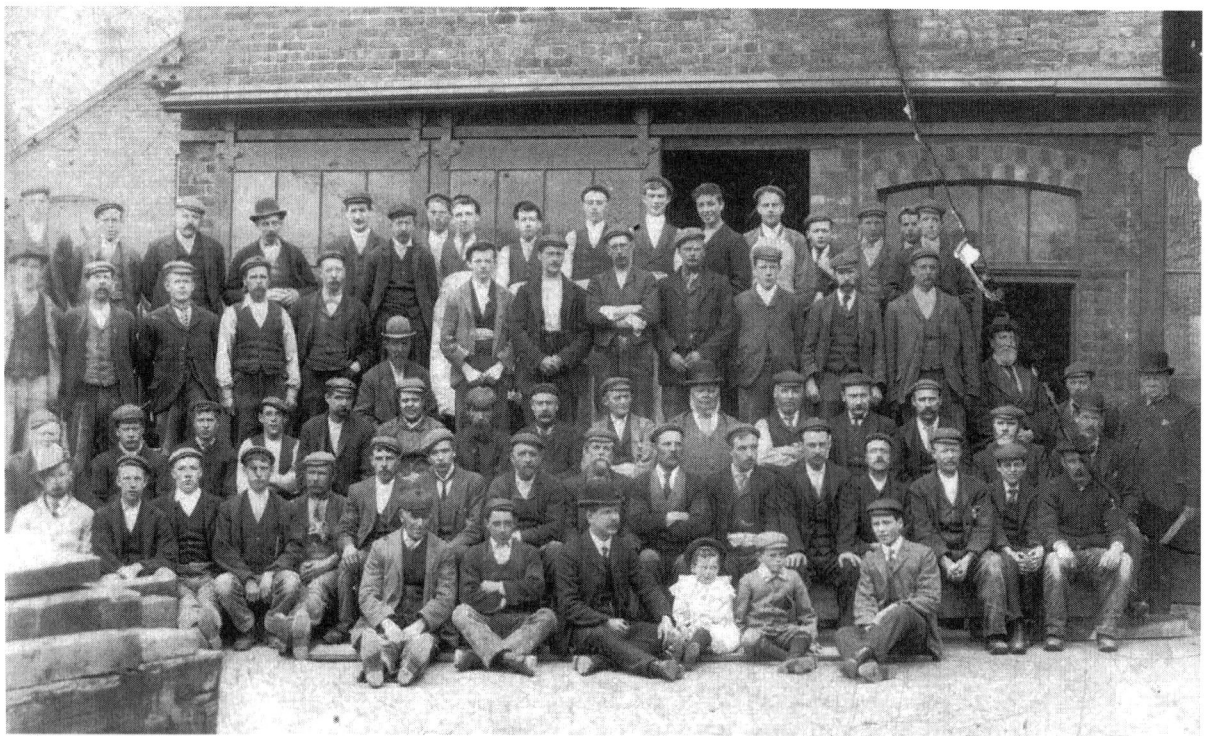

Figure 20.4. The staff of Isaac Massey's, taken outside one of their buildings, between 1895 and 1902.
Seated on the ground is Massey himself with his children; the foremen wear bowler hats, the others caps.

Photographer unknown; lent by Mrs Nellie Bowers, Alderley Edge.

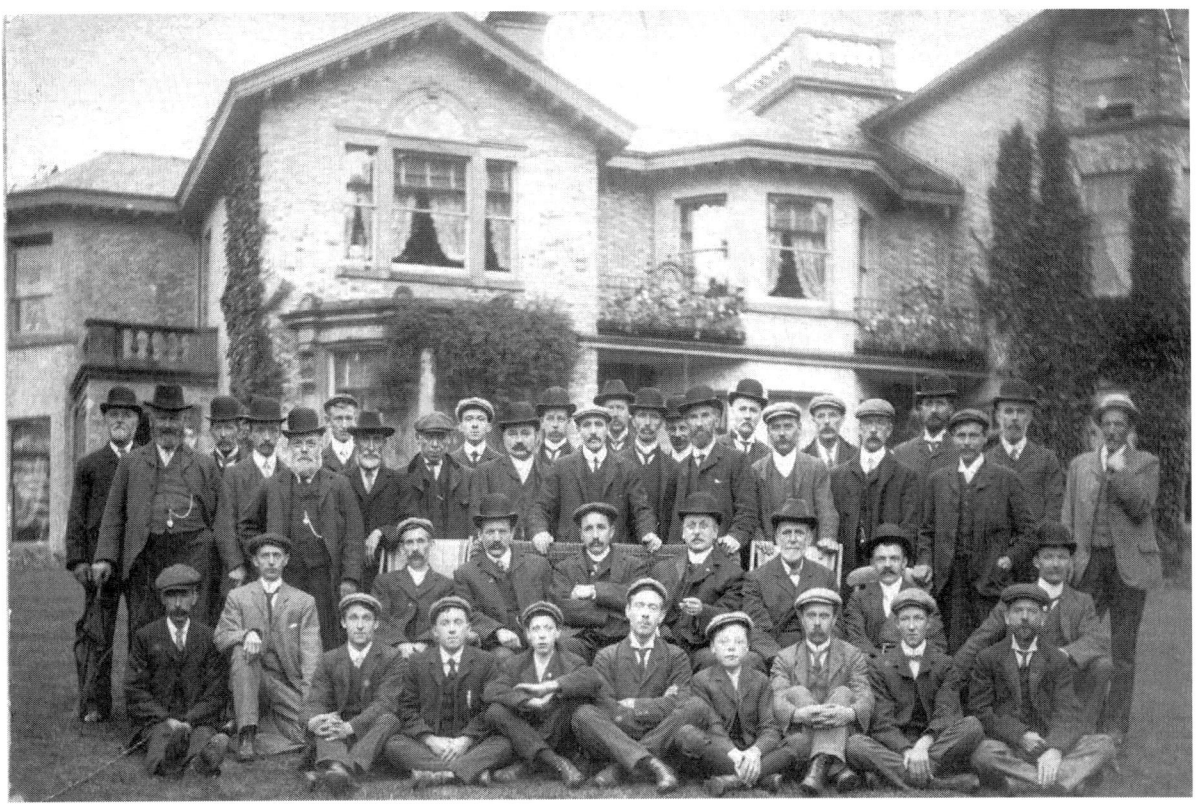

Figure 20.5. The Alderley Edge Gardeners' Society meeting at Beechfield *c.* 1912. The bearded figure in a bowler hat standing fifth from left is John Twigg (d. 1925), grandfather of George Twigg, who provided the image; Fred Dutton kneels in front of him in a flat cap and light-coloured suit.

Photographer unknown.

Beechfield indicates how many men were employed as gardeners to the big houses in Alderley Edge (Figure 20.5). This particular photograph has the added interest that it shows a view of the back of Beechfield, a house which no longer exists (see Chapter 23).

One of the most evocative documents of which we have a copy is a notebook giving a summary of the fires attended by 'Fire Brigade Wizard' from 1899 to 1921 (AELP Archive 72). The frequency of fires in hay, straw, stabling and thatched roofs reminds us that this was still largely an agricultural community (Figure 20.6).

Shopping patterns have changed greatly over the last fifty years, perhaps epitomised by the comments of George Twigg in the caption to Figure 20.1, and many small grocers' shops have disappeared and been replaced by one supermarket. The map presented in Figure 20.7 shows the shops in Alderley Edge village in 1928 as drawn by Alan Crossley, a former resident who emigrated to Canada and whose mother Amy wrote a guidebook to Alderley Edge in 1931 (Crossley, 1931). The Archive also

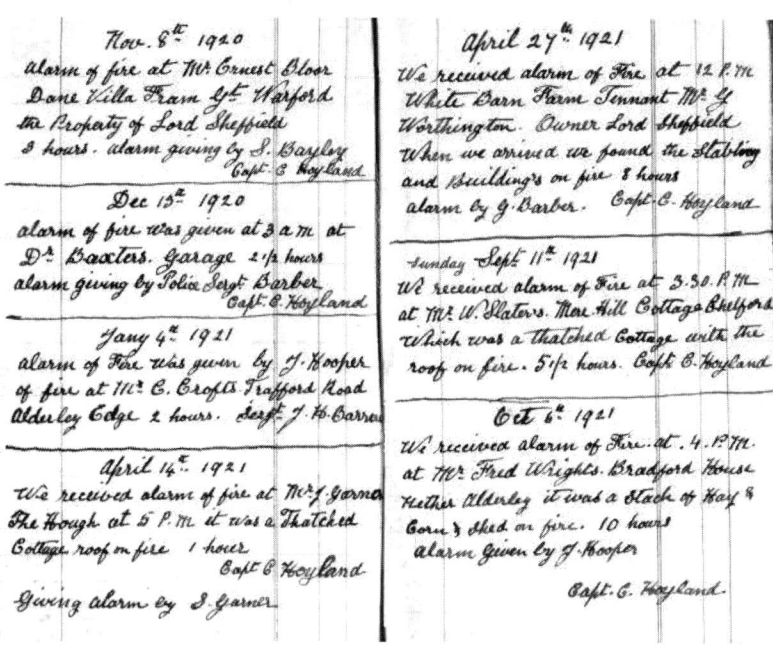

Figure 20.6. Pages 34 and 35 of the 'Summary of the Fires in the Alderley Edge A.D.C.' attended by the 'Fire Brigade Wizard' between 1899 and 1921. Compiled by Capt. J. Jaffrey, Capt. C. Hoyland and Sgt. J. H. Barrow, it lists the fires, the person who called the alarm, the time and place of the fire and insurance details. The document was given to Colin Garner in the Trafford Arms in the mid-1960s and donated to the Archive by his son Alan.

contains lists of shops drawn up by local residents at different periods between the late 1920s and 1999 (AELP Archive 87 and 316). A record of these, updated to November 2010, is found in Table 20.2, presented at the end of this chapter. The sound recordings in the Archive also include an account of the shops in Alderley Edge in the 1930s, given by a local resident, Bob Bancroft, who was able to recite the names of all the shops he remembered as a boy, starting at one end of the village and going right down one side of the main street and back up the other side.

The war years

During the 1914–18 war, Alderley Park became a military hospital and we were lent for copying a series of photographs showing servicemen, nurses and Voluntary Aid Detachment nurses (VADs) in the grounds and inside the old Hall. The stately surroundings make an incongruous background for men on crutches and with bandaged heads – indeed, at the time the contrast with normal service conditions must have been quite poignant. Seeing these photographs at a day school on the AELP, another resident was prompted to produce an autograph book she possessed in which some of the same servicemen had signed their names and given their regiments. In one particular case we were able to make a positive identification of one of the men in the photographs as a

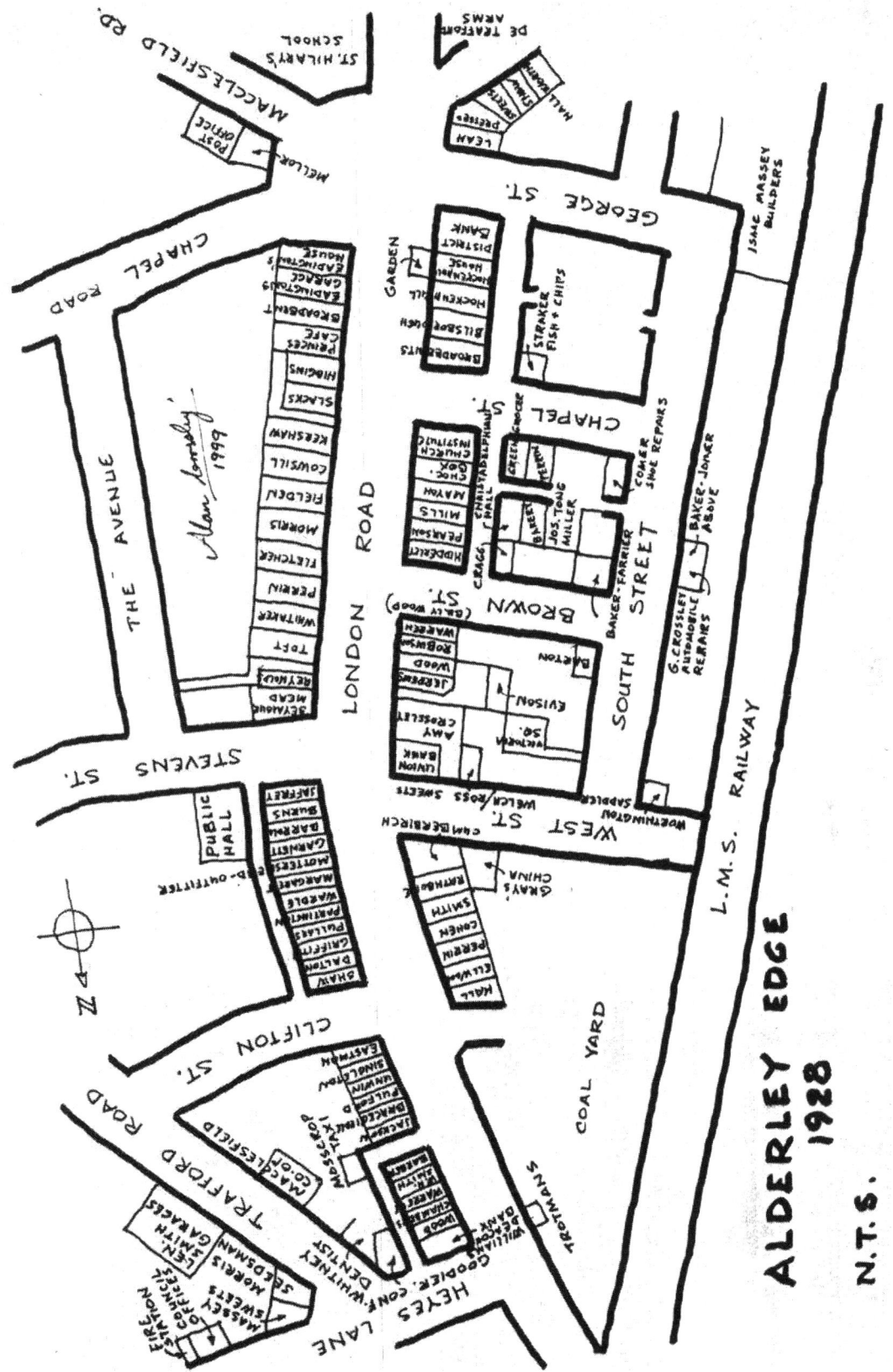

Figure 20.7. Sketch-map of the shops in Alderley Edge village in 1928, drawn from memory in 1999 by Alan Crossley. See also Table 20.2 (pp. 534–9).

result. This is one of many instances where records held by individuals can yield so much more information when they are viewed alongside other material.

During the 1939–45 war some of the big houses in Macclesfield Road were requisitioned and were used for billeting servicemen or as training headquarters. We have an account of one man returning after more than fifty years to the house he lived in at that time, together with a résumé of his war service thereafter.

Family history

Part of the collection of material supplied by Alan Garner concerns his own family. In addition to photographs there are notes on baptism and marriage registers, graveyard inscriptions and family trees, all of which combine to show the myriad connections of just one family. There is much material in the Archive for anyone similarly trying to trace their own family history: Census returns, tithe apportionment lists and other local documents can all help to build up a fuller picture than mere dates of birth and death. One particular item in the Archive which is a rich source of local family names, among other things, is the *Stanley Notebook*.

Stanley records

The book which we have called the *Stanley Notebook*, or more fully the *Stanley Genealogical Manuscript Book*, originally catalogued as AELP Archive 3, is a handsome volume of 464 pages bound in brown suede from the archive of St Mary's Church, Nether Alderley, which was lent to us by Brian Hobson (churchwarden 2000–04). It was found to contain copies of old records, genealogical tables and notes about the old buildings of the area. In 2010 it was placed with Cheshire Archives and Local Studies (CALS), where it was given the number D 8065/1 and where there is already a very similar notebook (probably the companion volume) (DSA 3752/1) which includes the legend of the Edge, as well as a series of notebooks (DSA 5/1–10) containing mainly genealogical information, often in several versions.

As the *Notebook* could not be photocopied without the risk of damage, a microfilm was made and prints made from this were used by volunteers to transcribe small sections at home. These were then entered in the FolioVIEWS database. The complete set of prints from the microfilm remains in the Archive for future use and the transcribed pages can be read in FolioVIEWS or printed out if required.

At first it was thought that the *Notebook* had been written by the Reverend Edward Stanley (1779–1849), Rector of Alderley, who later became Bishop of Norwich, but it became apparent when it was transcribed that this could not be so. It was an exciting moment when the transcription of page 222 of the manuscript proved beyond doubt who the writer was (Figure 20.8). He was describing the Park house and wrote: 'On the [old] hall being burnt [down] in 1779 Sir John S & Lady Stanley took possession of the best Rooms and lived in them [the whole] Summer of 1779. I was with them a Boy 13 years old I have made the house a Mansion…'. The only person who was thirteen years old in 1779 and who could have made changes to the Park house was John Thomas Stanley, the first Lord Stanley (1766–1850) (Figure 19.2, p. 465).

The value of the *Stanley Notebook* for elucidating the history of Alderley will already have become clear from Chapter 19. Between about 1830 and 1844, Lord Stanley copied out old records, including some of the Harleian records in London, parish records, churchwardens' accounts, tithe and Court Leet records; he drew genealogical tables and also described the old houses of the village (Nether Alderley, not the present Alderley Edge), detailing who had lived in them at various times. The book is an amazing potpourri of passages covering a wide variety of subjects. We do not know why he chose to copy out certain records (sometimes more than once!), although often it is clearly in order to establish the Stanley claim to certain lands. We know that he was a man who loved literature, a passion he shared with his wife Maria, and that he did not enjoy hunting and hounds like most other country gentlemen (Adeane, 1899: viii). When not dealing with estate matters, like many gentlemen of the period he therefore spent his spare time on more literary and scientific work and took an interest in antiquarian matters.

It is not difficult to guess why he copied out the records concerning the new pews in St Mary's Church in 1749, the meeting at which it was agreed to pay a Mr Lyon £150 for the re-pewing, and then the churchwardens' accounts for the following year, showing that in the end the total cost added up to £190.3s.6d!

The Court Leet records copied out by Lord Stanley date from the sixteenth to the eighteenth centuries, before the Edge was enclosed. They give a picture of the community in early modern times, before the changes created by the Agricultural and Industrial Revolutions. They record such things as fines for causing an affray (doubled if the record adds 'and did draw blood'), fines for not maintaining hedges and ditches (vital in an agricultural community) and fines for taking peat or grazing where it was not allowed. They are useful as a source of place and farm names and clues to agricultural practice. They also give the names of overseers and constables, as well as miscreants, with the same

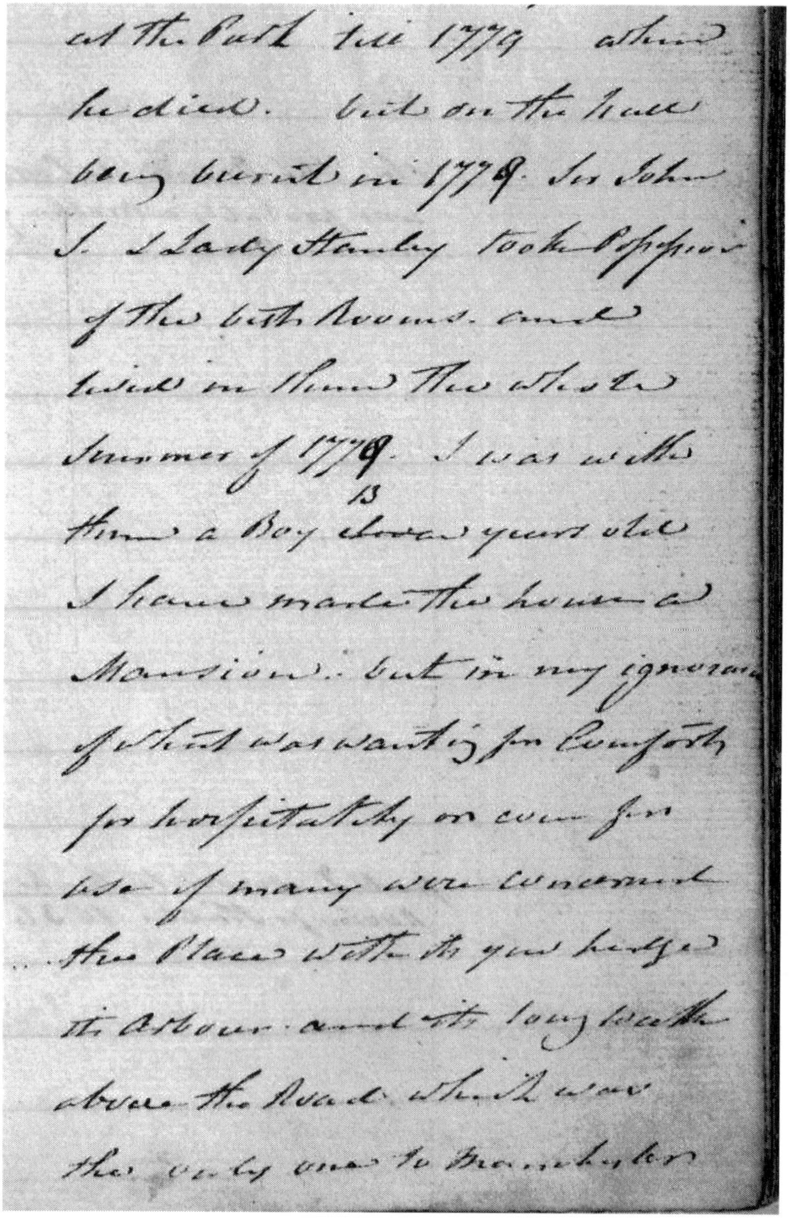

Figure 20.8. Part of page 222 of the *Stanley Notebook*: Lord Stanley describes the changes made to the house at Alderley Park.

Courtesy of Cheshire Archives and Local Studies (D 8065/1).

local family names constantly reappearing, and these will be a useful resource for anyone researching family history. Many of the names are familiar in Alderley Edge to this day – names such as Norbury, Massey, Henshall and Mottershead.

The Cheshire Record Office already had a number of similar manuscript books in its collection of Stanley family papers but this one filled a gap. One wonders if there are other documents relating to the Stanley estate 'out there'.

The Reverend Edward Stanley also wrote accounts of the parish when Rector of Alderley, and some of these are in the AELP Archive. A statistical report of the parish of Alderley, read before the Statistical Society of London on 20 April 1836 (AELP Archive 13; CALS P143/13/11), includes details of population, literacy, church and school attendance, agricultural stock and occupations. Another account (AELP Archive 16) gives the geographical and natural history of the area, its geology and mineralogy and shows the extremely detailed observations he made:

> The temperature of those springs which have come more immediately under observation varies from 43° to 56°. During a severe frost, when the external air was 26°, on breaking the ice over the deepest part of an extensive sheet of water, over a part about 12 feet deep, the temperature of the upper surface was 34° at the bottom 38°. In the same spot in the month of July when the external air was 70°, the upper surface of the water was 67° and the bottom 64°.

These statistics conjure up a wonderful picture of Edward Stanley actually making the observations.

He also throws light on why, to this day, St Mary's Alderley appoints three churchwardens rather than the usual two. He writes:

> The parish of Alderley like those on the most Northwestern part of England is composed of a certain number of sub divisions – called in the present instance of these, vis Nether Alderley, Over Alderley and Great Warford townships, each having their separate parochial jurisdiction, as regards to poor rate constables, by courtesy also church wardens are usually chosen for each, though really speaking they are for the general interest of the parish and have subordinate power in their respective townships.

Now that the parishes of Nether Alderley and Birtles (Over Alderley) have been united in one benefice, residents can feel happier for knowing that they are reverting to the former arrangement.

The newspapers

The newspaper part of the Archive records all the references to the Edge that could be found in the local papers, the *Stockport Advertiser* from 1822 to 1980 and the *Alderley and Wilmslow Advertiser* from 1897 to 1939 (although the Advertiser Group seems regularly to have changed the precise names of their various papers), available on microfilm in Stockport and Wilmslow Libraries respectively. Some stories also appeared in the *Manchester Evening News* and other papers which are available on microfilm in the Local Studies Library of the Manchester Central Reference Library. Some of these have also been transcribed.

We were particularly interested in finding stories about the mines, accidents and legal disputes, and people who were killed or committed suicide. Dramatic incidents of this kind have often been the basis for folktales and myths and so they are very much a part of the folklore history of the area, an essential strand of the Project.

The mines

In 1960 access to West Mine was closed by its new owner because of the danger to the public, and an article in the *Manchester Evening News* by James Lovelock, himself a speleologist, defended this action. He would have campaigned against any such plan a few years before, 'but', he wrote, 'I have just written a history of cave and potholing accidents during the past 60 years and I have found from my researches that there have been more accidents and deaths at Alderley than in any other cave or mine passage explored by potholers'. He went on to describe the first tragedy of the century:

> a young Ragged School lad, Alexander Rea … on a happy week-end outing with a master and other boys from the school … climbed into a passage and stepped under a beam intended to bar the way, slipped and fell headlong down a shaft. When finally he was hauled up the 84ft he was dead. (*Manchester Evening News*, 23 January 1960)

The 1920s seems to have been a particularly bad period for accidents in the mines, for in 1928 two men

> were lost in West Mine and were brought out scared stiff after 24 hours of wandering around aimlessly. A year later, three Manchester youths had a similar experience. They too, were lucky, they were found alive. The same year, Alfred Hadfield, aged 24, of Grenville Street, Stockport and George Etchells, aged 24, of Garden Street, Stockport, were not so lucky.
>
> They went into the mines in May. They were not seen again until September 7. They were dead and terribly decomposed.
>
> Hadfield was identified by his wallet and an envelope bearing his name and address … [he] had scribbled a note: 'Dear Mother, we are lost in the copper mines, I think we are done'. (*Manchester Evening News*, 23 January 1960)

The newspapers contain many more accounts of accidents and people getting lost in the mines and much argument as to whether they should be permanently closed for safety reasons, or kept open for the sake of their geological interest. Attempts to block off the entrances were not successful (*The Advertiser*, 14 April 1944). An article in *The Advertiser* of 10 April 1964 records that the demolition expert 'Blaster' Bates of Sandbach was called in to seal off Wood Mine. The present arrangement is that the Derbyshire Caving Club takes interested parties down the mines at regular intervals (see Chapter 17, p. 416).

Hallowe'en

It becomes evident from reading the local newspapers that the association of the Edge with Hallowe'en and witches is not of ancient origin at all. It stems from a piece of specious popular journalism in 1962 and we have found no references to it before that date. The picture editor, a photographer and a reporter from the *Saturday Chronicle and News* (i.e. *Manchester Evening News*) were persuaded to visit the Edge in the third week of September 1962 by Alex Sanders, a porter at the John Rylands Library who described himself as a 'High Priest' of the witches. He set up a fabricated incident purporting to show someone being raised from the dead and the newspaper ran headlines such as 'Amazing Black Magic Rites on Cheshire Hillside, "Dead Man" Comes to Life, Joins Witches' (15 September 1962). Sanders later added to this story by inviting the newspaper to attend 'the most remarkable witchcraft ritual ever performed in this country: the wedding of a High Priest and his Priestess'. They were to be married 'by ancient ritual' and the fact that the 'century-old rites' had just been invented did not stop the newspaper making the most of the incident and spreading the erroneous story of witches on Alderley Edge. Alan Garner has already touched on the after-effects of this piece of ill-researched journalism in Chapter 2.

Excursions

Another theme running through the newspaper part of the Archive is that of Alderley Edge as a place to visit on public holidays. It was one of the closest beauty spots to Manchester which was accessible by carriage, train or even cycle, and in those pre-smoke control days provided a welcome escape from the fumes and smoke of city chimneys. An article in the *Wilmslow and Alderley Advertiser* on 16 April 1897 describes Easter:

> The drive out from the city is one of the most popular drives in this part of the country, and on a Good Friday the traffic is simply enormous; indeed it seems to increase every year. If the man at the weather office is in good temper tomorrow, and the day is brilliantly fine, then we may expect to see another great rush, and we shall certainly not be surprised to see an extraordinary show of cycles.

In the event, the weather on Good Friday that year was rather poor and visitors were by no means as numerous as in many former seasons. On Easter Monday, however, a great deal of business was done, train after train depositing its living freight in the district until the many beautiful spots in the vicinity were alive with the moving figures of the excursionists. (*Wilmslow and Alderley Advertiser*, 23 April 1897)

The Edge was not only used as a picnic site; in 1897 the Manchester Wheelers held their hill-climbing competition up Macclesfield Road (*Wilmslow and Alderley Advertiser*, 28 May 1897 and 4 June 1897). Another newspaper article (*Manchester City News*, 8 May 1909) describes a visit to

Alderley, or Old Alderley as we prefer to call it, a contradiction to the aggregation of modern Swiss chalets, Italian villas, and imitation castles, which merchant princes have built for themselves on the wooded hill yclept Alderley Edge.

This description perhaps tells us more about the journalistic style of the period than it does about Alderley, but it shows the rift there has always been between the 'old' Alderley and the upstart Alderley Edge.

This next excerpt gives us some insight into the situation during the Second World War. People did not go to the coast for holidays because the beaches were mined and 'holidays at home' were encouraged to save fuel. The Edge provided an accessible alternative. The *Advertiser* of 14 April 1944 describes the holiday crowds over that wartime Easter weekend:

Thousands of visitors came by road and rail to Alderley Edge during the holiday weekend, but the roads were practically free from cars. It is many years since so many people were seen wandering through the woods, and on Monday afternoon the rocks at Stormy Point resembled a popular grand stand [*sic*] and for the time being people seemed to be without a care in the world.

Celebrations

The *Advertiser* of 25 June 1897 describes the celebrations on the Edge for Queen Victoria's Jubilee, when bonfires were lit, 'constructed by Lord Stanley's head carpenter and labourers from the estate'. Bonfires, this time prepared by the Scouts, were again lit on Stormy Point for King George V's Jubilee in 1935 (the photograph is AELP Archive 424) and for the coronation of George VI in 1937. In 1977 the Jubilee of Queen Elizabeth II was also celebrated with a bonfire on Stormy Point, although the sound part of the Archive contains a splendid song written by Stan Gee and sung by Steve Mills about the grey men in Whitehall who would not allow Alderley Edge to be an official Jubilee beacon.

There was also a party for the whole village in the Park. By contrast with 1897 this was under the auspices of the local authority (the parish council) and local traders and was organised by two residents, Mr and Mrs Nash (*Wilmslow and Alderley Advertiser*, 2 June 1977).

Local characters

John Evans

John Evans was a well known character who lived in a log cabin which he had built himself in Church Quarry. There are many stories about him, often contradicting one another. According to the newspaper accounts he was a former railway engineer, having retired through ill-health, and was very knowledgeable about minerals and the Alderley mines and used to take people into them, sometimes using a boat, remains of which were found in 1992 (*Manchester Evening News*, 1 September 1992). The recordings in the Sound Archive include an interview with Peter Kitching, who got to know him and visited him regularly in his Swiss-style log hut over a period of two or three years, and explored the mines with him. The relevant part of the interview is printed in the next chapter, and the appendix to that chapter contains a slightly fuller account of Evans's death and photographs (Figures 21.1, 21.2). The picture he paints is of a generous man with a keen interest in the Edge and the mines, who enjoyed sharing his knowledge with others, who did not like women but liked a drink perhaps too well. It appears he kept cyanide in the cabin to get rid of 'the odd rat or mice that got too nosey' and this might well have a bearing on the sad story reported in the newspapers in 1933. In July of that year a young man called Walter Whitelegg died while on a visit to Evans's cabin with a friend. When Evans failed to appear at the inquest, the police went to his hut and found him dead too. Many column inches of newsprint were expended on this story. Reports of the coroner's inquest held in the Church Institute, Alderley Edge, were carried by the local papers and the *Manchester Evening News*. The coroner was reported in the *Alderley and Wilmslow Advertiser* of 11 August 1933 as having recorded a verdict that Whitelegg's death was due to cyanide poisoning, that it was administered by John Evans in a glass of water at Bergli Hut on 21 July and that Whitelegg was killed accidentally or by misadventure. The *Manchester Evening News* of 25 July 1933 had reported: 'Second Hut Death Riddle Now Solved. Tenant's Poison Fate.... Suicide while of Unsound Mind.'

There were innuendos of suspected homosexuality in the newspaper reporting but Peter Kitching states that although he and a friend visited Evans for two or three years and often, with their parents' permission, stayed the night at weekends, there was never any suggestion of it.

A further article which appeared in 1989 (*Express Advertiser*, 5 January) put a totally different construction on the deaths of Whitelegg and Evans, suggesting that Evans died 'possibly from the same bronchial viral infection which was rampant in the area at the time'. Other friends and relatives of John Evans who are still alive hold differing views on the circumstances of this incident and are protective of his memory. The truth may never be known.

Lucy Lear (Louise Leah)

Another newspaper story was the murder of Lucy Lear by her father on 24 September 1926. His trial was reported in the *Wilmslow and Alderley Advertiser* in October that year. She was said to be his favourite daughter and when he found her packing up to leave home because of his autocratic ways and his violent temper, he attacked her with a knife and she later died from her wounds. He was hanged for the crime.

Amy Crossley

A less tragic character whose story is nevertheless of interest and who featured in the local newspapers is Amy Crossley, 'the most remarkable washer-up in the business' (Figure 20.9). Amy was born in Alderley Edge in 1887. She wrote a guidebook to the village and the Edge in 1931, of which very few copies now survive.

'I've gambled and won and gambled and lost', says Amy, now back at the kitchen sink washing restaurant dishes for £5 a week, and writing up her memoirs 'From Kitchen Sink to Claridges and Back Again' (cf. her article in the *Manchester City News*, 25 May 1935, AELP Archive 420). She became Britain's first woman auctioneer, took singing lessons with Enrico Caruso's widow, met Benito Mussolini and had tea with Franklin D. Roosevelt. Her career began in 1912 when her husband criticised her bad English. She began taking elocution lessons – and next day advertised herself as 'Madam Amy Crossley – Elocutionist'. Soon she had six pupils, whom she taught by keeping one lesson ahead.

She repaired bicycles and cars and in 1920 applied for an auctioneer's licence. Next day she astounded her husband by auctioning all the furniture at their cottage in Alderley Edge. Later she had twenty-nine shops throughout the north of England, went bankrupt, started again but lost again when her uninsured property was destroyed in the Blitz. (We are grateful to Mrs Skermer of Alderley Edge for these stories.)

Amy Crossley's son Alan, who moved to Ontario, has contributed several items to the Archive, particularly in relation to his mother. One of these, a reprint of an article about her from *Town and Country News* for 9 June 1934 (AELP Archive 425), includes her 'Philosophy':

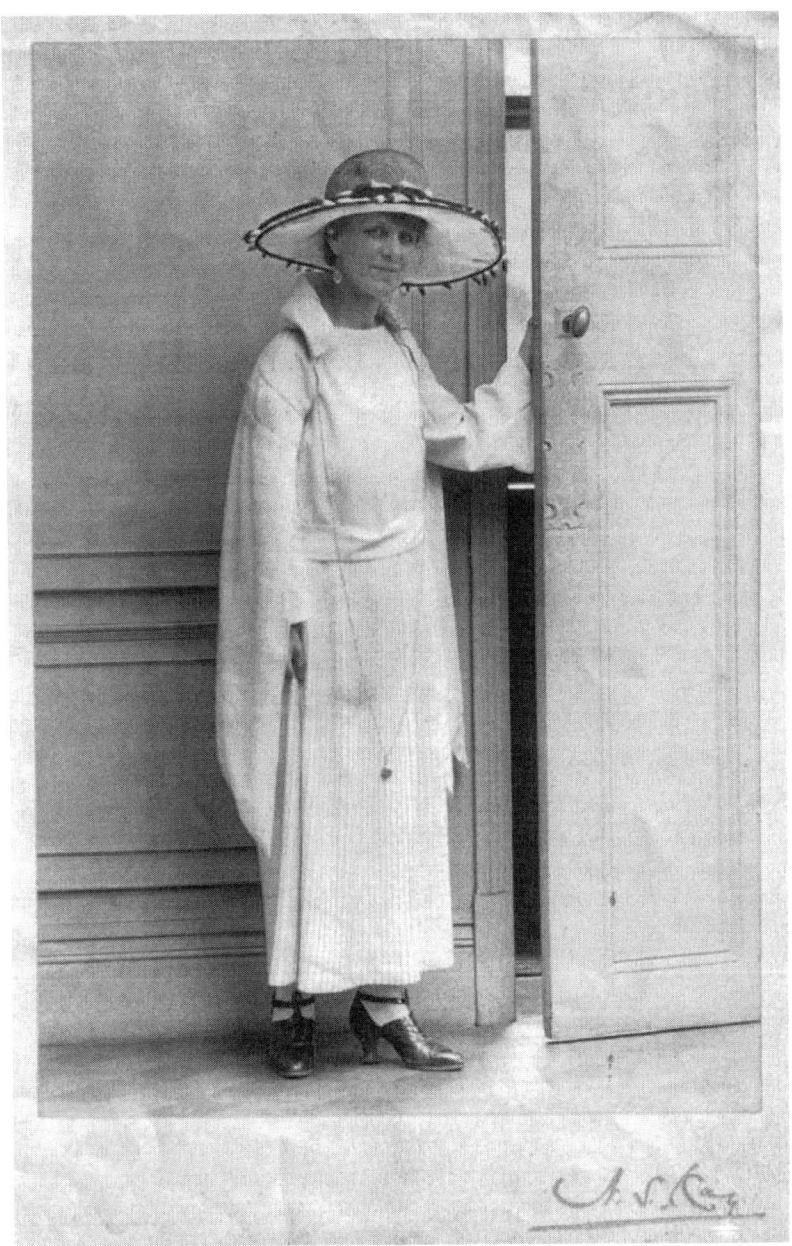

Figure 20.9. Amy Crossley in
Paris *c.* 1935.

Donated by Alan Crossley 1999.

Amy Crossley's Philosophy – Keep your chin up

I am going to tell you the truth about this naughty world, and the truth
is that whichever way you are going, everybody wants to help you along, if
you are going up, they all want to pull; if you are going down they all want
to push. That is what we call sympathy.

You hear complaints that the rich are getting richer and the poor poorer;
that has always been the case, simply because it is human nature. Society has
always been organised to increase the wealth of the wealthy and the power of
the powerful; also to make the weak weaker. There's no use whining about
it, it is simply one of the flinty laws of nature and the only thing to do with

Nature's laws is to adjust oneself to them and not to complain. This might be called the law of the inertia of prosperity.

You are guilty yourself – who do you want to see, the man everybody wants to see, and you read the book that everybody's reading, go to the store where it is the place to go; follow the crowds, the advertiser says with his shrewd knowledge of our make up. If you are fifty pounds ahead, to whom do you want to hand it – to the poor man who needs it? Not at all, but to the rich banker who does not need it. If I ask you for the loan of a pound you will pass it over without a word if you think it is a trifling matter to me, but if you suspect that I am in need of the pound to buy a little food with, that's quite another affair – you can't encourage that sort of thing. I must go to the Guild of the poor things.

Now the way to use this law is to feign prosperity, even if you have it not. Keep your chin up, wear good clothes, don't withdraw from the society of the prosperous. Look pleasant, don't let yourself get down at heel, don't get that poor beggar look on your face. It isn't hypocrisy, it isn't pretence, it is sheer courage, it is letting the world know that while you live you propose to fight, and you do not know when you are licked. Keep smiling, and an unfriendly universe will not know what to do with you, so it will crown you. Fate is a bluff, face her, defy her, and she will fawn on you – Fate is only cruel to the duffer.

Attention; Eyes front! Quick march! Keep your chin up!

The Garside papers

The Garside papers consist of 138 volumes held by the Manchester Central Library Local Studies Unit. Written between the early 1930s and the mid-1960s, they were the personal journals of the late Bob Garside of Burnage, Manchester (plus a few entries written by Brian Hampson and Dennis Smith). Primarily, the volumes are concerned with the rambling and pot-holing activities of Bob Garside and friends and his work with the Boy Scout movement. A substantial part is concerned with trips to, and exploration of, the Alderley Edge mines and the surrounding area. As well as written accounts, the volumes contain numerous newspaper cuttings, journal extracts, photographs, postcards, illustrations, maps, diagrams and plans.

Most, though not all, of the passages relating to Alderley have been photocopied and transcribed for the AELP Archive, and have been listed in the database (AELP Archive 380a, later renumbered 671), although of course anyone wishing to consult the Garside material should consult the originals in the Central Library. A brief description of photographs, diagrams and so on is given with the transcript, as are the newspaper titles and dates of all press cuttings. These cuttings have been transcribed and placed in the news section of the database. Volume and page references to those passages not held by the Archive can be found in the Garside database together with a brief description of their contents.

The greater part of the transcript is taken up with a description of the exploration and mapping of the mines but the transcript also includes accounts and discussion of local history and legends, especially that of the Wizard, as well as the geology of the Edge, accidents in the mines, and planning decisions regarding closure of the mines, the conservation of the Edge and its protection from development.

The sections relating to the mines give a detailed account of explorations in the West, Engine Vein and Wood Mines over a thirty-year period. Most of the explorations were systematically undertaken and are accompanied by plans, diagrams and illustrations of the routes taken or of the particular passages, shafts and galleries being discussed. The manner in which they performed their tasks is well illustrated by the following extract taken from the entry for 20 May 1944:

> Going out to Alderley on the 10–7 P.M. train from Mauldeth Rd, (as usual) we walked up to the West Mine and established Base in the Cavern of the Lion.
>
> The Agenda:
>
> 1) To investigate the Valley of the Dawn, to try and find the upper passages leading to the Chalk Ledge.
> 2) To explore the Squiggly Dragon (this being another part of the Mine we hadn't previously done).
> 3) To try and locate the top of Doctor's Shaft on the Surface.
> 4) To move over to Wood Mine to check up on certain points there.
>
> We had taken the two long ropes and the 30ft. ladder, so we were well equipped; and starting investigations in the Valley of the Dawn we succeeded in climbing up on to a ledge high up in the side above Trickle Down Again; we found that this ledge continued as a short tunnel above the main cavern, and then there was another flight of steps leading down the side of the great rock pillar in the middle of the Valley of the Dawn.

Most of the plans and diagrams were done by Brian Hampson, some of them revisions or corrections to earlier plans. He used the plans contained in the volumes as the basis for the large-scale coloured draft of 'The Land of the Dim Grey King' (i.e. West Mine), a copy of which is in the Archive (AELP Archive 298). It is such a large and complex item that it is impossible to reproduce it meaningfully here, but Figure 20.10, showing the detail of the mapping of what they called the H Planks and the Cavern of the Squiggly Dragon (mentioned above), gives a good sense of the whole concept. The names are interesting but with few exceptions have never been adopted by others. The Derbyshire Caving Club still use a few, such as the 'H Planks', but these are exceptions and the feature called the Dim Grey King (Box 20.3) has long been known as the Sphinx. The general shape of the plan is fairly good and shows

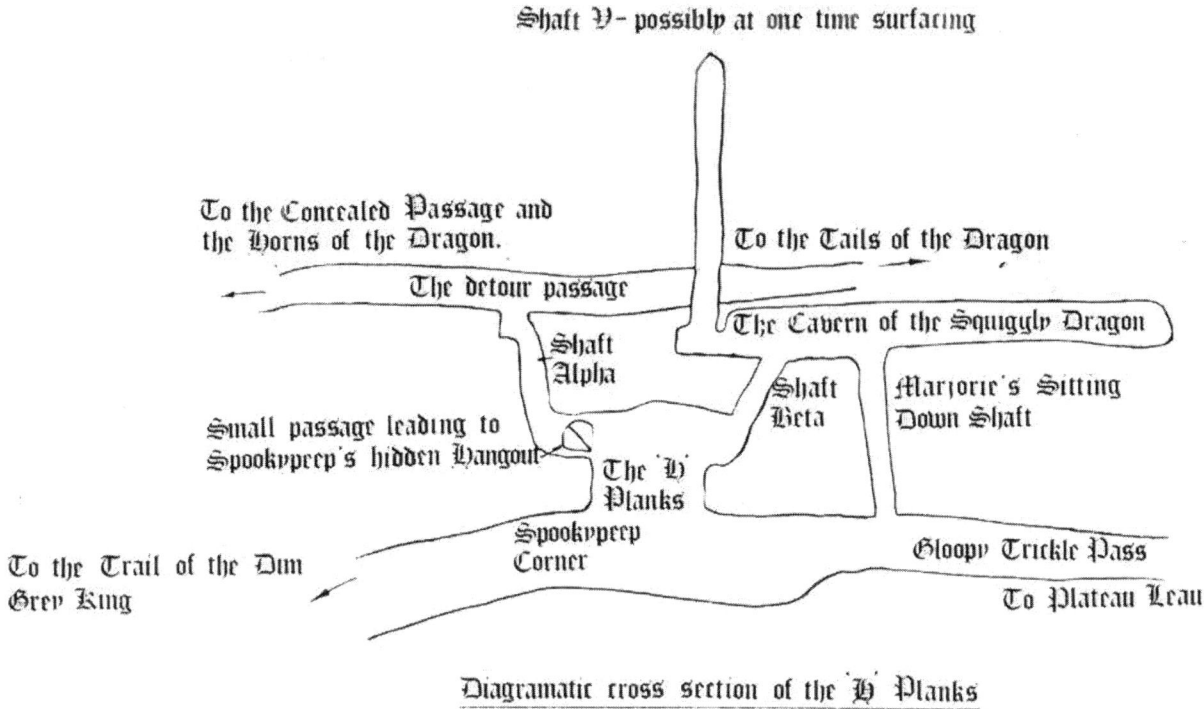

Figure 20.10. Detail of the map of the 'Land of the Dim Grey King' drawn by Brian Hampson, showing the section of the 'H Planks' and the Cavern of the Squiggly Dragon.

Photograph Nigel Dibben, from a copy given to the Project by Paul Sorensen.

evidence of having been based on an original version, although not the 1878 mine abandonment plan, as there are some significant differences.

Also of note in the Garside papers are the photographs taken in the mines, or at the entrances to them, and the numerous postcards containing views both of and from the Edge and of various locations in Alderley village.

However, the work has a greater content, appeal and value than would be the case were it simply a record of mine explorations. Humorous comments and asides permeate the text throughout and the pleasure

Box 20.3. Explanation on the Map of the Land of the Dim Grey King

If there is a purpose for all this – the chart, the innate wisdom of the nomenclature, the long, long hours of work – it belongs, an elusive myth, where it dwells in the dead Worlds beyond the light of the living, yet it is there in the tinkle of trickling water and in the fleeing shadows forever ahead; it is somewhere across the Devil's Causeway, and along the Road to Rome, it lurks in the Pass of Despondent Redemption, it is a soft whisper in the very silence of dark places; it is there, wherever yawning chasms go down in to unknown realms; it remains, yes, and it shall remain, unseen and unrealised, down all the long ages, in the brooding deeps of the darkness in the land of the Dim Grey King.

expressed at the start of one excursion echoes the feelings that many visitors, both past and present, hold towards Alderley Edge when the author writes of how, when reaching the foot of the escarpment, he and his associates 'then joined hands with the Wizard, & danced up his magnificent hill'.

Emotions felt towards the area are also made clear, in a very different way, in the reaction to the decision to use the entrance to West Mine as a landfill site:

> We walked uppy through the miserable drizzle past the Performing Seals and Abbot Brow to West Mine to survey the scene of devastation in the big open-cast where a sea of mud merged into a Corporation Muck Tip covering the entrance to the Land of the Dim Grey King.
> Accursed Be All Vandals!

To those who have seen photographs of the West Mine entrance and the gorge which lay in front of it, and also those who may remember it, the writer's indignation will surely be understandable. Certainly, at the present time and for the foreseeable future such an action would not be permitted, or very likely not even be considered, given the protection which the Edge now enjoys.

The volumes well illustrate some of the changes which have taken place in the decades since they were written, covering, as they do, a period prior to the mines being thoroughly sealed and when planning controls were less considerate towards the conservation and preservation of the Edge than they are now. Indeed, the timescale over which the volumes were written allows for reflection not just upon the changes that have taken place since then but also those taking place during the time of writing. The attraction of the mines to large numbers of the adventurous and curious of all ages prior to their closure is clearly evident, as was the unfortunate price that was paid with the frequent accidents and occasional deaths which resulted from their easy accessibility. The debate that took place regarding the closure of the mines figures prominently. Arguments, both for and against, are recorded. The dismay, noted above, provoked by the decision to use the entrance to West Mine as a site for a local authority refuse tip is later offset by the pleasure expressed at the successful efforts to protect and conserve the Edge, culminating in its designation as a Site of Special Scientific Interest and its purchase and transfer of ownership to the National Trust.

This sense of change is reflected not only in the transformations which take place within the landscape but also in the attitude of Bob Garside as his perception and interests shift over time. The youthful fascination with local legends and the attractions of adventure and, to an extent, the excitement of danger pervading his early experiences of the mines are, over time, replaced by the measured and purposeful manner of the later explorations and research into the geological and historical aspects of the mines.

The factual information, personal comment and quality of presentation, combined with the author's quirky yet very readable prose (which the numerous misspellings and defiance of the laws of composition and punctuation enhance rather than diminish), ensure that the importance of the content is enriched by the nature and individualistic style of the manuscript. Together, these extracts from the Garside papers constitute a unique and important document. Moreover, they illustrate the profound effect the Edge can have on the imagination. Many people know of the 'Weirdstone' through the books of Alan Garner, while very few have heard of the 'Land of the Dim Grey King', and yet both are examples of how this ancient and mysterious place can foster the creation of a fantasy world.

Project papers

In addition to the material presented to the Archive from outside sources, we have also built up a considerable archive of material produced by the Project itself. At the time of writing we have over 1,300 slides and 700 prints, over 100 maps, plans or drawings, and 50 reports. These cover such topics as the archaeological digs, the 'archaeology days', botany, the villas, the Project in action and topographical records. All these are entered in the Archive catalogue and can be accessed in FolioVIEWS. Furthermore, we have built up a vast amount of digital information, topographical, archaeological, botanical, geological and other, which is not covered by the catalogue.

Further investigation

As with any study of this nature, there is much scope for further research.

Education

How did the education provided at Alderley Edge Council School differ from what was provided elsewhere at the same period, for instance at St Hilary's? How did it compare with present-day education at the same school? What were the prospects of the children educated at Alderley Edge Council School in the first half of the twentieth century? What happened to all those children in the photographs taken between 1900 and the 1950s?

Employment

The whole question of the changing economic base of the area deserves further study. The Reverend Edward Stanley's accounts of occupations and the 1851 Census returns, for instance, give a picture very different from that provided by the photographs of Massey's workforce and the Gardeners' Society. Employment in the mines could be a study in itself.

And what of female employment? We have an account of life in domestic service at one of the big houses, and we have the example of the unconventional and enterprising Amy Crossley, but little else.

As the pattern of shopping in the village has changed, how has this affected local employment?

Wartime

There must be many more accounts and photographs of Alderley Edge during the 1914–18 and the 1939–45 wars which would add to our picture of life there in wartime. How is Alderley Edge remembered by the children from the Channel Islands who were evacuated there? We know of one who regularly returns. Are there any photographs or records of the National Fire Service training headquarters which is said to have been in one of the big houses on Macclesfield Road? Or photographs of other buildings which acquired a different identity in wartime?

Family history

There are many possibilities for further research into family history. Just as the Stanley papers, as well as tithe maps and Census returns, have provided much information about former landowners and occupiers, it can be expected that the de Trafford papers could equally furnish valuable details of their land holdings in the area. There are over 600 boxes of these papers in the Lancashire Archives in Preston, at present uncatalogued: an application for funding to catalogue both the de Trafford archive and the remaining Stanley papers to the Arts and Humanities Research Council in 2001 narrowly missed being approved.

Development and planning

The Archive has already been consulted not just by local people but by planners and planning consultants, Cheshire County Council and others in efforts to resolve some of the current problems facing the village. As one example, through the Project, planners were alerted to the existence of an ancient trackway on St Hilary's land and to the importance of some of the trees as well as buildings affected by any redevelopment of the site. There are likely to be other instances where the historical data built up by the Project can be used to help clarify rights of way, boundaries and other planning issues.

AELPHER 2000 (Alderley Edge Landscape Project Heritage and Education Resources)

The Archive formed the basis of this ground-breaking web-based educational project, largely funded by the Heritage Lottery Fund. When it was set up in 2003, large parts of the Archive became accessible on the internet, but unfortunately changes in University policy on the hosting and funding of websites not long afterwards meant that the crucial search facility ceased to function without modifications for which additional funding was not provided. Various options for reviving it have been mooted, and we still hope that one day we shall be able to restore it to its former strength. However, at the time of writing (2014) an archived version from 2008 is available on the British Library's website, and can be accessed at http://www.museum.manchester.ac.uk/community/alderleyedge/ by following the link to the Alderley Edge website. This works for everything except the link to the Project Archive. Alternatively go to www.webarchive.org.uk and then enter 'Alderley Edge Heritage' (not just Alderley Edge) into the Quick Search box and select the 'full text' option, and when the AELPHER site comes up select item 4. The sound archive can be found on another British Library website, cadensa.bl.uk/cgi-bin/webcat, via a search for 'Alderley Edge'.

Conclusion

The many and varied items we have in the Archive give only fascinating glimpses of life in Alderley Edge; we cannot lay any claim to completeness. We are aware of the existence of other 'personal' archives as well as the records of the Derbyshire Caving Club, which we hope will one day at least be linked to the AELP Archive. What we have is a random collection, built up from smaller collections which are themselves typical of those to be found in attics everywhere. On their own the information they can provide is fragmented, but in the overall context of the Archive they fall into place, and can fill lacunae in our record of the village's story. The more we can add to that record the more complete will be our picture of the life of Alderley Edge as it has changed over the years.

In 2000 the Archive was given the Jaffrey papers, a collection of a tradesman's accounts from Walter Jaffrey, plumber, glazier, gas fitter and decorator, of London Road, Alderley Edge, in the late nineteenth century. They were discovered in the loft by Mrs Anna Fern when she renovated her shop, Blue Lagoon, in 1990. They give a fascinating insight into life in Alderley Edge village in the heyday of the villa community, particularly into the relationships between tradesmen and their clients. When reading these accounts we discover that the vicar of Alderley Edge, James Consterdine, did not pay his bills to his plumber for over five years, and many only paid them annually. This puts a new complexion on the 'discriminating price-lists' for the owners of the big houses or for their servants, referred to by Katharine Chorley in her book *Manchester Made Them* (1950: 148), and more recently by Alan Fitchett when he was interviewed for our Project (Chapter 21, p. 548). If a tradesman was expected to wait so long to be paid, he could be forgiven for charging more in the first place.

Shortly afterwards Alan Garner deposited part of the archive of Bilsborough's, the firm of blacksmiths, ironmongers and locksmiths for which his grandfather had worked, and which, in the changed circumstances of the twenty-first century, are still in business as locksmiths in Chelford. How many more historical gems are hiding in the attics?

Editor's note

Perhaps more than other chapters this one may show the effects of the delay in publishing our results – through no fault of the author. However, apart from some very minor updating we have decided to leave it as it stood when Jean Wearne completed her final revision in 2006. The chief exception to this is the table of shops in Table 20.2, which has been brought up to November 2010, just before the long-awaited by-pass was opened: this was a historic moment in the life of Alderley Edge and how it will affect Alderley's shopping patterns remains to be seen, so it seemed to us that a permanent record of the shops as they were at that time could be of some interest, whereas an update to, for example, November 2012 would be too soon to have any particular significance. And as the world of computer databases developed and became more focused it was almost inevitable that our carefully chosen FolioVIEWS was threatened with obsolescence soon after we completed the main work of compiling the catalogue. Happily, an updated version now exists that is compatible with the updated versions of the Windows operating system and at present (2014) it still functions well, but the intention is to incorporate the records into Manchester Museum's comprehensive Ke EMu collections database as resources become available.

Table 20.2. The shops on London Road, 1928–2010: (a) east side

Compiled by Jean and Stephen Wearne

No.	1928	1948	1968	1999	2006	2008	2010
1	Williams Deacons' Bank	Williams Deacons' Bank	Williams & Glyns	Royal Bank of Scotland	Royal Bank of Scotland	Royal Bank of Scotland	Royal Bank of Scotland
	Bank	*Bank*	*Bank*	*Bank*	*Bank*	*Bank*	*Bank*
3	Wood	Wood	de Marco	Edge Interiors	Edge Interiors	Edge Interiors	Edge Interiors
	Electrical	*Electrical*	*Hairdresser*	*Interior design*	*Interior design*	*Interior design*	*Interior design*
5	Chambers	Chambers		Running Bear	Running Bear	Running Bear	Running Bear
	Grocers	*Grocers*	*(arts & crafts)*	*Sports footwear*	*Sports footwear*	*Sports footwear*	*Sports footwear*
7	Warren	Warren		Indian Experience	Balti	Balti	Balti
	Greengrocer and fishmonger	*Greengrocer and fishmonger*	*Ice cream, sweets, greengrocer*	*Takeaway restaurant*	*Restaurant and takeaway*	*Restaurant and takeaway*	*Restaurant and takeaway*
9	W. H. Smith & Sons	W. H. Smith & Sons	National Coal Board	Gascoigne Halman	Chafes	Fiorucci	Fiorucci
	Stationers	*Books and stationery*	*Harris or Allcock, newsagent*	*Estate agent*	*Solicitors*	*Hair*	*Hair*
11	Mrs Bray	Heywood	Pimlotts ?	Bridgfords	Bridgfords	Bridgfords	Bridgfords
	Hairdresser	*Gents hairdresser*	*Fish and chip bar*	*Estate agent*	*Estate agent*	*Estate agent*	*Estate agent*
11A*	Mosscrop	Mosscrop	Brooks		Power Engineering	Power Engineering	Power Engineering
	Taxis	*Taxis*	*Garden sundries and cycles*		*Engineering consultants*	*Engineering consultants*	*Engineering consultants*
13	Jackson	Brookes	Brooks	Potting Shed	Potting Shed	Potting Shed	Potting Shed
	Batteries and bicycles	*Cycles, etc.*	*Garden sundries and cycles*	*Gardening supplies*	*Gardening supplies*	*Gardening supplies*	*Gardening supplies*
15	Bracegirdle	Bracegirdle	Chaney	No 15 Wine Bar	No 15 Wine Bar	No 15 Wine Bar	vacant
	Butcher	*Butcher*	*Greengrocer*	*Restaurant*	*Restaurant*	*Restaurant*	
15A	Butcher's yard	Butcher's yard		The Paintspot	Rose	Tuula	vacant
				Decorative art	*Fashions*	*Fashions*	
15B	Pulford	Wright		Paul David	*unnamed*	*vacant*	vacant
	Toys, stationery	*Toys, stationery*	*Photographer*	*Jewellery*	*Gifts for home*		
17	Unwin	Unwin	Guy Busby	Men Only	*under redevelopment*		Entrance to offices over
	Jeweller and optician	*Jeweller*	*Antiques*	*Men's hairdresser*			
was 19	Singleton	Express Valet	Guy Busby	Encore	*under redevelopment*		Tesco Express
	Creamery	*Dry cleaners*	*Furnishings*	*Fashions*			*Supermarket*
was 21				*vacant (Eurofone soon after)*	*under redevelopment*		Tesco Express
							Supermarket
23	Eastman	Breeze		Timberland			vacant
	Butcher	*Butcher*	*Handbags & fancy goods*	*Wooden floors*			
Clifton Street							
25	Shaw	Shaw	Wienholt	Wienholt	Wienholt	Wienholt	Wienholt
	Confectionery	*Confectionery*	*Pastry cook*	*Pastry cook*	*Pastry cook*	*Pastry cook*	*Pastry cook*
27	Dalton	Dalton	Fitchett	Alan Jackson	Alan Jackson	Alan Jackson	Alan Jackson
	Greengrocer and game	*Greengrocer*	*Greengrocer and fishmonger*	*Butcher/ delicatessen*	*Butcher*	*Butcher*	*Butcher*

No.	1928	1948	1968	1999	2006	2008	2010
27A	Griffith	Griffith	Edna	R Taylor	Mundo	Konak	Konak
	Decorator and plumber	*Decorator and plumber*	*Hairdresser*	*Fishmonger*	*Tapas bar*	*Turkish restaurant*	*Turkish restaurant*
27B			Tweet				
			Barber				
29			Katie's	Brambles of Alderley	Pinks	La Vina	Stay
			Children's wear	*Florist*	*Restaurant*	*Restaurant*	*Restaurant and bar*
31	Pullars (Mrs Knowles)	Woolshop (Cooper)	The Wool Shop	Carrier Travel	Carrier Travel	Carrier Travel	Carrier
	Dyers and cleaners	*Knitting wools, etc.*	*Knitting/sewing*	*Travel Agent*	*Travel agent*	*Travel agent*	*Travel agent*
33	Partington	Partington	Partington	Alderley Village Butcher	Alderley Village Butcher	Alderley Village Butcher	Alderley Village Butcher
	Butcher	*Butcher*	*Butcher*	*(W Walton) Butcher*	*Butcher*	*Butcher*	*Butcher*
35	Wardle	Jamieson	Seaton	Teasel	Barnardos Store	Barnardos Store	Barnardos Store
	Sweets and tobacco	*Sweets and tobacco*	*Sweets/tobacco*	*Fashions*	*Charity shop and agency*	*Charity shop and agency*	*Charity shop and agency*
37	Margaret	Margaret		La Femme	Peter Saville	The Style Lounge	The Style Lounge
	Dress shop	*Dress shop*		*Beautician*	*Hairdresser*	*Hairdresser*	*Hairdresser*
39	Mottershead	Maison		Farmhouse Kitchen	Cinderella	Cinderella	Tuula
	Outfitters	*Milliner*	*Greengrocer*	*Health-food shop*	*Fashions*	*– closing down sale*	*Fashions*
41	Garnett	Household Stores		Ann Barnes	Box 2	Birdcage – closed	Runway
	Dress shop	*Household goods*		*Fashions*	*Fashions*		*Fashions*
43	Barrow	Barrow	Household Stores	Johnsons	Johnsons	Johnsons	Johnsons
	Shoes	*Shoes*	*Household and carpet store*	*Cleaners*	*Cleaners*	*Cleaners*	*Cleaners*
45	Burns	Burns		Post office and stationery	Post office and stationery	Post office and stationery	Post office (only)
	Sweets and tobacco	*Sweets and tobacco*					
47	Jaffrey	Eileen Elwood	Grill & Chicken	Siro	The Bubble Room	The Bubble Room	The Bubble Room
	Plumber and decorator	*Ladies hairdresser*	*Restaurant*	*Restaurant*	*Restaurant*	*Restaurant*	*Restaurant*
Stevens Street							
49	Seymour Mead	Seymour Mead	Seymour Mead	Wine Rack	Wine Rack	Wine Rack	- vacant -
	Grocer	*Grocer*	*Grocer*	*Wine*	*Wine*	*Wine*	
51	Reynolds	Whitworth	Massey	Massey	Henry Johnstone	Henry Johnstone	Henry Johnstone
		Cycles	*Jeweller*	*Jeweller*	*Jeweller*	*Jeweller*	*Jeweller*
53	Tofts Supper Rooms (Miss M E Chynoweth)	Tofts Café (Mrs Beatie)	Beattie	Stanley Racing	William Hill	William Hill	William Hill
	Sweets and café	*Café, groceries, sweets, cooked meats*	*Grocer/baker*	*Betting shop*	*Betting shop*	*Betting shop*	*Betting shop*

No.	1928	1948	1968	1999	2006	2008	2010
55	Whitaker	Boots	Boots	The Legend	*vacant*	World Wide Escapes	World Wide Escapes
		Chemist	*Chemist*	*Bookshop*		*Travel*	*Travel*
57	Perrin	Perrin	Acton	Acton	Arthouse	Arthouse	SieMatic
	Cake shop	*Cakes and bread*	*Baker*	*Baker*	*Creative interiors*	*Creative interiors*	*Creative interiors*
59	Fletcher	Fletcher	Dewhurst	Wood & Watson	Wood & Watson	Wood & Watson	Ruby & Ruby
	Butcher	*Butcher*	*Butcher*	*Optician*	*Optician*	*Optician*	*Optician, hearing aids*
61	Morris	Morris	Morris	Alderley Gallery	Colours & Crafts	Colours & Crafts	vacant
	Florist	*Florist and seedsman*	*Florist*	*Art/Picture Framing*	*Art shop*	*Art shop*	
63	Fielden	Alison	Robinsons ?	Wizard Cards	Martins	Martins	Martins
	Toys and newsagent	*Toys and newsagent*	*Newsagent*	*Newsagent*	*Newsagent*	*Newsagent*	*Newsagent*
65	Cowsill	Cowsill		Imperial Cancer Research Fund	Cancer Research UK	Cancer Research UK	Cancer Research UK
	Grocer	*Grocer*	*Grocer ? Estate agent ?*	*Charity shop*	*Charity shop*	*Charity shop*	*Charity shop*
67	Kershaw	Kershaw	Kershaw	Cedrics	Cedrics	Cedrics	Cedrics
	Chemist	*Chemist*	*Chemist*	*Chemist*	*Chemist*	*Chemist*	*Chemist*

Passageway to 69 Pannone – solicitors (office above 69A)

No.	1928	1948	1968	1999	2006	2008	2010
69A	Slacks	Slacks	Rawson Chad	Modische Schuhe	J P Connolly	J P Connolly	vacant
	Shoes	*Shoes*	*Shoes*	*Shoes*	*Jeweller*	*Jeweller*	
71	Higgins	Burgon	Nota Bene (later?)	La Casa Bella	S K Nine	Marie Curie Cancer Care	Marie Curie Cancer Care
	Grocer	*Grocer*	*China/kitchenware ?*	*China/ceramics*	*Sunspa*	*Charity shop*	*Charity shop*
73	Broadbent	Broadbent	Holding	Oddbins	Oddbins	Nicolas	Corks Out
	Drapers	*Drapers*	*Decorators*	*Wine*	*Wine*	*Wine*	*Wine*
75	Princes Café	Princes Café		Est Est Est	Est Est Est	Gusto	Gusto
	Café	*Cake shop and café*		*Restaurant*	*Restaurant*	*Restaurant*	*Restaurant*
77	Eadington	Eadington	Wallwork (Volvo)	Kinsey Jones	Chorlegh Grange	Chorlegh Grange	Chorlegh Grange
	Garage	*Garage*	*Garage and car showroom*	*Car showroom*	*Apartments*	*Apartments*	*Apartments*
	Eadington	Eadington		Kinsey Jones			
	House	*House*	*Garage*	*Car showroom*			

Chapel Road

No.	1928	1948	1968	1999	2006	2008	2010
79	Mellor	Mellor	Mellor	Hannah	Alderley Dental	Alderley Dental	Alderley Dental
	Grocer	*Grocer*	*Grocer*	*Dentist*	*Dentist*	*Dentist*	*Dentist*

*Access to 11A is by a passage between 11 and 13 London Road.

Table 20.2. The shops on London Road, 1928–2010: (b) west side

Compiled by Jean and Stephen Wearne

No.	1928	1948	1968	1999	2006	2008	2010
The Parade							
1	Trotman	Trotman (kiosk)		HSBC	HSBC	HSBC	HSBC
	Sweets	*Sweets and tobacco*		*Bank*	*Bank*	*Bank*	*Bank*
2+3		National Coal Board		Mandarin	Mandarin	Mandarin	Mandarin
		Coal office		*Restaurant*	*Restaurant*	*Restaurant*	*Restaurant*
4				Keith Barnes	Keith Barnes Ann Barnes	*vacant*	Jayne Connolly
				Menswear	*Menswear*		*Jeweller*
5		Coop		Alderley Veg	Fireworks	*vacant*	Fruitcake
		Coal office		*Greengrocer*	*Fireworks*		*Café*
6				Sketchley/ Supasnaps	Designs on the Edge	Somerfields	Cooperative Food
				Cleaners/photos	*Interiors*	*Supermarket*	*Supermarket*
7			H & C (later Liptons)	Kwiksave	Somerfields		
			Supermarket	*Supermarket*	*Supermarket*		
Entrance to coal yard – the Parade with the above shops and car park were built in the former coal yard							
6A					Murray's (daytime), Masala (evenings)	Murray's (daytime)	Murray's (daytime)
					Sandwich bar, Indian takeaway	*Sandwich bar ?*	*Sandwich bar*
6		Beatie		Artizanz of Alderley	Gascoigne Halman	Gascoigne Halman	Gascoigne Halman
		Coal office	*Coal office*	*Arts, crafts and gifts*	*Estate agent*	*Estate agent*	*Estate agent*
8	Hall	Anderson	Anderson	Andrew J Nowell	Andrew J Nowell	Andrew J Nowell	Andrew J Nowell
	Fine art dealer	*Electrical goods*	*Electricians*	*Estate agent*	*Estate agent*	*Estate agent*	*Estate agent*
10	Ellwood	Ellwood	Martins	Cheshire Building Society	*vacant*	Britannia Building	Britannia Building
	Shoes	*Shoe shop and cobblers*	*Bank*	*Building society*		*Society*	*Society*
12	Winnie Perrin	*vacant*		Culina	Lemon Tree	Ponto Fresco	Ponto Fresco
	Confectioners		*Dress shop*	*Delicatessen*	*Licensed coffee bar*	*Licensed coffee bar*	*Licensed coffee bar*
14	Cohen	Cohen	Duncan & Foster/Prices ?	Baker Antiques	Hi Ho Silver	Hi Ho Silver	Hi Ho Silver
	Jeweller	*Jeweller*	*Baker*	*Antiques*	*'Silver' goods*	*'Silver' goods*	*'Silver' goods*
16	Smith	Smith	Smith	Alderley Cheese Wedge	Alderley Cheese Wedge	Alderley Cheese Wedge	Alderley Cheese Wedge
	Cleaners	*Cleaners*	*Cleaners*	*Cheese*	*Cheese and cooked meats*	*Cheese and cooked meats*	*Cheese and cooked meats*
18	Rathbone	Lady Fair	Lady Fair	Beauty Works	Beauty Works	Beauty Works	Beauty Works
	Milliners and drapers	*Dress shop*	*Dress shop*	*Beauty*	*Beauty*	*Beauty*	*Beauty*

No.	1928	1948	1968	1999	2006	2008	2010
20	Cumberbirch	Cumberbirch	Charles Charnley	Charles Charnley	Cedrics Health/Beauty	Cedrics Health/Beauty	Cedrics Health/Beauty
	Chemist	*Chemist*	*Chemist*	*Chemist*	*Chemist*	*Chemist*	*Chemist*
West Street							
22	Union Bank	Union Bank	Barclays	Barclays	Barclays	Barclays	Barclays
	Bank	*Bank*	*Bank*	*Bank*	*Bank*	*Bank*	*Bank*
24	Amy Crossley	Arthur Royle	Central Garage	Royles	Costa Coffee	Costa Coffee	Costa Coffee
	Furniture and second-hand clothing	*Car sales*	*Car showroom*	*Car showroom*	*Coffee bar*	*Coffee bar*	*Coffee bar*

Cobblers Yard – access to what is now called Cobblers Yard is by a passage between 24 and 26 London Road

No.	1928	1948	1968	1999	2006	2008	2010
		Evison	*not recorded*	Cutting Edge	Cutting Edge	Cutting Edge	Cutting Edge
		Riding academy		*Hairdresser*	*Hairdresser*	*Hairdresser*	*Hairdresser*
			not recorded	Powell	Paperie	Paperie	Paperie
				Coffee, tea	*Cards, paper*	*Cards, paper*	*Cards, paper*
			not recorded	Pet Foods	(Alderley Flowers storage)	(Alderley Flowers storage)	(Alderley Flowers storage)
				Pet foods			
26		Cheney		Alderley Flowers	Alderley Flowers	Alderley Flowers	Alderley Flowers
		Fruit and vegetables		*Florist*	*Florist*	*Florist*	*Florist*
26A	Jerrems	Edith Dennett	Edith Dennett ?	Alan Jackson	Nailworx	Nailrooms	Nailrooms
	Milliner, wools	*Dress shop*	*Dress shop*	*Greengrocer*	*Manicure*	*Manicure*	*Manicure*
28	R. H. Wood	R. H. Wood	R. H. Wood	Travel by Design	Travel by Design	Travel by Design	Travel by Design
	Butcher	*Butcher*	*Butcher*	*Travel agent*	*Travel agent*	*Travel agent*	*Travel agent*
30	Robinson	Sidlows (Robinson)	Alderley Wine & Spirits	Marshall Rodgers	vacant	Tom Howley	Tom Howley
	Off-licence	*Off-licence*	*Off-licence*	*Estate agent*		*Bespoke furniture*	*Bespoke furniture*
32	Warren	Billy Woods	Fraser Lee	Chafes	Chafes	Chafes	Chafes
	Greengrocer	Greengrocer	Men's outfitters	Solicitors	Solicitors	Solicitors	Solicitors
Brown Street							
34	Hidderley	Hidderley	Alderley Rose	Alderley Rose	Alderley Rose	Alderley Rose	Alderley Rose
	Outfitter, draper	*Clothing, haberdashery*	*Restaurant*	*Restaurant*	*Restaurant*	*Restaurant*	*Restaurant*
36	Pearson	Pearson	Craggs	Wedding Shop	Wedding Shop	Wedding Shop	Wedding Shop
	Cobbler, bootmaker	*Cobbler*	*Baker*	*Bridal wear*	*Bridal wear*	*Bridal wear*	*Bridal wear*
38	Mills	Matley	Stearn	Forbuoys	World Wide Escapes	Posh	Posh
	Stationer	*Toys and newsagent*	*Newsagent and toys*	*Newsagent*	*Travel agent*	*Hairdresser*	*Hairdresser*
40	Mayoh	Mayoh	Mayoh	Marie Curie Cancer Care	Marie Curie Cancer Care	Deli Lavalle	Village Café
	Grocer and off-licence	*Grocer and off-licence*	*Grocer and off-licence*	*Charity shop*	*Charity shop*	*Delicatessen*	*Café*
42	Chocolate Box	Chocolate Box (Mrs Hulme)	*vacant*	Bag & Baggage	Chaos	Daniel	Daniel
	Sweets	*Sweets*		*Handbags etc.*	*Children's wear*	*Footwear*	*Footwear*

No.	1928	1948	1968	1999	2006	2008	2010
44	Church Institute	Church Institute	Church Institute	up for sale	Public Library *(apartments above)*	Public Library *(apartments above)*	Public Library

Chapel Street

No.	1928	1948	1968	1999	2006	2008	2010
46	Broadbents *Furniture and undertaker*	G W Broadbent *Furniture, funerals, upholsterers, cabinet makers, household removals*	G W Broadbent *Furniture and carpets*	Blue Lagoon *Fashions*	*vacant*	London Road *Restaurant and café*	London Road *Restaurant and café*
48A	Bilsborough *Hardware*	James Bilsborough *Ironmongers, locksmiths, mowing machine repairs*	Bilsborough *Ironmonger*	L'Azure *Fashions*	Sensory International *Custom installations*	Sensory International *Custom installations*	Sensory International *Custom installations*
48B	Hockenhull *Butcher*	Hockenhull *Butcher*	Edith Dennett ? *Dress shop*	Medicine Shop *Health*	Medicine Shop *Health*	Medicine Shop *Health*	Medicine Shop *Health*
50	Hockenhull *House*	Hockenhull *House*	Hockenhull *Butcher*	Mas Que Vada *Restaurant*	Alderley Bar & Grill *Restaurant*	Alderley Bar & Grill *Restaurant*	Alderley Bar & Grill *Restaurant*
52	District Bank *Bank*	District Bank *Bank*	National Westminster *Bank*	Nat West Bank *Bank*	Nat West Bank *Bank*	Nat West Bank *Bank*	Nat West Bank *Bank*

George Street

No.	1928	1948	1968	1999	2006	2008	2010
54	Leah *Mats and baskets*	Corner House *Delicatessen, ice cream, café*	The Corner House *Grocery, delicatessen, café*	Victoria Wine *Wine*	Thresher *Wine*	Thresher *Wine*	Portland Wine *Wine*

Sources:
1928 data: Map by Alan Crossley, dated 1999; emails with Alan Crossley, February and March 2006; Meetings with Alma Heath and Ruth Bracegirdle January 2006; Traders' advertisements in *Alderley Edge Parish Magazine*, May 1927 (lent by Hilda Gittins).
1948 data: Harold Smith.
1968, 1999 and 2006 data: private notes, Jean and Stephen Wearne and Brenda Roberts.
2008 and 2010 data: Jean and Stephen Wearne.

Note: *This column shows the property numbering along London Road in 2006. Some property numbers before 2006 may have been different before redevelopment.

21

Living memory: the people of the Edge

John L. Ecclestone

> Above all tell the children. Tell your children. Tell your grandchildren. They may not appear to listen, not want to hear, to be impatient. But tell them; and they will remember, and at some time in the future, if not now, the words and their importance will resurface and the story will go on.

Thus Alan Garner, in the final lecture in the series 'The Story of Alderley Edge', given at St Hilary's School in the autumn of 1998, laid upon his audience the duty to pass on their memories.

Mrs Edna Younger did it for her children. On tape she described the Miners' Cottages and what it was like to live there. Compared with today 'it was a different world, wasn't it?' she said. And her record is not just for her children and for future generations. It is also for me and my family. We lived in Alderley Edge for twenty years but the Miners' Cottages were long gone before we arrived. My impression is derived entirely from Mrs Younger's recording and the photographs she showed me.

By the time Alan Garner gave his lecture we had already made a good start. In the first two years of the Alderley Edge Landscape Project we made forty-seven recordings, the foundation of a sound archive of oral history. By the time the project finally ended this archive had grown to over 100 hours: we see it as one of the most important elements in the future of the Alderley Project. We intend to leave behind far more than our Bronze Age ancestors left for us!

Our descendants may well be surprised both by the variety of the material and by its recurring themes. We were privileged to be allowed into the homes of people who were willing to talk to us and answer our questions. Some took the initiative and contacted the Project to offer their memories; none that I can recall refused an invitation from us. Every interviewee had the opportunity to listen to the recording after it had been edited and each had the right to demand cuts and corrections. People were, after all, recalling events as far back as fifty or sixty years – or even further. Charlie Hayes had vivid memories of a military exercise around the mines on the Edge which took place during the First World War. Charlie was ninety-four years old. The rights of the interview were (and are) the property of the interviewee until they were happy to allow the National Trust and the Project to make use of it. Only when we had obtained their signature of confirmation could the tapes be heard by others, transcribed and copies placed in the National Sound Archive, and the archives of the National Trust and Manchester Museum.

In this way, through the generosity, patience and tolerance of individuals, we learned of, among many other things, what it was like to be 'in service' with the Stanleys, and of Lady Stanley's kindness to the children of one of their tenants; of the bodysnatchers of Whitebarn; of the generosity of John Evans, known as 'the Hermit', to the unemployed; of the gang of poachers from Macclesfield who invaded the territory of our own poachers on the Edge; and how schoolboys drove sheep from the railway station to Whitebarn all the way up London Road.

In addition to the individual interviews we recorded lectures and field trips. The lectures enabled us to record for posterity a more academic body of knowledge than the social history of individuals, but the field trips brought an element of actuality and spontaneity that often gives the listener the feeling of 'being there at the time'. The applause which greeted Simon Timberlake's successful smelting of copper by the methods which might have been used there 3,500 years ago was truly spontaneous, as was his unconcealed delight in the achievement. No less rewarding was the 'Evening with Steve Mills', when he sang many songs which touched on local history and folklore, including the Legend of Alderley Edge. Only in a recording can the atmosphere of such an occasion be captured, as it was in the Reading Room at Over Alderley that night.

Steve Mills is one of the people to whom acknowledgement must be made for making some of his own recordings available to us. He talked to Lady Worthington in the 1970s, and gave a running commentary on the festivities which took place on the Edge on the night of the Jubilee bonfire in 1977. We are also indebted to the Edge Association for a copy of a lecture given to the Association by Miss Margaret Pilkington in 1972 (of which more later in this chapter); to the late Mrs Marjorie Garner for a recording of the driver of that huge RAF lorry which crashed down the Macclesfield Road, across the Square, through Massey's yard and onto the railway line; and to several people who gave us tapes they recorded with Alec Barber, of mummers' fame.

So, on the one hand, our recordings cover a very wide range of memories but, on the other, the overlaps are equally fascinating. By overlaps I mean those events and occasions remembered by more than one person. There were those who slid down the Sandhills on tea trays, and those who slid down Lizzie Leah's Field on toboggans in the snow with real danger to life and limb from (and to!) the traffic on the Mottram Road. Several people described the fair at the Wizard and virtually everyone we spoke to had a memory, some good, some bad and some very bad, of their school days. We have an 'end of term report' on most teachers of the time!

Memories of childhood were almost always rosy in retrospect. For Doug Poyner 'the Edge was our playground'.

Mr Doug Poyner talking to John Ecclestone

Mr Doug Poyner: They used to catch rabbits and all sorts you know; that used to be a big sort of pastime in the old days.

John Ecclestone: Now you mentioned birdwatching. On the Edge?

DP: Well anywhere birdwatching, we'd go anywhere. We used to walk for miles, from Alderley to Prestbury there were footpaths all over the fields you see. We knew all the farms sort of thing and we'd go walking along the farms. We were a bit naughty: we used to go and get waterhen eggs and eat them!

JE: Where were the best places for waterhens?

DP: Well any pits;, there were loads of pits over the farms you know. We used to know all the pits. We used to track along – we used to have a big dessert spoon in your pocket and a long cane, and you whipped it on the end of the cane, pushed it out, get the eggs and whipped the cane back, like that see – and then we used to eat them! Unless they were hatching. We'd try one first – if it floated you'd put it back quick, if it sank they'd be all right to eat! Its illegal today, but nobody bothered about it in those days. It was just our playground for rambling and anything, you know.

JE: Animals? Foxes?…

DP: Foxes, rabbits. Later on we started ferreting rabbits. And then later on when we got older we got guns, and shot rabbits. It was just a nature thing like, you know. That was when the war time was on. And we got 3d for a netted rabbit – oh no, sorry, we got 3d for a shot rabbit and 6d for a netted rabbit – 3d for the shot ones and your cartridge cost 2d.…

JE: So you weren't making much on that!

DP: It was the adventure, it was the adventure sort of thing! And then one of the old poachers there taught us how to long-net. He used to take us along the woods at night to long-net the rabbits. It's illegal now!

He taught me how to catch partridge. Every farm in them days had at least two covers of partridge on, like, but today everything is ploughed in right away so that there is no stubble for them. He used to catch the partridge with a cider bottle – you know the flagon cider bottle? He used to get one of those and push it into the ground neck first about half way down and pull it out and it left the shape of the neck of a cider bottle; he used to do about half a dozen of these and he'd put a handful of corn in each one and scatter a lot round about. And sometimes you went the next day a partridge would be there – all you could see, they'd be upside down with their little feet going like that – they couldn't get back on their feet – it was a perfect fit round the wings and it definitely works because I've seen it happen.

And I always remember he taught us how to long-net. Yes, that was the in thing in those days. There were plenty of rabbits about in those days. Loads of them. You used to get that many rabbits that you had to gut them to cut the weight down to carry them back, you know.

It was just the adventure, something to do, you see.

'Poyner the Poacher'! So if that was what little boys were made of in those days, what about the girls? Edna Younger (née Barrow), at the age of five, walked from the Miners' Cottages, where she lived, to Nether Alderley, where she went to school.

Mrs Edna Younger talking to John Ecclestone

Mrs Edna Younger: Yes, down Artists' Lane, and then through the fields in the summertime, to school. That was wonderful, wonderful school days. Completely carefree, you know? I don't know if you've ever read *Lark Rise To Candleford*?

John Ecclestone: No.

EY: There, reminded me a bit of the days when we lived up there. Completely carefree. We could play in the woods; there were, of course there were other children there, just two next door to us, Roy and Molly Barber. It was a lovely community.

JE: So at five years old you would walk from the copper mines....

EY: Yes, to Nether Alderley school.

JE: Can you describe that journey for me?

EY: Oh yes.

JE: What was, what was the scenery like? What....

EY: Absolutely beautiful. In the wintertime, of course, it was snow, birds, robins, you know, all the things you get in the countryside. The two children next door walked with me, and we went to the farm on Artists Lane; then we were picked up by an older girl and her brother, the Owens, and they walked with us. Our mothers took us as far as that you see. And then we walked on to school. Oh the flowers in the spring, indescribable! Wood anemones, primroses, any of the spring flowers you could mention were on that walk; it was beautiful. In the summertime there was a walk, and it's still there now, halfway down Artists Lane, across the fields and it comes out at the back of the school. But you couldn't walk that in the wintertime because it was probably knee deep in snow you know, but it made no difference whether it was snowing or what, we went to school – and an excellent little school it was! Only three teachers, I think there was only about ninety children in the school.

And at Christmas time Lord Stanley used to give a party for all the children. Oh that was a great occasion. They had fireworks at the back of the lake and, of course, we never saw fireworks like those. You know, nursery rhymes and that sort of thing and, behind the lake, and presents off the Christmas tree. Lady Stanley used to, and her daughters, used to make a lot of the presents; I can remember them giving me a little cot with blankets on, just one to go in a doll's house, small cot, and as Lady Stanley handed it to me she said: 'I embroidered those'. Oh that meant the world to me. She put satin ribbon on them you see.

JE: Do you still have it?

EY: No, unfortunately. You don't keep things like that do you?

JE: Now you've mentioned the fireworks and things at the Hall. Were there any other occasions like that when…?

EY: Well, they had a tenants' party; that was after we'd had the children's party, and it was always in the Tenants' Hall, and they'd have a ball, and, oh yes, they treated the tenants very well, and we as schoolchildren were allowed to go anywhere in the Park; all the nature rambles were in the Park, and we were allowed to swim or paddle in the mere….

JE: Really?

EY: In the Park, oh yes. Yes.

JE: No one to chase you away or anything like that?

EY: Oh no, no, the children belonged, we were sort of belonging to them, you see?

JE: But the children of people who were not tenants would not have been allowed to….

EY: Oh no.

JE: No.

EY: No, not without permission. It was it was a lovely upbringing, as a child. But, I used to love going up there and, really living in Alderley and amongst those woods; it gave you a vivid imagination. It did.

JE: What were you imagining?

EY: Oh fairies and, you know, all sorts of things as a child. It was a, oh it was a child's dream really to live near those woods and the, you know, all the animals; the squirrels, the rabbits and, it was wonderful, wonderful place to live.

Mr Poyner and Mrs Younger have taken us back to their childhood some sixty years ago. But we can go back further than that. Miss Pilkington takes us back to the very beginning of the century.

Miss Margaret Pilkington speaking to the Edge Association in 1972

Miss Margaret Pilkington: A good many people have asked me what it was like to be a child in Alderley Edge. Well, that I cannot claim to have done because we lived in Fulford and I grew up to the sound of the mill sirens and I woke in the early morning to hear the clogs going along the streets to the mills.

I think I must tell you one rather funny incident. I was with my, the nurse, and my sister, who was two years younger than me, was in a perambulator and nurse suddenly rushed us into a side street, sweeping another nurse and another perambulator with her, and I heard the nurse say to her, the other nurse say to my nurse, 'why are we doing this?' 'Didn't you see, there was a woman with bloomers on, riding on a bicycle [laughter] I couldn't let the children see that'. When I went home I said to mother 'what's bloomers' [more laughter].

Well, we didn't come to Alderley until we were in our teens, and I remember the first day coming up here. Father had been out looking for a house and we came out on a lovely sunny day and walked up Woodbrook Road, and I remember both of us thinking that it was really rather like Italy, with the cobblestones and the sunshine and the fir trees.

In those days in Alderley it was very curious – how things have changed! We were thought to be quite moderate because we had five servants living in – a good many people had seven and eight servants living in, and when Dorothy and I used to go and stay with our uncle, father's eldest brother William Pilkington in St Helens, they had I think about ten or eleven.

In her talk Miss Pilkington paints a wonderful picture of life in the early years of the century: family prayers with the servants; the etiquette of 'calling' on neighbours. After you had called you asked people to dinner and she describes in mouth-watering detail very long dinner parties with up to thirteen courses – not forgetting, she says, 'the sorbet – to cool the tummy'.

And it wasn't just the food that was different.

Miss Margaret Pilkington: The traffic too, that's another thing I was thinking the other day. When we came here a certain old friend of ours, a Mrs Carver, came to live in Chapel Road and she was very crippled, and so on a Saturday morning I used to take her in her bath chair in the village to shop and she always made me push her bath chair in the middle of the road because she didn't like the camber, she said she fell over in her chair [laughter]. Well, I was a bit uneasy in the middle of the road but it was perfectly possible to do it, and on a Sunday Father and I used to go for her again and we pushed her all the way up Macclesfield Road up here in the middle of the road! Well there were very few motors then; it was mostly horse-drawn traffic.

We [Miss Pilkington and her sister] never had horses, the Crewdsons had horses, a lot of the people here had horses and carriages. Mother had a brougham and a victoria and we had the horses for them. Then of course the bread came round in a van and the milk cart – the milk carts were very nice open carts with big brass cans and they used to ladle the milk out into the bowls of people who came out to … bowls and jugs. And the coal carts of course were from the colliery, were all from my Father's colliery; all the coal carts were bright red, big square carts, and the horses were very splendid horses.

Most of the men of course went to town by train, practically all of them, and there were three trains that were most used and they were called Striving, Thriving and Thriven! Striving went about eight o'clock, seven-thirty or eight, and Thriving went about eight-thirty and Thriven went at nine or nine-thirty [laughter]. And they had their particular carriages; my Father always travelled in a carriage with certain people. Hubert Worthington who was in the Thriving set and Philip Godley they were about half an hour earlier and they had their special carriage; and if another person came in Father used to talk to them but some of the other people in the carriage wouldn't, you know; they'd sit behind their newspapers and wouldn't talk at all because there was a stranger in the carriage.

Nearly all these places were big houses then – now most of them have either been split up or made into flats, or houses pulled down and houses put in their places, but when we came I think the whole, all the Edge was big houses with gardens and the 'Hill' and the Village were two quite different things.

Miss Pilkington referred to the Hill and the Village as two quite different things. It's surprising how many people described that relationship with the words 'them and us'.

Mr Robert Bancroft talking to Matthew Hyde and John Ecclestone

Mr Robert (Bob) Bancroft: Most people were poor in the village end – I thought that was what you were going to ask me, the big divide in Alderley: there was a big divide, there was the Edge up there and then down in the village were the working-class people, which were the gardeners, the maids, the chauffeurs for the people on the Edge.

Matthew Hyde: But the one must have depended on the other, mustn't it?

RB: Yes

MH: I mean, in a way, you couldn't have one without the other?

RB: No, the village people relied on the work, very poorly paid but they relied on the job; probably the husband was chauffeur and his wife was say, housemaid or parlourmaid or cook, but I've known people on the Edge have four gardeners and possibly five maids and a chauffeur, not one family, many families up there. A very big divide; I mean, I could quote several instances where if you were waiting in a queue in a shop, there might be seven of us waiting in the fish shop, and if someone came down from the Edge they pulled up at the front and the lady came in and she didn't go to the queue, she went to the owner, gave you an order and out she went, and then ten minutes after the chauffeur came in, followed her you see, picked up the box and put it in the boot, and off. There was no queuing for the people on the Edge, because she's such a good customer, you know – money – I mean ours was probably a small piece of fish and theirs was probably five pieces. But it was quite distinct; you could feel it around. It was nothing to us because we were used to it, but it's amazing now: you never see it today, I don't think.

MH: Did you feel hostile about it? I mean did it annoy you?

RB: No.

MH: You just took it the way it was?

RB: Yes, way of life.

Without any difficulty Mr Bancroft gave us the names of all the grocers in the village in the 1930s. There were ten. I said to Mr Bancroft 'I bet you couldn't do that for the butchers' shops'. He did. All seven of them.

Returning to the theme of 'them and us', I wonder if Miss Pilkington realised that some people felt as strongly as Mr Fitchett.

Mr Alan Fitchett talking to Alan Garner and John Ecclestone

Alan Garner: Now Alan, everybody who had grown up in Alderley knows what the 'Back Streets' is.

Mr Alan Fitchett: Or were.

AG: Or were, or were. What would you define as the 'Back Streets'? What does it mean to you?

AF: To me it means the working, the people who used to work for 'them up there', if you understand what I mean by that. They were mainly gardeners, chauffeurs, whatever.

AG: Would you, and I don't put words into your mouth, would you say that there, it was a community of 'them and us'.

AF: Oh before the war yes, very much so; not after the war.

AG: Did Dawson's and Warren's [shops] have a different clientele?

AF: Oh yes. At one time it used to be 'them' went to Rupert Warren's, and 'us' had working class, because Rupert Warren's as well had another shop besides that one you know – he had Wood's shop, corner of Brown Street, which was Fraser Lee's. And he used to send his seconds into that, his old stock into that. Anyway we [our shop] came in between, at the same prices as the 'us' shop and snatched the trade.

AG: Why do you feel such a strong division?

AF: I don't now.

AG: Ah, but you did.

AF: I did yes, because we were brought up like that.

AG: How did it show itself?

AF: By being ignored by them. We literally were – they literally walked – they walked all over us. I'm sorry but it really was 'them and us', and they were a different period: they were Victorian in their attitude. And they made you feel nothing. There were 'them up top of the hill', there was the shopkeepers and there was the working people.

AG: And how did the shopkeepers react to the working people?

AF: They were a class above them. They just made themselves known that they were shopkeepers.

AG: Were they deferential towards the people on the Hill?

AF: Oh yes they were very servile, very. It was yes sir, no sir, three bags full sir. It was business!

John Ecclestone: Now Rupert Warren's two shops, they were selling the same sort of goods at different prices?

AF: Oh yes! One lot was the gentry from up the Hill; they'd got the stuff which the gentry wanted. They would ring up and say can you send me an order blah, blah, blah, and all the second and old stuff went into the other shop for the working class.

JE: But it was the same sort of....

AF: Oh yes, similar exactly.

JE: But depending on who I was, I would know which of Rupert Warren's shops I was to go to?

AF: Oh yes.

JE: That was quite clear.

AF: Oh yes, yes, yes. If you'd got the accent and the money you went to the shop at the end of the village.

Mr Fitchett and others were angry and resentful about the way some people treated others. This may make us feel uncomfortable today but if we are to present our findings honestly we must do so 'warts an' all'.

Mr John Hamnett also recognised that not everyone was equal – but he sees a lighter side.

Mr John Hamnett talking to Alan Garner and John Ecclestone

Alan Garner: Did you grow up with a feeling that there was a 'them and us'?

Mr John Hamnett: Oh definitely.

John Ecclestone: But where was the geographical divide that Alan is talking about. 'Them' who lived … and 'us' who lived….

JH: I see. Well I don't know. There was like three classes. There was an upper class that talked with like a plum in their mouth didn't they; I always pictured them like Margaret Thatcher – when I saw Margaret Thatcher I always thought that was typical of the ladies who lived up on Alderley Edge, you see. Then of course there was the middle class like this Mr Hitchen, who lived in the big houses down Heyes Lane; my father used to call them 'First Class Thirds' those sorts of people. We used to laugh and say they had their brief cases full of jam butties, jam sandwiches!

AG: My father used to say that they had their brief cases with their overalls in!

JH: Did he? Yes, well I think there was a bit of jealousy there!

It seems to me that 'them and us' is far too simple an approach to the class structure in Alderley Edge in the 1920s and 1930s. It was far more complicated than that. As I think is the answer to the question 'Why did the lifestyle of the people who lived on the Hill end?' I've been told many times that it was the two World Wars which put an end to domestic servants, but it was Mr Noel Swinfin, formerly a bank manager in Alderley Edge, and his son Mr Stephen Swinfin, secretary of the Edge Association, who opened my eyes to the wider issues.

Of course, they said, these big houses could not operate without servants but while domestic service was certainly one of the key job market areas in the nineteenth and early part of the twentieth century, the wars and changes in industry were also producing new job opportunities and labour-saving devices. In the 1950s there were very heavy levels of taxation, which restricted the ability to pay for servants. The cotton industry was declining and the population of the Edge was increasing as the big houses were replaced by smaller ones, whose new owners drove their own cars and cut their own lawns. But there was also the knock on the door.

Noel and Stephen Swinfin talking to John Ecclestone

John Ecclestone: Let me ask Noel, if I may. When these properties were being sold, while you were the bank manager, was it because the owners were facing financial difficulties, or was it because builders were coming along with offers that they couldn't refuse?

Noel Swinfin: I think it was because builders were coming – it was just at a time when land values were rising and builders were coming along with offers that they couldn't really refuse, bearing in mind the circumstances in which they found themselves at the time.

JE: With big houses, with no servants and with somebody knocking on the door and saying 'I will give you this for you house'?

NS: It's an obvious....

Stephen Swinfin: I think also there were some cases of older people, in some cases widows, were left with large properties, and perhaps their income derived from fixed-interest stocks, was beginning to suffer in a time of increasing inflation.

NS: Yes, it was the inflation....

SS: In the '30s government stocks provided a secure income. In the '50s and '60s it was the very worst possible thing to have, and I'm sure that some older people ran into this trap of steadily rising costs, and effectively reducing incomes, remembering that by the time that one had got into the late '50s a number of these properties were 100 years old and suddenly all sorts of repairs were coming due, especially roofs, this sort of thing, all sorts of repairs were coming due and there just wasn't, perhaps, the income to pay for them.

JE: And perhaps a feeling, on behalf of their children, that they just didn't want to live in that type of house?

SS: Yes.

NS: A recurring theme at this time I seem to remember was dry rot, you know, as Stephen said the properties were about, were 100 years old and dry rot was beginning to....

SS: But in some cases it was just the family dying out, effectively.

So was that the end of an era? Mr Noel Swinfin told me that he regarded Lady Chorley's book *Manchester Made Them* (1950) as a very accurate account of social life as it was still being lived in Alderley Edge and I hope it is not a presumption if I say that, in a way, I see Miss Pilkington's lecture in 1972 not only as an epilogue to Lady Chorley's book, but also as an acceptance, a cheerful acceptance I think in Miss Pilkington's case, that an era had indeed come to an end. 'How things have changed', she said, without, I think, any bitterness or regret. Just think, at the beginning of her life she was swept up and away from a lady cyclist wearing bloomers by one of her family's five live-in servants. Towards the end of her life her family presented the Edge to the National Trust for the benefit of all people (that story is set out in Chapter 29).

So back to the Edge itself. A quotation and witness reports help us to explore a question that is often asked – 'Is there anything up there?' By that we mean is there anything sinister, supernatural, benevolent or magical.

The first quotation is from Alan Garner's book *The Voice That Thunders* (1997: 4):

> The Edge is a beauty spot in summer and at weekends, but its long history and prehistory make it unsafe at all times. It is physically and emotionally dangerous. No one born to the Edge questions that, and we show it proper respect.

The first witness is James Vanden, a young man who frequently visited the Edge with his friends to 'mess about', as he put it. He told Dr George Bankes about a time when he and his mates got very frightened indeed. The party had split up when they heard the one left behind shouting in a way that made the others think he was scared about something.

Mr James Vanden talking to Dr George Bankes

Mr James Vanden: As we were running back we could still hear him shouting and the Edge, it looked as if it had actually physically shifted, although it hadn't but there was something different about it: it looked almost menacing in a way, and we ran up the hill and we got all the way up to Saddlebole, we ran all that way up and he was at the top, he was like that. We got to the top, he said, 'there's something watching me', he said, 'I don't know what it is, I was just stood there but there's something watching me'. And we noticed all the crows had started gathering in the trees above us, so I was like 'I don't know what it is, don't worry about it, we'll get the tin of beans open' and we sat there, but you could feel it. It was as if there was something. It was like a knife in your back. It was definitely something. It was as if it was looking through your soul in a way, it was strange, and we were sat there and we were getting the feeling that there was something behind us, at the side of us, and in the shadows you could just catch out of the corner of your eye slight movements within the shadows; you know, you get these shadows of the rocks, but within the shadows themselves there was like a deeper shadow, just a slight movement. You could just catch it out of the corner of your eye or behind the trees, and these crows had gathered in the tree above us by now and we were thinking it's getting a bit dodgy, this, and it was windy on the far side, the wind started blowing up and it was getting into twilight and we thought, we'll open this tin of beans and we'll eat them, 'cos you can eat them cold, obviously, and we were sat there thinking there's something going on here, don't like this, and we still got this feeling that there was something watching us, but it seemed to be getting closer and there was like a buzzing in the air then. It was like if you can imagine, like I said before, thousands of mosquitoes or something, and it was like a pressure was building up, and all of sudden fear took over and we said, right, we're getting out of here, we don't like this. We got over the top of Saddlebole, started running down the far side. We jumped over the fence in the middle and we got to the fence at the bottom where the rabbit warren is. As we were climbing over it, Chris said, he was panicking, 'Look at that behind us, there's something on the field'. There was me and him; we turned around. We looked at the field, and you could see the wood, the fence-line of where the woods were, you could see shadows moving along the inside of the fence and we were like, we'd seen these shadows when we were up at the top on Saddlebole. It started to get a bit weird then; we thought goblins or something after us and then they actually started coming out of the fence and coming into the field, by which time it was time to turn and run. And they must have got halfway across that field but we knew there was something odd about it because there was no sun in the sky. It was twilight. It was overcast, and I've got a photo of the day of when it was, and you can see on the photo that it's a completely overcast sky that night and it was, fear got into us and until we actually left Mottram Road and got out of the way. In fact we ran all the way to the train station and we stopped when we got to the train station – it was only then that we felt all right – but it was fear. There was a coldness that went with it as well, like something you get when you're a child and you get the old 'scared of the dark' syndrome. It was like that. But it was as if it was looking into you; there was definitely something there that I don't know, whether it wanted us to be there or didn't. I don't know whether it was menacing or not but at the time I thought, I'm not hanging around! Definitely got out of the way!

Nevertheless, despite that experience James Vanden also made it clear to us that for those who 'believe in the Edge', as he put it, it is benevolent and that if he had a problem, such as a career move, he would consult the Edge in the same way that another person might offer a prayer in a church.

One of James Vanden's mates was James Scott, also in his twenties. He told us 'The amazing and intriguing thing about the Edge is its atmosphere changes all the time. And it changes at the click of a finger and it's almost literally as if somebody turns a switch and the whole place switches off. The Edge does change rapidly and there's definitely some kind of presence there, or this is what people feel, there is some kind of presence at the Edge. Just what it is I don't as yet know'.

The Edge can also affect people over long distances. Two ladies who no longer lived there missed it terribly. Mrs Jean Harrison (née Street) now lived in Carlisle.

Mrs Jean Harrison talking to Alan Garner and John Ecclestone

Alan Garner: Now you have not lived in Alderley since 1960, is that so? Why do you keep coming back?

Mrs Jean Harrison: I have to come back to my tribal lands to cuddle trees!

AG: How often?

JH: Twice a year, hopefully.

AG: Why do you have to cuddle a tree?

JH: I don't know.

AG: What effect does it have on you?

JH: I've done it since I was a very small child – I don't know why I do it – it makes me feel good.

AG: Any tree, anywhere?

JH: No, one of the particular trees, one of the beech trees and my own little particular tree, or big particular tree, is tree number 135.

AG: Now I don't want to put words into your mouth but do you feel, you used the word tribal, do you feel that there is an affinity between you and the Edge?

JH: Yes.

AG: Would you say that the Edge has something that most other places don't?

JH: I always thought it had for me, but I think, and I always have thought, that it's a very special place that people didn't know about and I wondered if we were all too clever in keeping it quiet, but now it should be recognised.

AG: Go on.

JH: Well that's just it! It just has something. It's like a kind of mother; there is something about the Edge which gives some of us what we need. But I don't know what.

AG: Have you ever been frightened there?

JH: No.

John Ecclestone: And have you ever had that experience anywhere else?

JH: No.

AG: Now I am putting words, not in your mouth but in front of you: would you say that the people who claim to have had mystical experiences on the Edge have been trying so hard that they've missed it?

JH: I think that if you go up there and you are an innocent as children are, and you feel something, that's got to be true. But I think that it's got a mystery that people tap into and they want to become part of, and for them it's something, maybe, that they are willing too much for themselves. I have never felt that I would be hurt by the Edge. I feel warm with the Edge. I feel that the Edge gives something to me and I owe a lot to the Edge.

AG: Do you feel that you carry the Edge within you?

JH: Yes.

AG: Can you, when you need it, tap into it even when you are not there?

JH: Yes.

AG: Roy Pearson's sister, Jean, who is a GI bride, has exactly the same experience. She has to come all the way from Ohio every year and has done since the end of the war.

JH: It's like walking back onto the Edge and saying 'I'm here, I'm back!' It's like recharging your batteries so that you can go away and do all the other things in life, the exciting, mundane, whatever you have to do. I'm not making this up – this is….

AG: Well I know that….

JH: I know, but there are fanciful people out there, and I am capable of being fanciful but this has got to be truth, and this is the truth, this is what I wouldn't really talk to 99 per cent of the population about because they would ridicule me. But I can talk to you two because we're talking about the one thing that binds us, which is the Edge.

The other lady was 'GI bride' Mrs Parker (née Jean Pearson), who, as Alan said, now lived in Dayton, Ohio. She came back every year on what her friends called her 'pilgrimage'. She thought there is something magical about the Edge, the whole aura of the place. There seems to be a certain presence, she told us. (That word again, you notice.) Alan Garner asked her too, 'Can you carry the Edge within you when you are not there?' 'Oh absolutely', she said, 'it's always there. There's not a day goes by when I don't think about it'.

Just how and why some people are influenced by the Edge in a variety of ways is a mystery – and perhaps it always will be. And perhaps that's how it should be.

A different sort of mystery surrounds a death which occurred in John Evans's cabin in Church Quarry in the early 1930s, which has already been touched on in the previous chapter. John Evans was known as the Hermit. I've been told that he acted as a sort of warden on the Edge, keeping the woods tidy, building little bridges and steps; that he organised search parties when people got lost in the mines and took parties down himself, when he used magnesium flares to show up the mineralisation in the rocks.

Much has been written, and indeed was written at the time, about John Evans but I had the chance to talk to someone who, as a boy of ten to twelve years old, spent many hours with Evans on the Edge. He and his school friend often stayed in the cabin overnight.

Mr Peter Kitching talking to John Ecclestone

Mr Peter Kitching: Well, it was just like what I call a Swiss log cabin, all logs, built in Swiss style. And he'd got it so good inside, a big, I don't know whether he made it himself, stone fireplace, made with these round stones and bits of granite or whatever it was, quite big that, and he had all his climbing ropes hung round on pegs. He had climbs all round the Edge, and some of them were wonderful really, you were like a fly hung on a ceiling on some of them; he had to have the ropes on for those. He used to try them himself; he used to go to Switzerland a lot.

No, it…. You see it was just an adventure for us really. And all the birds and everything, they all seemed to accept him. I mean they'd come in his window, and eat off the table inside at breakfast and things like that. Blackbirds as far as I remember, and thrushes and things, and he used to have names for a lot of them. Ah he's, grand chap, but I think in the end, they used to call him 'the Hermit', the locals, and he must have appeared like a hermit to them, and he used to, when we stayed there for weekends he used to always used to go down into the village on a Saturday night, and used to come back quite tiddly! Yes, we'd be or pretending to be asleep, you know; he was happy any road, put it that way! That was on a Saturday night, it was always late so we were, been in bed a long time, but … and we, somehow or other, stopped going for a year or so, because of other activities, and we'd been, really were going there fairly steady for at least two or three years, and then we drifted away, then the next thing all this blew up about his problem of somebody dying in his cabin, and I never got the full story of it. Somebody said that, or it was in the press, I don't know, that the person who'd died had died of cyanide poisoning, and all we know about that: he used to have some cyanide in the cabin and he used to mix bread pellets in with the cyanide, and this was when the odd rat or mice got too nosey and started to come round, and he used to get rid of them that way. Soon got rid of them.

John Ecclestone: So he would put pellets with cyanide down inside the cabin?

PK: Yes.

JE: Yes. Not outside?

PK: No.

JE: No.

PK: Not outside. Well, wherever he thought. I don't know, he might have put some outside as well. Doubt whether he would outside because, other birds and animals…

JE: That's right, that's why I asked.

PK: … would have eaten it you see? So I think they were always inside. Because he was a nature lover, apart from when the rats became a nuisance! But they all, 'cause, like all little villages, as Alderley Edge was then, they all thought the worst, they all thought he was homosexual I think.

JE: Hmm.

PK: Er, that he'd been involved in the death.

JE: Now, you mentioned homosexuality. I take it from what you say that nothing improper ever occurred when you and your friend were there?

PK: He never laid a finger on, or any suggestion at all, never, and we went there for two or three years, and slept there. Never any suggestion of it.

Powerful testimony from just one of several people who met or knew John Evans. A fuller account of his life is given in Appendix 21.1.

The Second World War affected everyone in the village and is a good example of the way in which the evidence from different people overlaps to build up a composite picture of an event.

On Hocker Lane in December 1940 three people were killed at Acton Farm.

Mr Brian Hobson talking to Matthew Hyde and John Ecclestone

Mr Brian Hobson: 'Oh yes, it's still there, Acton Farm. It's been rebuilt. It's now a private house I think. But that was in 1940, December 1940 when the Manchester blitz was on. My father was an air-raid warden at the time, him and another chap, and I can remember it as clear as a bell: he came in that night, walked back in the house, he says there's something going to happen, he says there's something going on outside, and what it obviously was, was a plane that was damaged was circling or doing something and he let drive, and Acton Farm took a direct hit on the back doorstep. And there was five bombs right the way round it, but it picked the house up, virtually picked the house up, turned it upside down and put it back in the crater again. The roof was in the bottom of the hole when they came. But father and mother, they were sat by either side of the fire, by the side of the fireplace and they were both killed. The beam in the house dropped and killed them; it dropped across the table, under which the two sons were sheltering and they were okay. The two girls, Mary and Doris, they were in the pantry doing some baking or something or other when this happened, and the pantry saved them. Doris got crushed with the stone slab out of the pantry; she got a broken pelvis and legs and bad injuries, but she's, they were in that and that was a bad do. I remember that well; all our lights went out as that exploded I'll tell you. It was just up Hocker Lane.

In 1940 John Beswick was born at the Wizard. He has given the National Trust some important information about that building. But he has also very kindly made available to us some of his mother's papers, a diary, which, of course, takes us back one more generation. He has kindly agreed to let us quote from a wartime entry.

From the diary of Mrs May Beswick

The Manchester blitz was an unforgettable experience. On the day after, a Mr Holbury, a funeral director of Upper Brook Street, Manchester, came to ask if he could bring his cars and hearses onto the swing field, as he dare not leave them in Manchester, as he had so many funerals due to the blitz. He arrived with the cars, filled with almost demented people and babies and children, even in the hearses. We had over forty people and the smallest children slept in a row on the kitchen table, as the kitchen was warm, as we had a good fire with wood we had collected in the woods. Luckily, we could get milk from the farmers, so lots of cups of tea were made and drunk that night. The people were covered in rubble and dirt, and some had lost everything, but they laughed and made the best of things. Some went off the next day, and others stayed for a few days. On the second night, at about eight p.m., a bomb was dropped over Birtles and it struck a farmhouse and killed three people and a dog. The clock in the kitchen at the Wizard almost fell off the mantlepiece. It was an awful experience. We had two elderly ladies, whose home had been demolished, and one was an invalid, due to a weak heart. They stayed for a while, and then Mrs Ramage, of Bradford Lodge, offered to have them, until Mr Holbury found them a bungalow in Prestatyn.

To many in Alderley Edge the war must have seemed like one invasion after another. Three waves of evacuees, the Americans and the British army, which, I think, was here first.

Mr John Hamnett talking to Alan Garner and John Ecclestone

Mr John Hamnett: Now round the Circuit there was the Royal Army Service Corps with wagons, and they were all parked round the Circuit. Now we used to let the tyres down! And one day there was this soldier, I remember him as plain as anything, Bill his name, dark curly-haired chap, and he was in the back of the wagon and we didn't know, and he heard this 'hiss' and he leapt out and chased us!

And we used to pinch the 'jerry-cans' and build pontoon bridges across that brook, you know, down at the bottom.

And then the Yanks came. Well there was this Yankee sentry – he had his rifle against that wall and he was leaning on his hands on the other wall and we saw this officer come and so we thought 'oh he's going to get a right rocketing this chap'. And the officer just went 'Hi, Mac', 'Hi' – and he never got his backside off the wall this bloke! And from that day on I don't think we had any respect for the Yanks. Because when it snowed we used to snowball them and in the summer, on that big lawn on Annis Road, they used to have an instructor with an easel, and perhaps a machine-gun or something, and he'd have them all sat cross-legged on the lawn and we'd be wanging acorns at them, you know! And he'd detail a sergeant or something to clear us off and we'd all go running off down those fields.

But they were very generous, giving us sweets and gum.

Alan Garner: They were totally generous with comics, sweets….

JH: They used to sing all these dirty songs didn't they! They used to go to Horseshoe Lane for their dinner I think, for their meals; they used to have all these 'billy cans', they'd all be drumming and singing these dirty songs wouldn't they. They used to give kids condoms! Blow them up. They didn't know what they were did they – take them to school blowing them up!

But do you remember the parades they used to have. What would they be for?

AG: For everything. Dig for Victory, Save Russia.

JH: And do you remember the Wellington Bomber?

AG: The Wellington Bomber outside the station. I flew that miles!

JH: And that big bomb tied to the railway post. There was a LNWR sign on a post – the old LNWR [London and North-Western Railway]. And you had to buy a savings stamp and stick it on the bomb didn't you, to walk through the Wellington. It was supposed to have been over Berlin a dozen times!

AG: And the big poster outside the council houses with a bell – you moved the clapper every day.

JH: That's right. We used to knit, didn't we, squares for soldiers' blankets and we used to design posters and there would be a prize in the local paper for the child who designed the best 'Save for the War' effort and all these things, didn't we.

AG: And there is one thing which I think everybody I've spoken to will agree that if they have to say 'what is your memory of the war' they will always say 'the taste of a balaclava!'

JH: That's right!

AG: Because it got to the point where you had to keep sucking more and more of it to stop your lips from getting sore.

JH: That's right! It would be all dew on a frosty morning wouldn't it! I remember a lad said 'What's that you've got on? It looks like an unstitched football!' I always remember that. He was one of the bigger boys you know.

John Hamnett and Alan Garner re-living their misspent youth! Coming back to the Americans, I remember Alan Garner's mother, the late Mrs Marjorie Garner, telling me that one of her memories of the war was the 'swish, swish, swish' of the Americans as they came up behind you. They didn't have boots like our soldiers – they had crepe soles that went 'swish, swish, swish' when they walked.

Doug Poyner, as you might expect of our poacher extraordinary, did rather well out of the Americans.

Mr Doug Poyner talking to John Ecclestone

Mr Doug Poyner: We used to smoke in them days, I know we shouldn't have done, and going home from school and there was some big houses near there and they were full of Americans, American servicemen, you see, and I was going home from school one day and this Yank says 'Hey, son, can you take my pants home and get them pressed? I'll give you a carton of cigarettes.' Well my Dad smoked like a factory, so I took them back, a 250 carton, in twenty-packs of Camel and Lucky Strike and all that. Of course I was doing a shuttle service, and my dad was smoking like mad!

John Ecclestone: Where were those Americans based? Where was the base they were working from? Was it Ringway or....

DP: I can't think now. They were in those big houses round Horseshoe Lane. I think they were there just waiting to go abroad, just waiting to be shipped out. Because I got very friendly with two of them. I don't know what were their proper names. One was called Inko and one was called Dor, and they took my address to write to and they were shipped out abroad and I got a letter one day, I don't know how he got my address, the colonel, but they had both got killed on the landing. And one of them left me his ring. Actually, I give it to my nephew; he'll still have that.

They were quite good chaps really. They weren't very well liked in some respect because they pulled all the girls! Our lads in the forces were on twenty-one shillings a week. Now, a Yankee private was on eleven pounds, apart from what they were sent from home! And in the dance hall they would light a cigarette up take one puff and drop it – and we'd grab it! Its sounds stupid now but....

JE: And they had the nylons too, didn't they?

DP: Oh yeah. They were good old days really. You had a lot of fun. You had to make your own entertainment. You didn't have much money but at least you enjoyed yourself.

Cigarettes and nylons are all very well but many of us will remember that most foodstuffs were rationed during the war and we needed coupons for petrol. Mrs Margaret Shaak came back to live in Artists Lane after they'd been bombed out in Moss Side but her husband continued to work in Manchester. I asked her if the travelling was difficult for him during the war.

Mrs Margaret Shaak talking to John Ecclestone

Mrs Margaret Shaak: Not really, you see he had to get a bus to – oh no – they provided him with a car then, the garage did, yes.

John Ecclestone: Did he get petrol in coupons and things?

MS: Yes, we never went short of anything! Never went short of anything.

JE: Tell me.

MS: I don't know how! We always knew someone that had something.

JE: I mean the fact that you were living in a farm cottage, did that help?

MS: I don't think so, no. There was always someone that had something that we wanted and we had something. I always remember the district nurse; she was so glad of my clothing coupons because we couldn't afford a lot of clothes; even though they were rationed we couldn't afford a lot, so she was very glad of my clothing coupons and she didn't take sugar, and those kind of things, you know!

JE: And you had lots of friends who had chickens?

MS: Yes, eggs and everything, yes. I never remember – even my husband smoked and he never went short of cigarettes either.

JE: And he got his petrol through the garage?

MS: Yes, through the garage!

JE: Jolly good!

MS: So, I've nothing to regret I don't think, during my life: it's all been happy, which is a lot to say, isn't it?

JE: Not everyone can say that.

MS: I don't think they can. I think I've been very fortunate. I mean, I could say a lot of things that haven't gone right but I don't dwell on those; I refuse to dwell on them.

JE: During the war did you come into contact with any of the Americans that were billeted here?

MS: No, but a lot of the young ones. I was married but my two sisters did!

JE: They were pleased to see the Americans?

MS: Oh yes, they were at Wilmslow. The RAF camp on the Manchester Road there, there was hundreds of them there, and of course my two sisters used to go to Wilmslow you see and you know there was plenty of fun and games down there, oh they had, they did, they had a lovely time, because they could provide nylons and cigarettes.

JE: Only I've been talking to people about how long the Americans were here and I get the impression they weren't here very long, that they were waiting as it were to go to Normandy. Is that your memory of it?

MS: It is, and yet it's vague because I never was part of that. I had my son, I think I'd got my young son you see, and I didn't go, I didn't go on those kind of do's. They had a marvellous time during the war, my two sisters, you see, but I was married then, so I couldn't have a marvellous time!

JE: You had to behave yourself!

MS: They behaved themselves. I mean there was nothing funny about it; neither of them married an American so....

JE: Now the other thing people have told me about during the war were the evacuees.

MS: Oh yes, my dad had an evacuee, yes, from Manchester and that was awful. There was a lot of discontent about that because you see my dad and two girls were in a two-bedroom cottage. They had to have an evacuee and yet a lot of the big houses never had them so there was a lot of, you know, people didn't like a lot of that. How they got out of it I don't know. I'm sure, you know, I'm not sure how it was arranged, but I mean I know that a lot of the big houses, because there are several in Nether Alderley you see. Bollington Grange, that's a very big house, they never had any, and they had three servants. Now that doesn't seem fair does it? That isn't fair.

Miss Turner was a teacher at the village school during the war and it was she who told me about the three waves of evacuees.

Miss Hope Turner talking to John Ecclestone

Miss Hope Turner: The first lot of evacuees we had in 1939 immediately were from Manchester, and it was a complete Catholic school with teachers. Well they wouldn't integrate with a Church of England, and we couldn't find room for them, so what we did was the Alderley children occupied the school in the morning one week, and the Catholic school occupied it in the afternoon and then the next week it was the other way around, and when you weren't in school, we used the Church Institute or the Methodist schoolroom.

John Ecclestone: And how long did that go on for?

HT: Well, they filtered away, the Manchester ones and the Catholic school took a big empty house in the end and took the pupils to there.

And then we had the Guernsey evacuees, not very many of them and they had two teachers, and they just mixed in with us.

And then, right at the end, was it 1944, when the V2 rockets on London, we got a huge number from London, and they were the ones who – they'd no teachers with them, and they sort of bumped our classes up to sixty.

But we had some funny ones. Being ten they must have been born round about when the Princess Marina was married, and I remember having five Marinas amongst my class! Yes!

Finally in this selection of wartime memories is Mrs Jean Parker (née Pearson), the GI bride. She had an interesting reaction to my suggestion that, *pace* the tragedy in Hocker Lane, a number of people in Alderley Edge actually enjoyed the war. But she also surprised us with her reaction to the Americans.

Mrs Jean Parker talking to Alan Garner and John Ecclestone

Alan Garner: Regardless of the fact that you married an American soldier, what are your memories overall of the arrival and 'occupation' by the Yanks?

Mrs Jean Parker: I was absolutely appalled! I've discussed this with my husband and he agrees with me. Appalled at their behaviour. I'd never been out with a boy. I didn't like them and I met him for the first time at church, well it was a chapel I should say. From there I met him at June Ward's house. Her parents were very good to a few American soldiers. They'd go there and they would be like parents to them, and let them take a hot bath. My husband was based down at that Hall between Alderley and Wilmslow and he wasn't here very long and then he went to Europe and then he was in the end of the Battle of the Bulge.

I was absolutely appalled by a lot of the behaviour of them, and I was frightened of them to be honest with you. So it is really strange how I came to marry one.

John Ecclestone: How did this behaviour show itself then?

JP: Oh they were noisy and rambunctious, and they seemed to, they didn't seem to pick very nice girls, and I was a nice girl! So it was really strange how it all happened. And incidentally, if you are interested, our initials are up on Castle Rock – I know we shouldn't have done it but he did! It's not nice to do those things.

JE: And before the Americans arrived what was the impact of the war either on your lives or on the village, or both?

JP: I think it made quite a difference in our lives. My mother, she was very good to evacuees. We always had evacuees. I never knew when I came home from work who was going to be living at the house! She was very good that way.

JE: Do you have any recollection of being short of things, with rationing?

JP: Oh yes, I do. I've still got my ration book! Oh yes and that was another thing that was hard on the mothers. They had to go and line up every day for food for whatever they could get. But my mother was a wonderful cook and she was very resourceful: she could make a meal out of nothing – everyone said that. She was great.

JE: And when you say line up you mean….

JP: Queue up, yes, sorry I probably used the American word! Yes but she would go up to the village every day like they all had to and queue up for a long long time.

JE: Without actually saying it, a number of people have – hinted – that they really rather enjoyed the war. It was a different sort of life after 1940.

JP: I'll say this, that it was not a miserable part of my life. There was a friendliness, of everybody working to get something done; we knew what we had to do and I've never encountered that feeling since. Never.

JE: People were less selfish, weren't they?

JP: Less selfish – they weren't selfish at all. They just didn't think about things like that. People were kinder to one another and I think that's what we greatly miss now. People aren't kind to each other.

JE: And do I get the impression from something you said to Alan earlier that you meet with other wives in America now?

JP: Yes, we have a very nice club in Dayton, our meetings we hold once a month and really we are all getting older now. Some are in their eighties, and that really, I think it's all helped us with our home-sickness. Because we're nearly all home-sick to some degree or another. Maybe not as advanced as I am!

A homesick Jean Parker. Mrs Parker was one of the last interviewees we spoke to before the first phase of the Project was completed. There was so much more to do to put on record the story of Alderley Edge, and we were able to continue putting living people's memory onto tape for several years in the hope of creating what could become one of the best-documented villages in the land.

In the meantime, let the last words of this chapter, as the first, come from Alan Garner's lecture.

> Many people do not appreciate the value of what they know. Yet our lives are composed of stories: some valuable in themselves; others filling out the completeness of a larger story or supplying a missing detail that explains a conundrum. We each have unique knowledge of importance, and if that knowledge is not passed on and recorded in some way it will disappear with us and be irretrievable. There is an African proverb that says it all. 'When someone dies, a library burns.'

Author's note

Here there has been space to present only a small selection of the contents of the Project's Archive. The extracts in this chapter are those I used in the lecture I gave at St Hilary's School in November 1998. In that lecture I gave the following explanation for my choice, and the reason why the extracts had been re-edited:

> Before I go on let me say that it really has been a frightful job deciding what to include and what to leave out. I have deliberately excluded the interviews we have done with those who are also giving lectures in this series. I have also tried not to use the extracts you can hear when you go to the Museum exhibition. But in order to include the voices of as many people as possible, I have had to make selections, and re-edit the recordings. In the re-editing, just for tonight, I hope I have never distorted what anyone said, and I do assure you that the original recordings, which you approved, are untouched, and those are the ones that are preserved in the National Sound Archive.

For this chapter the extracts have been transcribed 'as spoken' at the time the recording was made. Only punctuation has been added.

Editor's note

In the time that it has taken to bring this book to publication, nature has taken its course and many of the people whose memories are described in this chapter are no longer with us, including, sadly, John Ecclestone himself, but I have not made any substantial changes to the text, which he completed in 1999. On the positive side, we are left with the realisation that we were very fortunate to have been making these recordings while there were still people alive who witnessed the great changes in Alderley and who remembered them for us. Since we started our Project, the history and memories of other villages in Britain have been studied in similar detail – one thinks for example of Michael Wood's television series *The Story of England*, which focused on Kibworth in Leicestershire (Wood, 2010).

Readers will have noticed that this chapter does not have any illustrations: we asked the interviewees if they would like photographs of themselves included, but they all preferred to be remembered by their words alone. The delay has also enabled us to add two appendices to this chapter, one filling out the unhappy story of John Evans, 'the Hermit of the Edge', the other inspired by the discovery of a recording of an Alderley man in the remarkable Berlin Sound Archive.

Those who wish to listen to the actual interviews will find them most readily in the British Library Sound Archive Catalogue (search for 'Alderley Edge' at cadensa.bl.uk).

Further reading

Chorley, K. 1940. *Manchester Made Them*. London: Faber and Faber (republished Hale: Silk Press, 2001).

Garner, A. 1997. *The Voice That Thunders*. London: Harvill (most recent reprint 2010).

Wood, M. 2010. *The Story of England*. London: Viking Penguin.

22

The graffiti on stone and wood

Carolanne King, Clare Pye, Nigel Dibben, Simon Timberlake and Alan Garner

Graffiti at ground level: quarries, mine entrances and rock faces

Carolanne King with Clare Pye

The rock of Alderley Edge is exposed in three ways: the original face of the escarpment, made by the geological fault along the north-west ridge; the water-eroded valleys of Waterfall Wood and Brynlow Dell, dating from the end of the Ice Age; and man-made rock faces caused by mining and quarrying since prehistoric times. The Alderley Edge sandstone invites people to cut into it, whether to extract the stone by quarrying or to inscribe graffiti.

All these quarries, mines and rock faces have been very tempting for people (men's names are more common than women's) to leave their mark in the form of graffiti. There is an irony here: the softer rocks are easier to inscribe but the more public and visible sites are also more vulnerable to erosion. In sheltered damp parts of the Edge many carvings will be covered and obscured by moss in a remarkably short time. Trees bear graffiti permanently, although the expansion of the bark blurs the work over the years, but carvings on soft stone can be rubbed out and destroyed. This is perhaps contrary to what we might expect, as wood is generally thought to be a less permanent material than stone.

Most of the surviving graffiti, where they can be dated, seem to come from the 1940s and later; whether this reflects the erosion suffered by older markings, or the accessibility of the whole Edge area once the National Trust opened it up, it is difficult to say. Earlier graffiti do survive but in sheltered, less visited places and on inaccessible parts of the rock face. The earliest date, 1666, is in Waterfall Wood; nearby is the record of a late eighteenth-century tryst, a heart containing the initials AWG, both of them in lettering that is characteristic for the time. Three other probable eighteenth-century carvings, found in Over Alderley and Church Quarries, which may have direct links with the quarrying activities there, have already been described in Chapter 18 (pp. 450, 453, and Figures 18.9, 18.13). However, the earliest stone carving is probably much older: on Saddlebole there is a parish merestone marking the point where Nether Alderley and Over Alderley meet Chorley which is inscribed with a cross to denote its significance. This could be as old as the mid-sixteenth century, when the parish boundaries were marked out (CALS DLT A75/5). It is untypical of the carvings on the Edge as it is cut into the hard conglomerate and is an official marker rather than a graffito in the pejorative sense (see also Chapter 27).

Graffiti are often clustered in particular places. This grouping is interesting, but it is difficult to say whether it is no more than the syndrome of the dog and the well visited lamp-post, a response to the malleability of particular beds of sandstone, or reflects the perceived mythic importance of the site. There is a greater tendency to inscribe names and/or initials than everything else. Many of the initials and names are records of trysts, including some modern same-sex ones. Dates beside the initials are rarer, as if, having registered their personal presence in a permanent manner, people see less need to record the date. They were there on the day and marked the place as their own; the time was less relevant. Nevertheless, some names belong to particular eras; the changing fashions in first names means it may be assumed that ALF immortalised himself some years before WAYNE. Affiliations are also uncommon; however, the Edge has not escaped the ubiquitous MUFC, carved in Brynlow Dell fairly recently. Pictograms, too, are relatively rare and tend to be found in particular areas or sites.

As with the tree graffiti, the inscriptions come in waves, and are to be found in particular places. The area of the Wizard's Well and Castle Rock is especially rich in nineteenth-century graffiti, for this was on the public path through the de Trafford woods up onto the Edge. Above the well is carved a head and the poem

DRINK OF
THIS AND
TAKE THY
FILL FOR THE
WATER FALLS
BY THE
WIZHARDS
WILL

The spelling of 'Wizhard' is unusual and attempts to find an authentic source for it have proved fruitless. The Wizard's Well has the longest inscription on the Edge (Figure 2.7, p. 34).

The accessible soft sandstone at Castle Rock is covered with graffiti; to survive, inscriptions have to be high up and away from the path. At Castle Rock, the earliest date, 1916, is well out of the way; down by the path, where the stone is easier to carve, the earliest clear date is 1986 and later generations have obscured any earlier work. Between Castle Rock and the Wizard's Well is a moss-covered 1868 beside an anchor; this could have been a sailor home on leave. Nearby is a HOBSON, perhaps one of the Hobsons of Nether Alderley, and at least one Victorian child took the trouble to inscribe his name in copper-plate script which, with the curves of the letters, demands skill and patience. Wartime encouraged people to leave their mark; at a time when everything could change so quickly and perhaps tragically, there must have been an even greater urge to record something permanent. This was not confined to the local inhabitants. In Waterfall Wood there is a MITCH dated 1943, almost certainly an American serviceman billeted in the area. There were many Americans stationed in Alderley Edge and there was at least one GI bride (see Chapter 21, p. 562), so we could expect the GIs to record their presence on the Edge as they walked their dates through the woods, perhaps just before they left for good. Such graffiti are also found carved into the trees of the Edge and they are discussed in the third section of this chapter ('The distribution of tree graffiti').

Pillar Mine attracted attention from visitors as soon as they were able to go there; as at Castle Rock, the soft sandstone is particularly tempting. One neat group of six pairs of initials is dated 1922; this has survived so long because it is carved in one of the vertical faces of harder rock. One would like to know who AB, MH, AO, MY, NH and MC were and why they decided to record their friendship on the rock at this time. Pillar Mine became a popular area towards the end of the twentieth century, a favourite spot to indulge in various 'new age' rituals, sleep out illicitly and see the dawn come up, when people have the time really to make their mark, but it had to be fenced off when some of these visitors set a large tyre alight in the mine, killed all the bats and made the roof unsafe. The soft sandstone here means there is an abundance of initials, names and miniature relief carvings, much of it superimposed on earlier work. As a result even deeply inscribed work is often ephemeral; a well cut horned devil's face recorded by the Landscape Project in May 1998 had been erased eighteen months later. Pillar Mine is a favourite area for heads of all types. Most are faces roughly cut on angled rocks and are probably twentieth century in date; they include the classic three-hole death's head and a 'smiley face'. Other pictograms include pentangles in circles, the odd political emblem and a deeply carved clenched fist.

The graffiti continue down into the mine, becoming sparser with the increasing darkness, although there is a collection of heads carved at the far end.

Carved stone heads are associated with Celtic and other myths; they are the subject of much speculation, and their use has been adopted by various 'new age' groups who invest their own meaning into them. The heads are often quite modern, but, especially in the upland areas of northern England, they are traditionally associated with Celtic shrines such as water sources, and Manchester Museum has been involved in long-term research into the heads carved in stone in the north-west. In Celtic belief, heads held the essence or soul of both the person and god and were thus appropriate guardians of holy or significant places. As in other parts of northern England, they can be found by the wells on the Edge, but there is also a tendency to carve heads at the entrances to caves and mines, seemingly to look after the boundary between light and dark, the earth above ground and the underworld below.

Since many of these heads are relatively modern, their placing on the Edge can be difficult to interpret. Some scholars such as Ronald Hutton, while accepting the survival of vernacular superstition and tradition, doubt whether there was any genuine continuity of pagan religion from Celtic times to today, and say that many 'traditional Celtic' ideas and ritual, Wicca and the like, are constructs that go back no further than the start of the twentieth century (e.g. Hutton, 2001). Modern archaeologists and anthropologists also play their part: by investigating and describing what people once thought, they may encourage a revival of those beliefs. However, this does not mean that people today may not genuinely believe in these ideas and their actions are accordingly honest; they have left signs on the Edge of rituals associated with such beliefs but, overall, they respect the environment and their actions are benign.

Even without believing in paganism as such, people may feel that in an area associated with a legend that may be very old indeed it is right that illustrative material should be in keeping with the perceived character of the place, and so they incorporate what they think are appropriate symbols and motifs within the landscape. In such cases, carving and placing these heads is more of an educated and self-conscious reaction than a religious response. It is in this context that one might see the Stanleys' landscaping of the Edge, given the publicity which they were ready to give to the Legend and their probable embellishment of it with Arthurian overtones. One notable exception to the mysterious origin of the faces is the one carved on a gatepost near the Old Quarry which bears a marked similarity to Mussolini and a suitable caption below (Figure 22.1; the post is no. 26 in the discussion of the stones of Alderley by Jeremy Milln and John Adams, Chapter 27). This, we are reliably told, was carved during the Second World War.

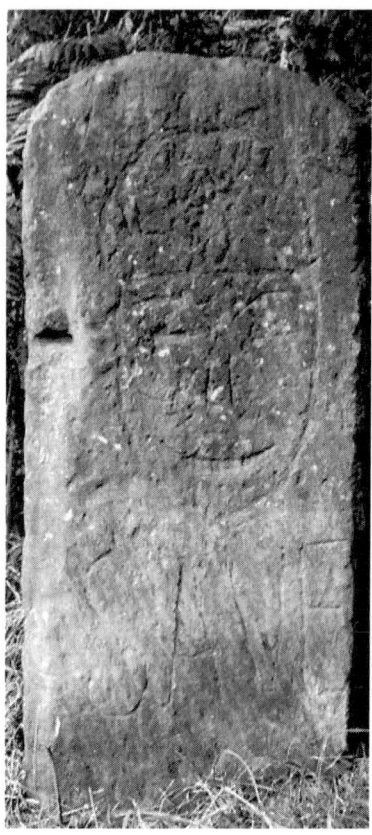

Figure 22.1. Carving said to be the likeness of Mussolini, the Italian dictator of the 1930s and '40s, with the word 'SAVE' beneath.

Photograph AELP.

The nearness of Lindow Moss, where the remains of bodies preserved in the peat-bog were found in the 1980s, meant that the Landscape Project paid special attention to the heads on the Edge and to any rituals which they may reflect. Most of the existing heads have been carved in the last 200 years, but the vegetation and the softness of the stone mean that it takes the eye of faith to see an ancient head in the lumps and bumps of moss-covered rock beside the wells on the Edge. Nevertheless, there are some interesting faces, many of them near the Wizard's Well – a rather jolly bewigged eighteenth-century gentleman's head, a suitably hoary face above the well itself (Figure 2.7) and a face carved on the corner of a rock between the well and Castle Rock. All of these seem to be part of the romanticisation of the Edge in the eighteenth and nineteenth centuries, and were probably carved under the auspices of the Stanleys and de Traffords. Alan Garner's family tradition (described in Chapter 2) includes his mason great-great-grandfather as one of the carvers. However, the more recent heads, especially those at the mine entrances, seem to be part of modern 'new age' traditions developed since the Second World War, and are examples of how old themes are part of a continuously developing story.

The Holy Well and de Trafford's Well have few visible carvings round the well areas themselves, although they are often decorated with flower offerings and other temporary additions at key times of the year. The abundant moss round the water sources will obscure any carvings very quickly anyway. Above the wells it is different: the rocks are covered with graffiti, initials mostly, although there is a 'Tom' carefully inscribed and a couple of pentagrams.

There are other pictograms on the Edge, all undated. They include a horse's head by the entrance to the rock shelter on Saddlebole, which could be a reference to the white mare in the Legend of the Edge (for some, this spot might be where the Iron Gates of the legend are). A phallus is erect on a rock at the north-west end of Waterfall Wood and drooping in Brynlow Dell. Stormy Point has a selection, including a flower/sun motif, a radioactive warning pictogram and some 'runes'. Attempts to decipher these runes have failed and they appear to be somebody's private version of the alphabet. Pentagrams in circles are common by Pillar Mine and there are some political symbols on the Edge, including CND, Anarchists and an occasional swastika; most of these are inside the caves and mines.

Just as the beech trees in Artists Lane have attracted graffiti, so has the adjacent Brynlow Dell. There seems to be a concentration in the 1950s and 1960s; in 1957, David Christian Ellis decided to inscribe his complete name in Straight Mine, but there are few modern graffiti here as this now seems to be a less well visited part of the Edge despite its closeness to the road.

If one was to date the shifting popularity of various areas of the Edge from the evidence of the graffiti one would probably come to the conclusion that certain areas, such as Castle Rock, have always been popular. Visitors in the nineteenth century appear to have been more common in the accessible areas on the de Trafford side of the Edge, and visitors today with unfettered access to almost all of the Edge can be found everywhere but often choose a favourite spot to make their mark, such as Pillar Mine.

The 'Druids' Circle' or 'Druid Stones', despite their known nineteenth-century origin, also attract modern 'new age' visitors and their graffiti. Some of the inscriptions here are very recent, including an M+L 99, seen in the September of that year. A few of the stones have been 'de-paganised' with crosses, but most of the graffiti at the Druids' Circle are ephemeral, done in chalk or charcoal. This use of temporary marking can be seen elsewhere on the Edge; a chalk mark or scratch on the surface will soon disappear. Painted graffiti are uncommon: perhaps people are environmentally aware, or they may think a stone place warrants carving rather than daubing, or perhaps they are just reluctant to lug around leaky pots or aerosols; the result, thankfully, is a notable absence of paint, although sadly we noted at least one carved graffito which had been defaced with a red-painted scrawl.

As with the tree graffiti, there seems to have been a falling off in rock graffiti from the 1980s on. One reason may be that people no longer regularly carry knives, so they lack a handy cutting tool to make a deep long-lasting mark. They may well write on the rock in some way, but their efforts disappear in a short time. Anybody visiting the Edge can see many of these short-term scratches and inscriptions, so there is probably little or no falling off in the well established habit of making a mark in a place significant to the person concerned, but now it is less likely to create a permanent inscription on the rock.

The graffiti carved on the stone of the Edge and included in the National Trust Sites and Monuments Record are listed in Table 18.1 (p. 437).

Graffiti in the mines

Nigel Dibben

The preceding section refers to graffiti at ground level and in mine entrances but probably the largest amount of graffiti at Alderley Edge is out of sight except to those who explore the mines. Unlike the surface graffiti, underground graffiti have a far longer life; indeed, they could remain there permanently unless destroyed intentionally. The graffiti range from 1764 to the twenty-first century.

Figure 22.2a shows the 1764 marking from Brynlow Mine, where we also find 1805 and GL 1866 marked. The remaining illustrations except possibly Figures 22.4c and 22.4d show graffiti that were created while the mines were closed. Five main types of graffiti have been identified.

1 Memento – to record, probably mainly for the benefit of the writer, that he or she has been to a particular place. Memento graffiti are often found in extreme locations (for example in the far end of West Mine), notable places (the start of the flooded section of the Hough Level from the Engine Vein end, Figure 22.2c) or alternatively just inside an entrance (Graffiti Chamber in Wood Mine, Figure 22.3d). Memento graffiti are often dated and would probably be written to reflect a sense of achievement by the writer. Some areas have a number of graffiti close together (e.g. Figure 22.2b), probably to record an extreme or notable place but just as probably as a copy-cat reaction to seeing other graffiti. In the class

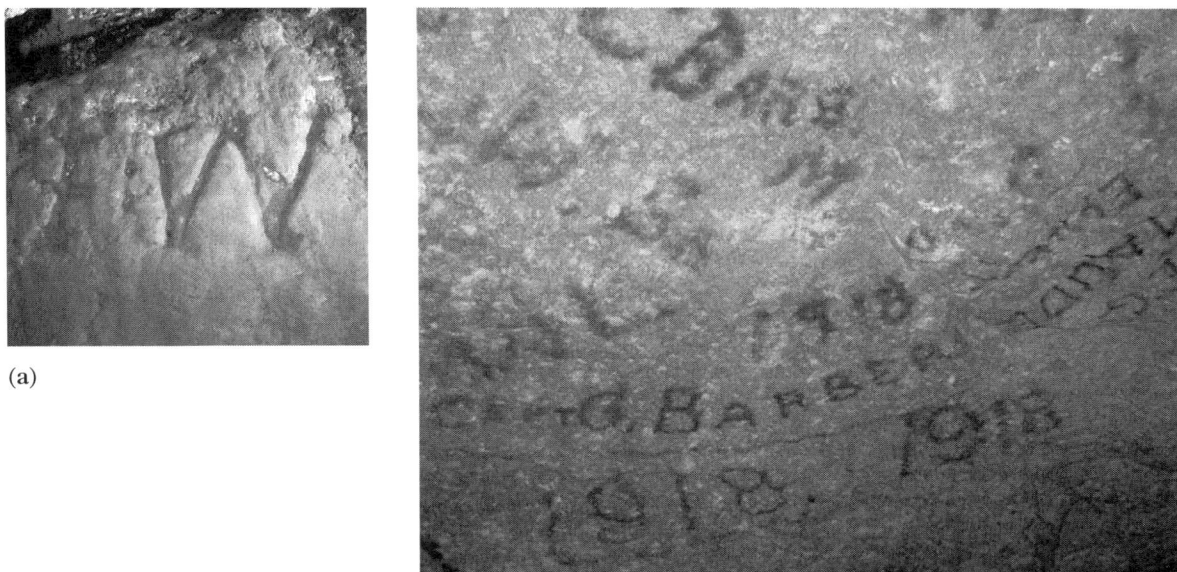

(a)

(b)

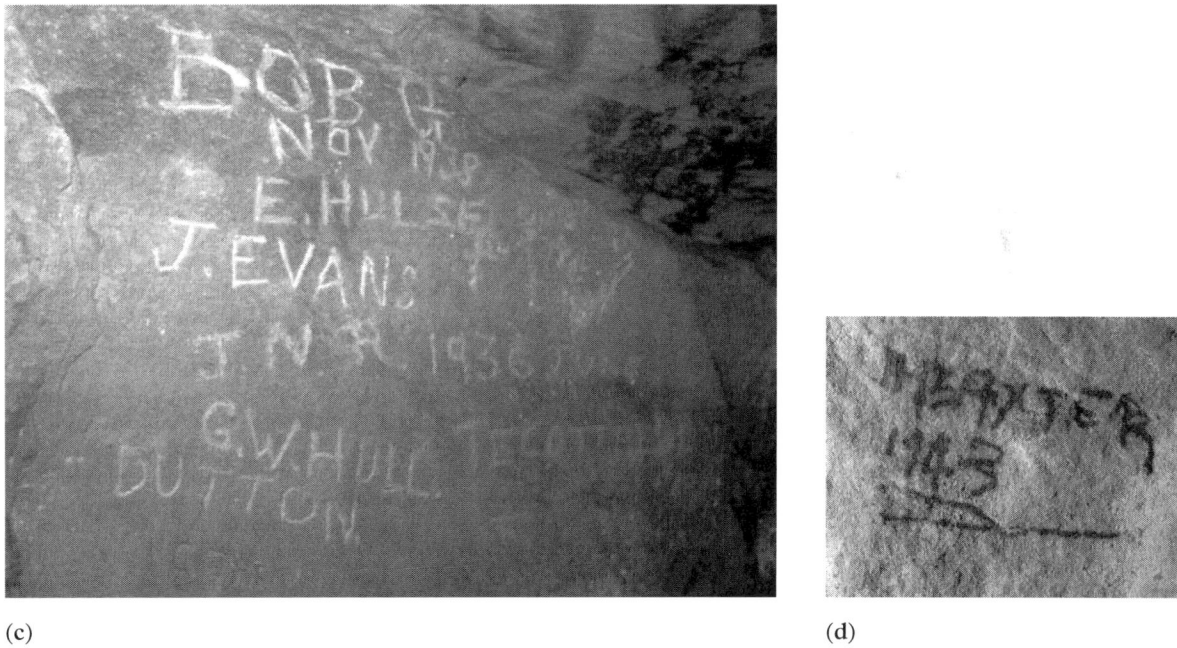

(c)

(d)

Figure 22.2. Graffiti in the mines 1. (a) JW in Brynlow Mine (carved 1764). Probably Josiah Wagstaff, who managed the mine for Charles Roe (see p. 378). (b) Captain Barber and others in West Mine (candle soot, 1918). Two George Barbers lived at the mine cottages. (c) John Evans in the Hough Level (carved 1936 or 1938). Evans lived in Church Quarry. (d) H. Baxter in West Mine (pencil, 1943). We have no further information.

Photographs Nigel Dibben.

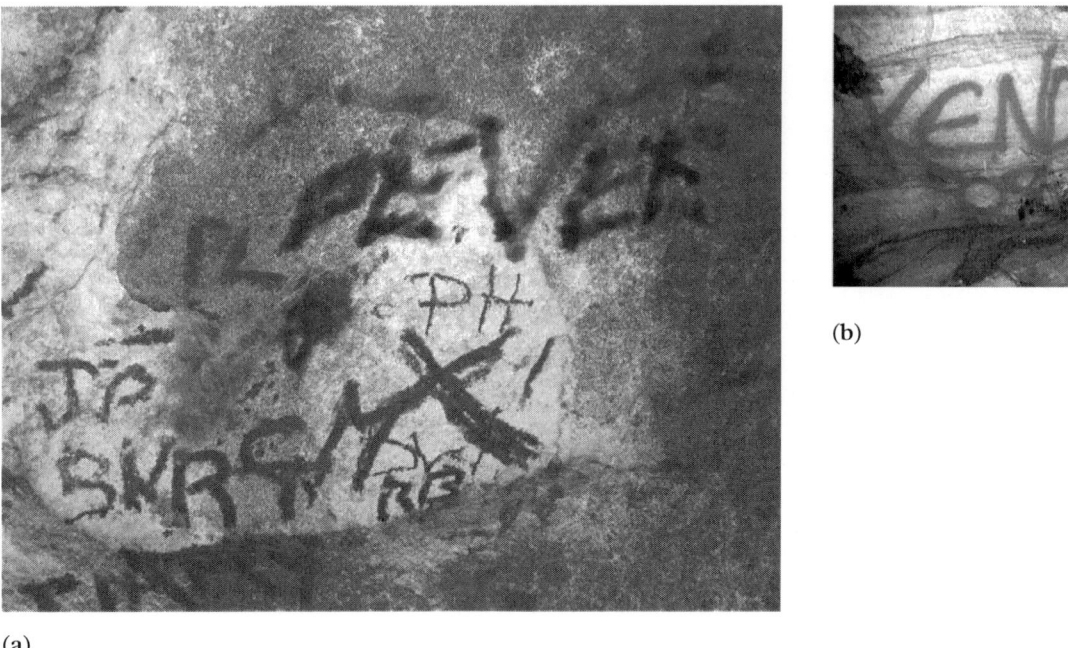

(a)

(b)

(c)

(d)

Figure 22.3. Graffiti in the mines 2. (a) PEVEE (probably carbide lamp soot, undated) and others in Wood Mine (fungi, undated). PEVEE signs his name in at least two other places in West Mine using the same distinctive 'logo'. (b) Kendo in West Mine (paint, 2009). Kendo was a trespasser as well as a vandal and was reported to the police. (c) Spike and Billy the Kid in West Mine (scratched, undated but probably 1950s or 1960s). The names of Spike Mycroft and his brother Doc Mycroft crop up elsewhere. (d) Graffiti chamber in Wood Mine (fungi, many dates). This chamber was a very short way into the mine, accessed from the Wood Mine quarry.

Photographs Nigel Dibben.

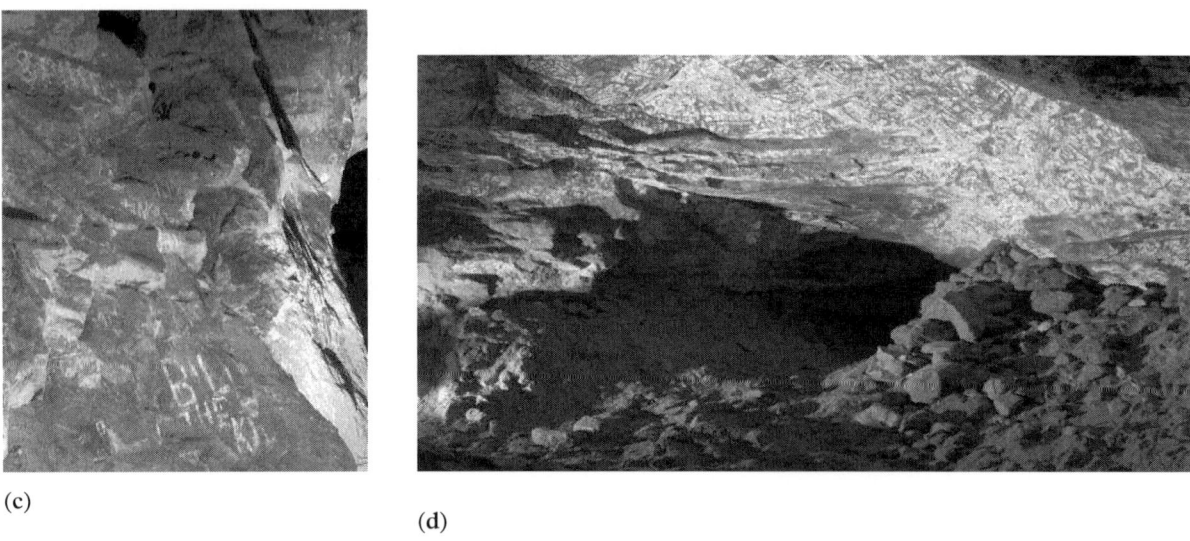

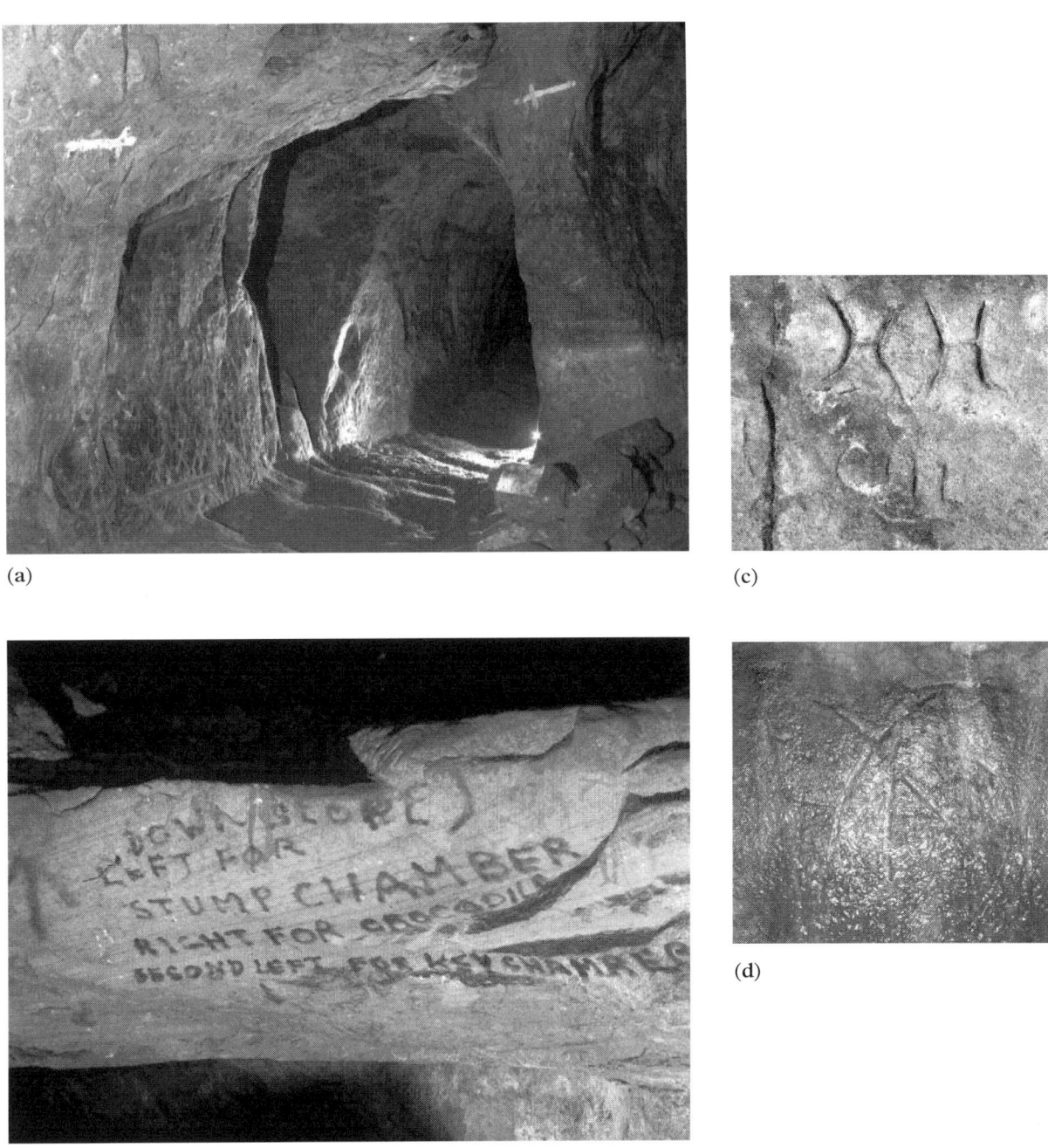

Figure 22.4. Graffiti in the mines 3. (a) Direction marking in West Mine (paint, undated). The white marks are highly distinctive but there are also a number of arrows and a cross on the right of the picture. (b) Route marking in Wood Mine (candle soot, undated). Wood Mine is uncommon in having so many places named in the mine. (c) 'HH' in West Mine (carved, undated). Potentially a miner's mark – note the vertical line to the left which may indicate the start or end of HH's work area. (d) A cross or triangle alongside a circle, carved on the fault wall in the Hough Level south of Brynlow Mine, probably marking the start or end of a section of working (scratched, undated).

Photographs Nigel Dibben.

of 'memento' graffiti we have examples dating back to 1764 (JW in Brynlow, Figure 22.2a), 1866 (GL almost certainly displaying the copy-cat type alongside JW – see also p. 378), 1907 (A. Long in West Mine), 1918 (G. Barber in West Mine, Figure 22.2b), 1936–38 (J. Evans and others in Hough Level, Figure 22c) right up to May 2009, when intruders in West Mine spray-painted on the walls in Sphinx Chamber (Figure 22.3b).

2 Territorial – to record an individual with a claim to a particular area or mine. This could be a subset of the memento graffiti except that the purpose is not so much for the individual concerned but to inform or warn others. Although it is hard to identify territorial marks from general memento ones, it is likely that 'Billy the Kid' and 'Spike' in Lion Chamber in West Mine (Figure 22.3c) fall into this category, as they are reputed to have been 'gang' members from Manchester. 'Club' initials such as NCC (Northern Caving Club), OCC (Openshaw Caving Club) and WCC (Wilmslow Caving Club) are also found.

3 Informative – especially in Wood Mine, there are a number of carefully carved or carbide-written (see below) names in distinct places such as North End Chambers (erroneously named West End Chamber), the Caveman Caverns, Chain Steps, Junction Shaft, Shamiri Chamber and Venus Hall/Mycroft's Chamber/ Rabbit Caverns. Presumably, these helped the explorers in the 1940s, 1950s and 1960s to find their way around the mine. Figure 22.4b shows that quite elaborate instructions were marked on the roof at times.

4 Directional – as a subset of the former, a considerable amount of graffiti are in the form of arrows. Presumably most of these were marked on the way into the mine to show the way out, but, although some have the words 'way out' alongside them, many do not and at complex junctions it is not uncommon to find arrows pointing in opposite directions. Arrows are sometimes marked in soot and sometimes chalk. Chalk has an obvious advantage in that it is quick to apply and different colours can be used to reduce ambiguity. One notable form of directional marking in West Mine is a cross with a long left or right arm pointing the way out, presumably designed to be distinctive. The markings are white-painted (Figure 22.4a) and represent someone's conscious effort to help others.

5 Recording – last but not least, there are a few examples of marking which may not strictly be graffiti. These are made by miners or others for a specific licit purpose. One example is the marking of the identity of survey stations so that they can be relocated in future, as can be seen on the extreme left of Figure 22.4b. Another

suspected example is a series of marks on the fault wall in the Hough Level south of Brynlow Mine. In one case, there is what appears to be a cross or triangle alongside a circle (Figure 22.4d). This is surmised to mark the start or end of a section of working. Another mark not far away consists of four small circles marked by a few minutes of drilling. In the main chamber of West Mine there is a vertical line about 40 cm long and close to it the initials HH (Figure 22.4c). These could mark the start of a particular miner's area of working; it is nice to think that this may be where Henry Harvey – a copper and lead miner from Buckfastleigh in Devon – was working in the early 1860s.

The methods of marking the graffiti have changed over time. Examples can be found of the following:

1 Engraving – from 1764 (Figure 22.2a and 22.2c) onwards up to recently.
2 Soot (roof) – from at least 1918 such as Capt. G. Barber (Figure 22.2b) and the Wood Mine directions (Figure 22.4b). Soot on the roof is usually applied with a candle or oil-filled lamp and so generally indicates earlier rather than later marking.
3 Soot (wall) – after carbide lamps became available to cavers, graffiti become common on vertical walls as the lamp lends itself to use as a writing implement (e.g. 'PEVEE' in West Mine and Wood Mine, Figure 22.3a).
4 Paint – there is relatively little graffiti using paint but examples include the arrows referred to above (Figure 22.4a) and the spray-painting in 2009 (Figure 22.3b).
5 Chalk – examples are not uncommon, especially as directional arrows and less so as personal marks, initials or dates.
6 Pencil – the smooth rock faces in some parts of West Mine in particular are marked neatly in pencil. Some of the graffiti are grey and some purple (the writing shown in Figure 22.2d is so coloured), which could be a sign that a 'permanent' pencil was used, that is, one containing methyl violet, which leaves a characteristic mark when wet.
7 Fungus – a feature of the near-entrance sections of the mines is the growth of white fungus on roof and walls. In more recent years, temporary marks have been left, illicitly, by visitors writing with a finger in the white fungus, revealing the darker rock surface (Figure 22.3a, 22.3d).
8 Mud – there are not a great many places where there is a smooth surface of mud but where it exists graffiti are occasionally found, either in the mud or using the mud on rock walls.

What do the graffiti tell us about the mines? Apart from showing how far people travelled into the mines, ranging from just out of daylight (e.g. Graffiti Chamber in Wood Mine) to the furthest extremity (e.g. West Mine), we are able to obtain a few dates for the working of specific parts of the mines. For instance, Brynlow is quite confidently dated to 1764 or earlier, while the western extension of Engine Vein has what appears to be 1874 carved through an old surface layer, suggesting the tunnel was originally earlier but was revisited in 1874. Another message is provided by locations such as Sphinx Chamber in West Mine, where there is candle-writing on the ceiling above the Sphinx Rock, which must have been put there when the rock reached close to the roof, before it was broken down some time in the 1950s. The white-painted arrows in West Mine show how someone was sufficiently concerned about others getting lost that he or she went to the trouble of clearly marking the main route, even though the mines had officially been closed since the 1920s. In Wood Mine, the naming of chambers with graffiti is a particular characteristic and gives us a picture of the usage of the mines at the time the chambers were named. There is no suggestion that the naming is original: it is far more likely to have been carried out in the 1940s or 1950s as a means of helping people find their way around the mine, which is particularly complex in parts. Names found include the Caveman Caverns, West End Chamber, Shamiri Chamber, Junction Shaft, Venus Hall, the Seed Bed and Chain Steps. These names and more also appear on a mine survey ascribed to JNR-AW-DT-GW and dated 1970, so were presumably present when the survey was made, which is believed to be in the early 1960s.

The marks by miners in the Hough Level, if they are indeed original marks, could tell us more about the driving of the level. We know that teams of men (pares) were allocated sections to work and could drive about two fathoms (roughly 4 m) in a week. A thorough study of the fault wall where the marks have been found (Figure 22.4d) may reveal more marks and the distance between them may tell us about working practices. The south wall of the main chamber in West Mine contains not only the HH inscription but also scratched crosses and lines, which appear to be below the layer of soot and dust that arises from active mining. Analysis of these graffiti would need to be combined with information from the wages books for the period, which, sadly, have been kept in private hands.

One feature that has not been observed underground is the carving of anything but initials, names, place names and dates. The author has not observed any faces, 'mystic symbols' or similar markings deep in any of the mines.

In conclusion, the underground graffiti tell us a considerable amount about the people who visited the mines as well as a little about the people who worked in them. Further detailed recording of the location and types of graffiti may add to the knowledge of the mines' various histories.

The distribution of tree graffiti

Simon Timberlake

The map accompanying the survey of the trees (Plate 20) provides us with an interesting correlation between mature beech trees and graffiti. This in itself is not surprising, since beech trees, with their smooth bark, have long been considered a source of inspiration. As Mabey (1996) points out, the Romans had both a tradition and a proverb for the practice of tree graffiti: 'crescunt illae; crescant amores' ('as these letters grow, so may our love'). The latter is in fact a good description of the effect of the growth of the beech trunk upon graffiti carved into it. In the beech woods of Alderley Edge generations of initials and dates have expanded into illegibility over a period of several hundred years.

Tree graffiti have been recorded from a number of well loved and ancient beech woods in southern Britain, although northern examples are rather less well known. At Frithsden Beeches in Hertfordshire, ancient pollarded beeches are covered with over 100 years of graffiti, from Victorian initials to messages carved by visiting Americans. Wittenham Clumps in Oxfordshire, the dramatic beech plantation crowning an Iron Age hill-fort made famous by Paul Nash's paintings, boasts the 'Poem Tree', bearing the verse carved by Joseph Tubb in 1844 celebrating the surrounding landscape.

Some 95 per cent of the graffiti trees on Alderley Edge are beech, the remaining 5 per cent being silver birch, rowan and a smaller number of Scots pine. Because of their thick corrugated bark, very few oaks were found with any sort of graffiti on them, and most of those detected were quite illegible. The legibility of graffiti on beech trees depends very largely upon the age of the tree, depth of carving and position on the trunk. In the case of furrowed trunks, some areas of bark may become considerably more distorted than others. Nevertheless, the main problem has often been the sheer volume of graffito cover, much of it written over earlier messages, defacing them and destroying the bark skin. Examples of trees of over 2.5 m girth with more than 100 items of carved graffiti covering the circumference up to a height of 2 m above ground level are not unknown in Mottram Wood. Some beech trees appear to have suffered deformities and still others may have become diseased following this defacement, although most cope well with these attentions.

The highest incidence of graffiti-covered trees is to be found in Mottram Wood (100 or more). The distribution of these trees closely mirrors the gradient of the slopes, and hence the beeches growing on the steepest slopes above the main footpath are almost completely devoid of graffiti. The second-largest concentration is to be found in Brynlow Wood, in particular on some the largest trees above Artists Lane. A similar dense concentration is found on Glaze Hill, with smaller numbers of inscribed trees around the Beacon, and finally in an outlier of tall beeches at the north end of Waterfall Wood.

Graffito dates and verse on trees

Some common thread in both content and style is detectable in graffiti of all ages. In terms of their content, in order of importance come: initials (often multiple), year, month, first name, surname, an indication of a tryst or love match, home town, regiment (if applicable) and, in the case of more recent graffiti, football team! Much of what is left survives as abbreviations and a good deal of that is impossible to interpret out of context. Legibility sometimes makes the interpretation arbitrary. Nevertheless, graffiti provide an important record of the names of visitors to the Edge over a 100-year period, as well as providing some insight into changes in popular working-class culture, recorded by day-trippers picnicking, hiking or playing on the Edge.

As with the graffiti cut in stone, a study of recorded dates on trees gives the impression of several 'waves' of tourism. While the earliest date found was 1627, the earliest genuine dates appear to fall within the period 1880–1900 (the oldest credible date recorded was from the early 1870s). Another grouping of dates falls within the years of the Great War (particularly 1916–18). While this latter period seems unlikely to have seen much tourism on the Edge, the carving of dates and initials might represent the brief visits of soldiers on leave from active service or recuperating in the hospital set up by the Red Cross in the village at Brookdale, or even perhaps a memorial for men lost or away from home. Yet another wave of visitors (many of whom could have been locals) is reflected by an increase in the number of dates between the years 1919 and 1927. Very few graffiti date to the 1930s, but the war years 1940–45 are quite a different matter. Great attention seems to have been paid to the Edge at this time. This may have been for similar reasons to those suggested for the Great War, but the effect of an increase in local population due to the influx of evacuees and American servicemen and the like will surely have had an additional impact. The importance of 'living in the moment' during times of uncertainty, and the need to record or else leave some mark of one's presence for the future, may also have encouraged the writing of graffiti. A walk on the Edge could well have seemed a great escape from the pressures and worries of war. A recent study of the 'arborglyphs' on the 'culturally modified trees' of Salisbury Plain has shown how important the action of leaving one's name could be for soldiers about to go on campaign (Summerfield, 2013).

The biggest proportion of graffiti post-dates the Second World War. The period 1948 up to the early 1950s is commonly represented, although from this period onwards the 'quality' of the graffiti and writing deteriorates. A massive increase in graffiti dates from the early 1960s. The 'modern period' ranges from this date through to the late 1970s, but tails off quite dramatically after that. It is tempting to link this drop with current social and political changes, and it is perhaps no coincidence that graffiti, at least those out here in the woods, decline at the beginning of the Thatcher years!

The making of trysts, whether marking a friendship, an engagement, marriage or an anniversary, is one important use of a tree. At the end of the nineteenth century this was probably taken quite seriously. The subject of most of the late Victorian graffiti relates to trysts (much of it unfortunately now illegible, either as a result of bark overgrowth or else because of concealment beneath the work of generations of later writers). The earliest tryst inscription found was carved on a beech tree growing on a tip of mine spoil on the eastern slope of Glaze Hill (SJ 8603 7797): '1882 George Matilda' (Figure 22.5). Typically, many such

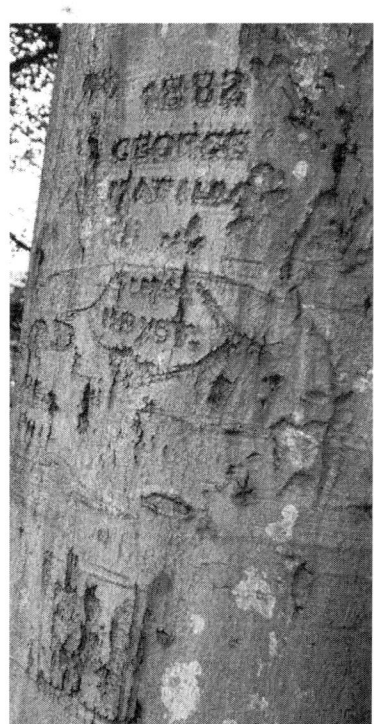

Figure 22.5. '1882 George Matilda': an example of a 'tryst' graffito on an old beech tree, dating from 1882.

Photograph Sean Edwards.

inscriptions would be associated with the carving of hearts, and exact dates would also be recorded, and occasionally the words 'forever' or 'until death do us part'. Certain trees appear to have been favoured for tryst-making graffiti.

Some of the named graffiti were clearly the work of groups of friends, invariably men. Sometimes these inscriptions were executed with amazing detail and precision, involving upwards of eight or more people. Usually, personal names were written by the individuals concerned, and precise dates given. Once again, the overall impression was of some sort of 'bonding experience'. It was clear in some instances that such friends or colleagues were soldiers while a number were sailors – both merchant seamen and Royal Navy.

Several of the inscriptions noted were cut in memory of a dead relative or friend. At least one found in the Mottram beech wood (approx. SJ 8515 7827) included a detailed eulogy to a loved one (Figure 22.6).

Most of the cruder vernacular graffiti appear to be rather less than twenty-five years old. Phallic symbols, as well as the embellishment of vulva-shaped orifices within the bark of some beech trunks, are common within some areas of the woods.

Thematic mapping of the dates of graffiti might show some clustering of data, revealing specific areas of Alderley Edge or else groups of trees on which graffiti have been scrawled at different periods during the Edge's recent history.

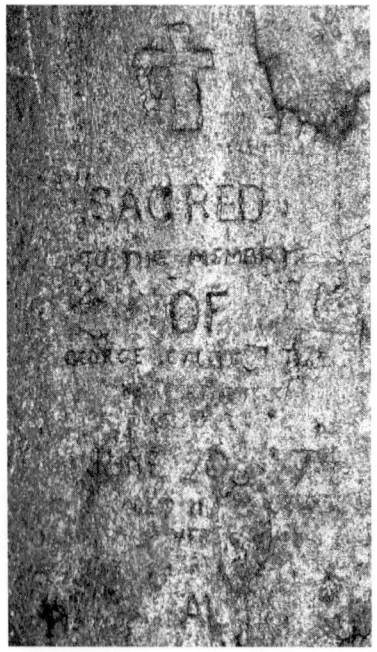

Figure 22.6. Graffito in Mottram Wood. The lettering appears to read 'SACRED TO THE MEMORY OF GEORGE CALID... | ... | JUNE 20 [?] [18]74 | AGED 11... | ... | IN MEMORIAM [?]'.

Photograph Sean Edwards.

Evidence for magic and ritual associated with trees

In spite of considerable excitement associated with the use of the Edge for witchcraft practices during the 1960s and 1970s, and recently for the rather more public, albeit discouraged, celebration of Hallowe'en, there are few overt signs of Wicca or 'new age' ritual here today. However, some quiet and unpublicised ritual persists, associated with the veneration of trees, rocks and in particular the wells of the Edge. In some cases this is the continuation or revival of folk custom and earlier cult practices associated with wells and trees which coexisted with Christianity in many rural areas of Britain up until the early twentieth century. Today, spring and well 'worship' persists in the guise of well dressing ceremonies in the neighbouring Peak District of Derbyshire.

Apart from numerous documentary references to the waters of the Holy Well being a cure for barrenness and as a receptacle for offerings in the form of coins and bent pins (Roeder, 1901; Roeder and Graves, 1905a; Potter, 1970), there is also local tradition for there having been an accompanying tree, reputedly a holly bush, which at times was be-decked with offerings of rags (Graves, 1905; A. Garner, personal communication). The custom of pinning rags to a thorn tree growing beside a 'holy well' or 'wishing well' is an interesting one, and according to Jones (1992) is often associated with venerated wells, and is found in all parts of the British Isles, Europe, Asia, Africa and South America. It has been suggested, among other things, that the rags represent the survival of the custom of leaving the whole garment of a diseased person, whereby the disease will be carried away in the discarded clothes – that is, the rags represent riddances. Alternatively, it has been suggested that the rags simply represent clothes, hence an offering, or else that these were the signs of expiation, and thus an expression of penance. At Ffynnon Cae Moch in Glamorgan, the visitor stood in the well, bathed the wound with the rag that formerly bound it, then applied a fresh bandage, and hung the discarded rag on a nearby thorn tree. Although the Holy Well on Alderley Edge was not, in recorded memory or tradition, ever used for the healing of wounds, pinning rags to a holly bush may likewise relate to offerings associated with drinking or bathing in its healing waters.

A recent revival in this 'rag well' custom has been noticed at certain times of the year on the Edge. Both in 1997 and 1998 rags were seen pinned to a small holly bush to the left of the track below Holy Well (SJ 8587 7785). This would seem, therefore, to represent the continuity of a much earlier tree-dressing tradition, of whose true significance the current perpetrators of this ritual may in fact be unaware.

Other tree ceremonies whose results can be seen at different times of the year appear not to be associated with the wells. Trees growing within some of the earth circles on the Edge, such as that on Stormy Point (SJ 8606 7784), have been seen bedecked with flowers and plants and with their branches woven together, presumably following night-time ceremonies (D. Cartilage, personal communication). Offerings of flowers are also found at various other spots around the Edge, but almost invariably these offerings are associated with trees.

Many of these ritualistic practices still carried out on the Edge appear to take place at Hallowe'en, or at least at the celebration of the Celtic festival of Samhain (1 November), and so this may be the work of neo-pagans rather than individuals interested purely in the veneration of trees or water, or indeed the locality or 'presence' of the Edge.

Note on the rock graffiti

Alan Garner and Nigel Dibben

The graffiti are mainly of the 'memento' type, saying nothing more than 'I was here'. They have been done with no care or thought for the rock, but are hacked and scratched and daubed. A second kind is quite different and less common. Here the work is incised with skill and respect, and, in the underground instances, with difficulty yet with no loss of precision. The conditions under which they were cut, in darkness by candlelight, would have been dangerous and frightening, yet they are not hurried. Unlike the 'memento' crudities, they are integral to the rock; they are a part of the making.

Examples of those found so far may be seen in Church Quarry, the Old Quarry and Brynlow Mine. In the quarries they take the form of a 'crossed I' or J, and in Brynlow there is added a W, which may be read as M when inverted (Figure 22.2a). These have been interpreted as personal initials, but their occurrence is widespread in natural caves and old workings, singly or together, and the W occurs on late Medieval and early Modern millstones. The W is often formed by interlocked Vs. It is standard in the fourteenth and fifteenth centuries on lead ampullae that pilgrims used for carrying holy water from the Shrine of Our Lady of Walsingham. The same letters are found in the timbers of secular and religious buildings from at least the sixteenth century to the eighteenth, where they occur at points of 'spiritual weakness': doors, windows, thresholds and chimneys. They are especially common on chimneys, since the chimney is a double danger, open to the outside world at the top and a fire hazard at the bottom. From around 1550 the letters appear on cast-iron firebacks (Hodgkinson, 2013). And in the case of the pre-Reformation church at Hemingston, Suffolk, an interlocked W and three crosses, using differently coloured bricks, are built into the north porch. At all periods such marks are likely to have been made by people who could not read, who would have seen them as symbols, not script.

The current interpretation of these letters, whether read as I, J, M or W, are that they invoke the protection of Jesus, *Virgo Virginum* ('Virgin of Virgins') and Mary (Binding and Wilson, 2010; Lord and Howard, 2013). They are not detached claims of ownership but are supplications to protect those exposed to physical risk and to other kinds of threat. If this reading is correct then the comment in the text above about mystic symbols and the attribution of the initials to Josiah Wagstaff (see p. 378) may prove to be incorrect.

23

Alderley Edge: the villas and the village

Matthew Hyde

The name Alderley Edge belongs properly to an outrigger of the Pennines jutting abruptly from the Cheshire Plain. There was no settlement called Alderley Edge, just a scattering of cottages round Five Lane Ends on the present A34/B5369, and a fine hall which gives the district its pre-railway name of Chorley. When a station was opened in 1842 on the new Manchester and Birmingham Railway the company cast around for a name to call it. Chorley could cause confusion with Chorley in Lancashire – as Adlington still does – and so the name Alderley Edge was appropriated, first to the station and its attendant hotel, and then to the residential district for affluent Mancunians which grew up in its wake.

The new name caused considerable annoyance to the Stanleys of Alderley, a wordy family whose estate included most of Alderley Edge proper, or as we should now have to call it Alderley Edge Edge.

> An interest almost national, owing to the notice taken by the London press, was in the year 1863, excited by the refusal of the post office authorities to recognise the existence of any such place as Alderley Edge, and the consequent non-delivery, until after much delay, of letters thus addressed. Meetings were held, and memorials were sent up in vain, until at last, a formidable guarantee fund was subscribed, for compelling the post office to send letters direct to the place, for which they knew only too well that such letters were intended. Perseverance prevailed, and Alderley Edge is now recognised by the post office authorities.

This is from Thomas Morris & Co.'s *Directory* of 1874. The effect of this bizarre state of affairs is apparent even today to researchers, who will search in vain for the Census returns for Alderley Edge. You must look under Chorley. Edward John, second Lord Stanley of Alderley, was behind this vendetta. He was Postmaster General. Fletcher Moss has the neatest comment on the affair, simply reminding us of the good baron's epitaph (Moss, 1903: 2): '[He] was always distinguished by clearness of judgement and by uncompromising public spirit'. Quite so.

No account of the villas of Alderley Edge is complete without reference to Katherine Chorley and her book *Manchester Made Them* (1950). The reader is also referred to *The Villas of Alderley Edge* by Matthew Hyde (1999).

Alderley Edge is a villa colony. The villas fall into three distinct waves of development.

The first wave

The first wave owes its origin to a rapprochement between the railway company and the other major landowning family. The de Trafford lands on the west slope of the Edge down to the station offered wonderful sites for villas, romantic, wooded, with far-reaching views, which, as absentee landlords, they were happy to see developed. As for the railway company, which needed to drum up custom, not only did it build a splendid hotel for would-be villa builders but it also offered a generous financial inducement in the form of a first-class pass to the head of any household building a new house exceeding a certain value: a villa.

One or two villas had anticipated the railway's arrival, but by and large building started soon after 1842 and the Victorian quarter, round the station and up the leafy heights of Woodbrook and Macclesfield Roads, was complete by about 1870.

The land was divided for development into four- and five-acre plots (Figure 19.15, p. 496). A few were then occupied by a single superior villa: Ferns, Croston Towers, Springfield. More commonly two villas, occasionally three or four, were built on each plot, with the apportionment of land diminishing accordingly. Often the pairs are in contrasting styles: St Mary's Cliffe and Redclyffe Grange; Broomfield and The Whins; Hazelcroft and Beechfield. Economically, they were built with their service quarters close together, allowing drainage and services to be shared but leaving maximum land for the all-important garden and drive (see Figure 20.5, p. 513, and Figure 23.1). The style is variegated: Italianate, Tudor, Gothic, castellated, Swiss; their finish yellow or red brick, render, or stone. Under the skin, however, they vary little – Figure 23.2 shows a typical plan. They feature handsomely proportioned rooms with high ceilings. Typically, a broad hallway will lead to a male-influenced dining room, all dark colours and hard surfaces, a female-oriented drawing room in lighter colours and softer textures,

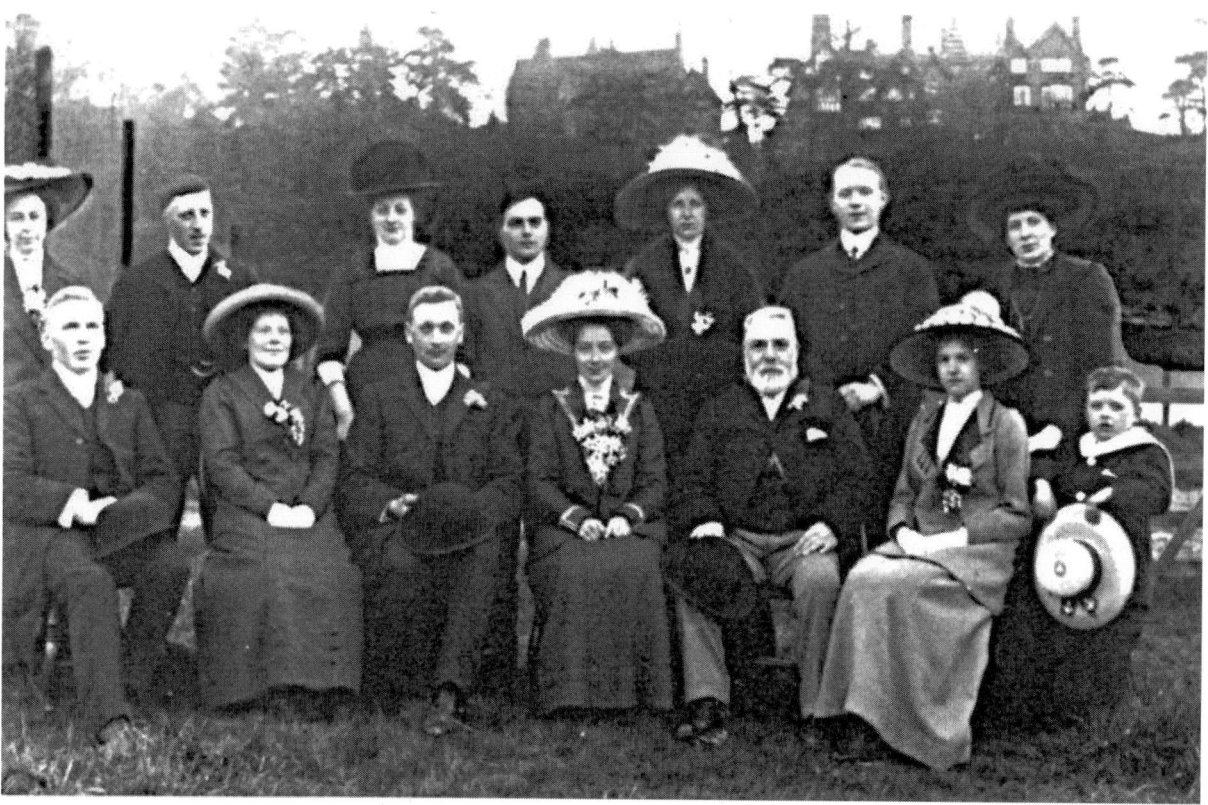

Figure 23.1. The wedding of Ernest Kennedy and Ethel Twigg, 17 April 1912. This photograph was taken on the cricket field, Moss Lane. In the background loom the silhouettes of Redclyffe Grange and St Mary's Cliffe.

After Hyde (1999: 109); courtesy of George Twigg.

and a somewhat smaller sunny breakfast room. A good staircase rises between dining and drawing room. Under the stair is the 'green baize door', sometimes literally that, sometimes frosted, that gives onto a region of plain cream walls and deal doors. Here is the big kitchen looking out into a narrow yard, a scullery and a couple of pantries, the cellar steps and maybe a narrow back stair to the upper floors.

Upstairs are the bedrooms and the nursery, often a dressing room, certainly a bathroom. Sometimes a bathroom was provided for the maids as well. Most houses had two or three living-in servants, almost exclusively female. Census returns show that they were recruited from all over the country. Although a butler's pantry was generally provided there was seldom an actual butler.

The garden was an important setting, well planted and making the most of the rock outcrops and quarry faces of the Edge. Maps and descriptions indicate extensive and choice glasshouses. There were

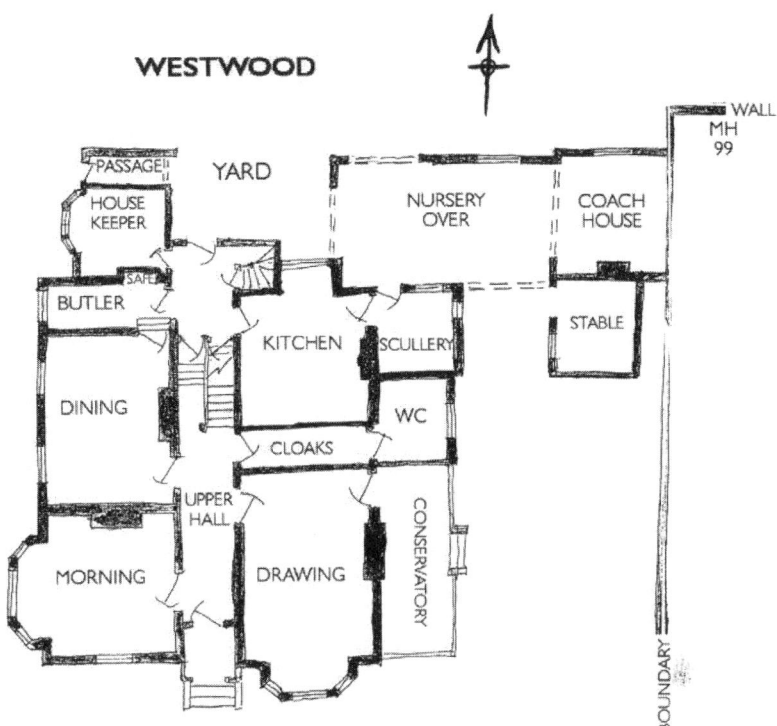

Figure 23.2. Plan of Westwood, a typical Alderley villa.

After Hyde (1999: 115).

usually a vegetable patch, some fruit trees, sometimes a hen run and bees. The gardeners, unlike the live-in servants, were local and continued to live in the village or down at the Hough. Only Ferns and Hazelcroft sported a lodge. Stables were sometimes down at the bottom of the hill too (St Mary's Cliffe, Firwood), but in any case carriages and horses were often hired.

Socially, Alderley Edge was never quite as grand as Bowdon. The typical incomer was self-made, intelligent, entrepreneurial, socially aware. In concept these first villas are country houses writ small, with best rooms and service quarters, stable-yards and kitchen gardens, shrubberies and lawns. The gracious environment they created was greater than the sum of its parts.

The second wave

This is an early twentieth-century phenomenon involving the belated development of parts of the Stanley estate. Until the turn of the century the Stanleys of Alderley Park resisted the blandishments of railway directors, ignored as far as possible the new settlers or 'Cottentots' (their nickname) and even disregarded their own agent, who urged them to do some profitable villa-building. Only three villas – Barnfield, West Bank

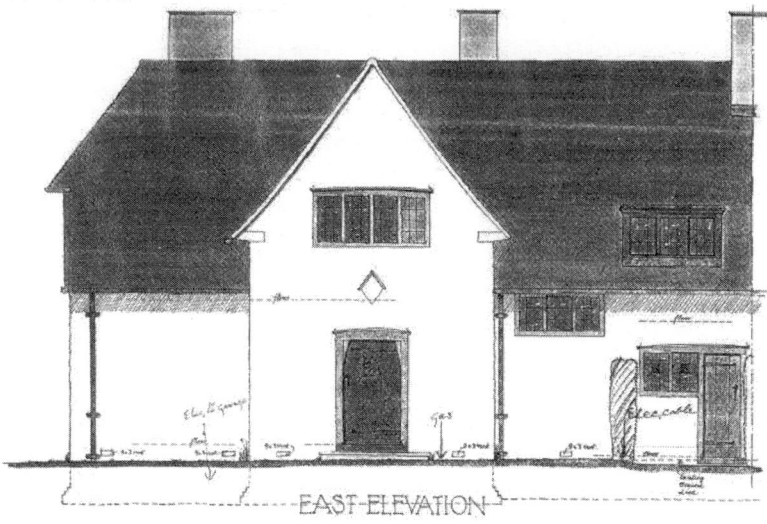

(a)

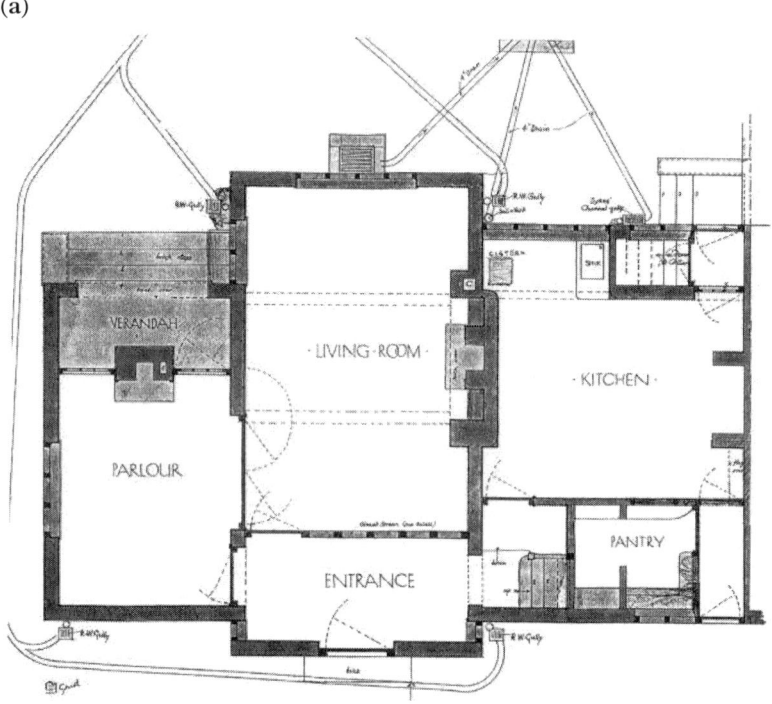

(b)

Figure 23.3. Hill Cottage:
(a) elevation; (b) ground-floor
plan; (c, *opposite*) first-floor plan.
Note the glazed screen and the
folding doors of the living room
which allow the internal space to
flow, and the parlour is opened
up to the verandah and garden.

Drawn by Matthew Hyde; after Hyde
(1999: 147–9).

and Oakwood – were built on the anomalous finger of Stanley land
mentioned in Chapter 19 which points down between de Trafford lands
to Alderley Cottage (Figure 19.5, p. 470).

Henry, third Baron Stanley, awkward with his sharp-witted family
(though he was no fool himself), had little to do with Alderley. He was
more interested in his estates at Tilston and in Anglesey, where there
are some interesting examples of his patronage. Only with his death in

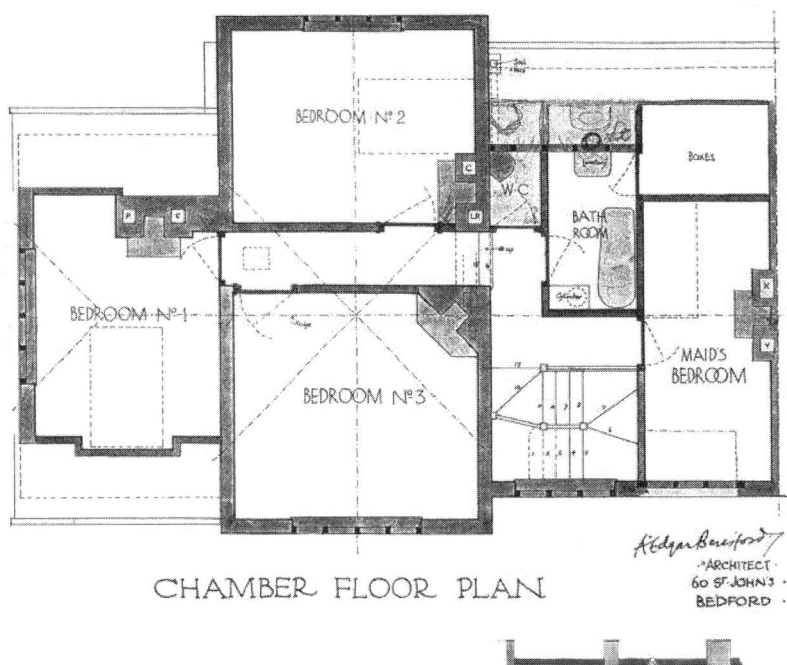

CHAMBER FLOOR PLAN

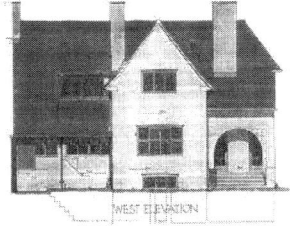

(c)

1903, to be followed as fourth Baron by his more progressive brother Edward Lyulph, did things begin to change. In landscape terms this second wave does not add up to much: ribbon development along the Congleton Road and the lanes off it, a neatly manicured enclave on Whitebarn Road, and three or four extra villas at the top of Macclesfield Road (e.g. Hill Cottage, Figure 23.3). In terms of design and craftsmanship, however, it is more distinguished than the first wave, for this was a golden age of English domestic architecture. The houses are more comfortable than the first lot, warmer, less labour-intensive, more relaxed, the rooms flowing internally and out into the landscape. Their architecture starts from a new premise: the cottage. Admittedly no real cottage was ever half so comfortable, so roomy or gracious, but the cottage influence shows in the catslide roofs of stone or tile rather than mechanical-looking slate, in the white roughcast walls, the homely latticed windows and plank doors, the inglenooks, low ceilings and cozy room sizes, and restricted service quarters. Clearly there are different social connotations too, reflecting Lyulph Stanley's radical views; deeds show that he personally vetted each design. Alderley Edge could now offer home-grown architects too, in particular the Worthington brothers and the Fairhurst dynasty, and the excellent building firm of Isaac Massey and Sons was at its peak.

The third wave

A third major phase of house-building started in the late 1990s. It gathered pace in 2000 with the loss of a crucial planning appeal (verbal information from planning officer) and was in full swing by 2009 in spite of a general downturn in the economy. Prestbury, Alderley Edge, Knutsford Legh Road, Hale and Bowdon are the Cheshire hotspots. The type is as characteristic of what the newspapers are calling the noughties as the earlier phases are to their times.

There was a housing moratorium. Planning restrictions prohibited new-build. This had an unintentional effect, in that every new house had to replace an existing one, so they were in a sense cannibalistic. Decent houses could be seen empty and awaiting their fate; often they were of the 1960s or 1970s, and so of styles which had fallen out of favour, but casualties also included farms such as Findlow's Bower and original villas such as Oak Bank, on Brook Lane, upon which the description above is based. It was worth doing only if the new-build would have double or treble the value of the old, either by squeezing in a block of flats or by building a footballer's mansion, to use a generic term.

The type is easily recognised. The combination of ostentation coupled with insecurity is unmistakeable. They differ from their nineteenth-century or early twentieth-century predecessors in several significant ways. Maximisation of square footage is the aim, to achieve a property worth several million pounds at current prices on a relatively modest plot. The deep-plan house will fill most of the plot, so the garden is shrunk to insignificance. Indeed, the house is likely to be even bigger than it looks because much of it is underground. This is to sidestep planning restrictions, though it is promoted on the grounds of energy efficiency and privacy. The basement will be for leisure – pool, jacuzzi, steam room, plant room, media room, gym. Services such as laundry room are often removed to the attic floor, but in the modern way the kitchen will be one of the main living rooms. Bedrooms will all have bathrooms en suite, the master bedroom probably with a complete suite of dressing room and bathroom for him and another for her. The house will be extensively automated and programmable – lift, pool, lighting, video and audio, security. A machine for living in.

As for architectural style, it generally refers back to the Arts and Crafts movement. Indeed, these houses often display a genuinely high level of craftsmanship. C. F. A. Voysey is the favoured model (see the perambulation, below), but the low roofs of Frank Lloyd Wright's Prairie style may be employed if there are restrictions on height. The architects Fallows Gowen of Davyhulme perfected the type and are the most prolific designers. The few neo-Georgian or Victorian pastiches are less successful. A whiff of modernism may be ventured here and there, such as fully glazed gables, but thoroughgoing modernism – flat roofs and sheet glass – is rare, and apparently hard to sell. The first of the genre, George Best's 1969 house in Bramhall, by Frazer Crane of Wilmslow, was as modern as could be, but has tellingly been toned down and traditionalised since.

The village

The village was essentially subservient to the villas, and its development followed a step behind; indeed, the 1872 Ordnance Survey shows a villa with a spacious garden occupying part of the present street frontage. The village street, called London Road but once Street Lane, still wears a prosperous late-Victorian air, though by 2009 it was wearing a little thin (Figures 20.1 and 20.2 show it in Edwardian guise, pp. 507, 508). Banks provide the dominating accents, not pubs, as would have been the case in a genuine old village: the excellent Arts and Crafts **District Bank** of 1903–04 is by Percy Scott Worthington.

The most interesting building on the main street was the **Institute** of 1878, knocked down in 2003 for the new library and flats, shortly before the end of the Landscape Project. Its unspoken purpose was to keep the servants out of the pub in their time off, although apparently they preferred to walk into Wilmslow. The facade was of red brick and terracotta, with some fancy detail, but inside it was strictly utilitarian. The deeds record in typical unpunctuated style:

> George Railton stock broker William Coulborn manufacturer James Broomfield Insurance broker Ernest Crewdson accountant and Mary Kennedy spinster as its promoters ... to be called The Alderley Edge Temperance and Mission Hall.... Public Temperance Coffee and News Room for the working classes.... No lecture meetings of a political character and no ball dancing or theatrical performance no wine spirits cider perry or any intoxicating liquor or for any entertainment at which gambling spiritualism or necromancy will be practised. (Deeds held by the Secretary of the Alderley Edge Institute Trust at the Festival Hall, Talbot Road, Alderley Edge, Cheshire East SK9 7HR)

Between London Road and the railway line were the premises of Isaac Massey and Sons, high-class builders, also now gone. The largest employer, with as many as 120 men in its heyday, its one o'clock hooter regulated village life. Office and manager's house on George Street fronted the yard, which stretched out along the railway line.

The station (Figure 19.16, p. 497), built in 1842, at the north end of the village, is a disappointing little set of buildings considering it is the *fons et origo* of the colony. However, it should be seen in conjunction with the Queen's Hotel, built by the railway company in 1845. In a showy Jacobean style with strapwork and shaped gables, this is a major statement, especially if it is imagined brand new in a purely rural setting. Today we perceive the hotel, now offices, as a short front to the road and a long side to the railway, but of course it was designed the other way round. There is evidence of the covered terrace that once linked it with the platform. A poignant relic is the line of rings on the retaining wall of the station approach, where waiting horses were tethered.

The new community must have its church, and it must be of the best kind, following the principles of the Oxford Movement and the Ecclesiologists. **St Philip's Church** (Figure 23.4), with its rocketing spire, multiple roofs and richly traceried windows, clearly ought to be the focus of the new Alderley Edge. Somehow, however, it got itself built in the wrong place. It is the wrong side of the railway, neither easy nor pleasant to access from the village or the main crop of villas. This can be explained by the 'course of new road' marked on the deeds of the Meadows (1854) and other houses, which was planned to run due south from St Philip's on the west side of the tracks. Here it was anticipated, no doubt, that the new village would grow. In 2010 the new road was finally built much further to the west – following roughly the line proposed in 1938 on the Stanley sale maps.

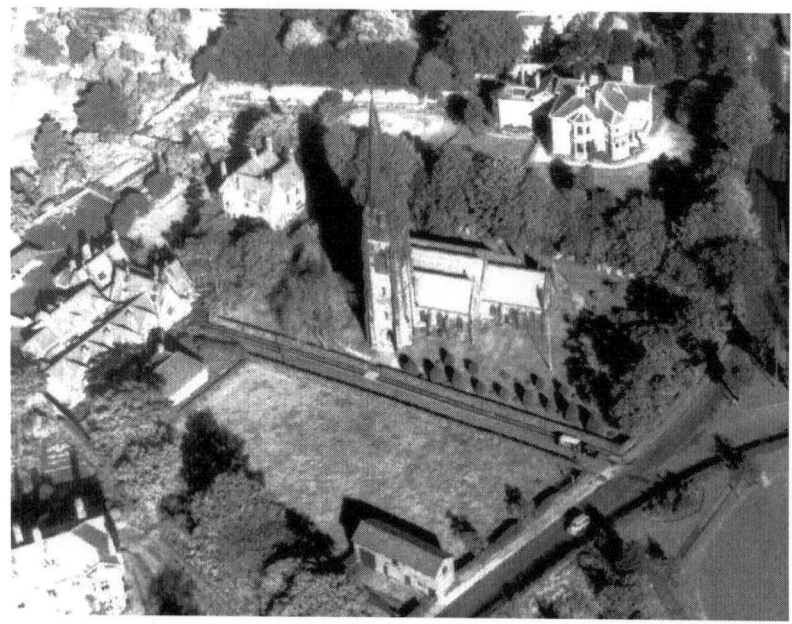

Figure 23.4. Aerial photo of St Philip's Church, probably taken in the 1950s. At the end of the road running in front of the church is the village school, and next to the shadow of the spire is the old vicarage (now demolished); behind the trees north of the church is Brookdale which was later incorporated into Mount Carmel School (now Alderley Edge School for Girls). Ryleys Lane runs from the bottom of the picture to join London Road east of the church, passing the field with a barn where the present (1968) vicarage now stands.

Source unknown.

The design was by Joseph Stretch Crowther of Manchester, a young architect keen to make his name. This was his first independent work.

The church was built in two stages: first, in 1851–52, the chancel, the nave, a north aisle, a porch on the south, and a miniature spire perched on the west gable; then, in 1856–57, a new south aisle, and almost free-standing outside it the splendid steeple with its broach spire, and an extra west bay right across. It is obvious looking at the church today that all this must have been planned from the beginning. A little imagination shows how it was done. A heating grid inside, the centre line of the original building, shows that the new south arcade was built inside the earlier wall, which could then be demolished for the new aisle. The south porch was re-erected on the north (where it was of little use, though providing shelter for several years for a wandering tramp), and it seems probable that the top of the present spire is the original spirelet re-erected. Inside again, the carved faces of the arcades, clearly by two hands, reflect exactly the two phases of construction.

The Decorated style used here was considered at the time to represent the best of Medieval Gothic, which thereafter suffered a catastrophic decline to the 'immeasurably inferior' (Crowther's phrase) Perpendicular and Tudor. Unfortunately, Cheshire can offer very little genuine Decorated. St Mary's Alderley was no use as a model, being typically in the 'debased' Perpendicular style. Instead, Crowther took the flowing tracery and ogee hoodmoulds, scaled down, from Nantwich and from Chester cathedral, and the rocketing steeple with its three-tier broached spire from Lincolnshire via his own *Churches of the Middle Ages* (Bowman and Crowther, 1845).

Forming a pretty group with St Philip's is the **village school**. The first part, with its belfry-topped gable and traceried window, is contemporary with phase one of the church and also by J. S. Crowther. A further phase may also be by him, but the third phase, with its row of gables, is Cheshire County Council.

The third member of the group has gone. This was the original vicarage, by John Lowe, not Crowther, although like the school built in header bond brick.

By the lych gate is Alderley Edge's War Memorial, an aedicule cross on an octagonal base, with a ring of stone columns to carry the names. An extra inscription at its foot commemorates Emily Hutton of Woodlands, who ran an auxiliary hospital at Brookdale immediately north of the church, but died in 1919.

Characteristically, Alderley Edge **Methodist church** has a good spire too – and a clock. Built in 1863 by Hayley and Sons, it is unusually churchy for the Methodists, with Decorated tracery. It has a broad unobstructed interior under a light, notched collar-truss roof. Pews and dais have gone but the big pitch-pine pulpit and organ case remain.

Nearby is **Orchard Green,** a charming close of gardeners' houses by Hubert Worthington, 1920. It was paid for by a consortium of the Cottentots – such a useful word – called the Alderley Edge Public Utility Society.

The villas and the village in 2009 – a perambulation

In 1999, at the time of the Alderley Edge Landscape Project, villas and village presented a stable picture and could be recorded with equanimity. Thereafter, the third phase of building meant that Alderley Edge often resembled a building site. It is very difficult to give a reasoned assessment of its architectural value. Therefore the following snapshot is offered, in the form of a walk from London Road up Woodbrook Road and back down Macclesfield Road.

The village street in 2009 was still the A34, the legionary road from Manchester to Oxford and Southampton – but not for much longer. A by-pass was at last under construction, cutting through the dull country to the west of Alderley Edge. Smart bars and eateries line the street, with seating on the wide pavement – a relic of when the earliest houses had front gardens – yards from the stalled traffic. Several high-class food shops survive: it is doubtful whether they have different prices for locals and incomers, as was once the case.

Stevens Street leads off the London Road opposite Percy Scott Worthington's District Bank of 1903. Here on the east side of the main road, but before starting to ascend, is a district of middle-quality middle-management houses. Social gradations were acute when these were built, even within the village, those living here looking down on those in the tightly packed streets, now mostly cleared, on the west side of the street. Also on Stevens Street is the Union Club, with its bowling green. Facing Stevens Street in **Trafford Road** is No. 29, Alan Garner's childhood home, an aboriginal cottage of the late seventeenth or early eighteenth century, of brick, nicely proportioned, and tiny (Figure 23.5). Alan recalls how, even in so tiny a house, the front parlour was sacrosanct, cold, kept for best.'

Turning right and across the Mottram Road is **Lake House,** built in an old quarry. A long drive winds up to **Woodbrook,** a yellow brick villa built in about 1850 on one of the finest sites. In 1905 and 1914–18, C. F. A. Voysey made some alterations, mainly internal but with a few outside bits finished in white roughcast with flush-mullioned windows. A major architect, much revered and imitated today, but a minor work.

Woodbrook Road, partly cut into the bedrock, starts to climb the hill. Immediately on the left is **The Ridge,** under construction in 2009, a modernist essay by Stephenson Bell offering a subterranean pool, spa

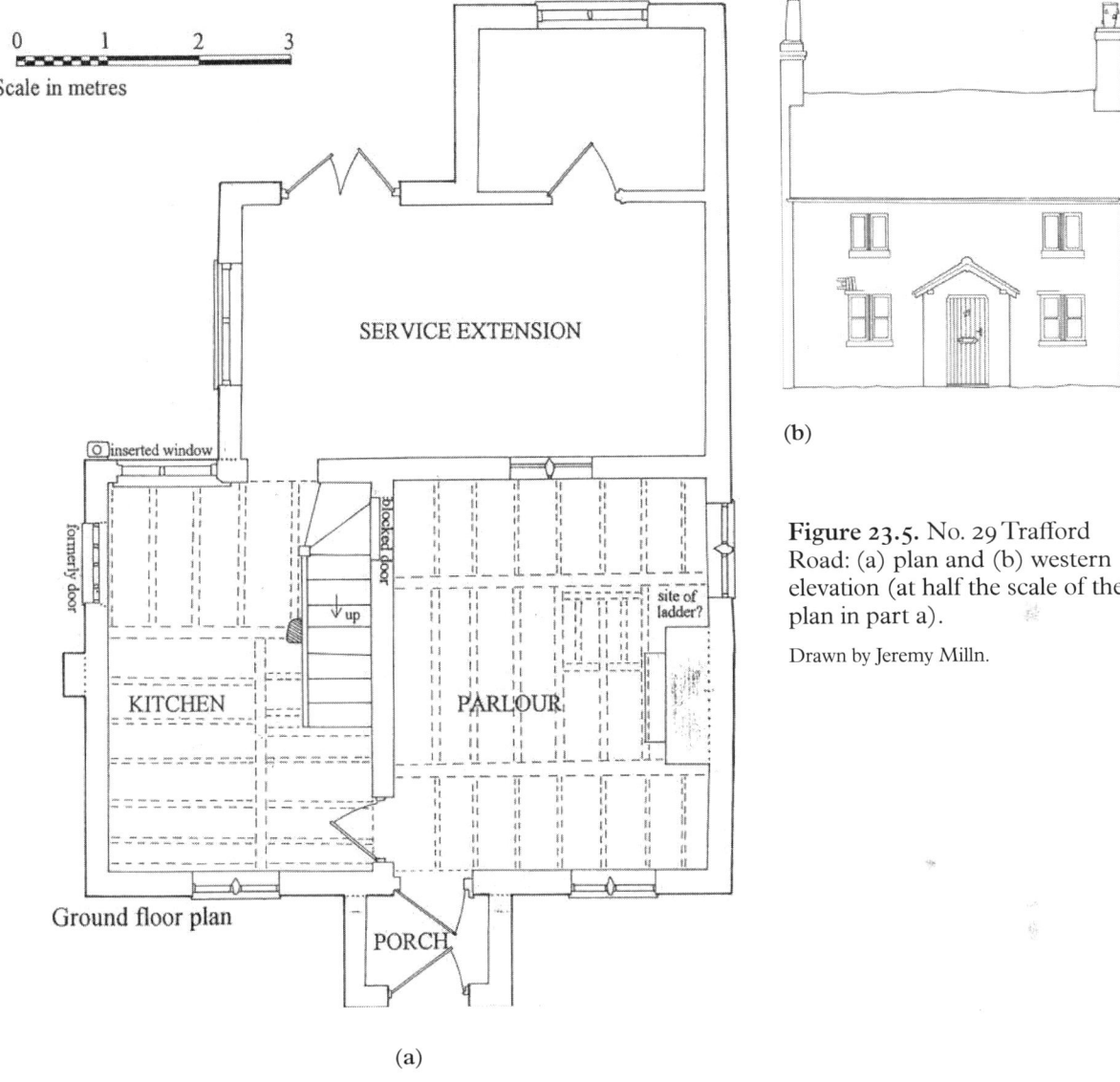

(b)

Figure 23.5. No. 29 Trafford Road: (a) plan and (b) western elevation (at half the scale of the plan in part a).

Drawn by Jeremy Milln.

and cinema, a huge garage and floating above them a double-height living space flowing into dining, kitchen and family areas. **The Hollies** is an early villa, partly 1840s, white and amateurishly Gothic. Inside, a charming bit of stained glass shows the Beacon on the Edge and the Spanish Armada. An unexpected delight is the maids' bathroom, complete. Above that is **Jaysholme**, a ranch-style house of *c.* 1972, the sort of house on which 2009 redevelopers set their sights. This occupies the site of St Mary's Cliffe, which was a spooky J. S. Crowther house of 1851 bristling with spire roofs, tall chimneys and spiky finials. It burnt out in 1971, leaving only the incomplete inscription from above the front door '+GODS:PROVIDENCE:IS:MINE:INHER[ITANCE…]'. Next

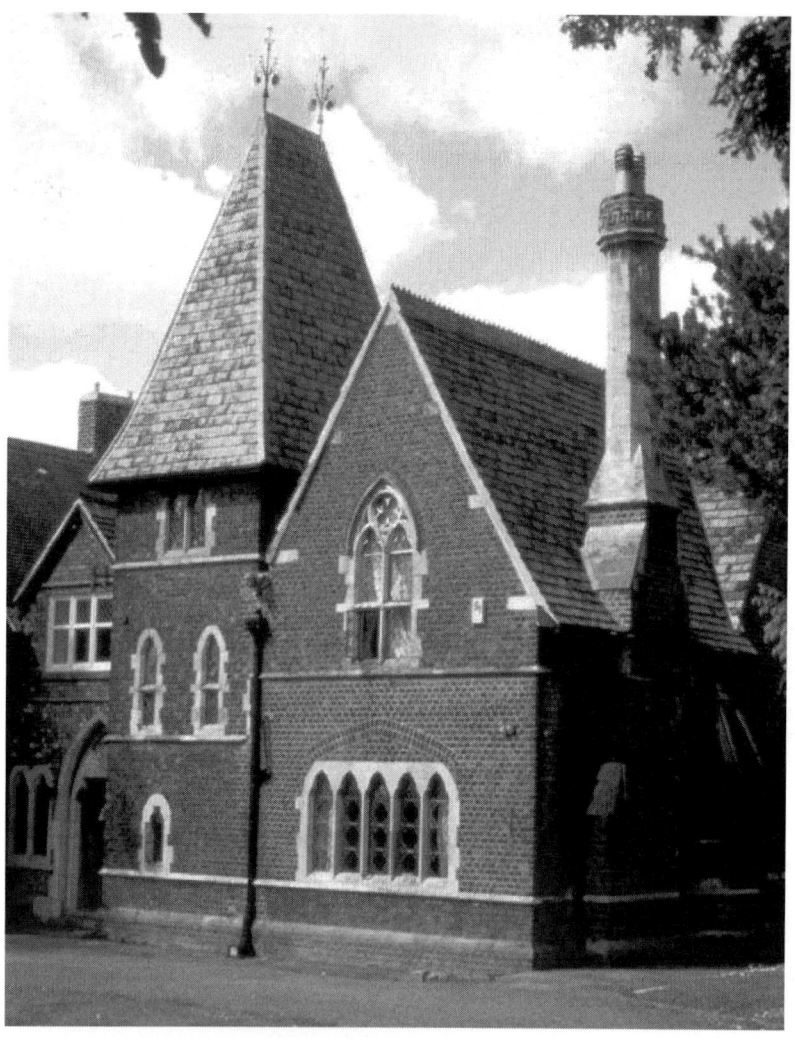

Figure 23.6. Redclyffe Grange, by J. S. Crowther.

Photograph Matthew Hyde.

door however is **Redclyffe Grange**, a complete J. S. Crowther house, indeed his own (Figure 23.6, also Figure 23.1), apparently named after Charlotte M. Yonge's novel *The Heir of Redclyffe* (1853). It is likely that he bought one of the original plots and built two houses on it, one for himself and one to sell. To the followers of the Oxford Movement, it was not only a beautiful story, but also a confession of faith, a noble picture of an ideal life. Redclyffe Grange is the manifesto of a modern Gothic man, showing forth in its outer form the mullioned and occasionally traceried windows of true Gothic, the over-steep roofs defining each component, the over-tall chimneys, and a carved gargoyle or two. Inside, Gothic arches articulating the stairs paraphrase the screens passage arches of a Medieval house like Chorley Hall (see Chapter 24 on the Stanley estate, pp. 614–16, including Figures 24.7 and 24.8).

After that is **Firwood**, now called **The Cedars**, which was designed by John Gregan for John Heugh but is remembered as the Pilkingtons' house. It looks down on the **Cricket/Tennis Club** below (1891, by Thomas Worthington and Sons), which was the social centre of Alderley Edge in its Edwardian heyday. Firwood is large, Italianate, of yellow brick with a tower. It lost its name in the 1960s when Margaret Pilkington built a new, more convenient Firwood in a detached piece of her garden across the road. This retains a magical hidden dell of a garden, a real bit of Alderley Edge romance. Next, Fern Cottage and **Woodbrook Place**, a range of fake stables of *c.* 2000 in timber-framing. **Underwood** is a big Italianate villa built in header bond brick with yellow accents. Its big roof looks like a 1930s alteration. **Fernhill** was the home of John Ramsbottom, Chief Mechanical Engineer of the London and North Western Railway, the successor to the Manchester and Birmingham: an unspoilt villa, yellow and Italianate, with an open balcony. Opposite, however, **The Larches**, by J. S. Crowther, with its famous garden, was redeveloped as long ago as 1935. One of the 1935 infill houses was itself replaced *c.* 2005 in Frank Lloyd Wright style. At the top is **Bollin Tower** (Figure 23.7): a great sight, rock-faced, picturesque and castellated, with a tower and higher turret poking out of the trees. The earliest directories list an Alderley Castle and Mr John Rogers as architect. 'Went over to Alderley Edge to look over a piece of land bought by Mr Rogers' writes the de Trafford steward in his diary of 11 October 1843 (in the de Trafford papers at the Lancashire Archives in Preston). The name Alderley Castle is confirmed by the deeds. It looks as though this is the very first villa. The martial aspect is all bluff – at the back and inside it is a perfectly ordinary villa. The Stanley 'brid and babby' emblem on the facade is discussed by John Adams in Chapter 28, p. 713. Beside it is **The Gables**, perhaps originally a staff cottage, and beyond that **Earnscliff**, built on the same original plot but in a contrasting white Italianate style.

This is the top of the de Trafford estate. Beyond is Stanley land, and the opportunity to weigh up a couple of houses of the second wave of development (see above). **Penn**, by Percy Scott Worthington, was built in 1912 for Walter and Dorothy Milne. Date and initials appear on an oval cartouche. It is white and Georgian, with a graded Coniston slate roof and sliding sashes. Its rhododendron garden was regularly open to the public, but at the time of the perambulation it was a building site with a huge conservatory or pool extension under construction. Nearby on Macclesfield Road is **Abbot Brow**, by his half-brother, Hubert Worthington. Dated 1923 on its cartouche, it is very similar to Penn, while differing in almost every particular. The style is Queen Anne rather than Georgian, the walling is fine red brick not roughcast, the roof tile not slate, the windows casements rather than sashes. This is a subtle

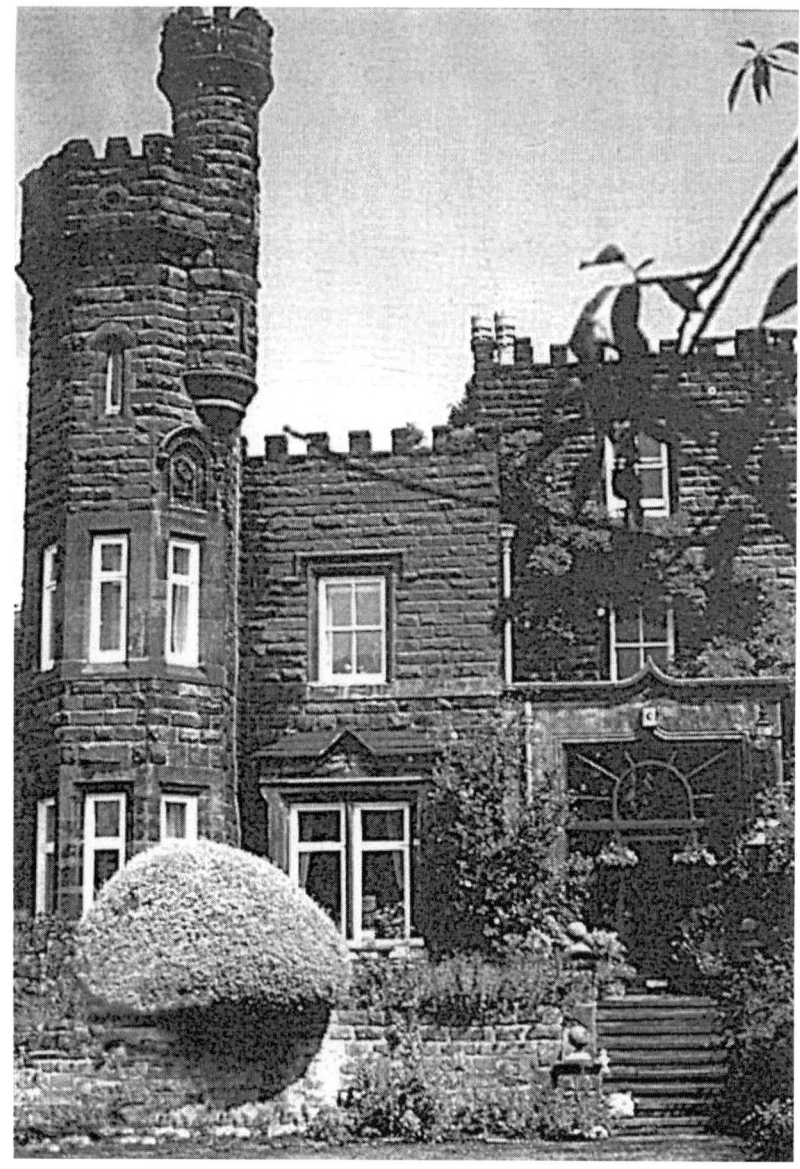

Figure 23.7. Bollin Tower by John Rogers, once apparently known as Alderley Castle.

After Hyde (1999: 71).

design achieving considerable presence, even grandeur, with surprisingly modest interiors. The effect is managed by the big simple hipped roof and powerful chimneys, the careful symmetry, and the smaller than usual scale of doors, windows and even bricks, which deceives the eye into thinking the building is bigger than it really is. Every detail is thought out – there are no visible drainpipes for example – and the specification is so good that Massey's (which built both houses) used to bring apprentices out to see how it should be done. These two houses are rather more formal than their brethren on Congleton Road.

Descending now, and back in de Trafford territory.

In the loop between Macclesfield Road and Woodbrook Road stood **Croston Towers**, named after a Lancashire estate of the de Traffords. It was a big villa with extensive gardens, redeveloped in the 1960s and again in 2007–09. On Woodbrook Road we might have noticed **Overwood**, an olde Cheshire manor complete with graded (reconstituted) stone roofs and black windows. This has been reconstructed from a Spanish ranch called Mirador, a typically cheap-looking white-painted 1960s house with fancy ironwork, picture windows and a monopitch roof. **Broadwood**, a suave homage to Voysey, exemplifies the third-wave villas. It also incorporates Croston Towers' original rock-faced gardener's cottage.

Descending Macclesfield Road, **Cherrytree** is a late villa, or early infill, of 1892, by George T. Redmayne (who lived on Ryleys Lane) for Charles Railton, in rather hard materials. The Railtons came to Alderley Edge in 1860 and lived in several houses in turn before building Cherrytree. Reid Railton was a lover of fast machines, and Railton Specials took several world speed records in the 1930s. **Cherrydene** of 1985 or so is in front, infilling the infill. Next, **Eden Park** is the site of **Oatlands**. This was demolished in the 1960s for eight smaller houses, but they are all doomed in their turn. On one corner, however, is **Manden House**, completed in 2009, unusually in a modern idiom, by McHugh Stoppard of Liverpool: a cube of fine ashlar, glass-ended and floating on a recessed base, linked by a glass foyer to a dark brick block with monopitch roof. Here too is **Witches' Gate**, a 1960s house rebuilt in an unadventurous modern style, but huge. The said gate, underneath it, is the old garden gate to Oatlands. **Springfield**, opposite, was one of the finest of the 1850s villas, built of fine ashlar stone in a French style. Though truncated now, it has considerable presence.

Below Witches' Gate is another large development site, called **Edenhouse**. This is the plot belonging to **The Whins**, by Henry Bowman *c.* 1845, a yellow brick villa in a classical rather than Italianate style. The house was trashed for redevelopment in 2009, leaving nothing but the roofless outer walls. On the other half of the plot, Bowman handed the designing of **Broomfield**, 1845–47, to his young apprentice Thomas Worthington, who showed what he could do in the Gothic style. In 1869, by a curious turn of fate, Worthington was able to buy it himself. He extended it and then in 1873 married his second wife, Edith Emma Swanwick, the daughter of the original client, reputed to be the first Cottentot baby of Alderley Edge. Worthington's spread-out family was prominent on Alderley Edge life for many years.

Now **Thornfield**, another redevelopment redeveloped. The original villa, yellow and Italianate, was demolished in 1969 for four new houses by Derek Cobb. These have gone in their turn. One of the replacements is the new Thornfield, *c.* 2005, unusually styled Victorian, with barge-boards and sash windows, though in red brick. Opposite is the lodge to **Franklyn**. This house, invisible from the road, replaced **Ferns**, which is central to the Alderley Edge story because Edwardian life there was so vividly remembered in Katharine Chorley's book *Manchester Made Them* (1950). Ferns was of rough stone with a tower, and stood on the largest plot, five and half acres.

The 'Elizabethian' **Hollybank**, with its tall star chimneys, is on the corner of Trafford Road. The last descent to the village passes the **Alderley Edge Hotel**, formerly **Ashfield** of *c.* 1850, and **Beech Manor**, another twenty-first-century attempt at Victorian, this time in yellow brick. At the bottom is another tiny aboriginal cottage, now called **Wizard's Thatch**. At the six-ways junction a fake Italianate tower signals the site of **St Hilary's School**, which grew up around two villas called Westwood and Barnfield. These are preserved to their outer appearance only, and surrounded by flats.

As a postscript, one ought to venture out into the boringly flat country south and west of Alderley Edge, to the non-village of Great Warford. Not good villa country. Instead, there is an extraordinary plethora of out-of-town hospitals, caring for the needy of Manchester. They are here at least in part because of the philanthropic consciences of the ladies of Alderley Edge. Katherine Chorley's *Manchester Made Them* makes clear the obligation felt by the fortunate villa-dwellers of Alderley Edge to the city that had nurtured them, an obligation which many tried to repay by good works in the slums. Building a hospital in Warford made it all much easier. The slum-dwellers gained by the clean air and pleasant surroundings; the good ladies gained by being able to do good deeds on the doorstep. The **David Lewis Hospital** for epileptics still flourishes, whereas the **Mary Dendy Psychiatric Hospital** of 1902 etc. has gone, except for a secure unit on Chelford Road. **Ancoats Hospital Convalescent Home** and its handsome **Lodge** of 1903–04 are now flats. For women and children, it was supported especially by Mrs Crossley, whose wealth came from east Manchester. The architect was Percy Scott Worthington, and some of its details, especially the carving over the entrance, are reminiscent of his District Bank in Alderley Edge.

Further reading

Hyde, M. 1999. *The Villas of Alderley Edge*. Altrincham: Silk Press.
Also useful are the sections on Alderley Edge and Great Warford in Hartwell, C., Hyde, M. and Pevsner, N. 2011. *Cheshire: The Buildings of England* (Pevsner Architectural Guides: Buildings of England). London: Penguin.

24

The Stanley estate

Matthew Hyde

The Stanleys of Alderley can trace their descent from Sir John Stanley (d. 1485), brother of Sir Thomas who was created first Earl of Derby at the Battle of Bosworth, and of Elizabeth Weever, heiress of Weaver and of Over Alderley (the family tree appears in Figure 19.6, p. 473). The family held the estates in Over Alderley and later Nether Alderley until 11–14 October 1938, when the whole lot was put up for sale by auction: 4,624 acres, 4 lesser halls, 77 farms and 166 houses and cottages came under the hammer, together with what was left of the old hall and of Alderley Park, the family seat. The sale was highly traumatic for all concerned, as is described in this chapter. The 100-page *Sale Catalogue*, with its three fold-out maps, is the key to rural Alderley (*Sale Catalogue* lot numbers quoted hereafter refer to the catalogue; the large fold-out plan no. 1 in the catalogue makes clear the layout and the relationship of the different buildings, especially those within Alderley Park; plan no. 2, reproduced in part as Figure 19.19, p. 501, shows the lots along Macclesfield Road and on the top of the Edge).

Alderley Old Hall

The original seat of the Stanleys, Alderley Old Hall stood in a moat on a last outlier of the Edge, by the old mill and the London Road, near St Mary's. The first Lord Stanley tells us in one of his notebooks (CALS DSA 5/10) that there were two bridges over the moat, which served both for defence and as a reservoir to supply the mill. The oldest buildings were at the back. The great hall was built in the ancient style of Cheshire, 'with beams crossing each other and plaster filling up panels or squares left between them', which sounds like timber-framing, although in paintings it looks like stone. It had a very large fireplace and a gallery communicating with the rooms of the upper floor. On the east were the offices of brick and stone, with mullioned windows, which are still standing, but are not shown on his plan. On the west side, forming three sides of a courtyard, stood the latest parts, the last built being the grand west front, which was a handsome architectural elevation of brick with stone quoins and window surrounds and a pair of giant Corinthian pilasters framing the door. A balustrade hid the roof. Stanley gives no date, but the brick facade looks *c.* 1710 English Baroque, having been added to an older house, parts of which must have dated from the seventeenth century. From this front a bridge of two arches crossed to a terrace; then there were steps down to a garden or court and a handsome ornamented archway to the high road (Figure 19.1, p. 464).

Alderley Old Hall burnt down in 1779. At the time, the family were at their town house in Chester, the still-extant Stanley Palace at the lower end of Watergate Street. As Lord Stanley recalls, 'Very little of the furniture was saved and all the papers excepting a few leases in the Steward's Room were lost'. Some time afterwards he made the sketch and plan of the old place illustrated at Figure 19.1 from memory. These seem to form the basis of the surviving paintings of the hall, all of which depict it from the same impossible angle; in other words, all the images of it are posthumous.

The site today seems at first to bear no relation to Stanley's description and sketches: no gate, no steps, no bridge, no new front and no old back. What does remain is the moat, a second bridge not visible in the picture but shown on the plan and clearly ancient, and a brick service wing of the seventeenth century, which annoyingly is not shown on either. It must have been aligned with the kitchen wing but may have been detached from the main block or nearly so.

However, covered in ivy and hidden in the trees are the two outer piers of the terrace garden – just enough to be able to accept the picture as true. The abutments of the west bridge can also be found. The offices which still stand are at least mentioned by Stanley, if not indicated on his plan, and he does speculate that the remaining bridge, leading to the stables (demolished 1806), was the original access. On the north side of the remaining bridge there is much to be found. The seventeenth-century walled garden is well preserved and very fine: a beautiful tall wall of brick with triangular buttresses on the inside alternating with the square ones outside, a central rectangular canal, and two pretty corner pavilions with pyramid roofs, all indicating that it was primarily ornamental, unlike a Victorian kitchen garden. Both pavilions are now dwellings, and much extended. The Apple House has a well in the vaulted cellar and a stone outer stair to the main floor like that to the Stanley pew at St Mary's. Alderley Mill Cottage in the opposite corner has a slow clear spring in the cellar and curved steps to a terrace in front.

Alderley Park

To the south and east of the Old Hall lay the deer park. In about 1750 a fort-like 'deer house' was built by Radnor Mere – a big walled shelter, open to the sky though perhaps having some lean-to roofing inside. It was in the Gothick style, like the existing one at Sudbury in Derbyshire, and appears in the background in a charming portrait of about 1810 of the twins, Edward and William Stanley, aged about eight (Figure 19.11, p. 487). Also in the park was a plain obelisk topped by the Eagle and Child and dated 1750, still visible from the Old Hall. Park House was occupied by a family called Deane de Park, recorded by inscriptions on the school and the Eagle and Child Inn, but also sometimes used by the Stanleys as a dower house, as is clear from an inscription on the large upright stone below the Stanley pew.

After the fire of 1779 the Stanley family moved to the Park House (Figure 24.1). Temporary became permanent and Alderley Park became the Stanley seat for 160 years, although in 1809 they bought Winnington

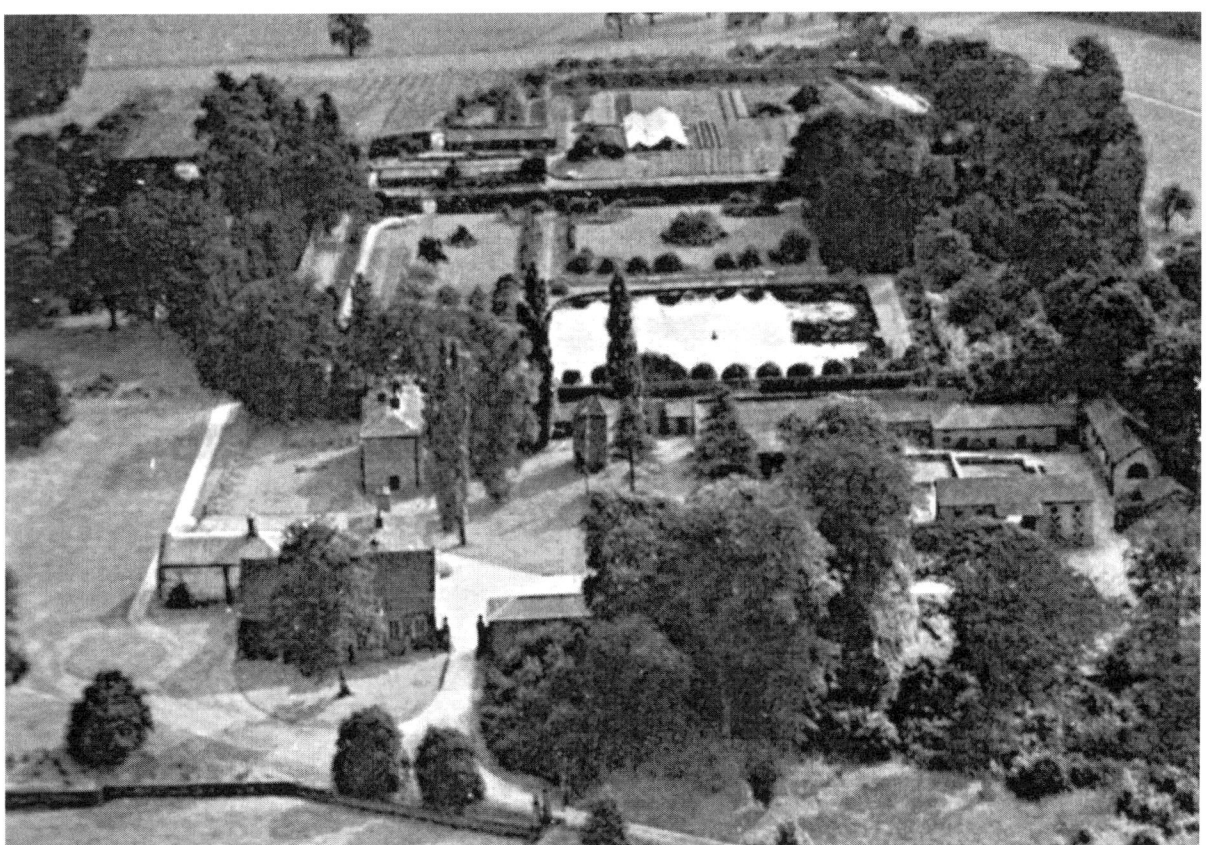

Figure 24.1. Aerial view of Alderley Park.

From *Sale Catalogue* (lot 126A).

Hall, near Northwich, which was a favoured residence for some years: the family occupied it while the house at Alderley was being rebuilt and later used it as a dower house.

The garden at Park House was taken in hand first, and then the old house itself was gradually enlarged and modernised, starting in 1817, into a substantial and rambling country house, which by the Stanleys' own assessment had no great architectural merit. Again, it is possible only to reconstruct it from photographs and memories and the scanty evidence on site; in fact it is harder to reconstruct mentally than the Old Hall. Some of it looks like the work of one of the Wyatt clan, probably Samuel, who did so much in Cheshire. The taller range to the right of the main entrance, with carved (or Coade stone) plaques above the ground-floor windows, is a good candidate. The canted bays on either side of the entrance portico are less convincing.

A different attribution is suggested by Church Lodge, dated 1817. This is a strange little house, like three child's building blocks of different sizes, each topped with a Chinese pagoda roof in lead. It is nothing like the classical Wyatt lodges of Tatton or Heaton, but does resemble the twin towers, also pagoda-roofed, of Toft Hall near Knutsford. These are the work of Samuel Pepys Cockerell, who reconstructed Toft in 1810–13. Not a dull architect: his exotic onion-domed house at Sezincote in Gloucestershire places him in the same league as John Nash at Hafod and Brighton Pavilion. The Leycesters of Toft were close friends of the Stanleys of Alderley, unlike the Leicesters of Tabley – the relationships between the families have been described by Clare Pye in Chapter 19.

The older parts of the Park House were of brick and similar in style to the remaining hexagonal dovecote. There was a large tenants' hall as at Tatton, rebuilt in 1904 to a dull historical design, and still standing. A small portion of the link building also remains which presents a windowless wall of finest ashlar – perhaps the backing to a conservatory.

The house at Alderley Park burnt down in 1931 and was demolished in 1933.

The stable-yard is substantially preserved but not particularly eloquent. The large walled garden adjoining is interesting, however, in that it seems to be a deliberate echo of the one they had left behind at the Old Hall. It has a large square ornamental pool in the middle, and can never have been a utilitarian kitchen garden, which makes it something of an anachronism. Moreover, the corner pavilions at the old hall are echoed in the gardener's house and the brewery house in the stable-yard.

S. P. Cockerell may have been responsible for Beechtree Lodge too, which is very distinctive, with its heavy horizontals and massive stonework. In the paddock behind it is a pretty, though surprisingly impoverished-looking, kennel, dated 1867, in brick with crow-stepped gable. Beacon Lodge up on the Edge, dated 1845, is of stone, originally with two gables. It has been extended to make three equal gables, giving it a fortuitous resemblance to Soss Moss, Chorley and Heawood Halls. Bradford Lodge is a gauche historicist design in stone with mullioned windows, *c.* 1840. Bollington and Whirley Lodges, with their shaped gables, belong to the 1870s and Henry, third Lord Stanley; they are by John Birch 'from his Lordship's rough sketches', as were for instance the Picturesque cottages on Welsh Row (Figure 24.5f, p. 610).

The Stanleys and St Mary's Church

Church, school and mausoleum stand in one pretty and well groomed churchyard (Figures 19.4, 19.17, pp. 469, 499). The church is of typical east Cheshire Perpendicular type, weighed down by its heavy stone roof, which precludes parapets and keeps the clerestory low and sparsely windowed. The tower is a very fine piece of construction, stately, carefully proportioned and enlivened with gruesome gargoyles. Its similarity to Mobberley suggests a date close to 1533 and common authorship by the master-mason recorded there, Richard Plat. However, it looks as though the Mobberley tower was built outside the church, which was then extended to meet it. Here it seems the tower was built inside the west end of the church, and the westernmost arches of the arcades had to be shortened to suit.

An unusual feature is the domestic-looking two-storey transept projecting on the south. This is the Jacobean Stanley pew. Elevated inside like an opera box, and just as plushy, it is the result of a protracted lawsuit in the sixteenth century between the Fittons and Stanleys that was resolved in the diocesan law courts. The outside stair used by the family is very similar to the steps of the corner pavilions of the walled garden. On the other side is a seventeenth-century dormer window, presumably to light the pulpit. Its proportions and its central placing allow it to be read like a pediment (Figure 24.2). This is such a common vernacular feature of the area, appearing in timber, in stone as here, and in brick, that the AELP surveyors coined the term 'Stanley gable' or 'Stanley dormer' as a shorthand. The Medieval chancel was taken down and rebuilt in 1856 by Cuffley and Starkey, who were involved in villa-building at the Edge, in a Victorian Decorated style. A study of the proportions suggests that the Medieval chancel was somewhat longer.

Underneath it is the Stanley burial vault.

More restoration by Paley and Austin of Lancaster in 1877–88 included retooling all the interior stonework, presumably to remove plaster. The fine pews date from this period; they were made by Joseph Foden from estate oak, with different carving on every bench end.

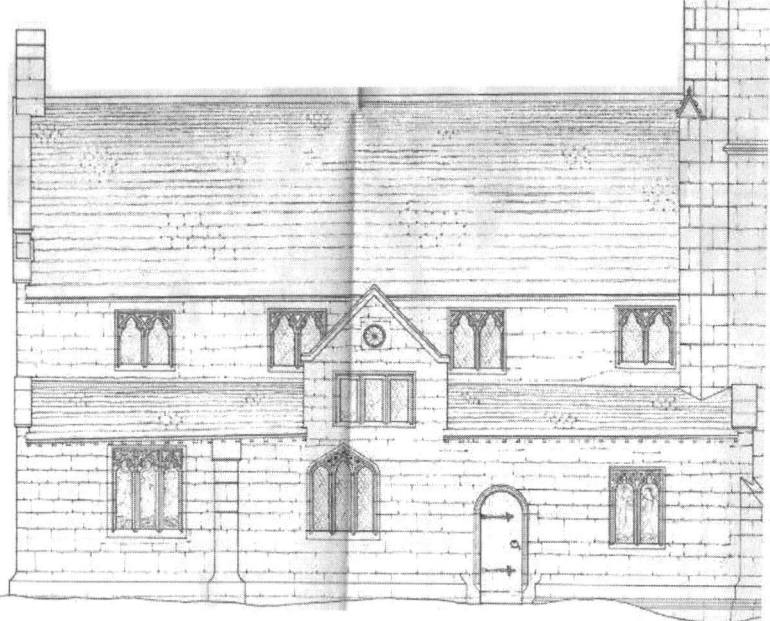

Figure 24.2. St Mary's Church, Nether Alderley. North elevation of the nave, showing the 'Stanley dormer' lighting the pulpit.

Drawn by G. D. Boddington and Harry M. Fairhurst, 1944–45.

Tomb recesses were built into both sides of the new chancel. In the right-hand one is John Thomas, first Lord Stanley, builder of the chancel, who died in 1856. His effigy is by the younger Richard Westmacott. On the other side is Edward John, the second Lord Stanley, who died in 1869. His alabaster effigy, signed George Nelson, 1872, rests on a tomb-chest which has Cosmati-style inset decoration. Could the twirly Cosmati colonettes be genuine? On the side of the tomb is a magnificent brass portraying the mourning family, each dressed according to profession and character and identified by enamelled heraldry.

Further memorials are on the walls: the provocative John Constantine Stanley 1878 (the Stanley children seem to have taken the greatest delight in needling each other); Henrietta Maria Stanley, brass 1895 by Philip Webb.

Lyulph, fourth Lord Stanley, built the mausoleum outside in 1909, architect Paul Phipps, presumably for himself and many future generations (Figure 19.18). In the event it houses only his own monument, a white marble tomb chest, and in any case he was cremated (1925). Like many of his family he was agnostic and fiercely anti-clerical.

Notably missing is Henry, third Baron Stanley, who died in 1903. Brilliant but eccentric, and made lonely by his deafness, he travelled widely, in the course of which he had espoused the Muslim faith. Henry was buried according to the Muslim rite in a lonely copse by Bollington Grange, an evocative spot, dank, overgrown with rhododendrons, with a large badger sett for company. His memorial is a tall thin stone of frilled

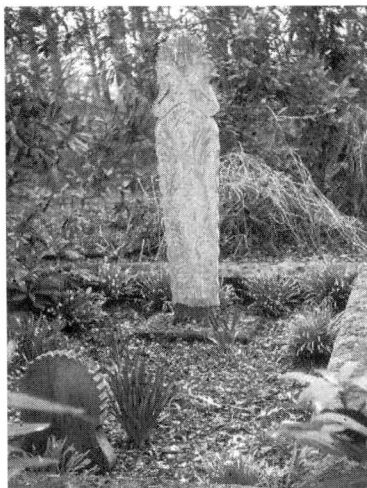

Figure 24.3. The grave of Henry, third Lord Stanley, near Bollington Grange.

Photograph Matthew Hyde.

outline with a chrysanthemum arrayed like a sunburst and climbing plants below. A smaller footstone (if he is buried upright, should there be one?) carries a lightly cut inscription (Figure 24.3).

Also in the churchyard, by the church gate, is the old school (Figure 24.4). An inscription tells us that it was built by Hugh Shaw, clerk, in 1628, and endowed by Thomas Deane 1694. An engaging little building, small and square, schoolroom below, master's lodging above. Raised dormers placed centrally – the Stanley dormer, no less – light the upper floor. Attached at the back is a large hall added in 1817 by the Reverend Edward Stanley. One of the most interesting of the clan, he was a clergyman of scientific bent and unusually liberal views, and was appointed Bishop of Norwich in 1837. Owen Stanley, his eldest son, was the great explorer; Arthur Penrhyn Stanley, another son and also a great traveller, was a distinguished and liberal Dean of Westminster.

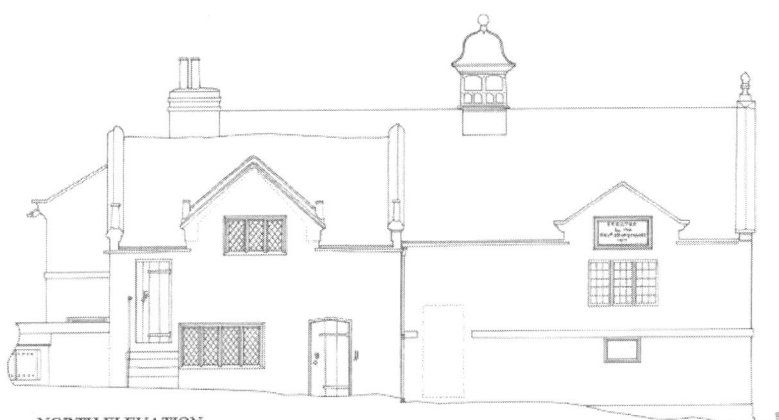

Figure 24.4. Front elevation of the old school by St Mary's Church.

Drawn by Matthew Hyde.

NORTH ELEVATION

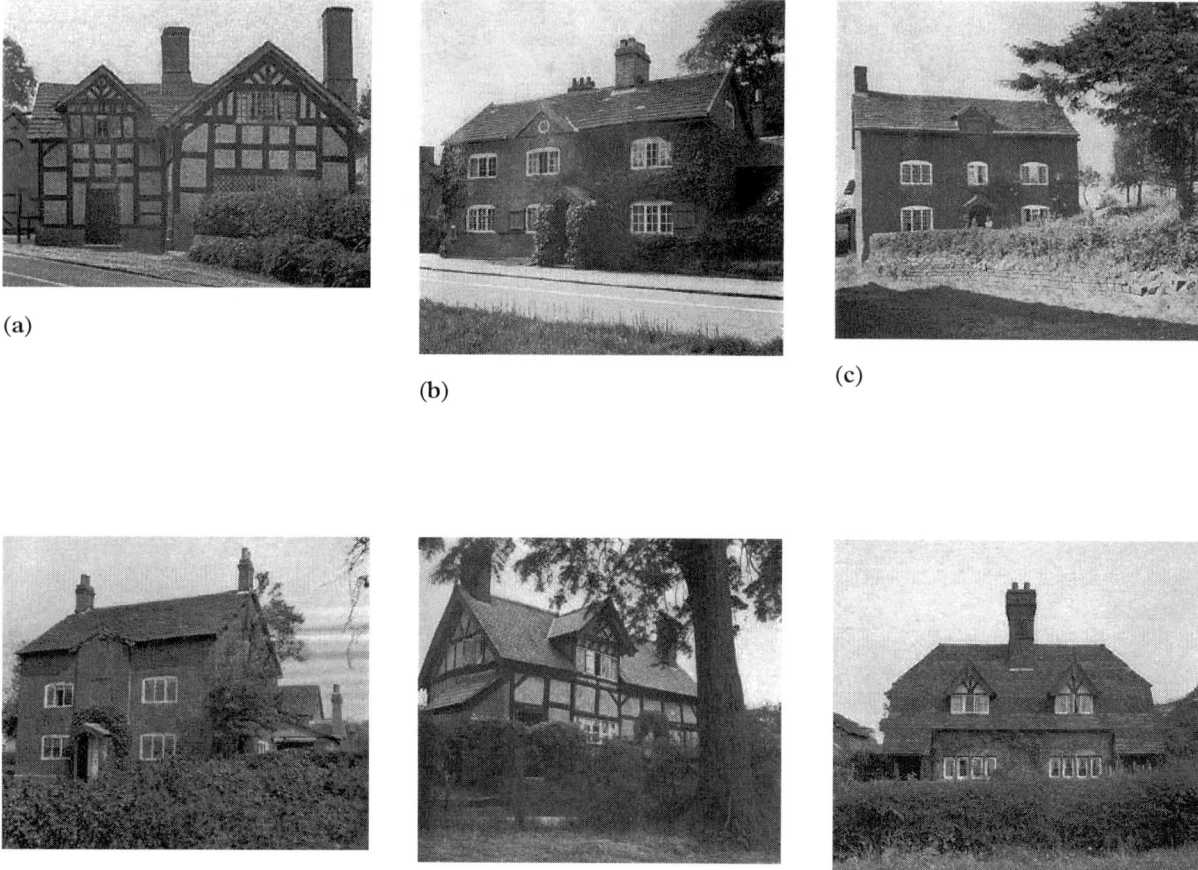

Figure 24.5. Examples of the 'Stanley gable': (a) the Eagle and Child cottage (lot 145 in the 1938 *Sale Catalogue*); (b) Millbrook (lot 149); (c) Bradford House Farm (lot 377); (d) Higher House Farm (lot 584); (e) Yew Tree Cottage (lot 354); (f) a pair of cottages on Welsh Row (lot 283).

From the 1938 *Sale Catalogue*.

Edward Stanley also rebuilt the former rectory on the other side of the lane, *c.* 1810. It has the vaguely Tudor dripmoulds and bargeboards of the time, and an enormous scarlet rhododendron embellishes the garden. The rector now lives in part of the stable block.

On the corner of the lane and the main road is the Eagle and Child Cottage (lot 145 in the 1938 *Sale Catalogue*) (Figure 24.5a), timber-framed, with a decorative dormer with quatrefoils on the cove, 'TD 1688' on ornamental lead gutter. This too has a decorative dormer, with quatrefoils on the cove, to light the upper floor. For the story behind its rather curious name, see Chapter 28, p. 713. Opposite is Millbrook Cottage (lot 149), of late seventeenth-century brick (Figure 24.5b). Formerly a shop, it now offers bed and breakfast. Here again we have a central dormer or gable. So we have seen the Stanley dormer or gable in brick, timber and twice in stone.

The Mill, east of the church, is on the main road. It is a sixteenth-century water-mill with restored machinery. It has a big sweep of stone-flagged roof with small dormers. This is fully described and illustrated by Mike Redfern in the next chapter of this book, where the Old Hall is also discussed further, in particular in its historical and topographic relationship to the Mill.

Architectural progression

Many of the following houses are described, with measured drawings by Jeremy Milln, in the Vernacular Architecture Group's spring conference book for 2000 (Cleverdon *et al.*, 2000).

Unlike many landed families the Stanleys never carried out wholesale rebuilding on their estate, but rather made piecemeal improvements here and there. So the buildings are often preserved in their original form, or have been repaired in such a way that the original form can be recognised.

When looking at the old farmhouses it is possible to see a scale of size, attuned to the size of the landholding, ranging from the miniscule **Hocker Lane Farm** with eleven acres (lot 633) to the relatively splendid **Hayman's Farm** (lot 474), which has 105 acres. Within this graduation a system can be discerned, a common formula which can be expanded or contracted as required.

Hocker Lane Farm has two heated rooms either side of a stack with a tiny unheated room at the downhill end. The door is at the side of the stack, a so-called baffle-entry. The house is less than twelve feet wide outside and the height to the ridge of the roof is not a lot more. An alternative design, almost as small, is exemplified by **Findlow's Bower Farm** (lot 421). This time the house is T-shaped. The houseplace has a big stone fireplace in the end wall, leaving a space for the main entry in front of it, that is, in the baffle position. The second room has become a cross-piece divided into two by a timber partition, with a tight stair to the rooms in the roof above. **Wyche's Farm** (lot 81), which has the same plan, was built in timber framing as late as 1725.

At **Clock House Farm** (lot 431) these two plans are added together (Figure 24.6). There are two heated rooms each side of a central stack (although one has fallen down) with a pair of rooms beyond the larger, forming a T. The entry, protected by a rudimentary porch, is not really in the baffle position but just behind the stack, so that you enter the main living room or house round the far side of the fireplace. This is the standard plan in wet and windy Cumbria. Curiously, the porch still

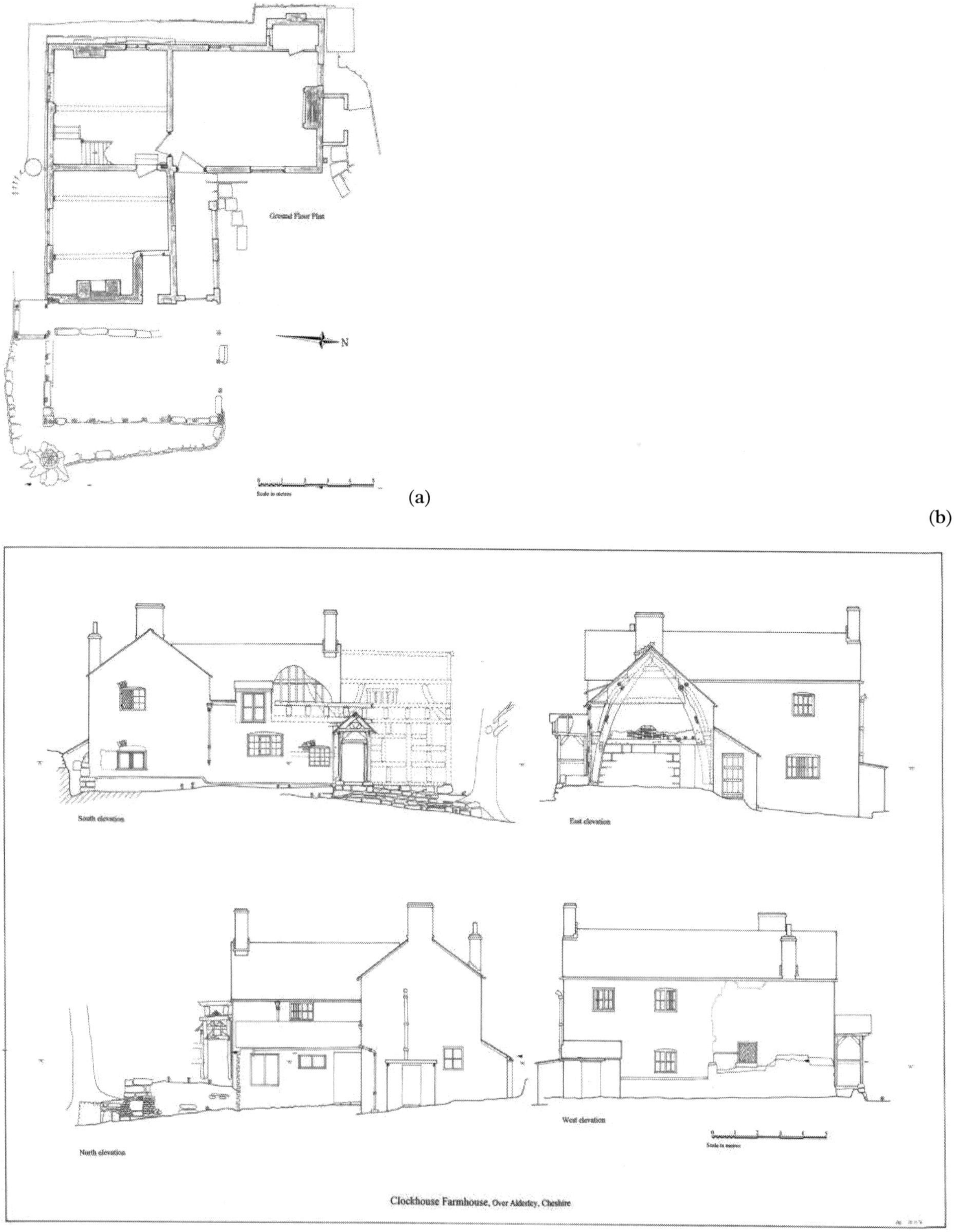

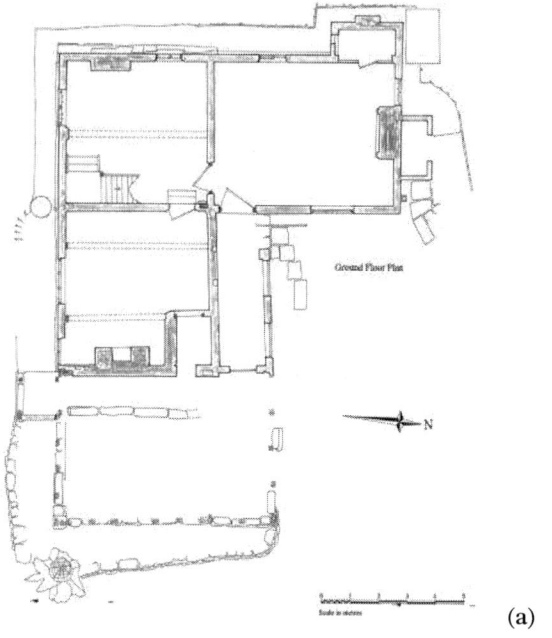

(a)

(b)

Figure 24.6. Clock House Farm: (a) plan and (b) section/elevation.

Drawn by Jeremy Milln.

stands, while the room it entered has fallen down, leaving its chimney jammed in the fork of a tree. Clock House is the only cruck-framed house currently known in the area, and stands in a curiously unfavourable situation under the north face of the scarp.

Hayman's Farm is a bit bigger still, with basically the same plan as Clock House but the porch has become something of a feature, with an upper room, though still opening straight onto the side of the stack. At the back is a long lean-to outshut. Both ends of the house are roofed transversely, so this is the first appearance of the classic H-shape.

The next step can be seen at **Soss Moss Hall** (lot 56), a fine old black-and-white hall of classic Cheshire H-shape, but with the centre given a third gable (Figure 24.7). Once again, the entrance is in baffle position. Soss Moss is signed and dated 'T Wyche 1583' on the mighty stone stack at the service end of the house. The stack doubles as both chimney and garderobe tower, a most sophisticated conceit. Two little windows light 'his and hers' openings off the two upper chambers between the two fireplaces, although there must have been little more than a curtain between them. An opening at the foot was for digging out. A second sophistication shows in the upper floor level of the house, which rises up several steps to allow for a central hall of sufficiently imposing height to recall the old open hall but without the discomfort of an open hearth and roof. The iron fireback here is an anomaly, because it carries the Stanley Eagle and Child with the date 1583, whereas Sir Edward Stanley acquired Soss Moss only in 1753: a fake, presumably. The Wyches moved then to the modest holding of Wyche's farm, seemingly taking their fireback with them.

The kitchen of Soss Moss Hall was Nether Alderley Methodist church from 1835 to 1940. Photographs and cuttings preserved at the Hall record the simple furnishings of the chapel, and the wiliness of the early travelling ministers in circumventing the Stanleys' disapproval.

For a screens passage entry we can stray from the Stanley estate to look at **Lower House Farm** on Mottram Road. Along with Higher House nearby this was the seat of the Mottersheads, an armigerous family related to the Wyches of Soss Moss (Earwaker, 1880: 356). Both farms passed eventually to the Mottram Hall estate, not to Stanleys or de Traffords. It is interesting to note that neither shows any of the Stanley characteristics of plan or design. It is a beautiful house, H-shaped like Soss Moss but with the stacks differently disposed to allow a screens passage between kitchen wing and hall. Timber-framing still shows in the high end wing, but the rest was built away in brick and stone *c.* 1600, with a splendid run of mullions on two floors along the front. Inside there is a remnant of decorative wall-painting, and a magnificent deeply moulded timber re-used over the kitchen fireplace shows that this has always been a high-status property. A curious feature is the numerous

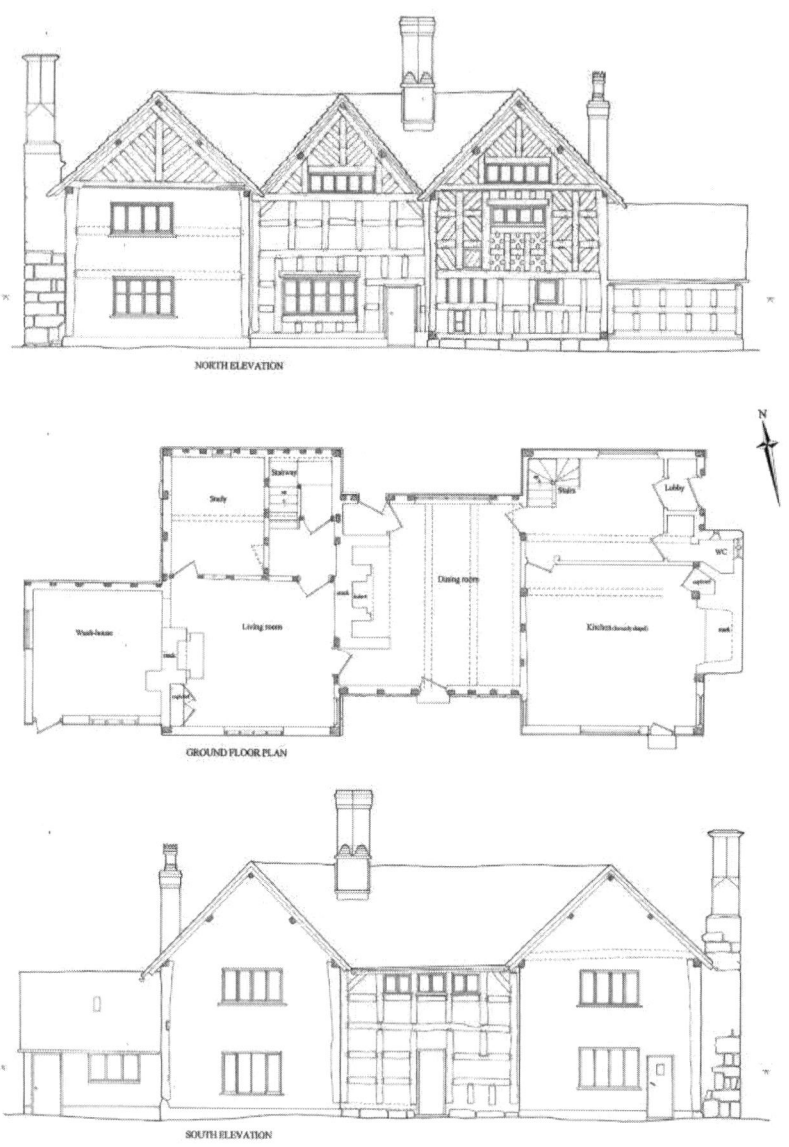

NORTH ELEVATION

GROUND FLOOR PLAN

SOUTH ELEVATION

SCALE IN METRES

Figure 24.7. Soss Moss Hall.

Drawn by Jeremy Milln.

initials and dates, mostly eighteenth century, deeply cut around the door; more of the same can be seen at the Mill.

A classic open-hall house (although an upper floor has been inserted) with full screens passage is **Chorley Hall** (lot 20; Figure 24.8). It is older than any of the others, none of which are likely to be much older than sixteenth century. Chorley dates back to about 1300, making it the oldest substantially extant building in the area of study. It is also probably the one of highest quality. The nearest comparison is with Baguley Hall, a few miles to the north, where the open hall can be seen entire. Chorley is moated, like Alderley Old Hall. The platform is rectangular

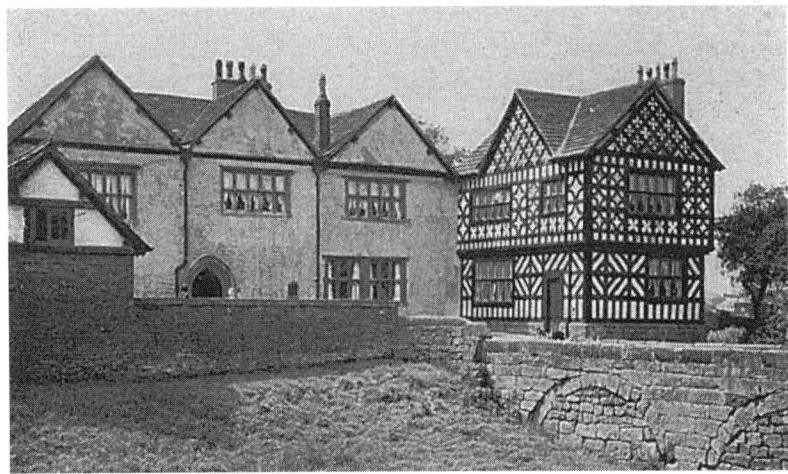

(a)

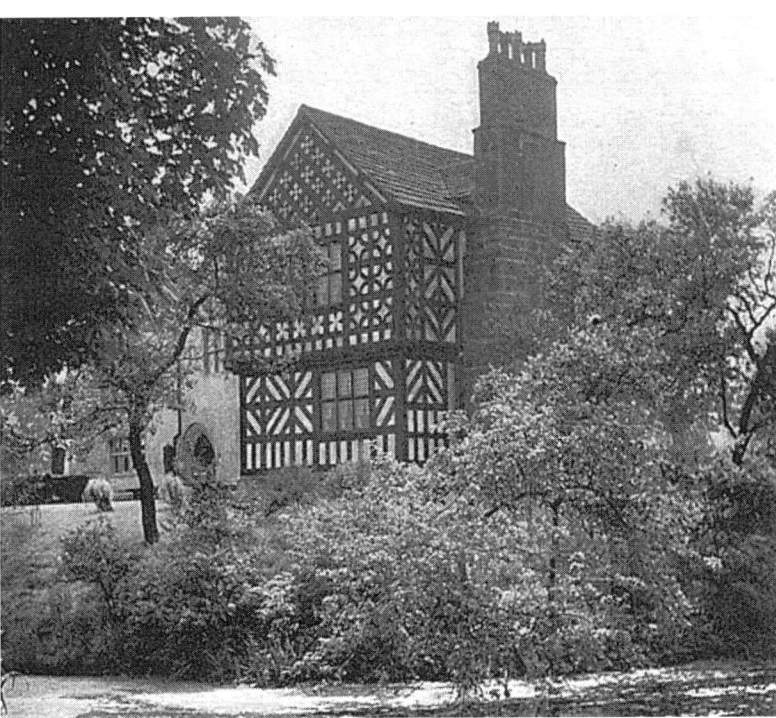

Figure 24.8. Chorley Hall:
(a) whole building, and
(b) Tudor wing.

From *Sale Catalogue* (lot 20).

(b)

but the moat widens out greatly at one corner and, like Alderley Hall, the farm buildings are outside the moat on *terra firma*. Here too there is evidence of complex water engineering, in this case probably for a series of fishponds. Facing the bridge over the moat is a three-gabled facade of stone and brick, with a showy timber-framed Tudor wing standing forward on the west side. Ignoring that for now, the facade hides an exceptionally fine and early open hall and single cross-wing of timber, with a magnificent spere truss and windbraced roof, although these can be seen only in instalments among the present disposition of rooms. The house is a condensation of the classic Medieval H plan – the single wing housed service quarters below but a family solar above. There are, unusually, not three but four doorways in a row along the screens passage. Now they all lead into the same big sitting-room, but they once led to the buttery, kitchen passageway, pantry and a stone turning-stair to the solar above.

The Elizabethan wing is a separate building – just – which was then linked across to the main hall by a temporary-looking outshut. It makes entertaining use of the Cheshire style, with many variations upon quatrefoils within a square grid frame, but when examined after the main house it shows a notable decline in quality. It is constructed of many short timbers of small scantling and shallow jointing, whereas the ancient hall utilised relatively few timbers of mighty size, jointed by enormous tenons and rows of pegs.

Chorley Hall was restored by Lyulph Stanley in 1915, during the lean years. Massey's were the builders, employing older skilled men while the younger ones were away at the Front. The architect was Edmund L. Warre. It would be nice to make the final link with Alderley Hall, but in its absence we can simply say that an H-shaped house can be extended at both ends and then linked across to make a courtyard. At Adlington is a complete courtyard house made up of ranges of disparate age and style, as must have been the case at Alderley.

Later farms

A number of farmhouses were newly built or rebuilt in brick in the seventeenth and early eighteenth centuries. There seem to be two plans; the smaller one has three equal rooms in a row on three storeys, with the stairs in the central one and the top floor lit by a 'Stanley dormer'. Bradford House (Figure 24.5c), Gatley Green, Dean Green Farms are like this. The larger plan is a double-pile, quite sophisticated if one accepts the date 1631 on Fitton Town Farm as a marker. **Higher House Farm** on Hocker Lane is a good example; it is interesting that the Stanley dormer here is just for looks, with no window; big windows in the gable ends light the third floor. It looks as though the Miners' Cottages, lots 499 and 500, were to the same design but minus a storey (Figure 19.22, p. 881).

Higher House (lot 584; Figure 24.5d) is worth describing in some detail because in 1999 it was sold to developers and was gutted. The front door, which is the only panelled door in the house and is and probably always has been virtually unused, opens straight into a big square parlour which has a built-in corner cupboard and a longcase clock that is sunk into the floor to accommodate its height. There is another large plain living-room at the front, and behind are a smaller kitchen, larders and a press-room and a plain wooden stair in the centre, lit by a tall narrow window. An outshut contains the dairy, which has been tiled with blue and white dairymaid tiles. Upstairs on two floors are large airy bedrooms and a bathroom over the outshut. All the original plank doors with their latches and iron latticed windows with heart-shaped openers were preserved at the time of the Project. Behind the house is an older timber-framed barn of four bays with an early brick wing, intriguing because provided with domestic windows but no fireplace. The timber barn at Clock House is likewise puzzling because it has a central Stanley dormer window on both sides, but no sign of heating. At right angles to the timber barn is a newer brick shippon, and there are three piggeries. This seems to be a fairly standard provision. The seventy-one-acre farm is given over to potatoes and pasture. It is a sobering thought that, just as in 1938, the 4,000 acres of the Stanley estate were no longer sufficient to support Alderley Park, so in 1999 seventy Cheshire acres could not support a viable family farm.

The cottages listed in the Stanley *Sale Catalogue*, such as **Yewtree Cottage** on Artists Lane or **Alderley Cottage**, are either good-quality small old dwellings, with an acre or two of land, and which have been steadily improved over the years, or are quite modern, such as the fussily Victorian pair on Welsh Row (Figure 24.5f). In other words, the real cottages of the past have gone. The 'Stanley dormer' is displayed on many of these smaller houses, often providing their one touch of class.

The sale

The sale has already been mentioned by Clare Pye her account of the history of Alderley in Chapter 19, but it is worth returning to it here in the context of the estate.

What was the reason for the sale? Many ancestral estates came up for disposal at this time because changes in agriculture, taxation, the balance of power and attitudes towards service had weakened the aristocracy and the value of land. In this case there were extra causes. Lyulph, who initiated the development of the estate, had died in 1925 and his son Arthur, the fifth baron, only six years later, in 1931. So Edward, the sixth baron Stanley, inherited an estate encumbered with two lots of death duties. According to family reminiscence he was a wastrel: drinker, gambler and womaniser and bad at all three. His marriage on 3 March 1931 to Lady Victoria Chetwynd-Talbot, sister of the Earl of Shrewsbury, was short-lived and they soon separated. Divorce followed in 1936. There were to be three more marriages. The hall at Alderley

Park, far too big now and expensive to run, burnt in 1931. The ruin was demolished and cleared by Massey's in 1933, leaving only the Tenants' Hall and attached Green Room.

The sale was a fiasco, so much so that it made national news. 'More Stonewalling at Alderley Auction' ran the headline in the *Daily Herald* for 13 October 1938. 'Second day's play in the four-day Test Match between the Yeomen of Cheshire and the Auctioneers of England continued dour and grim'. A significant reason for the general unwillingness to bid was the way in which hundreds of building plots had been hived off along every public road, taking the frontage off almost every farm. We may thank our stars that they did not sell, for instead of the present-day pleasures of walking and driving over the Edge there would be suburban ribbon development almost everywhere (Figure 19.19. p. 501). In the event only fourteen lots out of nearly 200 sold on the first day of the sale. Altogether, of the 664 lots offered only 58 sold, raising £45,580. Private treaties brought the total to just about £100,000. Many reasons can be suggested for the failure – powerful passive hostility of the tenants, the greedily insensitive way in which their lands had been carved up for sale, the unpropitiousness of the times – but it remains something of a mystery and one of the most remarkable episodes in the story of the Edge.

After the Stanleys

Alderley Park failed to sell in the 1938 sale. It was retained by the agents until 1950, when it was bought by ICI for £55,000 for its Pharmaceutical Research Division, and then AstraZeneca. Trafford Park had sold for £360,000 in 1896. The lead architect in the first phase was Harry Fairhurst (Harry S. Fairhurst and Sons), contractors John Laing and Co. Harry Fairhurst was born in one of the second wave of villas (see Chapter 23). Little sentiment was shown to the remaining buildings but the ambience of the Park was carefully preserved, even enhanced.

The seventeenth-century Deer House shown in the portrait of the Stanley twins (Figure 19.11) was demolished in 1955 and the first new research buildings, called **Mereside**, erected on the site. On the site of the hall is **Alderley House**, the main office complex, of 1963–64. Round it are the remains of Stanley occupation, though the seventeenth-century farmhouse and the matching brewhouse have gone. The **Tenants' Hall** of 1904 by Paul Phipps and the adjacent **Green Room** survive. Nineteenth-century stables and barns, all dated, surround two yards and a hexagonal **Dovecot**. Through a small Doric temple is the **Walled Garden**, *c.* 1798, clearly ornamental rather than simply productive, with its square lily-pond in the middle. A pair of pavilion-like houses clearly echo the garden at the Old Hall. The eighteenth-century **gates** are from Winnington Hall. Overlooking the pool ICI built a zigzag-fronted **Restaurant**, by H. S. Fairhurst and Sons again, 1968.

Since the early ICI phase, the research complex in the park has developed continuously, and some 5,000–6,000 people were employed at the site in 2007. The early buildings have either been replaced or radically face-lifted. In 1999 Gert Wingardh of Sweden gave the AstraZeneca sites here and in Macclesfield a change of style, encouraging a campus-like feel. Radnor Reception (architects AMEC and Stevenson Bell) and the attendant Conference Centre, opened in 2008 (Alderson Design), develops this theme. Inside is a spectacular longitudinal atrium or internal street with glass walkways and bridges. Business clichés such as 'blue sky thinking' and 'outside the box' take built form as suspended breakout pods. **Parklands** (2003 by Lovelock Mitchell Partners) is another very large building in the same mode. The future of the park consequent upon AstraZeneca's move to Cambridge in 2013 and the sale to Manchester Science Parks (renamed Manchester Science Partnerships in 2014) is touched on in Chapter 28 (pp. 683–4).

After the failure of the 1938 sale many of the farms were bought by private treaty by their tenants or at a second auction, held at Crewe in January 1939, when the developers dropped their plans for wholesale residential development, and farmed as before. Others were bought by incomers and gradually gentrified. Nothing was too sudden, until the late 1990s, when the third Alderley Edge boom came along. This hit the country farms and cottages as much as the villas of the Edge. The same planning restrictions applied and the same combination of extreme wealth and developer pressure was equally good at circumventing them.

A curious addendum is **Hill House**, on Nursery Lane near Soss Moss. A fine old timber-framed house, it had the misfortune to stand in the way of Manchester Airport's second runway, in Mobberley. It was dismantled in *c.* 1998, the bits put in storage, and eventually something partially resembling the original was rebuilt there by James Brotherhood and partners. By then few of the timbers were much use. Only the left wing has much old timbering in it. The fancy gable in the middle is recognisable, as is the inscription '1620 RR' on a beam at the back. It is interesting to note the bleakness of the site; the oldest houses really did take the most favourable sites, and there are none left.

Further reading

Hyde, M. 1999. *The Villas of Alderley Edge*. Altrincham: Silk Press.
Also useful are the sections on Alderley Edge and Great Warford in Hartwell, C., Hyde, M. and Pevsner, N. 2011. *Cheshire: The Buildings of England* (Pevsner Architectural Guides: Buildings of England). London: Penguin.

25

Nether Alderley Mill: a historical and architectural study

Mike Redfern

The early history of the Mill and the Old Hall

The Mill is located on the only suitable stream in the township of Nether Alderley (SJ 8434 7923). It sits in a short, steep-sided narrow valley running east–west, although immediately west of the Mill the valley widens considerably. It has been suggested that the position of the Mill took advantage of a natural break in the streambed which formed a waterfall. There are other instances of water-powered mills built in front of waterfalls: two that come to mind are Heron Corn Mill, Beetham, Cumbria (SD 496 799) and the former Rutter Mill, Great Asby, Cumbria (NY 609 107). The stream at this point cuts into the natural bedrock of sandstone and the faulting of these layers may well have produced such a feature, although this cannot be confirmed.

The earliest mention of a mill at Nether Alderley occurs in 1391, but little is known of the building and no trace of machinery survives from this date. The next confirmed reference to the Mill occurs in 1591, in an inquisition post-mortem (inquiry into property and effects) held on the death of Thomas Stanley, when both the manor house and the watermill are recorded (Earwaker, 1880: 596, 598).

Nether Alderley Mill and the Stanley family

The story of the Stanley family at Alderley is recounted in Chapter 19, so it is only necessary to summarise it here where it affects the history of the Mill. The Stanleys of Alderley dated from 1450, when Thomas de Stanley acquired the manor of Nether Alderley by marriage. The land passed to Sir William Stanley of Holt and a descendant of the Arderne family married a later John Stanley, bringing Over Alderley and Weever family lands as a dowry. The Stanleys were based at Weever for most of the sixteenth century but in the 1580s Thomas Stanley built a new home by the Mill at Nether Alderley. His grandson, another Thomas, inherited the Nether Alderley estate in 1595. The Nether Alderley estate remained in the family's hands until 1938, when it was auctioned.

The flooded valley formed by the millpond of Nether Alderley Mill created a peninsula of rising ground jutting into the northern side of the millpond. It was on this spit of land that the Stanleys had built their manor house and by cutting a channel across the narrow strip of connecting land turned the site into an island. The narrow channel served as a moat, crossed by a stone bridge. The house and Mill are therefore not so much separated by the lake as linked by it. The lake is not only a reservoir for the Mill, but also a protective barrier and a visual amenity for the house. It was lucrative to retain a mill on the estate due to Medieval soke rights; tenants were compelled to have their corn ground there and pay a toll for the privilege or have it milled elsewhere and pay a fine.

The house was extended in 1660 and again in 1754, but following a fire in 1779 most of the house was destroyed and a majority of estate documents were lost. The present Old Hall is only a fragment of the mansion that burned in 1779. It was divided into at least two tenements and at one time the miller and his family occupied one of the tenements.

After the fire, the family moved temporarily into the Park House, their bailiff's home, but never left – it was probably much more comfortable than the Old Hall. However, in 1931 the Park House was so badly damaged by fire that it was demolished in 1933 and the family moved to the adjacent estate farmhouse. Coming on top of two sets of death duties after the deaths of the fourth and fifth Barons in 1925 and 1931 and the lavish lifestyle of Edward, the sixth Baron Alderley, who seems to have had little interest in the estate, the decision was taken to sell the property. As described in Chapter 24, the auction on 11–14 October 1938 was a failure and only 58 of the 664 lots were sold. Some of the farms were purchased using a government low-cost mortgage scheme for tenants to buy their properties. The Old Hall and the Mill were bought by the Hall's tenant, Mr John Armitage Shelmerdine. Following a local appeal, the Mill was reroofed in 1946 and in 1950 Mr and Mrs Shelmerdine donated the Mill to the National Trust.

Alderley Park itself was sold to a London-based property company that intended to develop the site for housing. It was unable to implement these plans before the outbreak of war and with the introduction of Green Belt Acts by the first postwar government its plans were thwarted. In 1950 ICI's Pharmaceuticals Division bought it for its Research Department. The changes of ownership in more recent times are described in Chapter 28 (pp. 683–4, 693).

The development of Nether Alderley Mill

Although we know that a mill existed at Nether Alderley in 1391, there is no evidence of its appearance or of the machinery. An inspection of the Mill with Ivan Hradil, an archaeological timber specialist at the University of Manchester Archaeological Unit, identified several timbers as probably being older than the 1598 rebuilding.

The Medieval Mill would fit easily within the limits of the present ground floor and basement. It probably consisted of the waterwheel, pit wheel, wallower and great spur wheel on a vertical shaft to drive one or two pairs of stones through stone nuts (the gears that take the drive to the millstones). The lower courses of stonework in the gables, to front sill beam level, probably date from this period (Figure 25.1). Some of the stone for the earliest building was probably quarried on site, notably in the basement and wheelpit. Among the timbers thought to be re-used was the half-timbering in the gables. There is also evidence that very early sill beams are incorporated in the present front wall and intermediate wall, where there is evidence of recesses for at least three rafters.

A manuscript bound into the 'Family Memoranda' of the Stanleys of Alderley (1590–1601 and 1621–27) records that 'Alderley milnes were begune in 1595' and that in 1597 'Alderley milnes were finished before Xtmas this yeare' (Lawson, 1922: 84; the manuscript cited by

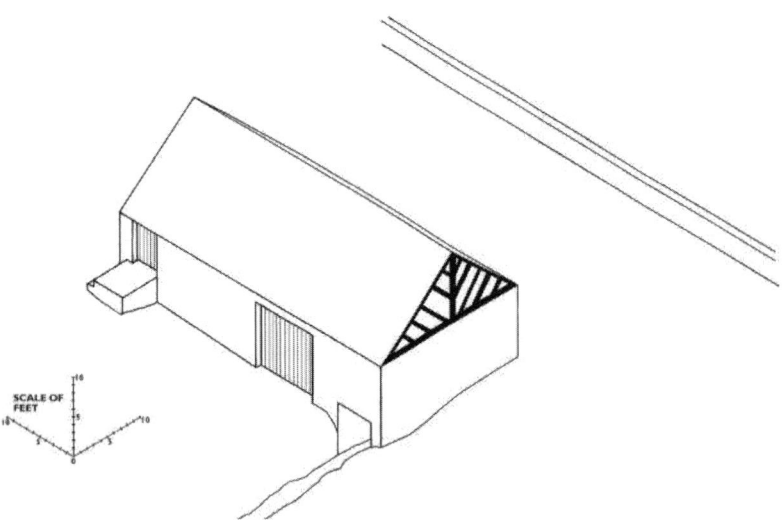

SCALE OF
FEET

Figure 25.1. The earliest reference to a mill at Nether Alderley is dated 1391. Based on evidence remaining in the present building, it was about 20 feet × 40 feet and would probably have looked something like this isometric view.

Drawn by Mike Redfern.

Lawson was then in the library of the Chester Archaeological Society but its present whereabouts are unknown). Entries in the same manuscript from 1590 to 1601 are in the handwriting of Thomas Stanley, of Alderley, who was knighted at Worksop Manor, 21 April 1603, and who died 21 November 1605, aged twenty-eight.

It appears that an earlier building was extended upwards and backwards. The dam was also raised so that in effect the back of the Mill is built into the dam. The raised water level was fed to an additional waterwheel above the level of the earlier single wheel.

The walls of the Mill are built of a warm red sandstone, believed to have come from several small quarries around Nether Alderley. It is soft, evenly textured, easily cut and yet weathers well. Two major periods of stonework can be seen to best effect on the northern gable end. The lower courses, to the level of the front sill beam, are approximately two feet thick; those above are about half that thickness and have been identified as typical of the sixteenth century (M. Nevell, personal communication, October 2002). From the tooling on the surface of the stones lining the tailrace (not accessible to the public), it appears that this is contemporary with the rebuilding of the Mill in the 1590s. The quality of the stonework suggests the work of an experienced mason, who, being proud of his workmanship, would want to 'sign' his work. On the ninth stone course up of the southern gable, next to the drying kiln wall, is a carved five-pointed star, believed to be a mason's mark.

There is evidence of two mullioned windows in the southern gable end. The upper one was later converted into a doorway by crudely cutting away the top and bottom stonework and extending the aperture to the size of the present doorway. The lower window frame can be seen on the inside wall above the lower wheelpit. Its stone lintel can also be seen just above the present floor level outside the back door. The doorway to the upper wheelpit still exists as the access from the furnace anteroom.

The half-timbered gables were once filled with wattle and daub but latterly this has been replaced with lath and cement.

Because the Mill is built up against the dam, there is only a short roof-slope on that side, but on the road side the roof has a long sweep broken by four dormer windows. The roof is covered with stone flags (from quarries at Kerridge, near Macclesfield) which are reputed to weigh about 200 tons.

Inside, the great feature of the building is the framed oak woodwork. Two heavy vertical posts rise from close to the ground floor in the middle of the Mill to support one side of two oak 'collar and tiebeam' trusses, which are supported at the other side by the low rear wall. These trusses in turn support the purlins, wind braces and rafters, all secured not by iron nails but by wooden pins or 'trenails'. The roof trusses are tied to the vertical posts by arch braces. Collar and tiebeam trusses were of the Medieval period and so were probably old-fashioned when these were erected in the 1590s, but one can imagine local builders working in a style that they had learned from their predecessors and which continued to be serviceable (McKenna, 1994: 9).

The two principal rafters, which are not part of the roof trusses but support the roof between those trusses and the front eaves, show evidence of earlier use. They have empty mortises, trenail holes and sockets for studs and laths associated with wattle and daub infilling. One face of each rafter has considerable surface 'hacking', indicating that at some time these timbers were plastered over. It is tempting to suggest that they may be reused timbers from the Old Hall, but there is no evidence for that. These principal rafters have had purlins trenched into them, resulting in serious weakening. At some time, the northern rafter has been iron-plated on each side to strengthen it, but the southern rafter had ironwork attached only on its underside. With time this has bent as the timber has been further stressed and in early 2006 the rafter was gauntleted with further steel reinforcing plates.

The front walls of the building show evidence of several changes which it has not been possible to date. It seems likely that an early doorway in the vicinity of the present front window gave access to the basement. A buttress to the front wall was added later but not tied into the stonework of the earlier building, nor into the still later outshut (Boucher, 1989). The stonework is neatly cut behind the buttress so could be original but the buttress and outshut display very poor-quality stonework. It is possible that more convenient access to the basement was needed, probably because the earlier access was restricted by being too close to the lower mill-gearing and mill stones. Before cutting the new access, while leaving the old one in use, it was probably thought necessary to provide additional support for the front wall, hence the buttress.

It is possible that the supposed third waterwheel was added during this phase, on the outside of the building and enclosed only later. Cyril Boucher (1989) wrote:

At some time between dates I am unable to give there was a third water-wheel. A portion of the stone at the front was cut away. The cutting was never trimmed down and is very roughly done. The wheelpit was extended and all this was done to house another wheel. This wheel was a smaller but wider one put in to drive some auxiliary machinery. The wheel was not fed from the lower wheel, because it was at the same level, but it is believed that a separate wooden pipe led to the penstock. Although no trace of this wheel remains, the place created for it, and the holes through which the axle passed, and the space created for the machine it drove are there for all to see. Moreover, once when I was talking to Mr Orme of Siddington

Mill, now deceased, who was born around 1903, he volunteered without my mentioning the subject that he remembered it used to have a third wheel which he had seen, and described to me.

It is difficult to understand how a 'smaller but wider' wheel 'at the same level' could be fitted. The tailrace in front of the lower wheel is only two feet wide.

At some time before the drying kiln was built, a structure was added to the southern gable end. The evidence for this is the six holes at two-foot centres, just above the present kiln floor level. They were probably mortises for floor joists and have been crudely filled, one with stone and five with brick. There is no other evidence for the structure, nor for its purpose or extent.

From evidence of the bricks used, the drying kiln was built some time between about 1690 and 1720. It is probable that the bricks were made on the estate using local clay and red sand. As well as estate use, they were also sold. An estate map of 1798 shows 'Brick Kiln Pits' and an estate account book held by Cheshire Archives and Local Studies (CALS) records that on 4 September 1798 'the second kiln of brick fired in the Calf Coat Field produced 34,625 bricks' (CALS DSA 241/1A).

About six feet south of the kiln is a culvert originally intended for draining the lake, but now blocked and disused. This has an arched entry with a keystone dated 'AD 17 4', interpreted as 1704. Stylistically, the construction of the culvert and of the drying kiln are very similar. It is tempting to date the kiln also to 1704 (Dr M. Nevell, University of Manchester Archaeology Unit, personal communication, December 2003). Could it be that a culvert for this purpose was originally sited where the drying kiln now stands and was relocated when the kiln was built? The dates attributed to this building make this a particularly early drying room (Peter Crew, Snowdonia National Park Authority Archaeologist, personal communication).

The details of the construction of the kiln before its collapse were never recorded and so can only be surmised from the remaining structure and practice elsewhere, because most kilns followed the same principle, with a fireplace below a floor of perforated tiles or plates totalling around thirty-five square feet. Although the Mill is built entirely of stone for the walls, brick was used for the kiln. As brick was not generally used for building kilns until the late nineteenth century, Nether Alderley's is particularly notable.

The kiln structure below first-floor level is like an inverted concave-sided funnel springing from a closed brick fireplace and extending to the walls just below the drying floor. This design gives a half-vaulted passage around the fireplace and makes most of the lower floor available for fuel storage. Attention was paid to even airflow through the floor, with a diffuser plate over the fire to prevent a 'hotspot'. There would have been fireproof iron doors between the furnace and the Mill – remains of the hinges for this can be seen. Ventilation above the drying floor was often left to chance – no more than a few roof slates lifted at the lower edge by battens to form primitive louvres or, as appears to have been the case at Nether Alderley, vents along the roof ridge.

The drying floor was composed of kiln tiles, usually about two inches thick, twelve inches square, supported on cast-iron or wrought-iron beams with subsidiary beams to carry the span of the tiles. The backs of the tiles are roughly punched so that a deep hole penetrates nearly to the face. The remaining thickness of the tile is then punched with a pattern of small holes at the crown of each deep hole. Samples of two types of tiles two inches thick and one sample of an early three-quarter-inch tile have been found around the Mill but dating these has not been possible. Some mills used perforated iron plates rather than ceramic tiles.

It is not known what fuel was used in the kiln at Nether Alderley. At various times it might have been oat husks, dried timber, oak charcoal, Welsh anthracite, coke or peat. Anyone who has ever smelled the pungency of burning peat might doubt its suitability for this process, but at mills that used peat it was a matter of pride to millers that they could enhance the flavour, not spoil it. Eskdale Mill at Boot in Cumbria used peat until the drying kiln fell out of use in the 1930s. The peat is still present.

The hot air and smoke would rise from the furnace, through the perforations in the tiles to the drying room floor, where the grain would be spread three to four inches deep. It would be turned regularly with a wooden meal shovel to ensure even drying. Traditionally, meal shovels were carved from a single piece of sycamore, because that timber resists splitting in a hot moist atmosphere. The heat, fumes and moisture would escape through vents in the roof ridge. Working in the drying room would have been very unpleasant – hot, humid and smelly.

Almost all wind and water-powered mills have a hurst frame, usually constructed of substantial timbers, to enclose and support the driving gears, support the millstones and the bridging timbers by which the upper millstone is tentered (i.e. adjusted). In addition, the hurst frame has to isolate the vibration of milling from the mill building and transmit it safely down to the ground (Watts, 2002: 97, 137).

From the evidence of the date cut into its stone pedestal, the hurst frame at Nether Alderley was fitted in 1877. It is a complex iron casting which appears to be unique in surviving mills but must have been an adaptation of a standard cast-iron hurst frame, probably installed specifically to link the auxiliary engine's drive to the milling machinery.

A photograph reproduced on the cover of early editions of the Mill guidebook and reputed to have been taken in 1880 shows the portable auxiliary engine outside the Mill. It was manufactured by Robey's of Lincoln and was probably of about ten horsepower (Boucher, 1978, 1989).

Since the 1760s it had become the practice for hurst frames to be built with a central vertical shaft, extending upwards from the great spur wheel, to drive ancillary machines (Ferguson, 1760). This was not required at Nether Alderley but the vertical shaft provided an ingenious millwright with a handy solution to the drive problem. Visitors to the Mill can still see the drive shaft on the top floor and where it was connected to the hurst frame's vertical shaft. A pulley and bevel mortise wheel associated with this drive survive in the Mill basement.

During the 1890s the Mill reached its greatest extent, with a lean-to wooden building added against the northern gable to house the portable steam engine (Figure 25.2; Figure 25.3 shows what remains today). This is shown in a photograph by Francis Frith of the Mill, dated 1896 (no. 37478 in the Frith collection, Gillingham, Dorset, http://www.francisfrith.com; Hardy, 1999: 56). Another view, dated 1903 and taken by Fletcher Moss's travelling companion James Watts of Abney Hall, Cheadle, shows the shed with the drive to an external pulley covered by a sheeted extension to the roof (Moss, 1903: 11; also Norris, 1969: fig. 4). The Mill in this form is shown on the 1909 twenty-five inch Ordnance Survey map.

The Mill continued to use steam and water power until some time before the First World War. It is listed as 'John Hogg Rawlins (miller, water & steam)' in Kelly's Directories for 1892, 1902 and 1906. The 1914 *Directory* lists only 'John Hogg Rawlins (miller, water)', so the assumption must be that the engine had worn out and the low level of

Figure 25.2. The Mill was greatly extended between 1595 and 1597 and the brick-built grain-drying kiln was added on the southern gable end between 1690 and 1720. From about 1880 the Mill had a steam engine as a supplementary power source and this was enclosed in a wooden shed during the 1890s. This isometric view shows the mill at its greatest extent.

Drawn by Mike Redfern.

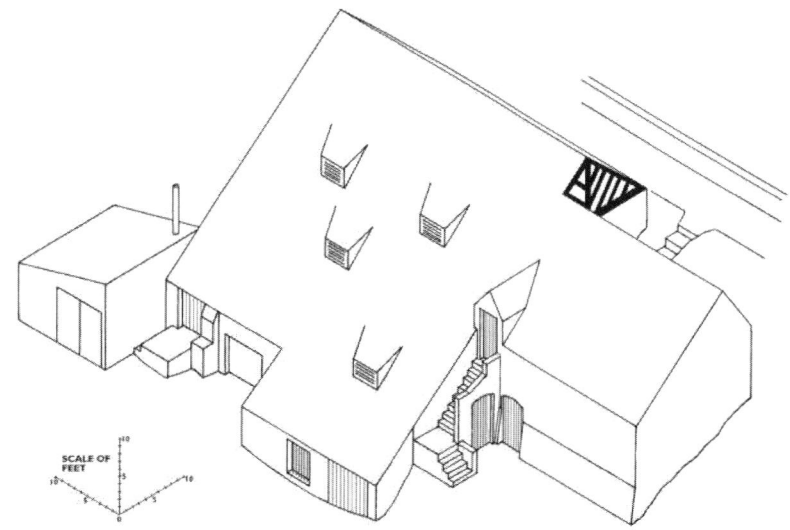

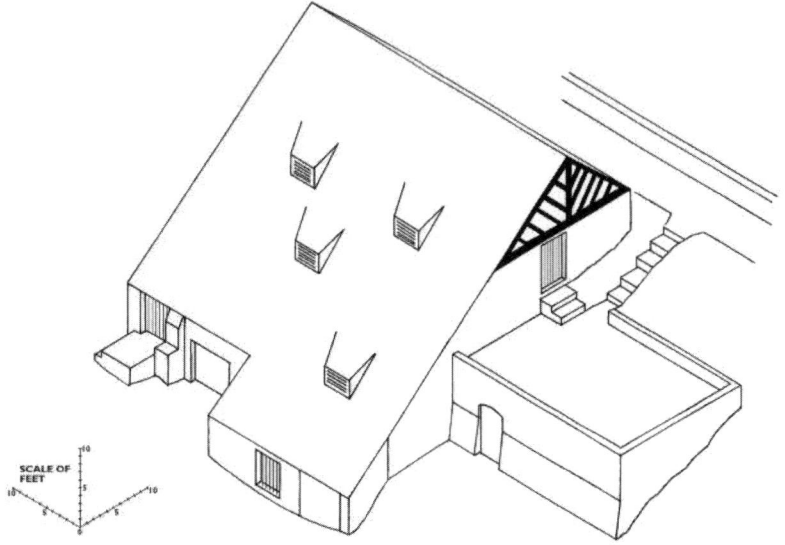

SCALE OF
FEET

Figure 25.3. An isometric view of the Mill as it appears today. The roof of the drying kiln collapsed c. 1940 and the former drying floor was concreted over and the outside steps removed some time after 1950, when the building was given to the National Trust.

Drawn by Mike Redfern.

business could not justify the cost of a replacement (Figure 25.4). John Hogg Rawlins died of congestion of the lungs, an occupational hazard for a miller. He was succeeded by John Jr, who continued the family tradition until some time in the early 1930s. He was in turn succeeded by his younger brother Ernest, the last miller at Nether Alderley.

The Mill remained part of the Stanley estate until the sale of October 1938. Mr J. A. Shelmerdine, the tenant of the Old Hall, bought his home and the Mill (*Sale Catalogue*, lot 148).

It is believed that the collapse of the lower waterwheel precipitated the closure of the Mill, but it is not known when this occurred. The Mill is described in the 1938 auction catalogue as 'still used for grinding corn'. The Mill guidebook states that it closed in 1939 and others have repeated this (Boucher, 1978); however, it is not listed in Kelly's *Directory* for 1939, which would have been compiled in 1938. Joyce Shone, daughter of John Rawlins Jr, interviewed for the AELP, associated the closing of the Mill with the birth of her sister Beryl in 1937 (AELP Sound Archive no. 88 = no. 13 on the British Library archive website, http://www/cadensa bl.ac.uk, and search for Alderley Edge).

After the Mill closed, the machinery soon become so derelict that it could no longer be worked. The wooden axle of the lower wheel had rotted and the wheel leaned against the walls, immovable. Expensive repairs were necessary but the Mill remained derelict and unusable. The wooden culvert conveying water to the wheels rotted away and was eventually removed and the dam was sealed off with clay. The roof and upper walls of the drying room collapsed in about 1940 (Brian Hobson, personal communication), probably because the roof timbers had been

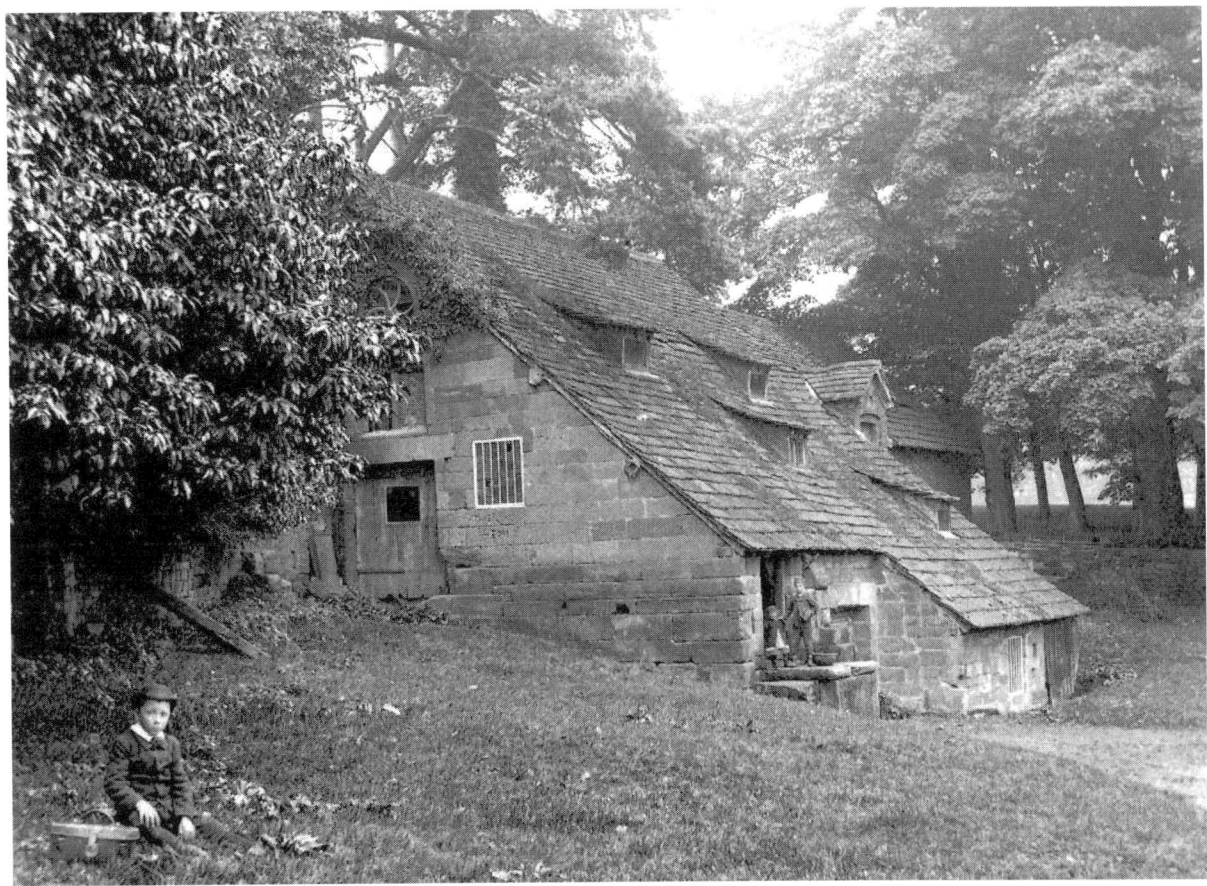

Figure 25.4. An undated photograph showing the Mill between 1906 and 1914. The engine has been removed, probably worn out, but the pulley that took the power into the Mill remains high on the gable end, and the drying kiln to the south is still intact. The boy in the foreground is looking after the photographer's case of glass plate negatives.

Photograph courtesy of Michael Gittins.

subjected to almost 240 years of moisture rising from the grain-drying process. At some time after the collapse, the front wall at least was tidied up at waist height and the void between the furnace and the drying floor was filled with the building's rubble and capped with concrete.

There is a newspaper report on the Mill, with photograph, from 1946:

> The fifteenth-century Old Mill, at Alderley, Cheshire, which the owner, Major J. A. Shelmerdine, has offered to the National Trust. About a year ago the East Cheshire branch of the Council for the Preservation of Rural England, the Lancashire & Cheshire Antiquarian Society, the Ancient Monuments Society, and the Royal Manchester Institution made a joint appeal for funds to put the mill into a state of repair which would enable the National Trust to take it over. So far £718 has been subscribed towards the target figure of £1,000, and the balance is urgently required in order

that the mill may be handed to the National Trust in good condition. The roof and gable ends are now completely restored. As a first step towards repairing the machinery of the mill a new water inlet gate is to be erected. The old one permits considerable water seepage. The treasurer of the fund is Mr A. V. Sugden, District Bank, Alderley Edge. (*Manchester Guardian*, Thursday 2 May 1946)

Shortly before being acquired by the National Trust in 1950, some renovation work was carried out. The brickwork around the former drying-room floor was tidied up and capped with stone sections. The former wooden panelling (or wooden door) above the tailrace was bricked up. Probably also at this time, the outside steps to the first floor of the drying room were removed and the doorway to the furnace anteroom bricked up. Inside, some stonework, noticeable because it is not local stone, was built near the lower wheel to give additional support to a sill beam. The work was carried out under the direction of Sir Hubert Worthington and Mr P. G. Fairhurst, FRIBA, both notable architects of the period, and the Mill when restored was presented to the National Trust by Mr and Mrs J. A. Shelmerdine.

The machinery remained idle until the Trust asked Dr Cyril Boucher to submit a report and estimate for the restoration of the Mill to working order. It was finally agreed that he should carry out the work, assisted by his two sons, and other helpers, including a Mr Drewery. The work was carried out between 1967 and 1970.

The upper wheel was first rebuilt with completely new woodwork and the machinery was eased, repaired and repainted. This included the renewal of the wooden cogs, the bevel cogs being cut with seven angles. The teeth were made from well seasoned beech and were then artificially dried down to a very low moisture content. In this shrunken state they were driven hard into their mortises and pinned. The natural moisture content in the Mill is around 25 per cent, so the teeth then swelled and became locked in position.

The next stage was the repair of the lower wheel with a new axle, six-sided through the wheel, but eight-sided where the pit wheel is mounted on it, and twelve feet long. The piece of oak from which it was prepared cost £20 in 1967. Iron cross-tailed gudgeons were mortised into each end and secured by three iron bands, which were shrunk on after being heated in a fire and driven on with sledgehammers.

In each set of stones the upper stone or runner was turned over and the underside and the bedstone re-cut. A stone must be perfectly flat, but is intersected by furrows; the flat surfaces, called 'lands', are then serrated or 'stitched' to grind the corn. The work was done in past days by travelling stone dressers, who took about four days to dress a pair of stones by hand using the mill bill and thrift, as the chisel and its handle were called, and the process was revived for the dressing of the stones at

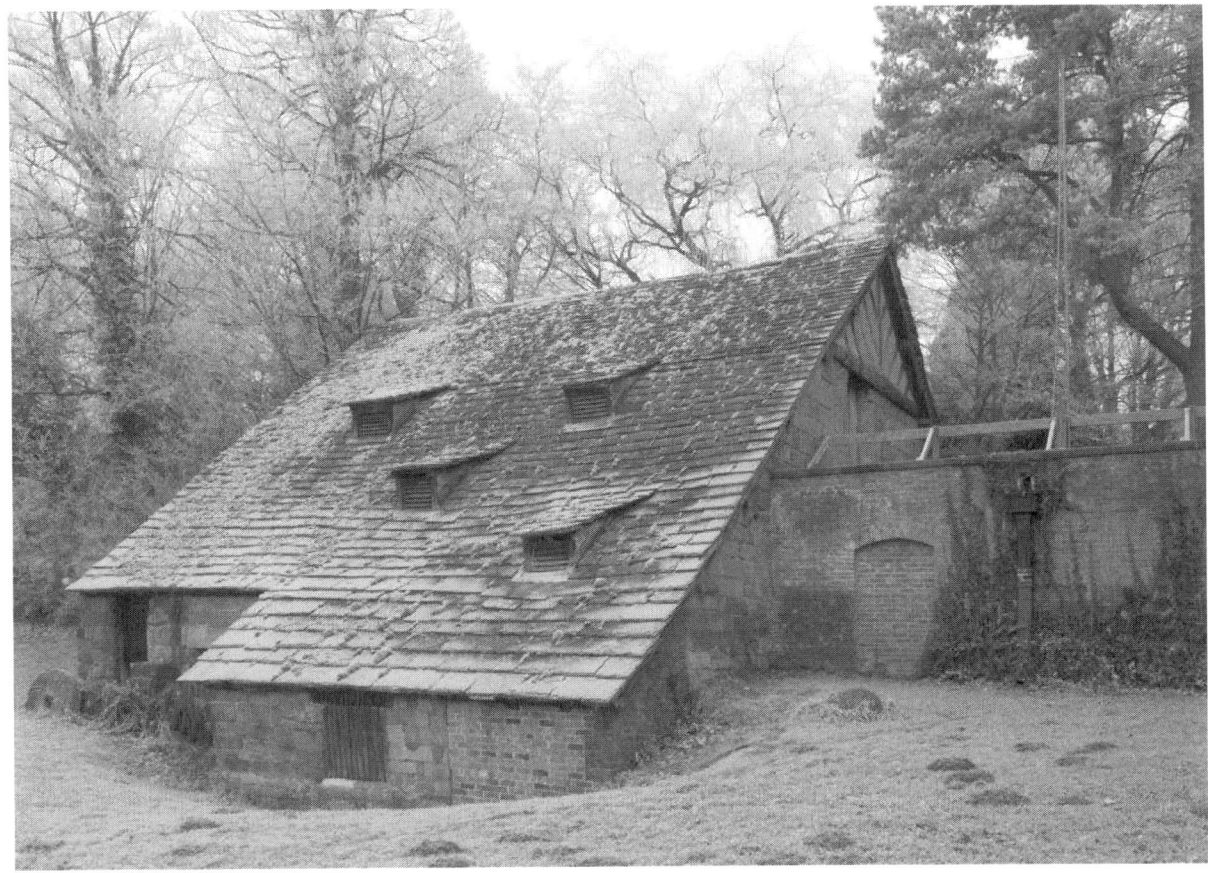

Figure 25.5. The Mill from the south in its present condition, during a heavy frost. The area outside the back door was the drying-kiln floor and the bricked-up doorway gave access to the kiln anteroom.

Photograph Mike Redfern.

Nether Alderley. Finally, the stones were reassembled, corn was placed in the hoppers and in the eye, and the water was turned on. The stones – one set at a time – began to revolve, and the meal came pouring out. The Mill was alive again (Boucher, 1978; Figures 25.3, 25.5).

Unfortunately, since Dr Boucher completed the restoration of the Mill in 1970, only basic maintenance has been carried out. The condition of various parts of the Mill give cause for concern and milling is no longer carried out, though the water does turn the wheels to give something of the atmosphere of a working mill.

(Since Mike Redfern completed this chapter in 2006 the National Trust has been able to carry out further restoration work, as described in the editorial note at the end of the chapter. Ed.)

The milling process

Corn is the generic term for several grain crops and is generally applied to the predominant crop of an area. In upland areas of England and in Wales and Scotland the term is generally applied to oats. Along the east coast of England it might be barley, but for most of lowland England up to the north Midlands it is wheat, though yields decrease the further north it is grown. If nineteenth-century parallels are relevant, yields of grain crops in Cheshire may have always been low by national standards (Higham, 1993: 14). In North America and Australasia corn is maize, which is how we come to have sweetcorn and cornflakes.

Wheat is composed of three principal parts. The bran (about 18 per cent) is the outer covering of the kernel, composed of cellulose fibres in several layers to protect the seed. The endosperm (about 80 per cent) is enclosed inside it, and contains starches and protein. The germ (about 2 per cent) is the embryo of the seed and contains fat. The tip of the grain is covered by stiff hairs, known as the brush. For white flour, the bran and germ must be separated from the endosperm. The germ, if ground in with the flour, reduces its keeping quality, particularly in warm weather.

The sacks of wheat brought to the Mill were raised by the sack hoist – powered by the waterwheel – up to the garner floor, also known as the bin floor or granary, in the roof (Figure 25.6). Although the hoist was available to lift the heavy sacks of grain, the miller or an assistant had to go to the garner floor to tip the sacks into the grain bin. Most millers were expert at arranging labour-saving working practices, but their ingenuity failed them here. They had to climb the steps near the penstock on the top floor, stand precariously on a wooden plank, before 'flopping' through a gap in the roof truss. The wear on alternate steps of the stairs and on the plank at the top can still be seen.

The wheat was placed in the grain bin, down which it flowed into the hopper and out into the shoe, the shallow trough that feeds it into stones. The shoe is shaken by the 'chattering' damsel, a four-pronged spindle rather ungallantly given that name by millers because it never stops its noise (though it has been said in defence that while it chatters it never stops working). As the grain is shaken down the shoe it falls into the eye of the runner (the top stone) revolving at about 110 revolutions per minute and is ground between that and the stationary bedstone (the lower stone).

The milling faces of the two stones are cut with a particular pattern of grooves which aid the milling process. The action of the milling faces shears the grain and as the grain is driven towards the circumference by centrifugal force the increasing surface speed mills it finer and finer. It is usual for the gap between the two working faces to decrease towards

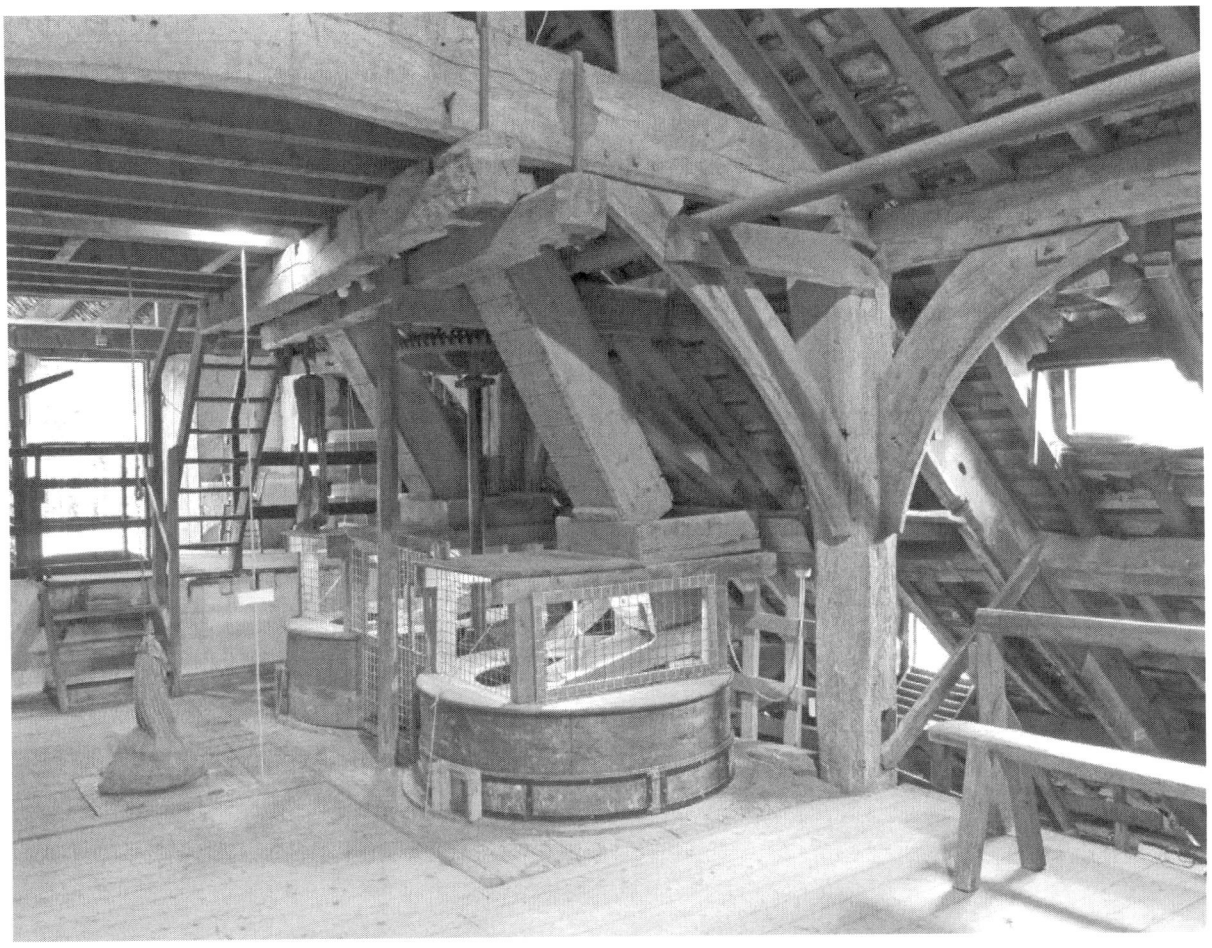

Figure 25.6. The upper floors of the Mill showing the heavy timber trusses dating from the rebuilding of 1595–97, although some timbers may be older and re-used. Grain was hoisted to the garner floor at the top of the Mill, where it was stored in grain bins, and would then flow down chutes to the stones, enclosed in a wooden vat (in the centre of the picture). The milled grain would then go to the ground floor to be bagged.

Photograph Mike Redfern.

the periphery to allow the material to be drawn in at the centre and be reduced in particle size as milling progresses. While milling, the only thing that prevents the stones from touching is the meal between them. Many mills had safeguards to notify the miller when the grain was about to run out, because the stones must never be run 'dry'. Flour dust is explosive and it would only need a spark from a pair of stones to cause a conflagration.

When the grain had been milled, the product was correctly called meal until it had been sieved to produce flour. The meal came out at the perimeter of the stones and a brush or wiper drove it down the chute to the sacks on the floor below. It would surprise most people to feel that the meal was warm from the grinding process. In her interview for the AELP, Joyce Shone (née Rawlins) recalled going to the Mill as a young girl in the 1930s. Uncle Ernest was the miller and he was careful about where she put her hands because there were no safety guards around the machinery. She was, however, allowed to put a hand into the flow of meal from the stones, which she said 'felt like warm silk'.

The meal would be put through a mechanical sifter to bolt (or boult) the meal. This removed most of the bran and wheat germ (which would be used as an animal feed) and produced perhaps two grades of flour, varied by their fineness. An early sifter or wire machine of a type invented and patented by a man named Milne in the 1760s is still in the Mill. It was manufactured by George Artingstall & Co. of Warrington (the date of manufacture is not known) and consists of an openwork cylinder lined with gauze (originally made of linen or silk) of varying degrees of fineness, and inside this revolving arms tipped with brushes. The cylinder was inclined and as meal was introduced at the upper end it was swept over the screens by the brushes as it descended, so sieving it into the required grades. The flour produced was not the fine bleached white flour so popular today. It was creamy white and still contained a small amount of wheat germ and bran. The modern sifter on the mezzanine floor, built by Thomas Robinson's of Rochdale and donated by Ranks, the millers, would have graded the milled wheat into fine flour, coarse meal or sharps, and husks, but this is not contemporary with the Mill and, so far as is known, never worked here.

In 1914, the charge at a similar mill for grinding was 11s.2d per stone. Extra would be charged if the miller had to dry the grain as he would have to purchase fuel for the kiln and spend more time handling the grain. Grain keeps better than flour, so most customers would keep the corn and have it ground only as required, usually one sack at a time. There was little need for bulk storage since every sack was a separate transaction. By the early twentieth century most customers expected while-you-wait service. A pair of millstones would grind up to two hundredweight of wheat per hour, but it was rarely possible to run the stones continuously all day because of the danger of overheating. One hundredweight of wheat would yield about 100 lb of flour.

Until about 100 years ago oats were milled at Nether Alderley as well as wheat for flour. Oats were an important foodstuff for horses, and horses were the principal motive force. It is probable that more time was spent milling oats than wheat. Milling of oats differed considerably from that for wheat. An essential part of the oatmeal process was grain drying to a very low moisture content, to enable the husk to be split off readily. This required kiln drying even after a dry harvest. The drying period and the temperature depended on the type, condition and intended use of the grain, and varied from less than twenty-four hours to several days. As with wheat, millers could charge extra for drying oats because they had to purchase fuel and spend more time.

After drying, the oats were 'shelled' between a pair of plain stones (i.e. without the pattern of grooves found on most millstones) with about a fifth of an inch clearance between bedstone and runner, to crack off the husk. The dust from this process was separated through a sieve, and the whole kernels and the husks were separated by an air blast. The kernels were then ground with a second pair of stones. At some mills, the same pair of stones could be used for both processes, resetting the distance between them for each operation. The resulting meal was sifted into oatmeal (or perhaps coarse and fine oatmeal) and the largest particles were returned to the stones to be reground. In addition to oatmeal for human consumption, oats were coarsely ground for horse feed or ground to a fine meal for poultry.

Barley might also be ground to meal, mainly as an animal feed, or might be left as large grains with only the husk removed (pearl barley). Barley was, and still is, used for fattening prize livestock, particularly on the Alderley estate for hogs (large, castrated male pigs), and for feeding the pigeons. The columbarium or dovecot (which still stands in the stable area at the south end of Alderley Park) was a source of fresh meat and eggs all year.

Cyril Boucher wrote (1978):

> At the turn of the century (i.e. nineteenth into twentieth) there were two more sets of stones at a lower level motivated by overdrift stone nuts and quants, as the driving shafts are called, running on the side teeth of the great spur wheel. The wooden floor at the entrance did not then exist and the stones were mounted just above the wallower, the big horizontal gear wheel in the basement. All this machinery was dismantled soon after, but it was never taken out of the mill, and still lies in parts in the basement. The term 'overdrift' indicates that the driving mechanism is mounted up above the stones. A stone nut has recently been retoothed and the quant on which it is mounted replaced in its original top bearing to run on the side of the great spur wheel and thus illustrate the layout described as 'overdrift'.

The stone nut (timber-cogged mortise gear wheel) and quant referred to by Boucher drove the shelling stones. To disengage the drive, the quant could be released from its upper bearing and leant over with the stone nut clear of the spur wheel, as in windmill practice. The quant for the oat milling stones is longer, indicating that those stones must have been positioned about three or four feet off the basement floor. This quant, with evidence of its timber-cogged mortise gear wheel, and the shelling and milling stones lie in the Mill basement.

Because overdrift is usually associated with windmills, its use in watermills is comparatively rare. The only sites known in Cheshire, apart from Nether Alderley, are Acton Mill (SJ 588 747), which contains both overdrift and underdrift, Church Minshull Mill (SJ 667 608) and Darnhall Mill (SJ 635 633).

In addition to the pulley and bevel gear wheel associated with the auxiliary steam engine, several rynds have been preserved at the mill. These are the iron fittings that serve to support the upper millstone of a pair on its quant and transmit the drive from quant to stone. There are two-armed and four-armed stiff rynds which fitted rigidly to the spindle. They required careful setting in the stone, and resetting after a few dressings, as well as the spindle being set square to the bedstone face to keep the grinding faces parallel. As the runner had to be put back in place for each test, and lifted again for each correction, this adjustment – 'changing the stones' – could be very time-consuming (Jones, 1977).

More elaborate designs followed, to provide flexibility in two axes, such as the gimbal rynd. These were introduced in the late nineteenth century and so were mainly used in steam-powered town mills. The example at Nether Alderley was on a large oat-milling stone and shows very little wear. As it literally 'hung' the runner rather than holding it parallel to the bedstone, the balance of the stone was critical and so it was probably not successful.

Dynamic balance was certainly understood (very likely the phenomenon of dynamic balance was discovered by millers) and many surviving millstones have balance boxes to adjust this: these were three or four recesses in the upper face of the stone near the rim, containing weights which could be changed to adjust the static balance, and moved vertically to adjust the dynamic balance. However, difficulties still arose when stones were worked with a large clearance. Under these conditions, balance could be so critical as to make it easier to revert to the fixed rynd. This is made evident by the practice in the Isle of Man, where mills with three pairs of stones generally have two pairs on balance rynds and the oatmeal stone on a fixed rynd (Jones, 1977).

The water supply

The stream that drives the Mill is an exceptionally small one and the flow of water is quite inadequate to drive a watermill. The Elizabethan millwrights overcame this difficulty by building a large dam across the valley, the back of the Mill forming part of the dam wall. This reservoir was filled day and night by the small stream. Thus, in the morning the dam would be full and for a period of eight hours the millers could draw off three times the volume of water flowing in. This quantity was sufficient to drive the machinery and do useful work during a normal working day.

The impounding reservoir does not allow for periods of drought, when the flow is so reduced that it is incapable of filling the reservoir each day, nor is it large enough to store winter floods against dry spells. It was probably for this purpose that Radnor Mere was constructed by Sir Thomas Stanley (1597–1672), and ultimately a further three reservoirs, Lady's Upper, Lady's Lower and Wood End. Radnor Mere was widened by Sir John Thomas Stanley in 1826 by around sixty yards, nearly doubling its width. Although the mere covers almost twenty-four acres, it is nowhere more than a few feet deep. All that comes from Radnor Mere nowadays is the overflow from the small stream that fills it. Wood End reservoir is now a depression where cattle graze and the two Lady's reservoirs have dried up.

Winter floods were stored and then let down to replenish the lower reservoir as occasion demanded. Obtaining sufficient water to run the Mill seems always to have been a problem. Apart from storing and feeding the water from ponds and reservoirs into the millpond, there is evidence that water from nearby springs was also fed to the Mill, for it sits at the foot of an escarpment that in places rises almost 300 feet, and along this hillside is a spring line with at least five springs, two of which supplied domestic water to the village and the estate before mains water was available. The supply to the estate still runs into the water garden in AstraZeneca's grounds.

The spring water from the north of the area is channelled by several miles of fieldside ditches into a cross-contour channel from Flume Cottage on Artists Lane into the rear of the millpond. The mystery is when this water course was built. It is shown on an estate map prepared in December 1799 for the re-alignment of local roads (QJF 227/3), but no map has been found to confirm an earlier date. Water also flows from a spring north of Beechtree Lodge on Hocker Lane, through Parkhead Pond to join the cross-contour channel just north of the millpond.

After passing through the mill, the water joins the Pedley Brook and in earlier times drove two further mills at Warford, Peck Mill (SJ 809 760) and Coulthurst or Sandlebridge Mill (SJ 808 769, which is described further below). The stream is a tributary of the River Bollin, which joins the River Mersey north of Lymm.

The waterwheels

Nether Alderley Mill is believed to be unique in having two waterwheels, one above the other, working in tandem. Many mills have (or had) two wheels (e.g. Stretton Mill in southern Cheshire) but none has this layout. The two overshot waterwheels are of composite iron and timber construction. The top wheel is thirteen feet in diameter by four feet wide with thirty buckets and is mounted on a cruciform-section iron shaft. The lower wheel is thirteen feet in diameter by three feet wide with forty-two buckets, mounted on a six-sided oak axle, which changes to eight-sided to carry the lower cast-iron pitwheel. The power generated by the Nether Alderley wheels has been variously calculated at between seven and ten horsepower when working at full capacity.

The water enters from the lake, to the top of the upper wheel, filling each bucket in succession as the wheel revolves. At the bottom the water drops off and runs along a short wooden trough and onto the top of the lower wheel. At the bottom of this wheel it falls off again, having made a total descent of thirty-two feet, and runs away in a deep culvert under the road and rejoins the brook. The wheels are coupled together by a lay shaft, which runs with one wooden cogged pinion on top of the composite great spur wheel and another coupling into the motion from the upper wheel.

John Smeaton (1724–92) experimented with forms of waterwheels. He ascertained that undershot wheels were 20–25 per cent efficient and that overshot wheels such as those at Nether Alderley were 60–65 per cent efficient. Lightweight iron suspension wheels, such as that working at Quarry Bank Mill can be up to 80 per cent efficient (Jones, 1973).

The mill gearing

The usual watermill gear surviving today, that is waterwheel–pit wheel–wallower–great spur wheel–under-driven stone nuts, must have originated quite early in the eighteenth century. The earliest published description in English dates from 1760, but John Smeaton used it for his two earliest mill designs in 1753 (Jones, 1977). The present machinery at Nether Alderley dates from between 1850 and 1877, but the original Elizabethan machinery would have been entirely of wood and has long disappeared. It is not possible to be certain about the layout. Various holes in the stonework indicating former axles or parts show that the original machinery may have differed, in detail at least, from the present arrangement.

Until cheap, plentiful cast iron became available in the eighteenth century, mill mechanisms could only be of wood, and certainly this limited their size and power. Cast iron liberated waterpower after 1750, enabling the construction of great watermills with several sets of millstones (Holt, 1990: 50–8).

'Teeth' or 'cogs'? Teeth are so called when they are an integral part of a wheel, as in a completely cast-iron gear. A cog is always an insertion in a mortise wheel. A fine-grained timber would be used for the cogs – apple, pear or cherry wood, or, in southern England, hornbeam. As flour dust is so combustible, installing iron gearing contributed to the problem of friction (metal meshing with metal) and thereby increased the risk of fire. To eliminate that risk, alternate gears were fitted with wooden cogs. At Nether Alderley there are only three iron-to-iron gear pairs in the Mill, which generate most of the noise. All the other gear pairs are wooden cogs to iron teeth, much quieter than iron to iron. Wooden cogs also break sooner than expensive cast-iron gear wheels, so providing a useful safety valve. Before modern lubricants were developed, goose grease or horse grease was used on bearings and gears.

The sack hoist

The miller would try to avoid carrying sacks of grain and flour up and down the stairs and so used a sack hoist. In addition to the one still in place that connects the rear ground floor (the meal floor) with the floor above and the granary, there is considerable evidence (former flap-doors and rope holes in timbers) of another hoist connecting the basement with the sifting floor.

The hoist ran through hinged one-way flap-doors that were opened by a sack travelling upwards, but bang closed when the sack had passed through. By listening for the flap-doors banging, the miller would know how far up the sack had travelled. The surviving hoist is operated by a rope running through holes in the floors. On pulling this down, the rope, which is threaded through structural timbers, lifts a beam on which are a mounted a wooden pulley and a winding drum. Around the wooden pulley is a flat belt that hangs down loosely around a pulley that is turning whenever the waterwheels are working. Pulling the control rope lifts the beam, tightens the slack belt around the pulleys and drives the winding drum. A rope around the winding drum also threads through holes in the structural timbers and hoists the sacks. When the control rope is released, the beam carrying the pulley and drum falls and movement is stopped by a drum brake rubbing on another beam. With fine handling of the control rope, it is possible to lift the beam sufficiently to stop the friction between the drum brake and the beam, but not tighten the drive belt, and so lower sacks down through the Mill.

The millstones

It has been estimated that some millstones wear by about a quarter of an inch per year when used to their full capacity, although this would vary depending on the hardness of the millstones and of the grain milled (Bonson, 2003: 156).

The two pairs of milling stones now at Nether Alderley are French burr stones. These are assembled from pieces of metaquartzite, a hard rock with pockets, very good at removing bran and therefore prized for their ability to grind wheat into fine flour. The stone came from La Ferté-Sous-Jouarre in the Paris basin or from Epernon, southwest of Paris. The individual pieces were shaped and fitted together, cemented, then bound with iron hoops and cosmetically finished on the backs with plaster of Paris. French stones were almost always constructed in this way and were used for milling fine wheat flour. French stones have been imported since about 1330, many of them assembled in England from imported pieces, and were particularly fashionable from about 1758. Peak stones are made of millstone grit, typically from the Chatsworth Grits at Stanage Edge or from quarries around Mow Cop. They are usually made in one piece, though the Mow Cop stones in the Mill are, very unusually, segmental stones.

The top stone is the runner and the bottom stone the bedstone. The millstones weigh between one and one and a half tons each. To clean or re-dress the grinding face, the top stone must be lifted with tackle and hoist above the stone and then turned. It would take at least a day and sometimes up to a week to re-dress the stone. Furrows and lands cut into the working surfaces of the stones were important for removing bran. Smaller cuts between furrows and lands are 'stitches'. From about the third quarter of the nineteenth century, the runners would be dynamically balanced with lead weights, usually in a pocket with a swivelling cover, to make sure they ran true, much in the way that car wheels are still balanced. The Nether Alderley stones do not have balance weights, which would seem to indicate that they pre-date this development

The stone was often dressed by itinerant stone-dressers. Before engaging them, the astute miller would ask to see their forearms. If they were unblemished they was obviously inexperienced. If their forearms were pock marked by the chips of stone or splinters of iron from the dressing operation, they had had years of experience. To protect their eyes, the dressers would wear plain glass glasses. The tool used for dressing the stone was a mill bill and thrift – a long, stretched-diamond-shaped hammerhead that was fixed into the thrift (the handle) with a wooden wedge. Stones were run in with sharp sand when new or after re-cutting. A stone could last up to sixty years, but over the years it would gradually wear down until it was too thin to re-dress.

Gordon Tucker has written of Mow Cop:

> This sharp-peaked hill of millstone grit, standing high above the Cheshire plain and distinguished by the large stone folly on its peak, is reckoned to have been a source of querns in ancient times. The making of millstones there probably started in medieval times, and certainly there was much cutting of millstones in the eighteenth and nineteenth centuries. John

Farey ('Derbyshire' Vol. 1, pp. 220–1), in 1811, referred to 'Molecopt south of Congleton in Cheshire' as a place where Peak millstones were formerly made; note the word 'formerly', suggesting that the activity had then temporarily ceased. Millstones built of segments of Mow Cop stone were used at Nether Alderley (Cheshire); Brindley's Mill, Leek; and Brund Mill, Sheen (Staffs). Millstone making at Mow Cop was evidently at a good level of activity in the second half of the nineteenth century; with both F. Stonier of Scholar Green and Wm. Jamieson of Mow Cop as makers of Mow Cop millstones. Below the folly on the east there can still be seen a half-hewn millstone only partially cut out from the parent rock, and on the south-west side of the folly there are several cavities where millstones have evidently been excavated. The half-hewn millstone blank is about 4ft 8in diameter, so that allowing for trimming, the finished millstone was evidently intended to be between 4 ft 0 in and 4 ft 6 in diameter with sharp sand – well within the range of sizes of nineteenth-century millstones. (Tucker, 1987)

The end of milling at Nether Alderley

The traditional milling industry probably reached its peak in Britain in the middle of the nineteenth century with about 10,000 mills. By the time of the 1851 Census there were 37,268 millers, 125 millstone makers and 9,953 millwrights in the country (Gifford, 1999: 5). Today, about 100 mills produce flour for a population about two and a half times larger. There were several factors that led to this change.

With the breakdown of the manorial system, soke rights, which compelled inhabitants to grind their corn at the lord's mill, were repealed. This made millers and their customers subject to commercial pressures rather than feudal obligations. When this change occurred at Nether Alderley is not known, but soke rights were certainly still in operation at nearby Adlington Mill in 1808 (Bruckshaw, 1982: 92).

After the introduction of the Corn Laws in 1436, the supply and price of grain was controlled, which incidentally made milling very profitable. When the Corn Laws were repealed in 1846, many small mills began to suffer. From the early nineteenth century the population, largely concentrated in urban areas, rose dramatically. Manchester's population increased from 84,000 in 1801 to 460,000 by 1861. Lancashire's population increased by almost 700 per cent in the nineteenth century – double the increase in Britain as a whole. This hugely increased population needed water, as did the factories in which they worked. As more water was extracted, the water-table dropped. It has been estimated that the water-table in the Mersey Basin has fallen by about six feet since 1800. As the water-table fell, so did the level of rivers and streams, in some cases by several feet (M. Nevell, personal communication).

From about the middle of the nineteenth century, many mills that depended on water for their power were finding it increasingly difficult to keep running and many closed. From about 1860 onwards some mills converted to water turbines that could generate the same power as waterwheels, but with half the water (e.g. Warburton Mill, on the River Bollin west of Altrincham; Bosley Old Mill, south of Macclesfield; Siddington Mill, a few miles south of Nether Alderley; Northenden Mill, on the River Mersey; and Quarry Bank Mill, at Styal) (Gilbert Gilkes and Gordon Ltd, 1951).

Another alternative was to install a steam engine or, later, an internal combustion engine. This could complement the waterwheel or in some instances replace it.

The major threat which led to a majority of rural mills closing in the late nineteenth century and the first half of the twentieth century was the introduction of roller milling to Britain. This development became popular after a demonstration of new flour-milling techniques at Islington Agricultural Hall in 1878, by Henry Simon, a prominent Manchester-based millwright. He subsequently completed a mill for McDougalls in Manchester. The incentive was the increased (and fashionable) demand for white flour. Mills such as Nether Alderley had difficulty producing white flour, if they could do it at all. Hard North American wheats were best but were too hard for conventional millstones (Jones, 2001: 11). Roller milling, where the grain is passed through a succession of parallel steel rollers (rather like old-fashioned mangles), first to break the grain, then to grind it to increasingly finer grades, could handle hard wheats. Increasingly, steam-powered roller mills were sited on quaysides in ports, or in towns or cities, where bulk grain could be taken directly from ship to mill.

By 1887 Henry Simon was able to claim that roller milling had already effectively replaced stone milling. He worked as an agent for Continental firms from a small shop in East Street, Manchester, and later from larger premises in Mount Street. By 1892 he had built more than 400 roller mills in different parts of the world and the growth of the business in the early twentieth century led to the building of a new works at Cheadle Heath, Stockport, in 1923–26.

Nether Alderley millers

The Mill was worked by a long line of country millers over the centuries. The earliest so far identified by the National Trust is John Burgess, whose name occurs for the first time in 1736. Peter Mottram was the miller in 1811. In most areas, the 1811 Census gave only the numbers of males, females and a total. We are fortunate that in Nether Alderley the Census was taken by the rector, Reverend Edward Stanley, the younger brother of Sir John Thomas Stanley. Edward Stanley, whose career has been summarised in Chapter 11, was the Rector of Alderley for thirty-two years; he had an interest in the village and recorded the names, occupations and residences in addition to the required statistics.

Peter Mottram's sons Peter Jr and James also became millers. James is recorded living at Nether Alderley in 1821 and 1831, though there is no specific evidence that they were millers in their own right. It is known that a John Bradley was the miller in 1828, when Pigot's *National Commercial Directory* lists 'John Bradley, miller, Alderley Mills' (J. Pigot and Co., 1828).

James Mottram's son William, born *c.* 1810, was the miller at Birtles in 1841 but had moved to Nether Alderley as the miller by 1850 (Bagshaw's *Directory* for that year lists 'Wm Mottram, corn miller, Nether Alderley'), when he was assisted by his brother James (1851 Census). By 1861, William was living at Manchester Road, Wilmslow, described as a corn miller employing one man, presumably at Bollin Mill, Wilmslow. In 1871, now living in Church Street, Wilmslow, he was a grocer and flour dealer. William Mottram died on 23 December 1883. He was buried at St Bartholomew's, Wilmslow, on 27 December 1883 (information about the Mottram family from Raymond Mottram).

James Pickering was the miller in 1860 (White's *Directory* for 1860 lists 'William Pickering, corn miller, Nether Alderley'). In 1874 William Davis was the miller, and in 1881 the Mill was run by the brothers Frederick and Frank Blease, originating from Cranage, where their family were millers.

It was no longer a manorial mill when John Hogg Rawlins (1860–1924) moved to Nether Alderley in 1884. He had been given the lease as a wedding gift from his father, the miller at Great Warford, who had bought it for £100. The mill at Warford has been known as Great Warford Mill, though it was actually in Little Warford, and has also been referred to as Sandlebridge Mill, Colthurst Mill and Coulthurst Mill. It was next to the smithy at Sandlebridge (SJ 80707688) and was demolished sometime after the Second World War.

John and his new wife Elizabeth moved into a tenement at the Old Hall as tenants of Lord Stanley. Here they raised six children: Alice (b. 1885), William Henry (b. 1887), Walter (1889–1916), Ethel (1892–1975), John (1893–1967) and Ernest (b. 1896). Elizabeth was proud of the fact that after bearing six children she still had a twenty-inch waist. In 1920 Lord Stanley built Mill House, near the village school on Bradford Lane, for the Rawlins family, surrounded by about eight acres for their cows and vegetables (information about the Rawlins family from AELP interviews with Joyce Shone and Beryl Bardsley, neé Rawlins, daughters of John Rawlins, 1893–1967). John Hogg Rawlins worked the Mill until he died in 1924 and John Jr and Ernest continued his work with Ernest as the miller for at least the last five years before the Mill closed in 1937.

The timber marks

Adjacent to the top of the stairs to the granary floor, there are several strange marks on a roof purlin. The marks are not assembly marks, though these appear on other timbers in the Mill, generally as Roman numerals. Similar marks have been found on timbers at Standen Mill, near Eccleshall, Staffordshire (SJ 823 351), and in the kiln roof at Trafford Mill, Mickle Trafford, near Chester (SJ 451 708), both corn mills, and also at Murray's Mill, a cotton spinning mill of *c.* 1798, in Manchester (SJ 851 986). Marks of similar appearance have been found on timbers in the 1830 warehouse at Liverpool Road Station, Manchester. Based on research at the 1830 warehouse, these marks relate to the trade in timber with ports on the Baltic (Greene, 1995: 117–28). The timber is not oak and is one of two large, post-Elizabethan, replacement purlins. It is probably European pine (*Pinus sylvestris*): pine was being imported from the Baltic (a term generally used to cover the Scandinavian peninsula as well as the mainland as far as timber is concerned) at least as early as the mid-eighteenth century, but it is not possible yet to date this timber based on these marks.

The graffiti

William Henry Rawlins carved his initials on the southern roof truss at the top of the steps to the granary, and on the side framing of the dormer near the modern sifter on the mezzanine floor. Ernest Rawlins was sixteen years old when he carved his name and the date on the north-western arch brace in the middle of a summer afternoon in 1912. It is possible to be this specific because there is only enough light for him to have carved this (and to see it now) when, for a short time on a summer afternoon, the light from a dormer illuminates the location. There are two styles of 'JR' carved on the northern front-door post. It is not known which were carved by John Hogg Rawlins and which by his son, John. There are several other instances of Rawlins graffiti around the Mill.

In the top left-hand corner of the front door are the carved initials 'WM JM'. William Mottram was the miller by 1850 and in the 1851 Census is recorded living in the Old Hall with his wife, two children and his brother James, also a miller. In 1841 he was at Birtles Mill and by 1861 he was at Bollin Mill, Wilmslow, so the carving must have been done between these dates.

On the inside of the northern wall, just a few feet inside the door, is the rather indistinct 'PM 1816' and, almost hidden behind a modern fire extinguiser, just inside the front door there is a 'PM'. These are almost certainly William's and James's grandfather, Peter, who was recorded in the 1811 Census.

The northern gable end of the Mill has a large amount of graffiti carved into the lower stones. 'AH JH mh 1775' implies a milling family but no evidence of their name has yet been found. Note that 'I' with a crossbar carved here is typically an eighteenth-century way of showing 'J'. The lower case 'mh' probably indicates a child and the carving to the right is possibly '12' – the child's age? There are several other instances of 'IH' (JH) around the Mill. Nearby is 'T: Burgeſs' (i.e. Burgess). John Burgess was the miller in 1736; perhaps this is a relative. The style of the engraving and the use of 'ſ' (the 'long s') is also typical of the period. There is also a 'WB 1736' (another relative?) carved nearby on a buttress of the dam wall. Next to the top door of the Mill in the southern gable is 'IB 1736'. John Burgess was the miller in the 1730s and these 1736 initials are the earliest graffiti in the Mill to which names can be ascribed.

On the inside of the northern gable wall, below the mezzanine floor window, are some particularly intriguing graffiti. They are unlike any of the other graffiti in the Mill and appear to include the initials 'JB'. There is a similar style of graffito at Brindley Mill, Leek – 'TI 1752 JB' – which is believed to represent Thomas Joliffe, a Leek landowner who commissioned the rebuilding of that mill in 1752, and James Brindley, the millwright supposed to have done the rebuilding. Unfortunately there is no documentary evidence that James Brindley ever did any work at Nether Alderley but there are no other graffiti remotely similar to these JBs in either mill.

James Brindley's journals provide the principal source for the work he did but they do not provide a complete record because only fourteen of his notebooks survive (held by Brindley Mill Trust at Brindley Mill, Leek), mainly from his later period, when he was mainly concerned with canal building. Between 1733 and 1742 he was apprenticed to Abraham Bennett at Sutton, near Macclesfield. During this period he worked on a silk mill at Macclesfield (1735) and a paper mill at Wildboarclough (1737). In 1742 he became a millwright in Leek on his own account. Subsequent work included: the corn mill at Leek in 1752; corn mills at Wheelock, Codan, Ashbourne, Marchant Brooks and Trentham and a silk mill at Congleton in 1755; a corn mill at Abbey Hulton, and a flint mill at Bucknall, both near Burslem, and Antrobus's corn mill at Congleton in 1756; a flint mill at Matherso in 1757; flint mills at Trentham and Burslem in 1758; Tatton Mill, for Samuel Egerton, in 1760; and Wilton Mill in 1762 (Boucher, 1968; Bode, 1999). It will be seen that he was a notable and well travelled millwright during the 1750s and early 1760s. Mills would require regular rebuilding internally as the wooden machinery wore out and it is tempting to suppose that if Sir Edward Stanley or his son Sir John Thomas Stanley (the fifth and sixth

Baronets) had required the rebuilding of the Mill during this period, they might have turned to James Brindley. As the estate papers for the period were lost in the 1779 house fire and none of Brindley's surviving notebooks mentions Nether Alderley, we shall probably never know for certain.

Editor's note

The Mill was never part of the Project's remit, but it does lie within the hinterland area, and when at the end of 2004 the opportunity arose to include an account of its history by someone who had recently re-searched it, this seemed too good to miss. The version printed here was basically ready in 2006, and the fact that it has been delayed until now is in no way the author's fault. In 2012 the National Trust carried out a major project to secure the roof; at the same time the internal structures were also examined and repaired, as were the moving parts of the Mill. In 2013 the Mill re-opened as a visitor attraction. The machinery has been restored and the Mill is capable of milling – and has recently done so.

Further reading

Davies, D. L. 1997. *Watermill: Life Story of a Welsh Cornmill*. Llangollen: Ceiriog Press. (A wonderfully readable gem – the history of a Welsh mill with information that is relevant to many British mills of the nineteenth century.)

Watts, M. 2002. *The Archaeology of Mills and Milling*. Stroud: Tempus. (A good general-purpose introduction to mills and milling by an acknowledged authority. Martin Watts was also involved in the recent restoration of the Mill.)

26

Crossing the Edge

Clare Pye with Simon Timberlake and Carolanne King

Roads, routes, highways, paths, tracks: they all have to be considered in a variety of ways. The first question to be asked is 'what is their function?', from which follows 'who needs to go from A to B and for what purpose?', and finally 'how are they getting there?' The last question can usually be settled if one knows the answer to the first two. There are two other considerations: not only do people need to travel, but goods have to be transported, two requirements that can lead to different solutions.

The purpose of this survey is to consider the tracks and routes in Alderley Edge from the evidence of the remains on the ground together with the documentary evidence of what local people did with these roads and paths to meet the changing needs of their community. Because of the fire at Alderley Old Hall in 1779, which destroyed most of the Stanley estate archive, there are large gaps in our information about Nether Alderley and the Edge before it was enclosed, and so some of our conclusions about the early route system have had to remain tentative. Nevertheless, routes change and develop as part of the total landscape, often as much by default as by design, although any major change tells one much about the extent of the local power structures and their ability or otherwise to manipulate the area and control access. However, this survey is not an attempt to define the present legal status of these routes: that is the concern of the county council highways authority (Cheshire East Highways) or ultimately of the courts.

Just as the roads themselves change over time, so do their names. In the case of new roads, the owner of the land or the developer chooses these names but then has to have them approved by local government and the Post Office; no one wants two Edgeview Roads in the same area. Occasionally street and road names are changed to honour famous people or events or to respect local sensitivities. Old road names are more uncertain, except to say that if an old document names a road, it is probably a very old route. In the past, most road names would have been the concern of the locals, who would have seen little need for uniformity of name or regularity of spelling when they wrote them down, and consequently phonetic variations abound in the records. Any outside officials who needed to record local place names often had to penetrate the Cheshire dialect before they could put them in writing. Nowadays, where place names or spelling are uncertain, the final arbiter is the owner of the land. Consequently, the precise spelling of a name has little significance and helps to explain why Brindlow, Brinlough, Brinlow, Bryndlow and so on (all of which appear in the Court Leets) has settled down to Brynlow, the spelling used by the owner, the National Trust.

The modern Artists Lane is probably one of the best examples in the Alderley area of a shifting name change. In the early nineteenth century, the western end was called Welsh Row or sometimes Upper Welsh Row, and occasionally the stretch of road past the Butts was called Butts Lane and the eastern end up on the Edge was known as Brynlow Lane. Even the location of places can change: the parish animal pound or pinfold, originally at Butts Farm, fell into disuse after enclosure and by the mid-nineteenth century its position had shifted in people's minds to the little quarry higher up, which is where archaeologists Roeder and Graves located it at the end of the century, following village oral tradition (see Roeder and Graves, 1905a: 27). All this shows how place and road names cannot be taken as immovable fixtures but are organically related to the landscape and the people using it.

In a rural community like Alderley, travel can be divided into two types: there are local, short-distance journeys, occasioned by the needs of agriculture or other exploitation of local resources, the business of the local community; and there is long-distance travel, usually caused by commerce and generally undertaken by people passing through the area. The former create routes that are likely to shift according to changing circumstances and to be less well defined; their precise legal status may be the subject of argument but they have left a legacy of footpaths and rights of way which can be seen on the map as evidence of past patterns of life and employment. The latter are the major through-routes. In Medieval times, they included drovers' roads, salters' ways and packhorse routes, which often followed the lines of the old Roman roads. Since then, these main roads have often been made by outside planners, and include eighteenth-century turnpikes and today's motorways, their line and status created and defined by Act of Parliament. As the controversy over the Alderley by-pass has shown, making these new routes is a subject of hot debate as conflicting interests jostle to be heard.

As mentioned in Chapter 14, there has been some discussion over whether Alderley had a Roman road, a theory occasioned by such place name evidence as Street Lane Ends by the de Trafford Arms in

Alderley Edge village and Walton Farm in Nether Alderley, and the topic comes up again in Chapter 28 in the context of these names (see also Timberlake in *ArchAE*: 17–18). Certainly, the line of the present A34/B5087 is in an appropriate place, below the steep Edge but above the mosses of the Cheshire Plain. The Landscape Project looked at the remains of the road by Church Lodge, Alderley Park, but as this is the 1780 turnpike, originally built in a straight line across the Park, it is impossible to say if there is anything obscured underneath (Figure 26.1). Unfortunately, although Roman remains have been found on top of the Edge, no Roman artefact has yet been found in Nether Alderley along the line of this supposed road to support the theory. The alignment of the Medieval fields in the Crossley (CALS P 143/14/1) and tithe maps (CALS IR 35) do not point to a pre-existing road as a feature in the landscape, as both the modern road and the eighteenth-century turnpike cross existing field boundaries, and so are later than the fields.

However, the Roman mine at Engine Vein, discovered and dated by the Landscape Project to the first century AD, would have used a road of some sort whether it was pre-existing or made for it. From place name evidence, Devil's Lane (suggesting an old road in existence before the Saxons arrived) is a candidate. This ran from Finlow Hill to Hocker Lane and, following the field and park boundaries, the general south-westerly direction takes one towards Peover and Middlewich, where Margary identified a Roman road running from Byley to Bradshaw House, Peover, the present B5081 (Margary, 1957: 112). Such a road on Alderley Edge could also have served whatever settlement produced the scattered finds such as the brooches and coins from the first and second

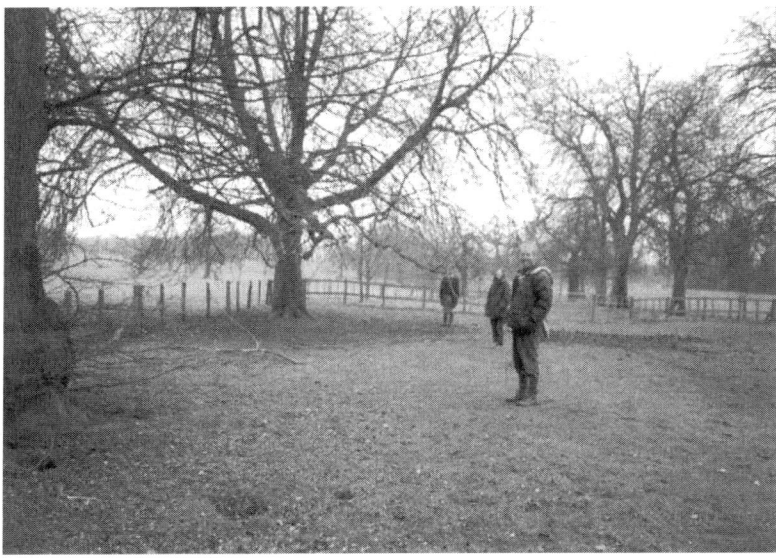

Figure 26.1. View looking south along the line of the old turnpike road in Alderley Park.

Photograph John Adams.

centuries and the fourth-century coin hoard (Chapter 14, pp. 331–2). Again, this theory remains speculative until there is archaeological evidence to confirm or deny it.

The line of the main road through Alderley Edge village and south to Monksheath before the building of the Alderley by-pass (the old A34) was developed as a turnpike in 1780. The original road ran close to both Stanley houses in Nether Alderley. On the 1787 Crossley map (CALS DSA 238/P143/14/1) and the 1799 highway diversion map (CALS QJF 227/3) the turnpike is shown taking a sharp bend by Sand Lane, coming up the present Old Hall drive and then taking another turn to the north to run immediately in front of the old smithy (Figure 19.13, p. 489). By 1800, when the Stanleys re-organised the roads in the area, the road had its bends straightened out and took the line it follows today (CALS QJF 228/1). Further south it ran very close to the Stanleys' enlarged house at Alderley Park, so the road was shifted in 1815 to its present alignment (*Stanley Notebook*); the line of the old route can be seen in an avenue in the Park. Old Sir John Stanley was one of the heaviest subscribers to this turnpike trust when it started and bequeathed his investment to his younger son, the Reverend Edward Stanley, who became one of the most assiduous of the trustees in the early nineteenth century (CALS DCB 1179/70). At the same time Edward Stanley oversaw the Nether Alderley township accounts for the bye-ways for which it was responsible (CALS P143/15/2).

Before this turnpike was built, the position of the Medieval cross by Welsh Row suggests that any north–south road was aligned a little more north-west–south-east (see Chapter 19, p. 468; Figure 19.3) and, indeed, Welsh Row and Sand Lane may have been more prominent as routes at this former time. The present east–west main route, the Knutsford–Macclesfield road, was turnpiked earlier than the north–south route. It was constructed in 1740 to the south of Alderley, straightening out the old meandering route, traces of which can still be seen in the 1872 Ordnance Survey map; one of this road's chief promoters was 'Squire Darcy' of Monksheath.

Long-distance routes over the Edge itself are more problematical. Common sense tells us that unless it meant a great saving in time, long-distance travellers with heavy loads to transport are not going to go up and over the steep escarpment if they can go round instead. Any route between the different communities is more likely to be across the shoulder of the hill than over the steepest part. It has been suggested that a longitudinal depression in Waterfall Wood is the relic of an old hollow way (Alan Garner, personal communication), but nothing conclusive has been found to confirm this. The hollow way by Thieves' Hollow does appear to align with a longitudinal depression on the top of Brynlow near Armstrong Farm, which in turn may have connected through to the path that followed the huge parish boundary bank between Barnfield and Westwood houses in Alderley Edge village. This route, coming down to the Congleton Road at this point, may be the predecessor of the present B5087 and, indeed, it provides a more gradual ascent of the Edge than the modern road.

The presence on the ground of linear hollows that bear little resemblance to the modern route system supports the likely discontinuity of settlement in the area. Despite the Saxon place names, there is little documentary evidence for the organisation of the landscape in these times, as Higham found when discussing the old Hamestan hundred (Higham, 1993: 171–6). Domesday, however, records the waste and under-population of the area at the end of the eleventh century. Although the bones of a pre-existing landscape may have been there when the area was resettled, field-name evidence, with the mention of town and church fields, and numerous heys (enclosures) and riddings (clearances of wooded land), suggests the piecemeal development of an enclosed 'ancient' countryside during the Middle Ages. By the beginning of the fourteenth century, the peak of population growth before the Black Death, these fields had climbed up the hill. The zigzag township boundary on Finlow Hill, created by 1328, respects these pre-existing enclosures.

An extensive lane system would have developed to serve these fields, allowing people, animals and carts to move between the farmsteads and the parish's communal assets, such as Soss Moss, Broadheath and Alderley Edge. Down on the plain, some of the sinuous detail of these roads was ironed out by the later turnpike, but Sand Lane and Welsh Row still serve the community of Nether Alderley, and traces of the old system, such as Clay Lane and the Town Field Lane mentioned in the Court Leets in the early seventeenth century, can be seen in the field boundaries on the 1787 Crossley map of the Stanley estate. In the late sixteenth and seventeenth centuries, the Court Leets records are full of references to maintenance irregularities affecting these low-lying lanes: the problems of drainage meant that they could easily become impassable unless the frontagers cleared out the ditches regularly as they were supposed to do (*Stanley Notebook*).

In the days when Alderley Edge was an open common, villagers needed to have access from the enclosed fields to exploit the communal assets there. As part of the parish's common land there was no need to define the routes on the Edge and, indeed, people and animals would have struck out in a variety of directions, creating the characteristic funnel- or horn-shaped entries to the common land (Rackham, 1994: 144). However, any mining or quarrying on the Edge needed better tracks, as ore and other heavy loads had to be transported. This would encourage more metalled surfaces and therefore a greater definition of the route, although once work ceased in a certain area there would be little incentive to keep up these service routes. Nevertheless, heavy use over even a short time left its mark on the landscape: the soft sandstone of the Edge means that any well used path or track quickly becomes eroded and starts to etch itself into the ground. Most of the routes up to the Edge create these hollow ways as they climb between the enclosed fields up to the higher ground.

The oldest documentary mention of a road on the Edge comes in a charter from the reign of Edward II in the early fourteenth century, which mentions a road running up to the Saddle and from there to the 'Pykedlowe' (probably Glaze Hill or Stormy Point) and on towards 'Fytone stryste' (Ormerod, 1880: 584). This could very well be a route running along the parish boundary up Red Lane towards Saddlebole, from there past the Iron Gates, up to Stormy Point and then on over the Edge past Edge House Farm into Over Alderley and on to Fitton Town. By the Iron Gates the sandstone has been cut into to make the road easier. It may have been used as a sledge road serving the mines or quarries at Stormy Point, the loaded sledges carried down the hill by gravity (Figure 26.2).

The earliest detailed map of Alderley is the 1636 Leycester map of the Broadheath area of Over Alderley (now in private possession; here Plate 61). Peter Leycester of Tabley, when in dispute with Thomas Stanley over manorial rights in the township (described in Chapter 19, p. 471), had a detailed survey done of his lands in the area, which included the roads as well as the fields and tenements. The resulting map shows the routes east to Macclesfield and Prestbury, including the complex lane systems by Adshead Green and by the Over Alderley smithy, Hocker Lane to the south, Birtles Lane on the east and Slade

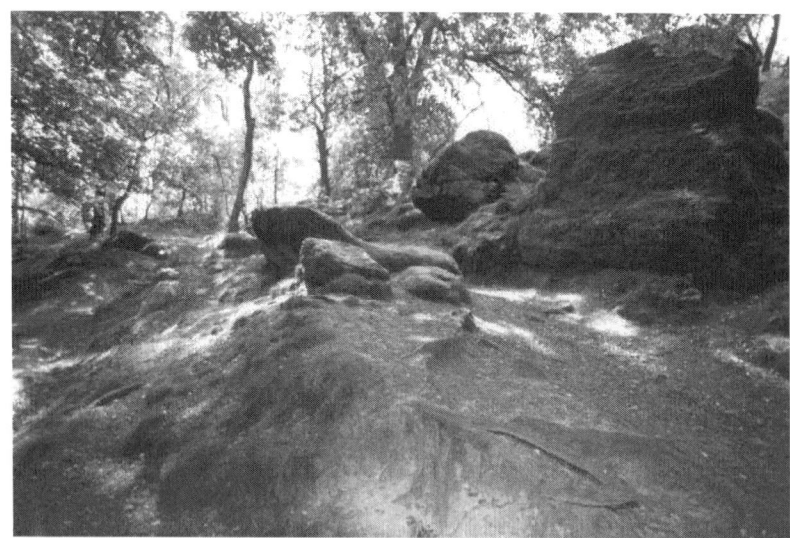

Figure 26.2. The route of what may have been a sledge road, past the Iron Gates on Glaze Hill.

Photograph Sean Edwards.

Lane on the west. Slade Lane and School Lane formed the boundary between the Stanley and the Leycester estates until the latter was sold off in 1797. The merestones that marked the start of the common land at Broadheath can still be seen at the point where Hocker Lane crosses Birtles Lane (see Chapter 27, p. 673). Once a cross marked this spot, but that had gone by 1590 (CALS DLT A75/5).

From this map it would appear that the road system in Over Alderley had been largely created and defined by the seventeenth century. The Landscape Project researchers were able to go round Broadheath using copies of the 1636 map and a 1590 perambulation, still finding many of the original features mentioned in these records. The gradual and piecemeal enclosure of any open land in the township meant that the new boundaries respected original features such as roads and paths, rather than changing them as happened elsewhere during the later period of parliamentary enclosure. Another reason for the stability of the route system in Over Alderley is that lordship of the manor was divided, and so there was no single controlling landowner in the township with the power to alter roads and paths for personal convenience, unlike Nether Alderley, where the Stanleys were so dominant.

Old hollow ways are still in use, the depth of some of them suggesting they have been routes for hundreds of years. The old route over the Edge between Hill Top and Clockhouse Farms is a good example. Now a footpath, in the early 1930s it was still the only access route to Clockhouse; it is very deep, 5 metres in places, the species count in the hedgerow is high and at one point there is a row of regularly spaced 200-year-old mature oaks halfway down the bank. This suggests the route has been there for centuries, and there is an oral tradition that such a route was still used in the mid-nineteenth century for packmen to take their goods from the Hough to Macclesfield (Garner, 1992: 10). Sadly, the section between Higher Farm and Clockhouse Farm was filled in during the foot-and-mouth epidemic in 2001 while public footpaths were closed to the public. It is typical of the hollow ways coming onto the Edge from the Hough side; Red Lane by Mottram Quarry, the parish boundary between Alderley and Chorley, is a similarly deep lane still in use as a footpath (Figure 26.3).

Hocker Lane is also a deep hollow way as it breasts Finlow Hill towards Shaw Cross. It is the original route from Nether Alderley to Over Alderley, Macclesfield and Prestbury, identified as such on the map of 1799 (CALS QJF 227/3); it is a steady climb in a reasonably straight line which avoids the worst of the steep hill, an all-weather route between the communities pre-dating the Knutsford–Macclesfield turnpike. It would also have provided access to Broadheath for the farmers on that side of Over Alderley before the area became the subject of legal argument in the late sixteenth century.

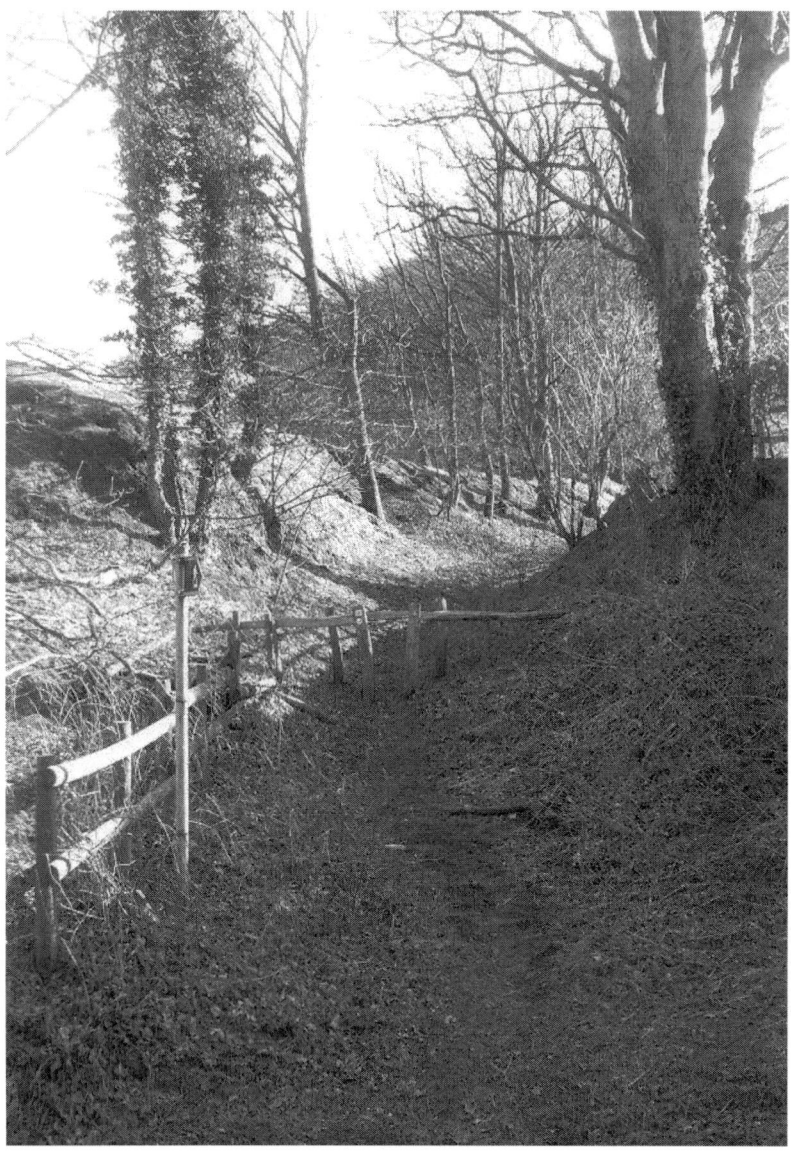

Figure 26.3. Red Lane by Mottram Quarry, looking north from the Hough Road

Photograph Clare Pye.

Slade Lane is another old route, the boundary between the Stanleys and the Leycesters. One can still stand at the top of the rise of Slade Lane at the point where, in 1696, according to the evidence sworn about the miners' riot that year, three Alderley miners, smoking their pipes and enjoying the view at the end of the day's work, saw Hugh Horden and William Sellars coming up Hocker Lane, their voices audible in the clear evening air as they talked about forcing the gate to the mine (Chester Quarter Sessions, 1559–1760 – Bennett and Dewhurst, 1940).

Other hollow ways, like the one at Thieves' Hollow, have fallen into disuse, sometimes so long ago that they do not appear on any map, although the line of the route can still be traced on the ground. At the bottom of Waterfall Wood there is whole group of disused hollow ways which can be traced coming across the fields, into the woods and going on up over the shoulder of the Edge. These routes could be very old indeed; they bear little relation to the existing route system or the land divisions created in the early Middle Ages; some could even be as early as the Bronze Age, since the only features on the landscape which they do seem to respect are high points on the Edge with their enigmatic circular earthworks. One of these routes in Waterfall Wood includes the so-called Sven's Way (Alan Garner, personal communication). It could have been along these disused routes that, according to an oral tradition recorded by Louisa Stanley, the people of Alderley went to hide in the woods from Bonnie Prince Charlie's army in 1745 as the Scottish high-landers passed from Stockport to Macclesfield (Stanley, 1843: 30–1).

The routes from the enclosed farmland in Nether Alderley up onto the old common land of the Edge can tell us a great deal. The typical concave outline of the common land as it funnels down the access routes suggests that Slade Lane, Devil's Lane, Brynlow Lane/Artists Lane and Hagg Lane/Whitebarn Road are old routes up onto the Edge from the south and east (Rackham, 1994: 144). In 1611 the Mottersheads at what is now Whitebarn Farm were reprimanded for not clearing the ditches on their farm, making it dangerous for their neighbours' cattle, although whether this was beside a road or at the edge of the common land is unclear (*Stanley Notebook*: 174). Interestingly, the present road to Macclesfield, now the B5087, did not exist in 1600; at least the parish perambulation of 1598 does not mention it. However, by the time of the perambulation in 1763 it is recorded (*Stanley Notebook*: 142), and in 1775 it is clearly shown on the Enclosure Award map for the Edge (CALS DSA 1919/33; Figure 19.7, p. 480).

However, the 1598 perambulation cited in Chapter 19 (p. 477) does mention a 'wain way' going from Lingard's Farm past the Goldenstone to the Beacon, and a trackway that went towards the mine holes (*Stanley Notebook*: 133). As a 'wain way', this road must have been capable of taking wheeled traffic; however, the actual line it took over the common land is uncertain, although to the south it probably aligns fairly closely to the present footpath past Edge House Farm, which is shown as a fenced track on the 1787 Crossley map.

Artists Lane, or Brynlow Lane as it is called on the 1775 Enclosure Award map, is interesting. It is clearly one of the main routes from the plain to the Edge, one that was used frequently by the villagers; according to the Court Leet records, in the days before enclosure the parish pinfold, the animal pound to keep strays found on the Edge, was at Butts Farm. Artists Lane was much wider then than it is now, because animals would have grazed on the verges as they went along

the route, which would have been just a rough track. By Brynlow Farm
there is evidence of braiding (multiple routes), shown on the 1839–40
Ordnance Survey drawing, where the actual line of the track became
confused as people varied the path slightly looking for better ground
(British Library, BLNIL O.S. NW, 81 A2; a photocopy is in the AELP
Archive, no. 36). This phenomenon can be seen on any overused eroded
path. Down near the crossroads, there appear to be cases of *purpresture*,
encroachment on the side of the road where squatters built cottages
along the verges; typically, the holdings are long narrow strips parallel
to the road.

However, the upper end of Bradford Lane, branching off Hocker
Lane, was originally built as Hall Lane, a private carriage-road made by
Sir James Stanley in the 1740s to allow him to drive from the Old Hall
up to the Edge (*Stanley Notebook*: 243; Figure 26.4). The western end
of Hocker Lane by Nether Alderley was altered by John Stanley in 1799.
The original route came down the hill, joining the main road in front

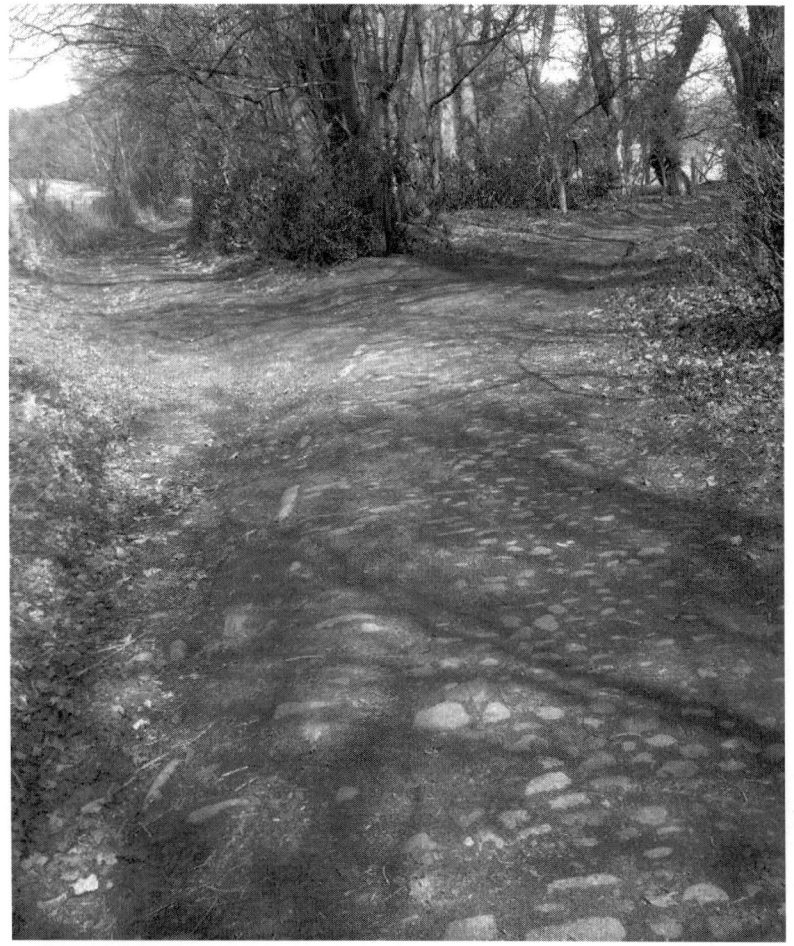

Figure 26.4. Looking east on
Bradford Lane, with the track to
Hayman's Farm branching off to
the right. The cobbled surface of
both roads is clear to see.

Photograph Clare Pye.

of the Old Hall and then went west to become Sand Lane. After the Stanleys extended the park northwards, they extinguished this section, diverting the route and creating a new footpath to reach the turnpike between the smithy and Wych's Farm, the present line of Bradford Lane (CALS QJF 227/3) (Figure 19.13). Their intention was to make Bradford Lane and Hocker Lane behind their park into a local footpath and thus prevent strangers from using it as a through-route. However, they had to allow their tenants vehicular access to the farms along these old roads, and it clearly became a well used local track, for in 1837 the turnpike trustees were contemplating putting a chain and a gate across the end of the lane to protect the turnpike road. The date of the cobbled surface is uncertain: the upper part may date from the mid-eighteenth century, but the western end was probably laid 100 years later, to make it easier to bring the stone out of Hayman's Quarry. In 1839 Edward Davenport made an *ex gratia* payment of £20 to the turnpike trust to compensate for any damage he might have done to the turnpike hauling stone from Hayman's to rebuild Capesthorne (CALS DCB 1179/71/1).

The 1775 Enclosure Award map (Figure 19.7, p. 480) is the nearest thing we have to a legal map of the eighteenth-century roads in Nether Alderley. The township was enclosed by agreement rather than by Act of Parliament. The map and related documents have as much legal validity as any other property conveyance; however, in practice, especially where a landowner had complete control over an area, as Sir John Stanley had on the Edge, they expressed intention, and details on the ground did vary later. The map shows only the common land that is to be enclosed and the public highways that now had to be defined once the land on each side became private property; it does not show any of the road network in the old enclosed fields in the rest of the parish. Looking at the map, one can see the roads and paths which the enclosure intended to define and their relationship to the modern highway system. The accompanying documentation goes into great detail about the expected width of these new roads, and how ditches and banks were to be constructed on each side of the road. The wider routes, such as the Macclesfield Road over the Edge, would be expected to carry more traffic.

However, even a brief glance can reveal that the Enclosure Award map did not stabilise the highway system. On the Edge, one of the most obvious alterations is the cut through at the top of Artists Lane to the Wizard. This had been done by 1787, when the Crossley map was drawn. Once the Stanleys gained control over the land, apart from the main Macclesfield Road, nearly all the minor roads and paths saw some changes after 1775. The Stanley wage books (CALS DSA 241/1) show that John Stanley was building and repairing roads on the Edge in the early years of the nineteenth century, about the time Ashton was starting his mining development up there (see Chapter 16, p. 381;

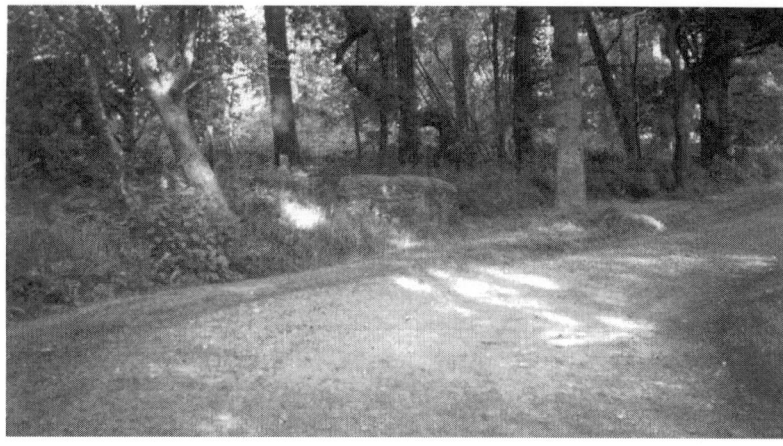

(a)

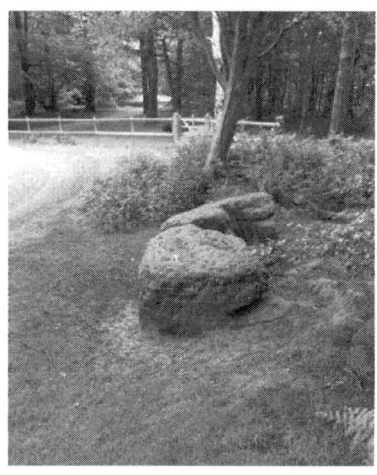

(b)

Figure 26.5. The tracks by the Goldenstone. (a) The track from the Wizard Inn that runs below the eastern side of the Edge as it passes the Goldenstone. (b) The Goldenstone looking north-west, showing the meeting of the paths from Engine Vein, Stormy Point, Adders Moss and Clockhouse Farm.

Photographs Simon Timberlake (a) and Jeremy Milln (b).

they may have been making the track that goes from the Wizard to the Goldenstone, past the bottom of Engine Vein (Figure 26.5). This track appears in pencil on the Crossley map, showing it post-dates the time of the original survey in 1787 (Figure 19.9, p. 484).

Once the Stanleys controlled the Edge, Quarry Road also ceased being a vehicular through-route, although there are signs on the ground that, earlier, the sandstone was cut into at the sides to make enough width for a cart. The development of Hayman's Quarry in the 1830s meant that the Old Quarry on the Edge no longer needed to be used and the Stanleys could close off the track for vehicles as part of their policy of restricting access. Beacon or Keeper's Lodge became the narrow-gated entry point onto the Edge, and anyone visiting the Edge in the nineteenth century on one of the Stanleys' open days had to pass through here on foot.

The Stanleys certainly stopped or diverted other routes. The 1787 Crossley map clearly shows the fenced track called Devil's Lane running between Finlow Hill Farm and Finlow Hill Cottage and going straight over the hill to the south-east side of Hayman's Farm (then called Byron's), and then down the present farmhouse drive to Hocker Lane. When Lord Stanley bought Finlow Hill Cottage in 1832 and re-organised the tenancies up there, the lane was 'filled up and levelled' (*Stanley Notebook*: 247). This had been done by the time of the 1839–40 Ordnance Survey drawing, although the footpath on this map, drawn at two inches to the mile, is still shown as a straight line, and the 1842 tithe map (CALS IR 30/5) shows a fenced track going past the two farms for a couple of fields until it peters out into an unfenced route along the side of the field. The present right of way follows this route until it reaches Hayman's Quarry, where it jinks right then left to come down to Hocker Lane along the township boundary. Devil's Lane no longer exists as a defined and direct hollow way providing access from Finlow Hill to Hocker Lane, despite the name that suggests it had very ancient origins.

As far as Chorley is concerned, the 1842 tithe map gives the best idea of what the route structure in the two communities of Chorley and Street Lane Ends looked like on the verge of the nineteenth-century development, when they were just two more farming communities on the east Cheshire Plain. The modern London Road was the main north–south route, a continuation of the turnpike running north from Nether Alderley to the Bollin Bridge in Wilmslow. A bye-way went off towards Chelford down modern Ryleys Lane, and Chorley Hall Lane connected the two roads from the bottom of Macclesfield Hill. Heyes Lane, known in 1825 as Jenny Heyes or Jennings Heath Lane, also existed as a route through the farmland to Hough Green (CALS DCB 1179/71/1). The road to Mottram running through Kirkleyditch under the north side of the Edge was there, as were the modern Trafford and Woodbrook Roads, which provided access to the Edge from the Wilmslow side. It would appear that the nineteenth-century villa development respected these original routes, including the network of footpaths and rights of way threading between the villas to the south of the Macclesfield Road. In many places the building plots used the old field boundaries, and the modern appearance of Woodbrook Road as a private road serving these houses disguises its original role as an access route from the Plain to the higher ground. Fortunately, Woodbrook Road and its adjacent branches have largely kept the original nineteenth-century cobbles and stone boundary walls to the villas, although the lamp standards are modern replicas (Figures 26.6).

The route starting with Trafford Road continues over the Macclesfield Road in the same cobbled fashion as Woodbrook Road, following the

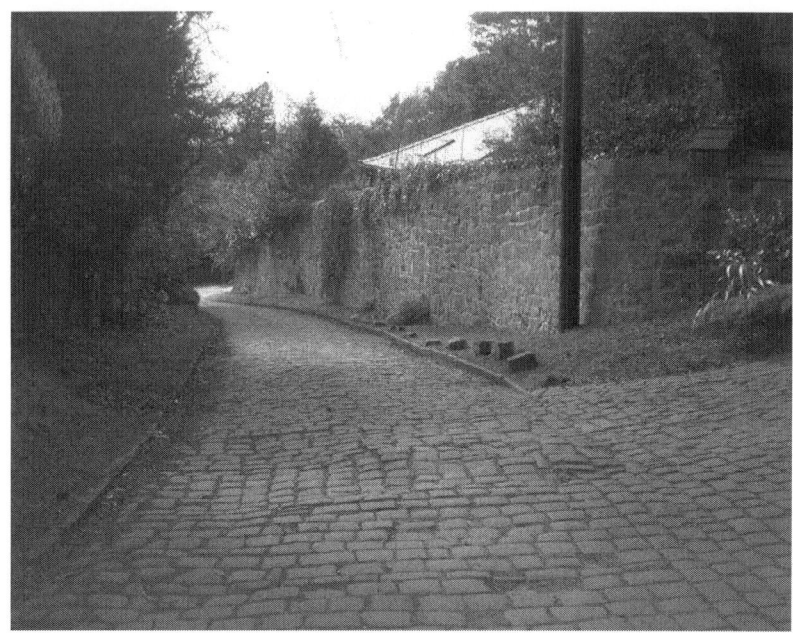

Figure 26.6. Looking down
Woodbrook Road, showing the
cobbles

Photograph Clare Pye.

right of way that goes along the contour line through to Bradford
Lane in Nether Alderley. Older members of the Alderley community
remember this was the path used by the nineteenth-century miners
living in Alderley Edge village to reach the Alderley mines (AELP
Oral Archive 22, interview with Noel and Stephen Swinfin). Other old
routes are still there as footpaths. For instance, Red Lane, the boundary
between Alderley and Chorley, continues over the Mottram Road, still
forming a parish boundary, this time between Chorley and Mottram.

Other routes which are now through-roads were little more than
access lanes for local farmers to get to communal assets. Brook Lane,
for instance, existed as a route to reach the peat of Lindow Moss, and
in 1842 the whole road system through to Mobberley was a jumble of
interconnecting lanes running between the farmhouses. The peculiari-
ties of Moss Lane show the way in which modern Alderley Edge village
gradually encroached on and developed the boggy place known in the
nineteenth century as Lifeless Moss. Moss Lane was originally just an
access lane to this peat moss. Heyes Lane existed as a through-road, and
it was from Heyes Lane that Duke Street and the area round the Moss
Rose public house was developed in the later nineteenth century. After
the Second World War, the Lifeless Moss area itself was built up, using
Moss Lane as the access road, but there is still no vehicular connection
between Duke Street and Marlborough Drive, and Moss Lane itself
turns sharp right to come up to the Mottram Road, emphasising the
piecemeal development of this area.

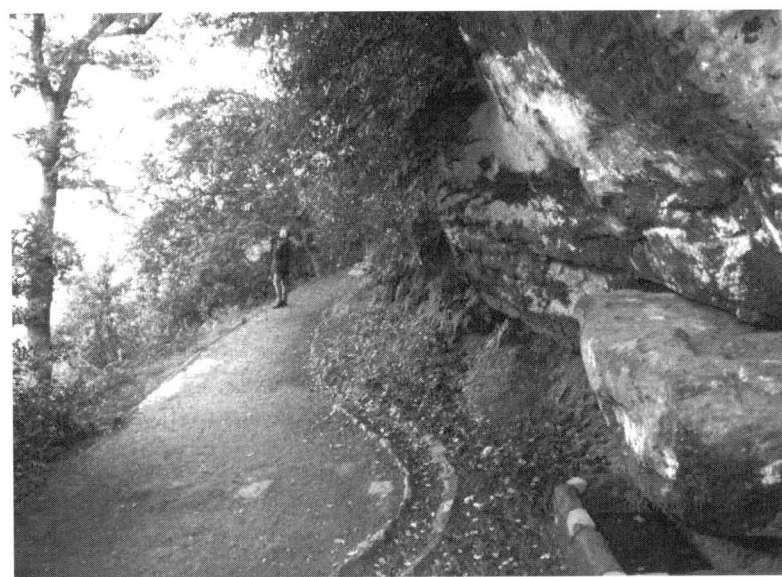

Figure 26.7. The path by the Wizard's Well.

Photograph Sean Edwards.

Up on the Edge itself, the paths used by visitors walking in the National Trust areas are the result of a complicated development over the years – for example, the path running past the Wizard's Well (Figure 26.7). Some are the remnants of the ancient path and highway system over the old common land and the tracks developed by the miners; some were built by the Stanleys as they landscaped the land for their own enjoyment, and by the de Traffords and the railway company as they developed the Victorian community in Alderley Edge village; some were laid by John Evans, the recluse who lived in his 'Bergli Hut' in Church Quarry and acted as an unofficial warden on the Edge in the 1920s and early 1930s (Appendix 21.1); and some have been made by the National Trust since it took over in 1948.

The surveys done by the Landscape Project also revealed a complicated network of unofficial paths created by visitors and their dogs as they take short cuts from one part of the Edge to another. Just as in the Middle Ages, when the Edge had been open common land, routes now vary and multiply to meet the convenience of the user. With the popularity of the area for recreation, Alderley Edge probably has more feet pounding the surface of its ground than ever before. The erosion problem thus created and the impact this has on the ecology and archaeology of the Edge were among the reasons for setting up the Landscape Project in the first place. One of the results of that work has been an evolving management plan to help the National Trust deal with the situation and organise for the future; how the Trust is carrying this through is described in Chapter 29.

Further reading

Maps

The Leycester map of Over Alderley, 1636: now in private possession, but there are high-quality scans in Chester (CALS, uncatalogued) and in the AELP Archive (no. 394) (Plate 61).

Enclosure Award map of Nether Alderley (CALS DSA 1919/33), 1775 (Figure 19.7).

The Crossley map of the Stanley estate (CALS P 143/14/1), 1787: portions are illustrated in Figures 19.5, 19.9, 19.13.

Tithe maps of Alderley (CALS IR 35) and Chorley (CALS IR 30/5), 1841.

Various editions of the Ordnance Survey maps, especially the 1839–40 surveyor's drawing (British Library, BLNIL O.S. NW, 81 A2) and the 1872 edition. The modern Landranger, Pathfinder and Explorer series all show rights of way.

Other sources

Cheshire Archives and Local Studies (CALS), based at Cheshire Record Office (CRO) in Chester, has most of the relevant records, including the collections from the Stanley (CALS DSA) and Leicester (CALS DLT) estates. It also has parish (CALS P 143), quarter sessions (CALS QJF) and turnpike (CALS DCB 1179) records. The Alderley Edge Landscape Project has also collected its own archive (AELP Archive) that includes copies of the Stanley manuscript book (*Stanley Notebook*: AELP no. 3) and the 1636 Leycester map (AELP no. 394).

A leaflet describing *Alderley Parish Paths with Nether Alderley and Over Alderley* is available from Alderley Edge Parish Council, Festival Hall, Talbot Road, Alderley Edge, Cheshire, SK9 7HR (tel. 01625 582150, email clerk@alderleyedge-pc.gov.co.uk).

27

Round the ragged Edge: recumbent rocks and standing stones

Jeremy Milln and John Adams

Individual stones at Alderley

(The numbers in parentheses after the description of each stone refer to the list in Table 27.1, presented at the end of the chapter, pp. 678–9.)

Peculiar stones with arresting shapes or at significant sites have always exercised fascination. The antiquarians William Camden (1551–1623) and later William Stukeley (1687–1765) wondered what drove the Wessex prehistoric cultures to drag huge sarsen boulders large distances across the Wiltshire downs. We, in a more modest way, are puzzled by large stones and hoary rocks sometimes seen on their own at the sides of lanes or in hedge banks on and around Alderley Edge.

Stukeley explored megalithic Avebury and Stonehenge. Alderley has its own diminutive version of Avebury in the faux Druids' Circle or Druid Stones (3) (Figure 2.10, p. 41) between Stormy Point and Beacon Hill, but it also has a number of individual stones at sites of genuine antiquity. Some have been hewn and shaped for their purpose, while others are found in their natural state and have simply been hauled to, or hailed at, a boundary or track.

Those known around Alderley Edge were recorded by the Landscape Project (Timberlake *et al.* in *ArchAE*: 154–5). Let us look at them together and explore the nature, origin and purpose of stones used mainly to mark the way of lanes and boundaries, rather than define ceremonial or funerary sites.

Definition and variety

There is much variation in the geology, situation and date of stones found around Alderley, and it is their geography and function which define them as a group. Some are rough-hewn boulders of sandstone or pebbly conglomerate quarried from the Triassic outcrops of the Edge. Others are rounded 'erratics'; that is, they are foreigners of Cumbrian granite or similar hard rock left by retreating glaciers. Most stones are recumbent while others have clearly been stood up on an end, or set atop banks and along roadways to mark boundaries and routes. Few are marked, let alone inscribed, yet most speak of the significance of territories, particularly parishes, and the roads between them.

Standing stones

Standing stones may be gateposts, war memorials, menhirs, obelisks, wayside crosses, orthostats, rubbing stones, grave and mile markers. At Alderley some are small enough for a person to lift, while the Golden Stone (1) weighs about thirty tons (Figures 2.13, 26.5, pp. 45, 658). The smaller ones tend to be glacial, while the larger stones are usually of the local conglomerate and derived from the sandstone of the Edge itself.

Locally quarried sandstone was also used for gateposts and mileposts at Alderley. These are characteristically flat faced and finely dressed, with rolled or rounded tops, and belong to the processes of enclosure and turnpike improvement. Rougher stones standing in open areas, of the type which in Wales or the West Country might be prehistoric, today rubbed by stock, are absent at Alderley, perhaps because the local sandstone has not endured so well.

Age and origin

Definition by age is most uncertain. A stone-marked boundary mentioned in a sixteenth-century perambulation may have originated much earlier. A stone gatepost may have evidence of earlier hangings or of conversion from a different purpose altogether.

While milestones, tombstones, memorials and the like will be easy to date (indeed, some are obligingly dated by inscription), Alderley's boundary stones, or 'merestones', are much older and more enigmatic. There is growing evidence of the antiquity of many pre-enclosure boundaries in the western half of England and parish boundaries are likely to be in excess of 1,000 years old, their markers dating from when they were first established.

With archaeological skill, the purpose of most stones will be apparent. It is a common thread that all the curious and solitary stones of Alderley Edge which have been recruited by human agency have been required to mark the way. Most were used to denote – and many still do denote – the course of administrative, tenancy or ownership boundaries. Others mark (or at least are found adjacent to) roads and tracks, while yet others denote nothing more significant than a gateway to a field.

Stones marking boundaries

So the Alderley stones are by and large the markers of estates, parishes and fields and the course of route-ways. The Edge was an area of ancient common land shared by civil parishes but disputed between landowners. One may imagine the fun of 'beating the bounds' during Rogation Week where natural features were scarce and boundaries followed man-made ones over open ground. The common lands of Alderley were sandy heaths with extensive pockets of glacial clays forming peat bogs. It was also an area where, until enclosure – a process completed by 1780 – the routes of tracks across the common may have required definition.

Significantly, many large merestones are found at changes of boundary direction, the spaces between having been open ground lacking permanent features. Ill-defined boundaries could lead to disputes, especially as the complex rights over mineral extraction, grazing and turf cutting held by commoners and landowners will have been jealously protected. We recognise this still in the modern use of awkward irregular rocks to protect private verges and gardens from motor vehicles.

So, early boundary stones played an important part in agreements for the transfer of land or rights. In the Medieval period the practice of assarting, that is, the clearing or 'ridding' of patches of woodland for agriculture, will have been marked. So too the limits of turbary in – or 'intake' of – the moss, that is, the taking of turf from the bog. Early boundary stones therefore played an important part in agreements for the transfer of land or rights. An individual's 'intake' of the bog, and around Alderley there were many mosses, was a similarly marked patch of ground. In a 'moss room' individuals exercised the right of turbary, for taking or storing turf used as fuel where firewood or coal was scarce. At Alderley it is known that occasionally the 'room' marker stones were removed illegally, to the consternation of the owner of the turf, although one would suppose them to be just as liable to sink into the ground. An entry in the Court Leet for 1611 records a tenant being fined for moving and destroying one or more merestones for the moss rooms nearby on Soss Moss (*Stanley Notebook*). This despite the Biblical injunction:

'Thou shalt not remove thy neighbour's landmark' (*Deuteronomy* 19:14). A turf room on Soss Moss to the west of Alderley Edge was marked with merestones belonging to the Rectory in 1771.

Stones marking the way

The former A34 road running north through Alderley Edge towards Manchester is marked by a Medieval preaching cross where it is met by Artists Lane in Nether Alderley (11) (Figure 19.3, p. 468). This stone cross, weathered to a stump, atop a stepped plinth much repaired from vehicle damage, is a rare survivor, for other wayside crosses in oak-rich Cheshire were probably timber. More modern are the milestones marking the way on the A34 and the A537, which crosses it at Monksheath to the south of Alderley Park. These include a Cheshire County Council casting of 1896 (24) and an 'open book' post of *c.* 1820 (23) (Figure 27.1).

The Golden Stone

Alderley's chief landowning family, the Stanleys, saw their family archives burnt by disastrous fires in 1779 and 1931 and it is possible we have lost the evidence of others, but the Golden Stone (1) (Figures 2.13, 26.5, pp. 45, 658) happily remains well known. The stone itself sits high on the Edge, at a place where paths from Engine Vein, Stormy Point,

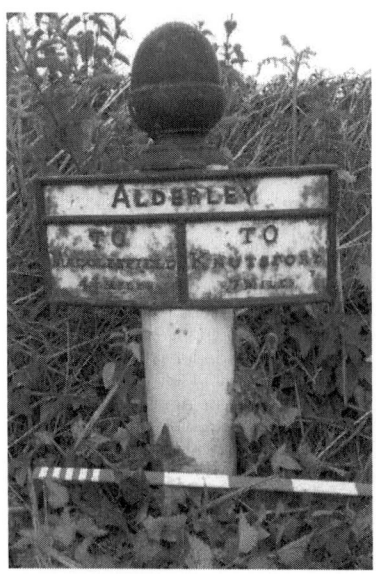

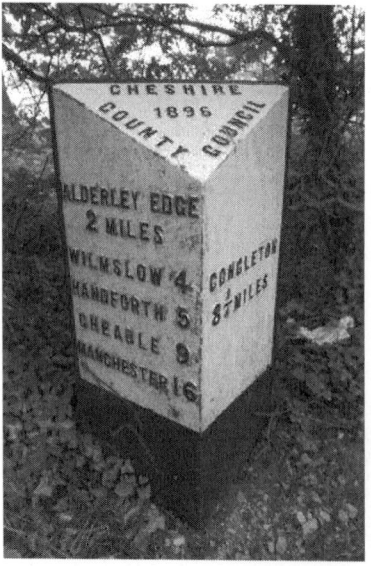

Figure 27.1. More modern A-road milestones. (a) Milestone on A537 just east of Monksheath cross-roads: cast iron open book and acorn post, *c.* 1820. The inscription reads 'TO MACCLESFIELD 4½ MILES | TO KNUTSFORD 7 MILES' (no. 23 in Table 27.1). (b) Cast iron Cheshire County Council milestone (1896) on the former A34 close to Alderley Park (no. 24 in Table 27.1).

Photographs Jeremy Milln.

(a)   (b)

Adders Moss and Clockhouse Farm all meet. It marks an angle in the Over Alderley/Nether Alderley parish boundary and is itself bench-marked by the Ordnance Survey at 606' 10" (184.96 m). This long low un-golden green-grey monster is some three yards in length, a yard high and more than a yard deep.

The origin of its superb name is a mystery, but a great cleft across its middle, as though a deliberate attempt had been made to open it up, might offer a clue. A large chunk is missing and a hole, recognis-able from the mines nearby, has been drilled as though for an explosive charge. We owe its recognition to Alan Garner, who, in 1955, began to research the legend of Alderley. Garner recalls that an oak tree had long rooted in the cleft, so its assault had not been a recent event.

In the legend, the Golden Stone is one of the fixed points on the path of the Wizard as he makes his way to a secret cave barred by iron gates wherein lies a host of mounted warriors in enchanted sleep, ready to save their king at his hour of peril. Romanticised, as such traditions came to be, the warriors became Arthurian knights on milk-white steeds, the wizard Merlin and the name Iron Gates became attached to a mining cave that is unlikely to pre-date the Tudor period.

The name can probably not now be explained, but it is worth evoking some possibilities. Are the Golden Stone and Shining Tor, visible in the distance, linked by connotations of light? Alternatively, like the Cheshire settlement of Guilden Sutton (Dodgson, 1972: 126–7), could the name refer optimistically to richness, splendour or fertility? Perhaps the stone is a prayer to good fortune for the Alderley copper mines and those who worked in them.

(The story of his recognition of the Golden Stone, its place in the landscape and possible interpretations of the name are discussed in greater detail in the context of the legend by Alan Garner in Chapters 2 and 30, and also in Garner, 1997: 69–70).

Stones of the 1598 perambulation

Certainly the 'Golden Stone' name is old enough. It is mentioned in a perambulation of the 'Meares of Alderley Edge' made in 1598, the fortieth year of the reign of Elizabeth: 'and so to a great stone called the Golden Stone'. In this document (cited in full in Chapter 19, p. 477) some eighteen boundary stones are mentioned, including the Castle Stone, which probably equates to a boulder or now lost standing stone at Castle Rock, or indeed the Rock itself, about half a mile to the north-west. The perambulation goes on to state tantalisingly, 'and so to another merestone which many of the jury do remember stood on the end and is now fallen down'.

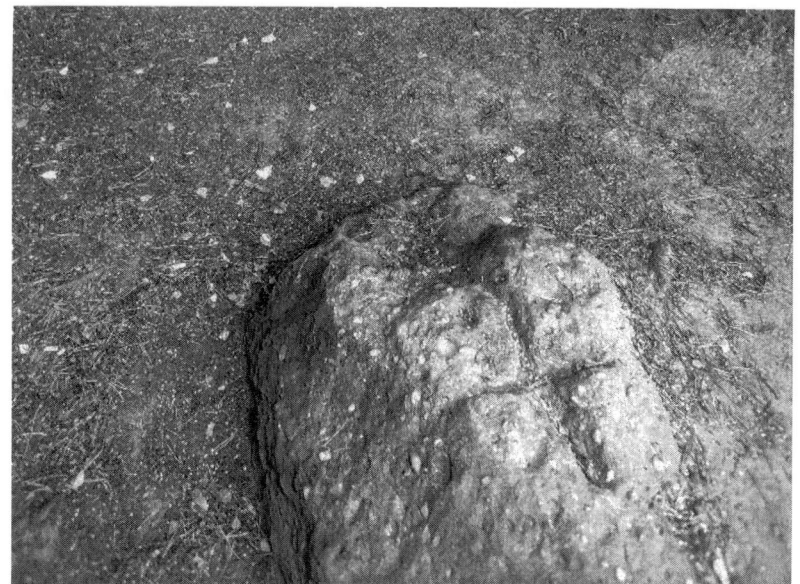

Figure 27.2. The Saddlebole stone: a large conglomerate boulder with an equal-armed cross deeply incised into the top. Set into an ancient boundary bank at the junction of Over/Nether Alderley/Wilmslow parishes (no. 2).

Photograph Sean Edwards.

Mention is also made of a stone at the top of a ridge known as the Saddlebole (2) (Figure 27.2). This stone marks both the boundary between the parishes of Chorley and Over Alderley and the lands respectively of Trafford and Stanley. Befitting its double function, it is large and, as excavation has shown, well embedded into the boundary bank (Milln *et al.* in *ArchAE*: 171–6, fig. 8.20a; see also Alan Garner's discussion of the place of Saddlebole in the Legend of Alderley in Chapter 30). The perambulation mentions 'crists' (crosses) marking the stones or trees and the cross carved on the Saddlebole stone, also mentioned in a perambulation of 1763 (*Stanley Notebook*), is still visible. It is of equal-armed form, suggested by Winchester to be perhaps Medieval in date (Winchester, 1990: especially 41–4).

The 1598 perambulation mentions a stone on Finlow Hill. It is by the side of Finlow Hill Lane, where it is crossed by the parish boundary to the south-east of Mottram House (6). Looking to the west, the bank of the old boundary between the enclosed fields and the common lands of Alderley Edge is still visible, but it is absent to the north-east, where it crossed open ground.

It is intriguing to note that at the end of the 1598 perambulation one reaches 'the hedge between the Inheritance of Sir Edward Ffitton [*sic*] in the holding of Reginald Ffindlow and the lands of Edmond Trafford Esq.' The merestones were in fact only part of a system of land definition which included significant or cross-marked trees and named features such as the Beacon at Alderley identified by Saxton in his map of 1577.

Recumbent erratics

Most of the erratic boulders are hard igneous rock from Cumbria. Although often weighing well over a ton, they were carried to Alderley Edge from the area of today's Lake District by ice-sheets during the Devensian glaciation, 25,000–13,000 years ago.

Following the Nether Alderley–Over Alderley parish boundary due south from the Golden Stone, a large lump of igneous rock is found jammed between an oak tree and a clutter of modern service indicator posts by the B5087 Macclesfield Road (4) (Figure 27.3). Here the boundary turns sharply east on the northern edge of Finlow Hill Wood. The rock, which is identified with the word 'stone' on the 1842 tithe map for Nether Alderley, is of a purplish porphyritic andesite carried to the site during the Devensian glaciation (David Thompson, personal communication, 1998; see also Chapters 5 and 6).

Following the boundary south-west into the large Finlow Hill Wood field is a large hog-backed erratic of pinkish porphyritic andesite from the Borrowdale volcanic series (5) (Figure 27.4). It is a little to the south of today's Nether Alderley–Over Alderley parish boundary, having been

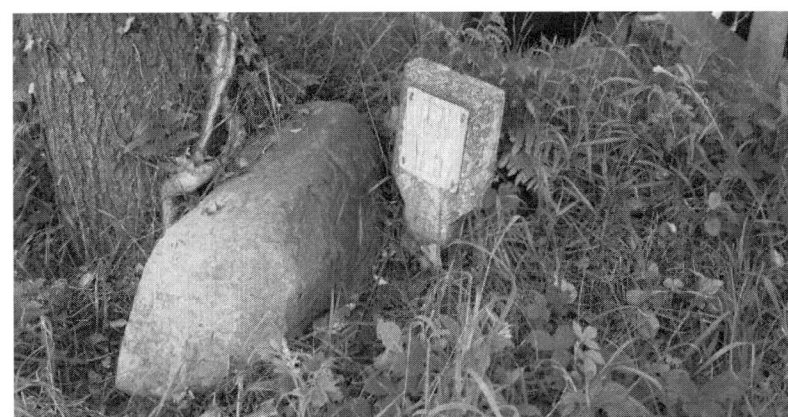

Figure 27.3. Over Alderley–Nether Alderley parish boundary stone: a granite erratic set beside the road at the corner of Finlow Hill Wood (no. 4 in Table 27.1).

Photograph Jeremy Milln.

Figure 27.4. Recumbent pinkish stone of local sandstone conglomerate in a field west of Finlow Hill Wood – perhaps a former enclosure boundary (no. 5 in Table 27.1).

Photograph Jeremy Milln.

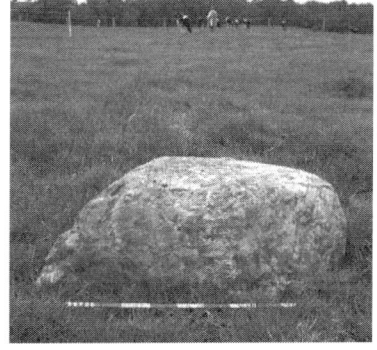

incorporated into an area of pony paddocks, but it seems likely to have acted as an important marker (Timberlake *et al.* in *ArchAE*: 155, fig. 8.20b).

Next in this series comes number 6, which is of native rock. In the corner of a field at Bradford Lane is another very large dark granitic stone weighing over two tons (10), the Bloomery Stone. Its purpose is more obscure, but it lies adjacent to an early metal-working site where it appears to delimit a slag-rich area of smelting from an early water-powered bloomery furnace.

Other, smaller erratic boulders around the Edge are found pushed to the edges of fields following land clearance for cultivation or enclosure. On Bradford Lane, not far from the Bloomery Stone (10), a resident has observed a group of probable field boundary stones roughly the size of rugby balls as they were unearthed while digging for a telecom cable. However, a series along Birtles Lane (now barely visible in the grass and undergrowth) (17–20) would seem to denote the limits of Broadheath Common with numbers 17 and 18 sentinel either side of Hocker Lane at the junction of the two roads. Perhaps the largest erratic boundary marker of Broadheath Common is the huge lump which stands guard by the path into Hare Hill Park from the National Trust's car park (25) (Figure 27.5).

Sir Peter Leicester's 1636 map of Over Alderley is a key document to understanding why, with multiple landed interests in this parish, there are so many more merestones than in Nether Alderley, where Lord Stanley's interest went unchallenged (Plate 61).

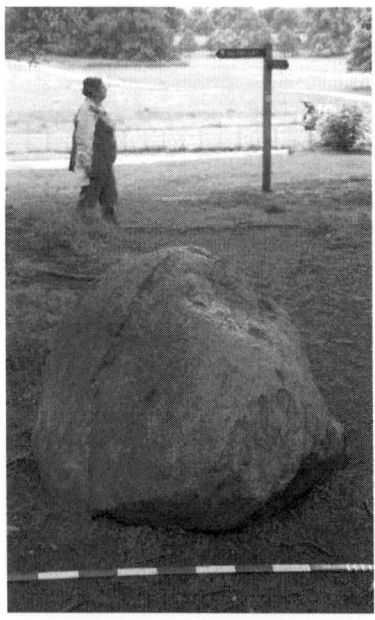

Figure 27.5. Large glacial granite erratic at Hare Hill Park, close to the National Trust car park, marking the boundary of Broadheath Common and an old track (no. 25 in Table 27.1).

Photograph Jeremy Milln.

Shaped and standing sandstones

Dunge Farm on the Macclesfield Road, south-east of the Edge, was formerly also part of Broadheath Common. Enclosed from 1661, a stone just across the road opposite the buildings survives (8). Resembling a small grave-marker this stands upright in, and parallel to, the hedge line (Figure 27.6). A second stone (9), seen on the right-hand side of the gateway to the farm, given its unusual form and pyramidal top, may be later.

The Dunge Farm stones seem to mark the location of an entrance way to the Common recorded on the 1636 map (Plate 61). This extraordinarily detailed map provides a *terminus post quem* for enclosure of Broadheath Common and therefore, by inference, for their openings and gate furniture, which should all be later.

Huge slabs of bedded sandstones, fashioned to act as gateposts by tracks and at the entrance of fields, occur at Alderley, some stranded by removal of associated hedgerows, most generally with relict iron pintles. Most will date from the 1780s enclosure, recognisable by their tooled faces and rounded tops such as those at Engine Vein (26), said to portray the Italian dictator Mussolini (see Chapter 22, p. 569, and Figure 22.1, p. 570), and a matching pair at Hare Hill (27). Another pair of stone gateposts – in this case rather unlike one another – may be seen further along the Macclesfield Road, at Hare's Chase (28), apparently also coincident with a gateway shown on the Leicester map of 1636 (Plate 61).

Much smaller are the pair of tiny early nineteenth-century boundary stones (21, 22) (Figure 27.7) standing outside the eastern entrance to

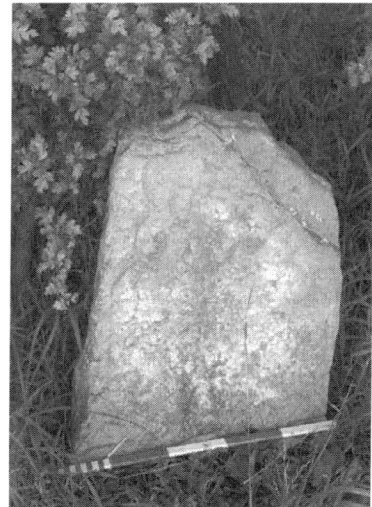

Figure 27.6. Standing stone beside the road opposite Dunge Farm on B5087. A land ownership boundary apparently marking the edge of Broadheath Common in the seventeenth century (no. 8 in Table 27.1).

Photograph Jeremy Milln.

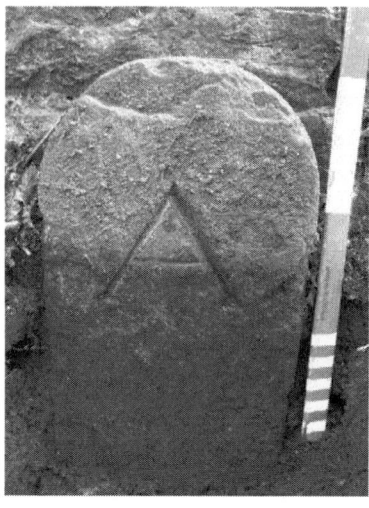

Figure 27.7. Parish boundary stone by Hare Hill Garden Lodge, marking the junction of Over Alderley, Prestbury and Macclesfield parishes: a small finely made early nineteenth-century stone with 'A' (Alderley) on one side and 'P' (Prestbury) on the other (no. 21 in Table 27.1).

Photograph Jeremy Milln.

Hare Hill Park where meet the parishes of (Over) Alderley, Prestbury and Macclesfield. The letters 'A', 'P' and 'M' are crisply inscribed on their faces according to their setting.

Three large worn sandstone ashlar blocks, one atop the other two and set within a modern timber stile, are seen at the side of Finlow Hill Lane (15) (Figure 27.8). Resembling a mounting block, they give access to the Finlow Hill Wood and are known as the 'Pea Steps' (Garner, personal communication, 1 March 2002; see also Chapter 28). The 1840s tithe map shows that the field opposite is called 'The Piece', a common enough field name, so evidently the original name was 'the Piece Steps'.

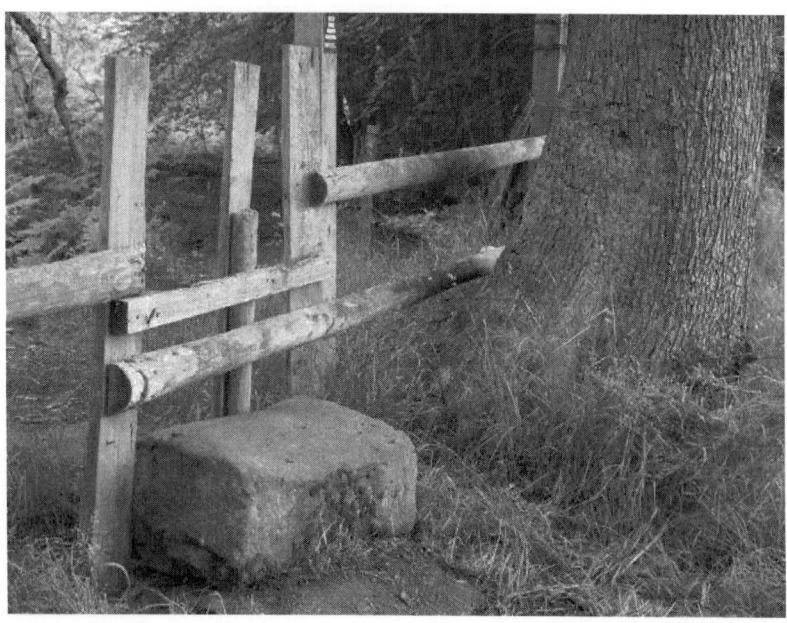

Figure 27.8. The 'Piece Steps' stepping stones: three large shaped and heavily worn sandstone steps forming a stile (the third stone can just be seen beyond the post on the left) (no. 15 in Table 27.1).

Photograph Jeremy Milln.

Stones in maps and documents

Maps are an essential tool to the stone-hunter. Most valuable in the understanding of the bounds of the Common of Broadheath is the map of Over Alderley commissioned by Peter Leicester of Tabley in 1636 (Plate 61). This was originally linked to a series of documents, described by Peter Leicester as a 'bundle of old suits', now held by Cheshire Archives and Local Studies (CALS DLT 75) (see Clare Pye's account of the history of the Edge in Chapter 19, and Plate 61).

Although the Leicester map does not depict merestones, it has been possible, through its delineation of ways and properties, to identify a number of previously unrecognised stones, particularly around Broadheath and at the corners of lanes already extant in the 1630s (17, 18). In contrast to Nether Alderley, where the Stanley family controlled the township and could order boundaries as they wished, Over Alderley had multiple lord and land ownerships, which seems to have worked to the benefit of the survival of merestones in this area.

A few stones, such as number 4, on the Macclesfield Road, appear on the tithe maps of c. 1842, but maps of the Ordnance Survey are by far the most valuable. At its larger scales and earlier editions, contemporary boundary stones and milestones were conveniently marked where they were known at the time. The first edition of the twenty-five inch to one mile series of the 1870s and 1880s is most valuable, although the example shown on the Nether Alderley–Over Alderley boundary in Alderley Park (7), now occupied by a pharmacology research unit, could not be found in the deep undergrowth.

Documentary sources can also provide primary evidence for stones. The finding of the two stones (17, 18) at the junction of Birtles and Hocker Lanes, which may once have been an important crossroads, was implied by the 1590 perambulation of Broadheath, which mentions that there was once a cross here, held in local memory as a marker in the landscape (CALS DLT A75/5).

A manuscript ledger book compiled in the 1830s by Sir John Thomas Stanley, the first Lord Stanley, also survives (*Stanley Notebook*). Effectively a compilation from earlier sources now lost, it refers to a charter of 22 Ed I, that is, the year 1294, which refers to intakes of common land, which will have been marked out with stones. It is noteworthy that the enclosures and use of merestones came at a time of population growth just prior to the Black Death:

> Agreement between John de Arderene and Hugh de Birchall and others. Roger Hugh and others concede to John A[rderne] 40 acres of Land and Wood ... in common between said John Aderne & his tenants in Nether Alderley and said Roger Hugh and others tenants on Over Alderley and marked out by mere stones.

Finally, a small footnote and map in a cramped hand in Sir John Thomas Stanley's 1830 ledger book (part of the *Stanley Notebook*) records a stone on the Chelford and Nether Alderley Parish boundary at Knowlsley Farm (16). (This is probably the erratic by the gatepost opposite the Farm that was noted in 1998 and 2013 but unlikely to be there still.)

Stones as memorials

No prehistoric stone cairn or chamber seems to survive at Alderley. However, such stones are believed to have been used to mark the grave of Ellen 'Nell' Beck, as recounted by Lord Stanley's daughter Louisa (1843). Nell was reported to have taken her own life in the previous century and was denied a consecrated burial. Instead, she was interred in a field under a 'hollow bank' near Brindlow Wood:

> Ellen's Grave is well known by all the people thereabouts – any one will point it out. Some years ago three upright stones marked the spot, but one Dewsbury took them up and threw them into the lane – they are no longer to be seen.

Sadly, the folk tradition has passed out of local memory, for nobody attending the local history meetings about the Landscape Project in Alderley in 1998 could locate her grave.

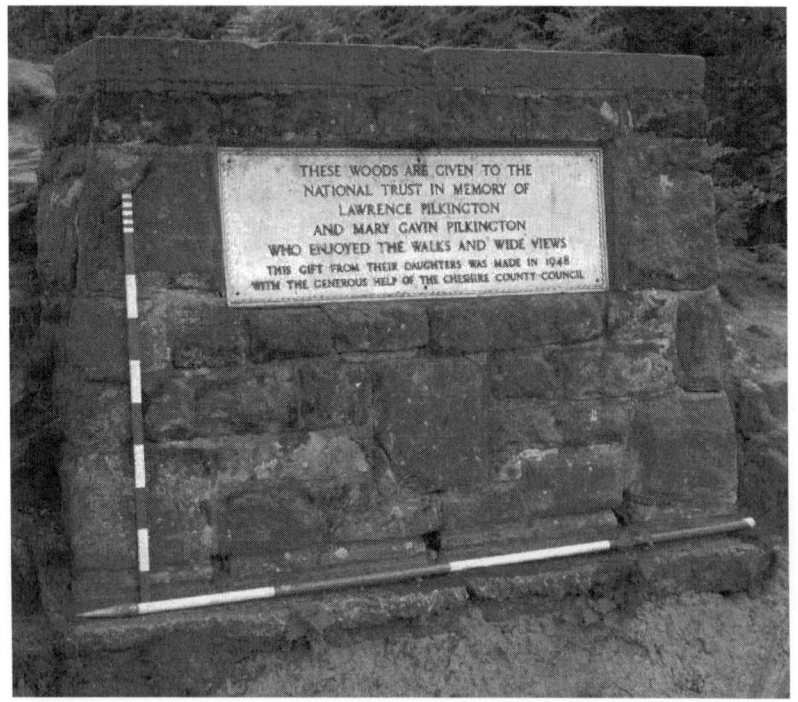

Figure 27.9. The Pilkington memorial stone at Stormy Point, commemorating the donation of Alderley Edge to the National Trust in 1948 (no. 13 in Table 27.1).

Photograph Jeremy Milln.

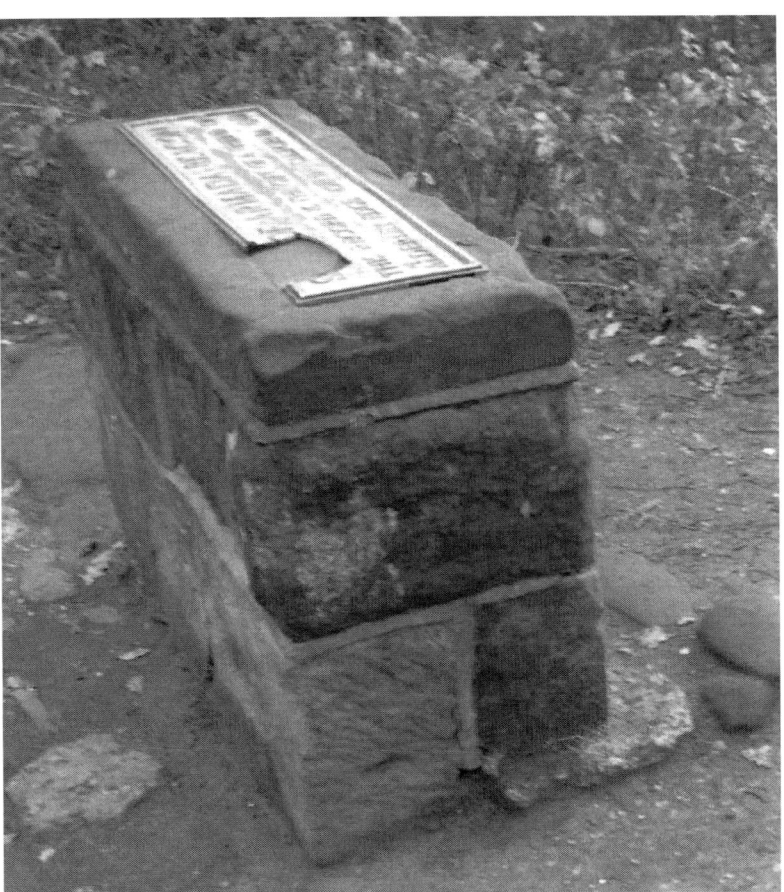

Figure 27.10. The Beacon cairn with a (damaged) plaque reading 'SITE OF ARMADA BEACON...' (see text) (no. 14 in Table 27.1).

Photograph Jeremy Milln.

There is record of a curious, but sadly mislaid, stone on Lindow Common, a little outside Alderley proper. It is mentioned by Christina Hole in *Traditions and Customs of Cheshire* (Hole, 1937). Engraved only 'E. S. 1665', it is taken to be the last resting place of a woman, the unfortunate E. Stonaw, whose name appears in the parish registers as dying on 17 July that year. She was buried 'at her own house, she being suspected to dye of the plague, shee but coming home the day before'.

Most recent of all the stones on the Edge are the two built memorials. The first is on Stormy Point, which commemorates the donation of the Alderley Edge property to the National Trust, erected by the Pilkington family in 1948 (13) (Figure 27.9). The second is perched atop the old Beacon mound, a mortared cairn of stones recovered from the sixteenth-century fire-beacon tower which collapsed in 1931 (see Appendix 19.1) (14) (Figure 27.10). The cairn, erected in 1961, has on its top surface a damaged metal plaque with the words:

SITE OF ARMADA BEACON THIS RECORD IS THE GIFT OF A FRIEND OF ALDERLEY EDGE NOW IN CALIFORNIA 1961.

Other stones of tradition and association

We sometimes find that certain rocks (and trees) of great age, association or landscape value have names of their own and some that have been borrowed by the local settlement or even public house, with many a Royal Oak or Longstone Inn. One such on White Moor in north Yorkshire is known as the Blue Man (from *Plu men*) I' th' Moss, a parish boundary stone, although in origin a prehistoric standing stone. 'Hoar stone' is a name frequently occurring in England. There are hoar stones at Chirbury, a stone circle in Shropshire and at Enstone in Oxfordshire, in origin a Neolithic chamber tomb. A 'hoarstone' at Caterham, in Surrey, used to be rolled annually by its menfolk. 'Hoar' here is usually held to imply that the stone was 'aged', 'hairy', such as could be said of one which had developed a good covering of lichens. The word also occurs fixed to the names of woods, valleys and fields, and at Alderley we may have it in Hare Hill, Harden Park, Harepasture and Harebarrow Farms.

The rather eerie Trafford Stone of Destiny, not far from Alderley, was, by tradition, held to tie the fate and prosperity of the Traffords, neighbours of the Stanleys of Alderley. Once it was moved in the 1890s the estate, theirs for a thousand years, was sold, and the Hall closed up.

Further along the B5087 road towards Macclesfield is a finely shaped stone little more than three feet tall (12). It is on the edge of Spenser Brook near to Trugs-i'-th'-Hole and marked 'BS' on the 1:25,000 Ordnance Survey map. It carries the inscription 'M' and a date – 1789. Local tradition – mentioned by John Adams in Chapter 28 (p. 700) – has it that it marks the grave of a drayhorse, for 'trugs' were hitched for extra power to wagons climbing out of this rather steep and sharp little valley. 'Trugs' is figured in the wind-vane of the house at this spot. Dodgson's *Place-Names of Cheshire*, however, equates 'trugs' with 'troughs' (Dodgson', 1970: 102, 184). There may of course be some truth in the story of an extra horse being kept here, and perhaps over time the colloquialism converted to a name. More prosaically, the primary purpose of the stone is to mark the boundary of Macclesfield and Alderley.

Finally, mention must be made of the 'Druids' Circle' or 'Druid Stones' near Stormy Point (3), although already discussed by Alan Garner in Chapter 2 (Figure 2.10, p. 41). This group of twelve large undressed stones arranged in a circle twenty-three feet in diameter owes its origin to the use of the Edge as an extension of Alderley Park. Here the Stanleys would enjoy picnics or games in the style of *fêtes champêtres*, popular in the Georgian and early Victorian periods. So the circle is pure fancy and the rocks of which it is comprised came most likely from Church Quarry nearby.

Louisa Stanley commented: 'an author, who was writing some account of Cheshire, put down in his book these stones as real remains of antiquity, and was far from being well pleased when he was undeceived'. That author was surely the Reverend William Marriott, who in 1810 published an illustrated description of the stones in *The Antiquities of Lyme and Its Vicinity,* and who had presumably visited the Edge early in the nineteenth century when Louisa was perhaps ten or twelve years old (Stanley, 1843: 18, quoted in Chapter 2, p. 41; also Chapter 19, p. 483).

Nonetheless, the stones, unimpeded by their pseudo-history, have entered modern folklore and constitute one of the most popular destinations for visitors to the Edge.

In conclusion

The evidence is that individual stones on the Edge have an overwhelmingly utilitarian purpose. 'Good fences make good neighbours', as Robert Frost said. From the evidence of Sir Peter Leicester and the perambulation, the conglomerate boulders of the Golden Stone and Saddlebole and the parish boundary erratics have been in place for hundreds of years. Whether their arrival was a response to pressure on land in the Medieval period prior to the Black Death or as the population recovered in the sixteenth century is a matter of debate. Certainly the finer and inscribed stones of quarried sandstone are later and answer more purposes, as milestones, gateposts and memorials as well as marking boundaries.

Acknowledgements

Special thanks go to Alan Garner, particularly for his illuminating comments on the Golden Stone; to Clare Pye for helping to verify many of the stones on the ground; to the AELPHER Project for invaluable background; and to the late David Thompson for commenting on the geology of some of the glacially derived merestones. We are indebted David Green for much other geological data used in this chapter.

Further reading

Winchester, A. 1990. *Discovering Parish Boundaries*. Princes Risborough: Shire Publications.

Table 27.1. Alderley stones

No.	Name and place	NGR	Type or purpose	Description	Figure nos
1	Golden Stone, Alderley Edge	8621 7763	Parish boundary	Enormous conglomerate boulder on Over Alderley/ Nether Alderley parish boundary	2.13, 26.5
2	Saddlebole Stone	8602 7806	Parish boundary	Large conglomerate boulder with an equal-armed cross deeply incised into the top. Set into ancient and badly eroded boundary bank at junction of Over/Nether Alderley/Wilmslow parishes	27.2
3	'Druids' Circle' or 'Druid Stones', Alderley Edge	8603 7778	Folly	Small 19th-century circle of large rough-hewn sandstone boulders	2.10
4	Stone beside road at corner of Finlow Hill Wood	8626 7696	Parish boundary	Granite erratic. Over Alderely/Nether Alderley parish boundary stone (next to modern service indicator post)	27.3
5	Recumbent pinkish stone in field to the west of Finlow Hill Wood	8612 7675	Former enclosure boundary?	Local sandstone conglomerate about 40 m south of the Over/Nether Alderley Parish boundary, now an area of pony paddocks	27.4
6	Stone in ditch at Finlow	8603 7678	Parish boundary	Natural sandstone rock outcrop perhaps once noted as on Over/Nether Alderley Parish boundary	Not illustrated
7	Alderley Park stone	8527 7524	Parish boundary	Over/Nether Alderley Parish boundary. Identified by Ordnance Survey 1st edition 1:2,500 map but now lost	Not illustrated
8	Standing stone beside road opposite Dunge Farm on B5087	8702 7633	Land ownership boundary	Local grit-stone slab like a grave-marker, slightly damaged. Apparently marking the edge of Broadheath Common in the seventeenth century	27.6
9	Standing stone on the right-hand side of the gateway to Dunge farm	8703 7636	Land ownership boundary	Sedimentary rock in the form of a large hewn cube with a pyramidal head, c. 30 inches (75 cm) high (not found when checked in June 2013)	Not illustrated
10	Corner of field next to Bloomery site, Bradford Lane	8516 7670	Land ownership boundary?	Large, dark-coloured granitic erratic boulder	Not illustrated
11	Cross at Nether Alderley, junction former A34 and Welsh Row	8435 7692	Wayside preaching cross	Large stepped sandstone base to Medieval wayside cross of which the stump only now survives	19.3
12	Stone at Spenser Brook, Whirley Grove, close to B5087	8850 7540	Parish boundary	Over Alderley/Macclesfield parish boundary stone. Finely made and lettered, dated 1789	Not illustrated
13	Pilkington Memorial stone, Stormy Point	8602 7794	Built memorial	Commemorates donation of Alderley Edge to the National Trust in 1948	27.9
14	Beacon cairn, Alderley Edge	8586 7773	Memorial	Bears an alloy plaque reading: 'SITE OF ARMADA BEACON THIS RECORD IS THE GIFT OF A FRIEND OF ALDERLEY EDGE NOW IN CALIFORNIA 1961'	27.10
15	The 'Piece Steps'	8640 7676	Stepping stones	Three large shaped and heavily worn sandstone steps forming a stile	27.8
16	Stone on A537 at Knowlsley Farm	8280 7430	Parish boundary	Modest granite erratic boulder on Nether Alderley/ Chelford parish boundary	Not illustrated
17	Junction Birtles and Hocker Lanes	8713 7558	Land ownership boundary	Small smooth black granitic stone. Boundary of Broadheath Common, defining Leycester and Stanley lands	Not illustrated
18	Junction Birtles and Hocker Lanes	8715 7559	As above	Small brown stone, as above	Not illustrated
19	Junction of Birtles and Wrigley Lane, Windmill Farm	8740 7583	Route marker?	Small granitic erratic boulder in roadside verge	Not illustrated

No.	Name and place	NGR	Type or purpose	Description	Figure nos
20	Birtles Lane, by chapel	8743 7591	As above	Another, as above	Not illustrated
21	By Hare Hill Garden Lodge, right-hand side of drive entry	8794 7668	Parish boundary	Small finely made early 19th-century stone with an 'A' on one side and a 'P' on the other, marking the junction of Over Alderley/Prestbury/Macclesfield parishes	27.7
22	By Hare Hill Garden Lodge, left hand side of drive entry	8794 7667	Parish boundary	As above, but with an 'A' and possibly an 'M' on other side	
23	On A537 just east of Monksheath cross-roads	8479 7415	Milestone	Cast iron open book and acorn post of *c.* 1820: 'TO MACCLESFIELD 4½ MILES TO KNUTSFORD 7 MILES'	27.1a
24	On former A34 close to the Alderley Park site	8410 7523	Milestone	Cast iron Cheshire County Council post of 1896	27.1b
25	Hare Hill Park, close to National Trust car park	8737 7678	Land ownership boundary	Large glacial granitic erratic marking boundary of Broadheath Common and old track	27.5
26	Engine vein Mine, Alderley Edge	8616 7756	Gatepost	Tall and broad upright stone inscribed with the head of a man, believed to be a portrayal of Mussolini, the Italian dictator	22.1
27	Withinlee Farm, Hare Hill	8794 7670	Gateposts	Pair of tall sandstone gateposts standing at field entrance almost opposite eastern Lodge to Hare Hill. Iron gate hangings	Not illustrated
28	Hare's Chase, Over Alderley	8775 7602	Gateposts	Pair of squat sandstone gateposts with rounded tops: 940 × 355 × 240 mm and 1090 × 330 × 140 mm	Not illustrated

NGR: National Grid reference (all start SJ).
Source: National Trust Sites and Monuments Record (NTSMR), supplemented by AELP fieldwork

28

Alderley: the names of street, house and field

John Adams

Alderley, as in Nether Alderley and Over Alderley, Alderley Edge, Alderley Park, Alderley Field, Alderley Cottage and Alderley Cross, together with the recent outlier Alderley Edge railway station, lends itself kindly to the study of its names. Although there is no written record of names from before the Norman conquest, Alderley itself appears in the Domesday Book and regularly thereafter, and there are a number of perambulations, with estate and field maps, from 1590 onwards. These, together with the map of the Leycester lands in Over Alderley drawn by Hibbert and Overton in 1636 for Peter Leycester (Plate 61), father of the more famous and quarrelsome Sir Peter Leicester (*sic*) (on the Leycester/Leicester family see Appendix 19.1) and the tithe maps of the 1840s yield some 1,500 names in the study area. These have been extensively examined (Dodgson, 1970: especially 94–105, 225–7, 230; Rumble, 1997, which is the index volume to Dodgson's *The Place-Names of Cheshire*; see also Ekwall, 1960; Gelling and Cole, 2000; Watts, 2004). In the discussion that follows, references to the tithe maps include the field number prefixed by 'NA' for Nether Alderley and 'OA' for Over Alderley.

Even today there are still fewer than 100 named streets and roads in the Alderley area; and of the 5,000 or so houses, perhaps only 10 per cent are named. The total amount of examinable name material is therefore probably of the manageable order of fewer than 3,000 items. This is over a recorded time length of 900 years since the first written record, namely the Domesday Book. We can only regret that, at the burning of the Old Hall in 1779, the cook saved precious jars of jam, but the steward let the irreplaceable and uncatalogued Stanley archives and library be consumed by the flames.

Many of Alderley's names are now preserved only in the written rather than the oral record. In 1842 every field had a name, and it was probably known and used by the tenant and the landowner. By the time of the catalogue for the fiasco of the Stanley estate auction of 1938 (see Chapter 24, pp. 617–18), the names of the fields, in use for centuries, had been dispensed with, perhaps in that eclipse of folk memory that was the Great War. Names were no longer considered necessary: there is not a single example of a field being named in the 664 auction lots.

This was an immense erasure; we are the poorer for it. A scant few fields live on in house names, treated below, or occasionally in the speech of local farmers but most have gone forever from common parlance. A measure of this loss can be seen in the continuity between the run of consecutive field names and sizes of the 1636 Leycester estate book and map and the 1842 tithe assessment for Over Alderley, shown in Table 28.1. If such ephemera as these rather simple names can be sustained over two centuries, it is not altogether improbable that we are in some cases looking through a very distant window of great age, onto the Norman conquest and before.

Table 28.1. Field names in the Leycester estate book and map (1636) and the tithe assessment for Over Alderley (1842)

1636 Leycester map	1842 Over Alderley tithe assessment (field number)
The further Yate	Further Gate Meadow (522)
The further ffoxley croft	High Foxley (523)
The nearer ffoxley croft	Near Foxley (524)
The Blacke Croft	Black Croft (525)
The Calfe Wood	Calves Wood (575)
The Stichings	Stichings (578)
The Broken Cliffe	Near Broken Cliff (280)
The higher B[roken Cliffe]	Far Broken Cliff (281)

Compiled by the author from the Leycester estate book and map (1636) and the tithe assessment for Over Alderley (1842), held by Cheshire Archives and Local Studies, Chester.

The owners of the land

The derivation of the place name Alderley itself, discussed in detail below, is either **Alðryð**, an Old English feminine personal name, or else **Aldred**, a man's name. We know nothing else about this tenant or owner, the form of whose name is merely imputed from documents which begin at the Domesday Book (Williams and Martin, 2003). The personal name is a common thread in many English place names, and has been seen as evidence of seignorial activity in the organisation of rural activity – and in Anglo-Saxon times women as well as men were active both economically and militarily.

As noted in Chapter 19, at the time of Domesday Alderley was already apparently split into Over and Nether. A freeman called **Brun** had held Over Alderley prior to the Norman conquest, and it is not impossible, but very uncertain, that we still see his name reflected in **Brynlow**. Nether Alderley was held, at some point prior to 1066, by a **Godwine** – also a freeman and holding yet more land in Congleton, but leaving no local name trace. Apart from this, we know little about the people who held Alderley in Saxon and early Norman times. There is mention (Dodgson, 1970) of a disappeared **Avardshache** – Aelfward's gate or 'hatch', usually into a woodland. Aelfward is a good Saxon name (Elf Guardian); it is the name of both a local landowner mentioned in Cheshire's Domesday and one of those licensed to mint coins at Chester, although that may be mere coincidence. In any case, his place name is long extinct.

Domesday mentions 'a hide' at both Nether Alderley and Over Alderley. This measure (fiscal or real) should be treated with care, but in general refers to 120 acres; this might imply that there were 120 named 'fields' at Alderley. We do not know what the field names were, though they are likely to have been of the simple English forms so frequent at Alderley. Certainly the obsolete **mean** (common) looks like an early contender (NA 431, 509 and 546, associated with hey, ley and croft).

Somewhat later, we do know that the Ardernes ('of Aldford, Alderligh and Eccles') held lands at Nether Alderley and Over Alderley from about 1220 until 1446, when they disappear, leaving their name to perhaps only **Harden Park** to the north of present-day Alderley (SJ 844 794). We have one very specific date: on 22 March 1254 the right to a market at Nether Alderley was granted to Wakelin de Arderne (*Gascon Rolls*, 1242–54, no. 4151; *Calendar of Patent Rolls*, 1247–58: 339). Alderley also appears around 1300, when we meet **Actons** at Acton Farm, described as being next to Alderley (see below in the discussion of Alderley deer park).

By 1446 John Stanley appears in Over Alderley. The Manor of Nether Alderley had been split off and variously held by a Brereton (1495–1535), an Edward Peckham and a Margaret Moreton. By 1557 it had fallen to Edward Fitton of Gawseworth, who finally sold it to the Stanleys in 1602, thus re-uniting the manors of Over Alderley and Nether Alderley under one lordship. In the 1630s there was a dispute concerning the commons at Over Alderley with the Leycesters of Tabley – here again, despite the 353 wide Cheshire acres which they held locally, the name of the Leycesters has left no local trace in either form (in the later seventeenth century the family reverted to the original spelling of its name with an 'i' – see Appendix 19.1).

The Fittons too, despite their epithet ('the Fighting Fittons'), left only a small imprint on the landscape. There is **Fitton Town Farm**

(SJ 878 757), before AD 1330, where the Fittons had a hunting lodge, and there is the viewpoint **Fitton's Chair** (in an old quarry by Castle Stone Field at SJ 856 779), though this site name is perhaps now in abeyance – it was already mistakenly recorded by William Marriott (1810) as 'Fitting's Chair'.

Lord Stanley, recording a conversation from the 1790s in the *Stanley Notebook* fifty years later, mentions a local oral tradition that a local carpenter gave his name to the site:

> Thomas Ridgway's father (William Ridgeway) told him that a Man named Fitton a Carpenter or Wheelwright lived at the house he now inhabits (Mountain of Poverty) & cut the rock called Fitton's Chair into its present shape.

A nineteenth-century place name on the Edge, **Fitton's Bower**, has similarly now disappeared. It has perhaps a late romantic feel to it. However, the word 'bower' is attested from the 1350s as a shelter or bothy, and from 1523 in the sense of a place sheltered by trees – and thus could conceivably fall into the Fitton ownership of the Alderley estates. There was also a **Virgin's Bower** in Over Alderley, near to Windmill Farm, but this name, recorded in the 1840s, may also be lost.

The imprint of the **Stanleys** on the place names is also modest, as we shall see below, being limited to a mausoleum, a pew and a modern public house.

The park at Alderley and also Monk's Heath were reported by Louisa Stanley to have belonged to Dieulacres, a Cistercian Abbey near Leek (Stanley, 1843). Whatever the influence of Dieulacres at Alderley over the centuries, they too have left only the single name **Monk's Heath** (spelled thus by the Ordnance Survey but the traditional local preference was for Monksheath).

Alderley has also seen a major change in the power over naming in the past 170 years: the arrival of Manchester merchants from the 1840s and the influx of footballers from the 1960s brought new naming habits to the streets and particularly to the houses; the Stanley estate sale of 1938 created 200 new landowners, who were joined in 1948 by the National Trust and two years later ICI Pharmaceuticals (later Zeneca and then AstraZeneca). By the early twenty-first century there was also a working population of 4,000 at AstraZeneca, which had placed its own kind of imprint on naming in the grounds of the former park (see below) as well as its own guidebook (Hill, 2003). However, on 21 March 2013 AstraZeneca announced the ending of all its research and development at Alderley Park and a move to a new facility in Cambridge, although about 700 out of nearly 3,000 staff were to remain at Alderley. The whole of the site except for Little Clays Field across the A34 was sold to a consortium called Manchester Science Parks, led by Bruntwood and including among its principal stakeholders the University of Manchester. In October 2014 it was announced that the consortium's name was being changed to Manchester Science Partnerships, and the association of incoming (small) companies in the new science park is known as the BioHub. The further effects on local nomenclature remain unpredictable, especially as part of the Park is to be opened up for housing and other developments. The story of the Park up to and including AstraZeneca's tenure and the plans for the future are described in George B. Hill's *Alderley Park Discovered* (Hill, 2016).

It should also be remembered that Alderley is a literary landscape, from at least as early as 1805: a long press article on the Legend of Alderley Edge in the *Manchester Mail* was published on 19 May that year, during the build-up to the Battle of Trafalgar, and this was reinforced in 1843 by Louisa Stanley's guide, *Alderley Edge and Its Neighbourhood*, as well as more recently in the works of Alan Garner and others. Literature tends to have a subtle series of effects: it fixes and places the memory of an imagined landscape (which readers may never visit) at the disposal of a large number of people, who may feel that they own it, in some protective fashion. Literature may also generate its own folklore and nomenclature: there are a number of local names at Alderley, mainly for passing trade, such as the **Wizard of Edge** (restaurant and tearooms), **Brasingamens** (a wine bar now mutated into the **Braz**) and the **Merlin** (now a large road house but formerly a Quaker school) which play off this literary resonance. These are covered further below.

The shape of the landscape and local place names

In many of her books (e.g. *The Landscape of Place-Names*; Gelling and Cole, 2000), the place name expert Margaret Gelling has explored how the geography of a landscape dictates many of the technical words used to describe it. Much of the following draws on her excellent work. It is however useful to remember that each generation sees the kind of landscape it wishes to see: Marriott (1810), for example, saw in the Edge a Roman-style military landscape of 'fosses' and 'aggers'. Many modern visitors see it as a kind of sacred Arthurian landscape.

The topography of the Alderley area is relatively simple: **Alderley Edge** (the steep eminence at SJ 859 779) rises up from what must have been until quite recently, on all sides, a morass of bogs and streams, reflected in the place names – to the west lie **Sossmoss** (sodden bog, SJ 829 759, generally taken to be the *profundam mossam* or 'deep bog' mentioned in 1271), **Lindow Moss** (SJ 824 796, Lindow being sometimes parsed as Celtic 'black lake', Welsh llyn + du, but more likely Old English 'lime tree hill', lind + hōh: see Dodgson, 1970: 230; Ross, 1986: 169) and the

Common Carr (SJ 834 786, a common land of brushwood in a marsh). To the south, there is a series of Cheshire meres, beginning with **Radnor Mere** in Alderley Park grounds (SJ 847 758, perhaps named by the Stanleys for their Welsh antecedents), and culminating below the A537 in **Redes Mere**, which forced the north–south A34 into a sharp dogleg (SJ 846 722). North and east, the wetlands of the eponymous **Lifeless Moss** (SJ 850 781) are drained by the **River Bollin** and numerous small brooks. To the south-east lies **Adders Moss** (SJ 868 770 – containing the word 'adsheads', the headlands where the ploughman turned the ox-team). Further in the same direction the Spencer Brook, in its deep declivity, also forms a kind of terminus to Alderley, where **Alderley Field** (SJ 884 754) marks the end of Over Alderley parish and the beginning of Macclesfield. Parts of the wetlands of Over Alderley, like Lindow Moss, were used for cutting peat for household fuel (turbary). The local name for a section is a 'room'.

A walk up to the Edge from **St Mary's Church** (SJ 841 761) at the centre of old Alderley proper passes the water-driven **Alderley Mill** (Chapter 25) and the moated **Alderley Old Hall**. Going up the gentle slope of **Bradford Lane** (first mention 1208 – see Dodgson, 1970: 95) or more steep **Artists Lane** one is always struck by the amount of water coming in the opposite direction – there was a fulling mill with millpond on Artists Lane, and even the top of Alderley Edge is a wet, boggy place. The mines contain varying amounts of water – in some shafts one can look down into many metres of flooded workings. The eerie precipitous abandoned quarry at **Finlow Hill Farm** (SJ 857 765) lying exactly athwart the boundary between Over Alderley and Nether Alderley townships is also completely flooded.

There are three main watercourses in the area – the **Spencer** and **Whitehall** Brooks, and the **River Bollin**. The origins of their names are unclear, though Spencer is probably a personal name, Whitehall is clearly a place name, but yet to be identified, and Bollin is disputed – it may or may not be 'eel torrent'.

On the east and north-east of the Edge proper, and at Castle Rock Field, the bare red sandstone of Alderley is exposed, and the landscape falls dramatically and indeed dangerously away. This vertiginous effect of the Edge, scarcely 200 m high, is perhaps achieved by the fact that the surrounding land is hardly more than 60 m above sea level, and the Edge allows views to distant Manchester and over much of north Cheshire. The exception is the **Hough**, or heel (SJ 856 784), where the land slides away more gradually from the Edge. (It is also possible that this is a local Cheshire usage, extended to meaning an embayment or valley running into a hillside. This would also fit the topography.)

At Alderley we can only guess from the many local place names ending in -ley (Old English *lēah* – a woodland clearing) that the area might have been still wooded when the English-speaking population arrived. Or possibly they took over clearings that had been there for many centuries. The element *lēah* in place names had its heyday in the period 750 to 950, and it seems likely that the area around Alderley was settled (if not actually cleared) by English-speakers in this period – perhaps when the formidable Æthelfleada, Lady of the Mercians, helped push out the Vikings in the period up to 919, the year King Edward the Elder finally signed one of his charters from Manchester – 'in Northumbria', a salutary reminder that everything was different then.

Cheshire itself as a place name does not appear before 980 – it was carved administratively and rather late out of other areas. Chester was the local seat of administration, but only when it was not being sacked by the Vikings and abandoned. Cheshire also looked further north than today – as far as to the Ribble in Lancashire – and it also took in Flintshire and Denbighshire, at least for tax records. But for ecclesiastical purposes, parishes like Alderley looked south to the Diocese of Lichfield, until they were transferred to Chester in 1541.

The origins of Alderley

The first mention of **Alderley** appears in the Domesday Book of 1086, and it has had at least thirty different spellings over time. **Over Alderley** appears by the late twelfth century in Latin as 'superior', in English by 1315; **Nether Alderley**, also in Latin as 'inferior' by 1285, in English by 1315. The administrative 'hundred' in which they were located, **Hamestan**, is no longer exactly identifiable but it covered a large area, from Stockport to Macclesfield. There is no mention at Alderley of a mill or any mines (unlike Domesday entries for Derbyshire, which list lead mines). The parish of Alderley was not created until about 1300.

The meaning of the name Alderley is subtly different to what one might expect (it has nothing to do with alder trees or the lee side of a hill). It means, according to Dodgson (1970: 95), the *lēah*, here woodland clearing, of Alðryð. Now Alðryð is an Old English feminine personal name, which raises intriguing questions about female land ownership – Domesday, for example, records at least one woman who separated from her husband and 'withdrew all her land and possessed it as a lady'. The total number of female names in place names in Cheshire comes in at only about 5 per cent, making Alderley rather special.

It should however be mentioned that there are differing views on the personal name to be found in Alderley, with Ekwall (1960) preferring the male name 'Aldred'. There do not appear to be many other extant feminine place names in Alderley – apart from **Jenny Heyes Lane, St Mary's** Church (Nether Alderley) and **St Catherine's** Church

(Birtles), the villa **St Mary's Cliffe** and the now defunct **La Femme** shop. In Alderley Park grounds there is recorded from 1798 onwards **Lady Margaret's Walk**, which is an avenue of mature cypresses down to the **Water Garden**. This commemorates Margaret Owen (died 1819) of Penrhos, the wife of the sixth Baronet Stanley, and mother of the first Lord Stanley. St Hilary (of the former **St Hilary's Girls' School**, now St Hilary's Park apartments, SJ 843 781) was a man – most probably St Hilary (Hilarius) of Poitiers.

Did Alðryð live at Alderley, perhaps as a tenant, or did she own it as an estate? It is impossible to know at this distance in time. Was there a previous British or Viking resident who cleared the land, only to have it usurped by the incoming Mercian Anglo-Saxons in the 900s? Again, history is silent. There is however one curious modern survival: a Cheshire dialect dictionary (Leigh, 1877), under local place name pronunciations, cites 'Awtherley' for Alderley – a variant also cited a little later by Fletcher Moss (Moss, 1898), and perhaps closer to the Anglo-Saxon personal name. A report of the notorious 'Iron Bottle' exorcism in the early 1800s (described at the end of Chapter 11), written in a mock dialect and probably conducted by the rector at St Mary's, Edward Stanley, says 'a gamekeeper with a black dog used to walk at **Authorley**, till th' passon [parson] laid 'im'. The 'Awthorley' pronunciation is perhaps extinct today – probably under the influence of the written form. Local queries in 2005 failed to elicit it, or any living memory of it. It did however fool the collector of the 1851 Census data, who accepted a John Brocklehurst of Odd Rode in Cheshire as being born in 'Ortherley' – presumably our Alderley.

Leaving aside the problem of the correct personal name and its pronunciation, the 'ley' or *lēah* element in Alderley for 'woodland clearing' is one of the most common in place name elements in both Britain and Cheshire. The neighbouring area affords us also **Mobberley**, being the 'meeting mound clearing', and **Chorley**, now effectively part of Alderley village (SJ 835 780), being the 'churls' clearing', where churls were a class of free peasants, also mirrored by **Chorlton**, further north on the Mersey, and the Prestbury field name **choke churl**, presumably poor or bad land and doing just what it says. However, Bentley House (SJ 841 756), opposite Alderley Park grounds on the old A34, is most likely named after the Bentley family, who lived in Park House in Alderley Park grounds until 1695. There is also a **Bentley Brook** (Bently on a 1798 estate map) flowing through the Park (Houghton, 1986).

Other local examples are perhaps **Highleas** (from 1320), **Withinlee Farm** (SJ 883 769), **Gatley Green Farm** (SJ 836 764, some evidence from 1391 for this name), **Knowsley Farm** (SJ 826 741), **Shrigley Fold Farm**, **Baguley Farm**, **Whirley Grove** (from 1348 at SJ 886 751) and **Stanley Green** (if this is not a Stanley family name, rather than a stony lea); **Heatherley** (OA 620, possibly as early as 1285) as a field name; possibly **Kirkleyditch**, unless this is a confusion with church fields or leas – but Kirkley has been written **Keighley** (probably a personal name + *lēah*) in the past. Similarly, **Ryleys Lane** in Alderley may be a *lēah*-type clearing, but is more likely a crop of rye on the leas (fields) of the Common Carr. (Rye was more productive than wheat, giving a sevenfold yield, against five for wheat.)

The current view is that *lēahs* were perhaps not new settlements by the incoming English-speakers, but older settlements which had perhaps existed for many years, centuries even. In general terms *lēahs* are places of minor settlement. In north-east Cheshire, however, it may still have been the case that these were in fact new English settlements: the land was intractable and settled late. Gelling suggests that the whole area was perhaps a large forest, with settlements on its fringes. Its northerly boundary would be Cheadle (containing British *cēd*, 'forest' – cf. modern Welsh *coed*). In this thesis Macclesfield to the south was at the other end of the forest – the *feld* here is open countryside, in opposition to woodland.

It is unclear to what use these *lēah* clearings were put locally at Alderley. They may have been for pasture on the less fertile ground, or for the plough in the richer soil of Nether Alderley. Certainly by the eighteenth century the rolling reforested 'Repton' style of Alderley Park grounds lent itself mainly to pasture. The word *lēah* or 'ley' has had a good currency: it was still used until recently in the extended sense of 'to pasture cattle' – as late as 1920 the Alderley estate manager commented on the land in Alderley Park: 'It is very undulating, has many trees upon it … impossible to do anything with it other than take in [live]stock to ley'.

With a long history of local copper and lead mining, there is also the possibility that at least some of the many *lēahs* at Alderley were cleared for fuel for smelting. For example, although the occurrence of Medieval mining at Alderley is poorly understood, the area below Bradford House on Bradford Lane has yielded a vast amount of slag, probably Medieval if pottery found in association with it is taken into account. This smelting would have required a considerable consumption of wood or charcoal, presumably from the surrounding area. It may therefore be that the *lēah* clearings at Alderley reflect both agricultural and mining activity. We can also guess that the **Hagg** (SJ 855 776 – an area of coppiced woodland) may also have been associated with smelting – see below, and also Warrington's account of mining in the historic period (Chapter 16) and Clare Pye's summary of recent work at the Hagg Cottages (Appendix 19.3).

A *lēah* and a derogatory feminine motif is contained in **Corbishley** (at SJ 828 757, first mention 1200), 'cur bitch clearing': we can probably imagine what kind of land that was to clear, situated in the middle of Soss Moss. It has also generated a local surname, suggesting that the derogatory term was in widespread Medieval usage – an example of a vulgar place name which has not been edited out of existence by the bowdlerising Victorian Ordnance Survey. It has also attached itself to Corbishley Bridge. It has generated a local surname – Curbushley occurs in a will at Chorley by 1655.

The process of denuding Alderley of its tree cover for agriculture or mining was probably continuous over a long period, depending on population and climatic fluctuations. What is also certain is that the accumulation of large estates by the Stanleys and the utterly bare nature of the Edge by 1745 allowed them to replant large areas, for both aesthetic and economic reasons, with oak, spruce, willow and of course the beeches now at their climax, for which Alderley remains famous. Lord Stanley gives an interesting set of place names and dates for the re-afforestation of the Alderley estates (the word 'plantation' occurring seventy-three times in the tithe assessment) (*Stanley Notebook*):

> 1802. A field of Downes farm called *[illegible]* was planted. The first tree was put in ye ground by Sir Will Clinton and the plantation was given ye name of Clinton hill.

> 1810. Dumvilles Plantation bordering on Fernhill … spring of 1810

The former is at SJ 862 760. The name **Clinton hill** is still extant, but the area is no longer wooded, whereas in the latter case both the name **Dumvilles** and the plantation are still extant (at SJ 847 743). There was a numerous Dumville family at Alderley from at least 1703, and the wood is also mentioned by name in Alan Garner's *The Weirdstone of Brisingamen* (1960: 172).

Patterns of settlement: 'common', 'hey' and 'ridding' (Figure 28.1)

The classic opposition to *lēah* is the *tūn,* modern '-ton'. The *tūn* is usually taken to be an unwooded area, associated with an estate or farm, but perhaps with a stronger meaning than just a farm or settlement. At Alderley there are two on or near the route of the old A34: we have both **Hoblington** (NA 231 Hoblington Meadow; SJ 848 751) and **Worthington** (NA 8; SJ 842 758) as field names, in the immediate vicinity of Alderley Park grounds– these are discussed below.

Doubtless the formation of parishes and the building of parish churches helped the process of fixing names, since these were important

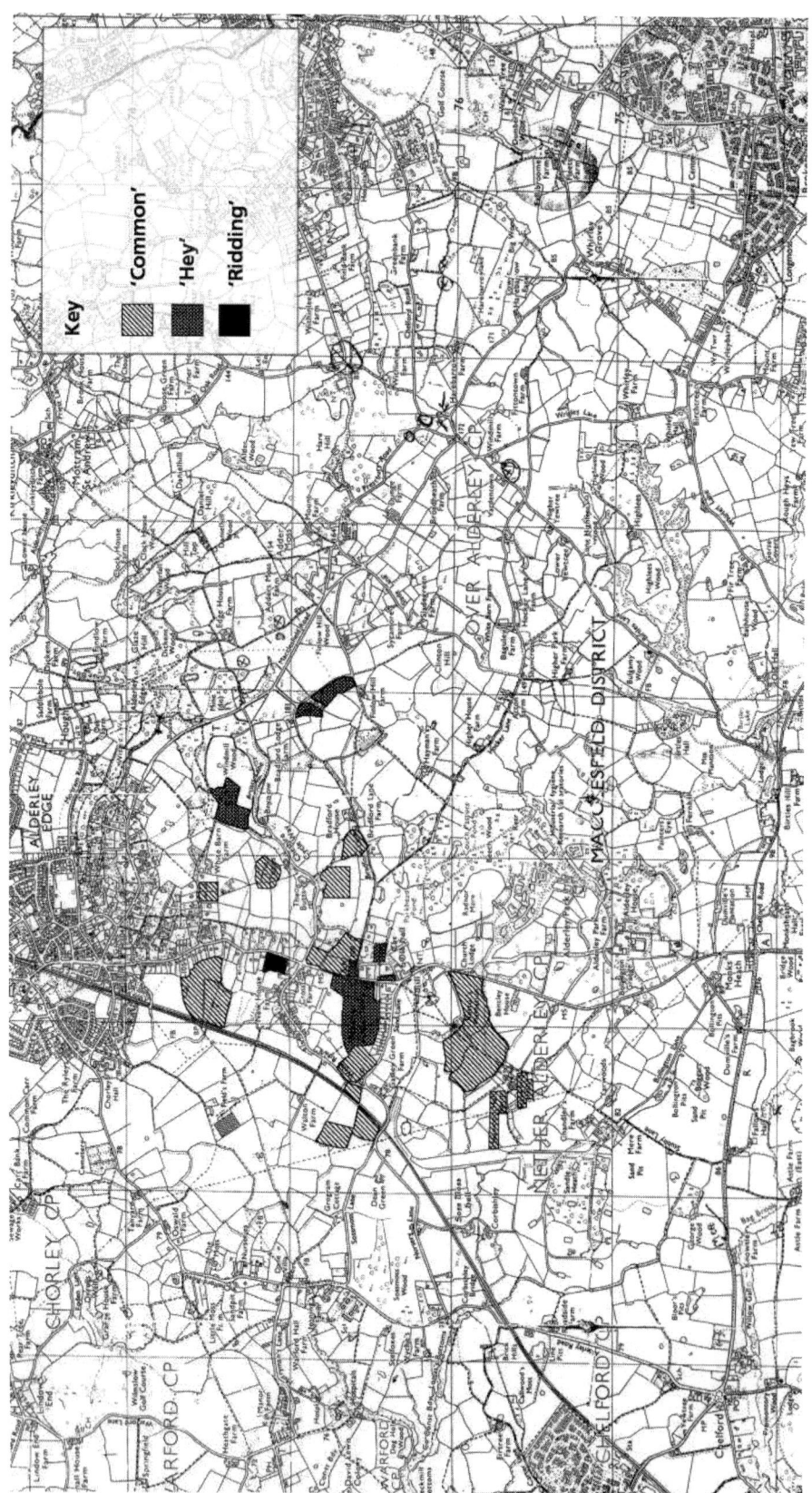

Figure 28.1. Map 1. Patterns of settlement: 'common', 'hey' and 'ridding'.

Based on the 1992 Ordnance Survey 1:25,000 Pathfinder map sheet 759 with the permission of the Controller of Her Majesty's Stationery Office, Crown copyright October 2013.

social, fiscal and indeed physical structures. Although Alderley dates from 1300 as a parish, Over Alderley had no church. **St Mary's** in Nether Alderley (Figure 19.4, p. 469), consecrated in about 1300 as the church for the three townships of Nether Alderley, Over Alderley and Great Warford, is a naming peculiarity – at some point after 1536 it gave up its original dedication of **St Lawrence**. It would be interesting to know the reason for this original dedication – St Lawrence is now the patron saint of miners and one could suggest a connection to the processing of ore. A more mundane explanation would be that the original Roman St Lawrence defended church property and the poor against rapacious officials and nobility. However, there is no written evidence to support either of these notions, and for the present they must remain specula- tion. It would also be interesting to know why there was a change to the Marian dedication after 1536, at or about the time of the Reformation, and in an increasingly puritan Cheshire.

Within the church and its grounds are two specific names: the **Stanley Mausoleum** (Figure 19.18) and the **Stanley pew**, which, although not strictly place names, are perhaps worth recording as the few places to which the Stanley name attaches locally – though the family have used neither since the sale of the estate in 1938, which severed the connection. We have already noted that the Stanleys were at Alderley from 1446, yet even then had arrived too late to impose their names on the landscape. It is also noticeable that the **Schoolhouse** (Figure 24.4, p. 609), also in the churchyard, although extended by Edward Stanley, is not referred to as a Stanley building – in fact, as the inscription narrates, 'Mr Hugh Shaw, Clerk, built this School Ano 1628. Mr Thomas Deane de Park Endow'd it Jan: ye 30th 1694'. Deane de Park has almost been written out of the linguistic record at Alderley. There is a **Dean Field** and **Meadow** (NA 228 and 230) next to the site of Alderley Park House. The area next to the Rectory called **Deans Tump** (no longer used) was levelled during the rebuilding in about 1819 – possibly also a much older mound.

Mention should also be made of the **Tenants' Hall** in Alderley Park – built in 1818, it was renamed in 1989 as the **Sir James Black Conference Centre** after a celebrated Alderley Park Nobel Prize-winning scientist, Sir James Whyte Black, the discoverer of beta-blockers. This area is shown on some Ordnance Survey maps as 'Industrial Hygiene Research Laboratories'. 'Central Toxicology Laboratory' occasionally surfaces on the internet.

The several more recent Methodist chapels, associated perhaps with the miners, carry no dedication at all. **St Philip's** is from 1852, though the intended resonances of this Apostle's name are unclear (see Matthew Hyde's account of the architecture of the village, Chapter 23, p. 595). Other minor landowners have left more traces: the surname Wiche for **Wyche's Farm** is extant in the 1300s (Hayes, 1998), while a

Lingard (as in **Lingard's Farm**) was extracting marl from the Edge in 1598, and a Rafe Lingart was farming in Over Alderley in 1636. Other personal names, doubtless equally ancient, are present, as in **Hayman's Farm** (SJ 854 761). We have lists of the major landowners and tenants from the 1636 map and the 1842 tithe maps – but surprisingly few of these appear to have left their names to local features.

Where is Alderley Edge?

There is a wide location of 'Alderley' names, from Alderley House in the south, to Alderley Edge in the north – a distance of some three miles, and a further two miles to the limits of Over Alderley. In fact, the physical location of 'Alderley' has shifted in the past 150 years. Before the railway arrived in 1842 it is clear that Alderley was the area around the church of St Mary. Even today the correct address for the church is plain 'Alderley'. Alderley Edge was the area at the top of the hill. The present village of Alderley Edge sits in an area formerly known as Chorley; a short walk along London Road in the modern village of Alderley Edge reveals that most shopkeepers still do not know where they are – The Edge, Alderley, Alderley Edge and Alderley Edge Village all feature in shop names. The people who should know are the Post Office and until 2013 their mail was sorted in the Edwardian **Alderley Edge Sorting Office** on the Macclesfield Road, now replaced by a new office, happily still in the village on West Street. Some of this confusion arises from the fact that the ancient village of Alderley centred on the church of St Mary – Over Alderley and Nether Alderley were not villages but locations.

If we take Alderley to be the two parishes of Over Alderley and Nether Alderley, there is a satisfying symmetry, since the furthest point west of Nether Alderley parish is **Alderley Cottage** (SJ 843 778), where a tongue of the Stanley lands protruded into those of the de Traffords (Figure 19.5, p. 470); and the furthest point east of Over Alderley is **Alderley Field** (SJ 884 753), still sporting a boundary stone dated 1789. This is now reputed to have a racehorse buried below it, whose initials were M.P. (perhaps, but more likely Macclesfield Parish).

Rather strangely, the Stanleys do not seem to have owned Alderley Park grounds until quite late. The old deer park is first mentioned glancingly in 1390, when the widow of Adam de Acton left all her lands in Over Alderley 'lying near the Park of the Lords of Alderley' to her son. The area was reputed by Louisa Stanley later to have been part of the local holdings of Dieulacres Monastery at Leek, until the Dissolution of the Monasteries in 1538 – the monastic name lingers in **Monks' Heath**.

After that, the lands in Alderley Park belonged to a number of people – Sheldons and Greenes and a Bentley family. The Park appears to have come into the ownership, but not the occupation, of the Stanleys by 1567. By 1668 Thomas Deane de Park (son of Thomas Bentley, Deane de Park) had built **Park House** on the site of the **Park Tenement** – presumably a field held from the Stanleys. It was he who endowed the school in 1694. By 1695 Park House was finally occupied by a branch of the Stanleys – William Stanley de Park, and by 1739 the Stanleys had actually bought Park House.

As described in Chapter 19, in 1779 the main Stanley family moved into Park House, after the disastrous fire at the Old Hall. In 1818 Park House was demolished to make way for a dwelling named **Alderley Park** (sometimes called Alderley Park House or Mansion). Alderley Park House also burnt down, in 1931, and was finally demolished in 1933. In 1963–64 ICI built a new **Alderley House** on the same site.

As can be seen, the Stanleys led a somewhat itinerant existence in variously named dwellings:

1602–1779	**Alderley Old Hall** (burnt down)
1780–1818	**Park House** (built 1668, demolished 1818)
1808–	**Winnington Hall** (winter residence)
1818–1931	**Alderley Park House** (burnt down 1931)
1903–29	**Penrhos, Anglesey** (residence of the fourth Lord Stanley)
1931–39	**'The Hall'** (opposite Tenants' Hall, demolished 1950)

The Park under ICI/Zeneca/AstraZeneca stewardship

1964–	**Alderley House** (built by ICI, on site of Alderley Park House)
2002–	**Parklands Office Block** (built by Zeneca)
2013	Alderley Park sold to Manchester Science Parks, renamed Manchester Science Partnership in 2014 (Hill, 2016)

The strange disappearance of Chorley

A major factor in fixing local names was the opening of stations through-out Britain in the railway mania of the 1840s. A station named **Alderley**, on the then Manchester–Crewe line, was opened on Wednesday 10 May 1842 (Figure 28.2). It was built, with surrounding houses, and no doubt profitably, on land owned by the de Traffords. The ostensible reason for choosing the Alderley name was that, although the station was actually in the village of Chorley, there might be confusion with Chorley in Lancashire. But perhaps Alderley carried a greater cachet among the wealthy Mancunians whom the railway wanted to attract. The Stanleys

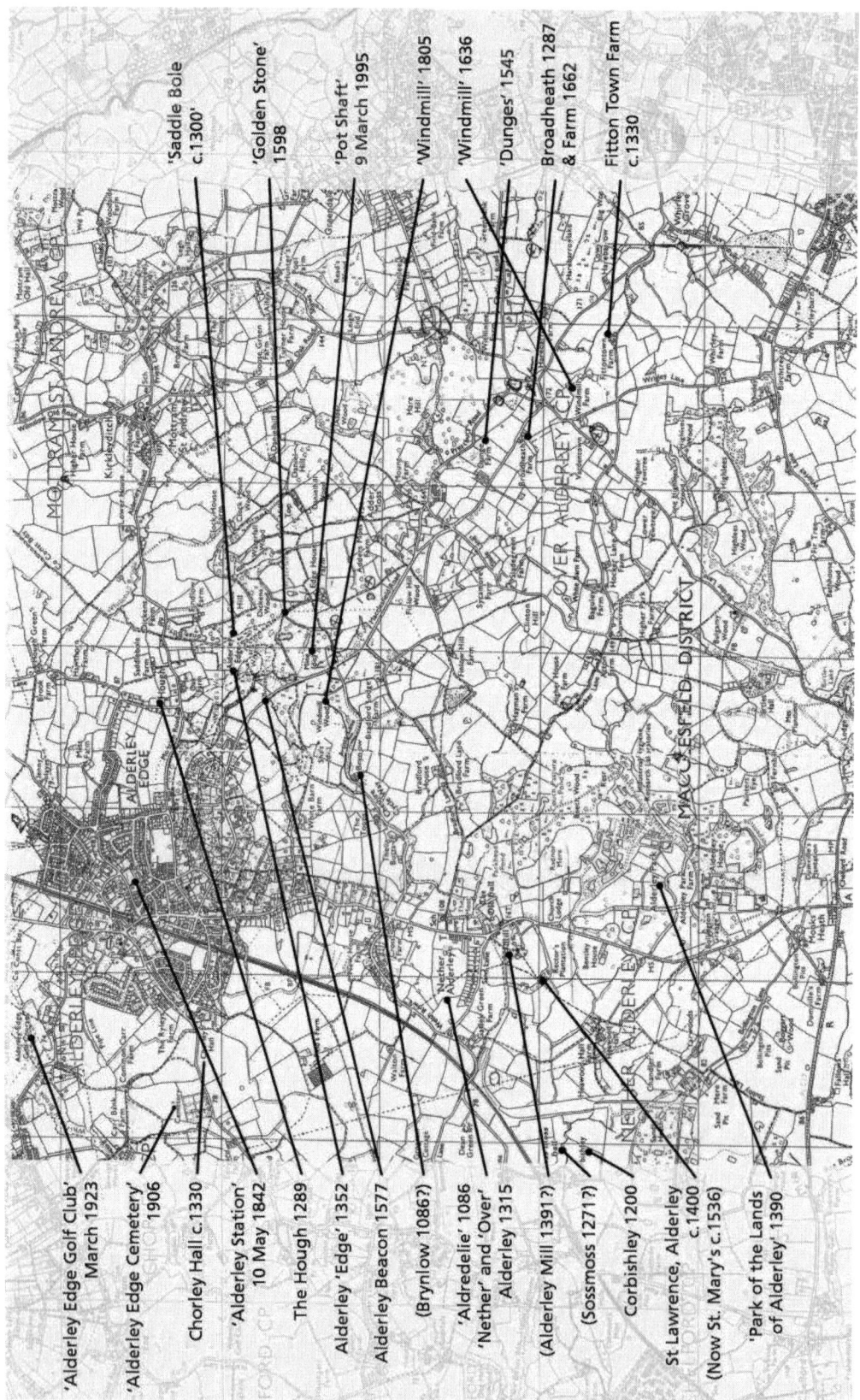

'Saddle Bole
c.1300'

'Golden Stone'
1598

'Pot Shaft'
9 March 1995

'Windmill' 1805

'Windmill' 1636

'Dunges' 1545

Broadheath 1287
& Farm 1662

Fitton Town Farm
c.1330

'Alderley Edge Golf Club'
March 1923

'Alderley Edge Cemetery'
1906

Chorley Hall c.1330

'Alderley Station'
10 May 1842

The Hough 1289

Alderley 'Edge' 1352

Alderley Beacon 1577

(Brynlow 1086?)

'Aldredelie' 1086
'Nether' and 'Over'
Alderley 1315

(Alderley Mill 1391?)

(Sossmoss 1271?)

Corbishley 1200

St Lawrence, Alderley
c.1400
(Now St. Mary's c.1536)

'Park of the Lands
of Alderley 1390

Figure 28.2. Map 2. Alderley: the earliest recorded names and dates.

Based on the 1992 Ordnance Survey 1:25,000 Pathfinder map sheet 759 with the permission of the Controller of Her Majesty's Stationery Office, Crown copyright October 2013.

objected to the name of the railway station and the pushy developers, the 'Railroadians'. The second Lord Stanley, as Postmaster General from 1860 to 1866, is said to have had letters addressed to 'Alderley' returned to the sender as 'address unknown' (Moss, 1903: 1–2; see also Chapter 19, p. 498).

Perhaps under this political pressure, the station name was changed to **Alderley and Chorley** in April 1853 – a name that would probably be meaningless today. It became **Alderley Edge** in March 1876, possibly as a marketing ploy when day trips by train from Manchester were becoming popular with the mill workers, and the Stanleys had opened up the Edge proper to visitors, at some considerable distance from the village (Peacock, 1860). **Alderley Edge High School** also opened in 1876; later renamed St Hilary's, these buildings are now apartments, but the name has been continued in **Alderley Edge School for Girls**, formed in September 1999 from the merger of St Hilary's with Mount Carmel School on the Mount Carmel site on Wilmslow Road.

Census and other data show, however, that local people thought they were living in **Chorley** for the purposes of births, deaths and marriages from the 1200s until at least the 1890s (Ekwall, 1960: 107). Even in 1912 a local newspaper advertisement refers to land on the corner of Macclesfield Road and Congleton Road as being in 'Chorley'. In addition, Chorley can claim the oldest manor house in Cheshire – **Chorley Old Hall** is from the 1330s, though owned by the Stanleys from at least the 1640s.

As late as 1882 the Ordnance Survey map was still referring to 'Alderley & Chorley Station', and showing the village now known as 'Alderley Edge' as 'Chorley', with Chorley Hall prominent nearby. Even in 1892 the Chorley Temperance Brass Band was being engaged for the Alderley wakes. By 1906 the battle might appear to have been finally over with the opening of **Alderley Edge Cemetery**, in Ryleys Lane (SJ 831 781). This cemetery is of course nowhere near the geographical Edge, nor indeed near the village of Alderley Edge, but lies on the poor lands of the Common Carr. This naming might look pretty conclusive, even terminal. However, the **Alderley Edge Golf Club** (SJ 834 792) took much longer to decide where it was. A club official writes:

> [It] was officially instituted in September 1907 and was originally known as Fulshaw Golf Club…. The club changed its name to Alderley Edge GC in March, 1923, but club minutes give absolutely no reason why the name was changed. (Dixon, 2007)

The ecclesiastical parish was even slower to change: it was 'The Parish of St Philip, Chorley' until the name was finally officially changed as late as 1990 to 'The Parish of St Philip, Alderley Edge'. By then the great majority of parishioners were probably unaware of its original correct name.

The **Edge** itself appears as a name by 1352 (and oddly as **le Hegge** too – perhaps an over-enthusiastic French clerk). According to Gelling there are many instances (including the well known example of Wenlock Edge) of the word being used, as here, of an escarpment or slope named from a nearby settlement (Gelling and Cole, 2000: 174). **Alderley becon** (the Beacon at SJ 857 777) appears on Saxton's map of Cheshire dated 1577 – thus predating by at least a decade the Spanish Armada, with which it is traditionally associated (see Appendix 19.2). **Alderley Mill** (SJ 843 762) appears only late in 1831, but is probably the '*molendinum aquaticum*' of a 1391 record (Chapter 25). **Nether Alderley Cross** (SJ 843 769; Figure 19.3, p. 468) does not appear in the written record till 1831, though it will be of equal antiquity to other names (or even greater, given the folklore that a Roman soldier sleeps beneath it). The Cross has had time to be beheaded – usually attributed to the period of James I. Nearby **Cross Farm** was certainly already there by 1735, according to its stone tablet.

Linguistic elements

British, Welsh, English, Viking and Norman sources

Alderley is in general terms a linguistic monoculture – mainly words of good Anglo-Saxon with very little of whatever Celtic language preceded that, and scarcely any evidence of Scandinavian or Norman French influence. We know the landscape of Alderley is ancient, with Bronze Age (*c.* 1900 BC) and Roman artefacts (first to fourth centuries AD). Nearby was found the famous Late Iron Age ('Celtic') bog body lying in the Lindow Moss – which, as noted above, has been variously parsed as Welsh for the 'black pool' or more likely 'lime tree hill' (*lind hōh/how*). It is possible that the Roman mines were worked by local people policed by Roman troops, but it is much more likely the Romans took over and maximised existing exploitation of the source: the problem of dating the 'Roman' workings ('Pot shaft') is fully discussed under 'Roman mining' in Chapter 15 (p. 355).

Yet at Alderley we can find only a few scattered and doubtful words of the ancient British tongue – perhaps in NA 512 **Maddocksfield**, an English genitive with Welsh personal name 'Madog'; **Grogrum** Field and Cottage (NA 402 'grug', Welsh for heather, and even here the 'rum' part is good old English 'room' in the sense of an open space or allocation in the turbary); and **Penter Croft** (NA 157), possibly from the Welsh *pentref*, manor house. The Welsh element in Cheadle has already been mentioned. Brynlow (discussed later) is another uncertain candidate for the Welsh *bryn* or hill – but is more probably 'brown' hill. There are probably more modern Celtic-style house names (listed below) in Alderley than ancient field or place names.

The Welsh were pushed back from Cheshire by the Northumbrians in 613, and again by the Mercians from the 650s onwards. Dodgson notes that the linguistic evidence shows no change in Welsh elements in place names from about 650 onwards, implying that they were retained as linguistic fossils by non-speakers, presumably the 'English'-speaking incomers.

In this early Mercian context, two local '*tūn*' curiosities are: **Hoblington Meadow** (NA 231) and similarly **Worthington Field** (NA 8). The latter is possibly Old English 'enclosure' (*worðing*). Both are intriguingly close to the centre of Nether Alderley, and generate a number of local family names. The *tūn* ending often marks the setting for a habitation that was on ground long cleared of forest, and in some parts of England stands in direct contrast to the *lēahs* which were still being hacked out of the woodland. Perhaps this is the contrast intended here, in farms taken on by incoming Mercians, rather than the wilder lands at Alderley, Mobberley, Chorley and Chorlton, the latter perhaps settled by tough 'churls'.

In the ninth century there followed the Viking and Irish Viking invasions of the area, but at Alderley the Scandinavian linguistic element is almost as sparse as the Celtic – two personal names which have not survived as place names, and a few Scandinavian terms for geographical features, which may have been common usage by English-speakers at the time they were adopted (such as *hulme*, *carr* and *moss* – see below). So we are faced with a study area that is a linguistic monoculture: very little but good English elements in the names of fields and places.

The settlement of Cheshire by English-speakers of some sort continued in the upheavals both before and after the Norman conquest. It may even have been resettled after the Conqueror laid waste the area in the winter of 1067/68 – we know that many parts of Cheshire were still wastelands twenty years later, at the time of Domesday in 1086 – 'wasta fuit et est' in the phrase of the scribe ('Was wasteland [not cultivated], and so it remains', sometimes translated as 'Was laid waste, and so it remains'). This reflects the Cheshire side-campaign of the Conqueror's 'Harrowing of the North' and the Cheshire uprising of Edric the Wild. So perhaps there were no longer any inhabitants, British, Welsh or Nordic, for the later English to dislodge at Alderley.

Intriguingly there was a **Brun** (Brown) holding Alderley before Domesday – 'et liber homo fuit' – a free man. **Brynlow** (SJ 852 771) is sometimes recorded as Brindlow, Brimelow (and as such also a local surname), or even Brownlow on older maps, and has a legend of buried treasure and of being haunted by the ghost of Nell Beck. It is usually parsed as Old English for 'Brown Hill'. Perhaps Brun gave his name to or took it from the hill. Or perhaps there was already a brown spoil heap from mining there. The 'brown hill' name would be curiously mirrored nearby by a **Whitlow** – a 'white hill' at SJ 836 740, said to be so named from the colour of the tumulus on it (on Brun and Brynlow and also on the 'waste' land, see also Chapter 19, p. 467).

Brun also held nearby Chelford, Bramhall and part of Stockport prior to Domesday, so that we may be looking at an original large pre-Norman landholding, of which Alderley was only part.

The place name 'Brown Low' is, however, too common generally in Britain for us to ascribe it to one family with any certainty. It also looks suspiciously like Welsh *bryn* (a hill) added to Anglo-Saxon *low*, usually meaning also an artificial hill or burial mound. Gelling has drawn attention to the fact that, south of the Mersey–Humber line, some *low* were in fact also 'non-sepulchral' meeting places. The presence of two such meeting places (at Mobberley and Mottram) on either side of Brynlow is therefore interesting. Furthermore, there are other 'lows' in the area – Bucklow and Wilmslow (the latter 'low' now buried under the railway line) – both attached to personal names. A **Pykedlowe** (SJ 860 779; also known as Pike's Low, Pikelow/Pike Low and Peaked Lowe) is recorded as early as AD 1230–50 near Saddlebole, and seems to have served as a meeting point of three parishes – see further Chapter 14, p. 320, and Alan Garner's discussion in the context of the Legend in Chapter 30 (see also *ArchAE*: 154, 158). Another local mound is near Monk's Heath – variously called **Sodger's Hump** or **Tump** (SJ 8427 3900), *sodger* being a version of soldier. A buried weapon is reputed to have been found below it.

Dating of place names

With regard to the dating of the Alderley place names, one can only guess that the mainly English names we find are probably not of the first wave of Germanic settlement, nor of great antiquity, though some may be celebrating their first millennium, and thus Old English. The majority of names may be later, when the peasants pushed out in the population expansion of the 1200s, and prior to the population collapse at the time of the Black Death in 1349 – and thus Middle English. From this period we find reference at Alderley not to *lēahs* but to intakes of the wastelands – *assartis in vastis*. The word *intake* and the rarer *intack* occur twenty-five times at Alderley, for about forty-five acres of ground. This probably reflects both expansion into the woodlands and also encroachment onto the mosses.

There appear to be very few post-conquest Norman French additions, though an innocuous and undateable word like 'pasture' has eighteen occurrences as field name, with several 'parks' and 'granges' and the possibly French-derived field name **Mountain of Poverty** (NA 599, at SJ 855 779). But, as in the case of Celtic elements, there are now more modern French-style house names in Alderley than there were ever French-derived field names.

Local dialect

It is probably safe to assume that the dialect spoken in Alderley at the time of the mainly English naming conformed in general terms to the Mercian form of English, with its own special north-west features. Northumbrian elements such as *lang* for 'long' are absent. It should, however, be stressed that by the time most field names were collected in the 1840s, dialect appears to be a small element in the overall naming – possibly because the tithe commissioners filtered it out, or possibly because the Stanleys and their land agents did not use local dialect. We cannot, for example, with certainty track in the place names the strong Scandinavian influence on vocabulary noted in fourteenth-century north-west poetry such as 'Sir Gawain and the Green Knight'.

It is also interesting that the local word *siche*, meaning a ditch or stream, also perhaps a drain from a mine, seems to have vanished between its recorded use in 1598 and the 1842 tithe registers, where it simply does not occur.

Sometimes what looks like dialect is mis-hearing: the land agents all fell for **Hure Wood** ('the higher wood'). Similarly, NA 87, **Daving Ditch**, must have been a mis-hearing of 'delving ditch' – also a field name, at NA 287 (and possibly a mining reference), while the 1842 **God's Knowl** (OA 409) was, we know from prior records, merely 'gorse knowl' in 1654. The inexplicable 1842 **Welley Hey** (OA 572) was in fact the more intelligible (and perhaps glottalised) Whitley Hey in 1636.

Mouse Ridding (OA 115) must be moss riddings (tree clearance – it comes in at five Cheshire acres). Similarly, the compilers of the tithe registers sometimes mis-spelt entries: **Higher Oldam** (*sic*) and **Lower Oldham** at NA 589 and 590, **Hollow** and **Holland** referring to the adjacent fields NA 178 and 179, occur within a line of each other in the registers. There is also a very weak, very olde, and very common plough-man's joke in the 1636 Over Alderley field name the **fowre day worke**, which is only just over one acre, and could be polished off, not in four days, but before daybreak ('afore day'). These miscomprehensions and leg-pulls are a salutary reminder of how corruptions creep in.

A good example of former local usage and accompanying recent folklore is the small farmstead called **Trugs-i'-th'-'ole**, which lies at the border between Macclesfield parish and the county constituency (SJ 884 753). This is an area of soft sand, where the Spencer Brook has cut deeply into the landscape. *Trug* is Old English for a valley or possibly here for a 'trough', with which it is cognate (Dodgson, 1970: 102). But local folklore has it that Trug was the name of the drayhorse which pulled the wagons up the steep slope – indeed, it must be so: he appears on the farm weather vane. Perhaps both are true.... The stone that is said to mark his grave has been discussed in the previous chapter (p. 676).

Clock House Farm (SJ 867 779) appears by 1787. Lord Stanley states simply that it was a 'Tenement below the Edge, so called from a Clock with a dial outside the house' (*Stanley Notebook*).

On Broadheath, when it was a common, there were a number of gates – presumably to keep the cattle on the heath. These were then called *yates*, though by the 1840s this pronunciation was being recorded as 'gate'.

Some names are utterly pedestrian: one tiny plot was called **Piece by Railroad** (NA 274), incorporating what is now an Americanism (though reminiscent of the Stanleys' dislike of the 'Railroadians') and cannot be earlier than 1840. There are also too many instances of Far Field, Middle Field, and Near Field for us to feel comfortable that this was anything but a convenience name from a hurried farmer to a pressed land surveyor. **Shippon**, the local word for a cattle shed, and still in use now by farmers (the author heard this in use in 2000 at **Mount Farm**, SJ 869 769), occurs only four times in the field names. Some Alderley items are of particular historical interest: for example, **Irons Farm, Welsh Row** (SJ 841 770), now gone, but still present in **Irons Cottage**, is, according to Dodgson, probably Old English *hyrne*, a corner (the road bends sharply here). We know that this word *hyrne* was already being misunderstood at Chester as the metal 'iron' by about 1350, when the Iron Bridge – i.e. at the bend of the River Dee – was rendered as 'pons ferreus' by a witty but locally uninformed scribe. The meaning of 'bend' was probably already obsolete by then. Local usage at Alderley presumably therefore predates 1350, though meanings can have a tenacious way of surviving in local usage.

The area carries a number of words that occur more in the north of England than elsewhere – *carr* (Old Norse import into English – hereafter ON – marsh with brushwood), *moss* (ON, bog), *flatts* (ON, level ground), *slack* (ON, a shallow valley), the delightful term *bongs* (NA 304a: Middle English – hereafter ME – banks), *clough* (ME, a ravine) and hough (Old English, the heel-shaped spur of a hill, which fits the topography here; hough is an early name – first reference at Alderley is from 1289); *intack* (ON, land enclosed, a very localised and rare form of 'intake' recorded as early as 1598), *hulme* (small river island – Old

Danish). There are also *pingots*, a *picker* and a *patch*, which mean in Middle English 'small enclosures'. At SJ 864 773 there are some stone steps at the edge of Finlow Hill Wood, usually parsed as the **Pea Steps** (Alan Garner, personal communication, March 1998). Investigation reveals that they face a field known as the **Piece** (see also Chapter 27). **Mickle** survives happily (with a similar meaning to 'great' and 'big'), for example in 'mickle hey'. There is only one northern *garth* (garden) in the field names. The ubiquitous alder trees appear variously as *oller* or *owler* locally – we know that the first Stanley to live at Alderley in the early 1600s hired a plumber from the Cloud (Bosley Cloud) to bring water to his offices (kitchens) in 'oller pipes' – alders are well known for their water-resistant properties.

Agriculture and milling

Over Alderley and Nether Alderley show a typical concentration of land-holding by 1842. Of the 1,523 or so acres then in Nether Alderley, some 1,350 were owned by the Stanleys (including a 100-acre park with lake). In Over Alderley, out of a total of 2,145 acres in the parish, the Stanleys had 992. By 1938, the total Stanley holdings had risen by some 1,000 acres to 4,500 acres in the whole area (i.e. including other parishes). The absence of any Stanley place name (apart from the modern **Stanley Arms** in the grounds of Alderley Park, and the Stanley Mausoleum and pew already mentioned) is therefore all the more striking.

Of the farm names around Alderley, **Fallows Hall** (from AD 1199; at SJ 833 741) appears to be the oldest in the written record, in 1199. Peculiarly, 'Fallows' here has the original meaning of 'ploughed fields', rather than the modern meaning of uncultivated land. The Halls at **Heawood** (AD 1286, a fenced wood), **Harebarrow** (AD 1220, possibly 'hoary' or ancient wood, and pre-Norman if the impressive and gloomy Big Wood at Harebarrow with its deep banks is the one mentioned in the Domesday Book) and **Birtles** (birch trees; at SJ 857 746) appear by the late 1200s. Birch trees may on occasion be an indicator of land that has already been cleared reverting to woodland. On recorded dating evidence, there was another minor expansion in farms in the 1300s – **Whirley Hall** (bog-myrtle clearing) in 1348, **Acton Farm** (oak farm) in 1352 and **Sossmoss Hall** (SJ 829 759; hall in the soaking swamp) in 1389. Even a modern-looking name like **Fernhill** appears in 1287. We also know for certain that **Broadheath Farm** (SJ 873 761) cannot be earlier than the 1662 enclosure of the common lands on the heath, which allowed its establishment.

Embedded in the field names are also relics of landholdings and tenancies: field names are attached to *church*, *parson*, *bailiff* and *school*, presumably as a way of generating income to support these offices. There is also at NA 32 a **copy field** (from the nature of the lease – presumably a written copy), as well as the unusual and perhaps early **oxter** (NA 528 and 543), interpreted by Dodgson as meaning land leased by swearing some form of loyalty with the hands of the lessee in the armpit ('oxter') of the lessor.

Elsewhere the area, on clay soil, was probably mainly subsistence corn, with cattle and dairying. Rye, however, also features in the field names (four items) and is now perpetuated in the **Ryleys** (1304) and the **Ryleys Farm**, though rye is probably no longer grown now. The unpromising **Field Back o'th' House, Field at door** and variants (eight field names) may conceal the agricultural practice of having a paddock into which cattle kept indoors in the winter were turned out at appropriate times of lease renewal. **Dunge Farm** (SJ 870 763) seems to be just that: there is a reference in 1545 and again on the 1636 Over Alderley estate map to 'the two dunges', i.e. dunghills, shown beside the road at this point.

Statistically, the most common field name element by 1842 is 'field' itself – 340 items. It is unlikely to be being used in the older sense of open country here (there are very few 'feld'-type names in Cheshire), though there may have been some fields which were not enclosed till late. The names in 'field' show some of the classic opposition of *white* (= infertile, seven items) and *black* (= fertile, nine items). The use of 'field' may, however, be more modern than we realise: since in the 1820s the same names and acreages were listed not as 'fields', but by the more ancient term, both in writing and usage, of 'names of clo∫ses'. Occasionally the archaic 'room' appears, as in **Moss Room** (e.g. NA 376) – here reflecting the allotment of the right to cut turf in the peat bog. In Alderley the term 'earth' in field names is most commonly tied to either 'black' or 'burnt', in both 1636 and 1842.

Next most common is 'meadow', at 160, reflecting the pasture aspect of the area. Then comes 'croft' (small enclosed field), with 133 occurrences. (In this context, it is interesting to note that in March 2007 a survey by the on-line survey company YouGov of Norwich Union's most common British house names revealed that 'The Croft' came twentieth in England, with the highest prevalence in Cheshire.) 'Plantation' seems to be more modern – it occurs by 1842 in the tithe registers, and has 73 mentions. But we know that plantations were being made earlier by the Stanleys on the Edge – see below. Then comes 'hey' (hedge), with 60 specimens. 'Moss' comes in at 53 – the boggy nature of the area being well reflected. The next most common items are 'well' at 35 names, and the same number for 'barn' and also 'riddings' – that is, trees being got rid of, as also in 'stubbing' (**Stubby Lane**), 'stitching' and 'stock'. 'Pit' comes with 25 examples – generally for marl, with the first record

Table 28.2. Statistical frequency of field names by number: 1636 for Over Alderley; 1842 for Over and Nether Alderley and Mottram St Andrew

Item	1636	% (129 fields)	1842	% (1,370 fields)
Field	26	20	340	25
White	(8)	6	(7)	<1
Black	(7)	5	(9)	<1
Burnt	(2)	2	(12)	<1
Meadow	6	5	160	12
Croft	35	27	133	10
Plantation	n.a.	–	73	5
Hey	4	3	60	4
Moss	2	2	53	4
Well	3	2	35	3
Barn	4	3	35	3
Riddings etc	3	2	35	3
Pit	n.a.	–	25	2
Intake/Intacke	2	2	25	2
Marl/Marled	5	4	20	1
Pasture	1	1	19	1
Heath	5	4	13	<1
Moor	5	4	6	<1
Earth	4	3	6	<1

Note: Since items occur in combination, totals are more than 100%.
Compiled by the author from the Leycester estate book and map (1636) and the tithe assessment for Over Alderley (1842), held by Cheshire Archives and Local Studies, Chester.

being **Marlpit** in 1598, a **Marled Field** in Over Alderley by 1636 and at Nether Alderley for **marl carts** in 1642 (Table 28.2).

There are 25 'intakes' (new land taken in – we have a 1598 dialect 'intack' on the Edge itself). This process must even then have been very old – documents of the 1200s already mention 'assartis in vastis' (assarts of the waste). On linguistic evidence the total acreage involved (intakes, stubbings, etc.) is not great – about eighty acres taken in, out of a total of 3,500 acres or so in the whole estate by 1938. But the amount will have been more important in the past, when the estate was smaller; and it represents the need to feed more mouths, with the average local population perhaps only ever a few hundred souls.

There are also four 'inclosures' – reflecting the removal of woods and the enclosure or encroachment on the waste and mosses. This is interesting given that most of Cheshire had already been enclosed by 1815, with most 'common' land at Alderley enclosed by 1775. The much older term for common land – 'mean' (cf. German *gemein*) – appears three times (NA 431, 509 and 546, with hey, ley and croft). Many of the common fields come in tellingly at near one Cheshire acre. The **Common Piece** (OA 449) comes in at almost exactly eight Cheshire acres. Even further back, an unpromisingly simple name such as **Dean Green** dates probably from 1286, and contains a geographical feature in 'dean', a valley, here between the Bollin and the Dean rivers, as well as a land use indicator, 'green': a common pasturage. 'Dale', possibly meaning here a portion (as in a 'dole') of common land, occurs once as a field name, significantly at one Cheshire acre (NA 199 as **Dale Field Meadow**). It is clear that at Over Alderley and Nether Alderley we now have enough linguistic evidence in the form of intakes, riddings, common land and heys to begin an assessment of the common fields and their location.

Other terms indicative of early land usage include 'butts' – a strip of land at the end of a field where the ox team turned during ploughing. This occurs in **burnt butts** (twice as field names, NA 289 and 303) as well **Butts Farm**. It also occurs possibly in **The Butts** at Alderley Cross, though this may have been the site of the archery butts at the bottom of the hill. There seems to be an opposition in the name **The Topps** at the higher end of Artists Lane. But Lord Stanley asserts that a family of that name had once lived there (*Stanley Notebook*). In the 1636 list, the term **Butty Croft** occurs as 'The Butty Croft between Lingart and Whitacres'. The meaning is not clear – a place where the plough turned, or merely a small field between the land of two other tenants.

On the question of ownership, it is interesting to note only one piece of contested land: **Barrat Meadow** (the Middle English *baret* means dispute) in Bollin Fee. This is surprising given that the Stanleys and Leycesters were often at loggerheads about the rights of the Manor of Over Alderley. There was also a **Barrat Farm** in Welsh Row – presumably where the bordering Trafford and Stanley estates were in dispute. **Four Day Math** (four day's mowing) occurs at Chorley Hall for a six-acre field: sometimes, however, this name is a jocular name for a small field – 'afore day(light) mowing'.

'Broom' and 'gorse' feature strongly at some fifteen entries each, though the older dialect form of 'gorse' as 'gorsty', found in the Stanley estate books, had been edited out by 1842 under the tithe commissioners. It should be remembered that until the commencement of plantations (particularly from the 1740s onwards), most of the Edge proper was covered in gorse. 'Rush' and 'thistle' and the name **Mountain of Poverty** (already mentioned and not uncommon elsewhere in England) reflect on the intractable nature of some of the fields on the Edge. 'Cow' and 'horse' both come in at ten, 'dog' at nine, including the enigmatic **dogholes** (NA 350) – even more enigmatically rented to a family of Stelfoxes. 'Ox' comes in at six, 'swine' at five but 'sheep' at only one. There is still an eighteenth-century brick dovecote, the **Columbarium**, in the Park. One oddity is the disappeared name **Elfgrenhoks** (or **Wlfgreneockes**) of a 1347 estate boundary: it contains a reference, according to Dodgson, to 'oaks at the wolf green': if correct, it is a rare mention of these creatures locally, but see also the discussion of this name by Alan Garner in Chapter 30, p. 773.

Oddly, there is only one Cheshire 'mere' (lake) recorded in 1842 – **Radnor Mere**, at SJ 847 759. It is sometimes referred to as Alderley Mere: Astra Zeneca, when it took over the Park, opened a **Mereview Restaurant** next to it, and the modern buildings are known as **Mereside**. There are no 'tofts' in Alderley (personal allotments around a village, usually Danish in origin) and, strangely for Cheshire, no references to cheese– though one solitary lease for a Stanley farm in 1827 included 'a cheese to be made in the later end of May'.

Tanyard Farm (OA 10) contains an interesting reflection on the oak wood and pastoral economy of the region, with bark used to cure the hides produced locally; glovers and tanners were one of the predominant trades of Medieval Chester. **Hemp Yard** appears in the Stanley estate book of 1820, but had gone by the 1842 tithe maps.

'Wheat' occurs only twice. There are 'bilberry', 'crabtree' and 'cherry' fields. There are only two bean fields, while **Turnip piece** appears only once (NA 584) – perhaps an indicator of an addition to agricultural practice in the 1700s as the Broad Heath was taken in hand. Finally, the prize for sheer charm must go to **Blue Button Field** (NA 171 – the blue button plant being *Scabiosa succisa*, also known as devil's bit).

Curiously, despite being planted in hedges and boundaries for centuries, 'hawthorn' is completely lacking from the 1842 inventory of field names (although occurring in the farm of that name in Hough Lane). Again, 'yew trees', despite being planted for many centuries (that at St Mary's, shown in Figure 10.20, p. 178, being perhaps 1,200 years old), are recorded only late in Cheshire place names, and in Over Alderley are represented by **Higher** and **Lower Yew Tree** (SJ 869 753). A millennial yew marks the end of Stanley lands in the grounds of Alderley Cottage, on the edge of a small cliff, unrecorded by any formal name, but also marking a mine adit and a possible toll road at **Lydiat Lane** (SJ 869 753) ('swing gate' lane).

The traditional pre-1824 statutory measure of land in Cheshire was the Cheshire acre: thus the field name **Four Acres** (OA 59) is four Cheshire acres and comes in at over nine statute acres. (The word 'acre' may also have the technical Old English meaning of 'arable land'). 'Intakes' were often one Cheshire acre in size, while rather satisfactorily the **Church Field** or **Glebe** (NA 6) at St Mary's Church also comes in at exactly one Cheshire acre.

There must also have been many names current only locally which disappeared before they took common parlance or could be recorded.

Stanley's description from 1835 of **Woodcock-glade** has been reproduced in Chapter 11 (p. 201), but alas this place is probably no longer identifiable. The area of trees near the Church is shown in 1842 as **Rector's Plantation** (SJ 840 759), probably to be associated with Edward Stanley. There is also a **Rector's Land** at OA 152, though this is probably more generic, in the sense of belonging to the incumbent.

Alderley had three mills at one point, but the Windmill in Over Alderley has long vanished – it was certainly there in 1594 when Thomas Stanley owned it as Lord of the Manor (**Windmill Farm** still exists at SJ 875 757); and an engine for crushing ore once stood in **Windmill Wood** (SJ 855 774) – built after 1805, it was certainly still active in 1810 when it was seen by Marriott (1810). The Water Mill has already been covered (see above, and Chapter 25) – this is now firmly listed by the National Trust as being in Nether Alderley, though the more correct location, as with St Mary's Church, must be plain 'Alderley'.

Finally, the **Common Carr** is to the west of Alderley Edge village (SJ 833 785), and contains an old Norse word (or its Anglicised version) for an area of scrub in marshy land. It has generated a number of names which must be later both linguistically and in terms of agricultural expansion onto the marsh – **Common Carr Farm** and **Carr Bank Farm**. On this poor land also lay **The Ryleys** – presumably here rye leas or fields. And also the Alderley Edge Cemetery.

The eighteenth-century trend to landscaping has also had an effect on Alderley, and an innocuous name such as **Beech Wood** in Alderley Park grounds (SJ 850 757) reveals a succession of beech tree plantings by the Stanleys, both in their park and on the Edge itself (which was previously denuded of tree cover, over a period of several centuries). This same process may also have given us the **Druids' Circle** (SJ 859 778), whose name, if not the stones, betrays a late date. Similarly, **Stormy Point** has too much of the romantic about it, and is difficult to date before the 1840s.

The Wizard's route to the Iron Gates

The legendary route taken by the farmer and his horse from Mobberley to Macclesfield when accosted by the Wizard of the Edge has been much debated (Figure 28.3): it is discussed fully by Alan Garner in Chapter 30, and here we only consider the names of the places involved. The classic tortuous route, given for example by Louisa Stanley in 1843, is as follows: **Thieves' Hollow** at SJ 860 773, **Seven Firs** by the adit entrance to Engine Vein at SJ 860 774; the **Golden Stone** on the track towards Edge House Farm at SJ 878 776; **Stormy Point** at SJ 860 778; **Saddlebole** at SJ 860 780; and the **Iron Gates**, whose location was

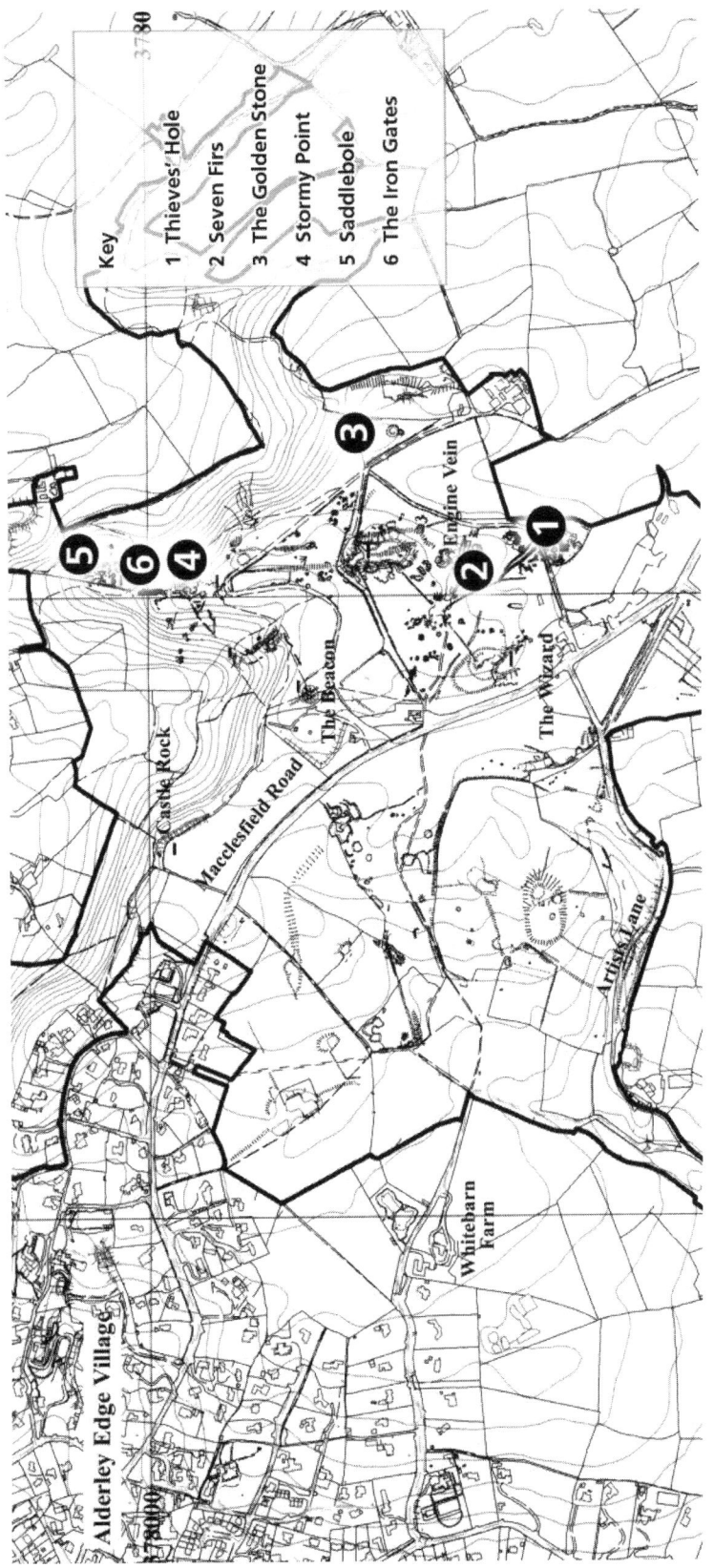

Figure 28.3. The Wizard's route to the Iron Gates.

Based on the 1992 Ordnance Survey 1:25,000 Pathfinder map sheet 759 with the permission of the Controller of Her Majesty's Stationery Office, Crown copyright October 2013.

known only to a few, including the doomed and betrayed Nell Beck. This route is so unlikely that some have suggested it refers to an underground mining route, though this too is difficult to square. Certainly some of the names are old – Saddlebole probably by the 1300s, and the Golden Stone by 1598 (its name is discussed in Chapter 27); Seven Firs, however, looks later, as does Stormy Point.

Around the same time that the Wizard legend was collected, the tragic story of Nell Beck also became current. She claimed to know the location of the Iron Gates and, in one version of her tale, died by drowning – the pool is in **Nell Beck's Wood** (SJ 856 776), though this name is now in abeyance: it last appeared on a map of Alderley from July 1965 drawn by the local Boy Scouts in July 1965 (now in the Project Archive, AELP 561). Similarly forgotten is the location of her grave in a field on **Armstrong Farm** (SJ 853 779) – as a *felo de se* she was denied burial in consecrated ground. She has not been seen to walk at Brynlow for several centuries.

Mining

Mining at Alderley was for a variety of metals over time – mainly copper, but also lead and cobalt in the eighteenth and nineteenth centuries. The mining process at Alderley went on sporadically for perhaps over 3,800 years (1900 BC or earlier to AD June 1919) but has left surprisingly few linguistic traces – certainly we do not know the Brythonic or the Roman names for the mines. It may be that because mining was intermittent no names were transmitted over time. There is no continuity of mine naming at Alderley from the Medieval period. We know of recorded mining only from 1693, but by name merely as 'Nether Alderley'. Another example is the **Hough Level** (SJ 8622 7781), with activity dating from the 1760s, but not appearing in the written record as a name until 1919 – at the very end of mining activity at Alderley.

In fact, most named shafts on the Edge are relatively late: **Wood Mine** (SJ 8544 7760), last worked in 1857–77, **West Mine** (SJ 8519 7760) also last worked 1857–77, **Brynlow Mine** (SJ 8555 7723) certainly worked by 1764. **Pillar** and **Doc Mines** (SJ 8610 7783) are possibly Bronze Age, but their names are new or obscure.

Engine Vein (SJ 8605 7747) is probably named from its being equipped with a horse engine or steam engine at some time. It is unknown when or where the engine was installed, and whether it was for pumping water or handling ore. A splendid name such as **Abbadine**, a mine owner as recently as 1708 (discussed in Chapter 16, p. 374), has also vanished without trace, though he had a smelter near to **Edge House**. His shafts can be identified, but no contemporary name survives. The name **Pot**

Shaft, however, the putative Roman trial next to Engine Vein, can be categorically dated to Thursday 9 March 1995, when a pot of Roman coins from around AD 340 was found by the Derbyshire Caving Club (Chapter 14, p. 331, and Figure 14.9, p. 332; also Chapter 15, p. 355). The shaft itself has been dated as probably from about AD 50, immediately after the Roman invasion, and thus marking a linguistic collision of the same magnitude as that accompanying the Norman conquest, but again with very few perceptible modern traces.

As described in Chapters 15 and 16, the whole Alderley area and beyond is pockmarked with adits, many now lost, some coming to light in unexpected and at times unwelcome places (below Artists Lane at Brynlow and under the National Trust information centre). There are at least two fields containing the element 'delving' (= diggings) and one **Bow graves** (NA 496 – also diggings). It would also be interesting to know if **Whirley Grove** (from 1348, at SJ 886 751) in fact conceals a mine digging – the word 'grove' is used locally in this context, and **Devil's Grave** at Stormy Point is also identified as **Devil's Grove** on old postcards from the 1920s. There is also a **South Grove** in Alderley village itself, which name sits oddly with the other street names – it would be interesting to know if this is a mining reference connected to the putative mine adit in nearby Lydiat Lane.

Similarly, it would be useful to know if **Painter's Eye** (SJ 851 746) and **Vardon Field** (OA 4) refer to the mine managers of those surnames active in the Alderley area in the 1750s under Charles Roe of Macclesfield. However, Verdon also occurs as a local name – a Susan Verdon was tenant in Over Alderley in 1842 (Bentley Smith, 2005) and there was a Payisters Eye at Fernhill in 1594, so perhaps the mining coincidence is fortuitous.

Copper mining at Alderley sits between two other ancient mining traditions – those of Derbyshire for lead and Cheshire for salt, both with their own terms and traditions. These terms do not seem to have carried over to Alderley in linguistic terms. In the 1750s Welsh copper miners, and from the 1860s Cornish tin miners, were brought in to Alderley, but again, apart from one Cornish surname (**Chynoweth** – see below) there appears to be no perceptible linguistic heritage. The laws applied to copper mining at Alderley in the eighteenth century were those of the Cornish tin Stannary, rather than the Barmote of Derbyshire lead mines – and Lord Stanley was technically 'The Lord of the Soil'. These legal provisions appear to have left no trace in local place names, unlike the diverse fossils of 'oxter', 'copy' and 'mean' from Medieval field-tenure systems.

Finlow Hill Farm (SJ 859 765) is 'heaped mound' (of mine spoil?) and appears by 1598 but already existed in the form of a local surname from 1342. There are also at OA 455 and 463 (SJ 863 785) fields called

Great and **Little Ox Mullock**, where mullock is a rubbish heap – again possibly from mine spoil. **Saddlebole** (SJ 860 780) as **Saddle boule** is extant by 1598, the bole being a 'wind-driven smelter'. **Sadel** occurs as early as the 1300s and probably refers to the shape of the land here, though there is also a track ascending the Edge at this point which has been called a saddle-road. Peculiarly, extensive searching has failed to find a *bole* at this spot, and the very name was nearly extinct by 1905, the area being known as Whinberry Hill (*Wilmslow Advertiser*, 1905). Next to West Mine is an area known as **The Hagg** (at SJ 865 775; Old Norse for 'a place set aside for the felling of trees' – presumably to fuel the furnaces or boles). **Windmill Wood** (SJ 855 773) refers to a device for crushing ore (see Chapter 16, p. 382). The straightforward **Cinder Hill** also occurs, but the significance of **Glaze Hill** (SJ 862 779) raises speculation. It has been suggested the name refers to a sheen of galena, but it could also be interpreted as referring to potter's glaze or else to glass-making. The Old English words glæs, 'glass', and *glæs, 'clear, bright, shining', cannot be distinguished formally, but the latter may enter into names such as Glascote (Tamworth) ('shed where glass is made') and Glass Houghton in west Yorkshire (Smith, 1961: 203). The earliest written reference to the name Glaze Hill appears to be in 1831, which is much too late to help with the etymology. In Chapter 15 (p. 362) Simon Timberlake suggests that it may allude to a particular form of soft but non-silver-bearing lead ore often described as 'potter's ore', which is referred to at other English lead-mining sites: this was used to give Medieval and early post-Medieval pottery its familiar green glaze. On the other hand, while there is no local oral tradition of a glass-making industry, in the early 1950s two pieces of white cullet were found by chance on separate occasions on the eastern side of the Saddlebole ridge, near the mine but in the beech wood; they were not pieces of broken glass that had melted in a grass or turf fire and must have been subjected to a sustained temperature of over 1,000°C. They have not been tested scientifically, but their presence could strengthen the case for glass manufacture nearby (Alan Garner, personal communication). One field, **lower oldham** (NA 590), carries the interesting annotation in the estate rent books for 1824 – 'about one Cheshire acre spoil'd by the miners' (CALS DSA 3752/2–4).

Nearby **Mottram Mine** has the distinction of having added a mineral name to the English language – mottramite: its discovery is described by David Green in Chapter 6 (pp. 98–9).

It is also possible that the **siche** or small stream of the 1598 perambulation of the Edge (quoted in Chapter 19, p. 477) is a mine drainage ditch, comparable to a mining 'sough' in Derbyshire. Brynlow Sough occurs in 1764, driven as a drain into **Brynlow Dell**, but both names subsequently fell out of use and the location of the Sough was lost.

It has been rediscovered and the name revived in recent years by the Derbyshire Caving Club. There is also a cognate **Sough Meadow** (1842) listed at OA 54.

There are thirteen 'smith' fields in the sample, though some may be 'smooth fields'; these are allied to seven 'oven houses' (= furnaces) and four 'kiln fields' (also furnaces, perhaps for brick-making). We probably have here a concentration of metal-working locations (or also brick-making), which will merit further examination.

Quarries

Alderley also yields stone for building and the word 'quarry' appears seven times as a field, once as a house name. We also have a **Church Quarry** at SJ 858 773 – it certainly appears vast enough to encompass St Mary's and probably also provided the stone for other local churches in the 1400s. The largest quarry on the Edge, the **Great Quarry** of the 1598 perambulation and now known as **Old Alderley Quarry**, lies between Quarry Road and Engine Vein (SJ 858 774) (Chapter 18, pp. 441–2). Another major quarry, still visible, is **Mottram Quarry** on the Mottram Road – this was exploited from 1870 to 1965, but is almost invisible in the records. It is also interesting to note that the innocuous **Sandle Heath** is a 'sand hill heath' and dates from 1208 – again this may be an indicator of early industrial activity in the area.

One satisfying discovery by the Alderley Edge Landscape Project was the Boy Scouts' map of Alderley from July 1965, which shows at SJ 866 773 both a **Chynoweth Field** and **Chynoweth Wood**. These are believed to have been named after a Cornish miner who came to Alderley in the nineteenth century and stayed. The name means 'new house' in Cornish.

It should also be remembered that there was a considerable brick-making industry in and near to Alderley Park grounds, with the 1842 tithe map still showing **clays one acre bricks** at NA 237 and 238 and a **Sandle Inclosure** (sand hill) at NA248. Furthermore, the loam of Alderley Park grounds covers a layer of marl – much extracted for fertiliser from the 1600s onwards (see Chapter 18). 'Marl' is reflected at Alderley in twenty field names.

Archaeological references

The disappointing lack of any Celtic elements in place names has been noted earlier. There are one or two enigmatic references to possible Roman remains: **Street Lane Ends** (now under London Road, the old A34) may be one, if 'street' is here associated with an undetected Roman road (see further Chapter 14, p. 330, but also, more particularly, Chapter 26, p. 468). It would be pleasant if **Walton Farm** (SJ 835 769) was a *tūn* of the *wealas* – often used by the Anglo-Saxons for sub-Roman settlements. It may, however, be that the farm was named for the Waltons who farmed there. There is also a **Folley field** at (OA 517, at SJ 871 774) – a word whose meaning is ill understood but statistically associated with Roman roads. It is, however, on an isolated dead end into **Daniel's Hill** (also a tenant in 1648) and is probably unconnected with any early road.

There is a reference in the Domesday Book to 'duas haias' at Alderley. Two hedged enclosures – were they clearings, defensive structures or deer parks? Was there one at Over and one at Nether Alderley? The grounds of Alderley were emparked by 1390, and hold the site of one deer park (with the now-vanished **Deer House**, built in 1750). It may also be relevant that of the 1,500 fields, sixty bore the hedge name in the form of 'hey', clustering along the railway line near Welsh Row and, significantly, near Heawood Hall. They occur also at the Over Alderley boundary with Macclesfield. Unfortunately, the promising **recabuck field** in the Hough is returned by Dodgson as of unknown origin, rather than anything to do with deer and 'bucks'.

In the centre of the land next to Welsh Row is a strange long T-shaped field (SJ 841 768). This, until the early 1800s, was part of a larger piece of land which bore the name **Town Field**. It sits near to an old ridge-and-furrow field system and may in fact represent the main area of open field whose name lived on.

Finally, it is curious that, apart from the **Golden Stone** (1598, at SJ 861 773) there appear to be almost no references to the merestones (parish and territorial boundary stones) in the names of Alderley. Only about half a dozen still appear to be extant, so perhaps their small number accounts for the absence of names. It is noted in the Court Leet for 1611 that:

> There is a piece of Land belonging to the Ladie of this Manor lying in the Tenement of John Bollington and Elizabeth his Mother the Meres thereof is not certainly known by reason of the removing of some Merestones destroyed. Therefore we are agreed to go to the place and make it perfect.

Marriott (1810), writing specifically of Alderley, states:

> The first enquiries for ancient stones from aged people produced the reply, that there were Mere, Meer, or boundary stones, which separated the townships.

This usage of the word 'mere' has not carried through into the records or local modern usage for either stones or place names at Alderley.

Finally, the Leycester map of 1636 returns a very interesting set of field names probably associated with brick making – the **Kilne Croft**, probably the same as Brick Kiln Wood (OA 590), to the east of which lies a series of **Burnt Earth** fields (OA 595–9). To the west there is an **Ashfield** (same as OA 585) and also a **Stiching** or wood clearance (same as OA 578).

Folklore

There is an undercurrent of the eerie and uncanny in some older names: we have **Boggart's Wood** (SJ 836 744 – a boggart being a rather nasty local ghost) as well as the Devil in various guises: **Devil's Grave** ('grave' here being possibly a reference to the Bronze Age mining at Stormy Point – Chapter 15), **Devil's Lane** (now lost as a name, but running from Hayman's Farm to Finlow Hill Lane – SJ 855 759 to 860 766); and possibly in a polite form for Old Nick – **Dickens Wood** (OA 441, SJ 862 777), though there was also a local tenant of that name, one Philip Dikins in 1648, as well as an existing farm of that name.

There was another level of mythical naming, for example in the name **Eagle and Child Public House**, now Eagle and Child Cottage and located at SJ 843 761 (see Chapter 24, p. 610, and Figure 24.5a). A swaddled baby held in the talons of an eagle forms part of the Stanley armorial crest and refers to the story of a child being seized and conveniently redeposited by that raptor where it could be found and adopted as an heir by a childless Stanley. The emblem was apparently called 'the brid and babby' locally, and appears on the facade of the first Victorian villa built in Alderley (Bollin Tower, at that time called Alderley Castle; see also Figure 23.7, p. 600), as well as inside Chorley Old Hall. Another less polite variant was sometimes 'the bird and b***ard', which, it is pleasing to note, is not yet entirely defunct. The Reverend Edward Stanley's genteel attempt to gloss over this aspect of his family history will be found in Chapter 11 (p. 188). What is extremely odd is that exactly the same crest (an eagle, wings elevated, preying on an infant proper swaddled) is listed in the Herald's visitation of Cheshire for 1580, but as belonging to the Fittons – when they owned Nether Alderley. So perhaps there are multiple origins for the Alderley usage.

The Stanleys themselves, as the great local landowners, appear to have left hardly one single local name. The de Traffords, the other great landowners, of course have a street in the present Alderley Edge village, as well as the **De Trafford Arms** (first recorded in 1802 – the 'de' was a noble Victorian addition to the family name) and a **Trafford House**.

The Wizard legend appears first in the name the **Iron Gates** public house (named by November 1805, at SJ 844 741, now gone) and **Wizard of the Edge** (by 1843, at SJ 859 773, still extant, though now a restaurant and the name has mutated on the signboard into **Wizard of Edge**, perhaps in imitation of *The Wizard of Oz*). The name **Wizard's Well** (SJ 855 780) is probably not much older than the 1860s (**Holy Well** at SJ 858 778 is first recorded in the 1770s). More recently there has been **Brasingamen's Restaurant** in the village, with the **Wizard Caravan Park** (SJ 858 770), the shop names **Wizard Cards** and **Wizard Video**, as well as the **Legend Bookshop** (by 2004 this latter had ceased trading). **Wizard Property Management** continues. Finally, the house name **Witch's Gate** on the Macclesfield Road provides a suitably ominous dark partner for the Wizard himself.

One non-barking dog is the absence of pagan names indicative of religious practice in the area (apart from the late, probably eighteenth-century name **Druids' Circle**). Gelling asserts: 'They [pagan place names] do not occur in Shropshire, Herefordshire and Cheshire, perhaps because there were never enough pagan Angles to establish centres of Germanic heathenism which were sufficiently notable'. Or perhaps the settlements by the 900s were late and Christian.

Alderley, unlike many Victorian developments, has none of the usual street name references to the Crimean War (1853) or the Indian 'Mutiny' (1857) – though Johnny Stanley, the irrepressible Stanley son, was present in both areas of conflict. There is a **Waterloo Barn** in Alderley Park grounds, though it may pre-date that battle by about a decade. **Jutland Cottage** near Alderley Edge village must post-date that ambiguous naval engagement in May 1916. (There is a local resonance: at this battle HMS *Southampton* was commanded by Sir William Goodenough, married to Margaret, daughter of Arthur, fifth Lord Stanley).

Street and road names

What do the street names of Alderley Edge reveal of its character? Firstly, most are of modern origin, that is, after the railway of 1842. There are only 100 or so. On the Edge itself, the present narrow grassy track past the Golden Stone was referred to in 1598 as the **Wain Way**. **Lydiat Lane** (= swing gate, possibly, toll gate) still exists, first mentioned in 1610. Some have been lost: **Street Lane Ends** at Alderley Cross has vanished since 1841, though the reliability of Burdett, the celebrated map maker who placed this on his maps of Cheshire in the late 1700s, has been called into question.

The modern obsession for street names is with trees: **Beech Close, Beech Cottages, Beech Road, Beechfield Road, Elm Grove, Hazlecroft Gardens, Maple Road, Oakfield Road, The Orchard, Orchard Green, Underwood Road, Wood Gardens, Woodbrook Road, Woodleigh Court.** Given that there are only some 100 street names in Alderley Edge, 14 per cent as trees is pretty impressive. Furthermore, Alderley, or at least the Edge, was described as being almost treeless in the 1760s. It is surprising that there is only one **Squirrel's Jump** in this plethora of foliage.

After this, the next major group of street names are lakes or rather the Lakes – **Windermere, Thirlmere, Grasmere** and **Redesmere**: these are all from a 1964–66 development by a Mr Cox. **Buttermere Drive, Coniston Close** and **Ullswater Drive** must almost complete the set.

Developers choose street names that have positive selling connotations: **Haddon, Sutton, Eaton** and **Wilton** were apparently all named after famous halls, by the developer, Mr McManus, in 1963. Similarly, **Devonshire** and **Marlborough** and **Talbot** were named after dukes by a Mr P. E. Jones in the 1970s, who wisely named the estate **Dukes' Meadows** (sometimes referred to locally as **The Dukeries**) rather than retain the original name of the site (**Lifeless Moss**). Only Moss Lane, Moss Road and Moss Farm and the use of the area for bowling and cricket now betray the true nature of this low-lying land. **Swiss Hill** (with of course **Swiss Cottage**) is a charming but perhaps exaggerated Victorian statement of the steepness of the Edge here.

There is also a modern tendency to use the word 'Close' for a small newish development (in contrast to its use for 'fields' in the past). These closes tend to be extensions of existing roads, and they use same name – thus Beech Close is off Beech Road, Annis Close is off Annis Road and so on.

Old maps show a familiar but in many ways totally different picture of the road network. On the Leycester map of Over Alderley in 1636, the one identified road, 'from Prestburie to Knuttesforde', is not the Prestbury Road (SJ 875 765) of today. The old road runs around Harebarrow (here 'Harborowe'). Conversely, there is a vanished road shown running from Windmill Farm to the site of **Broadheath Farm** (SJ 873 762) – the latter not yet present, of course, since no one could then build without permission on the common lands. But the **Broad Heath** itself was more ancient – first mentioned in 1287. The main road cutting across 'the Broad Heath' is also unnamed, but is certainly the present 'Macclesfield Road' from about **Dunge Farm** (SJ 870 763) to Whirley Grove, at that time shown with gates, to keep the animals on the common.

The area is of course now transected by major roads – the **A34** being the most notorious, the subject of many Alderley by-pass studies and since 2010 largely diverted onto the Alderley Edge by-pass (named **Melrose Way**, after Margaret Melrose, who started campaigning for this road forty-three years earlier). It was originally the A526 in the 1920s. To the north, the A34 or **Wilmslow Road** becomes (since 1992) the **Wilmslow by-pass** and the old A34 is now the **B5359**. The A535 to Holmes Chapel (**Ryleys Lane** at this point, and renumbered B5359 as far as Chelford in 2010) also adds to local congestion. To the south the course of the ex-A34 becomes interesting, beginning pretentiously as **London Road** but devolving into the **Congleton Road**. As described in Chapters 19 and 26, as it passes Alderley Park grounds it deviates to the west – the Stanleys had the road turnpiked in the nineteenth century and took the opportunity to divert it away from their residence in the grounds of Alderley Park. Since 2010 this stretch has been declassified from Street Lane Ends in Alderley Edge village to the junction with the by-pass (the new A34) north of Bollington Grange (SJ 842 752).

There were three drives up to Alderley Park House – each with a lodge: **Church Lodge** in the north (1817, and still standing), **Bollington Lodge** to the west and **Eagle Lodge** to the south, with this totemistic Stanley emblem on the capstones of the gates. **Beacon Lodge**, on the Macclesfield Road, has a plaque both dated (1837) and initialled by the first Lord and Lady Stanley (Church Lodge and Beacon Lodge are described briefly in Chapter 24, pp. 606, 607).

Lastly, the A34 comes to **Matthews' Garden Centre**, on the edge of the Park, named after the Park's head gardener under ICI (Fred Matthews). Near to this is the newer **Gauntlet Bird of Prey Centre**. Facing it is an isolated **Little Chef** – the modern descendant of the Iron Gates coaching inn at Monk's Heath and from whose signage the legend of the Wizard of Alderley was first noted in writing in 1805. This is a very long declension – Monk's Heath belonged to Dieulacres Abbey at Leek from the Middle Ages until the Dissolution in 1538, so perhaps there was a hostelry here even then.

Outside the Alderley area, and apart from the obvious connecting roads (e.g. to nearby Wilmslow), there are many roads in Britain called **Alderley Road, Alderley Terrace** and so on. Those in Cheshire and the north-west of England (there are thirteen in the Manchester area alone) may probably be attributed with some certainty to Alderley proper. That in Hoylake on the Wirral has or had houses looking like Alderley villas. This naming may be in part because of Alderley's distinct social cachet. 'Alderley Road' also occurs as far south as Bournemouth, and as far away as Auckland, New Zealand, and Victoria in British Columbia. Only local knowledge can say whether these are lineal descendants of Alderley proper, or of Alderley in Gloucestershire, or some other local name. It is noteworthy that **Alderley Edge Road** occurs only in the close vicinity of Alderley.

House names

The major expansion at Alderley was in the large Victorian houses of the Manchester 'Cottentots'. The first 'villa' may have been the one put up on the Edge in 1844–45 by the architect John Rogers, and now called **Bollin Tower**, after the local river. It is in appearance a Victorian castle and was perhaps the house listed in the early directories as **Alderley Castle**. The house presents one puzzle: the Stanley crest of eagle and child appears on the Tower, though this was Trafford land (Figure 23.7, p. 600). The de Traffords embraced the role of property developer – only three villas were built on Stanley land (**Barnfield**, **West Bank** and **Oakwood**). But the Stanleys could afford to hold off: they had a brief mining bonanza around this time, drawing £2,000 per annum from royalties on copper mining in the 1860s (see Chapters 16 and 19; and Bentley Smith, 2005).

At their Edwardian peak in 1909 there were some fifty villas off the Macclesfield Road. Even the Gothick spellings are resonant – **Redclyffe** (see below), but **Earnscliffe**, **Northcliffe**, then **St Mary's Cliffe** and **Beaucliff**. Fully one-third of the villa names are tree names. Like Medieval halls and ancient farms, these mansions have names but no numbers. Along the Macclesfield Road there is not a single numbered house in the sixty from the Wizard of Edge to the old sorting office in Alderley. The terraced houses below the De Trafford Arms are the exact opposite – in 150 years they have acquired hardly a name between them. Social class apart, we are dealing with long-term processes here: the time needed for a numbered house to acquire a name may be considerable. Of the sixteen new houses built in 1991 in **Orchard Crescent** off Welsh Row, only one was named at the time of a 1998 survey. Of the twenty houses in **Carlisle Street** from *c.* 1900, only four are named.

There also seem to be other undercurrents at work in house naming, where the name of the house and the location coincide: **Horseshoe Cottage** is in Horseshoe Lane, **Foden House** is in Foden Road. Similarly, some houses are easy to identify: the **Old Cottage** in Hough Lane is pretty self-explanatory, with its picture-book looks.

The **physical signing** of house names will almost certainly be of great interest to future archaeologists of Alderley, since, unlike field names, they tend to be affixed, often more than once (many four times) and in enduring manner, to the object that they signify: cut into stone tablets, and onto stone gateposts (unless these have been torn up to allow cars access), or set on cast-iron, wooden and plastic plaques. Only gravestones provide more permanent and publicly displayed information.

Holly Bank on the Macclesfield Road, for example, has fine Gothic lettering of probably the 1850s, cut into both stone posts, with traces of red colouring still visible. More recently, the coloured ceramic name-kits from DIY stores have given a new lease to house names, and many at Alderley appear to be from the last decade. These contrast with the restrained 1960s vogue for Eric Gill lettering, often gilt, on blue slate. The prize here must go to **Tara** in Welsh Row, with its fine gilt Celtic-style lettering and blue scrolls. There appear, however, to be no examples of house names in coloured glass at Alderley of the kind seen over doorways in London suburbia. Only the **Union Club** (coloured glass) and the **Alderley Edge Medical Practice** (frosted) exhibit any form of this most fragile of signifiers.

House names have also inherited the territory of field names: below Lydiat Lane there is a house called **Hillfield** – there was a field of that name there in 1840, now disappeared, but perpetuated. **Irons Cottage** is on the site of **Irons Farm** in Welsh Row. There are other examples, but, in general, the ancient fields and farms do not supply the names of local houses, at least at Alderley.

Alderley's house names, like its street names, are obsessed with trees: endless variations of 'oak', but also **Ash, Beech, Birch, Cherry Tree** (three), **Elmbank, Firwood, The Hollies, Hollybank, Hollytrees, The Larches, Maple Bank, Peartree, Pine, Sycamore, Thornfields** (two) and **Yewtree** (three) as well as **Whins** (three), **Bracken** and **Broom** (no monkey-puzzles – yet). A personal preference is the house name **Red Thorn**, on a sign affixed to a flourishing red hawthorn.

There are perhaps more Celtic references in the recent house names than in the much older field names: **Peninver, Penn, Tan-y-Rallt, Tara, Teigh beag** (the wee hoos – an ambiguous name) and **Trelawney**, neatly taking in Welsh, Irish, Scots Gaelic and Cornish. This may tell us more about either small-scale movement across the borders of individuals moving from Welsh areas into Cheshire, or Wales-loving holiday-makers, highlighting their affection through house names. There are also intrusive elements of English: **Langendale** oversteps the classic northern split of long/lang, while **Ellergarth** introduces the Old Norse *garth* – very rare in Cheshire place names. The element *lyn-* occurs frequently in house-name compounds (**Lyndhurst** etc.), with no apparent real meaning. But these are a pedant's quibbles – richness is all. **Netherly** provides a curious but satisfying hybrid of 'Nether' and 'Alderley' (similarly **Netherall**, and the new street name **Netherfields** off **Lydiat Lane**).

There is a modern in-fill called **Brasília**, correctly accented. There are a number of older foreign-style names, particularly French or Latinate (**Frog Castle** excepted): **Amalfi Cottage** and **Bel Air** sound fine, as do **Casa Bella** (house and shop), **Beaufort** and **Caudebec**. **Rosenau** is another; there is also the **Bergli Hut** (Figure 21.2, p. 892), a log cabin in the Wizard's Wood and the scene of two sudden deaths in 1933 (see Appendix 21.1).

The homecoming schoolboy in Alan Garner's *Elidor* (1965) tells off the Trafford Road house names 'Ivanhoe, Fern Bank, Strathdene, Rowena, Trelawney...': such are the touchstones of charm and incantation. The stone posts bearing **Ivanhoe** have gone, **Rowena** remains. **Cerinamroth** is straight from *The Lord of the Rings* and dates from 1972. **Redclyffe Grange** (Figures 23.1, 23.6, pp. 588, 598), with suitable Gothick spelling, was apparently so named in 1853 after a Victorian bestseller (now unreadable) called *The Heir of Redclyffe*. Other names appear unremarkable, but have internal resonance: **Fairfield**, for example, refers to the ancestral seat in the Lake District, looking onto Fairfield, of the Quaker Satterthwaite family, who had gradually moved to Alderley. Some of the names are hermetic and their meaning may already have been lost: **Manara, Quinta, Kamiros**, although the last of these is the name of one of the ancient Greek cities on Rhodes and presumably signals either an affection for the island or an affectation demonstrating a knowledge of ancient history. Finally, a fine study in toponymic confusion is provided by the name **Beyond The Edge**, in Chelford Road, which is, of course, in Alderley Edge.

Post-millennium new builds in Alderley Edge village follow a well established pattern: in Whitebarn Road these include **Silvertrees** and **Rocklands**. **Highgrove** in Ancoats Lane is perhaps hinting at Prince Charles's country house. It seems unlikely that **Beaufort Close** is, however, populated with supporters of the Beaufort Hunt. **Green Gables** (Croston Close) carries on a sub-literary horse-riding tradition. One might hope that **Micheldelving** in Davey Lane is also a literary conceit, rather than an actual mining name for 'much mining'.

Shop names and pub names

Shop names are a different kind of study in fashions and fads. Alderley has a fine selection of the foreign: **Est Est Est** (from the Latin) as well as **Modische Schuhe**, one of the few German names in the area, and perhaps still reflecting some antipathy. There are also **La Casa Bella** and the erstwhile **La Femme**. The shop **Teasels** has a fine pair of these plants in metal as signifiers over its door. There are several Chinese restaurants in Alderley – the **Alderley Rose** on London Road being signed 玫瑰 (pronounced méiguī) – 'rose' in Chinese. A brief comparison with the 1930s shows how much Alderley has changed in terms of types of shop and social structure: there were then two blacksmiths, six bootmakers, eight coal merchants and a solitary saddler. There were at least three smithies in the area on the 1910 map – but none today. Table 20.2 (pp. 534–9) and the accompanying discussion in Chapter 20 (pp. 513–14) illustrate this well.

Finally, it is striking that there are almost no public houses in the area, possibly because of Stanley opposition to public drunkenness among the miners. It is therefore perhaps ironic that AstraZeneca created a slightly mocking **Stanley Arms** in Alderley Park. The **Black Greyhound** (1831), the **Wizard of the Edge**, the **Eagle and Child** and the **Iron Gates** (1805) complete the tally, and of these only the Wizard is still extant (it was once known as **Pogmores** or the **Miner Inn** and sometimes as the **Miner on ye Edge** and then as the **Miner's Arms** – we have a close date for the renaming, for a new sign was up by 18 June 1843; see also Figure 16.6, p. 386). The **Royal Oak** is of course a more modern addition, with Civil War royalist pretensions. The **De Trafford Arms** lies, as one might expect, just outside the Stanley and inside the de Trafford lands, where the main highway enters the village. The **Drum and Monkey** is to the north of Alderley. The origin of its name is obscure (it occurs all over Britain, with a rich variety of explanations) but it has been suggested that as it was a miners' pub in the old days, the drum referred to the drum of the winding gear and the monkey was the trolley that went along the rails. Being on Lifeless Moss, it was for a time known as the **Moss Rose** – again, a not uncommon name for pubs in this wet area of the north-west.

Oblivion and memory

House building has of course been the *raison d'être* of Alderley Edge for over 160 years. The de Traffords struck a deal with the railway which allowed house-owners favourable fares, and the first dormitory suburb in the world was born. Houses are still being added at a fair pace – between 1996 and 2003 over 350 new dwellings were constructed. This is a 'net' figure – some of the large Victorian dwellings have now been demolished or converted. A contemporary witness states in a weblog in June 2004:

> Our final visit of the day was to Alderley Edge to look for 'Oak Bank' in Brook Lane, the home of Samuel Thorp of Alderley from about 1851 to 1889.
> We were hopeful of finding this house, as it was marked on an old A–Z map dated around 1980. However, we were to be disappointed, as it was just a building site, where a block of flats (or 'penthouses' as the sign grandly called them) were being built. It seems we were only a few months too late to see Oak Bank, which was a rather sad end to the trip.

Thorp was a ribbon manufacturer, and originally lived in Manchester, but had typically moved to Alderley and built Oak Bank, around 1850, extending it further around 1870. The new development on this site – described as having 'electric gates … a Ferrari hop from the centre of Alderley Edge' – is still called Oak Bank. This small area of Alderley was in fact heavily dotted with oak house names in the Victorian period – **Oakleigh, Oakhurst, Oakview, Oakfield** and, of course, **The Oaks**.

The vitality of the naming process

The process of naming is systematised and stabilised by the use of the written form. This process began with the tithe commissioners collecting the names of nearly every field in Britain, and continued with the emergence of postal addresses and railway platform signs confirming that one had indeed arrived at, and could send a postcard from, Alderley Edge (though one was nowhere near it in walking distance). It is prolonged by the power of local authorities and property developers to impress their own nomenclature on sites.

We have one very good example of naming in Over Alderley. On 20 November 1661 the fields at Broadheath were allocated to the twenty-one commoners or tenants. This generated a number of new field names, along the line of the current Macclesfield Road around **Dunge Farm** – itself a new creation. **Broadheath Farm** (SJ 873 762) is another new creation whose name betrays it. Nearby is a field called 'intake' on the 1842 tithe assessment (OA 315, SJ 873 863). If this is a new name from 1661, it shows a long run for this particular term. Behind Broadheath Farm are two other indicators – **Common Piece** and **Little Common Piece** (OA 338 and 339). Interestingly, the next field is the innocent-sounding **Clover Field** (OA 336), probably indicative of an early attempt to improve the soil of the heath by 'modern' methods. Seventeenth-century farmers experimented with both clover and turnips to safeguard supplies of cattle fodder – compare **Turnip piece** (NA 584) in Nether Alderley.

Lord Stanley passes on a series of notes on local names:

> White Barn: a Tenement halfway on the Western slope of the Edge formerly Mottersheds. It got the name of White Barn from a large Barn built near the house by Sir Edw. Stanley which, when whitened, became a very conspicuous object. (*Stanley Notebook*)

This kind of information is ephemeral in the extreme – with the added benefit that we have both the previous name and a tentative date.

Many names may well have been acquired purely as nicknames. **Welsh Row** (1831) may be one such example. Even in 1938 there was still a William Lewis, a Miss Owen and a Hugh Owen, Joseph and James Powell, all resident in Welsh Row. There was here a row of five cottages, reportedly built in 1747 for Welsh miners brought in to work the mines. These were demolished in the 1930s. They were possibly contemporaneous with two pairs of eighteenth-century dwellings called **Hagg Cottages** (also known as the **Miners' Cottages**) at The Hagg (see Appendix 19.3 and Figure 19.22, p. 881).

House naming, still a private process, is curiously anodyne for what should be free form: it tends towards the private, rustic and sylvan. Humour occasionally creeps in: a terraced villa at 19 Carlisle Street bears a simple sign saying **Number 10**; there is a weak rhyming joke in the shop name **Alderley Veg**. In 2013 a New York-style eatery opened in Alderley Edge, in a very suitable building – the circular Deco car showroom by the station and St Philip's; it is called the **Aldeli**, a rare German intruder making a curtailed local appearance – via 'Delikatessen'.

More anarchic, there exists a literal underground of oral naming, since recent creation of names within the Alderley mines has been largely in the gift of those who frequent them. Many people remember **Pillar Mine** as **Chocolate Mine**. More names, mainly descriptive, some whimsical, are still being given by the Derbyshire Caving Club to the adits, shafts and natural features of the mines. **Pot Shaft** (where the hoard of Roman coins was found: see Chapter 15 and Timberlake and Kidd in *ArchAE*: 79–97), **Graffiti Cavern** (covered in smoky names) and the **Land of the Dim Grey King** (Figure 20.10, p. 528) are but a few. The process is alive and uncontrolled.

One small mystery is the low level of 'Alderley' as a surname. There is a small scattering from the 1740s in the Sale area, and a blacksmith called Orderley in Ashton-on-Mersey in 1720. There appear to be no modern surnames current as Authorley.

There exist Alderleys as settlements in other parts of the world, notably in Dodge County, Wisconsin (where polite requests have yet to prove any link); and more notably as a very early suburb of Brisbane, built around **Alderley House**. Anthony Smith, of Alderley Creek Wines Pty Limited, wrote to say:

> This property was built in circa 1833 as Alderley Horse Station to house the farrier and convict workers for the Australian Agricultural Company. The home is typically colonial Georgian and was named by the daughter of Lord Stanley, Isabella, after her father's estate in England.

Envoi

This study was completed in 2006/07. Although there has been some updating to 2015 (especially with regard to the by-pass and Alderley Park), the increasing speed of development inevitably means that some aspects may be out of date. On the positive side, the report is already acquiring the character of a historical record and it is reassuring to know that, despite the departure of the great families such as the Stanleys and the de Traffords, the breaking up of the great estates, and the arrival of the National Trust, there are still Potts farming next to a brook on the parish boundary called the **Pott Brook**. As for the true location of Alderley Edge itself – it is in Macclesfield for the postal address and in Stockport (SK) for the postcode.

But Alderley's true location is in an Imagined Landscape of the Memory, and the Heart.

Further reading

Dodgson, J. McN. 1970. *The Place-Names of Cheshire. Part 1: County Name, Regional and Forest-Names, River-Names, Road-Names, The Place-Names of Macclesfield Hundred* (English Place-Name Society 44). Cambridge: Cambridge University Press.

Part VI

Looking back, looking forward

29

Close to the Edge – ensuring the future of the Edge for everyone

Christopher Widger

As we near the end of the book, this chapter sets out not so much to summarise what has come before as simply to recognise the remarkable work which has been undertaken over a period of a dozen or so years. It sets out to provide some idea of what it all means for the National Trust, through the eyes of the Property Manager, whose task is to bring it together into a plan for management and conservation. Not so much looking back, in fact, as thinking what lies ahead for Alderley Edge.

The National Trust was founded in 1895 by three Victorian philanthropists, Miss Octavia Hill, Sir Robert Hunter and Canon Hardwicke Rawnsley. Concerned about the impact of uncontrolled development and industrialisation, they set up the Trust to act as a guardian for the nation in the acquisition and protection of threatened coastline, countryside and buildings. The organisation grew out of a popular movement, when industrial change seemed to be challenging people's ability to stay in touch with the 'good' things in life. The Trust's 'statement of purpose' is summarised in the first National Trust Act of Parliament, from 1907:

> The National Trust shall be established for the purposes of promoting the permanent preservation for the benefit of the nation of land and tenements (including buildings) of beauty or historic interest and, as regards land, for the preservation (so far as practicable) of their natural aspect, features and animal and plant life.

More than a century later the core aim of the organisation remains the same: through ownership, management and covenants we now care for more than 252,000 hectares of countryside in England, Wales and Northern Ireland, well over 1,000 km of coastline, ancient monuments and gardens. Our built heritage is represented by more than 200 historic and important buildings dating from the Middle Ages to recent times. Most of these properties are held in perpetuity and so their future protection is secure. The vast majority are open to visitors and the organisation constantly explores ways in which it can improve public access and on-site facilities.

As a registered charity, the National Trust is independent of government completely, but therefore relies on the generosity of our subscribing members (in 2013 numbering around 4 million) and other supporters. As an organisation synonymous with 'heritage', representing the values of so many people, we have a responsibility as the mouthpiece of our membership to address those issues that are close to our hearts.

In an attempt to meet such obligations I believe the Trust is becoming more outward-focused. In looking after our own properties as well as influencing the management of the wider environment, it is vital that we help to shape policy which is generated externally, whether by European, national, regional or local decision-makers. The Trust is in a very special position to advocate environmental solutions to policy-makers on the basis of experience.

The Trust in the twenty-first century

If we are to succeed in our aims as an organisation we have to prioritise particular objectives. In today's climate of accountability and openness it is essential that we become a source of inspiration for others so that we can ensure that relationships with our core customer groups are as effective as possible, and that we make the most of the profile and influence of the properties and the individuals within the organisation.

For several years in the first decade of the twenty-first century the annual operating surplus was affected by issues such as the foot-and-mouth epidemic of 2002, when government restrictions closed many of our properties, along with rising insurance costs and poor returns on investment. Financial sustainability became crucial, and not just as a concept: it needed to be put into practice through policy and action. The spectre of operating at a deficit loomed all too clearly throughout those years and led to major efforts by the Trust to become more efficient, in which effective cost-control and increased revenue were fundamental.

Several areas have the potential for generating a greater surplus, such as increasing the contribution of the catering and retail areas of the Enterprises Department. Given trends over recent years we can also achieve an increase in membership. The fact that well over half of the Trust's total revenue is currently raised through this source is an important consideration for the future. Even by 2009 the drive of the previous few years to ensure a more sustainable financial position had begun to take dramatic effect – while many of our banks and financial institutions were being baled out by the taxpayer and both commercial and domestic borrowing saw restrictions, the Trust seemed to be able to capitalise on people's reduced capacity or desire to travel, which translated into higher than anticipated visitor numbers.

In its quest to become more businesslike in its functioning, the efficiency of the Trust's operations must be controlled and so management planning becomes important, focusing on conservation priorities through tight internal consultation. The need to build a risk management strategy into the regional business plans is perhaps now more pressing than at any other stage in the history of the organisation, especially given the ever-increasing litigious nature of society.

Though many might argue that the Trust has always been adept at ensuring a high profile and has been something of an inspiration to others, the organisation should aim to manage and share information both internally and externally in a way that ensures a culture of accountability and one where we can learn from our own experience and that of others without fear of reprisal.

For the Trust to achieve these objectives, the values by which we operate must be transparent. Our aim should be to ensure that, to the best of our ability, each and every encounter experienced by our supporters is an inspiring and positive experience, and that quality is second to none.

The organisation has been through considerable change in recent years. It has had to recognise and respond to a changing political and economic climate. The effect of rising costs required a re-assessment of its structure and priorities, and during 2002 the Trust undertook a major restructuring process. It realigned its regional boundaries to coincide more closely with political ones. Many of the traditional lines of authority were amended to provide greater clarity and also to harmonise with national policies. It has also proved necessary to scrutinise environmental and financial policies in order to re-establish both the Trust's fiscal sustainability and its position as an environmental advocate. The last two years of the first decade of the twenty-first century saw further transformation in the way that many of the property portfolios and operational teams were structured, with the aim of ensuring greater autonomy, faster and more locally driven decision-making and still further emphasis on visitor experience. Changes in functional support structures have been designed to support this.

National Trust strategy: '2010 and beyond'

In order to achieve its goals the Trust produced a framework, 'Our strategy to 2010 and beyond', setting out the way in which it will meet its long-term organisational aims. This superseded 'The National Trust strategic plan 2004–7' and has very much been a means by which the Trust has been able to consolidate its direction as an organisation. Put simply, it provides a means for employees and supporters to focus energy on our core objective – 'to look after special places for ever, for everyone'.

The strategy is broken down into four main areas. First and foremost is the need to build deeper relationships with the public by engaging with supporters. Second, we identify the aim of improving conservation performance with even more emphasis on tackling environmental issues. Third, in order to achieve this effectively we recognise that investment in the way our people are managed is crucial. Underlying all these objectives is the absolute necessity to establish a sustainable financial model for the future.

1. Engaging supporters

The National Trust cannot afford to take people's support for granted. To understand the interests and motivations of its supporters and to inspire, enthuse, involve and nurture their interest, not just in what it does, but also in what it stands for, the Trust must find means to ensure that it is recognised widely as a champion of a perpetual cause that today goes beyond conservation excellence and access but also embraces the critical matter of environmental sustainability.

2. Improving conservation and environmental performance

Clear conservation objectives exist for every property, though these will of course vary with local factors and the essential nature of the property. Until recently, it has been difficult to quantify performance in this area and thus to assess funding for improvements. What was needed was a conservation equivalent to the financial accounting process, which clearly conveys how well properties are performing against a set of agreed objectives, just as we would expect a series of budget spreadsheets to present our finances. To this end, the Trust introduced a 'Conservation Performance Indicator' (CPI) system during 2008, to be used at properties to indicate how well we are conserving their particular features of significance.

Closely linked with each property's Statement of Significance, the CPI measures the delivery of conservation objectives over time. These objectives are prioritised by property staff and local conservation specialists. The assessment of each objective leads to an overall CPI, expressed as a percentage score. However, rather than the individual score for each year it is the change in CPI over time that shows whether conservation is improving or failing overall, and which specific areas show a change. By considering and scoring the significance of each feature, the consequences of allowing it to deteriorate, and the urgency with which it needs to be addressed, we can rank and thus prioritise conservation objectives.

Ranked features as identified in the CPI for Alderley Edge are:

- industrial archaeology;
- archaeology;
- wider setting and views;
- geology;
- built structures;
- woodland and trees;
- landscape;
- nature conservation;
- archives and collection.

Not only should this system help guide property staff in recognising the key features at a property, it ensures that conservation matters can be prioritised more clearly, particularly when bidding for funding for improvements. This may appear to be a very bureaucratic approach, but it brings the great benefit that such cross-departmental input at the set-up stage leads to a consensus based on shared understanding of those features of a property which we should be striving to conserve and of their ranking in order of significance.

The year 2008 also saw the introduction of an environmental compliance audit. For the first time the Trust has succeeded in collating all relevant assets, such as water supply and sewage systems, oil and gas tanks, and heating systems. Their condition and their maintenance and replacement schedules have been plotted accordingly; the expectation is that a reduction in the environmental footprint and in the use of energy and water as well as in waste generation will follow in every case.

3. Investing in our people

The strategy responds to calls to improve decision-making, providing clearer accountability and simplified bureaucracy. It also recognises that in some areas salaries have not kept pace with the outside world. A range of innovative training and development programmes has been put in place, a number of which have been recognised outside the Trust as models of their type. A key advance is the delegation of authority to property managers in order to improve performance management for staff and volunteers.

4. Financing our future

There is a clear requirement to remain focused on income and managing costs, but to do so in a sustainable way by improving social and environmental as well as financial performance.

The financial recession which developed during the latter months of 2008, colloquially recognised as the 'credit crunch', did not leave the Trust unscathed. National operating results for financial year 2008/09 generally were very poor, in stark contrast to the previous few years. Membership recruitment held up well, and visitor numbers were by and large as expected. Secondary spend in shops and restaurants was hit hard, as people thought twice before spending. Poor investment return was also a factor. As a result, a 'head-count' policy was deployed which has affected the Cheshire countryside properties: our proposed and initially approved new position of Community Project and Volunteering Officer was withdrawn.

However, the head-count policy and the various mechanisms by which the organisation has sought to become more financially sustainable have not been unsuccessful. Perhaps ironically, while the nation struggled financially, the Trust's results for 2009 were remarkably good, our cost controls working together with higher than anticipated visitor numbers as the population collectively decide to 'holiday at home'.

National Trust policy

The Trust's Policy and Campaigns team play an important role in delivering these strategic objectives by aiming to influence decision-makers and by shaping public debate. Explaining why and what the Trust does is important in terms of helping to generate support for the organisation as a cause and also to demonstrate its relevance to politicians, funders and members. The public's love affair with history shows no sign of abating. Yet this passion for history and heritage has not necessarily grabbed the consciences of our politicians. While millions of people are tracing their family trees or buying the latest historical blockbuster, the government could be accused of turning a blind eye to the things we value from the past and casually dismantling its support for them – there is a perceived lack of investment in heritage, a reliance upon charitable organisations, relaxation of planning regulations and more. The future of our heritage is under threat on several fronts. In response to this, the Trust has developed a series of policy goals:

- to influence public policy in the most important areas for the Trust;
- to build better external partnerships;
- to show leadership in the countryside;
- to promote cultural heritage;
- to deliver a learning programme;
- to manage change in farming;
- to manage water and wildlife efficiently;
- to promote our countryside;
- to promote consumption of local food;
- to promote a cultural heritage programme;
- to improve understanding;
- to conserve assets;
- to improve interpretation;
- to develop skills;
- to recognise, adapt to and address climate change;
- to promote rural regeneration;
- to value our environment;
- to promote 'green' transport.

These campaign themes, which fall into three overall areas of Showing Leadership in the Countryside, Cultural Heritage, and Learning, all consider the delivery of the Trust's 'for everyone' purpose and concentrate on extending its appeal to both existing and new audiences. Considering the breadth of range of people who support the Trust, this means we have the potential to influence 'ordinary' people, not just 'environmentalists'.

The National Trust in the north-west of England

The north-west of England has some of Britain's most impressive scenery, as well as a fascinating industrial heritage. In the north, the dramatic grandeur of the Lake District offers great opportunities for outdoor recreation. To the south, the urban centres of Manchester and Liverpool are surrounded by unspoilt countryside.

Cheshire forms the southern part of the Trust's North-West Region, a region perhaps dominated by the Lake District both in terms of landscape and also because the main regional office is located at Grasmere. Until the organisational review of 2002, Cheshire fell into what until then was known as the Mercia Region, which included the more southerly counties of Shropshire and part of Staffordshire. For a time, until the review had 'bedded in' and the psychological and to some degree the geographical barrier of Greater Manchester had been overcome, the Cheshire staff remained somewhat isolated from their colleagues. I believe it is now true to say, however, that that isolation has generated a strong sense of identity and individuality, at least within the region. One theory is that the concentration of 'heavyweight' pay-to-enter properties such as Lyme Park, Quarry Bank Mill at Styal, Tatton Park and Dunham Massey, together with the iconic Little Moreton Hall, all of which Cheshire can boast, provide a distinct contrast to the essentially rural Lake District. Whatever the case, this individuality has bred a healthy rivalry which manifests itself in a concerted drive for efficiency and quality.

The National Trust in Cheshire

In Cheshire, the National Trust owns and manages over 8,000 acres. The open space properties in the county include Alderley Edge, Hare Hill, The Cloud, Mow Cop, Bickerton Hill, Bulkeley Hill, Helsby Hill, Mobberley Manor, Lewis Carroll's birthplace at Daresbury, and Maggoty Wood, all of which are administered from the Trust's Cheshire Countryside Office, which lies within the boundary of the Alderley Edge estate. The estates associated with the historically significant buildings south of Manchester such as Dunham Massey Hall, Tatton Park, Quarry Bank Mill and Lyme Hall each contribute many hundreds of acres to the total.

Alderley Edge forms the core of the Cheshire countryside properties, which are scattered widely across the county and include some of the most prominent and important areas of landscape as well as unique buildings of historical importance.

The National Trust at Alderley Edge

Clare Pye has described in Chapter 19 how the sale of the Stanley estate in 1938 saw the area which now falls within the National Trust boundary divided into 'parcels', each of which was destined to be sold in lot form as building development plots. After all, the gradual migration of the village up the hill towards the Edge in the form of new grand Victorian villas had been not only acceptable to previous generations but distinctly encouraged. However the value of the Edge was perceived at the time, it was obviously the case that strength of feeling manifested itself through the Pilkington sisters, Margaret and Dorothy, and their ability to raise the necessary funds to purchase those plots, the aim being the protection of the area from development.

The modern history of the Edge can perhaps be summarised as follows:

1700s	the Edge a treeless heath;
1745	pines planted;
1779	land enclosed, beech trees planted;
1842	railway to 'Alderley' built;
1850	public given access to the Edge;
1914–18	many trees felled;
1938	Stanley estate sold;
1946	the Edge earmarked for housing development;
1948	the Edge presented to the National Trust;
2005	Alderley Edge Landscape Project completed.

Alderley Edge – a summary of significance

Alderley Edge is a striking escarpment of sandstone rising some 150 m above the Cheshire Plain around 25 km south of Manchester. Its story has been described in some detail in the previous chapters, but a summary here will help to put the National Trust's role and responsibilities into context. Historically, it has been largely owned by a branch of one of England's greatest landed families, the Stanleys, who leased much of it for the mining of copper and other minerals during the eighteenth century. The common land at Alderley Edge was enclosed also from the eighteenth century, and was planted with beech and pine for ornament in an attempt to 'gentrify' the local landscape. It became, by custom, if not consent, a popular meeting place, with an alehouse; by the later nineteenth century the annual fair described in Chapter 19 had moved from Nether Alderley to the fields opposite the alehouse, which by then had become a tea-room, catering for the growing number of visitors to the Edge. With the coming of the railway, Alderley Edge was on the route to the south and it became an important 'green lung' for Manchester's citizens. Then in 1938 came the great sale of the Stanley estate, with 4,624 acres, 77 farms and 166 cottages going under the hammer. The *Sale Catalogue* shows the Edge identified for housing development and it seemed likely to be lost (Figure 19.19, p. 501). In the event little sold, such was the economic depression of the time, and the Pilkingtons, who lived at one of Alderley Edge's fine early Victorian villas, stepped in to save the Edge. With help from the County Council some 250 acres (just over 100 ha) were acquired for the National Trust. The property is held inalienably and continues to afford some of the finest views and loveliest walks in all Cheshire.

These might be reasons enough to cherish such a place, and indeed the National Trust has continued to recognise the importance of the Edge with subsequent acquisitions, lately through the annexation of land at the neighbouring Hill Top and Butts Farms. The research undertaken through the Alderley Edge Landscape Project (AELP) has shown how important the Edge is both scientifically and socially. Geologically the Edge is celebrated for its richly mineralised and intricately faulted Triassic sandstone and conglomerates, much of it being protected either as a Site of Special Scientific Interest (SSSI) or as a Regionally Important Geological and geomorphological Site (RIGS). Exposures of the ores of copper, lead, cobalt and rarer elements such as vanadium and arsenic in circumstances which suggest that they were introduced much later than the original fluvial deposition of the sediments in which they occur are recognised as being of considerable interest to scholars.

Alderley Edge is important internationally for its archaeology and at its highest point (197 m) a beacon was erected, which by the time of Saxton's 1577 map of Cheshire had been topped by a tower used to store the pitch and faggots needed for a fire beacon, apocryphally used to warn of the Armada. The beacon was erected on the site of a probable prehistoric barrow or burial mound that has recently been added to the list of scheduled monuments by English Heritage.

The Edge is now known to be one of the earliest metal-mining sites in England. Across the property there are remains of mining industry, which, at various times from prehistory to the twentieth century, exploited its valuable non-ferrous ores; some are now scheduled as Ancient Monuments. The site includes the only Roman mineshaft so far known in Britain, most probably dated to the first century AD. Radiocarbon dating of the miner's oak shovel, which miraculously survived in a back-filled shaft and was discovered in 1875 and then rediscovered by Alan Garner, showed that this activity began at least as early as 1750 BC, and work by the AELP took this back to around 1900 BC. In 1995 safety work on a shaft whose cap had begun to 'slump' produced a hoard of coins of the early fourth century AD, making Alderley Edge the only non-ferrous mining site in England known to have been worked in both the Bronze Age and the Roman period.

Medieval miners are probably responsible for some of the shallower, hand-picked workings. No documents survive from before the seventeenth century, when court records show a dispute between miners, and the later working has tended to mask the evidence of the earlier, even though this is less true than at equivalent sites elsewhere in the United Kingdom. Important episodes of mining in the historic period occurred in the eighteenth century under Charles Roe of Macclesfield, who operated a virtually unique sail-driven mill for the crushing of ore in Windmill Wood – hence the name. During the period 1857–78 the

Alderley Edge Mining Company extracted an estimated 200,000 tons of ore at West Mine. By 1860 the company had developed a successful leaching process to extract copper from relatively low-grade ore. Sand steeped in hydrochloric acid was a by-product of such quantities that its dumps became known locally as the Sandhills, until much of it was enterprisingly sold in the 1950s and early 1960s by a local firm for use in road and runway building.

Ecologically the Edge owes much to the geology, the effects of mining and other human activity. It offers variety and surprising interest in the range of woodland, meadows, sandy soils, rock outcrops and wet habitats that exist. Originally the Edge would presumably have formed part of the extensive oak forest that once covered much of Cheshire and the British Isles. Cheshire is said to have only 4 per cent of its land under woodland today, which is less than the national average of around 9 per cent. Within the property there is remnant ancient semi-natural woodland, indicated by ground flora at Waterfall Wood. Since pre-history, timber has been felled for use in buildings, mining and kilns or smelters and the majority of the Edge became an open heath. It is likely that the characteristic heathland vegetation of heathers, bilberry and gorse dominated the area until the Stanleys' planting of the area with beech and Scots pine in the mid to late eighteenth century. Today it supports a predominantly woodland community as the original deliberate planting of native deciduous species has been augmented by natural regeneration, and in living memory many of the heathland remnants have been shaded out. Intriguingly, areas of remnant heath still survive to the south of Macclesfield Road and dormant heather and gorse seed will on occasion still germinate when local conditions allow, typically following tree removal and opening up of the canopy. Specialised organisms have adapted to live in the unusual conditions and include threaded mosses, two new species of bramble first discovered on the Edge called *Rubus alderleyensis* ('the Alderley Edge Bramble') and *Rubus baileyi* (Bailey's Bramble) (Plate 15), the tiny Greater Copperwort and various slime moulds, bats and spiders (e.g. Plates 18, 19, 52–58).

Designations

It is clear that the Edge is significant to people for a multitude of reasons, but the site is formally recognised for geological interest through its designation as an SSSI (Figure 1.2, p. 9). This status was applied in the 1980s and in 1993 it was extended to cover the whole of West Mine, which lies just outside the Trust boundary. Natural England, which in 2006 took over from English Nature the responsibility as the government's environmental advisory body, administers such SSSIs. This process not only offers the site recognition for its significance, but it also affords protection. It is only with consent from Natural England that much of the work of maintaining and managing the site can be undertaken. It is, in essence, a statutory obligation for the Trust to manage the site in accordance with the interests of the SSSI.

The Alderley Edge escarpment is of unique geological importance as the only known area in Britain where the typical ore deposits of copper, lead, zinc, iron and others remain accessible together with the full local succession of sedimentary host rocks. These features of mineralisation and their relationship to the host sedimentary rocks are clearly evident in parts of the mines: at least 13 km of workings are known to exist and are currently accessible, and other passages which may exist and have not yet been made accessible may extend this to 14 km or more. Above ground much of this evidence has been lost or at least is much less evident, having been exposed to erosion and weathering.

In addition to the SSSI, scheduling protects five historically interesting locations at Alderley Edge as Scheduled Monuments (previously termed Scheduled Ancient Monuments, or SAMs), namely the Armada Beacon, Engine Vein Mine, the Goldenstone, the parish boundary marker at Saddlebole and the Wood Mine complex, with its cobalt works (SAM nos 33858–61 and 33863).

The National Trust Sites and Monuments Record

The National Trust Sites and Monuments Record (NTSMR) incorporates details from both the Trust's computer database and the Project Archive (Appendix 29.1). It is essentially a repository for information about the archaeology, the built environment and the historic landscapes in the care of the National Trust; as such it is a core tool for the management of the historic environment. The NTSMR currently holds approximately 50,000 monument records nationwide, although it is estimated that this is only one-third of the data that will be held when all historic landscape surveys have been completed and collated. The North-West Regional NTSMR already contains over 10,000 separate records for archaeological sites and features of historic interest, including details of over 1,400 individual buildings. This resource is constantly expanded and updated in order to provide the most relevant information on National Trust properties to both archaeologists and other property-based staff and regional managers. This database, with a wide scope of inclusion from the prehistoric to the recent past, includes information relating to all statutory designation sites, such as World Heritage Sites, Scheduled Monuments, Listed Buildings, Historic Parks and Gardens, Conservation Areas and Historic Battlefields as well as non-statutory sites, monuments and buildings. It is linked to a substantial archive of photographs, plans and historic landscape survey reports for various properties, together with other reports containing details of various forms of investigation such as geophysical survey, building survey, excavation and documentary research.

Threats and attractions at Alderley Edge

Extensive as this list is, all these designations were, however, applied well after the Trust acquired Alderley Edge. So what was it at the time which generated interest in protecting them? There is little question that even in 1948 the significance of Alderley as a place of historic interest was well understood; certainly the Legend of Alderley Edge was an additional factor in generating interest, as it continues to be to this day. Alderley Edge is commonly said to be one of the most haunted places in Cheshire. Somewhere beneath the Edge itself, behind the 'Iron Gates', are said to lie a king and his knights, waiting there to be called to save England in hour of need – see Alan Garner's account in the next chapter.

Since the advent of formal access when the Stanley family made the place available, initially on a limited basis during the mid-nineteenth century and latterly much more informally, the Edge has provided a means for simple recreation such as country walks and a venue for adventure for the young at heart. The coming of the railway made it much easier to reach the area and the associated development of the village of Alderley Edge provided an added dimension to the attraction of the destination for the visitor. The opportunity to seek refuge from the bustle of 'boomtown' Manchester has now existed for more than 170 years, but the numbers of visitors have steadily grown to levels which threaten much of the very value that people most associate with it. It cannot be denied that the pure landscape quality of the area is also in its favour, when one considers how people generally view and interact with their surroundings; it is not just the fact that Alderley is convenient.

Alderley Edge may be significant in terms of geology; the various designations reflect this fact. Generally speaking, though, it is neither the site's geological importance nor the relevance of the Pilkington sisters' interest in the prevention of the impending development which are the reason why people visit it. There is no question that the place appeals on a variety of levels and people come from far and wide to experience its special character. As with any site, one's reasons for visiting and the response one feels to a place will be a purely personal matter. A small survey of visitors to the Edge carried out during mid-2006 indicated that the main purpose for visits tended to be related to the availability of 'safe' countryside walks. The facility for walking the dog was also highly valued. These findings confirm those of an AELP survey in 1997. The term 'safe' should be taken as relative to, say, a walk in the neighbouring Peak District, which generally requires a somewhat more hardy approach, at least if one is to appreciate the typical moorland scenery at its best. We must therefore recognise the social value of a site, such as the Edge, which lies within easy reach of the Manchester conurbation and of several north Cheshire towns, and its appeal to large numbers of people who wish to experience the countryside in a way in which they feel comfortable and which they can reach without the need for expedition-like preparation.

It is evident, then, that the generally open access which is available in woodland that lies close to home is what attracts many to the place, although this in itself may represent something of a threat. Whether or not people recognise the complete range of interests which exists is open to question, if indeed it is possible ever to draw up a 'complete' list. It is possible, however, to identify at least some of the various reasons which make the place special simply because we, who represent the National Trust, interact with so many of those who come. So, what are those reasons? The series of photographs reproduced as Plates 62 and 63 and Figure 29.1 illustrates just some of the features that lead people to visit the Edge, at least those which we understand or of which we are aware. When it comes to wildlife, these images can be supplemented by all those used to illustrate Chapters 11–13, and Alan Garner talks about the 'mysterious' Druid Stones in Chapter 2 (see Figure 2.10, p. 41), while the ancient mines that people come to see are illustrated in Chapters 15–18.

Whatever moves people to visit the Edge is undoubtedly a subjective, personal matter, and no matter what the cause, it falls within the role of the National Trust to recognise, understand and accommodate these diverse viewpoints. Consider the full title of the organisation: the National Trust for Places of Historic Interest or Natural Beauty. Remember, through the 1907 Act of Parliament the Trust is tasked with 'permanent preservation for the benefit of the nation' or, in other words, 'for ever, for everyone'. No mean feat! Put yet another way, the multitude of reasons for which people value sites such as the Edge has to be considered while at the same time aiming to ensure the sustainable management of the site.

Currently we have no exact figure for the number of visitors to Trust property at the Edge, but certainly the number of car-park tickets sold remained roughly static for the six years prior to 2008. On average between 12,000 and 13,000 such tickets were purchased in each of the years between 2003 and 2008. Usually cars have at least two occupants, especially at the weekends. However, many more visitors park their cars at other nearby locations not owned by the Trust at which parking is free. Given that in recent years the number of National Trust members (who enjoy free parking) recruited locally has increased dramatically, and that during 2006 for the first time overall membership nationally exceeded 3.5 million people and in 2013 approached 4 million, we can only assume that the number of visitors to Alderley Edge is also increasing all the time. When the National Trust first received the proposal to establish the Landscape Project in 1995, visitor numbers were estimated to be 70,000 per year (Milln and Prag, 1995). Given more recent understanding, it would be a conservative estimate to suggest that at least 200,000 people currently visit each year.

The numerous and often eclectic ways in which people interact with the site can all be considered under a generic term: access. As has already been said, 'access' at the Edge might be for general enjoyment of landscape, or to interact freely with woodland, to take in the dramatic views, to be spiritually uplifted, to experience wildlife, to escape from suburbia, to learn, to study, to find tranquillity, a morning cup of coffee, to experience something new, to exercise the dog, a family day out, simple relaxation or for other reasons of which we may have no real idea. Access can therefore be considered as being a physical concept, a visual one or an intellectual one. A combination is eminently possible and indeed likely.

At the same time as recognising these factors, the Trust must aim to ensure effective conservation of the site. Pedestrian (and canine) pressure on the site is a considerable issue, especially with regard to erosion in the form of damage to vegetation and archaeological features. The processes of erosion are exacerbated by the weather. Surfaces devoid of vegetation, in many cases compacted by perpetual pedestrian pressures, are vulnerable to soil loss during rainfall, especially when it is severe. During periods of drought, similar losses can be induced by the wind. Frost adds to the problem: water penetrates the barren surface, freezes, expands and thus further destroys its structure, increasing the risk of loss from wind and rain. These problems can be bad enough in areas which are of interest purely for their vegetation; at the Edge, these processes are affecting features related to mining that include deposits of mine spoil which are of high archaeological value. These deposits may still conceal secrets related to the mining processes which took place at the site as far back as the Bronze Age. A postcard of Stormy Point from 1905 (Figure 29.2) and a photograph taken in 2006 (Figure 29.3) combine to show clearly the level of loss of ancient and Medieval mine spoil. Notice on the postcard the rock which penetrates the surface of the mine spoil. Could this be the same as the one on which the couple in the more recent photo sit? There is no question, however, that the rate of erosion of mine spoil at Stormy Point in particular has increased dramatically in recent years, though other locations suffer in the same

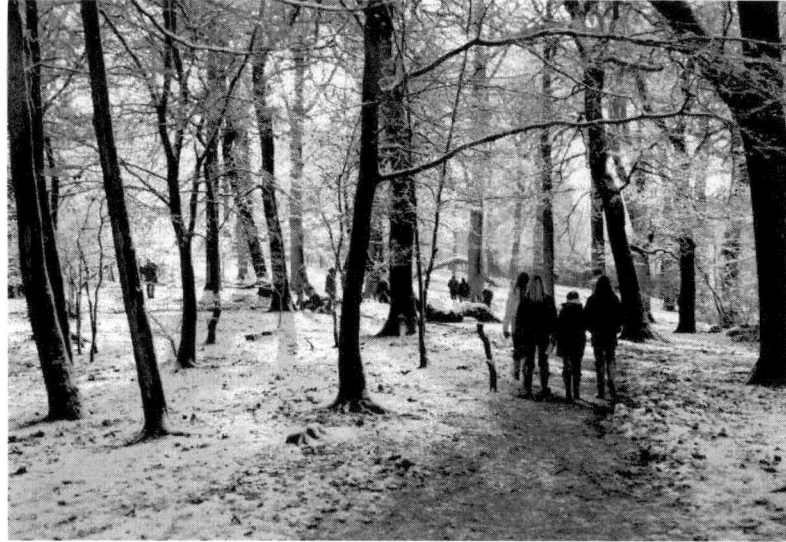

(a)

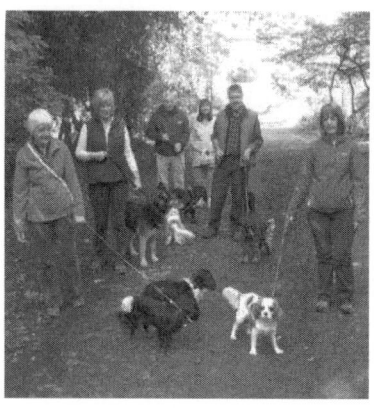

(b)

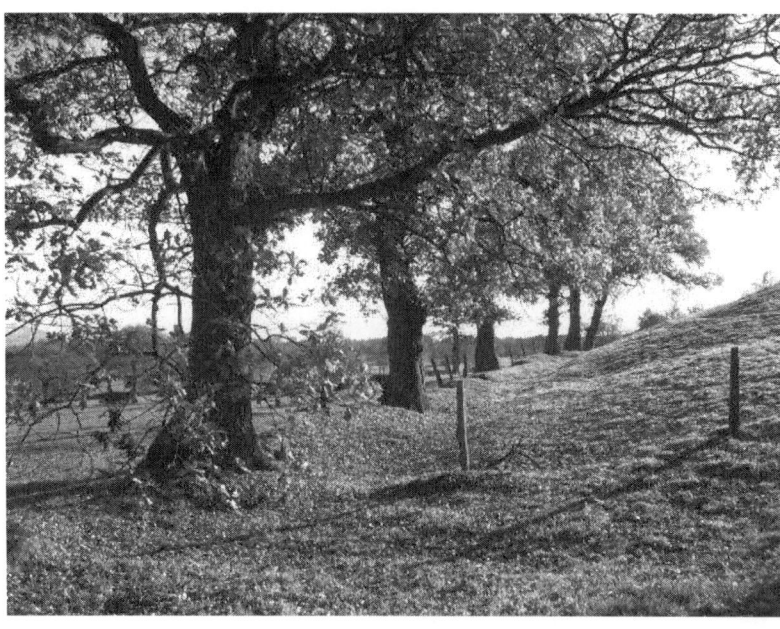

(c)

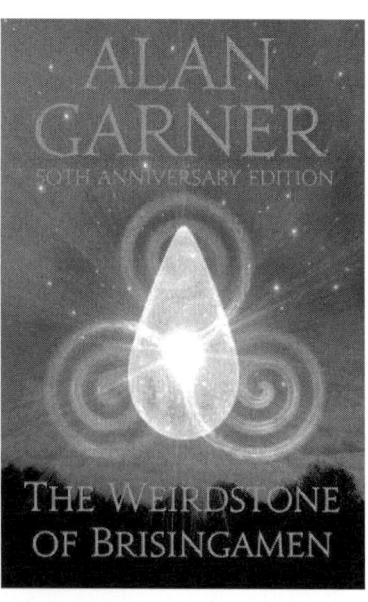

(d)

Figure 29.1. Most commonly reported reasons and features that lead people to visit Alderley Edge:
(a) walks – and (b) walking the dog; (c) open countryside; (d) literary connections; (e) tranquillity; (f) an ice cream; (g) views; (h) education – a group of 'gifted and talented' children being taught under the government's 'Excellence in Cities' scheme at Church Quarry in 2002; (i) picnics; (j) myths, legends and mysteries (the Druid Stones are illustrated in Figure 2.10); (k) history; (l) family fun.

Photographs Christopher Widger, except (d), courtesy of HarperCollins Publishers Ltd, © 1960, first publication/2010 Alan Garner, and (h) Alan Garner.

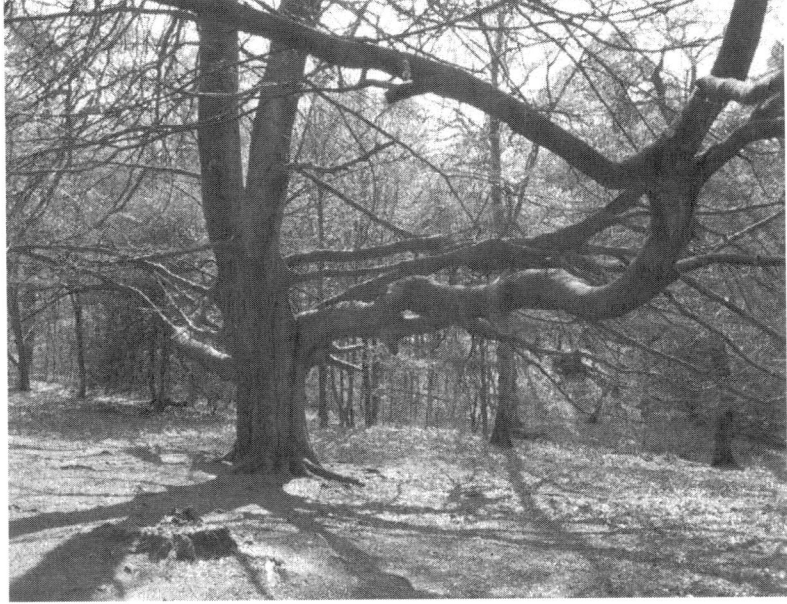

(e)

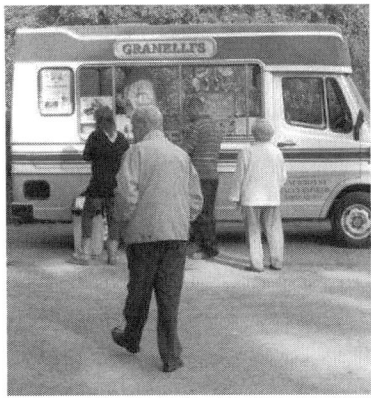

(f)

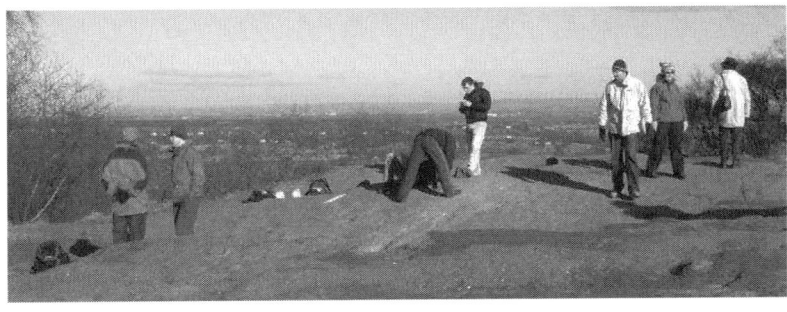

(g)

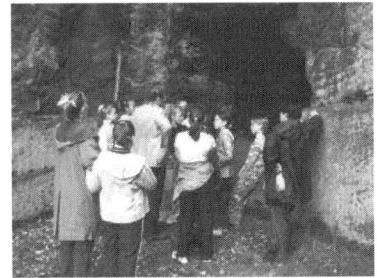

(h)

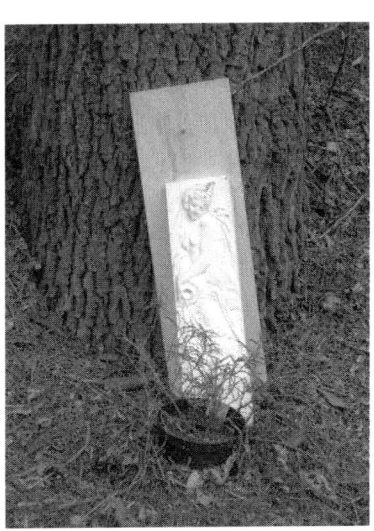

(j)

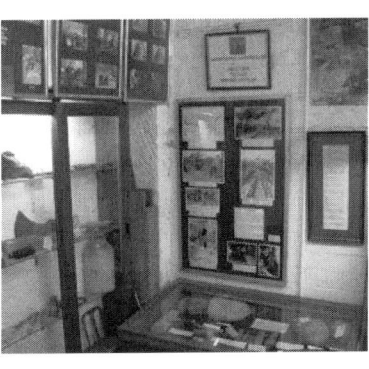

(k)

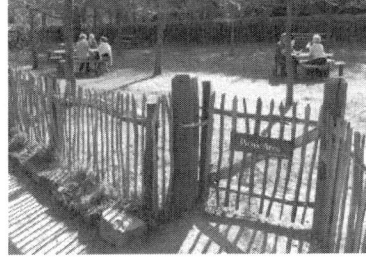

(i)

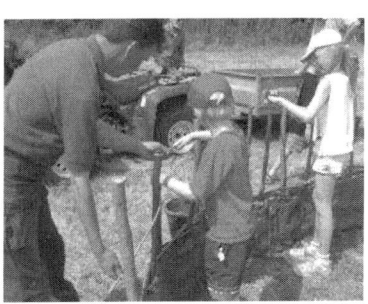

(l)

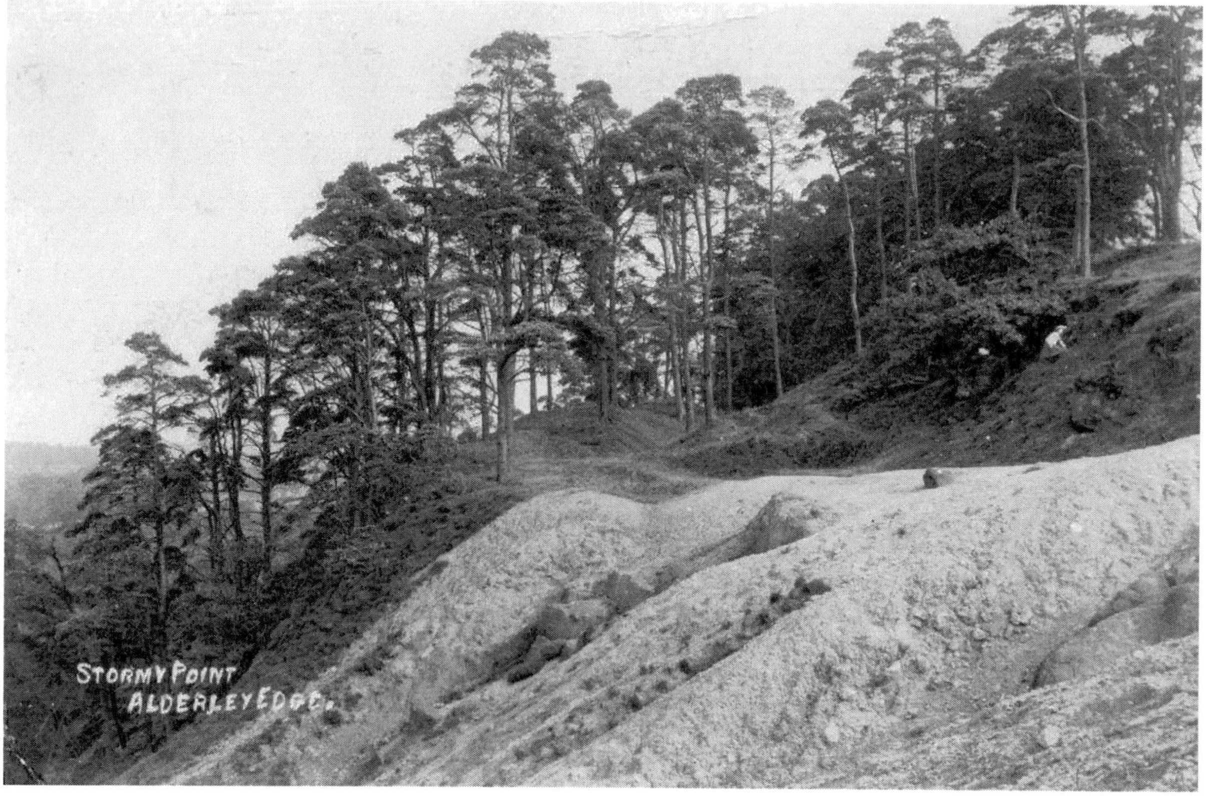

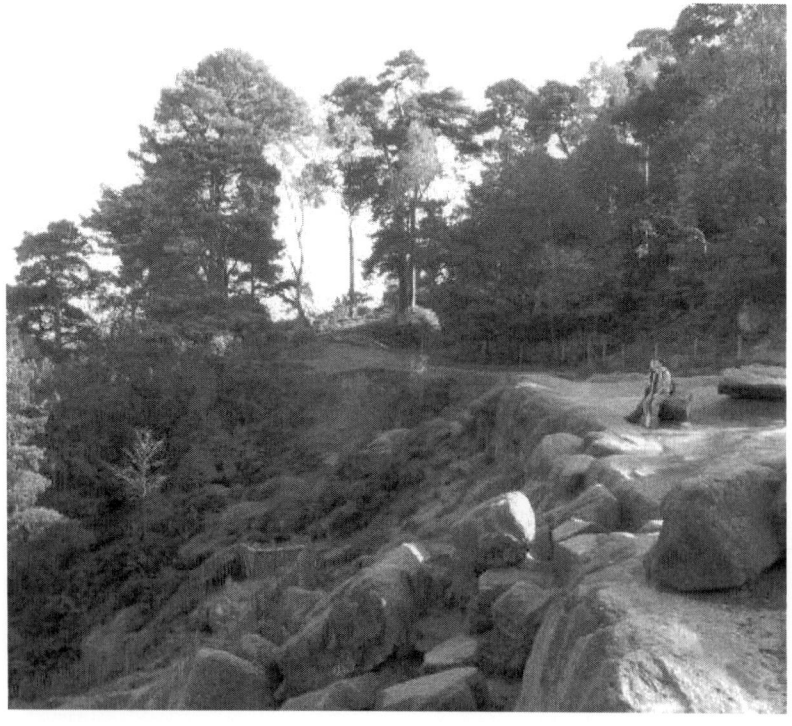

Figure 29.2. Postcard of Stormy Point in 1905.

Figure 29.3. Stormy Point in 2006.

Photograph Christopher Widger.

way. Much of the legacy of mining at Stormy Point has disappeared down the hill in torrents of water-borne silt over the last 100 years, yet early photographs show that it had for the most part lain reasonably intact since Medieval times. The Trust's archaeologists have identified features on the surface of the spoil which were not visible even in 2005.

Individual weather events cannot be directly blamed on climate change but various trends are becoming apparent which are consistent with the changes recorded in our climate over recent years. Severe winds in early 2007 brought down trees in their scores at the Edge and hundreds of others were damaged. This evidence – if evidence it is – together with the fact that several mature beech trees have died suddenly suggests a change in the typically seasonal responses by our landscape to the influence of the weather. These trees are not gracefully declining and showing the usual gradual increase in symptoms of ill-health and decay until eventually they become a hazard and have to be felled. Drought has to be a contributory factor in the rapid death of shallow-rooted beech trees. We have also experienced extreme though short incidents of summer rainfall on baked, dry and friable sandy soil and mine spoil, particularly through the summers of 2004–07. It may therefore be reasonable to suggest that subtle changes in the patterns of our weather are significantly affecting the historic and ecological resources at the site and are doing so at a hitherto unparalleled rate.

A major question that managers of a site which suffers not only from the intense impact of thousands of boots and shoes as well as the influence of the weather must ask is whether the provision of access, both physical and intellectual, is compatible with sustainable conservation. For the National Trust, tasked with managing places of historic interest and natural beauty for ever and for everyone, the answer is clear: yes, it has to be, because that in essence is what the organisation was established to do. Realistically, it would be neither acceptable nor desirable and certainly extremely difficult socially to protect the site by preventing access. Typically, only at sites designated as internationally significant has access been restricted. At Stonehenge, for example, even with the recent improvements, access to the stones themselves is available only on a licensed basis and at selected times of the year. Great have been the difficulties for the managers of the site in building up acceptance of this extreme measure.

It may not be unreasonable to consider management of such a site as balancing access with conservation. If one accepts this premise then increased access and thus physical pressure would surely manifest itself in a conservation compromise. One might suggest that if a percentage value is applied to the conservation importance of a site and the level of access increases, the percentage value of its conservation importance must decrease.

However, this is a somewhat simplistic view. It does not allow for the influence of successful communication between those involved in the management of a site and those who wish to access it. Effective, sustainable management should be possible if visitors to a site are able in some way to feel 'connected' to it. If they do indeed experience that connection then they are more likely to support the process of management, whether practically, vocally, physically, financially or purely emotionally. We cannot expect to deny the existence of the Edge as a destination for recreation, and it is preferable not to suppress the importance of such a place. Where simply by their presence and by indulging in the usual spectrum of recreational activities the numbers of visitors threaten to compromise the sustainable management of a conservation or heritage site, rather than adopting the futile approach of aiming to reduce impact by reducing visitor numbers, managers must endeavour to optimise conservation while at the same time also optimising access. The key here is to promote the means by which access is made possible. This can be achieved only by deploying techniques which effectively allow people to feel they understand the site, and of course the most effective way to promote that understanding is by involving them in a way in which they feel initially comfortable and are ultimately inspired actively to support management work. It is recognised that to fence and restrict access to sites of high amenity value such as Stormy Point without considerable explanation and interpretation would quite simply not be accepted by the thousands of visitors each year to what is for most people the focal point of the property. If people do not see and understand the need for change they will refuse to accept such change: in today's world of highly vocal comment, this will, in its turn, inevitably provoke a flood of adverse comment that could only impede progress. Bitter experience garnered in similar work elsewhere provides the lesson!

Management planning at the Edge

The resource that has accumulated through the research of the AELP, which has so evidently promoted understanding, together with local experience and expertise within the Trust and the environmental industry, have generally informed the preparation of a property management plan. The overall purpose of this management plan is to provide a long-term 'vision' of what the National Trust is seeking to achieve at Alderley Edge and to set medium-term and long-term objectives towards the fulfilment of this vision, in conjunction with a clear and achievable action plan. The primary intention of this management plan is to provide both direction and assistance for the National Trust's management of the Edge by:

1 describing the essential significance of the property, thus enabling continuity of purpose and management;

2 ensuring that management decisions at property level take account of national and regional strategies and policies by incorporating these throughout the plan;

3 providing a document for public consultation and information;

4 setting out a prioritised work programme.

First, a 'statement of significance' gives a context for the plan: much of this can be found in the paragraphs on 'The National Trust at Alderley Edge' above. Next a SWOT analysis is compiled – strengths, weaknesses, opportunities and threats – in this case mainly built on knowledge and experience accrued over time and once again drawing on the research of the Landscape Project (Box 29.1).

SWOT analysis of Alderley Edge

The material and understanding generated through the Landscape Project heavily influenced the thinking of our conservation managers in the drafting of the 'statement of significance' and this in turn drove the collation of the 'vision'. The 'vision' for the Cheshire countryside properties collectively is defined as follows:

> To ensure they will be loved by their local communities as places where people can re-connect with their natural environment. They will also provide inspiration for all new visitors as places where spiritual and emotional connections with the countryside can be made, and where a sense of wellbeing for all is assured.
>
> Cheshire Countryside Properties will also:
>
> 1. Be recognised within the Trust, the county and elsewhere, as a leader in engaging and involving people with their countryside, particularly by building upon and developing strong volunteering capabilities.
> 2. Be places where conservation features are managed in a sustainable way and which demonstrate exemplary methods of how access and conservation interests can together be optimised through successfully engaging supporters.
> 3. Be the first choice in the region for anyone wishing to become involved in the Trust's countryside work.

In turn, the 'vision' for Alderley Edge is one where:

> 1. As a 'green lung' for the bustling city, it provides access for everyone, physically, visually and intellectually, to a mixed landscape of woodland, farmland and remnant heathland with unspoilt views over the Cheshire plain.

Box 29.1. SWOT analysis of Alderley Edge

Strengths
- Located close to Manchester
- Well understood and documented history of past land use and archaeology
- SAM designations
- Link with Manchester University (Alderley Edge Landscape Project)
- Mining heritage of national importance
- Attractive woodland setting
- Impressive views
- Good range of access
- SSSI designation
- Popular family venue
- Strong link with Caving Club
- Dedicated staff and volunteers
- Diverse natural history
- Good relations with grazier
- Links with community groups

Opportunities
- Membership recruitment potential
- Wealthy local population
- Links with local people/groups
- To promote other NT properties, including countryside
- Links with local communities and companies
- Revision of the current scheduled status of archaeology on the property
- Development of archaeological research strategy for the property
- Opening of mines and charging for admission
- Raising NT profile through information point and site management
- Heathland restoration (particularly considering possible climate change)
- Formalised educational visits
- Potential for new and better interpretation including events
- Regulated riding routes
- Assume direct management control of tea-room on cessation of tenancy.
- AELPHER website link
- Improved access for disabled visitors
- Acquisition of neighbouring 'consolidation' property
- Better understanding of visitor numbers/ profile

Weaknesses
- Modest income stream
- Site abuse from some visitors
- Irresponsible dog walkers creating conflicts
- Levels of visitor usage causing erosion
- Reliance on Caving Club for management of mines
- Low appreciation of NT work in the countryside
- 24-hour access reduces overall control of activities on the property
- Isolated toilet facilities
- Busy road splits the property
- Limited NT information and interpretation facilities
- Low level of staffing
- Availability of non-NT parking nearby
- Large footpath network requiring regular maintenance
- Steep banks and rock edges
- Visitors likely to be critical of or resistant to change on the property
- Unclear access routes
- Beech woodland nearing maturity (decay and risk potential)
- Susceptibility of fragile vegetation and thus archaeological deposits to climate change
- No direct control over tea-room management

Threats
- Visitor pressure on ecology of site
- Visitor pressure (erosion) on archaeological sites
- Damage or loss of archaeological resource through natural erosion
- Failure to meet statutory management of designations objectives
- Potential risk of runoff pollution (minerals)
- Unregulated horse riding
- Mountain biking (conflict with pedestrians)
- Low income generation
- Urban development and threats to existing adjacent farmland
- High levels of dog faeces deposits
- Unregulated Hallowe'en activities
- Trespass/occupation (travellers)
- Beech woodland, effect on re-vegetation
- Steep banks and rock outcrops
- Encroachment of neighbouring gardens into woodland
- Abuse by night-time visitors
- Open access at all times
- Unregulated excavation of archaeology
- Ecological implications from climate change (effect on woodland habitat)

2. We understand, conserve and enhance the key features of archaeology and historic mining, geology, habitats and built structures, and ensure their sustainable management.
3. We interpret the story of how human activity over the last 4,000 years has shaped the character and landscape of the Edge.

The long-term conservation management objectives for Alderley Edge, which relate to the key features of the property as defined in its CPI (see above), are outlined under separate headings below. This series of aims for both the long term and the medium term has been incorporated into the work plan for the Edge. The CPI process has highlighted a number of priorities and objectives which in essence crystallise management aims into a fairly simply defined set of targets; their overarching concept remains sustainable access to the Edge, hand in hand with conservation of all the varied aspects of its heritage. To achieve this requires the support of the local community, which in turn is best achieved by promoting better understanding of both the problems and the plans for solving them.

Archaeology and industrial archaeology

All recorded industrial archaeology features and areas are present as identified in the Trust's Historic Landscape Survey, with no loss or preventable damage, their condition being at least as good as that recorded in the Historic Landscape Survey or other archaeological survey.

Wider settings and views

The identified key natural views are maintained and undiminished in quality as far as is practical (and where possible are enhanced).

Geology

The significant geological elements as described in the SSSI entry are present and monitored with no preventable loss or damage as recorded in the baseline (1997) photographic record and landscape map.

Built structures

All buildings and structures are present, as identified in the Trust's Quinquennial Building Survey and future Historic Buildings Surveys, and are in good structural and decorative order, with their architectural and historical significance intact, as identified in the Historic Buildings Survey.

Landscape

All the critical elements of the designed, farmed and historic landscapes are present, recognisable and as close to their original design, form and appearance as is possible, as identified in the Historic Landscape Survey.

Woodland and trees

The woodlands are managed according to National Trust guidelines. The current extent of ancient and semi-natural woodland, managed secondary woodland and notable specimens are maintained in line with the Woodland Management Plan 2009. All identified veteran trees within the woodland and wider landscape, as specified in the Veteran Survey, are managed under best-practice guidelines. The cultural and historic importance of the woodlands is understood and recorded in the Woodland Management Plan.

Archives and collection

The archive is fully catalogued, conserved, accessible and stored to British Standard 5454. The collection is managed according to National Trust guidelines.

Nature conservation

There is no loss or preventable deterioration of the habitats as defined in the Trust's regular biological surveys. All opportunities to expand and enhance habitats are taken where possible. No invasive non-native species are present as currently defined by English Nature. We shall also seek to:

- maintain and, where possible, improve the property's financial position;
- promote emotional 'engagement' with the property with as broad a range of elements of the community as possible;
- ensure that it continues to be a hub for partnership working with key organisations, for example the Derbyshire Caving Club, Manchester Museum and the University of Manchester;

- develop a research strategy to guide future investigations, deepen our understanding and facilitate partnership projects;
- ensure access to the underground features of the property is available;
- ensure visitors can enjoy the benefits of a 'green lung' experience and relative peace and quiet away from the bustling cityscape.

The future – optimising access, optimising conservation

Alderley Edge is faced with a number of conservation and communication issues. Ideally all of them require attention, but there are several key points:

- the need to address the serious and rapid erosion of highly significant archaeological deposits and features;
- the need to ensure the sustainable provision of physical access to the site;
- the potential risk to the Trust from failing to meet its statutory obligations with regard to the proper management of designated sites;
- the possible damage to visitor/member satisfaction, as well as loyalty levels from the perception of compromised conservation interests;
- the potential conflict between conservation measures and access;
- damage to archaeological features by tree roots;
- the potential effects of climate change on archaeological and ecological features.

In addressing both the need to stabilise the archaeological features and the difficulties which prevent the ecosystems of the site from thriving, the unavoidable closure of some parts of the Edge (even if only for the medium term) to assist in consolidation and restoration of the mine workings actually provides a crucial opportunity to improve the visual and intellectual access to these particular sites. In many respects a closure may lead to a heightened awareness of these areas. It is perfectly acceptable to generate the questions 'why are they fenced off and what is special about them?' The equivalent in a stately home might be a cordoned-off room, which one views with some awe. However, it is absolutely essential to gain public support for such actions. A rationale which is clear and lucid must provide the justification for the exclusion of the public and it has to be effectively conveyed; after all, open access has been available for many years and an expected and understandable response to change would be to question why.

In addressing a revision of access at critical sites such as Stormy Point, a number of factors need to be considered. First, the key points of vulnerability must be acknowledged. Then strategies come into play for preventing deterioration while still enabling public access, albeit with some essential controls. Thus improved visual, physical and intellectual access can lead to a raised awareness of the importance of the site as well of the challenges faced by the Trust that are the fundamental prerequisite of success.

Stormy Point – archaeological evaluation

In the wake of AELP's work, the Trust commissioned several detailed reports and surveys from 2004 on (e.g. Mottershead and King, 2005), and given our new-found general awareness of the significance of the site along with recognition of the vulnerability of the mine-spoil deposits at Stormy Point, in 2007 the Trust commissioned the University of Manchester Archaeological Unit to carry out a series of surveys and evaluation excavations (Mottershead and Wright, 2008). These have already been mentioned in Simon Timberlake's discussion of early mining at the Edge (Chapter 15) and we return to them here for their implications for the conservation and management of the Edge, for they were designed to fulfil two objectives:

1   The primary aim of the archaeological programme was to evaluate and record what would be lost through the continued destruction of the archaeological remains by the erosion of the site.
2   The programme of work should enable National Trust archaeologists to formulate a strategy for the management of the archaeological remains, including the promotion and presentation of the site as an archaeological resource.

If at all possible, preservation of the site in its present form would be the preferred option, though if this proved impossible we would implement an appropriate programme of mitigation to manage the threatened archaeological resource. The evaluation was also designed to determine the need for, and to inform a planning process for, full or partial excavation and recording of the site.

The Unit's report (Mottershead and Wright, 2008) concluded that, in many respects, Stormy Point is similar to Engine Vein (which had seen excavation during 1997). Bronze Age prospection pits were found at both sites, typically situated over the faults and following seams of baryte visible on the surface. Test pits suggest that further early workings of the metal-rich clays within the faults exist below the Devil's Grave working and elsewhere, and it seems that Bronze Age smelting may have taken place here too. The site appears to have been used for mining and processing intermittently, possibly from the early Bronze Age to the Medieval period and later. The area may have gained a reputation for metal processing, first using locally derived ores and later with material brought in from elsewhere – analysis shows that the crushed spoil material was not derived from the bedrock at Stormy Point. The discovery of iron-smithing slag, pieces of hearth base and hammer scale was unexpected. Although probably not *in situ*, the material is unlikely to have come from very far away and so it can be assumed that a Romano-British or Medieval smithing hearth existed in the local area. Indeed, it may be that by the Romano-British and Medieval periods the metal-processing reputation of the site was so well established that smithing was occurring in the area using iron brought in from elsewhere. If people were attracted to Stormy Point in order to exploit the bright red, green and yellow clays and marls for use as pigments, this may suggest that such activity occurred as far back as the Palaeolithic, Mesolithic and Neolithic and may have been the beginning of a reputation for the area for mineral exploitation.

The evaluation has shown that intact, archaeologically significant remains from the Early Bronze Age through to the early post-Medieval period exist *in situ* across the site, with features, structures and deposits preserved beneath the current ground surface. The site contains remains that are potentially of national importance, whose study could hugely increase our knowledge of mining and ore processing from the Early Bronze Age through to the Medieval period. These deposits are under very serious and constantly increasing threat from erosion and require action to preserve or at least record them.

Thus the report confirms and extends the need to address erosion, yet in our efforts to protect and conserve the site we are at the same time seeking to secure public appreciation, understanding and enjoyment. In many respects it is the issue of public access that forces us to address the conservation requirements. Access could therefore be said to be a means towards achieving conservation enhancement. In seeking to integrate public access with conservation, we should not aim to achieve a balance, but rather to find solutions that meet the needs of both. Indeed, the messages implicit in the need to manage such access are those which support and interpret the conservation message.

The re-vegetation of Engine Vein

As an initial step towards the conservation of *in situ* archaeological deposits, a project to promote the re-vegetation of the surface features at

Engine Vein was undertaken through 2006 and early 2007 (Figure 29.4). The concept of using a membrane (Figure 29.5) and imported material to limit loss of the surface and to promote the conditions necessary for the establishment of grasses or other ground vegetation is not new; indeed, it is a technique likely to be deployed by many property managers, especially at sites with concentrated visitor numbers or especially delicate habitat. In essence, if a sustainable form of vegetation can be established on the surface of an otherwise eroding land surface, then it will provide the necessary stability to ensure a dramatic reduction in soil movement. In most cases the type of vegetation required will be determined by local factors such as climate, altitude, soil type, anticipated usage and the presence of specific fauna. When considering the conservation of archaeological deposits, however, the type of vegetation is important for any of these reasons; nevertheless, plants with deep root systems should be discouraged because those roots can disturb buried features. Woodland grasses which eventually form a thick sward would be appropriate in our case (Figure 29.6).

Early photographs show that for many years – possibly as far back as the nineteenth century – it has been necessary to restrict access to the area immediately around Engine Vein for safety reasons. It is not certain whether the area has been continuously fenced, but it is true that over recent decades fences have been maintained purely as a safety consideration.

The system employed of late to address erosion at Engine Vein has been to start by removing much of the fencing which surrounded the site closely. Not only has this reduced the impact of pedestrian pressure

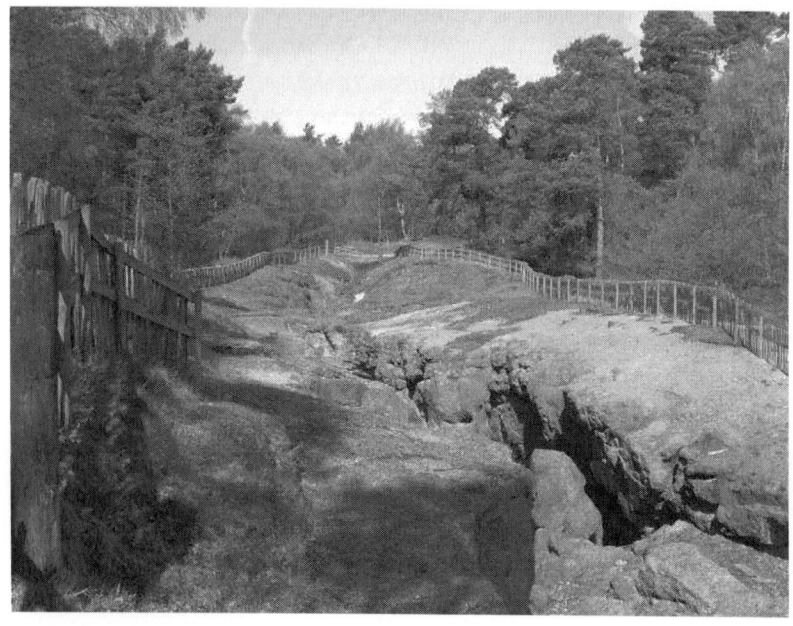

Figure 29.4. Engine Vein from the east, early 2006.

Photograph Christopher Widger.

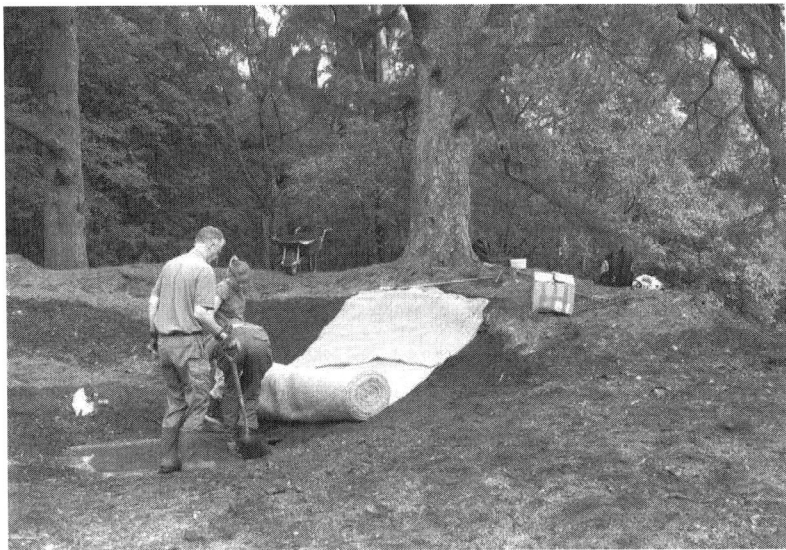

(a)

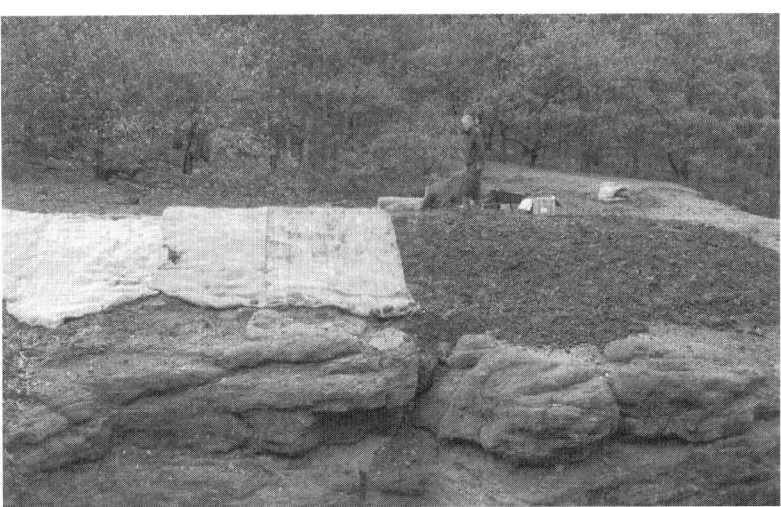

Figure 29.5. (a,b) Erosion prevention under way at Engine Vein, late 2006.

Photographs Christopher Widger.

(b)

on features along the northern side of the workings as well as around Seven Firs to the south-east, but it has also helped improve the aesthetic qualities of the area by removing much of the unnatural and incongruous visual intrusion produced by the substantial fencing. On the south of the Vein the heavy wooden fences which once intruded significantly into one's view have been replaced by wire ones, relocated and now hidden in the trees beyond.

The following stage involved 're-depositing' a layer of eroded material of around 10 cm in depth, collected from above the cap over the mine workings of the Vein and spread across those areas of the site which were

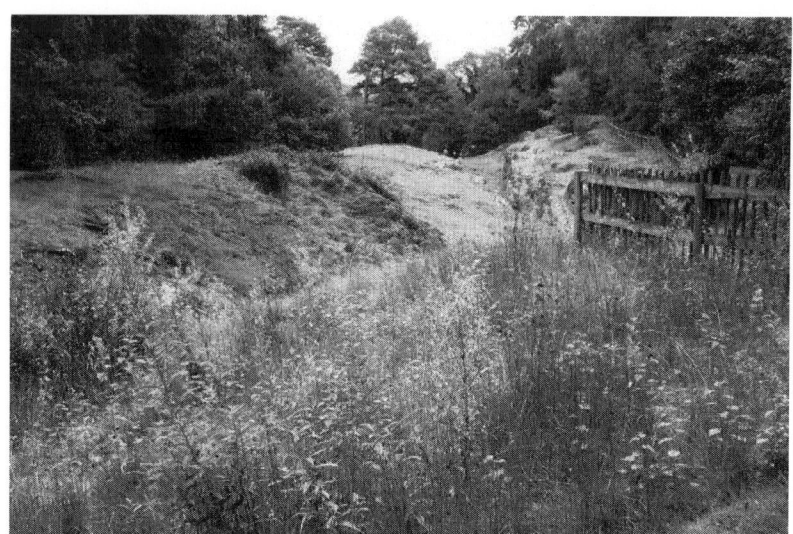

Figure 29.6. Well established vegetation at Engine Vein, 2010.

Photograph Christopher Widger.

devoid of grass but excluding bare rock. Over this layer a membrane of hessian was laid, on top of which was applied a further 8–10 cm of leaf mould; this is the nutrient-rich layer composed of decaying vegetable matter found at the surface of the surrounding woodland. A mix of grass seed rich in fescue and meadow grass which was sown into the leaf mould had already become well established at the time of writing. As the grass became established, the rapidity of movement of soil during heavy rain reduced dramatically. The aesthetic benefit of having re-sited the fencing is complemented by the reduction in the overall scarred appearance of the area as the healing contribution of the grasses increases. The sanctuary which these fences have created will, however, also help to create suitable conditions for an ecological succession process and we will need to intervene if we are to hold the area in equilibrium. It will become necessary to ensure that the natural germination and colonisation of certain woodland species such as Silver Birch (*Betula pendula*) is avoided, and burrowing rabbits will need to be controlled.

The transformation at Engine Vein has provided much-needed evidence that such a system can reduce loss of material. Archaeological deposits are protected and the future is assured, at least in terms of opportunities to learn further from this site.

Engine Vein was chosen as the pilot for this work at the Edge for a number of reasons. As we have noted, the Vein itself had been fenced for many years. This work might realistically have been expected to be less controversial, therefore, in that access was simply being modified, on a scale which would be perceived as modest. One small area within the original fence line had been treated with some success in 2003 using the methods described, and thus a means for conveying interpretation of the process was readily available while work was under way. Recognising the relative difficulty of using the same approach in treating other areas, such as Pillar Mine and Stormy Point, we felt that it would undoubtedly help to have an example of what might be achieved as demonstration material when faced with opposition to more obvious and intrusive access restrictions elsewhere. In short, Engine Vein provides a model for anticipated future plans.

Emotional engagement

Over recent years, warden staff at the Cheshire countryside properties have been extremely proactive in seeking out ways in which people might become involved in our conservation work. In 2006 volunteers contributed a total of around 15,000 hours to the properties, up on the previous year's 13,000. By 2008 the total had reached 18,000. There is recognition in the North-West Region that the Cheshire country-side properties are at the forefront of a drive to meet the Strategy's expectation to engage with groups and individuals from across society. Alderley Edge, situated as it is only a dozen miles or so from the centre of one of the country's largest and most cosmopolitan cities, is well placed geographically and fortunate in the local knowledge, experience, proactivity and enthusiasm of its staff: thus we are readily able to seek out opportunities to embark on new relationships. Of course, many of those who work alongside the regular staff are themselves endeavouring to acquire the necessary skills and recognition required to enter the environmental conservation industry. This is undoubtedly usual at many Trust properties, but it is perhaps less common to encounter

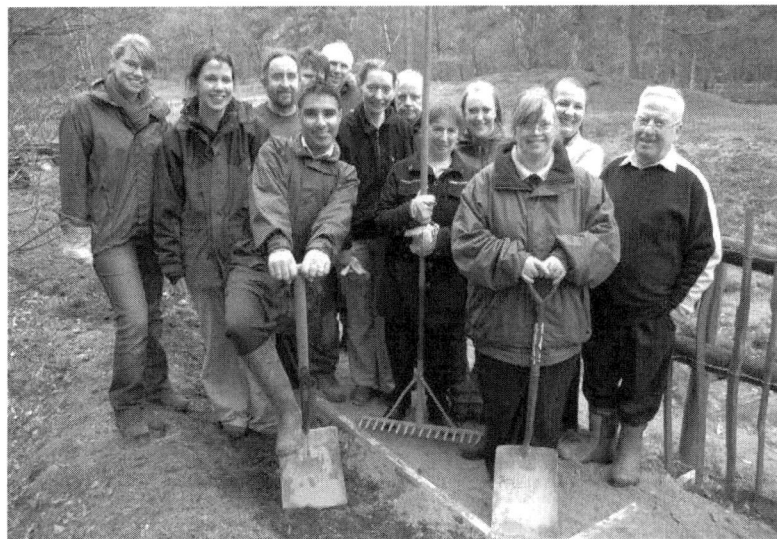

Figure 29.7. Wardens, volunteers with learning difficulties and their carers working on a path designed to protect archaeological deposits near Engine Vein.

Photograph Christopher Widger.

relationships with volunteers from centres for people with physical and learning disabilities, people undergoing rehabilitation from drugs or alcohol, from hostels for the homeless, the probation service, young people from socially underprivileged areas of the city, 'foundation study' students and so on. At Alderley Edge relationships such as these are the norm.

To a degree, the Trust's strategy is the driver for us, but the words 'engaging with supporters' feel somehow inadequate to describe both what takes place and the extensive mutual benefits that can be so effectively achieved through such relationships. Our partnership with Mencap, for example, has the potential to take on a special momentum, one which puts our often restrictive, bureaucratic and administrative treadmill into perspective (Figure 29.7).

What next?

In essence, a further project is required to address the future conservation of Alderley Edge. Work such as that undertaken at Engine Vein during 2006 and 2007 and the outcomes of the evaluation of Stormy Point provide a springboard for further, more extensive initiatives. It is only natural that the Alderley Edge Landscape Project, so thorough, extensive and enquiring, would raise almost as many questions as it answered. Where questions have been answered, our understanding of our heritage resource is enhanced, with the inevitable consequence that we know better how to respond to and act on those matters.

Early 2007 saw the drafting of a proposal designed to achieve the objectives set out in the management plan and to respond to our new-found understanding. The proposed project 'vision' was to provide sustainable access and enjoyment for all who visit the Edge, while promoting conservation through developing new opportunities for community involvement, emotional engagement and better understanding of what makes the site so special.

The project is envisaged as a two-stage process. The first stage would facilitate the development and design of a full project proposal; the second stage would implement those plans and the practical measures which had been developed in the first. These are set out below, as per the 2007 draft, with comments on progress since in italic:

Project development aims (stage 1)
- To carry out preliminary archaeological work at Stormy Point, including a sample excavation, analysis and recording (this project will have a community and education focus and will offer exciting opportunities for participation, education and outreach). *This*

work was indeed undertaken (as outlined above) later in the year; it was coordinated to coincide with National Archaeology Week and a series of family activities were designed to complement the archaeological excavation work.

- To carry out temporary archaeological stabilisation to curb the worst of the erosion for the short term. *Subsequently undertaken at Stormy Point.*
- To implement stabilisation and landscaping of other eroding sites of recognised archaeological importance, including but not exclusively Pillar Mine, Castle Rock and the site adjacent to the erstwhile sail-powered ore crusher in Windmill Wood. *Pillar Mine is now gated and the wider area of mine spoil fenced to ensure only formal access.*
- To carry out audience research including visitor survey, audience involvement and an engagement plan to build support for proposals.
- To develop an access plan.
- To develop an interpretation plan.
- To assess the potential impact of climate change.

Project implementation (stage 2)

- To implement archaeological excavation in areas which are under particular threat.
- To implement full stabilisation and landscaping at Stormy Point.
- To implement a comprehensive series of engagement programmes, including volunteers, events, training, learning, outreach, partnerships.
- To implement a comprehensive interpretation programme.
- To improve access to deal with current problems caused by erosion and to enhance access elsewhere around the site.
- To implement a programme of tree removal from archaeologically sensitive areas. *This programme of works commenced in 2007 as part of an English Woodland Grant Scheme (EWGS) in conjunction with the Forestry Commission.*

However, a significant hurdle for a major project lies in securing the internal 'match funds' necessary to draw potential revenue from external grant sources. Application for these funds was made to the Trust's North-West Regional Business Planning Group in 2007 but was unsuccessful – largely for the general economic reasons outlined above. In the meantime, however, there has been immediate need and opportunity to address elements of the work. By way of contingency, and to address short-term critical need, funds were sourced for the series of evaluation excavations at Stormy Point as identified in the project development plan and outlined above; interim erosion control measures have also been applied at Stormy Point, using the principles and elements of the technique already deployed at Engine Vein (Figures 29.4–29.6) but without the addition of fencing to protect it. We recognise that at Stormy Point vegetation is unlikely to take hold in this pressurised location without such provision, but at least for the time being the original surface is protected.

Early in 2009 there was a dramatic increase in the level of inappropriate activity at Pillar Mine, for which this location has become notorious in recent years. The mine entrance was often used as a venue for drugtaking and fires had been lit regularly. Pillar Mine had remained the last mine of any scale to which access was still unrestricted (at least as far as a blockage some 30 m in). The police were involved when the scale and frequency of fires lit within the mine caused sections of the roof to become unstable. It appears that several tyres had been brought to the site and set alight and a number of gas cylinders were then added to the blaze. As well as the structural damage to the rock, surfaces became covered with a thick black layer of tar-like residue. This activity brought forward the decision to exclude access to the mine with a heavy steel mesh. Before this work could be completed, a Scots pine of considerable age (probably a Stanley planting) which stood near the entrance to the mine was illegally felled by an unknown person. Again, the decision to fence the surrounding area – a measure included in the proposed project to protect surface archaeology – was brought forward and this fence is now in place.

So here we are: this is the situation at the time of writing, in January 2010. For the Trust's local managers and regional advisors the way ahead is to address critical elements of our objectives by approaching them through a major project. It remains necessary to go through a process of gaining internal Trust acceptance that the initiative fits with the priorities of the Regional Business Plan, simply because an element of match funding will be required for whatever grant funding might be raised.

We expect that a holistic development plan or 'masterplan' process will be embarked upon in 2017, which will aim to analyse the issues at the Edge from within various disciplines, such as conservation, curatorial, commercial and interpretative, and which explicitly includes physical and practical considerations related to the critical need to conserve the place while providing sustainable access. The masterplan should inform investment and long-term strategic planning and it is likely that the project outlined above will form a substantive element of the outcome. It is recognised that the project proposal pre-empts the masterplan to some degree but, given the experience of recent years, it is reasonable to expect it will be effective. Hopefully, approvals for the development project will be in place some time after this. The second or implementation stage would be expected to be carried out under a three-year programme starting a year later, with the archaeological work and with short-term interpretation to explain what is happening on site, followed by access work and longer-term interpretation. With the support of a proposed new Project Officer position, the community engagement element of the project would aim to deliver the conservation aspects of the project by building upon and extending relationships in the community which are so highly valued already. Should we fail in our attempts to achieve project funding, then we must devise a contingency plan. In such circumstances our approach should be to address the various objectives in piecemeal fashion – much as we have attempted to do already with elements of the development phase work. The crucial drawback in this method is, of course, that it restricts our ability to engage the public in the process because the Trust's project management role disappears and at the same time the task will take longer to complete.

Alderley Edge is a dramatic, wooded sandstone escarpment set in rolling Cheshire farmland just twelve miles south of Manchester. Its panoramic views, mature Scots pine and beech woods, intriguing legends and cat's cradle of paths, so many of which reflect routes related to ancient mining, have long attracted people, yet today the average visitor often appears to display only limited awareness of the fuller story of the place; indeed, it seems that they scarcely recognise the impact that their presence may have on the physical evidence beneath their feet. But in many ways, that's fine! After all, it is clear that the enigmatic qualities which the site possesses are, for a great many people, the very essence of its fundamental and perennial appeal. Although, as we have seen, the threat to the site is exacerbated by each foot that passes, combined with the rain falling upon it, and that certain deposits within this nationally significant site are disappearing at an alarming rate, much of it still retains the secrets it has kept for generations. In protecting these secrets the Trust, as custodian of the Edge, must aim to predict and to mitigate pressures and influencing factors, including now also potential climate change. It must endeavour to increase its understanding of the Edge while ensuring that the resource itself is effectively conserved for future generations. But however efficiently we address these targets, we must never lose sight of what it is that people want from the place. Should we fail to recognise the essential magic that it holds for so many people, then whatever we do we are to a degree compromising the very qualities that make it special. Yet while this is a dilemma for current and no doubt future managers, it should also perhaps remain a guiding principle.

30

By Seven Firs and Goldenstone: an account of the Legend of Alderley

Alan Garner

Landscapes can be deceptive.

Sometimes a landscape can seem to be less a setting for the life of its inhabitants than a curtain behind which their struggles, achievements and accidents take place.

For those who, with the inhabitants, are behind the curtain, landmarks are no longer only geographic but biographical and personal.

John Berger, *A Fortunate Man* (1967)

My grandfather told me this tale. He told it in the dark of his forge, and by the side of his hearth, and in his garden as we pulled rhubarb. He told it with simplicity, respect, authority; and he would not have brooked doubt. It was his truth, a part of him, which he passed on.

Here is how he told it. And it is the manner of the telling that is important.

There's a farmer living down Mobberley. And he has a white mare. And he must take the mare to sell her at Macclesfield market.

So he sets off one day at the back end of October; and just as it's coming light he's crossing the Edge, but when he gets to Thieves' Hole, the mare stops and won't budge, choose what he does. Against the side of the road he sees a tall old chap, thin as a rasher of wind; and he's got a proper sort of a stick in his hand.

'Oh,' he says, this chap, 'that's just the mare I'm after. How much do you want for her?'

'I'm not selling to the likes of you,' says the farmer. 'I'll get more at market.'

'You go your ways,' says the old chap. 'You'll not sell her. And I'll be waiting for you tonight.'

So off the farmer rides to market. And he sits there all day; but though everybody says she's a grand beast, no one offers to buy that mare. And at the finish, he has to get him back to Mobberley with her.

When he comes to Thieves' Hole it's fetching night. And there's the old chap waiting for him.

'Now will you sell?' he says.

'How much will you give?' says the farmer.

'Enough,' he says. 'You come with me.'

And off he tramps, with the farmer behind him.

They go from Thieves' Hole, by Seven Firs, and Goldenstone, to Stormy Point and Saddlebole. And on Saddlebole they come to a rock, big as our house nearly.

The old chap touches the rock with his stick, and the rock splits open, clatter. And behind the rock there's some iron gates. He touches them with his stick, and they open; and there's a rum sort of a hole going into the hill.

By this time the farmer, he's asking the old chap to let him go, and keep the mare. He wants no money for her.

But the old chap tells him he'll not come to no harm, he says. So the farmer takes the mare down into the hill, after him.

They come to a cave; and there, all around, are knights in armour and a big man with them, all asleep with their heads each against a white horse, except one, and he has nobbut a ruck of stones for rest on.

'This here,' says the old chap, 'is a sleeping army, with their Top Man and their horses, waiting on the last battle of the world, and whenever that day is I must wake them. But I'm one horse short, and yours will do nicely. Now you come with me.'

And he takes the farmer to another cave; and this one is full of gold and silver and all sorts. 'Have as much as you can carry,' he says, 'and we'll call that payment.'

Well, the farmer, he sets to and he crams his boots and his pockets, his britches and his shirt with the treasure; and his hat; and when he can hold no more, the old chap takes him back to the iron gates and shoves him through. Another clatter and a bang, and when the farmer turns him round, there's just the rock and it's dark as a bag outside.

Well, the farmer, he gets home as best he may and tells his tale; and the next morning him and his neighbours they go back to the Edge to fetch more treasure; but neither they nor any since have seen the iron gates again.

That is the tale my grandfather told; and it is, of course, the Legend of Alderley. What my grandfather did not know, and would not have cared if he had, is that the Legend, in various forms, occurs across at least the northern hemisphere, at all times and in many places. It is the myth of the Sleeping Hero. Aspects of it are in the earliest written record of any myth, *The Epic of Gilgamesh*, baked on clay tablets, some dating from the second millennium BC. Incidents differ, but, at their most simple and comprehensive, the stories involve the encounter of a mortal, through an intermediary, with an immortal, asleep under the ground in a special or sacred place.

Here, it is necessary to say what is meant by a legend in the study of folklore. The technical definition of a legend is: 'a fanciful story associated with a place and believed to be true by the people that live there.'

I remember, as a child during World War II, listening to adults joking, yet only half joking, and nervously, that if the knights were ever going to wake now was the time; but they would need white tanks not white horses. The story was fulfilling its definition of a legend.

The clearest statement is that of K. M. Briggs (1971). '[Folk Tale] is Folk Fiction, told for the edification, delight or amusement. Folk Legend was once believed to be true.... A difficulty arises when [legends] are handed on by people who no longer believe them, for entertainment or as curiosities. Then they begin to be embellished with picturesque touches, new circumstances, and the legend becomes a fiction.' More poetically, but no less cogently, John Maruskin writes: 'It is in the speech of carters and housewives, in the speech of blacksmiths and old women, that one discovers the magic that sings the claim of the voice in the shadow, or that chants the rhyme of the fish in the well' (Maruskin, 1980).

Both writers' words are exemplified by the early printed texts of the Legend. The first, recorded in *The Manchester Mail* in May 1805 is dull; the second is a bolted lettuce of verbiage, an example of how to make polite literature from the vulgar. It is nothing else.

> [The farmer] perceived a figure before him, of more than common height, clad in a sable vest, which enveloped his figure; over his head he wore a cowl, which bent over his ghastly visage, and screened not hid, the eyes, that sunken and scowling, were now fully bent upon the horseman; in his hand he held a staff of black wood, this he extended so as to prevent the horse from proceeding until he had addressed the rider. When he essayed to speak his countenance became more spectre-like, and in a hollow yet command-ing voice, he said, 'Listen, Cestrian! I know thee, whence thou comest, and what is thy errand to yonder fair! That errand shall be fruitless; thy steed is destined to fulfil a nobler fate'. (Anon., 1820)

Compare it with my grandfather's delivery.

The different forms of the theme have been much discussed, but for the purpose of the Legend of Alderley it is pertinent that the Greek historian, Plutarch, in his book *Concerning the Failure of Oracles* written in the first century AD, quotes the report of Dimitrios, who had been sent by the Emperor of Rome to gather information about the islands of Britain. 'There is, men said, an island in which Kronos is imprisoned with Briareus keeping guard over him as he sleeps. For, as they put it, Sleep is the bond forged for Kronos. They add that around him are many divine beings, his knights and his soldiers.'

Plutarch was using names that Romans and Greeks would recognise. What their British equivalents were we can only guess, but the names of individuals appear not to be important. In the Legend of Alderley, the old man is not at first called a wizard, and his name of Merlin and of Arthur for the Sleeping Hero are nineteenth-century decorations. In the Legend as it was told to me, they were simply an 'old chap' and a 'Top Man'.

I am not suggesting that Plutarch is referring to Alderley. There are at least eight versions of the Legend in the British Isles. What I am saying is that the story existed in this part of Europe in the Iron Age; and a question is: why should it occur on the Edge? An answer is: I do not know.

A bigger question would be how and why the legends, different yet the same, should have spread so far through space and time; but the Edge has enough of its own to challenge us. Why, when and how did the story start its journey to me through my grandfather's mouth and the mouths of others of the Edge?

The most reliable source to trace is oral, for the reasons given. The difference between the oral and the written is that the written is a fiction, whereas the oral, however changed, is, in its origin, an attempt to retain, perhaps to explain, a reality. It is news that time has warped: a game of Chinese Whispers passed from generation to generation, until the meaning may be lost, but the elements remain. How may we find them?

By the time I was eighteen I had learnt an important rule of research: Pursue the Anomaly. If something does not make sense, what is it saying? And there are anomalies in the truth my grandfather told me about the land he knew best.

Here is one.

In the Legend the old man stops the farmer at a place called Thieves' Hole (their route is shown in Figure 28.3, p. 707). To get from there to the spot where the old man opens the way to the cavern, at a rock known as the Iron Gates, the farmer is led by an illogical route: 'from Thieves' Hole, by Seven Firs, and Goldenstone, to Stormy Point and Saddlebole'.

Until the eighteenth century the Edge was an unenclosed, all but treeless 'dreary common.' The woods that we see now are the result of deliberate landscaping. Why, then, did the old man traipse the farmer across an open hillside in a zigzag that increased the journey by more than twenty per cent? What 'truth' was my grandfather remembering about the land he knew best?

I went to look for the Why and the What. And in trying to answer these questions I set out on a journey: a journey no less mysterious than the farmer's. It was a journey into the land, and the land was itself the telling of a story, the narration of a tale that followed a path and took its line from waymarkers, just as the Legend does.

At each of the named places on the route from Thieves' Hole to the Iron Gates I found interferences with the ground, in the form of earthworks, big stones, and, above all, ancient boundaries. I was confronted by something old, possibly prehistoric.

The places were important to my grandfather, and, even though he did not know the exact position of every one, the route was beyond doubt, and a search filled in the gaps. And since place names in England tend to be among the earliest survivors from the past, when names were descriptive only (and that is important), identifying what was then seen as fact, here was where to start to look for a clew through the temporal and physical maze. I began to question the names.

Most place name elements in Cheshire are Old English (the language of the Anglo-Saxons), Old Norse, Middle English or Old French in origin. That is, they were in the language by the end of the fourteenth century, at least in speech. They may turn up later in documents, but the document does not date the name. It records what exists.

The old man stopped the farmer at Thieves' Hole. Old English *hol* means 'valley', 'depression', or in describing roads, 'sunken'. Middle English *þef* is 'thief.' In modern Cheshire speech, 'hole' is qualified by an adjective, as in 'mine hole', 'sand hole', 'pit hole'. The Old English *pytt* is an excavated hole, where minerals or other materials are got. An example of this is the quarry in a larger depression below Bradford Lodge on the north side of Bradford Lane, known as Stonpit Hole (stone pit hole), which distinguishes between the two elements (SJ 845 768).

Were it not for etymology and usage, the 'hole' of 'Thieves' Hole' would be the small quarry close by; but that is not a 'hole'. It is a 'pit'. The 'hole' passes under a modern road as a double sunken depression.

Thieves' Hole could be both a road and a boundary; they are often one and the same. It is not a boundary of any existing land division at this point now, but it could have been used as such, whatever its original purpose, in the early Middle Ages for an estate now lost. A charter of 1008 for Rolleston, Staffordshire, describes one of the boundary marks as *ðan þorne þer ða þeofes licgað*, 'to the thorn where the thieves lie'. And at Witney, Oxfordshire, in 1044, there occurs *Of Æcenes felda ðær ða cnitas licgað*, 'From Æcen's field where the lads lie'. The Old English verb *licgan* means 'to lie', not in wait but to lie as a corpse. It indicates a place of execution and/or burial; and for this the Anglo-Saxons came to favour boundaries. It was not so at first. To begin with, the Anglo-Saxons' approach had more of the numinous than of dread. But with the introduction of Christianity there was a movement from pagan respect for the ancient to a God-goaded fear.

Thieves' Hole as a place name occurs four more times in Cheshire alone. In the township of Fallibroome, next to Alderley, it is the name of a field that lies between the confluence of two brooks, each arm of which forms the boundary with Prestbury. Three more occur in Hattersley, along the banks of the river Etherow, which until recently was here counted to be the Mersey, the meaning of which is 'boundary water'.

From Thieves' Hole, by Seven Firs, and Goldenstone, to Stormy Point and Saddlebole.

One of the enigmas of the Edge is the occurrence of artificial, flat-topped mounds of earth of no known age or purpose. They could be prehistoric burials; they could be more recent 'improvements' by the Stanleys for the romanticisation of the new woodland; they could be both, or almost anything. With one exception, they have no name, but the route from Thieves' Hole to Saddlebole takes in three of them, including the one exception, which is called Seven Firs. Only excavation would answer the question of what these circular features are, but a geophysical survey of Seven Firs has shown seven 'anomalies' in the mound, which could be the remains of tree roots. All over the country, especially in the eighteenth century, it was common for landscapes to be 'improved' aesthetically by the planting of clumps on old bumps.

From Thieves' Hole, by Seven Firs, and Goldenstone, to Stormy Point and Saddlebole.

The earliest surviving mention of Goldenstone is in a Perambulation of the boundary between Over Alderley and Nether Alderley of 1598: 'and so to a great stone called the golden stone on the north side of the wain way'.

Goldenstone, which marks a kink in the parish boundary, has the appearance of age and a chequered history (see also Chapter 27). It is a freestanding irregular but worked block of conglomerate sandstone, notable for its high content of quartz pebbles. It seems to have been shaped by battering; that is, not with metal tools. And it is not golden, it is grey. It has been badly used, in that a portion has been destroyed, and the traces of drill holes that remain suggest the use of explosives. But the rock has no useful purpose, and there is the finest freestone close by. At a comparatively recent date, within the past few centuries, someone tried to obliterate it. An earth bank covered it, and I exposed it again in 1955.

When complete, Goldenstone weighed about twelve tons and was hauled into place from some distance when there was plenty of other stone that would have served the purpose nearby. This, together with the nature of its tooling, is consistent with a prehistoric origin for its placement. But why is a grey stone golden?

There are many 'golden stones' in England. We need to look at language again.

In place names, Old English *gylden* can mean several things. 1) 'gold-coloured': plainly not the case here. 2) 'sacrifice.' 3) 'tribute, tax.' 4) 'treasure.' 5) 'wealthy.' 6) 'splendid.' It is a matter of choice unless other evidence turns up. I intuitively reject 'sacrifice,' and tend towards 'tribute.' A boundary is neutral, neither here nor there, a good symbolic place for the safe transfer of wealth, since, while it is on the boundary, the tribute is nowhere and can belong to no one. Behind Goldenstone is the second flat-topped mound.

From Thieves' Hole, by Seven Firs, and Goldenstone, to Stormy Point and Saddlebole.

The route from Goldenstone to Stormy Point follows the boundary between Over Alderley and Nether Alderley. As it reaches Stormy Point it passes by the third flat-topped mound.

Old English *stormig* is 'stormy.' Middle English, from Old French, *pointe* is 'a place having definite spatial position, but no extent, or of which the position alone is considered; a spot.' This may be convoluted, but it is an accurate description of Stormy Point; and there is much to note on its amorphous ground.

For the purpose of this chapter, there is the Devil's Grave: a small discoidal chamber entered by an open trench that runs along one side. In form it is unique on the Edge, unless it is the same type of working of which traces may be seen at Engine Vein, but almost destroyed there by the later cutting. 'Devil' is used frequently in the naming of strangeness, especially of early features in the landscape. The sense is that they are 'other': unsafe things from long ago and a different kind of time. Also, naming and renaming matters where places or things are already recognised, have meaning, and need to be dealt with; which is often done by demonisation of prehistoric remains at the time of conversion from paganism to Christianity. Old English *græf* is, essentially, 'something dug in stone: a cave, or a trench.' Again the description is apt: 'the tricky trench.'

Close by the Devil's Grave is a now inconspicuous circular mound: Pikelow. Old English *piced*, 'pointed,' and Old English *hlāw*, 'mound,' and, well attested as the most common meaning, 'artificial mound,' 'burial mound', 'barrow.' What makes Pikelow significant beyond its appearance is that the boundaries of three parishes and four townships meet at its centre.

Boundaries, of great age in themselves, when first defined often used visible, well-known aspects of the landscape as reference points. Natural features are common, as are pre-existing artificial ones, and also isolated trees. It is likely that Goldenstone was used because it was already there. Similarly, Pikelow was not built to be used as a boundary marker but was chosen because it was of importance and beyond dispute. The boundary was strung between.

From Thieves' Hole, by Seven Firs, and Goldenstone, to Stormy Point and Saddlebole.

We, and the farmer, are on the last leg of the journey; and it is the most intriguing one.

Saddlebole is a spur from Stormy Point, with a dip the shape of a saddle about half way along its length. The further summit ridge ends in a steep convex slope. Old English *sadol*. Old English *bol*, 'a smooth, rounded hill.'

There is another meaning for *bole* that may apply to this part of the Edge, where copper and lead have been worked from early periods, and amounts of iron, cobalt, manganese, sulphur, silver, mercury and tin occur. Old English *bolla* is 'a round hollow,' 'a bowl,' 'a crucible.'

Bole, as a mining term, is first found in print in *Fodinæ Regales, or the History, Laws and Places of the Chief Mines and Mineral Works in England, Wales, and the English Pale in Ireland, as also of the Mint and Mony. With a CLAVIS Explaining some difficult Words relating to Mines, &c.* By Sir John Pettus, Knight (London: printed by H.L. and R.B. for T. Basset, 1670).

Sir John was deputy governor of the royal mines, and his book was the standard treatise of the seventeenth century. In the clavis, there is the entry: 'Boles or Bolestids are places where in ancient time, before Smelting Mills were invented; the Miners did fine their lead.'

The spur of Saddlebole begins at Stormy Point. A preliminary excavation here in 2007 produced lead scoria and other smelting waste, together with broken lumps of unburnt lead ore, galena (see Chapter 15, p. 343). Future work will show whether or not boles are present. Certainly this part of the hill would suggest that they are. The concentration of metals in the soil here prohibits any kind of vegetation.

Saddlebole may have had an importance that anachronistic modern thought would miss. The *Fodinæ* is concerned not only with metallurgy but also with alchemy, and it should be remembered that the division between the two was once more permeable than it is today. Saddlebole may have been associated with a Mystery, to add to its other, ancient, otherness.

At the side of the track, which is another multiple boundary, descending from Stormy Point to the saddle, there is the dramatic rock of the Iron Gates. I have not seen the name identified as being that rock in any written or printed form. How, then, do I know that it is the Iron Gates of the Legend, the way to the Sleeping Hero? My grandfather told me. And how did he know? Someone told him; as they too had been told. Question or proof did not come into it.

Remember that we are dealing with legend, and legend is belief of truth. It is not fiction. It is not imagination. It is not invention. It is reportage. But why the Iron Gates? A solid rock should not need an iron gate.

In European legend, folklore and mythology, iron gates commonly occur as entrances to the Land of the Dead. These gates are found not so much in the depths of the earth as in hills and rocks that rise above the level ground. They are opened sometimes by touching them with a particular flower, but more often what translates as a 'wishing rod' is used, although there are other names, such as 'fire rod', 'burn rod', burst rod', and 'quake rod'. Descriptions of it vary, but it is most commonly a single, slender staff, the same as the 'proper sort of a stick' that the 'old chap' uses on the Edge.

So much for the zigzag journey. Yet there are questions to be asked of the Legend from the start.

Why was it that the old man stopped the farmer at Thieves' Hole? And what was a farmer travelling from Mobberley doing there in the first place? He could not have been on any modern road.

The double ditch has been interpreted as the 'braiding' of an ancient hollow way running from the north-west to the south-east along the ridge of the Edge and possibly prehistoric in origin (Timberlake *et al.*, *ArchAE*: 144–5). Beyond Thieves' Hole, in the right conditions, the track may be seen as a crop mark heading towards 'The Black Greyhound' on the B5087, from where there is a choice of roads to Macclesfield.

In the other direction, the track has been traced to the former A34 opposite Alderley Cottage. It does not end there. The line continues, with the immediate surface detail lost or obscured, across the former A34, along the side of the house and down to join Cuttlers (now Lydiat) Lane, from which it is visible as a hollow way in the lower part of the garden and as far as the hedge of the lane (SJ 84273 77956). Opposite Beechfield Road, itself parallel to the line of the bank and delineating the sides of the 'Stanley finger' *(ArchAE*: 155), but extending beyond, there is a footpath that also drops into Lydiat Lane (SJ 84241 77913).

From there, with a little jinking over the railway, paths and boundaries lead to and through Common Carr farm (its track a Civil Parish boundary and the find spot of a Bronze Age palstave – see Figure 14.7a, p. 326) to the B5085, which is the southern fringe of the ritual waters of Lindow Moss (with its Lindow Men – see Chapter 14, p. 329; and Turner and Scaife, 1995; Joy, 2009) and so to Mobberley. But why is Mobberley a part of the Legend?

Back at Thieves' Hole, we still have to cope with the old man. Why did he stop the mare here?

Today a farm road crosses the double ditch at right angles on its way from the B5087 to Edge House. It is along this road that the zigzag journey starts. On the earliest surviving Stanley Estate Map of 1787 (the 'Crossley map', Figure 19.9, p. 484) no road is shown. However, when dealing with cartography, we need to know what information the commissioner of the map wanted or needed to record. Only with the appearance of the Ordnance Survey's discipline is accuracy mandatory. Earlier, absence of evidence is not evidence of absence.

It is plausible to suppose that the 'missing' road was there, perhaps a little off its present course, before 1787. To the south and north of the hiatus, there are tracks, running in part along hollow ways, and they line up to cross the Edge at Thieves' Hole. It does not make sense for two track systems, approaching each other head on, to stop. But I may be pernickety. The tracks are climbing to open common and heath. Once there the ways would not be so confined, and what the Legend implies may be more accurately described as movement between known and named points.

If the various tracks do continue and cross over Thieves' Hole they should be the later feature. But roads are deceptive, in that their function alters through time, which causes changes in size and surface. In the archaeology of landscape, tarmac is the great deceiver of the eye. To determine what, if any, relationship may exist between the two ways their intersection would have to be excavated. Should there be a true relationship and intersection, then Thieves' Hole would have formed a crossroad; and crossroads share the uncertainty and the uncanny with boundaries, for the same reason: they are ambivalent. The centre of a crossroad leads nowhere, just as the centre of Pikelow, with its joined seven boundaries, occupies nowhere. Such liminal places are where space and time are weakened and other dimensions may break through. That is why, I suggest, boundaries play so great a part in the Legend.

I go further and say that if a crossroad did not exist at Thieves' Hole the old man would not have met the farmer there. And to find the place now would require the disciplines of archaeology and folklore working together; which is perhaps a difficult concept to swallow.

We, with our modern, materialistic minds, think of time and space linearly: that is, yesterday-today-tomorrow time, and behind-here-before-up-down space. With these views we form only a small part of human thought. The majority of the world, including many of the great religions, preliterate cultures, physicists and cosmologists (and these only as an example), have no difficulty in accepting multiple realities, which I shall call 'mythic' space and time.

'Myth' is an abused word, equated with 'untruth,' whereas it is the opposite. At our most profound, we can never say what we mean. The mirror that reflects meaning is metaphor and poetry, but what they reflect is truth. By 'myth' I do not imply 'fiction,' but more the weaving of patterns that we unconsciously recognise as the core of being, both within and without us. Myth is as near as words, through poetry and metaphor, can get to the wholeness of perfect truth.

In the Legend we are dealing with physical and spiritual mythic topography. Boundaries and centres are a large part of the structure.

They are 'betwixts-and-betweens', mid points or the midway line between opposites; neither this nor that. The dividing lines without breadth symbolise the supernatural in the realm of space. Temporally, the same phenomenon is represented as the juncture between years, seasons, days: 'today' (which never was and never will be, and yet is.) Both kinds of line are occupied by a mysterious power, which has a propensity both for good and evil. This supernatural power, when applied to time, breaks through in a most ominous way on November Eve and May Eve in 'Celtic', that is Iron Age, culture. They are the joints between the two great seasons of the year.

November Eve, called Samhain in Ireland, the start of winter and of the year, was a solemn and weird festival. The mounds were open and their inhabitants were abroad in a more real sense than on any other night. The boundary between the living and the dead was breached.

And which temporal boundary is 'at the back end of October', when the farmer goes out of his world to meet the Sleeping Hero? Consider, too, how the first meeting with the old man is at the boundary between night and day, dawn, and the second at dusk.

Boundaries between territories, like boundaries between time, are lines along which the supernatural intrudes through the surface of existence. The union of two opposites is symbolised by the line along which they impinge upon one another; and the reconciliation of three or more independent entities involves the discovery of the point at which they coincide.

The Legend speaks philosophy as story. It is why the old man has to meet the farmer at a crossroad, a road without direction or commitment, at a time when time is stopped. Once the farmer turns from his way home, he is entering another reality. The approach to the Sleeping Hero begins with the first step from Thieves' Hole, and with each step he moves out of his reality into another, to return for ever changed.

Surveys of physical boundaries are themselves often enigmatic. It is by no means easy to follow the Perambulation of 1598:

> And so lineally to a little mere-stone in the track way towards the mineholes and so to the mere-stone at the top of the hill and from thence on the north side [of] the minehole directly to the Saddlebole and so from the Saddlebole along under the great stones after the crest. And so back after the crest by the great stones to the two stones lying together over against the hanging stone on the slack....

The cause of confusion may be the combination of different factors, not least that the document is of its moment and not of ours, when the people concerned knew what was being referred to. They knew; but often knowledge has been lost, so that we have to look at the ground carefully, and sometimes guess. A particular hazard is the interpretation of individual names. The misunderstanding of a single letter or syllable can alter meaning. It may stretch belief that 'oaks at the wolf's green' could ever have been claimed as 'sandy ridge of the elves' or 'green ridge of the elf', but I once claimed it, and with reason, though that reasoning may have been wrong. I shall try to make more rigorous sense here, because there is the chance that something important is lurking in the word thicket.

The boundary on Saddlebole is particularly intriguing, not least for its being the earliest documented description of the topography of a part of the Edge.

It is a record, written in Medieval contracted Latin, of a grant of land dating from the thirteenth century. The text is corrupted in its printing, and I am grateful to Jonathan Prag and Paul Cavill for their opinions on the Latin.

Walking the land, I read the text as:

> Greetings. I, John of Arderne, lord of Alderley, gave and bequeathed to John, son of Edmund Fyton, and to his heirs all my land with the wood rising above the aforesaid land within these divisions; namely: taking to Elfgrenhoks by rising as far as the Sadel and from the Sadel following the one-time road as far as the Birchenegros and to the Pykedlowe and from the Pykedlowe and so on to Avardeshache and from there to Fytounes trystre, and so on.

The meaning of the marker names on Saddlebole would appear to be: Elfgrenhocks: 'Oaks at the wolf green'; Old English, *wulf*, 'wolf'; Old English *grēne*, 'a grassy place'; Old English *ac*, oak. (If the definition is accurate, Elfgrenhocks may still exist. On the line of the boundary, there is a single oak, and single oaks were often boundary markers. It could be the oldest tree on the Edge, since it attained its shape by growing at a time when there was no competition. It grew on the 'dreary common.' I am not claiming that the oak is eight hundred years old, though that is not impossible, but I do argue that it is in a place where an oak would have been handy; so it may be a replacement.) Sadel: 'Saddle.' Birchenegros: 'Birch grove'; Old English, *birchen*, 'birchen'; Old English *grāf*, 'copse'. Pykedlowe: 'Pikelow.' Avardeshache: 'Ælfweard's gate'; Old English personal name: *Ælfweard*; Old English *hæc*, 'gate'. Fytounes trystre: 'Fitton's hunting station'; Middle English personal name: *Fytoune*; Middle English *trystre*, 'hunting station.'

Ælfweard is a personal name, but it breaks down into two elements: Old English *ælf*, 'elf' (and in the Middle Ages an elf was no whimsy but a spiritual force); and Old English *weard*, 'ward'. I felt that this was too important a matter to risk, so I wrote to one of the most respected of English Language scholars, the late Professor R. W. V. Elliott, of the Australian National University. Here is his reply.

Auardeshacche/Avardeshache. Your suggestion that this is not Ælfweard's gate, but the elf-guard's gate is perfectly possible. In the West Midlands the words 'elf, elves' are recorded as 'alve, alven', according to the *Middle English Dictionary*, Part E.1, p.72. These words occur several times in Layamon's 'Brut', *c.* A.D.1200 according to C. S. Lewis's Introduction to G. L. Brook's edition (Brook, 1983). Thus 'the gate of the elf-guard' is a good West Midland reading, perfect for Alderley!

The Sleeping Hero could be called an elf in this context; and the old man his ward.

Boundaries can be among the longest surviving of our monuments. Many delineate Saxon estates, Roman and Iron Age structures, Bronze Age field systems and a few even the Neolithic; and some can be combined in the one feature. However, the majority of our old boundaries are of Saxon origin. The Anglo-Saxons developed an ambivalent attitude towards these spaceless spaces, as has been noted. They feared them, and yet employed them because of their liminality for such purposes as execution sites and for the safe disposal of 'deviants.' These negative associations came with Christianity. Earlier, they were in awe of monuments, especially of Bronze Age round barrows, which they took as marker points for the boundaries of their land divisions, intensifying that liminal force, and they re-used the barrows, inserting their dead into the realm of the more ancient. Even natural features that looked like barrows were used. Yet these places, dangerous because of their lack of contact with the world while yet defining it, and unknown to God, were chosen as meeting places for assemblies both political and social, perhaps for that very neutrality, where disputes of this world held no sway. Mobberley, which means 'the mound of the assembly', has its church sited on an artificial circular earthwork, which may be the eponymous mound. From it the Beacon barrow mound on the Edge, skirted by the prehistoric road to Thieves' Hole, would have been visible. If there was a connection between the Edge and the mound of Mobberley, has folk memory preserved it as the route taken by the farmer? And what connection could there have been? I suggest that the link between mounds, moss and hill point to a landscape of the sacred, and that the Legend records it.

The swing of beliefs increased the Anglo-Saxons' association of ancient burials and boundaries with the uncanny. The no-places became synonymous with the supernatural. It is clear in the earliest surviving English epic, *Beowulf*, which dates from an uncertain time, possibly the seventh or eighth centuries (see e.g. Jack, 1994). The poem is written from a Christian viewpoint, but its material is pagan.

Beowulf is a tale driven by boundaries and barrows. It contains the spatial topography understood by an eighth-century mind. Beowulf's first heroic victory is the killing of the monster Grendel, whose epithet is *mearc-stappa,* 'boundary-walker'; and his last victory, and his death, is in battle with a dragon from a mound. On boundaries and in barrows evil was confined until darkness dissolved the barriers from view.

Barrows, in tradition and in reality, could hold treasure, nowadays called 'grave goods', and the finding of them during secondary use of the barrow would give an extra bond with the past and add to the other-worldliness of the site. Here, by coincidence, yet not wholly coincidence, *Beowulf* and the Legend overlap. It is a part of the pattern of folklore to associate hollow hills, either natural or artificial, with the other world and with riches. It is as if the image were hardwired into our psyches. In *Beowulf* (lines 2212–14) the dragon is guarding a treasure in the mound.

> *Hord beweotode,*
> *Stānbeorh stēapne; stīg under læg*
> *Eldum uncūð*

'It watched over the hoard, in a stone-roofed barrow;
Men did not know the way to it under the ground.'

In the poem, a man discovers the hidden entrance and takes a goblet from the treasure. The comparison with the Mobberley farmer of the Legend is close.

Accounting for the nature of the Edge is not easy. The hill has been used since the end of the last Ice Age, about 10,000 years ago. Worked flint is found there. But the culture of the Mesolithic could not be expected to leave other traces. However, by the age of 21 I felt that the Legend of Alderley, as told by my grandfather, contained, as it were, a guide to an unrecognised Bronze Age, 4,000 years ago. I was nearly 60 before persistence won through and made the archaeologists look; which justified both grandfather and Legend. The Edge is the earliest dated site of metal mining in England. And that radiocarbon date is 4,000 years ago.

I would say that the Edge, crisscrossed with boundaries and earth-works, is itself liminal, a special, a holy, or a haunted place, dependent upon the historical moment of the viewer. It is a remarkable hill that was largely heath, another form of boundary, another no-man's-land, which stands out both from the plain and from the high ground to the east. And the nature and colours of its rock formations are striking. Such things would have been important at many levels of consciousness in earlier times, as they are, if to a lesser extent, today.

It may be that the Edge was first seen as a place of numen millennia before copper was worked here. Metallurgy has always been a magical and dangerous art, and its practitioners are magical and dangerous men. (Who else but the rightful king could draw the sword from the stone?) Yet before and after copper the Edge could have been valued and even revered more as a source of pigments for the decoration of the human body. Such practices are universal in space and time. Pigments were traded over distances, and their source was considered to be a place of power, a seat of spirituality. We, as children of the Edge, knew where to find our paint; the green, the red, the blue, the yellow, the white, the black; and how to mix them in a paste of precious lard and dripping stolen from our mothers' jars in World War II. John Hockenhull, the mildest of boys, when daubed became a god.

There is more in the Legend, when we listen: another question.

If some supernatural agency has gone to the trouble of creating a cavern to house an enchanted army against the day of ultimate trial, why is there the logistical error of being one horse short? Did no one count? And why is that required horse a mare? What is it the Sleeping Hero needs?

Mares were not used in battle. Stallions were. Why is there a milk-white mare on the Edge? What is it this Hero lacks? I knew that I knew. But what? Then I remembered Giraldus Cambrensis.

Giraldus was a Welsh monk writing in Latin in the late twelfth century. He starts Chapter 25 of the third part of his *History and Topography of Ireland*, which was intended, in part, to show the backwardness of the Irish, with these words: 'There are some things that, if the urgent demands of my account did not require it, shame would prevent their being described. But the severe discipline of history spares neither truth nor modesty.' He then relates a ritual alleged to be found in Donegal when a king assumes power (O'Meara, 1982: especially 134–5, n. 67).

At the inauguration, the king, before all the people, copulates – with a white mare. The mare is then killed (Figure 30.1). The mare is

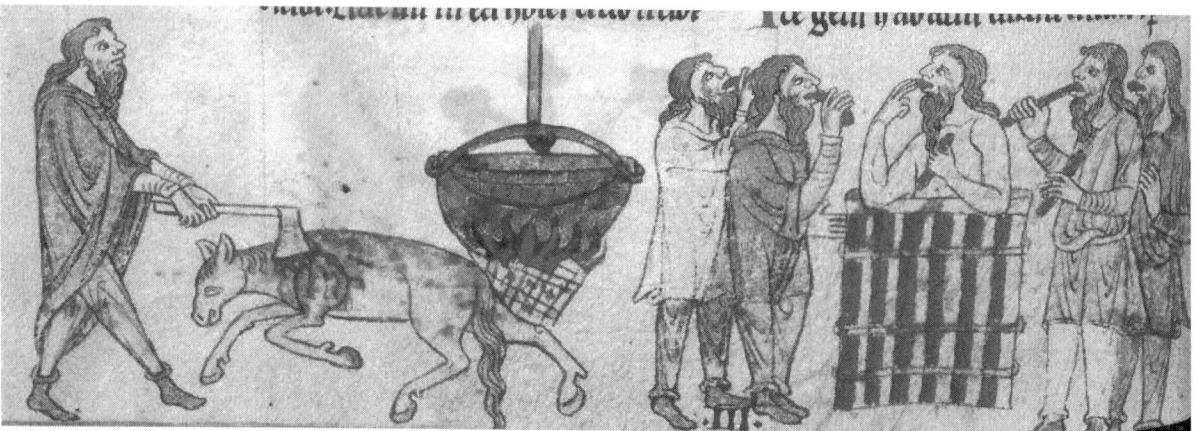

Figure 30.1. Detail of a miniature of the kingship ritual in Tirconnell of the killing of the white mare, the bath of a king in a stew of mare's meat and eating of the meat by the king's supporters.

British Library Royal 13 B VIII f. 28v (public domain image courtesy of the British Library).

butchered, and boiled. A bath is made for the king from the broth. He sits in the bath and partakes of the meat; and his immediate companions, his knights, if you like, eat also. Then, and only then, he enters into the kingship. The mare is the complement of his strength, the receptacle of his power. The act is a new Creation, a cleansing, a Eucharist, and a sacrament.

Yet can the ceremony be a survival spanning three millennia to Giraldus? I see no reason to reject the thought. Using a rough rule of thumb, the period represents about 120 generations; that is, 120 tellings, 120 rememberings. It is our ability to read that inhibits our capacity for retention.

Ireland was not troubled by the Roman Interlude in the way that Britain was, and its Iron Age progressed relatively undisturbed into the Middle Ages and is reflected in its literature.

Support for the argument for a Bronze Age survival in Ireland and, by inference, in the Legend comes from Scandinavia. At Bohuslän, in Sweden, there is Bronze Age rock art that depicts the copulation that Giraldus describes, which resolves the anomaly of the 'missing' horse in the Legend of Alderley with exuberant and explicit vigour (Plates 64 and 65).

I set out on a journey to find why my grandfather told me a story, and I have told that journey as a story. As with the farmer, it has been a long way to market. I found my answer in the land, because the land itself is a narrative, paths and waymarkers its stories. The reworking of oral tradition and the reworking of landscape go hand in hand; and the mare and the man are one.

Is it all coincidence? I think not. The story told to a child holds fragments of timelessness, embodying archaeological and spiritual truths, passed down in the memories of unlettered minds, the importance, if not the meaning and understanding, retained, faithfully, over 4,000 years. To me; and to my people.

31

Envoi

A. J. N. W. Prag

In Chapter 2 Alan Garner described an 'Approach to the Edge' that led to the top of the hill, step by step. Since then we have taken you on a perambulation of many parts of the Edge: it has been a long journey that has led down many avenues, and it has taken a long time, both in the research and in the writing up. Some avenues have opened on familiar vistas but have shown them in a new and more penetrating light; others have led in quite unexpected directions. Yet however hard we may have looked, one thing we know for sure is that there is still much more to be discovered.

During the fifteen years or so that we have been wandering round Alderley Edge and its story – a mere eye's blink in its ten millennia of human history – the Edge itself has continued to change and to develop: the long-awaited by-pass has finally been both planned and completed; many of the villas whose construction changed the face of Alderley in the nineteenth century have themselves changed out of all recognition as the people living in them and their style of living have changed. We have seen the seemingly barren and polluted waste of the Sandhills turn green again. The damage caused to the very fabric of the Edge by weather and by human feet is finally being brought under control, thanks in part to the National Trust's informed understanding of both the environmental and the archaeological issues that resulted from the Project's researches.

It has been an exciting journey, and happily it is not over yet. There is still much more to learn: as with all good research we have raised new questions as well as answering old ones. Directly or indirectly the Landscape Project produced a number of spin-offs, such as the educational and archival website (AELPHER) and the Sandhills excavations, and from the village itself the Alderley Edge History Group, and it brought some long-running research projects to their conclusion and publication – one example is Geoffrey Warrington's study of the mining history (Chapter 16) – while other aspects of the story have gone through a searching re-assessment, such as the insect life and even the legend (Chapters 13 and 30). In our account of the trees of Alderley we touched on the role that thematic distribution maps could play in future planning and management of the woodlands (Chapter 10). The National Trust's own understanding of the Edge has been deepened and there is a growing appreciation of the resources available close at hand in the University of Manchester. If the proposal by the Trust and the University to investigate further the archaeology of the landscape of Alderley has been put on hold for lack of resources, it is still there to be taken down and put into action when its time comes. If our own project provided a test-bed for investigative techniques that were new to archaeology (just as the miners of the Early Bronze Age were trying out and improving a completely new technology), so our future colleagues will be able to exploit methods about which we can only dream.

The village and its people have seen many changes over the past two centuries, many of them springing from the coming of the railway and then of the motor-car (and even, in one case, of a helicopter). Alderley is not the only village whose shops and social habits have been affected by the creation of out-of-town shopping malls and supermarkets at places like Handforth Dean. Now the cars have been led out of the village by the by-pass. Who in Alderley will benefit from this, and who suffer?

For many people an important element in Alderley's story is the legend of the old man, the king and his knights, and their white horses: a straightforward story, found in many other places in this island and further afield, its origins perhaps lost in the mists of time. For some it is no more than a good story, though one which became part of the 'romantic' landscape of the Edge in the eighteenth and nineteenth centuries; for others it is still very much alive and affects their lives – we were told by various people how they had been 'spooked' by the Edge. The dawn of the New Millennium in 2000 saw druid ceremonies and torchlight processions at Castle Rock and Stormy Point, while other somewhat anomalous groups appearing on the Edge have included men dressed as North American 'Indians' and a band of Saxon warriors.

John, the first Lord Stanley, had a deep and enduring affection for the Edge – he was, after all, in the very special position of owning and caring for much of it. We cannot doubt that it affected him in many ways, and we owe much to the notebooks in which he wrote down the stories and his thoughts and reflections. By the 1840s he had pondered on the legend for nearly half a century and it had developed a whole new significance for him: writing in his *Notebook*, he concluded that the story had grown out of a peasant reaction against priests and other corrupt Medieval practices, and that the social conditions of the time, especially in the towns, might suggest that knights were still needed to save the country (*Stanley Notebook*).

Lord Stanley is by no means the only person on whom the legend has grown in this way. To cite but one example, the members of the Derbyshire Caving Club have their own collection of tales mainly concerning exploits underground. At one time they even had their own Wizard, an aged veteran of the Club, white-haired and bearded, black-cloaked with staff, hat and magic stone – by no means the first such impersonation to walk the Edge. Stephen Mills has put many of these tales of the Edge into song, adding another element to the rich mythology of the Edge, while the map of 'The Land of the Dim Grey King' (Figure 20.10, p. 528) illustrates another take on the mysteries of the Edge.

And Alan Garner has told the version that was handed down to him by his grandfather. He too has thought long about the story, and delved into it with a historian's persistence, finding the roots of the story in prehistory; and he has also told us how the story did not die, how by the time of the Second World War the people of Alderley were looking for a king with his knights riding in white tanks. The threat of an invasion forms a strong undercurrent in the story and one commentator has noted that John Stanley collected the story in the late 1790s, when Britain was standing alone against Napoleon and invasion scares were plentiful. A story about the king rising with his knights to help England in its hour of need would have resonated, and explains why it had the same resonance with the situation in 1940. The story remains a real story, and like all good stories has many twists, depending on who is telling it, and when. And here it is the outsider's turn to tell it.

When (as we thought) our work was finished and our first book – *The Archaeology of Alderley Edge* – was about to be published in 2005, we held a 'thank you' event in the village at which the book was launched and at which contributors from our team and from the village spoke about their involvement in the Project in all its forms. As it was drawing to a close, a lady came up to me and said 'You know about the Americans, of course'. Yes, I knew about the American troops billeted in Alderley Edge during the war. 'You know that there were men from the US Air Force among them?' I did. 'Did you know the planes they flew were Mustangs?' No, I did not. That was exciting. Then I remembered something else, and the hairs on the back of my neck began to stand up. I remembered that their P-51 Mustang fighters, originally designed by the North American Aviation company for low-level reconnaissance and as fighter-bombers, were underpowered for the high-level flying which they were required to do in the European theatre, so they were fitted with a more powerful engine: the Rolls-Royce Merlin.

Appendices

Appendix 5.1

Reptilian tracks from the Hayman's Farm Borehole

John E. Pollard

In the early 1960s David Thompson discovered a remarkable assemblage of small reptilian tracks in the Wood Mine Conglomerate Member of the Helsby Sandstone Formation while he was logging a water borehole (diameter *c.* 38 cm) core at Hayman's Farm, Nether Alderley (SJ 8563 7633). This assemblage is now preserved in the Manchester Museum collections (LL 11902) (Figure 5.14). He recorded a detailed analysis of this specimen in his MSc thesis (Thompson, 1966: 185–9, plate 11), but a full description has never been published, although the discovery has been referred to by several workers on Triassic tracks (Warrington and Thompson, 1971; Demathieu and Haubold, 1972; Sarjeant, 1974; Haubold, 1984; Tresise and Sarjeant, 1997). It is highly appropriate, therefore, that this unique discovery in the Alderley Edge hinterland is documented and illustrated here.

The tracks cover a mudstone bedding plane surface within thin-bedded, fine-grained, ripple cross-laminated, red sandstones. They are preserved in positive (hypichnial) relief, representing footprints made in mud, or transmitted downwards through a thin layer of sand, naturally cast on the base of the overlying sandstone bed. More than twenty-five complete and partial tracks can be recognised in various orientations, varying in depth and quality of preserved detail (Figure 5.14). About twelve discrete footprints show a pentadactyl character of five delicate splayed digits with parallel straight sides and pointed or obliquely truncated distal ends (Figure 5.15). The length of the tracks is up to 40 mm, the width at proximal ends of the digits being 13–15 mm and at the distal ends 20–30 mm. Angles of divergence of digits I–IV are 25–50°; I–V 30–65°; I–II 10–20° (Table 5.1). Some of the digits (*c.* 2 mm wide) are slightly flexed but none is strongly curved. There is no indication of either slightly lobate impressions of phalangial pads, or interdigital

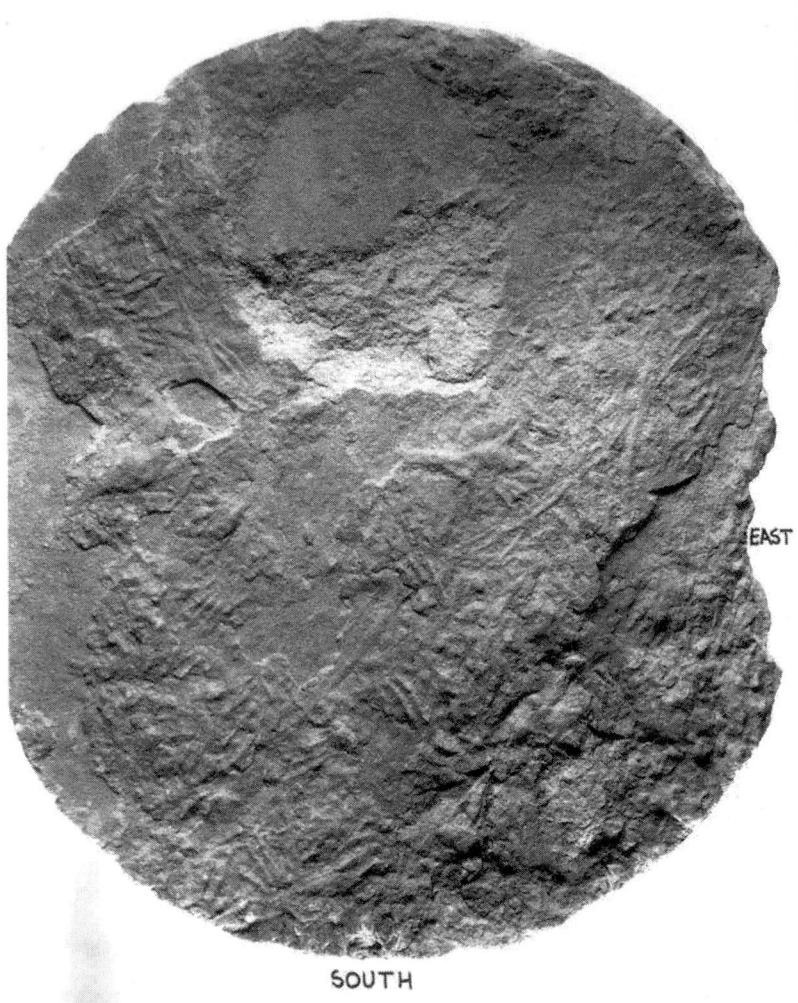

EAST

SOUTH

Figure 5.14. Footprints *Rhynchosauroides rectipes* Maidwell on lower surface of thin bed of red sandstone in a core from the Hayman's Farm Borehole, Nether Alderley (SJ 8563 7633). The core slab measures 38 cm top to bottom.

Manchester Museum LL 11902. From Thompson (1966: plate 11).

webbing. These features, however, may not be preserved on these transmitted tracks as distinct from those in true footprints.

The overall characters of the size and the morphological features of these tracks most closely approach those of the pes (hind feet) of the ichnospecies *Rhynchosauroides rectipes* Beasley and Maidwell (in Maidwell, 1914) (= *Rhynchosauroides* type D2 of Beasley, 1904: 227). The slender straight form of the digit imprints, the strong divergence, the lack of phalangial pad impressions and the common obliquely truncated distal ends distinguish this ichnospecies from *Rhynchosauroides articeps*, which could have been made by the fossil reptile *Rhynchosaurus articeps* Owen known from rocks of a similar age at Grinshill in Shropshire (Owen, 1842).

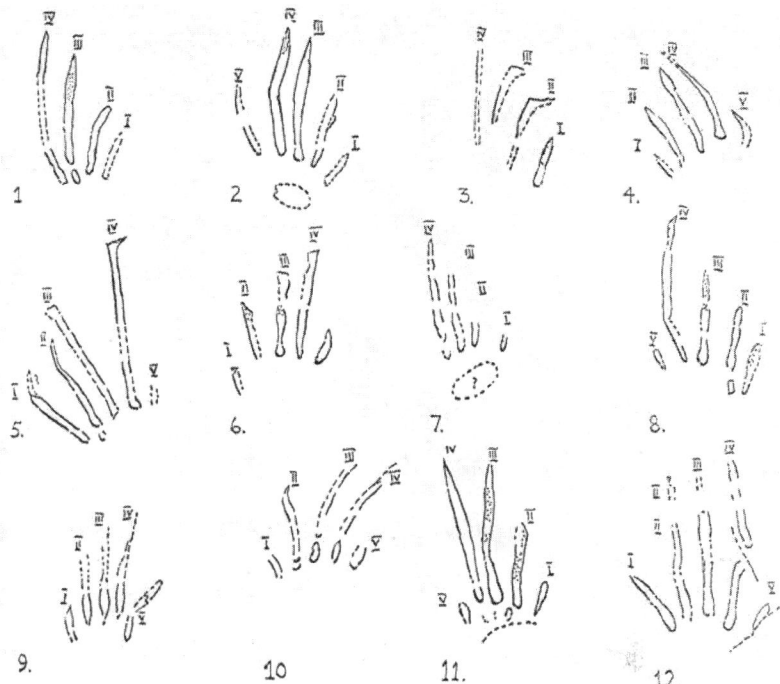

Figure 5.15. Twelve footprints *Rhynchosauroides* from the Hayman's Farm Borehole shown in Figure 5.14. For measurements and analysis see Table 5.1.

From Thompson (1966: fig. 110).

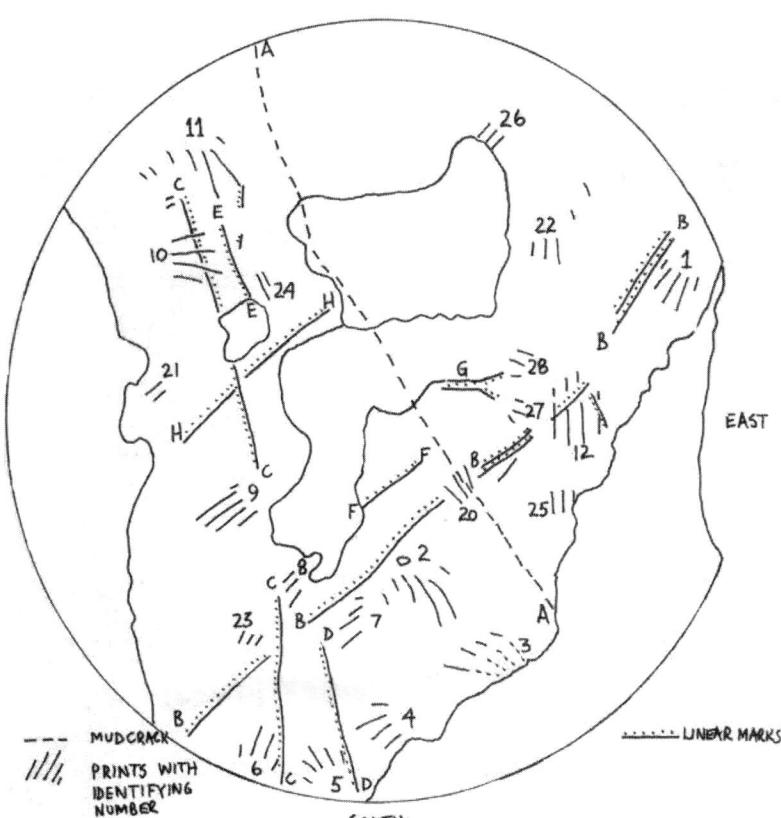

Figure 5.16. Location diagram (not to scale) for the footprints depicted in Figures 5.14 and 5.15.

From Thompson (1966: fig. 107).

Table 5.1. Measurements of the rhynchosaur footprints depicted in Figure 5.15 and comparison with ichnospecies of *Rhynchosauroides* (types D1 and D2 of Beasley, 1904)

1	2	3	4	5	6	7	8	9	10	11	12	13	14	15	16	17	18	19
Number of specimen	Digit I	Digit II	Digit III	Digit IV	Digit V	I–IV	I–V	I–II	II–IV	I–V								Diagnosis
1	?10	16	29	35	–	30°	–	<5°	0.20	–	0.80	–	11		×		×	Right pes D2
2	7	17	28	29	17	12°	65°	20°	0.22	0.50	1.07	17	14		×		×	Right pes D2
3	–	–	–	–	–	20°	–	0°	–	–	–	–	?14		×	×	×	Right pes D2
4	7	16	22	?23	8	18°	30°	12°	0.60	0.85	1.04	?21	15	×			×	Left pes or manus D2
5	18	23	30	40	?4	46°	55°	18°	0.30	0.44	1.01	?33	15	little	×		×	Left pes D2
6	6	14	19	25	8	29°	45°	10°	–	–	1.32	19	15		×		×	Left pes D2
7	?3	?5	?18	28	–	25°	–	10°	0.29	–	1.04	–	14				×	Right pes D2
8	12	21	21	34	5	23°	56°	10°	0.23	0.48	1.01	31	15		×		×	Right pes D2
9	?8	?17	?23	?25	5	22°	27°	5°	0.32	0.33	?1.12	?17	12					Probably left pes D2
10	5	18	24	27	5	59°	53°	20°	0.33	0.60	?1.26	?15	13	×			×	Left pes or manus D2
11	8	19	32	34	5	26°	40°	12°	0.28	0.44	1.06	33	13		×		×	Right pes D2
12	16	?30	?31	?38	?6	43°	63°	22°	0.31	0.51	0.92	34	14					Left pes D2
D1	6	14	21	24	6	<5°	10°	0°	0.46	0.60	0.92	26	15	×			×	Beasley type D1 (1904: 276)
D2	15	23	26	30	8	24°	43°	<5°	0.23	0.48	0.90	23	13		×			Beasley type D2 (1904: 277)
Ricketts D2	3	12	20	25	6	40°	57°		0.27	0.45	1.20	15	12.5					Dr Ricketts type D2 (Maidwell, 1914:144)
Manus D2	9	13	14	14.5	–	47°	–		0.29	–	1.38	–	10					D type manus (Maidwell, 1914: 152, plate IV fig. 1)
R. rectipes	10	13	20	24	10	29°	–		0.33	0.81	1.08	18	17.5	×			×	*R. rectipes* (Runcorn Free Library)

Columns 2–6: length of digits (mm).
Columns 7–9: angle of divergence.
Columns 10–11: width of base of digits, as a ratio to height.
Column 12: spread of digits at distal end compared with length of digit IV.
Column 13: distance distal end of digit IV to distal end of digit V.
Column 14: spread of digits at proximal ends of I–IV.
Column 15: × indicates presence of curvature of digits: typical of D1.
Column 16: × indicates presence of curvature of digits: typical of D2.
Column 17: × indicates presence of blunt termination.
Column 18: × indicates presence of sharp termination.

Thompson's analysis of the distribution of the tracks on the core slab (Figure 5.16) shows that it is very difficult to recognise paired prints of individual animals, prints of forelimbs (manus) or tail drag marks (Thompson, 1966). Rarely, tracks of paired left and right pes suggest a trackway width of about 7 cm and a stride of about 22 cm – both close to the dimensions reported by Beasley (1907) for this ichnospecies. Overall, the track assemblage appears to represent the activity of several individual animals moving in various directions, thus producing over-tracking.

These tracks are believed to have been made by the reptile *Rhynchosaurus*, which was about 0.25 m long and quadripedal, skeletons and tracks of which were known from the contemporaneous Grinshill

Sandstone of Shropshire (Owen, 1842; Benton, 1990). This fossil was once thought to be related to a 'living fossil', the Tuatara (*Sphenodon*) of New Zealand, but it is now regarded as more closely related to the stem reptiles, the archosaurs (Benton, 1990, 1997). The rhynchosaurs had crushing teeth in their lower jaws and on the roof of the mouth (palatal teeth), believed to have been used to shear tough vegetation as these small plant eaters may have fed on roots (Benton, 1990, 1997) and lived in herds on the edge of vegetated zones marginal to lakes or river channels (Demathieu, 1985).

This unique specimen, therefore, reveals interesting details of the palaeo-environmental context of small herbivorous reptiles living along margins of fluvial channels in Triassic times about 240 million years ago in the Alderley Edge area of an intraplate sedimentary desert basin (Plate 5).

Further reading

Brenchley, P. J. and Rawson P. F. (eds). 2006. *Geology of England and Wales* (2nd edition). London: Geological Society.

Tresise, G. and Sarjeant, W. A. S. 1997. *The Tracks of Triassic Vertebrates: Fossil Evidence from North-West England*. London: HMSO.

Appendix 6.1

Primary mineralisation at Alderley Edge

David I. Green

One of the aims of the Alderley Edge Landscape Project was to provide as comprehensive a record of the natural history of the area as possible. These tabulations of the mineral species go a considerable way towards this as far as the mineralogy of the ore deposits is concerned. Literature citations are given to allow the reader to judge the basis on which the identifications are made. Only the most useful references are given; no attempt has been made to cite every reference to every mineral that is reported.

The tabulation is based primarily on Braithwaite (1994) but includes more recent data from Plant *et al.* (1999), together with research carried out under the aegis of the Alderley Edge Landscape Project. Previous descriptions are examined critically, allowing mineral species that the authors feel have been listed from the area on a dubious or in some cases fraudulent basis to be discredited.

To be included in this summary, a mineral must be listed by Back and Mandarino (2008) as a valid species. Thus, varietal names such as bravoite (a nickel-rich variety of pyrite) and pisanite are not included. Limonite is assumed to be finely divided goethite (the name accepted by the IMA, the International Mineralogical Association) and native copper is described as copper (the IMA-approved name). Hydrocarbons, although known from most of the mines at Alderley Edge (e.g. Rowe and Burley, 1997), are excluded from the tables as they fall outside the strict definition of a mineral (Nickel, 1995).

Only mineral species associated with the ore deposits are tabulated. Rock-forming species such as quartz, clay minerals and feldspars which make up the clastic sedimentary rocks of Alderley Edge are excluded, as are species such as haematite, carbonates and various clays formed during the lithification of the sandstones. Information on these species can be found in Rowe and Burley (1997), Milodowski *et al.* (1999), Tindle (2008) and Warrington (2010). The minerals found in derived pebbles and in the soils are also excluded.

Abbreviations used generally throughout Tables 6.1–6.8 are as follows:

- ⋆   indicates the occurrence of a mineral
- U   indicates that the occurrence of a mineral is uncertain
- AE   the Alderley Edge area (including Mottram St Andrew)
- EV   Engine Vein (including the Opencast)
- WM   West Mine (including New Venture Level, North Mine, South Mine)
- WD   Wood Mine (excluding Brynlow levels)
- MM   Mottram Mine
- NHM   Natural History Museum
- SP   Stormy Point area (including Twin Shafts, Stormy Point, Doc Mine, Pillar Mine)

Note that 'first British occurrence' is geological terminology for first report or record of the mineral species noted, and so those in bold in the tables were first reported from those particular localities at Alderley.

Table 6.1. Minerals from the Alderley Edge and Mottram St Andrew mines; first British occurrences are indicated in bold

Mineral	AE	EV	WM	SP	WD	MM	Comment
Acanthite	★		★				Noted as argentite by Milodowski *et al.* (1999) in the West Mine Boundary Fault. Argentite, the high-temperature cubic polymorph of Ag₂S, is no longer recognised as a mineral species (e.g. Gaines *et al.*, 1997)
Anglesite	★	★	★	U	★	★	Widespread as minute inconspicuous crystals with oxidised galena (Braithwaite, 1994)
Antlerite	★	★					As greenish crusts (Braithwaite, 1994), rare
Asbolane	★	★	★	★	★	★	Common as black sooty patches and soft crusts. Figured in Sowerby (1811). Described from the Cobalt Mine by Timberlake and Mills (2003)
Aurichalcite	★				★	★	Very rare, as blue-green radiating blades with hemimorphite (Braithwaite, 1994)
Azurite	★	★	★	★	★	★	Very common, as blue encrustations and intergranular cements, and as small nodules (Tindle, 2008)
Baryte	★	★	★	★	★	★	Abundant. Cementing sandstone and as white to pinkish veins (Rowe and Burley, 1997; Milodowski *et al.*, 1999)
Beaverite	★			★			Probably common as a yellowish encrustation (Braithwaite, 1994; Lawton, 1994)
Beudantite	★		★				As yellow-brown coatings (Braithwaite, 1994)
Bornite	★	★	★	★			An alteration product of chalcopyrite produced by secondary supergene enrichment (Ixer and Vaughan, 1982)
Brochantite	★	★		★	★		Widespread but not common (Braithwaite, 1994)
Calcite	★	★					Cementing the grains in the sandstone (Rowe and Burley, 1997), commonly ferroan
Cerussite	★	★	★	★	★	★	Common as small inconspicuous crystals, most often with galena (Braithwaite, 1994)
Chalcocite	★	★	★		★		As black impregnations in sandstone (Ixer and Vaughan, 1982; Milodowski *et al.*, 1999)
Chalcopyrite	★	★	★	★	★		Widespread, commonly altering to other copper sulphides (Milodowski *et al.*, 1999)
Chrysocolla	★	★	★	★	★	★	A common component of bluish and greenish flowstone crusts (Braithwaite, 1994)
Cinnabar	★		★				A mercury sulphide (probably cinnabar) is present in the West Mine Boundary Fault (Milodowski *et al.*, 1999)
Cobaltite	★	U	★	U			As minute inclusions in quartz at West Mine (Milodowski *et al.*, 1999); also noted by Ixer and Vaughan (1982)
Connellite	U	U					Visually identified as minute, royal blue, radiating spherules (Braithwaite, 1994)
Copper	★	★			★		Uncommon; early reports refer to copper ore, not native copper (Braithwaite, 1994)
Covelline	★	★					Common as a bluish metallic coating on sulphides (Ixer and Vaughan, 1982)
Cuprite	★	★		U	★		Rare, as wine-red crystals with copper (Braithwaite, 1994)
Cyanotrichite	U	U					A possible component of a bluish gel (Braithwaite, 1994)
Dioptase	★		★				Noted without description by Milodowski *et al.* (1999)
Djurleite	★	★					The major black copper sulphide at Alderley Edge (Ixer and Vaughan, 1982). See also Thompson (1991)

Mineral	AE	EV	WM	SP	WD	MM	Comment
Duftite	★					★	As compositionally zoned black botryoidal crusts, visually similar to mottramite, and as minute green lenticular crystals (D. I. Green, unpublished data; Tindle, 2008)
Enargite	★	★					In alteration rims and as inclusions in galena (Ixer and Budd, 1998). The identification by Warrington (1965) was considered erroneous by Braithwaite (1994)
Erythrite	★	★		★	★		Widespread, but uncommon; first noted by Sowerby (1811). See also Tindle (2008)
Galena	★	★	★	★	★	★	Common, cementing sandstone and as a fault vein filling, the major ore of lead (Tindle, 2008)
Gersdorffite	★			U			As optically zoned crystals containing Ni, Co and Fe (Ixer and Vaughan, 1982)
Goethite	★	★	★	★	★	★	Blackish botryoidal at Mottram Mine. Ubiquitous as limonite (Milodowski et al., 1999)
Gold	★		★				As minute grains (Milodowski et al., 1999)
Gypsum	★	★			★		As post-mining efflorescences and coatings (Braithwaite, 1994)
Hemimorphite	★	★			★		Very rare as radiating sheaves of colourless crystals (Braithwaite, 1994)
Hydrocerussite	★		★				Noted without description by Milodowski et al. (1999)
Idaite	★	★					Chalcopyrite alters to a brown anisotropic phase chemically close to idaite (Ixer and Vaughan, 1982). See also Thompson (1991)
Jarosite	★	★					Probably widespread as a yellowish coating (Braithwaite, 1994)
Langite	★	★					Uncommon as blue pseudohexagonal crystals (Braithwaite, 1994)
Lavendulan	U			U			As microscopic blue needles, identified visually (Braithwaite, 1994)
Leadhillite	★	★					Very rare, as colourless to pale green, blocky hexagonal crystals (Braithwaite, 1994)
Linarite	★	★			★		Uncommon, but locally conspicuous, as impregnations and small blue crystals (Tindle, 2008)
Malachite	★	★	★	★	★	★	Common as a green impregnation in sandstone; a major copper ore (Tindle, 2008)
Marcasite	★	★		★			Traces with other sulphides (Ixer and Vaughan, 1982)
Melanterite	★	★					As blue-green efflorescences (Braithwaite, 1994). Noted as pisanite by Thompson (1991)
Mimetite	★	★	★			★	Common, but indistinguishable in hand specimen from pyromorphite (Braithwaite, 1994)
Minium	U	U					Rare (Thompson, 1970c), possibly formed by roasting galena and therefore perhaps artificial (Braithwaite, 1994)
Mottramite	★					★	As black botryoidal or, rarely, drusy crusts (Braithwaite, 1994)
Olivenite	★	U			★		Listed by Braithwaite (1994) but early references are questionable
Osarizawaite	★						As yellow-green crusts and impregnations in sandstone (Braithwaite, 1994)
Pararammelsbergite	★	U	★	U			As minute inclusions with other arsenides (Ixer and Vaughan, 1982; Milodowski et al., 1999)
Pharmacosiderite	★	★					Very rare, as minute orange-brown cubes (Braithwaite, 1994)
Planchéite	★	★					Specimens supposedly collected by Arthur Kingsbury at Alderley Edge were discredited by Ryback et al. (1998); however, Braithwaite (1994) notes a matrix-free spherule from Engine Vein which was not collected by Kingsbury
Plumbogummite	★					★	A powdery cream to brown encrustation on mottramite (D. I. Green, unpublished data)

Mineral	AE	EV	WM	SP	WD	MM	Comment
Posnjakite	★	★					Rare, as blue crusts: visually indistinguishable from langite (Braithwaite, 1994)
Pyrite	★	★		★	★		Widespread but uncommon (Mohr, 1964); nickel-rich (Ixer and Vaughan, 1982)
Pyromorphite	★	★	★	★	★	★	Common as colourless, yellow and green crusts and impregnations (Braithwaite, 1994)
Scorodite	U	U					Listed by Carlon (1979), but requires confirmation (Braithwaite, 1994)
Siderite	U	U					Listed as 'sparry iron ore' (Thompson, 1970c), but requires confirmation (Braithwaite, 1994)
Silver	★	★					Very rare, as minute dendrites (Braithwaite, 1994)
Smithsonite	★	★		U			Very rare (Ixer and Vaughan, 1982; Milodowski et al., 1999)
Sphalerite	★	★	★	★			Uncommon but widespread (Ixer and Vaughan, 1982)
Spionkopite	★						Alteration rims around tennantite-bearing chalcopyrite (Ixer and Stanley, 1998)
Sulphur	★	★					Widespread as small rounded crystals in galena; inconspicuous (Braithwaite, 1994)
Tetrahedrite	★	★		★			Microscopic argentian and zincian inclusions in galena (Ixer and Vaughan, 1982)
Tyrolite	★	★	★		★		Rare, as thin green blades, often with chrysocolla (Braithwaite, 1994). Sulphate-rich (Warrington, 2010)
Vanadinite	U	U				U	Listed by the Imperial Institute (1924) and subsequently noted by other authors; no specimens are known; requires confirmation (Braithwaite, 1994)
Wulfenite	★	★	★		★		Rare, but relatively widespread, in tiny yellow and orange tabular and pyramidal crystals (Braithwaite, 1994)

Table 6.2. Mineral species whose occurrence or claimed occurrence at Alderley Edge is fraudulent, or based on very poor evidence, or a misinterpretation of earlier reports. Claimed first British occurrences are given in bold

Mineral	Comment
Caledonite	Erroneously reported (Eagar and Broadhurst, 1959), discredited (Braithwaite, 1994)
Descloizite	A specimen in the Kingsbury collection (NHM) is fraudulently labelled (Ryback et al., 1998)
Heterogenite	A specimen in the Kingsbury collection (NHM) is fraudulently labelled (Ryback et al., 1998)
Libethenite	A highly questionable interpretation of early assays of bulk ore (Braithwaite, 1994)
Liroconite	Not confirmed by modern analyses, almost certainly an error (Braithwaite, 1994)
Massicot	Not confirmed by modern methods and easily confused with other minerals (Braithwaite, 1994)
Roscoelite	All published records are based on a misunderstanding of Roscoe (1876a)
Tennantite	Reports of tennantite from Alderley Edge (e.g. Ixer and Stanley, 1998; Tindle, 2008) appear to be in error: only tetrahedrite is known from the locality (Ixer and Budd, 1998)
Witherite	Recorded (Greenwood, 1919) on the basis of a trace of carbonate in a baryte-rich stratum

Table 6.3. Chemical formulae and parageneses of minerals from Alderley Edge and Mottram St Andrew. For further information on the parageneses of the major species consult Rowe and Burley (1997) or Plant, Ball *et al.* (1999) and references therein

Mineral	Formula	Paragenesis
Acanthite	Ag_2S	Primary
Anglesite	$PbSO_4$	Secondary
Antlerite	$Cu_3(SO_4)(OH)_4$	Post-mining
Asbolane	$(Co,Ni)_{1-y}(MnO_2)_{2-x}(OH)_{2-2y+2x}.nH_2O$	Secondary
Aurichalcite	$(Zn,Cu)_5(CO_3)_2(OH)_6$	Secondary
Azurite	$Cu_3(CO_3)_2(OH)_2$	Secondary and post-mining
Baryte	$BaSO_4$	Primary, minor secondary
Beaverite	$Pb(Cu,Fe,Al)_3(SO_4)_2(OH)_6$	Secondary
Beudantite	$PbFe_3([(As,S)O_4)]_2(OH,H_2O)_6$	Secondary
Bornite	Cu_5FeS_4	Primary?
Brochantite	$Cu_4(SO_4)(OH)_6$	Secondary
Calcite	$CaCO_3$	Primary
Cerussite	$PbCO_3$	Secondary
Chalcocite	Cu_2S	Primary
Chalcopyrite	$CuFeS_2$	Primary
Chrysocolla	$(Cu,Al)_2H_2Si_2O_5(OH)_4.nH_2O$	Secondary and post-mining
Cinnabar	HgS	Secondary
Cobaltite	$CoAsS$	Primary
Connellite	$Cu_{19}Cl_4(SO_4)(OH)_{32}.3H_2O$	Secondary
Copper	Cu	Secondary
Covelline	CuS	Secondary and post-mining
Cuprite	Cu_2O	Secondary
Cyanotrichite	$Cu_4Al_2(SO_4)(OH)$	Secondary
Dioptase	$Cu_6Si_6O_{18}.6H_2O$	Secondary
Djurleite	$Cu_{31}S_{16}$	Primary
Duftite	$PbCu(AsO_4)(OH)$	Secondary
Enargite	Cu_3AsS_4	Primary
Erythrite	$Co_3(AsO_4)_2.8H_2O$	Secondary
Galena	PbS	Primary
Gersdorffite	$NiAsS$	Primary
Goethite	$FeO(OH)$	Secondary
Gold	Au	Primary
Gypsum	$CaSO_4.2H_2O$	Post-mining
Hemimorphite	$Zn_4Si_2O_7(OH)_2.H_2O$	Secondary
Hydrocerussite	$Pb_3(CO_3)_2(OH)_2$	Secondary
Idaite	Cu_3FeS_4	Primary
Jarosite	$KFe_3(SO_4)_2(OH)_6$	Secondary and post-mining
Langite	$Cu_4(SO_4)(OH)_6.2H_2O$	Post-mining
Lavendulan	$NaCaCu_5(AsO_4)_4Cl.5H_2O$	Secondary
Leadhillite	$Pb_4(SO_4)(CO_3)_2(OH)_2$	Secondary
Linarite	$PbCu(SO_4)(OH)_2$	Secondary
Malachite	$Cu_2(CO_3)(OH)_2$	Secondary

Mineral	Formula	Paragenesis
Marcasite	FeS_2	Primary
Melanterite	$FeSO_4.7H_2O$	Post-mining
Mimetite	$Pb_5(AsO_4)_3Cl$	Secondary
Minium	Pb_3O_4	Secondary or post-mining?
Mottramite	$PbCu(VO_4)(OH)$	Secondary
Olivenite	$Cu_2(AsO_4)(OH)$	Secondary
Osarizawaite	$PbCuAl_2(SO_4)_2(OH)_6$	Secondary
Pararammelsbergite	$NiAs_2$	Primary
Pharmacosiderite	$KFe_4(AsO_4)_3(OH)_4.6-7H_2O$	Secondary
Planchéite	$Cu_8(Si_4O_{11})_2(OH)_4.H_2O$	Secondary
Plumbogummite	$PbAl_3(PO_4)_2(OH)_5.H_2O$	Secondary
Posnjakite	$Cu_4(SO_4)(OH)_6.H_2O$	Post-mining
Pyrite	FeS_2	Primary
Pyromorphite	$Pb_5(PO_4)_3Cl$	Secondary
Scorodite	$FeAsO_4.2H_2O$	Secondary
Siderite	$FeCO_3$	Primary
Silver	Ag	Secondary
Smithsonite	$ZnCO_3$	Secondary
Sphalerite	ZnS	Primary
Spionkopite	$Cu_{39}S_{28}$	Primary
Sulphur	S	Secondary
Tetrahedrite	$(Cu,Fe)_{12}Sb_4S_{13}$	Primary
Tyrolite	$CaCu_5(AsO_4)_2(SO_4,CO_3)(OH)_4.6H_2O$	Secondary
Vanadinite	$Pb_5(VO_4)_3Cl$	Secondary
Wulfenite	$PbMoO_4$	Secondary

Table 6.4. Minerals known to occur at Engine Vein Mine, with descriptions and literature references as appropriate. The identification methods are noted using the abbreviations: XRD, X-ray diffraction; IR, infra-red absorption spectroscopy

Mineral	Identification	Comment
Anglesite		Colourless elongated blades (Braithwaite, 1994; Eagar and Broadhurst, 1959)
Antlerite	XRD, IR	A greenish crust with posnjakite and langite (Braithwaite, 1994)
Asbolane		Black sooty patches (Braithwaite, 1994)
Azurite		As small crystals and blue nodules up to 10 mm (Braithwaite, 1994; Dewey and Eastwood, 1925)
Baryte		Common (Braithwaite, 1994)
Bornite		Widespread (Warrington, 1965; Thompson, 1970c; Braithwaite, 1994)
Brochantite	IR	As green crusts and crystals up to 0.2 mm (Braithwaite, 1994)
Calcite		Noted by Dewey and Eastwood (1925) and Braithwaite (1994)
Cerussite		Noted by Eagar and Broadhurst (1959). As tabular, prismatic and rod-like crystals (Braithwaite, 1994)
Chalcocite		Noted by Thompson (1991)
Chalcopyrite		Noted by Thompson (1991)
Chrysocolla	IR	In azurite-rich nodules (Dewey and Eastwood, 1925). As green (to bluish) crusts (Braithwaite, 1994)
Copper		In arborescent clusters to 3 mm (Braithwaite, 1994)
Covelline	XRD	As blue films on galena (Braithwaite, 1994)
Cuprite		As octahedral crystals to 0.5 mm with native copper (Braithwaite, 1994)
Djurleite		Noted by Thompson (1991)
Enargite		Noted by Ixer and Budd (1998)
Erythrite		Tiny pink radiating spherules (Warrington, 1965; Thompson, 1970c; Braithwaite, 1994)
Galena		Common (Eagar and Broadhurst, 1959; Braithwaite, 1994)
Goethite		Common
Gypsum	IR	As post-mining efflorescences (Mohr, 1964; Braithwaite, 1994)
Hemimorphite	IR	Tiny colourless radiating blades (Braithwaite, 1994)
Idaite		Noted by Thompson (1991)
Jarosite	IR	As a yellow brown powder (Braithwaite, 1994)
Langite	XRD, IR	As blue pseudohexagonal crystals to 3 mm (Braithwaite, 1994)
Leadhillite	IR	Colourless to pale green pearly pseudohexagonal crystals (Braithwaite, 1994)
Linarite		See Eagar and Broadhurst (1959). As blue blades up to 0.5 mm (Braithwaite, 1994)
Malachite		Common (Eagar and Broadhurst, 1959; Braithwaite, 1994)
Marcasite		Rare, with other sulphides (Ixer and Vaughan, 1982)
Melanterite		As blue-green efflorescences of post-mining origin (Eagar and Broadhurst, 1959)
Mimetite	IR	Phosphatian mimetite with a phosphorus:arsenic ratio of 1:3 (Braithwaite, 1994)
Minium		Very rare, bright red powdery in galena (Thompson, 1970c; Braithwaite, 1994) but possibly artificial
Pharmacosiderite	XRD	As orange-brown cubes up to 0.2 mm (Braithwaite, 1994)
Planchéite		A single matrix free spherule is probably genuine (Braithwaite, 1994)
Posnjakite	XRD	As thin blue crusts (Braithwaite, 1994)

Mineral	Identification	Comment
Pyrite		See Warrington (1965); some as the nickel-rich variety bravoite (Ixer and Vaughan, 1982)
Pyromorphite	IR	Small colourless, yellow and green crystals
Scorodite		Listed by Carlon (1979), but requires confirmation (Braithwaite, 1994)
Silver		As minute dendritic aggregates (Braithwaite, 1994)
Smithsonite		Noted by Thompson (1991)
Sphalerite		Uncommon (Dewey and Eastwood, 1925)
Sulphur		As small rounded crystals in galena (Braithwaite, 1994)
Tetrahedrite		Intergrown with galena (Ixer and Vaughan, 1982)
Tyrolite	XRD	As green masses of lath-like crystals (D. I. Green, unpublished data)
Wulfenite	XRD	As tiny yellow tabular crystals (Braithwaite, 1994)

Table 6.5. Mineral species known to occur at West Mine, with descriptions and literature references as appropriate. The identification methods are noted using the abbreviation BSEM (back-scattered electron microscopy)

Mineral	Identification	Comment
Acanthite		Noted by Milodowski et al. (1999) in the West Mine Boundary Fault, but described as argentite
Anglesite		Small blocky crystals with galena (D. I. Green, unpublished data)
Asbolane		Black sooty patches (Braithwaite, 1994)
Azurite		As blue impregnations in sandstone (Braithwaite, 1994)
Baryte		As opaque pinkish vein fillings, slickensided (Braithwaite, 1994)
Bornite		Noted by Thompson (1991)
Cerussite		An alteration product of galena (Eagar and Broadhurst, 1959; Braithwaite, 1994)
Chalcocite		Black impregnations in sandstone
Chalcopyrite		As patches in limonitic sandstone (Braithwaite, 1994)
Chrysocolla	BSEM	As green impregnations and crusts (Braithwaite, 1994; Milodowski et al., 1999)
Cinnabar		A mercury sulphide (probably cinnabar) is present in the West Mine Boundary Fault (Milodowski et al., 1999)
Cobaltite	BSEM	Noted by Milodowski et al. (1999)
Dioptase		Recorded without description from the West Mine Boundary Fault (Milodowski et al., 1999)
Galena		As impregnations in sandstone (Eagar and Broadhurst, 1959; Braithwaite, 1994)
Goethite		Noted by Milodowski et al. (1999)
Gold		As microscopic grains (Milodowski et al., 1999)
Hydrocerussite		Noted without description from the Chain Shaft Fault (Milodowski et al., 1999)
Malachite		As green crusts and impregnations (Eagar and Broadhurst, 1959; Braithwaite, 1994)
Mimetite	BSEM	Noted by Milodowski et al. (1999)
Pararammelsbergite		Noted by Milodowski et al. (1999)
Pyromorphite		Noted by Milodowski et al. (1999)
Sphalerite		Noted by Milodowski et al. (1999)
Tyrolite		One small specimen (Braithwaite, 1994)
Wulfenite		Tiny orange yellow tabular to prismatic crystals (Braithwaite, 1994)

Table 6.6. Mineral species known to occur at Wood Mine, with descriptions and literature references as appropriate. The identification methods are noted using the abbreviations XRD (X-ray diffraction), Chem (chemical methods), Mic (reflected light microscopy), IR (infra-red absorption spectroscopy)

Mineral	Identification	Comment
Anglesite		As tiny colourless blades with wulfenite (Braithwaite, 1994)
Asbolane		Black sooty patches (Braithwaite, 1994)
Aurichalcite	Chem	Pearly blue-green radiating blades with hemimorphite (Braithwaite, 1994)
Azurite		As small blue crystals and impregnations (Braithwaite, 1994)
Baryte		Opaque, pink (Warrington, 1965; Braithwaite, 1994)
Beaverite	XRD	As a powdery yellow mineral in sandstone (Lawton, 1994)
Brochantite		Minute crystals with wulfenite (Braithwaite, 1994)
Cerussite		Impregnations in sandstone and as small crystals (Mohr, 1964; Braithwaite, 1994)
Chalcocite	Mic	As grey patches (Braithwaite, 1994)
Chalcopyrite	Mic	Small scattered masses (Ixer and Vaughan, 1982; Braithwaite, 1994)
Chrysocolla	IR	As impregnations and green to blue rippled crusts (Warrington, 1965; Braithwaite, 1994)
Copper		Noted by Thompson (1991)
Cuprite		Noted by Thompson (1991)
Erythrite		Tiny pink radiating spherules (Braithwaite, 1994)
Galena		In faults and disseminations in the sandstone (Mohr, 1964; Braithwaite, 1994)
Goethite		Noted by Thompson (1991)
Gypsum		As post-mining efflorescences (Carlon, 1979)
Hemimorphite		Colourless sheaves with aurichalcite (Braithwaite, 1994)
Linarite		As minute royal-blue blades (Thompson, 1970c; Braithwaite, 1994)
Malachite		Common in green impregnations (Warrington, 1965; Braithwaite, 1994)
Olivenite		Very rare, with tyrolite (Thompson, 1970c; Braithwaite, 1994)
Pyrite	Mic	Noted by Ixer and Vaughan (1982), also as the nickel-rich variety bravoite
Pyromorphite	IR	Pale yellow crystals with wulfenite (Braithwaite, 1994)
Tyrolite	XRD	Sulphate-rich (possibly clinotyrolite), with chrysocolla, as fan-shaped aggregates (Braithwaite, 1994)
Wulfenite		Tiny bipyramidal orange-yellow crystals (Braithwaite, 1994)

Table 6.7. Mineral species known to occur at Mottram Mine, with descriptions and literature references as appropriate. The identification methods are noted using the abbreviations XRD (X-ray diffraction), IR (infra-red absorption spectroscopy), EDX (energy dispersive X-ray analysis)

Mineral	Identification	Comment
Anglesite		Noted by Thompson (1991)
Asbolane	EDX	Powdery to botryoidal, recorded as cobalt ore (Hull, 1864) and as asbolite (Warrington, 1965)
Aurichalcite		Noted by Thompson (1991)
Azurite		Recorded by (Braithwaite (1994) and Hull (1864)
Baryte		Noted by Carlon (1979)
Cerussite		Noted by Hull (1864)
Chrysocolla		In flowstone crusts (D. I. Green, unpublished data)
Duftite	XRD	As compositionally zoned black botryoidal crusts, visually similar to mottramite and as minute green lenticular crystals (Tindle, 2008). There are two distinct structural types, which have been labelled duftite-alpha and duftite-beta (D. I. Green, unpublished data); both occur at Mottram Mine
Galena		Recorded by Carlon (1979)
Goethite	XRD	As black botryoidal crusts with overgrowing duftite (D. I. Green, unpublished data)
Malachite		Hull (1864) noted green carbonate of copper (Warrington, 1965; Braithwaite, 1994)
Mimetite	IR	Calcium-rich pyromorphite forms shells around phosphatian calcium-rich mimetite (Braithwaite, 1994)
Mottramite	XRD, IR	Considered to be the type locality (Roscoe, 1876a); later workers suggested Pim Hill (Braithwaite, 1994)
Plumbogummite	XRD	As a brownish encrustation on mottramite-duftite (D. I. Green, unpublished data)
Pyromorphite	IR	Recorded by Warrington (1965). Calcium-rich pyromorphite forms shells around mimetite (Braithwaite, 1994)

Table 6.8. Mineral species known to occur in the Stormy Point area, with descriptions and literature references as appropriate. The identification methods are noted using the abbreviations XRD (X-ray diffraction), Mic (reflected light microscopy)

Mineral	Identification	Description
Anglesite		Possibly present (Ixer and Vaughan, 1982)
Asbolane		As black sooty patches (Braithwaite, 1994)
Azurite		Small crystals from Doc Mine (Eagar and Broadhurst, 1959)
Baryte		Common as pinkish vein fillings (Braithwaite, 1994)
Beudantite	XRD	A pale yellow to brownish coating on sandstone (Braithwaite, 1994)
Bornite		Noted without description by Warrington (1965) and Braithwaite (1994)
Brochantite		Bright green crystals from Doc Mine (Braithwaite, 1994)
Cerussite		Recorded by Mohr (1964)
Chalcopyrite		Noted by Warrington (1965)
Chrysocolla		As blue to green crusts and impregnations (Warrington, 1965; Braithwaite, 1994)
Cuprite		Possibly present (Thompson, 1991)
Erythrite		As tiny pink spherules (Warrington, 1965; Braithwaite, 1994)
Galena		Impregnating sandstone (Warrington, 1965)
Goethite		Noted by Thompson (1991)
Malachite		As impregnations (Warrington, 1965; Braithwaite, 1994)
Marcasite	Mic	Traces (Ixer and Vaughan, 1982)
Pyrite		Noted by Warrington (1965)
Pyromorphite		Noted by Warrington (1965). Virtually arsenate-free from Doc Mine (Braithwaite, 1994)
Smithsonite		Possibly present (Ixer and Vaughan, 1982)
Sphalerite	Mic	Intergrown with galena (Ixer and Vaughan, 1982)
Tetrahedrite		Noted by Thompson (1991)

Appendix 9.1

Inventory of vegetation recorded on the Edge

Sean R. Edwards

The Alderley Edge Landscape Project incorporated a survey of the vegetation. The results have been summarised in a series of tables that, in their full detailed form, do not lend themselves to presentation in print. They have therefore been made available in their original Excel database form on the publisher's website:

Table 9.1   Vascular plant survey, 1997–2003
Table 9.2a   Survey of brambles in the core area, 1997–98
Table 9.2b   Survey of brambles in the hinterland area
Table 9.3   Alga, liverwort and moss survey, 1997–2003
Table 9.4   Fungus survey, to summer 1998
Table 9.5   Lichen and lichenicolous fungus survey, 1997–2003

These may be downloaded from http://www.manchesteruniversitypress.co.uk/ThestoryofAlderlyAdditionalResources.

With the exception of Table 9.2b, they are all similar in format. As described in Chapter 9, the Project area was divided into a series of parcels, numbered from 1 to 30, but some with subdivisions. These tables list all the species recorded in each parcel; that is, the first column lists all the species, and then the next series of columns records their presence or absence in each of the parcels. The last four columns give:

- Parcels/sp.;
- DAFOR;
- % DAFOR flag;
- Comments.

The final rows provide some summary information:

- Species counts (total number);
- Parcel (total number 55);
- Survey levels of parcels;
- Survey level assessment of parcels (0 = no records; 1 = incidental records; 2 = passing through; 3 = casual survey; 4 = moderate survey; 5 = intensive survey).

The screen shot of Table 9.1 on the following page (Figure 9.9) shows the format of the presentation of the information available to the interested reader. A full list of the species recorded is given in the following section ('Inventory of plants, slime-moulds and fungi', p. 803).

Table 9.2a is rather different. It simply gives a listing of where and when *Rubus* was found, in the format shown in the following brief extract:

Date	Zone	Location	Comment
12/7/1998	Hinterland	Mottram St. Andrews	
11/7/1998	Hinterland	Nether Alderley	
12/6/1993	Hinterland	Over Alderley	
1993	Hinterland	Over Alderley	
12/07/1998	Hinterland	Mottram St. Andrews	
07/08/1998	Hinterland	A34, Mathew's Nursery (opposite)	Specimen at Manchester Museum
		Monks Heath	Specimen at Manchester Museum
12/07/1998	Hinterland	Mottram St. Andrews	
6/1993	Hinterland	Slade Lane, Over Alderley	Specimens at Bolton Museum
2/8/1998	Hinterland	Over Alderley	
6/93	Hinterland	Slade Lane, Over Alderley	Specimens at Bolton Museum, images held by DP Earl

The full table presents over 170 such records.

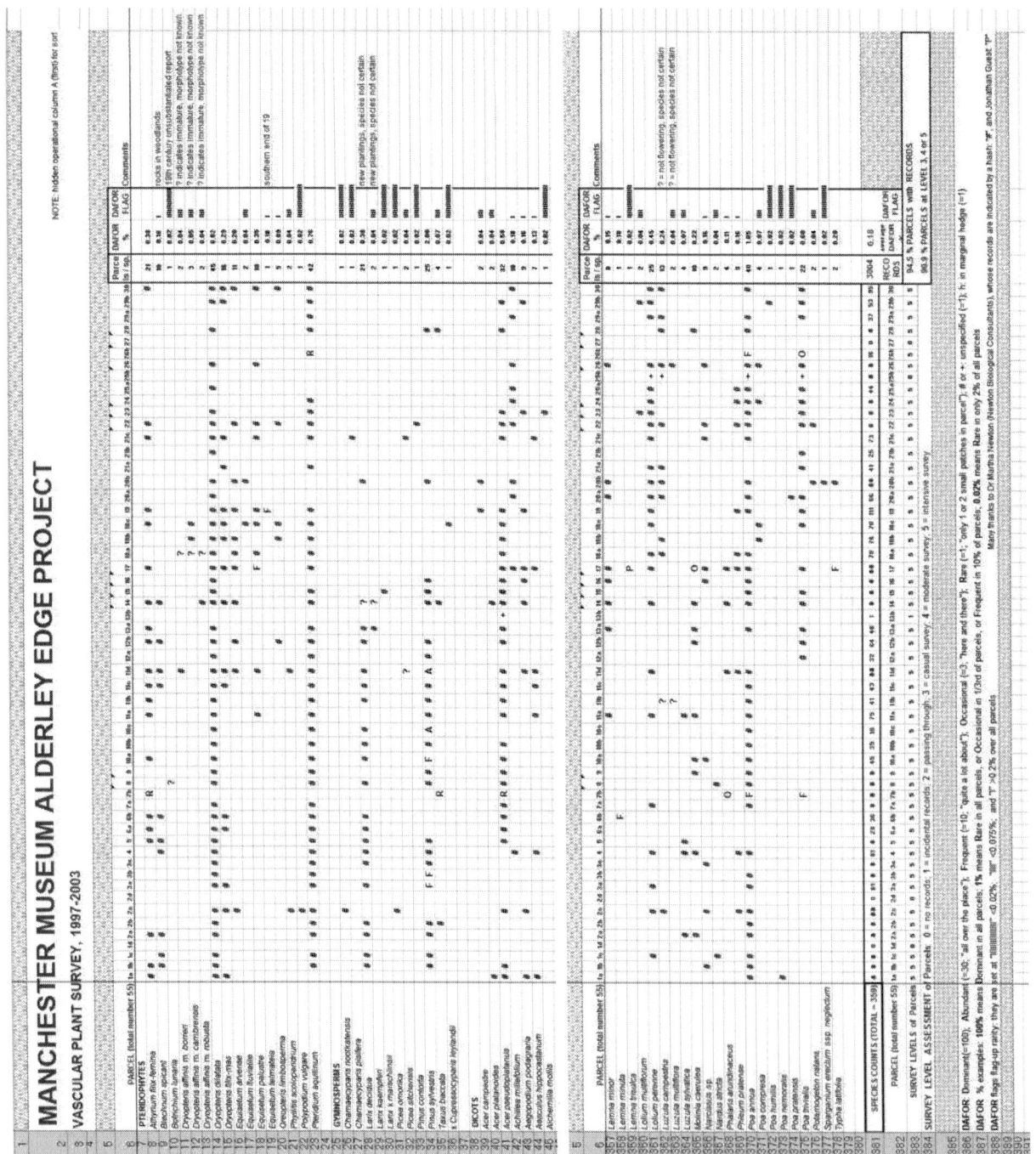

Figure 9.9. Screen shot of Table 9.1.

Inventory of plants, slime-moulds and fungi recorded on the Edge by the Alderley Edge Landscape Project, by Sean Edwards

This checklist is intended as a guide to the spreadsheets set out in Tables 9.1–9.5. Species noted by Dr Des Callaghan in his 2015 survey are marked with an asterisk (Callaghan, D. A. 2015. *Bryophyte Survey and Assessment of Alderley Edge, Cheshire.* Unpublished report to Natural England).

FUNGI: Agaricales
Agaricus vaporarius
Amanita citrina
Amanita citrina var. *alba*
Amanita muscaria
Amanita pantherina
Amanita rubescens
Amanitopsis fulva
Armillarea mellea agg. *rhizomorphs*
Armillaria mellea agg.
Armillaria mellia s. str.
Armillaria ostoyae
Baeospora myosura
Bolbitius vitellinus
Calocybe carnea
Calocybe gambosa
Cantherellula umbonata
Clitocybe cerussata
Clitocybe dealbata
Clitocybe dicolor
Clitocybe flaccida cf.
Clitocybe langei
Clitocybe nebularis
Clitocybe odora
Clitocybe phyllophyla
Clitocybe rivulosa
Clitocybe vibecina cf.
Collybia butyracea
Collybia confluens
Collybia dryophila
Collybia maculata
Collybia peronata
Conocybe pseudopilosella
Conocybe pubescens
Conocybe tenera
Coprinus (ozonium stage only)
Coprinus atramentarius
Coprinus comatus
Coprinus lagopides
Coprinus lagopus
Coprinus micaceus
Coprinus plicatilis
Cortinarius anomalus
Cortinarius elatior
Cortinarius grandicolor
Cortinarius hemitrichus
Cortinarius paleaceus
Cortinarius pseudosalor
Cystoderma amianthinum
Entoloma lucidum
Entoloma porphyraceum

Flammulina velutipes
Galerina hypnorum cf.
Galerina pumila
Galerina vittaeformis
Gymnopilus hybridus
Gymnopilus junonius (= *Gymnopilus spectabilis*)
Gymnopilus penetrans
Hebeloma crustuliniforme
Hebeloma mesophaeum
Hebeloma sacchariolens
Hebeloma strophosum
Hygrocybe conica
Hygrocybe nigrescens
Hygrocybe nivea
Hygrocybe psittacina
Hypholoma capnoides
Hypholoma elongatum
Hypholoma fasciculare
Hypholoma marginatum
Hypholoma myosotis
Hypholoma sublateritum
Inocybe flocculosa
Inocybe lacera
Inocybe lanuginella
Inocybe napipes
Inocybe umbrina
Kuehneromyces mutabilis
Laccaria amethystina
Laccaria laccata
Laccaria proxima
Laccaria tortilis
Lacrymaria velutina
Lepiota cristata
Lepiota sistrata
Lepista nuda
Leptonia lampropus
Leptonia poliopus
Leptonia poliopus var. *parvisporigerum*
Leptonia serrulata
Lyophyllum connatum
Lyophyllum decastes
Marasmius androsaceus
Marasmius oreades
Marasmius rotula
Melanoleuca grammopodia
Melanoleuca melaleuca
Melanotus horizontalis
Mycena alcalina
Mycena epipterygia
Mycena epipterygioides

Mycena filopes
Mycena galericulata
Mycena galopus
Mycena galopus var. *candida*
Mycena haematopus
Mycena inclinata
Mycena leptocephala
Mycena leucogala
Mycena maculata
Mycena metata
Mycena oortiana
Mycena polygramma
Mycena pura
Mycena sanguinolenta
Mycena tintinnabulum
Mycena uracea
Naucoria sumptuosa
Nolanea conferenda
Nolanea hirtipes
Nolanea sericea
Omphalina ericetorum
Oudmansiella radicata
Panaeolus rickenii
Panaeolus semiovatus
Panaeolus sphinctrinus
Panellus mitis
Panellus stipticus
Pholiota adiposa
Pholiota gummosa
Pholiota highlandensis
Pholiota squarrosa
Pluteus cervinus
Postia fragilis
Psathyrella artemisiae
Psathyrella candolleana
Psathyrella gracilis
Psathyrella hydrophylla
Psathyrella microrrhiza
Psathyrella pennata
Psathyrella sarcocephala
Psathyrella spadiceogrisea
Psilocybe semilanceata
Resupinatus applicatus
Rickenella fibula
Rickenella swartzii
Strobilurus stephanocystis
Stropharia aeruginosa
Stropharia semiglobata
Tephrocybe palustris
Tephrocybe tylicolor
Tricholoma fulva

Tricholoma terreum
Tricholoma virgatum
Tricholomopsis platyphylla
Tricholomopsis rutilans
Tubaria conspersa
Tubaria furfuracea
Tubaria pallidospora

FUNGI: Aphyllophorales
Athelia arachnoidea
Bjerkandera adusta
Cantharellus cibarius
Chondrostereum purpureum
Clavulina cristata
Clavulinopsis helvola
Coniophora puteana
Coriolus (= Trametes) versicolor
Crepidotus mollis
Crepidotus variabilis
Cylindrobasidium evolvens
Daedalea quercina
Daedaleopsis confragosa
Datronia mollis
Fibuloporia vaillantii
Fistulina hepatica
Ganoderma adspersum
Ganoderma applanatum
Gloeocystidiellum porosum
Grifola frondosa
Haemotostereum sanguinolentum
Heterobasidion annosum
Heteroporus biennis
Hyphoderma puberum
Inonotus hispidis
Inonotus radiatus
Laetiporus sulphureus
Lentinellus cochleatus
Lenzites betulina
Macrotyphula filiformis
Macrotyphula fistulosus
Meripilus giganteus
Merulius tremellosus
Oxyporus populinus
Peniophora quercina
Phlebia radiata (= Phlebia merismoides)
Piptoporus betulinus
Pleurotus ostreatus
Polyporus brumalis
Polyporus sulphureus
Postia caesia
Postia fragilis
Postia leucomellula
Pseudotrametes gibbosa
Radulomyces confluens
Schizopora paradoxa
Serpula himantioides
Stereum gausapatum
Stereum hirsutum
Stereum rugosum
Stereum sanguinolentum
Thelephora terrestris
Trichaptum abietinum
Tyromyces gloeocystidiatus
Vuilleminia comedens

FUNGI: Boletales
Boletus edulis
Boletus erythropus

Boletus luridus
Boletus rubellus
Hygrophoropsis aurantiaca
Leccinum holpopus
Leccinum scabrum
Leccinum variicolor
Paxillus involutus
Suillus grevillei
Tylopilus felleus
Xerocomus badius
Xerocomus chrysenteron
Xerocomus parasiticus
Xerocomus pruinatus
Xerocum subtomentosus

FUNGI: Dacrymycetales
Calocera cornea
Calocera pallidospathulata
Calocera viscosa
Dacrymyces stillatus
Exidia glandulosa
Hirneola auricula-judae

FUNGI: Diaporthales
Pseudovalsa lanciformis

FUNGI: Lycoperdales
Bovista plumbea
Handkea excipuliformis
Lycoperdon echinatum
Lycoperdon ericetorum
Lycoperdon foetidum
Lycoperdon nigrescens
Lycoperdon perlatum
Lycoperdon pyriforme
Vascellum pratense

FUNGI: Phallales
Phallus impudicus

FUNGI: Russulales
Lactarius blennius
Lactarius glyciosmus
Lactarius hepaticus
Lactarius quietus
Lactarius rufus
Lactarius subdulcis
Lactarius tabidus
Lactarius torminosus
Lactarius turpis
Lactarius vietus
Russula atropurpurea
Russula betularum
Russula brunneoviolacea
Russula claroflava
Russula cyanoxantha
Russula cyanoxantha var. *peltereaui*
Russula farinipes
Russula fellea
Russula foetens
Russula fragilis
Russula heterophylla
Russula knauthii
Russula krombholzii
Russula mairei
Russula nigricans
Russula nitida
Russula ochroleuca

Russula parazurea
Russula puellaris
Russula versicolor
Russula xerampelina

FUNGI: Sclerodermatales
Scleroderma citrinum
Scleroderma verrucosum
Sphaerobolus stellatus

FUNGI: Tremellales
Myxarium nucleatum
Tremella foliacea
Tremella mesenterica

FUNGI: Uredinales
Melampsoridium betulinum
Melampsoridium capraearum
Phragmidium violaceum
Puccinea lagenophorae
Puccinia poarum
Uromyces viciae-fabae

FUNGI: Ustilaginales
Urocystis ranunculi

FUNGI: Clavicipitales
Apocrea chrysosperma
Claviceps purpurea
Cordyceps militaris

FUNGI: Diatrypales
Diatrype disciformis
Diatrype stigma
Diatrypella favacea
Diatrypella quercina
Eutypa acharii
Eutypa spinosa
Eutypella acericola
Quaternaria quaternata (= Libertella faginea)

FUNGI: Dothidiales
Rhopographus filicinus

FUNGI: Elaphomycetales
Elaphomyces muricatus

FUNGI: Erysyphales
Erisyphe trifolii
Erysiphe heraclei
Erysiphe ranunculi
Microsphaera alphitoides
Podosphaera clandestina
Sphaerotheca fusca
Uncinula bicornis

FUNGI: Helotiales
Ascocoryne cylichnium
Ascocoryne sarcoides
Bulgaria inquinans
Calloria neglecta
Catinella olivacea
Ciboria americana
Ciboria batschiana
Cudoniella acicularis
Cudoniella clavus
Dasyscyphus apalus

Dasyscyphus virgineus
Diplocarpon rosae
Hymenoscyphus laetus
Lachnellula occidentalis
Leota lubrica
Mollisia cinerea
Orbilia xanthostigma
Phacidiostroma multivalve
Trochila ilicina

FUNGI: Hypocreales
Hypocrea pulvinata
Hypocrea rufa
Nectria cinnabarina
Nectria coccinea
Nectria episphaeria
Nectria myxomyceticola

FUNGI: Pezizales
Aleuria aurantia
Anthrocobia melaloma
Helvella crispa
Helvella lacunosa
Peziza badia
Peziza badioconfusa
Peziza petersii
Peziza praetervisa
Peziza repanda
Rhizina undulata
Scutellinia scutellata

FUNGI: Polystigmatales
Phyllachora junci

FUNGI: Rhytismatales
Rhytisma acerinum

FUNGI: Sphaeriales
Daldinia concentrica
Hypoxylon fragiforme
Hypoxylon multiforme
Rosellinia aquila
Ustulina deusta
Xylaria carpophila
Xylaria hypoxylon
Xylaria polymorpha

FUNGI: Taphrinales
Taphrina athyrii
Taphrina betulina
Taphrina populina

FUNGI: Sclerotiales
Poculum firmum

FUNGI: Zygomycetes
Spinellus fusiger

FUNGI: Hyphomycetes
Blistrum ovalisporum
Calcarispoum arbuscula
Gliocladium roseum
Libertella faginea
Monodictys lepraria
Trichoderma viride

SLIME-MOULDS: Ceratiomyxales
Ceratomyxia fruticulosa

SLIME-MOULDS: Lyciales
Cribraria rufa
Dictydiaethalium plumbeum
Enteridium lycoperdon
Lycogala epidendrum
Lycogala terrestre
Reticularia lobata
Tubifera ferruginea

SLIME-MOULDS: Physarales
Badhamia panicea
Badhamia utricularis
Didymium difforme
Didymium melanosporum
Fuligo septica
Leocarpus fragilis
Physarum cinereum
Physarum compressum
Physarum nutans
Physarum viride var. *incanum*

SLIME-MOULDS: Stemonitales
Comatrichia nigra
Comatrichia pulchella
Comatrichia typhodes
Stemonitis axifera
Stemonitis fusca

SLIME-MOULDS: Trichiales
Arcyria denudata
Arcyria incarnata
Arcyria nutans
Trichia varia

LICHENS
Acarospora fuscata
Agonimia tristicula
Bacidea cuprea
Baeomyces rufus
Buellia punctata
Calicium viride
Caloplaca citrina
Caloplaca holocarpa
Candelariella aurella
Candelariella vitellina
Chrysothrix candelaris
Cladonia chlorophaea
Cladonia coniocraea
Cladonia digitata
Cladonia fimbriata
Cladonia furcata
Cladonia macilenta
Cladonia ochrochlora
Cladonia polydactyla
Cladonia pyxidata
Cladonia ramulosa
Cladonia squamosa
Cladonia subulata
Evernia prunastri
Haematoma ochroleucum
Hypocenomyce scalaris
Hypogymnia physodes
Lecanora albescens
Lecanora conizeoides
Lecanora crenulata
Lecanora dispersa
Lecanora expallens
Lecanora fuscoatra

Lecanora muralis
Lecanora polytropa
Lecanora varia
Lecidella scaber
Lecidella stigmatea
Lepraria incana
Lepraria lobificans
Leproloma membranacea
Micarea bauschiana
Micarea botyoides
Micarea denigrata
Micarea lignaria
Micaria melina
Mycroblastus sterilis
Parmelia saxatilis
Parmelia subaurifera
Parmelia sulcata
Peltigera neckeri cf.
Peltigera lactucifolia
Phaeophyscia orbicularis
Physcia adscendens
Physcia caesia
Physcia tenella
Placynthiella icmalia
Porina chlorotica
Porpidia crustulosa
Porpidia macrocarpa
Porpidia soredizodes
Porpidia tuberculosa
Psilolechia lucida
Ramalina farinacea
Rhizocarpon furfurosum
Rhizocarpon obscuratum
Rinodina genarii
Sarcogyne regularis
Scoliciosporum chlorococcum
Scoliciosporum umbrinum
Stereocaulon dactylophyllum
Stereocaulon pileatum
Trapelia involuta
Trapeliopsis flexuosa
Trapeliopsis granulosa
Usnea subfloridana
Verrucaria hochstetteri
Verrucaria muralis
Verrucaria nigrescens
Xanthoria candelaria
Xanthoria parietina

LICHENICOLOUS FUNGI
Athelia arachnoides

ALGAE
Desmococcus olivaceum s. lat.
Euglena sanguinea
Microspora amoena cf.
Microspora stagnorum cf.
Microthamnoin kuetzingianum
Spirogyra nitida
Trentepohlia calamicola
Tribonema viride cf.
Ulothrix aequalis

LIVERWORTS: Jungermanniopsida
Aneura pinguis
Barbilophozia attenuata
Calypogeia arguta
Calypogeia fissa

Calypogeia integristipula
Calypogeia muelleriana
Calypogeia muelleriana
Calypogeia neesiana
Cephalozia bicuspidata var. *bicuspidata*
Cephalozia lunulifolia
Cephaloziella divaricata
Cephaloziella hampeana
Cephaloziella massalongi *
Cephaloziella nicholsonii
Cephaloziella sp.
Cephaloziella stellulifera
Chiloscyphus polyanthos
Cololejeunea minutissima *
Diplophyllum albicans
Fossombronia pusilla
Fossombronia sp.
Frullania dilatata *
Gymnocolea inflata
Jungermannia gracillima var. *gracillima*
(= *Solenostoma*)
Jungermannia sphaerocarpa
(= *Solenostoma*)
Lepidozia reptans
Leptobryum pyriforme *
Lophocolea bidentata var. *bidentata*
Lophocolea bidentata var. *rivularis*
Lophocolea heterophylla
Lophocolea semiteres *
Lophozia bicrenata
Lophozia ventricosa
Metzgeria consanguinea *
Metzgeria furcata *
Metzgeria violacea *
Nardia scalaris
Nowellia curvifolia
Pellia endiviifolia
Pellia epiphylla
Pellia neesiana
Radula complanata *
Riccardia incurvata
Riccardia palmata *
Riccia fluitans
Riccia rhenana
Ricia sorocarpa
Scapania irrigua *
Scapania nemorea *
Scapania scandica
Scapania undulata

LIVERWORTS: Marchantiopsida
Lunularia cruciata

MOSSES: Sphagnopsida
Sphagnum angustifolium *
Sphagnum denticulatum
Sphagnum fallax *
Sphagnum fimbriatum
Sphagnum flexuosum
Sphagnum inundatum *
Sphagnum palustre *
Sphagnum palustre form squarrosum
Sphagnum recurvum var. *mucronatum*
Sphagnum squarrosum

MOSSES: Polytrichopsida
Atrichum undulatum
Pogonatum aloides

Pogonatum urnigerum
Polytrichastrum formosum
Polytrichastrum longisetum
Polytrichum commune var. *commune*
Polytrichum juniperinum
Polytrichum piliferum

MOSSES: Bryopsida
Amblystegium riparium
Amblystegium serpens var. *serpens*
Amblystegium tenax
Aulocomnium androgynum
Barbula convoluta
Barbula tophacea
Barbula unguiculata
Brachythecium albicans
Brachythecium plumosum
Brachythecium populeum
Brachythecium rivulare
Brachythecium rutabulum
Brachythecium velutinum
Bryoerythrophyllum recurvirostrum
Bryum algovicum var. *rutheanum*
Bryum archangelicum (= *Bryum inclinatum*)
Bryum argenteum
Bryum caespiticium
Bryum capillare
Bryum dichotomum
Bryum dunense
Bryum intermedium
Bryum pallens
Bryum pseudotriquetrum
Bryum rubens *
Bryum ruderale *
Calliergon cordifolium
Calliergon stramineum
Calliergonella cuspidata
Campylopus flexuosus
Campylopus fragilis
Campylopus introflexus
Campylopus pyriformis
Ceratodon purpureus
Cratoneuron filicinum
Cryphaea heteromalla *
Ctenidium molluscum
Dichodontium pellucidum s. lat. *
Dicranella heteromalla
Dicranella rufescens *
Dicranella staphylina *
Dicranella varia
Dicranoweisia cirrata
Dicranum majus
Dicranum scoparium
Dicranum tauricum
Didymodon fallax
Didymodon insulanus
Didymodon luridus
Didymodon rigidulus
Didymodon tophaceus
Didymodon vinealis
Ditrichum cylindricum
Ditrichum heteromallum
Drepanocladus aduncus
Drepanocladus fluitans var. *fluitans*
Encalypta streptocarpa *
Eurhynchium striatum
Fissidens bryoides var. *bryoides*

Fissidens pusillus *
Fissidens taxifolius var. *taxifolius*
Fissidens viridulus
Funaria hygrometrica
Grimmia pulvinata
Homalothecium sericeum
Hylocomium splendens
Hypnum andoi
Hypnum cupressiforme s. str.
Hypnum jutlandicum
Hypnum resupinatum
Isopterygium elegans
Isothecium myosuroides var. *myosuroides*
Kindbergia praelonga var. *praelonga*
Kindbergia praelonga var. *stokesii*
Leptobryum pyriforme
Leptodontium flexifolium
Leucobryum glaucum
Mnium hornum
Orthodontium gracile *
Orthodontium lineare
Orthotrichum affine
Orthotrichum anomalum
Orthotrichum cupulatum var. *cupulatum*
Orthotrichum diaphanum
Orthotrichum lyellii *
Orthotrichum pulchellum
Orthotrichum pulchellum *
Orthotrichum striatum *
Orthotrichum tenellum *
Oxyrrhynchium hians *
Plagiomnium affine
Plagiomnium rostratum
Plagiomnium undulatum
Plagiothecium curvifolium
Plagiothecium denticulatum
Plagiothecium laetum
Plagiothecium nemorale
Plagiothecium succulentum
Plagiothecium undulatum
Platyhypnidium riparioides *
Pleurozium schreberi
Pohlia annotina
Pohlia camptotrachela
Pohlia carnea
Pohlia nutans
Pohlia nutans fm *gemmiclada* *
Pohlia wahlenbergii var. *wahlenbergii*
Pottia truncata
Pseudephmerum nitidum
Pseudocrossidium hornschuchianum
Pseudocrossidium revolutum
Pseudoscleropodium purum
Pseudotaxiphyllum elegans *
Ptychomitrium polyphyllum
Pylaisia polyantha *
Racomitrium aciculare
Racomitrium fasciculare
Rhizomnium punctatum
Rhynchostegiella tenella *
Rhynchostegium confertum
Rhynchostegium murale
Rhynchostegium riparioides
Rhytidiadelphus loreus
Rhytidiadelphus squarrosus
Schistidium apocarpum *
Schistidium apocarpum agg.
Schistidium crassipilum *

Schistostega pennata
Syntrichia papillosa ⋆
Tetrodontium brownianum
Tetraphis pellucida
Tortula intermedia
Tortula muralis var. aestiva
Tortula muralis var. muralis
Tortula ruralis
Ulota bruchii
Ulota crispa s. lat.
Ulota phyllantha ⋆
Weissia controversa var. controversa
Zygodon conoideus var. conoideus
Zygodon viridissimus var. viridissimus ⋆

PTERIDOPHYTES
Athyrium filix-femina
Blechnum spicant
Botrichium lunaria
Dryopteris affinis m. borreri
Dryopteris affinis m. cambrensis
Dryopteris affinis m. robusta
Dryopteris dilatata
Dryopteris filix-mas
Equisetum arvense
Equisetum fluviatile
Equisetum palustre
Equisetum telmateia
Oreopteris limbosperma
Phyllitis scolopendrium
Polypodium vulgare
Pteridium aquilinum

GYMNOSPERMS
Chamaecyparis nootkatensis
Chamaecyparis pisifera × Cupressocyparis
leylandii
Larix decidua
Larix kaempferi
Larix × marschlinsii
Picea omorika
Picea sitchensis
Pinus contorta
Pinus sylvestris
Taxus baccata

DICOTYLEDONS
Acer campestre
Acer platanoides
Acer pseudoplatanus
Achillea millefolium
Aegopodium podagraria
Aesculus hippocastanum
Alchemilla mollis
Alchemilla xanthochlora
Alliaria petiolata
Alnus glutinosa
Alnus incana
Angelica sylvestris
Anthriscus sylvestris
Arctium minus ssp. minus
Armoracea rusticana
Artemisia vulgaris
Aster × salignum cf.
Bellis perennis
Betula pendula
Betula pubescens
Bidens cernua

Brassica rapa ssp. campestris
Callitriche hamulata
Callitriche stagmalis
Calluna vulgaris
Caltha palustris
Calystegia sepium
Calystegia sylvatica
Campanula rotundifolia
Capsella bursa-pastoris
Cardamine flexuosa
Cardamine hirsuta
Cardamine pratensis
Carpinus betulus
Castanea sativa
Centaurea montana
Centaurea nigra
Centaurium erythraea
Cerastium fontanum
Cerastium glomeratum
Ceratocapnos claviculata
Chamerion angustifolium
Chelidonium majus
Chrysosplenium oppositifolium
Circaea lutetiana
Cirsium arvense
Cirsium palustre
Cirsium vulgare
Conopodium majus
Cornus sanguinea
Corylus avellana
Corylus maxima 'Purpurea' cf.
Crassula helmsii
Crataegus monogyna
Crepis capillaris
Digitalis purpurea
Epilobium ciliatum
Epilobium hirsutum
Epilobium montanum
Epilobium obscurum
Epilobium palustre
Epilobium parviflorum
Epilobium sp.
Epilobium tetragonum
Fagus sylvatica
Fallopia japonica
Filipendula ulmaria
Fragaria vesca
Fraxinus exselsior
Fumaria bastardii ssp bastardii
Galeopsis speciosa
Galeopsis tetrahit
Galium aparine
Galium palustre
Galium saxatile
Geranium dissectum
Geranium endressii
Geranium pusillum
Geranium robertianum
Geranium × magnificum
Geum urbanum
Gnaphalium uliginosum
Hebe sp.
Hedera helix
Heracleum sphondylium
Hieracium sect. Sabauda
Hieracium sp.
Hottonia palustris
Humulus lupulus

Hypericum androsaemum
Hypericum perforatum
Hypericum tetrapterum
Hypochaeris radicata
Ilex aquifolium
Impatiens glandulifrea
Lamiastrum galeobdolon ssp. argentatum
Lamium maculatum
Lamium purpureum
Lapsana communis ssp. communis
Lathyrus pratensis
Leontodon autumnalis
Leucanthemum vulgare
Ligustrum ovalifolium
Ligustrum vulgare
Lonicera periclymenium
Lotus corniculatus
Lotus pedunculatus
Lunaria annua
Lycopus europaeus
Lysimachia nemorum
Lysimachia punctata
Lysimachia vulgaris
Lythrum portula
Lythrum salicaria
Malus domestica
Malus sp.
Malus sylvestris
Matricaria discoidea
Meconopsis cambrica
Mentha aquatica
Mentha arvensis
Mentha spicata
Myosotis arvensis
Myosotis laxa
Myosotis scorpioides
Myosotos sylvatica
Odontites vera ssp. verna
Oenothera glazoviana
Ornithopus perpusillus
Oxalis acetosella
Papaver sp.
Pentaglottis sempervirens
Persicaria bistorta
Persicaria hydropiper
Persicaria lapathifolium
Persicaria maculosa
Petasites hybridus
Pilosella officinarum
Plantago lanceolata
Plantago major
Polygonum arenastrum
Polygonum aviculare
Populus alba
Populus nigra
Populus tremula
Populus × canadensis
Potentilla anglica
Potentilla anserina
Potentilla erecta
Potentilla reptans
Primula vulgaris
Prunella vulgaris
Prunus avium
Prunus domestica cf.
Prunus domestica ssp. institia
Prunus laurocerasus
Prunus padus

Prunus spinosa
Pulicaria dysenterica
Quercus robur
Ranunculus acris
Ranunculus bulbosus
Ranunculus ficaria
Ranunculus flammula
Ranunculus hederaceus
Ranunculus lingua
Ranunculus omiophyllus
Ranunculus repens
Reseda luteola
Rhinanthus minor ssp. *stenophyllus*
Rhododendron ponticum
Ribes nigrum
Ribes rubrum
Ribes sanguineum
Rosa arvensis
Rosa caesia
Rosa canina
Rosa 'Hollandica' cf.
Rosa virginiana cf.
Rosa × *alba* cf.
Rubus 'false-calvatus-1'
Rubus 'false-calvatus-2'
Rubus accrescens
Rubus accrescens × *sprengelii* cf.
Rubus adspersus
Rubus alderleyensis
Rubus alderleyensis var. *cuneatus*
Rubus armeniacus
Rubus baileyi
Rubus bartonii
Rubus calvatus
Rubus cardiophyllus
Rubus cardiophyllus var. *fallax* cf.
Rubus cissburiensis
Rubus dasyphyllus
Rubus distractiformis
Rubus eboracensis
Rubus euryanthemus
Rubus hindii
Rubus idaeus
Rubus idaeus
Rubus incurvatiformis
Rubus infestus
Rubus intensior
Rubus laciniatus
Rubus lindleianus
Rubus loganobaccus
Rubus mancuniensis
Rubus nemoralis
Rubus nemorosus
Rubus newbouldii
Rubus painteri
Rubus polyanthemus
Rubus robiae
Rubus sciocharis
Rubus scissus
Rubus spectabilis
Rubus sprengelii
Rubus tuberculatus
Rubus tuberculatus × *vestitus* cf.
Rubus ulmifolius
Rubus vestitus
Rubus vestitus hybrid
Rubus vestitus × *accrescens* cf.
Rubus vestitus × *distractiformis* cf.

Rubus warrenii
Rubus wirralensis
Rumex acetosa
Rumex acetosella
Rumex crispus
Rumex obtusifolius
Rumex sanguineus
Sagina procumbens
Salix caprea
Salix cinerea
Salix fragilis
Salix fragilis var. *fragilis*
Salix sp.
Sambucus nigra
Sanguisorba officinalis
Saxifraga × *urbium*
Scleranthus annuus ssp. *annuus*
Scrophularia nodosa
Sedum spurium
Senecio jacobaea
Senecio sylvaticus
Senecio vulgaris
Silene dioica
Sisymbrium officinale
Solanum dulcamara
Solanum tuberosum
Sonchus asper
Sonchus oleraceus
Sorbus aria agg.
Sorbus aucuparia
Sorbus intermedia agg.
Spiraea douglasii
Stachys palustris
Stachys sylvatica
Stellaria graminea
Stellaria holostea
Stellaria media
Stellaria uliginosa
Symphoricarpos albus
Symphytum × *uplandicum*
Syringa vulgaris
Tanecetum parthenium
Taraxacum
Teucrium scorodonia
Tilia × *vulgaris*
Trifolium dubium
Trifolium medium
Trifolium pratense
Trifolium repens
Tussilago farfara
Ulex europaeus
Ulex gallii
Urtica dioica
Vaccinium myrtillus
Valeriana officinalis
Veronica agrestis
Veronica arvensis
Veronica beccabunga
Veronica chamaedrys
Veronica filiformis
Veronica hederifolia
Veronica officinalis
Veronica serpyllifolia
Viburnum opulus
Viccia cracca
Viccia hirsuta
Viccia sativa
Viccia sepium

Viola palustris
Viola riviniana
Viola sp. (subg. *Melanium*)
Weigela florida

MONOCOTYLEDONS

Agrostis canina
Agrostis capillaris
Agrostis gigantea
Agrostis stolonifera
Aira praecox
Alisma plantago-aquatica
Allium ursinum
Alopecurus geniculatus
Alopecurus pratensis
Anisantha sterilis
Anthoxanthum odoratum
Arrhenatherum elatius
Bromus hordaceus ssp. *hordaceus*
Butomus umbellatus
Carex hirta
Carex nigra
Carex ovalis
Carex panicea
Carex pendula
Carex remota
Carex sp.
Catabrosa aquatica
Convalaria majalis
Crocosmia × *crocosmiflora*
Cynosurus cristatus
Cytisus scoparius
Dactylis glomerata
Dactylorhiza fuchsii
Dactylorhiza purpurella
Deschampsia cespitosa
Deschampsia flexuosa
Eleocharis palustris
Elodea canadensis
Elytrigia repens
Epipactis helleborine
Festuca arundinacea
Festuca longifolia cf.
Festuca gigantea
Festuca ovina
Festuca pratensis
Festuca rubra
Galanthus nivalis
Glyceria declinata
Glyceria fluitans
Glyceria plicata
Glyceria × *pedicellata*
Holcus lanatus
Holcus mollis
Hyacinthoides hispanica
Hyacinthoides non-scripta
Hyacinthoides non-scripta × *hispanica*
Iris pseudacorus
Isolepis setacea
Juncus acutiflorus
Juncus articulatus
Juncus bufonius
Juncus bulbosus
Juncus conglomeratus
Juncus effusus
Juncus inflexus
Juncus squarrosus
Juncus tenuis

Lemna minor
Lemna minuta
Lemna trisulca
Lolium multiflorum
Lolium perenne
Luzula campestris
Luzula multiflora
Luzula sylvatica

Molinia caerulea
Narcissus sp.
Nardus stricta
Phalaris arundinaceus
Phleum pratense
Poa annua
Poa compressa
Poa humilis

Poa nemoralis
Poa pratensis
Poa trivialis
Potamogeton natans
Sparganium erectum ssp. *neglectum*
Typha latifolia

Appendix 9.2

An account of the *Rubus* species of Alderley Edge

David P. Earl

The survey of the *Rubus* flora for the Alderley Edge Landscape Project clearly demonstrated the important links between historic landscape features and biodiversity. Twenty-one described *Rubus* species were found in the core study area together with a number of hitherto un-described brambles. We made an estimate of the relative frequency of each species within the majority of the parcels, and carried out a survey of the lanes and footpaths in the hinterland area, which also indicated the importance of woodlands, hedgerows and lanes for biodiversity: several additional bramble species were recorded in the hinterland.

Introduced species established at Alderley Edge

Several introduced *Rubus* species are established at Alderley Edge. In parcel 1a an ornamental raspberry, the Salmonberry *Rubus spectabilis*, is naturalised; originating from North America, the Salmonberry has attractive pale-purple flowers that appear as the leaves begin to emerge. Later in the year tasty raspberry-like 'berries' are produced. The extensively cultivated Himalayan Giant (*Rubus armeniacus*) had been established at five locations within the core study area. Recorded as rare to occasional at the time of the survey it is likely that the frequency of Himalayan Giant will have increased, as this species can soon become prolific once established. Plants often occur about the sites of former habitation or allotments but are also extensively naturalised by bird dispersal; thus, both brambles (*Rubus fruticosus*) and raspberries (*Rubus idaeus*) were found at the Hagg cottages (Casella and Croucher, 2010: 26). Within the hinterland area, other introduced brambles include the widely grown Loganberry (*Rubus loganobaccus*), found as a relic of cultivation, the Cut-leaved Bramble (*Rubus laciniatus*) and the Cissbury Bramble (*Rubus cissburiensis*). The last species is classed as native to the southern counties of England, with the type locality being the woodlands by the archaeological site Cissbury Ring in Sussex, but it is considered a horticultural escape elsewhere. *Rubus cissburiensis* is also established in Australia, having been introduced there by settlers from southern Britain.

Rubus biogeography and speciation

Many of the native bramble species that occur at Alderley Edge are widespread in north-west Europe and probably arrived in the south of Britain before the land bridges to Continental Europe disappeared due to rising sea levels. Several such bramble species were found to occur in the core study area at Alderley Edge, including *Rubus scissus*, *Rubus lindleianus*, *Rubus sciocharis*, *Rubus nemoralis*, *Rubus cardiophyllus*, *Rubus polyanthemus*, *Rubus sprengelii*, *Rubus ulmifolius*, *Rubus vestitus and Rubus dasyphyllus*. It is highly likely that these major species are the 'ancestral species' from which the diverse *Rubus* flora of the British Isles arose.

As the widespread north-west European bramble species migrated northwards across England, a grouping of species characteristic of the South and Midlands developed and passed through the lowlands between North Wales and the Peak District by way of what is referred to here as the Staffordshire–Shropshire–Cheshire migration gap. In addition to some of the native species mentioned above, 'South and Midlands brambles' that have reached Alderley Edge also include the following:

Rubus tuberculatus. This species occurs in many of the parcels and is often abundant in Cheshire hedgerows. It is an aggressive colonist of man-made habitats, particularly on derelict land and along railway embankments.

Rubus nemorosus. Occurring within the hinterland and characterised by large showy pale-pink flowers with red-base styles and hairy anthers, this species is locally frequent in parts of east Cheshire, particularly about Mobberley and the Dane Valley between Congleton and Holmes Chapel. Such populations are near to the northern limit for mainland Britain.

Rubus euryanthemus. A bramble at the northern limits of its species range, a few bushes of which were found under birch trees by Macclesfield

Road. Recently studies have shown this species to be locally abundant in parts of south and east Cheshire.

Rubus adspersus and *Rubus hindii*. A few bushes occur in hedgerows at Monks' Heath. Both these species have strongholds in East Anglia and recent studies indicate that they are locally frequent in east Cheshire.

In those parts of Britain bordering the Irish Sea another grouping of bramble species developed. As is to be expected, many of these species occur in Cheshire. Alderley Edge is within a zone where both the 'Irish Sea' and 'South and Midlands' brambles meet, adding to the diversity of the bramble species to be found in the Alderley Edge area. Not only are there additional 'Irish Sea' species occurring at Alderley Edge but a significant proportion of the additional species are endemic to the British Isles and include *Rubus robiae* (parcel 13a), *Rubus wirralensis* and a few plants of *Rubus bartonii* by the lodge at parcel 10a. The main populations of *Rubus bartonii* occur in Wales; the Alderley Edge plants may originate from the Bollin valley populations that occur about Bowdon and Hale, but may be of garden origin, as *Rubus bartonii* is also grown on allotments as 'Ashton Cross'. Another of the Irish Sea–South and Midlands endemics is *Rubus calvatus*, which has been recorded from Alderley Edge by Edees and Newton (1988).

Alderley Edge is at the western margins of the South Pennines and thus several bramble species that occur on both sides of the Pennine Chain are found at Alderley Edge, such as *Rubus infestus* and endemics that include 'The Yorkshire Bramble' *Rubus eboracensis*, *Rubus incurvatiformis*, *Rubus newbouldii* and 'Lord de Tabley's Bramble' *Rubus warrenii*.

A few plants of *Rubus intensior* (also endemic) occur at two parcels, one of these populations being along the edge of Windmill Wood by the Macclesfield Road. This species is thought to be a recent arrival to Alderley Edge and has probably originated from the major populations that occur about the Potteries district of north Staffordshire.

It should be noted that a regional grouping of species that are confined to the British Isles has been recognised, extending from near Stoke-on-Trent to north Derbyshire and Greater Manchester and known as the sub-Pennine endemic complex (Edees and Newton, 1988). The described species belonging to this grouping recorded for Alderley Edge include *Rubus accrescens*, *Rubus distractiformis* and *Rubus painteri*. Such species almost certainly evolved within the local region, as this is where the main populations occur, but it should be noted that they are expanding in range from their point of origin, with *Rubus accrescens* having recently been found in Flintshire, *Rubus painteri* near Abbeystead in Lancashire and *Rubus distractiformis* having been found in Northern Ireland.

The landscape features of Alderley Edge are particularly important for two undescribed bramble members of the sub-Pennine endemic complex, referred to as 'Bailey's Bramble' (*Rubus baileyi* DP Earl MS) (Plate 15). Research has shown that the main distribution of Bailey's Bramble is in east Cheshire, with additional populations about Greater Manchester, where a few bushes appropriately grow close to Bailey's former residence in Manchester, near College Road in Whalley Range.

Bailey's Bramble is particularly suited to heaths, woodland margins, old sand quarries, hedge-banks and river-valley slopes on sandy soils. The Alderley Edge Bramble is locally abundant along the lanes, hedgerows and in field scrub about Nether Alderley and Over Alderley and occurs again in local abundance at the former coal-mining areas of Poynton, especially along sections of the disused railway line and associated sidings that now form the Middlewood Way. With the Alderley Edge Bramble once again we see an endemic species that has almost certainly evolved locally, expanding in range from its core area to form small but expanding populations at Ashton-under-Lyne, Manchester and Cheddleton near Leek. This is also the case for the 'Manchester Bramble', an undescribed endemic species that often occurs in great abundance along the river valleys of Manchester and was discovered during the Alderley Edge survey at its present known southern limit, along wood borders at Monks' Heath.

In our present state of knowledge we do not know how the regional and local endemic species evolved. Our batologists are wandering within a time capsule of evolution here in the British Isles, observing thousands of years of evolution, describing a fraction of the well established forms which they encounter, and spotting the new forms that have evolved in recent times on whose origins we might speculate. In the hedgerows of Hocker Lane, Over Alderley, a dwarf form of *Rubus cardiophyllus* considered to be var. *fallax* was found. Such miniature forms are referred to micromorphs. Has this isolated bush arrived from a population elsewhere or is this a mutation arising from the localised plants of *Rubus cardiophyllus* that occur about Alderley Edge? There is also an assumed mutation of the Alderley Edge Bramble occurring along Birtles Lane at Over Alderley, which has non-characteristic cuneate (wedge-shaped) terminal leaflets, providing further evidence for speciation processes being at work at a local level. As I looked at the brambles which were to be found in the core area parcels and around the hinterland, I did find a number of plants that I was unable to name. There are nearly always a few localised un-named brambles to be found on explorations in those parts of the British Isles where brambles grow. The brambles that I describe in this appendix are mainly species with distributions extending over a significant area; only a few very distinct but localised brambles have been described previously, mainly during the Victorian era. From Table 9.2a (Appendix 9.1) it can be seen that I referred to two brambles as *Rubus 'false-calvatus-1'* and *Rubus 'false-calvatus-2'* and I speculated that some bushes found might be of hybrid origin: *Rubus accrescens* × *sprengelii?*, *Rubus tuberculatus* × *vestitus?*, *Rubus vestitus* × *accrescens?*, *Rubus vestitus* × *distractiformis?*.

Two of the suggested hybrids grow in association with the assumed parental species by Artists Lane, providing evidence that further speciation of the British *Rubus* flora is actually occurring within the Alderley Edge district. It is interesting to note that one of the suggested hybrids occurs at the edge of a wooded quarry, while the other is to be found along the old track to the Sandhills. The results of the survey strongly indicate the links that exist between key man-made landscape features and bio-diversity, and that the existence of habitats where related species occur together at Alderley Edge may have led to the evolution of new forms of bramble which may or may not occur at any other global locations. The results of the Alderley Edge bramble survey demonstrate that the sub-Pennine regional endemic complex is not merely a static entity but is continuing to evolve.

It is clear that there is a great deal of scope for further research, in particular the use of molecular tools to aid our understanding of the processes of regional evolution within the genus *Rubus*. I do not know of any published molecular ecological studies to date (July 2015) of the native species of *Rubus* occurring in the British Isles; however, such studies have been carried out by the Swedish geneticist Hilde Nybom and her associates, resulting in the evaluation of DNA profiles for several species which are widely distributed within north-west Europe. Indeed, studies carried out by Kraft *et al.* (1995) indicate that C. E. Gustafsson's suggestion that the bramble he named *Rubus vestervicensis* in 1938 as a possible hybrid of *Rubus pedemontanus* × *Rubus grabowskii* was indeed correct.

As several supposed hybrids were found to be growing in association with the assumed parental species at Alderley Edge we have the opportunity to apply molecular techniques to test such assumptions. If the assumptions of hybrid origin are found to be valid by scientific investigation, the results could be used as educational case studies to demonstrate the significance of man-made landscape features in the processes of evolution in the British Isles.

Ecological adaptation

Different species of *Rubus* are better adapted to some habitats than others. For example, *Rubus vestitus* and *Rubus ulmifolius* often occur in abundance on calcareous soils, while many other species are noticeably absent. Some interesting results of the survey include the abundance of *Rubus distractiformis* and *Rubus tuberculatus* in the scrub margins of the Sandhills (an old mine-working area) as well as among the seasonally flooded fields downstream of the Sandhills mine. Note that *Rubus* species are noticeably absent from open areas of the mine, where ionic toxicity is assumed to be high. It is not known at present whether these two species, which are aggressive colonists of derelict land, show any degree of tolerance to such ionic toxicity. Other species also occur in mining districts. In south Lancashire *Rubus criniger* is abundant around the fringes of colliery spoil heaps at Leigh, while *Rubus intensior* is a common species on waste ground in the Potteries and at Wigan. A Cornish endemic which is associated with tin mines was named *Rubus metallorum* (Margetts and Spurgin, 1991).

Some species of bramble can have a competitive advantage over others. At Alderley Edge *Rubus scissus*, a rhizomatous species of subsection *Rubus* which spreads through the peat soils rather like a raspberry, is confined to the winter-wet purple moor-grass areas of Finlow Hill birch wood, but two *Rubus* species which could be classified as members of the same subsection *Rubus accrescens* and 'Bailey's Bramble' occur in far greater abundance. *Rubus accrescens* and 'Bailey's Bramble' frequently spread by the arching and subsequent rooting of the stem tip. While rooting of the stem tip is common for most species of bramble which belong to the subsection *Hiemales*, the main mode of vegetative spread in subsection *Rubus* is by the rhizomatous spread of the root system. It is suggested that the *Rubus* species of subsection *Rubus* which spread by both stem-tip rooting and rhizomes, *Rubus accrescens* and 'Bailey's Bramble', are at a competitive advantage over other members of the same subsection, such as *Rubus scissus*, which spread by rhizomes only. It is plausible that *Rubus accrescens* and 'Bailey's Bramble' may be derived from hybridisation between members of subsection *Rubus* and subsection *Hiemales*.

This account may provide an insight into some of the factors that have to be considered with regard to *Rubus* speciation and ecological adaptability. It stresses the importance of key man-made features such as hedgerows, woodlands, unimproved fields, lane sides, bridle tracks, quarries and mine workings to evolutionary processes. At this stage British batologists can only speculate about the subject: in the future, further research techniques such as molecular studies may provide answers to what Charles Darwin viewed as a rather complex subject within the 'Mystery of Mysteries'.

Descriptions of two brambles

The Alderley Edge Bramble

This species of bramble is locally abundant along Slade Lane, Over Alderley, where the plants flower during the month of June. The stems are usually crimson in colour and are slightly furrowed.

There are about twelve to fifteen main prickles per 5 cm and these occur chiefly on the angles of the stem but with a few prickles also being present on the stem faces, which are clothed with scattered short simple hairs, numerous sessile glands, a variable number of short-stalked glands and numerous short to medium pricklets, a proportion of which are needle-like in form.

The leaves usually comprise five leaflets and tend not to overlap; they are thinly hairy above, more hairy below, with spreading hairs occurring along the leaf veins.

The terminal leaflet is often broader towards the apex, with a leaf tip that is about 1.5 cm in length and with a base that is slightly to entirely heart-shaped; coarse teeth occur along the edge of the leaflet and the principal teeth are prominent.

The flowering branch is pyramidal, with the side branches and the apex bearing numerous attractive pink flowers. The flowers are commonly 24–28 mm in diameter with bright pink petals, *c.* 13 mm long × 7 mm wide and broadest towards the tip; the petals are hairy along the margins and densely hairy beneath. The stamens have striking pink filaments that exceed the yellowish-green styles. The sepals are green with a narrow white border and are clothed with numerous hairs and stalked glands; they are long to leafy-pointed, initially turned downwards but later spreading outwards.

Bailey's Bramble

The species of bramble is locally common in woodlands, along country lanes, on heaths and along the margins of the former moss lands in East Cheshire, and flowers during June and July. The green stems are slightly furrowed. There are about five to eight main prickles per 5 cm occurring along the stem angles with occasional short-stalked glands and scattered very short needle-like pricklets occurring on the stem faces.

The leaves comprise four or five leaflets which do not overlap; they are thinly hairy above and densely hairy below. The terminal leaflets are broadly elliptical with a tapering apex, a slightly heart-shaped base and numerous deeply cut teeth along the margins.

The flowers are approximately 24 mm in diameter. The white petals are widely spaced, not overlapping, and are about 13 mm long by 9 mm wide, broadest towards the apex, which is frequently jagged or slightly notched; the petal margins appear to be without hairs but are thinly hairy beneath; the stamens have white filaments and are shorter than the yellow-green styles. The anthers are glabrous. The sepals are long-pointed and spreading, green with a narrow white border and are clothed with numerous hairs, scattered stalked glands and a few needle-like pricklets.

The main flowering branch is short and broad with the side branches and flower stalks often spreading at 90°. On the flower stalks there are several patent to slightly declining short pricklets approximately 0.5–3 mm long and some short stalked glands.

References and further reading

Because this appendix covers a very specialised topic, its bibliography is so specialised that it almost forms part of the study itself. For that reason it is printed here rather than with the main bibliographies; works mentioned in the text are marked with an asterisk. For more general reading on brambles the four books authored or co-authored by A. Newton are recommended.

Bennett, S. T., Kenton, A. Y. and Bennett, M. D. 1992. Genomic In Situ Hybridisation Reveals the Allopolyploid Nature of *Milium montianum* (Graminae). *Chromosoma*, 101: 420–4.

*Casella, E. C. and Croucher, S. K. 2010. *The Alderley Sandhills Project: An Archaeology of Community Life in (Post-)industrial England*. Manchester: Manchester University Press for English Heritage.

Datta, S. 1932. Some Chromosome Numbers in British Species of *Rubus*. *Memoirs and Proceedings of the Manchester Literary and Philosophical Society*, 76: 85–9.

Earl, D. P. In preparation. *The Rubus Flora of Cheshire* (in preparation as a pdf; images of *Rubus* species seen in Cheshire are due to be placed online).

*Edees, E. S. and Newton, A. 1988. *Brambles of the British Isles*. London: Ray Society.

Gustafsson, A. 1939. Differential Polyploidy Within the Blackberries. *Hereditas*, 25: 33–47.

Gustafsson, A. 1942. The Origin and Properties of the European Blackberry Flora. *Hereditas*, 28: 249–77.

Gustafsson A. 1943. The Genesis of the European Blackberry Flora. *Lunds Universitets Arsskrift*, 39(6): 1–200.

Gustafsson, C. E. 1920. *Rubus wahlbergii* Arrh. var. *vestervicensis* C.E. Gustafsson. *Botaniska Notiser (Lund)*, 20: 211–12.

*Gustafsson, C. E. 1938. Skandinaviens Rubusflora. *Botaniska Notiser (Lund)*, 38: 378–420.

Heslop-Harrison, Y. 1953. Cytological Studies in the Genus *Rubus* L., 1. Chromosome Studies in the British *Rubus* Flora. *The New Phytologist*, 52: 22–39.

Kraft, T. and Nybom, H. 1995. DNA Fingerprinting and Biometry Can Solve Some Taxonomic Problems in Apomictic Blackberries (*Rubus* subg. *Rubus, Rosaceae*). *Watsonia*, 20: 329–43.

*Kraft, T., Nybom, H. and Werlemark, G. 1995. *Rubus vestervicensis* (Rosaceae) – Its Hybrid Origin Revealed by DNA Fingerprinting. *Nordic Journal of Botany*, 15(3): 237–42.

*Margetts, L. J. and Spurgin, K. L. 1991. *Cornish Flora Supplement*. Zennor: Trendine Press.

Newton, A. 1971. *Flora of Cheshire*. Chester: Cheshire Community Council Publications Trust.

Newton, A., 1990. *Supplement to the Flora of Cheshire*. Leamington Spa: Alan Newton.

Newton, A. and Randall, R. D. 2004. *Atlas of the British and Irish Brambles*. London: Botanical Society of the British Isles.

Appendix 11.1

Alderley breeding birds, 1978–84 and 2004–06

Jonathan Guest

Between 1978 and 1984 (Guest *et al.*, 1992) and again between 2004 and 2006 (Norman, 2008), the breeding birds of Cheshire were mapped by amateur ornithologists. The recording unit used in each case was a tetrad of 2 km × 2 km, bounded by the grid-lines shown on 1:25,000 Ordnance Survey maps. Two of these tetrads include the majority of the Alderley Edge Landscape Project's survey area, namely SJ 87N with the grid-line intersection 8476 at its south-western corner, and SJ 87T lying to north and east of intersection 8676. The results of the two surveys are summarised in Table 11.1, which illustrates the composition of the breeding avifauna of the Edge and its hinterland. Three categories of evidence are employed for each species: 1, possible; 2, probable; and 3, confirmed breeding (e.g. by finding an occupied nest or seeing adult birds carrying food to their chicks).

Since the time and effort expended in each tetrad may have varied between the two surveys, the results are only broadly comparable. Table 11.1 therefore shows the number of tetrads (out of 670 in the county) with records of confirmed or probable breeding for each species in each of the two surveys. A regional trend is then deduced against which changes at Alderley can be set: + indicates an increase of at least 10 per cent in the number of occupied squares over the twenty-five years between the surveys; ++ more than 20 per cent increase; - at least 10 per cent decrease; and – a decrease of more than 20 per cent. Tree Pipit and Redstart were not found at the Edge during the recent survey but Wood Warblers are holding on and Pied Flycatchers were found to breed. Willow Warbler and Garden Warbler are much more thinly distributed than formerly. Note that Corncrake and Nightjar have ceased to breed in Cheshire. Table 11.1 excludes most waterfowl, which are represented chiefly at the northern end of Radnor Mere in Alderley Park, outside the AELP survey area. For more information readers are referred to Norman (2008).

Table 11.1. Alderley breeding birds, 1978–84 and 2004–06

| Species | 1978–84 | | 2004–06 | | Sum of probable + confirmed breeding records (Cheshire and Wirral) | | Trend |
					1978–84	2004–06	
Mallard	3	3	3	3	512	605	+
Red-legged Partridge			2	2	40	116	++
Grey Partridge				2	349	118	--
Pheasant	2	3	1	3	298	349	+
Sparrowhawk	3	3	1	2	181	235	+
Buzzard			1	3	2	436	++
Kestrel	1	1	3	3	338	307	-
Moorhen	3	3	3	3	583	536	
Lapwing	3	3		2	503	440	-
Woodcock	2	2		1	87	12	--
Feral Pigeon				1	191	226	+
Stock Dove	3	3	2	3	377	373	
Wood Pigeon	3	3	3	3	642	596	
Collared Dove	3		2	1	501	536	
Cuckoo	1		1	1	322	17	--
Little Owl	1	3	1	2	259	158	--
Tawny Owl	3	3	3	2	334	134	--
Kingfisher			3	2	100	63	--
Green Woodpecker	1	1	1	2	123	69	--
Great Spotted Woodpecker	2	3	3	3	397	432	
Lesser Spotted Woodpecker	3	2		1	133	28	--
Skylark		2			590	284	--
Sand Martin				1	82	47	--
Swallow	3	3	3	3	642	602	
House Martin	3	3	1	3	572	539	
Tree Pipit	3	3			68	5	--
Meadow Pipit				1	159	102	--
Grey Wagtail	1		1	1	123	183	++
Pied Wagtail	3	3	2	3	482	496	
Wren	3	3	3	3	643	563	-
Dunnock	3	3	3	3	641	557	-
Robin	3	3	3	3	647	596	
Redstart	2	2			51	24	--
Blackbird	3	3	3	3	658	620	

Species	1978–84		2004–06		Sum of probable + confirmed breeding records (Cheshire and Wirral)		Trend
					1978–84	2004–06	
Song Thrush	3	3	3	3	633	507	--
Mistle Thrush	3	3	3	2	594	482	--
Blackcap	2	3	3	2	454	353	--
Garden Warbler	3		2	2	214	77	--
Lesser Whitethroat	1				200	83	--
Whitethroat	1				434	388	-
Wood Warbler	2	3	1	3	59	5	--
Chiffchaff	2	3	3	2	376	327	--
Willow Warbler	3	3	3	3	615	218	--
Goldcrest	2	3	3	3	189	223	+
Spotted Flycatcher	3	3	2	3	345	145	--
Pied Flycatcher	2			3	11	23	++
Long-tailed Tit	3	3	3	3	389	539	++
Blue Tit	3	3	3	3	647	621	
Great Tit	3	3	3	3	630	614	
Coal Tit	3	3	3	3	324	292	-
Willow Tit	2				180	28	--
Marsh Tit	1				91	16	--
Nuthatch	3	3	3	3	269	305	+
Treecreeper	3	3	3	3	357	247	--
Jay	3	3	3	2	371	384	
Magpie	3	3	3	3	645	583	-
Jackdaw	3	3	3	3	388	486	++
Rook		3		3	278	209	--
Crow	3	3	3	3	627	580	
Raven				2	0	50	++
Starling	3	3	3	3	658	597	-
House Sparrow	3	3	3	3	646	598	
Tree Sparrow	3	3		1	432	270	--
Chaffinch	3	3	3	3	624	590	
Greenfinch	2	3	3	3	512	537	
Goldfinch	3	3	1	3	474	540	+
Siskin				2	0	15	++
Linnet	1	2		2	501	347	--
Redpoll	2	2		2	195	34	--
Crossbill				1	1	0	
Bullfinch	2		2	3	412	317	--
Yellowhammer	3	3			522	241	--
Reed Bunting	3			1	464	283	--

Source: Guest *et al.* (1992); Norman (2008).

Appendix 13.1

A checklist of the invertebrates of Alderley Edge

Dmitri V. Logunov

The checklist of 1,732 species of invertebrates found on Alderley Edge provided below has been compiled on the basis of several unpublished reports, the data released at our request by a number of organisations and county recorders, the collections and card indexes of Manchester Museum, and a number of publications. The names of colleagues or institutions whose data have been used are mentioned at the beginning of each section. Although this checklist is by no means complete (see also the Introduction to Chapter 13), it is the first ever to have been compiled for Alderley Edge. Further progress in extending it will depend on conducting a number of special and detailed inventories of the separate invertebrate groups listed below.

A note on scientific names

The checklist contains both scientific and common English names (if they exist). Biologists have divided the living world into groups of organisms, or taxa, which are usually arranged according to a series of levels known as a *taxonomic hierarchy*. The *species* is the basal element in this hierarchy, having typically the lowest taxonomic rank. However, some species include even lower taxonomic ranks, called *subspecies*. Related species are grouped into a *genus*, related genera into a *family*, families into an *order*, orders into a *class*, classes into a *phylum*. Families can be further subdivided into subfamilies, and genera into subgenera. Scientific names are assigned or reassigned according to the sets of rules called *codes of nomenclatures*, conventional among specialists. The *International Code of Zoological Nomenclature* (ICZN) is the one followed by the zoological disciplines. In the present checklist, the following taxonomic hierarchy is used (from bottom to top): subspecies – species – subgenus – genus – tribes – subfamily – family – order – class – subphylum – phylum. However, subspecies, subgenera and subfamilies are included only if it is thought appropriate. For some groups these names are not available, as their classification is still poorly developed. The publications mentioned at the beginning of each section will provide the complete classification of every large group in the present checklist (i.e. the order or class) and the detailed nomenclature of the taxa involved. Note that the references themselves are listed at the end of Chapter 13 itself (pp. 293–9).

Scientific species names are always Latinised, and each typically consists of four essential parts: *Genus, Species, Author's name* and *Date*. For instance, the scientific name of the Great Diving Beetle is *Dytiscus marginalis* Linnaeus, 1758. This shows that the species *marginalis* was described in the genus *Dytiscus* by Linnaeus in 1758. The author and date can be bracketed or not, depending on the original combination of a species name given by its author. If a species name was described in a particular genus and still remains in that genus, the author and date are given without brackets. If the species name has been transferred to another genus since its original description, the author and date are enclosed in curved brackets.

Genus and species names constitute a unique two-word (*binomial*) combination of a scientific name for every species. If a subgenus name is included, the combination will be *trinomial*. The current checklist contains both bi- and trinomial names, depending on availability and practicalities. The family names can be recognised by the standard ending '-*idae*'. Nomenclature of all listed groups is given in accordance with most up-to-date relevant catalogues, if available; all references are provided. It is beyond the scope of these brief notes to describe all existing nomenclatural rules. A brief account of the taxonomic nomenclature can be found in Cooter and Barclay (2006); one of the best and most comprehensive accounts of the practical taxonomy is a book by J. E. Winston, *Describing Species: Practical Taxonomic Procedure for Biologists* (1999).

Common English names have been provided for the majority of macro-Lepidoptera and for those groups where such names exist. For a fairly comprehensive synopsis of common English names of insects, as well of those from nine other European languages, see 'the Pherobase', online at http://www.pherobase.com/database/commonname/common-names-atoz-index.php. The meanings of the scientific names of the British butterflies and moths, as well as a brief history of the scientific nomenclature, were discussed by Emmet (1991). The scientific names of the British spiders and harvestmen were covered by Parker (1982, 1993).

If a species has remained undetermined, it is listed below as 'sp.', which means 'species'. In this case, the name of the most similar species is given followed by the word 'complex' (both in parentheses).

For simplicity, all taxa are arranged alphabetically within their parent group.

Phylum Arthropoda (Jointed-foot invertebrates: insects, arachnids, crustaceans, etc.) Subphylum Mandibulata

Class Insecta (Insects)

Order Coleoptera (Beetles; 363 species)

The checklist presented below includes 363 species and is mainly based on the unpublished report on terrestrial beetles prepared by Colin Johnson (Manchester). This report includes data on 264 species taken both from fieldwork on Alderley Edge which he carried out over a number of years and from the Lancashire and Cheshire Card Index by Harry Britten in Manchester Museum (extracted by Lai Mei Li, Wigan). The list of aquatic beetles of the families Dytiscidae, Haliplidae, Hydraenidae, Hydrophilidae, Gyrinidae, Paelobiidae, Scirtidae, Chrysomelidae, Coccinellidae and Noteridae (sixty-one species) is based on the unpublished reports of two aquatic invertebrate surveys undertaken by Ian Wallace from Liverpool Museum in 1996 and by Jonathan Guest in 1998 (the latter forms the basis for our Chapter 12 on the Alderley Edge pondlife). Thirty-eight additional species from the families Cantharidae, Carabidae, Cerambycidae, Chrysomelidae, Coccinellidae, Leiodidae, Rhynchitidae, Scarabaeidae and Staphylinidae were added from the 2002 unpublished report by Dmitri Logunov (Manchester Museum), the data released at our request by rECOrd, the Biodiversity Information System for Cheshire (courtesy of Tom Hunt) and by Don Stenhouse (Bolton Museum), the Cheshire County recorder for Coleoptera, and from the unpublished report on the National Trust Biological Survey by Jackson and Alexander in 1998.

Nomenclature is arranged in accordance with the latest checklist of beetles of the British Isles edited by Duff (2008), with tribes omitted.

Suborder Adephaga

Family CARABIDAE (41) – Ground Beetles
Subfamily Carabinae

Abax (Abax) parallelepipedus (Piller and Mitterpacher, 1783)
Agonum (Agonum) muelleri (Herbst, 1784)
Agonum (Europhilus) fuliginosum (Panzer, 1809)
Agonum (Europhilus) thoreyi Dejean, 1828
Amara (Zezea) plebeja (Gyllenhal, 1810)
Anchomenus dorsalis (Pontoppidan, 1763)
Bembidion (Metallina) lampros (Herbst, 1784)
Bembidion (Peryphus) tetracolum Say, 1823
Calathus (Amphyginus) rotundicollis Dejean, 1828
Calathus (Calathus) fuscipes (Goeze, 1777)
Calathus (Calathus) melanocephalus (Linnaeus, 1758)
Carabus (Archicarabus) nemoralis Müller, 1764
Carabus (Carabus) granulatus Linnaeus, 1758
Carabus (Mesocarabus) problematicus harcyniae Sturm, 1815
Clivina fossor (Linnaeus, 1758)
Cychrus caraboides (Linnaeus, 1758)
Dromius (Dromius) quadrimaculatus (Linnaeus, 1758)
Elaphrus (Neoelaphrus) cupreus Duftschmid, 1812
Leistus (Leistus) fulvibarbis Dejean, 1826
Leistus (Leistus) terminatus (Panzer, 1793)
Leistus (Pogonophorus) spinibarbis (Fabricius, 1775)
Loricera (Leistus) pilicornis (Fabricius, 1775)
Nebria (Boreonebria) rufescens (Strøm, 1768)
Nebria (Nebria) brevicollis (Fabricius, 1792)
Nebria (Nebria) salina Fairmaire and Laboulbène, 1854
Notiophilus aestuans Dejean, 1826
Notiophilus biguttatus (Fabricius, 1779)
Notiophilus rufipes Curtis, 1829
Ocys harpaloides (Audinet-Serville, 1821)
Paranchus albipes (Fabricius, 1796)
Patrobus atrorufus (Strøm, 1768)
Platynus (Platynus) assimilis (Paykull, 1790)
Pterostichus (Bothriopterus) quadrifoveolatus Letzner, 1852
Pterostichus (Morphosoma) melanarius (Illiger, 1798)
Pterostichus (Lagarus) vernalis (Panzer, 1795)
Pterostichus (Platysma) niger (Schaller, 1783)
Pterostichus (Phonias) diligens (Sturm, 1824)
Pterostichus (Phonias) strenuus (Panzer, 1796)
Pterostichus (Steropus) madidus (Fabricius, 1775) – 'Black Clock' in Surrey
Pterostichus sp. (*nigrita* complex)

Subfamily Cicindelinae

Cicindela (s.str.) *campestris* Linnaeus, 1758

Family DYTISCIDAE (30) – Diving Beetles

Acilius (Acilius) sulcatus (Linnaeus, 1758)
Agabus (Acatodes) sturmi (Gyllenhal in Schönherr, 1808)
Agabus (Gaurodytes) affinis (Paykull, 1798)
Agabus (Gaurodytes) bipustulatus (Linnaeus, 1767)
Agabus (Gaurodytes) guttatus (Paykull, 1798)
Agabus (Gaurodytes) nebulosus (Forster, 1771)
Colymbetes fuscus (Linnaeus, 1758)
Dytiscus marginalis Linnaeus, 1758 – Great Diving Beetle
Hydroporus angustatus Sturm, 1835
Hydroporus erythrocephalus (Linnaeus, 1758)
Hydroporus incognitus Sharp, 1869
Hydroporus gyllenhalii Schiødte, 1841
Hydroporus memnonius Nicolai, 1822
Hydroporus neglectus Schaum, 1845
Hydroporus nigrita (Fabricius, 1792)
Hydroporus obscurus Sturm, 1835
Hydroporus palustris (Linnaeus, 1761)

Hydroporus planus (Fabricius, 1781)
Hydroporus pubescens (Gyllenhal, 1808)
Hydroporus striola (Gyllenhall, 1862)
Hydroporus tessellates (Drapiez, 1819)
Hydroporus tristis (Paykull, 1798)
Hygrotus (Coelambus) impressopunctatus (Schaller, 1783)
Hygrotus (Hygrotus) inaequalis (Fabricius, 1777)
Hyphydrus ovatus (Linnaeus, 1761)
Ilybius ater (DeGeer, 1774)
Ilybius fuliginosus (Fabricius, 1792)
Ilybius quadriguttatus (Lacordaire, 1835)
Laccophilus minutus (Linnaeus, 1758)
Suphrodytes dorsalis (Fabricius, 1787)

Family HALIPLIDAE (3) – Crawling Water Beetles
Haliplus (Haliplinus) immaculatus Gerhardt, 1877
Haliplus (Haliplinus) ruficollis (DeGeer, 1774)
Haliplus (Haliplinus) sibiricus Motschulsky, 1860

Family GYRINIDAE (1) – Whirligig Beetles
Gyrinus substriatus Stephens, 1828

Family NOTERIDAE (1) – Burrowing Water Beetles
Noterus clavicornis (DeGeer, 1774)

Family PAELOBIIDAE (1) – Screech Beetles
Hygrobia hermanni (Fabricius, 1775)

Suborder Polyphaga

Family ANOBIIDAE (3) – Woodworm and Spider Beetles
Dryophilus pusillus (Gyllenhal, 1808)
Niptus hololeucus (Faldermann, 1835) – Golden Spider Beetle
Ptilinus pectinicornis (Linnaeus, 1758) – Fan-bearing Wood-borer

Family APIONIDAE (1) – Seed Weevils
Exapion (Ulapion) ulicis (Forster, 1771)

Family BYRRHIDAE (1) – Pill Beetles
Simplocaria semistriata (Fabricius, 1794)

Family BYTURIDAE (1) – Raspberry Beetles
Byturus tomentosus (DeGeer, 1774) – Raspberry Beetle

Family CANTHARIDAE (10) – Soldier Beetles
Cantharis decipiens Baudi, 1871
Cantharis nigra (DeGeer, 1774)
Cantharis nigricans (Müller, 1776)
Malthinus frontalis (Marsham, 1802)
Malthodes fuscus (Waltl, 1838)
Malthodes mysticus Kiesenwetter, 1852
Rhagonycha fulva (Scopoli, 1763) – Common Red Soldier Beetle
Rhagonycha lignosa (Müller, 1764)
Rhagonycha limbata (Thomson, 1864)
Rhagonycha testacea (Linnaeus, 1758)

Family CERAMBYCIDAE (4) – Long-horn Beetles

Clytus arietis (Linnaeus, 1758) – Wasp Beetle
Phymatodes testaceus (Linnaeus, 1758)
Tetropium gabrieli Weise, 1905
Saperda scalaris (Linnaeus, 1758)

Family CERYLONIDAE (2)

Cerylon ferrugineum Stephens, 1830
Cerylon histeroides (Fabricius, 1792)

Family CHRYSOMELIDAE (12) – Leaf and Flea Beetles

Altica lythri Aubé, 1843 – Willowherb Flea Beetle
Chaetocnema sp. (*concinna* complex)
Crepidodera fulvicornis (Fabricius, 1793)
Donacia vulgaris Zschach, 1788 – Reed Beetle
Hydrothassa marginella (Linnaeus, 1758)
Lochmaea caprea (Linnaeus, 1758)
Lochmaea crataegi (Forster, 1771)
Oulema sp. (*melanopus* complex)
Phaedon tumidulus (Germar, 1824) – Celery Leaf Beetle
Phratora laticollis (Suffrian, 1851)
Phyllotreta undulata Kutschera, 1860 – Lesser or Small Striped Flea Beetle
Prasocuris phellandrii (Linnaeus, 1758)

Family CIIDAE (5) – Minute Tree Fungus Beetles

Octotemnus glabriculus (Gyllenhal, 1827)
Cis bidentatus (Olivier, 1790)
Cis bilamellatus Wood, 1884
Cis boleti (Scopoli, 1763)
Cis fagi Waltl, 1839

Family COCCINELLIDAE (15) – Ladybirds

Adalia bipunctata (Linnaeus, 1758) – Two-spot Ladybird
Adalia decempunctata (Linnaeus, 1758) – Ten-spot Ladybird
Anatis ocellata (Linnaeus, 1758) – Eyed Ladybird
Anisosticta novemdecimpunctata (Linnaeus, 1758) – Nineteen-Spot Ladybird
Aphidecta obliterata (Linnaeus, 1758) – Larch Ladybird
Calvia quattuordecimguttata (Linnaeus, 1758) – Cream-spot Ladybird
Coccidula rufa (Herbst, 1783)
Coccinella septempunctata Linnaeus, 1758 – Seven-spot Ladybird
Coccinella undecimpunctata Linnaeus, 1758 – Eleven-spot Ladybird
Halyzia sedecimguttata (Linnaeus, 1758) – Sixteen-spot Ladybird
Myrrha octodecimguttata (Linnaeus, 1758) – Eighteen-spot Ladybird
Myzia oblongoguttata (Linnaeus, 1758) – Striped Ladybird
Propylea quattuordecimpunctata (Linnaeus, 1758)
Psyllobora vigintiduopunctata (Linnaeus, 1758) – Twenty-two-spot Ladybird
Scymnus (*Pullus*) *auritus* Thunberg, 1795

Family CRYPTOPHAGIDAE (8) – Silken Fungus Beetles

Atomaria (*Anchicera*) *lewisi* Reitter, 1877
Atomaria (*Anchicera*) *rubella* Heer, 1841
Cryptophagus dentatus (Herbst, 1793)
Cryptophagus denticulatus Heer, 1841
Cryptophagus lycoperdi (Scopoli, 1763)
Cryptophagus punctipennis Brisout de Barneville, 1863
Micrambe ulicis (Stephens, 1830)
Ootypus globosus (Waltl, 1838)

Family CURCULIONIDAE (25) – True Weevils and Bark Beetles

Subfamily Ceuthorhynchinae

Nedyus quadrimaculatus (Linnaeus, 1758)
Parethelcus pollinarius (Forster, 1771)
Sirocalodes mixtus (Mulsant and Rey, 1858)

Subfamily Cossoninae

Euophryum confine (Broun, 1881)

Subfamily Curculioninae

Archarius pyrrhoceras (Marsham, 1802)
Dorytomus rufatus (Bedel, 1888)
Orchestes (Salius) fagi (Linnaeus, 1758)

Subfamily Entiminae

Otiorhynchus singularis (Linnaeus, 1767) – Clay-coloured Weevil
Phyllobius (Dieletus) argentatus (Linnaeus, 1758)
Phyllobius (Metaphyllobius) glaucus (Scopoli, 1763)
Phyllobius (Phyllobius) pyri (Linnaeus, 1758) – Common Leaf Weevil
Polydrusus (Neoeustolus) cervinus (Linnaeus, 1758)
Sitona puncticollis Stephens, 1831
Sitona regensteinensis (Herbst, 1797)
Strophosoma capitatum (DeGeer, 1775)
Strophosoma melanogrammum (Forster, 1771)

Subfamily Scolytinae

Dryocoetinus villosus (Fabricius, 1792)
Hylurgops palliatus (Gyllenhal, 1813)
Hylastes ater (Paykull, 1792)
Hylastes opacus Erichson, 1836
Hylesinus sp. (*varius* complex)
Scolytus intricatus (Ratzeburg, 1837) – Oak Bark Beetle
Trypodendron domesticum (Linnaeus, 1758) – Ambrosia Beetle
Trypodendron lineatum (Olivier, 1795)
Trypodendron signatum (Fabricius, 1792)

Family DERMESTIDAE (1) – Skin, Carpet or Larder Beetles

Anthrenus (Florilinus) museorum (Linnaeus, 1761) – Museum Beetle

Family ELATERIDAE (5) – Click Beetles

Agriotes pallidulus (Illiger, 1807)
Athous (Athous) haemorrhoidalis (Fabricius, 1801)
Dalopius marginatus (Linnaeus, 1758)
Denticollis linearis (Linnaeus, 1758)
Melanotus sp. (*villosus* complex)

Family EROTYLIDAE (1) – Pleasing Fungus Beetles

Triplax aenea (Schaller, 1783)

Family GEOTRUPIDAE (3) – Dor Beetles

Anoplotrupes stercorosus (Scriba, 1791)
Geotrupes spiniger (Marsham, 1802)
Geotrupes stercorarius (Linnaeus, 1758) – Dumble-dor or Lousy Watchman

Family HELOPHORIDAE (4)

Helophorus (Atracthelophorus) brevipalpis Bedel, 1881
Helophorus (Helophorus) minutus Fabricius, 1775
Helophorus (Helophorus) obscurus Mulsant, 1844
Helophorus (Megahelophorus) grandis Illiger, 1798

Family HISTERIDAE (1) – Clown or Hister Beetles

Gnathoncus rotundatus (Kugelann, 1792)

Family HYDRAENIDAE (4)
Hydraena riparia Kugelann, 1794
Hydraena testacea Curtis, 1830
Limnebius truncatellus (Thunberg, 1794)
Ochthebius minimus (Fabricius, 1792)

Family HYDROPHILIDAE (19) – Scavenger Water Beetles
Subfamily Hydrophylinae
Anacaena globulus (Paykull, 1798)
Anacaena limbata (Fabricius, 1792)
Anacaena lutescens (Stephens, 1829)
Cymbiodyta marginellus (Fabricius, 1792)
Enochrus coarctatus (Gredler, 1863)
Enochrus testaceus (Fabricius, 1801)
Helochares lividus (Forster, 1771)
Hydrobius fuscipes (Linnaeus, 1758)
Laccobius bipunctatus (Fabricius, 1775)

Subfamily Sphaeridiinae
Cercyon (*Cercyon*) *convexiusculus* Stephens, 1829
Cercyon (*Cercyon*) *impressus* (Sturm, 1807)
Cercyon (*Cercyon*) *melanocephalus* (Linnaeus, 1758)
Cercyon (*Cercyon*) *pygmaeus* (Illiger, 1801)
Coelostoma orbiculare (Fabricius, 1775)
Cryptopleurum minutum (Fabricius, 1775)
Megasternum concinnum (Marsham, 1802)
Megasternum obscurum (Marsham, 1802)
Sphaeridium scarabaeoides (Linnaeus, 1758)
Sphaeridium sp. (*bipustulatum* complex)

Family KATERETIDAE (1) – Pollen Beetles
Brachypterus urticae (Fabricius, 1792)

Family LATRIDIIDAE (7) – Plaster Beetles
Cartodere (*Aridius*) *bifasciata* (Reitter, 1877)
Cartodere (*Aridius*) *nodifer* (Westwood, 1839)
Cortinicara gibbosa (Herbst, 1793)
Enicmus testaceus (Stephens, 1830)
Enicmus transversus (Olivier, 1790)
Latridius porcatus Herbst, 1793
Stephostethus lardarius (DeGeer, 1775)

Family LEIODIDAE (6) – Round Fungus Beetles
Agathidium (*Neoceble*) *nigripenne* (Fabricius, 1792)
Agathidium (*Neoceble*) *rotundatum* (Gyllenhal, 1827)
Anisotoma humeralis (Fabricius, 1792)
Leptinus testaceus Müller, 1817
Nargus (*Nargus*) *velox* (Spence, 1813)
Nargus (*Nargus*) *wilkini* (Spence, 1813)

Family LUCANIDAE (1) – Stag Beetles
Sinodendron cylindricum (Linnaeus, 1758) – Rhinoceros beetle

Family LYMEXYLIDAE (1) – Ship-timber Beetles
Hylecoetus dermestoides (Linnaeus, 1761)

Family MALACHIIDAE (1) – Soft-wing Flower Beetles
Malachius bipustulatus (Linnaeus, 1758)

Family MELANDRYIDAE (2) – False Darkling Beetles
Melandrya caraboides (Linnaeus, 1761)
Orchesia undulata Kraatz, 1853

Family MONOTOMIDAE (4) – Root-eating Beetles
Rhizophagus (*Eurhizophagus*) *depressus* (Fabricius, 1792)
Rhizophagus (*Rhizophagus*) *bipustulatus* (Fabricius, 1792)
Rhizophagus (*Rhizophagus*) *dispar* (Paykull, 1800)
Rhizophagus (*Rhizophagus*) *nitidulus* (Fabricius, 1798)

Family MYCETOPHAGIDAE (3) – Hairy Fungus Beetles
Litargus connexus (Geoffroy in Fourcroy, 1785)
Mycetophagus atomarius (Fabricius, 1787)
Mycetophagus quadripustulatus (Linnaeus, 1761)

Family NITIDULIDAE (7) – Pollen or Sap Beetles
Carpophilus marginellus Motschulsky, 1858
Cryptarcha strigata (Fabricius, 1787)
Epuraea (*Epuraea*) *pallescens* (Stephens, 1835)
Epuraea (*Epuraea*) *biguttata* (Thunberg, 1784)
Epuraea (*Micruria*) *melanocephala* (Marsham, 1802)
Glischrochilus (*Glischrochilus*) *quadriguttatus* (Fabricius, 1777)
Meligethes aeneus (Fabricius, 1775) – Bronzed Blossom, Blossom or Rape Blossom Beetles

Family PTILIIDAE (13) – Feather-winged Beetles
Acrotrichis (*Acrotrichis*) *atomaria* (DeGeer, 1774)
Acrotrichis (*Acrotrichis*) *cognata* (Matthews, 1877)
Acrotrichis (*Acrotrichis*) *danica* Sundt, 1958
Acrotrichis (*Acrotrichis*) *fascicularis* (Herbst, 1793)
Acrotrichis (*Acrotrichis*) *henrici* (Matthews, 1872)
Acrotrichis (*Acrotrichis*) *intermedia* (Gillmeister, 1845)
Ptenidium (*Gillmeisterium*) *nitidum* (Heer, 1841)
Ptenidium (*Matthewsium*) *laevigatum* Erichson, 1845
Ptenidium (*Ptenidium*) *formicetorum* Kraatz, 1851
Ptiliolum (*Ptenidium*) *fuscum* (Erichson, 1845)
Ptinella cavelli (Broun, 1893)
Ptinella denticollis (Fairmaire, 1858)
Ptinella errabunda Johnson, 1975

Family RHYNCHITIDAE (1)
Deporaus (*Deporaus*) *betulae* (Linnaeus, 1758)

Family SALPINGIDAE (2) – Narrow-waisted Bark Beetles
Salpingus planirostris (Fabricius, 1787)
Salpingus ruficollis (Linnaeus, 1761)

Family SCRAPTIIDAE (5)
Anaspis (*Anaspis*) *fasciata* (Forster, 1771)
Anaspis (*Anaspis*) *frontalis* (Linnaeus, 1758)
Anaspis (*Anaspis*) *maculata* Fourcroy, 1785 – Tumbling Flower Beetle
Anaspis (*Anaspis*) *regimbarti* Schilsky, 1895
Anaspis (*Nassipa*) *rufilabris* (Gyllenhal, 1827)

Family SCARABAEIDAE (7) – Dung Beetles and Chafers
Aphodius (*Agrilinus*) *ater* (DeGeer, 1774)
Aphodius (*Melinopterus*) *prodromus* (Brahm, 1790)
Aphodius (*Melinopterus*) *sphacelatus* (Panzer, 1798)
Aphodius (*Teuchestes*) *fossor* (Linnaeus, 1758)
Aphodius sp. (*fimetarius* complex)
Melolontha melolontha (Linnaeus, 1758) – Common Cockchafer or 'Maybug'
Phyllopertha horticola (Linnaeus, 1758) – Garden Chafer or Bracken-clock

Family SCIRTIDAE (3) – Marsh beetles
Cyphon coarctatus Paykull, 1799
Cyphon hilaris Nyholm, 1844
Scirtes hemisphaericus (Linnaeus, 1758)

Family SCYDMAENIDAE (2) – Ant-like Stone Beetles
Neuraphes (Neuraphes) elongatulus (Müller and Kunze, 1822)
Stenichnus collaris (Müller and Kunze, 1822)

Family SILPHIDAE (1) – Sexton and Carrion Beetles
Aclypea opaca (Linnaeus, 1758) – Beet Carrion Beetle

Family SPHINDIDAE (1) – Dry Fungus Beetles
Aspidiphorus orbiculatus (Gyllenhal, 1808)

Family STAPHYLINIDAE (90) – Rove Beetles
Subfamily Aleocharinae
Acrotona obfuscata (Gravenhorst, 1802)
Alaobia taxiceroides (Munster, 1932)
Aleochara (Xenochara) lanuginosa Gravenhorst, 1802
Aloconota (Aloconota) gregaria (Erichson, 1839)
Amischa analis (Gravenhorst, 1802)
Anomognathus cuspidatus (Erichson, 1839)
Atheta aquatica (Thomson, 1852)
Atheta aquatilis (Thomson, 1867)
Atheta britanniae (Bernhauer and Scheerpeltz, 1926)
Atheta castanoptera (Mannerheim, 1830)
Atheta crassicornis (Fabricius, 1792)
Atheta harwoodi Williams, 1930
Atheta vaga (Heer, 1839)
Atheta xanthopus (Thomson, 1856)
Autalia sp. (*impressa* complex)
Autalia rivularis (Gravenhorst, 1802)
Bolitochara obliqua Erichson, 1837
Cypha laeviuscula (Manerheim, 1830)
Datomicra celata (Erichson, 1837)
Datomicra dadopora (Thomson, 1867)
Dimetrota cinnamoptera (Thomson, 1856)
Dimetrota ischnocera (Thomson, 1870)
Dimetrota laevana (Mulsant and Rey, 1852)
Dimetrota marcida (Erichson, 1837)
Encephalus complicans Stephens, 1832
Haploglossa nidicola (Fairmaire, 1852)
Ischnoglossa prolixa (Gravenhorst, 1802)
Ischnoglossa turcica Wunderle, 1902
Geostiba circellaris (Gravenhorst, 1806)
Leptusa fumida Kraatz, 1856
Leptusa pulchella (Mannerheim, 1830)
Liogluta granigera (Kiesenwetter, 1850)
Mocyta amplicollis (Mulsant and Rey, 1873)
Mocyta fungi (Gravenhorst, 1806)
Mocyta sp. (*fungi* complex)
Oxypoda alternans (Gravenhorst, 1802)
Oxypoda brevicornis (Stephens, 1832)
Oxypoda elongatula Aubé, 1850
Philhygra palustris (Kiesenwetter, 1844)
Phloeopora corticalis (Gravenhorst, 1802)
Phloeopora testacea (Mannerheim, 1830)
Placusa depressa Mäklin, 1845
Placusa pumilio (Gravenhorst, 1802)

Subfamily Omaliinae
Anthobium atrocephalum (Gyllenhal, 1827)

Anthobium unicolor (Marsham, 1802)
Dropephylla vilis (Erichson, 1840)
Hapalaraea pygmaea (Paykull, 1800)
Lesteva longoelytrata (Goeze, 1777)
Olophrum piceum (Gyllenhal, 1810)
Omalium italicum Bernhauer, 1902
Omalium rivulare (Paykull, 1789)
Phloeonomus punctipennis Thomson, 1867

Subfamily Oxytelinae

Anotylus sculpturatus (Gravenhorst, 1806)
Anotylus tetracarinatus (Block, 1799)
Oxytelus laqueatus (Marsham, 1802)
Platystethus (Platystethus) arenarius (Fourcroy, 1785)
Syntomium aeneum (Müller, 1821)

Subfamily Pederinae

Lathrobium brunnipes (Fabricius, 1792)

Subfamily Proteininae

Proteinus ovalis Stephens, 1834

Subfamily Pselaphinae

Bibloporus bicolor (Denny, 1825)
Tychus niger (Paykull, 1800)

Subfamily Staphylininae

Bisnus fimetarius (Gravenhorst, 1802)
Dinothenarus pubescens (DeGeer, 1774)
Gabrius splendidulus (Gravenhorst, 1802)
Gyrohypnus fracticornis (Müller, 1776)
Nudobius lentus (Gravenhorst, 1806)
Ocypus (Ocypus) olens (Müller, 1764) – Devil's Coach-horse
Ontholestes tesellatus (Fourcroy, 1785)
Othius subuliformis Stephens, 1833
Philonthus cognatus Stephens, 1832
Philonthus nigrita (Gravenhorst, 1806)
Philonthus tenuicornis Mulsant and Rey, 1853
Philonthus varians (Paykull, 1783)
Philonthus varius (Gyllenhal, 1810)
Quedius (Microsaurus) cruentus (Olivier, 1795)
Quedius (Microsaurus) lateralis (Gravenhorst, 1802)
Quedius (Microsaurus) xanthopus Erichson, 1839
Quedius (Raphirus) fumatus (Stephens, 1833)
Quedius (Raphirus) maurorufus (Gravenhorst, 1806)

Subfamily Steninae

Stenus (Hemistenus) impressus Germar, 1824
Stenus (Metastenus) bifoveolatus Gyllenhal, 1827
Stenus (Metastenus) nitidiusculus Stephens, 1833

Subfamily Tachyporinae

Lordithon trinotatus (Erichson, 1839)
Tachinus humeralis Gravenhorst, 1802
Tachinus marginellus (Fabricius, 1781)
Tachinus proximus Kraatz, 1855
Tachinus rufipes (Linnaeus, 1758)
Tachyporus nitidulus (Fabricius, 1781)
Tachyporus obtusus (Linnaeus, 1767)
Tachyporus sp. (*chrysomelinus* complex)

Family TENEBRIONIDAE (1) – Darkling Beetles
Eledona agricola (Herbst, 1783)

Family TETRATOMIDAE (1)
Tetratoma fungorum Fabricius, 1790

Order Collembola (Springtails; 1 species)

The record is based on the slide collection of Collembola held in the Manchester Museum (courtesy of Phillip Rispin). Nomenclature follows Kloet and Hinks (1964).

Family ENTOMOBRYIDAE (1)
Entomobrya albocincta (Templeton, 1835) [ex Hedge Sparrow's nest]

Order Dermaptera (Earwigs; 1 species)

The record is taken from the unpublished report prepared by the Liverpool Museum staff and associates resulting from the Alderley Edge Invertebrate Survey undertaken by their team in 1996 (courtesy of Steve Judd, Liverpool). Nomenclature and common English names follow Marshall and Haes (1988).

Family FORFICULIDAE (1)
Forficula auricularia Linnaeus, 1758 – Common Earwig

Order Diplura (Two-pronged Bristletails; 1 species)

The record is taken from the Lancashire and Cheshire Card Index held in the Manchester Museum (courtesy of Phillip Rispin). Nomenclature follows Kloet and Hinks (1964).

Family CAMPODEIDAE (1)
Campodea plusiocheta Silvestri, 1912 [ex Robin's nest]

Order Diptera (True Flies; 216 species)

The checklist presented below includes 216 species and is mainly based on the unpublished report prepared by the Liverpool Museum staff and associates resulting from the Alderley Edge Invertebrate Survey undertaken by their team in 1996 (courtesy of Steve Judd, Liverpool). Diptera were collected by T. H. Mawdsley and identified by L. Clemons. Sixty-one additional records were taken from three publications (Britten, 1947; Kidd and Brindle, 1959; Chandler, 1991) and from the data extracted from the Lancashire and Cheshire Card Index of Harry Britten in the Manchester Museum (courtesy of Phillip Rispin). Seven species of Bolitophilidae and Mycetophilidae from Alderley Edge were kindly added by Peter Chandler (Melksham, UK), based on his examination of H. Britten's Diptera collection retained in the Manchester Museum. Two records of Conopidae were taken from the data released at our request by rECOrd, the Biodiversity Information System for Cheshire (courtesy of Tom Hunt), and five additional records from the unpublished report on the National Trust Biological Survey by Jackson and Alexander in 1998. The list of aquatic groups is mostly based on the unpublished reports of two aquatic invertebrate surveys undertaken by Ian Wallace from the Liverpool Museum in 1996 and by Jonathan Guest in 1998 (see Chapter 12). Nomenclature follows the checklist by Chandler (1998) and subsequent updates in *Dipterists Digest* (courtesy of Peter Chandler), with subfamilies and tribes omitted. A useful and fairly complete source of information about the British true flies, including the latest checklist of Diptera of the British Isles, is the Dipterist Forum, online at http://www.dipteristsforum.org.uk; the latest counts of the British Diptera fauna and much useful information on how to collect and study true flies can be found in the second edition of *A Dipterist's Handbook* (Chandler, 2010).

Suborder Lower Diptera (= Nematocera)

Family ANISOPODIDAE (2) – Window Gnats
Sylvicola cinctus (Fabricius, 1787)
Sylvicola fenestralis (Scopoli, 1763)

Family BIBIONIDAE (2) – St Mark's Flies
Bibio johannis (Linnaeus, 1767)
Dilophus febrilis (Linnaeus, 1758) – Fever-fly

Family BOLITOPHILIDAE (4) – Fungus Gnats
Bolitophila (Bolitophila) basicornis (Mayer, 1951)
Bolitophila (Bolitophila) cinerea Meigen, 1818
Bolitophila (Bolitophila) saundersii (Curtis, 1836)
Bolitophila (Cliopisa) hybrida (Meigen, 1818)

Family CECIDOMYIIDAE (1) – Gall Midges
Dasineura urticae (Perris, 1840)

Family CHAOBORIDAE (1) – Phantom Midges
Chaoborus sp.

Family CHIRONOMIDAE (1) – Non-biting Midges
Orthocladius (Eudactylocladius) fuscimanus (Kieffer in Kieffer and Thienemann, 1908)

Family CULICIDAE (3) – Mosquitoes
Culex (Culex) pipiens Linnaeus, 1758
Culiseta (Culiseta) morsitans (Theobald, 1901)
Ochlerotatus punctor (Kirby in Richardson, 1837)

Family DIXIDAE (3) – Meniscus Midges
Dixa maculata Meigen, 1818
Dixa nebulosa Meigen, 1830
Dixella aestivalis (Meigen, 1818)

Family KEROPLATIDAE (1) – Fungus Gnats
Macrocera phalerata Meigen, 1818

Family LIMONIIDAE (12) – Short-palped Craneflies
Austrolimnophila ochracea (Meigen, 1804)
Cheilotrichia (Empeda) cinerascens (Meigen, 1804)
Crypteria limnophiloides Bergroth, 1913
Dicranomyia (Dicranomyia) modesta (Meigen, 1881)
Dicranomyia (Numantia) fusca (Meigen, 1804)
Erioconopa trivialis (Meigen, 1881)
Erioptera (Erioptera) lutea Meigen, 1804
Limonia nubeculosa Meigen, 1804
Molophilus appendiculatus (Staeger, 1840)
Ormosia hederae (Curtis, 1935)
Rhipidia maculata Meigen, 1818
Rhypholophus varius (Meigen, 1818)

Family MYCETOPHILIDAE (29) – Fungus Gnats
Allodia (Allodia) lugens (Wiedemann, 1817)
Allodia (Allodia) truncata Edwards, 1921
Allodia zaitzevi Kurina, 1998
Boletina gripha Dziedzicki, 1885
Coelophthinia thoracica (Winnertz, 1863)
Cordyla brevicornis (Staeger, 1840)
Exechia contaminata Winnertz, 1863
Exechia dorsalis (Staeger, 1840)
Exechia fusca (Meigen, 1804)
Exechia parva Lundström, 1909
Exechia spinuligera Lundström, 1912
Exechiopsis hammi (Edwards, 1925)
Mycetophila finlandica Edwards, 1913
Mycetophila formosa Lundström, 1911
Mycetophila fraterna Winnertz, 1863
Mycetophila fungorum (De Geer, 1776)
Mycetophila ichneumonea Say, 1823
Mycetophila luctuosa Meigen, 1830
Mycetophila marginata Winnertz, 1863
Mycetophila ocellus Walker, 1848
Mycetophila signatoides Dziedzicki, 1884
Mycetophila vittipes Zetterstedt, 1852
Mycomya (Mycomya) annulata (Meigen, 1818)
Phronia cinerascens Winnertz, 1863
Phronia coritanica Chandler, 1992
Phronia nigricornis (Zetterstedt, 1852)
Platurocypta testata (Edwards, 1924)
Rymosia virens Dziedzicki, 1910
Tarnania fenestralis (Meigen, 1818)

Family PSYCHODIDAE (1) – Moth-flies
Psychoda sp.

Family PTYCHOPTERIDAE (2) – Fold-winged Craneflies
Ptychoptera albimana (Fabricius, 1787)
Ptychoptera contaminata (Linnaeus, 1758)

Family SCIARIDAE (3) – Black Fungus Gnats
Leptosciarella (Leptosciarella) rejecta (Winnertz, 1867)
Lycoriella (Hemineurina) modesta (Staeger, 1840)
Lycoriella (Lycoriella) ingenua (Dufour, 1839)

Family TIPULIDAE (10) – Long-palped Craneflies
Dolichopeza albipes (Stroem, 1768)
Nephrotoma appendiculata (Pierre, 1919)
Tipula (Acutipula) fulvipennis Degeer, 1776
Tipula (Acutipula) vittata Meigen, 1804
Tipula (Lunatipula) fascipennis Meigen, 1818
Tipula (Lunatipula) vernalis Meigen, 1804
Tipula (Savtshenkia) rufina Meigen, 1818
Tipula (Savtshenkia) staegeri Nielsen, 1922
Tipula (Tipula) oleracea Linnaeus, 1758
Tipula (Vestiplex) scripta Meigen, 1830

Family TRICHOCERIDAE (3) – Winter Gnats
Trichocera maculipennis Meigen, 1818
Trichocera regelationis (Linnaeus, 1758)
Trichocera saltator (Harris, 1776)

Suborder Brachycera

Family ANTHOMYIIDAE (4)
Chirosia flavipennis (Fallén, 1823)
Hydrophoria ruralis (Meigen, 1826)
Hylemya vagans (Panzer, 1798)
Lasiomma picipes (Migen, 1826)

Family BRACHYSTOMATIDAE (1)
Trichopeza longicornis (Meigen, 1822)

Family CALLIPHORIDAE (2) – Blowflies
Calliphora vicina Robineau-Desvoidy, 1830 – Bluebottle
Protocalliphora azurea (Fallén, 1817)

Family CHLOROPIDAE (1) – Grass Flies
Oscinella maura (Fallén, 1820)

Family CONOPIDAE (4) – Thick-headed Flies
Conops flavipes Linnaeus, 1758
Conops quadrifasciatus DeGeer, 1776
Leopoldius signatus (Wiedemann in Meigen, 1824)
Physocephala rufipes (Fabricius, 1781)

Family DOLICHOPODIDAE (10) – Long-legged Flies
Campsicnemus curvipes (Fallén, 1823)
Campsicnemus loripes (Haliday, 1832)
Campsicnemus scambus (Fallén, 1823)
Dolichopus trivialis Haliday, 1832
Dolichopus ungulatus (Linnaeus, 1758)
Gymnopternus aerosus (Fallén, 1823)
Gymnopternus cupreus (Fallén, 1823)
Gymnopternus metallicus (Stannius, 1831)
Rhaphium appendiculatum (Zetterstedt, 1849)
Sciapus platypterus (Fabricius, 1805)

Family DROSOPHILIDAE (1) – Fruit-flies
Scaptomyza (Parascaptomyza) pallida (Zetterstedt, 1847)

Family DRYOMYZIDAE (1)
Neuroctena anilis Fallén, 1820

Family EMPIDIDAE (9) – Dance or Dagger-flies
Chelifera precatoria (Fallén, 1816)
Empis (*Coptophlebia*) *hyalipennis* Fallén, 1816
Empis (*Empis*) *nuntia* Meigen, 1838
Empis (*Euempis*) *tessellata* Fabricius, 1794
Empis (*Xanthempis*) *punctata* Meigen, 1804
Empis (*Xanthempis*) *stercorea* Linnaeus, 1761
Hilara longifurca Strobl, 1892
Rhamphomyia (*Amydroneura*) *erythrophthalma* Meigen, 1830
Rhamphomyia (*Holoclera*) *caliginosa* Collin, 1902

Family EPHYDRIDAE (2) – Shore-flies
Hydrellia maura Meigen, 1839
Limnellia quadrata (Fallén, 1813)

Family FANNIIDAE (1) – Lesser Houseflies
Fannia aequilineata Ringdahl, 1945

Family HELEOMYZIDAE (8)
Heleomyza borealis Boheman, 1865
Heleomyza serrata (Linnaeus, 1758)
Suillia atricornis (Meigen, 1830)
Suillia bicolor (Zetterstedt, 1838)
Suilla fuscicornis (Zetterstedt, 1838)
Suilla laevifrons (Loew, 1862)
Suilla ustulata (Meigen, 1830)
Tephrochlamys rufiventris (Meigen, 1830)

Family HIPPOBOSCIDAE (1) – Keds or Louse Flies
Stenepteryx hirundinis (Linnaeus, 1758) [ex House Martin] – Swallow Ked

Family HYBOTIDAE (6) – Dance-flies
Hybos culiciformis (Fabricius, 1775)
Ocydromia glabricula (Fallén, 1816)
Platypalpus longiseta (Zetterstedt, 1842)
Platypalpus pallidiventris (Meigen, 1822)
Tachypeza nubila (Meigen, 1804)
Trichinomyia flavipes (Meigen, 1830)

Family LAUXANIIDAE (4)
Calliopum simillimum (Collin, 1933)
Meiosimyza rorida (Fallén, 1820)
Minettia (*Frendelia*) *longipennis* (Fabricius, 1794)
Minettia (*Minettia*) *inusta* (Meigen, 1826)

Family LONCHOPTERIDAE (2) – Lance-flies
Lonchoptera lutea Panzer, 1809
Lonchoptera tristis Meigen, 1824

Family MICROPEZIDAE (1) – Stilt Flies
Micropeza lateralis Meigen, 1826

Family MUSCIDAE (15) – Houseflies and allies

Coenosia tigrina (Fabricius, 1775)
Eudasyphora cyanella (Meigen, 1826)
Graphomya maculata (Scopoli, 1763)
Hebecnema nigricolor (Fallén, 1825)
Hebecnema umbratica (Meigen, 1826)
Hydrotaea cyrtoneurina (Zetterstedt, 1845)
Hydrotaea irritans (Fallén, 1823) – Sheep Headfly
Mesembrina meridiana (Linnaeus, 1758) – Noon Fly
Phaonia basalis (Zetterstedt, 1838)
Phaonia errans (Meigen, 1826)
Phaonia palpata (Stein, 1897)
Phaonia subventa (Harris, 1780)
Polietes lardarius (Fabricius, 1781)
Stomoxys calcitrans (Linnaeus, 1758) – Stablefly
Thricops semicinereus (Wiedeman, 1817)

Family OPOMYZIDAE (2)

Geomyza sp. (*hackmani* complex)
Opomyza germinationis (Linnaeus, 1758)

Family PALLOPTERIDAE (1) – Flutter-wing Flies

Palloptera ustulata Fallén, 1820

Family PIPUNCULIDAE (2) – Big-headed Flies

Chalarus spurius (Fallén, 1816)
Verrallia aucta (Fallén, 1817)

Family PSILIDAE (1) – Carrot Flies

Loxocera albiseta (Schrank, 1803)

Family RHAGIONIDAE (3) – Snipeflies

Chrysopilus cristatus (Fabricius, 1775)
Rhagio lineola Fabricius, 1794
Rhagio scolopaceus (Linnaeus, 1758)

Family SARCOPHAGIDAE (3) – Flesh-flies

Metopia argyrocephala (Meigen, 1824)
Sarcophaga (*Sarcophaga*) *carnaria* (Linnaeus, 1758)
Sarcophaga (*Sarcophaga*) *subvicina* Rohdendorf, 1937

Family SCATHOPHAGIDAE (2) – Yellow Dung-flies

Scathophaga stercoraria (Linnaeus, 1758)
Scathophaga inquinata Meigen, 1826

Family SCIOMYZIDAE (1) – Snail-killing Flies

Tetanocera elata (Fabricius, 1781)

Family SEPSIDAE (4) – Black Scavenger Flies

Sepsis fulgens Meigen, 1826
Sepsis cynipsea (Linnaeus, 1758)
Sepsis punctum (Fabricius, 1794)
Sepsis violacea Meigen, 1826

Family SPHAEROCERIDAE (8) – Lesser Dung-flies
Lotophila atra (Meigen, 1830)
Crumomyia nigra (Meigen, 1830)
Crumomyia nitida (Meigen, 1830)
Crumomyia notabilis (Collin, 1902)
Limosina silvatica (Meigen, 1830)
Spelobia (Spelobia) clunipes (Meigen, 1830)
Spelobia (Spelobia) manicata (Richards, 1927)
Sphaerocera curvipes Latreille, 1804

Family STRATIOMYIDAE (5) – Soldier-flies
Beris chalybata (Forster, 1771)
Beris fuscipes Meigen, 1820
Chloromyia formosa (Scopoli, 1763)
Sargus bipunctatus (Scopoli, 1763) - Twin-spot Centurion
Sargus iridatus (Scopoli, 1763)

Family SYRPHIDAE (21) – Hoverflies
Baccha elongata (Fabricius, 1775)
Brachypalpoides lentus (Meigen, 1822)
Cheilosia illustrata (Harris, 1780)
Episyrphus balteatus (DeGeer, 1776)
Epistrophe grossulariae (Meigen, 1822)
Eristalis nemorum (Linnaeus, 1758)
Eristalis intricaria (Linnaeus, 1758)
Eristalis pertinax (Scopoli, 1763)
Eupeodes corollae (Fabricius, 1794)
Eupeodes latifasciatus (Macquart, 1829)
Helophilus pendulus (Linnaeus, 1758)
Leucozona lucorum (Linnaeus, 1758)
Melanostoma scalare (Fabricius, 1794)
Myathropa florea (Linnaeus, 1758)
Platycheirus albimanus (Fabricius, 1781)
Scaeva pyrastri (Linnaeus, 1758)
Syrphus vitripennis Meigen, 1822
Syritta pipiens (Linnaeus, 1758)
Volucella pellucens (Linnaeus, 1758)
Xylota segnis (Linnaeus, 1758)
Xylota sylvarum (Linnaeus, 1758)

Family TABANIDAE (1) – Horseflies
Haematopota pluvialis (Linnaeus, 1758) – Common Clegg

Family TACHINIDAE (8) – Parasite Flies
Carcelia (Carcelia) gnava (Meigen, 1824)
Dexiosoma caninum (Fabricius, 1781)
Eriothrix rufomaculata (DeGeer, 1776)
Gymnocheta viridis (Fallén, 1810)
Pelatachina tibialis (Fallén, 1810)
Phebellia glauca (Meigen, 1824)
Siphona sp.
Tachina fera (Linnaeus, 1761)

Family TEPHRITIDAE (2) – Picture-winged Flies or Fruitflies
Acidia cognata (Wiedemann, 1817)
Trypeta sp.

Family XYLOPHAGIDAE (1) – Awl-flies
Xylophagus ater Meigen, 1804

Order Ephemeroptera (Mayflies; 1 species)

The record is taken from the unpublished report prepared by the Liverpool Museum staff and associates resulting from the Alderley Edge Invertebrate Survey undertaken by their team in 1996 (courtesy of Ian Wallace, Liverpool). Nomenclature follows Kloet and Hinks (1964).

Family BAETIDAE (1)
Cloeon dipterum (Linnaeus, 1761)

Order Hemiptera (Bugs; 126 species)

Based on the unpublished report prepared by the Liverpool Museum staff and associates resulting from the Alderley Edge Invertebrate Survey undertaken by their team in 1996 (courtesy of Steve Judd, Liverpool), on the paper by Judd (2012), and on the data extracted from the Lancashire and Cheshire Card Index of Harry Britten in the Manchester Museum, with sixteen additional species (courtesy of Phillip Rispin). Hemiptera were collected by S. Judd and C. Felton and identified by S. Judd; one species (*Aradus depressus*) was collected by C. Johnson (Manchester). The collection of voucher specimens is kept in the National Museums Liverpool. The list of aquatic groups is based on the unpublished reports of two aquatic invertebrate surveys undertaken by Ian Wallace from the Liverpool Museum in 1996 and by Jonathan Guest in 1998 (see Chapter 12). The list of Aphids (families Aphididae, Callaphididae, Lachnidae and Pemphigidae) is based in the data extracted from the corresponding slide collection and the Lancashire and Cheshire Card Index of H. Britten. Nomenclature of the suborders of Hemiptera follows Forero (2008; see also Dolling, 1991). The Heteroptera follow the revised checklist of British species by Nau (2006), but tribal names are omitted; the British Auchenorhyncha follow the updated checklist by Le Quesne and Payne (1981), but subfamily names are omitted and the Aphrophoridae is here considered a family rank, following Bantock and Botting (2010); families included in the suborder Sternorrhyncha are given given according to Kloet and Hinks (1964).

Suborder Auchenorrhyncha

Family APHROPHORIDAE (3) – Froghoppers or Spittlebugs
Aphrophora alni (Fallén, 1805)
Neophilaenus lineatus (Linnaeus, 1758)
Philaenus spumarius (Linnaeus, 1758) – Common Froghopper

Family CICADELLIDAE (26) – Leafhoppers
Adarrus ocellaris (Fallén, 1806)
Allygus mixtus (Fabricius, 1794)

Aphrodes albifrons (Linnaeus, 1758)
Cicadella viridis (Linnaeus, 1758) – Green Leafhopper
Cicadula quadrinotata (Fabricius, 1794)
Conosanus obsoletus (Kirschbaum, 1858)
Deltocephalus pulicaris (Fallén, 1806)
Elymana sulphurella (Zetterstedt, 1828)
Eupelix cuspidata (Fabricius, 1775)
Eupteryx aurata (Linnaeus, 1758)
Eupteryx urticae (Fabricius, 1803)
Eurhadina concinna (Germar, 1831)
Eurhadina pulchella (Fallén, 1806)
Euscelis lineolatus Brullé, 1832
Fagocyba carri (Edwards, 1914)
Fagocyba cruenta (Herrich-Schaeffer, 1838)
Iassus lanio (Linnaeus, 1761)
Jassargus distinguendus (Flor, 1861)
Linnavuoriana decempunctata (Fallén, 1806)
Linnavuoriana sexmaculata (Hardy, 1850)
Oncopsis flavicollis (Linnaeus, 1761)
Ribautiana scalaris (Ribaut, 1931)
Speudotettix subfusculus (Fallén, 1806)
Streptanus marginatus (Kirschbaum, 1858)
Streptanus sordidus (Zetterstedt, 1828)
Ulopa reticulata (Fabricius, 1794)

Family CIXIIDAE (2) – Planthoppers
Cixius nervosus (Linnaeus, 1758)
Tachycixius pilosus (Olivier, 1791)

Family DELPHACIDAE (3) – Planthoppers
Conomelus anceps (Germar, 1802)
Dicranotropis hamata (Boheman, 1849)
Hyledelphax elegantulus (Boheman, 1847)

Suborder Heteroptera – True Bugs

Family ACANTHOSOMATIDAE (3) – Shield Bugs
Acanthosoma haemorrhoidale (Linnaeus, 1758) – Hawthorn Shieldbug
Elasmostethus interstinctus (Linnaeus, 1758) – Birch Shieldbug
Elasmucha grisea (Linnaeus, 1758) – Parent Bug

Family ANTHOCORIDAE (4) – Flower or Minute Pirate Bugs
Anthocoris confusus Reuter, 1884
Anthocoris nemoralis (Fabricius, 1794)
Anthocoris nemorum (Linnaeus, 1761)
Tetraphleps bicuspis (Herrich-Schäffer, 1835)

Family ARADIDAE (1) – Flat or Bark Bugs
Aradus depressus (Fabricius, 1794)

Family CORIXIDAE (9)
Callicorixa praeusta (Fieber, 1860)
Corixa punctata (Illinger, 1807) – Common Water Boatman
Hesperocorixa sahlbergi (Fieber, 1848) – Lesser Water Boatman
Sigara distincta (Fieber, 1848)
Sigara dorsalis (Leach, 1817)
Sigara falleni (Fieber, 1848)
Sigara lateralis (Leach, 1817)
Sigara limitata (Fieber, 1848)
Sigara nigrolineata (Fieber, 1848)

Family GERRIDAE (1)
Gerris lacustris (Linnaeus, 1758) – Common Pond Skater

Family LYGAEIDAE (8) – Ground or Seed Bugs
Cymus claviculus (Fallén, 1807)
Drymus brunneus (Sahlberg, 1848)
Drymus sylvaticus (Fabricius, 1775)
Kleidocerys ericae (Horváth, 1910)
Kleidocerys resedae (Panzer, 1797) – Birch Catkin Bug
Scolopostethus decoratus (Hahn, 1833)
Stygnocoris sabulosus (Schilling, 1829)
Trapezonotus desertus Seidenstücker, 1951

Family MICROPHYSIDAE (2) – Minute Bugs
Loricula elegantula (Bärensprung, 1853)
Loricula pselaphifromis Curtis, 1833

Family MIRIDAE (45) – Capsid Bugs
Apolygus spinolae (Meyer-Dür, 1841)
Asciodema obsoleta (Fieber, 1864)
Atractotomus magnicornis (Fallén, 1807)
Blepharidopterus angulatus (Fallén, 1807) – Black-kneed Capsid
Bryocoris pteridis (Fallén, 1807) – Fern Bug
Calocoris alpestris (Meyer-Dür, 1843)
Campyloneura virgula (Herrich-Schäffer, 1836)
Closterotomus norvegicus (Gmelin, 1788) – Potato Caspid
Cyllecoris histrionicus (Linnaeus, 1767)
Cyrtorhinus caricis (Fallén, 1807)
Deraeocoris lutescens (Schilling, 1837)
Dicyphus pallicornis (Meyer-Dür in Fieber, 1861)
Dryophilocoris flavoquadrimacula (DeGeer, 1773)
Grypocoris stysi (Wagner, 1968)
Heterocordylus tibialis (Hahn, 1833)
Heterotoma planicornis (Pallas, 1772)
Leptopterna dolabrata (Linnaeus, 1758) – Meadow Plant Bug
Leptopterna ferrugata (Fallén, 1807)
Lygocoris pabulinus (Linnaeus, 1761) – Common Green Capsid
Lygocoris rugicollis (Fallén, 1829)
Liocoris tripustulatus (Fabricius, 1781)
Monalocoris filicis (Linnaeus, 1767) – Bracken Bug
Neolygus contaminatus (Fallén, 1807)
Notostira elongata (Geoffroy in Fourcroy, 1785)
Orthotylus ericetorum (Fallén, 1807)
Orthotylus marginalis Reuter, 1883
Orthotylus virescens (Douglas in Scott, 1865)
Phylus melanocephalus (Linnaeus, 1758)
Phylus palliceps Fieber, 1861
Phytocoris longipennis Flor, 1861
Phytocoris tiliae (Fabricius, 1776)
Phytocoris ulmi (Linnaeus, 1758)
Plagiognathus arbustorum (Fabricius, 1794)
Plagiognathus chrysanthemi (Wolff, 1804)
Psallus flavellus Stichel, 1933
Psallus haematodes (Gmelin, 1788)
Psallus mollis (Mulsant et Rey, 1852)
Psallus varians (Herrich-Schäffer, 1836)
Psallus wagneri Ossianilson, 1953
Rhabdomiris striatellus (Fabricius, 1794)
Stenodema calcarata (Fallén, 1807)
Stenodema holsata (Fabricius, 1787)
Stenodema laevigata (Linnaeus, 1758)
Stenotus binotatus (Fabricius, 1794)
Trigonotylus ruficornis (Geoffroy in Fourcroy, 1785)

Family NABIDAE (4) – Damsel Bugs
Himacerus major (Costa, 1842)
Nabis ferus (Linnaeus, 1758) – Field Damsel Bug
Nabis flavomarginatus Scholtz, 1847 – Broad Damsel Bug
Nabis limbatus Dahlbom 1851 – Marsh Damsel Bug

Family NAUCORIDAE (1)
Ilyocoris cimicoides (Linnaeus, 1758) – Saucer Bug

Family NEPIDAE (1) – Water Scorpions
Nepa cinerea Linnaeus, 1758 – Water Scorpion

Family NOTONECTIDAE (1) – Water Boatmen
Notonecta glauca Linnaeus, 1758 – Common Backswimmer

Family PENTATOMIDAE (2) – Shield Bugs
Piezodorus lituratus (Fabricius, 1794) – Gorse Shieldbug
Picromerus bidens (Linnaeus, 1758)

Family REDUVIIDAE (1) – Assassin Bugs
Empicoris vagabundus (Linnaeus, 1758)

Family SALDIDAE (3) – Shore Bugs
Chartoscirta cincta (Herrich-Schäffer, 1842)
Saldula orthochila (Fieber, 1859)
Saldula saltatoria (Linnaeus, 1758) – Common Shore Bug

Family TINGIDAE (2) – Lace Bugs
Dictyonota strichnocera Fieber, 1844 – Gorse Lacebug
Tingis ampliata (Herrich-Schäffer, 1838)

Family VELIIDAE (2)
Microvelia reticulata (Burmeister, 1835) – Lesser Water Cricket
Velia caprai Tamanini, 1947 – Water Cricket

Suborder Sternorrhyncha

Family APHIDIDAE (3)
Amphorophora ampullata Buckton, 1876
Aphis epilobii Kaltenbach, 1843
Cavariella aegopodii (Scopoli, 1763) – Willow-carrot Aphid

Family CALLAPHIDIDAE (2)
Euceraphis punctipennis (Zetterstedt, 1828) – European Birch Aphid
Myzocallis (*Agrioaphis*) *castanicola* Baker, 1917 – Oak Aphid

Family LACHNIDAE (2)
Protolachnus agilis (Kaltenbach, 1843)
Schizolachnus pineti (Fabricius, 1781) – Grey Pine Aphid

Family PEMPHIGIDAE (1) – Galling Aphids
Pemphigus sp.

Family PSYLLIDAE (2) – Jumping Plant Lice
Aphalara exilis (Weber and Mohr, 1804)
Psylla sorbi (Linnaeus, 1758)

Order Hymenoptera (wasps, bees and allies; 128 species)

The species list contains 128 species and is based on the unpublished report prepared by the Liverpool Museum staff and associates resulting from the Alderley Edge Invertebrate Survey undertaken by their team in 1996 (courtesy of Steve Judd, Liverpool). The Aculeata Hymenoptera were collected and identified by C. Clee and the Symphyta by T. Green. The collection of voucher specimens is kept in the National Museums Liverpool. Four additional species of the families Tenthredinidae and Cynipidae were added from the data released at our request by rECOrd, the Biodiversity Information System for Cheshire (courtesy of Tom Hunt), two species of Ichneumonidae and one of Pompilidae have been taken from Britten (1950) and Askew (1981), and thirty-three additonal records (mostly of the parasitic Hymenoptera, but also of the Andrenidae, Chrysididae, Cimbicidae, Halictidae and Tenthredinidae) were extracted from the Lancashire and Cheshire Card Index of H. Britten held in the Manchester Museum (courtesy of Phillip Rispin).

Nomenclature follows Fitton *et al.* (1978), but that of the Ichneumonidae is in accordance with Broad (in prep.).

Suborder Symphyta – Sawflies

Family CIMBICIDAE (2)
Cimbex femoratus (Linnaeus, 1758)
Trichosoma lucorum (Linnaeus, 1758)

Family TENTHREDINIDAE (9)
Aglaostigma aucupariae (Klug, 1814)
Ametastegia equiseti (Fallén, 1808)
Ametastegia glabrata (Fallén, 1808)
Dolerus ferrugatus Lepeletier, 1823
Dolerus nitens Zaddach, 1859
Eutomostethus luteiventris (Klug, 1814)
Loderus vestigialis (Klug, 1814)
Tenthredo arcuata Forster, 1771
Tenthredopsis nassata (Linnaeus, 1767)

Suborder Apocrita – Wasps, ants and bees

Family ANDRENIDAE (13) – Mining Bees
Andrena (Andrena) clarkella (Kirby, 1802)
Andrena (Andrena) fucata Smith, 1847
Andrena (Andrena) fulva (Müller in Allioni, 1766) – Tawny Mining Bee
Andrena (Andrena) lapponica Zetterestedt, 1838
Andrena (Euandrena) bicolor Fabricius, 1775 – Gwynne's Mining Bee
Andrena (Hoplandrena) jacobi Perkins, 1921
Andrena (Hoplandrena) scotica Perkins, 1921
Andrena (Leucandrena) barbilabris (Kirby, 1802)
Andrena (Melandrena) cineraria (Linnaeus, 1758) – Grey Mining Bee
Andrena (Melandrena) nigroaenea (Kirby, 1802)
Andrena (Micrandrena) subopaca Nylander, 1848
Andrena (Notandrena) chrysosceles (Kirby, 1802)
Andrena (Trachandrena) haemorrhoa (Fabricius, 1781) – Early Mining Bee

Family ANTHOPHORIDAE (5)
Nomada flava Panzer, 1798
Nomada goodeniana (Kirby, 1802) – Gooden's Nomad Bee
Nomada lathburiana (Kirby, 1802)
Nomada leucophthalma (Kirby, 1802)
Nomada panzeri Lepeletier, 1841

Family APIDAE (8) – Social Bees
Bombus (*Bombus*) *hortorum* (Linnaeus, 1761) – Small Garden Bumble Bee
Bombus (*Bombus*) *lapidarius* (Linnaeus, 1758) – Large Red-tailed Bumble Bee
Bombus (*Bombus*) *lucorum* (Linnaeus, 1761) – White-tailed Bumble Bee
Bombus (*Bombus*) *pascuorum* (Scopoli, 1763) – Common Carder Bee
Bombus (*Bombus*) *pratorum* (Linnaeus, 1761) – Early Bumble Bee
Bombus (*Bombus*) *terrestris* (Linnaeus, 1758) – Buff-tailed Bumble Bee
Bombus (*Psithyrus*) *sylvestris* Lepeletier, 1841 – Four-coloured Cuckoo Bee
Bombus (*Psithyrus*) *vestalis* (Geoffroy in Foucroy, 1785) – Vestal Cuckoo Bee

Family BRACONIDAE (3)
Aleiodes circumscriptus (Nees, 1834)
Ephedrus plagiator (Nees, 1811)
Macrocentrus infirmus (Nees, 1834)

Family CHRYSIDIDAE (3) – Ruby-tailed or Cuckoo Wasps
Chrysis (*Chrysis*) *ignita* (Linnaeus, 1758)
Elampus panzeri (Fabricius, 1804)
Omalus (*Notozus*) *panzeri* (Fabricius, 1804)

Family COLLETIDAE (2)
Hylaeus (*Hylaeus*) *communis* Nylander, 1852
Hylaeus (*Spatulariella*) *hyalinatus* Smith, 1803

Family CYNIPIDAE (1) – Gall Wasps
Andricus kollari (Hartig, 1843) – Oak Marble Gall

Family FORMICIDAE (7) – Ants
Formica fusca Linnaeus, 1758 – Negro Ant
Formica lemani Bondroit, 1917
Lasius niger (Linnaeus, 1758) – Black Garden Ant
Myrmica lobicornis Nylander, 1846
Myrmica rubra (Linnaeus, 1758) – Red Ant
Myrmica ruginodis Nylander, 1846
Myrmica scabrinodis Nylander, 1846

Family EUMENIDAE (2) – Potter and Mason Wasps
Ancistrocerus gazella (Panzer, 1798)
Ancistrocerus trifasciatus (Müller, 1776)

Family HALICTIDAE (13)
Halictus tumulorum (Linnaeus, 1758)
Lasioglossum (*Dialictus*) *leucopum* (Kirby, 1802)
Lasioglossum (*Dialictus*) *morio* (Fabricius, 1793)
Lasioglossum (*Dialictus*) *smeathmanellum* (Kirby, 1802)
Lasioglossum (*Evylaeus*) *albipes* (Fabricius, 1781)
Lasioglossum (*Evylaeus*) *calceatum* (Scopoli, 1763) – Slender Mining Bee
Lasioglossum (*Evylaeus*) *fratellum* (Pérez, 1903)
Lasioglossum (*Evylaeus*) *rufitarse* (Zetterstedt, 1838)
Lasioglossum (*Evylaeus*) *villosulum* (Kirby, 1802) – Shaggy Mining Bee
Sphecodes fasciatus von Hagens, 1882

Sphecodes gibbus (Linnaeus, 1758)
Sphecodes monilicornis (Kirby, 1802)
Sphecodes pellucidus Smith, 1845

Family ICHNEUMONIDAE (16) – Ichneumon or Scorpion Wasps
Agrypon clandestinum (Gravenhorst, 1829)
Amblyjoppa proteus (Christ, 1791) [ex Elephant Hawk-moth]
Campoplex difformis (Gmelin, 1790)
Cryptus titubator (Thunberg, 1824)
Diplazon laetatorius (Fabricius, 1781)
Epitomus infuscatus (Gravenhorst, 1829)
Gelis anthracinus (Förster, 1850)
Gelis areator (Panzer, 1804)
Gelis rufogaster Thunberg, 1827
Gregopimpla inquisitor (Scopoli, 1763)
Netelia (Bessobates) cristata (Thomson, 1888)
Phygadeuon troglodytes Gravenhorst, 1829
Rhembobius quadrispinus (Gravenhorst, 1829)
Scambus (Scambus) sagax (Harting, 1838)
Syrphoctonus pictus (Gravenhorst, 1829)
Xorides brachylabis (Kriechbaumer, 1889)

Family MEGACHILIDAE (2) – Leaf-cutting and Mason Bees
Megachile centuncularis (Linnaeus, 1758) – Patchwork Leaf-cutter Bee
Megachile willughbiella (Kirby, 1802) – Willughby's Leaf-cutter Bee

Family PLATYGASTRIDAE (1)
Metaclisis areolata (Haliday in Walker, 1835)

Family POMPILIDAE (7) – Spider-hunting Wasps
Anoplius (Anoplius) concinnus (Dahlbom, 1845)
Anoplius (Anoplius) nigerrimus (Scopoli, 1763)
Arachnospila spissa (Schiødte, 1837)
Dipogon variegatus (Linnaeus, 1758)
Evagetes crassicornis (Shuckard, 1837)
Priocnemis (Priocnemis) schioedtei Haupt, 1927
Priocnemis (Umbripennis) perturbator (Harris, 1780)

Family PROCTOTRUPIDAE (2)
Codrus confusus (Nixon, 1938)
Phaenoserphus calcar (Haliday, 1839)

Family PTEROMALIDAE (2)
Nasonia vitripennis (Walker, 1836)
Stenomalina gracilis (Walker, 1834)

Family SAPYGIDAE (1)
Sapyga quinquepunctata (Fabricius, 1781)

Family SPHECIDAE (24) – Digger Wasps
Argogorytes mystaceus (Linnaeus, 1761) – Field Digger Wasp
Crabro cribrarius (Linnaeus, 1758) – Slender-bodied Digger Wasp
Crabro peltarius (Schreber, 1784)
Crossocerus (Blepharipus) cetratus (Shuckard, 1837)
Crossocerus (Blepharipus) megacephalus (Rossius, 1790)
Crossocerus (Crossocerus) elongatulus (Vander Linder, 1829) – Slender Digger Wasp
Crossocerus (Crossocerus) pusillus Lepeletier et Brullé, 1834
Crossocerus (Crossocerus) tarsatus (Shuckard, 1837)

Crossocerus (*Crossocerus*) *varus* Lepeletier et Brullé, 1835
Crossocerus (*Crossocerus*) *wesmaeli* (Vander Linden, 1829) – Wesmael's Digger Wasp
Crossocerus (*Hoplocrabro*) *quadrimaculatus* (Fabricius, 1793) – Four-spotted Digger Wasp
Ectemnius cavifrons (Thomson, 1870)
Ectemnius cephalotes (Olivier, 1791)
Mellinus arvensis (Linnaeus, 1758) – Field Digger Wasp
Nysso spinosus (Forster, 1771) – Large Spurred Digger Wasp
Oxybelus uniglumis (Linnaeus, 1758) – Common Spiny Digger Wasp
Passaloecus corniger Shuckard, 1837 – Horned Black Wasp
Pemphredon (*Cemonus*) *inornatus* Say, 1824 – Shuckard's Wasp
Pemphredon (*Pemphredon*) *lugubris* (Fabricius, 1793) – Mournful Wasp
Podalonia hirsuta (Scopoli, 1763) – Hairy Sand Wasp
Psen (*Mimesa*) *equestris* (Fabricius, 1804)
Psen (*Mimesa*) *lutarius* (Fabricius, 1804)
Rhopalum (*Rhopalum*) *clavipes* (Linnaeus, 1758)
Trypoxylon attenuatum Smith, 1851 – Slender Wood Borer Wasp

Family TIPHIIDAE (1)
Myrmosa atra Panzer, 1801 – Black Headed Velvet Ant

Family VESPIDAE (5)
Dolichovespula norwegica (Fabricius, 1781) – Norwegian Wasp
Dolichovespula sylvestris (Scopoli, 1763) – Tree Wasp
Vespula (*Paravespula*) *germanica* (Fabricius, 1793) – German Wasp
Vespula (*Paravespula*) *vulgaris* (Linnaeus, 1758) – Common Wasp
Vespula (*Vespula*) *rufa* (Linnaeus, 1758) – Red Wasp

Order Lepidoptera (butterflies and moths; 616 species)

The species list given below is mainly based on the data provided by Shane Farrell, the Data Officer of the Cheshire Moth Group (http://www.consult-eco.ndirect.co.uk/lrc/cmg/cmg.htm), Steve Hind, the Cheshire (VC58) county micromoth recorder, and by Mr Kevin McCabe (Alderley Edge, UK), plus additional data taken from the published account by Ellis (1940), but with updated nomenclature, and from the data released at our request by rECOrd, the Biodiversity Information System for Cheshire (courtesy of Tom Hunt) and one additional record (*Odezia atrata*) from the unpublished report on the National Trust Biological Survey by Jackson and Alexander (1998). The list of the four butterfly families (Hesperidae, Lycaenidae, Nymphalidae and Pieriae) is based on the report by Roger Dennis (Wilmslow, UK) published as section C of Chapter 13 and on the data released by rECOrd.

Nomenclature and English common names are given according to the checklist by Bradley (2000); family composition follows Agassiz *et al.* (2013). Numbers in square brackets following the author name and year of description refer to the 'code numbers' given in Bradley (2000). Using this code, one can easily consult the information on feeding plants and biology of the corresponding species in the checklist by Bradley (2000).

Family ADELIDAE (3)
Adela reaumurella (Linnaeus, 1758) [150]
Nematopogon schwarziellus (Zeller, 1839) [141]
Nematopogon swammerdammella (Linnaeus, 1758) [140]

Family ALUCITIDAE (1)
Alucita hexadactyla Linnaeus, 1758 [1288] – Twenty-plume Moth

Family ARGYRESTHIIDAE (1)
Argyresthia trifasciata Staudinger, 1871 [409a]

Family BLASTOBASIDAE (2)
Blastobasis adustella Walsingham, 1894 [873]
Blastobasis lacticolella Rebel, 1940 [874]

Family BUCCULATRICIDAE (1)
Bucculatrix cidarella Zeller, 1839 [272]

Family CHOREUTIDAE (1)
Anthophila fabriciana (Linnaeus, 1767) [385] – Nettle-tap

Family COLEOPHORIDAE (10)
Coleophora albicosta (Haworth, 1828) [544]
Coleophora albidella (Denis et Schiffermüller, 1775) [532]
Coleophora alticolella Zeller, 1849 [584]
Coleophora caespititiella Zeller, 1839 [587]
Coleophora laricella (Hübner, 1817) [526] – Larch Case-bearer
Coleophora orbitella Zeller, 1849 [511]
Coleophora paripennella Zeller, 1839 [560]
Coleophora serratella (Linnaeus, 1761) [493]
Coleophora taeniipennella Herrich-Schäffer, 1855 [581]
Coleophora trifolii (Curtis, 1832) [516] – Large Clover Case-bearer

Family COSMOPTERIGIDAE (1)
Blastodacna hellerella (Duponchel, 1838) [905]

Family COSSIDAE (1)
Zeuzera pyrina (Linnaeus, 1761) [161] – Leopard Moth

Family CRAMBIDAE (3)
Catoptria falsella (Denis et Schiffermüller, 1775) [1316]
Dipleurina lacustrata (Panzer, 1804) [1338]
Scoparia pyralella (Denis et Schiffermüller, 1775) [1333]

Family DREPANIDAE (9)
Achlya flavicornis (Linnaeus, 1758) [1659] – Yellow Horned
Cilix glaucata (Scopoli, 1763) [1651] – Chinese Character
Falcaria lacertinaria (Linnaeus, 1758) [1645] – Scalloped Hook-tip
Drepana falcataria (Linnaeus, 1758) [1648] – Pebble Hook-tip
Habrosyne pyritoides (Hufnagel, 1766) [1653] – Buff Arches
Ochropacha duplaris (Linnaeus, 1761) [1657] – Common Lutestring
Tethea ocularis (Linnaeus, 1767) [1654] – Figure of Eighty
Thyatira batis (Linnaeus, 1758) [1652] – Peach Blossom
Watsonalla binaria (Hufnagel, 1767) [1646] – Oak Hook-tip

Family ELACHISTIDAE (6)
Cosmiotes freyerella (Hübner, 1825) [631]
Elachista albifrontella (Hübner, 1817) [601]
Elachista argentella (Clerck, 1759) [610]
Elachista canapennella (Hübner, 1813) [607]
Elachista humilis Zeller, 1850 [606]
Elachista rufocinerea (Haworth, 1828) [608]

Family EPERMENIIDAE (1)
Epermenia chaerophyllella (Goeze, 1783) [483]

Family EREBIDAE (10)
Arctia caja (Linnaeus, 1758) [2057] – Garden Tiger
Diaphora mendica (Clerck, 1759) [2063] – Muslin Moth
Eilema depressa (Esper, 1787) [2049] – Buff Footman
Eilema lurideola (Zincken, 1817) [2050] – Common Footman
Nudaria mundana (Linnaeus, 1761) [2038] – Muslin Footman
Orgyia antique (Linnaeus, 1758) [2026] – Vapourer
Phragmatobia fuliginosa (Linnaeus, 1758) [2064] – Ruby Tiger
Spilosoma lubricipeda (Linnaeus, 1758) [2060] – White Ermine
Spilosoma luteum (Hufnagel, 1766) [2061] – Buff Ermine
Tyria jacobaeae (Linnaeus, 1758) [2069] – Cinnabar

Family ERIOCRANIIDAE (3)
Eriocrania salopiella (Stainton, 1854) [10]
Eriocrania semipurpurella (Stephens, 1835) [13]
Eriocrania subpurpurella (Haworth, 1828) [6]

Family GELECHIIDAE (10)
Athrips mouffetella (Linnaeus, 1758) [762]
Brachmia blandella (Fabricius, 1798) [866]
Bryotropha affinis (Haworth, 1828) [779]
Bryotropha domestica (Haworth, 1828) [789]
Bryotropha terrella (Denis et Schiffermüller, 1775) [787]
Carpatolechia alburnella (Zeller, 1839) [771]
Carpatolechia fugitivella (Zeller, 1839) [772]
Helcystogramma rufescens (Haworth, 1828) [868]
Gelechia rhombella (Denis et Schiffermüller, 1775) [800]
Monochroa tenebrella (Hübner, 1817) [735]

Family GEOMETRIDAE (148)
Abraxas grossulariata (Linnaeus, 1758) [1884] – Magpie
Abraxas sylvata (Scopoli, 1763) [1885] – Clouded Magpie
Acasis viretata (Hübner, 1799) [1883] – Yellow-barred Brindle
Aethalura punctulata (Denis et Schiffermüller, 1775) [1951] – Grey Birch
Agriopis aurantiaria (Hübner, 1799) [1933] – Scarse Umber
Agriopis leucophaearia (Denis et Schiffermüller, 1775) [1932] – Spring Usher
Agriopis marginaria (Fabricius, 1777) [1934] – Dotted Border
Alcis repandata repandata (Linnaeus, 1758) [1941] – Mottled Beauty
Archiearis parthenias (Linnaeus, 1761) [1661] – Orange Underwing
Alsophila aescularia (Denis et Schiffermüller, 1775) [1663] – March Moth
Anticlea badiata (Denis et Schiffermüller, 1775) [1746] – Shoulder Stripe
Anticlea derivata (Denis et Schiffermüller, 1775) [1747] – Streamer
Apeira syringaria (Linnaeus, 1758) [1910] – Lilac Beauty
Aplocera plagiata (Linnaeus, 1758) [1867] – Treble-bar
Biston betularia (Linnaeus, 1758) [1931] – Peppered Moth
Biston strataria (Hufnagel, 1767) [1930] – Oak Beauty
Bupalus piniaria (Linnaeus, 1758) [1954] – Bordered White
Cabera exanthemata (Scopoli, 1763) [1956] – Common Wave
Cabera pusaria (Linnaeus, 1758) [1955] – Common White Wave
Campaea margaritata (Linnaeus, 1767) [1960] – Light Emerald

Camptogramma bilineata bilineata (Linnaeus, 1758) [1742] – Yellow Shell
Chesias legatella (Denis et Schiffermüller, 1775) [1864] – Streak
Chesias rufata (Fabricius, 1775) [1865] – Broom-tip
Chiasmia clathrata (Linnaeus, 1758) [1894] – Latticed Heath
Chloroclysta siterata (Hufnagel, 1767) [1760] – Red-green Carpet
Chloroclysta truncata (Hufnagel, 1767) [1764] – Common Marbled Carpet
Chloroclystis v-ata (Haworth, 1809) [1858] – V-Pug
Cidaria fulvata (Forster, 1771) [1765] – Barred Yellow
Colostygia multistrigaria (Haworth, 1809) [1775] – Mottled Grey
Colostygia pectinataria (Knoch, 1781) [1776] – Green Carpet
Colotois pennaria (Linnaeus, 1761) [1923] – Feathered Thorn
Comibaena bajularia (Denis et Schiffermüller, 1775) [1667] – Blotched Emerald
Cosmorhoe ocellata (Linnaeus, 1758) [1752] – Purple Bar
Crocallis elinguaria (Linnaeus, 1758) [1921] – Scalloped Oak
Cyclophora albipunctata (Hufnagel, 1767) [1677] – Birch Mocha
Cyclophora linearia (Hübner, 1799) [1681] – Clay Triple-lines
Dysstroma citrata (Linnaeus, 1761) [1762] – Dark Marbled Carpet
Ecliptopera silaceata (Denis et Schiffermüller, 1775) [1759] – Small Phoenix
Ectropis bistortata (Goeze, 1781) [1947] – Engrailed
Ectropis crepuscularia (Denis et Schiffermüller, 1775) [1948] – Small Engrailed
Electrophaes corylata (Thunberg, 1792) [1773] – Broken-barred Carpet
Ennomos alniaria (Linnaeus, 1758) [1913] – Canary-shouldered Thorn
Ennomos erosaria (Denis et Schiffermüller, 1775) [1915] – September Thorn
Ennomos fuscantaria (Haworth, 1809) [1914] – Dusky Thorn
Ennomos quercinaria (Hufnagel, 1767) [1912] – August Thorn
Epirrita autumnata (Borkhausen, 1794) [1797] – Autumnal Moth
Epirrita dilutata (Denis et Schiffermüller, 1775) [1795] – November Moth
Epirrita filigrammaria (Herrich-Schäffer, 1846) [1798] – Small Autumnal Moth
Euchoeca nebulata (Scopoli, 1763) [1874] – Dingy Shell
Eulithis mellinata (Fabricius, 1787) [1757] – Spinach
Eulithis testata (Linnaeus, 1761) [1755] – Chevron
Eupithecia abbreviata Stephens, 1831 [1852] – Brindled Pug
Eupithecia abietaria (Goeze, 1781) [1815] – Cloaked Pug
Eupithecia absinthiata (Clerck, 1759) [1830] – Wormwood Pug
Eupithecia assimilata Doubleday, 1856 [1832] – Currant Pug
Eupithecia centaureata (Denis et Schiffermüller, 1775) [1825] – Lime-speck Pug
Eupithecia dodoneata Guenée, 1858 [1853] – Oak-tree Pug
Eupithecia exiguata (Hübner, 1813) [1819] – Mottled Pug
Eupithecia icterata icterata (Villers, 1789) [1838] – Tawny Speckled Pug
Eupithecia indigata (Hübner, 1813) [1844] – Ochreous Pug
Eupithecia innotata (Hufnagel, 1767) [1848] – Angle-barred Pug
Eupithecia intricata (Zetterstedt, 1839) [1827] – Freyer's Pug
Eupithecia lariciata (Freyer, 1842) [1856] – Larch Pug
Eupithecia nanata (Hübner, 1813) [1846] – Narrow-winged Pug
Eupithecia pulchellata pulchellata Stephens, 1831 [1817] – Foxglove Pug
Eupithecia pusillata (Denis et Schiffermüller, 1775) [1854] – Juniper Pug
Eupithecia tantillaria Boisduval, 1840 [1857] – Dwarf Pug
Eupithecia tenuiata (Hübner, 1813) [1811] – Slender Pug
Eupithecia satyrata satyrata (Hübner, 1813) [1828] – Satyr Pug
Eupithecia subfuscata (Haworth, 1809) [1837] – Grey Pug
Eupithecia succenturiata (Linnaeus, 1758) [1839] – Bordered Pug
Eupithecia tripunctaria Herrich-Schäffer, 1852 [1835] – White-spotted Pug
Eupithecia virgaureata Doubleday, 1861 [1851] – Golden-rod Pug
Eupithecia vulgata (Haworth, 1809) [1834] – Common Pug
Entephria caesiata (Denis et Schiffermüller, 1775) [1744] – Grey Mountain Carpet
Epione repandaria (Hufnagel, 1767) [1907] – Bordered Beauty
Epirrhoe alternata alternata (Müller, 1764) [1738] – Common Carpet
Epirrhoe galiata (Denis et Schiffermüller, 1775) [1740] – Galium Carpet
Epirrita autumnata (Borkhausen, 1794) [1797] – Autumnal Moth
Epirrita dilutata (Denis et Schiffermüller, 1775) [1795] – November Moth
Epirrita filigrammaria (Herrich-Schäffer, 1846) [1798] – Small Autumnal Moth
Erannis defoliaria (Clerck, 1759) [1935] – Mottled Umber
Eulithis populata (Linnaeus, 1758) [1756] – Northern Spinach
Eulithis prunata (Linnaeus, 1758) [1754] – Phoenix
Eulithis pyraliata (Denis et Schiffermüller, 1775) [1758] – Barred Straw
Geometra papilionaria (Linnaeus, 1758) [1666] – Large Emerald
Gymnoscelis rufifasciata (Haworth, 1809) [1862] – Double-striped Pug
Hemithea aestivaria (Hübner, 1799) [1669] – Common Emerald

Hydrelia flammeolaria (Hufnagel, 1767) [1876] – Small Yellow Wave
Hydria cervinalis (Scopoli, 1763) [1788] – Scarce Tissue
Hydria undulata (Linnaeus, 1758) [1789] – Scallop Shell
Hydriomena furcata (Thunberg, 1784) [1777] – July Highflyer
Hydriomena impluviata (Denis et Schiffermüller, 1775) [1778] – May Highflyer
Hylaea fasciaria (Linnaeus, 1758) [1962] – Barred Red
Idaea aversata (Linnaeus, 1758) [1713] – Riband Wave
Idaea biselata (Hufnagel, 1767) [1702] – Small Fan-footed Wave
Idaea dimidiate (Hufnagel, 1767) [1708] – Single-dotted Wave
Idaea fuscovenosa (Goeze, 1781) [1705] – Dwarf Cream Wave
Idaea seriata (Schrank, 1802) [1707] – Small Dusty Wave
Jodis lactearia (Linnaeus, 1758) [1674] – Little Emerald
Lampropteryx suffumata (Denis et Schiffermüller, 1775) [1750] – Water Carpet
Lobophora halterata (Hufnagel, 1767) [1879] – Seraphim
Lomaspilis marginata (Linnaeus, 1758) [1887] – Clouded Border
Lomographa bimaculata (Fabricius, 1775) [1957] – White-pinion Spotted
Lomographa temerata (Denis et Schiffermüller, 1775) [1958] – Clouded Silver
Macaria liturata (Clerck, 1759) [1893] – Tawny-barred Angle
Macaria notata (Linnaeus, 1758) [1889] – Peacock Moth
Macaria wauaria (Linnaeus, 1758) [1897] – V-Moth
Menophra abruptaria (Thunberg, 1792) [1936] – Waved Umber
Mesoleuca albicillata (Linnaeus, 1758) [1748] – Beautiful Carpet
Mesotype didymata (Linnaeus, 1758) [1809] – Twin-spot Carpet
Odezia atrata (Linnaeus, 1758) – Chimney Sweeper
Odontopera bidentata (Clerck, 1759) [1920] – Scalloped Hazel
Operophtera brumata (Linnaeus, 1758) [1799] – Winter Moth
Operophtera fagata (Scharfenberg, 1805) [1800] – Northern Winter Moth
Opisthograptis luteolata (Linnaeus, 1758) [1906] – Brimstone Moth
Ourapteryx sambucaria (Linnaeus, 1758) [1922] – Swallow-tailed Moth
Pasiphila rectangulata (Linnaeus, 1758) [1860] – Green Pug
Pelurga comitata (Linnaeus, 1758) [1749] – Dark Spinach
Pennithera firmata (Hübner, 1822) [1767] – Pine Carpet
Peribatodes rhomboidaria (Denis et Schiffermüller, 1775) [1937] – Willow Beauty
Perizoma affinitata (Stephens, 1831) [1802] – Rivulet
Perizoma albulata (Denis et Schiffermüller, 1775) [1807] – Grass Rivulet
Perizoma alchemillata (Linnaeus, 1758) [1803] – Small Rivulet
Perizoma flavofasciata (Thunberg, 1792) [1808] – Sandy Carpet
Petrophora chlorosata (Scopoli, 1763) [1902] – Brown Silver-line
Phigalia pilosaria (Denis et Schiffermüller, 1775) [1926] – Pale Brindled Beauty
Plagodis dolabraria (Linnaeus, 1767) [1904] – Scorched Wing
Plemyria rubiginata (Denis et Schiffermüller, 1775) [1766] – Blue-bordered Carpet
Pseudoterpna pruinata (Walker, 1863) [1665] – Grass Emerald
Rheumaptera hastata (Linnaeus, 1758) [1787] – Argent and Sable
Rhodometra sacraria (Linnaeus, 1767) [1716] – The Vestal
Scopula floslactata (Haworth, 1809) [1693] – Cream Wave
Scotopteryx chenopodiata (Linnaeus, 1758) [1732] – Shaded Broad-bar
Scotopteryx mucronata (Heydemann, 1925) [1733] – Lead Belle
Selenia dentaria (Fabricius, 1775) [1917] – Early Thorn
Selenia lunularia (Hübner, 1788) [1918] – Lunar Thorn
Selenia tetralunaria (Hufnagel, 1767) [1919] – Purple Thorn
Thera britannica (Turner, 1925) [1769] – Spruce Carpet
Thera juniperata (Linnaeus, 1758) [1771] – Juniper Carpet
Thera obeliscata (Hübner, 1787) [1768] – Grey Pine Carpet
Theria primaria (Haworth, 1809) [1960] – Early Moth
Timandra comae (Schmidt, 1931) [1682] – Blood-vein
Trichopteryx carpinata (Borkhausen, 1794) [1881] – Early Tooth-striped
Triphosa dubitata (Linnaeus, 1758) [1790] – Tissue
Xanthorhoe designata (Hufnagel, 1767) [1722] – Flame Carpet
Xanthorhoe ferrugata (Clerck, 1759) [1725] – Dark-barred Twin-spot Carpet
Xanthorhoe fluctuata fluctuata (Linnaeus, 1758) [1728] – Garden Carpet
Xanthorhoe montanata montanata (Denis et Schiffermüller, 1775) [1727] – Silver-ground Carpet
Xanthorhoe spadicearia (Denis et Schiffermüller, 1775) [1724] – Red Twin-spot Carpet

Family GLYPHIPTERIGIDAE (2)
Glyphipteryx simpliciella (Stephens, 1834) [391] – Cocksfoot Moth
Glyphipterix thrasonella (Scopoli, 1763) [397]

Family GRACILLARIIDAE (34)

Aspilapteryx tringipennella (Zeller, 1839) [294]
Callisto denticulella (Thunberg, 1794) [310]
Caloptilia alchimiella (Scopoli, 1763) [286]
Caloptilia betulicola (Hering, 1927) [283]
Caloptilia elongella (Linnaeus, 1761) [282]
Caloptilia rufipennella (Hübner, 1796) [284]
Caloptilia stigmatella (Fabricius, 1781) [288]
Caloptilia syringella (Fabricius, 1794) [293]
Cameraria ohridella Deschka et Dimić, 1986 [366a] – Horse Chestnut Leaf-miner
Parornix anglicella (Stainton, 1850) [303]
Parornix betulae (Stainton, 1854) [301]
Parornix devoniella (Stainton, 1850) [304]
Phyllonorycter coryli (Nicelli, 1851) [342] – Nut Leaf Blister Moth
Phyllonorycter emberizaepenella (Bouché, 1834) [354]
Phyllonorycter froelichiella (Zeller, 1839) [358]
Phyllonorycter geniculella (Ragonot, 1874) [364]
Phyllonorycter harrisella (Linnaeus, 1761) [315]
Phyllonorycter hilarella (Zetterstedt, 1839) [337]
Phyllonorycter lautella (Zeller, 1846) [351]
Phyllonorycter leucographella (Zeller, 1850) [332a] – Firethorn Leaf Miner
Phyllonorycter maestingella (Müller, 1764) [341]
Phyllonorycter messaniella (Zeller, 1846) [321]
Phyllonorycter oxyacanthae (Frey, 1856) [323]
Phyllonorycter platani (Staudinger, 1870) [321a]
Phyllonorycter platanoidella (Joannis, 1920) [363]
Phyllonorycter quercifoliella (Zeller, 1839) [320]
Phyllonorycter quinnata (Geoffroy, 1785) [343]
Phyllonorycter rajella (Linnaeus, 1758) [345]
Phyllonorycter salictella viminiella (Sircom, 1848) [333]
Phyllonorycter sorbi (Frey, 1855) [324]
Phyllonorycter strigulatella (Lienig et Zeller, 1846) [344]
Phyllonorycter trifasciella (Haworth, 1828) [361]
Phyllonorycter tristrigella (Haworth, 1828) [356]
Phyllonorycter ulmifoliella (Hübner, 1817) [353]

Family HELIOZELIDAE (2)

Heliozela hammoniella Sorhagen, 1885 [157]
Heliozela sericiella (Haworth, 1828) [154]

Family HEPIALIDAE (5)

Hepialus humuli humuli (Linnaeus, 1758) [14] – Common Ghost Moth
Hepialus (Korscheltellus) lupulinus (Linnaeus, 1758) [17] – Common Swift
Hepialus (Pharmacis) fusconebulosa (DeGeer, 1778) [18] – Map-winged Swift
Hepialus (Triodia) sylvina (Linnaeus, 1761) [15] – Orange Swift
Phymatopus hecta (Linnaeus, 1758) [16] – Gold Swift

Family HESPERIIDAE (2)

Thymelicus sylvestris (Poda, 1761) [1526] – Small Skipper
Ochlodes faunus (Turani, 1905) [1531] – Large Skipper

Family LASIOCAMPIDAE (2)

Poecilocampa populi (Linnaeus, 1758) [1631] – December Moth
Saturnia pavonia (Linnaeus, 1758) [1643] – Emperor Moth

Family LYCAENIDAE (4)

Lycaena phlaeas eleus (Fabricius, 1798) [1561] – Small Copper
Neozephyrus quercus (Linnaeus, 1758) [1557] – Purple Hairstreak
Polyommatus icarus icarus (Rottemburg, 1775) [1574] – Common Blue
Celastrina argiolus brittanna (Verity, 1919) [1580] – Holly Blue

Family LYMANTRIIDAE (3)
Calliteara pudibunda (Linnaeus, 1758) [2028] – Pale Tussock
Euproctis similis (Fuessly, 1775) [2030] – Yellow-tail
Leucoma salicis (Linnaeus, 1758) [2031] – White Satin

Family LYONETIIDAE (3)
Leucoptera laburnella (Stainton, 1851) [254] – Laburnum Leaf Miner
Leucoptera spartifoliella (Hübner, 1813) [256]
Lyonetia clerkella (Linnaeus, 1758) [263] – Apple Leaf Miner

Family MICROPTERIGIDAE (1)
Micropterix aruncella (Scopoli, 1763) [4]

Family MOMPHIDAE (3)
Mompha epilobiella (Denis et Schiffermüller, 1775) [893]
Mompha raschkiella (Zeller, 1839) [883]
Mompha subbistrigella (Haworth, 1828) [892]

Family NEPTICULIDAE (28)
Bohemannia pulverosella (Stainton, 1849) [40]
Ectoedemia (Etainia) albifasciella (Heinemann, 1871) [37]
Ectoedemia (Etainia) angulifasciella (Stainton, 1849) [28]
Ectoedemia (Etainia) atricollis (Stainton, 1857) [29]
Ectoedemia (Etainia) intimella (Zeller, 1848) [25]
Ectoedemia (Etainia) minimella (Zetterstedt, 1839) [35]
Ectoedemia (Etainia) occultella (Linnaeus, 1767) [34]
Ectoedemia (Etainia) subbimaculella (Haworth, 1828) [38]
Ectoedemia (Fomoria) septembrella (Stainton, 1849) [42]
Stigmella anomalella (Goeze, 1783) [92] – Rose Leaf Miner
Stigmella aurella (Fabricius, 1775) [50]
Stigmella confusella (Wood, 1894) [117]
Stigmella floslactella (Haworth, 1828) [75]
Stigmella hemargyrella (Kollar, 1832) [81]
Stigmella hybnerella (Hübner, 1796) [99]
Stigmella lapponica (Wocke, 1862) [116]
Stigmella lemniscella (Zeller, 1839) [63]
Stigmella luteella (Stainton, 1857) [112]
Stigmella microtheriella (Stainton, 1854) [111]
Stigmella nylandriella (Tengsdtröm, 1848) [103]
Stigmella obliquella (Heinemann, 1862) [70]
Stigmella oxyacanthella (Stainton, 1854) [100]
Stigmella perpygmaeella (Doubleday, 1859) [79]
Stigmella ruficapitella (Haworth, 1828) [84]
Stigmella salicis (Stainton, 1854) [68]
Stigmella samiatella (Zeller, 1839) [88]
Stigmella sorbi (Stainton, 1861) [66]
Stigmella tityrella (Stainton, 1854) [77]

Family NOCTUIDAE (169)
Abrostola tripartita (Hufnagel, 1766) [2450] – Spectacle
Abrostola triplasia (Linnaeus, 1758) [2449] – Dark Spectacle
Acronicta alni (Linnaeus, 1767) [2281] – Alder Moth
Acronicta leporina (Linnaeus, 1758) [2280] – Miller
Acronicta rumicis (Linnaeus, 1758) [2289] – Knot Grass
Acronicta tridens (Denis et Schiffermüller, 1775) [2283] – Dark Dagger
Acronicta megacephala (Denis et Schiffermüller, 1775) [2278] – Poplar Grey
Acronicta psi (Linnaeus, 1758) [2284] – Grey Dagger
Agrochola circellaris (Hufnagel, 1766) [2262] – Brick
Agrochola helvola (Linnaeus, 1758) [2265] – Flounced Chestnut
Agrochola litura (Linnaeus, 1761) [2266] – Brown-spot Pinion
Agrochola lota (Clerck, 1759) [2263] – Red-line Quaker

Agrochola lychnidis (Denis et Schiffermüller, 1775) [2267] – Beaded Chestnut
Agrochola macilenta (Hübner, 1809) [2264] – Yellow-line Quaker
Agrotis exclamationis (Linnaeus, 1758) [2089] – Heart and Dart
Agrotis ipsilon (Hufnagel, 1766) [2091] – Dark Sword-grass
Agrotis segetum (Denis et Schiffermüller, 1775) [2087] – Turnip Moth
Agrotis trux trux Stephens, 1829 [2090] – Crescent Dart
Agrotis puta (Hübner, 1803) [2092] – Shuttle-shaped Dart
Allophyes oxyacanthae (Linnaeus, 1758) [2245] – Green-brindled Crescent
Amphipoea lucens (Freyer, 1845) [2357] – Large Ear
Amphipoea oculea (Linnaeus, 1761) [2360] – Ear Moth
Amphipyra berbera svenssoni Fletcher, 1968 [2298] – Svensson's Copper Underwing
Amphipyra pyramidea (Linnaeus, 1758) [2297] – Copper Underwing
Amphipyra tragopoginis (Clerck, 1759) [2299] – Mouse Moth
Anaplectoides prasina (Denis et Schiffermüller, 1775) [2138] – Green Arches
Anarta myrtilli (Linnaeus, 1761) [2142] – Beautiful Yellow Underwing
Anarta trifolii (Hufnagel, 1766) [2145] – Nutmeg
Anorthoa munda (Denis et Schiffermüller, 1775) [2189] – Twin-spotted Quaker
Antitype chi (Linnaeus, 1758) [2254] – Grey Chi
Apamea anceps (Denis et Schiffermüller, 1775) [2333] – Large Nutmeg
Apamea epomidion (Haworth, 1809) [2327] – Clouded Brindle
Apamea crenata (Hufnagel, 1766) [2326] – Clouded-bordered Brindle
Apamea lithoxylaea (Denis et Schiffermüller, 1775) [2322] – Light Arches
Apamea monoglypha (Hufnagel, 1766) [2321] – Dark Arches
Apamea remissa (Hübner, 1809) [2330] – Dusky Brocade
Apamea scolopacina (Esper, 1788) [2335] – Slender Brindle
Apamea sordens (Hufnagel, 1766) [2334] – Rustic Shoulder-knot
Apamea unanimis (Hübner, 1813) [2331] – Small Clouded Brindle
Atethmia centrago (Haworth, 1809) [2269] – Centre-barred Sallow
Aporophyla lutulenta (Denis et Schiffermüller, 1775) [2231] – Deep-brown Dart
Aporophyla nigra (Haworth, 1809) [2232] – Black Rustic
Autographa bractea (Denis et Schiffermüller, 1775) [2444] – Gold Spangle
Autographa gamma (Linnaeus, 1758) [2441] – Silver Y
Autographa jota (Linnaeus, 1758) [2443] – Plain Golden Y
Autographa pulchrina (Haworth, 1809) [2442] – Beautiful Golden Y
Axylia putris (Linnaeus, 1761) [2098] – Flame
Bena bicolorana (Linnaeus, 1758) [2421] – Scarce Silver-lines
Brachylomia viminalis (Fabricius, 1777) [2225] – Minor Shoulder-knot
Caradrina clavipalpis (Scopoli, 1763) [2389] – Pale Mottled Willow
Caradrina morpheus (Hufnagel, 1766) [2387] – Mottled Rustic
Catocala nupta (Linnaeus, 1767) [2452] – Red Underwing
Celaena haworthii (Curtis, 1829) [2367] – Haworth's Minor
Cerapteryx graminis (Linnaeus, 1758) [2176] – Antler Moth
Cerastis rubricosa (Denis et Schiffermüller, 1775) [2139] – Red Chestnut
Charanyca trigrammica (Hufnagel, 1766) [2380] – Treble Lines
Chortodes pygmina (Haworth, 1809) [2350] – Small Wainscot
Cirrhia gilvago (Denis et Schiffermüller, 1775) [2275] – Dusky-lemon Sallow
Coenobia rufa (Haworth, 1809) [2379] – Small Rufous
Conistra ligula (Esper, 1791) [2259] – Dark Chestnut
Conistra vaccinii (Linnaeus, 1761) [2258] – Chestnut
Cosmia affinis (Linnaeus, 1767) [2316] – Lesser-spotted Pinion
Cosmia trapezina (Linnaeus, 1758) [2318] – Dun-bar
Cryphia domestica (Hufnagel, 1766) [2293] – Marbled Beauty
Cucullia chamomillae (Denis et Schiffermüller, 1775) [2214] – Chamomile Shark
Cucullia umbratica (Linnaeus, 1758) [2216] - Shark
Diachrysia chrysitis (Linnaeus, 1758) [2434] – Burnished Brass
Diarsia brunnea (Denis et Schiffermüller, 1775) [2122] – Purple Clay
Diarsia dahlia (Hübner, 1813) [2121] – Barred Chestnut
Diarsia florida (Schmidt, 1859) [2124] – Fen Square-spot
Diarsia mendica mendica (Fabricius, 1775) [2120] – Ingrailed Clay
Diarsia rubi (Vieweg, 1790) [2123] – Small Square-spot
Dryobotodes eremita (Fabricius, 1775) [2248] – Brindled Green
Dypterygia scabriuscula (Linnaeus, 1758) [2301] – Bird's Wing
Enargia paleacea (Esper, 1788) [2313] – Angle-striped Sallow
Eugnorisma glareosa (Esper, 1788) [2117] – Autumnal Rustic
Euxoa tritici (Linnaeus, 1761) [2081] – White-line Dart
Euplexia lucipara (Linnaeus, 1758) [2305] – Small Angle Shades
Eupsilia transversa (Hufnagel, 1766) [2256] – Satellite
Euxoa nigricans (Linnaeus, 1761) [2082] – Garden Dart

Gortyna flavago (Denis et Schiffermüller, 1775) [2364] – Frosted Orange
Graphiphora augur (Fabricius, 1775) [2114] – Double Dart
Griposia aprilina (Linnaeus, 1758) [2247] – Merveille du Jour
Hada plebeja (Linnaeus, 1761) [2147] – Shears
Hadena bicruris (Hufnagel, 1766) [2173] – Lychnis
Hadena confusa (Hufnagel, 1766) [2171] – Marbled Coronet
Hadena perplexa (Denis et Schiffermüller, 1775) [2167] – Tawny Shears
Hecatera bicolorata (Hufnagel, 1766) [2164] – Broad-barred White
Helicoverpa armigera (Hübner, 1808) [2400] – Scarce Bordered Straw
Heliothis peltigera (Denis et Schiffermüller, 1775) [2403] – Bordered Straw
Herminia grisealis (Denis et Schiffermüller, 1775) [2492] – Small Fan-foot
Hoplodrina alsines (Brahm, 1791) [2381] – Uncertain
Hoplodrina blanda (Denis et Schiffermüller, 1775) [2382] – Rustic
Hydraecia micacea (Esper, 1789) [2361] – Rosy Rustic
Hypena proboscidalis (Linnaeus, 1758) [2477] – Snout
Ipimorpha subtusa (Denis et Schiffermüller, 1775) [2312] – Olive
Lacanobia oleracea (Linnaeus, 1758) [2160] – Bright-line Brown-eye
Lacanobia thalassina (Hufnagel, 1766) [2158] – Pale-shouldered Brocade
Lateroligia ophiogramma (Esper, 1794) [2336] – Double Lobed
Lithophane leautieri hesperica Boursin, 1957 [2240] – Blair's Shoulder-knot
Lithophane social (Hufnagel, 1766) [2236] – Pale Pinion
Luperina testacea (Denis et Schiffermüller, 1775) [2353] – Flounced Rustic
Lycophotia porphyrea (Denis et Schiffermüller, 1775) [2118] – True Lover's Knot
Mamestra brassicae (Linnaeus, 1758) [2154] – Cabbage Moth
Melanchra persicariae (Linnaeus, 1761) [2155] – Dot Moth
Melanchra pisi (Linnaeus, 1758) [2163] – Broom Moth
Mesapamea didyma (Esper, 1788) [2343a] – Lesser Common Rustic
Mesapamea secalis (Linnaeus, 1758) [2343] – Common Rustic
Mesoligia furuncula (Denis et Schiffermüller, 1775) [2341] – Cloaked Minor
Mesoligia literosa (Haworth, 1809) [2342] – Rosy Minor
Mniotype adusta (Esper, 1790) [2250] – Dark Brocade
Mythimna comma (Linnaeus, 1761) [2205] – Shoulder-striped Wainscot
Mythimna conigera (Denis et Schiffermüller, 1775) [2192] – Brown-line Bright-eye
Mythimna farrago (Fabricius, 1787) [2193] – Clay
Mythimna impura (Hübner, 1808) [2198] – Smoky Wainscot
Mythimna pallens (Linnaeus, 1758) [2199] – Common Wainscot
Naenia typica (Linnaeus, 1758) [2136] – Gothic
Noctua comes Hübner, 1813 [2109] – Lesser Yellow Underwing
Noctua fimbriata (Schreber, 1759) [2110] – Broad-bordered Yellow Underwing
Noctua interjecta caliginosa (Schawerda, 1919) [2112] – Least Yellow Underwing
Noctua janthe Borkhausen, 1792 [2111] – Lesser Broad-bordered Yellow Underwing
Noctua pronuba Linnaeus, 1758 [2107] – Large Yellow Underwing
Nonagria typhae (Thunberg, 1784) [2369] – Bulrush Wainscot
Ochropleura plecta (Linnaeus, 1761) [2102] – Flame Shoulder
Oligia fasciuncula (Haworth, 1809) [2340] – Middle-barred Minor
Oligia latruncula (Denis et Schiffermüller, 1775) [2339] – Tawny Marbled Minor
Oligia strigilis (Linnaeus, 1758) [2337] – Marbled Minor
Oligia versicolor (Borkhausen, 1792) [2338] – Rufous Minor
Omphaloscelis lunosa (Haworth, 1809) [2270] – Lunar Underwing
Orthosia cerasi (Fabricius, 1775) [2187] – Common Quaker
Orthosia cruda (Denis et Schiffermüller, 1775) [2182] – Small Quaker
Orthosia gothica (Linnaeus, 1758) [2190] – Hebrew Character
Orthosia gracilis (Denis et Schiffermüller, 1775) [2186] – Powdered Quaker
Orthosia incerta (Hufnagel, 1766) [2188] – Clouded Drab
Orthosia populeti (Fabricius, 1781) [2185] – Lead-coloured Drab
Panolis flammea (Denis et Schiffermüller, 1775) [2179] – Pine Beauty
Papestra biren (Goeze, 1781) [2162] – Glaucous Shears
Parastichtis suspecta (Hübner, 1817) [2268] – Suspected
Parastichtis ypsillon (Denis et Schiffermüller, 1775) [2314] – Dingy Shears
Peridroma saucia (Hübner, 1808) [2119] – Pearly Underwing
Phlogophora meticulosa (Linnaeus, 1758) [2306] – Angle Shades
Photedes minima (Haworth, 1809) [2345] – Small Dotted Buff
Plusia festucae (Linnaeus, 1758) [2439] – Gold Spot
Polia nebulosa (Hufnagel, 1766) [2150] – Grey Archer
Polychrysia moneta (Fabricius, 1787) [2437] – Golden Plusia
Pseudoips prasinana (Linnaeus, 1758) [2422] – Green Silver-lines
Rhizedra lutosa (Hübner, 1803) [2375] – Large Wainscot
Rhyacia simulans (Hufnagel, 1766) [2105] – Dotted Rustic

Rivula sericealis (Scopoli, 1763) [2474] – Straw Dot
Rusina ferruginea (Esper, 1785) [2302] – Brown Rustic
Scoliopteryx libatrix (Linnaeus, 1758) [2469] – Herald
Sideridis rivularis (Fabricius, 1775) [2166] – Campion
Thalpophila matura (Hufnagel, 1766) [2303] – Straw Underwing
Tholera cespitis (Denis et Schiffermüller, 1775) [2177] – Hedge Rustic
Tholera decimalis (Poda, 1761) [2178] – Feathered Gothic
Tiliacea citrago (Linnaeus, 1758) [2271] – Orange Sallow
Xanthia aurago (Denis et Schiffermüller, 1775) [2272] – Barred Sallow
Xanthia icteritia (Hufnagel, 1766) [2274] – Sallow
Xanthia togata (Esper, 1788) [2273] – Pink-barred Sallow
Xestia baja (Denis et Schiffermüller, 1775) [2130] – Dotted Clay
Xestia castanea (Esper, 1798) [2132] – Neglected Rustic
Xestia c-nigrum (Linnaeus, 1758) [2126] – Setaceous Hebrew Character
Xestia ditrapezium (Denis et Schiffermüller, 1775) [2127] – Triple-spotted Clay
Xestia sexstrigata (Haworth, 1809) [2133] – Six-striped Rustic
Xestia triangulum (Hufnagel, 1766) [2128] – Double Square-spot
Xestia xanthographa (Denis et Schiffermüller, 1775) [2134] – Square-spot Rustic
Xylena solidaginis (Hübner, 1803) [2233] – Golden-rod Brindle
Xylocampa areola (Esper, 1789) [2243] – Early Grey
Zanclognatha tarsipennalis (Treitschke, 1835) [2489] – Fan-foot

Family Nolidae (2)
Nola cucullatella (Linnaeus, 1758) [2077] – Short-cloaked Moth
Nycteola revayana (Scopoli, 1772) [2423] – Oak Nycteoline

Family Notodontidae (12)
Cerura vinula (Linnaeus, 1758) [1995] – Puss Moth
Diloba caeruleocephala (Linnaeus, 1758) [2020] – Figure of Eight
Drymonia ruficornis (Hufnagel, 1766) [2015] – Lunar Marbled Brown
Furcula bicuspis (Borkhausen, 1790) [1996] – Alder Kitten
Furcula bifida (Brahm, 1787) [1998] – Poplar Kitten
Notodonta dromedarius (Linnaeus, 1767) [2000] – Iron Prominent
Notodonta ziczac (Linnaeus, 1758) [2003] – Pebble Prominent
Phalera bucephala (Linnaeus, 1758) [1994] – Buff-tip
Pheosia gnoma (Fabricius, 1777) [2006] – Lesser Swallow Prominent
Pheosia tremula (Clerck, 1759) [2007] – Swallow Prominent
Pterostoma palpina (Clerck, 1759) [2011] – Pale Prominent
Ptilodon capucina (Linnaeus, 1758) [2008] – Coxcomb Prominent

Family Nymphalidae (10)
Aglais io (Linnaeus, 1758) [1597] – Peacock
Aglais urticae (Linnaeus, 1758) [1593] – Small Tortoiseshell
Coenonympha pamphilus pamphilus (Linnaeus, 1758) [1627] – Small Heath
Lasiommata megera (Linnaeus, 1758) [1615] – Wall
Maniola jurtina insularis Thomson, 1969 [1626] – Meadow Brown
Pararge aegeria tircis (Godart, 1821) [1614] – Speckled Wood
Polygonia c-album (Linnaeus, 1758) [1598] – Comma
Pyronia tithonus brittaniae (Verity, 1915) [1625] – Hedge Brown or Gatekeeper
Vanessa atalanta (Linnaeus, 1758) [1590] – Red Admiral
Vanessa cardui (Linnaeus, 1758) [1591] – Painted Lady

Family OECOPHORIDAE (11)
Agonopterix ciliella (Stainton, 1849) [689]
Agonopterix nervosa (Haworth, 1811) [706]
Batia unitella (Hübner, 1796) [642] – Golden-brown Tubic
Carcina quercana (Fabricius, 1775) [658]
Depressaria pastinacella (Duponchel, 1838) [672] – Parsnip Moth
Diurnea fagella (Denis et Schiffermüller, 1775) [663]
Diurnea lipsiella (Hübner, 1796) [664]
Endrosis sarcitrella (Linnaeus, 1758) [648] – White-shouldered House-moth
Hofmannophila pseudospretella (Stainton, 1849) [647] – Brown House Moth
Tachystola acroxantha (Meyrick, 1885) [656]

Semioscopis steinkellneriana (Denis et Schiffermüller, 1775) [667]

Family OPOSTEGIDAE (1)
Opostega salaciella (Treitschke, 1833) [119]

Family PARAMETRIOTIDAE (1)
Spuleria flavicaput (Haworth, 1828) [904]

Family PIERIDAE (6)
Anthocharis cardamines britannica Verity, 1908 [1553] – Orange-tip
Colias croceus (Geoffroy, 1785) [1545] – Clouded Yellow
Pieris brassicae (Linnaeus, 1758) [1549] – Large White
Pieris napi sabellicae Stephens, 1827 [1551] – Green-veined white
Pieris rapae (Linnaeus, 1758) [1550] – Small White
Gonepteryx rhamni rhamni (Linnaeus, 1758) [1546] – Brimstone

Family PTEROPHORIDAE (3)
Amblyptilia acanthadactyla (Hübner, 1813) [1497]
Gillmeria pallidactyla (Haworth, 1811) [1504]
Emmelina monodactyla (Linnaeus, 1758) [1524]

Family PYRALIDAE (32)
Acentria ephemerella (Denis et Schiffermüller, 1775) [1331] – Water Veneer
Agriphila straminella (Denis et Schiffermüller, 1775) [1304]
Agriphila tristella (Denis et Schiffermüller, 1775) [1305]
Aphomia sociella (Linnaeus, 1758) [1428] – Bee Moth
Cataclysta lemnata (Linnaeus, 1758) [1354] – Small China-mark
Catoptria pinella (Linnaeus, 1758) [1313]
Chrysoteuchia culmella (Linnaeus, 1758) [1293] – Garden Grass-veneer
Crambus lathoniellus (Zincken, 1817) [1301]
Crambus pascuella (Linnaeus, 1758) [1294]
Crambus perlella (Scopoli, 1763) [1302]
Dioryctria abietella (Denis et Schiffermüller, 1775) [1454]
Elophila nymphaeata (Linnaeus, 1758) [1345] – Brown China-mark
Eudonia angustea (Curtis, 1827) [1342]
Eudonia mercurella (Linnaeus, 1758) [1344]
Eudonia truncicolella (Stainton, 1849) [1340]
Eurrhypara hortulata (Linnaeus, 1758) [1376] – Small Magpie
Evergestis forficalis (Linnaeus, 1758) [1356] – Garden Pebble
Homoeosoma sinuella (Fabricius, 1794) [1481]
Hypsopygia costalis (Fabricius, 1775) [1413] – Gold Triangle
Nomophila noctuella (Denis et Schiffermüller, 1775) [1398] – Rush Veneer
Ortholepis betulae (Goeze, 1778) [1450]
Orthopygia glaucinalis (Linnaeus, 1758) [1415]
Pempelia palumbella (Denis et Schiffermüller, 1775) [1442]
Phycita roborella (Denis et Schiffermüller, 1775) [1452]
Pleuroptya ruralis (Scopoli, 1763) [1405] – Mother of Pearl
Pyla fusca (Haworth, 1811) [1451]
Pyralis farinalis (Linnaeus, 1758) [1417] – Meal Moth
Scoparia ambigualis (Treitschke, 1829) [1334]
Trachycera advenella (Zincken, 1818) [1439]
Udea ferrugalis (Hübner, 1796) [1395] – Rusty-dot Pearl
Udea lutealis (Hübner, 1809) [1388]
Udea prunalis (Denis et Schiffermüller, 1775) [1390]

Family SESIIDAE (1)
Synanthedon tipuliformis (Clerck, 1759) [373] – Currant Cleawing

Family SPHINGIDAE (8)
Agrius convolvuli (Linnaeus, 1758) [1972] – Convolvulus Hawk-moth

Deilephila elpenor (Linnaeus, 1758) [1991] – Elephant Hawk-moth
Deilephila porcellus (Linnaeus, 1758) [1992] – Small Elephant Hawk-moth
Hippotion celerio (Linnaeus, 1758) [1993] – Silver-striped Hawk-moth
Laothoe populi (Linnaeus, 1758) [1981] – Poplar Hawk-moth
Macroglossum stellatarum (Linnaeus, 1758) [1984] – Humming-bird Hawk-moth
Mimas tiliae (Linnaeus, 1758) [1979] – Lime Hawk-moth
Smerinthus ocellata (Linnaeus, 1758) [1980] – Eyed Hawk-moth

Family TINEIDAE (2)
Nemapogon cloacella (Haworth, 1828) [216] – Cork Moth
Tinea trinotella Thunberg, 1794 [247]

Family TISCHERIIDAE (2)
Emmetia marginea (Haworth, 1828) [125]
Tischeria ekebladella (Bjerkander, 1795) [123]

Family TORTRICIDAE (61)
Acleris ferrugana (Denis et Schiffermüller, 1775) [1044]
Acleris forsskaleana (Linnaeus, 1758) [1036]
Acleris holmiana (Linnaeus, 1758) [1037]
Acleris laterana (Fabricius, 1794) [1038]
Acleris rhombana (Denis et Schiffermüller, 1775) [1042] – Rhomboid Tortrix
Acleris sparsana (Denis et Schiffermüller, 1775) [1041]
Acleris variegana (Denis et Schiffermüller, 1775) [1048] – Garden Rose Tortrix
Aethes rubigana (Treitschke, 1830) [946]
Agapeta hamana (Linnaeus, 1758) [937]
Aleimma loeflingiana (Linnaeus, 1758) [1032]
Ancylis achatana (Denis et Schiffermüller, 1775) [1115]
Ancylis badiana (Denis et Schiffermüller, 1775) [1126]
Ancylis mitterbacheriana (Denis et Schiffermüller, 1775) [1120]
Apotomis betuletana (Haworth, 1811) [1093]
Apotomis turbidana (Hübner, 1825) [1092]
Archips podana (Scopoli, 1763) [977] – Large Fruit-tree Tortrix
Bactra lancealana (Hübner, 1799) [1111]
Celypha lacunana (Denis et Schiffermüller, 1775) [1076]
Clepsis consimilana (Hübner, 1817) [994]
Clepsis spectrana (Treitschke, 1830) [993] – Cyclamen Tortrix
Cnephasia asseclana (Denis et Schiffermüller, 1775) [1021] – Flax Tortrix
Cnephasia stephensiana (Doubleday, 1849) [1020] – Grey Tortrix
Cochylis nana (Haworth, 1811) [968]
Cydia pomonella (Linnaeus, 1758) [1261] – Codling Moth
Cydia splendana (Hübner, 1799) [1260]
Cydia ulicetana (Haworth, 1811) [1255]
Ditula angustiorana (Haworth, 1811) [1010] – Red-barred Tortrix
Epiblema cynosbatella (Linnaeus, 1758) [1174]
Epiblema uddmanniana (Linnaeus, 1758) [1175] – Bramble Shoot Moth
Epinotia abbreviana (Fabricius, 1794) [1150]
Epinotia bilunana (Haworth, 1811) [1133]
Epinotia brunnichana (Linnaeus, 1767) [1155]
Epinotia cruciana (Linnaeus, 1761) [1147] – Willow Tortrix
Epinotia tenerana (Denis et Schiffermüller, 1775) [1139] – Nut Bud Moth
Epiphyas postvittana (Walker, 1863) [998] – Light Brown Apple Moth
Eucosma cana (Denis et Schiffermüller, 1775) [1201]
Eucosma hohenwartiana (Denis et Schiffermüller, 1775) [1200]
Eulia ministrana (Linnaeus, 1758) [1015]
Gypsonoma dealbana (Frölich, 1828) [1069]
Hedya nubiferana (Haworth, 1811) [1083] – Marbled Orchard Tortrix
Lobesia littoralis (Humphreys and Westwood, 1845) [1109]
Lobesia reliquana (Hübner, 1825) [1106]
Lozotaenia forsterana (Fabricius, 1781) [1002]
Lozotaeniodes formosanus (Geyer, 1830) [1001]
Metendothenia atropunctana (Zetterstedt, 1840) [1085]
Orthotaenia undulana (Denis et Schiffermüller, 1775) [1087]
Pandemis cerasana (Hübner, 1786) [970] – Barred Fruit-tree Tortrix
Pandemis corylana (Fabricius, 1794) [969] – Chequered Fruit-tree Tortrix

Pandemis heparana (Denis et Schiffermüller, 1775) [972] – Dark Fruit-tree Tortrix
Pammene argyrana (Hübner, 1799) [1228]
Pammene fasciana (Linnaeus, 1761) [1236]
Pammene giganteana (Peyerimhoff, 1863) [1227]
Pammene rhediella (Clerck, 1759) [1239] – Fruitlet Mining Tortrix
Pammene splendidulana (Guenée, 1845) [1223]
Pseudargyrotoza conwagana (Fabricius, 1775) [1011]
Ptycholomoides aeriferana (Herrich-Schäffer, 1851) [987]
Rhopobota naevana (Hübner, 1817) [1159] – Holly Tortrix
Rhyacionia pinivorana (Lienig et Zeller, 1846) [1212] – Spotted Shoot Moth
Spilonota ocellana (Denis et Schiffermüller, 1775) [1205] – Bud Moth
Tortrix viridana Linnaeus, 1758 [1033] – Green Oak Tortrix
Zeiraphera isertana (Fabricius, 1794) [1165]

Family YPONOMEUTIDAE (19)
Argyresthia bonnetella (Linnaeus, 1758) [421]
Argyresthia brockeella (Hübner, 1813) [410]
Argyresthia conjugella Zeller, 1839 [418] – Apple Fruit Moth
Argyresthia goedartella (Linnaeus, 1758) [411]
Argyresthia pygmaeella (Denis et Schiffermüller, 1775) [412]
Argyresthia retinella Zeller, 1839 [415]
Argyresthia semitestacella (Curtis, 1833) [423]
Paraswammerdamia nebulella (Goeze, 1783) [441]
Plutella xylostella (Linnaeus, 1758) [464] – Diamond-back Moth
Prays fraxinella (Bjerkander, 1784) [449] – Ash Bud Moth
Swammerdamia caesiella (Hübner, 1796) [437]
Yponomeuta evonymella (Linnaeus, 1758) [424] – Bird-cherry Ermine
Yponomeuta padella (Linnaeus, 1758) [425] – Orchard Ermine
Ypsolopha nemorella (Linnaeus, 1758) [452]
Ypsolopha dentella (Fabricius, 1775) [453] – Honeysuckle Moth
Ypsolopha scabrella (Linnaeus, 1761) [455]
Ypsolopha parenthesella (Linnaeus, 1761) [460]
Ypsolopha ustella (Clerck, 1759) [461]
Ypsolopha vittella (Linnaeus, 1758) [463]

Family ZYGAENIDAE (2)
Zygaena filipendulae (Linnaeus, 1758) [169] – Six-spot Burnet
Zygaena lonicerae (Scheven, 1777) [171] – Narrow-bordered Five-spot Burnet

Order Mecoptera (Scorpion flies; 1 species)

The record is based on the data extracted from the Lancashire and Cheshire Card Index of H. Britten in the Manchester Museum (courtesy of Phillip Rispin). Nomenclature follows Kloet and Hinks (1964).

Family BOREIDAE (1) – Snow Scorpion-flies or Snow Fleas
Boreus hyemalis (Linnaeus, 1767)

Order Megaloptera (Alder flies and allies; 1 species)

The record is based on the data released at our request by rECOrd, the Biodiversity Information System for Cheshire (courtesy of Tom Hunt). Nomenclature follows Kloet and Hinks (1964).

Family SIALIDAE (1)

Sialis lutaria (Linnaeus, 1758)

Order Neuroptera (lacewings and allies; 1 species)

The record is based on the unpublished report prepared by the Liverpool Museum staff and associates resulting from the Alderley Edge Invertebrate Survey undertaken by their team in 1996 (courtesy of Ian Wallace, Liverpool). Nomenclature follows Kloet and Hinks (1964).

Family CHRYSOPIDAE (1) – Green Lacewings

Chrysoperla sp. (*carnea* group)

Order Odonata (Dragonflies and Damselflies; 9 species)

The list is based on the data released at our request by David Kitching, the Cheshire County recorder for Odonata, and also taken from the unpublished aquatic invertebrate survey undertaken by by Jonathan Guest in 1998 (see Chapter 12). Nomenclature and English common names follow Miller (1987). Complete information on the Dragonflies and Damselflies of Cheshire can be found in Gabb and Kitching (1992); a full checklist of the British Odonata and information about their biology and conservation are given on the website of the British Dragonfly Society (http://www.british-dragonflies.org.uk).

Family AESHNIDAE (2)

Aeshna cyanea (Müller, 1764) – Southern Hawker
Aeshna grandis (Linnaeus, 1758) – Brown Hawker

Family COENAGRIIDAE (4)

Coenagrion puella (Linnaeus, 1758) – Azure Damselfly
Enallagma cyathigerum (Charpentier, 1840) – Common Blue Damselfly
Ischnura elegans (van der Linden, 1820) – Blue-tailed Damselfly
Pyrrhosoma nymphula (Sulzer, 1776) – Large Red Damselfly

Family LIBELLULIDAE (3)

Libellula depressa Linnaeus, 1758 – Broad-bodied Chaser
Libellula quadrimaculata Linnaeus, 1758 – Four-spotted Chaser
Sympetrum (?) *striolatum* (Charpentier, 1840) – Common Darter

Order Orthoptera (Grasshoppers and Crickets; 2 species)

The list is based on the paper by Brindle (1971) and the data extracted from the Lancashire and Cheshire Card Index of H. Britten in the Manchester Museum (courtesy of Phillip Rispin). Nomenclature and common English names follow Marshall and Haes (1988).

Family ACRIDIDAE (2) – Grasshoppers
Chorthippus (Glyptobothrus) brunneus brunneus (Thunberg, 1815) – Field Grasshopper
Myrmeleotettix maculatus maculatus (Thunberg, 1815) – Mottled Grasshopper

Order Phthiraptera (True Lice; 7 species)

The list is based on the data extracted from the collection of British lice and from the Lancashire and Cheshire Card Index of H. Britten in the Manchester Museum (courtesy of Phillip Rispin). All recorded louse species belong to the chewing lice, sometimes called Mallophaga. Nomenclature follows Price *et al.* (2003).

Suborder Amblicera

Family MENOPONIDAE (2) – Chicken body lice
Kurodaia subpachygaster (Piaget, 1880) [ex Barn Owl]
Pseudomenopon pilosum (Scopoli, 1763) [ex Moorhen]

Suborder Ischnocera

Family PHILOPTERIDAE (4)
Brueellia domestica (Kellogg and Chapman, 1899) [ex House Martin]
Degeeriella fusca (Denny, 1842) [ex Hobby]
Philopterus atratus Nitzsch, 1818 [ex Barn Owl]
Strigiphilus rostratus (Burmeister, 1838) [ex Barn Owl]

Family TRICHODECTIDAE (1)
Stachiella mustelae (Schrank, 1803) [ex Stoat]

Order Plecoptera (Stoneflies; 1 species)

The record is taken from the unpublished aquatic invertebrate survey undertaken by by Jonathan Guest in 1998 (see Chapter 12). Nomenclature follows Kloet and Hinks (1964).

Family NEMOURIDAE (1)
Nemoura cinerea (Retzius, 1783)

Order Psocoptera (Barklice and Booklice; 5 species)

The list is based on the data extracted from the Lancashire and Cheshire Card Index of H. Britten in the Manchester Museum (courtesy of Phillip Rispin). Nomenclature follows New (2005). A complete checklist of the British Psocoptera (sixty-eight species) accounts for all the recorded species and much supporting information can be obtained from the website of National Barkfly Recording Scheme (http://www.brc.ac.uk/schemes/barkfly/homepage.htm).

Family CAECILIUSIDAE (1)
Enderleinella obsoleta (Stephens, 1836)

Family ECTOPSOCIDAE (1)
Ectopsocus briggsi McLachlan, 1899

Family ELIPSOCIDAE (1)
Elipsocus pumilis (Hagen, 1861)

Family PSOCIDAE (1)
Loensia fasciata (Fabricius, 1787)

Family STENOPSOCIDAE (1)
Graphopsocus cruciatus (Linnaeus, 1768)

Order Siphonaptera (Fleas; 9 species)

The list is based on the data released from the collection of British fleas held in the Manchester Museum (courtesy of Phillip Rispin). Nomenclature follows Whitaker (2007), but subfamilies and subgenera are omitted.

Family CERATOPHYLLIDAE (7)
Amalaraeus penicilliger mustelae (Dale, 1878) [ex Robin nest]
Ceratophyllus farreni farreni Rothschild, 1905 [ex House Martin nest]
Ceratophyllus fringillae (Walker, 1856) [ex Hedge Sparrow nest]
Ceratophyllus gallinae (Schrank, 1803) [ex Hedge Sparrow nest]
Ceratophyllus hirundinis (Curtis, 1826) [ex House Martin nest]
Ceratophyllus styx jordani Smit, 1955 [ex Sand Martin nest]
Dasypsyllus gallinulae gallinulae (Dale, 1878) [ex Snipes nest]

Family ISCHNOPSYLLIDAE (2)
Ischnopsyllus octactenus (Kolenati, 1856) [ex Whiskered Bat]
Ischnopsyllus simplex simplex Rothschild, 1906 [ex Whiskered Bat]

Order Trichoptera (Caddisflies; 13 species)

The record is taken from the unpublished report prepared by the Liverpool Museum staff and associates which resulted from the Alderley Edge Invertebrate Survey undertaken by their team in 1996 (courtesy of Ian Wallace, Liverpool), and from the unpublished aquatic invertebrate survey undertaken by by Jonathan Guest in 1998 (see Chapter 12). Nomenclature follows Kloet and Hinks (1964).

Family BERAEIDAE (1)
Beraea pullata (Curtis, 1834)

Family HYDROPTILIDAE (2)
Athripsodes aterrimus (Stephens, 1836)
Triaenodes bicolor (Curtis, 1834)

Family LEPTOCERIDAE (1)
Agraylea multipunctata Curtis, 1834

Family LIMNEPHILIDAE (9)
Anabolia nervosa (Curtis, 1834)
Glyphotaelius pellucidus (Retzius, 1783)
Limnephilus centralis Curtis, 1834
Limnephilus flavicornis (Fabricius, 1787)
Limnephilus lunatus Curtis, 1834
Limnephilus vittatus (Fabricius, 1798)
Limnephilus sp. (*flavicornis* or *marmoratus*)
Micropterna lateralis (Stephens, 1837)
Micropterna sequax (McLachlan, 1875)

Subphylum Chelicerata
Class Arachnida (Spiders, Harvestmen and allies; 164 species)
Subclass Acarina or Acari (Mites and Ticks)

The list of mites and ticks (Acarina) is based on the data extracted from the collections of the Manchester Museum. Composition of families is given in accordance with the *Biology Catalog* of J. Hallan (2008; at http://bug.tamu.edu/research/collection/hallan). The higher classification of the Acarina is still a matter of controversy and debate: we follow the review by Dunlop and Alberti (2008) and consider mites and ticks in two orders. However, many specialists place the Acarina at the rank of subclass within the class Arachnida, with seven orders recognised. For instance, suborders given in the present checklist are accepted as orders in Hallan (2008).

Order Actinotrichida (Mites; 15 species)

Suborder Actinedida (or Prostigmata)

Family CHEYLETIDAE (1)
Neocheyletiella microrhynchus (Berlese and Trouessart, 1889) [ex House Martin]

Family BDELLIDAE (1)
Bdella longicornis (Linneaus, 1758) [ex Greenfinch nest with Cuckoo]

Family MYOBIIDAE (1)
Acanthophtirius mystacinalis (Radford 1953) [ex Whiskered bat]

Family TETRANYCHIDAE (1)
Bryobia praetiosa Koch, 1836 [ex Thrushes nest] – Clover Mite

Family TROMBICULIDAE (1)
Neotrombicula autumnalis (Shaw, 1790) [ex Stoat] – Harvest Mite

Suborder Astigmata

Family ACARIDAE (2)
Acarus siro Linnaeus, 1758 [ex Brown Rat]
Tyrophagus longior (Gervais, 1844) (= *Coelognathus dimidiatus*) [ex Hedgesparrow nest]

Family ANALGIDAE (1)
Protalges attennatus (Buchholz, 1869) [ex Barn Owl]

Family AVENZOARIIDAE (1)
Pteronyssoides obscurus (Berlese, 1884) [ex House Martin]

Family GLYCYPHAGIDAE (2)
Glycyphagus domesticus (DeGeer, 1778) [ex Thrush's nest] – Grocer's Itch Mite or House Mite
Ctenoglyphus canestrinii Armanelli 1887 [ex hay detritus]

Family PSOROPTOIDIDAE (2)
Pandalura strigis-oti (Buchholz, 1869) [ex Barn Owl]
Pandalura subintegra (Berlese, 1883) [ex House Martin]

Family PTILOXENIDAE (1)
Ptiloxenus vanelli (Canestrini, 1878) [ex Peewit]

Family PYROGLYPHIDAE (1)
Hirstia chelidonis Hull, 1901 [ex Dead House Martin]

Suborder Oribatida – Beetle Mites

Family HERMANNIIDAE (1)
Hermannia scabra (Koch, 1879) [ex Moss]

Order Anactinotrichida (mites and ticks; 5 species)

Suborder Ixodida

Family IXODIDAE (1) – Hard Ticks
Ixodes (Pholeoixodes) hexagonus Leach, 1815 [ex Hedgehog nest] – Hedgehog Tick

Suborder Mesostigmata

Family CELAENOPSIDAE (1)
Celaenopsis cuspidata (Kramer, 1876) [ex Greenfinch nest with Cuckoo]

Family DERMANYSSIDAE (1)
Dermanyssus gallinae (DeGeer, 1778) [ex Dead House Martin] – Red Poultry Mite

Family PARASITIDAE (2)
Pergamasus crassipes (Linnaeus, 1758) [ex Redshank nest]
Phorytocarpais fimetorum (Berlese, 1903) [ex Peewit nest]

Order Araneae (spiders; 137 species)

The list of Spiders, Harvestmen and False-scorpions of Alderley Edge is primarily based on the list published by Logunov (2003), plus twenty-two additional spider species from the unpublished report prepared by the Liverpool Museum staff and associates resulting from the Alderley Edge Invertebrate Survey in 1996 (courtesy of S. Judd and C. Felton). Two more species (*Agroeca proxima* and *Walckenaeria unicornis*) were found in D. W. Mackie and H. W. Freston's spider reference collection held by the Manchester Museum. One species, *Agyneta jacksoni*, reported by Logunov (2003), is a misidentification and this record should in fact be assigned to *Meioneta rurestris*. Voucher specimens of the listed spider and opilionid species are kept in the National Museums Liverpool (UK), Manchester Museum (UK) and the Zoological Museum of the Moscow State University (Russia). A total of 137 spider, eleven Harvestman and one False-scorpion species has been recorded from Alderley Edge to date. In the list given below, the numbers in square brackets following names refer to the habitats surveyed: [1] in crevices of sandy gorges; [2] under bark of standing trees or of logs; [3] rocks (under dry ferns and grass clumps, in litter, moss and lichen); [4] secondary grasslands; [5] gorse shrubs (shaken off twigs); [6] damp meadow with rush; [7] heather–stony slope; [8] broad-leaved (holly–oak–beech) wood (in litter and on ferns); [9] moss–heather–bilberry heath in birch coppice (in litter); [10] open sandy heath (with sparse grassy vegetation); [11] pine forest (in litter and on ferns); [12] damp birch forest (under rotten logs and in litter).

Family AGELENIDAE (3) – Funnel Weavers
Cryphoeca silvicola (C. L. Koch, 1834) [3, 8, 11]
Tegenaria gigantea Chamberlin et Ivie, 1935 [1, 2]
Tegenaria silvestris L. Koch, 1872 [no data]

Family AMAUROBIIDAE (2) – Window Spiders
Amaurobius fenestralis (Stroem, 1768) [2, 3]
Amaurobius similis (Blackwall, 1861) [2]

Family ARANEIDAE (9) – Orb Weavers
Araneus diadematus Clerk, 1757 [4, 5] – Garden Cross Spider
Araneus marmoreus Clerk, 1757 [4] – Marbled Orb Weaver
Araneus quadratus Clerk, 1757 [4] – 4-spot Orb Weaver
Araniella cucurbitina (Clerck, 1757) [4] – Cucumber Green Spider
Cyclosa conica (Pallas, 1772) [6]
Larinioides cornutus (Clerck, 1757) [4]
Nuctenea umbratica (Clerck, 1757) [2] – Walnut Orb-weaver Spider
Zygiella atrica (C. L. Koch, 1845) [5]
Zygiella x-notata (Clerck, 1757) [6]

Family CLUBIONIDAE (8) – Sac Spiders
Clubiona brevipes Blackwall, 1841 [no data]
Clubiona compta C. L. Koch, 1839 [7, 8]
Clubiona corticalis (Walckenaer, 1802) [2]
Clubiona diversa O. Pickard-Cambridge, 1862 [9, 10]
Clubiona lutescens Westring, 1851 [3, 4, 5, 6, 8]
Clubiona neglecta O. Pickard-Cambridge, 1862 [no data]
Clubiona reclusa O. Pickard-Cambridge, 1863 [6]
Clubiona terrestris Westring, 1851 [no data]

Family DICTYNIDAE (1) – Hackled-web Spiders
Dictyna arundinacea (Linnaeus, 1758) [4]

Family DYSDERIDAE (1) – Sixeyed Spiders
Harpactea hombergi (Scopoli, 1763) [no data]

Family HAHNIIDAE (1) – One-row Spiders
Antistea elegans (Blackwall, 1841) [6]

Family LINYPHIIDAE (83) – Money Spiders and allies
Agyneta conigera (O. Pickard-Cambridge, 1863) [8]
Agyneta decora (O. Pickard-Cambridge, 1871) [no data]
Bathyphantes approximates (O. Pickard-Cambridge, 1871) [6]
Bathyphantes gracilis (Blackwall, 1841) [3, 4, 5, 6, 8, 9, 10]
Bathyphantes nigrinus (Westring, 1851) [6, 12]
Bolyphantes alticeps (Sundevall, 1833) [8]
Centromerita bicolour (Blackwall, 1833) [no data]
Centromerita concinna (Thorell, 1875) [8]
Centromerus dilutus (O. Pickard-Cambridge, 1875) [9]
Centromerus sylvaticus (Blackwall, 1841) [6, 9]
Ceratinella brevipes (Westring, 1851) [7, 9]
Ceratinella brevis (Wider, 1834) [6, 7, 8]
Ceratinella scabrosa (O. Pickard-Cambridge, 1871) [8]
Cnephalocotes obscurus (Blackwall, 1834) [7, 9]
Collinsia inerrans (O. Pickard-Cambridge, 1885) [4]
Dicymbium nigrum (Blackwall, 1834) [6]
Dicymbium tibiale (Blackwall, 1836) [no data]
Diplocephalus cristatus (Blackwall, 1833) [8]
Diplocephalus latifrons (O. Pickard-Cambridge, 1863) [6, 8, 12]
Diplocephalus picinus (Blackwall, 1841) [8]

Diplostyla concolor (Wider, 1834) [8, 11]
Dismodicus bifrons (Blackwall, 1841) [4, 6]
Entelecara congenera (O. Pickard-Cambridge, 1879) [5]
Erigone atra Blackwall, 1833: [3, 4, 5, 6, 8, 9, 10]
Erigone dentipalpis (Wider, 1834) [3, 4, 5, 8, 9, 10]
Erigone promiscua (O. Pickard-Cambridge, 1872) [10]
Erigonella hiemalis (Blackwall, 1841) [7, 9, 12]
Floronia bucculenta (Cleck, 1757) [6]
Gnathonarium dentatum (Wider, 1834) [6]
Gonatium rubens (Blackwall, 1833) [7]
Gongylidiellum vivum (O. Pickard-Cambridge, 1875) [4, 9, 12]
Gongylidium rufipes (Linnaeus, 1758) [9]
Helophora insignis (Blackwall, 1841) [8]
Hilaira excisa (O.Pickard-Cambridge, 1871) [11]
Hypomma bituberculatum (Wider, 1834) [6]
Kaestneria pullata (O. Pickard-Cambridge, 1863) [4]
Labulla thoracica (Wider, 1834) [3]
Lepthyphantes minutus (Blackwall, 1833) [3, 8]
Lessertia dentichelis (Simon, 1884) [no data]
Linyphia hortensis Sundevall, 1829 [9, 11]
Linyphia triangularis (Clerck, 1757) [4, 5, 6]
Lophomma punctatum (Blackwall, 1841) [6]
Maso sundevalli (Westring, 1851) [8, 9]
Meioneta rurestris (C.L. Koch, 1836) [9]
Meioneta saxatilis (Blackwall, 1844) [5, 6, 9]
Micrargus herbigradus (Blackwall, 1854) [4, 5, 7, 11]
Microlinyphia pusilla (Sundevall, 1830) [4, 9, 10]
Microneta viaria (Blackwall, 1841) [8]
Minyriolus pusillus (Wider, 1834) [7]
Monocephalus fuscipes (Blackwall, 1836) [6, 7, 8, 9, 11, 12]
Neriene clathrata (Sundevall, 1830) [4, 6, 9]
Neriene montana (Clerck, 1757) [4]
Neriene peltata (Wider, 1834) [8, 9]
Obscuriphantes obscurus (Blackwall, 1841) [5, 9]
Oedothorax fuscus (Blackwall, 1834) [4, 5, 6, 9, 10]
Oedothorax gibbosus (Blackwall, 1841) (including *O. g.* form *tuberosus*) [6]
Oedothorax retusus (Westring, 1851) [6, 10]
Palliduphantes ericaeus (Blackwall, 1853) [7]
Palliduphantes pallidus (O. Pickard-Cambridge, 1871) [9]
Pocadicnemis pumila (Blackwall, 1841) [6, 9, 12]
Poeciloneta variegata (Blackwall, 1841) [5]
Pelecopsis parallela (Wider, 1834) [10]
Saaristoa abnormis (Blackwall, 1841) [9]
Saaristoa firma (O. Pickard-Cambridge, 1905) [9]
Savignia frontata Blackwall, 1833: [3, 8]
Silometopus elegans (O. Pickard-Cambridge, 1872) [10]
Stemonyphantes lineatus (Linnaeus, 1758) [no data]
Tapinocyba pallens (O. Pickard-Cambridge, 1872) [7, 11]
Tenuiphantes alacris (Blackwall, 1853) [8, 9, 11]
Tenuiphantes cristatus (Menge, 1866) [6, 8, 9]
Tenuiphantes flavipes (Blackwall, 1854) [3, 6, 8]
Tenuiphantes mengei (Kulczyński, 1887) [6]
Tenuiphantes tenebricola (Wider, 1834) [8, 9]
Tenuiphantes tenuis (Blackwall, 1852) [4, 5, 8, 9, 10]
Tenuiphantes zimmermanni (Bertkau, 1890) [3, 6, 8, 9, 11, 12]
Thyreosthenius parasiticus (Westring, 1851) [12]
Tiso vagans (Blackwall, 1834) [6]
Walckenaeria acuminata Blackwall, 1833 [9]
Walckenaeria cucullata (C. L. Koch, 1836) [8, 11]
Walckenaeria cuspidata Blackwall, 1833 [3]
Walckenaeria nudipalpis (Westring, 1851) [9]
Walckenaeria unicornis O. Pickard-Cambridge, 1861 [no data]
Walckenaeria vigilax (Blackwall, 1853) [10]

Family LIOCRANIDAE (2) – Field or Foliage-running Spiders

Agroeca proxima (O. Pickard-Cambridge, 1871) [no data]
Scotina celans (Blackwall, 1841) [7]

Family LYCOSIDAE (7) – Wolf Spiders
Alopecosa pulverulenta (Clerck, 1757) [6]
Arctosa perita (Latreille, 1799) [10]
Pardosa amentata (Clerck, 1757) [6, 10]
Pardosa palustris (Linnaeus, 1758) [6, 10]
Pardosa pullata (Clerck, 1757) [4, 8, 9]
Pirata piraticus (Clerck, 1757) [6]
Trochosa terricola Thorell, 1856: [8, 9]

Family PISAURIDAE (1) – Nursery Web Spiders
Pisaura mirabilis (Clerck, 1757) [4]

Family PHILODROMIDAE (3) – Rapid-running Crab Spiders
Philodromus aureolus (Clerck, 1757) [5, 9]
Philodromus cespitum (Walckenaer, 1802) [5]
Tibellus oblongus (Walckenaer, 1802) [4]

Family SALTICIDAE (3) – Jumping Spiders
Euophrys frontalis (Walckenaer, 1802) [3, 4, 9, 10]
Neon reticulatus (Blackwall, 1853) [9]
Salticus scenicus (Clerck, 1757) outer house walls – Zebra Spider

Family SEGESTRIIDAE (1) – Six-eyed Tunnel Spiders
Segestria senoculata (Linnaeus, 1758) [2]

Family TETRAGNATHIDAE (8) – Long-jawed and Thick-jawed Spiders
Metellina mengei (Blackwall, 1869) [3, 5, 6, 8, 10, 12]
Metellina merianae (Scopoli, 1763) [2, 3, in mines (close to entrances)]
Metellina segmentata (Clerk, 1757) [4, 5, 6, 8]
Pachygnatha clercki Sundevall, 1823 [4, 6]
Pachygnatha degeeri Sundevall, 1830 [6, 10]
Tetragnatha extensa (Linnaeus, 1758) [4, 6]
Tetragnatha montana Simon, 1874 [9]
Tetragnatha obtusa C.L. Koch, 1837 [4, 6]

Family THERIDIIDAE (11) – Comb-footed Spiders
Anelosimus vittatus (C. L. Koch, 1836) [4]
Enoplognatha ovata (Clerck, 1757) [4, 5, 6, 8, 9]
Crustulina guttata (Wider, 1834) [no data]
Neottiura bimaculata (Linnaeus, 1767) [6]
Paidiscura pallens (Blackwall, 1834) [6, 7, 8, 9]
Phylloneta impressa L. Koch, 1881 [4]
Phylloneta sisyphia (Clerck, 1757) [4, 5, 9]
Platnickina tincta (Walckenaer, 1802) [5]
Steatoda bipunctata (Linnaeus, 1758) [around houses] – Rabbit Hutch Spider
Theridion mystaceum L. Koch, 1870 [3]
Theridion varians Hahn, 1833: [5]

Family THOMISIDAE (1) – Crab Spiders
Xysticus cristatus (Clerck, 1757) [4, 5, 10]

Family ZORIDAE (1) – Wandering or Spiny-leg Spiders
Zora spinimana (Sundevall, 1833) [9]

Order Opiliones (Harvestmen; 11 species)

Family LEIOBUNIDAE (1)
Leiobunum rotundum (Latreille, 1798) [3, 5]

Family NEMASTOMATIDAE (2)
Mitostoma chrysomelas (Hermann, 1804) [7]
Nemastoma bimaculatum (Fabricius, 1885) [4, 6, 8, 9, 12]

Family PHALANGIIDAE (8)
Lacinius ephippiatus (C. L. Koch, 1835) [4]
Megabunus diadema (Fabricius, 1779) [1, 3]
Mitopus morio (Fabricius, 1799) [3, 4, 5, 8, 9]
Oligolophus hanseni (Kraepelin, 1896) [5, 8]
Oligolophus tridens (L. Koch, 1836) [6]
Paroligolophus agrestis (Meade, 1855) [3, 5, 8]
Phalangium opilio Linnaeus, 1758 [5]
Platybunus triangularis (Herbst, 1799) [3, 6, 8, 9, 11]

Order Pseudoscorpiones (False-scorpions; 1 species)

Family NEOBISIIDAE (1)
Neobisium (*Neobisium*) *muscorum* (Leach, 1817) [8, 9]

Subphylum Crustacea

The list of woodlice (Onicsidea) is based on the 1996 unpublished report by a Manchester biology student, Alison Deen. The list of aquatic groups is based on the unpublished reports of two aquatic invertebrate surveys undertaken by Ian Wallace from the Liverpool Museum in 1996 and by Jonathan Guest in 1998 (see Chapter 12). Nomenclature of Isopoda follows the world checklist by Schotte *et al.* (1995 onwards). A checklist of all the freshwater Crustacea of north-west England ponds is given by Bentley (2008). All the British freshwater Malacostraca are considered by Glendhill *et al.* (1993).

Class Malacostraca (Woodlice, Shrimps, Crabs and allies; 10 species)

Order Amphipoda – Freshwater Shrimps and Sand Hoppers

Family CRANGONYCTIDAE (1)
Crangonyx pseudogracilis Bousfield, 1958 – American Freshwater Shrimp

Family GAMMARIDAE (1)
Gammarus pulex (Linnaeus, 1758) – Common Freshwater Shrimp

Order Isopoda – Woodlice and allies

Suborder Asellota

Family ASELLIDAE (2)
Asellus aquaticus (Linnaeus, 1758) – Common Hog-louse
Asellus meridianus Racovitza, 1919 – Lesser Hog-louse

Suborder Oniscidea – Woodlice

Family PORCELLIONIDAE (1) – Sow Bugs
Porcellio scaber Latreille, 1804 – Common Rough Woodlouse

Family PHILOSCIIDAE (1)
Philoscia muscorum (Scopoli 1763) – Common Striped Woodlouse

Family TRICHONISCIDAE (1)
Trichoniscus pusillus Brandt 1833 – Common Pygmy Woodlouse

Class Brachiopoda

Order Cladocera

Family CHYDORIDAE (1)
Erycercus lamellatus (Müller, 1776)

Family DAPHNIIDAE (2) – Water-Fleas and allies
Daphnia pulex Leydig, 1860
Simocephalus vetulus (Müller, 1776)

Subphylum Myriapoda

The species list is based on the Myriapoda collection made by Dmitri Logunov (Manchester Museum) in 2002, which has been identified by Graham Proudlove (Manchester Museum). The collection is kept in the Manchester Museum (UK). Nomenclature of Diplopoda follows the checklist by Lee (2006). Nomenclature and common English names of Chilopoda follow the latest systematic list of British Chilopoda by Barber (2008). A complete list of the Myriapoda of Lancashire and Cheshire is provided by Blower (1987).

Class Diplopoda (Millipedes; 9 species)

Order Glomerida

Family GLOMERIDAE (1) – Pill Millipedes
Glomeris marginata (Villers, 1789)

Order Julida

Family JULIDAE (4)
Cylindroiulus punctatus (Leach, 1815) – Blunt-tailed Snake Millipede
Julus scandinavius Latzel, 1884
Ophyiulus pilosus (Newport, 1843)
Tachypodoiulus niger (Leach, 1815) – White-legged Snake Millipede

Family BLANIULIDAE (1)
Proteroiulus fuscus (Am Stein, 1857)

Family NEMASOMATIDAE (1)
Nemasoma varicorne C.L. Koch, 1847

Order Polydesmida

Family POLYDESMIDAE (2)
Brachydesmus supesus Latzel, 1884
Polydesmus angustus Latzel, 1884 – Flat-backed Millipede

Class Chilopoda (Centipedes; 8 species)

Order Geophilomorpha – Earth Centipedes

Family GEOPHILIDAE (3)
Geophilus carpophagus Leach, 1814 – Luminous Centipede
Geophilus insculptus (Attems 1895) – Common Geophilus
Geophilus truncorum (Bergsoë and Meinert, 1886) – Small Geophilus

Family HIMANTARIIDAE (1)
Stigmatogaster subterranea (Shaw, 1789) – Western Yellow Centipede

Family LINTOTAENIIDAE (1)
Strigamia acuminata (Leach, 1814) – Shorter Red Centipede

Order Lithobiomorpha – Stone Centipedes

Family LITHOBIIDAE (3)
Lithobius crassipes L. Koch, 1862 – Thick-legged Lithobius
Lithobius forficatus (Linnaeus, 1758) – Common Lithobius or Brown Centipede
Lithobius variegates Leach, 1814 – Variegated Centipede

Phylum Mollusca

The list of terrestrial groups is based on unpublished data collected from Alderley Edge by a Manchester biology student, Alison Deen, who sampled soil invertebrates in October 1996 and February 1997, and by Dmitri Logunov (Manchester Museum), who sampled litter-dwelling invertebrates between March and October 2002. The list of aquatic groups is based on the unpublished reports of two aquatic invertebrate surveys undertaken by Ian Wallace from the Liverpool Museum in 1996 and by Jonathan Guest in 1998 (see Chapter 12).

Nomenclature follows the checklist of British non-marine Mollusca by Anderson (2011). A checklist of all the non-marine Mollusca of Cheshire can be found in Pettitt (1975); the list of aquatic molluscs of north-west England ponds is given by Bentley (2008). A useful resource for understanding and identifying all the British terrestrial, freshwater and marine molluscs is the website of Conchological Society of Great Britain and Ireland (http://www.conchsoc.org/index.php).

Class Gastropoda (Snails and slugs; 26 species)

Order Pulmonata

Family ACROLOXIDAE (1) – River Limpets
Acroloxus lacustris (Linnaeus, 1758) – Lake Limpet

Family AGRIOLIMACIDAE (1)
Deroceras laeve (Müller, 1774) – Meadow Slug

Family ARIONIDAE (4)
Arion (Arion) ater (Linnaeus, 1758) – Great Black Slug
Arion (Kobeltia) intermedius Normand, 1852 – Hedgehog Slug
Arion (Kobeltia) hortensis Férussac, 1819 – Southern Garden Slug
Arion (Mesarion) subfuscus (Draparnaud, 1805) – Dusky Slug

Family CLAUSILIIDAE (1) – Door Snails
Clausilia (Clausilia) bidentata bidentata (Ström, 1765) – Two-toothed Door Snail

Family EUCONULIDAE (1)
Euconulus (*Euconulus*) *fulvus* (Müller, 1774)

Family DISCIDAE (1)
Discus (*Gonyodiscus*) *rotundatus rotundatus* (Müller, 1774) – Discus Snail

Family LIMACIDAE (1) – Keelback Slugs
Limacus flavus Linnaeus, 1758 – Yellow Slug

Family LYMNAEIDAE (3) – Pond Snails
Galba (*Galba*) *truncatula* (Müller 1774) – Dwarf Pond Snail
Lymnaea (*Lymnaea*) *stagnalis* (Linnaeus, 1758) – Great Pond Snail
Radix balthica (Linnaeus, 1758) – Wandering Pond Snail

Family OXYCHILIDAE (1)
Oxychilus (*Oxychilus*) *alliarus* (Miller, 1822) – Garlic Snail

Family PLANORBIDAE (7) – Ramshorns
Anisus (*Disculifer*) *vortex* (Linnaeus 1758) – Whirlpool Ramshorn
Bathyomphalus contortus (Linnaeus, 1758) – Twisted Ramshorn
Hippeutis complanatus (Linnaeus 1758) – Flat Ramshorn
Gyraulus (*Armiger*) *crista* (Linnaeus, 1758) – Nautilus Ramshorn
Gyraulus (*Gyraulus*) *albus* (Müller, 1774) – White Ramshorn
Planorbarius corneus corneus (Linnaeus, 1758) – Great Ramshorn
Planorbis carinatus Müller, 1774 – Keeled Ramshorn

Class bivalvia (Oysters, clams and allies; 5 species)

Order Veneroida

Family SPHAERIIDAE (5) – Pea Mussels or Peaclams
Musculium lacustre (Müller, 1774) – Lake Orb Mussel
Pisidium milium Held, 1836 – Quadrangular Pillclam
Pisidium personatum Malm, 1855 – Red-crusted Pea Mussel
Pisidium sp. (not *milium*)
Sphaerium corneum (Linnaeus, 1758) – Horny Orb Mussel

Phylum Annelida (Earthworms, Leeches and allies; 7 species)

The list is based on the 1996 unpublished reports by Ian Wallace from the Liverpool Museum, by Jonathan Guest in 1998 (see Chapter 12) and on the data released at our request by rECOrd, the Biodiversity Information System for Cheshire (courtesy of Tom Hunt). Nomenclature follows Elliott and Mann (1979); the latter authors provided a complete account on the sixteen leech species known to occur in Britain.

Class Hirudinea (Leeches; 7 species)

Order Gnathobdellae

Family HIRUDINIDAE (1)
Haemopis sanguisuga (Linnaeus, 1758) – Horse Leech

Order Rhynchobdellae

Family GLOSSIPHONIIDAE (5)
Glossiphonia complanata (Linnaeus, 1758)
Glossiphonia heteroclita (Linnaeus, 1761)
Helobdella stagnalis (Linnaeus, 1758)
Hemiclepsis marginata (Müller, 1774) – Fish Leech
Theromyzon tessulatum (Müller, 1774) – Duck Leech

Order Pharyngobdellae

Family ERPOBDELLIDAE (1)
Erpobdella octoculata (Linnaeus, 1758)

Phylum Platyhelminthes (Flatworms; 1 species)

The record is taken from the 1996 unpublished report by Ian Wallace from the Liverpool Museum. A complete checklist and key for the freshwater triclads in Britain and Ireland (twelve species altogether) can be found in Reynoldson and Young (2000).

Class Turbellaria (1 species)

Order Tricladida – Flatworms

Family PLANARIIDAE (1)
Polycelis sp. (*nigra* or *tenuis*)

Appendix 13.2

The butterflies of Alderley Edge

Roger L. H. Dennis

Table 13.2, available on the publisher's website, gives the numbers of species recorded in each of over fifty survey parcels and sub-parcels on Alderley Edge. For each species in each parcel the following is shown: h, host plant present; a, adult butterfly record; b, breeding record. In addition, s indicates 1 ha squares intensively surveyed between 1996 and 1999; and row and column totals indicate the total numbers of species recorded. This is done (table rows) for the following twenty species:

- *Thymelicus sylvestris* (Small Skipper)
- *Ochlodes sylvanus* (Large Skipper)
- *Pieris brassicae* (Large White)
- *Pieris rapae* (Small White)
- *Pieris napi* (Green-veined White)
- *Anthocharis cardamines* (Orange-tip)
- *Gonepteryx rhamni* (Brimstone)
- *Favonius quercus* (Purple Hairstreak)
- *Lycaena phlaeas* (Small Copper)
- *Polyommatus icarus* (Common Blue)
- *Celastrina argiolus* (Holly Blue)
- *Vanessa atalanta* (Red Admiral)
- *Vanessa cardui* (Painted Lady)
- *Aglais urticae* (Small Tortoiseshell)
- *Aglais io* (Peacock)
- *Polygonia c-album* (Comma)
- *Pararge aegeria* (Specked Wood)
- *Lasiommata megera* (Wall)
- *Pyronia tithonus* (Gatekeeper)
- *Maniola jurtina* (Meadow Brown)

It may be downloaded from http://www.manchesteruniversitypress. co.uk/ThestoryofAlderlyAdditionalResources

Appendix 19.1

Leicesters or Leycesters?

Clare Pye

The Leicesters of Tabley were an old-established Cheshire family, resident in the county for almost exactly 700 years, from the end of the thirteenth century to the death of Colonel John Leicester-Warren, the last Leicester to own Tabley House, in 1975.

However, the family history is not simple, and in particular the spelling of the family's name changed over the years. In the fourteenth century, a cadet member of the family married the heiress to lands in Mobberley and set himself up at Toft. The Leycesters of Toft, whose estate is next to Tabley, consistently spelled their name with a 'y', and it was a girl from this family, Catherine (Kitty) Leycester, who married Edward Stanley, brother to the first Lord Stanley and Rector of Alderley. In the eighteenth century, the Stanleys and the Leycesters of Toft were great friends, often visiting each other's houses.

The Leicesters of Tabley, however, changed the spelling of their name in the middle of the seventeenth century. Sir Peter, a precise lawyer and historian who became the first baronet in 1660, discovered that the earliest family documents spelt the name with an 'i', like the city of the same name, so he decided to revert to this earlier version. Thereafter the Tabley Leicesters used this spelling. In the seventeenth century, Tabley Leicesters and Alderley Stanleys were not good friends. They were on opposite sides in the Civil War, and maintained a long legal battle over Broadheath in Over Alderley. During the 1670s, in the course of this dispute, Sir Peter put together *The Book of Evidences of Sir Peter Leycester* (*sic*) to support his case, a compilation of documents that included a map of 1636 (Plate 61), commissioned by his father. How he felt about the Stanleys is perhaps shown by his description of them as 'a bundle of old suits tied up in a bag' (CALS DLT A75/1-10).

However, in 1793, Sir John Fleming Leicester of Tabley sold his lands in Over Alderley, with the Stanleys acquiring a major share, and in the nineteenth century, as both families were Liberals, they were on more friendly terms. In particular, the daughters of the second Lord Stanley and the second Lord de Tabley saw a great deal of each other.

Incidentally, Sir Peter Leicester's father was also called Peter (often abbreviated to 'Piers'), but he would have styled himself Peter Leycester, Esq. It was this Peter Leycester who commissioned the map of his estates in Over Alderley in 1636 (Plate 61).

Appendix 19.2

A brief history of the Alderley Beacon

Jeremy Milln

Whether or not the Beacon, which occupies the highest point of Alderley Edge, was actually fired to warn of the Spanish Armada, we do not know; but the site had been established by the time William Saxton published his *Map of Cheshire* in 1578 and Camden his *Britannia* in 1586. The Beacon itself is likely to have been a simple wrought-iron brazier set upon a stout bear-pole which, in this case, was itself set upon an earth mound, perhaps originally a prehistoric tumulus.

Fire beacons like Alderley's generally consisted of two permanent elements: a pole-mounted brazier and a hut in which combustible materials were kept dry and in readiness. There would be faggots of sticks and straw for night-time use and pitch or tar for day-time, when smoke rather than flames was required for visibility. A warden appointed by the landowner on orders from the Crown had responsibility for looking after the Beacon, and a building was erected to store faggots and other combustibles.

This building comprised a single room, with a doorway to the south, constructed from large ashlar blocks of the native sandstone. Louisa Stanley, in her guide *Alderley Edge and Its Neighbourhood*, published in 1843, retells how one Thomas Ridgeway recalls it being a 'hollow square room with a door, and that an iron pot was kept in it for the purpose of holding pitch and tar'. The source for the story is unknown, but it also occurs in the second *Stanley Notebook* (CALS DSA 3752/1). Ridgeway, who was born in 1725, is describing a building which existed perhaps from about 1600 until about 1779, when it was given a pyramidal roof of brick and became an eye-catcher to be viewed distantly from Alderley Park (Figure 19.20). The first Lord Stanley apparently believed that it was his father who added the brick courses and pyramidal peak soon

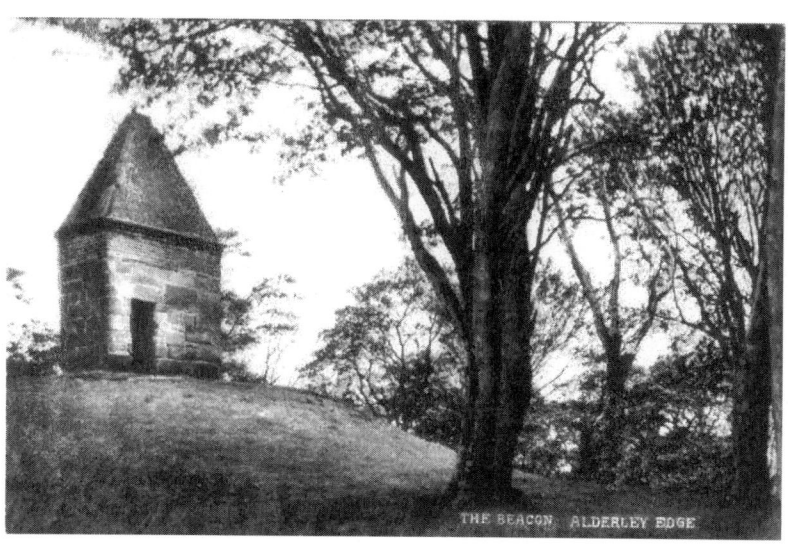

Figure 19.20. An old postcard of the Beacon, Alderley Edge, showing Sir John Stanley's alterations of the 1770s.

after the Edge was enclosed in the 1770s. This was during one of those times when little or no copper mining was taking place on the hill and its open heath had been enclosed and planted with clumps of ornamental pine and beech. Henceforward it was the more open Stormy Point which bore beacon bonfires.

Another early commentator, Samuel Finney of Fulshaw, writing in 1787, noted a

> small square stone building, now closed up on the top, in the form of a Pyramide, but was formerly open, with a small Aperture on the Side, just large enough for a man to enter. This Building stands upon the Confines of Alderley Parish, and is called the Beacon, from an old Angle-Saxon word which signifys to call or beckon. Its use, in the early times of the Heptarchy, was to fill it with combustibles, and set them on fire, to alarm the Country on the approach of an Enemy; its situation was well adapted for such a purpose, for the prospect from it to the west, north and south, is almost unbounded, and from whence you have a View of some Towns, many Gentleman's Seats, and of Lime Cage, which is said was formerly a prison for Macclesfield Forrest. (Cited in Barlow, 1853: 123–4)

The distinctive mound upon which the Beacon tower stood, recently scheduled as a probable prehistoric tumulus, caught the attention of early antiquarian eyes (Marriott, 1810: 196–207). After visiting the Druids' Circle and other antiquities he supposed to be prehistoric, Marriott was able to state that its tower 'is of modern construction, a small oblong storey of stone with an open door; from which rises pyramidically to a point a proportionate superstructure of brick'. Passing dismissively over the suggestion that it had been used as a sea-mark for the Liverpool channel, he was impressed by the evidence of its mound as a 'sepulchral monument'. Apparently, it is 'one hundred paces round its circumference' and has 'the vestiges of having been encompassed by a fosse'. Marriott concludes decisively that 'this mound must have been properly a barrow'.

Probably the nearest similar tower (just) visible from Alderley was that on Rivington Pike some twenty-two miles to the north-north-west. Here, a square tower of gritstone was erected in 1733 by one John Andrews on the site of an Armada beacon. However, the Rivington example has windows and is likely to have served principally as a landscape feature and lookout. It has also been suggested that the Rivington beacon tower had been built to resolve ownership of the common moor (Shawcross, 1933).

The use of fire-beacons for communicating warning generally did not outlast the Napoleonic period. In 1804 the Alderley site was assessed by the Duke of Gloucester as Commander-in-Chief of the district but was apparently talked out of recommissioning the Beacon. The grounds for this were that it might be wantonly set alight although, as the title page in Louisa Stanley's *Alderley Edge and Its Neighbourhood* shows, even as late as the 1840s the views were still clear of trees, so the risk (as later) was more from vandalism than fire (Figure 19.21). Indeed, Stanley's illustration, and others like it, demonstrate that by the mid-nineteenth century images of the Beacon had become iconic for the Edge.

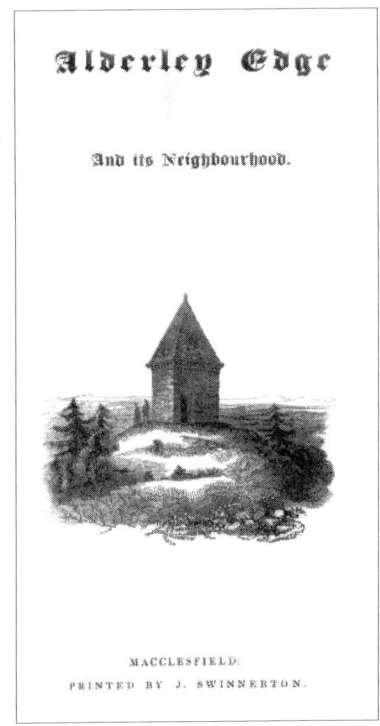

Figure 19.21. The title page of Louisa Stanley's *Alderley Edge and Its Neighbourhood* (1843), showing the Beacon mound still clear of trees.

The demise of the old Beacon building, long neglected and probably hastened by interference, came in 1931. Amy Crossley, in her guidebook to Alderley Edge published in that year, commented: 'the structure is now in a somewhat damaged condition. Two large stones are cut out of the wall at the back which allows a bulge as if it would collapse should any more stones be pulled out' (Crossley, 1931: 10). The 1779 building finally fell during a storm in December 1931. Much photographed (the postcard illustrated as Figure 19.20 is but one example), we know that it had in fact been rectangular and had been constructed from coursed sandstone ashlar, presumably from the nearby Church Quarry, and given a steeply pointed roof of brick over projecting dentilled eaves. It would seem that the stones of the lower part of the building belonged to the sixteenth-century structure and the brick to the 1779 rebuild. The earliest views suggest that originally it had been plastered and/or lime-washed, making it as visible from the Cheshire Plain as the Cage in Lyme Park. We learn from George Twigg, some of whose memories were recorded by the Alderley Edge Landscape Project in 1998, that, as a small boy, he was allowed to peep inside.

Alderley Edge's Stormy Point nearby has been host to two particularly spectacular beacon bonfires in recent times. Organised by the Derbyshire Caving Club, one marked the occasion of the Silver Jubilee of HM The Queen on 6 June 1977, accompanied by folk dancing displays by the Poynton Jemmers, and the other on 19 July 1988, to celebrate the quatercentenary of the Spanish Armada. These and other 'celebrations' on the Edge are also described in Chapter 20.

The Beacon site was surveyed and repaired by the National Trust in 2003 and a set of the drawings now forms part of the Project Archive (AELP 10156-8). It has long been suggested that at some suitable moment in the future the Trust might gather up and re-erect the fallen stones to recover this curious building.

Appendix 19.3

The Hagg Cottages: the historical background to the 2003 Alderley Sandhills Project excavation

Clare Pye

The Hagg Cottages, Nether Alderley, Cheshire (Figure 19.22), were part of the estate owned by the Stanleys of Alderley, who had been established in the north-east of the county since the fifteenth century. Sir John Stanley became Lord Stanley of Alderley in 1839. The sixth Lord Stanley sold the whole estate, including the Cottages, in 1938, and the houses themselves were demolished in the early 1950s by Thomas Neild, who had bought both them and the adjacent Sandhills.

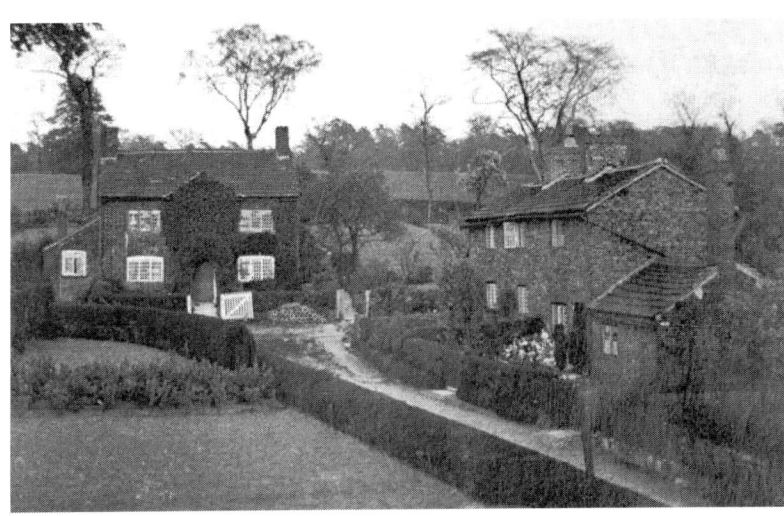

Figure 19.22. The Hagg Cottages, from the west, in the 1920s.

Photograph George Barber, courtesy of Roy Barber.

Tracing the history of the occupation of the Hagg is bedevilled by the patchy archival record. The Stanleys had the misfortune to suffer two fires, in 1779 and 1931, which severely depleted the estate archives. However, the earlier fire was remedied to some extent in the early nineteenth century by the first Lord Stanley's research, collected in a series of notebooks (CALS DSA 5/1–10 and DSA 3752/1), which are now held by Cheshire Archives and Local Studies in Chester, together with other surviving estate archives. There is only one estate document from before the 1779 fire, the 1775 Enclosure Award map for Alderley Edge (CALS DSA 1919/33; here Figure 19.7). This shows the open land to be enclosed, but not pre-existing fields, so it does not show the Hagg Cottages. Consequently, one has to rely on the Alderley parish records for glimpses into the situation before 1779.

In the *Stanley Notebook* Lord Stanley is quite clear about the building date for the eastern house; he says it was built for Daniel Dean in 1747. This is confirmed by the date plaque on the house remembered by people who knew the place. There is, however, evidence that there was a pre-existing building at the Hagg; the Poor Law assessment of 1735 mentions a Widow Dean of the Hagg (*ibid.*). Her house is assessed at 4s.1d, one of the smaller properties in the parish. Her neighbours had larger farms; White Barn was valued at 15s.11d, Brynlow at 17s.10d and Topps at 16s.4d. However, cottages are valued between 1s and 2s, suggesting that her social and economic position comes somewhere between the established tenant farmers and the labouring cottagers. The Alderley parish registers record the burial of a widow, Frances Dean of the Hagg, in 1745 (CALS P/143/1/1 mf65/1). The Deans were a multi-branched local family, and difficult to disentangle; there seem to have been at least two Daniels living in the Alderley parish in the middle of the eighteenth century.

In the late eighteenth century the Hagg was a small agricultural holding below the newly enclosed common of Alderley Edge. The Edge was in the process of being landscaped and having tree plantations established on it. There was one family living on the farm. Stanley said that a Frank Timperley married Daniel Dean's daughter and took over the Hagg tenement when his father-in-law died (*Stanley Notebook*). An estate book for 1800–08 records the farm at this time (*Stanley C7*) (Table 19.1). The Hagg tenement was small for the farms of this period; the average on the Stanley estate was about twice the size. However, most of the larger holdings were down on the plain, and tenements on the hill tended to have fewer acres.

In 1808, when Stanley's father died, this estate book was revised and it is clear that by now the Alderley Mining Company had been established, as it was renting the Hagg for £40 a year, double the amount for the original farm (*Stanley C7*). Fields 521–4 were at the centre of their

Table 19.1. The Hagg tenement, its fields and rental in 1800

Field number on estate map	Field name	Statute measure*	Cheshire measure*	Value per acre	Rent payable
222	Higher Pickin	1/2/25	0/3/5	£2.5.0	£1.15.1½
223	Lower Pickin	1/1/31	0/2/29	£2.14.0	£1.16.9½
519	Higher Riddings	2/2/37	1/1/6	£2.6.0	£2.19.2½
518	Lower Riddings	2/2/19	1/0/38	£2.0.0	£2.9.6
521	Lower Newfield	1/3/21	0/3/22	£2.10.0	£2.4.4½
522	Higher Newfield	2/2/30	1/1/3	£2.2.0	£2.13.3
523	Turnip Piece	1/2/20	0/3/3	£1.16.0	£1.7.8
524	Middle Piece	2/2/16	1/0/37	£2.6.0	£2.16.7¼
526	Wheat Field	2/1/7	1/0/13	£1.15.0	£1.17.10
527	Higher Croft	0/1/25	0/0/31	£2.10.0	£0.9.8½
528	Well Croft and Building	1/0/14	0/2/2		£2.0.0
	Total	21/0/5	9/3/29		£22.10.0¼

Note: *The units are acres – the three respective numbers are presumably acres, quarters and roods (typical of old records of land). Both statute and Cheshire acres were in use at the time, but the rental is calculated from the Cheshire measure.
Source: *Stanley Estate Book, 1800–1808* (Manchester Archives and Local Studies Centre: C7, mf2678) (*Stanley C7*).

opencast mining, so the farm was no longer a viable agricultural unit. It was at this time that the buildings at the farmstead were split up to accommodate four families (*Stanley Notebook*). The original farmhouse on the east was split into two and the building to the south was converted into two units. This is the occupation pattern for the rest of the buildings' life. The parish registers show that the Timperleys moved away, first to Manchester and then to Gatley; they still retained links with their old home as the family is buried at St Mary's, the Alderley parish church (CALS P 143/1/1).

Although the Stanleys had high hopes of the mines' profitability, especially after cobalt was discovered in 1806 (Lady Stanley to Serena Holroyd, in Adeane, 1899: 297), it appears the mining community was separate from the main estate. In 1810, at the time of George III's Golden Jubilee, the Stanleys entertained their tenants and estate workers to a great dinner at Alderley Park House, and then went up the Edge to eat with the miners and drink the King's health. They did not integrate the two events, but treated the two groups separately (Adeane, 1899: 324). This phase of mining on Alderley Edge ended in 1817; the resumption of peace and the restoration of imports of better-quality cobalt from the Continent meant the Alderley operations ceased to be profitable. However, the buildings at the Hagg did not revert to an independent agricultural holding but remained cottages tenanted by agricultural labourers and other estate workers.

During the nineteenth century, the main documents that deal specifically with the Hagg Cottages are a series of surviving estate rent books from 1825–48 (CALS DSA 3752/2–4) and Census returns, 1841–1901. The rent book has details of the tenants, their rent and, to a certain extent, information about the properties and their occupants (Table 19.2).

Table 19.2. Pattern of occupation at the Hagg Cottages, 1825–48

	East Cottage, northern end	East Cottage, southern end	South Cottage, western end	South Cottage, eastern end
Assessed value	£4	£4 (1834: £5)	£4	£3.15.0
1825	**John Acton**	Thomas Norbury New Tenant (late Jerome Cartright)	Vacant (late James Fisher)	Sarah Lowe
1826	John Acton	Thomas Norbury	**James Warren**	Sarah Lowe
1827	John Acton	**Widow Broadhurst**	James Warren	Sarah Lowe
1828	Vacant	Widow Broadhurst	James Warren went to Whirley Farm for a short time, but came back at the Hagg the next year	Sarah Lowe
1829	Vacant	**Charles Broadhurst**	James Warren	Sarah Lowe
1830	**Keay Owen**	Charles Broadhurst	James Warren	Sarah Lowe
1831	Keay Owen	Charles Broadhurst	**Thomas Henshall**	Sarah Lowe
1832	**Thomas Owen**	Charles Broadhurst	Thomas Henshall	Sarah Lowe
1833	Thomas Owen	**Joseph Clarke.** Moved to Beechtree Lodge, 1834. Cottage improved for next tenant.	Thomas Henshall	Sarah Lowe
1834	Thomas Owen	**Mrs Leighton**, paying £5 p.a. after the improvements	**William Thorley**	Sarah Lowe
1835	Thomas Owen	**Thomas Jackson**	Vacant	Sarah Lowe
1836	Thomas Owen	Thomas Jackson	**John Foden**	Sarah Lowe
1837	Thomas Owen	Thomas Jackson	John Foden	Sarah Lowe
1838	Thomas Owen	Thomas Jackson	*Vacant.*	When Sarah Lowe left, her home was rebuilt.
1839	**David Toft**	Thomas Jackson	**George Barton** for last half of year as the front wall was rebuilt and the roof replaced with Kerridge stone	**John Ellam**. Did not move in for the first part of the year as the front wall was rebuilt and the roof replaced with Kerridge stone.
1840	David Toft	Thomas Jackson	George Barton	John Ellam
1841*	David Toft	Thomas Jackson	George Barton	John Ellam
1842	Vacant	Thomas Jackson	George Barton	John Ellam
1843	**Mrs Clarke**	Thomas Jackson	George Barton	John Ellam
1844	Mrs Clarke	**John Clarke**	George Barton	John Ellam
1845	Mrs Clarke	John Clarke	George Barton	John Ellam
1846	Mrs Clarke	John Clarke	George Barton	John Ellam
1847	Mrs Clarke (Pimlott)	John Clarke	George Barton	John Ellam
1848		John Clarke	George Barton	Vacant

Notes: **Bold** type indicates new tenants.
* Census year.
Source of data: CALS DSA 3752/2–4.

These rent books show there was a steady turnover in tenancies, and some do not stay long. It is interesting to note that the southern pair of cottages had extensive repairs in 1839. Beechtree Lodge was the gamekeeper's lodge east of Alderley Park; the other keeper's house, the present Beacon Lodge on the Macclesfield Road, was built at the same time. Before this, the Stanleys did not have specially designed keepers' cottages, and the Hagg, conveniently situated between the Park and the newly landscaped Alderley Edge, could have been used by the gamekeepers before they got their own accommodation. The vacancy in 1848 in the cottage where the Ellams had lived may be explained by a reference in one of Lady Stanley's letters to her daughter-in-law, Henrietta, describing how she dealt with a smallpox outbreak on the Brynlow Hill area of the estate. She was clearly annoyed.

> I gathered up six children yesterday for vaccination – Nightingale was so stupid about it all. I had no trouble in persuading the woman at The Haggs to bring her 2 children or any other person. One of The Hagg inmates is in great disgrace & I shall probably send him about his business – John Ellam has thought proper to get a donkey to carry Nanny's washing home, which lives in the lanes, moreover he is accused of getting fern & heath at night from the Edge. (Lady Stanley to Henrietta Stanley, 14 March 1848, in Mitford, 1938: letter 229)

This rent book coincided with the 1841 Census (CALS 18/11mf), the first Census to detail people's occupations. All permanent residents at the Cottages in 1841 were agricultural labourers, but there was an anomaly: a separate entry for four single male stonecutters. They were part of the itinerant work force building the railway between Manchester and Crewe. All the parishes along the line of the railway showed this temporary increase in population in 1841, often, as here, living in makeshift accommodation next to other low-status housing. This railway opened the following year and transformed life in the north-east Cheshire countryside, not least as it was the direct cause of developing the wealthy commuter suburb of Alderley Edge village, bringing a flood of people into the area, and where the new villas inhabited by the Manchester mill-owners and other middle-class business people and professionals became an important source of service employment for the lower classes.

The beginnings of this impact can be seen in the 1851 Census (CALS 2/16mf). One of the tenants was a young married man, Benjamin Heywood from Poynton, who was a stonemason. His father, William, built the early villas, and the local trade directories (Thomas Morris and Co., 1874) show that Benjamin later took over his father's business. Another tenant was Samuel Oaks, again a young man with a family, including his sister, Sarah, who only a week before the Census was taken had given birth to an illegitimate daughter, Hannah. The Oakses came from the Hough, on other side of the Edge; presumably her brother was ready to give Sarah shelter during this difficult time and, acknowledging her debt, she named her daughter after her sister-in-law. In 1861 Hannah was still living with her uncle as a boarder; she had not been absorbed into Samuel's family but was supported separately (CALS 234/8mf). One presumes that Sarah had access to money and that she was either away in service, or in a relationship that precluded her daughter living with her (Table 19.3).

Table 19.3. Occupation of the Hagg Cottages from the Census, 1841–1901

Census	Head of household	Occupation of householder	Number in family
1841	Henry Jackson	Agricultural labourer	5
	David Toft	Agricultural labourer	4
	John Ellam	Agricultural labourer	2
	George Barton	Agricultural labourer	4
	Four stonecutters		
1851	Benjamin Heywood	Stonemason	2
	William Ridgeway	Labourer	3
	Samuel Oaks	Labourer	5
	John Clark	Gardener	5
1861	David Walston	Copper miner	5
	Samuel Oakes	Copper and lead miner	5
	Thomas Cooper	Engine feeder at the copper and lead works	5
	William Taylor	Mine labourer	2
1871	John Martin	Blacksmith	7
	William Davis	Copper miner	5
	George Layman	Mines agent	3
	Joseph Pliscombe	Copper miner	3
1881	David Ellam	Gardener	5
	Thomas Steele	Labourer, woodman	5
	John Leigh	Farm labourer	4
	George Leaman	Commercial agent for brewery	3
	Joseph Massey	Road man, High Road (*sic*)	5
1891	Joseph Massey	Labourer, road man	1
	Unoccupied		
	George Leaman	Brewer's representative	2
	George Barber	General labourer	5
	David Ellam	Gardener, domestic	4
1901	David Ellam	Gardener, domestic	3
	George Barber	Gardener, domestic	4
	Ernest Barber	Stone quarryman	3
	Joseph Massey	Township roadman	2

Source: CALS, Census returns, 1841–1901.

In 1861 Samuel Oaks had become a worker in the mines, the occupation for all the other tenants at the Hagg in that year. Two households came from outside the local area, the Coopers from Derbyshire and the Taylors from Yorkshire. The Alderley Edge Mining Company needed the Hagg Cottages to house its workers, especially the skilled men they brought in to head the mining teams. The 1871 Census confirms this; all the tenants worked in the mines and all came from outside the area (CALS 24/14mf). Three, William Davis, George Leaman and Joseph Pliscombe, came from the West Country; their skills as hard-rock ore miners were invaluable to the company.

The Alderley Edge Mining Company's effect on the landscape was significant. There were two main mines on the southern side of Alderley Edge, Wood and West Mines, both connected by a tramway to a central dressing area. Lead, cobalt and copper were all mined, but it was the last that had the most impact on the landscape. Over the twenty-one years of the lease, about 3,500 tons of copper were extracted from the sandstone by a leaching process using hydrochloric acid (see Chapter 16). This resulted in vast quantities of waste sand. Piled up, this became the Sandhills, a noted landmark on Alderley Edge until their final disappearance in the early 1960s. Everyone who grew up in the Alderley area in the 1940s and 1950s can remember them, especially as an area to play in when they were children.

However, the mines ceased operation in 1878, when the lease came to an end. There was an attempt to revive them during the First World War, and even a scheme to make copper sulphate for Bordeaux mixture, a pesticide used in the wine trade, but this came to nothing, and the mines were finally shut down and the equipment sold off in 1923 (Carlon and Dibben, 2012). For more information about the Alderley mines themselves, see Geoffrey Warrington's account of the history of the mines in Chapter 16.

Wages in the mines were not high. During the 1860s, the mines employed forty to fifty men and boys underground and on the dressing floor. In 1866, a David Walton, who may be the same man as the David Walston of the Census, had a team of two men and two boys. We know from the *Mines Setting Book*, an account book for the mines covering the years 1864–66 now in the AELP Archive (no. 6), that they were working on a cross-passage during February 1866, where they were paid at 22s a fathom dug, and managed to earn between £2.15s.0d and £3.4s.2d a week. This would have been shared out between them, and shows that this team was getting little more than they could have earned as agricultural labourers.

By 1881 the Alderley mines had closed and, with the exception of George Leaman who stayed on as a brewer's representative, all the tenants were again local labouring families. The mines office had been converted to residential use, a role it was to fill for the rest of its time (CALS 146/6mf). George Leaman's niece, Elizabeth Johns, was still living with him; she re-appears in 1891 as his housekeeper (CALS 265/10mf) and in 1901 as married to Ernest Barber and the mother of George Barber (CALS 34/38mf). At this time, Ernest Barber and his family appear to have occupied both sides of the eastern house. With George Barber we have reached the oral record, as he became the father of Roy and Molly Barber, two of the children who lived in the cottages in the 1920s. Molly Pitcher (née Barber) said that her grandmother died young and that Mr and Mrs Perrin then moved into the northern end of the house as Mrs Perrin was supposed to look after her brother Ernest and young George (AELP Oral Archive 17105).

The interviews given by Edna Younger, Roy Barber and Molly Pitcher (AELP Oral Archive, 17003, 17103, 17105–6, 17112–14) create a picture of growing up in the cottages in the 1920s. Edna lived with her parents, Mr and Mrs Barrow, in the eastern half of the southern pair of cottages, next door to old Mr Ellam and his two daughters. As a girl, Edna Barrow had lived in the converted office 100 yards away, where her parents still lived, while Mr Barrow was a joiner, working at Broadbents, the joiners, undertakers and furniture shop down in Alderley Edge village. Edna recalled the sense of security and freedom in her childhood, able to move easily round the little settlement by the Sandhills and the adjoining Alderley woods, with relatives and family friends close by. She was very sad to leave the Hagg and move down to Alderley Edge village at the end of the decade. Part of her interview is printed in Chapter 21 (p. 543).

Molly recalled that her mother was less happy living in the Hagg Cottages. She had come from Wilmslow to marry George Barber and found an isolated cottage with very few facilities and the work of caring for her father-in-law and the Perrins next door as well as her own children. As Edna said, the Cottages did have a water supply, but nothing else; only coal was delivered and everything else had to be carried up the hill. George Barber worked at Charnleys, the chemist in the village, and was responsible for the photographs of the Hagg Cottages and its inhabitants taken at this time. Working at the chemist meant he was vaguely connected to the medical profession, and he took the part of the doctor in the Barbers' performances of the mummers' play at Alderley Park. The Perrins were noted local characters. Mr Perrin had a series of odd jobs, including selling candles to people wanting to explore West Mine, and Mrs Perrin was apparently a sight to behold when she attended parish whist drives festooned with costume jewellery. She continued to live alone at the Cottages when everyone else left; even when James Neild cut off the water she used the spring by her back door. Eventually age and ill health took her into care when the Cottages were demolished.

George Barber and his family left Ernest Barber at the Hagg when they moved to Wilmslow in 1930. The 1938 sale catalogue for the auction of Stanley estate is the best record of the Cottages at the end of their occupancy and shows the last residents at the Hagg before old age and the Second World War removed them (sale catalogue: lots 497, 497a, 499, also lot 500). The Misses Ellam were still there and paid a rent of £6.10s a year; Mr Knight, who replaced the Barrows in 1930, paid £13 a year. Lot 499 shows the west-facing Stanley farmhouse; the developers put it up for sale as a single house although the sale details record the double tenancy: Ernest Barber paid £5.10s a year and Mrs Perrin £4.10s for their houses. This was only 10s a year more than the tenants of these two houses had paid a century before. The Stanleys had a reputation for charging low rents on the estate, although this was not the only factor in the decision to sell up in 1938. Double death duties, due to the fourth and fifth Lord Stanleys dying within six years of each other, together with the sixth Lord Stanley's extravagance, were the main reasons why the family could no longer afford to live at Alderley Park.

The Sandhills area, including the Cottages, was purchased by Thomas Neild, who ran a sand and gravel business from Whitebarn Farm. He was responsible for selling off the sand from the Sandhills and for demolishing the Hagg Cottages in the early 1950s, after they had fallen into disrepair and become a focus for vandals and for youths illicitly visiting the mines (Alan Garner and Harold Smith, personal communication).

In 2003, with the help of a grant from English Heritage, Dr Eleanor Casella of the Archaeology Department at the University of Manchester excavated the site of the Hagg Cottages, revealing the eastern pair of cottages to have been a typical eighteenth-century Stanley farmhouse adapted for two family units in the mid-nineteenth century (Casella and Croucher, 2010). The southern pair of cottages was more interesting. The nineteenth-century cottages had been razed to the ground, but this destruction uncovered signs of an earlier structure, perhaps the house where Widow Dean had lived in the early eighteenth century before the new farmhouse was built in 1747. Throughout the excavation the archaeologists were greatly helped by Roy Barber, Molly Pitcher and Edna Younger, who had lived in the cottages in the 1920s when they were children. Their recollections of the houses and their families' lives there informed the work done on the excavation as their memories were compared with the physical record of the archaeology (Casella and Croucher, 2010: 21–5, especially fig. 2.3).

Appendix 21.1

John Evans: the death of a hermit

Robin Salmon

Alderley Edge does not often feature in the national press, unless it is in an article about house prices. Or the WAGish activities of some of the newer residents. But in the mid-1930s two unnatural deaths in Church Quarry on the Edge were reported in no less a paper than *The Times*.

The central figure was John Evans, sometimes referred to, then and now, as the Hermit of Alderley Edge (Figure 21.1). This is a pity, as it conjures up a very false image. John Evans was well educated, well spoken and always well dressed – not at all the man we picture as a hermit. There are many accounts about him and the events that surrounded his death in 1933, at the age of fifty. Some are true, some clearly not. It has been said, for example, that he was poisoned, or killed by some mysterious virus (the 'bronchial viral infection which was rampant in the area

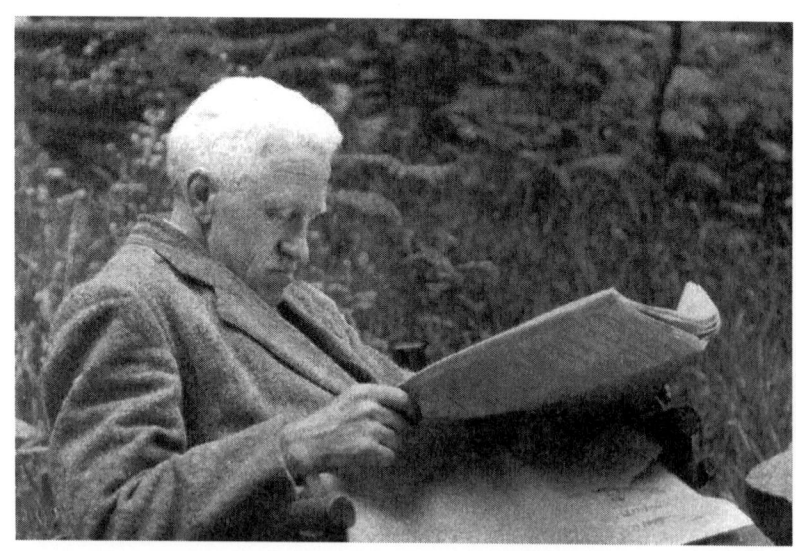

Figure 21.1. John Evans.

Derbyshire Caving Club archive.

at the time' mentioned in Chapter 20, p. 523). National Trust volunteers have been carrying out research into the man and his background, and the seventy-fifth anniversary of his death seemed an appropriate time to bring out as much of the truth as possible, and dispel some of the myths.

John Evans was born in Salford in the early 1880s, the son of a postal clerk. He worked for a local railway company from 1901 to 1915. At the age of eighteen, in 1901, he was working as a surveyor's clerk, but in 1915 he was described as a civil engineer. It has been said that he studied at the Camborne School of Mines, but its records show that he was never there (personal communication). He is also said to have worked in the gold mines in South Africa, but it is difficult to see how that could be true. His family was not rich and it is hard to imagine how such a trip could have been funded before he started work. Another suggestion has been that at some time he lectured at the University of Manchester on geology, or some related subject. However, the University Archivist can find no reference to him in any of the records where his name would be expected to be found (personal communication). Nor is he to be found in the records of the Manchester Municipal College of Technology.

It has been suggested that he had a fiancée who was lost on the *Titanic* in 1912. If that is true, it could have been what led to the mental health problems from which he suffered. In 1915 he had some sort of breakdown and was diagnosed as suffering from neurasthenia. He had to retire from work on health grounds aged thirty-three and was advised by his doctor to 'live among the pines'. Although he had signed a 'form of attestation' confirming that he was ready to serve in the forces if and when conscripted, Evans was in fact unable to do so because of his disability. So the suggestion that he was invalided out of the army with shellshock during the First World War is also untrue.

He went to live among the pines of the Edge, in Church Quarry, on the estate of the Stanley family, in a log cabin called the Bergli Hut (Figure 21.2). This was the name of a mountain refuge in the Swiss Alps, and the rent for it was set at the princely sum of 2s.6d per annum. He fitted out the Bergli Hut to a high standard and cultivated a garden, traces of which can still be made out. He was a respected member of the Climbing Club of the University of Manchester and was helpful to members of that club, and to all visitors to the Edge who wanted to improve their climbing skills on the many rocky outcrops. He was particularly helpful to youngsters who wanted to explore the Edge, especially to youth groups, and welcomed the many others who came to study the botany and geology of the area. He was rather hostile to women visitors, however, and would shoo them away from Church Quarry.

He used his mountaineering skills to great effect in the exploration and mapping of the miles of tunnels, a relic of the mining which had gone on under the Edge since the Bronze Age. He also helped the police

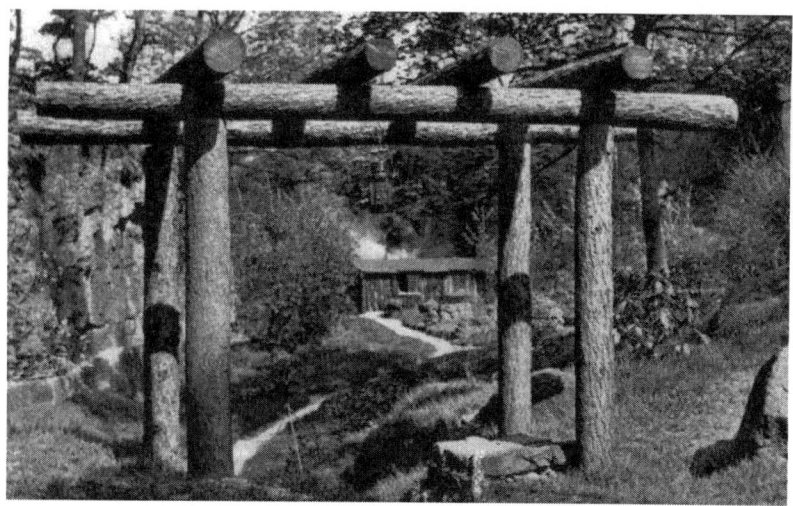

Figure 21.2. The Bergli Hut in Church Quarry.

Derbyshire Caving Club archive.

recover bodies when ill-equipped young lads from the area came to grief underground.

He was very well known and popular in the village, and would often go down in the evening to take a drink at the Queen's Hotel, near the station. Sometimes he would return with friends to continue their evening in the Quarry with a singsong, using a pedal organ which he had in the hut. It may be that this is what led the local children to refer to him as 'Juggy', for in those days it was normal for pubs to sell off-licence beer in the jugs which their customers brought with them, and it is quite likely that he and his friends took their drink up to Church Quarry in this way.

On Friday 21 July 1933, he returned from the Queen's Hotel with two young friends, but when the time came for them to return to Timperley they realised that they could not do so. Though they had a motorbike, they had no light for it. So they decided to stay the night, as several of John Evans's friends had done before. There were bunk beds in the Bergli Hut for overnight guests.

During the night the younger man, Walter Whitelegg, began to feel ill, and went outside to be sick. This was probably because the twenty-year-old came from a teetotal family and it was only the second time in his life that he had taken alcohol. John Evans got up and gave him a drink, but the young man's condition got worse and worse. Becoming concerned, John Evans went to the Wizard Temperance Inn and telephoned for the doctor, but it was too late. When he arrived Whitelegg was dead.

Because there was no obvious cause of death, an inquest was held, on Monday 24 July. The doctor stated that he could find no reason why the apparently healthy young man had died, and he was awaiting the results of further tests. John Evans was summoned as the key witness, but failed to appear. So the coroner adjourned the inquest and sent the police to find out why. The Bergli Hut was locked and there was no sign of life. The police summoned Walter Philipps, the gamekeeper, from nearby Beacon Lodge, and instructed him to break in. Inside, they found the Hut in good order, but John Evans was in his bed, and he, too, was dead.

There was an inquest into his death soon afterwards under the same coroner. The doctor who made the post-mortem examination stated that the cause of death was cyanide poisoning. 'The organs reeked of cyanide' – it had been a massive dose. The cyanide had come from a bottle which had been found within his reach, and as there were no indications to the contrary, the conclusion was that John Evans had taken his own life. Why he had done so was not clear, but the coroner was convinced that the dead man had been conducting a homosexual relationship with his young guests or, to use the modern term, was grooming them. To understand why he should make such a contentious and apparently unwarranted statement, we need to look at events which occurred earlier in the same year.

Towards the end of January, four men from Macclesfield had come to the Bergli Hut late at night, under the influence of drink. They 'demanded money with menaces' from John Evans. Their ages ranged from sixteen to thirty, and they managed to persuade him to part with a few shillings. They returned a few days later and repeated their demands. This time they used physical violence as well. He was so badly injured that he needed the help of Walter Philipps and his wife, and the police became involved. They arrested all four men and brought them before the police court, where they were remanded in custody. Three of them were sent for trial at the Chester Assizes in June, but for some reason no further action was taken against the fourth man.

During the Assizes trial it emerged that, in the attacks, they had threatened to spread a story that John Evans had made homosexual advances. He denied that he had ever done so, but they said that, true or not, this was the story they would spread. His reputation and his life would be ruined unless he paid up. The trial concluded with one of the men, Arthur Hill, being sentenced to fifteen months' hard labour. The other two were released without further punishment. The attack and trial seriously damaged John Evans's fragile mental health, as he later confessed to friends and to his sister.

At the inquest into the death of John Evans, one of the witnesses, Joseph Aymes, made a similar claim of homosexual advances. However, he was the fourth member of the gang who had carried out the attacks in January, but was not sent for trial at Chester. There is no indication that anyone at the inquest knew of his involvement in the attacks. Perhaps, if his membership of the gang had been known, then no one would have given his assertion any credence. But the coroner believed him, and associated his allegation with that of Arthur Hill at the Assizes trial. Everyone else who spoke at the inquest attested to John Evans's good character and denied any possibility of homosexual activity.

In spite of this, the coroner chose to accept the word of the two men. They were members of a gang who, as we have seen, had threatened, blackmailed and assaulted John Evans late at night at his home. They do not seem to be the kind of people who could be regarded as reliable witnesses in any circumstance. They clearly held a grudge against John Evans, who was responsible for their arrests and all that followed. It stretches credulity too far to accept that they could be relied upon for a truthful account of what had happened.

But the coroner believed them. He was unequivocal. He suggested that John Evans feared his alleged behaviour, illegal at the time, would come to light during the inquest. His life would be ruined, even if he escaped a jail sentence. He pronounced John Evans 'respectable by day, but a reprobate by night'. So he had killed himself to avoid ignominy.

There was a further shock to come. When Walter Whitelegg's inquest was resumed, the reason for his death was also found to be cyanide poisoning. According to the doctor who carried out the tests, he had consumed three times the amount of a fatal dose, apparently contained in the drink which John Evans had given him. No one could suggest why this should have been done deliberately and so the jury decided on a verdict of accidental death, by a majority of nine to two. How this accident came about was a mystery, but looking at the details in the accounts of what happened suggests several plausible explanations.

It is possible that John Evans gave Walter Whitelegg the cyanide as a medicine. Strange as it may seem today, cyanide could at the time be given to a patient to settle an upset stomach. This was asserted both by the chemist who sold John Evans the cyanide (for gold analysis, apparently) and the doctor who carried out the post-mortem examination. They stressed that it was dangerous, and should only be done by someone who knew what he was doing. John Evans was not a medical man, but perhaps he knew of this use of cyanide, and thought he could help the young man get over his nausea, but gave him a fatal dose.

Alternatively, he may have used it thinking it was sodium bromide, a common sedative at that time. For when the police found John Evans's body, the bottle containing the cyanide was labelled 'Sod. Bromide', not sodium cyanide. So John Evans could have given the young man what he believed to be something which would help him sleep, but in error gave him poison. Everyone has read of people being killed by weed-killer contained in a lemonade bottle and it is quite possible that this was a similar incident.

From different sources, we know that John Evans was rather cavalier in his use of cyanide. He is known to have given it to a camper on the

Edge to put in a wasps' nest. He also soaked bread in it to make rat poison for use in the Bergli Hut. Perhaps he was not careful enough in washing out the containers in which he had mixed the cyanide (there was no running water in the hut) and perhaps used a contaminated glass for Walter Whitelegg's drink.

There is a fourth possible explanation which deserves consideration. The jury and coroner were sure that John Evans had given Walter Whitelegg the poison in the drink he gave him. This may not have been so. After the young man's death, John Evans went to the police and gave an account of what had happened. He said that Walter Whitelegg complained of a 'burning sensation in his chest' and it was this which prompted him to give him the drink. This is exactly the kind of symptom one would expect with cyanide poisoning, according to a doctor recently consulted. So it seems quite possible that the burning sensation was caused by the action of the poison already in Walter Whitelegg's system. If this is true, then he must have taken it in before John Evans gave him the drink. He could have got up, without disturbing the others, and helped himself to a drink. Either he used a contaminated glass or he tried something from John Evans's stores thinking it would help settle him. From the account of the police interview it is clear they suspected that poison might be involved, and they asked John Evans if there was any poison in the Bergli Hut. He denied this (which was clearly untrue) but they still went on to search the Hut, without success.

The day after Walter Whitelegg's death, John Evans wrote a letter and a note to friends, which were found after his death. They were not suicide notes, but spoke of plans to meet the friends at a later date. So it is clear that, at that stage, he did not intend to kill himself. At some time later he must have come to a terrible realisation – he had been responsible for Walter Whitelegg's death, either directly or indirectly. He could not live with the thought that he had killed an innocent young man. And so he took his own life. He died, then, not from shame or fear, as the coroner had suggested, but from remorse.

Shortly after the inquests, the Bergli Hut was vandalised, and had to be taken down on safety grounds. We will never know for certain what happened there in the summer of 1933, nor the reasons why. But the memory of John Evans does not deserve to bear the opprobrium heaped upon him by a blinkered and prejudiced official. He deserves more than that. He at least deserves the benefit of the doubt, and our understanding and sympathy. For John Evans was a troubled, tormented and lonely man. May his soul rest in peace.

Editor's note

This account, which supplements the summary in Chapter 20, is based principally on reports of the deaths and of the trials in the *Chester Observer* (17 June 1933), the *Alderley and Wilmslow Express and Advertiser* (27 January, 28 July, 4 and 11 August 1933; 5 January 1989), the *Wilmslow Advertiser* (31 July 2008) and *The Times* (26 July and 5 August 1933), on the Stanley archive in the Chester Record Office, the *Journal of Manchester University Mountaineering Club* and the AELP Oral Archive, as well as official documents such as the Salford Census returns for 1891 and 1901 and Evans's and Whitelegg's death certificates. Some gaps in the story of Evans's life remain to be filled, and there are further papers in the Evans family archive to which the author did not have access, but we are including the account here as it stands to confirm Peter Kitching's account in Chapter 21 and to clear Evans's character.

Appendix 21.2

The voice of Philip Jarvis

John Adams with A. J. N. W. Prag

Suddenly, in 2005, a recording from 1917 of the voice of Philip Jarvis, a gamekeeper's son from Alderley Edge in Cheshire, was heard again. Thin and nervous, here was a prisoner of war (POW) in Germany, reciting with great pathos the parable of the Prodigal Son coming home, as no doubt he himself longed to do, from a foreign land to a feast at his father's table. The effect on many who have heard the recording is the same. Alan Garner has put it eloquently: 'At first the hairs stood up on the back of my neck; then the tears came...'. The Cheshire cadence and pronunciation he reckoned to be east Cheshire, within reach of Macclesfield market, but he also believed that the reader was trying to lessen his Cestrian phonetics.

Who was this speaker? How had this gamekeeper's son from Alderley Edge found himself standing in front of Alois Brandl, a renowned Professor of English Studies at a famous Berlin university, facing an early recording machine, in Münster POW Camp, on 20 March 1917?

For the answer we need to go back to the Alderley Edge Landscape Project: Heritage and Educational Resources (AELPHER). Part of the research involved a trawl of the catalogue of the British Library. This threw up a book entitled *Intonation und Vokalqualität dargestellt an der Mundart von Cheshire* – a guide in German to Cheshire dialect, dated 1938 (Büttner, 1938). On page 9 this publication referred intriguingly to recordings made of POWs in 1917. Correspondence with Berlin led to the amazing discovery that not only did three Cheshire recordings still exist, but that one of them was of a Philip Jarvis, from Alderley Edge. The Berlin Archive had then recently been digitised, and the relevant recordings were provided to Manchester Museum courtesy of the Humboldt University in Berlin.

The person who made the recordings, Alois Brandl (1855–1940), was an Austrian academic in Anglistik (English Studies) at the Friedrich-Wilhelms-University in Berlin, and he had written extensively on Chaucer, Shakespeare and Old English before the First

World War – hence his interest in Cheshire dialect. His autobiography, *Zwischen Inn und Themse* (*Between Inn and Thames*), published in 1936, gives much detail of his academic career (Brandl, 1936). For example, he and his students had trundled early recording equipment around most of Britain in the pre-1914 years, at times being taken for German spies. He had also studied in London and had had contact with Henry Sweet – the original Henry Higgins of *My Fair Lady* – who was collecting London dialects at around that time. Brandl also met Thomas Hardy and obtained sound samples of Wessex dialect. Brandl was still active in 1936, when he was the subject of an eightieth-birthday Festschrift. He also had that much desired linguist's gift: immortality in the common speech – the Brandlweg, a street named after him in his home town of Innsbruck in Austria.

Before the Great War, Brandl was also instrumental in setting up the Berlin Sound Archive (Das Berliner Lautarchiv), a worldwide collection of early spoken and musical recordings on wax cylinders, often sent in from far-flung parts of Africa and Asia by German missionaries. At the beginning of the war he became involved as the English expert in making recordings of all the dialects of English from POWs – with several hundred recordings still extant today and now available on the British Library website (http://sounds.bl.uk/Accents-and-dialects/ Berliner-Lautarchiv-British-and-Commonwealth-recordings). It is unclear if there was any sinister implication in this work, though it might have been of marginal use if a German invasion of Britain had occurred.

The recordings were made on wax, and then impressed onto shellac discs and stored in the Prussian State Library in Berlin (of which the Humboldt University is the successor). It is something of a miracle that they survived the interwar turmoil in Germany and the destruction of much of Berlin at the end of the Second World War – they are still lodged in green baize racks in their original purpose-built cabinets in the same building opposite the museums on the Pergamon Insel.

The rediscovery of the Berlin Archive recordings caused a small stir at the British Library National Sound Archive, which was unaware of their existence. It saw them as filling an important gap in its own recordings of English dialects from the 1950s and 2000. BBC Television also noted the rediscovery of the Archive and visited Berlin to film a programme entitled *How the Edwardians Spoke*. The BBC then managed to track down some of the descendants of the POWs, to compare how they spoke in 2007.

In fact, the recordings of 1917 are something of a peculiarity. Most use a text from the Gospel of St Luke, Chapter 15, 'The Prodigal Son'. But the text used is not that of any standard English translation of the Bible, and indeed seems closest to the Luther translation of 1534. The text has also been modified, probably by Brandl himself, to display what he considered typical elements of the individual speaker's accent or dialect. This aspect can be clearly demonstrated from the text used by Jarvis, which contains such phrases as 'in our house are many hired hands who have all the grub they want'. The word 'grub' occurs in no known canonical text, but perhaps struck Brandl as interesting for linguistic and dialect reasons. Other words also occur, such as 'feyther' for father; here one cannot be sure whether this is part of Philip Jarvis's dialect usage or has been incorporated at the wish of Brandl. There may be a forced element to the dialect. There are other interesting aspects to the recordings. For instance, they are accompanied by a phonetic transcription in a very early form of the International Phonetic Alphabet, before it had been standardised.

Perhaps the best that can be said of these recordings is that they are artefacts: they open a window onto how people spoke in the past, but the data must be treated with great caution. In contrast to many later recordings, when people tried to hide their accents under a veil of 'received pronunciation', here we have ordinary people encouraged to exaggerate their accent. And we are hearing for the first time, not recordings of kings or prime ministers, but the common man, who has stepped onto the world stage, and will shortly shake the world.

But what of Philip Jarvis? We know from the prisoner's questionnaire he filled out in 1917 that he was born in 1881, the son of a gamekeeper, in a cottage at Alderley. We know this to be Harebarrow Cottage on the Brocklehurst estate of Hare Hill, now also part of the National Trust's holding on the Edge. The Census returns show that he had moved away, and been in service with the Sawrey-Cookson family, which may have affected his accent. He could read and write, but had had only an elementary school education. While in service with the Sawrey-Cooksons he lived in Furness and in County Durham from his twenty-fifth to his thirtieth year, and then in London and probably Hertfordshire until he was thirty-four. In the German questionnaire his religion is given as Anglican, his profession as 'footman', though the Census for Broughton shows that he started as a gardener. He was about thirty-five at the time of the recording. He had lived away from Alderley for some time in Lancashire and in the north-east of England, and this may have affected his accent. His position as a footman would also have exposed him to other accents and classes of society – and also perhaps allowed him to experiment with 'producing' his own accent.

Philip Jarvis might have faded away, leaving only his voice and written record in the Berlin Sound Archive – a soldier from the Great War – but there is a bittersweet footnote. His voice was broadcast on local radio and television in Manchester in 2005, and within minutes there came a call from a householder in Alderley Edge to say that they had located part of the kerbstone from his grave in their garden. The inscription read, 'And of their dear son Philip Jarvis, died 22 December 1948 aged 67 years'. Jarvis had returned to Cheshire and had been buried in the grave of his parents – but presumably not in the garden of a house on the Congleton Road.

A search through the grave and burial registers of St Mary's Church and a visit to the burial ground with the parish clerk gradually led us to the truth. Plot 16 had been purchased on 16 March 1917 for the burial of Ann Jarvis the day before (this was a not uncommon practice). On 3 August 1926 her widower, John Jervis (*sic*), was buried next to her, and on 28 December 1948 their son Philip was interred in the same grave. Then in the 1950s it appears that the burial ground was running out of space, and in this corner a second layer of plots was added on top of the earlier ones as a temporary solution. Plot 16 was covered by plot 200, the grave of members of the Armstrong family, with gravestones to match. Shortly afterwards the parish council purchased part of the adjoining field and extended the burial ground into it, remodelling this corner of the old burial ground at the same time in order to provide access. It seems likely that when the extra layer of graves was added the stones were removed from the 'redundant' ones, probably to Massey's builders' yard nearby. This must have happened less than five years after Philip's burial, which would explain why the letters are so clear on the stone in the Congleton Road garden, while the fact that this house was once owned by Masseys might explain how the stone got there. However, Brian Hobson, one-time churchwarden at St Mary's, remarked 'Someone was trying to make a claim there'; sadly, he died before he could elucidate this cryptic comment. Of the stone with Ann and John's name there is no trace; possibly it was more weathered by the time of the re-ordering, and therefore not so attractive as a piece of garden furniture.

The surname is spelled in various ways even on official documents, as the burial records of Philip's parents demonstrate. The Census returns down to 1891 give the family name as Jervis. By 1901 Philip is in Furness working for the Sawrey-Cooksons and his name is spelled Jarvis in the Broughton Census. Perhaps we should assume that when he went into service away from home he or his employers found it simpler to spell the surname the way it was actually pronounced, a practice followed by the army and then naturally by his German captors. Chris Jervis (*sic*), a family historian, was able to confirm that no. 17292 Private Philip Jarvis had been a member of the Royal Berkshire Regiment: it is known that men from Hertfordshire (where the Sawrey-Cooksons had property) enlisted in the Royal Berkshires. Jarvis was taken prisoner of war on 3 March 1916, and had been demobilised into the army reserve on 19 March 1919. Chris Jervis also discovered the relevant birth and death certificates, firmly anchoring Philip Jarvis to Alderley. We also know that he had at least four siblings, one of whom followed his father as a gamekeeper, that he never married, and that he died in December 1948 St Thomas's Hospital, Shaw Heath, by then no longer the workhouse but the Stockport geriatric hospital. The fact that his body was brought from Bramhall for burial at Nether Alderley suggests that, at least at the end of his life, he was living not in his native Alderley but in the Stockport suburbs with his sister Mary Allen and her husband in Woodford Road.

For the historian the last word should go to Brandl, although it could equally be taken as referring to Jarvis. Brandl wrote that if the British should ever one day wish to know how their forefathers spoke in 1917, they would have to come to him. True indeed. Yet on a human level the real sorrow of the story of Philip Jarvis is marked by the dates of the events in 1917: that Philip, a prisoner far away in a foreign land, made the recording just at the time of his mother's death and burial; that the Prodigal Son was the text; that he lived and died a bachelor; that he rested at last with his parents, but that their memory was dismantled within five years; that he appears to be the sole survivor, as is his voice: here is poignant, immediate and lasting history.

Acknowledgements

Great and patient assistance was provided by Jürgen-K. Mahrenholz at the Berlin Sound Archive to the Alderley Edge Landscape Project, and to the BBC and to the British Library in their researches on this invaluable archive. In Alderley we are grateful to Gill Davies, Chris Jervis, Brian Hobson and Geoff Windsor for their watchfulness and their persistence in helping to put together Philip Jarvis's story.

Appendix 29.1

The National Trust Sites and Monuments Record (NTSMR)

Christopher Widger

Table 29.1 lists all those archaeological and historically significant sites, monuments and buildings at Alderley Edge recorded in the National Trust Sites and Monuments Record (NTSMR). Readers should note that the dates assigned to the periods are those used conventionally in sites and monuments records, and generally indicate an overall period rather than specific dates. There is, for instance, no evidence for Palaeolithic occupation at Alderley, while we cannot at present give a date to the gold bar (no. 57872); on the other hand the hoard of Roman coins (no. 57876) can be securely dated to *c.* AD 340.

Table 29.1. The National Trust Sites and Monuments Record (NTSMR)

	NGR	*Period*	*NTSMR no.*
Hollow Way at Waterfall Wood	8643 7806	Medieval to Post-Medieval – 1066 AD to 1900 AD	57700
Possible Rock Shelters, Waterfall Wood	8658 7764	Lower Palaeolithic to Modern – 500,000 BC to 2050 AD	57701
Possible Rock Shelters, Waterfall Wood	8658 7763	Lower Palaeolithic to Modern –500,000 BC to 2050 AD	57702
Excavated Hollow, Waterfall Wood	8658 7763	Medieval to Post-Medieval – 1066 AD to 1900 AD	57703
Graffiti, Waterfall Wood	8656 7764	Post-Medieval – 1664 AD to 1900 AD	57704
Rock Carvings, Waterfall Wood	8656 7765	Post-Medieval – 1540 AD to 1900 AD	57705
Possible Tramway, Waterfall Wood	8653 7773	Post-Medieval – 1540 AD to 1900 AD	57706
Stone Quarry and Borehole, Waterfall Wood	8643 7795	Post-Medieval 1540 – AD to 1900 AD	57707
Stone Quarry, Waterfall Wood	8655 7780	Post-Medieval – 1540 AD to 1900 AD	57708
Stone Quarry, Waterfall Wood	8644 7779	Post-Medieval – 1540 AD to 1900 AD	57709
Stone Quarry, Clock House Wood	8668 7795	Post-Medieval – 1540 AD to 1900 AD	57710
Stone Quarry and Spoil Heap, Dickens Wood	8637 7774	Post-Medieval – 1540 AD to 1900 AD	57711

	NGR	Period	NTSMR no.
Trackway, Dickens Wood	8628 7781	Medieval to Post-Medieval – 1066 AD to 1900 AD	57712
Earth Circle, Edge House Farm	8626 7758	Prehistoric – 500,000 BC to 42 AD	57713
Stone, Golden Stone	8622 7763	Lower Palaeolithic to Post-Medieval – 500,000 BC to 1900 AD	57714
Mine (Shaft), near Golden Stone	8625 7763	Post-Medieval – 1540 AD to 1900 AD	57715
Hollow Way, near Golden Stone	8629 7765	Medieval to Post-Medieval – 1066 AD to 1900 AD	57716
Mine (Workings), near Stormy Point	8608 7783	Post-Medieval – 1540 AD to 1900 AD	57717
Rock Shelter, near Stormy Point	8609 7782	Medieval – 1066 AD to 1539 AD	57718
Earthwork, Stormy Point	8606 7784	Prehistoric – 500,000 BC to 42 AD	57719
Mine (Level), Stormy Point	8608 7786	Medieval – 1066 AD to 1539 AD	57720
Mine, Stormy Point	8608 7786	Post-Medieval – 1540 AD to 1900 AD	57721
Opencast Working, Pillar Mine	8611 7783	Lower Palaeolithic to Post-Medieval – 500,000 BC to 1900 AD	57722
Pit Workings, Pillar Mine	8612 7783	Medieval to Post-Medieval – 1066 AD to 1900 AD	57723
Mine, Pillar Mine	8613 7782	Medieval to Post-Medieval – 1066 AD to 1900 AD	57724
Mine (Adit), near Pillar Mine	8623 7783	Post-Medieval – 1700 AD to 1900 AD	57725
Possible Mines, near Pillar Mine	8620 7784	Medieval to Post-Medieval – 1066 AD to 1900 AD	57726
Possible Mine Working, Stormy Point	8610 7787	Lower Palaeolithic to Post-Medieval – 500,000 BC to 1900 AD	57727
Possible Mine Working, Stormy Point	8608 7787	Lower Palaeolithic to Post-Medieval – 500,000 BC to 1900 AD	57728
Stone Dressing Floor, Devil's Grave	8601 7789	Lower Palaeolithic to Post-Medieval – 500,000 BC to 1900 AD	57729
Mine (Adit), Doc Mine	8610 7730	Post-Medieval to Modern – 1540 AD to 2050 AD	57730
Mine, Devil's Grave	8601 7788	Medieval to Post-Medieval – 1066 AD to 1900 AD	57731
Possible Mound, Pike's Low	8601 7790	Bronze Age – 2350 BC to 701 BC	57732
Stone, Memorial Stone	8602 7791	Modern – 1930 AD to 1939 AD	57733
Stone Quarry, Stormy Point	8603 7788	Medieval to Post-Medieval – 1066 AD to 1900 AD	57734
Stone Quarry, Stormy Point	8602 7791	Medieval to Post-Medieval – 1066 AD to 1900 AD	57735
Parish Boundary, near Stormy Point	8601 7794	Medieval to Post-Medieval – 1066 AD to 1900 AD	57736
Trackway, Glaze Hill	8604 7795	Medieval – 1066 AD to 1539 AD	57737
Stone, Glaze Hill	8601 7797	(Natural feature date unknown)	57738
Trackway, Saddlebole	8601 7802	Medieval to Post-Medieval – 1066 AD to 1900 AD	57739
Mine (Adit), Glaze Hill	8608 7793	Post-Medieval – 1540 AD to 1888 AD	57740
Possible Ore Preparation, Glaze Hill	8616 7796	Medieval to Post-Medieval – 1066 AD to 1900 AD	57741
Stone, Saddlebole	8603 7808	Medieval to Post-Medieval – 1066 AD to 1900 AD	57742
Mine Workings, Saddlebole	8603 7807	Medieval to Post-Medieval – 1066 AD to 1900 AD	57743
Smelting Site, Saddlebole	8605 7810	Medieval to Post-Medieval – 1066 AD to 1900 AD	57744
Blade, Saddlebole	8603 7807	Mesolithic – 10,000 BC to 4001 BC	57745
Boundary Stone, Saddlebole	8607 7814	Medieval to Post-Medieval – 1066 AD to 1900 AD	57746
Sandstone Quarry, near Dickens Farm	86107830	Post-Medieval to Modern – 1872 AD to 1965 AD	57747
Quarry, Glaze Hill	85987798	Post-Medieval – 1540 AD to 1900 AD	57748
Mine, near Holy Well	85927794	Post-Medieval – 1540 AD to 1900 AD	57749
Mine, near Holy Well,	85957794	Post-Medieval – 1540 AD to 1900 AD	57750
Shaft, near Devil's Grave	85987791	Post-Medieval – 1540 AD to 1900 AD	57751
Well, Holy Well	85917786	Early Medieval/Dark Ages to Medieval – 410 AD to 1539 AD	57752

	NGR	Period	NTSMR no.
Stones, Holy Well	85917788	(Natural feature date unknown)	57753
Well, De Trafford's Well	85887786	Post-Medieval – 1540 AD to 1900 AD	57754
Mine (Adit), Well Rocks	85887786	Post-Medieval – 1540 AD to 1900 AD	57755
Stone Quarry, Well Rocks	85917783	Modern – 1901 AD to 2050 AD	57756
Stone Quarry, near Holy Well	85947779	Post-Medieval – 1540 AD to 1900 AD	57757
Mine (Adit), Armada Beacon	85877777	Post-Medieval – 1540 AD to 1900 AD	57758
Beacon, Armada Beacon	85847773	Post-Medieval – 1540 AD to 1900 AD	57759
Possible House Platform, Bent Field	85727793	Post-Medieval – 1540 AD to 1900 AD	57760
Possible Mine Workings, near Castle Rock	85757784	Post-Medieval – 1540 AD to 1900 AD	57761
Graffiti, Castle Rock	85607798	Post-Medieval – 1540 AD to 1900 AD	57762
Possible Rock Shelter, Castle Rock	85557800	(Natural feature date unknown)	57763
Stone Quarry, Castle Rock	85537798	Medieval to Post-Medieval – 1066 AD to 1900 AD	57764
Stone Quarry, near Wizard's Well	85537803	Post-Medieval – 1540 AD to 1900 AD	57765
Well, Wizard's Well	85487803	Post-Medieval – 1540 AD to 1900 AD	57766
Mine (Adit), Wizard's Well	85477801	Post-Medieval – 1540 AD to 1900 AD	57767
Sandstone Quarry, Mottram Road	85377827	Post-Medieval – 1540 AD to 1900 AD	57768
Possible Mineshafts, Beech Wood	85347827	Medieval to Post-Medieval – 1066 AD to 1900 AD	57769
Refuse Disposal Site, Woodbrook Road	85257821	Post-Medieval – 1540 AD to 1900 AD	57770
Earthwork, near Castle Rock	85537793	Prehistoric – 500,000 BC to 42 AD	57771
Earthwork, Castle Stone Field	85557794	Medieval to Post-Medieval – 1066 AD to 1900 AD	57772
Stone Alignment, Castle Field	85607790	Early Iron Age to Post-Medieval – 700 BC to 1700 AD	57773
Flint Scatter, Castle Rock	85577797	Mesolithic – 10,000 BC to 4001 BC	57774
Reservoir, near Armada Beacon	85807770	Post-Medieval – 1540 AD to 1900 AD	57775
Gamekeepers Lodge, Beacon Lodge	85807755	Post-Medieval – 1540 AD to 1900 AD	57776
Mine, Beacon Lodge	85887757	Post-Medieval – 1540 AD to 1900 AD	57777
Mine Workings, near Engine Vein	85887757	Post-Medieval – 1540 AD to 1900 AD	57778
Prospecting Trench, near Engine Vein	85927753	Post-Medieval – 1540 AD to 1900 AD	57779
Earthwork, Engine Vein	85857751	Post-Medieval – 1540 AD to 1900 AD	57780
Mine Workings, near Engine Vein	85957751	Post-Medieval – 1540 AD to 1900 AD	57781
Earthwork, Church Quarry	85897744	Medieval to Post-Medieval – 1066 AD to 1900 AD	57782
Earthwork, Church Quarry Hill	8587 7749	Medieval to Post-Medieval – 1066 AD to 1900 AD	57783
Hollow Way, east of Macclesfield Road	8583 7754	Medieval to Post-Medieval – 1066 AD to 1900 AD	57784
Stone Quarry with graffiti, Church Quarry	8589 7740	Post-Medieval - 1540 AD to 1900 AD	57785
Powder Magazine, Church Quarry	8592 7736	Post-Medieval – 1540 AD to 1900 AD	57786
Log Cabin (Site of), Church Quarry	8589 7741	Modern – 1920 AD to 1939 AD	57787
Well, Wizard Inn	8593 7734	Modern – 1901 AD to 1949 AD	57788
Inn, Wizard Inn	8592 7731	Post-Medieval to Modern – 1540 AD to 1998 AD	57789
Mine, Cobalt Mine	8593 7732	Post-Medieval – 1810 AD to 1820 AD	57790
Marlpits, NT visitors' car park	8614 7713	Post-Medieval – 1540 AD to 1900 AD	57791
Stone Quarry, Thieves' Hole	8608 7730	Post-Medieval – 1540 AD to 1900 AD	57792
Well, Warden's Cottage	8598 7739	Medieval to Post-Medieval – 1066 AD to 1900 AD	57793
Stone Quarry, near Warden's Cottage	8605 7735	Post-Medieval – 1540 AD to 1900 AD	57794
Earthwork, Engine Vein	8607 7744	Post-Medieval – 1540 AD to 1900 AD	57795
Adit, Engine Vein	8610 7746	Post-Medieval – 1540 AD to 1900 AD	57796
Stone Quarry, near Engine Vein	8609 7739	Post-Medieval – 1540 AD to 1900 AD	57797
Open Cast, Engine Vein	8606 7747	Post-Medieval – 1540 AD to 1900 AD	57798

	NGR	Period	NTSMR no.
Stone Quarry, Engine Vein	860 77749	Post-Medieval – 1540 AD to 1900 AD	57799
Stone Quarry, near Engine Vein	8605 7755	Post-Medieval – 1540 AD to 1900 AD	57800
Stone Quarry, Old Alderley Quarry	8607 7764	Post-Medieval – 1540 AD to 1900 AD	57801
Road, Old Alderley Quarry	8605 7767	Post-Medieval – 1540 AD to 1900 AD	57802
Open Cast, Canyon Mine	8609 7771	Medieval – 1066 AD to 1539 AD	57803
Mine Workings, near Canyon Mine	8613 7769	Medieval – 1066 AD to 1539 AD	57804
Mine Workings, Old Alderley Quarry	8610 7765	Medieval – 1066 AD to 1539 AD	57805
Level, near Engine Vein	8610 7755	Post-Medieval – 1800 AD to 1900 AD	57806
Graffiti, near Engine Vein	8614 7754	Modern – 1940 AD to 1950 AD	57807
Possible Boundary Stone, near Engine Vein	8612 7752	Post-Medieval – 1540 AD to 1900 AD	57808
Stone Circle, near Old Alderley Quarry,	8602 7774	Post-Medieval – 1540 AD to 1900 AD	57809
Mesolithic Flint	8600 7700	Mesolithic – 10,000 BC to 4001 BC	57810
Site of Building, Macclesfield Road	8572 7767	Post-Medieval – 1540 AD to 1900 AD	57811
Possible Reservoirs, Windmill Wood	8564 7766	Post-Medieval – 1540 AD to 1900 AD	57812
Shafts, Windmill Wood	8569 7757	Post-Medieval – 1540 AD to 1900 AD	57813
Site of Windmill, Windmill Wood	8563 7763	Post-Medieval – 1540 AD to 1900 AD	57814
Possible Mine Workings, north-west of Windmill Wood	8557 7757	Post-Medieval – 1540 AD to 1900 AD	57815
Open Cast, Windmill Wood	8554 7764	Bronze Age – 2350 BC to 701 BC	57816
Earthwork, Windmill Wood	8557 7763	Lower Palaeolithic to Post-Medieval – 500,000 BC to 1900 AD	57817
Earthwork, Windmill Wood	8561 7753	Lower Palaeolithic to Post-Medieval – 500,000 BC to 1900 AD	57818
Hollow Ways, Haglane Road	8548 7754	Post-Medieval – 1540 AD to 1900 AD	57819
Smelting House (site of), The Hagg	8545 7755	Post-Medieval – 1540 AD to 1900 AD	57820
Shafts, near Wood Mine	8550 7754	Post-Medieval – 1540 AD to 1900 AD	57821
Mine (Adit), Wood Mine	8546 7760	Medieval to Post-Medieval – 1066 AD to 1900 AD	57822
Tramway, Wood Mine	8546 7760	Post-Medieval – 1540 AD to 1900 AD	57823
Mesolithic Flints (Flint scatter), Whitebarn Farm	8512 7763	Mesolithic – 10,000 BC to 4001 BC	57824
Trackway, near Brynlow Farm	8516 7726	Post-Medieval – 1540 AD to 1900 AD	57825
Pound, Pick Hill Lane	8511 7716	Post-Medieval – 1540 AD to 1900 AD	57826
Well, Brynlow	8514 7714	Medieval to Post-Medieval – 1066 AD to 1900 AD	57827
Adit, Brynlow Farm	8514 7714	Medieval to Post-Medieval – 1066 AD to 1900 AD	57828
Hollow Ways, Artists Lane	8535 7722	Medieval – 1066 AD to 1539 AD	57829
Shaft, Artist's Lane	8550 7714	Post-Medieval – 1540 AD to 1900 AD	57830
Possible Marlpit, Artists Lane	8559 7716	Post-Medieval – 1540 AD to 1900 AD	57831
Adit, Brynlow Dell	8547 7724	Post-Medieval – 1540 AD to 1900 AD	57832
Mine, Brynlow Dell	8548 7722	Post-Medieval – 1800 AD to 1900 AD	57833
Mine (Adit), Brynlow Dell	8553 7721	Post-Medieval – 1540 AD to 1900 AD	57834
Adit, Brynlow Dell	8555 7723	Post-Medieval – 1540 AD to 1900 AD	57835
Mine Workings, Brynlow Dell	8564 7726	Post-Medieval – 1540 AD to 1900 AD	57836
Shaft, near Brynlow Dell	8568 7723	Medieval to Post-Medieval – 1066 AD to 1900 AD	57837
Shafts, west of Cow Lane	8572 7730	Post-Medieval – 1540 AD to 1900 AD	57838
Mine Workings, Cow Lane	8572 7734	Post-Medieval – 1540 AD to 1900 AD	57839
Building Foundations, Cow Lane	8578 7725	Post-Medieval – 1540 AD to 1900 AD	57840
Stone Posts, Brynlow Field	8571 7737	Post-Medieval – 1540 AD to 1900 AD	57841

	NGR	Period	NTSMR no.
Shafts, Cow Lane Fault	8573 7742	Medieval to Post-Medieval – 1066 AD to 1900 AD	57842
Settlement (site of), Windmill Wood	8575 7753	(Unconfirmed site, date unknown)	57843
Open Cast, Brynlow Field	8550 7735	Post-Medieval – 1540 AD to 1900 AD	57844
Shaft, Brynlow Field	8548 7732	Post-Medieval – 1540 AD to 1900 AD	57845
Shaft, near Brynlow Field	8540 7740	Post-Medieval – 1870 AD to 1880 AD	57846
Shafts, near Brynlow Field	8545 7745	Post-Medieval – 1860 AD to 1880 AD	57847
Pit Workings (including hammer stones and wooden shovel), Brynlow Field	8552 7735	Early Bronze Age to Post-Medieval – 2350 BC to 1900 AD	57848
Possible Marlpits, Brynlow Field	8553 7745	Post-Medieval – 1540 AD to 1900 AD	57849
Ridge and Furrow, Brynlow Field	8545 7745	Medieval – 1066 AD to 1539 AD	57850
Building Platform, Brynlow Field	8550 7744	Post-Medieval – 1540 AD to 1850 AD	57851
Hollow Way, near Armstrong Farm	8565 7769	Medieval – 1066 AD to 1539 AD	57852
Possible Shaft, near West Mine	8542 7774	Post-Medieval – 1540 AD to 1900 AD	57853
Possible Open Cast, near West Mine	8540 7775	Post-Medieval – 1540 AD to 1900 AD	57854
Old Hedgerow, near West Mine	8538 7773	Post-Medieval – 1540 AD to 1900 AD	57855
Mine Workings, Armstrong Farm	8545 7784	Post-Medieval - 1800 AD to 1900 AD	57856
Earthworks, near West Mine	8510 7782	Post-Medieval – 1540 AD to 1900 AD	57857
Marlpits, near West Mine	8516 7776	Post-Medieval - 1850 AD to 1900 AD	57858
Ditch, The Hurst	8523 7790	Medieval to Post-Medieval – 1066 AD to 1900 AD	57859
Hollow Way, Cherry Tree House	8504 7785	Medieval to Post-Medieval – 1066 AD to 1900 AD	57860
Earthworks, near West Mine	8524 7765	Post-Medieval – 1540 AD to 1900 AD	57861
Mine (Shaft), New Venture Mine	8520 7764	Post-Medieval - 1870 AD to 1880 AD	57862
Field, Fair Field	8585 7731	Post-Medieval to Modern - 1540 AD to 1939 AD	57863
Building, Old Vet Surgery	8586 7731	Post-Medieval to Modern - 1807 AD to 1998 AD	57864
Road, Cow Lane	8580 7724	Post-Medieval – 1775 AD to 1787 AD	57865
Shaft, Bradford Lodge Wood	8584 7716	Post-Medieval – 1800 AD to 1900 AD	57866
Shaft, Bradford Lane	8601 7710	Post-Medieval – 1810 AD to 1820 AD	57867
Shafts, Finlow Hill Wood	8603 7698	Post-Medieval – 1540 AD to 1900 AD	57868
Mine Workings, Finlow Hill Wood	8603 7696	Post-Medieval – 1810 AD to 1820 AD	57869
Adit, Finlow Hill Wood	8606 7698	Post-Medieval – 1810 AD to 1820 AD	57870
Mining Axe, Pillar Mine	8615 7784	Bronze Age – 2350 BC to 701 BC	57871
Gold bar, Artist's Lane	8564 7721	Probably prehistoric, 2350 BC to 42 AD	57872
Hammer Stone, near Stormy Point	8613 7786	Lower Palaeolithic to Medieval – 500,000 BC to 1539 AD	57873
Earth Circle, Engine Vein	8602 7753	Post-Medieval – 1540 AD to 1900 AD	57874
Roads	8597 7751	Post-Medieval – 1540 AD to 1900 AD	57875
Coin Hoard, Pot Shaft	8604 7749	Early Bronze Age to Medieval – 2350 BC to 1539 AD	57876
Hammer Stones, Finlow Hill Wood	8600 7700	Early Bronze Age to Medieval – 2350 BC to 1539 AD	57877
Coins, Finlow Hill Wood	8600 7700	Roman – 43 AD to 409 AD	57878
Bronze Sword, Finlow Hill Wood	8600 7700	Bronze Age – 2350 BC to 701 BC	57879
Mine Workings, near Old Alderley Quarry	8602 7760	Mesolithic – 10,000 BC to 4001 BC	57880
Stone Axe Hammer, near Saddlebole	8600 7800	Bronze Age – 2350 BC to 701 BC	57881
Pit Workings, Engine Vein	8605 7749	Medieval to Post-Medieval – 1066 AD to 1900 AD	57882
Pit Workings, Engine Vein	8605 7749	Medieval to Post-Medieval – 1066 AD to 1900 AD	57883
Possible Access Route, Engine Vein	8605 7749	Early Bronze Age – 2350 BC to 1501 BC	57884
Archaeological Excavation Trench, Engine Vein	8606 7747	Modern – 1901 AD to 2050 AD	57885

	NGR	Period	NTSMR no.
Archaeological Excavation Trench, Engine Vein	8605 7749	Modern – 1997 AD	57886
Shaft and Level, Engine Vein	8605 7749	Late Iron Age to Roman – 0 AD to 100 AD	57887
Shaft, Engine Vein	8607 7747	Medieval – 1066 AD to 1539 AD	57888
Mine Workings, Engine Vein	8605 7749	Medieval to Post-Medieval – 1066 AD to 1900 AD	57889
Stone Quarry, Engine Vein	8605 7749	Post-Medieval – 1540 AD to 1900 AD	57890
Mine Working, Engine Vein	8605 7749	Post-Medieval – 1540 AD to 1900 AD	57891
Mine Working, Engine Vein	8605 7749	Bronze Age – 2350 BC to 701 BC	57892
Mine Workings, Engine Vein	8605 7749	Post-Medieval – 1540 AD to 1900 AD	57893
Shaft, Engine Vein	8605 7749	Medieval to Post-Medieval – 1066 AD to 1900 AD	57894
Shaft, Engine Vein	8607 7747	Medieval to Post-Medieval – 1066 AD to 1900 AD	57895
Shaft, Engine Vein	8605 7749	Medieval to Post-Medieval – 1066 AD to 1900 AD	57896
Flint, Pillar Mine	8608 7783	Mesolithic – 10,000 BC to 4001 BC	57897
Flint, Druids' Circle	8601 7773	Early Mesolithic to Post-Medieval – 10000 BC to 1815 AD	57898
Flint, near Old Alderley Quarry	8606 7763	Early Mesolithic to Modern – 10,000 BC to 1901 AD	57899
Flint, on Quarry Road	8596 7762	Mesolithic – 10,000 BC to 4001 BC	57900
Spoil Heap, Alderley Edge	8610 7736	Modern – 1901 AD to 2050 AD	57901
Earthworks, Alderley Edge	8595 7715	Post-Medieval – 1540 AD to 1900 AD	57902
Network of land drains, Alderley Edge	85947707	Post-Medieval to Modern – 1540 AD to 2050 AD	57903
Shaft Head, Alderley Edge	8547 7748	Post-Medieval – 1540 AD to 1900 AD	57904
Shaft Head, Alderley Edge	8546 7747	Post-Medieval – 1540 AD to 1900 AD	57905
Shaft Head, Alderley Edge	8545 7747	Post-Medieval – 1540 AD to 1900 AD	57906
Shaft Head, Alderley Edge	8556 7765	Post-Medieval – 1540 AD to 1900 AD	57907
Spoil Heap, Alderley Edge	8559 7761	Post-Medieval – 1540 AD to 1900 AD	57908
Mining – open cast, Alderley Edge	8528 7768	Post-Medieval – 1540 AD to 1900 AD	57909
Hollow way/ditch, Alderley Edge	8521 7767	Post-Medieval to Modern – 1540 AD to 2050 AD	57910
Ridge and furrow, Alderley Edge	8544 7785	Post-Medieval to Modern – 1540 AD to 2050 AD	57911
Large Earthen Bank, Alderley Edge	8603 7775	Post-Medieval to Modern – 1540 AD to 2050 AD	57912
Large Earthwork ditch, Alderley Edge	8607 7774	Medieval to Post-Medieval – 1066 AD to 1900 AD	57913
Small quarry and associated spoil heap	8602 7771	Medieval – 1066 AD to 1539 AD	57914
Capped Mineshaft, Alderley Edge	8604 7773	Post-Medieval – 1540 AD to 1900 AD	57915
Pair of sunken mineshafts, Alderley Edge	8603 7773	Post-Medieval – 1540 AD to 1900 AD	57916
The 'New Road', Alderley Edge	8604 7768	Post-Medieval – 1540 AD to 1900 AD	57917
Mining Adit, Alderley Edge	86097745	Medieval to Post-Medieval – 1066 AD to 1900 AD	57918
Bear Shaft, Alderley Edge	8599 7751	Medieval to Post-Medieval – 1066 AD to 1900 AD	57919

NGR, national Grid reference (all begin SJ).

General glossary

A. J. N. W. Prag (ed.)

The sections on geology and mining in this book contain many specialised terms and so they have been given separate glossaries. This glossary covers all other specialised, technical, historical and local terms used in the book.

Aedicule Small shrine (in Latin *aedicula*) commonly framed by two columns supporting an entablature and pediment set in a temple and containing a statue. More loosely the term is applied to a type of door or window case comprising flanking columns, piers or pilasters supporting a gable, lintel, plaque or entablature.

Arthropod Invertebrate animal (without a backbone) having an external skeleton, a segmented body and jointed appendages. Arthropods make up 90 per cent of all animals on Earth and are classified in the phylum Arthropoda.

Ashlar Hewn blocks of masonry wrought to even faces and square edges and laid in horizontal courses with vertical joints, as distinct from rubble or undressed stone straight from the quarry.

Assart To convert land from forest to arable; a piece of land thus converted.

Baffle-entry Arrangement, generally in traditional houses of the seventeenth century, where the entrance is obstructed by a chimney stack set axially, so that it is necessary to turn immediately right or left to progress to the living spaces.

Bargeboard Board, often carved or fretted, fixed to the end of the purlins at a gable.

Bed stone The fixed bottom millstone of a pair (see also 'Runner stone').

Biotope Small area with uniform biological conditions of climate, soil, altitude and, especially, vegetation.

Broached spire Tall structure, usually octagonal in plan, placed upon a square tower – usually of a church – and rising without an intermediate parapet to a point. Each of the four angles of the tower not covered by the base of the spire is filled with an inclined mass of masonry or broach built into the oblique sides of the spire.

CAL AD, BC, BP Dates calculated by radiocarbon (C^{14}) analysis of organic material need to be calibrated against timber from a tree whose age has been calculated by tree-ring analysis (counting the growth rings). They are then expressed as CAL BC, CAL AD, CAL BP. Since both sets of measurements have only limited precision there will still be a range of possible calendar years.

Calcicolous Growing best in chalky soil.

Carr Wet boggy ground.

Coade stone Artificial cast stone invented and successfully marketed from 1769 by Mrs Eleanor Coade and later by Coade & Sealy of London. It was widely used in the late eighteenth century for statuary and ornamentation.

Collar-truss Type of rigid transverse framework constructed across a roof to carry longitudinal timbers that support rafters whose spread is resisted by a horizontal beam set mid-way between the feet and the apex of the principal rafters.

Court leet Local manorial court.

Cranked (oak etc.) Timber specially selected for its curved shape, often deliberately grown for the purpose.

Cruciform   Cross-shaped in cross-section; in the case of a cast-iron waterwheel shaft it is the strongest form using least metal.

Cruck(-framed)   Building constructed of timber about a frame whose chief support is derived from pairs of inclined, generally curved, blades. Such blades – very often the halves of a cranked oak – may be joined at the apex (full cruck) or at a collar (base cruck).

Cryptogamic   Plants without true flowers or seeds.

Damsel   Three- or four-sided spindle which agitates the shoe feeding grain to the millstones.

Dimorphic, dimorphism   Occurring in or representing two distinct forms (cf. polymorphic).

Double pile   Type of house two rooms deep, fashionable from the seventeenth century; the two rows of rooms were usually separated by a corridor running the length of the house.

Dripmould   Contoured or profiled element projecting from a wall face, the purpose of which is both to decorate and to deflect rainwater from the wall itself or from a window below it.

Ecotone   The boundary or transitional zone between adjacent vegetation communities (biotopes).

Fee   An estate of land, especially one held on condition of feudal service.

Forb   Herbaceous flowering plant other than grass.

Frass   Excrement or other refuse left by (wood-boring) insects and insect larvae.

Garderobe   From the French *garder* (to watch, to guard) and *robe* (clothing): a garderobe is properly a large cupboard, usually adjoining the chamber or solar of a medieval house and providing safe keeping for valuable clothes, plate or money. Later the term came to refer to a primitive lavatory in a building, usually a simple hole discharging to the outside (clothes moths do not like the smell any more than humans do and tend to stay away). Garderobes were provided for early factories such as cotton mills, where they were enclosed in towers serving a privy at each floor level.

Glabrous   Free from hair or down; smooth.

Gothick   The nineteenth-century fashion for imitation of Medieval Gothic but which parodied the pointed arch, ribbed vault, flying buttress and other features of the period.

Great spur wheel   The main driving wheel in a mill, mounted on an upright shaft and transmitting drive to the stones via stone nuts (q.v.).

Gudgeon   Iron assembly forming the bearing for a wooden shaft; the journal (q.v.) is often provided with wings to secure it to the end of a wooden shaft.

Habitat   The natural environment that is inhabited by a particular species of animal, plant or other type of organism.

Header and stretcher bond   In brickwork, a bond where the ends of the brick are visible is known as a 'header', and where the sides of the brick are visible, as stretcher bond. The two may be variously combined to produce other types of bond.

Hey   Enclosure.

Hoodmould   As dripmould, but here the projecting moulding is generally found on the face of a wall above an arch, doorway or window, usually following the form of the opening.

House-place   The main living area of a small medieval house that combined the functions of hall, kitchen and chamber found in larger houses.

Hurst   Heavy timber or iron framework supporting the millstones and enclosing the main gearing in a windmill or watermill.

Hyphae   The branching filaments that make up the mycelium or vegetative part of a fungus.

Intake (also locally **intacke**)   New land taken in.

Journal   The part of a shaft that rests on bearings.

Matrix   In natural history, any area outside any organism's habitat patch, typically regarded as vacant of resources in studies that focus on multiple population units (viz., metapopulations).

Mere   Boundary or boundary marker, from the Anglo-Saxon *gemaere*. See Chapter 27.

Metapopulations   Multiple interconnected but discrete populations occupying separate habitats on different sites.

Monopitch (roof)   Inclined roof of single plane, lacking a ridge or valley.

Mortise/mortice   A hole, usually oblong or square, cut through a piece of wood or other material, into which a tenon, for example, is secured.

Mortise wheel   Gear, the rim of which is formed with usually oblong holes into which wooden cogs are fitted; a cog is always an insertion in a mortise wheel.

Moss   Peat bog.

Mullion   Vertical bar between the panes of a window.

Mycorrhiza   Symbiotic association between a fungus and the roots of a vascular plant.

Obligate (of parasites)   Restricted to a particular function or mode of life.

Ogee   Double curved line comprising convex and concave elements in the form of a reversed 'S'. The ogee form was used in sixteenth-century houses to create decorative door lintels.

Oligophagous   Having a very restricted diet.

Outshot, outshut   Subsidiary compartment at the side or end of a house or barn, under a lean-to roof, to be distinguished from an aisle, which is open to the body of the building.

Overdrift   Runner stones (q.v.) driven from above by quants (q.v.) (see also 'Underdrift').

Palp   Each of a pair of elongated segmented appendages near the mouth of an arthropod, usually concerned with the senses of touch and taste.

Patent   Botanical term meaning protruding at right angles.

Penstock   Sluice gate controlling the flow of water to the waterwheel.

Perambulation   'Walking around': in traditional English law, determining the bounds of a legal area such as a parish by walking around it, beating the bounds.

Pinion   The smaller of a pair of gear wheels.

Pintle   Pivot pin (usually upright) on which another part turns.

Pit wheel   Mounted on the same shaft as the waterwheel, it is the first gear wheel in the drive train from the waterwheel to the millstones: waterwheel – pit wheel – wallower – great spur wheel – stone nuts – millstones.

Plumose   Having a feather-like structure.

Polymorphic, polymorphism   Occurring in several different forms (cf. dimorphic).

Possum-like behaviour   Postures adopted by individuals that feign death (also known as thanatosis).

Purlin   Horizontal beam along the length of a roof supporting the rafters or boards.

Quant   Vertical iron spindle carrying the stone nut to drive the runner stone from above (i.e. overdrift).

Raptorial   Predatory; adapted for seizing prey.

Ridding   Tree clearance, thus a cleared area, especially one cleared of trees.

Room   (In landscape description) a section of the moss used for turbary (q.v.), an open space or allocation in the turbary.

Ruderal (of plants)   Growing on waste ground or among rubbish.

Runner stone   The upper, driven millstone in a pair (see also 'Bed stone')

Rynd/rhynd   Device set across the eye of the runner stone to support the stone above the bed stone and transmit the drive; a balance rynd is two-armed and allows some flexibility; a fixed rynd is three- or four-armed and holds the runner stone more firmly; a gimbal rynd was introduced in the late nineteenth century and works like a universal joint to provide flexibility in two axes, mainly used in steam-powered mills.

Saprophyte   Plant, fungus or micro-organism that lives on decaying matter.

Scantling   The measured size or dimensions of a timber.

Screens passage   The linear space at the service end of a Medieval hall between the screen, which is usually a wooden partition, and the buttery, kitchen and pantry entrances.

Sessile   Attached directly, without a stalk.

Shippon   Cattle shed.

Soke   The right of the lord of the manor to demand that his tenants had their grain ground at his mill, with either a payment or a toll taken in kind.

Solar   From the Latin *solarium* (a sunny spot), the term refers to an upper living room at the high end of a Medieval house used as a private room or bed chamber.

Spere truss   Truss at the lower end of a Medieval hall which divides the cross entry or screens passage (if the space between the main spere posts was occupied by a moveable screen) from the hall proper.

Stitching   Tree clearance, thus a cleared area, especially one cleared of trees.

Stone nut   Small driven cog wheel or gear wheel.

Strapwork   Decoration originating in France and the Netherlands around 1540 and popular in Elizabethan England. It consists of interlaced bands and forms redolent of fretwork and was employed for ceilings, screens and funerary monuments.

Stubbing   Place where trees have been stubbed, that is, their stubs (stumps) grubbed up.

Substrate   Matter or surface on which an organism is observed.

Tenon   Projecting piece (usually of wood) made for insertion into a mortise in another piece.

Trenail/treenail   Wooden pin used for fastening timbers together.

Turbary   The legal right to cut turf or peat on common ground or on another's ground.

Turning-stair   Type of stairway which ascends not by flights but by turns. These will be about a central well or newel post, often leaving small quarter landings at each turn.

Underdrift   Millstone driven from below, the usual arrangement in a watermill (see also 'Overdrift').

Vagrant (in entomology)   Individuals occurring in areas (sites) lacking larval host plants.

Vascular   Flowering plants with a system of vessels for carrying sap, water etc.

Wallower   Gear wheel driven by the pit wheel, in turn driving (sometimes through intermediate gears) the great spur wheel.

Windbrace   Short, usually curved braces in the plane of a roof. They connect side purlins with principal rafters to provide lateral rigidity. In early and high-status roofs, they are sometimes cusped or decorated.

Geology glossary

Simon Timberlake, with Nigel Dibben, David I. Green and Geoffrey Warrington

The languages of geology and mining have much in common, and terms missing from one glossary will usually be found in the other. However, for the reader's convenience there is a small overlap between the two glossaries, particularly of those words that have a slightly different meaning in the different contexts. Further explanations of geological terms can be found in Chapter 4.

Aeolian   Sediments deposited after transport by wind.

Alluvial fan   Mass of sediment deposited at a decrease in gradient where a stream or river leaves a mountainous area and branches radially onto a plain.

Andesite   Fine-grained volcanic rock of intermediate composition containing the feldspars andesine or oligoclase.

Anticline   Arch-shaped ridge or fold of stratified rock formed by compressional stresses in the Earth's crust, in which the strata slope downwards, away from the crest and into adjoining trough-shaped folds or synclines.

Arthropod   An invertebrate (i.e. lacking a backbone) with jointed appendages, a segmented body and an external skeleton made of chitin or calcium carbonate; about 90 per cent of all described living animal species are arthropods, including insects, spiders, crustaceans and centipedes.

Asbolane (asbolite)   Amorphous (non-crystalline) mineral of uncertain composition, consisting mostly of manganese and some iron oxides, with variable amounts of cobalt and other elements. Mined as a cobalt ore.

Bar   Linear deposit of sand or gravel parallel to the sides (banks) of the river channel.

Baryte (barite)   Heavy sparry mineral composed of barium sulphate ($BaSO_4$), the most widespread mineral in the Alderley district.

Basal till   Till (q.v.) dropped from the melting base or bed of an ice-sheet.

Block   Another term for a horst: an area of rock lifted up between two parallel faults or a block of crust left standing after rocks either side have been downfaulted. It usually forms a topographic feature of elevated ground such as the Edge.

Borrowdale Volcanic Series   Series of slates and volcanic rocks (i.e. lavas and ashes) of Ordovician (Llandeilo) age from the Lake District, Cumbria. Many of the glacial erratics found in the Manchester–Stockport–Wilmslow area (including Alderley Edge) are composed of these.

Botryoidal   Shaped like a cluster of grapes.

Braided river/stream   River or stream consisting of interwoven channels constantly shifting through islands of alluvium and sandbanks. This occurs where gradients are steep, where there is a high rate of discharge (water flow) and where the channel banks are composed of easily erodable sediments.

Braidplain   Alluvial floodplain formed of braided stream channels.

Carboniferous   Period of the Upper Palaeozoic between 358.9 million and 298.9 million years ago.

Cataclastite   Mechanical fracture of rock along a zone of breakage. On Alderley Edge this is often shown by numerous small parallel faults or tensional fractures without any slippage but commonly infilled with baryte (q.v.).

Cementation   The mineral fusion of quartz grains within sandstone. These grains are sometimes replaced through physical and chemical alteration accompanying burial (diagenesis). Baryte (q.v.) has commonly replaced silica and calcite as a cementing mineral at Alderley, particularly in the vicinity of faults, but in some places it is the copper ore malachite which has locally impregnated the rock. Cementation with baryte occurred under conditions of low temperature and pressure accompanying early burial, specifically the circulation of barium- and sulphate-rich groundwater through the pores of the rock, and changes in acidity and oxygen content.

Cerussite   Lead carbonate, a secondary mineral, usually white.

Chalcopyrite   A copper-iron sulphide mineral, the most common ore of copper.

Chalybeate   Iron-rich spring water.

Channel-fill   Sedimentary deposits infilling a river channel(s).

Clast   Fragment of pre-existing rock, of which many types of sedimentary rocks are made. 'Clasts' may refer to sand grains, but is also used to describe larger fragments such as pebbles.

Combe (coombe)   Dry valley in fairly permeable rocks formed under periglacial conditions from snow-melt run-off over frozen ground.

Cretaceous   Geological period of time between *c.* 145 million and 66 million years ago.

Cross-bedding   Series of inclined beds of sandstone, often truncated by overlying beds, formed by drifting ripples of sand. These may be either wind-borne or water-lain. Their inclination and orientation relate to the direction of current flow, the angle of rest and the rate of sediment supply.

Current ripple   Surface undulation produced by fluid movement over sediment. The type of ripples produced by current flow in water depends on the particle size, and the speed of the current, its direction and constancy.

Desiccation crack   Mud crack representing the drying out of a watercourse, a temporary lake or a flooded river plain as a result of increased aridity (part of a drying upwards cycle). Dessication cracks are sometimes visible on the underside of bedding planes, e.g. polygonal cracks in red mudstone filled with sandstone.

Devensian   The last glaciation affecting the British Isles, dating from *c.* 70,000 to 10,000 years ago.

Diagenesis   See 'Cementation'.

Diamict   Poorly sorted glacial sediments.

Dip slope   A land surface which dips in the same direction as the dip of the underlying beds, from north-east to south-west at Alderley Edge, where the latter is steeper than the slope of the present land surface.

Displacement   Distance that beds recognisable on opposite sides of a fault have been moved relative to one another; may be vertical or lateral (or a combination).

Downwasting   Stationary melting of an ice mass, or else on a slowly advancing front, resulting in the reduction in height and area of the ice-sheet and the deposition of till *in situ*.

Dreikanter   Wind-faceted pebble. See also 'Ventifact'.

Drusy   Lined with a crust of projecting crystals.

Drying-upwards cycle   Repeated cycle of sedimentation and climatic change from humid flood conditions to dry and desiccating.

Englacial   Water flowing within an ice-sheet and depositing sediment.

Epigenetic   Mineralisation at a date later than the formation of the host rocks.

Erg   Broad, flat area of desert covered with wind-swept sand that may form dunes.

Erratic   Large pebble, cobble or boulder which has been transported some distance from its source; most commonly applied to glacially transported material.

Evaporite   Mineral resulting from the evaporation of saline water (rock salt, gypsum, etc.).

Fault   Fracture or slip-plane in the rock along which there has been an observable amount of movement.

Faulting   Fracturing or slipping of rock that has resulted in an observable amount of movement.

Fining upwards   Progressive upward change from coarser to finer sediment, commonly in repeated cycles.

Flow till   Saturated rock debris that has started to creep, slide and flow on the surface of ice.

Fluid inclusion   Microscopic bubble of liquid trapped within the crystal lattice of a mineral (fluorite, baryte, calcite, etc.) which contains some of the original crystallising solution. By heating and observing this it is possible to calculate the temperature at which the mineral crystallised.

Fluvio-glacial   Relating to the erosion or deposition and re-deposition caused by meltwater rivers flowing from glaciers and ice-sheets, which sorts undifferentiated till into sands, gravels, etc.

Footwall   The two sides of a non-vertical fault or vein are known as the hanging wall and footwall. The hanging wall is above the fault plane and the footwall below it. This terminology comes from mining: when working an inclined vein, miners stood with the footwall under their feet and with the hanging wall hanging above them.

Foresets (beds)   Series of parallel beds formed on the front slope of an advancing sand-ripple or dune (of cross-bedded sandstones).

Freestone   Fairly even-grained (i.e. non-pebbly) unjointed sandstone which may be cut in any direction and is not inclined to split into layers in the way of slate.

Frost pitting   Pitting or shallow scalloping effect present on the surface of lumps of hard crystalline rock or flint, caused by frost shatter or flaking following surface exposure to extreme periglacial conditions.

Galena   Lead sulphide, the principal lead ore.

Glaciation   The processes as well as the results (erosion and deposition) arising from the presence of a moving ice mass on a landscape.

Glacio-fluvial   See 'Fluvio-glacial'.

Goethite   An iron oxide/hydroxide mineral formed during the oxidation and breakdown of iron pyrite or chalcopyrite.

Graben   Fault-bounded trough or rift valley created by extensional tectonics.

Graded   A river is graded when it is transporting its entire sediment load.

Greywacke   Type of sandstone/gritstone composed of fine to coarse angular/sub-angular particles, themselves composed mostly of rock fragments.

Hanging wall   See 'Footwall'.

Hardegsen unconformity   Unconformity within the Sherwood Sandstone Group separating, at Alderley, the Anisian (Mid Triassic) Helsby Sandstone Formation from the older (Early Triassic) Wilmslow Sandstone Formation. It represents the breakup of Pangea during the Triassic and is recognised all over northern Europe. See also 'Unconformity'.

Horst   See 'Block'.

Ice-tectonic structure   Fold, small fault or thrust developed within a deposit of till or fluvio-glacial gravel or sand, presumably while frozen, as a result of the bulldozing effect of lateral compression following the re-advance of a glacier.

Incised (valley)   Entrenchment or downcutting of a stream to form a gorge or narrow valley, usually as a response to uplift of the land following the retreat of an ice-sheet.

Injection strata   Under certain circumstances it is possible for one layer of unconsolidated sediment to force its way upward into an overlying layer, and even occasionally to pierce it and flow out at the surface as a mud or sand volcano. Flash floods or earthquake shocks may provide the sudden pressure to squeeze sediment up through existing mud-cracks.

Interglacial   Extended phases of climate amelioration and glacier retreat during a major glacial episode.

Interstadial   Minor periods of climate amelioration and glacier retreat during the main phases in a major glacial episode.

Isotope   One of two or more forms of a chemical element with the same atomic number but which contain different numbers of neutrons and hence have slightly different atomic weights. There are naturally occurring stable isotopes as well as unstable ones (e.g. uranium) which undergo radioactive decay into stable ones (e.g. lead).

Jurassic   Geological period of time from 201 million to 145 million years ago.

Kame   Terrace or elongate mound of sand deposited by a river at the margin of ice-sheets, sometimes as a sinuous ridge.

Kame terrace   Terrace built up of kames, usually around the base of higher ground where the ice-sheets stagnated, supplying meltwater streams and debris.

Kettle-hole   Formed as a result of collapse of the top soil and/or rock caused by the slow melting of an isolated buried mass of stagnating ice. These depressions often become lakes and later bogs.

Lacustrine   Of or relating to lakes.

Laminae/lamination   Very fine bedding, usually in finer-grained sediments; may impart a fissile or shaley character to a rock.

Lycopod   Club moss, resembling mosses but with woody tissue and spore-bearing cones. Common plant fossils of the Late Palaeozoic to Early Mesozoic, sometimes forming large trees and extensive forests.

Micaceous   Laminae of mica flakes usually along bedding planes, which often grow *in situ* from clay minerals.

Miospore   Plant spore or pollen grain (in the size range 5–200 μm).

Monocline   An anticlinal fold with one short limb almost vertical and the other horizontal.

Moraine   Accumulation of rock debris transported or deposited by ice (on its surface, within it, or at its base). A 'ground moraine' is the debris left after the retreat of the ice.

Nunatak   Rock peak protruding above the ice-sheet around which the ice streams flow and may later converge.

Outlier   Outcrop of younger rocks completely surrounded by older rocks, produced by erosion, faulting or folding.

Palaeocurrent   Current direction in fossil river systems or on the sea floor calculated from the orientation of pebbles, ripples and bedding. See also 'Palaeowind direction'.

Palaeomagnetism   The position of the continents has changed relative to the Earth's magnetic poles through geological time. Some rocks acquire a permanent record of the Earth's magnetic field at the time they were laid down, by virtue of the iron minerals they contain. Some red sandstones which contain haematite (iron oxide) show this very strongly and it may thus be possible to determine the latitude at which they were deposited.

Palaeontology   The study of ancient life through fossils.

Palaeowind direction   Ancient wind direction suggested by the direction of bedding within fossil sand dunes (dune-bedding) in aeolian sandstones.

Periglacial   Climatic conditions in the vicinity of and/or influenced by the presence of ice-sheets or large temporary snow caps; these include cold tundra-like winds and freeze-thaw processes.

Permian   Period between 298.9 and 252.2 million years ago.

Pisolith   Pea-sized concentric sedimentary grain formed as a concretion, often found in carbonate rocks.

Planar bedding   Formed under conditions of fast current flow and thus flat and without ripple marks.

Pleistocene   Earlier part (epoch) of the Quaternary Period (2.59 million to 11,700 years ago). It included the most recent ice periods, and ended with the last retreat of the ice-sheets.

Prod and scour mark   Known as sole marks (sedimentary structures produced by current flow and preserved on the bottom surface of a bedding plane). Scour marks are erosional features on the underlying bed formed by fast or turbulent flow. Prod marks are formed by the 'bouncing' of a sharp object along a muddy channel bed.

Pro-glacial   Lake and fluvio-glacial sediments deposited in front of the melting edge of a glacier or ice-sheet.

Pseudomorph   The crystal form of a mineral preserved by another substance or mineral. For example, a cubic rock salt crystal may be dissolved and the resulting cavity then filled with another mineral such as calcite.

Pyromorphite   Secondary or supergene lead mineral (lead chlorophosphate), usually forming yellow to yellow-green powdery masses. Associated with variable amounts of lead arsenate at Alderley.

Reducing environment   A deoxygenated chemical environment present within sediments and rocks. In these situations reactions can take place reducing or removing oxygen, and/or combining with hydrogen, for example reducing sulphate to a sulphide.

Reservoir (of oil and gas)   In addition to the presence of an oil and gas trap there has to be a rock which is sufficiently porous and permeable to act as a reservoir rock and hold sufficient quantities to form a viable oil and gas field.

Reverse grading   Where the normal grading sequence within a well sorted sediment from coarse-grain to fine-grain sediments is reversed so that the fine grains are at the bottom and coarse at the top.

Rhyolite   Fine-grained glassy volcanic rock, chemically similar to granites/granodiorites.

Rolled-mud clast   Clast of dried mud ripped up by flooding, rolled by currents into a small pebble, incorporated within the bed-load of a channel, and deposited within coarse, unsorted sediments such as pebbly sandstone (known as conglomerate).

Rugose coral   Group of fossil corals of both solitary and colonial forms which became extinct at the end of the Permian period. The individual corallites possessed internal radial walls known as septa.

Secondary mineral   A mineral formed through alteration of another (primary) mineral.

Sinuosity   Meandering effect of channel which relates to energy and speed of water flow: hence 'low sinuosity' and 'high sinuosity'.

Slickenside Polish and striation formed on a fault plane as a result of the contact and pressure of the rocks on opposing sides of the fault sliding against each other.

Slumping The movement of a mass of incoherent sediment down a slope.

Spreading oceanic crust Where new crust wells up along mid-oceanic volcanic ridges and the plates move outwards (usually at rate of a few centimetres per year).

Spring line Line or horizon along which springs issue, usually located towards the base of a slope, but most commonly along a permeable layer of rock immediately above an impervious one such as clay.

Stratigraphy The study of stratified rocks, their sequence in time and the correlation of rock beds from different localities.

Striae Linear marks or grooves, especially those caused by glaciers as they pass over the underlying rock.

Sub-aerial exposure Exposure of water-lain sediments to the air, resulting in the formation of desiccation cracks (i.e. mud-cracks) under conditions of aridity.

Subglacial (of rivers) Flowing beneath the ice and depositing sediment.

Supergene mineral Secondary mineral deposited from downward-percolating groundwater following the oxidation of a primary ore mineral (usually a metal sulphide).

Supraglacial Meltwater rivers carrying sediment that flow over the surface of the ice.

Syncline See 'Anticline'.

Syngenetic Mineralisation at the same time as the formation of the host rocks.

Talus Synonym for scree.

Tertiary The period of time between the end of the Cretaceous (*c.* 66 million years ago) and the start of the Quaternary (*c.* 2.59 million years ago).

Till Unstratified, unsorted rock debris such as boulder clay dropped by a glacier or larger ice-sheet.

Throw The amount of displacement of beds on opposite sides of a fault.

Thrust Low-angle fault in which one set of beds has been thrown up (thrust) over another.

Trace fossil Structure in sedimentary rock, such as a burrow, track, footprint or feeding trail, resulting from biological activity.

Trap (oil and gas) A structure, either sedimentary or controlled by folds or faulting, in which an impermeable layer acts as a cap or seal, and beneath which migrating oil and gas can become trapped and accumulate.

Triassic Geological period of time between 252.2 and 201.3 million years ago. The rocks of Alderley Edge were formed during the earlier part.

Trough cross-bedding Represents the infill of isolated examples of stream channels or cosets (groups of units of cross-bedding) formed in migrating channels which roughly truncate evenly bedded or cross-bedded strata.

Unconformity A break in sedimentation over a period of time. This may involve the emergence of sediments or rocks, erosion, then their re-submergence and the continuation of sedimentation.

Ventifact Pebble faceted by the abrasive effects of wind-blown sand (see also 'Dreikanter').

Wave ripple mark Ripple form induced on the floor of a body of water by wave action.

Glossary of mining and quarrying terms

Simon Timberlake with Nigel Dibben, David I. Green and Geoffrey Warrington

The languages of geology and mining and quarrying have much in common, and terms missing from one glossary will usually be found in the other. However, for the reader's convenience there is a small overlap between the two glossaries, particularly of those words that have a slightly different meaning in the different contexts. Note that references in the text to the names of the mines at Alderley Edge are to the modern names, not those in use at the time of mining.

Acid-leaching process   Process for the chemical extraction of copper from ores containing as little as 1 per cent copper which was developed by William Henderson at the Alderley Edge Mining Co. Ltd from 1857 (see Chapter 16).

Adit   Level driven from/to the surface for drainage, haulage, or foot access. See also 'Drainage adit'.

Adventurer   Entrepreneur who put up money to finance a mining venture, probably pre-dating the cost book system and limited companies.

Anvil stone   Stone such as a large cobble, slab or bit of outcrop used for hand-crushing ore with metal or stone tools. Some anvil stones have slight mortar hollows. Probably prehistoric to early Medieval: some possible Bronze Age examples have been found on the Edge. See also 'Mortar stone'.

Asbolane, asbolite   Amorphous (non-crystalline) mineral of uncertain composition, consisting mostly of manganese and some iron oxides, with variable amounts of cobalt and other elements. Mined as a cobalt ore. See also 'Cobaltian wad'.

Assay   Quantitative chemical analysis of an ore undertaken to detect proportions of desirable/undesirable elements.

Assay channelling   Shallow groove or series of scrape marks cut into walls or roof of mine workings to remove samples for bulk assay. Usually vertical scrapes hand-cut by picks on walls of levels, often at junctions and in worked ground. Appearance fresh and obviously more recent than pick work for driving levels (good examples in Wood and West Mines). Late nineteenth to early twentieth centuries.

Assay house   Building on surface where chemical assays of ores were carried out (e.g. at the Alderley Edge Mining Co. Ltd works).

Assay width   Width of vein or mineralised wall-rock sampled to determine the width worth mining for reasons of economic concentration (e.g. the percentage of extractable copper).

Azurite   Copper ore; hydrated copper carbonate; found less often than malachite (q.v.), diffused in mineralised sandstone. The blue-coloured ore mined at Alderley Edge.

Back (of level or lode)   The roof of the level. Working upwards into a lode (vein) in the roof is overhand stoping.

Back end (of shot hole)   Narrow end or deepest point of a bored shot hole (for gunpowder blasting).

Backfill   General term for waste material of various kinds deposited in mine workings, passages or shafts to infill them after use, for example waste deads (q.v.) stacked in abandoned portions of a mine.

Bailing   Draining a shaft using bucket and windlass.

Barrow board   A single line of wooden planking laid down on the floor of a level as a wheelbarrow run.

Barrow drill   Rock drill powered by compressed air for drilling shot holes, first introduced in the 1870s, though there is no evidence at Alderley Edge before the twentieth century.

Barrow level   Level driven using a wheelbarrow to cart away waste rather than a tram on rails. Characteristic is a rounded or V-cut bottom profile wide enough to take a barrow and perhaps a less regular or steeper gradient.

Baryte (barite)   Barium sulphate, the most common vein mineral in the lodes, invariably discarded. It imparts a dense, heavy feel to the rock.

Beam engine   Vertical reciprocating steam engine operating pumps or flywheel by way of an overhead beam.

Bearer   Large timber in a wooden frame slotted into the side of a shaft to support it through loose ground such as mudstone beds.

Bench   Working level in a hard rock quarry worked from top to bottom. During underhand stoping (working downwards from a level) the ore was often worked in 'benches' to facilitate drilling and removal; benches were cut at intervals that enabled miners to climb up and down ('benching'). Nineteenth century.

Bing   Pile of ore, or place for piling ore from a particular vein or part of a vein, mined by a specific person or group of miners, so that shares and tithe duties can be calculated (seventeenth- to eighteenth-century term, unlikely later, common to Derbyshire but also used more widely).

Bingstead   Small wooden or drystone-walled enclosure enclosing a bing. These structures may have been located on the edge of a hand dressing-floor, perhaps built into the side of a spoil mound.

Black-damp   Miner's term for 'heavy air' or carbon dioxide which can settle in pockets within unventilated abandoned areas of the mines or at the end of poorly ventilated headings. A serious hazard even today.

Black lead (ore)   Miner's term for galena (q.v.).

Black powder   Gunpowder or 'blasting powder', composed of saltpetre (potassium nitrate), charcoal and sulphur – the most commonly used explosive in the Alderley Edge mines.

Blasting   Use of explosives in mining. See 'Black powder', 'Charge', 'Shot hole'.

Bleached horizon   Pale-coloured sandstone within red bed sequence which host the mineralisation and is thus a good mineral indicator for the miner.

Blind heading   Abandoned exploratory level.

Blocking out   In the course of development work or prospection underground, the payable ground or ore body might be 'blocked out' into sections by interconnecting levels and intermediate shafts (late nineteenth to early twentieth centuries).

Boat level   Partly and often intentionally flooded haulage or drawing level, most commonly at the lowest level of the mine, through which boats or barges are used for carrying ore to the adit mouth or to the bottom of a drawing shaft. The flooded level between Engine Vein and Brynlow Mine shows no signs of having been a boat level as it is flooded due to partial blockages.

Bob wall   Front wall of a pumping engine house, which supports the iron beam.

Boiler house   Building housing high-pressure boiler associated with engine house.

Bole   Primitive smelting hearth, driven by natural air blast. Usually for lead and situated in exposed and windy hilltop locations such as Saddlebole (a Derbyshire term).

Boler   Person working the bole site (Medieval to early Post-Medieval).

Bolt tunnel   Part of the mounting which survives in the concrete or masonry foundations of an engine house following the removal of machinery.

Bore   Diameter of the cylinder and hence size of steam engine in use at mine.

Borer   Another name for a drill steel.

Boring   Boring shot holes for blasting. Multi-handed boring (one miner holding and turning the steel with one or two miners hammering it) was probably the technique most commonly used, particularly with the long drill steels used in the latter part of the nineteenth century. Single-handed boring may have been used earlier with the short, narrow-bore steels used in the eighteenth and early nineteenth centuries, particularly in narrower workings.

Boundary   Stones, posts, field banks, or paths on surface used to mark the boundaries of a mineral claim ('sett' or 'mere'). Typical of medieval or early Post-Medieval mining practice and mining law; common in Derbyshire, possible at Alderley.

Bowl furnace   The most primitive furnace: a clay-lined pit in the ground, used from the pre-historic to Medieval periods.

Box hole   Small connection (interdrive) between immediately overlying stopes and working drivages in the roof of the main level, for carrying services (compressed air/water pipes) and ore chutes. Typical of late nineteenth-century and twentieth-century mining.

Brattice (bratticing)   Partition in a shaft or passage to separate a manway from an ore pass or to create a ventilation route.

Bucket   For hoisting ore, rock or water.

Bucket pump   Plunger-operated pump which 'lifted' water on the up-stroke of the pump rods: likely to have used in shallower mines such as those on the Edge, though there is no clear evidence from Alderley.

Bucking hammer   Flat-faced iron hammer used for hand-crushing ore.

Bucking stone   Large anvil stone, originally used in conjunction with iron bucking hammers (eighteenth to nineteenth centuries).

Buddle (for ore dressing)   Shallow, round (concave or convex) or square container, built of wood and/or brick. Ore concentrate (pulp) was fed in at the centre or top end, and lighter articles washed to the side and out, with the heavier particles (e.g. lead minerals) retained in baffles.

Buddling   See 'Buddle'.

Bunch   A rich shoot of ore.

Burr stone   Grinding stone for crushing lead ore, in particular white lead ore (cerussite in sandstone).

Cable man   Winder operating the gearing and brake mechanism of ore tubs on inclines.

Cache   Drystone wall built into the side of a spoil tip as a shelter (probably pre-nineteenth century).

Calcined   Roasted, as in 'roasted ore': a process designed to lower the sulphur content prior to smelting.

Calciner   Furnace in which ore is roasted.

Call   Demand for money from the shareholders to finance the operations of a cost book company. See also 'Cost book'.

Candle clay   Blob of clay pressed onto a hat or helmet into which the bottom end or edge of a candle was pressed. Sometimes these clay holders can be found stuck to the wall of a level (e.g. Brynlow exploratory adit). Fingerprints are sometimes visible in them.

Candle hole   Small niche pick-cut into wall of level at chest or head height large enough to take a candle. Sometimes bigger (over 30 cm) to help throw out more light. Candle stubs, wax, or burnt wicks can sometimes be found in their bases.

Candle stain   Small soot stain surviving in top of and above candle holes or elsewhere on walls and roofs of levels. Small and localised as compared with powder stain (q.v.).

Cap   Detonator for high-explosive charge (e.g. mercury fulminate in small crimped copper tube) on end of safety fuse. Late nineteenth century, early twentieth century.

Capstan   Windlass hoist for raising or lowering wooden pit-work or timbers.

Captain   See 'Mine captain'.

Carboy   Container for carrying acid to the ore treatment works. Carboys were made from gutta-percha or glass and were used to bring acid from St Helens and elsewhere (*c.* 1858–78).

Caunter lode   Lode (mineralised vein or fault) whose direction does not conform with the preferred direction of others in the locality. See 'Preferred direction'.

Cement (in a description of rocks)   The mineral cementing together the quartz grains in the sandstone. These are sometimes replaced during physical and chemical alteration accompanying burial (diagenesis). Baryte (barium sulphate) has commonly replaced silica and calcite as a cementing mineral at many horizons in Alderley, particularly in the vicinity of faults, but in some places it is the copper ore malachite that has locally impregnated the rock.

Cementation   Extraction process for copper in which the mine waters holding copper salts in solution are made to pass through a pit filled with scrap iron. The copper was brought out of solution and replaced with iron, the resultant precipitate being periodically dug out and treated to obtain the copper. Usually one-third of the iron was replaced by copper in this way. The main treatment on the Edge was similar (see 'acid leaching process').

Cerussite   An ore of lead (lead carbonate), less common than galena. It is a white mineral with a glassy lustre, heavier than baryte, but associated with galena, malachite and azurite cementing sandstone.

Chain (a) Unit of distance used in the original surveying and planning of underground workings. A miner's steel chain measures 10 fathoms (60 feet), while a land-surveyor's chain is 66 feet (22 yards) long. (b) Forged iron linked chain used by miners to ascend and descend internal shafts. See 'Man way'.

Charge Quantity of black powder in a shot hole.

Charger Metal charging spoon used to load standard powder charge into shot hole. If the shot hole was angled upwards this would usually be in a paper cartridge.

Chrysocolla Copper silicate mineral, usually found in an amorphous form as a secondary mineral (q.v.; see also 'Cupriferous flowstone').

Clay scrape Small excavation made within a clay or mudstone band underground (such as in the wall of a level), and worked for wet, mouldable clay to use in the stemming of shot holes and for holding candles.

Clay stemming Clay plug up to 1–2 inches long sealing the powder charge in a shot hole and rammed down ('tamped') with a tamping bar. The powder was tamped to ensure that when it exploded the rocks at the side of the hole would burst away.

Clayboard Miner's term for the thin clay or mudstone horizons or partings between sandstone beds, which they sometimes followed. These relatively impermeable layers sometimes capped the mineralised beds, but in other locations were a focus for secondary deposition of azurite and malachite nodules.

Claying bar Conical-ended iron rod used to ram down a ball of clay and seal a wet shot hole. The clay lining formed helped seal the water-bearing cracks and keep the powder charge dry.

Climbing foothold Pick-cut foothold, placed on each opposite side of a narrow climbing shaft. Typically mid-eighteenth century or earlier.

Climbing shaft Vertical or inclined shaft, usually of quite narrow diameter and sometimes with staging at intervals or sunk in offset sections, specifically for miners' access.

Climbing stemple Stemple (q.v.) jammed between walls of shaft at regular intervals, often at right angles to one another, used as a means of climbing.

Clinker Vitrified and often iron-rich fuel ash found at surface near old processing floors, deriving from smelting furnaces or the fire grates of stationary steam engines. Should not be confused with slag.

Clog Common as miner's footwear. Wooden soles with iron studs for grip and leather uppers (typically nineteenth century and popular with Cornish miners). Normal footwear for miners on the Edge during the period 1858–78: evidence has been found in Engine Vein.

Clog print Characteristic footprint formed by studded clogs. Clog prints can be seen, and should be looked for, on entering unexplored sealed workings.

Cobalt Extracted from the Alderley ores in mineral form *c.* 1800–15 to obtain a blue colourant for glass and as a blue glaze in the porcelain china industry, and later to obtain metal in the form of a roasted cobalt/nickel speiss.

Cobalt fracture Fracture subsidiary to a main fault carrying cobalt mineralisation. Generally devoid of other minerals apart from wad (q.v.), the source of most of the cobalt ore at Alderley.

Cobaltian wad Amorphous mixture of manganese and iron oxides and hydroxides, chemically complex and containing variable amounts of cobalt, with traces of nickel and sometimes vanadium. Variable in texture, but usually occurs as dull sooty encrustations along faults and associated fractures. See 'Asbolane, asbolite'.

Cobalt scraper Small hand-held scraper, usually made of iron but often improvised, used to scrape cobaltian wad (powder) out of faults and joints.

Cobalt tin Lidded tin used by cobalt miners in conjunction with scraper to collect wad powder; held close to walls and roof in order to catch the powder.

Cobble Large pebble from the boulder clay (drift) often washed down into shallow workings from the surface. Unmodified and unused, these should not be confused with mining mauls, even though these may derive from the same source.

Coe Miner's shelter over the shaft head to protect miners from wind and rain, often built of stone. There is some ground disturbance at Engine Vein which could be the outline of a coe (Derbyshire practice, seventeenth to nineteenth century).

Coffin level Narrow pick-cut level, so called because of the shape in vertical profile, widened at shoulder level to allow easier passage for miners. Some levels are only 18 inches wide and 5 foot 6 inches high. Typically of seventeenth to eighteenth century; examples of mid-eighteenth-century coffin levels in Brynlow Mine, Engine Vein and Hough Level.

Compressor pipe Steel pipe *c.* 3 inches in diameter joined in sections and suspended from the walls of levels on pipe brackets for compressed-air drills (late nineteenth or twentieth century). Not found underground on the Edge, although in places pipe brackets are still visible.

Concentrate   A payable grade of dressed ore after milling and buddling (concentrating), ready for the smelter. Term in use since the nineteenth century.

Condenser   Part of a steam engine, such as a Cornish Pumping Engine: a cooling cylinder which condenses the steam to form a partial vacuum, aiding the down-stroke of the engine.

Conglomerate   A rock with a finer-grained matrix such as sand but containing whole and broken pebbles which make it harder and less easy to work into neat blocks.

Copper cake   Copper metal cast into solid form after smelting, usually simply referred to as 'cake'.

Copper ore (at Alderley Edge)   Typically malachite and azurite (hydrous copper carbonates) with lesser amounts of chrysocolla, copper sulphides etc. Low-grade ore that was processed by acid-leaching was worked down to 1.5 to 1 per cent copper. See also 'Azurite', 'Malachite'.

Copperas   Crystalline iron sulphate – a possible by-product of the acid-leaching process using sulphuric acid.

Core   See 'Spell'.

Cornish pick   Single-ended, short-handled pick with a long point.

Cornish shovel   Wide-brimmed, rounded shovel with a pointed end and slightly arched wooden handle.

Corve   Wooden or basket-work sledge with runners for carrying ore. Corves were dragged from the working face of a level to a shaft for hauling to the surface. One has been found in Engine Vein. See also 'Sledge'.

Cost book   System of operating mines common in nineteenth-century England through setting up unlimited liability companies into which shareholders either paid 'calls' (demands for money) or shared profits, according to the prosperity of the mine. The mine also kept a 'cost book' which recorded in detail the expenses, dues and earnings of miners. However, the Alderley Edge Mining Co. of 1857–78 was a limited company, not a cost book company.

Costeaning   Shallow trenching or closely spaced pitting as a primitive prospection technique to locate and test the width and extent of the back of the lode. Used in the sixteenth to nineteenth centuries, although typically pre-1800.

Count house (account house)   Mine office where miners were paid, and outside which they gathered to bid for contracts or 'tributes'. The 'Surgery', opposite the Wizard Restaurant, may have been a count house. See 'Tributing'.

Country rock   Rock either side of a mineral vein.

Course   Horizontal extent of an ore body in a lode.

Cranch   Piece of ground left as a support for walls and roof. See 'Pillar'.

Cross-course   Mineralised fracture which cuts across the main vein or fault.

Cross-cut   Level put out at right angles to the main direction of work, to explore for fresh parallel lodes or to meet a known one. Cross-cuts are also employed for ventilation (q.v.).

Cross-fault   Fault that cuts across the general direction of the main mineralised faults. The fault may or may not be mineralised, and if so the mineralisation may be of a different type, or else of an earlier or later phase (see 'Cross-course'). Engine Vein contains a good example.

Crow bar   Steel bar used to provide leverage. Occasionally to be found amongst iron tools left underground. Used in stempling work, laying rail track etc.

Cupriferous   Copper-bearing.

Cupriferous flowstone   Secondary copper deposits formed since the mining period on walls or floors of levels and sides of shafts from precipitation from dripping or trickling water containing high amounts of dissolved copper. Deposits over several millimetres thick may show a flow or rippled surface texture. Amorphous rather than crystalline, and at Alderley consisting principally of chrysocolla.

Cupriferous water   Pools of still clear water to be found in some places underground, often in flooded shafts or stopes, with a characteristic pale turquoise tinge.

Cut   Hand-drilled shot holes had normally been used for individual shots placed to open up natural planes of weakness (as in the case of black powder blasting), but were also occasionally employed for multiple, simultaneous firings in predetermined patterns ('cuts') to shatter the rock face. With the advent of machine drilling of shot holes and the use of high explosives this practice became commonplace. There are examples in West Mine and elsewhere.

Damp   Seventeenth- to nineteenth-century miner's term for gas accumulating in underground workings. See also 'Fire-damp'.

Dead work Work that produces waste rock only; i.e. the driving of levels or sinking of shafts.

Deads Term for waste rock usually stacked in abandoned parts of mine workings such as widenings in stopes, unused levels and shafts or on wooden platforms or floors in stopes.

Dead(s) walling Drystone walling made of deads, used to provide a place to retain a stack of deads, to block entrances to abandoned passages and in some places as a roof support.

Detonator See 'Cap'.

Detonator box Small tin or iron box for detonator caps and safety fuses (late nineteenth to twentieth century).

Development work Shafts or levels driven, often through sterile rock, in order to assess the grade and extent of ore reserves and to open up access routes to the ore body. Carried out in advance of mining. Standard late-nineteenth-century to twentieth-century procedure.

Dial Surveying underground was carried out using a miner's dial, a simple instrument used to measure compass directions and angles by sighting. Surveying was often referred to as 'dialling' from at least the eighteenth century.

Dip (a) The angle of inclination of a mineral vein or bed of rock, measured from the horizontal. (b) The earliest lighting, prior to the use of candles, was probably by weak dips, i.e. strips of burning cloth in a saucer of tallow or oil.

Displacement The amount of throw, or vertical or lateral movement, on a fault (see 'Fault').

Divining Attempting to search for ore, faults, water, or cavities underground using rods, a split hazel twig or a pendulum.

Double-ended pick Although distinctly different, this is often mistaken as the classic shape for a mining pick. With sharp and slender points, the tool is ideal for channelling and cutting facing blocks at a quarry face (the technique produces classic herring-bone pick marks of quarrying). Also used by Alderley stonemasons for cutting and finishing blocks. Probable period of use: Medieval to twentieth century. See 'Miner's pick'.

Dowsing See 'Divining'.

Drainage adit Lowest adit level accessible from the surface, used to drain the workings naturally. Water from deeper parts of the mine could be pumped up to this level. On the Edge, the Hough Level was probably used as a drainage adit from Engine Vein to Dickens Wood and from Brynlow to Wood Mine, in addition to being a haulage way. See 'Adit'.

Drain channel Small channel cut into the rock floor of a main access or haulage level, usually on the right-hand side heading inbye (q.v.), to contain flowing water and thereby to assist drainage while keeping the access area relatively dry. Many appear to be contemporary with the original cutting of the level (eighteenth to twentieth century).

Drawing Hoisting or winding ore, waste rock, or water (in buckets or kibbles) up shafts and out of the mine. Often found in references to the costs.

Drawing shaft Shaft specifically used for drawing.

Dressing Treatment (sorting, cleaning, crushing, concentrating) of ores carried out at a mine.

Dressing floor Area on the surface where the dressing of ores is carried out (nineteenth-century term).

Dressing mill Mill for crushing and concentrating ore.

Drilling See 'Boring'.

Drill steel Drill bit or borer, hand-held or driven by compressed air. Hand-held drill steels were regularly sharpened and re-forged at the drill ends. They were hit with a sledge hammer or steel mallet. The nineteenth-century drills typically in use on the Edge ranged from 0.3 m to *c.* 1 m long, rarely more.

Drip basin Small basin cut into rock in wall or floor of level below a water seepage, to collect water, possibly to use in wetting the clay for stemming shot holes, washing, etc. (found e.g. in West Mine).

Drip ledge Ledge or gutter cut around outer rim of entrance to level or rock-cut opening, to channel drips away from those working underneath (found e.g. in Engine Vein). See also 'Garland'.

Drivage Driving of a mine passage.

Drum chamber Chamber cut into the side of an underground passage to hold a winding drum mounting (examples in Wood and West Mines).

Drum house Small building holding the drum and possibly the winding engine at the head of the main haulage incline (e.g. at West Mine). See 'Cable man', 'Winding engine', 'Winding house'.

Duck machine Simple device for ventilating the end of a level with poor air circulation, consisting of a wooden container sliding in and out of another sealed with water and equipped with flap valves, connected to a pipe.

Duty   Efficiency of a steam engine (foot-pounds of work done per bushel of coal burnt).

Dynamite   A high explosive, only used in blasting to drive levels in some of the later workings at Alderley (e.g. West Mine, Wood Mine and Engine Vein).

End   The end of a level, known as the 'heading'.

End-tipping wagon   Mine tub constructed of iron and wood, later of riveted iron sheeting, with bolted tip-up door at rear (mid to late nineteenth century).

Engine   Term used to describe any large stationary machine used for pumping, winding, or crushing. Engines may be steam powered, horse powered or man powered. Horse gin is a shortened version of horse engine.

Eye   Area of 'payable' (ore-bearing) ground in a mine blocked out during development work.

Farm ore   Medieval term for ore 'farmed' by the miners and not liable to duty. See also 'Lot ore'.

Fathom   Six feet (1.83 m), the underground unit of measurement in mining. Levels off shafts were referred to in fathom intervals (relative to adit level), as were rates of drivage. Eighteenth to nineteenth century.

Fault   Fracture or slip-plane in the rock along which there has been an observable amount of movement, the result of tensional or compressional forces. Ore minerals deposited on faults formed veins or lodes.

Feather-edging   The limits of rich ore-bearing pockets present within the cross-set beds in conglomerates and sandstones; this cut-off happens where such beds lens out, or where they are truncated by planar bedding.

Felt helmet   Miner's helmet in the nineteenth century, typically of resin-impregnated felt. Probably a Cornish introduction.

Filling   Task mentioned in the Alderley Edge Mines Settings Book for 1865–66, e.g. 'filling tanks' meaning the loading of crushed copper ore into the acid leaching tanks.

Fire-damp   Miner's term for the flammable gas methane. There is no record of its occurrence underground on the Edge, although the organic rubbish infill of shafts and openworks might well produce it.

Fire-setting   An aid to breaking rock, used in mining. A wood fire was made against a working face either underground or in an opencast working and allowed to burn out, weakening and cracking the rock in the process. Sometimes the hot rock was doused with water in order to increase the breakage. Prehistoric to modern, though only rarely found associated with Post-Medieval mining in this country.

Flange rail   Iron rail track with flanged sides having an 'L' shaped cross-section.

Flat   Horizontal or sub-horizontal workings in which the ore body, consisting of a mineralised bed, bedding plane or infilled horizontal fracture has been entirely removed, apart from cranches (pillars) of rock left for support. This was an eighteenth- to nineteenth-century method: examples are to be found in Wood and West Mines and in the eastern workings of Engine Vein, parts of Cobalt Mine and elsewhere on the Edge. See 'Longwall face', 'Pillar/pillar and stall'.

Flatrod   Reciprocating rod on rollers transmitting power horizontally from an engine to a pump, winding wheel, or crusher; nineteenth century .

Flywheel pit   Pit for mounting flywheel for rotative steam engine, powering a whim, crusher, or compressor; usually stone-lined.

Fold, folding   Bending or flexure of the beds or strata of rock or sediment caused by lateral compression.

Footwall   The two sides of an inclined fault or vein are known as the 'hanging wall' and 'footwall'. The hanging wall is above the fault plane and the footwall below it. This terminology comes from mining: when working an inclined vein, the miner stood with the footwall under his feet and with the hanging wall above him.

Forefield   Heading or end of a level being driven in mineralised ground.

Forging steel   Forging and re-sharpening drill steels was an essential and regular occupation for a mine blacksmith.

Foul   Impure or poor concentrate or ore; contamination of copper ores with lead, cobalt or arsenic would lead to metallurgical problems on smelting, and mines were penalised for sending such concentrates to the smelter.

Free face   When blasting with gunpowder and high explosives the shot holes were driven at an angle along lines of weakness rather than straight in, so that they could explode to a 'free face'.

Freestone   Fairly even-grained (i.e. non-pebbly), un-jointed stone which may be cut in any direction and is not inclined to split into layers in the way of slate.

Fuse For blasting. See 'Quill', 'Safety fuse'.

Gad Narrow iron wedge used for splitting rock, often with sharp pointed end and square or rectangular flattened cross-section. Used from the Roman period to the end of the nineteenth century. Traces of use in Cobalt Mine and elsewhere.

Galena The common ore of lead (lead sulphide) worked at Alderley Edge. Recognisable by its characteristic silvery grey metallic lustre when freshly broken, cubic cleavage, and heaviness.

Gangue Miner's term for the waste minerals and rock in which the ore occurs. A typical gangue mineral on the Edge is baryte.

Garland Drip ledge (q.v.) around the circumference of a shaft (e.g. in Engine Vein).

Gelatine (or **blasting gelatine**) A high explosive made from guncotton dissolved in nitro-glycerine; it required a detonator but weight for weight was about three times as effective as gunpowder. Introduced at the end of the nineteenth century .

Gig Another term for a wheeled ore skip hoisted up a vertical or inclined shaft, which could also carry men (late nineteenth century).

Gin Winding engine usually located near the top of a shaft and used for hoisting buckets of ore. The rope was wound onto a drum or 'whim', and this was then rotated by a horse walking in a circle (gin circle). See 'Engine', 'Whim'.

Ginging Drystone walling built up around the collar and/or upper part of a (usually) round or oval shaft as support in soft ground. Found in shafts at Engine Vein.

Grass Surface (e.g. in the expression 'bringing the ore to grass').

Griddle See 'Sieve'.

Grizzly Coarse grate, usually made of old rails, constructed over the mouth of an ore chute underground to hold back large lumps of rock for further breaking, and thus to avoid jamming or clogging the exit.

Guide A barely mineralised fracture or cross-course (q.v.) which could be followed to find a richer vein of ore.

Gunpowder See 'Black powder'.

Gutta-percha Rubber-like coagulated latex of Malaysian *Palaquium* trees. See 'Carboy'.

Hammer and gad Technique of driving levels developed before the advent of gunpowder using existing joints and fractures for wedging. Involved the use of gads (wedges), usually knocked in single-handedly by a miner with a small hammer or mallet, to break off flakes or larger chunks of rock. Suitable for working in tight places; usage continued into the nineteenth century (e.g. at Cobalt Mine).

Hammer stone Stone pebble hammer (maul) used as a primitive mining tool and associated with prehistoric (probably Bronze Age) pit workings. Several different types exist, usually grooved, originally hafted, and used for both mining and crushing (see *ArchAE*: 58–78).

Hand crushing-floor Area with surface evidence of considerable hand crushing activity (e.g. coarsely broken ore-stuff, mortar stones). Possible Post-Medieval hand crushing-floors are to be found in Windmill Wood (top end), and at Engine Vein.

Hand dressing Crushing and separating ore by hand.

Hand picking Levels or shafts might be wholly or partly hand-picked. Different ages of working can be recognised by different styles of picking and/or sizes of passage. The tool itself changed little over time, although the technique of using it will have evolved (left- and right-handed sweep-picking, coarse vertical picking, chip-picking). See 'Miner's pick'.

Hanging wall The rock on the overhanging side of an inclined fault above the lode or vein. See also 'Footwall'.

Haulage way Main underground level used for tramming ore tubs out of the mine or to a shaft bottom.

Head gear Structure over shaft for winding buckets etc., with capstan for raising or lowering pitwork. Also known as a 'headframe'.

Hoist Small mechanical whim, commonly with gearing to a stationary engine.

Hoisting Raising a kibble or ore bucket.

Horizontal engine Steam engine with horizontal cylinder.

Horse whim See 'gin'.

Horse whim circle Earth bank 10–13 feet wide around a level circle, inside which was located the horse walk and whim.

Inbye Leading towards the working area.

Incline sloping passage into mine, usually at shallow angle to allow easy access by men, horses and tubs.

Incline haulage way Incline with rails and usually an engine (whim) to haul up wagons (in use at West Mine 1860–1919).

Iron-wire rope   Rope for lowering and raising kibble buckets, pitwork, etc. and for hauling. A mid-nineteenth-century development at Alderley, and associated with mechanical whim, winding engine, or inclines with trucks. See also 'Rope groove'.

Jackhammer   Light hand-held drill powered by compressed air, developed in 1880s and designed for underhand stoping.

Jagger   Mining term for one who leads ore from the mine to the smelting place on the backs of packhorses along 'jagger tracks' (eighteenth to nineteenth century). Otherwise a northern word for peddler or packman who leads horses carrying commodities such as salt over a distance (sixteenth century).

Jagging board   Sloping surface or board at the head of a square buddle, used for gravity separation of ore.

Jaw crushers   Type of ore-crushing mechanism in common use by 1870 and up to the 1880s: large stones were squeezed and crushed between two metal plates worked by offset from an engine.

Jigging   See 'Sieve'.

Jockey wheel   Part of the roller mechanism on railway inclines such as that at West Mine *c.* 1870; probably a flanged wheel for the wire rope, at places where there was a change in the horizontal angle of the incline. See also 'Roller'.

Jumper bar (drill)   Nineteenth-century method of hand-drilling shot holes using long rods with a heavy bulge along the length to give added weight. It was employed by lifting and letting fall, turning at each drop to chip out a cylindrical hole.

Kibble   Barrel-shaped bucket of wood or iron used for hoisting ore.

Knock stone   Stone platform used for hand-crushing ore (Medieval to Post-Medieval).

Knocker   In mining superstition knockers were allegedly small grizzled figures perhaps two feet tall, never seen but only heard knocking to hinder a miner by leading him on a false trail, or to help him by guiding him to a rich vein or warning of an imminent rock fall; they could also be a death omen or even actively dangerous. Perhaps of German or Norse origin (from the German *knocken*) and common in Cornwall and Wales (Medieval to nineteenth century).

Labourer   Person usually employed on surface work and paid a fixed wage. Most pares in the nineteenth century included a labourer.

Ladder   Mid- to late-nineteenth-century mining ladders were constructed with wooden sides and iron rungs; earlier they were made of wood or possibly chain.

Ladderway   Route for ladders up an access or climbing shaft, usually with fixed ladders in four- or five-fathom sections (24 or 30 feet) between wooden staging.

Land   To 'land' – i.e. halt and empty – a skip at a shaft top.

Land agent   The landowner's representative overseeing the mine works and ensuring the property is not damaged and is later restored or made safe.

Lander   Miner responsible for landing the skip.

Launder   Wooden box-culvert, usually made of three strapped and caulked planks, in sections. Used for directing water to a waterwheel or around dressing floors; for drainage and re-cycling; and underground to carry water over a shaft or along the sides of a stope, usually so as to drain it from the mine (most common in the eighteenth to nineteenth centuries, although much earlier examples are known).

Law   Regulation governing the mining and prospection for ore(s), often locally or regionally based. See 'Mining law'.

Lead ore   Lead mined on the Edge was principally in the form of galena (lead sulphide), but to a lesser extent cerussite (lead carbonate) or pyromorphite (lead chlorophosphate).

Lead works   Specified dressing floors for crushing and separating lead ore.

Leat   Cut or embanked channel dug to bring water from a reservoir, stream, or strong spring source to the working floor of the mine, for the purposes of waterpower, washing ore, or supplying an engine.

Leavings   Low grade of copper ore requiring further treatment. Also sometimes used for the finest fraction of crushed waste following buddling ('slimes' or 'tailings').

Level   Horizontal or gently inclined gallery or tunnel in a mine.

Level interval   Standard interval, usually 5 or 10 fathoms, at which levels were driven off a shaft.

Limonite   Amorphous mineral composed of a mixture of iron oxides and hydroxides. See 'Ochre'.

Litharge   Lead oxide (brown to vermillion red colour). The product of roasting galena, possibly in attempts to extract silver. Can be associated with lead works and smelting sites (Roman to eighteenth and early nineteenth centuries).

Loading pocket   At the base of a sequence of ore passes, usually in one of the lowest levels, for loading ore into trams or tubs in the main haulage way.

Lode (or vein)   A well defined, often near-vertical zone of mineralisation. The 'lodes' of the Edge are generally less well defined, with more diffuse mineralisation spreading outwards to the side(s), although the richest primary minerals will often follow the fault closely, and were the first to be worked.

Lode-back pit   Shallow shaft or bell-pit sunk on the surface on the back of a lode. Approximately 3 m × 5 m across, situated close together with spoil spilling into each other. Good examples associated with the Peak lead rakes (fifteenth to eighteenth century) and some possible examples in small groups on the Edge.

Lode stuff   Good ore-bearing rock (Cornish term).

Longwall face   Working face produced by 'longwall working' along a seam (typical of coal mining) and sometimes by the working of flats (q.v.) to remove mineral from within the rock beds or a near-horizontal ore body. Typically a longwall face was little higher than the depth of the payable ore or bed, and was worked back and forth along the strike of the bed, progressing forwards up or down dip. The deads were backfilled behind to support the roof.

Lord's mineral   The 'lord's mineral' was the portion of ore or 'dues' owed by the miners as a tithe to the landowner (lord) who would also have owned the mineral rights: at Alderley this would involve payments to the Stanley Estate.

Lot ore   Ore taken as duty. Term found in medieval Derbyshire mining lore, but may also occur in other areas, and a useful indicator of mining in e.g. manorial records.

Malachite   Copper ore; hydrated copper carbonate; found disseminated in mineralised sandstone. The main green-coloured ore mined at Alderley Edge.

Mallet   Iron-headed mallet or sledgehammer ('cat's head mallet') commonly used for hitting the drill steel in two-handed boring.

Manganese wad   Amorphous mixtures of black powdery manganese oxides and hydroxides infilling joints and fault fractures on the Edge, associated with cobalt mineralisation. Manganese wad has the property of incorporating other transitional elements such as cobalt and nickel.

Man way   Route down or through the mine specifically designed for man access and not necessarily through ore-bearing ground (e.g. Chain Shaft in Wood Mine).

Marl   In geological terms, a mudstone rich in calcium carbonate. However, many of the Triassic 'marls' (including those found interbedded within the Alderley Edge sandstones) are lime-free and thus strictly speaking are mudstones, though these were sometimes referred to as 'marls'. On the other hand the local boulder clays are significantly more calcareous, and these were also referred to as marls since they were dug to be laid on the land to lime it.

Marlpit   Small quarry dug into some of the more substantial surface outcrops of glacial boulder clay. The marl was used agriculturally to lime and clay the sandy soils. Most of the small ponds on the Edge are in fact old water-filled marlpits, often re-used as reservoirs. Not to be confused with flooded mine-workings, of which there are only a few.

Maul   See 'Hammer stone'.

Meer   Medieval Derbyshire term, but probably with much wider and earlier use, referring to a piece of ground such as a mining claim. In mining law and custom a meer is approximately 30 yards long, although the measurement may vary from place to place. In a mineral vein, it signified ownership or rights to carry out work on a piece of land, and also defined tithes or dues owing to the landowner and/or crown as won ore. In Derbyshire and other Medieval mining customs it was normal to define a worked claim with boundary markers. See also 'Merestone'.

Merestone   Boundary stone, often mentioned in early land ownership documents on Alderley Edge demarcating parish and other boundaries; some may refer to mining or quarrying rights within their bounds (see Chapter 27).

Mill   Name given both to the crushing and processing of ore(s) as well as to the building or shed housing such machinery (late nineteenth to twentieth centuries).

Mine captain   Mine manager appointed by the adventurers or directors of the company. Nineteenth-century Cornish term but common in other areas. Mine captains were often Cornishmen, on Alderley Edge as elsewhere. A mine captain had experienced miners as underground captains or foremen below ground. See 'Underground captain'.

Mineral rights   Rights to ownership of the minerals in the ground (not necessarily the same as surface rights or land ownership).

Mineral solution   Mineral-bearing solution (usually brine) which percolated up faults and outwards into rocks to deposit minerals.

Miner's dry Shed or building common on all mines, in which the miners could hang up their wet and muddy work clothes.

Miner's pick The common miner's pick ('poll pick'), having a short iron head with one pick arm and a heavy butt-hammer end as counterweight, and a short wooden handle. Its design changed little from the Medieval period to the nineteenth century. See also 'Double-ended pick', 'Hand picking'.

Mining law Laws peculiar to a particular mining area (before and during the nineteenth century) and then the national statutes controlling mining, particularly with respect to recording abandoned mines. There are no peculiar mining laws relevant to Alderley Edge.

Mortar stone Flat, hard stone, with visible mortar hollows on its upper surface (sometimes more than one) and often on both surfaces. Usually associated with hand-crushing floors where they were used for breaking up ore, probably in conjunction with iron hammers. Used from Roman period to the first decades of the nineteenth century, and common up to the eighteenth century. See also 'Anvil stone'.

Mounting Bolt or similar projecting from masonry or concrete foundations of heavy machinery, and often the only surviving visible remains of its former presence.

Muriatic acid Hydrochloric acid (HCl) as used in the copper-leaching process in the late nineteenth century.

Myne Early spelling of 'mine'.

Nickel speiss A nickel-rich form of speiss (q.v.).

Ochre Amorphous mixture of iron oxides and hydroxides which occurs naturally underground on the Edge associated with mineral veins and faults (see 'Limonite'), but is more likely to have been formed as a waste product in the acid-leaching extraction process.

Opencast An open surface working, where the lode or vein has been quarried away. Sometimes, as on the Edge, this has the appearance of a quarry where the ore-bearing rock has been removed (e.g. the now infilled West Mine Quarry), but more commonly in mining practice opencasting was restricted to a trench excavation as at Engine Vein, whose form is typical in following the lode and fault downwards at a steep angle.

Opencut See 'Opencast'.

Openworks Series of opencast workings on a vein, often interconnected.

Ore Payable mineral.

Ore bin See 'Ore hopper'.

Ore chute Usually a wooden chute or slide for ore associated with a box hole or loading pocket at the base of a worked stope in the roof of a main haulage way or tramming level.

Ore hearth Type of smelting furnace.

Ore hopper Semi-circular structure, usually of stone, situated outside a mine at the head of the dressing floors, for storing mined ore prior to crushing and dressing. At the treatment works, there were probably distinct hoppers for both copper and lead ores.

Ore pass Small subsidiary interconnecting way down which ore could be tipped from the various working levels, leading to a loading pocket. See 'Box hole', 'Ore chute'.

Outbye Leading towards the entrance (by adit) or foot of a shaft to surface.

Outcrop Where the rock is exposed at the surface, breaking through the cover of soil and sand or showing on a vertical face.

Overburden The rock and soil of little value that overlies the valuable and workable material.

Overhand stoping Standard (Cornish) method of ore extraction used in metal mining during the eighteenth and nineteenth centuries, working upwards into the lode in the roof (back) of a level. Ore and sometimes waste were then dropped down into the level from the cavity above (cf. 'Underhand stoping').

Parcel Ore was sometimes dressed as parcels, i.e. heaps of ore dressed at the surface coming from different tributers, or destined for the mineral lord in royalties. See 'Tributing'.

Pare 'Gang' of men working on a tribute. A Cornish term and working practice (see 'Tributing'). A typical late-nineteenth-century pare would have two miners, a labourer, a youth and a young boy.

Payable Ore-bearing (ground).

Pick See 'Double-ended pick', 'Miner's pick'.

Pig Cast block of lead metal formed after smelting (seventeenth to nineteenth centuries).

Pile Pile of ore stocked by working tributers underground, and used for sampling to assess the quality of the lode being worked. See 'Tributing'.

Pillar/pillar and stall Small section of lode left as solid supporting ground between the stope walls and/or the bottom of the stope and the level beneath. Wherever possible the poorer sections of the lode were chosen, but sometimes pillars were rich and big enough to be worth taking out later, a process known as 'robbing the pillars'. Parts of the Alderley mines were worked by pillar-and-stall techniques – removing blocks of ground within an ore-bearing bed leaving pillars to support the roof.

Pitch Tributing miners bid against each other to work a pitch, or section of the lode. See 'Tributing'.

Pit fields A field name (Medieval or possibly early Post-Medieval) which may refer to the former existence here of some sort of mineral extraction.

Pit workings Primitive form of early mine-working peculiar to Alderley Edge, most likely of Bronze Age date (see Chapter 15).

Pitting Small sampling or prospection pits sunk along the back of a lode (Roman to Post-Medieval).

Pitwork Pumping and other equipment within a shaft.

Plug and feathers One of the earliest (and longest tried) methods for levering and wedging out rocks: a conical metal rod is driven between one or two thin metal wedges placed within a rock crack or drilled hole.

Plunger Part of a Cornish pumping engine.

Poling Method of driving through soft ground and previously back-filled areas using boards driven into the roof and supported by timber frames; there are good examples in Engine Vein.

Poll pick See 'Miner's pick'.

Powder stain Sooty black stain often seen lining the inside of a bisected shot hole exposed in the side of a level and as a light coating of the rock surface thereabouts, most typically along the initial (and weakest) plane of explosive breakage, along joints and fractures in the rock surrounding the hole, and away from the tamped end of the shot hole. Where blasting has been closely spaced and frequent, powder stain sometimes coats the whole passage – particularly noticeable in the later workings from *c.* 1870 on.

Preferred direction (of lodes) A tendency for particular ores to be deposited in lodes running roughly parallel with one another. On the Edge the lead lodes are generally oriented south-east to north-west, with cobalt both in these and in north–south cross-courses.

Prill Small particle of metal such as copper or lead found in slag and the products of smelting, typically from small primitive furnaces.

Primitive mine Mine worked using stone tools and fire-setting.

Prospecting The art of locating metal ores and mineral lodes.

Prospection pit Small rectangular pit sunk through the soil cover to prospect and follow the course of a lode, with crescent-shaped mounds downslope and at right angles to the expected lode.

Pulp Slurry of crushed ore before separation.

Quill Hollow goose quill cut and primed with gunpowder and used as a fuse. Used in powder blasting in the eighteenth to the early nineteenth centuries, before the introduction of the safety fuse.

Rag and chain (pump) Endless chain with bolts of rags lifting water through a pipe (Roman to the eighteenth century).

Ragging The process of initial hand-crushing large lumps of ore and gangue previously separated on a coarse sieve, using 10 lb hammers.

Reverberatory furnace Furnace having a curved roof or cupola which deflects heat onto the charge so that the fuel is not in direct contact with the ore.

Rise Shaft driven upwards connecting with a higher level.

Roadway See 'Haulage way'.

Rock-bridge Part of vein left unworked between both sides of a vertical stope as a natural support, with access both above and below.

Roller Wood or iron roller within the track base of an incline to support and guide the haulage rope, in particular where there was a change in the vertical angle of the track. See also 'Jockey wheel'.

Rope groove Polished groove up to 3 cm wide, cut into the rock of a level or shaft wall by the continual rubbing of what are usually iron wire ropes. Examples visible in the entrance chamber of West Mine, where the incline rope has rubbed into the side wall (see 'Iron-wire rope'). In many cases rope grooves on the edge of shafts are from post-mining visits.

Ropeway Route of rope in shaft or on surface from a mounted whim engine.

Rotative engine Beam or other type of steam engine with the beam connected to a crank and flywheel so as to drive machinery such as a crushing plant or winder.

Round Group of shot holes fired at the same time during the blasting of a rock face.

Safety fuse   Slower and safer-burning fuse for blasting, invented in 1831 by William Bickford, who built a factory for its manufacture in Tuckingmill, Cornwall. Made of spun rope, usually jute, with a core of gunpowder, and sealed in gutta-percha and sometimes bitumen. It burned at a standard rate of approximately 1 foot per 30 seconds, and was typically sold in 24-feet lengths. Lengths of fuse recovered from Wood and West Mines appear all to be of the standard type.

Sandhill   Mine waste tip composed largely of sand from the dumping of waste raked out of the acid-leaching tanks after the dissolution of copper carbonate cementing the sandstone.

Scrin vein   Small vein or veinlets with minerals, not usually worked, except when removed *en masse* with others in the rock (Derbyshire and/or Cornish term).

Secondary enrichment   Oxidation of the primary (sulphide) ores within the vein along the fault and the deposition of secondary enriched minerals (e.g. malachite, azurite, cuprite) in a zone either side. See 'Secondary mineral'.

Secondary mineral   Mineral deposited through secondary enrichment (q.v.), usually as a result of weathering of a primary mineral. Common secondary minerals found on the Edge include malachite, azurite, chrysocolla, pyromorphite and cerussite.

Sett   Parcel of mineral land divided up as a result of agreement reached between the mineral lord and adventurers.

Setting book   Record of the contracts agreed periodically between the miners working in groups and the management of the mine.

Setting day   Day on which tributing miners bid to work a section of the lode (see 'Pitch') (a Cornish working tradition). Bids were made outside the mine office. See 'Count house', 'Tributing'.

Settling tank   See 'Slimes pond'.

Shaft   Vertical or nearly vertical access route into a mine. Shafts can be square, round, oval or rectangular in cross-section, sometimes lined with drystone walling if these are cut through earth, clay, or fractured ground at the top. Shafts can be described according to use, as climbing shafts, drawing shafts, engine shafts, etc. Shafts on the Edge range from possible Roman date to the late nineteenth century.

Shaft collapse   Pronounced hollow, usually over 1 m deep, formed by a recent surface collapse into a part-buried shaft forming a 'shaft hollow'.

Shaft collar   Reinforced edge around a shaft top.

Shaft head   Portion of shaft which reaches surface; working area over the shaft.

Shaft rim mound   Small raised spoil mound (maximum 10–15 m in diameter) with a narrow, truncated rim, and invariably a cone-shaped depression (the shaft collapse) in the centre.

Shaft stroke   Stroke of a beam pumping-engine.

Shammelling   Step-by-step shovelling of loose spoil up to the surface: an early method of working shallow open-trenches on a vein.

Sheer legs   Pulley frame made of two or three beams (legs) joined at the apex and erected over the shaft head, for winding up buckets and lowering timbers and ironwork. Usually a temporary arrangement (nineteenth to twentieth centuries).

Shoot   Vertical extent of an ore body or of values in a lode.

Shooting the rocks   Seventeenth- to eighteenth-century term for tool-assisted and explosive breaking of rocks following boring, first through slow wedging and lime blasting, and later by means of gunpowder.

Shot hole   Hole drilled for packing with explosive to fire, blast, and remove rock. Most shot holes under the Edge were for gunpowder, since most of the sandstone could be moved easily without high explosives. Powder shot holes were usually driven on or to a line of weakness (see 'Free face') to facilitate and control breakage of rock on firing. At least three different types of shot hole have been recognised underground on the Edge, as well as a number of different methods of blasting a face. See also 'Boring', 'Drill steel', 'Black powder', etc.

Shovelling platform   Temporary platform constructed of wooden boards placed over rocky spoil for shovelling ore and waste rock underground, usually at the working face.

Sieve   Used for separating crushed from uncrushed ore or waste. A griddle is a coarse sieve. At its simplest, this developed into the practice of jigging, using gravity separation: after buddling, finely-crushed ore slimes were passed through a jigging sieve shaken up and down in a water-tank. Used widely for lead ore recovery. See also 'Tye', 'Tying'.

Single-ended pick   See 'Miner's pick'.

Sinking   Sinking a shaft or underhand stope by drilling and blasting.

Sized feed   Sorting the fragment sizes of crushed ore to facilitate buddling.

Skip   Sheet-iron container, usually a box, holding up to 1.5 tons of ore, for drawing ore up a shaft. It ran in wooden guides fixed to the side of the shaft, later on rails. Originally Cornish, introduced elsewhere after 1850.

Slag mound   Low mound of slag left from unspecified smelting activity.

Sledge   Wooden sledge for dragging ore, over short distances on the surface or underground, hauled by man or horse; generally no later than the seventeenth or eighteenth century, although one has been found in Engine Vein in early nineteenth-century workings. See 'Corve'.

Sledge route, sledgeway   Track for ore sledges over rough, steep, or boggy ground: there is a probable example at the Iron Gates between Stormy Point and Saddlebole.

Sleeper   Small wooden beam on floor of level to take railway track. Nineteenth-century mining used longitudinal wooden rails with sleepers at intervals – evidence in Wood Mine and Hough Level. Twentieth-century sleepers can be seen in Wood Mine adit.

Sleeper slot   Slot cut into the floor of a level to take a wooden sleeper for iron rails (nineteenth and early twentieth centuries).

Slickenside   Ground and polished surface visible on one or several slip planes of a fault. Formed under intense compressional or tensional stress, and usually having striations which indicate the direction of movement. Common; especially visible on the hanging walls of veins, and may be seen on the sides of old stope workings. Examples can be seen in most of the Alderley mines.

Slimes   The finest particle size of the crushed ores, difficult to catch and often carried away in the water flow, and thus one of the waste products of the crushing and concentrating process.

Slimes pond   Small reservoir located below the dressing floors used to catch the suspended fine material washing over the buddles. A probable example exists below the buddling floor at Wood Mine.

Smelting works   Site of smelter and associated buildings and floors, on or close to the mine (e.g. Abbadine's supposed smelting works at Edge House Farm *c.* 1706; works near the Wood Mine site *c.* 1805).

Smithy   Small blacksmith's shop at the mine for sharpening and re-forging drill steels, repairing machinery etc.

Spall   Hand-crushing small pieces of ore into finer fragments. Also refers to part of a wall or pillar breaking away due to pressure on the rock.

Spalling floor   Hand-crushing floor, paved with thick stone slabs or up-ended cobbles (late eighteenth to early nineteenth century in other mining areas such as Parys Mountain on Anglesey and in mid-Wales).

Spalling hammer   Sledgehammer for spalling, used mostly by women on the spalling floor.

Speiss   Cobalt-nickel residue produced in the Alderley Edge Mining Co.'s treatment works *c.* 1860–64 (see Chapter 16).

Spell (or **core**)   The usual time spent underground (a six- to eight-hour shift in the 1850s).

Stack   Chimney of an engine house.

Stamp   Form of crushing engine (stamping mill) that used a rotating cam powered by a waterwheel or steam engine to lift a row of iron-shod wooden beams known as stamps which dropped under their own weight onto mortar stones ('stamp stones') or an iron plate. Stamps were first recorded in use in British mines at the end of the seventeenth century, although they may be much earlier, and Cornish stamps were still in use at the beginning of the twentieth century.

Steam whim   Steam-operated winding engine.

Stemple   Brace jammed between opposite sides of a shaft or stope cavity as a support or step, usually of wood but sometimes of stone (the use of stone here appears to be a Derbyshire mining practice). Often placed to hold a platform of deads within an overhand stope, planking for a footway or barrows, or a drainage launder, but most commonly in the Edge mines as climbing stemples up a footway shaft. Also used at Alderley Edge to support a brattice in a shaft.

Stemple niche   Bevelled niche cut in the opposite wall into which the other end of the stemple can be knocked down and wedged. This simple technique of bracing can be found in mines from the Roman to the modern periods.

Stemple socket   Socket hole pick-cut into the side of a rock wall to take one end of a wooden stemple.

Stope   The working area in a lode, usually a cavity left underground where the lode has been removed *en masse*, above or below the level floor or roof. See 'Overhand stoping', 'Underhand stoping'.

Stoping   The action of removing the lode in mining.

Stowes   Early name for a wooden windlass, mentioned in medieval and early Post-Medieval documents which refer to mining. There is a reference to stowes in the account of the 1696 miners' riot on the Edge, though the word used there is a 'windglass'.

Stowes slot   Cutting in the rock at the head of a hand-picked underground shaft or winze, intended to take the vertical and cross-pieces of the windlass (there are eighteenth-century examples in the upper sections of Brynlow Mine).

Strapping plate   Iron fishplate, sometimes many feet long, used for connecting abutting timbers in driving machinery such as pump rods or waterwheel cranks.

Straw   Straw fuse for black powder blasting, used alongside quills before the advent of the safety fuse.

Strike   The main direction of a lode or of a bed of rock along a horizontal surface such as its outcrop on the ground, usually given as a compass bearing.

Sump   Lowest section of a shaft, often used as a drain to collect water, from where it could be pumped up to adit level or to the surface.

Survey pegging   While many survey tags and nails clearly belong to the modern period of exploration of the mines, in places bore holes in the roofs of levels contain the ends of large chamfered wooden pegs with old iron staples on their tips. These are late nineteenth or early twentieth century, relating to the mechanical drivage of levels or the abandonment plans (e.g. in Wood Mine and the Hough Level).

Sweep rod   Iron rod connecting the beam of a steam engine to a crank to give rotary action. Rotative engines could be used to drive machinery such as crushers and whims, and hoists on inclines.

Tailings   Waste from the dressing floors such as the waste gangue minerals from the crusher and buddles, or at the treatment works waste from the acid-leaching tanks (the 'Sandhills', q.v.).

Tallow candle   Miner's candle made from processed tallow (fat), such as those manufactured in the candle factory at The Topps, Brynlow, during the eighteenth and nineteenth centuries.

Tally-mark (tally)   One of a series of short, vertical pick-cut marks in walls of levels at head height, usually at an entrance or junction, sometimes crossed through. May refer to a miner's identity (like masons' marks), but most probably kept as a simple 'score-card' of activity, volume of ore, value of work, the number of men working, or time spent. Possible examples associated with eighteenth-century workings at Brynlow and Engine Vein.

Tamping bar   Thin iron bar with a small flange at the end used for ramming in the clay 'stemming' or plug to seal the powder charge in a shot hole, ensuring that the maximum explosive power is directed into the surrounding rocks. Wooden tampers were also used in the interests of safety.

Throw   See 'Displacement'.

Tie rod wall plate   Pair of iron plates bolted onto either side of a masonry or brick wall as reinforcement, particularly within a building such as an engine house subjected to heavy load-bearing stress and strong vibrations.

Timbering   Important underground activity, particularly in overhand stoping and creating a rise between levels, where mining commenced by working upwards from the back of the level, building stulls or platforms.

Trammel   Revolving iron sieve into which crushed ore was fed from the stamps or rolls for grading.

Tramming   (a) A task listed in tutwork (q.v.) contracts, usually tramming rubbish, i.e. filling and pushing tubs to the main haulage way or incline. (b) General term for pushing tubs, often by hand.

Trench mine   This type of working (see 'Opencast') can date to any time from the prehistoric to the Victorian period. On the Edge itself such workings appear most typically to date from the late eighteenth century to the end of the second decade of the nineteenth.

Tributing   Method of working popular in nineteenth-century Cornish-managed mines. On setting days tributing miners, usually working in pares (q.v.), bid against each other for the pitch they would work in the mine. The miners gathered outside the mine office (see 'Count house') and listened as the manager read out the working places available for tributing, asking for bids for the contract and the proportion of the value to be retained by the men. The system encouraged skill in the miners' ability to judge lode values. Usually the poorer the pitch, the higher the bid, thus unexpected finds could prove a particular bonus. The miners would aim to outwit the management. The mine owners provided the necessary materials – tools, candles, gunpowder – and their value was deducted at the end of the contract. This system of working, along with tutwork (q.v.), seems to have been in operation on Alderley Edge from 1858 onwards. See also 'Count house', 'Parcel', 'Pare', 'Pitch', 'Setting day'.

Trunking (a) A second washing of ore prior to further separation and dressing on frames. (b) Air trunking or ducting in the form of wooden box or galvanised iron pipes carrying forced air ventilation into blind headings and rises. Good examples of a course of air-trunking can be seen going up into the Probationers' Workings above the Hough Level in Wood Mine and in passages beyond Plank Shaft in West Mine. Trunking is often mounted high on the right hand wall (inbye) of a passage.

Trunking bracket Iron bracket fixed onto a rock wall to take trunking along the sides or roof of a level.

Tub See 'Wagon'.

Tutwork Another widely practised Cornish system of working: a form of piecework, the miners taking a contract and being paid a set amount per unit of work done. Payments could be per fathom advanced in a level of given size, per square fathom of lode stoped, or the actual weight mined. Tutwork appears to have been a common working practice in the Alderley mines in the 1860s for driving levels and shafts.

Tye Simple form of sieve machine (referred to in eighteenth- to nineteenth-century accounts).

Tying Jigging or sieving ore (Cornish term usually referring to tin, but also to the separation of other ores).

Underground captain Knowledgeable and experienced miner, appointed by the mine captain (q.v.), who was responsible to him for supervising the underground work (common Cornish mining practice).

Underhand stoping 'Stoping out' or removing the vein by working downwards from a level through a series of benches. Although less common than overhand stoping as a general mining practice during the nineteenth century, underhand stoping was the predominant method in the 1857–77 period at Alderley Edge. Stulls or false floors were similarly constructed between the footwall and hanging wall to carry over the haulage level, as evidenced in West Mine main chamber. In a much simpler fashion, underhand stoping was probably the earliest underground mining technique to be used.

Underlie The angle the lode makes with the vertical, at right angles to its strike (q.v.).

Upper hole Hole drilled into the side or roof of a shaft while driving upwards in a rise.

Value The value or potential value of ore won, also used in assessing the prices of contracts.

Valvebox Valves or 'door pieces' within the rising main pump pipes of a Cornish pump, also known as clack valves from the noise they made on seating.

Vein See 'Lode'.

Veinstuff The minerals of a mineral vein, both ore and gangue.

Ventilation The existence of several open shafts and levels into a working will assist proper circulation of air within the mine. On occasions natural ventilation requires assistance, with air being pumped in (see 'Trunking'). Fire baskets at the foot of open shafts also create air currents (e.g. probably in West Mine at the start of Twisted Pillar Chamber).

Ventilation door Wooden door to block off passages, and hence direct air and assist with ventilation. Remains of a door were found in Wood Mine and a replica has been constructed *in situ*.

Vugh Occasional empty cavity within the lode, sometimes lined with fine crystalline crusts or precipitated banded mineral.

Wad See 'Cobaltian wad', 'Manganese wad'.

Wagon Iron-rimmed wooden or iron tub fixed to an undercarriage with flanged wheels which sat on rails and was used for haulage underground and on the dressing floors at the surface. At Alderley wagons were hauled up an incline from underground at West Mine and the west end of the Hough Level.

Wash ore A separated gravel-sized fraction of hand-crushed and dressed ore. See 'Hand dressing'.

Wastrel Common land (found in early references to mines on land at Alderley Edge).

Water barrel Very basic method of drainage using a water barrel drawn up a shaft and emptied at the surface. It was an effective method, particularly to cope with flood water entering a mine.

Wheelbarrow Still the commonest vehicle at Alderley in the eighteenth to nineteenth centuries, for transporting ore and waste from the forefield in a level or a stope working face to the ore chute or a haulageway intersection.

Wheeling   The removal of waste from the mine face, or spoil from the dressing floors.

Whim   Winding drum used to raise or lower buckets in a shaft. Sometimes this refers to the winding engine itself, particularly when this was operated by steam.

White lead (ore)   Miner's term for cerussite (lead carbonate) (q.v.).

Windbore   Pipe up which water was drawn by suction on the up stroke of a pumping engine, then forced up the rising main on the down stroke (nineteenth century, Alderley Edge Mining Co. Ltd).

Winding   Contract or tutwork (q.v.) within the mine, to wind or hoist both ore and waste up shafts or an incline.

Winding engine   Usually refers to a steam whim, most commonly a rotative engine.

Winding house   The winding or drum house at the top of an incline, such as at the treatment works.

Windlass   Wood-framed hand-operated winch with a small wooden drum and wood or iron handle. See also 'Stowe'.

Winze   Underground shaft, sunk to a lower level within a mine, either exploratory or as a connection with a haulage level.

References

This, the main list of references, covers the works cited in all the chapters of this book except for Chapter 13 ('The insects and other invertebrates of Alderley Edge') and Appendix 9.2 ('An account of the *Rubus* species of Alderley Edge'): these both describe somewhat specialised topics, and thus their bibliographic references are also specialised and are linked closely to the discussion in the text. For that reason they are printed separately, with their respective texts.

Adeane, J. H. (ed.). 1899. *The Early Married Life of Maria Josepha Lady Stanley, with Extracts from Sir John Stanley's 'Praeterita' Edited by One of Their Grandchildren.* London: Longmans, Green.

Aikin, J. 1795. *A Description of the Country from Thirty to Forty Miles Around Manchester.* London: J. Stockdale (reprinted Newton Abbot: David and Charles, 1968).

Aitkenhead, N., Barclay, W. J., Brandon, A., Chadwick, R. A., Chisholm, J. I., Cooper, A. H. and Johnson, E. W. 2002. *British Regional Geology: The Pennines and Adjacent Areas* (4th edition). Keyworth: British Geological Survey.

Alty, S. W. 1926. The Petrographic Features of Keuper Rocks from a Boring at Wilmslow, Near Stockport, Cheshire. *Proceedings of the Liverpool Geological Society,* 14: 278–83.

Angus-Butterworth, L. M. 1932. *Old Cheshire Families and Their Seats.* Manchester: Sherratt and Hughes (reprinted by Morten, 1970).

Anon. 1665. A Way to Break Easily and Speedily the Hardest Rocks.... *Philosophical Transactions,* 1(5) (3 July).

Anon. 1820. *The Cheshire Enchanter, or, The Legend of the Iron Gates: Containing the Explanation of the Sign of the Public House at Monk's Heath, Near Macclesfield* (2nd edition). Manchester: G. Innes.

Anon. 1861. *Excursion to the Copper Mines, Alderley.* Leaflet for 31st Annual Meeting of the British Association at Manchester.

Anon. [Stephen Osborne]. 1863. Quarterly General Meeting Report. *Mining Journal,* 7 November.

Anon. 1864a. Alderley Edge mine setting book, dated 20 August 1864. Now held in the AELP Archive.

Anon. 1864b. Report of a Meeting of the Alderley Edge Mining Company, 29 January. *Mining Journal,* 34: 153.

Anon. 1865a. The Alderley Edge Mine – From a Correspondent. *Mining Journal,* 35: 499.

Anon. 1865b. Visit of Japanese to the Copper Mine at Alderley Edge. *Mining Journal,* No. 1569 (16 September): 606.

Anon. 1878. Mine plans of Wood Mine etc. in the hands of Mr A. Lowndes – see Carlon (1979).

Anon. 1913. The 'Wizard', Alderley Edge. *Cheshire Notes and Queries,* 9(1): 11–14.

Anon. 1949. *Mottram St. Andrew Recreation Centre. Souvenir Programme: Opening Ceremony of the Village Hall by Sir R. Noton Barclay. April 30th, 1949.*

Anon. 1964. Big Blast Ends Alderley Mine Hazard At Last. *Stockport Advertiser,* 10 April.

ArchAE – see Timberlake and Prag (2005).

Armstrong, A. and Brasier, M. 2004. *Microfossils* (2nd edition). Oxford: Blackwell.

Axon, W. E. A. 1884. *Cheshire Gleanings.* Manchester: Tubbs, Brooks and Chrystal; London: Simpkin, Marshall.

Back, M. E. and Mandarino, J. A. 2008. *Fleischer's Glossary of Mineral Species 2008*. Tucson, AZ: Mineralogical Record.

Bagshaw, S. 1850. *History, Gazetteer, and Directory of the County Palatine of Chester: Comprising a General Survey of the County: With a Variety of Historical, Statistical, Topographical, Commercial, and Agricultural Information*. Sheffield: G. Ridge.

Bainbridge, W. 1878. *A Practical Treatise on the Law of Mines and Minerals* (4th edition, ed. A. Brown). London: Butterworths.

Bakewell, R. 1811. Account of a Cobalt Mine in Cheshire (The Cobalt Mines at Alderley). *Monthly Magazine*, 31: 7–9.

Bakewell, R. 1813. *An Introduction to Geology*. London: J. Harding (and later editions by Longmans).

Barker, I. and Beck, J. S. 2010. *Caves of the Peak District*. Great Hucklow: Hucklow Publishing for Derbyshire Caving Association.

Barlow, T. W. (ed.). 1853. *The Cheshire and Lancashire Historical Collector*. Manchester: John Russell Smith; London: John Gray Bell.

Barnatt, J. 1999. Prehistoric and Roman Mining in the Peak District: Present Knowledge and Future Research. *Mining History (Bulletin of the Peak District Mines Historical Society)*, 14(2): 19–30.

Barnatt, J. and Thomas, G. 1998. Prehistoric Mining at Ecton, Staffordshire: A Dated Antler Tool and Its Context. *Mining History (Bulletin of the Peak District Mines Historical Society)*, 13(5): 72–8.

Barnatt, J. and Worthington, T. 2006. Using Coal to Mine Lead: Firesetting at Peak District Mines. *Mining History (Bulletin of the Peak District Mines Historical Society)*, 16(3): 1–94.

Beasley, H. C. 1904. Report on Footprints from the Trias, Part 1. *Report of the British Association for Advancement of Science (Southport 1903)*, 219–30.

Beasley, H. C. 1907. Report on Footprints from the Trias, Part 4. *Report of the British Association for Advancement of Science (York 1906)*, 229–301.

Bennett, J. H. E. and Dewhurst, J. C. (eds). 1940. *Cheshire Quarter Sessions Records (1559–1760), Vol. 1. Quarter Sessions Records with Other Records of the Justices of the Peace for the County Palatine of Chester, 1559–1760, Together with a Few Earlier Miscellaneous Records Deposited with the Cheshire County Council*. Manchester: Lancashire and Cheshire Record Society.

Bennett, M. R. and Glasser N. F. 1996. *Glacial Geology: Ice Sheets and Landforms*. Chichester: John Wiley.

Bentley Smith, D. 2005. *A Georgian Gent and Co. The Life and Times of Charles Roe*. Ashbourne: Landmark Publishing.

Benton, M. J. 1990. The Species of *Rhynchosaurus*, a Rhynchosaur (Reptilia, Diapsida) from the Middle Triassic Tetrapod Assemblages of England. *Philosophical Transactions of the Royal Society of London, B*, 328: 213–306.

Benton, M. J. 1997. *Vertebrate Palaeontology* (2nd edition). London: Chapman and Hall.

Benton, M. J., Warrington, G., Newell, A. J. and Spencer, P. S. 1994. A Review of the British Tetrapod Assemblages. In: Fraser, N. C. and Suess, D. (eds), *In the Shadow of the Dinosaurs*, 131–60. Cambridge: Cambridge University Press.

Berger, John. 1967. *A Fortunate Man*. London: Allen Lane, the Penguin Press.

Bevins, R. E. and Mason, J. S. 2010. Parys Mountain. In Bevins, R. E., Young, B., Mason, J. S., Manning, D. A. C. and Symes, R. F. (eds), *Mineralization of England and Wales* (Geological Conservation Review Series 36), 263–9. Peterborough: Joint Nature Conservation Committee.

Bick, D. E. 1977. *The Old Metal Mines of Mid-Wales. Part 4, West Montgomeryshire*. Newent: The Pound House.

Bick, D. E. and Wyn Davies, P. 1994. *Lewis Morris and the Cardiganshire Mines*. Aberystwyth: National Library of Wales.

Bidgood, S. 1978. A New Attribution for the 'Cambrian Pottery' Jug. *Leeds Arts Calendar*, 82: 26–31.

Binding, C. J. and Wilson, L. J. 2010. Ritual Protection Marks in Wookey Hole and Long Hole, Somerset. *Proceedings of the Spelaeological Society, University of Bristol*, 25(1): 47–73.

Blick, C. R. (ed.). 1991. *Early Metallurgical Sites in Great Britain: BC 2000 to AD 1500*. London: Institute of Metals.

Boase, G. C. and Courtney, W. P. 1874. *Bibliotheca Cornubiensis, Vol. 1: A–O*. London: Longmans, Green, Reader and Dyer.

Bode, H. 1999. *James Brindley*. Princes Risborough: Shire.

Bonson, T. 2003. *Driven by the Dane*. Congleton: Midland Wind and Water Mills Group.

Boothby, J. 1997. Ponds and Other Small Water-Bodies in North-West England: An Audit. In Boothby, J. (ed.), *British Pond Landscapes: Action for Protection and Enhancement. Proceedings of the UK Conference of the Pond Life Project, 1997*. Liverpool: John Moores University.

Boucher, C. T. G. 1968. *James Brindley, Engineer, 1716–1772*. Norwich: Goose and Son.

Boucher, C. T. G. 1978. *Nether Alderley Mill*. London: National Trust.

Boucher, C. T. G. 1989. Unpublished report on Nether Alderley Mill, for the National Trust. Held at the Trust's Cheshire Countryside Office, Forester's Lodge, Macclesfield Road, Nether Alderley, Cheshire SK10 4UB.

Bowman, H. and Crowther, J. S. 1845. *The Churches of the Middle Ages: Being Select Specimens of Early and Middle Pointed Structures*. London: George Bell (2nd edition 1853).

Boyd Dawkins, W. 1875. On the Stone Mining Tools from Alderley Edge. *Proceedings of the Literary and Philosophical Society of Manchester*, 14: 74–9. Reprinted as Boyd Dawkins, W. 1876. On the Stone Mining Tools from Alderley Edge. *Journal of the Anthropological Institute of Great Britain and Ireland*, 5: 2–5.

Bradley, R. 1984. *The Social Foundations of Prehistoric Britain*. London: Longman Archaeological Series.

Braithwaite, R. S. W. 1994. Mineralogy of the Alderley Edge – Mottram St Andrew Area, Cheshire, England. *Journal of the Russell Society*, 5(2): 91–102.

Brandl, Alois. 1936. *Zwischen Inn und Themse: Lebensbeobachtungen eines Anglisten*. Berlin: G. Grote'sche Verlagsbuchhandlung.

Brenchley, P. J. and Rawson P. F. (eds). 2006. *The Geology of England and Wales* (2nd edition). London: Geological Society.

Brennand, M. (ed.). 2006. *The Archaeology of North West England: An Archaeological Research Framework for the North West Region, Vol. 1: Resource Assessment – Archaeology North West*, 8 (issue 18 for 2006). Manchester: Council for British Archaeology North West.

Briggs, C. S. 1983. Copper Mining at Mount Gabriel, County Cork: Bronze Age Bonanza or Post-famine Fiasco? *Proceedings of the Prehistoric Society*, 49: 317–33.

Briggs, K. M. 1971. *A Dictionary of British Folk-Tales*. London: Routledge and Kegan Paul.

British Geological Survey. 1999. *Copper*. Keyworth: British Geological Survey.

Broadhurst, F. M., Eagar, R. M. C., Jackson, J. W., Simpson, I. M. and Thompson, D. B. (ed. Hester, S. W.). 1970. *The Area Around Manchester* (Geologists' Association Guide No. 7). Colchester: Benham.

Brockbank, W. 1891a. On the Discovery of *Estheria minuta*, var. *Brodieana* of Prof. Rupert Jones, F.R.S., by Mr. C. E. de Rance, F.G.S, in the Lower Keuper Sandstone of Alderley Edge. *Memoirs and Proceedings of the Manchester Literary and Philosophical Society* (Fourth Series), 34: 12–13.

Brockbank, W. 1891b. Additional Note on the Discovery of *Estheria minuta* var. *Brodieana* by Mr. C. E. de Rance, F.G.S. in the Lower Keuper Sandstone of Alderley Edge. *Memoirs and Proceedings of the Manchester Literary and Philosophical Society* (Fourth Series), 34: 31.

Brook, G. L. (ed.). 1983. *Selections from Layamon's Brut* (revised edition with an Introduction by C. S. Lewis). Exeter: University of Exeter.

Browne, T. 1995. The Mysteries of Alderley Edge. *North West Geologist*, 5: 18–21.

Bruckshaw, F. 1982. *Eadwulf's Farm*. Adlington: Adlington Civic Society.

Buckland, W. 1839. An Unapproved Palaeoenvironmental Interpretation of the *Chirotherium* Footprints of the Wirral. In Cunningham, J. An Account of the Impressions and Casts of Drops of Rain Discovered in the Quarries at Storeton Hill, Cheshire. *Proceedings of the Geological Society of London*, 3: 99–100.

Burnham, B. C. 1994. Dolaucothi revisited. In Ford, T. D. and Willies, L. (eds). *Peak District Mines Historical Society Bulletin*, 12 (3, *Mining Before Powder*), 41–7.

Büttner, K. 1938. *Intonation und Vokalqualität dargestellt an der Mundart von Cheshire* (Sprache und Kultur der Germanischen und Romanischen Völker, Anglistische Reihe 28). Breslau: Priebatschs Buchhandlung.

Callaghan, D. A. 2015. *Bryophyte Survey and Assessment of Alderley Edge, Cheshire*. Unpublished report to Natural England.

Camden, W. 1772. *Britannia, or a Chorographical Description of Great Britain and Ireland, Together with the Adjacent Islands* (4th edition, written in Latin by William Camden, Clarenceux King at Arms and translated into English with additions and improvements by Edmund Gibson, D.D., Late Lord Bishop of London, printed from a copy of 1722, left corrected by the Bishop for the press). London: printed for W. Bowyer *et al.*

Carlon, C. J. 1975. The Geology and Geochemistry of Some British Barite Deposits. PhD thesis, Manchester University.

Carlon, C. J. 1979. *The Alderley Edge Mines*. Altrincham: John Sherratt and Son.

Carlon, C. J. 1981. *The Gallantry Bank Copper Mine, Bickerton, Cheshire, With a Review of Mining in the Triassic Rocks of the Cheshire–Shropshire Basin* (British Mining 16). Sheffield: Northern Mine Research Society.

Carlon, C. J. and Dibben, N. J. 2012. *The Alderley Edge Mines*. Nantwich: Nigel Dibben.

Carlon, C. J. and Thompson, D. B. 1981. Aspects of the Mineralization Within the Cheshire Basin. *Journal of the Geological Society of London*, 138: 220.

Carter, C. F. (ed.). 1962. *Manchester and Its Region* (a survey prepared for the British Association for the Advancement of Science Manchester Meeting, 1962). Manchester: Manchester University Press.

Casella, E. C. and Croucher, S. K. 2010. *The Alderley Sandhills Project: An Archaeology of Community Life in (Post-)Industrial England*. Manchester: Manchester University Press for English Heritage.

Chadwick, R. A. 1997. Fault Analysis of the Cheshire Basin, NW England. In Meadows, N. S., Trueblood, S. P., Hardman, M. and Cowan, G. (eds), *Petroleum Geology of the Irish Sea and Adjacent Areas* (Geological Society Special Publication No. 124). London: Geological Society.

Chadwick, R. A., Evans, D. J., Rowley, W. J., Smith, N. J. P., Walker, A. S. D., Birch, B. and Bulat, J. 1999. Structure and Evolution of the Basin. In Plant, J. A., Jones, D. G. and Haslam, H. W. (eds), *The Cheshire Basin: Basin Evolution, Fluid Movement and Mineral Resources in a Permo-Triassic Rift Setting*, 41–89. Keyworth: British Geological Survey.

Chaloner, W. H. 1953. Charles Roe of Macclesfield (1715–81): An Eighteenth-Century Industrialist, Part 1. *Transactions of the Lancashire and Cheshire Antiquarian Society*, 62: 133–56.

Chaloner, W. H. 1954. Charles Roe of Macclesfield (1715–81): An Eighteenth-Century Industrialist, Part 2. *Transactions of the Lancashire and Cheshire Antiquarian Society*, 63: 52–86.

Cheshire Quarter Sessions Records (1559–1760), Vol. 1. See Bennett and Dewhurst (1940).

Chisholm, J. I., Charsley, T. J. and Aitkenhead, N. 1988. *Geology of the Country Around Ashbourne and Cheadle* (Memoirs of the British Geological Survey). London: HMSO.

Chorley, K. 1950. *Manchester Made Them*. London: Faber and Faber (republished Hale: Silk Press, 2001, the edition from which quotations in the text are taken).

Claughton, P. 1996. The Lumburn Leat – Evidence for New Pumping Technology at Bere Ferrers in the 15th Century. In Newman, P. (ed.), *The Archaeology of Mining and Metallurgy in South-West Britain*, 35–40. Matlock Bath: Peak District Mines Historical Society and the Historical Metallurgy Society.

Clegg, J. A., Almond, M. and Stubbs, P. H. S. 1954. The Remanent Magnetism of Some Sedimentary Rocks in Britain. *Philosophical Magazine*, 45: 538–98.

Clements, D., Scruby, M. and Lutley, W. 1985 (updated as Jackson, P. K., Lister J. A. and Alexander, K. N. A. 1997). *Biological Evaluation: The National Trust Biological Survey, Alderley Edge, Cheshire* (unpublished report). Cirencester: National Trust Estates Department.

Clemmensen, L. B., Oxnevad, E. I. E. and De Boer, P. L. 1994. Climatic Controls on Ancient Desert Sedimentation: Some Late Palaeozoic and Mesozoic Examples from NW Europe and the Western Interior of USA. *Special Publications of the International Association of Sedimentologists*, 19: 439–57.

Cleverdon, F., Meeson, R. A. and Milln, J. 2000. *Vernacular Architecture Group Spring Conference 2000: Staffordshire and Cheshire*. Vernacular Architecture Group (http://www.vag.org.uk).

Cobbing, A. 2000. *The Satsuma Students in Britain. Japan's Early Search for the 'Essence of the West'* (Japan Library, Meiji Series 9). Richmond: Curzon Press.

Cocker, M. and Mabey, R. 2005. *Birds Britannica*. London: Chatto and Windus.

Collins, J. H. 1893–94. The Economic Treatment of Low-Grade Copper Ores. *Transactions of the Institution of Mining and Metallurgy*, 2: 4–75.

Collinson, J. D., Mountney, N. P. and Thompson, D. B. 2006. *Sedimentary Structures* (3rd edition). Harpenden: Terra Publishing.

Cook, L. M. 2008. Diversity and Evenness from Sequential Sightings. *Insect Conservation and Diversity*, 1: 263–5.

Coope, G. R., Robinson, D. J. and Roe, F. E. S. 1988. The Petrological Identification of Stone Implements from Lancashire and Cheshire. In Clough, T. H. McK. and Cummins, W. A. (eds), *Stone Axe Studies Vol. 2: The Petrology of Prehistoric Stone Implements from the British Isles* (Research Report No. 67), 60–6. London: Council for British Archaeology.

Coward, T. A. 1903. *Picturesque Cheshire*. Manchester: Sherratt and Hughes (later editions London: Methuen).

Coward, T. A. and Oldham, C. 1900. *The Birds of Cheshire*. Manchester: Sherratt and Hughes.

Coward, T. A. and Oldham, C. 1910. *The Vertebrate Fauna of Cheshire and Liverpool Bay*. London: Witherby.

Cowell, M. R. and Craddock, P. T. 1995. Addendum: Copper in the Skin of Lindow Man. In Turner, R. C. and Scaife, R. G. (eds), *Bog Bodies: New Discoveries and New Perspectives*, 74–5. London: British Museum Press.

Craddock, P. 1986. Bronze Age Metallurgy in Britain. *Current Archaeology*, 99: 106–9.

Craddock, P. 2007. Introduction: Achievements and Challenges. In La Niece, S., Hook, D. and Craddock, P. (eds), *Metals and Mines: Studies in Archaeometallurgy*, ix–xii. London: Archetype Publications and the British Museum.

Craddock, P., Meeks, N. and Timberlake, S. 2007. On the Edge of Success: The Scientific Examination of the Products of the Early Mines Research Group Smelting Experiments. In La Niece, S., Hook, D. and Craddock, P. (eds), *Metals and Mines: Studies in Archaeometallurgy*, 37–45. London: Archetype Publications and the British Museum.

Crew, P. and Crew, S. (eds). 1990. *Early Mining in the British Isles: Proceedings of the Early Mining Workshop at Plas Tan y Bwlch Snowdonia National Park Study Centre, Maentwrog, 1989* (Occasional Paper No. 1). Maentwrog: Plas Tan y Bwlch.

Crofts, R. G., Hough, E. and Humpage, A. 2005. The Quaternary of the Rossendale Forest and Greater Manchester and Its Regional Setting Within North-West England and the Lancashire/Shropshire/Cheshire Plain. In Crofts, R. G. (ed.), *Quaternary of the Rossendale Forest and Greater Manchester* (Quaternary Research Association Field Guide), 1–10. London: Quaternary Research Association.

Crosby, A. 1996. *A History of Cheshire*. Chichester: Phillimore.

Crossley, A. 1931. *Amy Crossley's Guide to Alderley Edge and Old Alderley*. Alderley Edge: The author. A second printing (ed. Alan Crossley, 1989) has different pagination and end-matter.

Crossley, W. 1787. *A Map of the Estates Situate in Over Alderley, Nether Alderley, Chorley, in the County of Chester – The Property of Sir Thomas Stanley Baronet*. Held by Cheshire Archives and Local Studies (formerly Cheshire Records Office), Chester (DSA 238/P143/14/1).

Croston, J. 1883. *Historic Sites in Lancashire and Cheshire*. Manchester: John Heywood.

Cunningham, J. 1839. An Account of the Impressions and Casts of Drops of Rain Discovered in the Quarries at Storeton Hill, Cheshire. *Proceedings of the Geological Society of London*, 3: 99–100.

Davey, P. J. and Forster, E. 1975. *Bronze Age Metalwork from Lancashire and Cheshire* (Work Notes 1). Liverpool: University of Liverpool.

Davies, C. S. (ed.). 1961. *A History of Macclesfield*. Manchester: Manchester University Press.

Davies, D. L. 1997. *Watermill: Life Story of a Welsh Cornmill*. Llangollen: Ceiriog Press.

Davies, O. 1935. *Roman Mines in Europe*. Oxford: Clarendon Press.

Dawkins, W. Boyd – see Boyd Dawkins, W.

Delaney, C. 2003. The Last Glacial Stage (the Devensian) in Northwest England. *North West Geography*, 3(1): 27–7.

Demathieu, G. R. 1985. Trace Fossil Assemblages in Middle Triassic Marginal Marine Deposits, Eastern Border of the Massif Central, France. In Curran H. C. (ed.), *Biogenic Sedimentary Structures: Their Use in Interpreting Depositional Environments* (SEPM Special Publication No. 35), 53–66. Tulsa, OK: Society for Sedimentary Geology.

Demathieu, G. R. and Haubold, H. 1972. Stratigraphische Aussagen der Tetrapoden Färten aus der terrestischer Trias Europas. *Geologie*, 21: 806–40.

Department of the Environment. 1994. *The Reclamation and Management of Metalliferous Mining Sites*. London: HMSO.

de Rance, C. E. 1890. *Geological Map, Particularly of the Drift Deposits of Alderley Edge*. Keyworth: British Geological Survey (archives).

de Rance, C. E. 1891 – see Brockbank (1891a, 1891b).

de Tabley, J. B. L. W. 1899. *The Flora of Cheshire*, edited by Spencer Moore with a biographical notice of the author by Sir Mountstuart Grant Duff. London: Longmans, Green.

Dewey, E. and Eastwood, T. 1925. *Copper Ores of the Midlands, Wales, the Lake District and the Isle of Man* (Memoirs of the Geological Survey: Special Reports on the Mineral Resources of Great Britain 30). London: HMSO.

Dixon, J. 2007. *The First 100 Years of Alderley Edge Golf Club*. (No publisher given.)

Dodgson, J. McN. 1970. *The Place-Names of Cheshire. Part 1: County Name, Regional and Forest-Names, River-Names, Road-Names, the Place-Names of Macclesfield Hundred* (English Place-Name Society 44). Cambridge: Cambridge University Press.

Dodgson, J. McN. 1972. *The Place-Names of Cheshire, Part 4: The Place-Names of Broxton Hundred and Wirral Hundred* (English Place-Name Society 47). Cambridge: Cambridge University Press.

Donald, M. B. 1955. *Elizabethan Copper*. London: Pergamon Press.

Dore, R. N. 1966. *The Civil War in Cheshire. A History of Cheshire, Vol. 8*. Chester: Cheshire Community Council Publications Trust.

Dore, R. N. (ed.). 1983–84. *Letter Book of Sir William Brereton*. Manchester: Record Society of Lancashire and Cheshire (vol. 123).

Eagar, R. M. C. and Broadhurst, F. M. 1959. Itinerary IV: Alderley Edge, Cheshire. In Eagar, R. M. C., Broadhurst, F. M. and Jackson, J. W. *The Area Around Manchester* (Geologists' Association Guide No. 7), 18–22. Colchester: Benham.

Eagar, R. M. C. and Broadhurst, F. M., with contributions by Adams, A. E., Braithwaite, R. S. W., Johnson, R. H., Riley, K., Selden, P., Simpson, I. M. and Thompson, D. B. (ed. Greensmith, J. T.). 1991. *Geology of the Manchester Area* (Geologists' Association Guide No. 7) (2nd edition). London: Geologists' Association.

Eagar, R. M. C., Broadhurst, F. M. and Jackson, J. W. (ed. Wells, A. K.). 1959. *The Area Around Manchester* (Geologists' Association Guide No. 7). Colchester: Benham (later editions 1970, 1991).

Earwaker, J. P. 1877. *East Cheshire Past and Present, or, A History of the Hundred of Macclesfield, in the County Palatine of Chester. From Original Records, Vol. 1*. London: the author/Wyman and Sons.

Earwaker, J. P. 1880. *East Cheshire Past and Present, or, A History of the Hundred of Macclesfield, in the County Palatine of Chester. From Original Records, Vol. 2*. London: the author/Wyman and Sons.

Edees, E. S. and Newton, A. N. 1988. *Brambles of the British Isles*. London: Ray Society.

E.E.L. 1913. Alderley Edge Copper Mines. *Cheshire Notes and Queries*, 9(1): 19–23.

Ekwall, E. 1960. *The Concise Oxford Dictionary of English Place Names*. Oxford: Clarendon Press.

English Heritage. 1991. *Exploring Our Past: Strategies for the Archaeology of England*. London: Historic Buildings and Monuments Commission for England.

Evans, D. J., Rees, J. G. and Holloway, S. 1993. The Permian to Jurassic Stratigraphy and Structural Evolution of the Central Cheshire Basin. *Journal of the Geological Society of London*, 150: 857–70.

Evans, J. 1897. *The Ancient Stone Implements, Weapons, and Ornaments, of Great Britain* (2nd edition). London: Longmans, Green.

Evans, W. B., Wilson, A., Taylor, B. J. and Price, D. 1968. *Geology of the Country Around Macclesfield, Congleton, Crewe and Middlewich* (Memoirs of the Geological Survey of Great Britain) (2nd edition). London: HMSO, for the Institute of Geological Sciences and Natural Environment Research Council.

Evelyn, J. 1786. *Silva: or, a Discourse of Forest-Trees, and the Propagation of Timber in His Majesty's Dominions: Together with an Historical Account of the Sacredness and Use of Standing Groves. With Notes by A. Hunter*. York: A. Ward (first published 1776; numerous editions published York, London etc.).

Ferguson, J. 1760. *Lectures in Select Subjects in Mechanics etc*. London: printed for A. Murray (numerous editions, published London, Edinburgh, Dublin, etc.).

Fitzpatrick, B. 1935. Article in *Cheshire Life*, January.

Fluck, P. 1993. Montanarchäologische Forschungen in den Vogesen. In Steuer, H. and Zimmermann, U. (eds), *Montanarchäologie in Europa*, 267–89. Sigmaringen: J. Thorbecke Verlag.

Ford, T. D. and Rieuwerts, J. H. 1968. *Lead Mining in the Peak District*. Bakewell: Peak Park Planning Board.

Ford, T. D. and Willies L. (eds). 1994. *Peak District Mines Historical Society Bulletin*, 12 (3) (*Mining Before Powder*).

Foster, J. 1873. *Pedigrees of the County Families of England. Vol. 1: Lancashire*. London: Head, Hole.

Fowles, J. and Burley, S. D. 1994. Textural and Permeability Characteristics of Faulted, High Porosity Sandstones. *Marine and Petroleum Geology*, 11: 608–23.

Fox, B. W. and Guest, J. 2003. *The Lichen Flora of Cheshire and Wirral*. Frodsham: Nepa Books.

Fundación Rio Tinto. 1994. *La Comarca de Rio Tinto*. Huelva: Fundacion Rio Tinto.

Gaines, R. V., Skinner, H. C. W., Foord, E. E., Mason, B. and Rosenzweig, A. 1997. *Dana's New Mineralogy*. New York: John Wiley and Sons.

Gale, D. 1986. Recording an Elevation of a Copper Mining Face at Engine Vein, Alderley Edge. Undergraduate thesis, School of Archaeological Sciences, University of Bradford.

Gale, D. 1989. Evidence of Ancient Copper Mining at Engine Vein, Alderley Edge, Cheshire. *Bulletin of the Peak District Mines Historical Society*, 10(5): 266–73.

Gale, D. 1990. Prehistoric Stone Mining Tools from Alderley Edge. In Crew, P. and Crew, S. (eds), *Early Mining in the British Isles: Proceedings of the Early Mining Workshop at Plas Tan y Bwlch Snowdonia National Park Study Centre, Maentwrog, 1989* (Occasional Paper No. 1), 47–8. Maentwrog: Plas Tan y Bwlch.

Gale, D. 1993. Prehistoric Mining at Alderley Edge. *Cheshire Past,* 2: 6–7.

Gale, D. 1994. Alderley Edge Mines: Prehistoric Copper Mining – The 1991 Project. *National Trust Archaeological Review,* 3: 91–5.

Gale, D. 1995. Stone Tools Employed in Prehistoric Metal Mining. PhD thesis, University of Bradford.

Garner, A. 1960. *The Weirdstone of Brisingamen.* London: Collins (many reprints, most recently London: HarperCollins, 2010).

Garner, A. 1963. *The Moon of Gomrath.* London: Collins (many reprints, most recently London: HarperCollins, 2010).

Garner, A. 1965. *Elidor.* London: Collins (most recent reprint London: HarperCollins, 2008).

Garner, A. 1979. *The Stone Book Quartet.* London: William Collins (most recent reprint London: HarperCollins, 2010).

Garner, A. 1992. *Tom Fobble's Day.* London: HarperCollins (reprinted in Garner, A. 1979/2010. *The Stone Book Quartet,* q.v.).

Garner, A. 1997. *The Voice That Thunders.* London: Harvill (most recent reprint 2010).

Garner, A. 2012. *Boneland.* London: HarperCollins.

Garner, A., Prag, J. and Housley, R. 1994. The Alderley Edge Shovel. *Current Archaeology,* 12 (5): 172–5 (reprinted in Garner, 1997: 184–92).

Garner, D. J. 2001. The Bronze Age of Manchester Airport: Runway 2. In Bruck, J. (ed.), *Bronze Age Landscapes: Tradition and Transformation,* 41–56. Oxford: Oxbow Books.

Garner, D. J., Allen, C. S. M. and Wenban-Smith, F. F. 2007. *The Neolithic and Bronze Age Settlement at Oversley Farm, Styal, Cheshire: Excavations in Advance of Manchester Airport's Second Runway, 1997–8* (Gifford Archaeological Monographs No. 1; British Archaeological Reports (British Series) No. 435). Oxford: Archaeopress.

Gascon Rolls – see Renouard (1962).

Gelling, M. and Cole A. 2000. *The Landscape of Place-Names.* Stamford: Shaun Tyas.

Gifford, A. 1999. *Derbyshire Watermills: Corn Mills.* Congleton: Midland Wind and Water Mills Group.

Gilbert Gilkes and Gordon Ltd. 1951. *On the Development of Water Power.* Kendal: Gilbert Gilkes and Gordon Ltd.

Giraldus Cambrensis – see O'Meara (1982).

Graves, F. S. 1905. The Archaeology of Alderley Edge. *Stockport Advertiser,* 17 November.

Greene, J. P. 1995. An Archaeological Study of the 1830 Warehouse at Liverpool Road Station, Manchester. *Industrial Archaeology Review,* 17(2): 117–28.

Greenwell, G. C. 1864. On the Copper Sandstone of Alderley, Cheshire. *Proceedings of the South Wales Institute of Engineers,* 4: 44–50.

Greenwood, H. W. 1919. The Trias of the Macclesfield District with Notes on Its Relation to the Adjacent Carboniferous Rocks and the Trias of the Midlands. *Proceedings of the Liverpool Geological Society,* 12: 325–38.

Guest, J. P., Elphick, D., Hunter, J. S. A. and Norman, D. 1992. *The Breeding Birds of Cheshire and Wirral.* Chester: Cheshire and Wirral Ornithological Society.

Gunther, R. T. 1925. *Early Science in Oxford, Vol. 3.* Oxford: Oxford University Press.

Hallam, H. E. 1981. *Rural England, 1066–1348.* London: Fontana.

Hambrey, M. J. 1994. *Glacial Environments.* London: CRC Press; Vancouver: UBC Press.

Hambrey, M. J. and Alean, J. 2004. *Glaciers* (2nd edition). Cambridge: Cambridge University Press.

Hardy, C. 1999. *Francis Frith's Cheshire.* Salisbury: Frith.

Hare, A. J. C. 1872. *Memorials of a Quiet Life.* London: Strahan.

Hartwell, C., Hyde, M. and Pevsner, N. 2011. *Cheshire: The Buildings of England* (Pevsner Architectural Guides: Buildings of England). London: Penguin.

Harvey, A. 2012. *Introducing Geomorphology: A Guide to Landforms and Processes.* Edinburgh: Dunedin Academic Press.

Haubold, H. 1984. *Saurierfährten* (2nd edition). Wittenberg Lutherstadt: Ziemsen Verlag.

Hayes, R. 1998. *Wyches Farm and the Stanley Estate, 1726–1997.* Wilmslow: Wilmslow Historical Society.

Heck, L. 2005. Ägyptisch Blau in NORICUM – aus NORICUM? *Jahrbuch des Landesmuseums Kärnten,* 223–39.

Henderson, W. 1860a. The Economical Treatment of Poor Copper and Other Ores – No. I. *Mining Journal*, 30: 636.

Henderson, W. 1860b. The Economical Treatment of Poor Copper and Other Ores – No. II. *Mining Journal*, 30: 686.

Henderson, W. 1860c. The Economical Treatment of Poor Copper and Other Ores – No. III. *Mining Journal*, 30: 690.

Herries, R. 1997. Sedimentology of Continental Erg–Margin Interactions. PhD thesis, University of Aberdeen.

Higgs, S. 1858. Notice of the Copper Mines, at Alderley Edge, Cheshire. *Mining Magazine*, 16 October: 692.

Higham, N. J. 1993. *The Origins of Cheshire*. Manchester: Manchester University Press.

Highways Accounts. 1775. The Accounts of … Surveyors of the Highways … for Part of the Year 1774–75. In *Parish History Series, 1: Parish Church of St Mary Alderley, Roll 22, Part 1: Surveyors Accounts 1767–1821*. Published on CD by the Family History Society of Cheshire, undated.

Highways Accounts. 1821. *The Accounts of … Surveyors of the Highways 1768–1821…*. Published on CD by the Family History Society of Cheshire, undated.

Hill, G. B. 2003. *Alderley House Trail Circuit: Purple, Blue and Gold Routes*. Alderley: AstraZeneca.

Hill, G. B. 2016. *Alderley Park Discovered*. Lancaster: Carnegie Publishing.

Hill, M. O., Preston, C. D. and Smith, A. J. E. 1991. *Atlas of the Bryophytes of Britain and Ireland, Vol. 1*. Colchester: Harley Books.

Hodgkinson, J. 2013. Apotropaic Symbols on Cast-Iron Firebacks. *Journal of the Antique Metalware Society*, 21: 14–33.

Hodgson, J. and Brennand, M. 2006. The Prehistoric Period Resource Assessment. In Brennand, M. (ed.), *The Archaeology of North West England: An Archaeological Research Framework for the North West Region, Vol. 1: Resource Assessment – Archaeology North West* 8 (issue 18), 23–58. Manchester: Council for British Archaeology North West.

Hodson, H. 1978. *Cheshire 1660–1780* (A History of Cheshire 9). Chester: Cheshire Community Council Publications Trust.

Hole, C. 1937. *Traditions and Customs of Cheshire*. London: Williams and Norgate Ltd (2nd edition, Wakefield: S. R. Publishers, 1970).

Holland, H. 1808. *General View of the Agriculture of Cheshire*. London: Board of Agriculture (printed for Richard Phillips).

Holland, H. 1811. A Sketch of the Natural History of the Cheshire Rock-Salt District. *Transactions of the Geological Society of London* (Series 1), 1: 38–61.

Holloway, S. 2002. *The Historical Atlas of Breeding Birds in Britain and Ireland: 1875–1900*. London: T. and A. D. Poyser.

Holmes, I., Chambers, A. D., Ixer, R. A., Turner, P. and Vaughan, D. J. 1983. Diagenetic Processes and the Mineralization in the Triassic of Central England. *Mineralium Deposita*, 18: 365–77.

Holt, R. 1990. Milling Technology in the Middle Ages: The Direction of Recent Research. *Industrial Archaeology Review*, 13(1): 50–8.

Hough, R. 1994. *Captain James Cook*. London: Hodder and Stoughton.

Houghton, H. H. 1986. *The Changing Landscape of Alderley Park* (Project for Certificate of Landscape History). Manchester: Manchester University Department of Extra Mural Studies.

Howard, A. S., Warrington, G., Ambrose, K. and Rees, J. G. 2008. *A Formational Framework for the Mercia Mudstone Group of England and Wales* (British Geological Survey Research Report, RR/08/04). Keyworth: British Geological Survey.

Hull, E. 1860. On the New Subdivisions of the Triassic Rocks of the Central Counties. *Transactions of the Manchester Geological Society*, 2: 21–34.

Hull, E. 1861. *Geology of the Country Around Altrincham, Cheshire* (Memoirs of the Geological Survey of England and Wales). London: HMSO.

Hull, E. 1864. On the Copper-Bearing Rocks of Alderley Edge, Cheshire. *Geological Magazine*, 1(2): 65–9.

Hull, E. 1869. *The Triassic and Permian Rocks of the Midland Counties of England* (Memoirs of the Geological Survey of England and Wales). London: HMSO.

Hull, E. and Green, A. H. 1866. *The Geology of the Country Around Stockport, Macclesfield, Congleton and Leek* (Memoirs of the Geological Survey of England and Wales, Sheets 81 NW and 81 SW). London: Longmans, Green, Reader and Dyer.

Hunt, R. (ed.). 1875. *Ure's Dictionary of Arts, Manufactures and Mines, Volume 1* (7th edition). London: Longmans, Green.

Hunt, R. 1884. *British Mining*. London: Crosby Lockwood.

Hunter, J. 1982. The Bakumatsu Textile Industry – Continuity and Change. In Nish, I. (ed.), *Bakumatsu and Meiji: Studies in Japan's Economic and Social History*, 18–38. London: London School of Economics and Political Science.

Hutton, R. 2001. *The Triumph of the Moon: A History of Modern Pagan Witchcraft*. Oxford: Oxford University Press.

Hyde, M. 1999. *The Villas of Alderley Edge*. Altrincham: Silk Press.

Hyde, M. and Pemberton, C. 2002. *Lindow and the Bog Warriors*. Wilmslow: Rex Publishing.

Imperial Institute Mineral Resources Committee. 1924. *Vanadium Ores* (Monographs on Mineral Resources with Special Reference to the British Empire). London: John Murray.

Ireland, R. I., Pollard, J. E., Steel, R. J. and Thompson, D. B. 1978. Intertidal Sediments and Trace Fossils from the Waterstones (Scythian–?Anisian) at Daresbury, Cheshire. *Proceedings of the Yorkshire Geological Society*, 41: 399–436.

Ives, E. W. (ed.). 1976. *Letters and Accounts of William Brereton of Malpas*. Manchester: Record Society of Lancashire and Cheshire (vol. 116).

Ixer, R. A. and Budd, P. 1998. The Mineralogy and Parageneses of Bronze Age Copper Ores from the British Isles: Implications for the Composition of Early Metalwork. *Oxford Journal of Archaeology*, 17(1): 15–41.

Ixer, R. A. and Stanley, C. J. 1998. Enargite Group Minerals from Scaleber Bridge, North Yorkshire, England. *Journal of the Russell Society*, 7(1): 41–2.

Ixer, R. A. and Vaughan, D. J. 1982. The Primary Ore Mineralogy of the Alderley Edge Deposit, Cheshire. *Mineralogical Magazine*, 46: 485–92.

J. Pigot and Co. 1828. *National Commercial Directory: Cheshire, Derbyshire, Nottinghamshire, Shropshire*. Manchester: J. Pigot and Co. (facsimile edition, King's Lynn: Michael Winton, 1995).

Jack, G. (ed.). 1994. *Beowulf*. Oxford: Clarendon Press.

Jackson, J. W. 1966. Sir William Boyd Dawkins (1837–1929). A Biographical Sketch. *Cave Science: Journal of the British Speleological Association*, 5: 397–412.

Jackson, P. K. and Alexander, K. N. A. 1998. *The National Trust Biological Survey (Biological Evaluation), Alderley Edge, Cheshire* (unpublished report). Cirencester: National Trust (update of Clements and Scruby, 1985).

Jackson, P. K., Lister, J. A. and Alexander, K. N. A. 1997. *Biological Evaluation: The National Trust Biological Survey, Alderley Edge, Cheshire* (unpublished report). Cirencester: National Trust Estates Department.

Jeuda, B. 1984. *Railways of the Macclesfield District*. Skipton: Wyvern Publications.

John Pritchard and Co. (auctioneers). 1938. *Alderley Park Estates Sale Catalogue (Alderley Park: Illustrated Particulars with Plans and Conditions of Sale of the Alderley Park Estates)*. No place of publication given (abbreviated as *Sale Catalogue*).

Johnson, N. C. 1984a. Brynlow Mine, Alderley Edge – An Eighteenth-Century Working. *Journal of the Derbyshire Caving Club*: 8–13.

Johnson, N. C. 1984b. Wizard's Well Mine, Alderley Edge – Early Nineteenth-Century Cobalt Workings. *Journal of the Derbyshire Caving Club*: 17–21.

Johnson, O. (illus. More, D.). 2006. *Collins Tree Guide*. London: Collins.

Johnson, R. H. 1965. Glacial Geomorphology of the West Pennine Slopes Between Cliviger and Congleton. In Whittow, J. B. and Wood, P. D. (eds), *Essays in Geography for A. A. Miller*, 58–94. Reading: Reading University Press.

Johnson, R. H. 1985. The Imprint of Glaciation on the West Pennine Uplands. In R. H. Johnson (ed.), *Geomorphology of North-West England*, 237–62. Manchester: Manchester University Press.

Johnson, R. H. 2007. A Comment on the Quaternary of the Rossendale Forest and Greater Manchester. Field Guide and Field Meeting Report. *Quaternary Newsletter*, 111: 45–6.

Jones, D. H. 1973. The Moulin Pendant. In *Transactions of the Third International Molinological Symposion of the International Molinological Society, Netherlands, 1973*, 169–73. Compiled by M. van Hoogstraten. Oosterbeek: International Molinological Society.

Jones, D. H. 1977. The Water-Powered Cornmills of England, Wales and the Isle of Man. A Preliminary Account of their Development. In Jespersen, A. (ed.), *Transactions of the Second International Symposium of the International Molinological Society, Danmark, May 1969*, 303–54. Lyngby: Danske Møllers Venner in association with the International Molinological Society.

Jones, F. 1992. *The Holy Wells of Wales*. Cardiff: University of Wales Press.

Jones, G. 2001. *The Millers: A Story of Technological Endeavour and Industrial Success, 1870–2001*. Lancaster: Carnegie.

Joy, J. 2009. *Lindow Man*. London: British Museum Press.

Kargon, R. H. 1977. *Science in Victorian Manchester*. Manchester: Manchester University Press.

Kearey, P. 2003. *Penguin Dictionary of Geology*. Harmondsworth: Penguin Books.

Keys, R. and North Staffordshire Railway Society. 1974. *The Churnet Valley Railway*. Hartington: Moorland Publishing.

Kobayashi, T. 1954. Fossil Estherians and Allied Fossils. *Tokyo Imperial University Journal of the Faculty of Science*, 9: 1–192.

Korlin, G. 2010. Luxusgut Blau – Romischer Azuritbergbau in Wallerfangen/Saar. *Der Anschnitt* 62 (April): 174–88.

Lambeck, K. 1995. Late Devensian and Holocene Shorelines of the British Isles and North Sea from Models of Glacio-Hydrostatic Rebound. *Journal of the Geological Society of London*, 152: 437–8.

Lawrence, H. 1974. *Yorkshire Pots and Potteries*. Newton Abbot: David and Charles.

Lawson, P. H. 1922. Family Memoranda of the Stanleys of Alderley, 1590–1601 and 1621–1627. *Journal of the Chester Archaeological Society*, 24(2).

Lawton, A. 1994. Beaverite from Alderley Edge, Cheshire. *UK Journal of Mines and Minerals*, 14: 9.

Leah, M. D., Wells, C. E., Appleby, C. and Huckerby, E. 1997. *The Wetlands of Cheshire* (North West Wetlands Survey No. 4). Lancaster: Lancaster Archaeological Unit.

Leahy, C. 1986. A Dated Axe-Hammer from Cleethorpes, Lincolnshire. *Proceedings of the Prehistoric Society*, 52: 143–52.

Leigh, E. 1877. *A Glossary of Words Used in the Dialect of Cheshire, Founded on a Similar Attempt by Roger Wilbraham*. London: Hamilton, Adams; Chester: Minshull and Hughes.

Lewis, A. 1990a. Underground Exploration of the Great Orme Copper Mines. In Crew, P. and Crew, S. (eds), *Early Mining in the British Isles: Proceedings of the Early Mining Workshop at Plas Tan y Bwlch, Snowdonia National Park Study Centre, 17–19 November 1989* (Occasional Paper No. 1), 5–10. Plas Tan y Bwlch.

Lewis, A. 1990b. Fire-Setting Experiments on the Great Orme. In Crew, P. and Crew, S. (eds), *Early Mining in the British Isles: Proceedings of the Early Mining Workshop at Plas Tan y Bwlch Snowdonia National Park Study Centre, Maentwrog, 1989* (Occasional Paper No. 1), 55–6. Maentwrog: Plas Tan y Bwlch.

Lewis, A. 1996. Prehistoric Mining at the Great Orme: Criteria for the Identification of Early Mining. Unpublished MPhil thesis, University of Wales, Bangor.

Lewis, C. L. E., Green, P. F., Carter, A. and Hurford, A. 1992. Elevated K/T Palaeotemperatures Throughout Northern England: Three Kilometres of Tertiary Exhumation? *Earth and Planetary Science Letters*, 112: 131–45.

Lewis, P. R. 1977. The Ogofau Roman Gold Mines at Dolaucothi. In *National Trust Year Book 1976–77*. Llandeilo: Europa Publications.

Lewis, W. J. 1967. *Lead Mining in Wales*. Cardiff: University of Wales Press.

Leycester, P. 1589. *Deposition Concerning Alderley Edge and Over Alderley as a Resource of Freestone*. Held by Cheshire Archives and Local Studies (formerly Cheshire Records Office) (CALS DLT A 75/5), Chester.

Logunov, D. V. 2003. Preliminary Survey of the Spiders, Harvestmen and False-Scorpions of Alderley Edge, Cheshire. *Newsletter of the British Arachnological Society*, 98: 4–5.

Lomas, J. 1905. Note on the Occurrence and Habitat of *Estheria* in the Trias of Britain. *Report of the British Association for the Advancement of Science*, 166–8.

Longley, D. M. T. 1987. Prehistory. In Harris, B. E. and Thacker, A. T. (eds), *A History of the County of Chester, Vol. 1: The Victoria History of the Counties of England*, 36–114. London: Oxford University Press.

Lord, T. and Howard, J. 2013. Cave Archaeology. In Waltham, T. and Lowe, D. (eds), *Caves and Karst of the Yorkshire Dales, Vol. 1*, ch. 16. Great Hucklow: British Cave Research Association.

Lovelock, J. 1963. *Life and Death Underground*. London: Bell.

Lysons, D. and Lysons, S. 1810. *Magna Britannia, Vol. 2*. London: Cadell and Davies.

Mabey, R. 1996. *Flora Britannica*. London: Sinclair-Stevenson (later editions London: Chatto and Windus).

Magurran, A. E. 1991. *Ecological Diversity and Its Measurement*. London: Chapman and Hall.

Maidwell, F. T. 1914. Notes on Footprints from the Keuper II: The 'Fereday Smith' Footprint Slab in the Manchester Museum. *Proceedings of the Liverpool Geological Society*, 12: 53–71.

Manchester Field-Naturalists' and Archaeologists' Society. 1861. *Report and Proceedings*. Manchester: Manchester Field-Naturalists' and Archaeologists' Society.

Manning, D. A. C. 1990. The Copper Mineralisation of Alderley Edge. New Views on a Well Known Viewpoint. *Amateur Geologist*, 8: 50–2.

Manning, W. H. 1968. The Dolaucothi Gold Mines. *Antiquity*, 42: 299–303.

Margary, I. D. 1957. *Roman Roads in Britain, Vol. 2*. London: Phoenix House.

Marriott, W. 1810. *The Antiquities of Lyme and Its Vicinity*. Stockport: the author.

Maruskin, J. 1980. Listening to the Printed Text. *Folklore*, 91: 41–5.

Mattingly, H. and Sydenham, E. A. 1926. *Roman Imperial Coinage, Vol. 2: Vespasian to Hadrian*. London: Spink and Son (reprinted 1968, 1972, etc.).

McKee, E. D. and Bigarella, J. J. 1972. Deformational Structures in Brazilian Coastal Dunes. *Journal of Sedimentary Petrology*, 42(3): 670–81.

McKenna, L. 1994. *Timber Framed Buildings in Cheshire*. Chester: Cheshire County Council, Environmental Planning.

Meteyard, E. 1871. *A Group of Englishmen (1795–1815), Being Records of the Younger Wedgwoods and Their Friends*. London: Longmans Green.

Michell, J. 1846. On the Argentiferous Lead Mines of the Sierra Almagrera, on the South-East Coast of Spain. *Transactions of the Royal Geological Society of Cornwall*, 6: 308–15.

Michell, J. and the Govenors of Kings School, Macclesfield. 1860. *Indenture re the Lease of Lands at Kirkleyditch and Mottram St Andrew for Mining*. Macclesfield: Procter, Solicitor.

Middle English Dictionary. 1954–. Kurath, Hans and Kuhn, S. M. (eds). Ann Arbor, MI: University of Michigan Press.

Mikklesen, P. W. and Floodpage, J. B. 1997. The Hydrocarbon Potential of the Cheshire Basin. In Meadows, N. S., Trueblood, S. P., Hardman, M. and Cowan, G. (eds), *Petroleum Geology of the Irish Sea and Adjacent Areas* (Geological Society Special Publication No. 124), 161–83. London: Geological Society.

Milln, J. and Prag, J. 1995. *Alderley Edge Landscape Project: Research Proposal September 1995*. Shrewsbury: National Trust; Manchester: Manchester Museum.

Milln, J., King, C., Kidd, A. D., Taylor, E. and Woodside, R. 2005. Archaeological Excavation and Conservation at Saddlebole and on the Quarry Road, Alderley Edge. In Timberlake, S. and Prag, A. J. N. W. (eds), *The Archaeology of Alderley Edge: Survey, Excavation and Experiment in an Ancient Mining Landscape* (British Archaeological Reports, British Series 396), 169–87. Oxford: John and Erica Hedges.

Milodowski, A. E., Strong, G. E., Shepherd, T. J., Spiro, B., Kemp, S. J., Hyslop, E. K., Jones, D. G., Leng, M. J., Haslam, H. W., Bradley, A. D., Nicholson, R. A. and Warrington, G. 1999. Diagenesis of the Permo-Triassic Rocks. In Plant, J. A., Jones, D. G. and Haslam, H. W. (eds), *The Cheshire Basin: Basin Evolution, Fluid Movement and Mineral Resources in a Permo-Triassic Rift Setting*, 125–75. Keyworth: British Geological Survey.

Mining Records Office. 1878. *Abandonment Plan of the Alderley Edge Mines* (Plan 882/1) (retraced 1932 in the Mines Records Office). London: Mining Records Office.

Mitford, N. (ed.). 1938. *The Ladies of Alderley, Being the Letters Between Maria Josepha, Lady Stanley and Her Daughter-in-Law, Henrietta Maria Stanley (1841–1850)*. London: Chapman and Hall (2nd edition, London: Hamish Hamilton, 1967, from which quotations in the text are taken).

Mitford, N. (ed.). 1939. *The Stanleys of Alderley. Their Letters Between the Years 1851–1865*. London: Chapman and Hall (2nd edition, London: Hamish Hamilton, 1968, from which quotations in the text are taken).

Mohr, P. A. 1964. *On the Copper-Mineralised Sandstones of Alderley Edge, England, and of Chercher, Ethiopia, and the Problem of Their Genesis. An Essay on Red Bed Copper Deposits* (Contributions from the Geophysical Observatory). Addis Ababa: Haile Sellassie I University.

Morgan, V. B. and Paul, E. 2004. *Prehistoric Cheshire*. Ashbourne: Landmark Publishing.

Morgan Rees, D. 1975. *The Industrial Archaeology of Wales*. Newton Abbot: David and Charles.

Morrill, J. S. 1974. *Cheshire, 1630–1660. County Government and Society During the English Revolution*. London: Oxford University Press.

Morris, C. 1949. *The Journeys of Celia Fiennes*. London: Cresset Press.

Morris, J. (gen. ed.). 1978. *Domesday Book, Vol. 26: Cheshire* (ed. Morgan, P.). Chichester: Phillimore.

Moss, F. 1898. *Folk-Lore: Old Customs and Tales of My Neighbours*. Didsbury: the author.

Moss, F. 1903. *Pilgrimages to Old Homes Mostly on the Cheshire Border*. Didsbury: the author (reprinted 1972, Manchester: E. J. Morten).

Mottershead, G. and King, C. 2005 *Stormy Point and Pillar Mine, Alderley Edge, Cheshire: A Detailed Archaeological Survey*. University of Manchester Archaeological Unit Report (unpublished report to the National Trust, available from National Trust Cheshire and Wirral Countryside Office, Macclesfield Road, Nether Alderley, Macclesfield, Cheshire SK10 4UB, email alderleyedge@nationaltrust.org.uk).

Mottershead, G. and Wright, J. 2008. *Stormy Point, Alderley Edge, Cheshire: An Archaeological Evaluation.* University of Manchester Archaeological Unit Report (unpublished report to the National Trust, available from National Trust Cheshire and Wirral Countryside Office, Macclesfield Road, Nether Alderley, Macclesfield, Cheshire SK10 4UB, email alderleyedge@nationaltrust.org.uk).

Mountney, N. P. and Thompson, D. B. 2002. Stratigraphic Evolution and Preservation of Aeolian Dune and Damp/Wet Interdune Strata: An Example from the Triassic Helsby Sandstone Formation, Cheshire Basin, UK. *Sedimentology*, 49: 805–33.

Mundil, R., Pálfy, J., Renne, P. R. and Brack, P. 2010. *The Triassic Timescale: New Constraints and a Review of Geochronological Data* (Geological Society Special Publication No. 334): 41–60. London: Geological Society.

Naylor, H., Turner, P., Vaughan, D. J., Boyce, A. J. and Fallick, A. E. 1989. Genetic Studies of Red-Bed Mineralization in the Triassic of the Cheshire Basin, Northwest England. *Journal of the Geological Society, London*, 146(4): 685–99.

Needham, S. 1980. A Bronze from Winterfold Heath, Wonersh, and Its Place in the British Narrow-Bladed Palstave Sequence. *Surrey Archaeological Collections*, 72: 37–47.

Nevell, M. 1996a. The 'Pot Shaft' Roman Coin Hoard: A Preliminary Note. *Archaeology North West: The Bulletin of CBA North West*, 2(4): 96–8.

Nevell, M. 1996b. *The 'Pot Shaft' Hoard, Alderley Edge, Cheshire: Coins in Context.* University of Manchester Archaeological Unit, December (report 46).

Nevell, M. 1999. Iron Age and Romano-British Rural Settlement in North-West England: Theory, Marginality and Settlement. In Nevell, M. (ed.), *Living on the Edge: Models, Methodology and Marginality – Late Prehistoric and Romano-British Settlement in North West England. Archaeology North West* 3(13): 14–26. Manchester: CBA North West/University of Manchester Field Archaeology Centre; Chester: Chester Archaeology.

Newton, A. 1971. *Flora of Cheshire.* Chester: Cheshire Community Council Publications Trust.

Newton, A. 1990. *Supplement to the Flora of Cheshire.* Leamington Spa: Alan Newton.

Nickel, E. H. 1995. Definition of a Mineral. *Mineralogical Magazine*, 59(4): 767–8.

Norman, D. 2008. *Birds in Cheshire and Wirral.* Liverpool: Liverpool University Press.

Norris, J. H. 1969. *The Water-Powered Corn Mills of Cheshire.* Manchester: Lancashire and Cheshire Antiquarian Society.

Nudds, J. R. 1998. A Derived Coral Fauna in Triassic Sediments at Alderley Edge. *North West Geologist*, 8: 46–52.

O'Meara, J. J. (transl.). 1982. *The History and Topography of Ireland by Giraldus Cambrensis* (revised edition). Mountrath: Dolmen Press; Atlantic Highlands, NJ: Humanities Press.

Ormerod, G. 1882. *The History of the County Palatine and City of Chester, Vols 1–3* (3rd edition, ed. Helsby, T.). London: Routledge; Manchester: E. J. Morten (reprinted 1980).

Owen, P. 2001. *Report on St Hilary's Boundary Bank.* Chester: Gifford and Partners. Unpublished, copy in AELP Archive, no. 10553.

Owen, R. 1842. Description of the Extinct Lacertilian Reptile, *Rhynchosaurus articeps* Owen, of which the Bones and Footprints Characterise the Upper New Red Sandstone at Grinshill, Shropshire. *Proceedings of Cambridge Philosophical Society*, 7: 255–368.

Page, N. 2005. Industrial Complex and Timber Trackway at Llancynfelin, Ceredigion. *Archaeology in Wales*, 45: 103–4.

Paton, J. A. 1999. *The Liverwort Flora of the British Isles.* Colchester: Harley Books.

Peacock, W. F. 1860. *Our Pic-Nic Excursion to Alderley Edge.* Manchester: John Heywood.

Pettus, J. 1670. *Fodinae Regales.* London: Thomas Basset.

Phillips, J. A. 1896. *A Treatise on Ore Deposits* (2nd edition, rewritten and greatly enlarged by Henry Louis). London: Macmillan.

Pickford, D. 1992. *Myths and Legends of East Cheshire and the Moorlands: A Cabinet of Curiosities.* Wilmslow: Sigma Leisure.

Pickin, J. 1990. Stone Tools and Early Metal Mining in England and Wales. In Crew, P. and Crew, S. (eds), *Early Mining in the British Isles: Proceedings of the Early Mining Workshop at Plas Tan y Bwlch Snowdonia National Park Study Centre, Maentwrog, 1989* (Occasional Paper No. 1), 39–42. Maentwrog: Plas Tan y Bwlch.

Pickin, J. 1991. Site No. 8: Alderley Edge. In Blick, C. R. (ed.), *Early Metallurgical Sites in Great Britain: BC 2000 to AD 1500*, 66–71. London: Institute of Metals.

Plant, J. A., Ball, D. F., Bradley, A. D., Chadwick, R. A., Evans, D. J., Jones, D. G., Kirby, G. A., Milodowski, A. E., Nicholson, R. A., Shepherd, T. J., Smith, N. J. P., Warrington, G. and Wilson, A. A. 1999. Resources of the Basin: Base Metals, Industrial Mineral, Hydrocarbons and Groundwater. In Plant, J. A., Jones, D. G. and Haslam, H. W. (eds), *The Cheshire Basin:*

Basin Evolution, Fluid Movement and Mineral Resources in a Permo-Triassic Rift Setting, 210–39. Keyworth: British Geological Survey.

Plant, R. 1881. *History of Cheadle in Staffordshire, and Neighbouring Places.* Leek: William Clemesha.

Pocock, T. I. 1906. *The Geology of the Country Around Macclesfield, Congleton, Crewe and Middlewich* (Memoirs of the Geological Survey, England and Wales) (1st edition). London: HMSO.

Pocock, T. I. 1938. The Glacial Deposits Between North Wales and the Pennine Range. *Zeitschrift für Gletscherkunde,* 26: 52–69.

Pollard, J. E. 1981. A Comparison Between the Triassic Trace Fossils of Cheshire and South Germany. *Palaeontology,* 24: 555–88.

Pollard, J. E. 1985. *Isopodichnus,* Related Arthropod Trace Fossils and Notostracans from Triassic Fluvial Sediments. *Transactions of the Royal Society of Edinburgh: Earth Sciences,* 76: 273–85.

Portland, P. 2002. *Around Haunted Manchester.* Purley: AMCD Books.

Potter, F. 1970. A History of Alderley: The Mysterious Wizard and Holy Well. *Alderley and Wilmslow Advertiser,* 6 February, p. 26.

Prag, A. J. N. W. 1994. Note on a Bronze Age Shovel from Alderley Edge. In Hedges, R. E. M., Housley, R. A., Bronk Ramsey, C. and van Klinken, G. J. (eds), *Radiocarbon Dates from the Oxford AMS System: Archaeometry Datelist, Vol. 18. Archaeometry,* 36: 355–6.

Prag, J., Garner, A. and Housley, R. 1994. The Alderley Edge Shovel: An Epic in Three Acts. *Current Archaeology,* 12(5): 172–5 (reprinted in Garner 1997: 184–92).

Pyatt, F. B., Beaumont, E. H., Buckland, P. C., Lacy, D., Magilton, J. R. and Storey, D. M. 1995. Mobilisation of Elements from the Bog Bodies Lindow II and III and Some Observations on Bog Body Painting. In Turner, R. C. and Scaife R. G. (eds), *Bog Bodies: New Discoveries and New Perspectives,* 62–73. London: British Museum Press.

Quarter Sessions ... Chester, 1559–1760. See Bennett and Dewhurst (1940).

Rackham, O. 1994. *The Illustrated History of the Countryside.* London: Weidenfield and Nicholson.

Railton, C. W. 1935. A History of Alderley Edge (With Some Recollections of Old Days). In Railton, C. W. and Gravell, W. J. *The Story of Alderley Edge and Its Parish Church,* 5–20. Gloucester: British Publishing.

Railton, C. W. and Maltby, K. M. 1971. *The Story of Alderley Edge and Its Church* (2nd edition). Gloucester: British Publishing.

Raistrick, A. (ed.). 1967. *The Hatchett Diary.* Truro: D. Bradford Barton.

Raistrick, A. 1977. *Two Centuries of Industrial Welfare.* Hartington: Moorland Publishing.

Rees, W. 1968. *Industry Before the Industrial Revolution. Incorporating a Study of the Chartered Companies of the Society of Mines Royal and of Mineral and Battery Works, Vol. 2.* Cardiff: University of Wales Press.

Renouard, Y. (ed.). 1962. *Gascon Rolls Preserved in the Public Record Office.* London: HMSO.

Richardson, J. B. 1974. *Metal Mining* (Industrial Archaeology Series) (general ed. Rolt, L. T. C.). London: Allen Lane.

Roe, F. 1967. The Battle-Axes, Maceheads and Axe-Hammers from South-West Scotland. *Transactions of the Dumfries and Galloway Natural History and Antiquarian Society,* 44: 57–80.

Roe, F. 1979. Typology of Stone Implements with Shaft-Holes. In Clough, T. H. McK. and Cummins, W. A. (eds), *Stone Axe Studies, Vol. 1* (CBA Research Report 2), 23–48. London: Council for British Archaeology.

Roeder, C. 1901. Prehistoric and Subsequent Mining at Alderley Edge, with a Sketch of the Archaeological Features of the Neighbourhood. *Transactions of the Lancashire and Cheshire Antiquarian Society,* 19: 77–118.

Roeder, C. and Graves, F. S. 1905a. Recent Archaeological Discoveries at Alderley Edge. *Transactions of the Lancashire and Cheshire Antiquarian Society,* 23: 17–29.

Roeder, C. and Graves, F. S. 1905b. MSS papers ('the Roeder MSS'), Archives Department, Manchester Central Reference Library.

Rohl, B. and Needham, S. 1998. *The Circulation of Metal in the British Bronze Age: The Application of Lead Isotope Analysis* (Occasional Paper No. 102). London: British Museum.

Roman Imperial Coinage (RIC) – see Mattingly and Sydenham (1926).

Roscoe, H. E. 1868a. On Vanadium, One of the Trivalent Group of Elements. *Notices of Proceedings at the Meetings of the Members of the Royal Institution,* 5: 287–94.

Roscoe, H. E. 1868b. Researches on Vanadium. *Philosophical Transactions of the Royal Society of London,* 158: 1–27.

Roscoe, H. E. 1876a. On Two New Vanadium Minerals. *Proceedings of the Royal Society of London,* 25: 109–12.

Roscoe, H. E. 1876b. Recent Discoveries About Vanadium. *Notices of Proceedings at the Meetings of the Members of the Royal Institution*, 8: 221–30.

Roscoe, H. E. 1906. *The Life and Experiences of Sir Henry Enfield Roscoe, D.C.L., LL.D., F.R.S. Written by Himself.* London: Macmillan.

Ross, A. 1986. Lindow Man and the Celtic Tradition. In Stead, I. M., Bourke, J. B. and Brothwell, D. (eds). *Lindow Man: The Body in the Bog*, 162–9. London: British Museum Press.

Rowe, J. P. 1994. Evolution of Palaeofluid Flow in the East Irish Sea Basin and Its Margins. PhD thesis, University of Manchester.

Rowe, J. P. and Burley, S. D. 1997. Faulting and Porosity Modification in the Sherwood Sandstone at Alderley Edge, Northeastern Cheshire: An Exhumed Example of Fault-Related Diagenesis. In Meadows, N. S., Trueblood, S. P., Hardman, M. and Cowan, G. (eds), *Petroleum Geology of the Irish Sea and Adjacent Areas* (Geological Society Special Publication No. 124), 325–52. London: Geological Society.

Rowley, G. D. 1982. *Macclesfield in Prehistory.* Macclesfield: the author.

Rumble, A. R. 1997. *The Place-Names of Cheshire. Part V: 2. Introduction, Linguistic Notes and Indexes with Appendixes* (English Place-Name Society, 74). Cambridge: Cambridge University Press.

Russell, A. 1919. Report on the Mineralisation of Alderley Edge. Unpublished; typescript copy in Manchester Museum.

Ryback, G., Clark, A. M. and Stanley, C. J. 1998. Reexamination of the A. W. G. Kingsbury Collection of British Minerals at the Natural History Museum, London. *Geological Curator*, 6(9): 317–22.

Rylands, J. P. (ed.). 1882. *The Visitation of Cheshire 1580.* London: Harleian Society Publications.

Sainter, J. D. 1878. *The Jottings of Some Geological, Archaeological, Botanical, Ornithological and Zoological Rambles Round Macclesfield.* Macclesfield: Swinnerton and Brown.

Sale Catalogue – see John Pritchard and Co. (auctioneers) (1938).

Sarjeant, W. A. S. 1974. History and Bibliography of the Study of Fossil Vertebrate Footprints in the British Isles. *Palaeogeography, Palaeoclimatology, Palaeoecology*, 16: 265–379.

Schama, S. 1995. *Landscape and Memory.* London: HarperCollins.

Schunck, E. 1897. President's Address. *Journal of the Society of Chemical Industry*, 16: 586–94.

Selley, R. C. 1982. *An Introduction to Sedimentology* (2nd edition). London: Academic Press.

Shaw, M. 2009. *The Lead, Copper and Barytes Mines of Shropshire.* Woonton Almeley: Logaston Press.

Shawcross, G. N. 1933. The Building of the Beacon Tower on Rivington Pike. *Transactions of the Lancashire and Cheshire Antiquarian Society*, 44: 150–8.

Shimwell, D. W. and Hradil, I. W. 1998. Analysis of Environmental Samples from Excavations at Alderley Edge, unpublished report by the Palaeo-ecological Research Unit (PERU), Department of Geography, University of Manchester.

Shone, W. 1911. *Prehistoric Man in Cheshire.* Chester: Minshull and Meeson.

Smith, A. D., Green, D. I., Charnock, J. M., Pantos, E., Timberlake, S. and Prag, A. J. N. W. 2011. Natural Preservation Mechanisms at Play in a Bronze Age Wooden Shovel Found in the Copper Mines of Alderley Edge. *Journal of Archaeological Science*, 38(11): 3029–37 (doi:10.1016/j.jas.2011.06.036).

Smith, A. H. 1961. *English Place-Name Elements, Part 1* (English Place-Name Society, 25). Cambridge: Cambridge University Press.

Smith, A. J. E. 1982. *Bryophyte Ecology.* London: Chapman and Hall.

Smith, G. J. 1993. Green Fluorescence from the Hair of Lindow Man. *Antiquity*, 67(254): 117–19.

Smyth, W. W. 1846. *On the Mining District of Cardiganshire and Montgomeryshire* (Geological Survey of the United Kingdom. Memoirs of the Geological Survey, Vol. 2).

Sowerby, J. 1811. *British Mineralogy: Or Coloured Figures Intended to Elucidate the Mineralogy of Great Britain, Vol. 4.* London: Richard Taylor.

Stace, C. A. 1997. *A New Flora of the British Isles* (2nd edition). Cambridge: Cambridge University Press.

Stanier, P. 1985. *Quarries and Quarrying.* Princes Risborough: Shire Publications.

Stanier, P. 2000. *Stone Quarry Landscapes.* Stroud: Tempus Publishing.

Stanley, A. P. 1880. *Memoirs of Edward and Catherine Stanley.* London: John Murray.

Stanley, E. 1805–17. *Account Book.* Held by Cheshire Archives and Local Studies (formerly Cheshire Records Office), Chester (CALS P143/13/1).

Stanley, E. 1835. *A Familiar History of Birds.* London: J. W. Parker and Son (numerous editions, including the next entry, the last being London: Longmans, Green, 1902).

Stanley, E. 1881. *A Familiar History of Birds* (9th edition). London: Longmans, Green.

Stanley, J. T. 1830–44. *Genealogical Manuscript Book*. Copy in AELP archive, no. 3. Original held by St Mary's Church, Nether Alderley until 2011, now in Cheshire Archives and Local Studies (CALS) as D 8065/1 (abbreviated in this book as *Stanley Notebook*). A companion notebook is in the Stanley Archive in Cheshire Archives and Local Studies (CALS) as DSA 3752/1.

Stanley, L. D. 1843. *Alderley Edge and Its Neighbourhood*. Macclesfield: Swinnerton (published anonymously; republished Didsbury: E. Morten, 1972).

Stanley, T. (Lord Stanley of Alderley). 2002. *The Stanleys of Alderley 1927–2001* (revised edition). Purley: AMCD.

Stanley C7 – see *Stanley Estate Book, 1800–1808*.

Stanley Estate Book, 1800–1808 (includes Stanley, J. T. and Holland, J. 1807. *Survey and Valuation of Nether Alderley*). Manchester Archives and Local Studies Centre: C7, mf2678 (abbreviated in this book as *Stanley C7*).

Stanley Notebook – see Stanley (1830–44).

Stead, I. M., Bourke, J. B. and Brothwell, D. (eds). 1986. *Lindow Man: The Body in the Bog*. London: British Museum Press.

Steel, R. J. and Thompson, D. B. 1983. Structures and Textures in Triassic Braided Stream Conglomerates ('Bunter' Pebble Beds) in the Sherwood Sandstone Group, North Staffordshire, England. *Sedimentology*, 30: 341–67.

Sterry, P. 2007. *Collins Complete Guide to British Trees*. London: Collins.

Steuer, H. and Zimmermann, U. (eds). 1993. *Montanarchäologie in Europa: Berichte zum Internationalen Kolloquium 'Frühe Erzgewinnung und Verhüttung in Europa' in Freiburg im Breisgau vom 4. bis 7. Oktober 1990*. Sigmaringen: J. Thorbecke Verlag.

Summerfield, C. 2013. Landscape of Remembrance. *British Archaeology*, 128: 30–5.

Summerfield, M. A. 1991. *Global Geomorphology*. Harlow: Longman Scientific and Technical.

Sylvester, D. 1956. The Open Fields of Cheshire. *Transactions of the Historic Society of Lancashire and Cheshire*, 108: 1–33.

Sylvester, D. 1960. The Manor and the Cheshire Landscape. *Transactions of the Lancashire and Cheshire Antiquarian Society*, 70: 1–15.

Tait, J. 1916. *The Domesday Survey of Cheshire* (Remains Historical and Literary Connected with the Palatine Counties of Lancaster and Cheshire (New Series), 75). Manchester: Chetham Society.

Taylor, B. J. 1958. Cemented Shear Planes in the Pleistocene Middle Sands of Lancashire and Cheshire. *Proceedings of the Yorkshire Geological Society*, 31: 359–66.

Taylor, B. J., Price, R. H. and Trotter, F. M. 1963. *Geology of the Country Around Stockport and Knutsford* (One-Inch Geological Sheet 98, New Series) (Memoirs of the British Geological Survey). London: HMSO.

Taylor, G. and Beck, B. 1976. The Microbiology of West Mine at Alderley Edge. *North-Western Naturalist*, 47(24): 14–16.

Taylor, J. F. and Michell, J. 1860. *Indenture re the Lease of Lands at Kirkleyditch, Mottram St Andrew for Mining* (transcribed by N. Dibben). Macclesfield: Brocklehurst, Solicitors.

Thackray, C. (ed.). 1994. *The National Trust Annual Archaeological Review*, 3.

Thomas Morris and Co. 1874. *Morris and Co.'s Commercial Directory and Gazetteer of Cheshire*. Nottingham: Thomas Morris and Co.

Thompson, D. B. 1966. Some Aspects of the Stratigraphy and Sedimentology of the N.E. of the Permo-Triassic Cheshire Basin, with Special Reference to the Lower Keuper Sandstone Formation. MSc thesis, University of Manchester.

Thompson, D. B. 1969. Dome-Shaped Aeolian Dunes in the Frodsham Member of the So-Called 'Keuper' Sandstone Formation (Scythian–?Anisian; Triassic) at Frodsham, Cheshire, England. *Sedimentary Geology*, 3: 263–89.

Thompson, D. B. 1970a. The Stratigraphy of the So-Called Keuper Sandstone Formation in the Permo-Triassic Cheshire Basin. *Quarterly Journal of the Geological Society of London*, 126: 151–81.

Thompson, D. B. 1970b. Sedimentation of the Triassic (Scythian) Red Pebbly Sandstones in the Cheshire Basin and Its Margins. *Geological Journal*, 7: 183–216.

Thompson, D. B. 1970c. Triassic Itineraries. In Broadhurst, F. M., Eagar, R. M. C., Jackson, J. W., Simpson, I. M. and Thompson, D. B. (ed. Hester, S.W.). *The Area Around Manchester* (Geologists' Association Guide No. 7), 39–51. Colchester: Benham.

Thompson, D. B. 1984. *Field Excursion to the Permo-Triassic of the Cheshire, Irish Sea, Needwood and Stafford Basins* (Poroperm Excursion Guide No. 4). Chester: Poroperm Geochem.

Thompson, D. B. 1985. *Field Excursion to the Permo-Triassic of the Cheshire – East Irish Sea – Needwood and Stafford Basins* (Poroperm Excursion Guide No. 4) (3rd edition). Chester: Poroperm Geochem.

Thompson, D. B. 1991. Itineraries VIII–XI, Triassic Rocks of the Cheshire basin. In Eagar, R. M. C., Broadhurst, F. M., with contributions by Adams, A. E., Braithwaite, R. S. W., Johnson, R. H., Riley, K., Selden, P., Simpson, I. M. and Thompson, D. B. (ed. Greensmith, J. T.). *Geology of the Manchester Area* (Geologists' Association Guide No. 7) (2nd edition), 57–81. London: Geologists' Association.

Thompson, D. B. and Winchester, J. A. 1995. Field Relationships, Geochemistry, and Tectonic Context of the Tertiary Dyke Suites in Staffordshire and Shropshire, Central England. *Proceedings of the Yorkshire Geological Society*, 50: 191–208.

Thompson, D. B. and Worsley, P. 1966. A Late Pleistocene Marine Molluscan Fauna from the Drifts of the Cheshire Plain. *Geological Journal*, 5: 197–207.

Thompson, D. B and Worsley, P. 1967. Periods of Ventifact Formation in the Permo-Triassic and Quaternary of the North East Cheshire Basin. *Mercian Geologist*, 2: 279–98.

Timberlake, S. 2003. *Excavations on Copa Hill, Cwmystwyth (1986–1999). An Early Bronze Copper Mine Within the Uplands of Central Wales* (British Archaeological Reports, British Series 348). Oxford: John and Erica Hedges.

Timberlake, S. 2007. The Use of Experimental Archaeology/Archaeometallurgy for the Understanding and Reconstruction of Early Bronze Age Mining and Smelting Technology. In La Niece, S., Hook, D. and Craddock P. (eds), *Metals and Mines: Studies in Archaeometallurgy*, 27–36. London: Archetype Publications and British Museum.

Timberlake, S. 2009. Copper Mining and Production at the Beginning of the British Bronze Age. In Clark, P. (ed.), *Bronze Age Connections: Cultural Contact in Prehistoric Europe*, 94–121. Oxford: Oxbow Books.

Timberlake, S. 2010. Geological, Mineralogical and Environmental Controls on the Extraction of Copper Ores in the British Bronze Age. In Anreiter, P., Goldenberg, G., *et al.*, *Mining in European History and Its Impact on Environment and Human Societies: Proceedings for the 1st Mining in European History – Conference of the SFB-HIMAT, November 2009*. Innsbruck: Innsbruck University Press.

Timberlake, S. 2014. Prehistoric Copper Extraction in Britain: Ecton Hill, Staffordshire. *Proceedings of the Prehistoric Society*, 80: 159–206.

Timberlake, S. and Mills, S. 2003. The Use of a Portable XRF Within an Early Nineteenth Century Cobalt Mine of Alderley Edge, Cheshire. *Journal of Mines and Minerals*, 23: 41–6.

Timberlake, S. and Prag, A. J. N. W. (eds). 2005. *The Archaeology of Alderley Edge: Survey, Excavation and Experiment in an Ancient Mining Landscape* (British Archaeological Reports, British Series 396). Oxford: John and Erica Hedges (abbreviated throughout the text as *ArchAE*).

Tindall, A. 1995. Other News. *Cheshire Past*, 4: 23.

Tindle, A. G. 2008. *Minerals of Britain and Ireland*. Harpenden: Terra Publishing.

Todd, M. 1996. Ancient Mining on Mendip, Somerset: A Preliminary Report on Recent Work. In Newman, P. (ed.), *The Archaeology of Mining and Metallurgy in South West-Britain*, 47–51. Matlock Bath: Peak District Mines Historical Society and the Historical Metallurgy Society.

Tooke, A. W. 1837. The Mineral Topography of Great Britain. *Mining Review*, 4 (New Series 1) (9): 39–60.

Tresise, G. and Sarjeant, W. A. S. 1997. *The Tracks of Triassic Vertebrates: Fossil Evidence from North-West England*. London: HMSO.

Trotter, F. M. and Taylor, B. J. 1946–51, 1963. Six-Inch 1:10650 Geological Maps of the Alderley Edge Area: SJ 87 NW and NE. Keyworth: British Geological Survey archives.

Tucker, G. D. 1987. Millstone Making in England. *Industrial Archaeology Review*, 9(2): 167–88.

Turner, R. C. and Scaife, R. G. (eds). 1995. *Bog Bodies: New Discoveries and New Perspectives*. London: British Museum Press.

Walker, T. R. 1967. Formation of Red Beds in Modern and Ancient Deserts. *Bulletin of the Geological Society of America*, 78: 353–68.

Walker, T. R. 1976. Diagenetic Origin of Continental Red Beds. In Falke, H. (ed.), *The Continental Permian in Central, West and South Europe*. Dordrecht: D. Reidel.

Waltham, T. and Lowe, D. (eds). 2013. *Caves and Karst of the Yorkshire Dales, Vol. 1*. Great Hucklow: British Cave Research Association.

Ward, P. 1982. Mottram Mine, Cheshire. *Mineral Realm*, 2: 11–13.

Warrington, G. 1963. The Occurrence of the Branchiopod Crustacean *Euestheria* in the

Keuper Sandstone of Alderley Edge, Cheshire. *Liverpool and Manchester Geological Journal*, 3: 315–19.

Warrington, G. 1965. The Metalliferous Mining District of Alderley Edge, Cheshire, with a Note on Copper Production by Trevor Ford. *Mercian Geologist*, 1: 111–31.

Warrington, G. 1970. The 'Keuper' Series of the British Trias in the Northern Irish Sea and Neighbouring Areas. *Nature*, 226: 254–6.

Warrington, G. 1980. The Alderley Edge Mining District. *Amateur Geologist*, 8(1): 4–13.

Warrington, G. 1981. The Copper Mines of Alderley Edge and Mottram St Andrew, Cheshire. *Journal of the Chester Archaeological Society*, 64: 47–73.

Warrington, G. 1995. North Shropshire Copper Mines. In Pearce, A. (ed.), *Mining in Shropshire*, 19–26. Shrewsbury: Shropshire Books.

Warrington, G. 2010. Alderley Edge District, Cheshire. In Bevins, R. E., Young, B., Mason, J. S., Manning, D. A. C. and Symes, R. F. (eds), *Mineralization of England and Wales* (Geological Conservation Review Series 36), 182–90. Peterborough: Joint Nature Conservation Committee.

Warrington, G. and Ivimey-Cook, H. C. 1992. Triassic. In Cope, J. C. W., Ingham, J. K. and Rawson, P. F. (eds), *Atlas of Palaeogeography and Lithofacies* (Memoir 13), 97–106. London: Geological Society.

Warrington, G. and Thompson, D. B. 1971. The Triassic rocks of Alderley Edge, Cheshire. *Mercian Geologist*, 4: 69–72.

Warrington, G., Audley Charles, M. G., Elliott, R. E., Evans, W. B., Ivimey-Cook, H. C., Kent, P. E., Robinson, P. L., Shotton, F. W. and Taylor, F. M. 1980. *A Correlation of Triassic Rocks in the British Isles* (Special Report of the Geological Society of London, No. 13). Oxford: Blackwell.

Warrington, G., Wilson, A. A., Jones, N. S., Young, S. R. and Haslam, H. W. 1999. Stratigraphy and Sedimentology. In Plant, J. A., Jones, D. G. and Haslam, H. W. (eds), *The Cheshire Basin: Basin Evolution, Fluid Movement and Mineral Resources in a Permo-Triassic Rift Setting*, 10–40. Keyworth: British Geological Survey.

Watts, M. 2002. *The Archaeology of Mills and Milling*. Stroud: Tempus.

Watts, V. (ed.). 2004. *The Cambridge Dictionary of English Place-Names*. Cambridge: Cambridge University Press.

Wedepohl, K. H. 1978. *Handbook of Geochemistry*. Berlin: Springer.

White and Co. 1860. *History, Gazetteer and Directory of Cheshire: Comprising a General Survey of the County, with Separate Historical and Topographical Descriptions of All the Boroughs, Towns, Parishes, Chapelries, Townships, Villages, Hamlets and Extra-Parochial Liberties … with a Large Coloured Sheet Map of the County, from the Ordnance Survey, Engraved Expressly for the Work*. Sheffield: Francis White.

Whitten, D. G. A. and Brooks, J. R. V. 1972. *A Dictionary of Geology*. Harmondsworth: Penguin Books.

Williams, A. and Martin, G. H. (eds). 2003. *Domesday Book. A Complete Translation*. London: Alecto Historical Editions; Penguin Books.

Willies, L. 1975. The Washing of Lead Ore in Derbyshire During the Nineteenth Century. *Mining History (Bulletin of the Peak District Mines Historical Society)*, 6: 53–63.

Willies, L. 1990. Derbyshire Lead Smelting in the Eighteenth and Nineteenth Centuries. *Mining History (Bulletin of the Peak District Mines Historical Society)*, 11: 1–19.

Willies, L. 1997. Roman Mining at Rio Tinto, Huelva. *Mining History (Bulletin of the Peak District Mines Historical Society)*, 13(3): 1–17.

Wilson, A. A. 1993. The Mercia Mudstone Group (Trias) of the Cheshire Basin. *Proceedings of the Yorkshire Geological Society*, 49(3): 171–88.

Winchester, A. 1990. *Discovering Parish Boundaries*. Princes Risborough: Shire Publications.

Wood, M. 2010. *The Story of England*. London: Viking Penguin.

Woodcock, N. H. and Strachan, R. 2000. *Geological History of Britain and Ireland*. Oxford: Blackwell.

Worsley, P. 1985. Pleistocene History of the Cheshire–Shropshire Plain. In Johnson, R. H. (ed.), *The Geomorphology of North-West England*, 201–21. Manchester: Manchester University Press.

Worsley, P. 1991. Glacial Deposits of the Lowlands Between the Severn and Mersey Rivers. In Ehlers, J., Gibbard, P. L. and Rose, J. (eds), *Glacial Deposits in Great Britain and Ireland*, 203–12. Rotterdam: Balkema.

Worsley, P. 1992. A Pre-Devensian Mammoth from Arclid, Cheshire. *Proceedings of the Geologists Association*, 103(1): 75–7.

Worsley, P. 2005. Quaternary Geology of the Chelford Area. In Crofts, R. G. (ed.), *Quaternary of the Rossendale Forest and Greater Manchester: Field Guide*, 57–70. London: Quaternary Research Association.

Worthington, T. and Craddock, B. 1996. Modern Stone Tools. *Mining History (Bulletin of the Peak District Mines Historical Society)*, 13: 58.

Yaliz, A. M. 1997. The Douglas Oilfield. In Meadows, N. S., Trueblood, S. P., Hardman, M. and Cowan, G. (eds), *Petroleum Geology of the Irish Sea and Adjacent Areas* (Geological Society Special Publication No. 124), 399–416. London: Geological Society.

Index

Compiled by Simon Timberlake

Page numbers in upper case roman numerals letters refer to the plate section.